GEORGE ORWELL

GEORGE ORWELL

Down and Out in Paris and London

The Road to Wigan Pier

Homage to Catalonia

Essays and Journalism:
1931-1940

Essays and Journalism:
1940-1943

Essays and Journalism:
1944-1945

Essays and Journalism:
1945-1949

Secker & Warburg/Octopus

Down and Out in Paris and London first published in Great Britain 1933
by Victor Gollancz Limited

The Road to Wigan Pier first published in Great Britain 1973
by Victor Gollancz Limited

Homage to Catalonia first published in Great Britain 1938
by Martin Secker & Warburg Limited

Collected Essays, Journalism and Letters of George Orwell first published in Great Britain 1968
by Martin Secker & Warburg Limited

This edition first published in Great Britain 1980 by

Martin Secker & Warburg Limited
54 Poland Street
London W1

in association with

Octopus Books Limited
59 Grosvenor Street
London W1

ISBN 0 905712 45 5

Printed in the United States of America
by R. R. Donnelley and Sons Company

CONTENTS

Introduction

This volume contains all George Orwell's full-length works of non-fiction, the bulk of his essays, and a selection of his reviews and occasional journalism.

Down and Out in Paris and London, *Homage to Catalonia*, and *The Road to Wigan Pier* are classics of documentary, all three, in their different fashions, reports from the front line. But in their form, as in their impact, they transcend conventional reporting. By comparing the source material with the completed work – the Diary with *Wigan Pier*, 'Hop-Picking' and 'Clink' with *Down and Out* – the reader can trace the outlines of the process by which Orwell deployed his first-hand observation, marshalled his arguments and their mode of presentation, to create some of the most effective and sustained polemic of the first half of this century. *Down and Out* was a report from a period, after his return from Burma, when he tramped and worked with a social class he had not known before. *Homage to Catalonia* came from a very different front: Orwell, on active service with the POUM Militia of the government in the Spanish Civil War, reports what he saw and felt there. It was perhaps his life abroad, in Burma, in the northern mines round Wigan and in the Spanish Civil War, that made Orwell a political activist, pamphleteer and polemicist. In 1939, when he was rejected as unfit for military service, he had to fall back more into journalism to earn a living. But he also became a journalist because he wanted to be effective, to make his voice heard against the folly, stupidity and despair he saw around him, to struggle to keep alive the possibilities of a free, equal and decent society – possibilities he had briefly glimpsed in the early days of the Spanish Civil War.

It is difficult, and unnecessary, to pigeonhole Orwell's essays and journalism. Few of the pieces can easily be labelled. The categories merge and overlap, there is no simple distinction between the literary and the political. For Orwell the two were inseparable. What we hear in this volume is the voice of an individual, talking, on a number of levels, of the themes and events that most urgently concern him, arguing out and clarifying his own ideas in a variety of forms – in formal essays, in reviews, in front of a microphone, in his regular work as a columnist. It is a voice that is always relentlessly questioning, with an equal concern for man and for lanaguage, with a continual burning impatience of cant, hypocrisy, affectation and propaganda, continually seeking clarity and precision. It is the voice of a man arguing with himself in public: the voice of a man who, in his day-to-day journalism as in his great fiction, identified the needs of this century for honesty and directness in language, and who defined and provided the vocabulary when it was most needed. It is needed still.

DOWN AND OUT IN PARIS AND LONDON

Down and Out in Paris and London

'O scathful harm, condition of poverte!'
Chaucer

Chapter One

The Rue du Coq d'Or, Paris, seven in the morning. A succession of furious, choking yells from the street. Madame Monce, who kept the little hotel opposite mine, had come out onto the pavement to address a lodger on the third floor. Her bare feet were stuck into sabots and her grey hair was streaming down.

Madame Monce: 'Salope! Salope! How many times have I told you not to squash bugs on the wallpaper? Do you think you've bought the hotel, eh? Why can't you throw them out of the window like everyone else? *Putain! Salope!'*

The woman on the third floor: 'Vache!'

Thereupon a whole variegated chorus of yells, as windows were flung open on every side and half the street joined in the quarrel. They shut up abruptly ten minutes later, when a squadron of cavalry rode past and people stopped shouting to look at them.

I sketch this scene, just to convey something of the spirit of the Rue du Coq d'Or. Not that quarrels were the only thing that happened there – but still, we seldom got through the morning without at least one outburst of this description. Quarrels, and the desolate cries of street hawkers, and the shouts of children chasing orange-peel over the cobbles, and at night loud singing and the sour reek of the refuse-carts, made up the atmosphere of the street.

It was a very narrow street – a ravine of tall, leprous houses, lurching towards one another in queer attitudes, as though they had all been frozen in the act of collapse. All the houses were hotels and packed to the tiles with lodgers, mostly Poles, Arabs and Italians. At the foot of the hotels were tiny *bistros*, where you could be drunk for the equivalent of a shilling. On Saturday nights about a third of the male population of the quarter was drunk. There was fighting over women, and the Arab navvies who lived in the cheapest hotels used to conduct mysterious feuds, and fight them out with chairs and occasionally revolvers. At night the policemen would only come through the street two together. It was a fairly rackety place. And yet amid the noise and dirt lived the usual respectable French shopkeepers, bakers and laundresses and the like, keeping themselves to themselves and quietly piling up small fortunes. It was quite a representative Paris slum.

My hotel was called the Hôtel des Trois Moineaux. It was a dark, rickety warren of five storeys, cut up by wooden partitions into forty rooms. The rooms were small and inveterately dirty, for there was no maid, and Madame F., the *patronne*, had no time to do any sweeping. The walls were as thin as matchwood, and to hide the cracks they had been covered with layer after layer of pink paper, which had come loose and housed innumerable bugs. Near the ceiling long lines of bugs marched all day like columns of soldiers, and at night came down ravenously hungry, so that one had to get up every few hours and kill them in hecatombs. Sometimes when the bugs got too bad one used to burn sulphur and drive them into the next room; whereupon the lodger next door would retort by having *his* room sulphured, and drive the bugs back. It was a dirty place, but homelike, for Madame F. and her husband were good sorts.

The rent of the rooms varied between thirty and fifty francs a week.

The lodgers were a floating population, largely foreigners, who used to turn up without luggage, stay a week and then disappear again. They were of every trade – cobblers, bricklayers, stonemasons, navvies, students, prostitutes, rag-pickers. Some of them were fantastically poor. In one of the attics there was a Bulgarian student who made fancy shoes for the American market. From six to twelve he sat on his bed, making a dozen pairs of shoes and earning thirty-five francs; the rest of the day he attended lectures at the Sorbonne. He was studying for the Church, and books of theology lay face-down on his leather-strewn floor. In another room lived a Russian woman and her son, who called himself an artist. The mother worked sixteen hours a day, darning socks at twenty-five centimes a sock, while the son, decently dressed, loafed in the Montparnasse cafés. One room was let to two different lodgers, one a day worker and the other a night worker. In another room a widower shared the same bed with his two grown-up daughters, both consumptive.

There were eccentric characters in the hotel. The Paris slums are a gathering-place for eccentric people – people who have fallen into solitary, half-mad grooves of life and given up trying to be normal or decent. Poverty frees them from ordinary standards of behaviour, just as money frees people from work. Some of the lodgers in our hotel lived lives that were curious beyond words.

There were the Rougiers, for instance, an old, ragged, dwarfish couple who plied an extraordinary trade. They used to sell post cards on the Boulevard St Michel. The curious thing was that the post cards were sold in sealed packets as pornographic ones, but were actually photographs of chateaux on the Loire; the buyers did not discover this till too late, and of course never complained. The Rougiers earned about a hundred francs a week, and by strict economy managed to be always half starved and half drunk. The filth of their room was such that one could smell it on the floor below. According to Madame F., neither of the Rougiers had taken off their clothes for four years.

Or there was Henri, who worked in the sewers. He was a tall, melancholy man with curly hair, rather romantic-looking in his long, sewer-man's boots. Henri's peculiarity was that he did not speak, except for the purposes of work, literally for days together. Only a year before he had been a chauffeur in good employ and saving money. One day he fell in love, and when the girl refused him he lost his temper and kicked her. On being kicked the girl fell desperately in love with Henri, and for a fortnight they lived together and spent a thousand francs of Henri's money. Then the girl was unfaithful; Henri planted a knife in her upper arm and was sent to prison for six months. As soon as she had been stabbed the girl fell more in love with Henri than ever, and the two made up their quarrel and agreed that when Henri came out of jail he should buy a taxi and they would marry and settle down. But a fortnight later the girl was unfaithful again, and when Henri came out she was with child. Henri did not stab her again. He drew out all his savings and went on a drinking-bout that ended in another month's imprisonment; after that he went to work in the sewers. Nothing would induce Henri to talk. If you asked him why he worked in the sewers he never answered, but simply crossed his wrists to signify handcuffs, and jerked his head southward, towards the prison. Bad luck seemed to have turned him half-witted in a single day.

Or there was R., an Englishman, who lived six months of the year in Putney with his parents and six months in France. During his time in France he drank four litres of wine a day, and six litres on Saturdays; he had once travelled as far as the Azores, because the wine there is cheaper than anywhere in Europe. He was a gentle, domesticated creature, never rowdy or quarrelsome, and never sober. He would lie in bed till midday, and from then till midnight he was in his corner of the *bistro*, quietly and methodically soaking. While he soaked he talked, in a refined, womanish voice, about antique furniture. Except myself, R. was the only Englishman in the quarter.

There were plenty of other people who lived lives just as eccentric as these: Monsieur Jules, the Roumanian, who had a glass eye and would not admit it, Furex the Limousin stonemason, Roucolle the miser – he died before my time, though – old Laurent the rag-merchant, who used to copy his signature from a slip of paper he carried in his pocket. It would be fun to write some of their biographies, if one had time. I am trying to describe the people in our quarter, not for the mere curiosity, but because they are all part of the story. Poverty is what I am writing about, and I had my first contact with poverty in this slum. The slum, with its dirt and its queer lives, was first an object-lesson in poverty, and then the background of my own experiences. It is for that reason that I try to give some idea of what life was like there.

Chapter Two

Life in the quarter. Our *bistro*, for instance, at the foot of the Hôtel des Trois Moineaux. A tiny brick-floored room, half underground, with wine-sodden tables, and a photograph of a funeral inscribed '*Crédit est mort*'; and red-sashed workmen carving sausage with big jack-knives; and Madame F., a splendid Auvergnat peasant woman with the face of a strong-minded cow, drinking Malaga all day 'for her stomach'; and games of dice for *apéritifs*; and songs about '*Les Fraises et Les Framboises*', and about Madelon, who said, '*Comment épouser un soldat, moi qui aime tout le régiment?*'; and extraordinarily public love-making. Half the hotel used to meet in the *bistro* in the evenings. I wish one could find a pub in London a quarter as cheery.

One heard queer conversations in the *bistro*. As a sample I give you Charlie, one of the local curiosities, talking.

Charlie was a youth of family and education who had run away from home and lived on occasional remittances. Picture him very pink and young, with the fresh cheeks and soft brown hair of a nice little boy, and lips excessively red and wet, like cherries. His feet are tiny, his arms abnormally short, his hands dimpled like a baby's. He has a way of dancing and capering while he talks, as though he were too happy and too full of life to keep still for an instant. It is three in the afternoon, and there is no one in the *bistro* except Madame F. and one or two men who are out of work; but it is all the same to Charlie whom he talks to, so long as he can talk about himself. He declaims like an orator on a barricade, rolling the words on his tongue and gesticulating with his short arms. His small, rather piggy eyes glitter with enthusiasm. He is, somehow, profoundly disgusting to see.

He is talking of love, his favourite subject.

'*Ah, l'amour, l'amour! Ah, que les femmes m'ont tué!* Alas, *messieurs et dames*, women have been my ruin, beyond all hope my ruin. At twenty-two I am utterly worn out and finished. But what things I have learned, what abysses of wisdom have I not plumbed! How great a thing it is to have acquired the true wisdom, to have become in the highest sense of the word a civilized man, to have become *raffiné, vicieux,*' etc., etc.

'*Messieurs et dames,* I perceive that you are sad. *Ah, mais la vie est belle* – you must not be sad. Be more gay, I beseech you!

> '*Fill high ze bowl vid Samian vine,*
> *Ve vill not sink of semes like zese!*

'*Ah, que la vie est belle!* Listen, *messieurs et dames*, out of the fullness of my experience I will discourse to you of love. I will explain to you what is the true meaning of love – what is the true sensibility, the higher, more refined pleasure which is known to civilized men alone. I will tell you of the happiest day of my life. Alas, but I am past the time when I could know such happiness as that. It is gone for ever – the very possibility, even the desire for it, are gone.

'Listen, then. It was two years ago; my brother was in Paris – he is a lawyer – and my parents had told him to find me and take me out to dinner. We hate each other, my brother and I, but we preferred not to disobey my parents. We dined, and at dinner he grew very drunk upon three bottles of Bordeaux. I took him back to his hotel, and on the way I bought a bottle of brandy, and when we had arrived I made my brother drink a tumblerful of it – I told him it was something to make him sober. He drank it, and immediately he fell down like somebody in a fit, dead drunk. I lifted him up and propped his back against the bed; then I went through his pockets. I found eleven hundred francs, and with that I hurried down the stairs, jumped into a taxi, and escaped. My brother did not know my address – I was safe.

'Where does a man go when he has money? To the *bordels*, naturally. But you do not suppose that I was going to waste my time on some vulgar debauchery fit only for navvies? Confound it, one is a civilized man! I was fastidious, exigeant, you understand, with a thousand francs in my pocket. It was midnight before I found what I was looking for. I had fallen in with a very smart youth of eighteen, dressed *en smoking* and with his hair cut *à l'américaine*, and we were talking in a quiet *bistro* away from the boulevards. We understood one another well, that youth and I. We talked of this and that, and discussed ways of diverting oneself. Presently we took a taxi together and were driven away.

'The taxi stopped in a narrow, solitary street with a single gas-lamp flaring at the end. There were dark puddles among the stones. Down one side ran the high, blank wall of a convent. My guide led me to a tall, ruinous house with shuttered windows, and knocked several times at the door. Presently there was a sound of footsteps and a shooting of bolts, and the door opened a little. A hand came round the edge of it; it was a large, crooked hand, that held itself palm upwards under our noses, demanding money.

'My guide put his foot between the door and the step. "How much do you want?" he said.

' "A thousand francs," said a woman's voice. "Pay up at once or you don't come in."

'I put a thousand francs into the hand and gave the remaining hundred to my guide: he said good night and left me. I could hear the voice inside counting the notes, and then a thin old crow of a woman in a black dress put her nose out and regarded me suspiciously before letting me in. It was very dark inside: I could see nothing except a flaring gas-jet that illuminated a patch of plaster wall, throwing everything else into deeper shadow. There was a smell of rats and dust. Without speaking, the old woman lighted a candle at the gas-jet, then hobbled in front of me down a stone passage to the top of a flight of stone steps.

'"*Voilà!*" she said; "go down into the cellar there and do what you like. I shall see nothing, hear nothing, know nothing. You are free, you understand – perfectly free."

'Ha, *messieurs*, need I describe to you – *forcément*, you know it yourselves – that shiver, half of terror and half of joy, that goes through one at these moments? I crept down, feeling my way; I could hear my breathing and the scraping of my shoes on the stones, otherwise all was silence. At the bottom of the stairs my hand met an electric switch. I turned it, and a great electrolier of twelve red globes flooded the cellar with a red light. And behold, I was not in a cellar, but in a bedroom, a great, rich, garish bedroom, coloured blood red from top to bottom. Figure it to yourselves, *messieurs et dames!* Red carpet on the floor, red paper on the walls, red plush on the chairs, even the ceiling red; everywhere red, burning into the eyes. It was a heavy, stifling red, as though the light were shining through bowls of blood. At the far end stood a huge, square bed, with quilts red like the rest, and on it a girl was lying dressed in a frock of red velvet. At the sight of me she shrank away and tried to hide her knees under the short dress.

'I had halted by the door. "Come here, my chicken," I called to her.

'She gave a whimper of fright. With a bound I was beside the bed; she tried to elude me, but I seized her by the throat – like this, do you see? – tight! She struggled, she began to cry out for mercy, but I held her fast, forcing back her head and staring down into her face. She was twenty years old, perhaps; her face was the broad, dull face of a stupid child, but it was coated with paint and powder, and her blue, stupid eyes, shining in the red light, wore that shocked, distorted look that one sees nowhere save in the eyes of these women. She was some peasant girl, doubtless, whom her parents had sold into slavery.

'Without another word I pulled her off the bed and threw her onto the floor. And then I fell upon her like a tiger! Ah, the joy, the incomparable rapture of that time! There, *messieurs et dames*, is what I would expound to you; *voilà l'amour!* There is the true love, there is the only thing in the world worth striving for; there is the thing beside which all your arts and ideals, all your philosophies and creeds, all your fine words and high attitudes, are as pale and profitless as ashes. When one has experienced love – the true love – what is there in the world that seems more than a mere ghost of joy?

'More and more savagely I renewed the attack. Again and again the girl tried to escape; she cried out for mercy anew, but I laughed at her.

'"Mercy!" I said, "do you suppose I have come here to show mercy? Do you suppose I have paid a thousand francs for that?" I swear to you, *messieurs et dames*, that if it were not for that accursed law that robs us of our liberty, I would have murdered her at that moment.

'Ah, how she screamed, with what bitter cries of agony. But there was no one to hear them; down there under the streets of Paris we were as secure as at the heart of a pyramid. Tears streamed down the girl's face, washing away the powder in long, dirty smears. Ah, that irrecoverable time! You, *messieurs et dames*, you who have not cultivated the finer sensibilities of love, for you such pleasure is almost beyond conception. And I too, now that my youth is gone – ah, youth! – shall never again see life so beautiful as that. It is finished. 'Ah yes, it is gone – gone for ever. Ah, the poverty, the shortness, the disappointment of human joy! For in reality – *car en réalité*, what is the duration of the supreme moment of love? It is nothing, an instand, a second perhaps. A second of ecstasy, and after that – dust ashes, nothingness.

'And so, just for one instant, I captured the supreme happiness, the highest and most refined emotion to which human beings can attain. And in the same moment it was finished, and I was left – to what? All my savagery, my passion, were scattered like the petals of a rose. I was left cold and languid, full of vain regrets; in my revulsion I even felt a kind of pity for the weeping girl on the floor. Is it not nauseous, that we should be the prey of such mean emotions? I did not look at the girl again; my sole thought was to get away. I hastened up the steps of the vault and out into the street. It was dark and bitterly cold, the streets were empty, the stones echoed under my heels with a hollow, lonely ring. All my money was gone, I had not even the price of a taxi fare. I walked back alone to my cold, solitary room.

'But there, *messieurs et dames*, that is what I promised to expound to you. That is Love. That was the happiest day of my life.'

He was a curious specimen, Charlie. I describe him, just to show what diverse characters could be found flourishing in the Coq d'Or quarter.

Chapter Three

I lived in the Coq d'Or quarter for about a year and a half. One day, in summer, I found that I had just four hundred and fifty francs left, and beyond this nothing but thirty-six francs a week, which I earned by giving English lessons. Hitherto I had not thought about the future, but I now realized that I must do something at once. I decided to start looking for a job, and – very luckily, as it turned out – I took the precaution of paying two hundred francs for a month's rent in advance. With the other two hundred and fifty francs, besides the English lessons, I could live a month, and in a month I should probably find work. I aimed at becoming a guide to one of the tourist companies, or perhaps an interpreter. However, a piece of bad luck prevented this.

One day there turned up at the hotel a young Italian who called himself a compositor. He was rather an ambiguous person, for he wore side whiskers, which are the mark either of an apache or an intellectual, and nobody was quite certain in which class to put him. Madame F. did not like the look of him, and made him pay a week's rent in advance. The Italian paid the rent and stayed six nights at the hotel. During this time he managed to prepare some duplicate keys, and on the last night he robbed a dozen rooms, including mine. Luckily, he did not find the money that was in my pockets, so I was not left penniless. I was left with just forty-seven francs – that is, seven and tenpence.

This put an end to my plans of looking for work. I had now got to live at the rate of about six francs a day, and from the start it was too difficult to leave much thought for anything else. It was now that my experiences of poverty began – for six francs a day, if not actual poverty, is on the fringe of it. Six francs is a shilling, and you can live on a shilling a day in Paris if you know how. But it is a complicated business.

It is altogether curious, your first contact with poverty. You have thought so much about poverty – it is the thing you have feared all your life, the thing you knew would happen to you sooner or later; and it is all so utterly and prosaically different. You thought it would be quite simple; it is extraordinarily complicated. You thought it would be terrible; it is merely squalid and boring. It is the peculiar *lowness* of poverty that you discover first; the shifts that it puts you to, the complicated meanness, the crust-wiping.

You discover, for instance, the secrecy attaching to poverty. At a sudden stroke you have been reduced to an income of six francs a day. But of course you dare not admit it – you have got to pretend that you are living quite as usual. From the start it tangles you in a net of lies, and even with the lies you can hardly manage it. You stop sending clothes to the laundry, and the laundress catches you in the street and asks you why; you mumble something, and she, thinking you are sending the clothes elsewhere, is your enemy for life. The tobacconist keeps asking why you have cut down your smoking. There are letters you want to answer, and cannot, because stamps are too expensive. And then there are your meals – meals are the worst difficulty of all. Every day at meal-times you go out, ostensibly to a restaurant, and loaf an hour in the Luxembourg Gardens, watching the pigeons. Afterwards you smuggle your food home in your pockets. Your food is bread and margarine, or bread and wine, and even the nature of the food is governed by lies. You have to buy rye bread instead of household bread, because the rye loaves, though dearer, are round and can be smuggled in your pockets. This wastes you a franc a day. Sometimes, to keep up appearances, you have to spend sixty centimes on a drink, and go correspondingly short of food. Your linen gets filthy, and you run out of soap and razor-blades. Your hair wants cutting, and you try to cut it yourself, with such fearful results that you have to go to the barber after all, and spend the equivalent of a day's food. All day you are telling lies, and expensive lies.

You discover the extreme precariousness of your six francs a day. Mean disasters happen and rob you of food. You have spent your last eighty centimes on half a litre of milk, and are boiling it over the spirit lamp. While it boils a bug runs down your forearm; you give the bug a flick with your nail, and it falls, plop! straight into the milk. There is nothing for it but to throw the milk away and go foodless.

You go to the baker's to buy a pound of bread, and you wait while the girl cuts a pound for another customer. She is clumsy, and cuts more than a pound. '*Pardon, monsieur,*' she says, 'I suppose you don't mind paying two sous extra?' Bread is a franc a pound, and you have exactly a franc. When you think that you too might be asked to pay two sous extra, and would have to confess that you could not, you bolt in panic. It is hours before you dare venture into a baker's shop again.

You go to the greengrocer's to spend a franc on a kilogram of potatoes. But one of the pieces that make up the franc is a Belgium piece, and the shopman refuses it. You slink out of the shop, and can never go there again.

You have strayed into a respectable quarter, and you see a prosperous friend coming. To avoid him you dodge into the nearest café. Once in the café you must buy something, so you spend your last fifty centimes on a glass of black coffee with a dead fly in it. One could multiply these disasters by the hundred. They are part of the process of being hard up.

You discover what it is like to be hungry. With bread and margarine in your belly, you go out and look into the shop windows. Everywhere there is food insulting you in huge, wasteful piles; whole dead pigs, baskets of hot loaves, great yellow blocks of butter, strings of sausages, mountains of potatoes, vast Gruyère cheeses like grindstones. A snivelling self-pity comes over you at the sight of so much food. You plan to grab a loaf and run, swallowing it before they catch you; and you refrain, from pure funk.

You discover the boredom which is inseparable from poverty; the times when you have nothing to do and, being underfed, can interest yourself in nothing. For half a day at a time you lie on your bed, feeling like the *jeune squelette* in Baudelaire's poem. Only food could rouse you. You discover that a man who has gone even a week on bread and margarine is not a man any longer, only a belly with a few accessory organs.

This – one could describe it further, but it is all in the same style – is life on six francs a day. Thousands of people in Paris live it – struggling artists and students, prostitutes when their luck is out, out-of-work people of all kinds. It is the suburbs, as it were, of poverty.

I continued in this style for about three weeks. The forty-seven francs were soon gone, and I had to do what I could on thirty-six francs a week from the English lessons. Being inexperienced, I handled the money badly, and sometimes I was a day without food. When this happened I used to sell a few of my clothes, smuggling them out of the hotel in small packets and taking them to a second-hand shop in the Rue de la Montagne St Geneviève. The shopman was a red-haired Jew, and extraordinary disagreeable man, who used to fall into furious rages at the sight of a client. From his manner one would have supposed that we had done him some injury by coming to him '*Merde!*' he used to shout, '*you* here again? What do you think this is? A soup kitchen?' And he paid incredibly low prices. For a hat which I had bought for twenty-five shillings and scarcely worn he gave five francs; for a good pair of shoes, five francs; for shirts, a franc each. He always preferred to exchange rather than buy, and he had a trick of thrusting some useless article into one's hand and then pretending that one had accepted it. Once I saw him take a good overcoat from an old woman, put two white billiard-balls into her hand, and then push her rapidly out of the shop before she could protest. It would have been a pleasure to flatten the Jew's nose, if only one could have afforded it.

These three weeks were squalid and uncomfortable, and evidently there was worse coming, for my rent would be due before long. Nevertheless, things were not a quarter as bad as I had expected. For, when you are approaching poverty, you make one discovery which outweighs some of the others. You discover boredom and mean complications and the beginnings of hunger, but you also discover the great redeeming feature of poverty: the fact that it annihilates the future. Within certain limits, it is actually true that the less money you have, the less you worry. When you have a hundred francs in the world you are liable to the most craven panics. When you have only three francs you are quite indifferent; for three francs will feed you till tomorrow, and you cannot think further than that. You are bored, but you are not afraid. You think vaguely, 'I shall be starving in a day or two – shocking, isn't it?' And then the mind wanders to other topics. A bread and margarine diet does, to some extent, provide its own anodyne.

And there is another feeling that is a great consolation in poverty. I believe everyone who has been hard up has experienced it. It is a feeling of relief, almost of pleasure, at knowing yourself at last genuinely down and out. You have talked so often of going to the dogs – and well, here are the dogs, and you have reached them, and you can stand it. It takes off a lot of anxiety.

Chapter Four

One day my English lessons ceased abruptly. The weather was getting hot and one of my pupils, feeling too lazy to go on with his lessons, dismissed me. The other disappeared from his lodgings without notice, owing me twelve francs. I was left with only thirty centimes and no tobacco. For a day and a half I had nothing to eat or smoke, and then, too hungry to put it off any longer, I packed my remaining clothes into my suitcase and took them to the pawnshop. This put an end to all pretence of being in funds, for I could not take my clothes out of the hotel without asking Madame F.'s leave. I remember, however, how surprised she was at my asking her instead of removing the clothes on the sly shooting the moon being a common trick in our quarter.

It was the first time that I had been in a French pawnshop. One went through grandiose stone portals (marked, of course, '*Liberté, Égalité, Fraternite*' – they write that even over the police stations in France) into a large, bare room like a school classroom, with a counter and rows of benches. Forty or fifty people were waiting. One handed one's pledge over the counter and sat down. Presently, when the clerk had assessed its value he would call out, '*Numéro* such and such, will you take fifty francs?' Sometimes it was only fifteen francs, or ten, or five – whatever it was, the whole room knew it. As I came in the clerk called with an air of offence, '*Numéro* 83 – here!' and gave a little whistle and a beckon, as though calling a dog. *Numéro* 83 stepped to the counter; he was an old bearded man, with an overcoat buttoned up at the neck and frayed trouser-ends. Without a word the clerk shot the bundle across the counter – evidently it was worth nothing. It fell to the ground and came open, displaying four pairs of men's woollen pants. No one could help laughing. Poor *Numéro* 83 gathered up his pants and shambled out, muttering to himself.

The clothes I was pawning, together with the suitcase, had cost over twenty pounds, and were in good condition. I thought they must be worth ten pounds, and a quarter of this (one expects quarter value at a pawnshop) was two hundred and fifty or three hundred francs. I waited without anxiety, expecting two hundred francs at the worst.

At last the clerk called my number: '*Numéro* 97!'

'Yes,' I said, standing up.

'Seventy francs?'

Seventy francs for ten pounds' worth of clothes! But it was no use arguing; I had seen someone else attempt to argue, and the clerk had instantly refused the pledge. I took the money and the pawnticket and walked out. I had now no clothes except what I stood up in – the coat badly out at the elbow – an overcoat, moderately pawnable, and one spare shirt. Afterwards, when it was too late, I learned that it was wiser to go to the pawnshop in the afternoon. The clerks are French, and, like most French people, are in a bad temper till they have eaten their lunch.

When I got home, Madame F. was sweeping the *bistro* floor. She came up the steps to meet me. I could see in her eye that she was uneasy about my rent.

'Well,' she said, 'what did you get for your clothes? Not much, eh?'

'Two hundred francs,' I said promptly.

'*Tiens!*' she said, surprised; 'well, *that's* not bad. How expensive those English clothes must be!'

The lie saved a lot of trouble, and, strangely enough, it came true. A few days later I did receive exactly two hundred francs due to me for a newspaper article, and, though it hurt to do it, I at once paid every penny of it in rent. So, though I came near to starving in the following weeks, I was hardly ever without a roof.

It was now absolutely necessary to find work, and I remembered a friend of mine, a Russian waiter named Boris, who might be able to help me. I had first met him in the public ward of a hospital, where he was being treated for arthritis in the left leg. He had told me to come to him if I were ever in difficulties.

I must say something about Boris, for he was a curious character and my close friend for a long time. He was a big, soldierly man of about thirty-five, and had been good-looking, but since his illness he had grown immensely fat from lying in bed. Like most Russian refugees, he had had an adventurous life. His parents, killed in the Revolution, had been rich people, and he had served through the war in the Second Siberian Rifles, which, according to him, was the best regiment in the Russian Army. After the war he had first worked in a brush factory, then as a porter at Les Halles, then had become a dishwasher, and had finally worked his way up to be a waiter. When he fell ill he was at the Hôtel Scribe, and taking a hundred francs a day in tips. His ambition was to become a *maître d'hôtel*, save fifty thousand francs, and set up a small, select restaurant on the Right Bank.

Boris always talked of the war at the happiest time of his life. War and soldiering were his passion; he had read innumerable books of strategy and military history, and could tell you all about the theories of Napoleon, Kutuzof, Clausewitz, Moltke and Foch. Anything to do with soldiers pleased him. His favourite café was the Closerie des Lilas in Montparnasse, simply because the statue of Marshal Ney stands outside it. Later on, Boris and I sometimes went to the Rue du Commerce together. If we went by Metro, Boris always got out at Cambronne station instead of Commerce, though Commerce was nearer; he liked the association with General Cambronne, who was called on to surrender at Waterloo, and answered simply, '*Merde!*'

The only things left to Boris by the Revolution were his medals and some photographs of his old regiment; he had kept these when everything else went to the pawnshop. Almost every day he would spread the photographs out on the bed and talk about them:

'*Voilà, mon ami!* There you see me at the head of my company. Fine big men, eh? Not like these little rats of Frenchmen. A captain at twenty – not bad, eh? Yes, a captain in the Second Siberian Rifles; and my father was a colonel.

'*Ah, mais, mon ami*, the ups and downs of life! A captain in the Russian Army, and then, piff! the Revolution – every penny gone. In 1916 I stayed a week at the Hôtel Edouard Sept; in 1920 I was trying for a job as night watchman there. I have been night watchman, cellarman, floor scrubber, dishwasher, porter, lavatory attendant. I have tipped waiters, and I have been tipped by waiters.

'Ah, but I have known what it is to live like a gentleman, *mon ami*. I do not say it to boast, but the other day I was trying to compute how many mistresses I have had in my life, and I made it out to be over two hundred. Yes, at least two hundred ... Ah, well, *ça reviendra*. Victory is to him who fights the longest. Courage!' etc. etc.

Boris had a queer, changeable nature. He always wished himself back in the army, but he had also been a waiter long enough to acquire the waiter's outlook. Though he had never saved more than a few thousand francs, he took it for granted that in the end he would be able to set up his own restaurant and grow rich. All waiters, I afterwards found, talk and think of this; it is what reconciles them to being waiters. Boris used to talk interestingly about hotel life:

'Waiting is a gamble,' he used to say; 'you may die poor, you may make your fortune in a year. You are not paid wages, you depend on tips – ten per cent. of the bill, and a commission from the wine companies on champagne corks. Sometimes the tips are enormous. The barman at Maxim's, for instance, makes five hundred francs a day. More than five hundred, in the season ... I have made two hundred francs a day myself. It was at a hotel in Biarritz, in the season. The whole staff, from the manager down to the *plongeurs*, was working twenty-one hours a day. Twenty-one hours' work and two and a half hours in bed, for a month on end. Still, it was worth it, at two hundred francs a day.

'You never know when a stroke of luck is coming. Once when I was at the Hôtel Royal an American customer sent for me before dinner and ordered twenty-four brandy cocktails. I brought them all together on a tray, in twenty-four glasses. 'Now, *garçon*,' said the customer (he was drunk), 'I'll drink twelve and you'll drink twelve, and if you can walk to the door afterwards you get a hundred francs.' I walked to the door, and he gave me a hundred francs. And every night for six days he did the same thing; twelve brandy cocktails, then a hundred francs. A few months later I heard he had been extradited by the American Government – embezzlement. There is something fine, do you not think, about these Americans?'

I liked Boris, and we had interesting times together, playing chess and talking about war and hotels. Boris used often to suggest that I should become a waiter. 'The life would suit you,' he used to say; 'when you are in work, with a hundred francs a day and a nice mistress, it's not bad. You say you go in for writing. Writing is bosh. There is only one way to make money at writing, and that is to marry a publisher's daughter. But you would make a good waiter if you shaved that moustache off. You are tall and you speak English – those are the chief things a waiter needs. Wait till I can bend this accursed leg, *mon ami*. And then, if you are ever out of a job, come to me.'

Now that I was short of my rent, and getting hungry, I remembered Boris's promise, and decided to look him up at once. I did not hope to become a waiter so easily as he had promised, but of course I knew how to scrub dishes, and no doubt he could get me a job in the kitchen. He had said that dishwashing jobs were to be had for the asking during the summer. It was a great relief to remember that I had after all one influential friend to fall back on.

Chapter Five

A short time before, Boris had given me an address in the Rue du Marché des Blancs Manteaux. All he had said in his letter was that 'things were not marching too badly,' and I assumed that he was back at the Hôtel Scribe, touching his hundred francs a day. I was full of hope, and wondered why I had been fool enough not to go to Boris before. I saw myself in a cosy restaurant, with jolly cooks singing love-songs as they broke eggs into the pan, and five solid meals a day. I even squandered two francs-fifty on a packet of Gaulois Bleu, in anticipation of my wages.

In the morning I walked down to the Rue du Marché des Blancs Manteaux; with a shock, I found it a slummy back street as bad as my own. Boris's hotel was the dirtiest hotel in the street. From its dark doorway there came out a vile, sour odour, a mixture of slops and synthetic soup – it was Bouillon Zip, twenty-five centimes a packet. A misgiving came over me. People who drink Bouillon Zip are starving, or near it. Could Boris possibly be earning a hundred francs a day? A surly *patron*, sitting in the office, said to me, Yes, the Russian was at home – in the attic. I went up six flights of narrow, winding stairs, the Bouillon Zip growing stronger as one got higher. Boris did not answer when I knocked at his door, so I opened it and went in.

The room was an attic, ten feet square, lighted only by a skylight, its sole furniture a narrow iron bedstead, a chair, and a washhand-stand with one game leg. A long S-shaped chain of bugs marched slowly across the wall above the bed. Boris was lying asleep, naked, his large belly making a mound under the grimy sheet. His chest was spotted with insect bites. As I came in he woke up, rubbed his eyes, and groaned deeply.

'Name of Jesus Christ!' he exclaimed, 'oh, name of Jesus Christ, my back! Curse it, I believe my back is broken!'

'What's the matter?' I exclaimed.

'My back is broken, that is all. I have spent the night on the floor. Oh, name of Jesus Christ! If you knew what my back feels like!'

'My dear Boris, are you ill?'

'Not ill, only starving – yes, starving to death if this goes on much longer. Besides sleeping on the floor, I have lived on two francs a day for weeks past. It is fearful. You have come at a bad moment, *mon ami*.'

It did not seem much use to ask whether Boris still had his job at the Hôtel Scribe. I hurried downstairs and bought a loaf of bread. Boris threw himself on the bread and ate half of it, after which he felt better, sat up in bed, and told me what was the matter with him. He had failed to get a job after leaving the hospital, because he was still very lame, and he had spent all his money and pawned everything, and finally starved for several days. He had slept a week on the quay under the Pont d'Austerlitz, among some empty wine barrels. For the past fortnight he had been living in this room, together with a Jew, a mechanic. It appeared (there was some complicated explanation) that the Jew owed Boris three hundred francs, and was repaying this by letting him sleep on the floor and allowing him two francs a day for food. Two francs would buy a bowl of coffee and three rolls. The Jew went to work at seven in the mornings, and after that Boris would leave his sleeping-place (it was beneath the skylight, which let in the rain) and get into the bed. He could not sleep much even there owing to the bugs, but it rested his back after the floor.

It was a great disappointment, when I had come to Boris for help, to find him even worse off than myself. I explained that I had only about sixty francs left and must get a job immediately. By this time, however, Boris had eaten the rest of the bread and was feeling cheerful and talkative. He said carelessly:

'Good heavens, what are you worrying about? Sixty francs – why, it's a fortune! Please hand me that shoe, *mon ami*. I'm going to smash some of those bugs if they come within reach.'

'But do you think there's any chance of getting a job?'

'Chance? It's a certainty. In fact, I have got something already. There is a new Russian restaurant which is to open in a few days in the Rue du Commerce. It is *une chose entendue* that I am to be *maître d'hôtel*. I can easily get you a job in the kitchen. Five hundred francs a month and your food – tips, too, if you are lucky.'

'But in the meantime? I've got to pay my rent before long.'

'Oh, we shall find something. I have got a few cards up my sleeve. There are people who owe me money, for instance – Paris is full of them. One of them is bound to pay up before long. Then think of all the women who have been my mistress! A woman never forgets, you know – I have only to ask and they will help me. Besides, the Jew tells me he is going to steal some magnetos from the garage where he works, and he will pay us five francs a day to clean them before he sells them. That alone would keep us. Never worry, *mon ami*. Nothing is easier to get than money.'

'Well, let's go out now and look for a job.'

'Presently, *mon ami*. We shan't starve, don't you fear. This is only the fortune of war – I've been in a worse hole scores of times. It's only a question of persisting. Remember Foch's maxim: *'Attaquez! Attaquez! Attaquez!'*

It was midday before Boris decided to get up. All the clothes he now had left were one suit, with one shirt, collar and tie, a pair of shoes almost worn out, and a pair of socks all holes. He had also an overcoat which was to be pawned in the last extremity. He had a suitcase, a wretched twenty-franc cardboard thing, but very important, because the *patron* of the hotel believed that it was full of clothes – without that, he would probably have turned Boris out of doors. What it actually contained were the medals and photographs, various odds and ends, and huge bundles of love-letters. In spite of all this Boris managed to keep a fairly smart appearance. He shaved without soap and with a razor-blade two months old, tied his tie so that the holes did not show, and carefully stuffed the soles of his shoes with newspaper. Finally, when he was dressed, he produced an ink-bottle and inked the skin of his ankles where it showed through his socks. You would never have thought, when it was finished, that he had recently been sleeping under the Seine bridges.

We went to a small café off the Rue de Rivoli, a well-known rendezvous of hotel managers and employees. At the back was a dark, cave-like room where all kinds of hotel workers were sitting – smart young waiters, others not so smart and clearly hungry, fat pink cooks, greasy dishwashers, battered old scrubbing-women. Everyone had an untouched glass of black coffee in front of him. The place was, in effect, an employment bureau, and the money spent on drinks was the *patron*'s commission. Sometimes a stout, important-looking man, obviously a restaurateur, would come in and speak to the barman, and the barman would call to one of the people at the back of the café. But he never called to Boris or me, and we left after two hours, as the etiquette was that you could only stay two hours for one drink. We learned afterwards, when it was too late, that the dodge was to bribe the barman; if you could afford twenty francs he would generally get you a job.

We went to the Hôtel Scribe and waited an hour on the pavement, hoping that the manager would come out, but he never did. Then we dragged ourselves down to the Rue du Commerce, only to find that the new restaurant, which was being redecorated, was shut up and the *patron* away. It was now night. We had walked fourteen kilometres over pavement, and we were so tired that we had to waste one franc-fifty on going home by Metro. Walking was agony to Boris with his game leg, and his optimism wore thinner and thinner as the day went on. When he got out of the Metro at the Place d'Italie he was in despair. He began to say that it was no use looking for work – there was nothing for it but to try crime.

'Sooner rob than starve, *mon ami*. I have often planned it. A fat, rich American – some dark corner down Montparnasse way – a cobblestone in a stocking – bang! And then go through his pockets and bolt. It is feasible, do you not think? I would not flinch – I have been a soldier, remember.'

He decided against the plan in the end, because we were both foreigners and easily recognized.

When we had got back to my room we spent another one franc-fifty on bread and chocolate. Boris devoured his share, and at once cheered up like magic; food seemed to act on his system as rapidly as a cocktail. He took out a pencil and began making a list of the people who would probably give us jobs. There were dozens of them, he said.

'Tomorrow we shall find something, *mon ami*, I know it in my bones. The luck always changes. Besides, we both have brains – a man with brains can't starve.

'What things a man can do with brains! Brains will make money out of anything. I had a friend once, a Pole, a real man of genius; and what do you think he used to do? He would buy a gold ring and pawn it for fifteen francs. Then – you know how carelessly the clerks fill up the tickets – where the clerk hand written '*en or*' he would add '*et diamants*' and he would change 'fifteen francs' to 'fifteen thousand.' Neat, eh? Then, you see, he could borrow a thousand francs on the security of the ticket. That is what I mean by brains . . .'

For the rest of the evening Boris was in a hopeful mood, talking of the times we should have together when we were waiters together at Nice or Biarritz, with smart rooms and enough money to set up mistresses. He was too tired to walk the three kilometres back to his hotel, and slept the night on the floor of my room, with his coat rolled round his shoes for a pillow.

Chapter Six

We again failed to find work the next day, and it was three weeks before the luck changed. My two hundred francs saved me from trouble about the rent, but everything else went as badly as possible. Day after day Boris and I went up and down Paris, drifting at two miles an hour through the crowds, bored and hungry, and finding nothing. One day, I remember, we crossed the Seine eleven times. We loitered for hours outside service doorways, and when the manager came out we would go up to him ingratiatingly, cap in hand. We always got the same answer: they did not want a lame man, nor a man without experience. Once we were very nearly engaged. While we spoke to the manager Boris stood straight upright, not supporting himself with his stick, and the manager did not see that he was lame. 'Yes,' he said, 'we want two men in the cellars. Perhaps you would do. Come inside.' Then Boris moved, the game was up. 'Ah,' said the manager, 'you limp. *Malheureusement*——'

We enrolled our names at agencies and answered advertisements, but walking everywhere made us slow, and we seemed to miss every job by half an hour. Once we very nearly got a job swabbing out railway trucks, but at the last moment they rejected us in favour of Frenchmen. Once we answered an advertisement calling for hands at a circus. You had to shift benches and clean up litter, and, during the performance, stand on two tubs and let a lion jump through your legs. When we got to the place, an hour before the time named, we found a queue of fifty men already waiting. There is some attraction in lions, evidently.

Once an agency to which I had applied months earlier sent me a *petit bleu*, telling me of an Italian gentleman who wanted English lessons. The *petit bleu* said 'Come at once' and promised twenty francs an hour. Boris and I were in despair. Here was a splendid chance, and I could not take it, for it was impossible to go to the agency with my coat out at the elbow. Then it occurred to us that I could wear Boris's coat – it did not match my trousers, but the trousers were grey and might pass for flannel at a short distance. The coat was so much too big for me that I had to wear it unbuttoned and keep one hand in my pocket. I hurried out, and wasted seventy-five centimes on a bus fare to get to the agency. When I got there I found that the Italian had changed his mind and left Paris.

Once Boris suggested that I should go to Les Halles and try a job as a porter. I arrived at half-past four in the morning, when the work was getting into its swing. Seeing a short, fat man in a bowler hat directing some porters, I went up to him and asked for work. Before answering he seized my right hand and felt the palm.

'You are strong, eh?' he said.

'Very strong,' I said untruly.

'*Bien*. Let me see you lift that crate.'

It was a huge wicker basket full of potatoes. I took hold of it, and found that, so far from lifting it, I could not even move it. The man in the bowler hat watched me, then shrugged his shoulders and turned away. I made off. When I had gone some distance I looked back and saw *four* men lifting the basket onto a cart. It weighed three hundredweight, possibly. The man had seen that I was no use, and taken this way of getting rid of me.

Sometimes in his hopeful moments Boris spent fifty centimes on a stamp and wrote to one of his ex-mistresses, asking for money. Only one of them ever replied. It was a woman who, besides having been his mistress, owed him two hundred francs. When Boris saw the letter waiting and recognized the handwriting, he was wild with hope. We seized the letter and rushed up to Boris's room to read it, like a child with stolen sweets. Boris read the letter, then handed it silently to me. It ran:

> My Little Cherished Wolf,
>
> With what delight did I open thy charming letter, reminding me of the days of our perfect love, and of the so dear kisses which I have received from thy lips. Such memories linger for ever in the heart, like the perfume of a flower that is dead.
>
> As to thy request for two hundred francs, alas! it is impossible. Thou dost not know, my dear one, how I am desolated to hear of thy embarrassments. But what wouldst thou? In this life which is so sad, trouble comes to everyone. I too have had my share. My little sister has been ill (ah, the poor little one, how she suffered!) and we are obliged to pay I know not what to the doctor. All our money is gone and we are passing, I assure thee, very difficult days.
>
> Courage, my little wolf, always the courage! Remember that the bad days are not for ever, and the trouble which seems so terrible will disappear at last.
>
> Rest assured, my dear one, that I will remember thee always. And receive the most sincere embraces of her who has never ceased to love thee, thy
>
> Yvonne

This letter disappointed Boris so much that he went straight to bed and would not look for work again that day.

My sixty francs lasted about a fortnight. I had given up the pretence of going out to restaurants, and we used to eat in my room, one of us sitting on the bed and the other on the chair. Boris would contribute his two francs and I three or four francs, and we would buy bread, potatoes, milk and cheese, and make soup over my spirit lamp. We had a saucepan and a coffee-bowl and one spoon; every day there was a polite squabble as to who should eat out of the saucepan and who out of the coffee-bowl (the saucepan held more), and every day, to my secret anger, Boris gave in first and had the saucepan. Sometimes we had more bread in the evening, sometimes not. Our linen was getting filthy, and it was three weeks since I had had a bath; Boris, so he said, had not had a bath for months. It was tobacco that made everything tolerable. We had plenty of tobacco, for some time before Boris had met a soldier (the soldiers are given their tobacco free) and bought twenty or thirty packets at fifty centimes each.

All this was far worse for Boris than for me. The walking and sleeping on the floor kept his leg and back in constant pain, and with his vast Russian appetite he suffered torments of hunger, though he never seemed to grow thinner. On the whole he was surprisingly gay, and he had vast capacities for hope. He used to say seriously that he had a patron saint who watched over him, and when things were very bad he would search the gutter for money, saying that the saint often dropped a two-franc piece there. One day we were waiting in the Rue Royale; there was a Russian restaurant near by, and we were going to ask for a job there. Suddenly, Boris made up his mind to go into the Madeleine and burn a fifty-centime candle to his patron saint. Then, coming out, he said that he would be on the safe side, and solemnly put a match to a fifty-centime stamp, as a sacrifice to the immortal gods. Perhaps the gods and the saints did not get on together; at any rate, we missed the job.

On some mornings Boris collapsed in the most utter despair. He would lie in bed almost weeping, cursing the Jew with whom he lived. Of late the Jew had become restive about paying the daily two francs, and, what was worse, had begun putting on intolerable airs of patronage. Boris said that I, as an Englishman, could not conceive what torture it was to a Russian of family to be at the mercy of a Jew.

'A Jew, *mon ami*, a veritable Jew! And he hasn't even the decency to be ashamed of it. To think that I, a captain in the Russian Army – have I ever told you, *mon ami*, that I was a captain in the Second Siberian Rifles? Yes, a captain, and my father was a colonel. And here I am, eating the bread of a Jew. A Jew.

'I will tell you what Jews are like. Once, in the early months of the war, we were on the march, and we had halted at a village for the night. A horrible old Jew, with a red beard like Judas Iscariot, came sneaking up to my billet. I asked him what he wanted. "Your honour," he said, "I have brought a girl for you, a beautiful young girl only seventeen. It will only be fifty francs." "Thank you," I said, "you can take her away again. I don't want to catch any diseases." "Diseases!" cried the Jew, "*mais, monsieur le capitaine,* there's no fear of that. It's my own daughter!" That is the Jewish national character for you.

'Have I ever told you, *mon ami*, that in the old Russian Army it was considered bad form to spit on a Jew? Yes, we thought a Russian officer's spittle was too precious to be wasted on Jews ...' etc. etc.

On these days Boris usually declared himself too ill to go out and look for work. He would lie till evening in the greyish, verminous sheets, smoking and reading old newspapers. Sometimes we played chess. We had no board, but we wrote down the moves on a piece of paper, and afterwards we made a board from the side of a packing-case, and a set of men from buttons, Belgian coins and the like. Boris, like many Russians, had a passion for chess. It was a saying of his that the rules of chess are the same as the rules of love and war, and that if you can win at one you can win at the others. But he also said that if you have a chessboard you do not mind being hungry, which was certainly not true in my case.

Chapter Seven

My money oozed away – to eight francs, to four francs, to one franc, to twenty-five centimes; and twenty-five centimes is useless, for it will buy nothing except a newspaper. We went several days on dry bread, and then I was two and a half days with nothing to eat whatever. This was an ugly experience. There are people who do fasting cures of three weeks or more, and they say that fasting is quite pleasant after the fourth day; I do not know, never having gone beyond the third day. Probably it seems different when one is doing it voluntarily and is not underfed at the start.

The first day, too inert to look for work, I borrowed a rod and went fishing in the Seine, baiting with blue-bottles. I hoped to catch enough for a meal, but of course I did not. The Seine is full of dace, but they grew cunning during the seige of Paris, and none of them has been caught since, except in nets. On the second day I thought of pawning my overcoat, but it seemed too far to walk to the pawnshop, and I spent the day in bed, reading the *Memoirs of Sherlock Holmes*. It was all that I felt equal to, without food. Hunger reduces one to an utterly spineless, brainless condition, more like the after-effects of influenza than anything else. It is as though one had been turned into a jellyfish, or as though all one's blood had been pumped out and luke-warm water substituted. Complete inertia is my chief memory of hunger; that, and being obliged to spit very frequently, and the spittle being curiously white and flocculent, like cuckoo-spit. I do not know the reason for this, but everyone who has gone hungry several days has noticed it.

On the third morning I felt very much better. I realized that I must do something at once, and I decided to go and ask Boris to let me share his two francs, at any rate for a day or two. When I arrived I found Boris in bed, and furiously angry. As soon as I came in he burst out, almost choking:

'He has taken it back, the dirty thief! He has taken it back!'

'Who's taken what?' I said.

'The Jew! Taken my two francs, the dog, the thief! He robbed me in my sleep!'

It appeared that on the previous night the Jew had flatly refused to pay the daily two francs. They had argued and argued, and at last the Jew had consented to hand over the money; he had done it, Boris said, in the most offensive manner, making a little speech about how kind he was, and extorting abject gratitude. And then in the morning he had stolen the money back before Boris was awake.

This was a blow. I was horribly disappointed, for I had allowed my belly to expect food, a great mistake when one is hungry. However, rather to my surprise, Boris was far from despairing. He sat up in bed, lighted his pipe and reviewed the situation.

'Now listen, *mon ami*, this is a tight corner. We have only twenty-five centimes between us, and I don't suppose the Jew will ever pay my two francs again. In any case his behaviour is becoming intolerable. Will you believe it, the other night he had the indecency to bring a woman in here, while I was there on the floor. The low animal! And I have a worse thing to tell you. The Jew intends clearing out of here. He owes a week's rent, and his idea is to avoid paying that and give me the slip at the same time. If the Jew shoots the moon I shall be left without a roof, and the *patron* will take my suitcase in lieu of rent, curse him! We have got to make a vigorous move.'

'All right. But what can we do? It seems to me that the only thing is to pawn our overcoats and get some food.'

'We'll do that, of course, but I must get my possessions out of this house first. To think of my photographs being seized! Well, my plan is ready. I'm going to forestall the Jew and shoot the moon myself. *F—— le camp* – retreat, you understand. I think that is the correct move, eh?'

'But my dear Boris, how can you, in daytime? You're bound to be caught.'

'Ah well, it will need strategy, of course. Our *patron* is on the watch for people slipping out without paying their rent; he's been had that way before. He and his wife take it in turns all day to sit in the office – what misers, these Frenchmen! But I have thought of a way to do it, if you will help.'

I did not feel in a very helpful mood, but I asked Boris what his plan was. He explained it carefully.

'Now listen. We must start by pawning our overcoats. First go back to your room and fetch your overcoat, then come back here and fetch mine, and smuggle it out under cover of yours. Take them to the pawn-shop in the Rue des Francs Bourgeois. You ought to get twenty francs for the two, with luck. Then go down to the Seine bank and fill your pockets with stones, and bring them back and put them in my suitcase. You see the idea? I shall wrap as many of my things as I can carry in a newspaper, and go down and ask the *patron* the way to the nearest laundry. I shall be very brazen and casual, you understand, and of course the *patron* will think the bundle is nothing but dirty linen. Or, if he does suspect anything, he will do what he always does, the mean sneak; he will go up to my room and feel the weight of my suitcase. And when he feels the weight of stones he will think it is still full. Strategy, eh? Then afterwards I can come back and carry my other things out in my pockets.'

'But what about the suitcase?'

'Oh, that? We shall have to abandon it. The miserable thing only cost about twenty francs. Besides, one always abandons something in a retreat. Look at Napoleon at the Beresina! He abandoned his whole army.'

Boris was so pleased with this scheme (he called it *une ruse de guerre*) that he almost forgot being hungry. Its main weakness – that he would have nowhere to sleep after shooting the moon – he ignored.

At first the *ruse de guerre* worked well. I went home and fetched my overcoat (that made already nine kilometres, on an empty belly) and smuggled Boris's coat out successfully. Then a hitch occured. The receiver at the pawnshop, a nasty, sour-faced interfering, little man – a typical French official – refused the coats on the ground that they were not wrapped up in anything. He said that they must be put either in a valise or a cardboard box. This spoiled everything, for we had no box of any kind, and with only twenty-five centimes between us we could not buy one.

I went back and told Boris the bad news. '*Merde!*' he said, 'that makes it awkward. Well, no matter, there is always a way. We'll put the overcoats in my suitcase.'

'But how are we to get the suitcase past the *patron*? He's sitting almost in the door of the office. It's impossible!'

'How easily you despair, *mon ami*! Where is that English obstinacy that I have read of? Courage! We'll manage it.'

Boris thought for a little while, and then produced another cunning plan. The essential difficulty was to hold the *patron's* attention for perhaps five seconds, while we could slip past with the suitcase. But, as it happened, the *patron* had just one weak spot – that he was interested in *Le Sport*, and was ready to talk if you approached him on this subject. Boris read an article about bicycle races in an old copy of the *Petit Parisien*, and then, when he had reconnoitred the stairs, went down and managed to set the *patron* talking. Meanwhile, I waited at the foot of the stairs, with the overcoats under one arm and the suitcase under the other. Boris was to give a cough when he thought the moment favourable. I waited trembling, for at any moment the *patron's* wife might come out of the door opposite the office, and then the game was up. However, presently Boris coughed. I sneaked rapidly past the office and out into the street, rejoicing that my shoes did not creak. The plan might have failed if Boris had been thinner, for his big shoulders blocked the doorway of the office. His nerve was splendid, too; he went on laughing and talking in the most casual way, and so loud that he quite covered any noise I made. When I was well away he came and joined me round the corner, and we bolted.

And then, after all our trouble, the receiver at the pawnshop again refused the overcoats. He told me (one could see his French soul revelling in the pedantry of it) that I had not sufficient papers of identification; my *carte d'identité* was not enough, and I must show a passport or addressed envelopes. Boris had addressed envelopes by the score, but his *carte d'identité* was out of order (he never renewed it, so as to avoid the tax), so we could not pawn the overcoats in his name. All we could do was to trudge up to my room, get the necessary papers, and take the coats to the pawnshop in the Boulevard Port Royal.

I left Boris at my room and went down to the pawnshop. When I got there I found that it was shut and would not open till four in the afternoon. It was now about half-past one, and I had walked twelve kilometres and had no food for sixty hours. Fate seemed to be playing a series of extraordinarily unamusing jokes.

Then the luck changed as though by a miracle. I was walking home through the Rue Broca when suddenly, glittering on the cobbles, I saw a five-sou piece. I pounced on it, hurried home, got our other five-sou piece and bought a pound of potatoes. There was only enough alcohol in the stove to parboil them, and we had no salt, but we wolfed them, skins and all. After that we felt like new men, and sat playing chess till the pawnshop opened.

At four o'clock I went back to the pawnshop. I was not hopeful, for if I had only got seventy francs before, what could I expect for two shabby overcoats in a cardboard suitcase? Boris had said twenty francs, but I thought it would be ten francs, or even five. Worse yet, I might be refused altogether, like poor *Numéro* 83 on the previous occasion. I sat on the front bench, so as not to see people laughing when the clerk said five francs.

At last the clerk called my number: '*Numéro* 117!'

'Yes,' I said, standing up.

'Fifty francs?'

It was almost as great a shock as the seventy francs had been the time before. I believe now that the clerk had mixed my number up with someone else's, for one could not have sold the coats outright for fifty francs. I hurried home and walked into my room with my hands behind my back, saying nothing. Boris was playing with the chessboard. He looked up eagerly.

'What did you get?' he exclaimed. 'What, not twenty francs? Surely you got ten francs, anyway? *Nom de Dieu*, five francs – that is a bit too thick. *Mon ami, don't* say it was five francs. If you say it was five francs I shall really begin to think of suicide.'

I threw the fifty-franc note onto the table. Boris turned white as chalk, and then, springing up, seized my hand and gave it a grip that almost broke the bones. We ran out, bought bread and wine, a piece of meat and alcohol for the stove, and gorged.

After eating, Boris became more optimistic than I had ever known him. 'What did I tell you?' he said. 'The fortune of war! This morning with five sous, and now look at us. I have always said it, there is nothing easier to get than money. And that reminds me, I have a friend in the Rue Fondary whom we might go and see. He has cheated me of four thousand francs, the thief. He is the greatest thief alive when he is sober, but it is a curious thing, he is quite honest when he is drunk. I should think he would be drunk by six in the evening. Let's go and find him. Very likely he will pay up a hundred on account. *Merde!* He might pay two hundred. *Allons-y!*'

We went to the Rue Fondary and found the man, and he was drunk, but we did not get our hundred francs. As soon as he and Boris met there was a terrible altercation on the pavement. The other man declared that he did not owe Boris a penny, but that on the contrary Boris owed *him* four thousand francs, and both of them kept appealing to me for my opinion. I never understood the rights of the matter. The two argued and argued, first in the street, then in a *bistro*, then in a *prix fixe* restaurant where we went for dinner, then in another *bistro*. Finally, having called one another thieves for two hours, they went off together on a drinking bout that finished up the last sou of Boris's money.

Boris slept the night at the house of a cobbler, another Russian refugee, in the Commerce quarter. Meanwhile, I had eight francs left, and plenty of cigarettes, and was stuffed to the eyes with food and drink. It was a marvellous change for the better after two bad days.

Chapter Eight

We had now twenty-eight francs in hand, and could start looking for work once more. Boris was still sleeping, on some mysterious terms, at the house of the cobbler, and he had managed to borrow another twenty francs from a Russian friend. He had friends, mostly ex-officers like himself, here and there all over Paris. Some were waiters or dishwashers, some drove taxis, a few lived on women, some had managed to bring money away from Russia and owned garages or dancing-halls. In general, the Russian refugees in Paris are hard-working people, and have put up with their bad luck far better than one can imagine Englishmen of the same class doing. There are exceptions, of course. Boris told me of an exiled Russian duke whom he had once met, who frequented expensive restaurants. The duke would find out if there was a Russian officer among the waiters, and, after he had dined, call him in a friendly way to his table.

'Ah,' the duke would say, 'so you are an old soldier, like myself? These are bad days, eh? Well, well, the Russian soldier fears nothing. And what was your regiment?'

'The so-and-so, sir,' the waiter would answer.

'A very gallant regiment! I inspected them in 1912. By the way, I have unfortunately left my notecase at home. A Russian officer will, I know, oblige me with three hundred francs.'

If the waiter had three hundred francs he would hand it over, and, of course, never see it again. The duke made quite a lot in this way. Probably the waiters did not mind being swindled. A duke is a duke, even in exile.

It was through one of these Russian refugees that Boris heard of something which seemed to promise money. Two days after we had pawned the overcoats, Boris said to me rather mysteriously:

'Tell me, *mon ami*, have you any political opinions?'

'No,' I said.

'Neither have I. Of course, one is always a patriot; but still—— Did not

Moses say something about spoiling the Egyptians? As an Englishman you will have read the Bible. What I mean is, would you object to earning money from Communists?'

'No, of course not.'

'Well, it appears that there is a Russian secret society in Paris who might do something for us. They are Communists; in fact they are agents for the Bolsheviks. They act as a friendly society, get in touch with exiled Russians, and try to get them to turn Bolshevik. My friend has joined their society, and he thinks they would help us if we went to them.'

'But what can they do for us? In any case they won't help me, as I'm not a Russian.'

'That is just the point. It seems that they are correspondents for a Moscow paper, and they want some articles on English politics. If we go to them at once they may commission you to write the articles.'

'Me? But I don't know anything about politics.'

'*Merde!* Neither do they. Who *does* know anything about politics? It's easy. All you have to do is to copy it out of the English papers. Isn't there a Paris *Daily Mail*? Copy it from that.'

But the *Daily Mail* is a Conservative paper. They loathe the Communists.'

'Well, say the opposite of what the *Daily Mail* says, then you *can't* be wrong. We mustn't throw this chance away, *mon ami*. It might mean hundreds of francs.'

I did not like the idea, for the Paris police are very hard on Communists, especially if they are foreigners, and I was already under suspicion. Some months before, a detective had seen me come out of the office of a Communist weekly paper, and I had had a great deal of trouble with the police. If they caught me going to this secret society, it might mean deportation. However, the chance seemed too good to be missed. That afternoon Boris's friend, another waiter, came to take us to the rendezvous. I cannot remember the name of the street – it was a shabby street running south from the Seine bank, somewhere near the Chamber of Deputies. Boris's friend insisted on great caution. We loitered casually down the street, marked the doorway we were to enter – it was a laundry – and then strolled back again, keeping an eye on all the windows and cafés. If the place were known as a haunt of Communists it was probably watched, and we intended to go home if we saw anyone at all like a detective. I was frightened, but Boris enjoyed these conspiratorial proceedings, and quite forgot that he was about to trade with the slayers of his parents.

When we were certain that the coast was clear we dived quickly into the doorway. In the laundry was a Frenchwoman ironing clothes, who told us that 'the Russian gentlemen' lived up a staircase across the courtyard. We went up several flights of dark stairs and emerged onto a landing. A strong, surly-looking young man, with hair growing low on his head, was standing at the top of the stairs. As I came up he looked at me suspiciously, barred the way with his arm and said something in Russian.

'*Mot d'ordre!*' he said sharply when I did not answer.

I stopped, startled. I had not expected passwords.

'*Mot d'orde!*' repeated the Russian.

Boris's friend, who was walking behind, now came forward and said something in Russian, either the password or an explanation. At this, the surly young man seemed satisfied, and led us into a small, shabby room with frosted windows. It was like a very poverty-stricken office, with propaganda posters in Russian lettering and a huge, crude picture of Lenin tacked on the walls. At the table sat an unshaven Russian in shirt sleeves, addressing newspaper wrappers from a pile in front of him. As I came in he spoke to me in French, with a bad accent.

'This is very careless!' he exclaimed fussily. 'Why have you come here without a parcel of washing?'

'Washing?'

'Everybody who comes here brings washing. It looks as though they were going to the laundry downstairs. Bring a good, large bundle next time. We don't want the police on our tracks.'

This was even more conspiratorial than I had expected. Boris sat down in the only vacant chair, and there was a great deal of talking in Russian. Only the unshaven man talked; the surly one leaned against the wall with his eyes on me, as though he still suspected me. It was queer, standing in the little secret room with its revolutionary posters, listening to a conversation which I did not understand a word. The Russians talked quickly and eagerly, with smiles and shrugs of the shoulders. I wondered what it was all about. They would be calling each other 'little father', I thought, and 'little dove', and 'Ivan Alexandrovitch', like the characters in Russian novels. And the talk would be of revolutions. The unshaven man would be saying firmly, 'We never argue. Controversy is a bourgeois pastime. Deeds are our arguments.' Then I gathered that it was not this exactly. Twenty francs was being demanded, for an entrance fee apparently, and Boris was promising to pay it (we had just seventeen francs in the world). Finally Boris produced our precious store of money and paid five francs on account.

At this the surly man looked less suspicious, and sat down on the edge of the table. The unshaven one began to question me in French, making notes on a slip of paper. Was I a Communist? he asked. By sympathy, I answered; I had never joined any organization. Did I understand the political situation in England? Oh, of course, of course. I mentioned the names of various Ministers, and made some contemptuous remarks about the Labour Party. And what about *Le Sport*? Could I do articles on *Le Sport*? (Football and Socialism have some mysterious connection on the Continent.) Oh, of course, again. Both men nodded gravely. The unshaven one said:

'*Evidemment*, you have a thorough knowledge of conditions in England. Could you undertake to write a series of articles for a Moscow weekly paper? We will give you the particulars.'

'Certainly.'

'Then, comrade, you will hear from us by the first post tomorrow. Or possibly the second post. Our rate of pay is a hundred and fifty francs an article. Remember to bring a parcel of washing next time you come. *Au revoir*, comrade.'

We went downstairs, looked carefully out of the laundry to see if there was anyone in the street, and slipped out. Boris was wild with joy. In a sort of sacrificial ecstasy he rushed into the nearest tobacconist's and spent fifty centimes on a cigar. He came out thumping his stick on the pavement and beaming.

'At last! At last! Now, *mon ami*, our fortune really *is* made. You took them in finely. Did you hear him call you comrade? A hundred and fifty francs an article – *nom de Dieu*, what luck!'

Next morning when I heard the postman I rushed down to the *bistro* for my letter; to my disappointment, it had not come. I stayed at home for the second post; still no letter. When three days had gone by and I had not heard from the secret society, we gave up hope, deciding that they have found somebody else to do their articles.

Ten days later we made another visit to the office of the secret society, taking care to bring a parcel that looked like washing. And the secret society had vanished! The woman in the laundry knew nothing – she simply said that '*ees messieurs*' had left some days ago, after trouble about the rent. What fools we looked, standing there with our parcel! But it was a consolation that we had paid only five francs instead of twenty.

And that was the last we ever heard of the secret society. Who or what they really were, nobody knew. Personally I do not think they had anything to do with the Communist Party; I think they were simply swindlers, who preyed upon Russian refugees by extracting entrance fees to an imaginary society. It was quite safe, and no doubt they are still doing it in some other city. They were clever fellows, and played their part admirably. Their office looked exactly as a secret Communist office should look, and as for that touch about bringing a parcel of washing, it was genius.

Chapter Nine

For three more days we continued traipsing about looking for work, coming home for diminishing meals of soup and bread in my bedroom. There were now two gleams of hope. In the first place, Boris had heard of a possible job at the Hôtel X., near the Place de la Concorde, and in the second, the *patron* of the new restaurant in the Rue du Commerce had at last come back. We went down in the afternoon and saw him. On the way Boris talked of the vast fortunes we should make if we got this job, and on the importance of making a good impression on the *patron*.

'Appearance – appearance is everything, *mon ami*. Give me a new suit and I will borrow a thousand francs by dinner-time. What a pity I did not buy a collar when we had money. I turned my collar inside out this morning; but what is the use, one side is as dirty as the other. Do you think I look hungry, *mon ami*?'

'You look pale.'

'Curse it, what can one do on bread and potatoes? It is fatal to look hungry. It makes people want to kick you. Wait.'

He stopped at a jeweller's window and smacked his cheeks sharply to bring the blood into them. Then, before the flush had faded, we hurried into the restaurant and introduced ourselves to the *patron*.

The *patron* was a short, fattish, very dignified man with wavy grey hair, dressed in a smart, double-breasted flannel suit and smelling of scent. Boris told me that he too was an ex-colonel of the Russian Army. His wife was there too, a horrid, fat Frenchwoman with a dead-white face and scarlet lips, reminding me of cold veal and tomatoes. The *patron* greeted Boris genially, and they talked together in Russian for a few minutes. I stood in the background, preparing to tell some big lies about my experience as a dish-washer.

Then the *patron* came over towards me. I shuffled uneasily, trying to look servile. Boris had rubbed it into me that a *plongeur* is a slave's slave, and I expected the patron to treat me like dirt. To my astonishment, he seized me warmly by the hand.

'So you are an Englishman!' he exclaimed. 'But how charming! I need not ask, then, whether you are a golfer?'

'*Mais certainement,*' I said, seeing that this was expected of me.

'All my life I have wanted to play golf. Will you, my dear *monsieur*, be so kind as to show me a few of the principal strokes?'

Apparently this was the Russian way of doing business. The *patron* listened attentively while I explained the difference between a driver and an iron, and then suddenly informed me that it was all *entendu*; Boris was to be *maître d'hôtel* when the restaurant opened, and I *plongeur*, with a chance of rising to lavatory attendant if trade was good. When would the restaurant open? I asked. Exactly a fortnight from today,' the *patron* answered grandly (he had a manner of waving his hand and flicking off his cigarette ash at the same time, which looked very grand), 'exactly a fortnight from today, in time for lunch.' Then, with obvious pride, he showed us over the restaurant.

It was a smallish place, consisting of a bar, a dining-room, and a kitchen no bigger than the average bathroom. The *patron* was decorating it in a trumpery 'picturesque' style (he called it '*le Normand*'; it was a matter of sham beams stuck on the plaster, and the like) and proposed to call it the Auberge de Jehan Cottard, to give a medieval effect. He had a leaflet printed, full of lies about the historical associations of the quarter, and this leaflet actually claimed, among other things, that there had once been an inn on the site of the restaurant which was frequented by Charlemagne. The *patron* was very pleased with this touch. He was also having the bar decorated with indecent pictures by an artist from the Salon. Finally he gave us each an expensive cigarette, and after some more talk he went home.

I felt strongly that we should never get any good from this restaurant. The *patron* had looked to me like a cheat, and, what was worse, an incompetent cheat, and I had seen two unmistakable duns hanging about the back door. But Boris, seeing himself a *maître d'hôtel* once more, would not be discouraged.

'We've brought it off – only a fortnight to hold out. What is a fortnight? Food? *Je m'en f*——. To think that in only three weeks I shall have my mistress! Will she be dark or fair, I wonder? I don't mind, so long as she is not too thin.'

Two bad days followed. We had only sixty centimes left, and we spent it on half a pound of bread, with a piece of garlic to rub it with. The point of rubbing garlic on bread is that the taste lingers and gives one the illusion of having fed recently. We sat most of that day in the Jardin des Plantes. Boris had shots with stones at the tame pigeons, but always missed them, and after that we wrote dinner menus on the backs of envelopes. We were too hungry even to try and think of anything except food. I remember the dinner Boris finally selected for himself. It was: a dozen oysters, bortch soup (the red, sweet, beetroot soup with cream on top), crayfishes, a young chicken *en casserole*, beef with stewed plums, new potatoes, a salad, suet pudding and Roquefort cheese, with a litre of Burgundy and some old brandy. Boris had international tastes in food. Later on, when we were prosperous, I occasionally saw him eat meals almost as large without difficulty.

When our money came to an end I stopped looking for work, and was another day without food. I did not believe that the Auberge de Jehan Cottard was really going to open, and I could see no other prospect, but I was too lazy to do anything but lie in bed. Then the luck changed abruptly. At night, at about ten o'clock, I heard an eager shout from the street. I got up and went to the window. Boris was there waving his stick and beaming. Before speaking he dragged a bent loaf from his pocket and threw it up to me.

'*Mon ami, mon cher ami*, we're saved! What do you think?'

'Surely you haven't got a job!'

'At the Hôtel X., near the Place de la Concorde – five hundred francs a month, and food. I have been working there today. Name of Jesus Christ, how I have eaten!'

After ten or twelve hours' work, and with his game leg, his first thought had been to walk three kilometres to my hotel and tell me the good news! What was more, he told me to meet him in the Tuileries the next day during his afternoon interval, in case he should be able to steal some food for me. At the appointed time I met Boris on a public bench. He undid his waistcoat and produced a large, crushed, newspaper packet; in it were some minced veal, a wedge of Camembert cheese, bread and an éclair, all jumbled together.

'*Voilà!*' said Boris, 'that's all I could smuggle out for you. The doorkeeper is a cunning swine.'

It is disagreeable to eat out of a newspaper on a public seat, especially in the Tuileries, which are generally full of pretty girls, but I was too hungry to care. While I ate, Boris explained that he was working in the cafeterie of the hotel – that is, in English, the stillroom. It appeared that the cafeterie was the very lowest post in the hotel, and a dreadful come-down for a waiter, but it would do until the Auberge de Jehan Cottard opened. Meanwhile I was to meet Boris every day in the Tuileries, and he would smuggle out as much food as he dared. For three days we continued with this arrangement, and I lived entirely on the stolen food. Then all our troubles came to an end, for one of the *plongeurs* left the Hôtel X., and on Boris's recommendation I was given a job there myself.

Chapter Ten

The Hôtel X. was a vast, grandiose place with a classical façade, and at one side a little, dark doorway like a rat-hole, which was the service entrance. I arrived at a quarter to seven in the morning. A stream of men with greasy trousers were hurrying in and being checked by a doorkeeper who sat in a tiny office. I waited, and presently the *chef du personnel*, a sort of assistant manager, arrived and began to question me. He was an Italian, with a round, pale face, haggard from overwork. He asked whether I was an experienced dishwasher, and I said that I was; he glanced at my hands and saw that I was lying, but on hearing that I was an Englishman he changed his tone and engaged me.

'We have been looking for someone to practise our English on,' he said. 'Our clients are all Americans, and the only English we know is ——' He repeated something that little boys write on the walls in London. 'You may be useful. Come downstairs.'

He led me down a winding staircase into a narrow passage, deep underground, and so low that I had to stoop in places. It was stiflingly hot and very dark, with only dim, yellow bulbs several yards apart. There seemed to be miles of dark labyrinthine passages – actually, I suppose, a few hundred yards in all – that reminded one queerly of the lower decks of a liner; there were the same heat and cramped space and warm reek of food, and a humming, whirring noise (it came from the kitchen furnaces) just like the whirl of engines. We passed doorways which let out sometimes a shouting of oaths, sometimes the red glare of a fire, once a shuddering draught from an ice chamber. As we went along, something struck me violently in the back. It was a hundred-pound block of ice, carried by a blue-aproned porter. After him came a boy with a great slab of veal on his shoulder, his cheek pressed into the damp, spongy flesh. They shoved me aside with a cry of '*Sauve-toi, idiot!*' and rushed on. On the wall, under one of the lights, someone had written in a very neat hand: 'Sooner will you find a cloudless sky in winter, than a woman at the Hôtel X. who has her maidenhead.' It seemed a queer sort of place.

One of the passages branched off into a laundry, where an old, skulled-face woman gave me a blue apron and a pile of dishcloths. Then the *chef du personnel* took me to a tiny underground den – a cellar below a cellar, as it were – where there were a sink and some gas-ovens. It was too low for me to stand quite upright, and the temperature was perhaps 110 degrees Fahrenheit. The *chef du personnel* explained that my job was to fetch meals for the higher hotel employees, who fed in a small dining-room above, clean their room and wash their crockery. When he had gone, a waiter, another Italian, thrust a fierce, fuzzy head into the doorway and looked down at me.

'English, eh?' he said. 'Well, I'm in charge here. If you work well' – he made the motion of up-ending a bottle and sucked noisily. 'If you don't't' – he gave the doorpost several vigorous kicks. 'To me, twisting your neck would be no more than spitting on the floor. And is there's any trouble, they'll believe me, not you. So be careful.'

After this I set to work rather hurriedly. Except for about an hour, I was at work from seven in the morning till a quarter past nine at night; first at washing crockery, then at scrubbing the tables and floors of the employees' dining-room, then at polishing glasses and knives, then at fetching meals, than at washing crockery again, then at fetching more meals and washing more crockery. It was easy work, and I got on well with it except when I went to the kitchen to fetch meals. The kitchen was like nothing I had ever seen or imagined – a stifling, low-ceilinged inferno of a cellar, red-lit from the fires, and deafening with oaths and the clanging of pots and pans. It was so hot that all the metal-work except the stoves had to be covered with cloth. In the middle were furnaces, where twelve cooks skipped to and fro, their faces dripping sweat in spite of their white caps. Round that were counters where a mob of waiters and *plongeurs* clamoured with trays. Scullions, naked to the waist, were stoking the fires and scouring huge copper saucepans with sand. Everyone seemed to be in a hurry and a rage. The head cook, a fine, scarlet man with big moustachios, stood in the middle booming continuously, '*Ça marche deux œufs brouillés! Ça marche un Chateau-briand aux pommes sautées!*' except when he broke off to curse at a *plongeur*. There were three counters, and the first time I went to the kitchen I took my tray unknowingly to the wrong one. The head cook walked up to me, twisted his moustaches, and looked me up and down. Then he beckoned to the breakfast cook and pointed at me.

'Do you see *that*? That is the type of *plongeur* they send us nowadays. Where do you come from, idiot? From Charenton, I suppose?' (There is a large lunatic asylum at Charenton.)

'From England,' I said.

'I might have known it. Well, *mon cher monsieur l'Anglais*, may I inform you that you are the son of a whore? And now —— the camp to the other counter, where you belong.'

I got this kind of reception every time I went to the kitchen, for I always made some mistake; I was expected to know the work, and was cursed accordingly. From curiosity I counted the number of times I was called *maquereau* during the day, and it was thirty-nine.

At half-past four the Italian told me that I could stop working, but that it was not worth going out, as we began again at five. I went to the lavatory for a smoke; smoking was strictly forbidden, and Boris had warned me that the lavatory was the only safe place. After that I worked again till a quarter-past nine, when the waiter put his head into the doorway and told me to leave the rest of the crockery. To my astonishment, after calling me pig, mackerel, etc., all day, he had suddenly grown quite friendly. I realized that the curses I had met with were only a kind of probation.

'That'll do, *mon p'tit*,' said the waiter. '*Tu n'es pas débrouillard*, but you work all right. Come up and have your dinner. The hotel allows us two litres of wine each, and I've stolen another bottle. We'll have a fine booze.'

We had an excellent dinner from the leavings of the higher employees. The waiter, grown mellow, told me stories about his love-affairs, and about two men whom he had stabbed in Italy, and about how he had dodged his military service. He was a good fellow when one got to know him; he reminded me of Benvenuto Cellini, somehow. I was tired and drenched with sweat, but I felt a new man after a day's solid food. The work did not seem difficult, and I felt that this job would suit me. It was not certain, however, that it would continue, for I had been engaged as an 'extra' for the day only, at twenty-five francs. The sour-faced doorkeeper counted out the money, less fifty centimes which he said was for insurance (a lie, I discovered afterwards). Then he stepped out into the passage, made me take off my coat, and carefully prodded me all over, searching for stolen food. After this the *chef du personnel* appeared and spoke to me. Like the waiter, he had grown more genial on seeing that I was willing to work.

'We will give you a permanent job if you like,' he said. 'The head waiter says he would enjoy calling an Englishman names. Will you sign on for a month?'

Here was a job at last, and I was ready to jump at it. Then I remembered the Russian restaurant, due to open in a fortnight. It seemed hardly fair to promise working a month, and then leave in the middle. I said that I had other work in prospect – could I be engaged for a fortnight? But at that the *chef du personnel* shrugged his shoulders and said that the hotel only engaged men by the month. Evidently I had lost my chance of a job.

Boris, by arrangement, was waiting for me in the Arcade of the Rue de Rivoli. When I told him what had happened, he was furious. For the first time since I had known him he forgot his manners and called me a fool.

'Idiot! Species of idiot! What's the good of my finding you a job when you go and chuck it up the next moment? How could you be such a fool as to mention the other restaurant? You'd only to promise you would work for a month.'

'It seemed more honest to say I might have to leave,' I objected.

'Honest! Honest! Who ever heard of a *plongeur* being honest? *Mon ami*' –

suddenly he seized my lapel and spoke very earnestly – '*mon ami*, you have worked here all day. You see what hotel work is like. Do you think a *plongeur* can afford a sense of honour?'

'No, perhaps not.'

'Well, then, go back quickly and tell the *chef du personnel* you are quite ready to work for a month. Say you will throw the other job over. Then, when our restaurant opens, we have only to walk out.'

'But what about my wages if I break my contract?'

Boris banged his stick on the pavement and cried out at such stupidity. 'Ask to be paid by the day, then you won't lose a sou. Do you suppose they would prosecute a *plongeur* for breaking his contract? A *plongeur* is too low to be prosecuted.'

I hurried back, found the *chef du personnel*, and told him that I would work for a month, whereat he signed me on. This was my first lesson in *plongeur* morality. Later I realized how foolish it had been to have any scruples, for the big hotels are quite merciless towards their employees. the engage or discharge men as the work demands, and they all sack ten per cent or more of their staff when the season is over. Nor have they any difficulty in replacing a man who leaves at short notice, for Paris is thronged by hotel employees out of work.

Chapter Eleven

As it turned out, I did not break my contract, for it was six weeks before the Auberge de Jehan Cottard even showed signs of opening. In the meantime I worked at the Hôtel X., four days a week in the cafeterie, one day helping the waiter on the fourth floor, and one day replacing the woman who washed up for the dining-room. My day off, luckily, was Sunday, but sometimes another man was ill and I had to work that day as well. The hours were from seven in the morning till two in the afternoon, and from five in the evening till nine – eleven hours; but it was a fourteen-hour day when I washed up for the dining-room. By the ordinary standards of a Paris *plongeur*, these are exceptionally short hours. The only hardship of life was the fearful heat and stuffiness of these labyrinthine cellars. Apart from this the hotel, which was large and well organized, was considered a comfortable one.

Our cafeterie was a murky cellar measuring twenty feet by seven by eight high, and so crowded with coffee-urns, breadcutters and the like that one could hardly move without banging against something. It was lighted by one dim electric bulb, and four or five gas-fires that sent out a fierce red breath. There was a thermometer there, and the temperature never fell below 110 degrees Fahrenheit – it neared 130 at some times of the day. At one end were five service lifts, and at the other an ice cupboard where we stored milk and butter. When you went into the ice cupboard you dropped a hundred degrees of temperature at a single step; it used to remind me of the hymn about Greenland's icy mountains and India's coral strand. Two men worked in the cafeterie besides Boris and myself. One was Mario, a huge excitable Italian – he was like a city policeman with operatic gestures – and the other, a hairy, uncouth animal whom we called the Magyar; I think he was a Transylvanian, or something even more remote. Except the Magyar we were all big men, and at the rush hours we collided incessantly.

The work in the cafeterie was spasmodic. We were never idle, but the real work only came in bursts of two hours at a time – we called each burst '*un coup de feu.*' The first *coup de feu* came at eight, when the guests upstairs began to wake up and demand breakfast. At eight a sudden banging and yelling would break out all through the basement; bells rang on all sides, blue-aproned men rushed through the passages, our service lifts came down with a simultaneous crash, and the waiters on all five floors began shouting Italian oaths down the shafts. I don't remember all our duties, but they included making tea, coffee and chocolate, fetching meals from the kitchen, wines from the cellar and fruit and so forth from the dining-room, slicing bread, making toast, rolling pats of butter, measuring jam, opening milk-cans, counting lumps of sugar, boiling eggs, cooking porridge, pounding ice, grinding coffee – all this for from a hundred to two hundred customers. The kitchen was thirty yards away, and the dining-room sixty or seventy yards. Everything we sent up in the service lifts had to be covered by a voucher, and the vouchers had to be carefully filed, and there was trouble if even a lump of sugar was lost. Besides this, we had to supply the staff with bread and coffee, and fetch the meals for the waiters upstairs. All in all, it was a complicated job.

I calculated that one had to walk and run about fifteen miles during the day, and yet the strain of the work was more mental than physical. Nothing could be easier, on the face of it, than this stupid scullion work, but it is astonishingly hard when one is in a hurry. One has to leap to and fro between a multitude of jobs – it is like sorting a pack of cards against the clock. You are, for example, making toast, when bang! down comes a service lift with an order for tea, rolls and three different kinds of jam, and simultaneously bang! down comes another demanding scrambled eggs, coffee and grapefruit; you run to the kitchen for the eggs and to the dining-room for the fruit, going like lightning so as to be back before your toast burns, and having to remember about the tea and coffee, besides half a dozen other orders that are still pending; and at the same time some waiter is following you and making trouble about a lost bottle of soda-water, and you are arguing with him. It needs more brains than one might think. Mario said, no doubt truly, that it took a year to make a reliable cafetier.

The time between eight and half-past ten was a sort of delirium. Sometimes we were going as though we had only five minutes to live; sometimes there were sudden lulls when the orders stopped and everything seemed quiet for a moment. Then we swept up the litter from the floor, threw down fresh sawdust, and swallowed gallipots of wine or coffee or water – anything, so long as it was wet. Very often we used to break off chunks of ice and suck them while we worked. The heat among the gas-fires was nauseating; we swallowed quarts of drink during the day, and after a few hours even our aprons were drenched with sweat. At times we were hopelessly behind with the work, and some of the customers would have gone without their breakfast, but Mario always pulled us through. He had worked fourteen years in the cafeterie, and he had the skill that never wastes a second between jobs. The Magyar was very stupid and I was inexperienced, and Boris was inclined to shirk, partly because of his lame leg, partly because he was ashamed of working in the cafeterie after being a waiter; but Mario was wonderful. The way he would stretch his great arms right across the cafeterie to fill a coffee-pot with one hand and boil an egg with the other, at the same time watching toast and shouting directions to the Magyar, and between whiles singing snatches from *Rigoletto*, was beyond all praise. The *patron* knew his value, and he was paid a thousand francs a month, instead of five hundred like the rest of us.

The breakfast pandemonium stopped at half-past ten. Then we scrubbed the cafeterie tables, swept the floor and polished the brasswork, and, on good mornings, went one at a time to the lavatory for a smoke. This was our slack time – only relatively slack, however, for we had only ten minutes for lunch, and we never got through it uninterrupted. The customers' luncheon hour, between twelve and two, was another period of turmoil like the breakfast hour. Most of our work was fetching meals from the kitchen, which meant constant *engueulades* from the cooks. By this time the cooks had sweated in front of their furnaces for four or five hours, and their tempers were all warmed up.

At two we were suddenly free men. We threw off our aprons and put on our coats, hurried out of doors, and, when we had money, dived into the nearest *bistro*. It was strange, coming up into the street from those firelit cellars. The air seemed blindingly clear and cold, like arctic summer; and how sweet the petrol did smell, after the stenches of sweat and food! Sometimes we met some of our cooks and waiters in the *bistros*, and they were friendly and stood us drinks. Indoors we were their slaves, but it is an etiquette in hotel life that between hours everyone is equal, and the *engueulades* do not count.

At a quarter to five we went back to the hotel. Till half-past six there were no orders, and we used this time to polish silver, clean out the coffee-urns, and do other odd jobs. Then the grand turmoil of the day started – the dinner hour. I wish I could be Zola for a little while, just to describe that dinner hour. The essence of the situation was that a hundred or two hundred people were demanding individually different meals of five or six courses, and that fifty or sixty people had to cook and serve them and clean up the mess afterwards; anyone with experience of catering will know what that means. And at this time when the work was doubled, the whole staff was tired out, and a number of them were drunk. I could write pages about the scene without giving a true idea of it. The chargings to and fro in the narrow passages, the collisions, the yells, the struggling with crates and trays and blocks of ice, the heat, the darkness, the furious festering quarrels which there was no time to fight out – they pass description. Anyone coming into the basement for the first time would have thought himself in a den of maniacs. It was only later, when I understood the working of a hotel, that I saw order in all this chaos.

At half-past eight the work stopped very suddenly. We were not free till nine, but we used to throw ourselves full length on the floor, and lie there resting our legs, too lazy even to go to the ice cupboard for a drink. Sometimes the *chef du personnel* would come in with bottles of beer, for the hotel stood us an extra beer when we had had a hard day. The food we were given was no more than eatable, but the *patron* was not mean about drink; he allowed us two litres of wine a day each, knowing that if a *plongeur* is not given two litres he will steal three. We had the heeltaps of bottles as well, so that we often drank too much – a good thing, for one seemed to work faster when partially drunk.

Four days of the week passed like this; of the other two working days, one was better and one worse. After a week of this life I felt in need of a holiday. It was Saturday night, so the people in our *bistro* were busy getting drunk, and with a free day ahead of me I was ready to join them. We all went to bed, drunk, at two in the morning, meaning to sleep till noon. At half-past five I was suddenly awakened. A night-watchman, sent from the hotel, was standing at my bedside. He stripped the clothes back and shook me roughly.

'Get up!' he said. '*Tu t'es bien saoulé la gueule, eh?* Well, never mind that, the hotel's a man short. You've got to work today.'

'Why should I work?' I protested. 'This is my day off.'

'Day off, nothing! The work's got to be done. Get up!'

I got up and went out, feeling as though my back were broken and my skull filled with hot cinders. I did not think that I could possibly do a day's work. And yet after only an hour in the basement, I found that I was perfectly well. It seemed that in the heat of those cellars, as in a turkish bath, one could sweat out almost any quantity of drink. *Plongeurs* know this, and count on it. The power of swallowing quarts of wine, and then sweating it out before it can do much damage, is one of the compensations of their life.

Chapter Twelve

By far my best time at the hotel was when I went to help the waiter on the fourth floor. We worked in a small pantry which communicated with the cafeterie by service lifts. It was delightfully cool after the cellars, and the work was chiefly polishing silver and glasses, which is a humane job. Valenti, the waiter, was a decent sort, and treated me almost as an equal when we were alone, though he had to speak roughly when there was anyone else present, for it does not do for a waiter to be friendly with *plongeurs*. He used sometimes to tip me five francs when he had had a good day. He was a comely youth, aged twenty-four but looking eighteen, and, like most waiters, he carried himself well and knew how to wear his clothes. With his black tail-coat and white tie, fresh face and sleek brown hair, he looked just like an Eton boy; yet he had earned his living since he was twelve, and worked his way up literally from the gutter. Crossing the Italian frontier without a passport, and selling chestnuts from a barrow on the northern boulevards, and being given fifty days' imprisonment in London for working without a permit, and being made love to by a rich old woman in a hotel, who gave him a diamond ring and afterwards accused him of stealing it, were among his experiences. I used to enjoy talking to him, at slack times when we sat smoking down the lift shaft.

My bad day was when I washed up for the dining-room. I had not to wash the plates, which were done in the kitchen, but only the other crockery, silver, knives and glasses; yet, even so, it meant thirteen hours' work, and I used between thirty and forty dishcloths during the day. The antiquated methods used in France double the work of washing up. Plate-racks are unheard-of, and there are no soap-flakes, only the treacly soft soap, which refuses to lather in the hard, Paris water. I worked in a dirty, crowded little den, a pantry and scullery combined, which gave straight on the dining-room. Besides washing up, I had to fetch the waiters' food and serve them at table; most of them were intolerably insolent, and I had to use my fists more than once to get common civility. The person who normally washed up was a woman, and they made her life a misery.

It was amusing to look round the filthy little scullery and think that only a double door was between us and the dining-room. There sat the customers in all their splendour – spotless table-cloths, bowls of flowers, mirrors and gilt cornices and painted cherubim; and here, just a few feet away, we in our disgusting filth. For it really was disgusting filth. There was no time to sweep the floor till evening, and we slithered about in a compound of soapy water, lettuce-leaves, torn paper and trampled food. A dozen waiters with their coats off, showing their sweaty armpits, sat at the table mixing salads and sticking their thumbs into the cream pots. The room had a dirty, mixed smell of food and sweat. Everywhere in the cupboards, behind the piles of crockery, were squalid stores of food that the waiters had stolen. There were only two sinks, and no washing basin, and it was nothing unusual for a waiter to wash his face in the water in which clean crockery was rinsing. But the customers saw nothing of this. There were a coco-nut mat and a mirror outside the dining-room door, and the waiters used to preen themselves up and go in looking the picture of cleanliness.

It is an instructive sight to see a waiter going into a hotel dining-room. As he passes the door a sudden change comes over him. The set of his shoulders alters; all the dirt and hurry and irritation have dropped off in an instant. He glides over the carpet, with a solemn priest-like air. I remember our assistant *maître d'hôtel*, a fiery Italian, pausing at the dining-room door to address an apprentice who had broken a bottle of wine. Shaking his fist above his head he yelled (luckily the door was more or less soundproof):

'*Tu me fais* —— Do you call yourself a waiter, you young bastard? You a waiter! You're not fit to scrub floors in the brothel your mother came from. *Maquereau!*'

Words failing him, he turned to the door; and as he opened it he delivered a final insult in the same manner as Squire Western in *Tom Jones*.

Then he entered the dining-room and sailed across it dish in hand, graceful as a swan. Ten seconds later he was bowing reverently to a customer. And you could not help thinking, as you saw him bow and smile, with that benign smile of the trained waiter, that the customer was put to shame by having such an aristocrat to serve him.

This washing up was a thoroughly odious job – not hard, but boring and silly beyond words. It is dreadful to think that some people spend their whole decades at such occupations. The woman whom I replaced was quite sixty years old, and she stood at the sink thirteen hours a day, six days a week, the year round; she was, in addition, horribly bullied by the waiters. She gave out that she had once been an actress – actually, I imagine, a prostitute; most prostitutes end as charwomen. It was strange to see that in spite of her age and her life she still wore a bright blonde wig, and darkened her eyes and painted her face like a girl of twenty. So apparently even a seventy-eight-hour week can leave one with some vitality.

Chapter Thirteen

On my third day at the hotel the *chef du personnel*, who had generally spoken to me in quite a pleasant tone, called me up and said sharply:

'Here, you, shave that moustache off at once! *Nom de Dieu*, who ever heard of a *plongeur* with a moustache?'

I began to protest, but he cut me short. 'A *plongeur* with a moustache – nonsense! Take care I don't see you with it tomorrow.'

On the way home I asked Boris what this meant. He shrugged his shoulders. 'You must do what he says, *mon ami*. No one in the hotel wears a moustache, except the cooks. I should have thought you would have noticed it. Reason? There *is* no reason. It is the custom.'

I saw that it was an etiquette, like not wearing a white tie with a dinner-jacket, and shaved off my moustache. Afterwards I found out the explanation of the custom, which is this: waiters in good hotels do not wear moustaches, and to show their superiority they decree that *plongeurs* shall not wear them either; and the cooks wear their moustaches to show their contempt for the waiters.

This gives some idea of the elaborate caste system existing in a hotel. Our staff, amounting to about a hundred and ten, had their prestige graded as accurately as that of soldiers, and a cook or waiter was as much above a *plongeur* as a captain above a private. Highest of all came the manager, who could sack anybody, even the cooks. We never saw the *patron*, and all we knew of him was that his meals had to be prepared more carefully than that of the customers; all the discipline of the hotel depended on the manager. He was a conscientious man, and always on the lookout for slackness, but we were too clever for him. A system of service bells ran through the hotel, and the whole staff used these for signalling to one another. A long ring and a short ring, followed by two more long rings, meant that the manager was coming, and when we heard it we took care to look busy.

Below the manager came the *maître d'hôtel*. He did not serve at table, unless to a lord or someone of that kind, but directed the other waiters and helped with the catering. His tips, and his bonus from the champagne companies (it was two francs for each cork he returned to them), came to two hundred francs a day. He was in a position quite apart from the rest of the staff, and took his meals in a private room, with silver on the table and two apprentices in clean white jackets to serve him. A little below the head waiter came the head cook, drawing about five thousand francs a month; he dined in the kitchen, but at a separate table, and one of the apprentice cooks waited on him. Then came the *chef du personnel*; he drew only fifteen hundred francs a month, but he wore a black coat and did no manual work, and he could sack *plongeurs* and fine waiters. Then came the other cooks, drawing anything between three thousand and seven hundred and fifty francs a month; then the waiters, making about seventy francs a day in tips, besides a small retaining fee; then the laundresses and sewing women; then the apprentice waiters, who received no tips, but were paid seven hundred and fifty francs a month; then the *plongeurs*, also at seven hundred and fifty francs; then the chambermaids, at five or six hundred francs a month; and lastly the cafetiers, at five hundred a month. We of the cafeterie were the very dregs of the hotel, despised and *tutoied* by everyone.

There were various others – the office employees, called generally couriers, the storekeeper, the cellarman, some porters and pages, the ice man, the bakers, the night-watchman, the doorkeeper. Different jobs were done by different races. The office employees and the cooks and sewing-women were French, the waiters Italians and Germans (there is hardly such a thing as a French waiter in Paris), the *plongeurs* of every race in Europe, beside Arabs and negroes. French was the lingua franca, even the Italians speaking it to one another.

All the departments had their special perquisites. In all Paris hotels it is the custom to sell the broken bread to bakers for eight sous a pound, and the kitchen scraps to pigkeepers for a trifle, and to divide the proceeds of this among the *plongeurs*. There was much pilfering, too. The waiters all stole food – in fact, I seldom saw a waiter trouble to eat the rations provided for him by the hotel – and the cooks did it on a larger scale in the kitchen, and we in the cafeterie swilled illicit tea and coffee. The cellarman stole brandy. By a rule of the hotel the waiters were not allowed to keep stores of spirits, but had to go to the cellarman for each drink as it was ordered. As the cellarman poured out the drinks he would set aside perhaps a teaspoonful from each glass, and he amassed quantities in this way. He would sell you the stolen brandy for five sous a swig if he thought he could trust you.

There were thieves among the staff, and if you left money in your coat pockets it was generally taken. The doorkeeper, who paid our wages and searched us for stolen food, was the greatest thief in the hotel. Out of my five hundred francs a month, this man actually managed to cheat me of a hundred and fourteen francs in six weeks. I had asked to be paid daily, so the doorkeeper paid me sixteen francs each evening, and, by not paying for Sundays (for which of course payment was due), pocketed sixty-four francs. Also, I sometimes worked on a Sunday, for which, though I did not know it, I was entitled to an extra twenty-five francs. The doorkeeper never paid me this either, and so made away with another seventy-five francs. I only realized during my last week that I was being cheated, and, as I could prove nothing, only twenty-five francs were refunded. The doorkeeper played similar tricks on any employee who was fool enough to be taken in. He called himself a Greek, but in reality he was an Armenian. After knowing him I saw the force of the proverb 'Trust a snake before a Jew and a Jew before a Greek, but don't trust an Armenian.'

There were queer characters among the waiters. One was a gentleman – a youth who had been educated at a university, and had had a well-paid job in a business office. He had caught a venereal disease, lost his job, drifted, and now considered himself lucky to be a waiter. Many of the waiters had slipped into France without passports, and one or two of them were spies – it is a common profession for a spy to adopt. One day there was a fearful row in the waiters' dining-room between Morandi, a dangerous-looking man with eyes set too far apart, and another Italian. It appeared that Morandi had taken the other man's mistress. The other man, a weakling and obviously frightened of Morandi, was threatening vaguely.

Morandi jeered at him. 'Well, what are you going to do about it? I've slept with your girl, slept with her three times. It was fine. What can you do, eh?'

'I can denounce you to the secret police. You are an Italian spy.'

Morandi did not deny it. He simply produced a razor from his tail pocket and made two swift strokes in the air, as though slashing a man's cheeks open. Whereat the other waiter took it back.

The queerest type I ever saw in the hotel was an 'extra'. He had been engaged at twenty-five francs for the day to replace the Magyar, who was ill. He was a Serbian, a thick-set nimble fellow of about twenty-five, speaking six languages, including English. He seemed to know all about hotel work, and up till midday he worked like a slave. Then, as soon as it had struck twelve, he turned sulky, shirked his work, stole wine, and finally crowned all by loafing about openly with a pipe in his mouth. Smoking, of course, was forbidden under severe penalties. The manager himself heard of it and came down to interview the Serbian, fuming with rage.

'What the devil do you mean by smoking here?' he cried.

'What the devil do you mean by having a face like that?' answered the Serbian, calmly.

I cannot convey the blasphemy of such a remark. The head cook, if a *plongeur* had spoken to him like that, would have thrown a saucepan of hot soup in his face. The manager said instantly, 'You're sacked!' and at two o'clock the Serbian was given his twenty-five francs and duly sacked. Before he went out Boris asked him in Russian what game he was playing. He said the Serbian answered:

'Lood here, *mon vieux*, they've got to pay me a day's wages if I work up to midday, haven't they? That's the law. And where's the sense of working after I get my wages? So I'll tell you what I do. I go to a hotel and get a job as an extra, and up to midday I worked hard. Then, the moment it's struck twelve, I start raising such hell that they've no choice but to sack me. Neat, eh? Most days I'm sacked by half-past twelve; today it was two o'clock; but I don't care, I've saved four hours' work. The only trouble is, one can't do it at the same hotel twice.'

It appeared that he had played this game at half the hotels and restaurants in Paris. It was probably quite an easy game to play during the summer, though the hotels protect themselves against it as well as they can by means of a black list.

Chapter Fourteen

In a few days I had grasped the main principles on which the hotel was run. The thing that would astonish anyone coming for the first time into the service quarters of a hotel would be the fearful noise and disorder during the rush hours. It is something so different from the steady work in a shop or factory that it looks at first sight like mere bad management. But it is really quite unavoidable, and for this reason. Hotel work is not particularly hard, but by its nature it comes in rushes and cannot be economized. You cannot, for instance, grill a steak two hours before it is wanted; you have to wait till the last moment, by which time a mass of other work has accumulated, and then do it all together, in frantic haste. The result is that at meal-times everyone is doing two men's work, which is impossible without noise and quarrelling. Indeed the quarrels are a necessary part of the process, for the pace would never be kept up if everyone did not accuse everyone else of idling. It was for this reason that during the rush hours the whole staff raged and cursed like demons. At those times there was scarcely a verb in the hotel except *foutre*. A girl in the bakery, aged sixteen, used oaths that would have defeated a cabman. (Did not Hamlet say 'cursing like a scullion'? No doubt Shakespeare had watched scullions at work.) But we are not losing our heads and wasting time; we were just stimulating one another for the effort of packing four hours' work into two hours.

What keeps a hotel going is the fact that the employees take a genuine pride in their work, beastly and silly though it is. If a man idles, the others soon find him out, and conspire against him to get him sacked. Cooks, waiters and *plongeurs* differ greatly in outlook, but they are all alike in being proud of their efficiency.

Undoubtedly the most workmanlike class, and the least servile, are the cooks. They do not earn quite so much as waiters, but their prestige is higher and their employment steadier. The cook does not look upon himself as a servant, but as a skilled workman: he is generally called '*un ouvrier*', which a waiter never is. He knows his power – knows that he alone makes or mars a restaurant, and that if he is five minutes late everything is out of gear, He despises the whole non-cooking staff, and makes it a point of honour to insult everyone below the head waiter. And he takes a genuine artistic pride in his work, which demands very great skill. It is not the cooking that is so difficult, but the doing everything to time. Between breakfast and luncheon the head cook at the Hôtel X. would receive orders for several hundred dishes, all to be served at different times; he cooked few of them himself, but he gave instructions about all of them and inspected them before they were sent up. His memory was wonderful. The vouchers were pinned on a board, but the head cook seldom looked at them; everything was stored in his mind, and exactly to the minute, as each dish fell due, he would call out, '*Faites marcher une côtelette de veau*' (or whatever it was) unfailingly. He was an insufferable bully, but he was also an artist. It is for their punctuality, and not for any superiority in technique, that men cooks are preferred to women.

The waiter's outlook is quite different. He too is proud in a way of his skill, but his skill is chiefly in being servile. His work gives him the mentality, not of a workman, but of a snob. He lives perpetually in sight of rich people, stands at their tables, listens to their conversation, sucks up to them with smiles and discreet little jokes. He has the pleasure of spending money by proxy. Moreover, there is always the chance that he may become rich himself, for, though most waiters die poor, they have long runs of luck occasionally. At some cafés on the Grand Boulevard there is so much money to be made that the waiters actually pay the *patron* for their employment. The result is that between constantly seeing money, and hoping to get it, the waiter comes to identify himself to some extent with his employers. He will take pains to serve a meal in style, because he feels that he is participating in the meal himself.

I remember Valenti telling me of some banquet at Nice at which he had once served, and of how it cost two hundred thousand francs and was talked of for months afterwards. 'It was splendid, *mon p'tit, mais magnifique!* Jesus Christ! The champagne, the silver, the orchids – I have never seen anything like them, and I have seen some things. Ah, it was glorious!'

'But,' I said, 'you were only there to wait?'

'Oh, of course. But still it was splendid.'

The moral is, never be sorry for a waiter. Sometimes when you sit in a restaurant, still stuffing yourself half an hour after closing time, you feel that the tired waiter at your side must surely be despising you. But he is not. He is not thinking as he looks at you, 'What an overfed lout'; he is thinking, 'One day, when I have saved enough money, I shall be able to imitate that man.' He is ministering to a kind of pleasure he thoroughly understands and admires. And that is why waiters are seldom Socialists, have no effective trade union, and will work twelve hours a day – they work fifteen hours seven days a week, in many cafés. They are snobs, and they find the servile nature of their work rather congenial.

The *plongeurs*, again, have a different outlook. Theirs is a job which offers no prospects, is intensely exhausting, and at the same time has not a trace of skill or interest; the sort of job that would always be done by women if women were strong enough. All that is required of them is to be constantly on the run, and to put up with long hours and a stuffy atmosphere. They have no way of escaping from this life, for they cannot save a penny from their wages, and working from sixty to a hundred hours a week leaves them no time to train for anything else. The best they can hope for is to find a slightly softer job as night-watchman or lavatory attendant.

And yet the *plongeurs*, low as they are, also have a kind of pride. It is the pride of the drudge – the man who is equal to no matter what quantity of work. At that level, the mere power to go on working like an ox is about the only virtue attainable. *Débrouillard* is what every *plongeur* wants to be called. A *débrouillard* is a man who, even when he is told to do the impossible, will *se débrouiller* – get it done somehow. One of the kitchen *plongeurs* at the Hôtel X., a German, was well known as a *débrouillard*. One night an English lord came to the hotel, and the waiters were in despair, for the lord had asked for peaches, and there were none in stock; it was late at night, and the shops would be shut. 'Leave it to me,' said the German. He went out, and in ten minutes he was back with four peaches. He had gone into a neighbouring restaurant and stolen them. That is what is meant by a *débrouillard*. The English lord paid for the peaches at twenty francs each.

Mario, who was in charge of the cafeterie, had the typical drudge mentality. All he thought of was getting through the '*boulot*', and he defied you to give him too much of it. Fourteen years underground had left him with about as much natural laziness as a piston rod. '*Faut être dur*,' he used to say when anyone complained. You still often hear *plongeurs* boast, '*Je suis dur*' – as though they were soldiers, not male charwomen.

Thus everyone in the hotel had his sense of honour, and when the press of work came we were all ready for a grand concerted effort to get through it. The constant war between the different departments also made for efficiency, for everyone clung to his own privileges and tried to stop the others idling and pilfering.

This is the good side of hotel work. In a hotel a huge and complicated machine is kept running by an inadequate staff, because every man has a well-defined job and does it scrupulously. But there is a weak point, and it is this – that the job the staff are doing is not necessarily what the customer pays for. The customer pays, as he sees it, for good service; the employee is paid, as he sees it, for the *boulot* – meaning, as a rule, an imitation of good service. The result is that, though hotels are miracles of punctuality, they are worse than the worst private houses in the things that matter.

Take cleanliness, for example. The dirt in the Hôtel X., as soon as one penetrated into the service quarters, was revolting. Our cafeterie had year-old filth in all the dark corners, and the bread-bin was infested with cockroaches. Once I suggested killing these beasts to Mario. 'Why kill the poor animals?' he said reproachfully. The others laughed when I wanted to wash my hands before touching the butter. Yet we were clean where we recognized cleanliness as part of the *boulot*. We scrubbed the tables and polished the brasswork regularly, because we had orders to do that; but we had no orders to be genuinely clean, and in any case we had no time for it. We were simply carrying out our duties; and as our first duty was punctuality, we saved time by being dirty.

In the kitchen the dirt was worse. It is not a figure of speech, it is a mere statement of fact to say that a French cook will spit in the soup – that is, if he is not going to drink it himself. He is an artist, but his art is not cleanliness. To a certain extent he is even dirty because he is an artist, for food, to look smart, needs dirty treatment. When a steak, for instance, is brought up for the head cook's inspection, he does not handle it with a fork. He picks it up in his fingers and slaps it down, runs his thumb round the dish and licks it to taste the gravy, runs it round and licks again, then steps back and contemplates the piece of meat like an artist judging a picture, then presses it lovingly into place with his fat, pink fingers, every one of which he has licked a hundred times that morning. When he is satisfied, he takes a cloth and wipes his fingerprints from the dish, and hands it to the waiter. And the waiter, of course, dips *his* fingers into the gravy – his nasty, greasy fingers which he is for ever running through his brilliantined hair. Whenever one pays more than, say, ten francs for a dish of meat in Paris, one may be certain that it has been fingered in this manner. In very cheap restaurants it is different; there, the same trouble is not taken over the food, and it is just forked out of the pan and flung onto a plate, without handling. Roughly speaking, the more one pays for food, the more sweat and spittle one is obliged to eat with it.

Dirtiness is inherent in hotels and restaurants, because sound food is sacrificed to punctuality and smartness. The hotel employee is too busy getting food ready to remember that it is meant to be eaten. A meal is simply '*une commande*' to him, just as a man dying of cancer is simply '*a case*' to the doctor. A customer orders, for example, a piece of toast. Somebody, pressed with work in a cellar deep underground, has to prepare it. How can he stop and say to himself, 'This toast is to be eaten – I must make it eatable'? All he knows is that it must look right and must be ready in three minutes. Some large drops of sweat fall from his forehead onto the toast. Why should he worry? Presently the toast falls among the filthy sawdust on the floor. Why trouble to make a new piece? It is much quicker to wipe the sawdust off. On the way upstairs the toast falls again, butter side down. Another wipe is all it needs. And so with everything. The only food at the Hôtel X. which was ever prepared cleanly was the staff's, and the *patron*'s. The maxim, repeated by everyone, was: 'Look out for the *patron*, and for the clients, *s'en f —— pas mal!*' Everywhere in the service quarters dirt festered – a secret vein of dirt, running through the great garish hotel like the intestines through a man's body.

Apart from the dirt, the *patron* swindled the customers wholeheartedly. For the most part the materials of the food were very bad, though the cooks knew how to serve it up in style. The meat was at best ordinary, and as to the vegetables, no good housekeeper would have looked at them in the market.

The cream, by a standing order, was diluted with milk. The tea and coffee were of inferior sorts, and the jam was synthetic stuff out of vast, unlabelled tins. All the cheaper wines, according to Boris, were corked *vin ordinaire*. There was a rule that employees must pay for anything they spoiled, and in consequence damaged things were seldom thrown away. Once the waiter on the third floor dropped a roast chicken down the shaft of our service lift, where it fell into a litter of broken bread, torn paper and so forth at the bottom. We simply wiped it with a cloth and sent it up again. Upstairs there were dirty tales of once-used sheets not being washed, but simply damped, ironed and put back on the beds. The *patron* was as mean to us as to the customers. Throughout the vast hotel there was not, for instance, such a thing as a brush and pan; one had to manage with a broom and a piece of cardboard. And the staff lavatory was worthy of Central Asia, and there was no place to wash one's hands, except the sinks used for washing crockery.

In spite of all this the Hôtel X. was one of the dozen most expensive hotels in Paris, and the customers paid startling prices. The ordinary charge for a night's lodging, not including breakfast, was two hundred francs. All wine and tobacco were sold at exactly double shop prices, though of course the *patron* bought at the wholesale price. If a customer had a title, or was reputed to be a millionaire, all his charges went up automatically. One morning on the fourth floor an American who was on diet wanted only salt and hot water for his breakfast. Valenti was furious. 'Jesus Christ!' he said, 'what about my ten per cent? Ten per cent of salt and water!' And he charged twenty-five francs for the breakfast. The customer paid without a murmur.

According to Boris, the same kind of thing went on in all Paris hotels, or at least in all the big, expensive ones. But I imagine that the customers at the Hôtel X. were especially easy to swindle, for they were mostly Americans, with a sprinkling of English – no French – and seemed to know nothing whatever about good food. They would stuff themselves with disgusting American 'cereals', and eat marmalade at tea, and drink vermouth after dinner, and order a *poulet à la reine* at a hundred francs and then souse it in Worcester sauce. One customer, from Pittsburg, dined every night in his bedroom on grape-nuts, scrambled eggs and cocoa. Perhaps it hardly matters whether such people are swindled or not.

Chapter Fifteen

I heard queer tales in the hotel. There were tales of dope fiends, of old debauchees who frequented hotels in search of pretty page boys, of thefts and blackmail. Mario told me of a hotel in which he had been, where a chambermaid stole a priceless diamond ring from an American lady. For days the staff were searched as they left work, and two detectives searched the hotel from top to bottom, but the ring was never found. The chambermaid had a lover in the bakery, and he had baked the ring into a roll, where it lay unsuspected until the search was over.

Once Valenti, at a slack time, told me a story about himself.

'You know, *mon p'tit*, this hotel life is all very well, but it's the devil when you're out of work. I expect you know what it is to go without eating, eh? *Forcément*, otherwise you wouldn't be scrubbing dishes. Well, I'm not a poor devil of a *plongeur*; I'm a waiter, and *I* went five days without eating, once. Five days without even a crust of bread – Jesus Christ!

'I tell you, those five days were the devil. The only good thing was, I had my rent paid in advance. I was living in a dirty, cheap little hotel in the Rue Sainte Éloise up in the Latin quarter. It was called the Hôtel Suzanne May, after some famous prostitute of the time of the Empire. I was starving, and there was nothing I could do; I couldn't even go to the cafés where the hotel proprietors come to engage waiters, because I hadn't the price of a drink. All I could do was to lie in bed getting weaker and weaker, and watching the bugs running about the ceiling. I don't want to go through that again, I can tell you.

'In the afternoon of the fifth day I went half mad; at least, that's how it seems to me now. There was an old faded print of a woman's head hanging on the wall of my room, and I took to wondering who it could be; and after about an hour I realized that it must be Sainte Éloise, who was the patron saint of the quarter. I had never taken any notice of the thing before, but now, as I lay staring at it, a most extraordinary idea came into my head.

' "*Écoute, mon cher*," I said to myself, "you'll be starving to death if this goes on much longer. You've got to do something. Why not try a prayer to Sainte Éloise? Go down on your knees and ask her to send you some money. After all, it can't do any harm. Try it!"

'Mad, eh? Still, a man will do anything when he's hungry. Besides, as I said, it couldn't do any harm. I got out of bed and began praying. I said:

' "Dear Sainte Éloise, if you exist, please send me some money. I don't ask for much – just enough to buy some bread and a bottle of wine and get my strength back. Three or four francs would do. You don't know how grateful I'll be, Sainte Éloise, if you help me this once. And be sure, if you send me anything, the first thing I'll do will be to go and burn a candle for you, at your church down the street. Amen."

'I put in that about the candle, because I had heard that saints like having candles burnt in their honour. I meant to keep my promise, of course. But I am an atheist and I didn't really believe that anything would come of it.

'Well, I got into bed again, and five minutes later there came a bang at the door. It was a girl called Maria, a big fat peasant girl who lived at our hotel. She was a very stupid girl, but a good sort, and I didn't much care for her to see me in the state I was in.

'She cried out at the sight of me. "*Nom de Dieur!*" she said, "what's the matter with you? What are you doing in bed at this time of day? *Quelle mine que tu as!* You look more like a corpse than a man."

'Probably I did look a sight. I had been five days without food, most of the time in bed, and it was three days since I had had a wash or a shave. The room was a regular pigsty, too.

' "What's the matter?" said Maria again.

' "The matter!" I said; "Jesus Christ! I'm starving. I haven't eaten for five days. That's what's the matter."

'Maria was horrified. "Not eaten for five days?" she said. "But why? Haven't you any money, then?"

' "Money!" I said. "Do you suppose I should be starving if I had money? I've got just five sous in the world, and I've pawned everything. Look round the room and see if there's anything more I can sell or pawn. If you can find anything that will fetch fifty centimes, you're cleverer than I am."

'Maria began looking round the room. She poked here and there among a lot of rubbish that was lying about, and then suddenly she got quite excited. Her great thick mouth fell open with astonishment.

'"You idiot!" she cried out. "Imbecile! What's *this*, then?"

'I saw that she had picked up an empty oil *bidon* that had been lying in the corner. I had bought it weeks before, for an oil lamp I had before I sold my things.

'"That?" I said. "That's an oil *bidon*. What about it?"

'"Imbecile! Didn't you pay three francs fifty deposit on it?"

'Now, of course I had paid the three francs fifty. They always make you pay a deposit on the *bidon*, and you get it back when the *bidon* is returned. But I'd forgotten all about it.

'"Yes –" I began.

'"Idiot!" shouted Maria again. She got so excited that she began to dance about until I thought her sabots would go through the floor. "Idiot! *T'es fou! T'es fou!* What have you got to do but take it back to the shop and get your deposit back? Starving, with three francs fifty staring you in the face! Imbecile!"

'I can hardly believe now that in all those five days I had never once thought of taking the *bidon* back to the shop. As good as three francs fifty in hard cash, and it had never occurred to me! I sat up in bed. "Quick!" I shouted to Maria, "you take it for me. Take it to the grocer's at the corner – run like the devil. And bring back food!"

'Maria didn't need to be told. She grabbed the *bidon* and went clattering down the stairs like a herd of elephants, and in three minutes she was back with two pounds of bread under one arm and a half-litre bottle of wine under the other. I didn't stop to thank her; I just seized the bread and sank my teeth in it. Have you noticed how bread tastes when you have been hungry for a long time? Cold, wet, doughy – like putty almost. But, Jesus Christ, how good it was! As for the wine, I sucked it all down in one draught, and it seemed to go straight into my veins and flow round my body like new blood. Ah, that made a difference!

'I wolfed the whole two pounds of bread without stopping to take breath. Maria stood with her hands on her hips, watching me eat. "Well, you feel better, eh?" she said when I had finished.

'"Better!" I said. "I feel perfect! I'm not the same man as I was five minutes ago. There's only one thing in the world I need now – a cigarette."

'Maria put her hand in her apron pocket. "You can't have it," she said. "I've no money. This is all I had left out of your three francs fifty – seven sous. It's no good; the cheapest cigarettes are twelve sous a packet."

'"Then I can have them!" I said. "Jesus Christ, what a piece of luck! I've got five sous – it's just enough."

'Maria took the twelve sous and was starting out to the tobacconist's. And then something I had forgotten all this time came into my head. There was that cursed Sainte Éloise! I had promised her a candle if she sent me money; and really, who could say that prayer hadn't come true? "Three or four francs," I had said; and the next moment along came three francs fifty. There was no getting away from it. I should have to spend my twelve sous on a candle.

'I called Maria back. "It's no use," I said; "there is Sainte Eloise – I have promised her a candle. The twelve sous will have to go on that. Silly, isn't it? I can't have my cigarettes after all."

'"Sainte Éloise?" said Maria. "What about Sainte Éloise?"

'"I prayed to her for money and promised her a candle," I said. "She answered the prayer – at any rate, the money turned up. I shall have to buy that candle. It's a nuisance, but it seems to me I must keep my promise."

'"But what put Sainte Éloise into your head?" said Maria.

'"It was her picture," I said, and I explained the whole thing. "There she is, you see," I said, and I pointed to the picture on the wall.

'Maria looked at the picture, and then to my surprise she burst into shouts of laughter. She laughed more and more, stamping about the room and holding her fat sides as though they would burst. I thought she had gone mad. It was two minutes before she could speak.

'"Idiot!" she cried at last. "*T'es fou! T'es fou!* Do you mean to tell me you really knelt down and prayed to that picture? Who told you it was Sainte Éloise?"

'"But I made sure it was Sainte Éloise!" I said.

'"Imbecile! It isn't Sainte Éloise at all. Who do you think it is?"

'"Who?" I said.

'"It is Suzanne May, the woman this hotel is called after."

'I had been praying to Suzanne May, the famous prostitute of the Empire . . .

'But, after all, I wasn't sorry. Maria and I had a good laugh, and then we talked it over, and we made out that I didn't owe Sainte Éloise anything. Clearly it wasn't she who had answered the prayer, and there was no need to buy her a candle. So I had my packet of cigarettes after all.'

Chapter Sixteen

Time went on and the Auberge de Jehan Cottard showed no signs of opening. Boris and I went down there one day during our afternoon interval and found that none of the alterations had been done, except the indecent pictures, and there were three duns instead of two. The *patron* greeted us with his usual blandness, and the next instant turned to me (his prospective dishwasher) and borrowed five francs. After that I felt certain that the restaurant would never get beyond talk. The *patron*, however, again named the opening for 'exactly a fortnight from today', and introduced us to the woman who was to do the cooking, a Baltic Russian five feet tall and a yard across the hips. She told us that she had been a singer before she came down to cooking, and that she was very artistic and adored English literature, especially *La Case de l'Oncle Tom*.

In a fortnight I had got so used to the routine of a *plongeur*'s life that I could hardly imagine anything different. It was a life without much variation. At a quarter to six one woke with a sudden start, tumbled into grease-stiffened clothes, and hurried out with dirty face and protesting muscles. It was dawn, and the windows were dark except for the workmen's cafés. The sky was like a vast flat wall of cobalt, with roofs and spires of black paper pasted upon it. Drowsy men were sweeping the pavements with ten-foot besoms, and ragged families picking over the dustbins. Workmen, and girls with a piece of chocolate in one hand and a *croissant* in the other, were pouring into the Metro stations. Trams, filled with more workmen, boomed gloomily past. One hastened down to the station, fought for a place – one does literally have to fight on the Paris Metro at six in the morning – and stood jammed in the swaying mass of passengers, nose to nose with some hideous French face, breathing sour wine and garlic. And then one descended into the labyrinth of the hotel basement, and forgot daylight till two o'clock, when the sun was hot and the town black with people and cars.

After my first week at the hotel I always spent the afternoon interval in sleeping, or, when I had money, in a *bistro*. Except for a few ambitious waiters who went to English classes, the whole staff wasted their leisure in this way; one seemed too lazy after the morning's work to do anything better. Sometimes half a dozen *plongeurs* would make up a party and go to an abominable brothel in the Rue de Sieyès, where the charge was only five francs twenty-five centimes – tenpence half-penny. It was nicknamed '*le prix fixe*', and they used to describe their experiences there as a great joke. It was a favourite rendezvous of hotel workers. The *plongeurs*' wages did not allow them to marry, and no doubt work in the basement does not encourage fastidious feelings.

For another four hours one was in the cellars, and then one emerged, sweating, into the cool street. It was lamplight – that strange purplish gleam of the Paris lamps – and beyond the river the Eiffel Tower flashed from top to bottom with zigzag skysigns, like enormous snakes of fire. Streams of cars glided silently to and fro, and women, exquisite-looking in the dim light, strolled up and down the arcade. Sometimes a woman would glance at Boris or me, and then, noticing our greasy clothes, look hastily away again. One fought another battle in the Metro and was home by ten. Generally from ten to midnight I went to a little *bistro* in our street, an underground place frequented by Arab navvies. It was a bad place for fights, and I sometimes saw bottles thrown, once with fearful effect, but as a rule the Arabs fought among themselves and let Christians alone. Raki, the Arab drink, was very cheap, and the *bistro* was open at all hours, for the Arabs – lucky men – had the power of working all day and drinking all night.

It was the typical life of a *plongeur*, and it did not seem a bad life at the time. I had no sensation of poverty, for even after paying my rent and setting aside enough for tobacco and journeys and my food on Sundays, I still had four francs a day for drinks, and four francs was wealth. There was – it is hard to express it – a sort of heavy contentment, the contentment a well-fed beast might feel, in a life which had become so simple. For nothing could be simpler than the life of a *plongeur*. He lives in a rhythm between work and sleep, without time to think, hardly conscious of the exterior world; his Paris has shrunk to the hotel, the Metro, a few *bistros* and his bed. If he goes afield, it is only a few streets away, on a trip with some servant-girl who sits on his knee swallowing oysters and beer. On his free day he lies in bed till noon, puts on a clean shirt, throws dice for drinks, and after lunch goes back to bed again. Nothing is quite real to him but the *boulot*, drinks and sleep; and of these sleep is the most important.

One night, in the small hours, there was a murder just beneath my window. I was woken by a fearful uproar, and, going to the window, saw a man lying flat on the stones below; I could see the murderers, three of them, flitting away at the end of the street. Some of us went down and found that the man was quite dead, his skull cracked with a piece of lead piping. I remember the colour of his blood, curiously purple, like wine; it was still on the cobbles when I came home that evening, and they said the schoolchildren had come from miles round to see it. But the thing that strikes me in looking back is that I was in bed and asleep within three minutes of the murder. So were most of the people in the street; we just made sure that the man was done for, and went straight back to bed. We were working people, and where was the sense of wasting sleep over a murder?

Work in the hotel taught me the true value of sleep, just as being hungry had taught me the true value of food. Sleep had ceased to be a mere physical necessity; it was something voluptuous, a debauch more than a relief. I had no more trouble with the bugs. Mario had told me of a sure remedy for them, namely pepper, strewed thick over the bedclothes. It made me sneeze, but the bugs all hated it, and emigrated to other rooms.

Chapter Seventeen

With thirty francs a week to spend on drinks I could take part in the social life of the quarter. We had some jolly evenings, on Saturdays, in the little *bistro* at the foot of the Hôtel des Trois Moineaux.

The brick-floored room, fifteen feet square, was packed with twenty people, and the air dim with smoke. The noise was deafening, for everyone was either talking at the top of his voice or singing. Sometimes it was just a confused din of voices; sometimes everyone would burst out together in the same song – the 'Marseillaise', or the 'Internationale', or ' madelon', or 'Les Fraises et les Framboises'. Azaya, a great clumping peasant girl who worked fourteen hours a day in a glass factory, sang a song about, '*Il a per*du *ses pantalons, tout en dans*ant *le Charleston*'. Her friend Marinette, a thin, dark Corsican girl of obstinate virtue, tied her knees together and danced the *danse du ventre*. The old Rougiers wandered in and out, cadging drinks and trying to tell a long, involved story about someone who had once cheated them over a bedstead. R., cadaverous and silent, sat in his corner quietly boozing. Charlie, drunk, half danced, half staggered to and fro with a glass of sham absinthe balanced in one fat hand, pinching the women's breasts and declaiming poetry. People played darts and diced for drinks. Manuel, a Spaniard, dragged the girls to the bar and shook the dice-box against their bellies, for luck. Madame F. stood at the bar rapidly pouring *chopines* of wine through the pewter funnel with a wet dishcloth always handy, because every man in the room tried to make love to her. Two children, bastards of big Louis the bricklayer, sat in a corner sharing a glass of *sirop*. Everyone was very happy, overwhelmingly certain that the world was a good place and we a notable set of people.

For an hour the noise scarcely slackened. Then about midnight there was a piercing shout of '*Citoyens!*' and the sound of a chair falling over. A blond, red-faced workman had risen to his feet and was banging a bottle on the table. Everyone stopped singing; the word went round, 'Sh! Furex is starting!' Furex was a strange creature, a Limousin stonemason who worked steadily all the week and drank himself into a kind of paroxysm on Saturdays. He had lost his memory and could not remember anything before the war, and he would have gone to pieces through drink if Madame F. had not taken care of him. On

Saturday evenings at about five o'clock she would say to someone, 'Catch Furex before he spends his wages', and when he had been caught she would take away his money, leaving him enough for one good drink. One week he escaped, and, rolling blind drunk in the Place Monge, was run over by a car and badly hurt.

The queer thing about Furex was that, though he was a Communist when sober, he turned violently patriotic when drunk. He started the evening with good Communist principles, but after four or five litres he was a rampant Chauvinist, denouncing spies, challenging all foreigners to fight, and, if he was not prevented, throwing bottles. It was at this stage that he made his speech – for he made a patriotic speech every Saturday night. The speech was always the same, word for word. It ran:

'Citizens of the Republic, are there any Frenchmen here? If there are any Frenchmen here, I rise to remind them – to remind them in effect, of the glorious days of the war. When one looks back upon that time of comradeship and heroism – one looks back, in effect, upon that time of comradeship and heroism. When one remembers the heroes who are dead – one remembers, in effect, the heroes who are dead. Citizens of the Republic, I was wounded at Verdun –'

Here he partially undressed and showed the wound he had received at Verdun. There were shouts of applause. We thought nothing in the world could be funnier than this speech of Furex's. He was a well-known spectacle in the quarter; people used to come in from other *bistros* to watch him when his fit started.

The word was passed round to bait Furex. With a wink to the others someone called for silence, and asked him to sing the 'Marseillaise'. He sang it well, in a fine bass voice, with patriotic gurgling noises deep down in his chest when he came to '*Aux arrmes, citoyens! Forrmez vos bataillons!*' Veritable tears rolled down his cheeks; he was too drunk to see that everyone was laughing at him. Then, before he had finished, two strong workmen seized him by either arm and held him down, while Azaya shouted, '*Vive l'Allemagne!*' just out of his reach. Furex's face went purple at such infamy. Everyone in the *bistro* began shouting together, '*Vive l'Allemagne! A bas la France!*' while Furex struggled to get at them. But suddenly he spoiled the fun. His face turned pale and doleful, his limbs went limp, and before anyone could stop him he was sick on the table. Then Madame F. hoisted him like a sack and carried him up to bed. In the morning he reappeared quiet and civil, and bought a copy of *L'Humanité*.

The table was wiped with a cloth, Madame F. brought more litre bottles and loaves of bread, and we settled down to serious drinking. There were more songs. An itinerant singer came in with his banjo and performed for five-sou pieces. An Arab and a girl from the *bistro* down the street did a dance, the man wielding a painted wooden phallus the size of a rolling-pin. There were gaps in the noise now. People had begun to talk about their love-affairs, and the war, and the barbel fishing in the Seine, and the best way to *faire la révolution*, and to tell stories. Charlie, grown sober again, captured the conversation and talked about his soul for five minutes. The doors and windows were opened to cool the room. The street was emptying, and in the distance one could hear the lonely milk train thundering down the Boulevard St Michel. The air blew cold on our foreheads, and the coarse African wine still tasted good: we were still happy, but meditatively, with the shouting and hilarious mood finished.

By one o'clock we were not happy any longer. We felt the joy of the evening wearing thin, and called hastily for more bottles, but Madame F. was watering the wine now, and it did not taste the same. Men grew quarrelsome. The girls were violently kissed and hands thrust into their bosoms and they made off lest worse should happen. Big Louis, the bricklayer, was drunk, and crawled about the floor barking and pretending to be a dog. The others grew tired of him and kicked at him as he went past. People seized each other by the arm and began long rambling confessions, and were angry when these were not listened to. The crowd thinned. Manuel and another man, both gamblers, went across to the Arab *bistro*, where card-playing went on till daylight. Charlie suddenly borrowed thirty francs from Madame F. and disappeared, probably to a brothel. Men began to empty their glasses, call briefly, *''Sieurs, dames!'* and go off to bed.

By half-past one the last drop of pleasure had evaporated, leaving nothing but headaches. We perceived that we were not splendid inhabitants of a splendid world, but a crew of underpaid workmen grown squalidly and dismally drunk. We went on swallowing the wine, but it was only from habit, and the stuff seemed suddenly nauseating. One's head had swollen up like a balloon, the floor rocked, one's tongue and lips were strained purple. At last it was no use keeping it up any longer. Several men went out into the yard behind the *bistro* and were sick. We crawled up to bed, tumbled down half dressed, and stayed there ten hours.

Most of my Saturday nights went in this way. On the whole, the two hours when one was perfectly and wildly happy seemed worth the subsequent headache. For many men in the quarter, unmarried and with no future to think of, the weekly drinking-bout was the one thing that made life worth living.

Chapter Eighteen

Charlie told us a good story one Saturday night in the *bistro*. Try and picture him – drunk, but sober enought to talk consecutively. He bangs on the zinc bar and yells for silence:

'Silence, *messieurs et dames* – silence, I implore you! Listen to this story, that I am about to tell you. A memorable story, an instructive story, one of the souvenirs of a refined and civilized life. Silence, *messieurs et dames!*

'It happened at a time when I was hard up. You know what that is like – how damnable, that a man of refinement should ever be in such a condition. My money had not come from home; I had pawned everything, and there was nothing open to me except to work, which is a thing I will not do. I was living with a girl at the time – Yvonne her name was – a great half-witted peasant girl like Azaya there, with yellow hair and fat legs. The two of us had eaten nothing in three days. *Mon Dieu*, what sufferings! The girl used to walk up and down the room with her hands on her belly, howling like a dog that she was dying of starvation. It was terrible.

'But to a man of intelligence nothing is impossible. I propounded to myself the question, "What is the easiest way to get money without working?" And immediately the answer came: "To get money easily one must be a woman.

Has not every woman something to sell?" And then, as I lay reflecting upon the things I should do if I were a woman, an idea came into my head. I remembered the Government maternity hospitals – you know the Government maternity hospitals? They are places where women who are *enceinte* are given meals free and no questions are asked. It is done to encourage childbearing.

Any woman can go there and demand a meal, and she is given it immediately.

'"*Mon Dieu!*" I thought, "if only I were a woman! I would eat at one of those places every day. Who can tell whether a woman is *enceinte* or not, without an examination?"

'I turned to Yvonne. "Stop that insufferable bawling." I said, "I have thought of a way to get food."

'"How?" said she.

'"It is simple," I said. 'Go to the Government maternity hospital. Tell them you are *enceinte* and ask for food. They will give you a good meal and ask no questions.'

'Yvonne was appalled. "*Mais, mon Dieu,*" she cried, "I am not *enceinte*!"

'"Who cares?" I said. "That is easily remedied. What do you need except a cushion – two cushions if necessary? It is an inspiration from heaven, *ma chère*. Don't waste it."

'Well, in the end I persuaded her, and then we borrowed a cushion and I got her ready and took her to the maternity hospital. They received her with open arms. They gave her cabbage soup, a ragoût of beef, a purée of potatoes, bread and cheese and beer, and all kinds of advice about her baby. Yvonne gorged till she almost burst her skin, and managed to slip some of the bread and cheese into her pocket for me. I took her there every day until I had money again. My intelligence had saved us.

'Everything went well until a year later. I was with Yvonne again, and one day we were walking down the Boulevard Port Royal, near the barracks. Suddenly Yvonne's mouth fell open, and she began turning red and white, and red again.

'"*Mon Dieu!*" she cried, "look at that who is coming! It is the nurse who was in charge at the maternity hospital. I am ruined!"

'"Quick!" I said, "run!" But it was too late. The nurse had recognized Yvonne, and she came straight up to us, smiling. She was a big fat woman with a gold pince-nez and red cheeks like the cheeks of an apple. A motherly, interfering kind of woman.

'"I hope you are well, *ma petite?*" she said kindly. "And your baby, is he well too? Was it a boy, as you were hoping?"

'Yvonne had begun trembling so hard that I had to grip her arm. "No," she said at last.

'"Ah, then, *évidemment*, it was a girl?"

'Thereupon Yvonne, the idiot, lost her head completely. "No," she actually said again!

'The nurse was taken aback. "*Comment!*" she exclaimed, "neither a boy nor a girl! But how can that be?"

'Figure to yourselves, *messieurs et dames*, it was a dangerous moment. Yvonne had turned the colour of a beetroot and she looked ready to burst into tears; another second and she would have confessed everything. Heaven knows what might have happened. But as for me, I had kept my head; I stepped in and saved the situation.

'"It was twins," I said calmly.

'"Twins!" exclaimed the nurse. And she was so pleased that she took Yvonne by the shoulders and embraced her on both cheeks, publicly.

'Yes, twins . . .'

Chapter Nineteen

One day, when we had been at the Hôtel X. five or six weeks, Boris disappeared without notice. In the evening I found him waiting for me in the Rue de Rivoli. He slapped me gaily on the shoulder.

'Free at last, *mon ami!* You can give notice in the morning. The Auberge opens tomorrow.'

'Tomorrow?'

'Well, possibly we shall need a day or two to arrange things. But, at any rate, no more *cafeterie! Nous sommes lancés, mon ami!* My tail coat is out of pawn already.'

His manner was so hearty that I felt sure there was something wrong, and I did not at all want to leave my safe and comfortable job at the hotel. However, I had promised Boris, so I gave notice, and the next morning at seven went down to the Auberge de Jehan Cottard. It was locked, and I went in search of Boris, who had once more bolted from his lodgings and taken a room in the Rue de la Croix Nivert. I found him asleep, together with a girl whom he had picked up the night before, and who he told me was 'of a very sympathetic temperament'. As to the restaurant, he said that it was all arranged; there were only a few little things to be seen to before we opened.

At ten I managed to get Boris out of bed, and we unlocked the restaurant. At a glance I saw what the 'few little things' amounted to. It was briefly this: that the alterations had not been touched since our last visit. The stoves for the kitchen had not arrived, the water and electricity had not been laid on, and there was all manner of painting, polishing and carpentering to be done. Nothing short of a miracle could open the restaurant within ten days, and by the look of things it might collapse without even opening. It was obvious what had happened. The *patron* was short of money, and he had engaged the staff (there were four of us) in order to use us instead of workmen. He would be getting our services almost free, for waiters are paid no wages, and though he would have to pay me, he would not be feeding me till the restaurant opened. In effect, he had swindled us of several hundred francs by sending for us before the restaurant was open. We had thrown up a good job for nothing.

Boris, however, was full of hope. He had only one idea in his head, namely, that here at last was a chance of being a waiter and wearing a tail coat once more. For this he was quite willing to do ten days' work unpaid, with the chance of being left jobless in the end. 'Patience!' he kept saying. 'That will arrange itself. Wait till the restaurant opens, and we'll get it all back. Patience, *mon ami!*'

We needed patience, for days passed and the restaurant did not even progress towards opening. We cleaned out the cellars, fixed the shelves, distempered the walls, polished the woodwork, whitewashed the ceiling, stained the floor; but the main work, the plumbing and gasfitting and electricity, was still not done, because the *patron* could not pay the bills. Evidently he was almost penniless, for he refused the smallest charges, and he had a trick of swiftly disappearing when asked for money. His blend of shiftiness and aristocratic manners made him very hard to deal with. Melancholy duns came looking for him at all hours, and by instruction we always told them that he was at Fontainebleau, or Saint Cloud, or some other place that was safely distant. Meanwhile, I was getting hungrier and hungrier. I had left the hotel with thirty francs, and I had to go back immediately to a diet of dry bread. Boris had managed in the beginning to extract an advance of sixty francs from the *patron*, but he had spent half of it, in redeeming his waiter's clothes, and half on the girl of sympathetic temperament. He borrowed three francs a day from Jules, the second waiter, and spent it on bread. Some days we had not even money for tobacco.

Sometimes the cook came to see how things were getting on, and when she saw that the kitchen was still bare of pots and pans she usually wept. Jules, the second waiter, refused steadily to help with the work. He was a Magyar, a little dark, sharp-featured fellow in spectacles, and very talkative; he had been a medical student, but had abandoned his training for lack of money. He had a taste for talking while other people were working, and he told me all about himself and his ideas. It appeared that he was a Communist, and had various strange theories (he could prove to you by figures that it was wrong to work), and he was also, like most Magyars, passionately proud. Proud and lazy men do not make good waiters. It was Jules's dearest boast that once when a customer in a restaurant had insulted him, he had poured a plate of hot soup down the customer's neck, and then walked straight out without even waiting to be sacked.

As each day went by Jules grew more and more enraged at the trick the *patron* had played on us. He had a spluttering, oratorical way of talking. He used to walk up and down shaking his fist, and trying to incite me not to work:

'Put that brush down, you fool! You and I belong to proud races; we don't work for nothing, like these damned Russian serfs. I tell you, to be cheated like this is torture to me. There have been times in my life, when someone has cheated me even of five sous, when I have vomited – yes, vomited with rage.

'Besides, *mon vieux*, don't forget that I'm a Communist. *A bas la bourgeoisie!* Did any man alive ever see me working when I could avoid it? No. And not only I don't wear myself out working, like you other fools, but I steal, just to show my independence. Once I was in a restaurant where the *patron* thought he could treat me like a dog. Well, in revenge I found out a way to steal milk from the milk-cans and seal them up again so that no one should know. I tell you I just swilled that milk down night and morning. Every day I drank four litres of milk, besides half a litre of cream. The *patron* was at his wits' end to know where the milk was going. It wasn't that I wanted milk, you understand, because I hate the stuff; it was principle, just principle.

'Well, after three days I began to get dreadful pains in my belly, and I went to the doctor. "What have you been eating?" he said. I said: "I drink four litres of milk a day, and half a litre of cream." "Four litres!" he said. "Then stop it at once. You'll burst if you go on." "What do I care?" I said. "With me principle is everything. I shall go on drinking that milk, even if I do burst."

'Well, the next day the *patron* caught me stealing milk. "You're sacked," he said; "you leave at the end of the week." "*Pardon, monsieur,*" I said, "I shall leave this morning." "No, you won't," he said, "I can't spare you till Saturday." "Very well, *mon patron*," I thought to myself, "we'll see who gets tired of it first." And then I set to work to smash the crockery. I broke nine plates the first day and thirteen the second; after that the *patron* was glad to see the last of me.

'Ah, I'm not one of your Russian *moujiks* ...

Ten days passed. It was a bad time. I was absolutely at the end of my money, and my rent was several days overdue. We loafed about the dismal empty restaurant, too hungry even to get on with the work that remained. Only Boris now believed that the restaurant would open. He had set his heart on being *maître d'hôtel*, and he invented a theory that the *patron*'s money was tied up in shares and he was waiting a favourable moment for selling. On the tenth day I had nothing to eat or smoke, and I told the *patron* that I could not continue working without an advance on my wages. As blandly as usual, the *patron* promised the advance, and then, according to his custom, vanished. I walked part of the way home, but I did not feel equal to a scene with Madame F. over the rent, so I passed the night on a bench on the boulevard. It was very uncomfortable – the arm of the seat cuts into your back – and much colder than I had expected. There was plenty of time, in the long boring hours between dawn and work, to think what a fool I had been to deliver myself into the hands of these Russians.

Then, in the morning, the luck changed. Evidently the *patron* had come to an understanding with his creditors, for he arrived with money in his pockets, set the alterations going, and gave me my advance. Boris and I bought macaroni and a piece of horse's liver, and had our first hot meal in ten days.

The workmen were brought in and the alterations made, hastily and with incredible shoddiness. The tables, for instance, were to be covered with baize, but when the *patron* found that baize was expensive he bought instead disused army blankets, smelling incorrigibly of sweat. The table-cloths (they were check, to go with the 'Norman' decorations) would cover them, of course. On the last night we were at work till two in the morning, getting things ready. The crockery did not arrive till eight, and, being new, had all to be washed. The cutlery did not arrive till the next morning, nor the linen either, so that we had to dry the crockery with a shirt of the *patron*'s and an old pillowslip belonging to the concierge. Boris and I did all the work. Jules was skulking, and the *patron* and his wife sat in the bar with a dun and some Russian friends, drinking success to the restaurant. The cook was in the kitchen with her head on the table, crying, because she was expected to cook for fifty people, and there were not pots and pans enough for ten. About midnight there was a fearful interview with some duns, who came intending to seize eight copper saucepans which the *patron* had obtained on credit. They were bought off with half a bottle of brandy.

Jules and I missed the last Metro home and had to sleep on the floor of the restaurant. The first thing we saw in the morning were two large rats sitting on the kitchen table, eating from a ham that stood there. It seemed a bad omen, and I was surer than ever that the Auberge de Jehan Cottard would turn out a failure.

Chapter Twenty

The *patron* had engaged me as kitchen *plongeur*; that is, my job was to wash up, keep the kitchen clean, prepare vegetables, make tea, coffee and sandwiches, do the simpler cooking, and run errands. The terms were, as usual, five hundred francs a month and food, but I had no free day and no fixed working hours. At the Hôtel X. I had seen catering at its best, with unlimited money and good organization. Now, at the Auberge, I learned how things are done in a thoroughly bad restaurant. It is worth describing, for there are hundreds of similar restaurants in Paris, and every visitor feeds in one of them occasionally.

I should add, by the way, that the Auberge was not the ordinary cheap eating-house frequented by students and workmen. We did not provide an adequate meal at less than twenty-five francs, and we were picturesque and artistic, which sent up our social standing. There were the indecent pictures in the bar, and the Norman decorations – sham beams on the walls, electric lights done up as candlesticks, 'peasant' pottery, even a mounting-block at the door – and the *patron* and the head waiter were Russian officers, and many of the customers titled Russian refugees. In short, we were decidedly chic.

Nevertheless, the conditions behind the kitchen door were suitable for a pigsty. For this is what our service arrangements were like.

The kitchen measured fifteen feet long by eight broad, and half this space was taken up by the stoves and tables. All the pots had to be kept on shelves out of reach, and there was only room for one dustbin. This dustbin used to be crammed full by midday, and the floor was normally an inch deep in a compost of trampled food.

For firing we had nothing but three gas-stoves, without ovens, and all joints had to be sent out to the bakery.

There was no larder. Our substitute for one was a half-roofed shed in the yard, with a tree growing in the middle of it. The meat, vegetables and so forth lay there on the bare earth, raided by rats and cats.

There was no hot water laid on. Water for washing up had to be heated in pans, and, as there was no room for these on the stoves when meals were cooking, most of the plates had to be washed in cold water. This, with soft soap and the hard Paris water, meant scraping the grease off with bits of newspaper.

We were so short of saucepans that I had to wash each one as soon as it was done with, instead of leaving them till the evening. This alone wasted probably an hour a day.

Owing to some scamping of expense in the installation, the electric light usually fused at eight in the evening. The *patron* would only allow us three candles in the kitchen, and the cook said three were unlucky, so we had only two.

Our coffee-grinder was borrowed from a *bistro* near by, and our dustbin and brooms from the concierge. After the first week a quantity of linen did not come back from the wash, as the bill was not paid. We were in trouble with the inspector of labour, who had discovered that the staff included no Frenchmen; he had several private interviews with the *patron*, who, I believe, was obliged to bribe him. The electric company was still dunning us, and when the duns found that we would buy them off with *apéritifs*, they came every morning. We were in debt at the grocery, and credit would have been stopped, only the grocer's wife (a moustachio'd woman of sixty) had taken a fancy to Jules, who was sent every morning to cajole her. Similarly I had to waste an hour every day haggling over vegetables in the Rue du Commerce, to save a few centimes.

These are the results of starting a restaurant on insufficient capital. And in these conditions the cook and I were expected to serve thirty or forty meals a day, and would later on be serving a hundred. From the first day it was too much for us. The cook's working hours were from eight in the morning till midnight, and mine from seven in the morning till half-past twelve the next morning – seventeen and a half hours, almost without a break. We never had time to sit down till five in the afternoon, and even then there was no seat except the top of the dustbin. Boris, who lived near by and had not to catch the last Metro home, worked from eight in the morning till two the next morning – eighteen hours a day, seven days a week. Such hours, though not usual, are nothing extraordinary in Paris.

Life settled at once into a routine that made the Hôtel X. seem like a holiday. Every morning at six I drove myself out of bed, did not shave, sometimes washed, hurried up to the Place d'Italie and fought for a place on the Metro. By seven I was in the desolation of the cold, filthy kitchen, with the potato skins and bones and fishtails littered on the floor, and a pile of plates, stuck together in their grease, waiting from overnight. I could not start on the plates yet, because the water was cold, and I had to fetch milk and make coffee, for the others arrived at eight and expected to find coffee ready. Also, there were always several copper saucepans to clean. Those copper saucepans are the bane of a *plongeur*'s life. They have to be scoured with sand and bunches of chain, ten minutes to each one, and then polished on the outside with Brasso. Fortunately, the art of making them has been lost and they are gradually vanishing from French kitchens, though one can still buy them second-hand.

When I had begun on the plates the cook would take me away from the plates to begin skinning onions, and when I had begun on the onions the *patron* would arrive and send me out to buy cabbages. When I came back with the cabbages the *patron*'s wife would tell me to go to some shop half a mile away and buy a pot of rouge; by the time I came back there would be more vegetables waiting, and the plates were still not done. In this way our incompetence piled one job on another throughout the day, everything in arrears.

Till ten, things went comparatively easily, though we were working fast, and no one lost his temper. The cook would find time to talk about her artistic nature, and say did I not think Tolstoi was *épatant*, and sing in a fine soprano voice as she minced beef on the board. But at ten the waiters began clamouring for their lunch, which they had early, and at eleven the first customers would be arriving. Suddenly everything became hurry and bad temper. There was not the same furious rushing and yelling as at the Hôtel X., but an atmosphere of muddle, petty spite and exasperation. Discomfort was at the bottom of it. It was unbearably cramped in the kitchen, and dishes had to be put on the floor, and one had to be thinking constantly about not stepping on them. The cook's vast buttocks banged against me as she moved to and fro. A ceaseless, nagging chorus of orders streamed from her:

'Unspeakable idiot! How many times have I told you not to bleed the beetroots? Quick, let me get to the sink! Put those knives away; get on with the potatoes. What have you done with my strainer? Oh, leave those potatoes alone. Didn't I tell you to skim the *bouillon*? Take that can of water off the stove. Never mind the washing up, chop this celery. No, not like that, you fool, like this. There! Look at you letting those peas boil over! Now get to work and scale these herrings. Look, do you call this plate clean? Wipe it on your apron. Put that salad on the floor. That's right, put it where I'm bound to step in it! Look out, that pot's boiling over! Get me down that saucepan. No, the other one. Put this on the grill. Throw those potatoes away. Don't waste time, throw them on the floor. Tread them in. Now throw down some sawdust; this floor's like a skating-rink. Look, you fool, that steak's burning! *Mon Dieu*, why did they send me an idiot for a *plongeur*? Who are you talking to? Do you realize that my aunt was a Russian countess?' etc., etc., etc.

This went on till three o'clock without much variation, except that about eleven the cook usually had a *crise de nerfs* and a flood of tears. From three to five was a fairly slack time for the waiters, but the cook was still busy, and I was working my fastest, for there was a pile of dirty plates waiting, and it was a race to get them done, or partly done, before dinner began. The washing up was doubled by the primitive conditions – a cramped draining-board, tepid water, sodden cloths, and a sink that got blocked once in an hour. By five the cook and I were feeling unsteady on our feet, not having eaten or sat down since seven. We used to collapse, she on the dustbin and I on the floor, drink a bottle of beer, and apologize for some of the things we had said in the morning. Tea was what kept us going. We took care to have a pot always stewing, and drank pints during the day.

At half-past five the hurry and quarrelling began again, and now worse than before, because everyone was tired out. The cook had a *crise de nerfs* at six and another at nine; they came on so regularly that one could have told the time by them. She would flop down on the dustbin, begin weeping hysterically, and cry out that never, no, never had she thought to come to such a life as this; her nerves would not stand it; she had studied music at Vienna; she had a bedridden husband to support, etc., etc. At another time one would have been sorry for her, but, tired as we all were, her whimpering voice merely infuriated us. Jules used to stand in the doorway and mimic her weeping. The *patron*'s wife nagged, and Boris and Jules quarrelled all day, because Jules shirked his work, and Boris, as head waiter, claimed the larger share of the tips. Only the second day after the restaurant opened, they came to blows in the kitchen over a two-franc tip, and the cook and I had to separate them. The only person who never forgot his manners was the *patron*. He kept the same hours as the rest of us, but he had no work to do, for it was his wife who really managed things. His sole job, besides ordering the supplies, was to stand in the bar smoking cigarettes and looking gentlemanly, and he did that to perfection.

The cook and I generally found time to eat our dinner between ten and eleven o'clock. At midnight the cook would steal a packet of food for her husband, stow it under her clothes, and make off, whimpering that these hours would kill her and she would give notice in the morning. Jules also left at midnight, usually after a dispute with Boris, who had to look after the bar till two. Between twelve and half-past I did what I could to finish the washing up. There was no time to attempt doing the work properly, and I used simply to rub the grease off the plates with table-napkins. As for the dirt on the floor, I let it lie, or swept the worst of it out of sight under the stoves.

At half-past twelve I would put on my coat and hurry out. The *patron*, bland as ever, would stop me as I went down the alley-way past the bar. '*Mais mon cher monsieur*, how tired you look! Please do me the favour of accepting this glass of brandy.'

He would hand me the glass of brandy as courteously as though I had been a Russian duke instead of a *plongeur*. He treated all of us like this. It was our compensation for working seventeen hours a day.

As a rule the last Metro was almost empty – a great advantage, for one could sit down and sleep for a quarter of an hour. Generally I was in bed by half-past one. Sometimes I missed the train and had to sleep on the floor of the restaurant, but it hardly mattered, for I could have slept on cobblestones at that time.

Chapter Twenty-one

This life went on for about a fortnight, with a slight increase of work as more customers came to the restaurant. I could have saved an hour a day by taking a room near the restaurant, but it seemed impossible to find time to change lodgings – or, for that matter, to get my hair cut, look at a newspaper, or even undress completely. After ten days I managed to find a free quarter of an hour, and wrote to my friend B. in London asking him if he could get me a job of some sort – anything, so long as it allowed more than five hours sleep. I was simply not equal to going on with a seventeen-hour day, though there are plenty of people who think nothing of it. When one is overworked, it is a good cure for self-pity to think of the thousands of people in Paris restaurants who work such hours, and will go on doing it, not for a few weeks, but for years. There was a girl in a *bistro* near my hotel who worked from seven in the morning till midnight for a whole year, only sitting down to her meals. I remember once asking her to come to a dance, and she laughed and said that she had not been further than the street corner for several months. She was consumptive, and died about the time I left Paris.

After only a week we were all neurasthenic with fatigue, except Jules, who skulked persistently. The quarrels, intermittent at first, had now become continuous. For hours one would keep up a drizzle of useless nagging, rising into storms of abuse every few minutes. 'Get me down that saucepan, idiot!' the cook would cry (she was not tall enough to reach the shelves where the saucepans were kept). 'Get it down yourself, you old whore,' I would answer. Such remarks seemed to be generated spontaneously from the air of the kitchen.

We quarrelled over things of inconceivable pettiness. The dustbin, for instance, was an unending source of quarrels – whether it should be put where I wanted it, which was in the cook's way, or where she wanted it, which was between me and the sink. Once she nagged and nagged until at last, in pure spite, I lifted the dustbin up and put it out in the middle of the floor, where she was bound to trip over it.

'Now, you cow,' I said, 'move it yourself.'

Poor old woman, it was too heavy for her to lift, and she sat down, put her head on the table and burst out crying. And I jeered at her. This is the kind of effect that fatigue has upon one's manners.

After a few days the cook had ceased talking about Tolstoi and her artistic nature, and she and I were not on speaking terms, except for the purposes of work, and Boris and Jules were not on speaking terms, and neither of them was on speaking terms with the cook. Even Boris and I were barely on speaking terms. We had agreed beforehand that the *engueulades* of working hours did not count between times; but we had called each other things too bad to be forgotten – and besides, there were no between times. Jules grew lazier and lazier, and he stole food constantly – from a sense of duty, he said. He called the rest of us *jaune* – blackleg – when we would not join with him in stealing. He had a curious, malignant spirit. He told me, as a matter of pride, that he had sometimes wrung a dirty dishcloth into a customer's soup before taking it in, just to be revenged upon a member of the bourgeoisie.

The kitchen grew dirtier and the rats bolder, though we trapped a few of them. Looking round that filthy room, with raw meat lying among refuse on the floor, and cold, clotted saucepans sprawling everywhere, and the sink blocked and coated with grease, I used to wonder whether there could be a restaurant in the world as bad as ours. But the other three all said that they had been in dirtier places. Jules took a positive pleasure in seeing things dirty. In the afternoon, when he had not much to do, he used to stand in the kitchen doorway jeering at us for working too hard:

'Fool! Why do you wash that plate? Wipe it on your trousers. Who cares about the customers? *They* don't know what's going on. What is restaurant work? You are carving a chicken and it falls on the floor. You apologize, you bow, you go out; and in five minutes you come back by another door – with the same chicken. That is restaurant work,' etc.

And, strange to say, in spite of all this filth and incompetence, the Auberge de Jehan Cottard was actually a success. For the first few days all our customers were Russians, friends of the *patron*, and these were followed by Americans and other foreigners – no Frenchmen. Then one night there was tremendous excitement, because our first Frenchman had arrived. For a moment our quarrels were forgotten and we all united in the effort to serve a good dinner. Boris tiptoed into the kitchen, jerked his thumb over his shoulder and whispered conspiratorially:

'*Sh! Attention, un Français!*'

A moment later the *patron*'s wife came and whispered:

'*Attention, un Français!* See that he gets a double portion of all vegetables.'

While the Frenchman ate, the *patron*'s wife stood behind the grille of the kitchen door and watched the expression of his face. Next night the Frenchman came back with two other Frenchmen. This meant that we were earning a good name; the surest sign of a bad restaurant is to be frequented only by foreigners. Probably part of the reason for our success was that the *patron*, with the sole gleam of sense he had shown in fitting out the restaurant, had bought very sharp tableknives. Sharp knives, of course, are *the* secret of a successful restaurant. I am glad that this happened, for it destroyed one of my illusions, namely, the idea that Frenchmen know good food when they see it. Or perhaps we *were* a fairly good restaurant by Paris standards; in which case the bad ones must be past imagining.

In a very few days after I had written to B. he replied to say that there was a job he could get for me. It was to look after a congenital imbecile, which sounded a splendid rest cure after the Auberge de Jehan Cottard. I pictured myself loafing in the country lanes, knocking thistle-heads off with my stick, feeding on roast lamb and treacle tart, and sleeping ten hours a night in sheets smelling of lavender. B. sent me a fiver to pay my passage and get my clothes out of the pawn, and as soon as the money arrived I gave one day's notice and left the restaurant. My leaving so suddenly embarrassed the *patron*, for as usual he was penniless, and he had to pay my wages thirty francs short. However he stood me a glass of Courvoisier '48 brandy, and I think he felt that this made up the difference. They engaged a Czech, a thoroughly competent *plongeur*, in my place and the poor old cook was sacked a few weeks later. Afterwards I heard that, with two first-rate people in the kitchen, the *plongeur*'s work had been cut down to fifteen hours a day. Below that no one could have cut it, short of modernizing the kitchen.

Chapter Twenty-two

For what they are worth I want to give my opinions about the life of a Paris *plongeur*. When one comes to think of it, it is strange that thousands of people in a great modern city should spend their waking hours swabbing dishes in hot dens underground. The question I am raising is why this life goes on – what purpose it serves, and who wants it to continue, and why. I am not taking the merely rebellious, *fainéant* attitude. I am trying to consider the social significance of a *plongeur*'s life.

I think one should start by saying that a *plongeur* is one of the slaves of the modern world. Not that there is any need to whine over him, for he is better off than many manual workers, but still, he is no freer than if he were bought and sold. His work is servile and without art; he is paid just enough to keep him alive; his only holiday is the sack. He is cut off from marriage, or if he marries, his wife must work too. Except by a lucky chance, he has no escape from this life, save into prison. At this moment there are men with university degrees scrubbing dishes in Paris for ten or fifteen hours a day. One cannot say that it is mere idleness on their part, for an idle man cannot be a *plongeur*; they have simply been trapped by a routine which makes thought impossible. If *plongeurs* thought at all, they would long ago have formed a union and gone on strike for better treatment. But they do not think, because they have no leisure for it; their life has made slaves of them.

The question is, why does this slavery continue? People have a way of taking it for granted that all work is done for a sound purpose. They see somebody else doing a disagreeable job, and think that they have solved things by saying that the job is necessary. Coal-mining, for example, is hard work, but it is necessary – we must have coal. Working in the sewers is unpleasant, but somebody must work in the sewers. And similarly with a *plongeur*'s work. Some people must feed in restaurants, and so other people must swab dishes for eighty hours a week. It is the work of civilization, therefore unquestionable. This point is worth considering.

Is a *plongeur*'s work really necessary to civilization? We have a feeling that it must be 'honest' work, because it is hard and disagreeable, and we have made a sort of fetish of manual work. We see a man cutting down a tree, and we make sure that he is filling a social need, just because he uses his muscles; it does not occur to us that he may only be cutting down a beautiful tree to make room for a hideous statue. I believe it is the same with a *plongeur*. He earns his bread in the sweat of his brow, but it does not follow that he is doing anything useful; he may be only supplying a luxury which, very often, is not a luxury.

As an example of what I mean by luxuries which are not luxuries, take an extreme case, such as one hardly sees in Europe. Take an Indian rickshaw puller, or a gharry pony. In any Far Eastern town there are rickshaw pullers by the hundred, black wretches weighing eight stone, clad in loin-cloths. Some of them are diseased; some of them are fifty years old. For miles on end they trot in the sun or rain, head down, dragging at the shafts, with the sweat dripping from their grey moustaches. When they go too slowly the passenger calls them *bahinchut*. They earn thirty or forty rupees a month, and cought their lungs out after a few years. The gharry ponies are gaunt, vicious things that have been sold cheap as having a few years' work left in them. Their master looks on the whip as a substitute for food. Their work expresses itself in a sort of equation – whip plus food equals energy; generally it is about sixty per cent whip and forty per cent food. Sometimes their necks are encircled by one vast sore, so that they drag all day on raw flesh. It is still possible to make them work, however; it is just a question of thrashing them so hard that the pain behind outweighs the pain in front. After a few years even the whip loses its virtue, and the pony goes to the knacker. These are instances of unnecessary work, for there is no real need for gharries and rickshaws; they only exist because Orientals consider it vulgar to walk. They are luxuries, and, as anyone who has ridden in them knows, very poor luxuries. They afford a small amount of convenience, which cannot possibly balance the suffering of the men and animals.

Similarly with the *plongeur*. He is a king compared with a rickshaw puller or a gharry pony, but his case is analogous. He is the slave of a hotel or a restaurant, and his slavery is more or less useless. For, after all, where is the *real* need of big hotels and smart restaurants? They are supposed to provide luxury, but in reality they provide only a cheap, shoddy imitation of it. Nearly everyone hates hotels. Some restaurants are better than others, but it is impossible to get as good a meal in a restaurant as one can get, for the same expense, in a private house. No doubt hotels and restaurants must exist, but there is no need that they should enslave hundreds of people. What makes the work in them is not the essentials; it is the shams that are supposed to represent luxury. Smartness, as it is called, means, in effect, merely that the staff work more and the customers pay more; no one benefits except the proprietor, who will presently buy himself a striped villa at Deauville. Essentially, a 'smart' hotel is a place where a hundred people toil like devils in order that two hundred may pay through the nose for things they do not really want. If the nonsense were cut out of hotels and restaurants, and the work done with simple efficiency, *plongeurs* might work six or eight hours a day instead of ten or fifteen.

Suppose it is granted that a *plongeur*'s work is more or less useless. Then the question follows, Why does anyone want him to go on working? I am trying to go beyond the immediate economic cause, and to consider what pleasure it can give anyone to think of men swabbing dishes for life. For there is no doubt that people – comfortably situated people – do find a pleasure in such thoughts. A slave, Marcus Cato said, should be working when he is not sleeping. It does not matter whether his work is needed or not, he must work, because work in itself is good – for slaves, at least. This sentiment still survives, and it has piled up mountains of useless drudgery.

I believe that this instinct to perpetuate useless work is, at bottom, simply fear of the mob. The mob (the thought runs) are such low animals that they would be dangerous if they had leisure; it is safer to keep them too busy to think. A rich man who happens to be intellectually honest, if he is questioned about the improvement of working conditions, usually says something like this:

'We know that poverty is unpleasant; in fact, since it is so remote, we rather enjoy harrowing ourselves with the thought of its unpleasantness. But don't expect us to do anything about it. We are sorry for you lower classes, just as we are sorry for a cat with the mange, but we will fight like devils against any improvement of your condition. We feel that you are much safer as you are. The present state of affairs suits us, and we are not going to take the risk of setting you free, even by an extra hour a day. So, dear brothers, since evidently you must sweat to pay for our trips to Italy, sweat and be damned to you.'

This is particularly the attitude of intelligent, cultivated people; one can read the substance of it in a hundred essays. Very few cultivated people have less than (say) four hundred pounds a year, and naturally they side with the rich, because they imagine that any liberty conceded to the poor is a threat to their own liberty. Foreseeing some dismal Marxian Utopia as the alternative, the educated man prefers to keep things as they are. Possibly he does not like his fellow-rich very much, but he supposes that even the vulgarest of them are less inimical to his pleasures, more his kind of people, than the poor, and that he had better stand by them. It is this fear of a supposedly dangerous mob that makes nearly all intelligent people conservative in their opinions.

Fear of the mob is a superstitious fear. It is based on the idea that there is some mysterious, fundamental difference between rich and poor, as though they were two different races, like negroes and white men. But in reality there is no such difference. The mass of the rich and the poor are differentiated by their incomes and nothing else, and the average millionaire is only the average dishwasher dressed in a new suit. Change places, and handy dandy, which is the justice, which is the thief? Everyone who has mixed on equal terms with the poor knows this quite well. But the trouble is that intelligent, cultivated people, the very people who might be expected to have liberal opinions, never do mix with the poor. For what do the majority of educated people know about poverty? In my copy of Villon's poems the editor has actually thought it necessary to explain the line '*Ne pain ne voyent qu'aux fenestres*' by a footnote; so remote is even hunger from the educated man's experience. From this ignorance a superstitious fear of the mob results quite naturally. The educated man pictures a horde of submen, wanting only a day's liberty to loot his house, burn his books, and set him to working minding a machine or sweeping out a lavatory. 'Anything,' he thinks, 'any injustice, sooner than let that mob loose.' He does not see that since there is no difference between the mass of rich and poor, there is no question of setting the mob loose. The mob is in fact loose now, and – in the shape of rich men – is using its power to set up enormous treadmills of boredom, such as 'smart' hotels.

To sum up. A *plongeur* is a slave, and a wasted slave, doing stupid and largely unnecessary work. He is kept at work, ultimately, because of a vague feeling that he would be dangerous if he had leisure. And educated people, who should be on his side, acquiesce in the process, because they know nothing about him and consequently are afraid of him. I say this of the *plongeur* because it is his case I have been considering; it would apply equally to numberless other types of worker. These are only my own ideas about the basic facts of a *plongeur*'s life, made without reference to immediate economic questions, and no doubt largely platitudes. I present them as a sample of the thoughts that are put into one's head by working in a hotel.

Chapter Twenty-three

As soon as I left the Auberge de Jehan Cottard I went to bed and slept the clock round, all but one hour. Then I washed my teeth for the first time in a fortnight, bathed and had my hair cut, and got my clothes out of pawn. I had two glorious days of loafing. I even went in my best suit to the Auberge, leant against the bar and spent five francs on a bottle of English beer. It is a curious sensation, being a customer where you have been a slave's slave. Boris was sorry that I had left the restaurant just at the moment when we were *lancés* and there was a chance of making money. I have heard from him since, and he tells me that he is making a hundred francs a day and has set up a girl who is *très serieuse* and never smells of garlic.

I spent a day wandering about our quarter, saying good-bye to everyone. It was on this day that Charlie told me about the death of old Roucolle the miser, who had once lived in the quarter. Very likely Charlie was lying as usual, but it was a good story.

Roucolle died, aged seventy-four, a year or two before I went to Paris, but the people in the quarter still talked of him while I was there. He never equalled Daniel Dancer or anyone of that kind, but he was an interesting character. He went to Les Halles every morning to pick up damaged vegetables, and ate cat's meat, and wore newspaper instead of underclothes, and used the wainscoting of his room for firewood, and made himself a pair of trousers out of a sack – all this with half a million francs invested. I should like very much to have known him.

Like many misers, Roucolle came to a bad end through putting his money into a wildcat scheme. One day a Jew appeared in the quarter, an alert, business-like young chap who had a first-rate plan for smuggling cocaine into England. It is easy enough, of course, to buy cocaine in Paris, and the smuggling would be quite simple in itself, only there is always some spy who betrays the plan to the customs or the police. It is said that this is often done by the very people who sell the cocaine, because the smuggling trade is in the hands of a large combine, who do not want competition. The Jew, however, swore that there was no danger. He knew a way of getting cocaine direct from Vienna, not through the usual channels, and there would be no blackmail to pay. He had got into touch with Roucolle through a young Pole, a student at the Sorbonne, who was going to put four thousand francs into the scheme if Roucolle would put six thousand. For this they could buy ten pounds of cocaine, which would be worth a small fortune in England.

The Pole and the Jew had a tremendous struggle to get the money from between old Roucolle's claws. Six thousand francs was not much – he had more than that sewn into the mattress in his room – but it was agony for him to part with a sou. The Pole and the Jew were at him for weeks on end, explaining, bullying, coaxing, arguing, going down on their knees and imploring him to produce the money. The old man was half frantic between greed and fear. His bowels yearned at the thought of getting, perhaps, fifty thousand francs' profit, and yet he could not bring himself to risk the money. He used to sit in a corner with his head in his hands, groaning and sometimes yelling out in agony, and often he would kneel down (he was very pious) and pray for strength, but still he couldn't do it. But at last, more from exhaustion than anything else, he gave in quite suddenly; he slit open the mattress where his money was concealed and handed over six thousand francs to the Jew.

The Jew delivered the cocaine the same day, and promptly vanished. And meanwhile, as was not surprising after the fuss Roucolle had made, the affair had been noised all over the quarter. The very next morning the hotel was raided and searched by the police.

Roucolle and the Pole were in agonies. The police were downstairs, working their way up and searching every room in turn, and there was the great packet of cocaine on the table, with no place to hide it and no chance of escaping down the stairs. The Pole was for throwing the stuff out of the window, but Roucolle would not hear of it. Charlie told me that he had been present at the scene. He said that when they tried to take the packet from Roucolle he clasped it to his breast and struggled like a madman, although he was seventy-four years old. He was wild with fright, but he would go to prison rather than throw his money away.

At last, when the police were searching only one floor below, somebody had an idea. A man on Roucolle's floor had a dozen tins of face-powder which he was selling on commission; it was suggested that the cocaine could be put into the tins and passed off as face-powder. The powder was hastily thrown out of the window and the cocaine substituted, and the tins were put openly on Roucolle's table, as though there were nothing to conceal. A few minutes later the police came to search Roucolle's room. They tapped the walls and looked up the chimney and turned out the drawers and examined the floorboards, and then, just as they were about to give it up, having found nothing, the inspector noticed the tins on the table.

'*Tiens,*' he said, 'have a look at those tins. I hadn't noticed them. What's in them, eh?'

'Face-powder,' said the Pole as calmly as he could manage. But at the same instant Roucolle let out a loud groaning noise, from alarm, and the police became suspicious immediately. They opened one of the tins and tipped out the contents, after smelling it, the inspector said that he believed it was cocaine. Roucolle and the Pole began swearing on the names of the saints that it was only face-powder; but it was no use, the more they protested the more suspicious the police became. The two men were arrested and led off to the police station, followed by half the quarter.

At the station, Roucolle and the Pole were interrogated by the Commissaire while a tin of the cocaine was sent away to be analysed. Charlie said that the scene Roucolle made was beyond description. He wept, prayed, made contradictory statements and denounced the Pole all at once, so loud that he could be heard half a street away. The policemen almost burst with laughing at him.

After an hour a policeman came back with the tin of cocaine and a note from the analyst. He was laughing.

'This is not cocaine, *monsieur,*' he said.

'What, not cocaine?' said the Commissaire. '*Mais, alors* – what is it, then?'

'It is face-powder.'

Roucolle and the Pole were released at once, entirely exonerated but very angry. The Jew had double-crossed them. Afterwards, when the excitement was over, it turned out that he had played the same trick on two other people in the quarter.

The Pole was glad enough to escape, even though he had lost his four thousand francs, but poor old Roucolle was utterly broken down. He took to his bed at once, and all that day and half the night they could hear him thrashing about, mumbling, and sometimes yelling out at the top of his voice:

'Six thousand francs! *Nom de Jésus-Christ!* Six thousand francs!'

Three days later he had some kind of stroke, and in a fortnight he was dead – of a broken heart, Charlie said.

Chapter Twenty-four

I travelled to England third class via Dunkirk and Tilbury, which is the cheapest and not the worst way of crossing the Channel. You had to pay extra for a cabin, so I slept in the saloon, together with most of the third-class passengers. I find this entry in my diary for that day:

'Sleeping in the saloon, twenty-seven men, sixteen women. Of the women, not a single one has washed her face this morning. The men mostly went to the bathroom; the women merely produced vanity cases and covered the dirt with powder. *Q.* A secondary sexual difference?'

On the journey I fell in with a couple of Roumanians, mere children, who were going to England on their honeymoon trip. They asked innumerable questions about England, and I told them some startling lies. I was so pleased to be getting home, after being hard up for months in a foreign city, that England seemed to me a sort of Paradise. There are, indeed, many things in England that make you glad to get home; bathrooms, armchairs, mint sauce, new potatoes properly cooked, brown bread, marmalade, beer made with veritable hops – they are all splendid, if you can pay for them. England is a very good country when you are not poor; and, of course, with a tame imbecile to look after, I was not going to be poor. The thought of not being poor made me very patriotic. The more questions the Roumanians asked, the more I praised England; the climate, the scenery, the art, the literature, the laws – everything in England was perfect.

Was the architecture in England good? the Roumanians asked. 'Splendid!' I said. 'And you should just see the London statues! Paris is vulgar – half grandiosity and half slums. But London –'

Then the boat drew alongside Tilbury pier. The first building we saw on the waterside was one of those huge hotels, all stucco and pinnacles, which stare from the English coast like idiots staring over an asylum wall. I saw the Roumanians, too polite to say anything, cocking their eyes at the hotel. 'Built by French architects,' I assured them; and even later, when the train was crawling into London through the eastern slums, I still kept it up about the beauties of English architecture. Nothing seemed too good to say about England, now that I was coming home and was not hard up any more.

I went to B.'s office, and his first words knocked everything to ruins. 'I'm sorry,' he said; 'your employers have gone abroad, patient and all. However, they'll be back in a month. I suppose you can hang on till then?'

I was outside in the street before it even occurred to me to borrow some more money. There was a month to wait, and I had exactly nineteen and sixpence in hand. The news had taken my breath away. For a long time I could not make up my mind what to do. I loafed the day in the streets, and at night, not having the slightest notion of how to get a cheap bed in London, I went to a 'family' hotel, where the charge was seven and sixpence. After paying the bill I had ten and twopence in hand.

By the morning I had made my plans. Sooner or later I should have to go to B. for more money, but it seemed hardly decent to do so yet, and in the meantime I must exist in some hole-and-corner way. Past experience set me against pawning my best suit. I would leave all my things at the station cloakroom, except my second-best suit, which I could exchange for some cheap clothes and perhaps a pound. If I was going to live a month on thirty shillings I must have bad clothes – indeed, the worse the better. Whether thirty shillings could be made to last a month I had no idea, not knowing London as I knew Paris. Perhaps I could beg, or sell bootlaces, and I remember articles I had read in the Sunday papers about beggars who have two thousand pounds sewn in their trousers. It was, at any rate, notoriously impossible to starve in London, so there was nothing to be anxious about.

To sell my clothes I went down into Lambeth, where the people are poor and there are a lot of rag shops. At the first shop I tried the proprietor was polite but unhelpful; at the second he was rude; at the third he was stone deaf, or pretended to be so. The fourth shopman was a large blond young man, very pink all over, like a slice of ham. He looked at the clothes I was wearing and felt them disparagingly between thumb and finger.

'Poor stuff,' he said, 'very poor stuff, that is.' (It was quite a good suit.) 'What yer want for 'em?'

I explained that I wanted some older clothes and as much money as he could spare. He thought for a moment, then collected some dirty-looking rags and threw them onto the counter. 'What about the money?' I said, hoping for a pound. He pursed his lips, then produced *a shilling* and laid it beside the clothes. I did not argue – I was going to argue, but as I opened my mouth he reached out as though to take up the shilling again; I saw that I was helpless. He let me change in a small room behind the shop.

The clothes were a coat, once dark brown, a pair of black dungaree trousers, a scarf and a cloth cap; I had kept my own shirt, socks and boots, and I had a comb and razor in my pocket. It gives one a very strange feeling to be wearing such clothes. I had worn bad enough things before, but nothing at all like these; they were not merely dirty and shapeless, they had – how is one to express it? – a gracelessness, a patina of antique filth, quite different from mere shabbiness. They were the sort of clothes you see on a bootlace seller, or a tramp. An hour later, in Lambeth, I saw a hang-dog man, obviously a tramp, coming towards me, and when I looked again it was myself, reflected in a shop window. The dirt was plastering my face already. Dirt is a great respecter of persons; it lets you alone when you are well dressed, but as soon as your collar is gone it flies towards you from all directions.

I stayed in the streets till late at night, keeping on the move all the time. Dressed as I was, I was half afraid that the police might arrest me as a vagabond, and I dared not speak to anyone, imagining that they must notice a disparity between my accent and my clothes. (Later I discovered that this never happened.) My new clothes had put me instantly into a new world. Everyone's demeanour seemed to have changed abruptly. I helped a hawker pick up a barrow that he had upset. 'Thanks, mate,' he said with a grin. No one had called me mate before in my life – it was the clothes that had done it. For the first time I noticed, too, how the attitude of women varies with a man's clothes. When a badly dressed man passes them they shudder away from him with a quite frank movement of disgust, as though he were a dead cat. Clothes are powerful things. Dressed in a tramp's clothes it is very difficult, at any rate for the first day, not to feel that you are genuinely degraded. You might feel the same shame, irrational but very real, your first night in prison.

At about eleven I began looking for a bed. I had read about doss-houses (they are never called doss-houses, by the way), and I supposed that one could get a bed for fourpence or thereabouts. Seeing a man, a navvy or something of the kind, standing on the kerb in the Waterloo Road, I stopped and questioned him. I said that I was stony broke and wanted the cheapest bed I could get.

'Oh,' said he, 'you go to that 'ouse across the street there, with the sign "Good Beds for Single Men". That's a good kip [sleeping place], that is. I bin there myself on and off. You'll find it cheap *and* clean.'

It was a tall, battered-looking house, with dim lights in all the windows, some of which were patched with brown paper. I entered a stone passage-way, and a little etiolated boy with sleepy eyes appeared from a door leading to a cellar. Murmurous sounds came from the cellar, and a wave of hot air and cheese. The boy yawned and held out his hand.

'Want a kip? That'll be a 'og, guv'nor.'

I paid the shilling, and the boy led me up a rickety unlighted staircase to a bedroom. I had a sweetish reek of paregoric and foul linen; the windows seemed to be tight shut, and the air was almost suffocating at first. There was a candle burning, and I saw that the room measured fifteen feet square by eight high, and had eight beds in it. Already six lodgers were in bed, queer lumpy shapes with all their own clothes, even their boots, piled on top of them. Someone was coughing in a loathsome manner in one corner.

When I got into the bed I found that it was as hard as a board, and as for the pillow, it was a mere hard cylinder like a block of wood. It was rather worse than sleeping on a table, because the bed was not six feet long, and very narrow, and the mattress was convex, so that one had to hold on to avoid falling out. The sheets stank so horribly of sweat that I could not bear them near my nose. Also, the bedclothes only consisted of the sheets and a cotton counterpane, so that though stuffy it was none too warm. Several noises recurred throughout the night. About once in an hour the man on my left – a sailor, I think – woke up, swore vilely, and lighted a cigarette. Another man, victim of a bladder disease, got up and noisily used his chamber-pot half a dozen times during the night. The man in the corner had a coughing fit once in every twenty minutes, so regularly that one came to listen for it as one listens for the next yap when a dog is baying the moon. It was an unspeakably repellent sound; a foul bubbling and retching, as though the man's bowels were being churned up within him. Once when he struck a match I saw that he was a very old man, with a grey, sunken face like that of a corpse, and he was wearing his trousers wrapped round his head as a nightcap, a thing which for some reason disgusted me very much. Every time he coughed or the other man swore, a sleepy voice from one of the other beds cried out:

'Shut up! Oh, for Christ's —— *sake* shut up!'

I had about an hour's sleep in all. In the morning I was woken by a dim impression of some large brown thing coming towards me. I opened my eyes and saw that it was one of the sailor's feet, sticking out of bed close to my face. It was dark brown, quite dark brown like an Indian's, with dirt. The walls were leprous, and the sheets, three weeks from the wash, were almost raw umber colour. I got up, dressed and went downstairs. In the cellar were a row of basins and two slippery roller towels. I had a piece of soap in my pocket, and I was going to wash, when I noticed that every basin was streaked with grime – solid, sticky filth as black as boot-blacking. I went out unwashed. Altogether, the lodging-house had not come up to its description as cheap *and* clean. It was however, as I found later, a fairly representative lodging-house.

I crossed the river and walked a long way eastward, finally going into a coffee-shop on Tower Hill. An ordinary London coffee-shop, like a thousand others, it seemed queer and foreign after Paris. It was a little stuffy room with the high-backed pews that were fashionable in the 'forties, the day's menu written on a mirror with a piece of soap, and a girl of fourteen handling the dishes. Navvies were eating out of newspaper parcels, and drinking tea in vast saucerless mugs like china tumblers. In a corner by himself a Jew, muzzle down in the plate, was guiltily wolfing bacon.

'Could I have some tea and bread and butter?' I said to the girl.

She stared. 'No butter, only marg,' she said, surprised. And she repeated the order in the phrase that is to London what the eternal *coup de rouge* is to Paris: 'Large tea and two slices!'

On the wall beside my pew there was a notice saying 'Pocketing the sugar not allowed', and beneath it some poetic customer had written:

> He that takes away the sugar,
> Shall be called a dirty –

but someone else had been at pains to scratch out the last word. This was England. The tea-and-two-slices cost threepence halfpenny, leaving me with eight and twopence.

Chapter Twenty-five

The eight shillings lasted three days and four nights. After my bad experience in the Waterloo Road[1] I moved eastward, and spent the next night in a lodging-house in Pennyfields. This was a typical lodging-house, like scores of others in London. It had accommodation for between fifty and a hundred men, and was managed by a 'deputy' – a deputy for the owner, that is, for these lodging-houses are profitable concerns and are owned by rich men. We slept fifteen or twenty in a dormitory; the beds were again cold and hard, but the

[1] It is a curious but well-known fact that bugs are much commoner in south than north London. For some reason they have not yet crossed the river in any great numbers.

sheets were not more than a week from the wash, which was an improvement. The charge was ninepence or a shilling (in the shilling dormitory the beds were six feet apart instead of four) and the terms were cash down by seven in the evening or out you went.

Downstairs there was a kitchen common to all lodgers, with free firing and a supply of cooking-pots, tea-basins, and toasting-forks. There were two great clinker fires, which were kept burning day and night the year through. The work of tending the fires, sweeping the kitchen and making the beds was done by the lodgers in rotation. One senior lodger, a fine Norman-looking stevedore named Steve, was known as 'head of the house', and was arbiter of disputes and unpaid chuckerout.

I liked the kitchen. It was a low-ceiled cellar deep underground, very hot and drowsy with coke fumes, and lighted only by the fires, which cast black velvet shadows in the corners. Ragged washing hung on strings from the ceiling. Red-lit men, stevedores mostly, moved about the fires with cooking-pots; some of them were quite naked, for they had been laundering and were waiting for their clothes to dry. At night there were games of nap and draughts, and songs – 'I'm a chap what's done wrong by my parents', was a favourite, and so was another popular song about a shipwreck. Sometimes late at night men would come in with a pail of winkles they had bought cheap, and share them out. There was a general sharing of food, and it was taken for granted to feed men who were out of work. A little pale, wizened creature, obviously dying, referred to as 'pore Brown, bin under the doctor and cut open three times', was regularly fed by the others.

Two or three of the lodgers were old-age pensioners. Till meeting them I had never realized that there are people in England who live on nothing but the old-age pension of ten shillings a week. None of these old men had any other resource whatever. One of them was talkative, and I asked him how he managed to exist. He said:

'Well, there's ninepence a night for yer kip – that's five an' threepence a week. Then there's threepence on Saturday for a shave – that's five an' six. Then say you 'as a 'aircut once a month for sixpence – that's another three'apence a week. So you 'as about four an' fourpence for food an' bacca.'

He could imagine no other expenses. His food was bread and margarine and tea – towards the end of the week dry bread and tea without milk – and perhaps he got his clothes from charity. He seemed contented, valuing his bed and fire more than food. But, with an income of ten shillings a week, to spend money on a shave – it is awe-inspiring.

All day I loafed in the streets, east as far as Wapping, west as far as Whitechapel. It was queer after Paris; everything was so much cleaner and quieter and drearier. One missed the scream of the trams, and the noisy, festering life of the back streets, and the armed men clattering through the squares. The crowds were better dressed and the faces comelier and milder and more alike, without that fierce individuality and malice of the French. There was less drunkenness, and less dirt, and less quarrelling, and more idling. Knots of men stood at the corners, slightly underfed, but kept going by the tea-and-two-slices which the Londoner swallows every two hours. One seemed to breathe a less feverish air than in Paris. It was the land of the tea urn and the Labour Exchange, as Paris is the land of the *bistro* and the sweatshop.

It was interesting to watch the crowds. The East London women are pretty (it is the mixture of blood, perhaps), and Limehouse was sprinkled with

Orientals – Chinamen, Chittagonian lascars, Dravidians selling silk scarves, even a few Sikhs, come goodness knows how. Here and there were street meetings. In Whitechapel somebody called The Singing Evangel undertook to save you from the hell for the charge of sixpence. In the East India Dock Road the Salvation Army were holding a service. They were singing 'Anybody here like sneaking Judas?' to the tune of 'What's to be done with a drunken sailor?' On Tower Hill two Mormons were trying to address a meeting. Round their platform struggled a mob of men, shouting and interrupting. Someone was denouncing them for polygamists. A lame, bearded man, evidently an atheist, had heard the word God and was heckling angrily. There was a confused uproar of voices.

'My dear friends, if you would only let us finish what we were saying – ! – That's right, give 'em a say. Don't get on the argue! – No, no, you answer me. Can you *show* me God? You *show* 'im me, then I'll believe in 'im – Oh, shut up, don't keep interrupting of 'em! – Interrupt yourself! —— polygamists! – Well, there's a lot to be said for polygamy. Take the —— women out of industry, anyway. – My dear friends, if you would just —— – No, no, don't you slip out of it. 'Ave you *seen* God? 'Ave you *touched* 'im? 'Ave you shook *'ands* with 'im? – Oh, don't get on the argue, for Christ's sake don't get on the *argue!*' etc., etc. I listened for twenty minutes, anxious to learn something about Mormonism, but the meeting never got beyond shouts. It is the general fate of street meetings.

In Middlesex Street, among the crowds at the market, a draggled, down-at-heel woman was hauling a brat of five by the arm. She brandished a tin trumpet in its face. The brat was squalling.

'Enjoy youself!' yelled the mother. 'What yer think I brought yer out 'ere for an' bought y'a trumpet an' all? D'ya want to go across my knee? You little bastard, you *shall* enjoy yerself!'

Some drops of spittle fell from the trumpet. The mother and the child disappeared, both bawling. It was all very queer after Paris.

The last night that I was in the Pennyfields lodging-house there was a quarrel between two of the lodgers, a vile scene. One of the old-age pensioners, a man of about seventy, naked to the waist (he had been laundering), was violently abusing a short thickset stevedore, who stood with his back to the fire. I could see the old man's face in the light of the fire, and he was almost crying with grief and rage. Evidently something very serious had happened.

The old-age pensioner: 'You ——!'

The stevedore: 'Shut yer mouth, you ole ——, afore I set about yer!'

The old-age pensioner: 'Jest you try it on, you ——! I'm thirty year older'n you, but it wouldn't take much to make me give you one as'd knock you into a bucketful of piss!'

The stevedore: 'Ah, an' then p'raps I wouldn't smash you up after, you ole ——!'

Thus for five minutes. The lodgers sat round, unhappy, trying to disregard the quarrel. The stevedore looked sullen, but the old man was growing more and more furious. He kept making little rushes at the other, sticking out his face and screaming from a few inches distant like a cat on a wall, and spitting. He was trying to nerve himself to strike a blow, and not quite succeeding. Finally he burst out:

'A ——, that's what you are, a —— ——! Take that in your dirty gob and suck it, you ——! By ——, I'll smash you afore I've done with you. A ——, that's what you are, a son of a —— whore. Lick that, you ——! That's what I think of you, you ——, you ——, you —— you BLACK BASTARD!'

Whereat he suddenly collapsed on a bench, took his face in his hands, and began crying. The other man seeing that public feeling was against him, went out.

Afterwards I heard Steve explaining the cause of the quarrel. It appeared that it was all about a shilling's worth of food. In some way the old man had lost his store of bread and margarine, and so would have nothing to eat for the next three days, except what the others gave him in charity. The stevedore, who was in work and well fed, had taunted him; hence the quarrel.

When my money was down to one and fourpence I went for a night to a lodging house in Bow, where the charge was only eightpence. One went down an area and through an alley-way into a deep, stifling cellar, ten feet square. Ten men, navvies mostly, were sitting in the fierce glare of the fire. It was midnight, but the deputy's son, a pale, sticky child of five, was there playing on the navvie's knees. An old Irishman was whistling to a blind bullfinch in a tiny cage. There were other songbirds there – tiny, faded things, that had lived all their lives underground. The lodgers habitually made water in the fire, to save going across a yard to the lavatory. As I sat at the table I felt something stir near my feet, and, looking down, saw a wave of black things moving slowly across the floor; they were blackbeetles.

There were six beds in the dormitory, and the sheets, marked in huge letters 'Stolen from No. —— Road', smelt loathsome. In the next bed to me lay a very old man, a pavement artist, with some extraordinary curvature of the spine that made him stick right out of bed, with his back a foot or two from my face. It was bare, and marked with curious swirls of dirt, like a marble table-top. During the night a man came in drunk and was sick on the floor, close to my bed. There were bugs too – not so bad as in Paris, but enough to keep one awake. It was a filthy place. Yet the deputy and his wife were friendly people, and ready to make one a cup of tea at any hour of the day or night.

Chapter Twenty-six

In the morning after paying for the usual tea-and-two-slices and buying half an ounce of tobacco, I had a halfpenny left. I did not care to ask B. for more money yet, so there was nothing for it but to go to a casual ward. I had very little idea how to set about this, but I knew that there was a casual ward at Romton, so I walked out there, arriving at three of four in the afternoon. Leaning against the pigpens in Romton market-place was a wizened old Irishman, obviously a tramp. I went and leaned beside him, and presently offered him my tobacco-box. He opened the box and looked at the tobacco in astonishment:

'By God,' he said, 'dere's sixpennorth o' good baccy here! Where de hell d'you get hold o' dat? *You* ain't been on de road long.'

'What, don't you have tobacco on the road?' I said.

'Oh, we *has* it. Look.'

He produced a rusty tin which had once held Oxo Cubes. In it were twenty or thirty cigarette ends, picked up from the pavement. The Irishman said that he rarely got any other tobacco; he added that, with care, one could collect two ounces of tobacco a day on the London pavements.

'D'you come out o' one o' de London spikes [casual wards], eh?' he asked me.

I said yes, thinking this would make him accept me as a fellow tramp, and asked him what the spike at Romton was like. He said:

'Well, 'tis a cocoa spike. Dere's tay spikes, and cocoa spikes, and skilly spikes. Dey don't give you skilly in Romton, t'ank God – leastways, dey didn't de last time I was here. I been up to York and round Wales since.'

'What is skilly?' I said.

'Skilly? A can o' hot water wid some bloody oatmeal at de bottom; dat's skilly. De skilly spikes is always de worst.'

We stayed talking for an hour or two. The Irishman was a friendly old man, but he smelt very unpleasant, which was not surprising when one learned how many diseases he suffered from. It appeared (he described his symptoms fully) that taking him from top to bottom he had the following things wrong with him: on his crown, which was bald, he had eczema; he was short-sighted, and had no glasses; he had chronic bronchitis; he had some undiagnosed pain in the back; he had dyspepsia; he had urethritis; he had varicose veins, bunions and flat feet. With this assemblage of diseases he had tramped the roads for fifteen years.

At about five the Irishman said, 'Could you do wid a cup o' tay? De spike don't open till six.'

'I should think I could.'

'Well, dere's a place here where dey gives you a free cup o' tay and a bun. *Good* tay it is. Dey makes you say a lot o' bloody prayers after; but hell! It all passes de time away. You come wid me.'

He led the way to a small tin-roofed shed in a side-street, rather like a village cricket pavilion. About twenty-five other tramps were waiting. A few of them were dirty old habitual vagabonds, the majority decent-looking lads from the north, probably miners or cotton operatives out of work. Presently the door opened and a lady in a blue silk dress, wearing gold spectacles and a crucifix, welcomed us in. Inside were thirty or forty hard chairs, a harmonium, and a very gory lithograph of the Crucifixion.

Uncomfortably we took off our caps and sat down. The lady handed out the tea, and while we ate and drank she moved to and fro, talking benignly. She talked upon religious subjects – about Jesus Christ always having a soft spot for poor rough men like us, about how quickly the time passed when you were in church, and what a difference it made to a man on the road if he said his prayers regularly. We hated it. We sat against the wall fingering our caps (a tramp feels indecently exposed with his cap off), and turning pink and trying to mumble something when the lady addressed us. There was no doubt that she meant it all kindly. As she came up to one of the north country lads with the plate of buns, she said to him:

'And you, my boy, how long is it since you knelt down and spoke with your Father in Heaven?'

Poor lad, not a word could he utter; but his belly answered for him, with a disgraceful rumbling which it set up at sight of the food. Thereafter he was so overcome with shame that he could scarcely swallow his bun. Only one man managed to answer the lady in her style, and he was a spry, red-nosed fellow looking like a corporal who had lost his stripe for drunkenness. He could pronounce the words 'the dear Lord Jesus' with less shame than anyone I ever saw. No doubt he had learned the knack in prison.

Tea ended, and I saw the tramps looking furtively at one another. An unspoken thought was running from man to man – could we possibly make off before the prayers started? Someone stirred in his chair – not getting up actually, but with just a glance at the door, as though half suggesting the idea of departure. The lady quelled him with one look. She said in a more benign tone than ever:

'I don't think you need go *quite* yet. The casual ward doesn't open till six, and we have time to kneel down and say a few words to our Father first. I think we should all feel better after that, shouldn't we?'

The red-nosed man was very helpful, pulling the harmonium into place and handing out the prayer-books. His back was to the lady as he did this, and it was his idea of a joke to deal the books like a pack of cards, whispering to each man as he did so, 'There y'are, mate, there's a —— nap 'and for yer! Four aces and a king!' etc.

Bareheaded, we knelt down among the dirty teacups and began to mumble that we had left undone those things that we ought to have done, and done those things that we ought not to have done, and there was no health in us. The lady prayed very fervently, but her eyes roved over us all the time, making sure that we were attending. When she was not looking we grinned and winked at one another, and whispered bawdy jokes, just to show that we did not care; but it stuck in our throats a little. No one except the red-nosed man was self-possessed enough to speak the responses above a whisper. We got on better with the singing, except that one old tramp knew no tune but 'Onward, Christian soldiers', and reverted to it sometimes, spoiling the harmony.

The prayers lasted half an hour, and then, after a handshake at the door, we made off. 'Well,' said somebody as soon as we were out of hearing, 'the trouble's over. I thought them —— prayers was never goin' to end.'

'You 'ad your bun,' said another; 'you got to pay for it.'

'Pray for it, you mean. Ah, you don't get much for nothing. They can't even give you a twopenny cup of tea without you go down on you —— knees for it.'

There were murmurs of agreement. Evidently the tramps were not grateful for their tea. And yet it was excellent tea, as different from coffee-shop tea as good Bordeaux is from the muck called colonial claret, and we were all glad of it. I am sure too that it was given in a good spirit, without any intention of humiliating us; so in fairness we ought to have been grateful – still, we were not.

Chapter Twenty-seven

At about a quarter to six the Irishman led me to the spike. It was a grim, smoky yellow cube of brick, standing in a corner of the workhouse grounds. With its rows of tiny, barred windows, and a high wall and iron gates separating it from the road, it looked much like a prison. Already a long queue of ragged men had formed up, waiting for the gates to open. They were of all kinds and ages, the youngest a fresh-faced boy of sixteen, the oldest a doubled-up, toothless mummy of seventy-five. Some were hardened tramps, recognizable by their sticks and billies and dust-darkened faces; some were factory hands out of work, some agricultural labourers, one a clerk in collar and tie, two certainly imbeciles. Seen in the mass, lounging there, they were a disgusting sight; nothing villainous or dangerous, but a graceless, mangy crew, nearly all ragged and palpably underfed. They were friendly, however, and asked no questions. Many offered me tobacco – cigarette ends, that is.

We leaned against the wall, smoking, and the tramps began to talk about the spikes they had been in recently. It appeared from what they said that all spikes are different, each with its peculiar merits and demerits, and it is important to know these when you are on the road. An old hand will tell you the peculiarities of every spike in England, as: at A you are allowed to smoke but there are bugs in the cells; at B the beds are comfortable but the porter is a bully; at C they let you out early in the morning but the tea is undrinkable; at D the officials steal your money if you have any – and so on interminably. There are regular beaten tracks where the spikes are within a day's march of one another. I was told that the Barnet–St Albans route is the best, and they warned me to steer clear of Billericay and Chelmsford, also Ide Hill in Kent. Chelsea was said to be the most luxurious spike in England; someone, praising it, said that the blankets there were more like prison than the spike. Tramps go far afield in summer, and in winter they circle as much as possible round the large towns, where it is warmer and there is more charity. But they have to keep moving, for you may not enter any one spike, or any two London spikes, more than once in a month, on pain of being confined for a week.

Some time after six the gates opened and we began to file in one at a time. In the yard was an office where an official entered in a ledger our names and trades and ages, also the places we were coming from and going to – this last is intended to keep a check on the movements of tramps. I gave my trade as 'painter'; I had painted water-colours – who has not? The official also asked us whether we had any money, and every man said no. It is against the law to enter the spike with more than eightpence, and any sum less than this one is supposed to hand over at the gate. But as a rule the tramps prefer to smuggle their money in, tying it tight in a piece of cloth so that it will not chink. Generally they put it in the bag of tea and sugar that every tramp carries, or among their 'papers'. The 'papers' are considered sacred and never searched.

After registering at the office we were led into the spike by an official known as the Tramp Major (his job is to supervise casuals, and he is generally a workhouse pauper) and a great bawling ruffian of a porter in a blue uniform, who treated us like cattle. The spike consisted simply of a bathroom and lavatory, and, for the rest, long double rows of stone cells, perhaps a hundred cells in all. It was a bare, gloomy place of stone and whitewash, unwillingly clean, with a smell which, somehow, I had foreseen from its appearance; a smell of soft soap, Jeyes' fluid and latrines – a cold, discouraging, prisonish smell.

The porter herded us all into the passage, and then told us to come into the bathroom six at a time, to be searched before bathing. The search was for money and tobacco, Romton being one of those spikes where you can smoke once you have smuggled your tobacco in, but it will be confiscated if it is found on you. The old hands had told us that the porter never searched below the knee, so before going in we had all hidden our tobacco in the ankles of our boots. Afterwards, while undressing, we slipped it into our coats, which we were allowed to keep, to serve as pillows.

The scene in the bathroom was extraordinarily repulsive. Fifty dirty, stark-naked men elbowing each other in a room twenty feet square , with only two bathtubs and two slimy roller towels between them all. I shall never forget the reek of dirty feet. Less than half the tramps actually bathed (I heard them saying that hot water is 'weakening' to the system), but they all washed their faces and feet, and the horrid greasy little clouts known as toe-rags which they bind round their toes. Fresh water was only allowed for men who were having a complete bath, so many men had to bathe in water where others had washed their feet. The porter shoved us to and fro, giving the rough side of his tongue when anyone wasted time. When my turn came for the bath, I asked if I might swill out the tub, which was streaked with dirt, before using it. He answered simply, 'Shut yer —— mouth and get on with yer bath!' That set the social tone of the place, and I did not speak again.

When we had finished bathing, the porter tied our clothes in bundles and gave us workhouse shirts – grey cotton things of doubtful cleanliness, like abbreviated nightgowns. We were sent along to the cells at once, and presently the porter and the Tramp Major brought our supper across from the workhouse. Each man's ration was a half-pound wedge of bread smeared with margarine, and a pint of bitter sugarless cocoa in a tin billy. Sitting on the floor we wolfed this in five minutes, and at about seven o'clock the cell doors were locked on the outside, to remain locked till eight in the morning.

Each man was allowed to sleep with his mate, the cells being intended to hold two men apiece. I had no mate, and was put in with another solitary man, a thin scrubby-faced fellow with a slight squint. The cell measured eight feet by five by eight high, was made of stone, and had a tiny barred window high up in the wall and a spyhole in the door, just like a cell in a prison. In it were six blankets, a chamber-pot, a hot water pipe, and nothing else whatever. I looked round the cell with a vague feeling that there was something missing. Then, with a shock of surprise, I realized what it was, and exclaimed:

'But I say, damn it, where are the beds?'

'*Beds?*' said the other man, surprised. 'There aren't no beds! What yer expect? This is one of them spikes where you sleeps on the floor. Christ! Ain't you got used to that yet?'

It appeared that no beds was quite a normal condition in the spike. We rolled up our coats and put them against the hot-water pipe, and made ourselves as comfortable as we could. It grew foully stuffy, but it was not warm enough to allow of our putting all the blankets underneath, so that we could only use one to soften the floor. We lay a foot apart, breathing into one another's face, with our naked limbs constantly touching, and rolling against one another whenever we fell asleep. One fidgeted from side to side, but it did not do much good; whichever way one turned there would be first a dull numb feeling, then a sharp ache as the hardness of the floor wore through the blanket. One could sleep, but not for more than ten minutes on end.

About midnight the other man began making homosexual attempts upon me – a nasty experience in a locked, pitch-dark cell. He was a feeble creature and I could manage him easily, but of course it was impossible to go to sleep again. For the rest of the night we stayed awake, smoking and talking. The man told me the story of his life – he was a fitter, out of work for three years. He said that his wife had promptly deserted him when he lost his job, and he had been so long away from women that he had almost forgotten what they were like. Homosexuality is general among tramps of long standing, he said.

At eight the porter came along the passage unlocking the doors and shouting 'All out!' The doors opened, letting out a stale, fetid stink. At once the passage was full of squalid, grey-shirted figures, each chamber-pot in hand, scrambling for the bathroom. It appeared that in the morning only one tub of water was allowed for the lot of us, and when I arrived twenty tramps had already washed their faces; I took one glance at the black scum floating on the water, and went unwashed. After this we were given a breakfast identical with the previous night's supper, our clothes were returned to us, and we were ordered out into the yard to work. The work was peeling potatoes for the pauper's dinner, but it was a mere formality, to keep us occupied until the doctor came to inspect us. Most of the tramps frankly idled. The doctor turned up at about ten o'clock and we were told to go back to our cells, strip and wait in the passage for the inspection.

Naked and shivering, we lined up in the passage. You cannot conceive what ruinous, degenerate curs we looked, standing there in the merciless morning light. A tramp's clothes are bad, but they conceal far worse things; to see him as he really is, unmitigated, you must see him naked. Flat feet, pot bellies, hollow chests, sagging muscles – every kind of physical rottenness was there. Nearly everyone was under-nourished, and some clearly diseased; two men were wearing trusses, and as for the old mummy-like creature of seventy-five, one wondered how he could possibly make his daily march. Looking at our faces, unshaven and creased from the sleepless night, you would have thought that all of us were recovering from a week on the drink.

The inspection was designed merely to detect smallpox, and took no notice of our general condition. A young medical student, smoking a cigarette, walked rapidly along the line glancing us up and down, and not inquiring whether any man was well or ill. When my cell companion stripped I saw that his chest was covered with a red rash, and, having spent the night a few inches away from him, I fell into a panic about smallpox. The doctor, however, examined the rash and said that it was due merely to under-nourishment.

After the inspection we dressed and were sent into the yard, where the porter called our names over, gave us back any possessions we had left at the office, and distributed meal tickets. These were worth sixpence each, and were directed to coffee-shops on the route we had named the night before. It was interesting to see that quite a number of the tramps could not read, and had to apply to myself and other 'scholars' to decipher their tickets.

The gates were opened, and we dispersed immediately. How sweet the air does smell – even the air of a back street in the suburbs – after the shut-in, subfaecal stench of the spike! I had a mate now, for while we were peeling potatoes I had made friends with an Irish tramp named Paddy Jacques, a melancholy pale man who seemed clean and decent. He was going to Edbury spike, and suggested that we should go together. We set out, getting there at three in the afternoon. It was a twelve-mile walk, but we made it fourteen by getting lost among the desolate north London slums. Our meal tickets were directed to a coffee-shop in Ilford. When we got there, the little chit of a serving-maid, having seen our tickets and grasped that we were tramps, tossed her head in contempt and for a long time would not serve us. Finally she slapped on the table two 'large teas' and four slices of bread and dripping – that is, eightpenny-worth of food. It appeared that the shop habitually cheated the tramps of twopence or so on each ticket; having tickets instead of money, the tramps could not protest or go elsewhere.

Chapter Twenty-eight

Paddy was my mate for about the next fortnight, and, as he was the first tramp I had known at all well, I want to give an account of him. I believe that he was a typical tramp and there are tens of thousands in England like him.

He was a tallish man, aged about thirty-five, with fair hair going grizzled and watery blue eyes. His features were good, but his cheeks had lanked and had that greyish, dirty in the grain look that comes of a bread and margarine diet. He was dressed, rather better than most tramps, in a tweed shooting-jacket and a pair of old evening trousers with the braid still on them. Evidently the braid figured in his mind as a lingering scrap of respectability, and he took care to sew it on again when it came loose. He was careful of his appearance altogether, and carried a razor and bootbrush that he would not sell, though he had sold his 'papers' and even his pocket-knife long since. Nevertheless, one would have known him for a tramp a hundred yards away. There was something in his drifting style of walk, and the way he had of hunching his shoulders forward, essentially abject. Seeing him walk, you felt instinctively that he would sooner take a blow than give one.

He had been brought up in Ireland, served two years in the war, and then worked in a metal polish factory, where he had lost his job two years earlier. He was horribly ashamed of being a tramp, but he had picked up all a tramp's ways. He browsed the pavements unceasingly, never missing a cigarette end, or even an empty cigarette packet, as he used the tissue paper for rolling cigarettes. On our way into Edbury he saw a newspaper parcel on the pavement, pounced on it, and found that it contained two mutton sandwiches, rather frayed at the edges; these he insisted on my sharing. He never passed an automatic machine without giving a tug at the handle, for he said that sometimes they are out of order and will eject pennies if you tug at them. He had no stomach for crime, however. When we were in the outskirts of Romton, Paddy noticed a bottle of milk on a doorstep, evidently left there by mistake. He stopped, eyeing the bottle hungrily.

'Christ!' he said, 'dere's good food goin' to waste. Somebody could knock dat bottle off, eh? Knock it off easy.'

I saw that he was thinking of 'knocking it off' himself. He looked up and down the street; it was a quiet residential street and there was nobody in sight. Paddy's sickly, chap-fallen face yearned over the milk. Then he turned away, saying gloomily:

'Best leave it. It don't do a man no good to steal. T'ank God, I ain't never stolen nothin' yet.'

It was funk, bred of hunger, that kept him virtuous. With only two or three sound meals in his belly, he would have found courage to steal the milk.

He had two subjects of conversation, the shame and come-down of being a tramp, and the best way of getting a free meal. As we drifted through the streets he would keep up a monologue in this style, in a whimpering, self-pitying Irish voice.

'It's hell bein' on de road, eh? It breaks yer heart goin' into dem bloody spikes. But what's a man to do else, eh? I ain't had a good meat meal for about two months, an' me boots is getting bad, an' – Christ! How'd it be if we was to try for a cup o' tay at one o' dem convents on de way to Edbury? Most times dey're good for a cup o' tay. Ah, what'd a man do widout religion, eh? I've took cups o' tay from de convents, an' de Baptists, an' de Church of England, an' all sorts. I'm a Catholic meself. Dat's to say, I ain't been to confession for about seventeen year, but still I got me religious feelin's, y'understand. An' dem convents is always good for a cup o' tay . . .' etc. etc. He would keep this up all day, almost without stopping.

His ignorance was limitless and appalling. He once asked me, for instance, whether Napoleon lived before Jesus Christ or after. Another time, when I was looking into a bookshop window, he grew very very perturbed because one of the books was called *Of the Imitation of Christ*. He took this for blasphemy. 'What de hell do dey want to go imitatin' of *Him* for?' he demanded angrily. He could read, but he had a kind of loathing for books. On our way from Romton to Edbury I went into a public library, and, though Paddy did not want to read, I suggested that he should come in and rest his legs. But he preferred to wait on the pavement. 'No,' he said, 'de sight of all dat bloody print makes me sick.'

Like most tramps, he was passionately mean about matches. He had a box of matches when I met him, but I never saw him strike one, and he used to lecture me for extravagance when I struck mine. His method was to cadge a light from strangers, sometimes going without a smoke for half an hour rather than strike a match.

Self-pity was the clue to his character. The thought of his bad luck never seemed to leave him for an instant. He would break long silences to exclaim, apropos of nothing, 'It's hell when yer clo'es begin to go up de spout, eh?' or 'Dat tay in de spike ain't tay, it's piss,' as though there was nothing else in the world to think about. And he had a low, worm-like envy of anyone who was better off – not of the rich, for they were beyond his social horizon, but of men in work. He pined for work as an artist pines to be famous. If he saw an old man working he would say bitterly, 'Look at dat old —— keepin' able-bodied men out o' work'; or if it was a boy, 'It's dem young devils what's takin' de bread out of our mouths.' And all foreigners to him were 'dem bloody dagoes' – for, according to his theory, foreigners were responsible for unemployment.

He looked at women with a mixture of longing and hatred. Young, pretty women were too much above him to enter into his ideas, but his mouth watered at prostitutes. A couple of scarlet-lipped old creatures would go past; Paddy's face would flush pale pink, and he would turn and stare hungrily after the women. 'Tarts!' he would murmur, like a boy at a sweetshop window. He told me once that he had not had to do with a woman for two years – since he had lost his job, that is – and he had forgotten that one could aim higher than prostitutes. He had the regular character of a tramp – abject, envious, a jackal's character.

Nevertheless, he was a good fellow, generous by nature and capable of sharing his last crust with a friend; indeed he did literally share his last crust with me more than once. He was probably capable of work too, if he had been well fed for a few months. But two years of bread and margarine had lowered his standards hopelessly. He had lived on this filthy imitation of food till his own mind and body were compounded of inferior stuff. It was malnutrition and not any native vice that had destroyed his manhood.

Chapter Twenty-nine

On the way to Edbury I told Paddy that I had a friend from whom I could be sure of getting money, and suggested going straight into London rather than face another night in the spike. But Paddy had not been in Edbury spike recently, and, tramp-like, he would not waste a night's free lodging. We arranged to go into London the next morning. I had only a halfpenny, but Paddy had two shillings, which would get us a bed each and a few cups of tea.

The Edbury spike did not differ much from the one at Romton. The worst feature was that all tobacco was confiscated at the gate, and we were warned that any man caught smoking would be turned out at once. Under the Vagrancy Act tramps can be prosecuted for smoking in the spike – in fact, they can be prosecuted for almost anything; but the authorities generally save the trouble of a prosecution by turning disobedient men out of doors. There was no work to do, and the cells were fairly comfortable. We slept two in a cell, 'one up, one down' – that is, one on a wooden shelf and one on the floor, with straw palliasses and plenty of blankets, dirty but not verminous. The food was the same as at Romton, except that we had tea instead of cocoa. One could get extra tea in the morning, as the Tramp Major was selling it at a halfpenny a mug, illicitly no doubt. We were each given a hunk of bread and cheese to take away for our midday meal.

When we got into London we had eight hours to kill before the lodging-houses opened. It is curious how one does not notice things. I had been in London innumerable times, and yet till that day I had never noticed one of the worst things about London – the fact that it costs money even to sit down. In Paris, if you had no money and could not find a public bench, you would sit on the pavement. Heaven knows what sitting on the pavement would lead to in London – prison, probably. By four we had stood five hours, and our feet seemed red-hot from the hardness of the stones. We were hungry, having eaten our ration as soon as we left the spike, and I was out of tobacco – it mattered less to Paddy, who picked up cigarette ends. We tried two churches and found them locked. Then we tried a public library, but there were no seats in it. As a last hope Paddy suggested trying a Rowton House; by the rules they would not let us in before seven, but we might slip in unnoticed. We walked up the magnificent doorway (the Rowton Houses really are magnificent) and very casually, trying to look like regular lodgers, began to stroll in. Instantly a man lounging in the doorway, a sharp-faced fellow, evidently in some position of authority, barred the way.

'You men sleep 'ere last night?'

'No.'

'Then —— off.'

We obeyed, and stood two more hours on the street corner. It was unpleasant, but it taught me not to use the expression 'street corner loafer', so I gained something else from it.

At six we went to a Salvation Army shelter. We could not book beds till eight and it was not certain that there would be any vacant, but an official, who called us 'Brother', let us in on the condition that we paid for two cups of tea. The main hall of the shelter was a great white-washed barn of a place, oppressively clean and bare, with no fires. Two hundred decentish, rather subdued-looking people were sitting packed on long wooden benches. One or two officers in uniform prowled up and down. On the wall were pictures of General Booth, and notices prohibiting cooking, drinking, spitting, swearing, quarrelling and gambling. As a specimen of these notices, here is one that I copied word for word:

> 'Any man found gambling or playing cards will be expelled and will not be admitted under any circumstances.
>
> 'A reward will be given for information leading to the discovery of such persons.
>
> 'The officers in charge appeal to all lodgers to assist them in keeping this hostel free from the DETESTABLE EVIL OF GAMBLING.'

'Gambling or playing cards' is a delightful phrase.

To my eye these Salvation Army shelters, though clean, are far drearier than the worst of the common lodging-houses. There is such a hopelessness about some of the people there – decent, broken-down types who have pawned their collars but are still trying for office jobs. Coming to a Salvation Army shelter, where it is at least clean, is their last clutch at respectability. At the next table to me were two foreigners, dressed in rags but manifestly gentlemen. They were playing chess verbally, not even writing down the moves. One of them was blind, and I heard them say that they had been saving up for a long time to buy a board, price half a crown, but could never manage it. Here and there were clerks out of work, pallid and moody. Among a group of them a tall, thin, deadly pale young man was talking excitedly. He thumped his fist on the table and boasted in a strange, feverish style. When the officers were out of hearing he broke out into startling blasphemies:

'I tell you what, boys, I'm going to get that job tomorrow. I'm not one of your bloody down-on-the-knee brigade; I can look after myself. Look at that — — notice there! "The Lord will provide!" A bloody lot He's ever provided me with. You don't catch me trusting to the —— Lord. You leave it to me, boys. *I'm going to get that job*,' etc., etc.

I watched him, struck by the wild, agitated way in which he talked; he seemed hysterical, or perhaps a little drunk. An hour later I went into a small room, apart from the main hall, which was intended for reading. It had no books or papers in it, so few of the lodgers went there. As I opened the door I saw the young clerk in there all alone; he was on his knees, *praying*. Before I shut the door again I had time to see his face, and it looked agonized. Quite suddenly I realized, from the expression of his face, that he was starving.

The charge for beds was eightpence. Paddy and I had fivepence left, and we spent it at the 'bar', where food was cheap, though not so cheap as in some common lodging-houses. The tea appeared to be made with tea *dust*, which I fancy had been given to the Salvation Army in charity, though they sold it at three-halfpence a cup. It was foul stuff. At ten o'clock an officer marched round the hall blowing a whistle. Immediately everyone stood up.

'What's this for?' I said to Paddy, astonished.

'Dat means you has to go off to bed. An' you has to look sharp about it, too.'

Obediently as sheep, the whole two hundred men trooped off to bed, under the command of the officers.

The dormitory was a great attic like a barrack room, with sixty or seventy beds in it. They were clean and tolerably comfortable, but very narrow and very close together, so that one breathed straight into one's neighbour's face. Two officers slept in the room, to see that there was no smoking and no talking after lights-out. Paddy and I had scarcely a wink of sleep, for there was a man near us who had some nervous trouble, shell-shock perhaps, which made him cry out 'Pip!' at irregular intervals. It was a loud, startling noise, something like the toot of a small motor-horn. You never knew when it was coming, and it was a sure preventer of sleep. It appeared that Pip, as the others called him, slept regularly in the shelter, and he must have kept ten or twenty people awake every night. He was an example of the kind of thing that prevents one from ever getting enough sleep when men are herded as they are in these lodging-houses.

At seven another whistle blew, and the officers went round shaking those who did not get up at once. Since then I have slept in a number of Salvation Army shelters, and found that, though the different houses vary a little, this semi-military discipline is the same in all of them. They are certainly cheap, but they are too like workhouses for my taste. In some of them there is even a compulsory religious service once or twice a week, which the lodgers must attend or leave the house. The fact is that the Salvation Army are so in the habit of thinking themselves a charitable body that they cannot even run a lodging-house without making it stink of charity.

At ten I want to B.'s office and asked him to lend me a pound. He gave me two pounds and told me to come again when necessary, so that Paddy and I were free of money troubles for a week at least. We loitered the day in Trafalgar Square, looking for a friend of Paddy's who never turned up, and at night went to a lodging-house in a back alley near the Strand. The charge was elevenpence, but it was a dark, evil-smelling place, and a notorious haunt of the 'nancy boys'. Downstairs, in the murky kitchen, three ambiguous-looking youths in smartish blue suits were sitting on a bench apart, ignored by the other lodgers. I suppose they were 'nancy boys'. They looked the same type as the apache boys one sees in Paris, except that they wore no side-whiskers. In front of the fire a fully dressed man and a stark-naked man were bargaining. They were newspaper sellers. The dressed man was selling his clothes to the naked man. He said:

''Ere y'are, the best rig-out you ever 'ad. A tosheroon [half a crown] for the coat, two 'ogs for the trousers, one and a tanner for the boots, and a 'og for the cap and scarf. That's seven bob.'

'You got a 'ope! I'll give yer one and a tanner for the coat, a 'og for the trousers, and two 'ogs for the rest. That's four and a tanner.'

'Take the 'ole lot for five and a tanner, chum.'

'Right y'are, off with 'em. I got to get out to sell my late edition.'

The clothed man stripped, and in three minutes their positions were reversed; the naked man dressed, and the other kilted with a sheet of the *Daily Mail.*

The dormitory was dark and close, with fifteen beds in it. There was a horrible hot reek of urine, so beastly that at first one tried to breathe in small, shallow puffs, not filling one's lungs to the bottom. As I lay down in bed a man loomed out of the darkness, leant over me and began babbling in an educated, half-drunken voice:

'An old public school boy, what? [He had heard me say something to Paddy.] Don't meet many of the old school here. I am an old Etonian. You know – twenty years hence this weather and all that.' He began to quaver out the Eton boating-song, not untunefully:

> '*Jolly boating weather,*
> *And a hay harvest* ——'

'Stop that —— noise!' shouted several lodgers.

'Low types,' said the old Etonian, 'very low types. Funny sort of place for you and me, eh? Do you know what my friends say to me? They say, 'M——, you are past redemption.' Quite true, I *am* past redemption. I've come down in the world; not like these ——s here, who couldn't come down if they tried. We chaps who have come down ought to hang together a bit. Youth will be still in our faces – you know. May I offer you a drink?'

He produced a bottle of cherry brandy, and at the same moment lost his balance and fell heavily across my legs. Paddy, who was undressing, pulled him upright.

'Get back to yer bed, you silly ole ——!'

The old Etonian walked unsteadily to his bed and crawled under the sheets with all his clothes on, even his boots. Several times in the night I heard him murmuring, 'M——, you are past redemption,' as though the phrase appealed to him. In the morning he was lying asleep fully dressed, with the bottle clasped in his arms. He was a man of about fifty, with a refined, worn face, and, curiously enough, quite fashionably dressed. It was queer to see his good patent-leather shoes sticking out of that filthy bed. It occurred to me, too, that the cherry brandy must have cost the equivalent of a fortnight's lodging, so he could not have been seriously hard up. Perhaps he frequented common lodging-houses in search of the 'nancy boys'.

The beds were not more than two feet apart. About midnight I woke up to find that the man next to me was trying to steal the money from beneath my pillow. He was pretending to be asleep while he did it, sliding his hand under the pillow as gently as a rat. In the morning I saw that he was a hunchback, with long, apelike arms. I told Paddy about the attempted theft. He laughed and said:

'Christ! You got to get used to dat. Dese lodgin' houses is full o' thieves. In some houses dere's nothin' safe but to sleep wid all yer clo'es on. I seen 'em steal a wooden leg off a cripple before now. Once I see a man – fourteen stone man he was – come into a lodgin'-house wid four pound ten. He puts it under his mattress. "Now," he says, "any —— dat touches dat money does it over my body," he says. But dey done him all de same. In de mornin' he woke up on de floor. Four fellers had took his mattress by de corners an' lifted him off as light as a feather. He never saw his four pound ten again.'

Chapter Thirty

The next morning we began looking once more for Paddy's friend, who was called Bozo, and was a screever – that is, a pavement artist. Addresses did not exist in Paddy's world, but he had a vague idea that Bozo might be found in Lambeth, and in the end we ran across him on the Embankment, where he had established himself not far from Waterloo Bridge. He was kneeling on the pavement with a box of chalks, copying a sketch of Winston Churchill from a penny note-book. The likeness was not at all bad. Bozo was a small, dark, hook-nosed man, with curly hair growing low on his head. His right leg was dreadfully deformed, the foot being twisted heel forward in a way horrible to see. From his appearance one could have taken him for a Jew, but he used to deny this vigorously. He spoke of his hook-nose as 'Roman', and was proud of his resemblance to some Roman Emperor – it was Vespasian, I think.

Bozo had a strange way of talking, Cockneyfied and yet very lucid and expressive. It was as though he had read good books but had never troubled to correct his grammar. For a while Paddy and I stayed on the Embankment, talking, and Bozo gave us an account of the screeving trade. I repeat what he said more or less in his own words.

'I'm what they call a serious screever. I don't draw in blackboard chalks like these others, I use proper colours the same as what painters use; bloody expensive they are, especially the reds. I use five bobs' worth of colours in a long day, and never less than two bobs' worth.[1] Cartoons is my line – you know, politics and cricket and that. Look here' – he showed me his note-book – 'here's likenesses of all the political blokes, what I've copied from the papers. I have a different cartoon every day. For instance, when the Budget was on I had one of Winston trying to push an elephant marked "Debt", and underneath I wrote, "Will he budge it?" See? You can have cartoons about any of the parties, but you mustn't put anything in favour of Socialism, because the police won't stand it. Once I did a cartoon of a boa constrictor marked Capital swallowing a rabbit marked Labour. The copper came along and saw it, and he says, "You rub that out, and look sharp about it," he says. I had to rub it out. The copper's got the right to move you on for loitering, and it's no good giving them a back answer.'

I asked Bozo what one could earn at screeving. He said:

'This time of year, when it don't rain, I take about three quid between Friday and Sunday – people get their wages Fridays, you see. I can't work when it rains; the colours get washed off straight away. Take the year round, I make about a pound a week, because you can't do much in the winter. Boat Race day, and Cup Final day, I've took as much as four pounds. But you have to *cut* it out of them, you know; you don't take a bob if you just sit and look at them. A halfpenny's the usual drop [gift], and you don't get even that unless you give them a bit of backchat. Once they've answered you they feel ashamed

[1] Pavement artists buy their colours in the form of powder, and work them into cakes with condensed milk.

not to give you a drop. The best thing's to keep changing your picture, because when they see you drawing they'll stop and watch you. The trouble is, the beggars scatter as soon as you turn round with the hat. You really want a nobber [assistant] at this game. You keep at work and get a crowd watching you, and the nobber comes casual-like round the back of them. They don't know he's the nobber. Then suddenly he pulls his cap off, and you got them between two fires like. You'll never get a drop of real toffs. It's shabby sort of blokes you get most off, and foreigners. I've had even sixpences off Japs, and blackies, and that. They're not so bloody mean as what an Englishman is. Another thing to remember is to keep your money covered up, except perhaps a penny in the hat. People won't give you anything if they see you got a bob or two already.'

Bozo had the deepest contempt for the other screevers on the Embankment. He called them 'the salmon platers'. At that time there was a screever almost every twenty-five yards along the Embankment – twenty-five yards being the recognized minimum between pitches. Bozo contemptuously pointed out an old white-bearded screever fifty yards away.

'You see that silly old fool? He's bin doing the same picture every day for ten years. "A faithful friend" he calls it. It's of a dog pulling a child out of the water. The silly old bastard can't draw any better than a child of ten. He's learned just that one picture by rule of thumb, like you learn to put a puzzle together. There's a lot of that sort about here. They come pinching my ideas sometimes; but I don't care; the silly ——s can't think of anything for themselves, so I'm always ahead of them. The whole thing with cartoons is being up to date. Once a child got its head stuck in the railings of Chelsea Bridge. Well, I heard about it, and my cartoon was on the pavement before they'd got the child's head out of the railings. Prompt, I am.'

Bozo seemed an interesting man, and I was anxious to see more of him. That evening I went down to the Embankment to meet him, as he had arranged to take Paddy and myself to a lodging-house south of the river. Bozo washed his pictures off the pavement and counted his takings – it was about sixteen shillings, of which he said twelve or thirteen would be profit. We walked down into Lambeth. Bozo limped slowly, with a queer crablike gait, half sideways, dragging his smashed foot behind him. He carried a stick in each hand and slung his box of colours over his shoulder. As we were crossing the bridge he stopped in one of the alcoves to rest. He fell silent for a minute or two, and to my surprise I saw that he was looking at the stars. He touched my arm and pointed to the sky with his stick.

'Say, will you look at Aldebaran! Look at the colour. Like —— great blood orange!'

From the way he spoke he might have been an art critic in a picture gallery. I was astonished. I confessed that I did not know which Aldebaran was – indeed, I had never even noticed that the stars were of different colours. Bozo began to give me some elementary hints on astronomy, pointing out the chief constellations. He seemed concerned at my ignorance. I said to him, surprised:

'You seem to know a lot about stars.'

'Not a great lot. I know a bit, though. I got two letters from the Astronomer Royal thanking me for writing about meteors. Now and again I go out at night and watch for meteors. The stars are a free show; it don't cost anything to use your eyes.'

'What a good idea! I should never have thought of it.'

'Well, you got to take an interest in something. It don't follow that because a man's on the road he can't think of anything but tea-and-two-slices.'

'But isn't it very hard to take an interest in things – things like stars – living this life?'

'Screeving, you mean? Not necessarily. It don't need turn you into a bloody rabbit – that is, not if you set you mind to it.'

'It seems to have that effect on most people.'

'Of course. Look at Paddy – tea-swilling old moocher, only fit to scrounge for fag-ends. That's the way most of them go. I despise them. But you don't *need* to get like that. If you've got any education, it don't matter to you if you're on the road for the rest of your life.'

'Well, I've found just the contrary,' I said. 'It seems to me that when you take a man's money away he's fit for nothing from that moment.'

'No, not necessarily. If you set yourself to it, you can live the same life, rich or poor. You can still keep on with your books and your ideas. You just got to say to yourself, "I'm a free man in here"' – he tapped his forehead – 'and you're all right.'

Bozo talked further in the same strain, and I listened with attention. He seemed a very unusual screever, and he was, moreover, the first person I had heard maintain that poverty did not matter. I saw a good deal of him during the next few days, for several times it rained and he could not work. He told me the history of his life, and it was a curious one.

The son of a bankrupt bookseller, he had gone to work as a house-painter at eighteen, and then served three years in France and India during the war. After the war he had found a house-painting job in Paris, and had stayed there several years. France suited him better than England (he despised the English), and he had been doing well in Paris, saving money, and engaged to a French girl. One day the girl was crushed to death under the wheels of an omnibus. Bozo went on the drink for a week, and then returned to work, rather shaky; the same morning he fell from a stage on which he was working, forty feet onto the pavement, and smashed his right foot to pulp. For some reason he received only sixty pounds compensation. He returned to England, spent his money in looking for jobs, tried hawking books in Middlesex Street market, then tried selling toys from a tray, and finally settled down as a screever. He had lived hand to mouth ever since, half starved throughout the winter, and often sleeping in the spike or on the Embankment. When I knew him he owned nothing but the clothes he stood up in, and his drawing materials and a few books. The clothes were the usual beggar's rags, but he wore a collar and tie, of which he was rather proud. The collar, a year or more old, was constantly 'going' round the neck, and Bozo used to patch it with bits cut from the tail of his shirt so that the shirt had scarcely any tail left. His damaged leg was getting worse and would probably have to be amputated, and his knees, from kneeling on the stones, had pads of skin on them as thick as boot-soles. There was, clearly, no future for him but beggary and a death in the workhouse.

With all this, he had neither fear, nor regret, nor shame, nor self-pity. He had faced his position, and made a philosophy for himself. Being a beggar, he said, was not his fault, and he refused either to have any compunction about it or to let it trouble him. He was the enemy of society, and quite ready to take to crime if he saw a good opportunity. He refused on principle to be thrifty. In the summer he saved nothing, spending his surplus earnings on drink, as he did not care about women. If he was penniless when winter came on, then society must look after him. He was ready to extract every penny he could from charity, provided that he was not expected to say thank you for it. He avoided religious charities, however, for he said that it stuck in his throat to sing hymns for buns. He had various other points of honour; for instance, it was his boast that never in his life, even when starving, had he picked up a cigarette end. He considered himself in a class above the ordinary run of beggars, who, he said, were an abject lot, without even the decency to be ungrateful.

He spoke French passably, and had read some of Zola's novels, all Shakespeare's plays, *Gulliver's Travels*, and a number of essays. He could describe his adventures in words that one remembered. For instance, speaking of funerals, he said to me:

'Have you ever seen a corpse burned? I have, in India. They put the old chap on the fire, and the next moment I almost jumped out of my skin, because he'd started kicking. It was only his muscles contracting in the heat – still, it give me a turn. Well, he wriggled about for a bit like a kipper on hot coals, and then his belly blew up and went off with a bang you could have heard fifty yards away. It fair put me against cremation.'

Or, again, apropos of his accident:

'The doctor says to me, "You fell on one foot, my man. And bloody lucky for you you didn't fall on both feet," he says. "Because if you had of fallen on both feet you'd have shut up like a bloody concertina, and your thigh bones'd be sticking out of your ears!"'

Clearly the phrase was not the doctor's but Bozo's own. He had a gift for phrases. He had managed to keep his brain intact and alert, and so nothing could make him succumb to poverty. He might be ragged and cold, or even starving, but so long as he could read, think and watch for meteors, he was, as he said, free in his own mind.

He was an embittered atheist (the sort of atheist who does not so much disbelieve in God as personally dislike Him), and took a sort of pleasure in thinking that human affairs would never improve. Sometimes, he said, when sleeping on the Embankment, it had consoled him to look up at Mars or Jupiter and think that there were probably Embankment sleepers there. He had a curious theory about this. Life on earth, he said, is harsh because the planet is poor in the necessities of existence. Mars, with its cold climate and scanty water, must be far poorer, and life correspondingly harsher. Whereas on earth you are merely imprisoned for stealing sixpence, on Mars you are probably boiled alive. This thought cheered Bozo, I do not know why. He was a very exceptional man.

Chapter Thirty-one

The charge at Bozo's lodging-house was ninepence a night. It was a large, crowded place, with accommodation for five hundred men, and a well-known rendezvous of tramps, beggars and petty criminals. All races, even black and white, mixed in it on terms of equality. There were Indians there, and when I spoke to one of them in bad Urdu he addressed me as 'tum' – a thing to make one shudder, if it had been in India. We had got below the range of colour prejudice. One had glimpses of curious lives. Old 'Grandpa', a tramp of seventy who made his living, or a great part of it, by collecting cigarette ends and selling the tobacco at threepence an ounce. 'The Doctor' – he was a real doctor, who had been struck off the register for some offence, and besides selling newspapers gave medical advice at a few pence a time. A little Chittagonian lascar, barefoot and starving, who had deserted his ship and wandered for days through London, so vague and helpless that he did not even know the name of the city he was in – he thought it was Liverpool, until I told him. A begging-letter writer, a friend of Bozo's, who wrote pathetic appeals for aid to pay for his wife's funeral, and, when a letter had taken effect, blew himself out with huge solitary gorges of bread and margarine. He was a nasty, hyena-like creature. I talked to him and found that, like most swindlers, he believed a great part of his own lies. The lodging-house was an Alsatia for types like these.

While I was with Bozo he taught me something about the technique of London begging. There is more in it than one might suppose. Beggars vary greatly, and there is a sharp social line between those who merely cadge and those who attempt to give value for money. The amounts that one can earn by the different 'gags' also vary. The stories in the Sunday papers about beggars who die with two thousand pounds sewn into their trousers are, of course, lies; but the better-class beggars do have runs of luck, when they earn a living wage for weeks at a time. The most prosperous beggars are street acrobats and street photographers. On a good pitch – a theatre queue, for instance – a street acrobat will often earn five pounds a week. Street photographers can earn about the same, but they are dependent on fine weather. They have a cunning dodge to stimulate trade. When they see a likely victim approaching, one of them runs behind the camera and pretends to take a photograph. Then as the victim reaches them, they exclaim:

'There y'are, sir, took yer photo lovely. That'll be a bob.'

'But I never asked you to take it,' protests the victim.

'What, you didn't want it took? Why, we thought you signalled with your 'and. Well, there's a plate wasted! That's cost us sixpence, that 'as.'

At this the victim usually takes pity and says he will have the photo after all. The photographers examine the plate and say that it is spoiled, and that they will take a fresh one free of charge. Of course, they have not really taken the first photo; and so, if the victim refuses, they waste nothing.

Organ-grinders, like acrobats, are considered artists rather than beggars. An organ-grinder named Shorty, a friend of Bozo's, told me all about his trade. He and his mate 'worked' the coffee-shops and public-houses round Whitechapel and the Commercial Road. It is a mistake to think that organ-grinders earn their living in the street; nine-tenths of their money is taken in coffee-shops and pubs – only the cheap pubs, for they are not allowed into the good-class ones. Shorty's procedure was to stop outside a pub and play one tune, after which his mate, who had a wooden leg and could excite compassion, went in and passed round the hat. It was a point of honour with Shorty always to play another tune after receiving the 'drop' – an encore, as it were; the idea being that he was a genuine entertainer and not merely paid to go away. He and his mate took two or three pounds a week between them, but, as they had to pay fifteen shillings a week for the hire of the organ, they only averaged a pound a week each. They were on the streets from eight in the morning till ten at night, and later on Saturdays.

Screevers can sometimes be called artists, sometimes not. Bozo introduced me to one who was a 'real' artist – that is, he had studied art in Paris and submitted pictures to the Salon in his day. His line was copies of Old Masters, which he did marvellously, considering that he was drawing on stone. He told me how he began as a screever.

'My wife and kids were starving. I was walking home late at night, with a lot of drawings I'd been taking round the dealers, and wondering how the devil to raise a bob or two. Then, in the Strand, I saw a fellow kneeling on the pavement drawing, and people giving him pennies. As I came past he got up and went into a pub. "Damn it," I thought, "if he can make money at that, so can I." So on the impulse I knelt down and began drawing with his chalks. Heaven knows how I came to do it; I must have been light-headed with hunger. The curious thing was that I'd never used pastels before; I had to learn the technique as I went along. Well, people began to stop and say that my drawing wasn't bad, and they gave me ninepence between them. At this moment the other fellow came out of the pub. "What in —— are you doing on my pitch?" he said. I explained that I was hungry and had to earn something. "Oh," said he, "come and have a pint with me." So I had a pint, and since that day I've been a screever. I make a pound a week. You can't keep six kids on a pound a week, but luckily my wife earns a bit taking in sewing.

'The worst thing in this life is the cold, and the next worst is the interference you have to put up with. At first, not knowing any better, I used sometimes to copy a nude on the pavement. The first I did was outside St Martin's-in-the-Fields church. A fellow in black – I suppose he was a churchwarden or something – came out in a tearing rage. "Do you think we can have that obscenity outside God's holy house?" he cried. So I had to wash it out. It was a copy of Botticelli's Venus. Another time I copied the same picture on the Embankment. A policeman passing looked at it, and then, without a word, walked onto it and rubbed it out with his great flat feet.'

Bozo told the same tale of police interference. At the time when I was with him there had been a case of 'immoral conduct' in Hyde Park, in which the police had behaved rather badly. Bozo produced a cartoon of Hyde Park with policemen concealed in the trees, and the legend, 'Puzzle, find the policemen'. I pointed out to him how much more telling it would be to put, 'Puzzle, find the immoral conduct', but Bozo would not hear of it. He said that any policeman who saw it would move him on, and he would lose his pitch for good.

Below screevers come the people who sing hymns, or sell matches, or bootlaces, or envelopes containing a few grains of lavender – called, euphemistically, perfume. All these people are frankly beggars, exploiting an appearance of misery, and none of them takes on an average more than half a crown a day. The reason why they have to pretend to sell matches and so forth instead of begging outright is that this is demanded by the absurd English law about begging. As the law now stands, if you approach a stranger and ask him for twopence, he can call a policeman and get you seven days for begging. But if you make the air hideous by droning 'Nearer, my god, To Thee', or scrawl some chalk daubs on the pavement, or stand about with a tray of matches – in short, if you make a nuisance of youself – you are held to be following a legitimate trade and not begging. Match-selling and street-singing are simply legalized crimes. Not profitable crimes, however; there is not a singer or match-seller in London who can be sure of £50 a year – a poor return for standing eighty-four hours a week on the kerb, with the cars grazing your backside.

It is worth saying something about the social position of beggars, for when one has consorted with them, and found that they are ordinary human beings, one cannot help being struck by the curious attitude that society takes towards them. People seem to feel that there is essential difference between beggars and ordinary 'working' men. They are a race apart – outcasts, like criminals and prostitutes. Working men 'work', beggars do not 'work'; they are parasites, worthless in their very nature. It is taken for granted that a beggar does not 'earn' his living, as a bricklayer or a literary critic 'earns' his. He is a mere social excrescence, tolerated because we live in a humane age, but essentially despicable.

Yet if one looks closely one sees that there is no *essential* difference between a beggar's livelihood and that of numberless respectable people. Beggars do not work, it is said; but, then, what is *work?* A navvy works by swinging a pick. An accountant works by adding up figures. A beggar works by standing out of doors in all weathers and getting varicose veins, chronic bronchitis, etc. It is a trade like any other; quite useless, of course – but, then, many reputable trades are quite useless. And as a social type a beggar compares well with scores of others. He is honest compared with the sellers of most patent medicines, high-minded compared with a Sunday newspaper proprietor, amiable compared with a hire-purchase tout – in short, a parasite, but a fairly harmless parasite. He seldom extracts more than a bare living from the community, and, what should justify him according to our ethical ideas, he pays for it over and over in suffering. I do not think there is anything about a beggar that sets him in a different class from other people, or gives most modern men the right to despise him.

Then the question arises, Why are beggars despised? – for they are despised, universally. I believe it is for the simple reason that they fail to earn a decent living. In practice nobody cares whether work is useful or useless, productive or parasitic; the sole thing demanded is that it shall be profitable. In all the modern talk about energy, efficiency, social service and the rest of it, what meaning is there except 'Get money, get it legally, and get a lot of it'? Money has become the grand test of virtue. By this test beggars fail, and for this they are despised. If one could earn even ten pounds a week at begging, it would become a respectable profession immediately. A beggar, looked at realistically, is simply a business man, getting his living, like other business men, in the way that comes to hand. He has not, more than most modern people, sold his honour; he has merely made the mistake of choosing a trade at which it is impossible to grow rich.

Chapter Thirty-two

I want to put in some notes, as short as possible, on London slang and swearing. These (omitting the ones that everyone knows) are some of the cant words now used in London:

A gagger – beggar or street performer of any kind. A moocher – one who begs outright, without pretence of doing a trade. A nobbler – one who collects pennies for a beggar. A chanter – a street singer. A clodhopper – a street dancer. A mugfaker – a street photographer. A glimmer – one who watches vacant motor-cars. A gee (or jee – it is pronounced jee) – the accomplice of a cheapjack, who stimulates trade by pretending to buy something. A split – a detective. A flattie – a policeman. A dideki – a gypsy. A toby – a tramp.

A drop – money given to a beggar. Funkum – lavender or other perfume sold in envelopes. A boozer – a public-house. A slang – a hawker's licence. A kip – a place to sleep in, or a night's lodging. Smoke – London. A judy – a woman. The spike – the casual ward. The lump – the casual ward. A tosheroon – a half-crown. A deaner – a shilling. A hog – a shilling. A sprowsie – a sixpence. Clods – coppers. A drum – a billy can. Shackles soup. A chat – a louse. Hard-up – tobacco made from cigarette ends. A stick or cane – a burglar's jemmy. A peter – a safe. A bly – a burglar's oxy-acetylene blow-lamp.

To bawl – to suck or swallow. To know off – to steal. To skipper – to sleep in the open.

About half of these words are in the larger dictionaries. It is interesting to guess at the derivation of some of them, though one or two – for instance, 'funkum' and 'tosheroon' – are beyond guessing. 'Deaner' presumably comes from 'denier'. 'Glimmer' (with the verb 'to glim') may have something to do with the old word 'glim', meaning a light, or another old word 'glim', meaning a glimpse; but it is an instance of the formation of new words, for in its present sense it can hardly be older than motor-cars. 'Gee' is a curious word; conceivably it has arisen out of 'gee', meaning horse, in the sense of stalking horse. The derivation of 'screever' is mysterious. It must come ultimately from *scribo*, but there has been no similar word in English for the past hundred and fifty years; nor can it have come directly from the French, for pavement artists are unknown in France. 'Judy' and 'bawl' are East End words, not found west of Tower Bridge. 'Smoke' is a word used only by tramps. 'Kip' is Danish. Till quite recently the word 'doss' was used in this sense, but it is now quite obsolete.

London slang and dialect seem to change very rapidly. The old London accent described by Dickens and Surtees, with v for w and w for v and so forth, has now vanished utterly. The Cockney accent as we know it seems to have come up in the 'forties (it is first mentioned in an American book, Herman Melville's *White Jacket*), and Cockney is already changing; there are few people now who say 'fice' for 'face', 'nawce' for 'nice' and so forth as consistently as they did twenty years ago. The slang changes together with the accent. Twenty-five or thirty years ago, for instance, the 'rhyming slang' was all the rage in London. In the 'rhyming slang' everything was named by something rhyming with it – a 'hit or miss' for a kiss, 'plates of meat' for feet, etc. It was so common that it was even reproduced in novels; now it is almost extinct.[1] Perhaps all the words I have mentioned above will have vanished in another twenty years.

The swear words also change – or, at any rate, they are subject to fashions. For example, twenty years ago the London working classes habitually used the word 'bloody'. Now they have abandoned it utterly, though novelists still represent them as using it. No born Londoner (it is different with people of Scotch or Irish origin) now says 'bloody', unless he is a man of some education. The word has, in fact, moved up in the social scale and ceased to be a swear word for the purposes of the working classes. The current London adjective, now tacked on to every noun, is ——. No doubt in time ——, like 'bloody', will find its way into the drawing-room and be replaced by some other word.

[1] It survives in certain abbreviations, such as 'use your twopenny' or 'use your head'. 'Twopenny' is arrived at like this: head – loaf of bread – twopenny loaf – twopenny.

The whole business of swearing, especially English swearing, is mysterious. Of its very nature swearing is as irrational as magic – indeed, it is a species of magic. But there is also a paradox about it, namely this: Our intention in swearing is to shock and wound, which we do by mentioning something that should be kept secret – usually something to do with the sexual functions. But the strange thing is that when a word is well established as a swear word, it seems to lose its original meaning; that is, it loses the thing that made it into a swear word. A word becomes an oath because it means a certain thing, and, because it has become an oath, it ceases to mean that thing. For example, ——. The Londoners do now use, or very seldom use, this word in its original meaning; it is on their lips from morning till night, but it is a mere expletive and means nothing. Similarly with ——, which is rapidly losing its original sense. One can think of similar instances in French – for example, ——, which is now a quite meaningless expletive. The word ——, also is still used occasionally in Paris, but the people who use it, or most of them, have no idea of what it once meant. The rule seems to be that words accepted as swear words have some magical character, which sets them apart and makes them useless for ordinary conversation.

Words used as insults seem to be governed by the same paradox as swear words. A word becomes an insult, one would suppose, because it means something bad; but in practice its insult-value has little to do with its actual meaning. For example, the most bitter insult one can offer to a Londoner is 'bastard' – which, taken for what it means, is hardly an insult at all. And the worst insult to women, either in London or Paris, is 'cow'; a name which might even be a compliment, for cows are among the most likeable of animals. Evidently a word is an insult simply because it is meant as an insult, without reference to its dictionary meaning; words, especially swear words, being what public opinion chooses to make them. In this connection it is interesting to see how a swear word can change character by crossing a frontier. In England you can print '*Je m'en fous*' without protest from anybody. In France you have to print it '*Je m'en f——*.' Or, as another example, take the words 'barnshoot' – a corruption of the Hindustani word *bahinchut*. A vile and unforgiveable insult in India, this word is a piece of gentle badinage in England. I have even seen it in a school text-book; it was in one of Aristophanes' plays, and the annotator suggested it as a rendering of some gibberish spoken by a Persian ambassador. Presumably the annotator knew what *bahinchut* meant. But, because it was a foreign word, it had lost its magical swear-word quality and could be printed.

One other thing is noticeable about swearing in London, and that is that the men do not usually swear in front of the women. In Paris it is quite different. A Parisian workman may prefer to suppress an oath in front of a woman, but he is not at all scrupulous about it, and the women themselves swear freely. The Londoners are more polite, or more squeamish, in this matter.

These are a few notes that I have set down more or less at random. It is a pity that someone capable of dealing with the subject does not keep a year-book of London slang and swearing, registering the changes accurately. It might throw useful light upon the formation, development and obsolescence of words.

Chapter Thirty-three

The two pounds that B. had given me lasted about ten days. That it lasted so long was due to Paddy, who had learned parsimony on the road and considered even one sound meal a day a wild extravagance. Food, to him, had come to mean simply bread and margarine – the eternal tea-and-two-slices, which will cheat hunger for an hour or two. He taught me how to live, food, bed, tobacco and all, at the rate of half a crown a day. And he managed to earn a few extra shillings by 'glimming' in the evenings. It was a precarious job, because illegal, but it brought in a little and eked out our money.

One morning we tried for a job as sandwich men. We went at five to an alleyway behind some offices, but there was already a queue of thirty or forty men waiting, and after two hours we were told that there was no work for us. We had not missed much, for sandwich men have an unenviable job. They are paid about three shillings a day for ten hours' work – it is hard work, especially in windy weather, and there is no skulking, for an inspector comes round frequently to see that the men are on their beat. To add to their troubles, they are only engaged by the day, or sometimes for three days, never weekly, so that they have to wait hours for their job every morning. The number of unemployed men who are ready to do the work makes them powerless to fight for better treatment. The job all sandwich men covet is distributing handbills, which is paid for at the same rate. When you see a man distributing handbills you can do him a good turn by taking one, for he goes off duty when he has distributed all his bills.

Meanwhile we went on with the lodging-house life – a squalid, eventless life of crushing boredom. For days together there was nothing to do but sit in the underground kitchen, reading yesterday's newspaper, or, when one could get hold of it, a back number of the *Union Jack*. It rained a great deal at this time, and everyone who came in steamed, so that the kitchen stank horribly. One's only excitement was the periodical tea-and-two-slices. I do not know how many men are living this life in London – it must be thousands at the least. As to Paddy, it was actually the best life he had known for two years past. His interludes from tramping, the times when he had somehow laid hands on a few shillings, had all been like this; the tramping itself had been slightly worse. Listening to his whimpering voice – he was always whimpering when he was not eating – one realized what torture unemployment must be to him. People are wrong when they think that an unemployed man only worries about losing his wages; on the contrary, an illiterate man, with the work habit in his bones, needs work even more than he needs money. An educated man can put up with enforced idleness, which is one of the worst evils of poverty. But a man like Paddy, with no means of filling up time, is as miserable out of work as a dog on the chain. That is why it is such nonsense to pretend that those who have 'come down in the world' are to be pitied above all others. The man who really merits pity is the man who has been down from the start, and faces poverty with a blank, resourceless mind.

It was a dull time, and little of it stays in my mind, except for talks with Bozo.

Once the lodging-house was invaded by a slumming-party. Paddy and I had been out, and, coming back in the afternoon, we heard sounds of music downstairs. We went down to find three gentle-people, sleekly dressed, holding a religious service in our kitchen. They were a grave and reverend seignior in a frock coat, a lady sitting at a portable harmonium, and a chinless youth toying with a crucifix. It appeared that they had marched in and started to hold the service, without any kind of invitation whatever.

It was a pleasure to see how the lodgers met this intrusion. They did not offer the smallest rudeness to the slummers; they just ignored them. By common consent everyone in the kitchen – a hundred men, perhaps – behaved as though the slummers had not existed. There they stood patiently singing and exhorting, and no more notice was taken of them than if they had been earwigs. The gentleman in the frock coat preached a sermon, but not a word of it was audible; it was drowned in the usual din of songs, oaths and the clattering of pans. Men sat at their meals and card games three feet away from the harmonium, peaceably ignoring it. Presently the slummers gave it up and cleared out, not insulted in any way, but merely disregarded. No doubt they consoled themselves by thinking how brave they had been, 'freely venturing into the lowest dens', etc. etc.

Bozo said that these people came to the lodging-house several times a month. They had influence with the police, and the 'deputy' could not exclude them. It is curious how people take it for granted that they have a right to preach at you and pray over you as soon as your income falls below a certain level.

After nine days B.'s two pounds was reduced to one and ninepence. Paddy and I set aside eighteenpence for our beds, and spent threepence on the usual tea-and-two-slices, which we shared – an appetizer rather than a meal. By the afternoon we were damnably hungry and Paddy remembered a church near King's Cross Station where a free tea was given once a week to tramps. This was the day, and we decided to go there. Bozo, though it was rainy weather and he was almost penniless, would not come, saying that churches were not his style.

Outside the church quite a hundred men were waiting, dirty types who had gathered from far and wide at the news of a free tea, like kites round a dead buffalo. Presently the doors opened and a clergyman and some girls shepherded us into a gallery at the top of the church. It was an evangelical church, gaunt and wilfully ugly, with texts about blood and fire blazoned on the walls, and a hymn-book containing twelve hundred and fifty-one hymns; reading some of the hymns, I concluded that the book would do as it stood for an anthology of bad verse. There was to be a service after the tea, and the regular congregation were sitting in the well of the church below. It was a week-day, and there were only a few dozen of them, mostly stringy old women who reminded one of boiling-fowls. We ranged ourselves in the gallery pews and were given our tea; it was a one-pound jam-jar of tea each, with six slices of bread and margarine. As soon as tea was over, a dozen tramps who had stationed themselves near the door bolted to avoid the service; the rest stayed, less from gratitude than lacking the cheek to go.

The organ let out a few preliminary hoots and the service began. And instantly, as though at a signal, the tramps began to misbehave in the most outrageous way. One would not have thought such scenes possible in a church. All round the gallery men lolled in their pews, laughed, chattered, leaned over and flicked pellets of bread among the congregation; I had to restrain the man next to me, more or less by force, from lighting a cigarette. The tramps treated the service as a purely comic spectacle. It was, indeed, a sufficiently ludicrous service – the kind where there are sudden yells of 'Hallelujah!' and endless extempore prayers – but their behaviour passed all bounds. There was one old fellow in the congregation – Brother Bootle or some such name – who was often called on to lead us in prayer, and whenever he stood up the tramps would begin stamping as though in a theatre; they said that on a previous occasion he had kept up an extempore prayer for twenty-five minutes, until the minister had interrupted him. Once when Brother Bootle stood up a tramp called out, 'Two to one 'e don't beat seven minutes!' so loud that the whole church must hear. It was not long before we were making far more noise than the minister. Sometimes somebody below would send up an indignant 'Hush!' but it made no impression. We had set ourselves to guy the service, and there was no stopping us.

It was a queer, rather disgusting scene. Below were the handful of simple, well-meaning people, trying hard to worship; and above were the hundred men whom they had fed, deliberately making worship impossible. A ring of dirty, hairy faces grinned down from the gallery, openly jeering. What could a few women and old men do against a hundred hostile tramps? They were afraid of us, and we were frankly bullying them. It was our revenge upon them for having humiliated us by feeding us.

The minister was a brave man. He thundered steadily through a long sermon on Joshua, and managed almost to ignore the sniggers and chattering from above. But in the end, perhaps goaded beyond endurance, he announced loudly:

'I shall address the last five minutes of my sermon to the *unsaved* sinners!'

Having said which, he turned his face to the gallery and kept it so for five minutes, lest there should be any doubt about who were saved and who unsaved. But much we cared! Even while the minister was threatening hell fire, we were rolling cigarettes, and at the last amen we clattered down the stairs with a yell, many agreeing to come back for another free tea next week.

The scene had interested me. It was so different from the ordinary demeanour of tramps – from the abject worm-like gratitude with which they normally accept charity. The explanation, of course, was that we outnumbered the congregation and so were not afraid of them. A man receiving charity practically always hates his benefactor – it is a fixed characteristic of human nature; and, when he has fifty or a hundred others to back him, he will show it.

In the evening, after the free tea, Paddy unexpectedly earned another eighteenpence at 'glimming'. It was exactly enough for another night's lodging, and we put it aside and went hungry till nine the next evening. Bozo, who might have given us some food, was away all day. The pavements were wet, and he had gone to the Elephant and Castle, where he knew of a ptich under shelter. Luckily I still had some tobacco, so that the day might have been worse.

At half-past eight Paddy took me to the Embankment, where a clergyman was known to distribute meal tickets once a week. Under Charing Cross Bridge fifty men were waiting, mirrored in the shivering puddles. Some of them were truly appalling specimens – they were Embankment sleepers, and the Embankment dredges up worse types than the spike. One of them, I remember, was dressed in an overcoat without buttons, laced up with rope, a pair of ragged trousers, and boots exposing his toes – not a rag else. He was bearded like a fakir, and he had managed to streak his chest and shoulders with some horrible black filth resembling train oil. What one could see of his face under the dirt and hair was bleached white as paper by some malignant disease. I heard him speak, and he had a goodish accent, as of a clerk or shopwalker.

Presently the clergyman appeared and the men ranged themselves in a queue in the order in which they had arrived. The clergyman was a nice, chubby, youngish man, and, curiously enough, very like Charlie, my friend in Paris. He was shy and embarrassed, and did not speak except for a brief good evening; he simply hurried down the line of men, thrusting a ticket upon each, and not waiting to be thanked. The consequence was that, for once, there was genuine gratitude, and everyone said that the clergyman was a —— good feller. Someone (in his hearing, I believe) called out: 'Well, *he'll* never be a —— bishop!' – this, of course, intended as a warm compliment.

The tickets were worth sixpence each, and were directed to an eating-house not far away. When we got there we found that the proprietor, knowing that the tramps could not go elsewhere, was cheating by only giving four pennyworth of food for each ticket. Paddy and I pooled our tickets, and received food which we could have got for sevenpence or eightpence at most coffee-shops. The clergyman had distributed well over a pound in tickets, so that the proprietor was evidently swindling the tramps to the tune of seven shillings or more a week. This kind of victimization is a regular part of a tramp's life, and it will go on as long as people continue to give meal tickets instead of money.

Paddy and I went back to the lodging-house and, still hungry, loafed in the kitchen, making the warmth of the fire a substitute for food. At half-past ten Bozo arrived, tired out and haggard, for his mangled leg made walking an agony. He had not earned a penny at screeving, all the pitches under shelter being taken, and for several hours he had begged outright, with one eye on the policemen. He had amassed eightpence – a penny short of his kip. It was long past the hour for paying, and he had only managed to slip indoors when the deputy was not looking; at any moment he might be caught and turned out, to sleep on the Embankment. Bozo took the things out of his pockets and looked them over, debating what to sell. He decided on his razor, took it round the kitchen, and in a few minutes he had sold it for threepence – enough to pay his kip, buy a basin of tea, and leave a halfpenny over.

Bozo got his basin of tea and sat down by the fire to dry his clothes. As he drank the tea I saw that he was laughing to himself, as though at some good joke. Surprised, I asked him what he had to laugh at.

'It's bloody funny!' he said. 'It's funny enough for *Punch*. What do you think I been and done?'

'What?'

'Sold my razor without having a shave first: Of all the —— fools!'

He had not eaten since the morning, had walked several miles with a twisted leg, his clothes were drenched, and he had a halfpenny between himself and starvation. With all this, he could laugh over the loss of his razor. One could not help admiring him.

Chapter Thirty-four

The next morning, our money being at an end, Paddy and I set out for the spike. We went southward by the Old Kent Road, making for Cromley; we could not go to a London spike, for Paddy had been in one recently and did not care to risk going again. It was a sixteen-mile walk over asphalt, blistering to the heels, and we were acutely hungry. Paddy browsed the pavement, laying up a store of cigarette ends against his time in the spike. In the end his perseverance was rewarded, for he picked up a penny. We bought a large piece of stale bread, and devoured it as we walked.

When we got to Cromley, it was too early to go to the spike, and we walked several miles farther, to a plantation beside a meadow, where one could sit down. It was a regular caravanserai of tramps – one could tell it by the worn grass and the sodden newspaper and rusty cans that they had left behind. Other tramps were arriving by ones and twos. It was jolly autumn weather. Near by, a deep bed of tansies was growing; it seems to me that even now I can smell the sharp reek of those tansies, warring with the reek of tramps. In the meadow two carthorse colts, raw sienna colour with white manes and tails, were nibbling at a gate. We sprawled about on the ground, sweaty and exhausted. Someone managed to find dry sticks and get a fire going, and we all had milkless tea out of a tin 'drum' which was passed round.

Some of the tramps began telling stories. One of them, Bill, was an interesting type, a genuine sturdy beggar of the old breed, strong as Hercules and a frank foe of work. He boasted that with his great strength he could get a navvying job any time he liked, but as soon as he drew his first week's wages he went on a terrific drunk and was sacked. Between whiles he 'mooched', chiefly from shopkeepers. He talked like this:

'I ain't goin' far in —— Kent. Kent's a tight county, Kent is. There's too many bin' moochin' about 'ere. The —— bakers get so as they'll throw their bread away sooner'n given it you. Now Oxford, that's the place for moochin', Oxford is. When I was in Oxford I mooched bread, and I mooched bacon, and I mooched beef, and every night I mooched tanners for my kip off of the students. The last night I was twopence short of my kip, so I goes up to a parson and mooches 'im for threepence. He give me threepence, and the next moment he turns round and gives me in charge for beggin'. "You bin beggin'," the copper says. "No I ain't," I says, "I was askin' the gentlemen the time," I says. The copper starts feelin' inside my coat, and he pulls out a pound of meat and two loaves of bread. "Well, what's all this, then?" he says. "You better come 'long to the station," he says. The beak give me seven days. I don't mooch from no more —— parsons. But Christ! what do I care for a lay-up of seven days?' etc., etc.

It seemed that his whole life was this – a round of mooching, drunks and lay-ups. He laughed as he talked of it, taking it all for a tremendous joke. He looked as though he made a poor thing out of begging, for he wore only a corduroy suit, scarf and cap – no socks or linen. Still, he was fat and jolly, and he even smelt of beer, a most unusual smell in a tramp nowadays.

Two of the tramps had been in Cromley spike recently, and they told a ghost story connected with it. Years ealier, they said, there had been a suicide there. A tramp had managed to smuggle a razor into his cell, and there cut his throat. In the morning, when the Tramp Major came round, the body was jammed against the door, and to open it they had to break the dead man's arm. In revenge for this, the dead man haunted his cell, and anyone who slept there was certain to die within the year; there were copious instances, of course. If a cell door stuck when you tried to open it, you should avoid that cell like the plague, for it was the haunted one.

Two tramps, ex-sailors, told another grisly story. A man (they swore they had known him) had planned to stow away on a boat bound for Chile. It was laden with manufactured goods packed in big wooden crates, and with the help of a docker the stowaway had managed to hide himself in one of these. But the docker had made a mistake about the order in which the crates were to be loaded. The crane gripped the stowaway, swung him aloft, and deposited him – at the very bottom of the hold, beneath hundreds of crates. No one discovered what had happened until the end of the voyage, when they found the stowaway rotting, dead of suffocation.

Another tramp told the story of Gilderoy, the Scottish robber. Gilderoy was the man who was condemned to be hanged, escaped, captured the judge who had sentenced him, and (splendid fellow!) hanged him. The tramps liked the story, of course, but the interesting thing was to see that they had got it all wrong. Their version was that Gilderoy escaped to America, whereas in reality he was recaptured and put to death. The story had been amended, no doubt deliberately; just as children amend the stories of Samson and Robin Hood, giving them happy endings which are quite imaginary.

This set the tramps talking about history, and a very old man declared that the 'one bite law' was a survival from days when the nobles hunted men instead of deer. Some of the others laughed at him, but he had the idea firm in his head. He had heard, too, of the Corn Laws, and the *jus primae noctis* (he believed it had really existed); also of the Great Rebellion, which he thought was a rebellion of poor against rich – perhaps he had got it mixed up with the peasant rebellions. I doubt whether the old man could read, and certainly he was not repeating newspaper articles. His scraps of history had been passed from generation to generation of tramps, perhaps for centuries in some cases. It was oral tradition lingering on, like a faint echo from the Middle Ages.

Paddy and I went to the spike at six in the evening, getting out at ten in the morning. It was much like Romton and Edbury, and we saw nothing of the ghost. Among the casuals were two young men named William and Fred, ex-fishermen from Norfolk, a lively pair and fond of singing. They had a song called 'Unhappy Bella' that is worth writing down. I heard them sing it half a dozen times during the next two days, and I managed to get it by heart, except a line or two which I have guessed. It ran:

Bella was young and Bella was fair
With bright blue eyes and golden hair,
O unhappy Bella!
Her step was light and her heart was gay,
But she had no sense, and one fine day
She got herself put in the family way
By a wicked, heartless, cruel deceiver.

Poor Bella, was young, she didn't believe
That the world is hard and men deceive,
O unhappy Bella!
She said, 'My man will do what's just,
He'll marry me now, because he must;'
Her heart was full of loving trust
In a wicked, heartless, cruel deceiver.

She went to his house; that dirty skunk
Had packed his bags and done a bunk,
O unhappy Bella!
Her landlady said, 'Get out, you whore,
I won't have your sort a-darkening my door.'
Poor Bella was put to affliction sore
By a wicked, heartless, cruel deceiver.

All night she tramped the cruel snows,
What she must have suffered nobody knows,
O unhappy Bella!
And when the morning dawned so red,
Alas, alas, poor Bella was dead,
Sent so young to her lonely bed
By a wicked, heartless, cruel deceiver.

So thus, you see, do what you will,
The fruits of sin are suffering still,
O unhappy Bella!
As into the grave they laid her low,
The men said, 'Alas, but life is so,'
But the women chanted, sweet and low,
'It's all the men, the dirty bastards!'

Written by a woman, perhaps.

William and Fred, the singers of this song, were thorough scallywags, the sort of men who get tramps a bad name. They happened to know that the Tramp Major at Cromley had a stock of old clothes, which were to be given at need to casuals. Before going in William and Fred took off their boots, ripped the seams and cut pieces off the soles, more or less ruining them. Then they applied for two pairs of boots, and the Tramp Major, seeing how bad their boots were, gave them almost new pairs. William and Fred were scarcely outside the spike in the morning before they had sold these boots for one and ninepence. It seemed to them quite worth while, for one and ninepence, to make their own boots practically unwearable.

Leaving the spike, we are started southward, a long slouching procession, for Lower Binfield and Ide Hill. On the way there was a fight between two of the tramps. They had quarrelled overnight (there was some silly *casus belli* about one saying to the other 'Bull shit', which was taken for Bolshevik – a deadly insult), and they fought it out in a field. A dozen of us stayed to watch them. The scene sticks in my mind for one thing – the man who was beaten going down, and his cap falling off and showing that his hair was quite white. After that some of us intervened and stopped the fight. Paddy had meanwhile been making inquiries, and found that the real cause of the quarrel was, as usual, a few pennyworth of food.

We got to Lower Binfield quite early, and Paddy filled in the time by asking for work at back doors. At one house he was given some boxes to chop up for firewood, and, saying he had a mate outside, he brought me in and we did the work together. When it was done the householder told the maid to take us out a cup of tea. I remember the terrified way in which she brought it out, and then, losing her courage, set the cups down on the path and bolted back to the house, shutting herself in the kitchen. So dreadful is the name of 'tramp'. They paid us sixpence each, and we bought a threepenny loaf and half an ounce of tobacco, leaving fivepence.

Paddy though it wiser to bury our fivepence, for the Tramp Major at Lower Binfield was renowned as a tyrant and might refuse to admit us if we had any money at all. It is quite a common practice of tramps to bury their money. If they intend to smuggle at all a large sum into the spike they generally sew it into their clothes, which may mean prison if they are caught, of course. Paddy and Bozo used to tell a good story about this. An Irishman (Bozo said it was an Irishman; Paddy said an Englishman), not a tramp, and in possession of thirty pounds, was stranded in a small village where he could not get a bed. He consulted a tramp, who advised him to go to the workhouse. It is quite a regular proceeding, if one cannot get a bed elsewhere, to get one at the workhouse, paying a reasonable sum for it. The Irishman, however, thought he would be clever and get a bed for nothing, so he presented himself at the workhouse as an ordinary casual. He had sewn the thirty pounds into his clothes. Meanwhile the tramp who had advised him had seen his chance, and that night he privately asked the Tramp Major for permission to leave the spike early in the morning, as he had to see about a job. At six in the morning he was released, and went out – in the Irishman's clothes. The Irishman complained of the theft, and was given thirty days for going into a casual ward under false pretences.

Chapter Thirty-five

Arrived at Lower Binfield, we sprawled for a long time on the green, watched by cottagers from their front gates. A clergyman and his daughter came and stared silently at us for a while, as though we had been aquarium fishes, and then went away again. There were several dozen of us waiting. William and Fred were there, still singing, and the men who had fought, and Bill the moocher. He had been mooching from bakers, and had quantities of stale bread tucked away between his coat and his bare body. He shared it out, and we were all glad of it. There was a woman among us, the first woman tramp I had ever seen. She was a fattish, battered, very dirty woman of sixty, in a long, trailing black skirt. She put on great airs of dignity, and if anyone sat down near her she sniffed and moved farther off.

'Where you bound for, missis?' one of the tramps called to her.

The woman sniffed and looked into the distance.

'Come on, missis,' he said, 'cheer up. Be chummy. We're all in the same boat 'ere.'

'Thank you,' said the woman bitterly, 'when I want to get mixed up with a set of *tramps*, I'll let you know.'

I enjoyed the way she said *tramps*. It seemed to show you in a flash the whole of her soul; a small, blinkered, feminine soul, that had learned absolutely nothing from years on the road. She was, no doubt, a respectable widow woman, become a tramp through some grotesque accident.

The spike opened at six. This was Saturday, and we were to be confined over the week-end, which is the usual practice; why, I do not know, unless it is from a vague feeling that Sunday merits something disagreeable. When we registered I gave my trade as 'journalist'. It was truer than 'painter', for I had sometimes earned money from newspaper articles, but it was a silly thing to say, being bound to lead to questions. As soon as we were inside the spike and had been lined up for the search, the Tramp Major called my name. He was a stiff, soldierly man of forty, not looking the bully he had been represented, but with an old soldier's gruffness. He said sharply:

'Which of you is Blank?' (I forget what name I had given.)

'Me, sir.'

'So you are a journalist?'

'Yes, sir,' I said, quaking. A few questions would betray the fact that I had been lying, which might mean prison. But the Tramp Major only looked me up and down and said:

'Then you are a gentleman?'

'I suppose so.'

He gave me another long look. 'Well, that's bloody bad luck, guv'nor,' he said; 'bloody bad luck that is.' And thereafter he treated me with unfair favouritism, and even with a kind of deference. He did not search me, and in the bathroom he actually gave me a clean towel to myself – an unheard-of luxury. So powerful is the word 'gentleman' in an old soldier's ear.

By seven we had wolfed our bread and tea and were in our cells. We slept one in a cell, and there were bedsteads and straw palliasses, so that one ought to have had a good night's sleep. But no spike is perfect, and the peculiar shortcoming at Lower Binfield was the cold. The hot pipes were not working, and the two blankets we had been given were thin cotton things and almost useless. It was only autumn, but the cold was bitter. One spent the long twelve-hour night in turning from side to side, falling asleep for a few minutes and waking up shivering. We could not smoke, for our tobacco, which we had managed to smuggle in, was in our clothes and we should not get these back till the morning. All down the passage one could hear groaning noises, and sometimes a shouted oath. No one, I imagine, got more than an hour or two of sleep.

In the morning, after breakfast and the doctor's inspection, the Tramp Major herded us all into the dining-room and locked the door upon us. It was a limewashed, stone-floored room, unutterably dreary, with its furniture of deal boards and benches, and its prison smell. The barred windows were too high to look out of, and there were no ornaments save a clock and a copy of the workhouse rules. Packed elbow to elbow on the benches, we were bored already, though it was barely eight in the morning. There was nothing to do, nothing to talk about, not even room to move. The sole consolation was that one could smoke, for smoking was connived at so long as one was not caught in the act. Scotty, a little hairy tramp with a bastard accent sired by Cockney out of Glasgow, was tobaccoless, his tin of cigarette ends having fallen out of his boot during the search and been impounded. I stood him the makings of a cigarette. We smoked furtively, thrusting our cigarettes into our pockets, like schoolboys, when we heard the Tramp Major coming.

Most of the tramps spent ten continuous hours in this comfortless, soulless room. Heaven knows how they put up with it. I was luckier than the others, for at ten o'clock the Tramp Major told off a few men for odd jobs, and he picked me out to help in the workhouse kitchen, the most coveted job of all. This, like the clean towel, was a charm worked by the word 'gentleman'.

There was no work to do in the kitchen, and I sneaked off into a small shed used for storing potatoes, where some workhouse paupers were skulking to avoid the Sunday morning service. There were comfortable packing-cases to sit on, and some back numbers of the *Family Herald*, and even a copy of *Raffles* from the workhouse library. The paupers talked interestingly about workhouse life. They told me, among other things, that the thing really hated in the workhouse, as a stigma of charity, is the uniform; if the men could wear their own clothes, or even their own caps and scarves, they would not mind being paupers. I had my dinner from the workhouse table, and it was a meal fit for a boa-constrictor – the largest meal I had eaten since my first day at the Hôtel X. The paupers said that they habitually gorged to the bursting-point on Sunday and were underfed the rest of the week. After dinner the cook set me to do the washing up, and told me to throw away the food that remained. The wastage was astonishing and, in the circumstances, appalling. Half-eaten joints of meat, and bucketfuls of broken bread and vegetables, were pitched away like so much rubbish and then defiled with tea-leaves. I filled five dustbins to overflowing with quite eatable food. And while I did so fifty tramps were sitting in the spike with their bellies half filled by the spike dinner of bread and cheese, and perhaps two cold boiled potatoes each in honour of Sunday. According to the paupers, the food was thrown away from deliberate policy, rather than that it should be given to the tramps.

At three I went back to the spike. The tramps had been sitting there since eight, with hardly room to move an elbow, and they were now half mad with boredom. Even smoking was at an end, for a tramp's tobacco is picked-up cigarette ends, and he starves if he is more than a few hours away from the pavement. Most of the men were too bored even to talk; they just sat packed on the benches, staring at nothing, their scrubby faces split in two by enormous yawns. The room stank of *ennui*.

Paddy, his backside aching from the hard bench, was in a whimpering mood, and to pass the time away I talked with a rather superior tramp, a young carpenter who wore a collar and tie and was on the road, he said, for lack of a set of tools. He kept a little aloof from the other tramps, and held himself more like a free man than a casual. He had literary tastes, too, and carried a copy of *Quentin Durward* in his pocket. He told me that he never went into a spike unless driven there by hunger, sleeping under hedges and behind ricks in preference. Along the south coast he had begged by day and slept in bathing-huts for weeks at a time.

We talked of life on the road. He criticized the system that makes a tramp spend fourteen hours a day in the spike, and the other ten in walking and dodging the police. He spoke of his own case – six months at the public charge for want of a few pounds' worth of tools. It was idiotic, he said.

Then I told him about the wastage of food in the workhouse kitchen, and what I thought of it. And at that he changed his tone instantly. I saw that I had awakened the pew-renter who sleeps in every English workman. Though he had been famished along with the others, he at once saw reasons why the food should have been thrown away rather than given to the tramps. He admonished me quite severely.

'They have to do it,' he said. 'If they made these places too comfortable, you'd have all the scum of the country flocking into them. It's only the bad food as keeps all that scum away. These here tramps are too lazy to work, that's all that's wrong with them. You don't want to go encouraging of them. They're scum.'

I produced arguments to prove him wrong, but he would not listen. He kept repeating:

'You don't want to have any pity on these here tramps – scum, they are. You don't want to judge them by the same standards as men like you and me. They're scum, just scum.'

It was interesting to see the subtle way in which he disassociated himself from 'these here tramps'. He had been on the road six months, but in the sight of God, he seemed to imply, he was not a tramp. I imagine there are quite a lot of tramps who thank God they are not tramps. They are like the trippers who say such cutting things about trippers.

Three hours dragged by. At six supper arrived, and turned out to be quite uneatable; the bread, tough enough in the morning (it had been cut into slices on Saturday night), was now as hard as ship's biscuit. Luckily it was spread with dripping, and we scraped the dripping off and ate that alone, which was better than nothing. At a quarter-past six we were sent to bed. New tramps were arriving, and in order not to mix the tramps of different days (for fear of infectious diseases) the new men were put in the cells and we in dormitories. Our dormitory was a barn-like room with thirty beds close together, and a tub to serve as a common chamber-pot. It stank abominably, and the older men coughed and got up all night. But being so many together kept the room warm, and we had some sleep.

We dispersed at ten in the morning, after a fresh medical inspection, with a hunk of bread and cheese for our midday dinner. William and Fred, strong in the possession of a shilling, impaled their bread on the spike railings – as a protest, they said. This was the second spike in Kent that they had made too hot to hold them, and they thought it a great joke. They were cheerful souls, for tramps. The imbecile (there is an imbecile in every collection of tramps) said that he was too tired to walk and clung to the railings, until the Tramp Major had to dislodge him and start him with a kick. Paddy and I turned north, for London. Most of the others were going on to Ide Hill, said to be about the worst spike in England.[1]

Once again it was jolly autumn weather, and the road was quiet, with few cars passing. The air was like sweet-briar after the spike's mingled stenches of sweat, soap and drains. We two seemed the only tramps on the road. Then I heard a hurried step behind us, and someone calling. It was little Scotty, the Glasgow tramp, who had run after us panting. He produced a rusty tin from his pocket. He wore a friendly smile, like someone repaying an obligation.

'Here y'are, mate,' he said cordially. 'I owe you some fag ends. You stood me a smoke yesterday. The Tramp Major give me back my box of fag ends when we come out this morning. One good turn deserves another – here y'are.'

And he put four sodden, debauched, loathly cigarette ends into my hand.

[1] I have been in it since, and it is not so bad.

Chapter Thirty-six

I want to set down some general remarks about tramps. When one comes to think of it, tramps are a queer product and worth thinking over. It is queer that a tribe of men, tens of thousands in number, should be marching up and down England like so many Wandering Jews. But though the case obviously wants considering, one cannot even start to consider it until one has got rid of certain prejudices. These prejudices are rooted in the idea that every tramp, *ipso facto*, is a blackguard. In childhood we have been taught that tramps are blackguards, and consequently there exists in our minds a sort of ideal or typical tramp – a repulsive, rather dangerous creature, who would die rather than work or wash, and wants nothing but to beg, drink and rob hen-houses. This tramp-monster is no truer to life than the sinister Chinaman of the magazine stories, but he is very hard to get rid of. The very word 'tramp' evokes his image. And the belief in him obscures the real questions of vagrancy.

To take a fundamental question about vagrancy: Why do tramps exist at all? It is a curious thing, but very few people know what makes a tramp take to the road. And, because of the belief in the tramp-monster, the most fantastic reasons are suggested. It is said, for instance, that tramps tramp to avoid work, to beg more easily, to seek opportunities for crime, even – least probable of reasons – because they like tramping. I have even read in a book of criminology that the tramp is an atavism, a throw-back to the nomadic stage of humanity. And meanwhile the quite obvious cause of vagrancy is staring one in the face. Of course a tramp is not a nomadic atavism – one might as well say that a commercial traveller is an atavism. A tramp tramps, not because he likes it, but for the same reason as a car keeps to the left; because there happens to be a law compelling him to do so. A destitute man, if he is not supported by the parish, can only get relief at the casual wards, and as each casual ward will only admit him for one night, he is automatically kept moving. He is a vagrant because, in the state of the law, it is that or starve. But people have been brought up to believe in the tramp-monster, and so they prefer to think that there must be some more or less villainous motive for tramping.

As a matter of fact, very little of the tramp-monster will survive inquiry. Take the generally accepted idea that tramps are dangerous characters. Quite apart from experience, one can say *a priori* that very few tramps are dangerous, because if they were dangerous they would be treated accordingly. A casual ward will often admit a hundred tramps in one night, and these are handled by a staff of at most three porters. A hundred ruffians could not be controlled by three unarmed men. Indeed, when one sees how tramps let themselves be bullied by the workhouse officials, it is obvious that they are the most docile, broken-spirited creatures imaginable. Or take the idea that all tramps are drunkards – an idea ridiculous on the face of it. No doubt many tramps would drink if they got the chance, but in the nature of things they cannot get the chance. At this moment a pale watery stuff called beer is sevenpence a pint in England. To be drunk on it would cost at least half a crown, and a man who can command half a crown at all often is not a tramp. The idea that tramps are impudent social parasites ('sturdy beggars') is not absolutely unfounded, but it is only true in a few per cent of the cases. Deliberate, cynical parasitism, such as one reads of in Jack London's books on American tramping, is not in the English character. The English are a conscience-ridden race, with a strong sense of the sinfulness of poverty. One cannot imagine the average Englishman deliberately turning parasite, and this national character does not necessarily change because a man is thrown out of work. Indeed, if one remembers that a tramp is only an Englishman out of work, forced by law to live as a vagabond, then the tramp-monster vanishes. I am not saying, of course, that most tramps are ideal characters; I am only saying that they are ordinary human beings, and that if they are worse than other people it is the result and not the cause of their way of life.

It follows that the 'Serve them damned well right' attitude that is normally taken towards tramps is no fairer than it would be towards cripples or invalids. When one has realized that, one begins to put oneself in a tramp's place and understand what his life is like. It is an extraordinarily futile, acutely unpleasant life. I have described the casual ward – the routine of a tramp's day – but there are three especial evils that need insisting upon. The first is hunger, which is the almost general fate of tramps. The casual ward gives them a ration which is probably not even meant to be sufficient, and anything beyond this must be got by begging – that is, by breaking the law. The result is that nearly every tramp is rotted by malnutrition; for proof of which one need only look at the men lining up outside any casual ward. The second great evil of a tramp's life – it seems much smaller at first sight, but it is a good second – is that he is entirely cut off from contact with women. This point needs elaborating.

Tramps are cut off from women, in the first place, because there are very few women at their level of society. One might imagine that among destitute people the sexes would be as equally balanced as elsewhere. But it is not so; in fact, one can almost say that below a certain level society is entirely male. The following figures, published by the L.C.C. from a night census taken on 13 February 1931, will show the relative numbers of destitute men and destitute women:

Spending the night in the streets, 60 men, 18 women.[1]
In shelters and homes not licensed as common lodging-houses, 1,057 men, 137 women.
In the crypt of St Martin's-in-the-Fields Church, 88 men, 12 women.
In L.C.C. casual wards and hostels, 674 men, 15 women.

It will be seen from these figures that at the charity level men outnumber women by something like ten to one. The cause is presumably that unemployment affects women less than men; also that any presentable woman can, in the last resort, attach herself to some man. The result, for a tramp, is that he is condemned to perpetual celibacy. For of course it goes without saying that if a tramp finds no women at his own level, those above – even a very little above – are as far out of his reach as the moon. The reasons are not worth discussing, but there is no doubt that women never, or hardly ever, condescend to men who are much poorer than themselves. A tramp, therefore, is a celibate from the moment when he takes to the road. He is absolutely without hope of getting

[1] This must be an underestimate. Still, the proportions probably hold good.

a wife, a mistress, or any kind of woman except – very rarely, when he can raise a few shillings – a prostitute.

It is obvious what the results of this must be: homosexuality, for instance, and occasional rape cases. But deeper than these there is the degradation worked in man who knows that he is not even considered fit for marriage. The sexual impulse, not to put it any higher, is a fundamental impulse, and starvation of it can be almost as demoralizing as physical hunger. The evil of poverty is not so much that it makes a man suffer as that it rots him physically and spiritually. And there can be no doubt that sexual starvation contributes to this rotting process. Cut off from the whole race of women, a tramp feels himself degraded to the rank of a cripple or a lunatic. No humiliation could do more damage to a man's self-respect.

The other great evil of a tramp's life is enforced idleness. By our vagrancy laws things are so arranged that when he is not walking the road he is sitting in a cell; or, in the intervals, lying on the ground waiting for the casual ward to open. It is obvious that this is a dismal, demoralizing way of life, especially for an uneducated man.

Besides these one could enumerate scores of minor evils – to name only one, discomfort, which is inseparable from life on the road; it is worth remembering that the average tramp has no clothes but what he stands up in, wears boots that are ill-fitting, and does not sit in a chair for months together. But the important point is that a tramp's sufferings are entirely useless. He lives a fantastically disagreeable life, and lives it to no purpose whatever. One could not, in fact invent a more futile routine than walking from prison to prison, spending perhaps eighteen hours a day in the cell and on the road. There must be at the least several tens of thousands of tramps in England. Each day they expend innumerable foot-pounds of energy – enough to plough thousands of acres, build miles of road, put up dozens of houses – in mere, useless walking. Each day they waste between them possibly ten years of time in staring at cell walls. They cost the country at least a pound a week a man, and give nothing in return for it. They go round and round, on an endless boring game of general post, which is of no use, and is not even meant to be of any use to any person whatever. The law keeps this process going, and we have got so accustomed to it that we are not surprised. But it is very silly.

Granting the futility of a tramp's life, the question is whether anything could be done to improve it. Obviously it would be possible, for instance, to make the casual wards a little more habitable, and this is actually being done in some cases. During the last year some of the casual wards have been improved – beyond recognition, if the accounts are true – and there is talk of doing the same to all of them. But this does not go to the heart of the problem. The problem is how to turn the tramp from a bored, half alive vagrant into a self-respecting human being. A mere increase of comfort cannot do this. Even if the casual wards became positively luxurious (they never will)[1] a tramp's life would still be wasted. He would still be a pauper, cut off from marriage and home life, and a dead loss to the community. What is needed is to depauperize him, and this can only be done by finding him work – not work for the sake of working, but work of which he can enjoy the benefit. At present, in the great

[1] In fairness it must be added that a few of the casual wards have been improved recently, at least from the point of view of sleeping accommodation. But most of them are the same as ever, and there has been no real improvement in the food.

majority of casual wards, tramps do no work whatever. At one time they were made to break stones for their food, but this was stopped when they had broken enough stone for years ahead and put the stone-breakers out of work. Nowadays they are kept idle, because there is seemingly nothing for them to do. Yet there is a fairly obvious way of making them useful, namely this: Each workhouse could run a small farm, or at least a kitchen garden, and every able-bodied tramp who presented himself could be made to do a sound day's work. The produce of the farm or garden could be used for feeding the tramps, and at the worst it would be better than the filthy diet of bread and margarine and tea. Of course, the casual wards could never be quite self-supporting, but they could go a long way towards it, and the rates would probably benefit in the long run. It must be remembered that under the present system tramps are as dead a loss to the country as they could possibly be, for they do not only do no work, but they live on a diet that is bound to undermine their health; the system, therefore, loses lives as well as money. A scheme which fed them decently, and made them produce at least a part of their own food, would be worth trying.

It may be objected that a farm or even a garden could not be run with casual labour. But there is no real reason why tramps should stay a day at each casual ward; they might stay a month or even a year, if there were work for them to do. The constant circulation of tramps is something quite artificial. At present a tramp is an expense to the rates, and the object of each workhouse is therefore to push him on to the next; hence the rule that he can stay only one night. If he returns within a month he is penalized by being confined for a week, and, as this is much the same as being in prison, naturally he keeps moving. But if he represented labour to the workhouse, and the workhouse represented sound food to him, it would be another matter. The workhouses would develop into partially self-supporting institutions, and the tramps, settling down here or there according as they were needed, would cease to be tramps. They would be doing something comparatively useful, getting decent food, and living a settled life. By degrees, if the scheme worked well, they might even cease to be regarded as paupers, and be able to marry and take a respectable place in society.

This is only a rough idea, and there are some obvious objections to it. Nevertheless, it does suggest a way of improving the status of tramps without piling new burdens on the rates. And the solution must, in any case, be something of this kind. For the question is, what to do with men who are underfed and idle; and the answer – to make them grow their own food – imposes itself automatically.

Chapter Thirty-seven

A word about the sleeping accommodation open to a homeless person in London. At present it is impossible to get a *bed* in any non-charitable institution in London for less than sevenpence a night. If you cannot afford sevenpence for a bed, you must put up with one of the following substitutes:

1. The Embankment. Here is the account that Paddy gave me of sleeping on the Embankment:

'De whole t'ing wid de Embankment is gettin' to sleep early. You got to be on your bench by eight o'clock, because dere ain't too many benches and sometimes dey're all taken. And you got to try to get to sleep at once. 'Tis too cold to sleep much after twelve o'clock, an' de police turns you off at four in de mornin'. It ain't easy to sleep, dough, wid dem bloody trams flyin' past your head all de time, an' dem sky-signs across de river flickin' on an' off in your eyes. De cold's cruel. Dem as sleeps dere generally wraps demselves up in newspaper, but it don't do much good. You'd be bloody lucky if you got t'ree hours' sleep.'

I have slept on the Embankment and found that it corresponded to Paddy's description. It is, however, much better than not sleeping at all, which is the alternative if you spend the night in the streets, elsewhere than on the Embankment. According to the law in London, you may sit down for the night, but the police must move you on if they see you asleep; the Embankment and one or two odd corners (there is one behind the Lyceum Theatre) are special exceptions. This law is evidently a piece of wilful offensiveness. Its object, so it is said, is to prevent people from dying of exposure; but clearly if a man has no home and is going to die of exposure, die he will, asleep or awake. In Paris there is no such law. There, people sleep by the score under the Seine bridges, and in doorways, and on benches in the squares, and round the ventilating shafts of the Metro, and even inside the Metro stations. It does no apparent harm. No one will spend a night in the street if he can possibly help it, and if he is going to stay out of doors he might as well be allowed to sleep, if he can.

2. The Twopenny Hangover. This comes a little higher than the Embankment. At the Twopenny Hangover, the lodgers sit in a row on a bench; there is a rope in front of them, and they lean on this as though leaning over a fence. A man, humorously called the valet, cuts the rope at five in the morning. I have never been there myself, but Bozo had been there often. I asked him whether anyone could sleep in such an attitude, and he said that it was more comfortable than it sounded – at any rate, better than the bare floor. There are similar shelters in Paris, but the charge there is only twenty-five centimes (a halfpenny) instead of twopence.

3. The Coffin, at fourpence a night. At the Coffin you sleep in a wooden box, with a tarpaulin for covering. It is cold, and the worst thing about it are the bugs, which, being enclosed in a box, you cannot escape.

Above this come the common lodging-houses, with charges varying between sevenpence and one and a penny a night. The best are the Rowton Houses, where the charge is a shilling, for which you get a cubicle to yourself, and the use of excellent bathrooms. You can also pay half a crown for a 'special', which is practically hotel accommodation. The Rowton Houses are splendid buildings, and the only objection to them is the strict discipline, with rules against cooking, card-playing, etc. Perhaps the best advertisement for the Rowton Houses is the fact that they are always full to overflowing. The Bruce Houses, at one and a penny, are also excellent.

Next best, in point of cleanliness, are the Salvation Army hostels, at sevenpence or eightpence. They vary (I have been in one or two that were not very unlike common lodging-houses), but most of them are clean, and they have good bathrooms; you have to pay extra for a bath, however. You can get a cubicle for a shilling. In the eightpenny dormitories the beds are comfortable, but there are not so many of them (as a rule at least forty to a room), and so close together, that it is impossible to get a quiet night. The numerous restrictions stink of prison and charity. The Salvation Army hostels would only appeal to people who put cleanliness before anything else.

Beyond this there are the ordinary common lodging-houses. Whether you pay sevenpence or a shilling, they are all stuffy and noisy, and the beds are uniformly dirty and uncomfortable. What redeems them are their *laissez-faire* atmosphere and the warm homelike kitchens where one can lounge at all hours of the day or night. They are squalid dens, but some kind of social life is possible in them. The women's lodging-houses are said to be generally worse than the men's, and there are very few houses with accommodation for married couples. In fact, it is nothing out of the common for a homeless man to sleep in one lodging-house and his wife in another.

At this moment at least fifteen thousand people in London are living in common lodging-houses. For an unattached man earning two pounds a week, or less, a lodging-house is a great convenience. He could hardly get a furnished room so cheaply, and the lodging-house gives him free firing, a bathroom of sorts, and plenty of society. As for the dirt, it is a minor evil. The really bad fault of lodging-houses is that they are places in which one pays to sleep, and in which sound sleep is impossible. All one gets for one's money is a bed measuring five feet six by two feet six, with a hard convex mattress and a pillow like a block of wood, covered by one cotton counterpane and two grey, stinking sheets. In winter there are blankets, but never enough. And this bed is in a room where there are never less than five, and sometimes fifty or sixty beds, a yard or two apart. Of course, no one can sleep soundly in such circumstances. The only other places where people are herded like this are barracks and hospitals. In the public wards of a hospital no one even hopes to sleep well. In barracks the soldiers are crowded, but they have good beds, and they are healthy; in a common lodging-house nearly all the lodgers have chronic coughs, and a large number have bladder diseases which make them get up at all hours of the night. The result is a perpetual racket, making sleep impossible. So far as my observation goes, no one in a lodging-house sleeps more than five hours a night – a damnable swindle when one has paid sevenpence or more.

Here legislation could accomplish something. At present there is all manner of legislation by the L.C.C. about lodging-houses, but it is not done in the interests of the lodgers. The L.C.C. only exert themselves to forbid drinking, gambling, fighting, etc. etc. There is no law to say that the beds in a lodging-house must be comfortable. This would be quite an easy thing to enforce – much easier, for instance, than restrictions upon gambling. The lodging-house keepers should be compelled to provide adequate bedclothes and better mattresses, and above all to divide their dormitories into cubicles. It does not matter how small a cubicle is, the important thing is that a man should be alone when he sleeps. These few changes, strictly enforced, would make an enormous difference. It is not impossible to make a lodging-house reasonably comfortable at the usual rates of payment. In the Croydon municipal lodging-house, where the charge is only ninepence, there are cubicles, good beds, chairs (a very rare luxury in lodging-houses), and kitchens above ground instead of in a cellar. There is no reason why every ninepenny lodging-house should not come up to this standard.

Of course, the owners of lodging-houses would be opposed *en bloc* to any improvement, for their present business is an immensely profitable one. The average house takes five or ten pounds a night, with no bad debts (credit being strictly forbidden), and except for rent the expenses are small. Any improvement would mean less crowding, and hence less profit. Still, the excellent municipal lodging-house at Croydon shows how well one *can* be served for ninepence. A few well-directed laws could make these conditions general. If the authorities are going to concern themselves with lodging-houses at all, they ought to start by making them more comfortable, not by silly restrictions that would never be tolerated in a hotel.

Chapter Thirty-eight

After we left the spike at Lower Binfield, Paddy and I earned half a crown at weeding and sweeping in somebody's garden, stayed the night at Cromley, and walked back to London. I parted from Paddy a day or two later. B. lent me a final two pounds, and, as I had only another eight days to hold out, that was the end of my troubles. My tame imbecile turned out worse than I had expected, but not bad enough to make me wish myself back in the spike or the Auberge de Jehan Cottard.

Paddy set out for Portsmouth, where he had a friend who might conceivably find work for him, and I have never seen him since. A short time ago I was told that he had been run over and killed, but perhaps my informant was mixing him up with someone else. I had news of Bozo only three days ago. He is in Wandsworth – fourteen days for begging. I do not suppose prison worries him very much.

My story ends here. It is a fairly trivial story, and I can only hope that it has been interesting in the same way as a travel diary is interesting. I can at least say, Here is the world that awaits you if you are ever penniless. Some day I want to explore that world more thoroughly. I should like to know people like Mario and Paddy and Bill the moocher, not from casual encounters, but intimately; I should like to understand what really goes on in the souls of *plongeurs* and tramps and Embankment sleepers. At present I do not feel that I have seen more than the fringe of poverty.

Still I can point to one or two things I have definitely learned by being hard up. I shall never again think that all tramps are drunken scoundrels, nor expect a beggar to be grateful when I give him a penny, nor be surprised if men out of work lack energy, nor subscribe to the Salvation Army, nor pawn my clothes, nor refuse a handbill, nor enjoy a meal at a smart restaurant. That is a beginning.

THE ROAD TO WIGAN PIER

Chapter One

The first sound in the mornings was the clumping of the mill-girls' clogs down the cobbled street. Earlier than that, I suppose, there were factory whistles which I was never awake to hear.

There were generally four of us in the bedroom, and a beastly place it was, with that defiled impermanent look of rooms that are not serving their rightful purpose. Years earlier the house had been an ordinary dwelling-house, and when the Brookers had taken it and fitted it out as a tripe-shop and lodging-house, they had inherited some of the more useless pieces of furniture and had never had the energy to remove them. We were therefore sleeping in what was still recognizably a drawing-room. Hanging from the ceiling there was a heavy glass chandelier on which the dust was so thick that it was like fur. And covering most of one wall there was a huge hideous piece of junk, something between a sideboard and a hall-stand, with lots of carving and little drawers and strips of looking-glass, and there was a once-gaudy carpet ringed by the slop-pails of years, and two gilt chairs with burst seats, and one of those old-fashioned horsehair armchairs which you slide off when you try to sit on them. The room had been turned into a bedroom by thrusting four squalid beds in among this other wreckage.

My bed was in the right-hand corner on the side nearest the door. There was another bed across the foot of it and jammed hard against it (it had to be in that position to allow the door to open) so that I had to sleep with my legs doubled up; if I straightened them out I kicked the occupant of the other bed in the small of the back. He was an elderly man named Mr Reilly, a mechanic of sorts and employed 'on top' at one of the coal-pits. Luckily he had to go to work at five in the morning, so I could uncoil my legs and have a couple of hours' proper sleep after he was gone. In the bed opposite there was a Scotch miner who had been injured in a pit accident (a huge chunk of stone pinned him to the ground and it was a couple of hours before they could lever if off), and had received five hundred pounds compensation. He was a big handsome man of forty, with grizzled hair and a clipped moustache, more like a sergeant-major than a miner, and he would lie in bed till late in the day, smoking a short pipe. The other bed was occupied by a succession of commercial travellers, newspaper-canvassers and hire-purchase touts who generally stayed for a couple of nights. It was a double bed and much the best in the room. I had slept in it myself my first night there, but had been manoeuvred out of it to make room for another lodger. I believe all newcomers spent their first night in the double bed, which was used, so to speak, as bait. All the windows were kept tight shut, with a red sandbag jammed in the bottom, and in the morning the room stank like a ferret's cage. You did not notice it when you got up, but if you went out of the room and came back, the smell hit you in the face with a smack.

I never discovered how many bedrooms the house contained, but strange to say there was a bathroom, dating from before the Brookers' time. Downstairs there was the usual kitchen living-room with its huge open range burning night and day. It was lighted only by a skylight, for on one side of it was the shop and on the other the larder, which opened into some dark subterranean place where the tripe was stored. Partly blocking the door of the larder there was a shapeless sofa upon which Mrs Brooker, our landlady, lay permanently ill, festooned in grimy blankets. She had a big pale yellow, anxious face. No one knew for certain what was the matter with her; I suspect that her only real trouble was over-eating. In front of the fire there was almost always a line of damp washing, and in the middle of the room was the big kitchen table at which the family and all the lodgers ate. I never saw this table completely uncovered, but I saw its various wrappings at different times. At the bottom there was a layer of old newspaper stained by Worcester Sauce; above that a sheet of sticky white oil-cloth; above that a green serge cloth; above that a coarse linen cloth, never changed and seldom taken off. Generally the crumbs from breakfast were still on the table at supper. I used to get to know individual crumbs by sight and watch their progress up and down the table from day to day.

The shop was a narrow, cold sort of room. On the outside of the window a few white letters, relics of ancient chocolate advertisements, were scattered like stars. Inside there was a slab upon which lay the great white folds of tripe, and the grey flocculent stuff known as 'black tripe', and the ghostly translucent feet of pigs, ready boiled. It was the ordinary 'tripe and pea' shop, and not much else was stocked except bread, cigarettes and tinned stuff. 'Teas' were advertised in the window, but if a customer demanded a cup of tea he was usually put off with excuses. Mr Brooker, though out of work for two years, was a miner by trade, but he and his wife had been keeping shops of various kinds as a side-line all their lives. At one time they had had a pub, but they had lost their licence for allowing gambling on the premises. I doubt whether any of their businesses had ever paid; they were the kind of people who run a business chiefly in order to have something to grumble about. Mr Brooker was a dark, small-boned, sour, Irish-looking man, and astonishingly dirty. I don't think I ever once saw his hands clean. As Mrs Brooker was now an invalid he prepared most of the food, and like all people with permanently dirty hands he had a peculiarly intimate, lingering manner of handling things. If he gave you a slice of bread-and-butter there was always a black thumb-print on it. Even in the early morning when he descended into the mysterious den behind Mrs Brooker's sofa and fished out the tripe, his hands were already black. I heard dreadful stories from the other lodgers about the place where the tripe was kept. Blackbeetles were said to swarm there. I do not know how often fresh consignments of tripe were ordered, but it was at long intervals, for Mrs Brooker used to date events by it. 'Let me see now, I've had in three lots of froze (frozen tripe) since that happened,' etc., etc. We lodgers were never given tripe to eat. At the time I imagined that this was because tripe was too expensive; I have since thought that it was merely because we knew too much about it. The Brookers never ate tripe themselves, I noticed.

The only permanent lodgers were the Scotch miner, Mr Reilly, two old-age pensioners and an unemployed man on the P.A.C. named Joe – he was the kind of person who has no surname. The Scotch miner was a bore when you got to know him. Like so many unemployed men he spent too much time reading newspapers, and if you did not head him off he would discourse for hours about such things as the Yellow Peril, trunk murders, astrology, and the conflict between religion and science. The old-age pensioners had, as usual, been driven from their homes by the Means Test. They handed their weekly ten shillings over to the Brookers and in return got the kind of accommodation you would expect for ten shillings; that is, a bed in the attic and meals chiefly of bread-and-butter. One of them was of 'superior' type and was dying of some malignant disease – cancer, I believe. He only got out of bed on the days when he went to draw his pension. The other, called by everyone Old Jack, was an ex-miner aged seventy-eight who had worked well over fifty years in the pits. He was alert and intelligent, but curiously enough he seemed only to remember his boyhood experiences and to have forgotten all about the modern mining machinery and improvements. He used to tell me tales of fights with savage horses in the narrow galleries underground. When he heard that I was arranging to go down several coal mines he was contemptuous and declared that a man of my size (six feet two and a half) would never manage the 'travelling'; it was no use telling him that the 'travelling' was better than it used to be. But he was friendly to everyone and used to give us all a fine shout of 'Good night, boys!' as he crawled up the stairs to his bed somewhere under the rafters. What I most admired about Old Jack was that he never cadged; he was generally out of tobacco towards the end of the week, but he always refused to smoke anyone else's. The Brookers had insured the lives of both old-age pensioners with one of the tanner-a-week companies. It was said that they were overheard anxiously asking the insurance-tout 'how long people lived when they've got cancer'.

Joe, like the Scotchman, was a great reader of newspapers and spent almost his entire day in the public library. He was the typical unmarried unemployed man, a derelict-looking, frankly ragged creature with a round, almost childish face on which there was a naïvely naughty expression. He looked more like a neglected little boy than a grown-up man. I suppose it is the complete lack of responsibility that makes so many of these men look younger than their ages. From Joe's appearance I took him to be about twenty-eight, and was amazed to learn that he was forty-three. He had a love of resounding phrases and was very proud of the astuteness with which he had avoided getting married. He often said to me, 'Matrimonial chains is a big item', evidently feeling this to be a very subtle and portentous remark. His total income was fifteen shillings a week, and he paid out six or seven to the Brookers for his bed. I sometimes used to see him making himself a cup of tea over the kitchen fire, but for the rest he got his meals somewhere out of doors; it was mostly slices of bread-and-marg and packets of fish and chips, I suppose.

Besides these there was a floating clientele of commercial travellers of the poorer sort, travelling actors – always common in the North because most of the larger pubs hire variety artists at the week-ends – and newspaper-canvassers. The newspaper-canvassers were a type I had never met before. Their job seemed to me so hopeless, so appalling that I wondered how anyone could put up with such a thing when prison was a possible alternative. They were employed mostly by weekly or Sunday papers, and they were sent from town to town, provided with maps and given a list of streets which they had to 'work' each day. If they failed to secure a minimum of twenty orders a day, they got the sack. So long as they kept up their twenty orders a day they received a small salary – two pounds a week, I think; on any order over the twenty they drew a tiny commission. The thing is not so impossible as it sounds, because in working-class districts every family takes in a twopenny weekly paper and changes it every few weeks; but I doubt whether anyone keeps a job of that kind long. The newspapers engage poor desperate wretches, out-of-work clerks and commercial travellers and the like, who for a while make frantic efforts and keep their sales up to the minimum; then as the deadly work wears them down they are sacked and fresh men are taken on. I got to know two who were employed by one of the more notorious weeklies. Both of them were middle-aged men with families to support, and one of them was a grandfather. They were on their feet ten hours a day, 'working' their appointed streets, and then busy late into the night filling in blank forms for some swindle their paper was running – one of those schemes by which you are 'given' a set of crockery if you take out a six weeks' subscription and send a two-shilling postal order as well. The fat one, the grandfather, used to fall asleep with his head on a pile of forms. Neither of them could afford the pound a week which the Brookers charged for full board. They used to pay a small sum for their beds and make shame-faced meals in a corner of the kitchen off bacon and bread-and-margarine which they stored in their suit-cases.

The Brookers had large numbers of sons and daughters, most of whom had long since fled from home. Some were in Canada – 'at Canada', as Mrs Brooker used to put it. There was only one son living near by, a large pig-like young man employed in a garage, who frequently came to the house for his meals. His wife was there all day with the two children, and most of the cooking and laundering was done by her and by Emmie, the fiancée of another son who was in London. Emmie was a fair-haired, sharp-nosed, unhappy-looking girl who worked at one of the mills for some starvation wage, but nevertheless spent all her evenings in bondage at the Brookers' house. I gathered that the marriage was constantly being postponed and would probably never take place, but Mrs Brooker had already appropriated Emmie as a daughter-in-law, and nagged her in that peculiar watchful, loving way that invalids have. The rest of the housework was done, or not done, by Mr Brooker. Mrs Brooker seldom rose from her sofa in the kitchen (she spent the night there as well as the day) and was too ill to do anything except eat stupendous meals. It was Mr Brooker who attended to the shop, gave the lodgers their food and 'did out' the bedrooms. He was always moving with incredible slowness from one hated job to another. Often the beds were still unmade at six in the evening, and at any hour of the day you were liable to meet Mr Brooker on the stairs, carrying a full chamber-pot which he gripped with his thumb well over the rim. In the mornings he sat by the fire with a tub of filthy water, peeling potatoes at the speed of a slow-motion picture. I never saw anyone who could peel potatoes with quite such an air of brooding resentment. You could see the hatred of this 'bloody woman's work', as he called it, fermenting inside him, a kind of bitter juice. He was one of those people who can chew their grievances like a cud.

Of course, as I was indoors a good deal, I heard all about the Brookers' woes, and how everyone swindled them and was ungrateful to them, and how the shop did not pay and the lodging-house hardly paid. By local standards they were not so badly off, for, in some way I did not understand, Mr Brooker was dodging the Means Test and drawing an allowance from the P.A.C., but their chief pleasure was talking about their grievances to anyone who would listen. Mrs Brooker used to lament by the hour, lying on her sofa, a soft mound of fat and self-pity, saying the same things over and over again. 'We don't seem to get no customers nowadays. I don't know 'ow it is. The tripe's just a-laying there day after day – such beautiful tripe it is, too! It does seem 'ard, don't it now?' etc., etc., etc. All Mrs Brooker's laments ended with 'It does seem 'ard, don't it now?' like the refrain of a ballade. Certainly it was true that the shop did not pay. The whole place had the unmistakable dusty, flyblown air of a business that is going down. But it would have been quite useless to explain to them *why* nobody came to the shop, even if one had had the face to do it; neither was capable of understanding that last year's dead blue-bottles supine in the shop window are not good for trade.

But the thing that really tormented them was the thought of those two old-age pensioners living in their house, usurping floor-space, devouring food and paying only ten shillings a week. I doubt whether they were really losing money over the old-age pensioners, though certainly the profit on ten shillings a week must have been very small. But in their eyes the two old men were a kind of dreadful parasite who had fastened on them and were living on their charity. Old Jack they could just tolerate, because he kept out-of-doors most of the day, but they really hated the bedridden one, Hooker by name. Mr Brooker had a queer way of pronouncing his name, without the H and with a long U – 'Uker'. What tales I heard about old Hooker and his fractiousness, the nuisance of making his bed, the way he 'wouldn't eat' this and 'wouldn't eat' that, his endless ingratitude and, above all, the selfish obstinacy with which he refused to die! The Brookers were quite openly pining for him to die. When that happened they could at least draw the insurance money. They seemed to feel him there, eating their substance day after day, as though he had been a living worm in their bowels. Sometimes Mr Brooker would look up from his potato-peeling, catch my eye and jerk his head with a look of inexpressible bitterness towards the ceiling, towards old Hooker's room. 'It's a b——, ain't it?' he would say. There was no need to say more; I had heard all about old Hooker's ways already. But the Brookers had grievances of one kind and another against all their lodgers, myself included, no doubt. Joe, being on the P.A.C., was practically in the same category as the old-age pensioners. The Scotchman paid a pound a week, but he was indoors most of the day and they 'didn't like him always hanging round the place', as they put it. The newspaper-canvassers were out all day, but the Brookers bore them a grudge for bringing in their own food, and even Mr Reilly, their best lodger, was in disgrace because Mrs Brooker said that he woke her up when he came downstairs in the mornings. They couldn't, they complained perpetually, get the kind of lodgers they wanted – good-class 'commercial gentlemen' who paid full board and were out all day. Their ideal lodger would have been somebody who paid thirty shillings a week and never came indoors except to sleep. I have noticed that people who let lodgings nearly always hate their lodgers. They want their money but they look on them as intruders and have a curiously watchful, jealous attitude which at bottom is a determination not to let the lodger make himself too much at home. It is an inevitable result of the bad system by which the lodger has to live in somebody else's house without being one of the family.

The meals at the Brookers' house were uniformly disgusting. For breakfast you got two rashers of bacon and a pale fried egg, and bread-and-butter which had often been cut overnight and always had thumb-marks on it. However tactfully I tried, I could never induce Mr Brooker to let me cut my own bread-and-butter; he *would* hand it to me slice by slice, each slice gripped firmly under that broad black thumb. For dinner there were generally those threepenny steak puddings which are sold ready-made in tins – these were part of the stock of the shop, I think – and boiled potatoes and rice pudding. For tea there was more bread-and-butter and frayed-looking sweet cakes which were probably bought as 'stales' from the baker. For supper there was the pale flabby Lancashire cheese and biscuits. The Brookers never called these biscuits biscuits. They always referred to them reverently as 'cream crackers' – 'Have another cream cracker, Mr Reilly. You'll like a cream cracker with your cheese' – thus glozing over the fact that there was only cheese for supper. Several bottles of Worcester Sauce and a half-full jar of marmalade lived permanently on the table. It was usual to souse everything, even a piece of cheese, with Worcester Sauce, but I never saw anyone brave the marmalade jar, which was an unspeakable mass of stickiness and dust. Mrs Brooker had her meals separately but also took snacks from any meal that happened to be going, and manoeuvred with great skill for what she called 'the bottom of the pot', meaning the strongest cup of tea. She had a habit of constantly wiping her mouth on one of her blankets. Towards the end of my stay she took to tearing off strips of newspaper for this purpose, and in the morning the floor was often littered with crumpled-up balls of slimy paper which lay there for hours. The smell of the kitchen was dreadful, but, as with that of the bedroom, you ceased to notice it after a while.

It struck me that this place must be fairly normal as lodging-houses in the industrial areas go, for on the whole the lodgers did not complain. The only one who ever did so to my knowledge was a little black-haired sharp-nosed Cockney, a traveller for a cigarette firm. He had never been in the North before, and I think that till recently he had been in better employ and was used to staying in commercial hotels. This was his first glimpse of really low-class lodgings, the kind of place in which the poor tribe of touts and canvassers have to shelter upon their endless journeys. In the morning as we were dressing (he had slept in the double bed, of course) I saw him look round the desolate room with a sort of wondering aversion. He caught my eye and suddenly divined that I was a fellow-Southerner.

'The filthy bloody bastards!' he said feelingly.

After that he packed his suit-case, went downstairs and, with great strength of mind, told the Brookers that this was not the kind of house he was accustomed to and that he was leaving immediately. The Brookers could never understand why. They were astonished and hurt. The ingratitude of it! Leaving them like that for no reason after a single night! Afterwards they discussed it over and over again, in all its bearings. It was added to their store of grievances.

On the day when there was a full chamber-pot under the breakfast table I decided to leave. The place was beginning to depress me. It was not only the dirt, the smells and the vile food, but the feeling of stagnant meaningless decay, of having got down into some subterranean place where people go creeping round and round, just like the blackbeetles, in an endless muddle of slovened jobs and mean grievances. The most dreadful thing about people like the Brookers is the way they say the same things over and over again. It gives you the feeling that they are not real people at all, but a kind of ghost for ever rehearsing the same futile rigmarole. In the end Mrs Brooker's self-pitying talk – always the same complaints, over and over, and always ending with the tremulous whine of 'It does seem 'ard, don't it now?' – revolted me even more than her habit of wiping her mouth with bits of newspaper. But it is no use saying that people like the Brookers are just disgusting and trying to put them out of mind. For they exist in tens and hundreds of thousands; they are one of the characteristic by-products of the modern world. You cannot disregard them if you accept the civilization that produced them. For this is part at least of what industrialism has done for us. Columbus sailed the Atlantic, the first steam engines tottered into motion, the British squares stood firm under the French guns at Waterloo, the one-eyed scoundrels of the nineteenth century praised God and filled their pockets; and this is where it all led – to labyrinthine slums and dark back kitchens with sickly, ageing people creeping round and round them like blackbeetles. It is a kind of duty to see and smell such places now and again, especially smell them, lest you should forget that they exist; though perhaps it is better not to stay there too long.

The train bore me away, through the monstrous scenery of slag-heaps, chimneys, piled scrap-iron, foul canals, paths of cindery mud criss-crossed by the prints of clogs. This was March, but the weather had been horribly cold and everywhere there were mounds of blackened snow. As we moved slowly through the outskirts of the town we passed row after row of little grey slum houses running at right angles to the embankment. At the back of one of the houses a young woman was kneeling on the stones, poking a stick up the leaden waste-pipe which ran from the sink inside and which I suppose was blocked. I had time to see everything about her – her sacking apron, her clumsy clogs, her arms reddened by the cold. She looked up as the train passed, and I was almost near enough to catch her eye. She had a round pale face, the usual exhausted face of the slum girl who is twenty-five and looks forty, thanks to miscarriages and drudgery; and it wore, for the second in which I saw it, the most desolate, hopeless expression I have ever seen. It struck me then that we are mistaken when we say that 'it isn't the same for them as it would be for us,' and that people bred in the slums can imagine nothing but the slums. For what I saw in her face was not the ignorant suffering of an animal. She knew well enough what was happening to her – understood as well as I did how dreadful a destiny it was to be kneeling there in the bitter cold, on the slimy stones of a slum backyard, poking a stick up a foul drain-pipe.

But quite soon the train drew away into open country, and that seemed strange, almost unnatural, as though the open country had been a kind of park; for in the industrial areas one always feels that the smoke and filth must go on for ever and that no part of the earth's surface can escape them. In a crowded, dirty little country like ours one takes defilement almost for granted. Slag-heaps and chimneys seem a more normal, probable landscape than grass and trees, and even in the depths of the country when you drive your fork into the ground you half expect to lever up a broken bottle or a rusty can. But out here the snow was untrodden and lay so deep that only the tops of the stone boundary-walls were showing, winding over the hills like black paths. I remembered that D. H. Lawrence, writing of this same landscape or another near by, said that the snow-covered hills rippled away into the distance 'like muscle'. It was not the simile that would have occurred to me. To my eye the snow and the black walls were more like a white dress with black piping running across it.

Although the snow was hardly broken the sun was shining brightly, and behind the shut windows of the carriage it seemed warm. According to the almanac this was spring, and a few of the birds seemed to believe it. For the first time in my life, in a bare patch beside the line, I saw rooks treading. They did it on the ground and not, as I should have expected, in a tree. The manner of courtship was curious. The female stood with her beak open and the male walked round her and appeared to be feeding her. I had hardly been in the train half an hour, but it seemed a very long way from the Brookers' back-kitchen to the empty slopes of snow, the bright sunshine and the big gleaming birds.

The whole of the industrial districts are really one enormous town, of about the same population as Greater London but, fortunately, of much larger area; so that even in the middle of them there is still room for patches of cleanness and decency. That is an encouraging thought. In spite of hard trying, man has not yet succeeded in doing his dirt everywhere. The earth is so vast and still so empty that even in the filthy heart of civilization you find fields where the grass is green instead of grey; perhaps if you looked for them you might even find streams with live fish in them instead of salmon tins. For quite a long time, perhaps another twenty minutes, the train was rolling through open country before the villa-civilization began to close in upon us again, and then the outer slums, and then the slag-heaps, belching chimneys, blast-furnaces, canals and gasometers of another industrial town.

Chapter Two

Our civilization, *pace* Chesterton, *is* founded on coal, more completely than one realizes until one stops to think about it. The machines that keep us alive, the machines that make the machines, are all directly or indirectly dependent upon coal. In the metabolism of the Western world the coal-miner is second in importance only to the man who ploughs the soil. He is a sort of grimy caryatid upon whose shoulders nearly everything that is *not* grimy is supported. For this reason the actual process by which coal is extracted is well worth watching, if you get the chance and are willing to take the trouble.

When you go down a coal-mine it is important to try and get to the coal face when the 'fillers' are at work. This is not easy, because when the mine is working visitors are a nuisance and are not encouraged, but if you go at any other time, it is possible to come away with a totally wrong impression. On a Sunday, for instance, a mine seems almost peaceful. The time to go there is when the machines are roaring and the air is black with coal dust, and when you can actually see what the miners have to do. At those times the place is like hell, or at any rate like my own mental picture of hell. Most of the things one imagines in hell are there – heat, noise, confusion, darkness, foul air, and, above all, unbearably cramped space. Everything except the fire, for there is no fire down there except the feeble beams of Davy lamps and electric torches which scarcely penetrate the clouds of coal dust.

When you have finally got there – and getting there is a job in itself: I will explain that in a moment – you crawl through the last line of pit props and see opposite you a shiny black wall three or four feet high. This is the coal face. Overhead is the smooth ceiling made by the rock from which the coal has been cut; underneath is the rock again, so that the gallery you are in is only as high as the ledge of coal itself, probably not much more than a yard. The first impression of all, overmastering everything else for a while, is the frightful, deafening din from the conveyor belt which carries the coal away. You cannot see very far, because the fog of coal dust throws back the beam of your lamp, but you can see on either side of you the line of half-naked kneeling men, one to every four or five yards, driving their shovels under the fallen coal and flinging it swiftly over their left shoulders. They are feeding it on to the conveyor belt, a moving rubber belt a couple of feet wide which runs a yard or two behind them. Down this belt a glittering river of coal races constantly. In a big mine it is carrying away several tons of coal every minute. It bears it off to some place in the main roads where it is shot into tubs holding half a ton, and thence dragged to the cages and hoisted to the outer air.

It is impossible to watch the 'fillers' at work without feeling a pang of envy for their toughness. It is a dreadful job that they do, an almost superhuman job by the standards of an ordinary person. For they are not only shifting monstrous quantities of coal, they are also doing it in a position that doubles or trebles the work. They have got to remain kneeling all the while – they could hardly rise from their knees without hitting the ceiling – and you can easily see by trying it what a tremendous effort this means. Shovelling is comparatively easy when you are standing up, because you can use your knee and thigh to drive the shovel along; kneeling down, the whole of the strain is thrown upon your arm and belly muscles. And the other conditions do not exactly make things easier. There is the heat – it varies, but in some mines it is suffocating – and the coal dust that stuffs up your throat and nostrils and collects along your eyelids, and the unending rattle of the conveyor belt, which in that confined space is rather like the rattle of a machine gun. But the fillers look and work as though they were made of iron. They really do look like iron – hammered iron statues – under the smooth coat of coal dust which clings to them from head to foot. It is only when you see miners down the mine and naked that you realize what splendid men they are. Most of them are small (big men are at a disadvantage in that job) but nearly all of them have the most noble bodies; wide shoulders tapering to slender supple waists, and the small pronounced buttocks and sinewy thighs, with not an ounce of waste flesh anywhere. In the hotter mines they wear only a pair of thin drawers, clogs and knee-pads; in the hottest mines of all, only the clogs and knee-pads. You can hardly tell by the look of them whether they are young or old. They may be any age up to sixty or even sixty-five, but when they are black and naked they all look alike. No one could do their work who had not a young man's body, and a figure fit for a guardsman at that; just a few pounds of extra flesh on the waist-line, and the constant bending would be impossible. You can never forget that spectacle once you have seen it – the line of bowed, kneeling figures, sooty black all over, driving their huge shovels under the coal with stupendous force and speed. They are on the job for seven and a half hours, theoretically without a break, for there is no time 'off'. Actually they snatch a quarter of an hour or so at some time during the shift to eat the food they have brought with them, usually a hunk of bread and dripping and a bottle of cold tea. The first time I was watching the 'fillers' at work I put my hand upon some dreadful slimy thing among the coal dust. It was a chewed quid of tobacco. Nearly all the miners chew tobacco, which is said to be good against thirst.

Probably you have to go down several coal-mines before you can get much grasp of the processes that are going on round you. This is chiefly because the mere effort of getting from place to place makes it difficult to notice anything else. In some ways it is even disappointing, or at least is unlike what you have expected. You get into the cage, which is a steel box about as wide as a telephone box and two or three times as long. It holds ten men, but they pack it like pilchards in a tin, and a tall man cannot stand upright in it. The steel door shuts upon you, and somebody working the winding gear above drops you into the void. You have the usual momentary qualm in your belly and a bursting sensation in the ears, but not much sensation of movement till you get near the bottom, when the cage slows down so abruptly that you could swear it is going upwards again. In the middle of the run the cage probably touches sixty miles an hour; in some of the deeper mines it touches even more. When you crawl out at the bottom you are perhaps four hundred yards underground. That is to say you have a tolerable-sized mountain on top of you; hundreds of yards of solid rock, bones of extinct beasts, subsoil, flints, roots of growing things, green grass and cows grazing on it – all this suspended over your head and held back only by wooden props as thick as the calf of your leg. But because of the speed at which the cage has brought you down, and the complete blackness through which you have travelled, you hardly feel yourself deeper down than you would at the bottom of the Piccadilly tube.

What *is* surprising, on the other hand, is the immense horizontal distances that have to be travelled underground. Before I had been down a mine I had vaguely imagined the miner stepping out of the cage and getting to work on a ledge of coal a few yards away. I had not realized that before he even gets to his work he may have to creep through passages as long as from London Bridge to Oxford Circus. In the beginning, of course, a mine shaft is sunk somewhere near a seam of coal. But as that seam is worked out and fresh seams are followed up, the workings get further and further from the pit bottom. If it is a mile from the pit bottom to the coal face, that is probably an average distance; three miles is a fairly normal one; there are even said to be a few mines where it is as much as five miles. But these distances bear no relation to distances above ground. For in all that mile or three miles as it may be, there is hardly anywhere outside the main road, and not many places even there, where a man can stand upright.

You do not notice the effect of this till you have gone a few hundred yards. You start off, stooping slightly, down the dim-lit gallery, eight or ten feet wide and about five high, with the walls built up with slabs of shale, like the stone walls in Derbyshire. Every yard or two there are wooden props holding up the beams and girders; some of the girders have buckled into fantastic curves under which you have to duck. Usually it is bad going underfoot – thick dust or jagged chunks of shale, and in some mines where there is water it is mucky as a farmyard. Also there is the track for the coal tubs, like a miniature railway track with sleepers a foot or two apart, which is tiresome to walk on. Everything is grey with shale dust; there is a dusty fiery smell which seems to be the same in all mines. You see mysterious machines of which you never learn the purpose, and bundles of tools slung together on wires, and sometimes mice darting away from the beam of the lamps. They are surprisingly common, especially in mines where there are or have been horses. It would be interesting to know how they got there in the first place; possibly by falling down the shaft – for they say a mouse can fall any distance uninjured, owing to its surface area being so large relative to its weight. You press yourself against the wall to make way for lines of tubs jolting slowly towards the shaft, drawn by an endless steel cable operated from the surface. You creep through sacking curtains and thick wooden doors which, when they are opened, let out fierce blasts of air. These doors are an important part of the ventilation system. The exhausted air is sucked out of one shaft by means of fans, and the fresh air enters the other of its own accord. But if left to itself the air will take the shortest way round, leaving the deeper workings unventilated; so all short cuts have to be partitioned off.

At the start to walk stooping is rather a joke, but it is a joke that soon wears off. I am handicapped by being exceptionally tall, but when the roof falls to four feet or less it is a tough job for anybody except a dwarf or a child. You have not only got to bend double, you have also got to keep you head up all the while so as to see the beams and girders and dodge them when they come. You have, therefore, a constant crick in the neck, but this is nothing to the pain in your knees and thighs. After half a mile it becomes (I am not exaggerating) an unbearable agony. You begin to wonder whether you will ever get to the end – still more, how on earth you are going to get back. Your pace grows slower and slower. You come to a stretch of a couple of hundred yards where it is all exceptionally low and you have to work yourself along in a squatting position. Then suddenly the roof opens out to a mysterious height – scene of an old fall of rock, probably – and for twenty whole yards you can stand upright. The relief is overwhelming. But after this there is another low stretch of a hundred yards and then a succession of beams which you have to crawl under. You go down on all fours; even this is a relief after the squatting business. But when you come to the end of the beams and try to get up again, you find that your knees have temporarily struck work and refuse to lift you. You call a halt, ignominiously, and say that you would like to rest for a minute or two. Your guide (a miner) is sympathetic. He knows that your muscles are not the same as his. 'Only another four hundred yards,' he says encouragingly; you feel that he might as well say another four hundred miles. But finally you do somehow creep as far as the coal face. You have gone a mile and taken the best part of an hour; a miner would do it in not much more than twenty minutes. Having got there, you have to sprawl in the coal dust and get your strength back for several minutes before you can even watch the work in progress with any kind of intelligence.

Coming back is worse than going, not only because you are already tired out but because the journey back to the shaft is probably slightly up hill. You get through the low places at the speed of a tortoise and you have no shame now about calling a halt when your knees give way. Even the lamp you are carrying becomes a nuisance and probably when you stumble you drop it; whereupon, if it is a Davy lamp, it goes out. Ducking the beams becomes more and more of an effort, and sometimes you forget to duck. You try walking head down as the miners do, and then you bang your backbone. Even the miners bang their backbones fairly often. This is the reason why in very hot mines, where it is necessary to go about half naked, most of the miners have what they call 'buttons down the back' – that is, a permanent scab on each vertebra. When the track is down hill the miners sometimes fit their clogs, which are hollow underneath, on to the trolley rails and slide down. In mines where the 'travelling' is very bad all the miners carry sticks about two and a half feet long, hollowed out below the handle. In normal places you keep your hand on top of the stick and in the low places you slide your hand down into the hollow. These sticks are a great help, and the wooden crash-helmets – a comparatively recent invention – are a godsend. They look like a French or Italian steel helmet, but they are made of some kind of pith and very light, and so strong that you can take a violent blow on the head without feeling it. When finally you get back to the surface you have been perhaps three hours underground and travelled two miles, and you are more exhausted than you would be by a twenty-five-mile walk above ground. For a week afterwards your thighs are so stiff that coming downstairs is quite a difficult feat; you have to work your way down in a peculiar sidelong manner, without bending the knees. Your miner friends notice the stiffness of your walk and chaff you about it. ('How'd ta like to work down pit, eh?' etc.) Yet even a miner who has been long away from work – from illness, for instance – when he comes back to the pit, suffers badly for the first few days.

It may seem that I am exaggerating, though no one who has been down an old-fashioned pit (most of the pits in England are old-fashioned) and actually gone as far as the coal face, is likely to say so. But what I want to emphasize is this. Here is this frightful business of crawling to and fro, which to any normal person is a hard day's work in itself; and it is not part of the miner's work at all, it is merely an extra, like the City man's daily ride in the Tube. The miner does that journey to and fro, and sandwiched in between there are seven and a half hours of savage work. I have never travelled much more than a mile to the coal face; but often it is three miles, in which case I and most people other than coal-miners would never get there at all. This is the kind of point that one is always liable to miss. When you think of a coal-mine you think of depth, heat, darkness, blackened figures hacking at walls of coal; you don't think, necessarily, of those miles of creeping to and fro. There is the question of time, also. A miner's working shift of seven and a half hours does not sound very long, but one has got to add on to it at least an hour a day for 'travelling', more often two hours and sometimes three. Of course, the 'travelling' is not technically work and the miner is not paid for it; but it is as like work as makes no difference. It is easy to say that miners don't mind all this. Certainly, it is not the same for them as it would be for you or me. They have done it since childhood, they have the right muscles hardened, and they can move to and fro underground with a startling and rather horrible agility. A miner puts his head down and *runs,* with a long swinging stride, through places where I can only stagger. At the workings you see them on all fours, skipping round the pit props almost like dogs. But it is quite a mistake to think that they enjoy it. I have talked about this to scores of miners and they all admit that the 'travelling' is hard work; in any case when you hear them discussing a pit among themselves the 'travelling' is always one of the things they discuss. It is said that a shift always returns from work faster than it goes; nevertheless the miners all say that it is the coming away, after a hard day's work, that is especially irksome. It is part of their work and they are equal to it, but certainly it is an effort. It is comparable, perhaps, to climbing a smallish mountain before and after your day's work.

When you have been down two or three pits you begin to get some grasp of the processes that are going on underground. (I ought to say, by the way, that I know nothing whatever about the technical side of mining: I am merely describing what I have seen.) Coal lies in thin seams between enormous layers of rock, so that essentially the process of getting it out is like scooping the central layer from a Neapolitan ice. In the old days the miners used to cut straight into the coal with pick and crowbar – a very slow job because coal, when lying in its virgin state, is almost as hard as rock. Nowadays the preliminary work is done by an electrically-driven coal-cutter, which in principle is an immensely tough and powerful band-saw, running horizontally instead of vertically, with teeth a couple of inches long and half an inch or an inch thick. It can move backwards or forwards on its own power, and the men operating it can rotate it this way and that. Incidentally it makes one of the most awful noises I have ever heard, and sends forth clouds of coal dust which make it impossible to see more than two or three feet and almost impossible to breathe. The machine travels along the coal face cutting into the base of the coal and undermining it to the depth of five feet or five feet and a half; after this it is comparatively easy to extract the coal to the depth to which it has been undermined. Where it is 'difficult getting', however, it has also to be loosened with explosives. A man with an electric drill, like a rather smaller version of the drills used in street-mending, bores holes at intervals in the coal, inserts blasting powder, plugs it with clay, goes round the corner if there is one handy (he is supposed to retire to twenty-five yards distance) and touches off the charge with an electric current. This is not intended to bring the coal out, only to loosen it. Occasionally, of course, the charge is too powerful, and then it not only brings the coal out but brings the roof down as well.

After the blasting has been done the 'fillers' can tumble the coal out, break it up and shovel it on to the conveyor belt. It comes out at first in monstrous boulders which may weigh anything up to twenty tons. The conveyor belt shoots it onto tubs, and the tubs are shoved into the main road and hitched onto an endlessly revolving steel cable which drags them to the cage. Then they are hoisted, and at the surface the coal is sorted by being run over screens, and if necessary is washed as well. As far as possible the 'dirt' – the shale, that is – is used for making the roads below. All that cannot be used is sent to the surface and dumped; hence the monstrous 'dirt-heaps', like hideous grey mountains, which are the characteristic scenery of the coal areas. When the coal has been extracted to the depth to which the machine has cut, the coal face has advanced by five feet. Fresh props are put in to hold up the newly exposed roof, and during the next shift the conveyor belt is taken to pieces, moved five feet forward and re-assembled. As far as possible the three operations of cutting, blasting and extraction are done in three separate shifts, the cutting in the afternoon, the blasting at night (there is a law, not always kept, that forbids its being done when there are other men working near by), and the 'filling' in the morning shift, which lasts from six in the morning until half past one.

Even when you watch the process of coal-extraction you probably only watch it for a short time, and it is not until you begin making a few calculations that you realize what a stupendous task the 'fillers' are performing. Normally each man has to clear a space four or five yards wide. The cutter has undermined the coal to the depth of five feet, so that if the seam of coal is three or four feet high, each man has to cut out, break up and load onto the belt something between seven and twelve cubic yards of coal. This is to say, taking a cubic yard as weighing twenty-seven hundredweight, that each man is shifting coal at a speed approaching two tons an hour. I have just enough experience of pick and shovel work to be able to grasp what this means. When I am digging trenches in my garden, if I shift two tons of earth during the afternoon, I feel that I have earned my tea. But earth is tractable stuff compared with coal, and I don't have to work kneeling down, a thousand feet underground, in suffocating heat and swallowing coal dust with every breath I take; nor do I have to walk a mile bent double before I begin. The miner's job would be as much beyond my power as it would be to perform on the flying trapeze or to win the Grand National. I am not a manual labourer and please God I never shall be one, but there are some kinds of manual work that I could do if I had to. At a pitch I could be a tolerable road-sweeper or an inefficient gardener or even a tenth-rate farm hand. But by no conceivable amount of effort or training could I become a coal-miner; the work would kill me in a few weeks.

Watching coal-miners at work, you realize momentarily what different universes different people inhabit. Down there where coal is dug it is a sort of world apart which one can quite easily go through life without ever hearing about. Probably a majority of people would even prefer not to hear about it. Yet it is the absolutely necessary counterpart of our world above. Practically everything we do, from eating an ice to crossing the Atlantic, and from baking a loaf to writing a novel, involves the use of coal, directly or indirectly. For all the arts of peace coal is needed; if war breaks out it is needed all the more. In time of revolution the miner must go on working or the revolution must stop, for revolution as much as reaction needs coal. Whatever may be happening on the surface, the hacking and shovelling have got to continue without a pause, or at any rate without pausing for more than a few weeks at the most. In order that Hitler may march the goose-step, that the Pope may denounce Bolshevism, that the cricket crowds may assemble at Lord's, that the Nancy poets may scratch one another's backs, coal has got to be forthcoming. But on the whole we are not aware of it; we all know that we 'must have coal', but we seldom or never remember what coal-getting involves. Here am I, sitting writing in front of my comfortable coal fire. It is April but I still need a fire. Once a fortnight the coal cart drives up to the door and men in leather jerkins carry the coal indoors in stout sacks smelling of tar and shoot it clanking into the coal-hole under the stairs. It is only very rarely, when I make a definite mental effort, that I connect this coal with that far-off labour in the mines. It is just 'coal' – something that I have got to have; black stuff that arrives mysteriously from nowhere in particular, like manna except that you have to pay for it. You could quite easily drive a car right across the North of England and never once remember that hundreds of feet below the road you are on the miners are hacking at the coal. Yet in a sense it is the miners who are driving your car forward. Their lamp-lit world down there is as necessary to the daylight world above as the root is to the flower.

It is not long since conditions in the mines were worse than they are now. There are still living a few very old women who in their youth have worked underground, with a harness round their waists and a chain that passed between their legs, crawling on all fours and dragging tubs of coal. They used to go on doing this even when they were pregnant. And even now, if coal could not be produced without pregnant women dragging it to and fro, I fancy we should let them do it rather than deprive ourselves of coal. But most of the time, of course, we should prefer to forget that they were doing it. It is so with all types of manual work; it keeps us alive, and we are oblivious of its existence. More than anyone else, perhaps, the miner can stand as the type of the manual worker, not only because his work is so exaggeratedly awful, but also because it is so vitally necessary and yet so remote from our experience, so invisible, as it were, that we are capable of forgetting it as we forget the blood in our veins. In a way it is even humiliating to watch coal-miners working. It raises in you a momentary doubt about your own status as an 'intellectual' and a superior person generally. For it is brought home to you, at least while you are watching, that it is only because miners sweat their guts out that superior persons can remain superior. You and I and the editor of the *Times Lit. Supp.*, and the Nancy poets and the Archbishop of Canterbury and Comrade X, author of *Marxism for Infants* – all of us *really* owe the comparative decency of our lives to poor drudges underground, blackened to the eyes, with their throats full of coal dust, driving their shovels forward with arms and belly muscles of steel.

Chapter Three

When the miner comes up from the pit his face is so pale that it is noticeable even through the mask of coal dust. This is due to the foul air that he has been breathing, and will wear off presently. To a Southerner, new to the mining districts, the spectacle of a shift of several hundred miners streaming out of the pit is strange and slightly sinister. Their exhausted faces, with the grime clinging in all the hollows, have a fierce, wild look. At other times, when their faces are clean, there is not much to distinguish them from the rest of the population. They have a very upright square-shouldered walk, a reaction from the constant bending underground, but most of them are shortish men and their thick ill-fitting clothes hide the splendour of their bodies. The most definitely distinctive thing about them is the blue scars on their noses. Every miner has blue scars on his nose and forehead, and will carry them to his death. The coal dust of which the air underground is full enters every cut, and then the skin grows over it and forms a blue stain like tattooing, which in fact it is. Some of the older men have their foreheads veined like Roquefort cheeses from this cause.

As soon as the miner comes above ground he gargles a little water to get the worst of the coal dust out of his throat and nostrils, and then goes home and either washes or does not wash according to his temperament. From what I have seen I should say that a majority of miners prefer to eat their meal first and wash afterwards, as I should do in their circumstances. It is the normal thing to see a miner sitting down to his tea with a Christy-minstrel face, completely black except for very red lips which become clean by eating. After his meal he takes a largish basin of water and washes very methodically, first his hands, then his chest, neck and armpits, then his forearms, then his face and scalp (it is on the scalp that the grime clings thickest), and then his wife takes the flannel and washes his back. He has only washed the top half of his body and probably his navel is still a nest of coal dust, but even so it takes some skill to get passably clean in a single basin of water. For my own part I found I needed two complete baths after going down a coal-mine. Getting the dirt out of one's eyelids is a ten minutes' job in itself.

At some of the larger and better appointed collieries there are pithead baths. This is an enormous advantage, for not only can the miner wash himself all over every day, in comfort and even luxury, but at the baths he has two lockers where he can keep his pit clothes separate from his day clothes, so that within twenty minutes of emerging as black as a negro he can be riding off to a football match dressed up to the nines. But it is only comparatively because a seam of coal does not last for ever, so that it is not necessarily worth building a bath every time a shaft is sunk. I cannot get hold of exact figures, but it seems likely that rather less than one miner in three has access to a pithead bath. Probably a large majority of miners are completely black from the waist down for at least six days a week. It is almost impossible for them to wash all over in their own homes. Every drop of water has got to be heated up, and in a tiny living-room which contains, apart from the kitchen range and a quantity of furniture, a wife, some children and probably a dog, there is simply not room to have a proper bath. Even with a basin one is bound to splash the furniture. Middle-class people are fond of saying that the miners would not wash themselves properly even if they could, but this is nonsense, as is shown by the fact that where pithead baths exist practically all the men use them. Only among the very old men does the belief still linger that washing one's legs 'causes lumbago'. Moreover the pithead baths, where they exist, are paid for wholly or partly by the miners themselves, out of the Miners' Welfare Fund. Sometimes the colliery company subscribes, sometimes the Fund bears the whole cost. But doubtless even at this late date the old ladies in Brighton boarding-houses are saying that 'if you give those miners baths they only use them to keep coal in'.

As a matter of fact it is surprising that miners wash as regularly as they do, seeing how little time they have between work and sleep. It is a great mistake to think of a miner's working day as being only seven and a half hours. Seven and a half hours is the time spent actually on the job, but, as I have already explained, one has got to add on to this time taken up in 'travelling', which is seldom less than an hour and may often be three hours. In addition most miners have to spend a considerable time in getting to and from the pit. Throughout the industrial districts there is acute shortage of houses, and it is only in the small mining villages, where the village is grouped round the pit, that the men can be certain of living near their work. In the larger mining towns where I have stayed, nearly everyone went to work by bus; half-a-crown a week seemed to be the normal amount to spend on fares. One miner I stayed with was working on the morning shift, which was from six in the morning till half-past one. He had to be out of bed at a quarter to four and got back somewhere after three in the afternoon. In another house where I stayed a boy of fifteen was working on the night shift. He left for work at nine at night and got back at eight in the morning, had his breakfast and them promptly went to bed and slept till six in the evening; so that his leisure time amounted to about four hours a day – actually a good deal less, if you take off the time for washing, eating and dressing.

The adjustments a miner's family have to make when he is changed from one shift to another must be tiresome in the extreme. If he is on the night shift he gets home in time for breakfast, on the morning shift he gets home in the middle of the afternoon, and on the afternoon shift he gets home in the middle of the night; and in each case, of course, he wants his principal meal of the day as soon as he returns. I notice that the Rev. W. R. Inge, in his book *England,* accuses the miners of gluttony. From my own observation I should say that they eat astonishingly little. Most of the miners I stayed with ate slightly less than I did. Many of them declare that they cannot do their day's work if they have had a heavy meal beforehand, and the food they take with them is only a snack, usually bread-and-dripping and cold tea. They carry it in a flat tin called a snap-can which they strap to their belts. When a miner gets back late at night his wife waits up for him, but when he is on the morning shift it seems to be the custom for him to get his breakfast for himself. Apparently the old superstition that it is bad luck to see a woman before going to work on the morning shift is not quite extinct. In the old days, it is said, a miner who happened to meet a woman in the early morning would often turn back and do no work that day.

Before I had been in the coal areas I shared the widespread illusion that miners are comparatively well paid. One hears it loosely stated that a miner is paid ten or eleven shillings a shift, and one does a small multiplication sum and concludes that every miner is earning round about £3 a week or £150 a year. But the statement that a miner receives ten or eleven shillings a shift is very misleading. To begin with, it is only the actual coal 'getter' who is paid at this rate; a 'dataller', for instance, who attends to the roofing, is paid at a lower rate, usually eight or nine shillings a shift. Again, when the coal 'getter' is paid piecework, so much per ton extracted, as is the case in many mines, he is dependent on the quality of the coal; a breakdown in the machinery or a 'fault' – that is, a streak of rock running through the coal seam – may rob him of his earnings for a day or two at a time. But in any case one ought not to think of the miner as working six days a week, fifty-two weeks a year. Almost certainly there will be a number of days when he is 'laid off'. The average earning per shift worked for every mine-worker, of all ages and both sexes, in Great Britain in 1934, was 9*s*. $1\frac{3}{4}$*d*.[1] If everyone were in work all the time, this would mean that the mine-worker was earning a little over £142 a year, or nearly £2 15*s*. a week. His real income, however, is far lower than this, for the 9*s*. $1\frac{3}{4}$*d*. is merely an average calculation on shifts actually worked and takes no account of blank days.

I have before me five pay-checks belonging to a Yorkshire miner, for five weeks (not consecutive) at the beginning of 1936. Averaging them up, the gross weekly wages they represent is £2 15*s*. 2*d*.; this is an average of nearly 9*s*. $2\frac{1}{2}$*d*. a shift. But these pay-checks are for the winter, when nearly all mines are running full time. As spring advances the coal trade slacks off and more and more men are 'temporarily stopped', while others still technically in work are laid off for a day or two in every week. It is obvious therefore that £150 or even £142 is an immense over-estimate for the mine-worker's yearly income. As a matter of fact, for the year 1934 the average gross earnings of all miners throughout Great Britain was only £115 11*s*. 6*d*. It varied considerably from district to district, rising as high as £133 2*s*. 8*d*. in Scotland, while in Durham it was a little under £105 or barely more than £2 a week. I take these figures from *The Coal Scuttle*, by Mr Joseph Jones, Mayor of Barnsley, Yorkshire. Mr Jones adds:

> 'These figures cover the earnings of youths as well as adults and of the higher as well as the lower-paid grades ... any particularly high earning would be included in these figures, as would the earnings of certain officials and other higher-paid men as well as the higher amounts paid for overtime work ...
>
> '*The figures, being averages, fail ... to reveal the position of thousands of adult workers whose earnings were substantially below the average and who received only 30s. to 40s. or less per week.*'

Mr Jones's italics. But please notice that even these wretched earnings are *gross* earnings. On top of this there are all kinds of stoppages which are deducted from the miner's wages every week. Here is a list of weekly stoppages which was given me as typical in one Lancashire district:

[1] From the *Colliery Year Book and Coal Trades Directory* for 1935.

	s.	d.
Insurance (unemployment and health)	1	5
Hire of lamp		6
For sharpening tools		6
Check-weighman		9
Infirmary		2
Hospital		1
Benevolent Fund		6
Union fees		6
Total	4	5

Some of these stoppages, such as the Benevolent Fund and the union fees, are, so to speak, the miner's own responsibility, others are imposed by the colliery company. They are not the same in all districts. For instance, the iniquitous swindle of making the miner pay for the hire of his lamp (at sixpence a week he buys the lamp several times over in a single year) does not obtain everywhere. But the stoppages always seem to total up to about the same amount. On the Yorkshire miner's five pay-checks, the average gross earning per week is £2 15*s.* 2*d.*; the average net earning, after the stoppages have come off, is only £2 11*s.* 4*d.* – a reduction of 3*s.* 10*d.* a week. But the pay-check, naturally, only mentions stoppages which are imposed by or paid through the colliery company; one has got to add the union fees, bringing the total reduction up to something over four shillings. Probably it is safe to say that stoppages of one kind and another cut four shillings or thereabouts from *every* adult miner's weekly wage. So that the £115 11*s.* 6*d.* which was the mine-worker's average earning throughout Great Britain in 1934 should really be something nearer £105. As against this, most miners receive allowances in kind, being able to purchase coal for their own use at a reduced rate, usually eight or nine shillings a ton. But according to Mr Jones, quoted above, 'the average value of all allowances in kind for the country as a whole is only fourpence a day.' And this fourpence a day is offset, in many cases, by the amount the miner has to spend on fares in getting to and from the pit. So, taking the industry as a whole, the sum the miner can actually bring home and call his own does not average more, perhaps slightly less, than two pounds a week.

Meanwhile, how much coal is the average miner producing?

The tonnage of coal raised yearly per person employed in mining rises steadily though rather slowly. In 1914 every mine-worker produced, on an average, 253 tons of coal; in 1934 he produced 280 tons.[1] This of course is an average figure for mine-workers of all kinds; those actually working at the coal face extract an enormously greater amount – in many cases, probably, well over a thousand tons each. But taking 280 tons as a representative figure, it is worth noticing what a vast achievment this is. One gets the best idea of it by comparing a miner's life work with somebody else's. If I live to be sixty I shall probably have produced thirty novels, or enough to fill two medium-sized library shelves. In the same period the average miner produces 8,400 tons of coal; enough coal to pave Trafalgar Square nearly two feet deep or to supply seven large families with fuel for over a hundred years.

Of the five pay-checks I mentioned above, no less than three are rubber-

[1] *The Coal Scuttle.* The *Colliery Year Book and Coal Trades Directory* gives a slightly higher figure.

stamped with the words 'death stoppage'. When a miner is killed at work it is usual for the other miners to make up a subscription, generally of a shilling each, for his widow, and this is collected by the colliery company and automatically deducted from their wages. The significant detail here is the *rubber stamp*. The rate of accidents among miners is so high, compared with that in other trades, that casualties are taken for granted almost as they would be in a minor war. Every year one miner in about nine hundred is killed and one in about six is injured; most of these injuries, of course, are petty ones, but a fair number amount to total disablement. This means that if a miner's working life is forty years the chances are nearly seven to one against his escaping injury and not much more than twenty to one against his being killed outright. No other trade approaches this in dangerousness; the next most dangerous is the shipping trade, one sailor in a little under 1,300 being killed every year. The figures I have given apply, of course, to mine-workers as a whole; for those actually working underground the proportion of injuries would be very much higher. Every miner of long standing that I have talked to had either been in a fairly serious accident himself or had seen some of his mates killed, and in every mining family they tell you tales of fathers, brothers or uncles killed at work. ('And he fell seven hundred feet, and they wouldn't never have collected t'pieces only he were wearing a new suit of oil-skins,' etc., etc., etc.) Some of these tales are appalling in the extreme. One miner, for instance, described to me how a mate of his, a 'dataller', was buried by a fall of rock. They rushed to him and managed to uncover his head and shoulders so that he could breathe, and he was alive and spoke to them. Then they saw that the roof was coming down again and had to run to save themselves; the 'dataller' was buried a second time. Once again they rushed to him and got his head and shoulders free, and again he was alive and spoke to them. Then the roof came down a third time, and this time they could not uncover him for several hours, after which, of course, he was dead. But the miner who told me the story (he had been buried himself on one occasion, but he was lucky enough to have his head jammed between his legs so that there was a small space in which he could breathe) did not think it was a particularly appalling one. Its significance, for him, was that the 'dataller' had known perfectly well that the place where he was working was unsafe, and had gone there in daily expectation of an accident. 'And it worked on his mind to that extent that he got to kissing his wife before he went to work. And she told me afterwards that it were over twenty year since he'd kissed her.'

The most obviously understandable cause of accidents is explosions of gas, which is always more or less present in the atmosphere of the pit. There is a special lamp which is used to test the air for gas, and when it is present in at all large quantities it can be detected by the flame of an ordinary Davy lamp burning blue. If the wick can be turned up to its full extent and the flame is still blue, the proportion of gas is dangerously high; it is, nevertheless, difficult to detect, because it does not distribute itself evenly throughout the atmosphere but hangs about in cracks and crevices. Before starting work a miner often tests for gas by poking his lamp into all the corners. The gas may be touched off by a spark during blasting operations, or by a pick striking a spark from a stone, or by a defective lamp, or by 'gob fires' – spontaneously generated fires which smoulder in the coal dust and are very hard to put out. The great mining disasters which happen from time to time, in which several hundred men are killed, are usually caused by explosions; hence one tends to think of explosions as the chief danger of mining. Actually, the great majority of accidents are due to the normal everyday dangers of the pit; in particular, to falls of roof. There are, for instance, 'pot-holes' – circular holes from which a lump of stone big enough to kill a man shoots out with the promptitude of a bullet. With, so far as I can remember, only one exception, all the miners I have talked to declared that the new machinery, and 'speeding up' generally, have made the work more dangerous. This may be partly due to conservatism, but they can give plenty of reasons. To begin with, the speed at which the coal is now extracted means that for hours at a time a dangerously large stretch of roof remains unpropped. Then there is the vibration, which tends to shake everything loose, and the noise, which makes it harder to detect signs of danger. One must remember that a miner's safety underground depends largely on his own care and skill. An experienced miner claims to know by a sort of instinct when the roof is unsafe; the way he puts it is that he 'can feel the weight on him'. He can, for instance, hear the faint creaking of the props. The reason why wooden props are still generally preferred to iron girders is that a wooden prop which is about to collapse gives warning by creaking, whereas a girder flies out unexpectedly. The devastating noise of the machines makes it impossible to hear anything else, and thus the danger is increased.

When a miner is hurt it is of course impossible to attend to him immediately. He lies crushed under several hundredweight of stone in some dreadful cranny underground, and even after he has been extricated it is necessary to drag his body a mile or more, perhaps, through galleries where nobody can stand upright. Usually when you talk to a man who has been injured you find that it was a couple of hours or so before they got him to the surface. Sometimes, of course, there are accidents to the cage. The cage is shooting several hundred yards up or down at the speed of an express train, and it is operated by somebody on the surface who cannot see what is happening. He has very delicate indicators to tell him how far the cage has got, but it is possible for him to make a mistake, and there have been cases of the cage crashing into the pit-bottom at its very maximum speed. This seems to me a dreadful way to die. For as that tiny steel box whizzes through the blackness there must come a moment when the ten men who are locked inside it *know* that something has gone wrong; and the remaining seconds before they are smashed to pieces hardly bear thinking about. A miner told me he was once in a cage in which something went wrong. It did not slow up when it should have done, and they thought the cable must have snapped. As it happened they got to the bottom safely, but when he stepped out he found that he had broken a tooth; he had been clenching his teeth so hard in expectation of that frightful crash.

Apart from accidents miners seem to be healthy, as obviously they have got to be, considering the muscular efforts demanded of them. They are liable to rheumatism and a man with defective lungs does not last long in that dust-impregnated air, but the most characteristic industrial disease is nystagmus. This is a disease of the eyes which makes the eyeballs oscillate in a strange manner when they come near a light. It is due presumably to working in half-darkness, and sometimes results in total blindness. Miners who are disabled in this way or any other way are compensated by the colliery company, sometimes with a lump sum, sometimes with a weekly pension. This pension never amounts to more than twenty-nine shillings a week; if it falls below fifteen shillings the disabled man can also get something from the dole or the P.A.C. If I were a disabled miner I should very much prefer the lump sum, for then at any rate I should know that I had got my money. Disability pensions are not guaranteed by any centralized fund, so that if the colliery company goes bankrupt that is the end of the disabled miner's pension, though he does figure among the other creditors.

In Wigan I stayed for a while with a miner who was suffering from nystagmus. He could see across the room but not much further. He had been drawing compensation of twenty-nine shillings a week for the past nine months, but the colliery company were now talking of putting him on 'partial compensation' of fourteen shillings a week. It all depended on whether the doctor passed him as fit for light work 'on top'. Even if the doctor did pass him there would, needless to say, be no light work available, but he could draw the dole and the company would have saved itself fifteen shillings a week. Watching this man go to the colliery to draw his compensation, I was struck by the profound differences that are still made by *status*. Here was a man who had been half blinded in one of the most useful of all jobs and was drawing a pension to which he had a perfect right, if anybody has a right to anything. Yet he could not, so to speak, *demand* this pension – he could not, for instance, draw it when and how he wanted it. He had to go to the colliery once a week at a time named by the company, and when he got there he was kept waiting for hours in the cold wind. For all I know he was also expected to touch his cap and show gratitude to whoever paid him; at any rate he had to waste an afternoon and spend sixpence in bus fares. It is very different for a member of the bourgeoisie, even such a down-at-heel member as I am. Even when I am on the verge of starvation I have certain rights attaching to my bourgeois status. I do not earn much more than a miner earns, but I do at least get it paid into my bank in a gentlemanly manner and can draw it out when I choose. And even when my account is exhausted the bank people are still passably polite.

This business of petty inconvenience and indignity, of being kept waiting about, of having to do everything at other people's convenience, is inherent in working-class life. A thousand influences constantly press a working man down into a *passive* rôle. He does not act, he is acted upon. He feels himself the slave of mysterious authority and has a firm conviction that 'they' will never allow him to do this, that and the other. Once when I was hop-picking I asked the sweated pickers (they earn something under sixpence an hour) why they did not form a union. I was told immediately that 'they' would never allow it. Who were 'they'? I asked. Nobody seemed to know; but evidently 'they' were omnipotent.

A person of bourgeois origin goes through life with some expectation of getting what he wants, within reasonable limits. Hence the fact that in times of stress 'educated' people tend to come to the front; they are no more gifted than the others and their 'education' is generally quite useless in itself, but they are accustomed to a certain amount of deference and consequently have the cheek necessary to a commander. That they *will* come to the front seems to be taken for granted, always and everywhere. In Lissagaray's *History of the Commune* there is an interesting passage describing the shootings that took place after the Commune had been suppressed. The authorities were shooting the ringleaders, and as they did not know who the ringleaders were, they were picking them out on the principle that those of better class would be the ringleaders. An officer walked down a line of prisoners, picking out likely-looking types. One man was shot because he was wearing a watch, another because he 'had an intelligent face'. I should not like to be shot for having an intelligent face, but I do agree that in almost any revolt the leaders would tend to be people who could pronounce their aitches.

Chapter Four

As you walk through the industrial towns you lose yourself in labyrinths of little brick houses blackened by smoke, festering in planless chaos round miry alleys and little cindered yards where there are stinking dustbins and lines of grimy washing and half-ruinous w.c's. The interiors of these houses are always very much the same, though the number of rooms varies between two or five. All have an almost exactly similar living-room, ten or fifteen feet square, with an open kitchen range; in the larger ones there is a scullery as well, in the smaller ones the sink and copper are in the living-room. At the back there is the yard, or part of a yard shared by a number of houses, just big enough for the dustbin and the w.c. Not a single one has hot water laid on. You might walk, I suppose, through literally hundreds of miles of streets inhabited by miners, every one of whom, when he is in work, gets black from head to foot every day, without ever passing a house in which one could have a bath. It would have been very simple to install a hot-water system working from the kitchen range, but the builder saved perhaps ten pounds on each house by not doing so, and at the time when these houses were built no one imagined that miners wanted baths.

For it is to be noted that the majority of these houses are old, fifty or sixty years old at least, and great numbers of them are by any ordinary standard not fit for human habitation. They go on being tenanted simply because there are no others to be had. And that is the central fact about housing in the industrial areas; not that the houses are poky and ugly, and insanitary and comfortless, or that they are distributed in incredibly filthy slums round belching foundries and stinking canals and slag-heaps that deluge them with sulphurous smoke – though all this is perfectly true – but simply that there are not enough houses to go round.

'Housing shortage' is a phrase that has been bandied about pretty freely since the war, but it means very little to anyone with an income of more than £10 a week, or even £5 a week for that matter. Where rents are high the difficulty is not to find houses but to find tenants. Walk down any street in Mayfair and you will see 'To Let' boards in half the windows. But in the industrial areas the mere difficulty of getting hold of a house is one of the worst aggravations of poverty. It means that people will put up with anything – any hole and corner slum, any misery of bugs and rotting floors and cracking walls, any extortion of skinflint landlords and blackmailing agents – simply to get a roof over their heads. I have been into appalling houses, houses in which I would not live a week if you paid me, and found that the tenants had been there twenty and thirty years and only hoped they might have the luck to die there. In general these conditions are taken as a matter of course, though not always. Some people hardly seem to realize that such things as decent houses exist and look on bugs and leaking roofs as acts of God; others rail bitterly against their landlords; but all cling desperately to their houses lest worse should befall. So long as the housing shortage continues the local authorities cannot do much to make existing houses more livable. They can 'condemn' a house, but they cannot order it to be pulled down till the tenant has another house to go to; and so the condemned houses remain standing and are all the worse for being condemned, because naturally the landlord will not spend more than he can help on a house which is going to be demolished sooner or later. In a town like Wigan, for instance, there are over two thousand houses standing which have been condemned for years, and whole sections of the town would be condemned *en bloc* if there were any hope of other houses being built to replace them. Towns like Leeds and Sheffield have scores of thousands of 'back to back' houses which are all of a condemned type but will remain standing for decades.

I have inspected great numbers of houses in various mining towns and villages and made notes on their essential points. I think I can best give an idea of what conditions are like by transcribing a few extracts from my notebook, taken more or less at random. They are only brief notes and they will need certain explanations which I will give afterwards. Here are a few from Wigan:

> 1. House in Wallgate quarter. Blind back type. One up, one down. Living-room measures 12 ft. by 10 ft., room upstairs the same. Alcove under stairs measuring 5 ft. by 5 ft. and serving as larder, scullery and coal hole. Windows will open. Distance to lavatory 50 yards. Rent 4*s*. 9*d*., rates 2*s*. 6*d*., total 7*s*. 3*d*.
>
> 2. Another near by. Measurements as above, but no alcove under stairs, merely a recess two feet deep containing the sink – no room for larder, etc. Rent 3*s*. 2*d*., rates 2*s*., total 5*s*. 2*d*.
>
> 4. House in Scholes quarter. Condemned house. One up, one down. Rooms 15 ft. by 15 ft. Sink and copper in living-room, coal hole under stairs. Floor subsiding. No windows will open. House decently dry. Landlord good. Rent 3*s*. 8*d*., rates 2*s*. 6*d*., total 6*s*. 2*d*.
>
> 5. Another near by. Two up, two down and coal hole. Walls falling absolutely to pieces. Water comes into upstairs rooms in quantities. Floor lopsided. Downstairs windows will not open. Landlord bad. Rent 6*s*., rates 3*s*. 6*d*., total 9*s*. 6*d*.
>
> 6. House in Greenough's Row. One up, two down. Living-room 13 ft. by 8 ft. Walls coming apart and water comes in. Back windows will not open, front ones will. Ten in family with eight children very near together in age. Corporations are trying to evict them for overcrowding but cannot find another house to send them to. Landlord bad. Rent 4*s*., rates 2*s*. 3*d*., total 6*s*. 3*d*.

So much for Wigan. I have pages more of the same type. Here is one from Sheffield – a typical specimen of Sheffield's several score thousand 'back to back' houses:

> House in Thomas Street. Back to back, two up, one down (i.e. a three-storey house with one room on each storey). Cellar below. Living-room 14 ft. by 10 ft., and rooms above corresponding. Sink in living-room. Top floor has no door but gives on open stairs. Walls in living-room slightly damp, walls in top rooms coming to pieces and oozing damp on all sides. House is so dark that light has to be kept burning all day. Electricity estimated at 6*d*. a day (probably an exaggeration). Six in family, parents and four children. Husband (on P.A.C.) is tuberculous. One child in hospital, the others appear healthy. Tenants have been seven years in this house. Would move, but no other house available. Rent 6*s*. 6*d*.,

rates included.

Here are one or two from Barnsley:

1. House in Wortley Street. Two up, one down. Living-room 12 ft. by 10 ft. Sink and copper in living-room, coal hole under stairs. Sink worn almost flat and constantly overflowing. Walls not too sound. Penny in slot, gas-light. House very dark and gas-light estimated 4*d.* a day. Upstairs rooms are really one large room partitioned into two. Walls very bad – wall of back room cracked right through. Window-frames coming to pieces and have to be stuffed with wood. Rain comes through in several places. Sewer runs under house and stinks in summer but Corporation 'says they can't do nowt'. Six people in house, two adults and four children, the eldest aged fifteen. Youngest but one attending hospital – tuberculosis suspected. House infested by bugs. Rent 5*s.* 3*d.*, including rates.

2. House in Peel Street. Back to back, two up, two down and large cellar. Living-room 10 ft. square with copper and sink. The other downstairs room the same size, probably intended as parlour but used as bedroom. Upstairs rooms the same size as those below. Living-room very dark. Gas-light estimated at 4½*d.* a day. Distance to lavatory 70 yards. Four beds in house for eight people – two old parents, two adult girls (the eldest aged twenty-seven), one young man and three children. Parents have one bed, eldest son another, and remaining five people share the other two. Bugs very bad – 'You can't keep 'em down when it's 'ot.' Indescribable squalor in downstairs room and smell upstairs almost unbearable. Rent 5*s.* 7½*d.*, including rates.

3. House in Mapplewell (small mining village near Barnsley). Two up, one down. Living-room 14 ft. by 12 ft. Sink in living-room. Plaster cracking and coming off walls. No shelves in oven. Gas leaking slightly. The upstairs rooms each 10 ft. by 8 ft. Four beds (for six persons, all adult), but 'one bed does nowt', presumably for lack of bedclothes. Room nearest stairs has no door and stairs have no banister, so that when you step out of bed your foot hangs in vacancy and you may fall ten feet onto stones. Dry rot so bad that one can see through the floor into the room below. Bugs, but 'I keeps 'em down with sheep dip'. Earth road past these cottages is like a muck-heap and said to be almost impassable in winter. Stone lavatories at ends of gardens in semi-ruinous condition. Tenants have been twenty-two years in this house. Are £11 in arrears with rent, and have been paying an extra 1*s.* a week to pay this off. Landlord now refuses this and has served orders to quit. Rent 5*s.*, including rates.

And so on and so on and so on. I could multiply examples by the score – they could be multiplied by the hundred thousand if anyone chose to make a house to house inspection throughout the industrial districts. Meanwhile some of the expressions I have used need explaining. 'One up, one down' means one room on each storey – i.e. a two-roomed house. 'Back to back' houses are two houses built in one, each side of the house being somebody's front door, so that if you walk down a row of what is apparently twelve houses you are in reality seeing not twelve houses but twenty-four. The front houses give on the street and the back ones on the yard, and there is only one way out of each house. The effect of this is obvious. The lavatories are in the yard at the back, so that if you live on the side facing the street, to get to the lavatory or the dust-bin you have to go out of the front door and walk round the end of the block – a distance that may be as much as two hundred yards; if you live at the back, on the other hand, your outlook is on to a row of lavatories. There are also houses of what is called the 'blind back' type, which are single houses, but in which the builder has omitted to put in a back door – from pure spite, apparently. The windows which refuse to open are a peculiarity of old mining towns. Some of these towns are so undermined by ancient workings that the ground is constantly subsiding and the houses above slip sideways. In Wigan you pass whole rows of houses which have slid to startling angles, their windows being ten or twenty degrees out of the horizontal. Sometimes the front wall bellies outward till it looks as though the house were seven months gone in pregnancy. It can be refaced, but the new facing soon begins to bulge again. When a house sinks at all suddenly its windows are jammed for ever and the door has to be refitted. This excites no surprise locally. The story of the miner who comes home from work and finds that he can only get indoors by smashing down the front door with an axe is considered humorous. In some cases I have noted 'Landlord good' or 'Landlord bad', because there is great variation in what the slum-dwellers say about their landlords. I found – one might expect it, perhaps – that the small landlords are usually the worst. It goes against the grain to say this, but one can see why it should be so. Ideally, the worst type of slum landlord is a fat wicked man, preferably a bishop, who is drawing an immense income from extortionate rents. Actually, it is a poor old woman who has invested her life's savings in three slum houses, inhabits one of them and tries to live on the rent of the other two – never, in consequence, having any money for repairs.

But mere notes like these are only valuable as reminders to myself. To me as I read them they bring back what I have seen, but they cannot in themselves give much idea of what conditions are like in those fearful northern slums. Words are such feeble things. What is the use of a brief phrase like 'roof leaks' or 'four beds for eight people'? It is the kind of thing your eye slides over, registering nothing. And yet what a wealth of misery it can cover! Take the question of overcrowding, for instance. Quite often you have eight or even ten people living in a three-roomed house. One of these rooms is a living-room, and as it probably measures about a dozen feet square and contains, besides the kitchen range and the sink, a table, some chairs and a dresser, there is no room in it for a bed. So there are eight or ten people sleeping in two small rooms, probably in at most four beds. If some of these people are adults and have to go to work, so much the worse. In one house, I remember, three grown-up girls shared the same bed and all went to work at different hours, each disturbing the others when she got up or came in; in another house a young miner working on the night shift slept by day in a narrow bed in which another member of the family slept by night. There is an added difficulty when there are grown-up children, in that you cannot let adolescent youths and girls sleep in the same bed. In one family I visited there were a father and mother and a son and daughter aged round about seventeen, and only two beds for the lot of them. The father slept with the son and the mother with the daughter; it was the only arrangement that ruled out the danger of incest. Then there is the misery of leaking roofs and oozing walls, which in winter makes some rooms almost uninhabitable. Then there are bugs. Once bugs get into a house they are in it till the crack of doom; there is no sure way of exterminating them. Then there are the windows that will not open. I need not point out what this must mean, in summer, in a tiny stuffy living-room where the fire, on which all the cooking is done, has to be kept burning more or less constantly. And there are the special miseries attendant upon back to back houses. A fifty yards' walk to the lavatory or the dust-bin is not exactly an inducement to be clean. In the front houses – at any rate in a side-street where the Corporation don't interfere – the women get into the habit of throwing their refuse out of the front door, so that the gutter is always littered with tea-leaves and bread crusts. And it is worth considering what it is like for a child to grow up in one of the back alleys where its gaze is bounded by a row of lavatories and a wall.

In such places as these a woman is only a poor drudge muddling among an infinity of jobs. She may keep up her spirits, but she cannot keep up her standards of cleanliness and tidiness. There is always something to be done, and no conveniences and almost literally not room to turn round. No sooner have you washed one child's face than another's is dirty; before you have washed the crocks from one meal the next is due to be cooked. I found great variation in the houses I visited. Some were as decent as one could possibly expect in the circumstances, some were so appalling that I have no hope of describing them adequately. To begin with, the smell, the dominant and essential thing, is indescribable. But the squalor and the confusion! A tub full of filthy water here, a basin full of unwashed crocks there, more crocks piled in any odd corner, torn newspaper littered everywhere, and in the middle always the same dreadful table covered with sticky oilcloth and crowded with cooking pots and irons and half-darned stockings and pieces of stale bread and bits of cheese wrapped round with greasy newspaper! And the congestion in a tiny room where getting from one side to the other is a complicated voyage between pieces of furniture, with a line of damp washing getting you in the face every time you move and the children as thick underfoot as toadstools! There are scenes that stand out vividly in my memory. The almost bare living-room of a cottage in a little mining village, where the whole family was out of work and everyone seemed to be underfed; and the big family of grown-up sons and daughters sprawling aimlessly about, all strangely alike with red hair, splendid bones and pinched faces ruined by malnutrition and idleness; and one tall son sitting by the fireplace, too listless even to notice the entry of a stranger, and slowly peeling a sticky sock from a bare foot. A dreadful room in Wigan where all the furniture seemed to be made of packing cases and barrel staves and was coming to pieces at that; and an old woman with a blackened neck and her hair coming down denouncing her landlord in a Lancashire-Irish accent; and her mother, aged well over ninety, sitting in the background on the barrel that served her as a commode and regarding us blankly with a yellow, cretinous face. I could fill up pages with memories of similar interiors.

Of course the squalor of these people's houses is sometimes their own fault. Even if you live in a back to back house and have four children and a total income of thirty-two and sixpence a week from the P.A.C., there is no *need* to have unemptied chamber-pots standing about in your living-room. But it is equally certain that their circumstances do not encourage self-respect. The determining factor is probably the number of children. The best-kept interiors I saw were always childless houses or houses where there were only one or two children; with, say, six children in a three-roomed house it is quite impossible to keep anything decent. One thing that is very noticeable is that the worst squalors are never downstairs. You might visit quite a number of houses, even among the poorest of the unemployed, and bring away a wrong impression. These people, you might reflect, cannot be so badly off if they still have a fair amount of furniture and crockery. But it is in the rooms upstairs that the gauntness of poverty really discloses itself. Whether this is because pride makes people cling to their living-room furniture to the last, or because bedding is more pawnable, I do not know, but certainly many of the bedrooms I saw were fearful places. Among people who have been unemployed for several years continuously I should say it is the exception to have anything like a full set of bedclothes. Often there is nothing that can be properly called bedclothes at all – just a heap of old overcoats and miscellaneous rags on a rusty iron bedstead. In this way overcrowding is aggravated. One family of four persons that I knew, a father and mother and two children, possessed two beds but could only use one of them because they had not enough bedding for the other.

Anyone who wants to see the effects of the housing shortage at their very worst should visit the dreadful caravan-dwellings that exist in numbers in many of the northern towns. Ever since the war, in the complete impossibility of getting houses, parts of the population have overflowed into supposedly temporary quarters in fixed caravans. Wigan, for instance, with a population of about 85,000, has round about 200 caravan-dwellings with a family in each – perhaps somewhere near 1,000 people in all. How many of these caravan-colonies exist throughout the industrial areas it would be difficult to discover with any accuracy. The local authorities are reticent about them and the census report of 1931 seems to have decided to ignore them. But so far as I can discover by enquiry they are to be found in most of the larger towns in Lancashire and Yorkshire, and perhaps further north as well. The probability is that throughout the North of England there are some thousands, perhaps tens of thousands of *families* (not individuals) who have no home except a fixed caravan.

But the word 'caravan' is very misleading. It calls up a picture of a cosy gypsy-encampment (in fine weather, of course) with wood fires crackling and children picking blackberries and many-coloured washing fluttering on the lines. The caravan-colonies in Wigan and Sheffield are not like that. I had a look at several of them, I inspected those in Wigan with considerable care, and I have never seen comparable squalor except in the Far East. Indeed when I saw them I was immediately reminded of the filthy kennels in which I have seen Indian coolies living in Burma. But, as a matter of fact, nothing in the East could ever be quite as bad, for in the East you haven't our clammy, penetrating cold to contend with, and the sun is a disinfectant.

Along the banks of Wigan's miry canal are patches of waste ground on which the caravans have been dumped like rubbish shot out of a bucket. Some of them are actually gypsy caravans, but very old ones and in bad repair. The majority are old single-decker buses (the rather smaller buses of ten years ago) which have been taken off their wheels and propped up with struts of wood. Some are simply wagons with semi-circular slats on top, over which canvas is stretched, so that the people inside have nothing but canvas between them and the outer air. Inside, these places are usually about five feet wide by six high (I could not stand quite upright in any of them) and anything from six to fifteen feet long. Some, I suppose, are inhabited by only one person, but I did not see any that held less than two persons, and some of them contained large families. One, for instance, measuring fourteen feet long, had seven people in it – seven people in about 450 cubic feet of space; which is to say that each person had for his entire dwelling a space a *good deal* smaller than one compartment of a public lavatory. The dirt and congestion of these places is such that you cannot well imagine it unless you have tested it with your own eyes and more particularly your nose. Each contains a tiny cottage kitchener and such furniture as can be crammed in – sometimes two beds, more usually one, into which the whole family have to huddle as best they can. It is almost impossible to sleep on the floor, because the damp soaks up from below. I was shown mattresses which were still wringing wet at eleven in the morning. In winter it is so cold that the kitcheners have to be kept burning day and night, and the windows, needless to say, are never opened. Water is got from a hydrant common to the whole colony, some of the caravan-dwellers having to walk 150 or 200 yards for every bucket of water. There are no sanitary arrangements at all. Most of the people construct a little hut to serve as a lavatory on the tiny patch of ground surrounding their caravan, and once a week dig a deep hole in which to bury the refuse. All the people I saw in these places, especially the children, were unspeakably dirty, and I do not doubt that they were lousy as well. They could not possibly be otherwise. The thought that haunted me as I went from caravan to caravan was, What can happen in those cramped interiors when anybody dies? But that, of course, is the kind of question you hardly care to ask.

Some of the people have been in their caravans for many years. Theoretically the Corporation are doing away with the caravan-colonies and getting the inhabitants out into houses; but as the houses don't get built, the caravans remain standing. Most of the people I talked to had given up the idea of ever getting a decent habitation again. They were all out of work, and a job and a house seemed to them about equally remote and impossible. Some hardly seemed to care; others realized quite clearly in what misery they were living. One woman's face stays by me, a worn skull-like face on which was a look of intolerable misery and degradation. I gathered that in that dreadful pigsty, struggling to keep her large brood of children clean, she felt as I should feel if I were coated all over with dung. One must remember that these people are not gypsies; they are decent English people who have all, except the children born there, had homes of their own in their day; besides, their caravans are greatly inferior to those of gypsies and they have not the great advantage of being on the move. No doubt there are still middle-class people who think that the Lower Orders don't mind that kind of thing and who, if they happened to pass a caravan-colony in the train, would immediately assume that the people lived there from choice. I never argue nowadays with that kind of person. But it is worth noticing that the caravan-dwellers don't even save money by living there, for they are paying about the same rents as they would for houses. I could not hear of any rent lower than five shillings a week (five shillings for 200 cubic feet of space!) and there are even cases where the rent is as high as ten shillings. Somebody must be making a good thing out of those caravans! But clearly their continued existence is due to the housing shortage and not directly to poverty.

Talking once with a miner I asked him when the housing shortage first became acute in his district; he answered, 'When we were told about it', meaning that till recently people's standards were so low that they took almost any degree of overcrowding for granted. He added that when he was a child his family had slept eleven in a room and thought nothing of it, and that later, when he was grown-up, he and his wife had lived in one of the old-style back to back houses in which you not only had to walk a couple of hundred yards to the lavatory but often had to wait in a queue when you got there, the lavatory being shared by thirty-six people. And when his wife was sick with the illness that killed her, she still had to make that two hundred yards' journey to the lavatory. This, he said, was the kind of thing people would put up with 'till they were told about it'.

I do not know whether that is true. What is certain is that nobody *now* thinks it bearable to sleep eleven in a room, and that even people with comfortable incomes are vaguely troubled by the thought of 'the slums'. Hence the clatter about 'rehousing' and 'slum clearance' which we have had at intervals ever since the war. Bishops, politicians, philanthropists and what not enjoy talking piously about 'slum clearance', because they can thus divert attention from more serious evils and pretend that if you abolish the slums you abolish poverty. But all this talk has led to surprisingly small results. So far as one can discover, the congestion is no better, perhaps slightly worse, than it was a dozen years ago. There is certainly great variation in the speed at which the different towns are attacking their housing problem. In some towns building seems to be almost at a standstill, in others it is proceeding rapidly and the private landlord is being driven out of business. Liverpool, for instance, has been very largely rebuilt, mainly by the efforts of the Corporation. Sheffield, too, is being torn down and rebuilt pretty fast, though perhaps, considering the unparalleled beastliness of its slums, not quite fast enough.[1]

Why rehousing has on the whole moved so slowly, and why some towns can borrow money for building purposes so much more easily than others, I do not know. Those questions would have to be answered by someone who knows more about the machinery of local government than I do. A Corporation house costs normally somewhere between three and four hundred pounds; it costs rather less when it is built by 'direct labour' than when built by contract. The rent of these houses would average something over twenty pounds a year not counting rates, so one would think that, even allowing for overhead expenses and interest on loans, it would pay any Corporation to build as many houses as could be tenanted. In many cases, of course, the houses would have to be inhabited by people on the P.A.C., so that the local bodies would merely be taking money out of one pocket and putting it into another – i.e. paying out money in the form of relief and taking it back in the form of rent. But they have got to pay the relief in any case, and at present a proportion of what they pay is being swallowed up by private landlords. The reasons given for the slow rate of building are lack of money and the difficulty of getting hold of sites – for Corporation houses are not erected piecemeal but in 'estates', sometimes of hundreds of houses at a time. One thing that always strikes me as mysterious is that so many of the northern towns see fit to build themselves immense and luxurious public buildings at the same time as they are in crying need of dwelling houses. The town of Barnsley, for instance, recently spent close on £150,000 on a new town hall, although admittedly needing at least 2,000 new working-class houses, not to mention public baths. (The public baths in Barnsley contain *nineteen* men's slipper baths – this in a town of 70,000 inhabitants, largely miners, not one of whom has a bath in his house!) For

[1] The number of Corporation houses in process of construction in Sheffield at the beginning of 1936 was 1,398. To replace the slum areas entirely Sheffield is said to need 100,000 houses.

£150,000 it could have built 350 Corporation houses and still had £10,000 to spend on a town hall. However, as I say, I do not pretend to understand the mysteries of local government. I merely record the fact that houses are desperately needed and are being built, on the whole, with paralytic slowness.

Still, houses *are* being built, and the Corporation building estates, with their row upon row of little red houses, all much liker than two peas (where did that expression come from? Peas have great individuality) are a regular feature of the outskirts of the industrial towns. As to what they are like and how they compare with the slum houses, I can best give an idea by transcribing two more extracts from my diary. The tenants' opinions of their houses vary greatly, so I will give one favourable extract and one unfavourable. Both of these are from Wigan and both are the cheaper 'non-parlour type' houses:

1. House in Beech Hill Estate.

Downstairs. Large living-room with kitchener fireplace, cupboards and fixed dresser, composition floor. Small hallway, largish kitchen. Up to date electric cooker hired from Corporation at much the same rate as a gas cooker.

Upstairs. Two largish bedrooms, one tiny one – suitable only for a box-room or temporary bedroom. Bathroom, w.c., with hot and cold water.

Smallish garden. These vary throughout the estate, but mostly rather smaller than an allotment.

Four in family, parents and two children. Husband in good employ. Houses appear well built and are quite agreeable to look at. Various restrictions, e.g. it is forbidden to keep poultry or pigeons, take in lodgers, sublet or start any kind of business without leave from the Corporation. (This is easily granted in the case of taking in lodgers, but not in any of the others.) Tenant very well satisfied with house and proud of it. Houses in this estate all well kept. Corporation are good about repairs, but keep tenants up to the mark with regard to keeping the place tidy, etc.

Rent 11*s*. 3*d*. including rates. Bus fare into town 2*d*.

2. House in Welly Estate.

Downstairs. Living-room 14 ft. by 10 ft., kitchen a good deal smaller, tiny larder under stairs, small but fairly good bathroom. Gas cooker, electric lighting. Outdoor w.c.

Upstairs. One bedroom 12 ft. by 10 ft. with tiny fireplace, another the same size without fireplace, another 7 ft. by 6 ft. Best bedroom has small wardrobe let into wall.

Garden about 20 yards by 10.

Six in family, parents and four children, eldest son nineteen, eldest daughter twenty-two. None in work except eldest son. Tenants very discontented. Their complaints are: 'House is cold, draughty and damp. Fireplace in living-room gives out no heat and makes room very dusty – attributed to its being set too low. Fireplace in best bedroom too small to be of any use. Walls upstairs cracking. Owing to uselessness of tiny bedroom, 5 are sleeping in one bedroom, 1 (the eldest son) in the other.'

Gardens in this estate all neglected.

Rent 10*s*. 3*d*., inclusive. Distance to town a little over a mile – there is no bus here.

I could multiply examples, but these two are enough, as the types of Corporation houses being built do not vary greatly from place to place. Two things are immediately obvious. The first is that at their very worst the Corporation houses are better than the slums they replace. The mere possession of a bathroom and a bit of garden would outweigh almost any disadvantage. The other is that they are much more expensive to live in. It is common enough for a man to be turned out of a condemned house where he is paying six or seven shillings a week and given a Corporation house where he has to pay ten. This only affects those who are in work or have recently been in work, because when a man is on the P.A.C. his rent is assessed at a quarter of his dole, and if it is more than this he gets an extra allowance; in any case, there are certain classes of Corporation houses to which people on the dole are not admitted. But there are other ways in which life in a Corporation estate is expensive, whether you are in work or out of it. To begin with, owing to the higher rents, the shops in the estate are much more expensive and there are not so many of them. Then again, in a comparatively large, detached house, away from the frowzy huddle of the slum, it is much colder and more fuel has to be burnt. And again there is the expense, especially for a man in work, of getting to and from town. This last is one of the more obvious problems of rehousing. Slum clearance means diffusion of the population. When you rebuild on a large scale, what you do in effect is to scoop out the centre of the town and redistribute it on the outskirts. This is all very well in a way; you have got the people out of fetid alleys into places where they have room to breathe; but from the point of view of the people themselves, what you have done is to pick them up and dump them down five miles from their work. The simplest solution is flats. If people are going to live in large towns at all they must learn to live on top of one another. But the northern working people do not take kindly to flats; even where flats exist they are contemptuously named 'tenements'. Almost everyone will tell you that he 'wants a house of his own', and apparently a house in the middle of an unbroken block of houses a hundred yards long seems to them more 'their own' than a flat situated in mid-air.

To revert to the second of the two Corporation houses I have just mentioned. The tenant complained that the house was cold, damp, and so forth. Perhaps the house was jerry-built, but equally probably he was exaggerating. He had come there from a filthy hovel in the middle of Wigan which I happened to have inspected previously; while there he had made every effort to get hold of a Corporation house, and he was no sooner in the Corporation house than he wanted to be back in the slum. This looks like mere captiousness but it covers a perfectly genuine grievance. In very many cases, perhaps in half the cases, I found that the people in Corporation houses don't really like them. They are glad to get out of the stink of the slum, they know that it is better for their children to have space to play about in, but they don't feel really at home. The exceptions are usually people in good employ who can afford to spend a little extra on fuel and furniture and journeys, and who in any case are of 'superior' type. The others, the typical slum-dwellers, miss the frowzy warmth of the slum. They complain that 'out in the country', i.e. on the edge of the town, they are 'starving' (freezing). Certainly most Corporation estates are pretty bleak in winter. Some I have been through, perched on treeless clayey hillsides and swept by icy winds, would be horrible places to live in. It is not that slum-dwellers want dirt and congestion for their own sakes, as the fat-bellied bourgeoisie love to believe. (See for instance the conversation about slum-clearance in Galsworthy's *Swan Song*, where the rentier's cherished belief that the slum-dweller makes the slum, and not vice versa, is put into the mouth of a philanthropic Jew.) Give people a decent house and they will soon learn to keep it decent. Moreover, with a smart-looking house to live up to they improve in self-respect and cleanliness, and their children start life with better chances. Nevertheless, in a Corporation estate there is an uncomfortable, almost prison-like atmosphere, and the people who live there are perfectly well aware of it.

And it is here that one comes on the central difficulty of the housing problem. When you walk through the smoke-dim slums of Manchester you think that nothing is needed except to tear down these abominations and build decent houses in their place. But the trouble is that in destroying the slum you destroy other things as well. Houses are desperately needed and are not being built fast enough; but in so far as rehousing is being done, it is being done – perhaps it is unavoidable – in a monstrously inhuman manner. I don't mean merely that the houses are new and ugly. All houses have got to be new at some time, and as a matter of fact the type of Corporation house now being built is not at all offensive to look at. On the outskirts of Liverpool there are what amount to whole towns consisting entirely of Corporation houses, and they are quite pleasing to the eye; the blocks of workers' flats in the centre of the town, modelled, I believe, on the workers' flats in Vienna, are definitely fine buildings. But there is something ruthless and soulless about the whole business. Take, for instance, the restrictions with which you are burdened in a Corporation house. You are not allowed to keep your house and garden as you want them – in some estates there is even a regulation that every garden must have the same kind of hedge. You are not allowed to keep poultry or pigeons. The Yorkshire miners are fond of keeping homer pigeons; they keep them in the back yard and take them out and race them on Sundays. But pigeons are messy birds and the Corporation suppresses them as a matter of course. The restrictions about shops are more serious. The number of shops in a Corporation estate is rigidly limited, and it is said that preference is given to the Co-op. and the chain stores; this may not be strictly true, but certainly those are the shops that one usually sees there. This is bad enough for the general public, but from the point of view of the independent shopkeeper it is a disaster. Many a small shopkeeper is utterly ruined by some rehousing scheme which takes no notice of his existence. A whole section of the town is condemned *en bloc*; presently the houses are pulled down and the people are transferred to some housing estate miles away. In this way all the small shopkeepers of the quarter have their whole clientele taken away from them at a single swoop and receive not a penny of compensation. They cannot transfer their business to the estate, because even if they can afford the move and the much higher rents, they would probably be refused a licence. As for pubs, they are banished from the housing estates almost completely, and the few that remain are dismal sham-Tudor places fitted out by the big brewery companies and very expensive. For a middle-class population this would be a nuisance – it might mean walking a mile to get a glass of beer; for a working-class population, which uses the pub as a kind of club, it is a serious blow at communal life. It is a great achievement to get slum-dwellers into decent houses, but it is unfortunate that, owing to the peculiar temper of our time, it is also considered necessary to rob them of the last vestiges of their liberty. The people themselves feel this, and it is this feeling that they are rationalizing when they complain that their new houses – so much better, *as* houses, than those they have come out of – are cold and uncomfortable and 'unhomelike'.

I sometimes think that the price of liberty is not so much eternal vigilance as eternal dirt. There are some Corporation estates in which new tenants are systematically deloused before being allowed into their houses. All their possessions except what they stand up in are taken away from them, fumigated and sent on to the new house. This procedure has its points, for it *is* a pity that people should take bugs into brand new houses (a bug will follow you about in your luggage if he gets half a chance), but it is the kind of thing that makes you wish that the word 'hygiene' could be dropped out of the dictionary. Bugs are bad, but a state of affairs in which men will allow themselves to be dipped like sheep is worse. Perhaps, however, when it is a case of slum clearance, one must take for granted a certain amount of restrictions and inhumanity. When all is said and done, the most important thing is that people shall live in decent houses and not in pigsties. I have seen too much of slums to go into Chestertonian raptures about them. A place where the children can breathe clean air, and women have a few conveniences to save them from drudgery, and a man has a bit of garden to dig in, *must* be better than the stinking backstreets of Leeds and Sheffield. On balance, the Corporation Estates are better than the slums; but only by a small margin.

When I was looking into the housing question I visited and inspected numbers of houses, perhaps a hundred or two hundred houses altogether, in various mining towns and villages. I cannot end this chapter without remarking on the extraordinary courtesy and good nature with which I was received everywhere. I did not go alone – I always had some local friend among the unemployed to show me round – but even so, it is an impertinence to go poking into strangers' houses and asking to see the cracks in the bedroom wall. Yet everyone was astonishingly patient and seemed to understand almost without explanation why I was questioning them and what I wanted to see. If any unauthorized person walked into *my* house and began asking me whether the roof leaked and whether I was much troubled by bugs and what I thought of my landlord, I should probably tell him to go to hell. This only happened to me once, and in that case the woman was slightly deaf and took me for a Means Test nark; but even she relented after a while and gave me the information I wanted.

I am told that it is bad form for a writer to quote his own reviews, but I want here to contradict a reviewer in the *Manchester Guardian* who says apropos of one of my books:

> 'Set down in Wigan or Whitechapel Mr Orwell would still exercise an unerring power of closing his vision to all that is good in order to proceed with his wholehearted vilification of humanity.'

Wrong. Mr Orwell was 'set down' in Wigan for quite a while and it did not inspire him with any wish to vilify humanity. He liked Wigan very much – the people, not the scenery. Indeed, he has only one fault to find with it, and that is in respect of the celebrated Wigan Pier, which he had set his heart on seeing. Alas! Wigan Pier has been demolished, and even the spot where it used to stand is no longer certain.

Chapter Five

When you see the unemployment figures quoted at two millions, it is fatally easy to take this as meaning that two million people are out of work and the rest of the population is comparatively comfortable. I admit that till recently I was in the habit of doing so myself. I used to calculate that if you put the registered unemployed at round about two millions and threw in the destitute and those who for one reason and another were not registered, you might take the number of underfed people in England (for *everyone* on the dole or thereabouts is underfed) as being, at the very most, five millions.

This is an enormous under-estimate, because, in the first place, the only people shown on unemployment figures are those actually drawing the dole – that is, in general, heads of families. An unemployed man's dependants do not figure on the list unless they too are drawing a separate allowance. A Labour Exchange officer told me that to get at the real number of people *living on* (not drawing) the dole, you have got to multiply the official figures by something over three. This alone brings the number of unemployed to round about six millions. But in addition there are great numbers of people who are in work but who, from a financial point of view, might equally well be unemployed, because they are not drawing anything that can be described as a living wage.[1] Allow for these and their dependants, throw in as before the old-age pensioners, the destitute and other nondescripts, and you get an *underfed* population of well over ten millions. Sir John Orr puts it at twenty millions.

Take the figures for Wigan, which is typical enough of the industrial and mining districts. The number of insured workers is round about 36,000 (26,000 men and 10,000 women). Of these, the number unemployed at the beginning of 1936 was about 10,000. But this was in winter when the mines are working full time; in summer it would probably be 12,000. Multiply by three, as above, and you get 30,000 or 36,000. The total population of Wigan is a little under 87,000; so that at any moment more than one person in three out of the whole population – not merely the registered workers – is either drawing or living on the dole. Those ten or twelve thousand unemployed contain a steady core of from four to five thousand miners who had been continuously unemployed for the past seven years. And Wigan is not especially badly off as industrial towns go. Even in Sheffield, which has been doing well for the last year or so because of wars and rumours of war, the proportion of unemployment is about the same – one in three of registered workers unemployed.

When a man is first unemployed, until his insurance stamps are exhausted, he draws 'full benefit', of which the rates are as follows:

	per week
Single man	17*s.*
Wife	9*s.*
Each child below 14	3*s.*

[1] For instance, a recent census of the Lancashire cotton mills revealed the fact that over 40,000 *full-time* employees receive less than thirty shillings a week each. In Preston, to take only one town, the number receiving *over* thirty shillings a week was 640 and the number receiving *under* thirty shillings was 3,113.

Thus in a typical family of parents and three children of whom one was over 14, the total income would be 32*s*. per week, plus anything that might be earned by the eldest child. When a man's stamps are exhausted, before being turned over to the P.A.C. (Public Assistance Committee), he receives twenty-six weeks' 'transitional benefit' from the U.A.B. (Unemployment Assistance Board), the rates being as follows:

	per week
Single man	15*s*.
Man and wife	24*s*.
Children, 14–18	6*s*.
Children, 11–14	4*s*. 6*d*.
Children, 8–11	4*s*.
Children, 5–8	3*s*. 6*d*.
Children, 3–5	3*s*.

Thus on the U.A.B. the income of the typical family of five persons would be 37*s*. 6*d*. a week if no child was in work. When a man is on the U.A.B. a quarter of his dole is regarded as rent, with a minimum of 7*s*. 6*d*. a week. If the rent he is paying is more than a quarter of his dole he receives an extra allowance, but if it is less than 7*s*. 6*d*., a corresponding amount is deducted. Payments on the P.A.C. theoretically come out of the local rates, but are backed by a central fund. The rates of benefit are:

	per week
Single man	12*s*. 6*d*.
Man and wife	23*s*.
Eldest child	4*s*.
Any other child	3*s*.

Being at the discretion of the local bodies these rates vary slightly, and a single man may or may not get an extra 2*s*. 6*d*. weekly, bringing his benefit up to 15 *s*. As on the U.A.B., a quarter of a married man's dole is regarded as rent. Thus in the typical family considered above the total income would be 33*s*. a week, a quarter of this being regarded as rent. In addition, in most districts a coal allowance of 1*s*. 6*d*. a week (1*s*. 6*d*. is equivalent to about a hundredweight of coal) is granted for six weeks before and six weeks after Christmas.

It will be seen that the income of a family on the dole normally averages round about thirty shillings a week. One can write at least a quarter of this off as rent, which is to say that the average person, child or adult, has got to be fed, clothed, warmed, and otherwise cared-for for six or seven shillings a week. Enormous groups of people, probably at least a third of the whole population of the industrial areas, are living at this level. The Means Test is very strictly enforced, and you are liable to be refused relief at the slightest hint that you are getting money from another source. Dock-labourers, for instance, who are generally hired by the half day, have to sign on at a Labour Exchange twice daily; if they fail to do so it is assumed that they have been working and their dole is reduced correspondingly. I have seen cases of evasion of the Means Test, but I should say that in the industrial towns, where there is still a certain amount of communal life and everyone has neighbours who know him, it is much harder than it would be in London. The usual method is for a young man who is actually living with his parents to get an accommodation address, so that supposedly he has a separate establishment and draws a separate allowance. But there is much spying and tale-bearing. One man I knew, for instance, was seen feeding his neighbour's chickens while the neighbour was away. It was reported to the authorities that he 'had a job feeding chickens' and he had great difficulty in refuting this. The favourite joke in Wigan was about a man who was refused relief on the ground that he 'had a job carting firewood'. He had been seen, it was said, carting firewood at night. He had to explain that he was not carting firewood but doing a moonlight flit. The 'firewood' was his furniture.

The most cruel and evil effect of the Means Test is the way in which it breaks up families. Old people, sometimes bedridden, are driven out of their homes by it. An old age pensioner, for instance, if a widower, would normally live with one or other of his children; his weekly ten shillings goes towards the household expenses, and probably he is not badly cared for. Under the Means Test, however, he counts as a 'lodger' and if he stays at home his children's dole will be docked. So, perhaps at seventy or seventy-five years of age, he has to turn out into lodgings, handing his pension over to the lodging-house keeper and existing on the verge of starvation. I have seen several cases of this myself. It is happening all over England at this moment, thanks to the Means Test.

Nevertheless, in spite of the frightful extent of unemployment, it is a fact that poverty – extreme poverty – is less in evidence in the industrial North than it is in London. Everything is poorer and shabbier, there are fewer motor-cars and fewer well-dressed people; but also there are fewer people who are obviously destitute. Even in a town the size of Liverpool or Manchester you are struck by the fewness of the beggars. London is a sort of whirlpool which draws derelict people towards it, and it is so vast that life there is solitary and anonymous. Until you break the law nobody will take any notice of you, and you can go to pieces as you could not possibly do in a place where you had neighbours who knew you. But in the industrial towns the old communal way of life has not yet broken up, tradition is still strong and almost everyone has a family – potentially, therefore, a home. In a town of 50,000 or 100,000 inhabitants there is no casual and as it were unaccounted-for population; nobody sleeping in the streets, for instance. Moreover, there is just this to be said for the unemployment regulations, that they do not discourage people from marrying. A man and wife on twenty-three shillings a week are not far from the starvation line, but they can make a home of sorts; they are vastly better off than a single man on fifteen shillings. The life of a single unemployed man is dreadful. He lives sometimes in a common lodging-house, more often in a 'furnished' room for which he usually pays six shillings a week, finding himself as best he can on the other nine (say six shillings a week for food and three for clothes, tobacco and amusements). Of course he cannot feed or look after himself properly, and a man who pays six shillings a week for his room is not encouraged to be indoors more than is necessary. So he spends his days loafing in the public library or any other place where he can keep warm. That – keeping warm – is almost the sole pre-occupation of a single unemployed man in winter. In Wigan a favourite refuge was the pictures, which are fantastically cheap there. You can always get a seat for fourpence, and at the matinée at some houses you can even get a seat for twopence. Even people on the verge of starvation will readily pay twopence to get out of the ghastly cold of a winter afternoon. In Sheffield I was taken to a public hall to listen to a lecture by a clergyman, and it was by a long way the silliest and worst-delivered lecture I have ever heard or ever expect to hear. I found it physically impossible to sit it out, indeed my feet carried me out, seemingly of their own accord, before it was half way through. Yet the hall was thronged with unemployed men; they would have sat through far worse drivel for the sake of a warm place to shelter in.

At times I have seen unmarried men on the dole living in the extreme of misery. In one town I remember a whole colony of them who were squatting, more or less illicitly, in a derelict house which was practically falling down. They had collected a few scraps of furniture, presumably off refuse-tips, and I remember that their sole table was an old marble-topped wash-hand-stand. But this kind of thing is exceptional. A working-class bachelor is a rarity, and so long as a man is married unemployment makes comparatively little alteration in his way of life. His home is impoverished but it is still a home, and it is noticeable everywhere that the anomalous position created by unemployment – the man being out of work while the woman's work continues as before – has not altered the relative status of the sexes. In a working-class home it is the man who is the master and not, as in a middle-class home, the woman or the baby. Practically never, for instance, in a working-class home, will you see the man doing a stroke of the housework. Unemployment has not changed this convention, which on the face of it seems a little unfair. The man is idle from morning to night but the woman is as busy as ever – more so, indeed, because she has to manage with less money. Yet so far as my experience goes the women do not protest. I believe that they, as well as the men, feel that a man would lose his manhood if, merely because he was out of work, he developed into a 'Mary Ann'.

But there is no doubt about the deadening, debilitating effect of unemployment upon everybody, married or single, and upon men more than upon women. The best intellects will not stand up against it. Once or twice it has happened to me to meet unemployed men of genuine literary ability; there are others whom I haven't met but whose work I occasionally see in the magazines. Now and again, at long intervals, these men will produce an article or a short story which is quite obviously better than most of the stuff that gets whooped up by the blurb-reviewers. Why, then, do they make so little use of their talents? They have all the leisure in the world; why don't they sit down and write books? Because to write books you need not only comfort and solitude – and solitude is never easy to attain in a working-class home – you also need peace of mind. You can't settle to anything, you can't command the spirit of *hope* in which anything has got to be created, with that dull evil cloud of unemployment hanging over you. Still, an unemployed man who feels at home with books can at any rate occupy himself by reading. But what about the man who cannot read without discomfort? Take a miner, for instance, who has worked in the pit since childhood and has been trained to be a miner and nothing else. How the devil is he to fill up the empty days? It is absurd to say that he ought to be looking for work. There is no work to look for, and everybody knows it. You can't go on looking for work every day for seven years. There are allotments, which occupy the time and help to feed a family, but in a big town there are only allotments for a small proportion of the people. Then there are the occupational centres which were started a few years ago to help the unemployed. On the whole this movement has been a failure, but some of the centres are still flourishing. I have visited one or two of them. There are shelters where the men can keep warm and there are periodical classes in carpentering, boot-making, leather-work, handloom-weaving, basket-work, sea-grass work, etc., etc.; the idea being that the men can make furniture and so forth, not for sale but for their own homes, getting tools free and materials cheaply. Most of the Socialists I have talked to denounce this movement as they denounce the project – it is always being talked about but it never comes to anything – to give the unemployed small-holdings. They say that the occupational centres are simply a device to keep the unemployed quiet and give them the illusion that something is being done for them. Undoubtedly that *is* the underlying motive. Keep a man busy mending boots and he is less likely to read the *Daily Worker*. Also there is a nasty Y.M.C.A. atmosphere about these places which you can feel as soon as you go in. The unemployed men who frequent them are mostly of the cap-touching type – the type who tells you oilily that he is 'Temperance' and votes Conservative. Yet even here you feel yourself torn both ways. For probably it is better that a man should waste his time even with such rubbish as sea-grass work than that for years upon end he should do absolutely *nothing*.

By far the best work for the unemployed is being done by the N.U.W.M. – National Unemployed Workers' Movement. This is a revolutionary organization intended to hold the unemployed together, stop them blacklegging during strikes and give them legal advice against the Means Test. It is a movement that has been built out of nothing by the pennies and efforts of the unemployed themselves. I have seen a good deal of the N.U.W.M., and I greatly admire the men, ragged and underfed like the others, who keep the organization going. Still more I admire the tact and patience with which they do it; for it is not easy to coax even a penny-a-week subscription out of the pockets of people on the P.A.C. As I said earlier, the English working class do not show much capacity for leadership, but they have a wonderful talent for organization. The whole trade union movement testifies to this; so do the excellent working-men's clubs – really a sort of glorified co-operative pub, and splendidly organized – which are so common in Yorkshire. In many towns the N.U.W.M. have shelters and arrange speeches by Communist speakers. But even at these shelters the men who go there do nothing but sit round the stove and occasionally play a game of dominoes. If this movement could be combined with something along the lines of the occupational centres, it would be nearer what is needed. It is a deadly thing to see a skilled man running to seed, year after year, in utter, hopeless idleness. It ought not to be impossible to give him the chance of using his hands and making furniture and so forth for his own home, without turning him into a Y.M.C.A. cocoa-drunkard. We may as well face the fact that several million men in England will – unless another war breaks out – never have a real job this side the grave. One thing that probably could be done and certainly ought to be done as a matter of course is to give every unemployed man a patch of ground and free tools if he chose to apply for them. It is disgraceful that men who are expected to keep alive on the P.A.C. should not even have the chance to grow vegetables for their families.

To study unemployment and its effects you have got to go to the industrial area. In the South unemployment exists, but it is scattered and queerly unobtrusive. There are plenty of rural districts where a man out of work is almost unheard-of, and you don't anywhere see the spectacle of whole blocks of cities living on the dole and the P.A.C. It is only when you lodge in streets where nobody has a job, where getting a job seems about as probable as owning an aeroplane and much *less* probable than winning fifty pounds in the Football Pool, that you begin to grasp the changes that are being worked in our civilization. For a change *is* taking place, there is no doubt about that. The attitude of the submerged working class is profoundly different from what it was seven or eight years ago.

I first became aware of the unemployment problem in 1928. At that time I had just come back from Burma, where unemployment was only a word, and I had gone to Burma when I was still a boy and the post-war boom was not quite over. When I first saw unemployed men at close quarters, the thing that horrified and amazed me was to find that many of them were *ashamed* of being unemployed. I was very ignorant, but not so ignorant as to imagine that when the loss of foreign markets pushes two million men out of work, those two million are any more to blame that the people who draw blanks in the Calcutta Sweep. But at that time nobody cared to admit that unemployment was inevitable, because this meant admitting that it would probably continue. The middle classes were still talking about 'lazy idle loafers on the dole' and saying that 'these men could all find work if they wanted to,' and naturally these opinions percolated to the working class themselves. I remember the shock of astonishment it gave me, when I first mingled with tramps and beggars, to find that a fair proportion, perhaps a quarter, of these beings whom I had been taught to regard as cynical parasities, were decent young miners and cotton-workers gazing at their destiny with the same sort of dumb amazement as an animal in a trap. They simply could not understand what was happening to them. They had been brought up to work, and behold! it seemed as if they were never going to have the chance of working again. In their circumstances it was inevitable, at first, that they should be haunted by a feeling of personal degradation. That was the attitude towards unemployment in those days: it was a disaster which happened to *you* as an individual and for which *you* were to blame.

When a quarter of a million miners are unemployed, it is part of the order of things that Alf Smith, a miner living in the back streets of Newcastle, should be out of work. Alf Smith is merely one of the quarter million, a statistical unit. But no human being finds it easy to regard himself as a statistical unit. So long as Bert Jones across the street is still at work, Alf Smith is bound to feel himself dishonoured and a failure. Hence that frightful feeling of impotence and despair which is almost the worst evil of unemployment – far worse than any hardship, worse than the demoralization of enforced idleness, and only less bad than the physical degeneracy of Alf Smith's children, born on the P.A.C. Everyone who saw Greenwood's play *Love on the Dole* must remember that dreadful moment when the poor, good, stupid working man beats on the table and cries out, 'O God, send me some work!' This was not dramatic exaggeration, it was a touch from life. That cry must have been uttered, in almost those words, in tens of thousands, perhaps hundreds of thousands of English homes, during the past fifteen years.

But, I think not again – or at least, not so often. That is the real point: people are ceasing to kick against the pricks. After all, even the middle classes – yes, even the bridge clubs in the country towns – are beginning to realize that there is such a thing as unemployment. The 'My dear, I don't *believe* in all this nonsense about unemployment. Why, only last week we wanted a man to weed the garden, and we simply couldn't get one. They don't *want* to work, that's all it is!' which you heard at every decent tea-table five years ago, is growing perceptibly less frequent. As for the working class themselves, they have gained immensely in economic knowledge. I believe that the *Daily Worker* has accomplished a great deal here: its influence is out of all proportion to its circulation. But in any case they have had their lesson well rubbed into them, not only because unemployment is so widespread but because it has lasted so long. When people live on the dole for years at a time they grow used to it, and drawing the dole, though it remains unpleasant, ceases to be shameful. Thus the old, independent, workhouse-fearing tradition is undermined, just as the ancient fear of debt is undermined by the hire-purchase system. In the back streets of Wigan and Barnsley I saw every kind of privation, but I probably saw much less *conscious* misery than I should have seen ten years ago. The people have at any rate grasped that unemployment is a thing they cannot help. It is not only Alf Smith who is out of work now; Bert Jones is out of work as well, and both of them have been 'out' for years. It makes a great deal of difference when things are the same for everybody.

So you have whole populations settling down, as it were, to a lifetime on the P.A.C. And what I think is admirable, perhaps even hopeful, is that they have managed to do it without going spiritually to pieces. A working man does not disintegrate under the strain of poverty as a middle-class person does. Take, for instance, the fact that the working class think nothing of getting married on the dole. It annoys the old ladies in Brighton, but it is a proof of their essential good sense, they realize that losing your job does not mean that you cease to be a human being. So that in one way things in the distressed areas are not so bad as they might be. Life is still fairly normal, more normal than one really has the right to expect. Families are impoverished, but the family-system has not broken up. The people are in effect living a reduced version of their former lives. Instead of raging against their destiny they have made things tolerable by lowering their standards.

But they don't necessarily lower their standards by cutting out luxuries and concentrating on necessities; more often it is the other way about – the more natural way, if you come to think of it. Hence the fact that in a decade of unparalleled depression, the consumption of all cheap luxuries has increased. The two things that have probably made the greatest difference of all are the movies and the mass-production of cheap smart clothes since the war. The youth who leaves school at fourteen and gets a blind-alley job is out of work at twenty, probably for life; but for two pounds ten on the hire-purchase system he can buy himself a suit which, for a little while and at a little distance, looks as though it had been tailored in Savile Row. The girl can look like a fashion plate at an even lower price. You may have three halfpence in your pocket and not a prospect in the world, and only the corner of a leaky bedroom to go home to; but in your new clothes you can stand on the street corner, indulging in a private daydream of yourself as Clark Gable or Greta Garbo, which compensates you for a great deal. And even at home there is generally a cup of tea going – a 'nice cup of tea' – and Father, who has been out of work since 1929, is temporarily happy because he has a sure tip for the Cesarewitch.

Trade since the war has had to adjust itself to meet the demands of underpaid, underfed people, with the result that a luxury is nowadays almost always cheaper than a necessity. One pair of plain solid shoes costs as much as two ultra-smart pairs. For the price of one square meal you can get two pounds of cheap sweets. You can't get much meat for threepence, but you can get a lot of fish-and-chips. Milk costs threepence a pint and even 'mild' beer costs fourpence, but aspirins are seven a penny and you can wring forty cups of tea out of a quarter-pound packet. And above all there is gambling, the cheapest of all luxuries. Even people on the verge of starvation can buy a few days' hope ('Something to live for', as they call it) by having a penny on a sweepstake. Organized gambling has now risen almost to the status of a major industry. Consider, for instance, a phenomenon like the Football Pools, with a turnover of about six million pounds a year, almost all of it from the pockets of working-class people. I happened to be in Yorkshire when Hitler re-occupied the Rhineland. Hitler, Locarno, Fascism and the threat of war aroused hardly a flicker of interest locally, but the decision of the Football Association to stop publishing their fixtures in advance (this was an attempt to quell the Football Pools) flung all Yorkshire into a storm of fury. And then there is the queer spectacle of modern electrical science showering miracles upon people with empty bellies. You may shiver all night for lack of bedclothes, but in the morning you can go to the public library and read the news that has been telegraphed for your benefit from San Francisco and Singapore. Twenty million people are underfed but literally everyone in England has access to a radio. What we have lost in food we have gained in electricity. Whole sections of the working class who have been plundered of all they really need are being compensated, in part, by cheap luxuries which mitigate the surface of life.

Do you consider all this desirable? No, I don't. But it may be that the psychological adjustment which the working class are visibly making is the best they could make in the circumstances. They have neither turned revolutionary nor lost their self-respect; merely they have kept their tempers and settled down to make the best of things on a fish-and-chip standard. The alternative would be God knows what continued agonies of despair; or it might be attempted insurrections which, in a strongly governed country like England, could only lead to futile massacres and a régime of savage repression.

Of course the post-war development of cheap luxuries has been a very fortunate thing for our rulers. It is quite likely that fish-and-chips, art-silk stockings, tinned salmon, cut-price chocolate (five two-ounce bars for sixpence), the movies, the radio, strong tea and the Football Pools have between them averted revolution. Therefore we are sometimes told that the whole thing is an astute manoeuvre by the governing class – a sort of 'bread and circuses' business – to hold the unemployed down. What I have seen of our governing class does not convince me that they have that much intelligence. The thing has happened, but by an unconscious process – the quite natural interaction between the manufacturer's need for a market and the need of half-starved people for cheap palliatives.

Chapter Six

When I was a small boy at school a lecturer used to come once a term and deliver excellent lectures on famous battles of the past, such as Blenheim, Austerlitz, etc. He was fond of quoting Napoleon's maxim 'An army marches on its stomach,' and at the end of his lecture he would suddenly turn to us and demand 'What's the most important thing in the world?' We were expected to shout 'Food!' and if we did not do so he was disappointed.

Obviously he was right in a way. A human being is primarily a bag for putting food into; the other functions and faculties may be more godlike, but in point of time they come afterwards. A man dies and is buried, and all his words and actions are forgotten, but the food he has eaten lives after him in the sound or rotten bones of his children. I think it could be plausibly argued that changes of diet are more important than changes of dynasty or even of religion. The Great War, for instance, could never have happened if tinned food had not been invented. And the history of the past four hundred years in England would have been immensely different if it had not been for the introduction of root-crops and various other vegetables at the end of the Middle Ages, and a little later the introduction of non-alcoholic drinks (tea, coffee, cocoa) and also of distilled liquors to which the beer-drinking English were not accustomed. Yet it is curious how seldom the all-importance of food is recognized. You see statues everywhere to politicians, poets, bishops, but none to cooks or bacon-curers or market-gardeners. The Emperor Charles V is said to have erected a statue to the inventor of bloaters, but that is the only case I can think of at the moment.

So perhaps the really important thing about the unemployed, the really basic thing if you look to the future, is the diet they are living on. As I said earlier, the average unemployed family lives on an income of round about thirty shillings a week, of which at least a quarter goes in rent. It is worth considering in some detail how the remaining money is spent. I have here a budget which was made out for me by an unemployed miner and his wife. I asked them to make a list which represented as exactly as possible their expenditure in a typical week. This man's allowance was thirty-two shillings a week, and besides his wife he had two children, one aged two years and five months and the other ten months. Here is the list:

		s.	*d.*
Rent		9	0½
Clothing Club		3	0
Coal		2	0
Gas		1	3
Milk		0	10½
Union fees		0	3
Insurance (on the children)		0	2
Meat		2	6
Flour (2 stone)		3	4
Yeast		0	4
Potatoes		1	0
Dripping		0	10
Margarine		0	10
Bacon		1	2
Sugar		1	9
Tea		1	0
Jam		0	7½
Peas and cabbage		0	6
Carrots and onions		0	4
Quaker oats		0	4½
Soap, powders, blue, etc.		0	10
Total	£1	12	0

In addition to this, three packets of dried milk were supplied weekly for the baby by the Infants' Welfare Clinic.

One or two comments are needed here. To begin with the list leaves out a great deal – blacking, pepper, salt, vinegar, matches, kindling-wood, razor blades, replacements of utensils and wear and tear of furniture and bedding, to name the first few that come to mind. Any money spent on these would mean reduction on some other item. A more serious charge is tobacco. This man happened to be a small smoker, but even so his tobacco would hardly cost less than a shilling a week, meaning a further reduction on food. The 'clothing clubs' into which unemployed people pay so much a week are run by big drapers in all the industrial towns. Without them it would be impossible for unemployed people to buy new clothes at all. I don't know whether or not they buy bedding through these clubs. This particular family, as I happen to know, possessed next to no bedding.

In the above list, if you allow a shilling for tobacco and deduct this and the other non-food items, you are left with sixteen and fivepence halfpenny. Call it sixteen shillings and leave the baby out of account – for the baby was getting its weekly packets of milk from the Welfare Clinic. This sixteen shillings has got to provide the entire nourishment, *including fuel*, of three persons, two of them adult. The first question is whether it is even theoretically possible for three persons to be properly nourished on sixteen shillings a week. When the dispute over the Means Test was in progress there was a disgusting public wrangle about the minimum weekly sum on which a human being could keep alive. So far as I remember, one school of dietitians worked it out at five and ninepence, while another school, more generous, put it at five and ninepence halfpenny. After this there were letters to the papers from a number of people who claimed to be feeding themselves on four shillings a week. Here is a weekly budget (it was printed in the *New Statesman* and also in the *News of the World*) which I picked out from among a number of others:

	s.	*d.*
3 wholemeal loves	1	0
½ lb. margarine	0	2½
½ lb. dripping	0	3
1 lb. cheese	0	7
1 lb. onions	0	1½
1 lb. carrots	0	1½
1 lb. broken biscuits	0	4
2 lb. dates	0	6
1 tin evaporated milk	0	5
10 oranges	0	5
Total	3	11½

Please notice that this budget contains *nothing for fuel*. In fact, the writer explicitly stated that he could not afford to buy fuel and ate all his food raw. Whether the letter was genuine or a hoax does not matter at the moment. What I think will be admitted is that this list represents about as wise an expenditure as could be contrived; if you *had* to live on three and elevenpence halfpenny a week, you could hardly extract more food-value from it than that.

So perhaps it is possible to feed yourself adequately on the P.A.C. allowance if you concentrate on essential foodstuffs; but not otherwise.

Now compare this list with the unemployed miner's budget that I gave earlier. The miner's family spend only tenpence a week on green vegetables and tenpence halfpenny on milk (remember that one of them is a child less than three years old), and nothing on fruit; but they spend one and nine on sugar (about eight pounds of sugar, that is) and a shilling on tea. The half-crown spent on meat *might* represent a small joint and the materials for a stew; probably as often as not it would represent four or five tins of bully beef. The basis of their diet, therefore, is white bread and margarine, corned beef, sugared tea and potatoes – an appalling diet. Would it not be better if they spent more money on wholesome things like oranges and wholemeal bread or if they even, like the writer of the letter to the *New Statesman*, saved on fuel and ate their carrots raw? Yes, it would, but the point is that no ordinary human being is ever going to do such a thing. The ordinary human being would sooner starve than live on brown bread and raw carrots. And the peculiar evil is this, that the less money you have, the less inclined you feel to spend it on wholesome food. A millionaire may enjoy breakfasting off orange juice and Ryvita biscuits; an unemployed man doesn't. Here the tendency of which I spoke at the end of the last chapter comes into play. When you are unemployed, which is to say when you are underfed, harassed, bored and miserable, you don't *want* to eat dull wholesome food. You want something a little bit 'tasty'. There is always some cheaply pleasant thing to tempt you. Let's have three pennorth of chips! Run out and buy us a twopenny ice-cream! Put the kettle on and we'll all have a nice cup of tea! *That* is how your mind works when you are at the P.A.C. level. White bread-and-marg and sugared tea don't nourish you to any extent, but they are *nicer* (at least most people think so) than brown bread-and-dripping and cold water. Unemployment is an endless misery that has got to be constantly palliated, and especially with tea, the Englishman's opium. A cup of tea or even an aspirin is much better as a temporary stimulant than a crust of brown bread.

The results of all this are visible in a physical degeneracy which you can study directly, by using your eyes, or inferentially, by having a look at the vital statistics. The physical average in the industrial towns is terribly low, lower even than in London. In Sheffield you have the feeling of walking among a population of troglodytes. The miners are splendid men, but they are usually small, and the mere fact that their muscles are toughened by constant work does not mean that their children start life with a better physique. In any case the miners are physically the pick of the population. The most obvious sign of under-nourishment is the badness of everybody's teeth. In Lancashire you would have to look for a long time before you saw a working-class person with good natural teeth. Indeed, you see very few people with natural teeth at all, apart from the children; and even the children's teeth have a frail bluish appearance which means, I suppose, calcium deficiency. Several dentists have told me that in industrial districts a person over thirty with any of his or her own teeth is coming to be an abnormality. In Wigan various people gave me their opinion that it is best to 'get shut of' your teeth as early in life as possible. 'Teeth is just a misery,' one woman said to me. In one house where I stayed there were, apart from myself, five people, the oldest being forty-three and the youngest a boy of fifteen. Of these the boy was the only one who possessed a single tooth of his own, and his teeth were obviously not going to last long. As for the vital statistics, the fact that in any large industrial town the death rate and infant mortality rate of the poorest quarters are always about double those of the well-to-do residential quarters – a good deal more than double in some cases – hardly needs commenting on.

Of course one ought not to imagine that the prevailing bad physique is due solely to unemployment, for it is probable that the physical average has been declining all over England for a long time past, and not merely among the unemployed in the industrial areas. This cannot be proved statistically, but it is a conclusion that is forced upon you if you use your eyes, even in rural places and even in a prosperous town like London. On the day when King George V's body passed through London on its way to Westminster, I happened to be caught for an hour or two in the crowd in Trafalgar Square. It was impossible, looking about one then, not to be struck by the physical degeneracy of modern England. The people surrounding me were *not* working-class people for the most part; they were the shopkeeper-commercial-traveller type, with a sprinkling of the well-to-do. But what a set they looked! Puny limbs, sickly faces, under the weeping London sky! Hardly a well-built man or a decent-looking woman, and not a fresh complexion anywhere. As the King's coffin went by, the men took off their hats, and a friend who was in the crowd at the other side of the Strand said to me afterwards, 'The only touch of colour anywhere was the bald heads.' Even the Guards, it seemed to me – there was a squad of guardsmen marching beside the coffin – were not what they used to be. Where are the monstrous men with chests like barrels and moustaches like the wings of eagles who strode across my childhood's gaze twenty or thirty years ago? Buried, I suppose, in the Flanders mud. In their place there are these pale-faced boys who have been picked for their height and consequently look like hop-poles in overcoats – the truth being that in modern England a man over six feet high is usually skin and bone and not much else. If the English physique has declined, this is no doubt partly due to the fact that the Great War carefully selected the million best men in England and slaughtered them, largely before they had had time to breed. But the process must have begun earlier than that, and it must be due ultimately to unhealthy ways of living, i.e. to industrialism. I don't mean the habit of living in towns – probably the town is healthier than the country, in many ways – but the modern industrial technique which provides you with cheap substitutes for everything. We may find in the long run that tinned food is a deadlier weapon than the machine gun.

It is unfortunate that the English working class – the English nation generally, for that matter – are exceptionally ignorant about and wasteful of food. I have pointed out elsewhere how civilized is a French navvy's idea of a meal compared with an Englishman's, and I cannot believe that you would ever see such wastage in a French house as you habitually see in English ones. Of course, in the very poorest homes, where everybody is unemployed, you don't see much actual waste, but those who can afford to waste food often do so. I could give startling instances of this. Even the Northern habit of baking one's own bread is slightly wasteful in itself, because an overworked woman cannot bake more than once or, at most, twice a week and it is impossible to tell beforehand how much bread will be wanted, so that a certain amount generally has to be thrown away. The usual thing is to bake six large loaves and twelve small ones at a time. All this is part of the old, generous English attitude to life, and it is an amiable quality, but a disastrous one at the present moment.

English working people everywhere, so far as I know, refuse brown bread; it is usually impossible to buy wholemeal bread in a working-class district. They sometimes give the reason that brown bread is 'dirty'. I suspect the real reason is that in the past brown bread has been confused with black bread, which is traditionally associated with Popery and wooden shoes. (They have plenty of Popery and wooden shoes in Lancashire. A pity they haven't the black bread as well!) But the English palate, especially the working-class palate, now rejects good food almost automatically. The number of people who *prefer* tinned peas and tinned fish to real peas and real fish must be increasing every year, and plenty of people who could afford real milk in their tea would much sooner have tinned milk – even that dreadful tinned milk which is made of sugar and cornflour and has UNFIT FOR BABIES on the tin in huge letters. In some districts efforts are now being made to teach the unemployed more about food-values and more about the intelligent spending of money. When you hear of a thing like this you feel yourself torn both ways. I have heard a Communist speaker on the platform grow very angry about it. In London, he said, parties of Society dames now have the cheek to walk into East End houses and give shopping-lessons to the wives of the unemployed. He gave this as an instance of the mentality of the English governing class. First you condemn a family to live on thirty shillings a week, and then you have the damned impertinence to tell them how they are to spend their money. He was quite right – I agree heartily. Yet all the same it *is* a pity that, merely for the lack of a proper tradition, people should pour muck like tinned milk down their throats and not even know that it is inferior to the product of the cow.

I doubt, however, whether the unemployed would ultimately benefit if they learned to spend their money more economically. For it is only the fact that they are *not* economical that keeps their allowances so high. An Englishman on the P.A.C. gets fifteen shillings a week because fifteen shillings is the smallest sum on which he can conceivably keep alive. If he were, say, an Indian or Japanese coolie, who can live on rice and onions, he wouldn't get fifteen shillings a week – he would be lucky if he got fifteen shillings a month. Our unemployment allowances, miserable though they are, are framed to suit a population with very high standards and not much notion of economy. If the unemployed learned to be better managers they would be visibly better off, and I fancy it would not be long before the dole was docked correspondingly.

There is one great mitigation of unemployment in the North, and that is the cheapness of fuel. Anywhere in the coal areas the retail price of coal is about one and sixpence a hundredweight; in the South of England it is about half a crown. Moreover, miners in work can usually buy coal direct from the pit at eight or nine shillings a ton, and those who have a cellar in their homes sometimes store a ton at a time and sell it (illicitly, I suppose) to those who are out of work. But apart from this there is immense and systematic thieving of coal by the unemployed. I call it thieving because technically it is that, though it does no harm to anybody. In the 'dirt' that is sent up from the pits there is a certain amount of broken coal, and unemployed people spend a lot of time in picking it out of the slag-heaps. All day long over those strange grey mountains you see people wandering to and fro with sacks and baskets among the sulphurous smoke (many slag-heaps are on fire under the surface), prising out the tiny nuggets of coal which are buried here and there. You meet men coming away, wheeling strange and wonderful home-made bicycles – bicycles made of rusty parts picked off refuse-tips, without saddles, with chains and almost always without tyres – across which are slung bags containing perhaps half a hundredweight of coal, fruit of half a day's searching. In times of strikes, when everybody is short of fuel, the miners turn out with pick and shovel and burrow into the slag-heaps, whence the hummocky appearance which most slag-heaps have. During long strikes, in places where there are outcrops of coal, they have sunk surface mines and carried them scores of yards into the earth.

In Wigan the competition among unemployed people for the waste coal has become so fierce that it has led to an extraordinary custom called 'scrambling for the coal', which is well worth seeing. Indeed I rather wonder that it has never been filmed. An unemployed miner took me to see it one afternoon. We got to the place, a mountain range of ancient slag-heaps with a railway running through the valley below. A couple of hundred ragged men, each with a sack and coal-hammer strapped under his coat-tails, were waiting on the 'broo'. When the dirt comes up from the pit it is loaded on to trucks and an engine runs these to the top of another slag-heap a quarter of a mile away and there leaves them. The process of 'scrambling for the coal' consists in getting on to the train while it is moving; any truck which you have succeeded in boarding while it is in motion counts as 'your' truck. Presently the train hove in sight. With a wild yell a hundred men dashed down the slope to catch her as she rounded the bend. Even at the bend the train was making twenty miles an hour. The men hurled themselves upon it, caught hold of the rings at the rear of the trucks and hoisted themselves up by way of the bumpers, five or ten of them on each truck. The driver took no notice. He drove up to the top of the slag-heap, uncoupled the trucks and ran the engine back to the pit, presently returning with a fresh string of trucks. There was the same wild rush of ragged figures as before. In the end only about fifty men had failed to get on to either train.

We walked up to the top of the slag-heap. The men were shovelling the dirt out of the trucks, while down below their wives and children were kneeling, swiftly scrabbling with their hands in the damp dirt and picking out lumps of coal the size of an egg or smaller. You would see a woman pounce on a tiny fragment of stuff, wipe it on her apron, scrutinize it to make sure it was coal and pop it jealously into her sack. Of course, when you are boarding a truck you don't know beforehand what is in it; it may be actual 'dirt' from the roads or it may merely be shale from the roofing. If it is a shale truck there will be no coal in it, but there occurs among the shale another inflammable rock called cannel, which looks very like ordinary shale but is slightly darker and is known by splitting in parallel lines, like slate. It makes tolerable fuel, not good enough to be commercially valuable but good enough to be eagerly sought after by the unemployed. The miners on the shale trucks were picking out the cannel and splitting it up with their hammers. Down at the bottom of the 'broo' the people who had failed to get on to either train were gleaning the tiny chips of coal that came rolling down from above – fragments no bigger than a hazel nut, these, but the people were glad enough to get them.

We stayed there till the train was empty. In a couple of hours the people had picked the dirt over to the last grain. They slung their sacks over shoulder or bicycle, and started on the two-mile trudge back to Wigan. Most of the families had gathered about half a hundredweight of coal or cannel, so that between them they must have stolen five or ten tons of fuel. This business of robbing the dirt trains takes place every day in Wigan, at any rate in winter, and at more collieries than one. It is of course extremely dangerous. No one was hurt the afternoon I was there, but a man had had both his legs cut off a few weeks earlier, and another man lost several fingers a week later. Technically it is stealing but, as everybody knows, if the coal were not stolen it would simply be wasted. Now and again, for form's sake, the colliery companies prosecute somebody for coal-picking, and in that morning's issue of the local paper there was a paragraph saying that two men had been fined ten shillings. But no notice is taken of the prosecutions – in fact, one of the men named in the paper was there that afternoon – and the coal-pickers subscribe among themselves to pay the fines. The thing is taken for granted. Everyone knows that the unemployed have got to get fuel somehow. So every afternoon several hundred men risk their necks and several hundred women scrabble in the mud for hours – and all for half a hundredweight of inferior fuel, value ninepence.

That scene stays in my mind as one of my pictures of Lancashire: the dumpy, shawled women, with their sacking aprons and their heavy black clogs, kneeling in the cindery mud and the bitter wind, searching eagerly for tiny chips of coal. They are glad enough to do it. In winter they are desperate for fuel; it is more important almost than food. Meanwhile all round, as far as the eye can see, are the slag-heaps and hoisting gear of collieries, and not one of those collieries can sell all the coal it is capable of producing. This ought to appeal to Major Douglas.

Chapter Seven

As you travel northward your eye, accustomed to the South or East, does not notice much difference until you are beyond Birmingham. In Coventry you might as well be in Finsbury Park, and the Bull Ring in Birmingham is not unlike Norwich Market, and between all the towns of the Midlands there stretches a villa-civilization indistinguishable from that of the South. It is only when you get a little further north, to the pottery towns and beyond, that you begin to encounter the real ugliness of industrialism – an ugliness so frightful and so arresting that you are obliged, as it were, to come to terms with it.

A slag-heap is at best a hideous thing, because it is so planless and functionless. It is something just dumped on the earth, like the emptying of a giant's dust-bin. On the outskirts of the mining towns there are frightful landscapes where your horizon is ringed completely round by jagged grey mountains, and underfoot is mud and ashes and overhead the steel cables where tubs of dirt travel slowly across miles of country. Often the slag-heaps are on fire, and at night you can see the red rivulets of fire winding this way and that, and also the slow-moving blue flames of sulphur, which always seem on the point of expiring and always spring out again. Even when a slag-heap sinks, as it does ultimately, only an evil brown grass grows on it, and it retains its hummocky surface. One in the slums of Wigan, used as a playground, looks like a choppy sea suddenly frozen; 'the flock mattress', it is called locally. Even centuries hence when the plough drives over the places where coal was once mined, the sites of ancient slag-heaps will still be distinguishable from an aeroplane.

I remember a winter afternoon in the dreadful environs of Wigan. All round was the lunar landscape of slag-heaps, and to the north, through the passes, as it were, between the mountains of slag, you could see the factory chimneys sending out their plumes of smoke. The canal path was a mixture of cinders and frozen mud, criss-crossed by the imprints of innumerable clogs, and all round, as far as the slag-heaps in the distance, stretched the 'flashes' – pools of stagnant water that has seeped into the hollows caused by the subsidence of ancient pits. It was horribly cold. The 'flashes' were covered with ice the colour of raw umber, the bargemen were muffled to the eyes in sacks, the lock gates wore beards of ice. It seemed a world from which vegetation had been banished; nothing existed except smoke, shale, ice, mud, ashes and foul water. But even Wigan is beautiful compared with Sheffield. Sheffield, I suppose, could justly claim to be called the ugliest town in the Old World: its inhabitants, who want it to be pre-eminent in everything, very likely do make that claim for it. It has a population of half a million and it contains fewer decent buildings than the average East Anglian village of five hundred. And the stench! If at rare moments you stop smelling sulphur it is because you have begun smelling gas. Even the shallow river that runs through the town is usually bright yellow with some chemical or other. Once I halted in the street and counted the factory chimneys I could see; there were thirty-three of them, but there would have been far more if the air had not been obscured by smoke. One scene especially lingers in my mind. A frightful patch of waste ground (somehow, up there, a patch of waste ground attains a squalor that would be impossible even in London) trampled bare of grass and littered with newspapers and old saucepans. To the right an isolated row of gaunt four-roomed houses, dark red, blackened by smoke. To the left an interminable vista of factory chimneys, chimney beyond chimney, fading away into a dim blackish haze. Behind me a railway embankment made of the slag from furnaces. In front, across the patch of waste ground, a cubical building of red and yellow brick, with the sign 'Thomas Grocock, Haulage Contractor'.

At night, when you cannot see the hideous shapes of the houses and the blackness of everything, a town like Sheffield assumes a kind of sinister magnificence. Sometimes the drifts of smoke are rosy with sulphur, and serrated flames, like circular saws, squeeze themselves out from the beneath the cowls of the foundry chimneys. Through the open doors of foundries you see fiery serpents of iron being hauled to and fro by redlit boys, and you hear the whizz and thump of steam hammers and the scream of the iron under the blow. The pottery towns are almost equally ugly in a pettier way. Right in among the rows of tiny blackened houses, part of the street as it were, are the 'pot banks' – conical brick chimneys like gigantic burgundy bottles buried in the soil and belching their smoke almost in your face. You come upon monstrous clay chasms hundreds of feet across and almost as deep, with little rusty tubs creeping on chain railways up one side, and on the other workmen clinging like samphire-gatherers and cutting into the face of the cliff with their picks. I passed that way in snowy weather, and even the snow was black. The best thing one can say for the pottery towns is that they are fairly small and stop abruptly. Less than ten miles away you can stand in undefiled country, on the almost naked hills, and the pottery towns are only a smudge in the distance.

When you contemplate such ugliness as this, there are two questions that strike you. First, is it inevitable? Secondly, does it matter?

I do not believe that there is anything inherently and unavoidably ugly about industrialism. A factory or even a gasworks is not obliged of its own nature to be ugly, any more than a palace or a dog-kennel or a cathedral. It all depends on the architectural tradition of the period. The industrial towns of the North are ugly because they happen to have been built at a time when modern methods of steel-construction and smoke-abatement were unknown, and when everyone was too busy making money to think about anything else. They go on being ugly largely because the Northerners have got used to that kind of thing and do not notice it. Many of the people in Sheffield or Manchester, if they smelled the air along the Cornish cliffs, would probably declare that it had no taste in it. But since the war, industry has tended to shift southward and in doing so has grown almost comely. The typical post-war factory is not a gaunt barrack or an awful chaos of blackness and belching chimneys; it is a glittering white structure of concrete, glass and steel, surrounded by green lawns and beds of tulips. Look at the factories you pass as you travel out of London on the G.W.R.; they may not be aesthetic triumphs but certainly they are not ugly in the same way as the Sheffield gasworks. But in any case, though the ugliness of industrialism is the most obvious thing about it and the thing every newcomer exclaims against, I doubt whether it is centrally important. And perhaps it is not even desirable, industrialism being what it is, that it should learn to disguise itself as something else. As Mr Aldous Huxley has truly remarked, a dark Satanic mill ought to look like a dark Satanic mill and not like the temple of mysterious and splendid gods. Moreover, even in the worst of the industrial towns one sees a great deal that is not ugly in the narrow aesthetic sense. A belching chimney or a stinking slum is repulsive chiefly because it implies warped lives and ailing children. Look at it from a purely aesthetic standpoint and it may have a certain macabre appeal. I find that anything outrageously strange generally ends by fascinating me even when I abominate it. The landscapes of Burma, which, when I was among them, so appalled me as to assume the qualities of nightmare, afterwards stayed so hauntingly in my mind that I was obliged to write a novel about them to get rid of them. (In all novels about the East the scenery is the real subject-matter.) It would probably be quite easy to extract a sort of beauty, as Arnold Bennett did, from the blackness of the industrial towns; one can easily imagine Baudelaire, for instance, writing a poem about a slag-heap. But the beauty or ugliness of industrialism hardly matters. Its real evil lies far deeper and is quite ineradicable. It is important to remember this, because there is always a temptation to think that industrialism is harmless so long as it is clean and orderly.

But when you go to the industrial North you are conscious, quite apart from the unfamiliar scenery, of entering a strange country. This is partly because of certain real differences which do exist, but still more because of the North-South antithesis which has been rubbed into us for such a long time past. There exists in England a curious cult of Northernness, a sort of Northern snobbishness. A Yorkshireman in the South will always take care to let you know that he regards you as an inferior. If you ask him why, he will explain that it is only in the North that life is 'real' life, that the industrial work done in the North is the only 'real' work, that the North is inhabited by 'real' people. The South merely by rentiers and their parasites. The Northerner has 'grit', he is grim, 'dour', plucky, warm-hearted and democratic; the Southerner is snobbish, effeminate and lazy – that at any rate is the theory. Hence the Southerner goes north, at any rate for the first time, with the vague inferiority-complex of a civilized man venturing among savages, while the Yorkshireman, like the Scotchman, comes to London in the spirit of a barbarian out for loot. And feelings of this kind, which are the result of tradition, are not affected by visible facts. Just as an Englishman five feet four inches high and twenty nine inches round the chest feels that as an Englishman he is the physical superior of Carnera (Carnera being a Dago), so also with the Northerner and the Southerner. I remember a weedy little Yorkshireman, who would almost certainly have run away if a fox-terrier had snapped at him, telling me that in the South of England he felt 'like a wild invader'. But the cult is often adopted by people who are not by birth Northerners themselves. A year or two ago a friend of mine, brought up in the South but now living in the North, was driving me through Suffolk in a car. We passed through a rather beautiful village. He glanced disapprovingly at the cottages and said:

> 'Of course most of the villages in Yorkshire are hideous; but the Yorkshiremen are splendid chaps. Down here it's just the other way about – beautiful villages and rotten people. All the people in those cottages there are worthless, absolutely worthless.'

I could not help enquiring whether he happened to know anybody in that village. No, he did not know them; but because this was East Anglia they were obviously worthless. Another friend of mine, again a Southerner by birth, loses no opportunity of praising the North to the detriment of the South. Here is an extract from one of his letters to me:

> 'I am in Clitheroe, Lancs. ... I think running water is much more attractive in moor and mountain country than in the fat and sluggish South. "The smug and silver Trent," Shakespeare says; and the South-er the smugger, I say.'

Here you have an interesting example of the Northern cult. Not only are you and I and everyone else in the South of England written off as 'fat and sluggish', but even water, when it gets north of a certain latitude, ceases to be H_2O and becomes something mystically superior. But the interest of this passage is that its writer is an extremely intelligent man of 'advanced' opinions who would have nothing but contempt for nationalism in its ordinary form. Put to him some such proposition as 'One Britisher is worth three foreigners,' and he would repudiate it with horror. But when it is a question of North versus South, he is quite ready to generalize. *All* nationalistic distinctions – all claims to be better than somebody else because you have a different-shaped skull or speak a different dialect – are entirely spurious, but they are important so long as people believe in them. There is no doubt about the Englishman's inbred conviction that those who live to the south of him are his inferiors; even our foreign policy is governed by it to some extent. I think, therefore, that it is worth pointing out when and why it came into being.

When nationalism first became a religion, the English looked at the map, and, noticing that their island lay very high in the Northern Hemisphere, evolved the pleasing theory that the further north you lived the more virtuous you become. The histories I was given when I was a little boy generally started off by explaining in the naïvest way that a cold climate made people energetic while a hot one made them lazy, and hence the defeat of the Spanish Armada. This nonsense about the superior energy of the English (actually the laziest people in Europe) has been current for at least a hundred years. 'Better is it for us,' writes a Quarterly Reviewer of 1827, 'to be condemned to labour for our country's good than to luxuriate amid olives, vines and vices.' 'Olives, vines and vices' sums up the normal English attitude towards the Latin races. In the mythology of Carlyle, Creasey, etc., the Northerner ('Teutonic', later 'Nordic') is pictured as a hefty, vigorous chap with blond moustaches and pure morals, while the Southerner is sly, cowardly and licentious. This theory was never pushed to its logical end, which would have meant assuming that the finest people in the world were the Eskimos, but it did involve admitting that the people who lived to the north of us were superior to ourselves. Hence, partly, the cult of Scotland and of Scotch things which has so deeply marked English life during the past fifty years. But it was the industrialization of the North that gave the North-South antithesis its peculiar slant. Until comparatively recently the northern part of England was the backward and feudal part, and such industry as existed was concentrated in London and the South-East. In the Civil War, for instance, roughly speaking a war of money versus feudalism, the North and West were for the King and the South and East for the Parliament. But with the increasing use of coal industry passed to the North, and there grew up a new type of man, the self-made Northern business man – the Mr Rouncewell and Mr Bounderby of Dickens. The Northern business man, with his hateful 'get on or get out' philosophy, was the dominant figure of the nineteenth century, and as a sort of tyrannical corpse he rules us still. This is the type deified by Arnold Bennett – the type who starts off with half a crown and ends up with fifty thousand pounds, and whose chief pride is to be an even greater boor after he has made his money than before. On analysis his sole virtue turns out to be a talent for making money. We were bidden to admire him because though he might be narrow-minded, sordid, ignorant, grasping and uncouth, he had 'grit', he 'got on'; in other words, he knew how to make money.

This kind of cant is nowadays a pure anachronism, for the Northern business man is no longer prosperous. But traditions are not killed by facts, and the tradition of Northern 'grit' lingers. It is still dimly felt that a Northerner will 'get on', i.e. make money, where a Southerner will fail. At the back of the mind of every Yorkshireman and every Scotchman who comes to London is a sort of Dick Whittington picture of himself as the boy who starts off by selling newspapers and ends up as Lord Mayor. And that, really, is at the bottom of his bumptiousness. But where one can make a great mistake is in imagining that this feeling extends to the genuine working class. When I first went to Yorkshire, some years ago, I imagined that I was going to a country of boors. I was used to the London Yorkshireman with his interminable harangues and his pride in the supposed raciness of his dialect (' "A stitch in time saves nine," as we say in the West Riding'), and I expected to meet with a good deal of rudeness. But I met with nothing of the kind, and least of all among the miners. Indeed the Lancashire and Yorkshire miners treated me with a kindness and courtesy that were even embarrassing; for if there is one type of man to whom I do feel myself inferior, it is a coal-miner. Certainly no one showed any sign of despising me for coming from a different part of the country. This has its importance when one remembers that the English regional snobberies are nationalism in miniature; for it suggests that place-snobbery is not a working-class characteristic.

There is nevertheless a real difference between North and South, and there is at least a tinge of truth in that picture of Southern England as one enormous Brighton inhabited by lounge-lizards. For climatic reasons the parasitic dividend-drawing class tend to settle in the South. In a Lancashire cotton-town you could probably go for months on end without once hearing an 'educated' accent, whereas there can hardly be a town in the South of England where you could throw a brick without hitting the niece of a bishop. Consequently, with no petty gentry to set the pace, the bourgeoisification of the working class, though it is taking place in the North, is taking place more slowly. All the Northern accents, for instance, persist strongly, while the Southern ones are collapsing before the movies and the B.B.C. Hence your 'educated' accent stamps you rather as a foreigner than as a chunk of the petty gentry; and this is an immense advantage, for it makes it much easier to get into contact with the working class.

But is it ever possible to be really intimate with the working class? I shall have to discuss that later; I will only say here that I do not think it is possible. But undoubtedly it is easier in the North than it would be in the South to meet working-class people on approximately equal terms. It is fairly easy to live in a miner's house and be accepted as one of the family; with, say, a farm labourer in the Southern counties it probably would be impossible. I have seen just enough of the working class to avoid idealizing them, but I do know that you can learn a great deal in a working-class home, if only you can get there. The essential point is that your middle-class ideals and prejudices are tested by contact with others which are not necessarily better but are certainly different.

Take for instance the different attitude towards the family. A working-class family hangs together as a middle-class one does, but the relationship is far less tyrannical. A working-man has not that deadly weight of family prestige hanging round his neck like a millstone. I have pointed out earlier that a middle-class person goes utterly to pieces under the influence of poverty; and this is generally due to the behaviour of his family – to the fact that he has scores of relations nagging and badgering him night and day for failing to 'get on'. The fact that the working class know how to combine and the middle class don't is probably due to their different conceptions of family loyalty. You cannot have an effective trade union of middle-class workers, because in times of strikes almost every middle-class wife would be egging her husband on to blackleg and get the other fellow's job. Another working-class characteristic, disconcerting at first, is their plain-spokenness towards anyone they regard as an equal. If you offer a working man something he doesn't want, he tells you that he doesn't want it; a middle-class person would accept it to avoid giving offence. And again, take the working-class attitude towards 'education'. How different it is from ours, and how immensely sounder! Working people often have a vague reverence for learning in others, but where 'education' touches their own lives they see through it and reject it by a healthy instinct. The time was when I used to lament over quite imaginary pictures of lads of fourteen dragged protesting from their lessons and set to work at dismal jobs. It seemed to me dreadful that the doom of a 'job' should descend upon anyone at fourteen. Of course I know now that there is not one working-class boy in a thousand who does not pine for the day when he will leave school. He wants to be doing real work, not wasting his time on ridiculous rubbish like history and geography. To the working class, the notion of staying at school till you are nearly grown-up seems merely contemptible and unmanly. The idea of a great big boy of eighteen, who ought to be bringing a pound a week home to his parents, going to school in a ridiculous uniform and even being caned for not doing his lessons! Just fancy a working-class boy of eighteen allowing himself to be caned! He is a man when the other is still a baby. Ernest Pontifex, in Samuel Butler's *Way of All Flesh*, after he had had a few glimpses of real life, looked back on his public school and university education and found it a 'sickly, debilitating debauch'. There is much in middle-class life that looks sickly and debilitating when you see it from a working-class angle.

In a working-class home – I am not thinking at the moment of the unemployed, but of comparatively prosperous homes – you breathe a warm, decent, deeply human atmosphere which it is not so easy to find elsewhere. I should say that a manual worker, if he is in steady work and drawing good wages – an 'if' which gets bigger and bigger – has a better chance of being happy than an 'educated' man. His home life seems to fall more naturally into a sane and comely shape. I have often been struck by the peculiar easy completeness, the perfect symmetry as it were, of a working-class interior at its best. Especially on winter evenings after tea, when the fire glows in the open range and dances mirrored in the steel fender, when Father, in shirt-sleeves, sits in the rocking chair at one side of the fire reading the racing finals, and Mother sits on the other with her sewing, and the children are happy with a pennorth of mint humbugs, and the dog lolls roasting himself on the rag mat – it is a good place to be in, provided that you can be not only in it but sufficiently *of* it to be taken for granted.

This scene is still reduplicated in a majority of English homes, though not in so many as before the war. Its happiness depends mainly upon one question – whether Father is in work. But notice that the picture I have called up, of a working-class family sitting round the coal fire after kippers and strong tea, belongs only to our own moment of time and could not belong either to the future or the past. Skip forward two hundred years into the Utopian future, and the scene is totally different. Hardly one of the things I have imagined will still be there. In that age when there is no manual labour and everyone is 'educated', it is hardly likely that Father will still be a rough man with enlarged hands who likes to sit in shirt-sleeves and says 'Ah wur coomin' oop street.' And there won't be a coal fire in the grate, only some kind of invisible heater. The furniture will be made of rubber, glass and steel. If there are still such things as evening papers there will certainly be no racing news in them, for gambling will be meaningless in a world where there is no poverty and the horse will have vanished from the face of the earth. Dogs, too, will have been suppressed on grounds of hygiene. And there won't be so many children, either, if the birth-controllers have their way. But move backwards into the Middle Ages and you are in a world almost equally foreign. A windowless hut, a wood fire which smokes in your face because there is no chimney, mouldy bread, 'Poor John', lice, scurvy, a yearly childbirth and a yearly child-death, and the priest terrifying you with tales of Hell.

Curiously enough it is *not* the triumphs of modern engineering, nor the radio, nor the cinematograph, nor the five thousand novels which are published yearly, nor the crowds at Ascot and the Eton and Harrow match, but the memory of working-class interiors – especially as I sometimes saw them in my childhood before the war, when England was still prosperous – that reminds me that our age has not been altogether a bad one to live in.

Chapter Eight

The road from Mandalay to Wigan is a long one and the reasons for taking it are not immediately clear.

In the earlier chapters of this book I have given a rather fragmentary account of various things I saw in the coal areas of Lancashire and Yorkshire. I went there partly because I wanted to see what mass-unemployment is like at its worst, partly in order to see the most typical section of the English working class at close quarters. This was necessary to me as part of my approach to Socialism. For before you can be sure whether you are genuinely in favour of Socialism, you have got to decide whether things at present are tolerable or not tolerable, and you have got to take up a definite attitude on the terribly difficult issue of class. Here I shall have to digress and explain how my own attitude towards the class question was developed. Obviously this involves writing a certain amount of autobiography, and I would not do it if I did not think that I am sufficiently typical of my class, or rather sub-caste, to have a certain symptomatic importance.

I was born into what you might describe as the lower-upper-middle class. The upper-middle class, which had its heyday in the 'eighties and 'nineties, with Kipling as its poet laureate, was a sort of mound of wreckage left behind when the tide of Victorian prosperity receded. Or perhaps it would be better to change the metaphor and describe it not as a mound but as a layer – the layer of society lying between £2,000 and £300 a year: my own family was not far from the bottom. You notice that I define it in terms of money, because that is always the quickest way of making yourself understood. Nevertheless, the essential point about the English class-system is that it is *not* entirely explicable in terms of money. Roughly speaking it is a money-stratification, but it is also interpenetrated by a sort of shadowy caste-system; rather like a jerry-built modern bungalow haunted by medieval ghosts. Hence the fact that the upper-middle class extends or extended to incomes as low as £300 a year – to incomes, that is, much lower than those of merely middle-class people with no social pretensions. Probably there are countries where you can predict a man's opinions from his income, but it is never quite safe to do so in England; you have always got to take his traditions into consideration as well. A naval officer and his grocer very likely have the same income, but they are not equivalent persons and they would only be on the same side in very large issues such as a war or a general strike – possibly not even then.

Of course it is obvious now that the upper-middle class is done for. In every country town in Southern England, not to mention the dreary wastes of Kensington and Earl's Court, those who knew it in the days of its glory are dying, vaguely embittered by a world which has not behaved as it ought. I never open one of Kipling's books or go into one of the huge dull shops which were once the favourite haunt of the upper-middle class, without thinking

'Change and decay in all around I see.' But before the war the upper-middle class, though already none too prosperous, still felt sure of itself. Before the war you were either a gentleman or not a gentleman, and if you were a gentleman you struggled to behave as such, whatever your income might be. Between those with £400 a year and those with £2,000 or even £1,000 a year there was a great gulf fixed, but it was a gulf which those with £400 a year did their best to ignore. Probably the distinguishing mark of the upper-middle class was that its traditions were not to any extent commercial, but mainly military, official, and professional. People in this class owned no land, but they felt that they were landowners in the sight of God and kept up a semi-aristocratic outlook by going into the professions and the fighting services rather than into trade. Small boys used to count the plum stones on their plates and foretell their destiny by chanting, 'Army, Navy, Church, Medicine, Law'; and even of these 'Medicine' was faintly inferior to the others and only put in for the sake of symmetry. To belong to this class when you were at the £400 a year level was a queer business, for it meant that your gentility was almost purely theoretical. You lived, so to speak, at two levels simultaneously. Theoretically you knew all about servants and how to tip them, although in practice you had one or, at most, two resident servants. Theoretically you knew how to wear your clothes and how to order a dinner, although in practice you could never afford to go to a decent tailor or a decent restaurant. Theoretically you knew how to shoot and ride, although in practice you had no horses to ride and not an inch of ground to shoot over. It was this that explained the attraction of India (more recently Kenya, Nigeria, etc.) for the lower-upper-middle class. The people who went there as soldiers and officials did not go there to make money, for a soldier or an official does not make money; they went there because in India, with cheap horses, free shooting, and hordes of black servants, it was so easy to play at being a gentleman.

In the kind of shabby-genteel family that I am talking about there is far more *consciousness* of poverty than in any working-class family above the level of the dole. Rent and clothes and school-bills are an unending nightmare, and every luxury, even a glass of beer, is an unwarrantable extravagance. Practically the whole family income goes in keeping up appearances. It is obvious that people of this kind are in an anomalous position, and one might be tempted to write them off as mere exceptions and therefore unimportant. Actually, however, they are or were fairly numerous. Most clergymen and schoolmasters, for instance, nearly all Anglo-Indian officials, a sprinkling of soldiers and sailors and a fair number of professional men and artists, fall into this category. But the real importance of this class is that they are the shock-absorbers of the bourgeoisie. The real bourgeoisie, those in the £2,000 a year class and over, have their money as a thick layer of padding between themselves and the class they plunder; in so far as they are aware of the Lower Orders at all they are aware of them as employees, servants and tradesmen. But it is quite different for the poor devils lower down who are struggling to live genteel lives on what are virtually working-class incomes. These last are forced into close and, in a sense, intimate contact with the working class, and I suspect it is from them that the traditional upper-class attitude towards 'common' people is derived.

And what is this attitude? An attitude of sniggering superiority punctuated by bursts of vicious hatred. Look at any number of *Punch* during the past thirty years. You will find it everywhere taken for granted that a working-class person, as such, is a figure of fun, except at odd moments when he shows signs of being too prosperous, whereupon he ceases to be a figure of fun and becomes a demon. It is no use wasting breath in denouncing this attitude. It is better to consider how it has arisen, and to do that one has got to realize what the working classes look like to those who live among them but have different habits and traditions.

A shabby-genteel family is in much the same position as a family of 'poor whites' living in a street where everyone else is a negro. In such circumstances you have got to cling to your gentility because it is the only thing you have; and meanwhile you are hated for your stuck-up-ness and for the accent and manners which stamp you as one of the boss class. I was very young, not much more than six, when I first became aware of class-distinctions. Before that age my chief heroes had generally been working-class people, because they always seemed to do such interesting things, such as being fishermen and blacksmiths and bricklayers. I remember the farm hands on a farm in Cornwall who used to let me ride on the drill when they were sowing turnips and would sometimes catch the ewes and milk them to give me a drink; and the workmen building the new house next door, who let me play with the wet mortar and from whom I first learned the word 'b——'; and the plumber up the road with whose children I used to go out bird-nesting. But it was not long before I was forbidden to play with the plumber's children; they were 'common' and I was told to keep away from them. This was snobbish, if you like, but it was also necessary, for middle-class people cannot afford to let their children grow up with vulgar accents. So, very early, the working class ceased to be a race of friendly and wonderful beings and became a race of enemies. We realized that they hated us, but we could never understand why, and naturally we set it down to pure, vicious malignity. To me in my early boyhood, to nearly all children of families like mine, 'common' people seemed almost sub-human. They had coarse faces, hideous accents and gross manners, they hated everyone who was not like themselves, and if they got half a chance they would insult you in brutal ways. That was our view of them, and though it was false it was understandable. For one must remember that before the war there was much more *overt* class-hatred in England than there is now. In those days you were quite likely to be insulted simply for looking like a member of the upper classes; nowadays, on the other hand, you are more likely to be fawned upon. Anyone over thirty can remember the time when it was impossible for a well-dressed person to walk through a slum street without being hooted at. Whole quarters of big towns were considered unsafe because of 'hooligans' (now almost an extinct type), and the London gutter-boy everywhere, with his loud voice and lack of intellectual scruples, could make life a misery for people who considered it beneath their dignity to answer back. A recurrent terror of my holidays, when I was a small boy, was the gangs of 'cads' who were liable to set upon you five or ten to one. In term time, on the other hand, it was we who were in the majority and the 'cads' who were oppressed; I remember a couple of savage mass-battles in the cold winter of 1916–17. And this tradition of open hostility between upper and lower class had apparently been the same for at least a century past. A typical joke in *Punch* in the 'sixties is a picture of a small, nervous-looking gentleman riding through a slum street and a crowd of street-boys closing in on him with shouts ''Ere comes a swell! Let's frighten 'is 'oss!' Just fancy the street boys trying to frighten his horse now! They would be much likelier to hang round him in vague hopes of a tip. During the past dozen years the English working class have grown servile with a rather horrifying rapidity. It was bound to happen, for the frightful weapon of unemployment has cowed them. Before the war their economic position was comparatively strong, for though there was no dole to fall back upon, there was not much unemployment, and the power of the boss class was not so obvious as it is now. A man did not see ruin staring him in the face every time he cheeked a 'toff', and naturally he did cheek a 'toff' whenever it seemed safe to do so. G. J. Renier, in his book on Oscar Wilde, points out that the strange, obscene burst of popular fury which followed the Wilde trial was essentially social in character. The London mob had caught a member of the upper classes on the hop, and they took care to keep him hopping. All this was natural and even proper. If you treat people as the English working class have been treated during the past two centuries, you must expect them to resent it. On the other hand the children of shabby-genteel families could not be blamed if they grew up with a hatred of the working class, typified for them by prowling gangs of 'cads'.

But there was another and more serious difficulty. Here you come to the real secret of class-distinctions in the West – the real reason why a European of bourgeois upbringing, even when he calls himself a Communist, cannot without a hard effort think of a working man as his equal. It is summed up in four frightful words which people nowadays are chary of uttering, but which were bandied about quite freely in my childhood. The words were: *The lower classes smell.*

That was what we were taught – *the lower classes smell.* And here, obviously, you are at an impassable barrier. For no feeling of like or dislike is quite so fundamental as a *physical* feeling. Race hatred, religious hatred, differences of education, of temperament, of intellect, even differences of moral code, can be got over; but physical repulsion cannot. You can have an affection for a murderer or a sodomite, but you cannot have an affection for a man whose breath stinks – habitually stinks, I mean. However well you may wish him, however much you may admire his mind and character, if his breath stinks he is horrible and in your heart of hearts you will hate him. It may not greatly matter if the average middle-class person is brought up to believe that the working classes are ignorant, lazy, drunken, boorish and dishonest; it is when he is brought up to believe that they are dirty that the harm is done. And in my childhood we *were* brought up to believe that they were dirty. Very early in life you acquired the idea that there was something subtly repulsive about a working-class body; you would not get nearer to it than you could help. You watched a great sweaty navvy walking down the road with his pick over his shoulder; you looked at his discoloured shirt and his corduroy trousers stiff with the dirt of a decade; you thought of those nests and layers of greasy rags below, and, under all, the unwashed body, brown all over (that was how I used to imagine it), with its strong, bacon-like reek. You watched a tramp taking off his boots in a ditch – ugh! It did not seriously occur to you that the tramp might not enjoy having black feet. And even 'lower-class' people whom you knew to be quite clean – servants, for instance – were faintly unappetizing. The smell of their sweat, the very texture of their skins, were mysteriously different from yours.

Everyone who has grown up pronouncing his aitches and in a house with a bathroom and one servant is likely to have grown up with these feelings; hence the chasmic, impassable quality of class-distinctions in the West. It is queer how seldom this is admitted. At the moment I can think of only one book where it is set forth without humbug, and that is Mr Somerset Maugham's *On a Chinese Screen*. Mr Maugham describes a high Chinese official arriving at a wayside inn and blustering and calling everybody names in order to impress upon them that he is a supreme dignitary and they are only worms. Five minutes later, having asserted his dignity in the way he thinks proper, he is eating his dinner in perfect amity with the baggage coolies. As an official he feels that he has got to make his presence felt, but he has no feeling that the coolies are of different clay from himself. I have observed countless similar scenes in Burma. Among Mongolians – among all Asiatics, for all I know – there is a sort of natural equality, an easy intimacy between man and man, which is simply unthinkable in the West. Mr Maugham adds:

> 'In the West we are divided from our fellows by our sense of smell. The working man is our master, inclined to rule us with an iron hand, but it cannot be denied that he stinks: none can wonder at it, for a bath in the dawn when you have to hurry to your work before the factory bell rings is no pleasant thing, nor does heavy labour tend to sweetness; and you do not change your linen more than you can help when the week's washing must be done by a sharp-tongued wife. I do not blame the working man because he stinks, but stink he does. It makes social intercourse difficult to persons of sensitive nostril. The matutinal tub divides the classes more effectually than birth, wealth or education.'

Meanwhile, *do* the 'lower classes' smell? Of course, as a whole, they are dirtier than the upper classes. They are bound to be, considering the circumstances in which they live, for even at this late date less than half the houses in England have bathrooms. Besides, the habit of washing yourself all over every day is a very recent one in Europe, and the working classes are generally more conservative than the bourgeoisie. But the English are growing visibly cleaner, and we may hope that in a hundred years they will be almost as clean as the Japanese. It is a pity that those who idealize the working class so often think it necessary to praise every working-class characteristic and therefore to pretend that dirtiness is somehow meritorious in itself. Here, curiously enough, the Socialist and the sentimental democratic Catholic of the type of Chesterton sometimes join hands; both will tell you that dirtiness is healthy and 'natural' and cleanliness is a mere fad or at best a luxury.[1] They seem not to see that they are merely giving colour to the notion that working-class people are dirty from choice and not from necessity. Actually, people who have access to a bath will generally use it. But the essential thing is that middle-class people *believe* that the working class are dirty – you see from the passage quoted above that Mr Maugham himself believes it – and, what is worse, that they are somehow *inherently* dirty. As a child, one of the most dreadful things I could imagine was to drink out of a bottle after a navvy. Once when I was thirteen, I was in a train coming from a market town, and the third-class carriage was packed full of shepherds and pig-men who had been selling their beasts. Somebody produced a quart bottle of beer and passed it round; it

[1] According to Chesterton, dirtiness is merely a kind of 'discomfort' and therefore ranks as self-mortification. Unfortunately, the discomfort of dirtiness is chiefly suffered by other people. It is not really very uncomfortable to be dirty – not nearly so uncomfortable as having a cold bath on a winter morning.

travelled from mouth to mouth to mouth, everyone taking a swig. I cannot describe the horror I felt as that bottle worked its way towards me. If I drank from it after all those lower-class male mouths I felt certain I should vomit; on the other hand, if they offered it to me I dared not refuse for fear of offending them – you see here how the middle-class squeamishness works both ways. Nowadays, thank God, I have no feelings of that kind. A working-man's body, as such, is no more repulsive to me than a millionaire's. I still don't like drinking out of a cup or bottle after another person – another man, I mean: with women I don't mind – but at least the question of class does not enter. It was rubbing shoulders with the tramps that cured me of it. Tramps are not really very dirty as English people go, but they have the name for being dirty, and when you have shared a bed with a tramp and drunk tea out of the same snuff-tin, you feel that you have seen the worst and the worst has no terrors for you.

I have dwelt on these subjects because they are vitally important. To get rid of class-distinctions you have got to start by understanding how one class appears when seen through the eyes of another. It is useless to say that the middle classes are 'snobbish' and leave it at that. You get no further if you do not realize that snobbishness is bound up with a species of idealism. It derives from the early training in which a middle-class child is taught almost simultaneously to wash his neck, to be ready to die for his country, and to despise the 'lower classes'.

Here I shall be accused of being behind the times, for I was a child before and during the war and it may be claimed that children nowadays are brought up with more enlightened notions. It is probably true that class-feeling is for the moment a very little less bitter than it was. The working class are submissive where they used to be openly hostile, and the post-war manufacture of cheap clothes and the general softening of manners have toned down the surface differences between class and class. But undoubtedly the essential feeling is still there. Every middle-class person has a dormant class-prejudice which needs only a small thing to arouse it; and if he is over forty he probably has a firm conviction that his own class has been sacrificed to the class below. Suggest to the average unthinking person of gentle birth who is struggling to keep up appearances on four or five hundred a year that he is a member of an exploiting parasite class, and he will think you are mad. In perfect sincerity he will point out to you a dozen ways in which he is worse-off than a working man. In his eyes the workers are not a submerged race of slaves, they are a sinister flood creeping upwards to engulf himself and his friends and his family and to sweep all culture and all decency out of existence. Hence that queer watchful anxiety lest the working class shall grow too prosperous. In a number of *Punch* soon after the war, when coal was still fetching high prices, there is a picture of four or five miners with grim, sinister faces riding in a cheap motor-car. A friend they are passing calls out and asks them where they have borrowed it. They answer, 'We've bought the thing!' This, you see, is 'good enough for *Punch*'; for miners to buy a motor-car, even one car between four or five of them, is a monstrosity, a sort of crime against nature. That was the attitude of a dozen years ago, and I see no evidence of any fundamental change. The notion that the working class have been absurdly pampered, hopelessly demoralized by doles, old age pensions, free education, etc., is still widely held; it has merely been a little shaken, perhaps, by the recent recognition that unemployment does exist. For quantities of middle-class people, probably for a large majority of those over fifty, the typical working man still rides to the Labour Exchange on a motor-bike and keeps coal in his bath-tub: 'And, if you'll believe it, my dear, they actually *get married* on the dole!'

The reason why class-hatred seems to be diminishing is that nowadays it tends not to get into print, partly owing to the mealy-mouthed habits of our time, partly because newspapers and even books now have to appeal to a working-class public. As a rule you can best study it in private conversations. But if you want some printed examples, it is worth having a look at the *obiter dicta* of the late Professor Saintsbury. Saintsbury was a very learned man and along certain lines a judicious literary critic, but when he talked of political or economic matters he only differed from the rest of his class by the fact that he was too thick-skinned and had been born too early to see any reason for pretending to common decency. According to Saintsbury, unemployment insurance was simply 'contributing to the support of lazy ne'er-do-weels', and the whole trade union movement was no more than a kind of organized mendicancy:

> '"Pauper" is almost actionable now, is it not, when used as a word? though to *be* paupers, in the sense of being wholly or partly supported at the expense of other people, is the ardent, and to a considerable extent achieved, aspiration of a large proportion of our population, and of an entire political party.'
>
> (*Second Scrap Book.*)

It is to be noticed, however, that Saintsbury recognizes that unemployment is bound to exist, and, in fact, thinks that it ought to exist, so long as the unemployed are made to suffer as much as possible:

> 'Is not "casual" labour the very secret and safety-valve of a safe and sound labour-system generally?
>
> '... In a complicated industrial and commercial state constant employment at regular wages is impossible; while dole-supported unemployment, at anything like the wages of employment, is demoralizing to begin with and ruinous at its more or less quickly arriving end.'
>
> (*Last Scrap Book.*)

What exactly is to happen to the 'casual labourers' when no casual labour happens to be available is not made clear. Presumably (Saintsbury speaks approvingly of 'good Poor Laws') they are to go into the workhouse or sleep in the streets. As to the notion that every human being ought as a matter of course to have the chance of earning at least a tolerable livelihood, Saintsbury dismisses it with contempt:

> 'Even the "right to live" ... extends no further than the right to protection against murder. Charity certainly will, morality possibly may, and public utility perhaps ought to add to this protection supererogatory provision for continuance of life; but it is questionable whether strict justice demands it.
>
> 'As for the insane doctrine that being born in a country gives some right to the possession of the soil of that country, it hardly requires notice.'
>
> (*Last Scrap Book.*)

It is worth reflecting for a moment upon the beautiful implications of this last passage. The interest of passages like these (and they are scattered all through Saintsbury's work) lies in their having been printed at all. Most people are a little shy of putting that kind of thing on paper. But what Saintsbury is saying here is what any little worm with a fairly safe five hundred a year *thinks*, and therefore in a way one must admire him for saying it. It takes a lot of guts to be *openly* such a skunk as that.

This is the outlook of a confessed reactionary. But how about the middle-class person whose views are not reactionary but 'advanced'? Beneath his revolutionary mask, is he really so different from the other?

A middle-class person embraces Socialism and perhaps even joins the Communist Party. How much real difference does it make? Obviously, living within the framework of capitalist society, he has got to go on earning his living, and one cannot blame him if he clings to his bourgeois economic status. But is there any change in his tastes, his habits, his manners, his imaginative background – his 'ideology', in Communist jargon? Is there *any* change in him except that he now votes Labour, or, when possible, Communist at the elections? It is noticeable that he still habitually associates with his own class; he is vastly more at home with a member of his own class, who thinks him a dangerous Bolshie, than with a member of the working class who supposedly agrees with him; his tastes in food, wine, clothes, books, pictures, music, ballet, are still recognizably bourgeois tastes; most significant of all, he invariably marries into his own class. Look at any bourgeois Socialist. Look at Comrade X, member of the C.P.G.B. and author of *Marxism for Infants*. Comrade X, it so happens, is an old Etonian. He would be ready to die on the barricades, in theory anyway, but you notice that he still leaves his bottom waistcoat button undone. He idealizes the proletariat, but it is remarkable how little his habits resemble theirs. Perhaps once, out of sheer bravado, he has smoked a cigar with the band on, but it would be almost physically impossible for him to put pieces of cheese into his mouth on the point of his knife, or to sit indoors with his cap on, or even to drink his tea out of the saucer. Perhaps table-manners are not a bad test of sincerity. I have known numbers of bourgeois Socialists, I have listened by the hour to their tirades against their own class, and yet never, not even once, have I met one who had picked up proletarian table-manners. Yet, after all, why not? Why should a man who thinks all virtue resides in the proletariat still take such pains to drink his soup silently? It can only be because in his heart he feels that proletarian manners are disgusting. So you see he is still responding to the training of his childhood, when he was taught to hate, fear, and despise the working class.

Chapter Nine

When I was fourteen of fifteen I was an odious little snob, but no worse than other boys of my own age and class. I suppose there is no place in the world where snobbery is quite so ever-present or where it is cultivated in such refined and subtle forms as in an English public school. Here at least one cannot say that English 'education' fails to do its job. You forget your Latin and Greek within a few months of leaving school – I studied Greek for eight or ten years, and now, at thirty-three, I cannot even repeat the Greek alphabet – but your snobbishness, unless you persistently root it out like the bindweed it is, sticks by you till your grave.

At school I was in a difficult position, for I was among boys who, for the most part, were much richer than myself, and I only went to an expensive public school because I happened to win a scholarship. This is the common experience of boys of the lower-upper-middle class, the sons of clergymen, Anglo-Indian officials, etc., and the effects it had on me were probably the usual ones. On the one hand it made me cling tighter than ever to my gentility; on the other hand it filled me with resentment against the boys whose parents were richer than mine and who took care to let me know it. I despised anyone who was not describable as a 'gentleman', but also I hated the hoggishly rich, especially those who had grown rich too recently. The correct and elegant thing, I felt, was to be of gentle birth but to have no money. This is part of the *credo* of the lower-upper-middle class. It has a romantic, Jacobite-in-exile feeling about it which is very comforting.

But those years, during and just after the war, were a queer time to be at school, for England was nearer revolution than she has been since or had been for a century earlier. Throughout almost the whole nation there was running a wave of revolutionary feeling which has since been reversed and forgotten, but which has left various deposits of sediment behind. Essentially, though of course one could not then see it in perspective, it was a revolt of youth against age, resulting directly from the war. In the war the young had been sacrificed and the old had behaved in a way which, even at this distance of time, is horrible to contemplate; they had been sternly patriotic in safe places while their sons went down like swathes of hay before the German machine guns. Moreover, the war had been conducted mainly by old men and had been conducted with supreme incompetence. By 1918 everyone under forty was in a bad temper with his elders, and the mood of anti-militarism which followed naturally upon the fighting was extended into a general revolt against orthodoxy and authority. At that time there was, among the young, a curious cult of hatred of 'old men'. The dominance of 'old men' was held to be responsible for every evil known to humanity, and every accepted institution from Scott's novels to the House of Lords was derided merely because 'old men' were in favour of it. For several years it was all the fashion to be a 'Bolshie', as people then called it. England was full of half-baked antinomian opinions. Pacifism, internationalism, humanitarianism of all kinds, feminism, free love, divorce-reform, atheism, birth-control – things like these were getting a better hearing than they would get in normal times. And of course the revolutionary mood extended to those who had been too young to fight, even to public schoolboys. At that time we all thought of ourselves as enlightened creatures of a new age, casting off the orthodoxy that had been forced upon us by those detested 'old men'. We retained, basically, the snobbish outlook of our class, we took it for granted that we should continue to draw our dividends or tumble into soft jobs, but also it seemed natural to us to be 'agin the government'. We derided the O.T.C., the Christian religion, and perhaps even compulsory games and the Royal Family, and we did not realize that we were merely taking part in a world-wide gesture of distaste for war. Two incidents stick in my mind as examples of the queer revolutionary feeling of that time. One day the master who taught us English set us a kind of general knowledge paper of which one of the questions was, 'Whom do you consider the ten greatest men now living?' Of sixteen boys in the class (our average age was about seventeen) fifteen included Lenin in their list. This was at a snobbish expensive public school, and the date was 1920, when the horrors of the Russian Revolution were still fresh in everyone's mind. Also there were the so-called peace celebrations in 1919. Our elders had decided for us that we should celebrate peace in the traditional manner by whooping over the fallen foe. We were to march into the school-yard, carrying torches, and sing jingo songs of the type of 'Rule, Britannia'. The boys – to their honour, I think – guyed the whole proceeding and sang blasphemous and seditious words to the tunes provided. I doubt whether things would happen in quite that manner now. Certainly the public schoolboys I meet nowadays, even the intelligent ones, are much more right-wing in their opinions than I and my contemporaries were fifteen years ago.

Hence, at the age of seventeen or eighteen, I was both a snob and a revolutionary. I was against all authority. I had read and re-read the entire published works of Shaw, Wells, and Galsworthy (at that time still regarded as dangerously 'advanced' writers), and I loosely described myself as a Socialist. But I had not much grasp of what Socialism meant, and no notion that the working class were human beings. At a distance, and through the medium of books – Jack London's *The People of the Abyss*, for instance – I could agonize over their sufferings, but I still hated them and despised them when I came anywhere near them. I was still revolted by their accents and infuriated by their habitual rudeness. One must remember that just then, immediately after the war, the English working class were in a fighting mood. That was the period of the great coal strikes, when a miner was thought of as a fiend incarnate and old ladies looked under their beds every night lest Robert Smillie should be concealed there. All through the war and for a little time afterwards there had been high wages and abundant employment; things were now returning to something worse than normal, and naturally the working class resisted. The men who had fought had been lured into the army by gaudy promises, and now they were coming home to a world where there were no jobs and not even any houses. Moreover, they had been at war and were coming home with the soldier's attitude to life, which is fundamentally, in spite of discipline, a lawless attitude. There was a turbulent feeling in the air. To that time belongs the song with the memorable refrain:

There's nothing sure but
The rich get richer and the poor get children;

In the mean time,
In between time,
Ain't we got fun?

People had not yet settled down to a lifetime of unemployment mitigated by endless cups of tea. They still vaguely expected the Utopia for which they had fought, and even more than before they were openly hostile to the aitch-pronouncing class. So to the shock-absorbers of the bourgeoisie, such as myself, 'common people' still appeared brutal and repulsive. Looking back upon that period, I seem to have spent half the time in denouncing the capitalist system and the other half in raging over the insolence of bus-conductors.

When I was not yet twenty I went to Burma, in the Indian Imperial Police. In an 'outpost of Empire' like Burma the class-question appeared at first sight to have been shelved. There was no obvious class-friction here, because the all-important thing was not whether you had been to one of the right schools but whether your skin was technically white. As a matter of fact most of the white men in Burma were not of the type who in England would be called 'gentlemen', but except for the common soldiers and a few nondescripts they lived lives appropriate to 'gentlemen' – had servants, that is, and called their evening meal 'dinner' – and officially they were regarded as being all of the same class. They were 'white men', in contradistinction to the other and inferior class, the 'natives'. But one did not feel towards the 'natives' as one felt towards the 'lower classes' at home. The essential point was that the 'natives', at any rate the Burmese, were not felt to be physically repulsive. One looked down on them as 'natives', but one was quite ready to be physically intimate with them; and this, I noticed, was the case even with white men who had the most vicious colour prejudice. When you have a lot of servants you soon get into lazy habits, and I habitually allowed myself, for instance, to be dressed and undressed by my Burmese boy. This was because he was a Burman and undisgusting; I could not have endured to let an English man-servant handle me in that intimate manner. I felt towards a Burman almost as I felt towards a woman. Like most other races, the Burmese have a distinctive smell – I cannot describe it: it is a smell that makes one's teeth tingle – but this smell never disgusted me. (Incidentally, orientals say that *we* smell. The Chinese, I believe, say that a white man smells like a corpse. The Burmese say the same – though no Burman was ever rude enough to say so to me.) And in a way my attitude was defensible, for if one faces facts one must admit that most Mongolians have much nicer bodies than most white men. Compare the firm-knit silken skin of the Burman, which does not wrinkle at all till he is past forty, and then merely withers up like a piece of dry leather, with the coarse-grained, flabby, sagging skin of the white man. The white man has lank ugly hair growing down his legs and the backs of his arms and in an ugly patch on his chest. The Burman has only a tuft or two of stiff black hair at the appropriate places; for the rest he is quite hairless and is usually beardless as well. The white man almost always goes bald, the Burman seldom or never. The Burman's teeth are perfect, though generally discoloured by betel juice, the white man's teeth invariably decay. The white man is generally ill-shaped, and when he grows fat he bulges in improbable places; the Mongol has beautiful bones and in old age he is almost as shapely as in youth. Admittedly the white races throw up a few individuals who for a few years are supremely beautiful; but on the whole, say what you will, they are far less comely than orientals. But it was not of this that

I was thinking when I found the English 'lower classes' so much more repellent than Burmese 'natives'. I was still thinking in terms of my early-acquired class-prejudice. When I was not much past twenty I was attached for a short time to a British regiment. Of course I admired and liked the private soldiers as any youth of twenty would admire and like hefty, cheery youths five years older than himself with the medals of the Great War on their chests. And yet, after all, they faintly repelled me; they were 'common people' and I did not care to be too close to them. In the hot mornings when the company marched down the road, myself in the rear with one of the junior subalterns, the steam of those hundred sweating bodies in front made my stomach turn. And this, you observe, was pure prejudice. For a soldier is probably as inoffensive, physically, as it is possible for a male white person to be. He is generally young, he is nearly always healthy from fresh air and exercise, and a rigorous discipline compels him to be clean. But I could not see it like that. All I knew was that it was *lower-class* sweat that I was smelling, and the thought of it made me sick.

When later on I got rid of my class-prejudice, or part of it, it was in a roundabout way and by a process that took several years. The thing that changed my attitude to the class-issue was something only indirectly connected with it – something almost irrelevant.

I was in the Indian Police five years, and by the end of that time I hated the imperialism I was serving with a bitterness which I probably cannot make clear. In the free air of England that kind of thing is not fully intelligible. In order to hate imperialism you have got to be part of it. Seen from the outside the British rule in India appears – indeed, it *is* – benevolent and even necessary; and so no doubt are the French rule in Morocco and the Dutch rule in Borneo, for people usually govern foreigners better than they govern themselves. But it is not possible to be part of such a system without recognizing it as an unjustifiable tyranny. Even the thickest-skinned Anglo-Indian is aware of this. Every 'native' face he sees in the street brings home to him his monstrous intrusion. And the majority of Anglo-Indians, intermittently at least, are not nearly so complacent about their position as people in England believe. From the most unexpected people, from gin-pickled old scoundrels high up in the Government service, I have heard some such remark as: 'Of course we've no right in this blasted country at all. Only now we're here for God's sake let's stay here.' The truth is that no modern man, in his heart of hearts, believes that it is right to invade a foreign country and hold the population down by force. Foreign oppression is a much more obvious, understandable evil than economic oppression. Thus in England we tamely admit to being robbed in order to keep half a million worthless idlers in luxury, but we would fight to the last man sooner than be ruled by Chinamen; similarly, people who live on unearned dividends without a single qualm of conscience, see clearly enough that it is wrong to go and lord it in a foreign country where you are not wanted. The result is that every Anglo-Indian is haunted by a sense of guilt which he usually conceals as best he can, because there is no freedom of speech, and merely to be overheard making a seditious remark may damage his career. All over India there are Englishmen who secretely loathe the system of which they are part; and just occasionally, when they are quite certain of being in the right company, their hidden bitterness overflows. I remember a night I spent on the train with a man in the Education Service, a stranger to myself whose name I never discovered. It was too hot to sleep and we spent the night talking. Half an hour's cautious questioning decided each of us that the other was 'safe'; and then for hours, while the train jolted slowly through the pitch-black night, sitting up in our bunks with bottles of beer handy, we damned the British Empire – damned it from the inside, intelligently and intimately. It did us both good. But we had been speaking forbidden things, and in the haggard morning light when the train crawled into Mandalay, we parted as guiltily as any adulterous couple.

So far as my observation goes nearly all Anglo-Indian officials have moments when their conscience troubles them. The exceptions are men who are doing something which is demonstrably useful and would still have to be done whether the British were in India or not: forest officers, for instance, and doctors and engineers. But I was in the police, which is to say that I was part of the actual machinery of despotism. Moreover, in the police you see the dirty work of Empire at close quarters, and there is an appreciable difference between doing dirty work and merely profiting by it. Most people approve of capital punishment, but most people wouldn't do the hangman's job. Even the other Europeans in Burma slightly looked down on the police because of the brutal work they had to do. I remember once when I was inspecting a police station, an American missionary whom I knew fairly well came in for some purpose or other. Like most Nonconformist missionaries he was a complete ass but quite a good fellow. One of my native sub-inspectors was bullying a suspect (I described this scene in *Burmese Days*). The American watched it, and then turning to me said thoughtfully, 'I wouldn't care to have your job.' It made me horribly ashamed. So *that* was the kind of job I had! Even an ass of an American missionary, a teetotal cock-virgin from the Middle West, had the right to look down on me and pity me! But I should have felt the same shame even if there had been no one to bring it home to me. I had begun to have an indescribable loathing of the whole machinery of so-called justice. Say what you will, our criminal law (far more humane, by the way, in India than in England) is a horrible thing. It needs very insensitive people to administer it. The wretched prisoners squatting in the reeking cages of the lock-ups, the grey cowed faces of the long-term convicts, the scarred buttocks of the men who had been flogged with bamboos, the women and children howling when their menfolk were led away under arrest – things like these are beyond bearing when you are in any way directly responsible for them. I watched a man hanged once; it seemed to me worse than a thousand murders. I never went into a jail without feeling (most visitors to jails feel the same) that my place was on the other side of the bars. I thought then – I think now, for that matter – that the worst criminal who ever walked is morally superior to a hanging judge. But of course I had to keep these notions to myself, because of the almost utter silence that is imposed on every Englishman in the East. In the end I worked out an anarchistic theory that all government is evil, that the punishment always does more harm than the crime and that people can be trusted to behave decently if only you will let them alone. This of course was sentimental nonsense. I see now as I did not see then, that it is always necessary to protect peaceful people from violence. In any state of society where crime can be profitable you have to to have a harsh criminal law and administer it ruthlessly; the alternative is Al Capone. But the feeling that punishment is evil arises inescapably in those who have to administer it. I should expect to find that even in England many policemen, judges, prison warders, and the like are haunted by a secret horror of what they do. But in Burma it was a double oppression that we were committing. Not only were we hanging people and putting them in jail and so forth; we were doing it in the capacity of unwanted foreign invaders. The Burmese themselves never really recognized our jurisdiction. The thief whom we put in prison did not think of himself as a criminal justly punished, he thought of himself as the victim of a foreign conqueror. The thing that was done to him was merely a wanton meaningless cruelty. His face, behind the stout teak bars of the lock-up and the iron bars of the jail, said so clearly. And unfortunately I had not trained myself to be indifferent to the expression of the human face.

When I came home on leave in 1927 I was already half determined to throw up my job, and one sniff of English air decided me. I was not going back to be a part of that evil despotism. But I wanted much more than merely to escape from my job. For five years I had been part of an oppressive system, and it had left me with a bad conscience. Innumerable remembered faces – faces of prisoners in the dock, of men waiting in the condemned cells, of subordinates I had bullied and aged peasants I had snubbed, of servants and coolies I had hit with my fist in moments of rage (nearly everyone does these things in the East, at any rate occasionally: orientals can be very provoking) – haunted me intolerably. I was conscious of an immense weight of guilt that I had got to expiate. I suppose that sounds exaggerated; but if you do for five years a job that you thoroughly disapprove of, you will probably feel the same. I had reduced everything to the simple theory that the oppressed are always right and the oppressors are always wrong: a mistaken theory, but the natural result of being one of the oppressors yourself. I felt that I had got to escape not merely from imperialism but from every form of man's dominion over man. I wanted to submerge myself, to get right down among the oppressed, to be one of them and on their side against their tyrants. And, chiefly because I had had to think everything out in solitude, I had carried my hatred of oppression to extraordinary lengths. At that time failure seemed to me to be the only virtue. Every suspicion of self-advancement, even to 'succeed' in life to the extent of making a few hundreds a year, seemed to me spiritually ugly, a species of bullying.

It was in this way that my thoughts turned towards the English working class. It was the first time that I had ever been really aware of the working class, and to begin with it was only because they supplied an analogy. They were the symbolic victims of injustice, playing the same part in England as the Burmese played in Burma. In Burma the issue had been quite simple. The whites were up and the blacks were down, and therefore as a matter of course one's sympathy was with the blacks. I now realized that there was no need to go as far as Burma to find tyranny and exploitation. Here in England, down under one's feet, were the submerged working class, suffering miseries which in their different way were as bad as any an oriental ever knows. The word 'unemployment' was on everyone's lips. That was more or less new to me, after Burma, but the drivel which the middle classes were still talking ('These unemployed are all unemployables', etc., etc.) failed to deceive me. I often wonder whether that kind of stuff deceives even the fools who utter it. On the other hand I had at that time no interest in Socialism or any other economic theory. It seemed to me then – it sometimes seems to me now, for that matter – that economic injustice will stop the moment we want it to stop, and no sooner, and if we genuinely want it to stop the method adopted hardly matters.

But I knew nothing about working-class conditions. I had read the unemployment figures but I had no notion of what they implied; above all, I did not know the essential fact that 'respectable' poverty is always the worst. The frightful doom of a decent working man suddenly thrown on the streets after a lifetime of steady work, his agonized struggles against economic laws which he does not understand, the disintegration of families, the corroding sense of shame – all this was outside the range of my experience. When I thought of poverty I thought of it in terms of brute starvation. Therefore my mind turned immediately towards the extreme cases, the social outcasts: tramps, beggars, criminals, prostitutes. These were 'the lowest of the low', and these were the people with whom I wanted to get in contact. What I profoundly wanted, at that time, was to find some way of getting out of the respectable world altogether. I meditated upon it a great deal, I even planned parts of it in detail; how one could sell everything, give everything away, change one's name and start out with no money and nothing but the clothes one stood up in. But in real life nobody ever does that kind of thing; apart from the relatives and friends who have to be considered, it is doubtful whether an educated man *could* do it if there were any other course open to him. But at least I could go among these people, see what their lives were like and feel myself temporarily part of their world. Once I had been among them and accepted by them, I should have touched bottom, and – this is what I felt: I was aware even then that it was irrational – part of my guilt would drop from me.

I thought it over and decided what I would do. I would go suitably disguised to Limehouse and Whitechapel and such places and sleep in common lodging-houses and pal up with dock labourers, street hawkers, derelict people, beggars, and, if possible, criminals. And I would find out about tramps and how you got in touch with them and what was the proper procedure for entering the casual ward; and then, when I felt that I knew the ropes well enough, I would go on the road myself.

At the start it was not easy. It meant masquerading and I have no talent for acting. I cannot, for instance, disguise my accent, at any rate not for more than a very few minutes. I imagined – notice the frightful class-consciousness of the Englishman – that I should be spotted as a 'gentleman' the moment I opened my mouth; so I had a hard luck story ready in case I should be questioned. I got hold of the right kind of clothes and dirtied them in appropriate places. I am a difficult person to disguise, being abnormally tall, but I did at least know what a tramp looks like. (How few people do know this, by the way! Look at any picture of a tramp in *Punch*. They are always twenty years out of date.) One evening, having made ready at a friend's house, I set out and wandered eastward till I landed up at a common lodging-house in Limehouse Causeway. It was a dark, dirty-looking place. I knew it was a common lodging-house by the sign 'Good Beds for Single Men' in the window. Heavens, how I had to screw up my courage before I went in! It seems ridiculous now. But you see I was still half afraid of the working class. I wanted to get in touch with them, I even wanted to become one of them, but I still thought of them as alien and dangerous; going into the dark doorway of that common lodging-house seemed to me like going down into some dreadful subterranean place – a sewer full of rats, for instance. I went in fully expecting a fight. The people would spot that I was not one of themselves and immediately infer that I had come to spy on them; and then they would set upon me and throw me out – that was what I expected. I felt that I had got to do it, but I did not enjoy the prospect.

Inside the door a man in shirt-sleeves appeared from somewhere or other. This was the 'deputy', and I told him that I wanted a bed for the night. My accent did not make him stare, I noticed; he merely demanded ninepence and then showed me the way to a frowzy firelit kitchen underground. There were stevedores and navvies and a few sailors sitting about and playing draughts and drinking tea. They barely glanced at me as I entered. But this was Saturday night and a hefty young stevedore was drunk and was reeling about the room. He turned, saw me and lurched towards me with broad red face thrust out and a dangerous-looking fishy gleam in his eyes. I stiffened myself. So the fight was coming already! The next moment the stevedore collapsed on my chest and flung his arms round my neck. ''Ave a cup of tea, chum!' he cried tearfully; ''ave a cup of tea!'

I had a cup of tea. It was a kind of baptism. After that my fears vanished. Nobody questioned me, nobody showed offensive curiosity; everybody was polite and gentle and took me utterly for granted. I stayed two or three days in that common lodging-house, and a few weeks later, having picked up a certain amount of information about the habits of destitute people, I went on the road for the first time.

I have described all this in *Down and Out in Paris and London* (nearly all the incidents described there actually happened, though they have been re-arranged) and I do not want to repeat it. Later I went on the road for much longer periods, sometimes from choice, sometimes from necessity. I have lived in common lodging-houses for months together. But it is that first expedition that sticks most vividly in my mind, because of the strangeness of it – the strangeness of being at last down there among 'the lowest of the low', and on terms of utter equality with working-class people. A tramp, it is true, is not a typical working-class person; still, when you are among tramps you are at any rate merged in one section – one sub-caste – of the working class, a thing which so far as I know can happen to you in no other way. For several days I wandered through the northern outskirts of London with an Irish tramp. I was his mate, temporarily. We shared the same cell at night, and he told me the history of his life and I told him a fictitious history of mine, and we took it in turns to beg at likely-looking houses and divided up the proceeds. I was very happy. Here I was, among 'the lowest of the low', at the bedrock of the Western world! The class-bar was down, or seemed to be down. And down there in the squalid and, as a matter of fact, horribly boring sub-world of the tramp I had a feeling of release, of adventure, which seems absurd when I look back, but which was sufficiently vivid at the time.

Chapter Ten

But unfortunately you do not solve the class problem by making friends with tramps. At most you get rid of some of your own class-prejudice by doing so.

Tramps, beggars, criminals and social outcasts generally are very exceptional beings and no more typical of the working class as a whole than, say, the literary intelligentsia are typical of the bourgeoisie. It is quite easy to be on terms of intimacy with a foreign 'intellectual', but it is not at all easy to be on terms of intimacy with an ordinary respectable foreigner of the middle class. How many Englishmen have seen the inside of an ordinary French bourgeois family, for instance? Probably it would be quite impossible to do so, short of marrying into it. And it is rather similar with the English working class.

Nothing is easier than to be bosom pals with a pickpocket, if you know where to look for him; but it is very difficult to be bosom pals with a bricklayer.

But why is it so easy to be on equal terms with social outcasts? People have often said to me, 'Surely when you are with the tramps they don't really accept you as one of themselves? Surely they notice that you are different – notice the difference of accent?' etc., etc. As a matter of fact, a fair proportion of tramps, well over a quarter I should say, notice nothing of the kind. To begin with, many people have no ear for accent and judge you entirely by your clothes. I was often struck by this fact when I was begging at back doors. Some people were obviously surprised by my 'educated' accent, others completely failed to notice it; I was dirty and ragged and that was all they saw. Again, tramps come from all parts of the British Isles and the variation in English accents is enormous. A tramp is used to hearing all kinds of accents among his mates, some of them so strange to him that he can hardly understand them, and a man from, say, Cardiff or Durham or Dublin does not necessarily know which of the south English accents is an 'educated' one. In any case men with 'educated' accents, though rare among tramps, are not unknown. But even when tramps are aware that you are of different origin from themselves, it does not necessarily alter their attitude. From their point of view all that matters is that you, like themselves, are 'on the bum'. And in that world it is not done to ask too many questions. You can tell people the history of your life if you choose, and most tramps do so on the smallest provocation, but you are under no compulsion to tell it and whatever story you tell will be accepted without question. Even a bishop could be at home among tramps if he wore the right clothes; and even if they knew he was a bishop it might not make any difference, provided that they also knew or believed that he was genuinely destitute. Once you are in that world and seemingly *of* it, it hardly matters what you have been in the past. It is a sort of world-within-a-world where everyone is equal, a small squalid democracy – perhaps the nearest thing to a democracy that exists in England.

But when you come to the normal working class the position is totally different. To begin with, there is no short cut into their midst. You can become a tramp simply by putting on the right clothes and going to the nearest casual ward, but you can't become a navvy or a coal-miner. You couldn't get a job as a navvy or a coal-miner even if you were equal to the work. Via Socialist politics you can get in touch with the working-class intelligentsia, but they are hardly more typical than tramps or burglars. For the rest you can only mingle with the working class by staying in their houses as a lodger, which always has a dangerous resemblance to 'slumming'. For some months I lived entirely in coal-miners' houses. I ate my meals with the family, I washed at the kitchen sink, I shared bedrooms with miners, drank beer with them, played darts with them, talked to them by the hour together. But though I was among them, and I hope and trust they did not find me a nuisance, I was not one of them, and they knew it even better than I did. However much you like them, however interesting you find their conversation, there is always that accursed itch of class-difference, like the pea under the princess's mattress. It is not a question of dislike or distaste, only of *difference*, but it is enough to make real intimacy impossible. Even with miners who described themselves as Communists I found that it needed tactful manoeuvrings to prevent them from calling me 'sir'; and all of them, except in moments of great animation, softened their northern accents for my benefit. I liked them and hoped they liked me; but I went among them as a foreigner, and both of us were aware of it. Whichever way you turn, this curse of class-difference confronts you like a wall of stone. Or rather it is not so much like a stone wall as the plate-glass pane of an aquarium; it is so easy to pretend that it isn't there, and so impossible to get through it.

Unfortunately it is nowadays the fashion to pretend that the glass is penetrable. Of course everyone knows that class-prejudice exists, but at the same time everyone claims that *he*, in some mysterious way, is exempt from it. Snobbishness is one of those vices which we can discern in everyone else but never in ourselves. Not only the *croyant et pratiquant* Socialist, but every 'intellectual' takes it as a matter of course that *he* at least is outside the class-racket; *he*, unlike his neighbours, can see through the absurdity of wealth, ranks, titles, etc., etc. 'I'm not a snob' is nowadays a kind of universal *credo*. Who is there who has not jeered at the House of Lords, the military caste, the Royal Family, the public schools, the huntin' and shootin' people, the old ladies in Cheltenham boarding-houses, the horrors of 'county' society and the social hierarchy generally? To do so has become an automatic gesture. You notice this particularly in novels. Every novelist of serious pretensions adopts an ironic attitude towards his upper-class characters. Indeed when a novelist has to put a definitely upper-class person – a duke or a baronet or whatnot – into one of his stories he guys him more or less instinctively. There is an important subsidiary cause of this in the poverty of the modern upper-class dialect. The speech of 'educated' people is now so lifeless and characterless that a novelist can do nothing with it. By far the easiest way of making it amusing is to burlesque it, which means pretending that every upper-class person is an ineffectual ass. The trick is imitated from novelist to novelist, and in the end becomes almost a reflex action.

And yet all the while, at the bottom of his heart, everyone knows that this is humbug. We all rail against class-distinctions, but very few people seriously want to abolish them. Here you come upon the important fact that every revolutionary opinion draws part of its strength from a secret conviction that nothing can be changed.

If you want a good illustration of this, it is worth studying the novels and plays of John Galsworthy, keeping one eye on their chronology. Galsworthy is a very fine specimen of the thin-skinned, tear-in-the-eye, pre-war humanitarian. He starts out with a morbid pity-complex which extends even to thinking that every married woman is an angel chained to a satyr. He is in a perpetual quiver of indignation over the sufferings of overworked clerks, of under-paid farm hands, of fallen women, of criminals, of prostitutes, of animals. The world, as he sees it in his earlier books (*The Man of Property*, *Justice*, etc.), is divided into oppressors and oppressed, with the oppressors sitting on top like some monstrous stone idol which all the dynamite in the world cannot overthrow. But is it so certain that he really wants it overthrown? On the contrary, in his fight against an immovable tyranny he is upheld by the consciousness that it *is* immovable. When things happen unexpectedly and the world-order which he has known begins to crumble, he feels somewhat differently about it. So, having set out to be the champion of the under-dog against tyranny and injustice, he ends by advocating (*vide The Silver Spoon*) that the English working class, to cure their economic ills, shall be deported to the colonies like batches of cattle. If he had lived ten years longer he would quite probably have arrived at some genteel version of Fascism. This is the inevitable fate of the sentimentalist. All his opinions change into their opposites at the first brush of reality.

The same streak of soggy half-baked insincerity runs through all 'advanced' opinion. Take the question of imperialism, for instance. Every left-wing 'intellectual' is, as a matter of course, an anti-imperialist. He claims to be outside the empire-racket as automatically and self-righteously as he claims to be outside the class-racket. Even the right-wing 'intellectual', who is not definitely in revolt against British imperialism, pretends to regard it with a sort of amused detachment. It is so easy to be witty about the British Empire. The White Man's Burden and 'Rule, Britannia' and Kipling's novels and Anglo-Indian bores – who could even mention such things without a snigger? And is there any cultured person who has not at least once in his life made a joke about that old Indian havildar who said that if the British left India there would not be a rupee or a virgin left between Peshawar and Delhi (or wherever it was)? That is the attitude of the typical left-winger towards imperialism, and a thoroughly flabby, boneless attitude it is. For in the last resort, the only important question is, Do you want the British Empire to hold together or do you want it to disintegrate? And at the bottom of his heart no Englishman, least of all the kind of person who is witty about Anglo-Indian colonels, does want it to disintegrate. For, apart from any other consideration, the high standard of life we enjoy in England depends upon our keeping a tight hold on the Empire, particularly the tropical portions of it such as India and Africa. Under the capitalist system, in order that England may live in comparative comfort, a hundred million Indians must live on the verge of starvation – an evil state of affairs, but you acquiesce in it every time you step into a taxi or eat a plate of strawberries and cream. The alternative is to throw the Empire overboard and reduce England to a cold and unimportant little island where we should all have to work very hard and live mainly on herrings and potatoes. That is the very last thing that any left-winger wants. Yet the left-winger continues to feel that he has no moral responsibility for imperialism. He is pefectly ready to accept the products of Empire and to save his soul by sneering at the people who hold the Empire together.

It is at this point that one begins to grasp the unreality of most people's attitude towards the class question. So long as it is merely a question of ameliorating the worker's lot, every decent person is agreed. Take a coal-miner, for example. Everyone, barring fools and scoundrels, would *like* to see the miner better off. If, for instance, the miner could ride to the coal face in a comfortable trolley instead of crawling on his hands and knees, if he could work a three-hour shift instead of seven and a half hours, if he could live in a decent house with five bedrooms and a bathroom and have ten pounds a week wages – splendid! Moreover, anyone who uses his brain knows perfectly well that this is within the range of possibility. The world, potentially at least, is immensely rich; develop it as it might be developed, and we could all live like princes, supposing that we wanted to. And to a very superficial glance the social side of the question looks equally simple. In a sense it is true that almost everyone would like to see class-distinctions abolished. Obviously this perpetual uneasiness between man and man, from which we suffer in modern England, is a curse and a nuisance. Hence the temptation to believe that it can be shouted out of existence with a few scoutmasterish bellows of good-will. Stop calling me 'sir', you chaps! Surely we're all men? Let's pal up and get our shoulders to the wheel and remember that we're all equal, and what the devil does it matter if I know what kind of ties to wear and you don't, and I drink my soup comparatively quietly and you drink yours with the noise of water going down a waste-pipe – and so on and so on and so on; all of it the most pernicious rubbish, but quite alluring when it is suitably expressed.

But unfortunately you get no further by merely wishing class-distinctions away. More exactly, it *is* necessary to wish them away, but your wish has no efficacy unless you grasp what it involves. The fact that has got to be faced is that to abolish class-distinctions means abolishing a part of yourself. Here am I, a typical member of the middle class. It is easy for me to say that I want to get rid of class-distinctions, but nearly everything I think and do is a result of class-distinctions. All my notions – notions of good and evil, of pleasant and unpleasant, of funny and serious, of ugly and beautiful – are essentially *middle-class* notions; my taste in books and food and clothes, my sense of honour, my table-manners, my turns of speech, my accent, even the characteristic movements of my body, are the products of a special kind of upbringing and a special niche about half-way up the social hierarchy. When I grasp this I grasp that it is no use clapping a proletarian on the back and telling him that he is as good a man as I am; if I want real contact with him, I have got to make an effort for which very likely I am unprepared. For to get outside the class-racket I have got to suppress not merely my private snobbishness, but most of my other tastes and prejudices as well. I have got to alter myself so completely that at the end I should hardly be recognizable as the same person. What is involved is not merely the amelioration of working-class conditions, nor an avoidance of the more stupid forms of snobbery, but a complete abandonment of the upper-class and middle-class attitude to life. And whether I say Yes or No probably depends upon the extent to which I grasp what is demanded of me.

Many people, however, imagine that they can abolish class-distinctions without making any uncomfortable change in their own habits and 'ideology'. Hence the eager class-breaking activities which one can see in progress on all sides. Everywhere there are people of good will who quite honestly believe that they are working for the overthrow of class-distinctions. The middle-class Socialist enthuses over the proletariat and runs 'summer schools' where the proletarian and the repentant bourgeois are supposed to fall upon one another's necks and be brothers for ever; and the bourgeois visitors come away saying how wonderful and inspiring it has all been (the proletarian ones come away saying something different). And then there is the outer-suburban creeping Jesus, a hangover from the William Morris period, but still surprisingly common, who goes about saying 'Why must we level *down?* Why not level *up?*' and proposes to level the working class 'up' (up to his own standard) by means of hygiene, fruit-juice, birth-control, poetry, etc. Even the Duke of York (now King George VI) runs a yearly camp where public-school boys and boys from the slums are supposed to mix on exactly equal terms, and *do* mix for the time being, rather like the animals in one of those 'Happy Family' cages where a dog, a cart, two ferrets, a rabbit and three canaries preserve an armed truce while the showman's eye is on them.

All such deliberate, conscious efforts at class-breaking are, I am convinced, a very serious mistake. Sometimes they are merely futile, but where they do show a definite result it is usually to *intensify* class-prejudice. This, if you come to think of it, is only what might be expected. You have forced the pace and set up an uneasy, unnatural equality between class and class; the resultant friction brings to the surface all kinds of feelings that might otherwise have remained buried, perhaps for ever. As I said apropos of Galsworthy, the opinions of the sentimentalist change into their opposites at the first touch of reality. Scratch the average pacifist and you find a jingo. The middle-class I.L.P.'er and the bearded fruit-juice drinker are all for a classless society so long as they see the proletariat through the wrong end of the telescope; force them into any *real* contact with a proletarian – let them get into a fight with a drunken fish-porter on Saturday night, for instance – and they are capable of swinging back to the most ordinary middle-class snobbishness. Most middle-class Socialists, however, are very unlikely to get into fights with drunken fish-porters; when they do make a genuine contact with the working class, it is usually with the working-class intelligentsia. But the working-class intelligentsia is sharply divisible into two different types. There is the type who remains working-class – who goes on working as a mechanic or a dock-labourer or whatever it may be and does not bother to change his working-class accent and habits, but who 'improves his mind' in his spare time and works for the I.L.P. or the Communist Party; and there is the type who does alter his way of life, at least externally, and who by means of State scholarships succeeds in climbing into the middle class. The first is one of the finest types of man we have. I can think of some I have met whom not even the most hidebound Tory could help liking and admiring. The other type, with exceptions – D. H. Lawrence, for example – is less admirable.

To begin with, it is a pity, though it is a natural result of the scholarship system, that the proletariat should tend to interpenetrate the middle class via the literary intelligentsia. For it is not easy to crash your way into the literary intelligentsia if you happen to be a decent human being. The modern English literary world, at any rate the highbrow section of it, is a sort of poisonous jungle where only weeds can flourish. It is just possible to be a literary gent and to keep your decency if you are a definitely *popular* writer – a writer of detective stories, for instance; but to be a highbrow, with a footing in the snootier magazines, means delivering yourself over to horrible campaigns of wire-pulling and backstairs-crawling. In the highbrow world you 'get on', if you 'get on' at all, not so much by your literary ability as by being the life and soul of cocktail parties and kissing the bums of verminous little lions. This, then, is the world that most readily opens its doors to the proletarian who is climbing out of his own class. The 'clever' boy of a working-class family, the sort of boy who wins scholarships and is obviously not fitted for a life of manual labour, may find other ways of rising into the class above – a slightly different type, for instance, rises via Labour Party politics – but the literary way is by far the most usual. Literary London now teems with young men who are of proletarian origin and have been educated by means of scholarships. Many of them are very disagreeable people, quite unrepresentative of their class, and it is most unfortunate that when a person of bourgeois origin does succeed in meeting a proletarian face to face on equal terms, this is the type he most commonly meets. For the result is to drive the bourgeois, who has idealized the proletariat so long as he knew nothing about them, back into frenzies of snobbishness. The process is sometimes very comic to watch, if you happen to be watching it from the outside. The poor well-meaning bourgeois, eager to embrace his proletarian brother, leaps forward with open arms; and only a little while later he is in retreat, minus a borrowed five pounds and exclaiming dolefully, 'But, dash it, the fellow's not a gentleman!'

The thing that disconcerts the bourgeois in a contact of this kind is to find certain of his own professions being taken seriously. I have pointed out that the left-wing opinions of the average 'intellectual' are mainly spurious. From pure imitativeness he jeers at things which in fact he believes in. As one example out of many, take the public-school code of honour, with its 'team spirit' and 'Don't hit a man when he's down', and all the rest of that familiar bunkum. Who has not laughed at it? Who, calling himself an 'intellectual', would dare *not* to laugh at it? But it is a bit different when you meet somebody who laughs at it *from the outside*; just as we spend our lives in abusing England but grow very angry when we hear a foreigner saying exactly the same things. No one has been more amusing about the public schools than 'Beachcomber' of the *Express*. He laughs, quite rightly, at the ridiculous code which makes cheating at cards the worst of all sins. But would 'Beachcomber' like it if one of his own friends was caught cheating at cards? I doubt it. It is only when you meet someone of a different culture from yourself that you begin to realize what your own beliefs really are. If you are a bourgeois 'intellectual' you too readily imagine that you have somehow become unbourgeois because you find it easy to laugh at patriotism and the C. of E. and the Old School Tie and Colonel Blimp and all the rest of it. But from the point of view of the proletarian 'intellectual', who at least by origin is genuinely outside the bourgeois culture, your resemblances to Colonel Blimp may be more important than your differences. Very likely he looks upon you and Colonel Blimp as practically equivalent persons; and in a way he is right, though neither you nor Colonel Blimp would admit it. So that the meeting of proletarian and bourgeois, when they do succeed in meeting, is not always the embrace of long-lost brothers; too often it is the clash of alien cultures which can only meet in war.

I have been looking at this from the point of view of the bourgeois who finds his secret beliefs challenged and is driven back to a frightened conservatism. But one has also got to consider the antagonism that is aroused in the proletarian 'intellectual'. By his own efforts and sometimes with frightful agonies he has struggled out of his own class into another where he expects to find a wider freedom and a greater intellectual refinement; and all he finds, very often, is a sort of hollowness, a deadness, a lack of any warm human feeling – of any real life whatever. Sometimes the bourgeoisie seem to him just dummies with money and water in their veins instead of blood. This at any rate is what he *says*, and almost any young highbrow of proletarian origin will spin you this line of talk. Hence the 'proletarian' cant from which we now suffer. Everyone knows, or ought to know by this time, how it runs: the bourgeoisie are 'dead' (a favourite word of abuse nowadays and very effective because meaningless), bourgeois culture is bankrupt, bourgeois 'values' are despicable, and so on and so forth; if you want examples, see any number of the *Left Review* or any of the younger Communist writers such as Alec Brown, Philip Henderson, etc. The sincerity of much of this is suspect, but D. H. Lawrence, who was sincere, whatever else he may not have been, expresses the same thought over and over again. It is curious how he harps upon that idea that the English bourgeoisie are all *dead*, or at least gelded. Mellors, the gamekeeper in *Lady Chatterley's Lover* (really Lawrence himself) has had the opportunity to get out of his own class and does not particularly want to return to it, because English working people have various 'disagreeable habits'; on the other hand the bourgeoisie, with whom he has also mixed to some extent, seem to him half dead, a race of eunuchs. Lady Chatterley's husband, symbolically, is impotent in the actual physical sense. And then there is the poem about the young man (once again Lawrence himself) who 'got up to the top of the tree' but came down saying:

Oh you've got to be like a monkey
if you climb up the tree!
You've no more use for the solid earth
and the lad you used to be.
You sit in the boughs and gibber
with superiority.

They all gibber and gibber and chatter,
and never a word they say
comes really out of their guts, lad,
they make it up half way. . . .

I tell you something's been done to 'em,
to the pullets up above;
there's not a cock bird among 'em, etc., etc.

You could hardly have it in plainer terms than that. Possibly by the people at 'the top of the tree' Lawrence only means the real bourgeoisie, those in the £2,000 a year class and over, but I doubt it. More probably he means everyone who is more or less within the bourgeois culture – everyone who was brought up with a mincing accent and in a house where there were one or two servants. And at this point you realize the danger of the 'proletarian' cant – realize, I mean, the terrible antagonism that it is capable of arousing. For when you come to such an accusation as this, you are up against a blank wall. Lawrence tells me that because I have been to a public school I am a eunuch. Well, what about it? I can produce medical evidence to the contrary, but what good will that do? Lawrence's condemnation remains. If you tell me I am a scoundrel I may mend my ways, but if you tell me I am a eunuch you are tempting me to hit back in any way that seems feasible. If you want to make an enemy of a man, tell him that his ills are incurable.

This then is the net result of most meetings between proletarian and bourgeois: they lay bare a real antagonism which is intensified by the 'proletarian' cant, itself the product of forced contacts between class and class. The only sensible procedure is to go slow and not force the pace. If you secretly think of yourself as a gentleman and as such the superior of the greengrocer's errand boy, it is far better to say so than to tell lies about it. Ultimately you have got to drop your snobbishness, but it is fatal to pretend to drop it before you are really ready to do so.

Meanwhile one can observe on every side that dreary phenomenon, the middle-class person who is an ardent Socialist at twenty-five and a sniffish Conservative at thirty-five. In a way his recoil is natural enough – at any rate, one can see how his thoughts run. Perhaps a classless society *doesn't* mean a beatific state of affairs in which we shall all go on behaving exactly as before except that there will be no class-hatred and no snobbishness; perhaps it means a bleak world in which all our ideals, our codes, our tastes – our 'ideology', in fact – will have no meaning. Perhaps this class-breaking business isn't so simple as it looked! On the contrary, it is a wild ride into the darkness, and it may be that at the end of it the smile will be on the face of the tiger. With loving though slightly patronizing smiles we set out to greet our proletarian brothers, and behold! our proletarian brothers – in so far as we understand them – are not asking for our greetings, they are asking us to commit suicide. When the bourgeois sees it in *that* form he takes to flight, and if his flight is rapid enough it may carry him to Fascism.

Chapter Eleven

Meanwhile, what about Socialism?

It hardly needs pointing out that at this moment we are in a very serious mess, so serious that even the dullest-witted people find it difficult to remain unaware of it. We are living in a world in which nobody is free, in which hardly anybody is secure, in which it is almost impossible to be honest and to remain alive. For enormous blocks of the working class the conditions of life are such as I have described in the opening chapters of this book, and there is no chance of those conditions showing any fundamental improvement. The very best the English working class can hope for is an occasional temporary decrease in unemployment when this or that industry is artificially stimulated by, for instance, rearmament. Even the middle classes, for the first time in their history, are feeling the pinch. They have not known actual hunger yet, but more and more of them find themselves floundering in a sort of deadly net of frustration in which it is harder and harder to persuade yourself that you are either happy, active or useful. Even the lucky ones at the top, the real bourgeoisie, are haunted periodically by a consciousness of the miseries below, and still more by fears of the menacing future. And this is merely a preliminary stage, in a country still rich with the loot of a hundred years. Presently there may be coming God knows what horrors – horrors of which, in this sheltered island, we have not even a traditional knowledge.

And all the while everyone who uses his brain knows that Socialism, as a world-system and wholeheartedly applied, is a way out. It would at least ensure our getting enough to eat even if it deprived us of everything else. Indeed, from one point of view, Socialism is such elementary common sense that I am sometimes amazed that it has not established itself already. The world is a raft sailing through space with, potentially, plenty of provisions for everybody; the idea that we must all co-operate and see to it that everyone does his fair share of the work and gets his fair share of the provisions seems so blatantly obvious that one would say that no one could possibly fail to accept it unless he had some corrupt motive for clinging to the present system. Yet the fact that we have got to face is that Socialism is *not* establishing itself. Instead of going forward, the cause of Socialism is visibly going back. At this moment Socialists almost everywhere are in retreat before the onslaught of Fascism, and events are moving at terrible speed. As I write this the Spanish Fascist forces are bombarding Madrid, and it is quite likely that before the book is printed we shall have another Fascist country to add to the list, not to mention a Fascist control of the Mediterranean which may have the effect of delivering British foreign policy into the hands of Mussolini. I do not, however, want here to discuss the wider political issues. What I am concerned with is the fact that Socialism is losing ground exactly where it ought to be gaining it. With so much in its favour – for every empty belly is an argument for Socialism – the *idea* of Socialism is less widely accepted than it was ten years ago. The average thinking person nowadays is not merely not a Socialist, he is actively hostile to Socialism. This must be due chiefly to mistaken methods of propaganda. It means that Socialism, in the form in which it is now presented to us, has about it something inherently distasteful – something that drives away the very people who ought to be flocking to its support.

A few years ago this might have seemed unimportant. It seems only yesterday that Socialists, especially orthodox Marxists, were telling me with superior smiles that Socialism was going to arrive of its own accord by some mysterious process called 'historic necessity'. Possibly that belief still lingers, but it has been shaken, to say the least of it. Hence the sudden attempts of Communists in various countries to ally themselves with democratic forces which they have been sabotaging for years past. At a moment like this it is desperately necessary to discover just *why* Socialism has failed in its appeal. And it is no use writing off the current distaste for Socialism as the product of stupidity or corrupt motives. If you want to remove that distaste you have got to understand it, which means getting inside the mind of the ordinary objector to Socialism, or at least regarding his viewpoint sympathetically. No case is really answered until it has had a fair hearing. Therefore, rather paradoxically, in order to defend Socialism it is necessary to start by attacking it.

In the last three chapters I tried to analyse the difficulties that are raised by our anachronistic class-system; I shall have to touch on that subject again, because I believe that the present intensely stupid handling of the class-issue may stampede quantities of potential Socialists into Fascism. In the chapter following this one I want to discuss certain underlying assumptions that alienate sensitive minds from Socialism. But in the present chapter I am merely dealing with the obvious, preliminary objections – the kind of thing that the person who is not a Socialist (I don't mean the 'Where's the money to come from?' type) always starts by saying when you tax him on the subject. Some of these objections may appear frivolous or self-contradictory, but that is beside the point; I am merely discussing symptoms. Anything is relevant which helps to make clear why Socialism is not accepted. And please notice that I am arguing *for* Socialism, not *against* it. But for the moment I am *advocatus diaboli*. I am making out a case for the sort of person who is in sympathy with the fundamental aims of Socialism, who has the brains to see that Socialism would 'work', but who in practice always takes to flight when Socialism is mentioned.

Question a person of this type, and you will often get the semi-frivolous answer: 'I don't object to Socialism, but I do object to Socialists.' Logically it is a poor argument, but it carries weight with many people. As with the Christian religion, the worst advertisement for Socialism is its adherents.

The first thing that must strike any outside observer is that Socialism in its developed form is a theory confined entirely to the middle class. The typical Socialist is not, as tremulous old ladies imagine, a ferocious-looking working man with greasy overalls and a raucous voice. He is either a youthful snob-Bolshevik who in five years' time will quite probably have made a wealthy marriage and been converted to Roman Catholicism; or, still more typically, a prim little man with a white-collar job, usually a secret teetotaller and often with vegetarian leanings, with a history of Nonconformity behind him, and, above all, with a social position which he has no intention of forfeiting. This last type is surprisingly common in Socialist parties of every shade; it has perhaps been taken over *en bloc* from the old Liberal Party. In addition to this there is the horrible – the really disquieting – prevalence of cranks wherever Socialists are gathered together. One sometimes gets the impression that the mere words 'Socialism' and 'Communism' draw towards them with magnetic force every fruit-juice drinker, nudist, sandal-wearer, sex-maniac, Quaker, 'Nature Cure' quack, pacifist and feminist in England. One day this summer I was riding through Letchworth when the bus stopped and two dreadful-looking old men got on to it. They were both about sixty, both very short, pink and chubby, and both hatless. One of them was obscenely bald, the other had long grey hair bobbed in the Lloyd George style. They were dressed in pistachio-coloured shirts and khaki shorts into which their huge bottoms were crammed so tightly that you could study every dimple. Their appearance created a mild stir of horror on top of the bus. The man next to me, a commercial traveller I should say, glanced at me, at them, and back again at me, and murmured, 'Socialists', as who should say, 'Red Indians'. He was probably right – the I.L.P. were holding their summer school at Letchworth. But the point is that to him, as an ordinary man, a crank meant a Socialist and a Socialist meant a crank. Any Socialist, he probably felt, could be counted on to have *something* eccentric about him. And some such notion seems to exist even among Socialists themselves. For instance, I have here a prospectus from another summer school which states its terms per week and then asks me to say 'whether my diet is ordinary or vegetarian'. They take it for granted, you see, that it is necessary to ask this question. This kind of thing is by itself sufficient to alienate plenty of decent people. And their instinct is perfectly sound, for the food-crank is by definition a person willing to cut himself off from human society in hopes of adding five years on to the life of his carcase; that is, a person out of touch with common humanity.

To this you have got to add the ugly fact that most middle-class Socialists, while theoretically pining for a classless society, cling like glue to their miserable fragments of social prestige. I remember my sensations of horror on first attending an I.L.P. branch meeting in London. (It might have been rather different in the North, where the bourgeoisie are less thickly scattered.) Are *these* mingy little beasts, I thought, the champions of the working class? For every person there, male and female, bore the worst stigmata of sniffish middle-class superiority. If a real working man, a miner dirty from the pit, for instance, had suddenly walked into their midst, they would have been embarrassed, angry, and disgusted; some, I should think, would have fled holding their noses. You can see the same tendency in Socialist literature, which, even when it is not openly written *de haut en bas,* is always completely removed from the working class in idiom and manner of thought. The Coles, Webbs, Stracheys, etc., are not *exactly* proletarian writers. It is doubtful whether anything describable as proletarian literature now exists – even the *Daily Worker* is written in standard South English – but a good music-hall comedian comes nearer to producing it than any Socialist writer I can think of. As for the technical jargon of the Communists, it is as far removed from the common speech as the language of a mathematical text-book. I remember hearing a professional Communist speaker address a working-class audience. His speech was the usual bookish stuff, full of long sentences and parentheses and 'Notwithstanding' and 'Be that as it may', besides the usual jargon of 'ideology' and 'class-consciousness' and 'proletarian solidarity' and all the rest of it. After him a Lancashire working man got up and spoke to the crowd in their own broad lingo. There was not much doubt which of the two was nearer to his audience, but I do not suppose for a moment that the Lancashire working man was an orthodox Communist.

For it must be remembered that a working man, so long as he remains a genuine working man, is seldom or never a Socialist in the complete, logically consistent sense. Very likely he votes Labour, or even Communist if he gets the chance, but his conception of Socialism is quite different from that of the book-trained Socialist higher up. To the ordinary working man, the sort you would meet in any pub on Saturday night, Socialism does not mean much more than better wages and shorter hours and nobody bossing you about. To the more revolutionary type, the type who is a hunger-marcher and is blacklisted by employers, the word is a sort of rallying-cry against the forces of oppression, a vague threat of future violence. But, so far as my experience goes, no genuine working man grasps the deeper implications of Socialism. Often, in my opinion, he is a truer Socialist than the orthodox Marxist, because he does remember, what the other so often forgets, that Socialism means justice and common decency. But what he does not grasp is that Socialism cannot be narrowed down to mere economic justice and that a reform of that magnitude is bound to work immense changes in our civilization and his own way of life. His vision of the Socialist future is a vision of present society with the worst abuses left out, and with interest centring round the same things as at present – family life, the pub, football, and local politics. As for the philosophic side of Marxism, the pea-and-thimble trick with those three mysterious entities, thesis, antithesis, and synthesis, I have never met a working man who had the faintest interest in it. It is of course true that plenty of people of working-class *origin* are Socialists of the theoretical bookish type. But they are never people who have *remained* working men; they don't work with their hands, that is. They belong either to the type I mentioned in the last chapter, the type who squirms into the middle class via the literary intelligentsia, or the type who becomes a Labour M.P. or a high-up trade-union official. This last type is one of the most desolating spectacles the world contains. He has been picked out to fight for his mates, and all it means to him is a soft job and the chance of 'bettering' himself. Not merely while but *by* fighting the bourgeoisie he becomes a bourgeois himself. And meanwhile it is quite possible that he has remained an orthodox Marxist. But I have yet to meet a *working* miner, steel-worker, cotton-weaver, docker, navvy or whatnot who was 'ideologically' sound.

One of the analogies between Communism and Roman Catholicism is that only the 'educated' are completely orthodox. The most immediately striking thing about the English Roman Catholics – I don't mean the real Catholics, I mean the converts: Ronald Knox, Arnold Lunn *et hoc genus* – is their intense self-consciousness. Apparently they never think, certainly they never write, about anything but the fact that they *are* Roman Catholics; this single fact and the self-praise resulting from it form the entire stock-in-trade of the Catholic literary man. But the really interesting thing about these people is the way in which they have worked out the supposed implications of orthodoxy until the tiniest details of life are involved. Even the liquids you drink, apparently, can be orthodox or heretical; hence the campaigns of Chesterton, 'Beachcomber', etc., against tea and in favour of beer. According to Chesterton, tea-drinking is 'pagan', while beer-drinking is 'Christian', and coffee is 'the puritan's opium'. It is unfortunate for this theory that Catholics abound in the 'Temperance' movement and the greatest tea-boozers in the world are the Catholic Irish; but what I am interested in here is the attitude of mind that can make even food and drink an occasion for religious intolerance. A working-class Catholic would never be so absurdly consistent as that. He does not spend his time in brooding on the fact that he is a Roman Catholic, and he is not particularly conscious of being different from his non-Catholic neighbours. Tell an Irish dock-labourer in the slums of Liverpool that his cup of tea is 'pagan', and he will call you a fool. And even in more serious matters he does not always grasp the implications of his faith. In the Roman Catholic homes of Lancashire you see the crucifix on the wall and the *Daily Worker* on the table. It is only the 'educated' man, especially the literary man, who knows how to be a bigot. And, *mutatis mutandis*, it is the same with Communism. The creed is never found in its pure form in a genuine proletarian.

It may be said, however, that even if the theoretical book-trained Socialist is not a working man himself, at least he is actuated by a love of the working class. He is endeavouring to shed his bourgeois status and fight on the side of the proletariat – that, obviously, must be his motive.

But is it? Sometimes I look at a Socialist – the intellectual, tract-writing type of Socialist, with his pullover, his fuzzy hair, and his Marxian quotation – and wonder what the devil his motive really *is*. It is often difficult to believe that it is a love of anybody, especially of the working class, from whom he is of all people the furthest removed. The underlying motive of many Socialists, I believe, is simply a hypertrophied sense of order. The present state of affairs offends them not because it causes misery, still less because it makes freedom impossible, but because it is untidy; what they desire, basically, is to reduce the world to something resembling a chess-board. Take the plays of a lifelong Socialist like Shaw. How much understanding or even awareness of working-class life do they display? Shaw himself declares that you can only bring a working man on the stage 'as an object of compassion'; in practice he doesn't bring him on even as that, but merely as a sort of W. W. Jacobs figure of fun – the ready-made comic East Ender, like those in *Major Barbara* and *Captain Brassbound's Conversion*. At best his attitude to the working class is the sniggering *Punch* attitude, in more serious moments (consider, for instance, the young man who symbolizes the dispossessed classes in *Misalliance*) he finds them merely contemptible and disgusting. Poverty and, what is more, the habits of mind created by poverty, are something to be abolished *from above*, by violence if necessary; perhaps even preferably by violence. Hence his worship of 'great' men and appetite for dictatorships, Fascist or Communist; for to him, apparently (*vide* his remarks apropos of the Italo-Abyssinian war and the Stalin-Wells conversations), Stalin and Mussolini are almost equivalent persons. You get the same thing in a more mealy-mouthed form in Mrs Sidney Webb's autobiography, which gives, unconsciously, a most revealing picture of the high-minded Socialist slum-visitor. The truth is that to many people, calling themselves Socialists, revolution does not mean a movement of the masses with which they hope to associate themselves; it means a set of reforms which 'we', the clever ones, are going to impose upon 'them', the Lower Orders. On the other hand, it would be a mistake to regard the book-trained Socialist as a bloodless creature entirely incapable of emotion. Though seldom giving much evidence of affection for the exploited, he is perfectly capable of displaying hatred – a sort of queer, theoretical, *in vacuo* hatred – against the exploiters. Hence the grand old Socialist sport of denouncing the bourgeoisie.

It is strange how easily almost any Socialist writer can lash himself into frenzies of rage against the class to which, by birth or by adoption, he himself invariably belongs. Sometimes the hatred of bourgeois habits and 'ideology' is so far-reaching that it extends even to bourgeois characters in books. According to Henri Barbusse, the characters in the novels of Proust, Gide, etc., are 'characters whom one would dearly love to have at the other side of a barricade'. 'A barricade', you observe. Judging from *Le Feu*, I should have thought Barbusse's experience of barricades had left him with a distaste for them. But the imaginary bayoneting of 'bourgeois', who presumably don't hit back, is a bit different from the real article.

The best example of bourgeois-baiting literature that I have yet come across is Mirsky's *Intelligentsia of Great Britain.* This is a very interesting and ably-written book, and it should be read by everyone who wants to understand the rise of Fascism. Mirsky (formerly Prince Mirsky) was a White Russian *émigré* who came to England and was for some years a lecturer in Russian literature at London University. Later he was converted to Communism, returned to Russia, and produced this book as a sort of 'show-up' of the British intelligentsia from a Marxist standpoint. It is a viciously malignant book, with an unmistakable note of 'Now I'm out of your reach I can say what I like about you' running all through it, and apart from a general distortion it contains some quite definite and probably intentional misrepresentation: as, for instance, when Conrad is declared to be 'no less imperialist than Kipling', and D. H. Lawrence is described as writing 'bare-bodied pornography' and as having 'succeeded in erasing all clues to his proletarian origin' – as though Lawrence had been a pork-butcher climbing into the House of Lords! This kind of thing is very disquieting when one remembers that it is addressed to a Russian audience who have no means of checking its accuracy. But what I am thinking of at the moment is the effect of such a book on the English public. Here you have a literary man of aristocratic extraction, a man who had probably never in his life spoken to a working man on anything approaching equal terms, uttering venomous screams of libel against his 'bourgeois' colleagues. Why? So far as appearances go, from pure malignity. He is battling *against* the British intelligentsia, but what is he battling *for?* Within the book itself there is no indication. Hence the net effect of books like this is to give outsiders the impression that there is nothing in Communism except *hatred.* And here once again you come upon that queer resemblance between Communism and (convert) Roman Catholicism. If you want to find a book as evil-spirited as *The Intelligentsia of Great Britain,* the likeliest place to look is among the popular Roman Catholic apologists. You will find there the same venom and the same dishonesty, though, to do the Catholic justice, you will not usually find the same bad manners. Queer that Comrade Mirsky's spiritual brother should be Father —— ——! The Communist and the Catholic are not saying the same thing, in a sense they are even saying opposite things, and each would gladly boil the other in oil if circumstances permitted; but from the point of view of an outsider they are very much alike.

The fact is that Socialism, *in the form in which it is now presented,* appeals chiefly to unsatisfactory or even inhuman types. On the one hand you have the warm-hearted unthinking Socialist, the typical working-class Socialist, who only wants to abolish poverty and does not always grasp what this implies. On the other hand, you have the intellectual, book-trained Socialist, who understands that it is necessary to throw our present civilization down the sink and is quite willing to do so. And this type is drawn, to begin with, entirely from the middle class, and from a rootless town-bred section of the middle class at that. Still more unfortunately, it includes – so much so that to an outsider it even appears to be composed of – the kind of people I have been discussing; the foaming denouncers of the bourgeoisie, and the more-water-in-your-beer reformers of whom Shaw is the prototype, and the astute young social-literary climbers who are Communists now, as they will be Fascists five years hence, because it is all the go, and all that dreary tribe of high-minded women and sandal-wearers and bearded fruit-juice drinkers who come flocking towards the smell of 'progress' like bluebottles to a dead cat. The ordinary decent person, who is in sympathy with the *essential* aims of Socialism, is given the impression that there is no room for his kind in any Socialist party that means business. Worse, he is driven to the cynical conclusion that Socialism is a kind of doom which is probably coming but must be staved off as long as possible. Of course, as I have suggested already, it is not strictly fair to judge a movement by its adherents; but the point is that people invariably do so, and that the popular conception of Socialism is coloured by the conception of a Socialist as a dull or disagreeable person. 'Socialism' is pictured as a state of affairs in which our more vocal Socialists would feel thoroughly at home. This does great harm to the cause. The ordinary man may not flinch from a dictatorship of the proletariat, if you offer it tactfully; offer him a dictatorship of the prigs, and he gets ready to fight.

There is a widespread feeling that any civilization in which Socialism was a reality would bear the same relation to our own as a brand-new bottle of colonial burgundy bears to a few spoonfuls of first-class Beaujolais. We live, admittedly, amid the wreck of a civilization, but it has been a great civilization in its day, and in patches it still flourishes almost undisturbed. It still has its bouquet, so to speak; whereas the imagined Socialist future, like the colonial burgundy, tastes only of iron and water. Hence the fact, which is really a disastrous one, that artists of any consequence can never be persuaded into the Socialist fold. This is particularly the case with the writer whose political opinions are more directly and obviously connected with his work than those of, say, a painter. If one faces facts one must admit that nearly everything describable as Socialist literature is dull, tasteless, and bad. Consider the situation in England at the present moment. A whole generation has grown up more or less in familiarity with the idea of Socialism; and yet the higher-water mark, so to speak, of Socialist literature is W. H. Auden, a sort of gutless Kipling,[1] and the even feebler poets who are associated with him. Every writer of consequence and every book worth reading is on the other side. I am willing to believe that it is otherwise in Russia – about which I know nothing, however – for presumably in post-revolutionary Russia the mere violence of events would tend to throw up a vigorous literature of sorts. But it is certain that in Western Europe Socialism has produced no literature worth having. A little while ago, when the issues were less clear, there were writers of some vitality who called themselves Socialists, but they were using the word as a vague label. Thus, if Ibsen and Zola described themselves as Socialists, it did not mean much more than that they were 'progressives', while in the case of Anatole France it meant merely that he was an anticlerical. The real Socialist writers, the propagandist writers, have always been dull, empty windbags – Shaw,

[1] Orwell somewhat retracted this remark later. See 'Inside the Whale', p. 494 (Publisher's note).

Barbusse, Upton Sinclair, William Morris, Waldo Frank, etc., etc. I am not, of course, suggesting that Socialism is to be condemned because literary gents don't like it; I am not even suggesting that it ought necessarily to produce literature on its own account, though I do think it a bad sign that it has produced no songs worth singing. I am merely pointing to the fact that writers of genuine talent are usually indifferent to Socialism, and sometimes actively and mischievously hostile. And this is a disaster, not only for the writers themselves, but for the cause of Socialism, which has great need of them.

This, then, is the superficial aspect of the ordinary man's recoil from Socialism. I know the whole dreary argument very thoroughly, because I know it from both sides. Everything that I say here I have both said to ardent Socialists who were trying to convert me, and had said to me by bored non-Socialists whom I was trying to convert. The whole thing amounts to a kind of *malaise* produced by dislike of individual Socialists, especially of the cocksure Marx-quoting type. Is it childish to be influenced by that kind of thing? Is it silly? Is it even contemptible? It is all that, but the point is that *it happens*, and therefore it is important to keep it in mind.

Chapter Twelve

However, there is a much more serious difficulty than the local and temporary objections which I discussed in the last chapter.

Faced by the fact that intelligent people are so often on the other side, the Socialist is apt to set it down to corrupt motives (conscious or unconscious), or to an ignorant belief that Socialism would not 'work', or to a mere dread of the horrors and discomforts of the revolutionary period before Socialism is established. Undoubtedly all these are important, but there are plenty of people who are influenced by none of them and are nevertheless hostile to Socialism. Their reason for recoiling from Socialism is spiritual, or 'ideological'. They object to it not on the ground that it would not 'work', but precisely because it would 'work' too well. What they are afraid of is not the things that are going to happen in their own lifetime, but the things that are going to happen in the remote future when Socialism is a reality.

I have very seldom met a convinced Socialist who could grasp that thinking people may be repelled by the *objective* towards which Socialism appears to be moving. The Marxist, especially, dismisses this kind of thing as bourgeois sentimentality. Marxists as a rule are not very good at reading the minds of their adversaries; if they were, the situation in Europe might be less desperate than it is at present. Possessing a technique which seems to explain everything, they do not often bother to discover what is going on inside other people's heads. Here, for instance, is an illustration of the kind of thing I mean. Discussing the widely held theory – which in one sense is certainly true – that Fascism is a product of Communism, Mr N. A. Holdaway, one of the ablest Marxist writers we possess, writes as follows:

> 'The hoary legend of Communism leading to Fascism ... The element of truth in it is this: that the appearance of Communist activity warns

> the ruling class that democratic Labour Parties are no longer capable of holding the working class in check, and that capitalist dictatorship must assume another form if it is to survive.'

You see here the defects of the method. Because he has detected the underlying economic cause of Fascism, he tacitly assumes that the spiritual side of it is of no importance. Fascism is written off as a manoeuvre of the 'ruling class', which at bottom it is. But this in itself would only explain why Fascism appeals to capitalists. What about the millions who are not capitalists, who in a material sense have nothing to gain from Fascism and are often aware of it, and who, nevertheless, are Fascists? Obviously their approach has been purely along the ideological line. They could only be stampeded into Fascism because Communism attacked or seemed to attack certain things (patriotism, religion, etc.) which lay deeper than the economic motive; and in *that* sense it is perfectly true that Communism leads to Fascism. It is a pity that Marxists nearly always concentrate on letting economic cats out of ideological bags; it does in one sense reveal the truth, but with this penalty, that most of their propaganda misses its mark. It is the spiritual recoil from Socialism, especially as it manifests itself in sensitive people, that I want to discuss in this chapter. I shall have to analyse it at some length, because it is very widespread, very powerful and, among Socialists, almost completely ignored.

The first thing to notice is that the idea of Socialism is bound up, more or less inextricably, with the idea of machine-production. Socialism is essentially an *urban* creed. It grew up more or less concurrently with industrialism, it has always had its roots in the town proletariat and the town intellectual, and it is doubtful whether it could ever have arisen in any but an industrial society. Granted industrialism, the idea of Socialism presents itself naturally, because private ownership is only tolerable when every individual (or family or other unit) is at least moderately self-supporting; but the effect of industrialism is to make it impossible for anyone to be self-supporting even for a moment. Industrialism, once it rises above a fairly low level, *must* lead to some form of collectivism. Not necessarily to Socialism, of course; conceivably it might lead to the Slave-State of which Fascism is a kind of prophecy. And the converse is also true. Machine-production suggests Socialism, but Socialism as a world-system implies machine-production, because it demands certain things not compatible with a primitive way of life. It demands, for instance, constant intercommunication and exchange of goods between all parts of the earth; it demands some degree of centralized control; it demands an approximately equal standard of life for all human beings and probably a certain uniformity of education. We may take it, therefore, that any world in which Socialism was a reality would be at least as highly mechanized as the United States at this moment, probably much more so. In any case, no Socialist would think of denying this. The Socialist world is always pictured as a completely mechanized, immensely organized world, depending on the machine as the civilizations of antiquity depend on the slave.

So far so good, or so bad. Many, perhaps a majority, of thinking people are not in love with machine-civilization, but everyone who is not a fool knows that it is nonsense to talk at this moment about scrapping the machine. But the unfortunate thing is that Socialism, as usually presented, is bound up with the idea of mechanical progress, not merely as a necessary development but as an end in itself, almost as a kind of religion. This idea is implicit in, for instance, most of the propagandist stuff that is written about the rapid mechanical advance in Soviet Russia (the Dneiper dam, tractors, etc., etc.). Karel Capek hits it off well enough in the horrible ending of *R.U.R.*, when the Robots, having slaughtered the last human being, announce their intention to 'build many houses' (just for the sake of building houses, you see). The kind of person who most readily accepts Socialism is also the kind of person who views mechanical progress, *as such,* with enthusiasm. And this is so much the case that Socialists are often unable to grasp that the opposite opinion exists. As a rule the most persuasive argument they can think of is to tell you that the present mechanization of the world is as nothing to what we shall see when Socialism is established. Where there is one aeroplane now, in those days there will be fifty! All the work that is now done by hand will then be done by machinery: everything that is now made of leather, wood or stone will be made of rubber, glass or steel; there will be no disorder, no loose ends, no wildernesses, no wild animals, no weeds, no disease, no poverty, no pain – and so on and so forth. The Socialist world is to be above all things an *ordered* world, an *efficient* world. But it is precisely from that vision of the future as a sort of glittering Wells-world that sensitive minds recoil. Please notice that this essentially fat-bellied version of 'progress' is not an integral part of Socialist doctrine; but it has come to be thought of as one, with the result that the temperamental conservatism which is latent in all kinds of people is easily mobilized against Socialism.

Every sensitive person has moments when he is suspicious of machinery and to some extent of physical science. But it is important to sort out the various motives, which have differed greatly at different times, for hostility to science and machinery, and to disregard the jealousy of the modern literary gent who hates science because science has stolen literature's thunder. The earliest full-length attack on science and machinery that I am acquainted with is in the third part of *Gulliver's Travels*. But Swift's attack, though brilliant as a *tour de force,* is irrelevant and even silly, because it is written from the standpoint – perhaps this seems a queer thing to say of the author of *Gulliver's Travels* – of a man who lacked imagination. To Swift, science was merely a kind of futile muckraking and the machines were nonsensical contraptions that would never work. His standard was that of practical usefulness, and he lacked the vision to see that an experiment which is not demonstrably useful at the moment may yield results in the future. Elsewhere in the book he names it as the best of all achievements 'to make two blades of grass grow where one grew before'; not seeing, apparently, that this is just what the machine can do. A little later the despised machines began working, physical science increased its scope, and there came the celebrated conflict between religion and science which agitated our grandfathers. That conflict is over and both sides have retreated and claimed a victory, but an anti-scientific bias still lingers in the minds of most religious believers. All through the nineteenth century protesting voices were raised against science and machinery (see Dickens's *Hard Times,* for instance), but usually for the rather shallow reason that industrialism in its first stages was cruel and ugly. Samuel Butler's attack on the machine in the well-known chapter of *Erewhon* is a different matter. But Butler himself lived in a less desperate age than our own, an age in which it was still possible for a first-rate man to be a dilettante part of the time, and therefore the whole thing appeared to him as a kind of intellectual exercise. He saw clearly enough our abject dependence on the machine, but instead of bothering to work out its consequences he preferred to exaggerate it for the sake of what was not much more than a joke. It is only in our own age, when mechanization has finally triumphed, that we can actually *feel* the tendency of the machine to make a fully human life impossible. There is probably no one capable of thinking and feeling who has not occasionally looked at a gas-pipe chair and reflected that the machine is the enemy of life. As a rule, however, this feeling is instinctive rather than reasoned. People know that in some way or another 'progress' is a swindle, but they reach this conclusion by a kind of mental shorthand; my job here is to supply the logical steps that are usually left out. But first one must ask, what is the function of the machine? Obviously its primary function is to save work, and the type of person to whom machine-civilization is entirely acceptable seldom sees any reason for looking further. Here for instance is a person who claims, or rather screams, that he is thoroughly at home in the modern mechanized world. I am quoting from *World Without Faith,* by Mr John Beevers. This is what he says:

> 'It is plain lunacy to say that the average £2 10*s*. to £4 a week man of today is a lower type than an eighteenth-century farm labourer. Or than the labourer or peasant of any exclusively agricultural community now or in the past. It just isn't true. It is so damn silly to cry out about the civilizing effects of work in the fields and farmyards as against that done in a big locomotive works or an automobile factory. Work is a nuisance. We work because we have to and all work is done to provide us with leisure and the means of spending that leisure as enjoyably as possible.'

And again:

> 'Man is going to have time enough and power enough to hunt for his own heaven on earth without worrying about the supernatural one. The earth will be so pleasant a place that the priest and the parson won't be left with much of a tale to tell. Half the stuffing is knocked out of them by one neat blow.' Etc., etc., etc.

There is a whole chapter to this effect (Chapter IV of Mr Beevers's book), and it is of some interest as an exhibition of machine-worship in its most completely vulgar, ignorant and half-baked form. It is the authentic voice of a large section of the modern world. Every aspirin-eater in the outer suburbs would echo it fervently. Notice the shrill wail of anger ('It just isn't troo-o-o!' etc.) with which Mr Beevers meets the suggestion that his grandfather may have been a better man than himself; and the still more horrible suggestion that if we returned to a simpler way of life he might have to toughen his muscles with a job of work. Work, you see, is done 'to provide us with leisure'. Leisure for what? Leisure to become more like Mr Beevers, presumably. Though as a matter of fact, from that line of talk about 'heaven on earth', you can make a fairly good guess at what he would like civilization to be; a sort of Lyons Corner House lasting *in saecula saeculorum* and getting bigger and noisier all the time. And in any book by anyone who feels at home in the machine-world – in any book by H. G. Wells, for instance – you will find passages of the same kind. How often have we not heard it, that glutinously uplifting stuff about 'the machines, our new race of slaves, which will set humanity free', etc., etc., etc. To these people, apparently, the only danger of the machine is its possible use for destructive purposes; as, for instance, aeroplanes are used in war. Barring wars and unforeseen disasters, the future is envisaged as an ever more rapid march of mechanical progress; machines to save work, machines to save thought, machines to save pain, hygiene, efficiency, organization, more hygiene, more efficiency, more organization, more machines – until finally you land up in the by now familiar Wellsian Utopia, aptly caricatured by Huxley in *Brave New World,* the paradise of little fat men. Of course in their day-dreams of the future the little fat men are neither fat nor little; they are Men Like Gods. But why should they be? All mechanical progress is towards greater and greater efficiency; ultimately, therefore, towards a world in which *nothing goes wrong*. But in a world in which nothing went wrong, many of the qualities which Mr Wells regards as 'godlike' would be no more valuable than the animal faculty of moving the ears. The beings in *Men Like Gods* and *The Dream* are represented, for example, as brave, generous and physically strong. But in a world from which physical danger had been banished – and obviously mechanical progress tends to eliminate danger – would physical courage be likely to survive? *Could* it survive? And why should physical strength survive in a world where there was never the need for physical labour? As for such qualities as loyalty, generosity, etc., in a world where nothing went wrong, they would be not only irrelevant but probably unimaginable. The truth is that many of the qualities we admire in human beings can only function in opposition to some kind of disaster, pain or difficulty; but the tendency of mechanical progress is to eliminate disaster, pain and difficulty. In books like *The Dream* and *Men Like Gods* it is assumed that such qualities as strength, courage, generosity, etc., will be kept alive because they are comely qualities and necessary attributes of a full human being. Presumably, for instance, the inhabitants of Utopia would create artificial dangers in order to exercise their courage, and do dumb-bell exercises to harden muscles which they would never be obliged to use. And here you observe the huge contradiction which is usually present in the idea of progress. The tendency of mechanical progress is to make your environment safe and soft; and yet you are striving to keep yourself brave and hard. You are at the same moment furiously pressing forward and desperately holding back. It is as though a London stockbroker should go to his office in a suit of chain mail and insist on talking medieval Latin. So in the last analysis the champion of progress is also the champion of anachronisms.

Meanwhile I am assuming that the tendency of mechanical progress *is* to make life safe and soft. This may be disputed, because at any given moment the effect of some recent mechanical invention may appear to be the opposite. Take for instance the transition from horses to motor vehicles. At a first glance one might say, considering the enormous toll of road deaths, that the motor-car does not exactly tend to make life safer. Moreover it probably needs as much toughness to be a first-rate dirt-track rider as to be a bronco-buster or to ride in the Grand National. Nevertheless the *tendency* of all machinery is to become safer and easier to handle. The danger of accidents would disappear if we chose to tackle our road-planning problem seriously, as we shall do sooner or later; and meanwhile the motor-car has evolved to a point at which anyone who is not blind or paralytic can drive it after a few lessons. Even now it needs far less nerve and skill to drive a car ordinarily well than to ride a horse ordinarily well; in twenty years' time it may need no nerve or skill at all. Therefore, one must say that, taking society as a whole, the result of the transition from horses to cars has been an increase in human softness. Presently somebody comes along with another invention, the aeroplane for instance, which does not at first sight appear to make life safer. The first men who went up in aeroplanes were superlatively brave, and even today it must need an exceptionally good nerve to be a pilot. But the same tendency as before is at work. The aeroplane, like the motor-car, will be made foolproof; a million engineers are working, almost unconsciously, in that direction. Finally – this is the objective, though it may never quite be reached – you will get an aeroplane whose pilot needs no more skill or courage than a baby needs in its perambulator. And all mechanical progress is and must be in this direction. A machine evolves by becoming more efficient, that is, more foolproof; hence the objective of mechanical progress is a foolproof world – which may or may not mean a world inhabited by fools. Mr Wells would probably retort that the world can never become foolproof, because, however high a standard of efficiency you have reached, there is always some greater difficulty ahead. For example (this is Mr Wells's favourite idea – he has used it in goodness knows how many perorations), when you have got this planet of ours perfectly into trim, you start upon the enormous task of reaching and colonizing another. But this is merely to push the objective further into the future; the objective itself remains the same. Colonize another planet, and the game of mechanical progress begins anew; for the foolproof world you have substituted the foolproof solar system – the foolproof universe. In tying yourself to the ideal of mechanical efficiency, you tie yourself to the ideal of softness. But softness is repulsive; and thus all progress is seen to be a frantic struggle towards an objective which you hope and pray will never be reached. Now and again, but not often, you meet somebody who grasps that what is usually called progress also entails what is usually called degeneracy, and who is nevertheless in favour of progress. Hence the fact that in Mr Shaw's Utopia a statue was erected to Falstaff, as the first man who ever made a speech in favour of cowardice.

But the trouble goes immensely deeper than this. Hitherto I have only pointed out the absurdity of aiming at mechanical progress and also at the preservation of qualities which mechanical progress makes unnecessary. The question one has got to consider is whether there is *any* human activity which would not be maimed by the dominance of the machine.

The function of the machine is to save work. In a fully mechanized world all the dull drudgery will be done by machinery, leaving us free for more interesting pursuits. So expressed, this sounds splendid. It makes one sick to see half a dozen men sweating their guts out to dig a trench for a water-pipe, when some easily devised machine would scoop the earth out in a couple of minutes. Why not let the machine do the work and the men go and do something else. But presently the question arises, what else are they to do? Supposedly they are set free from 'work' in order that they may do something which is not 'work'. But what is work and what is not work? Is it work to dig, to carpenter, to plant trees, to fell trees, to ride, to fish, to hunt, to feed chickens, to play the piano, to take photographs, to build a house, to cook, to sew, to trim hats, to mend motor bicycles? All of these things are work to somebody, and all of them are play to somebody. There are in fact very few activities which cannot be classed either as work or play according as you choose to regard them. The labourer set free from digging may want to spend his leisure, or part of it, in playing the piano, while the professional pianist may be only too glad to get out and dig at the potato patch. Hence the antithesis between work, as something intolerably tedious, and not-work, as something desirable, is false. The truth is that when a human being is not eating, drinking, sleeping, making love, talking, playing games or merely lounging about – and these things will not fill up a lifetime – he needs work and usually looks for it, though he may not call it work. Above the level of a third- or fourth-grade moron, life has got to be lived largely in terms of effort. For man is not, as the vulgarer hedonists seem to suppose, a kind of walking stomach; he has also got a hand, an eye and a brain. Cease to use your hands, and you have lopped off a huge chunk of your consciousness. And now consider again those half-dozen men who were digging the trench for the water-pipe. A machine has set them free from digging, and they are going to amuse themselves with something else – carpentering, for instance. But whatever they want to do, they will find that another machine has set them free from *that*. For in a fully mechanized world there would be no more need to carpenter, to cook, to mend motor bicycles, etc., than there would be to dig. There is scarcely anything, from catching a whale to carving a cherry stone, that could not conceivably be done by machinery. The machine would even encroach upon the activities we now class as 'art'; it is doing so already, via the camera and the radio. Mechanize the world as fully as it might be mechanized, and whichever way you turn there will be some machine cutting you off from the chance of working – that is, of living.

At a first glance this might not seem to matter. Why should you not get on with your 'creative work' and disregard the machines that would do it for you? But it is not so simple as it sounds. Here am I, working eight hours a day in an insurance office; in my spare time I want to do something 'creative', so I choose to do a bit of carpentering – to make myself a table, for instance. Notice that from the very start there is a touch of artificiality about the whole business, for the factories can turn me out a far better table than I can make for myself. But even when I get to work on my table, it is not possible for me to feel towards it as the cabinet-maker of a hundred years ago felt towards his table, still less as Robinson Crusoe felt towards his. For before I start, most of the work has already been done for me by machinery. The tools I use demand the minimum of skill. I can get, for instance, planes which will cut out any moulding; the cabinet-maker of a hundred years ago would have had to do the work with chisel and gouge, which demanded real skill of eye and hand. The boards I buy are ready planed and the legs are ready turned by the lathe. I can even go to the wood-shop and buy all the parts of the table ready-made and only needing to be fitted together; my work being reduced to driving in a few pegs and using a piece of sandpaper. And if this is so at present, in the mechanized future it will be enormously more so. With the tools and materials available *then*, there will be no possibility of mistake, hence no room for skill. Making a table will be easier and duller than peeling a potato. In such circumstances it is nonsense to talk of 'creative work'. In any case the arts of the hand (which have got to be transmitted by apprenticeship) would long since have disappeared. Some of them have disappeared already, under the competition of the machine. Look round any country churchyard and see whether you can find a decently-cut tombstone later than 1820. The art, or rather the craft, of stonework has died out so completely that it would take centuries to revive it.

But it may be said, why not retain the machine *and* retain 'creative work'? Why not cultivate anachronisms as a spare-time hobby? Many people have played with this idea; it seems to solve with such beautiful ease the problems set by the machine. The citizen of Utopia, we are told, coming home from his daily two hours of turning a handle in the tomato-canning factory, will deliberately revert to a more primitive way of life and solace his creative instincts with a bit of fretwork, pottery-glazing or handloom-weaving. And why is this picture an absurdity – as it is, of course? Because of a principle that is not always recognized, though always acted upon: that so long as the machine *is there*, one is under an obligation to use it. No one draws water from the well when he can turn on the tap. One sees a good illustration of this in the matter of travel. Everyone who has travelled by primitive methods in an undeveloped country knows that the difference between that kind of travel and modern travel in trains, cars, etc., is the difference between life and death. The nomad who walks or rides, with his baggage stowed on a camel or an ox-cart, may suffer every kind of discomfort, but at least he is living while he is travelling; whereas for the passenger in an express train or a luxury liner his journey is an interregnum, a kind of temporary death. And yet so long as the railways exist, one has got to travel by train – or by car or aeroplane. Here am I, forty miles from London. When I want to go up to London why do I not pack my luggage on to a mule and set out on foot, making a two days' march of it? Because, with the Green Line buses whizzing past me every ten minutes, such a journey would be intolerably irksome. In order that one may enjoy primitive methods of travel, it is necessary that no other method should be available. No human being ever wants to do anything in a more cumbrous way than is necessary. Hence the absurdity of that picture of Utopians saving their souls with fretwork. In a world where everything could be done by machinery, everything would be done by machinery. Deliberately to revert to primitive methods, to use archaic tools, to put silly little difficulties in your own way, would be a piece of dilettantism, of pretty-pretty arty and craftiness. It would be like solemnly sitting down to eat your dinner with stone implements. Revert to handwork in a machine age, and you are back in Ye Olde Tea Shoppe or the Tudor villa with the sham beams tacked to the wall.

The tendency of mechanical progress, then, is to frustrate the human need for effort and creation. It makes unnecessary and even impossible the activities of the eye and the hand. The apostle of 'progress' will sometimes declare that this does not matter, but you can usually drive him into a corner by pointing out the horrible lengths to which the process can be carried. Why, for instance, use your hands at all – why use them even for blowing your nose or sharpening a pencil? Surely you could fix some kind of steel and rubber contraption to your shoulders and let your arms wither into stumps of skin and bone? And so with every organ and every faculty. There is really no reason why a human being should do more than eat, drink, sleep, breathe and procreate; *everything* else could be done for him by machinery. Therefore the logical end of mechanical progress is to reduce the human being to something resembling a brain in a bottle. That is the goal towards which we are already moving, though, of course, we have no intention of getting there; just as a man who drinks a bottle of whisky a day does not actually intend to get cirrhosis of the liver. The implied objective of 'progress' is – not *exactly*, perhaps, the brain in the bottle, but at any rate some frightful subhuman depth of softness and helplessness. And the unfortunate thing is that at present the word 'progress' and the word 'Socialism' are linked inseparably in almost everyone's mind. The kind of person who hates machinery also takes it for granted to hate Socialism; the Socialist is always in favour of mechanization, rationalization, modernization – or at least thinks that he ought to be in favour of them. Quite recently, for instance, a prominent I.L.P.'er confessed to me with a sort of wistful shame – as though it were something faintly improper – that he was 'fond of horses'. Horses, you see, belong to the vanished agricultural past, and all sentiment for the past carries with it a vague smell of heresy. I do not believe that this need necessarily be so, but undoubtedly it is so. And in itself it is quite enough to explain the alienation of decent minds from Socialism.

A generation ago every intelligent person was in some sense a revolutionary; nowadays it would be nearer the mark to say that every intelligent person is a reactionary. In this connection it is worth comparing H. G. Wells's *The Sleeper Awakes* with Aldous Huxley's *Brave New World*, written thirty years later. Each is a pessimistic Utopia, a vision of a sort of prig's paradise in which all the dreams of the 'progressive' person come true. Considered merely as a piece of imaginative construction *The Sleeper Awakes* is, I think, much superior, but it suffers from vast contradictions because of the fact that Wells, as the arch-priest of 'progress', cannot write with any conviction *against* 'progress'. He draws a picture of a glittering, strangely sinister world in which the privileged classes live a life of shallow gutless hedonism, and the workers, reduced to a state of utter slavery and sub-human ignorance, toil like troglodytes in caverns underground. As soon as one examines this idea – it is further developed in a splendid short story in *Stories of Space and Time* – one sees its inconsistency. For in the immensely mechanized world that Wells is imagining, why should the workers have to work harder than at present? Obviously the tendency of the machine is to eliminate work, not to increase it. In the machine-world the workers might be enslaved, ill-treated and even underfed, but they certainly would not be condemned to ceaseless manual toil; because in that case what would be the function of the machine? You can have machines doing all the work or human beings doing all the work, but you can't have both. Those armies of underground workers, with their blue uniforms and their debased, half-human language, are only put in 'to make your flesh creep'. Wells wants to suggest that 'progress' might take a wrong turning; but the only evil he cares to imagine is inequality – one class grabbing all the wealth and power and oppressing the others, apparently out of pure spite. Give it quite a small twist, he seems to suggest, overthrow the privileged class – change over from world-capitalism to Socialism, in fact – and all will be well. The machine-civilization is to continue, but its products are to be shared out equally. The thought he dare not face is that the machine itself may be the enemy. So in his more characteristic Utopias (*The Dream*, *Men Like Gods*, etc.), he returns to optimism and to a vision of humanity, 'liberated' by the machine, as a race of enlightened sunbathers whose sole topic of conversation is their own superiority to their ancestors. *Brave New World* belongs to a later time and to a generation which has seen through the swindle of 'progress'. It contains its own contradictions (the most important of them is pointed out in Mr John Strachey's *The Coming Struggle for Power*), but it is at least a memorable assault on the more fat-bellied type of perfectionism. Allowing for the exaggerations of caricature, it probably expresses what a majority of thinking people feel about machine-civilization.

The sensitive person's hostility to the machine is in one sense unrealistic, because of the obvious fact that the machine has come to stay. But as an attitude of mind there is a great deal to be said for it. The machine has got to be accepted, but it is probably better to accept it rather as one accepts a drug – that is, grudgingly and suspiciously. Like a drug, the machine is useful, dangerous and habit forming. The oftener one surrenders to it the tighter its grip becomes. You have only to look about you at this moment to realize with what sinister speed the machine is getting us into its power. To begin with, there is the frightful debauchery of taste that has already been effected by a century of mechanization. This is almost too obvious and too generally admitted to need pointing out. But as a single instance, take taste in its narrowest sense – the taste for decent food. In the highly mechanized countries, thanks to tinned food, cold storage, synthetic flavouring matters, etc., the palate is almost a dead organ. As you can see by looking at any greengrocer's shop, what the majority of English people mean by an apple is a lump of highly-coloured cotton wool from America or Australia; they will devour these things, apparently with pleasure, and let the English apples rot under the trees. It is the shiny, standardized, machine-made look of the American apple that appeals to them; the superior taste of the English apple is something they simply do not notice. Or look at the factory-made, foil-wrapped cheese and 'blended' butter in any grocer's; look at the hideous rows of tins which usurp more and more of the space in any food-shop, even a dairy; look at a sixpenny Swiss roll or a twopenny ice-cream; look at the filthy chemical by-product that people will pour down their throats under the name of beer. Wherever you look you will see some slick machine-made article triumphing over the old-fashioned article that still tastes of something other than sawdust. And what applies to food applies also to furniture, houses, clothes, books, amusements and everything else that makes up our environment. There are now millions of people, and they are increasing every year, to whom the blaring of a radio is not only a more acceptable but a more *normal* background to their thoughts than the lowing of cattle or the song of birds. The mechanization of the world could never proceed very far while taste, even the taste-buds of the tongue, remained uncorrupted, because in that case most of the products of the machine would be simply unwanted. In a healthy world there would be no demand for tinned food, aspirins, gramophones, gaspipe chairs, machine guns, daily newspapers, telephones, motor-cars, etc., etc.; and on the other hand there would be a constant demand for the things the machine cannot produce. But meanwhile the machine is here, and its corrupting effects are almost irresistible. One inveighs against it, but one goes on using it. Even a bare-arse savage, given the chance, will learn the vices of civilization within a few months. Mechanization leads to the decay of taste, the decay of taste leads to the demand for machine-made articles and hence to more mechanization, and so a vicious circle is established.

But in addition to this there is a tendency for the mechanization of the world to proceed as it were automatically, whether we want it or not. This is due to the fact that in modern Western man the faculty of mechanical invention has been fed and stimulated till it has reached almost the status of an instinct. People invent new machines and improve existing ones almost unconsciously, rather as a somnambulist will go on working in his sleep. In the past, when it was taken for granted that life on this planet is harsh or at any rate laborious, it seemed the natural fate to go on using the clumsy implements of your forefathers, and only a few eccentric persons, centuries apart, proposed innovations; hence throughout enormous ages such things as the ox-cart, the plough, the sickle, etc., remained radically unchanged. It is on record that screws have been in use since remote antiquity and yet that it was not till the middle of the nineteenth century that anyone thought of making screws with points on them; for several thousand years they remained flat-ended and holes had to be drilled for them before they could be inserted. In our own epoch such a thing would be unthinkable. For almost every modern Western man has his inventive faculty to some extent developed; the Western man invents machines as naturally as the Polynesian islander swims. Give a Western man a job of work and he immediately begins devising a machine that would do it for him; give him a machine and he thinks of ways of improving it. I understand this tendency well enough, for in an ineffectual sort of way I have that type of mind myself. I have not either the patience or the mechanical skill to devise any machine that would work, but I am perpetually seeing, as it were, the ghosts of possible machines that might save me the trouble of using my brain or muscles. A person with a more definite mechanical turn would probably construct some of them and put them into operation. But under our present economic system, whether he constructed them – or rather, whether anyone else had the benefit of them – would depend upon whether they were commercially valuable. The Socialists are right, therefore, when they claim that the rate of mechanical progress will be much more rapid once Socialism is established. Given a mechanical civilization the process of invention and improvement will always continue, but the tendency of capitalism is to slow it down, because under capitalism any invention which does not promise fairly immediate profits is neglected; some, indeed, which threaten to reduce profits are suppressed almost as ruthlessly as the flexible glass mentioned by Petronius.[1] Establish Socialism – remove the profit principle – and the inventor will have a free hand. The mechanization of the world, already rapid enough, would be or at any rate could be enormously accelerated.

And this prospect is a slightly sinister one, because it is obvious even now that the process of mechanization is out of control. It is happening merely because humanity has got the habit. A chemist perfects a new method of synthesizing rubber, or a mechanic devises a new pattern of gudgeon-pin. Why? Not for any clearly understood purpose, but simply from the impulse to invent and improve, which has now become instinctive. Put a pacifist to work in a bomb-factory and in two months he will be devising a new type of bomb. Hence the appearance of such diabolical things as poison gases, which are not expected even by their inventors to be beneficial to humanity. Our attitude towards such things as poison gases *ought* to be the attitude of the king of Brobdingnag towards gunpowder; but because we live in a mechanical and scientific age we are infected with the notion that, whatever else happens, 'progress' must continue and knowledge must never be suppressed. Verbally, no doubt, we would agree that machinery is made for man and not man for machinery; in practice any attempt to check the development of the machine appears to us as an attack on knowledge and therefore a kind of blasphemy. And even if the whole of humanity suddenly revolted against the machine and decided to escape to a simpler way of life, the escape would still be immensely difficult. It would not do, as in Butler's *Erewhon,* to smash every machine invented after a certain date; we should also have to smash the habit of mind that would, almost involuntarily, devise fresh machines as soon as the old ones were smashed. And in all of us there is at least a tinge of that habit of mind. In every country in the world the large army of scientists and technicians, with the rest of us panting at their heels, are marching along the road of 'progress' with the blind persistence

[1] For example: Some years ago someone invented a gramophone needle that would last for decades. One of the big gramophone companies bought up the patent rights, and that was the last that was ever heard of it.

of a column of ants. Comparatively few people want it to happen, plenty of people actively want it *not* to happen, and yet it is happening. The process of mechanization has itself become a machine, a huge glittering vehicle whirling us we are not certain where, but probably towards the padded Wells-world and the brain in the bottle.

This, then, is the case against the machine. Whether it is a sound or unsound case hardly matters. The point is that these or very similar arguments would be echoed by every person who is hostile to machine-civilization. And unfortunately, because of that nexus of thought, 'Socialism - progress - machinery - Russia - tractor - hygiene - machinery - progress', which exists in almost everyone's mind, it is usually the *same* person who is hostile to Socialism. The kind of person who hates central heating and gaspipe chairs is also the kind of person who, when you mention Socialism, murmurs something about 'beehive state' and moves away with a pained expression. So far as my observation goes, very few Socialists grasp why this is so, or even that it *is* so. Get the more vocal type of Socialist into a corner, repeat to him the substance of what I have said in this chapter, and see what kind of answer you get. As a matter of fact you will get several answers; I am so familiar with them that I know them almost by heart.

In the first place he will tell you that it is impossible to 'go back' (or to 'put back the hand of progress' – as though the hand of progress hadn't been pretty violently put back several times in human history!), and will then accuse you of being a medievalist and begin to descant upon the horrors of the Middle Ages, leprosy, the Inquisition, etc. As a matter of fact, most attacks upon the Middle Ages and the past generally by apologists of modernity are beside the point, because their essential trick is to project a modern man, with his squeamishness and his high standards of comfort, into an age when such things were unheard of. But notice that in any case this is not an answer. For a dislike of the mechanized future does not imply the smallest reverence for any period of the past. D. H. Lawrence, wiser than the medievalist, chose to idealize the Etruscans about whom we know conveniently little. But there is no need to idealize even the Etruscans or the Pelasgians, or the Aztecs, or the Sumerians, or any other vanished and romantic people. When one pictures a desirable civilization, one pictures it merely as an objective; there is no need to pretend that it has ever existed in space and time. Press this point home, explain that you wish merely to aim at making life simpler and harder instead of softer and more complex, and the Socialist will usually assume that you want to revert to a 'state of nature' – meaning some stinking palaeolithic cave: as though there were nothing between a flint scraper and the steel mills of Sheffield, or between a skin coracle and the *Queen Mary*!

Finally, however, you will get an answer which is rather more to the point and which runs roughly as follows: 'Yes, what you are saying is all very well in its way. No doubt it would be very noble to harden ourselves and do without aspirins and central heating and so forth. But the point is, you see, that nobody seriously wants it. It would mean going back to an agricultural way of life, which means beastly hard work and isn't at all the same thing as playing at gardening. I don't want hard work, you don't want hard work – nobody wants it who knows what it means. You only talk as you do because you've never done a day's work in your life,' etc., etc.

Now this in a sense is true. It amounts to saying, 'We're soft – for God's sake let's stay soft!' which at least is realistic. As I have pointed out already, the machine has got us in its grip and to escape will be immensely difficult. Nevertheless this answer is really an evasion, because it fails to make clear what we mean when we say that we 'want' this or that. I am a degenerate modern semi-intellectual who would die if I did not get my early morning cup of tea and my *New Statesman* every Friday. Clearly I do not, in a sense, 'want' to return to a simpler, harder, probably agricultural way of life. In the same sense I don't 'want' to cut down my drinking, to pay my debts, to take enough exercise, to be faithful to my wife, etc., etc. But in another and more permanent sense I do want these things, and perhaps in the same sense I want a civilization in which 'progress' is not definable as making the world safe for little fat men. These that I have outlined are practically the only arguments that I have been able to get from Socialists – thinking, book-trained Socialists – when I have tried to explain to them just *how* they are driving away possible adherents. Of course there is also the old argument that Socialism is going to arrive anyway, whether people like it or not, because of that trouble-saving thing, 'historic necessity'. But 'historic necessity', or rather the belief in it, has failed to survive Hitler.

Meanwhile the thinking person, by intellect usually left-wing but by temperament often right-wing, hovers at the gate of the Socialist fold. He is no doubt aware that he *ought* to be a Socialist. But he observes first the dullness of individual Socialists, then the apparent flabbiness of Socialist ideals, and veers away. Till quite recently it was natural to veer towards indifferentism. Ten years ago, even five years ago, the typical literary gent wrote books on baroque architecture and had a soul above politics. But that attitude is becoming difficult and even unfashionable. The times are growing harsher, the issues are clearer, the belief that nothing will ever change (i.e. that your dividends will always be safe) is less prevalent. The fence on which the literary gent sits, once as comfortable as the plush cushion of a cathedral stall, is now pinching his bottom intolerably; more and more he shows a disposition to drop off on one side or the other. It is interesting to notice how many of our leading writers, who a dozen years ago were art for art's saking for all they were worth and would have considered it too vulgar for words even to vote at a general election, are now taking a definite political standpoint; while most of the younger writers, at least those of them who are not mere footlers, have been 'political' from the start. I believe that when the pinch comes there is a terrible danger that the main movement of the intelligentsia will be towards Fascism. Just how soon the pinch will come it is difficult to say; it depends, probably, upon events in Europe; but it may be that within two years or even a year we shall have reached the decisive moment. That will also be the moment when every person with any brains or any decency will know in his bones that he ought to be on the Socialist side. But he will not necessarily come there of his own accord; there are too many ancient prejudices standing in the way. He will have to be persuaded, and by methods that imply an understanding of his viewpoint. Socialists cannot afford to waste any more time in preaching to the converted. Their job now is to make Socialists as rapidly as possible; instead of which, all too often, they are making Fascists.

When I speak of Fascism in England, I am not necessarily thinking of Mosley and his pimpled followers. English Fascism, when it arrives, is likely to be of a sedate and subtle kind (presumably, at any rate at first, it won't be *called* Fascism), and it is doubtful whether a Gilbert and Sullivan heavy dragoon of Mosley's stamp would ever be much more than a joke to the majority of

English people; though even Mosley will bear watching, for experience shows (*vide* the careers of Hitler, Napoleon III) that to a political climber it is sometimes an advantage not to be taken too seriously at the beginning of his career. But what I am thinking of at this moment is the Fascist attitude of mind, which beyond any doubt is gaining ground among people who ought to know better. Fascism as it appears in the intellectual is a sort of mirror-image – not actually of Socialism but of a plausible travesty of Socialism. It boils down to a determination to do the *opposite* of whatever the mythical Socialist does. If you present Socialism in a bad and misleading light – if you let people imagine that it does not mean much more than pouring European civilization down the sink at the command of Marxist prigs – you risk driving the intellectual into Fascism. You frighten him into a sort of angry defensive attitude in which he simply refuses to listen to the Socialist case. Some such attitude is already quite clearly discernible in writers like Pound, Wyndham Lewis, Roy Campbell, etc., in most of the Roman Catholic writers and many of the Douglas Credit group, in certain popular novelists and even, if one looks below the surface, in so-superior conservative highbrows like Eliot and his countless followers. If you want some unmistakable illustrations of the growth of Fascist feeling in England, have a look at some of the innumerable letters that were written to the Press during the Abyssinian war, approving the Italian action, and also the howl of glee that went up from both Catholic and Anglican pulpits (see the *Daily Mail* of 17 August 1936) over the Fascist rising in Spain.

In order to combat Fascism it is necessary to understand it, which involves admitting that it contains some good as well as much evil. In practice, of course, it is merely an infamous tyranny, and its methods of attaining and holding power are such that even its most ardent apologists prefer to talk about something else. But the underlying feeling of Fascism, the feeling that first draws people into the Fascist camp, may be less contemptible. It is not *always*, as the *Saturday Review* would lead one to suppose, a squealing terror of the Bolshevik bogey-man. Everyone who has given the movement so much as a glance knows that the rank-and-file Fascist is often quite a well-meaning person – quite genuinely anxious, for instance, to better the lot of the unemployed. But more important than this is the fact that Fascism draws its strength from the good as well as the bad varieties of conservatism. To anyone with a feeling for tradition and for discipline it comes with its appeal ready-made. Probably it is very easy, when you have had a bellyful of the more tactless kind of Socialist propaganda, to see Fascism as the last line defence of all that is good in European civilization. Even the Fascist bully at his symbolic worst, with rubber truncheon in one hand and castor oil bottle in the other, does not necessarily feel himself a bully; more probably he feels like Roland in the pass at Roncevaux, defending Christendom against the barbarian. We have got to admit that if Fascism is everywhere advancing, this is largely the fault of Socialists themselves. Partly it is due to the mistaken Communist tactic of sabotaging democracy, i.e. sawing off the branch you are sitting on; but still more to the fact that Socialists have, so to speak, presented their case wrong side foremost. They have never made it sufficiently clear that the essential aims of Socialism are justice and liberty. With their eyes glued to economic facts, they have proceeded on the assumption that man has no soul, and explicitly or implicitly they have set up the goal of a materialistic Utopia. As a result Fascism has been able to play upon every instinct that revolts against hedonism and a cheap conception of 'progress'. It has been able to pose as the upholder of the European tradition, and to appeal to Christian belief, to patriotism and to the military virtues. It is far worse than useless to write Fascism off as 'mass sadism', or some easy phrase of that kind. If you pretend that it is merely an aberration which will presently pass off of its own accord, you are dreaming a dream from which you will awake when somebody coshes you with a rubber truncheon. The only possible ccurse is to examine the Fascist case, grasp that there is something to be said for it, and then make it clear to the world that whatever good Fascism contains is also implicit in Socialism.

At present the situation is desperate. Even if nothing worse befalls us, there are the conditions which I described in the earlier part of this book and which are not going to improve under our present economic system. Still more urgent is the danger of Fascist domination in Europe. And unless Socialist doctrine, in an effective form, can be diffused widely and very quickly, there is no certainty that Fascism will ever be overthrown. For Socialism is the only real enemy that Fascism has to face. The capitalist-imperialist governments, even though they themselves are about to be plundered, will not fight with any conviction against Fascism as such. Our rulers, those of them who understand the issue, would probably prefer to hand over every square inch of the British Empire to Italy, Germany and Japan than to see Socialism triumphant. It was easy to laugh at Fascism when we imagined that it was based on hysterical nationalism, because it seemed obvious that the Fascist states, each regarding itself as the chosen people and patriotic *contra mundum*, would clash with one another. But nothing of the kind is happening. Fascism is now an international movement, which means not only that the Fascist nations can combine for purposes of loot, but that they are groping, perhaps only half consciously as yet, towards a world-system. For the vision of the totalitarian state there is being substituted the vision of the totalitarian world. As I pointed out earlier, the advance of machine-technique must lead ultimately to some form of collectivism, but that form need not necessarily be equalitarian; that is, it need not be Socialism. *Pace* the economists, it is quite easy to imagine a world-society, economically collectivist – that is, with the profit principle eliminated – but with all political, military and educational power in the hands of a small caste of rulers and their bravos. That or something like it is the objective of Fascism. And that, of course, is the slave-state, or rather the slave-world; it would probably be a stable form of society, and the chances are, considering the enormous wealth of the world if scientifically exploited, that the slaves would be well-fed and contented. It is usual to speak of the Fascist objective as the 'beehive state', which does a grave injustice to bees. A world of rabbits ruled by stoats would be nearer the mark. It is against this beastly possibility that we have got to combine.

The only thing *for* which we can combine is the underlying ideal of Socialism; justice and liberty. But it is hardly strong enough to call this ideal 'underlying'. It is almost completely forgotten. It has been buried beneath layer after layer of doctrinaire priggishness, party squabbles and half-baked 'progressivism' until it is like a diamond hidden under a mountain of dung. The job of the Socialist is to get it out again. Justice and liberty! *Those* are the words that have got to ring like a bugle across the world. For a long time past, certainly for the last ten years, the devil has had all the best tunes. We have reached a stage when the very word 'Socialism' calls up, on the one hand, a picture of aeroplanes, tractors and huge glittering factories of glass and concrete; on the other, a picture of vegetarians with wilting beards, of

Bolshevik commissars (half gangster, half gramophone), of earnest ladies in sandals, shock-headed Marxists chewing polysyllables, escaped Quakers, birth-control fanatics and Labour Party backstairs-crawlers. Socialism, at least in this island, does not smell any longer of revolution and the overthrow of tyrants; it smells of crankishness, machine-worship and the stupid cult of Russia. Unless you can remove that smell, and very rapidly, Fascism may win.

Chapter Thirteen

And finally, is there anything one can do about it?

In the first part of this book I illustrated, by a few brief sidelights, the kind of mess we are in; in this second part I have been trying to explain why, in my opinion, so many normal decent people are repelled by the only remedy, namely by Socialism. Obviously the most urgent need of the next few years is to capture those normal decent ones before Fascism plays its trump card. I do not want to raise here the question of parties and political expedients. More important than any party label (though doubtless the mere menace of Fascism will presently bring some kind of Popular Front into existence) is the diffusion of Socialist doctrine in an effective form. People have got to be made ready to *act* as Socialists. There are, I believe, countless people who, without being aware of it, are in sympathy with the essential aims of Socialism, and who could be won over almost without a struggle if only one could find the word that would move them. Everyone who knows the meaning of poverty, everyone who has a genuine hatred of tyranny and war, is on the Socialist side, potentially. My job here, therefore, is to suggest – necessarily in very general terms – how a reconciliation might be effected between Socialism and its more intelligent enemies.

First, as to the enemies themselves – I mean all those people who grasp that capitalism is evil but who are conscious of a sort of queasy, shuddering sensation when Socialism is mentioned. As I have pointed out, this is traceable to two main causes. One is the personal inferiority of many individual Socialists; the other is the fact that Socialism is too often coupled with a fat-bellied, godless conception of 'progress' which revolts anyone with a feeling for tradition or the rudiments of an aesthetic sense. Let me take the second point first.

The distaste for 'progress' and machine-civilization which is so common among sensitive people is only defensible as an attitude of mind. It is not valid as a reason for rejecting Socialism, because it presupposes an alternative which does not exist. When you say, 'I object to mechanization and standardization – therefore I object to Socialism', you are saying in effect, 'I am free to do without the machine if I choose', which is nonsense. We are all dependent upon the machine, and if the machines stopped working most of us would die. You may hate the machine-civilization, probably you are right to hate it, but for the present there can be no question of accepting or rejecting it. The machine-civilization *is here*, and it can only be criticized from the inside, because all of us are inside it. It is only romantic fools who flatter themselves that they have escaped, like the literary gent in his Tudor cottage with bathroom h. and c., and the he-man who goes off to live a 'primitive' life in the jungle with a Mannlicher rifle and four wagon-loads of tinned food. And almost certainly the machine-civilization will continue to triumph. There is no reason to think that it will destroy itself or stop functioning of its own accord. For some time past it has been fashionable to say that war is presently going to 'wreck civilization' altogether; but, though the next full-sized war will certainly be horrible enough to make all previous ones seem a joke, it is immensely unlikely that it will put a stop to mechanical progress. It is true that a very vulnerable country like England, and perhaps the whole of western Europe, could be reduced to chaos by a few thousand well-placed bombs, but no war is at present thinkable which could wipe out industrialism in all countries simultaneously. We may take it that the return to a simpler, freer, less mechanized way of life, however desirable it may be, is not going to happen. This is not fatalism, it is merely acceptance of facts. It is meaningless to oppose Socialism on the ground that you object to the beehive state, for the beehive state *is here*. The choice is not, as yet, between a human and an inhuman world. It is simply between Socialism and Fascism, which at its very best is Socialism with the virtues left out.

The job of the thinking person, therefore, is not to reject Socialism but to make up his mind to humanize it. Once Socialism is in a way to being established, those who can see through the swindle of 'progress' will probably find themselves resisting. In fact, it is their special function to do so. In the machine-world they have got to be a sort of permanent opposition, which is not the same thing as being an obstructionist or a traitor. But in this I am speaking of the future. For the moment the only possible course for any decent person, however much of a Tory or an anarchist by temperament, is to work for the establishment of Socialism. Nothing else can save us from the misery of the present or the nightmare of the future. To oppose Socialism *now*, when twenty million Englishmen are underfed and Fascism has conquered half Europe, is suicidal. It is like starting a civil war when the Goths are crossing the frontier.

Therefore it is all the more important to get rid of that mere nervous prejudice against Socialism which is not founded on any serious objection. As I have pointed out already, many people who are not repelled by Socialism are repelled by Socialists. Socialism, as now presented, is unattractive largely because it appears, at any rate from the outside, to be the plaything of cranks, doctrinaires, parlour Bolsheviks and so forth. But it is worth remembering that this is only so because the cranks, doctrinaires, etc., have been allowed to get there first; if the movement were invaded by better brains and more common decency, the objectionable types would cease to dominate it. For the present one must just set one's teeth and ignore them; they will loom much smaller when the movement has been humanized. Besides, they are irrelevant. We have got to fight for justice and liberty, and Socialism does mean justice and liberty when the nonsense is stripped off it. It is only the essentials that are worth remembering. To recoil from Socialism because so many individual Socialists are inferior people is as absurd as refusing to travel by train because you dislike the ticket-collector's face.

And secondly, as to the Socialist himself – more especially the vocal, tract-writing type of Socialist.

We are at a moment when it is desperately necessary for left-wingers of all complexions to drop their differences and hang together. Indeed this is already happening to a small extent. Obviously, then, the more intransigent kind of

Socialist has now got to ally himself with people who are not in perfect agreement with him. As a rule he is rightly unwilling to do so, because he sees the very real danger of watering the whole Socialist movement down to some kind of pale-pink humbug even more ineffectual than the parliamentary Labour Party. At the moment, for instance, there is great danger that the Popular Front which Fascism will presumably bring into existence will not be genuinely Socialist in character, but will simply be a manoeuvre against German and Italian (not English) Fascism. Thus the need to unite against Fascism might draw the Socialist into alliance with his very worst enemies. But the principle to go upon is this: that you are never in danger of allying yourself with the wrong people provided that you keep the essentials of your movement in the foreground. And what are the essentials of Socialism? What is the mark of a real Socialist? I suggest that the real Socialist is one who wishes – not merely conceives it as desirable, but actively wishes – to see tyranny overthrown. But I fancy that the majority of orthodox Marxists would not accept that definition, or would only accept it very grudgingly. Sometimes, when I listen to these people talking, and still more when I read their books, I get the impression that, to them, the whole Socialist movement is no more than a kind of exciting heresy-hunt – a leaping to and fro of frenzied witch-doctors to the beat of tom-toms and the tune of 'Fee fi, fo, fum, I smell the blood of a right-wing deviationist!' It is because of this kind of thing that it is so much easier to feel yourself a Socialist when you are among working-class people. The working-class Socialist, like the working-class Catholic, is weak on doctrine and can hardly open his mouth without uttering a heresy, but he has the heart of the matter in him. He does grasp the central fact that Socialism means the overthrow of tyranny, and the 'Marseillaise', if it were translated for his benefit, would appeal to him more deeply than any learned treatise on dialectical materialism. At this moment it is waste of time to insist that acceptance of Socialism means acceptance of the philosophic side of Marxism, plus adulation of Russia. The Socialist movement has not time to be a league of dialectical materialists; it has got to be a league of the oppressed against the oppressors. You have got to attract the man who means business, and you have got to drive away the mealy-mouthed Liberal who wants foreign Fascism destroyed in order that he may go on drawing his dividends peacefully – the type of humbug who passes resolutions 'against Fascism and Communism', i.e. against rats and rat-poison. Socialism means the overthrow of tyranny, at home as well as abroad. So long as you keep *that* fact well to the front, you will never be in much doubt as to who are your real supporters. As for minor differences – and the profoundest philosophical difference is unimportant compared with saving the twenty million Englishmen whose bones are rotting from malnutrition – the time to argue about them is afterwards.

I do not think the Socialist need make any sacrifice of essentials, but certainly he will have to make a great sacrifice of externals. It would help enormously, for instance, if the smell of crankishness which still clings to the Socialist movement could be dispelled. If only the sandals and the pistachio-coloured shirts could be put in a pile and burnt, and every vegetarian, teetotaller and creeping Jesus sent home to Welwyn Garden City to do his yoga exercises quietly! But that, I am afraid, is not going to happen. What *is* possible, however, is for the more intelligent kind of Socialist to stop alienating possible supporters in silly and quite irrelevant ways. There are so many minor priggishnesses which could so easily be dropped. Take for instance the dreary attitude of the typical Marxist towards literature. Out of the many that come into my mind, I will give just one example. It sounds trivial, but it isn't. In the old *Worker's Weekly* (one of the forerunners of the *Daily Worker*) there used to be a column of literary chat of the 'Books on the Editor's Table' type. For several weeks running there had been a certain amount of talk about Shakespeare; whereupon an incensed reader wrote to say, 'Dear Comrade, we don't want to hear about these bourgeois writers like Shakespeare. Can't you give us something a bit more proletarian?' etc., etc. The editor's reply was simple. 'If you will turn to the index of Marx's *Capital,*' he wrote, 'you will find that Shakespeare is mentioned several times.' And please notice that this was enough to silence the objector. Once Shakespeare had received the benediction of Marx, he became respectable. *That* is the mentality that drives ordinary sensible people away from the Socialist movement. You do not need to care about Shakespeare to be repelled by that kind of thing. Again, there is the horrible jargon that nearly all Socialists think it necessary to employ. When the ordinary person hears phrases like 'bourgeois ideology' and 'proletarian solidarity' and 'expropriation of the expropriators', he is not inspired by them, he is merely disgusted. Even the single word 'Comrade' has done its dirty little bit towards discrediting the Socialist movement. How many a waverer has halted on the brink, gone perhaps to some public meeting and watched self-conscious Socialists dutifully addressing one another as 'Comrade', and then slid away, disillusioned, into the nearest four-ale bar! And his instinct is sound; for where is the sense of sticking on to yourself a ridiculous label which even after long practice can hardly be mentioned without a gulp of shame? It is fatal to let the ordinary enquirer get away with the idea that being a Socialist means wearing sandals and burbling about dialectical materialism. You have got to make it clear that there is room in the Socialist movement for human beings, or the game is up.

And this raises a great difficulty. It means that the issue of class, as distinct from mere economic status, has got to be faced more realistically than it is being faced at present.

I devoted three chapters to discussing the class-difficulty. The principal fact that will have emerged, I think, is that though the English class-system has outlived its usefulness, it *has* outlived it and shows no signs of dying. It greatly confuses the issue to assume, as the orthodox Marxist so often does (see for instance Mr Alec Brown's in some ways interesting book, *The Fate of the Middle Classes*), that social status is determined solely by income. Economically, no doubt, there are only two classes, the rich and the poor, but socially there is a whole hierarchy of classes, and the manners and traditions learned by each class in childhood are not only very different but – this is the essential point – generally persist from birth to death. Hence the anomalous individuals that you find in every class of society. You find writers like Wells and Bennett who have grown immensely rich and have yet preserved intact their lower-middle-class Nonconformist prejudices; you find millionaires who cannot pronounce their aitches; you find petty shopkeepers whose income is far lower than that of the bricklayer and who, nevertheless, consider themselves (and are considered) the bricklayer's social superiors; you find board-school boys ruling Indian provinces and public-school men touting vacuum cleaners. If social stratification corresponded precisely to economic stratification, the public-school man would assume a cockney accent the day his income dropped below £200 a year. But does he? On the contrary, he immediately becomes twenty times more Public School than before. He clings to the Old School Tie as to a life-line. And even the aitchless millionaire, though sometimes he goes to an elocutionist and learns a B.B.C. accent, seldom succeeds in disguising himself as completely as he would like to. It is in fact very difficult to escape, culturally, from the class into which you have been born.

As prosperity declines, social anomalies grow commoner. You don't get more aitchless millionaires, but you do get more and more public-school men touting vacuum cleaners and more and more small shopkeepers driven into the workhouse. Large sections of the middle class are being gradually proletarianized; but the important point is that they do not, at any rate in the first generation, adopt a proletarian outlook. Here am I, for instance, with a bourgeois upbringing and a working-class income. Which class do I belong to? Economically I belong to the working class, but it is almost impossible for me to think of myself as anything but a member of the bourgeoisie. And supposing I had to take sides, whom should I side with, the upper class which is trying to squeeze me out of existence, or the working class whose manners are not my manners? It is probable that I personally, in any important issue, would side with the working class. But what about the tens or hundreds of thousands of others who are in approximately the same position? And what about that far larger class, running into millions this time – the office-workers and black-coated employees of all kinds – whose traditions are less definitely middle class but who would certainly not thank you if you called them proletarians? All of these people have the same interests and the same enemies as the working class. All are being robbed and bullied by the same system. Yet how many of them realize it? When the pinch came nearly all of them would side with their oppressors and against those who ought to be their allies. It is quite easy to imagine a middle class crushed down to the worst depths of poverty and still remaining bitterly anti-working-class in sentiment; this being, of course, a ready-made Fascist Party.

Obviously the Socialist movement has got to capture the exploited middle class before it is too late; above all it must capture the office-workers, who are so numerous and, if they knew how to combine, so powerful. Equally obviously it has so far failed to do so. The very last person in whom you can hope to find revolutionary opinions is a clerk or a commercial traveller. Why? Very largely, I think, because of the 'proletarian' cant with which Socialist propaganda is mixed up. In order to symbolize the class war, there has been set up the more or less mythical figure of a 'proletarian', a muscular but downtrodden man in greasy overalls, in contradistinction to a 'capitalist', a fat, wicked man in a top hat and fur coat. It is tacitly assumed that there is no one in between; the truth being, of course, that in a country like England about a quarter of the population is in between. If you are going to harp on the 'dictatorship of the proletariat', it is an elementary precaution to start by explaining who the proletariat *are*. But because of the Socialist tendency to idealize the manual worker as such, this has never been made sufficiently clear. How many of the wretched shivering army of clerks and shopwalkers, who in some ways are actually worse off than a miner or a dock-hand, think of themselves as proletarians? A proletarian – so they have been taught to think – means a man without a collar. So that when you try to move them by talking about 'class war', you only succeed in scaring them; they forget their incomes and remember their accents, and fly to the defence of the class that is exploiting them.

Socialists have a big job ahead of them here. They have got to demonstrate, beyond possibility of doubt, just where the line of cleavage between exploiter and exploited comes. Once again it is a question of sticking to essentials; and the essential point here is that all people with small, insecure incomes are in the same boat and ought to be fighting on the same side. Probably we could do with a little less talk about 'capitalist' and 'proletarian' and a little more about the robbers and the robbed. But at any rate we must drop that misleading habit of pretending that the only proletarians are manual labourers. It has got to be brought home to the clerk, the engineer, the commercial traveller, the middle-class man who has 'come down in the world', the village grocer, the lower-grade civil servant and all other doubtful cases that they *are* the proletariat, and that Socialism means a fair deal for them as well as for the navvy and the factory-hand. They must not be allowed to think that the battle is between those who pronounce their aitches and those who don't; for if they think that, they will join in on the side of the aitches.

I am implying that different classes must be persuaded to act together without, for the moment, being asked to drop their class-differences. And that sounds dangerous. It sounds rather too like the Duke of York's summer camp and that dismal line of talk about class-co-operation and putting our shoulders to the wheel, which is eyewash or Fascism, or both. There can be no co-operation between classes whose real interests are opposed. The capitalist cannot co-operate with the proletarian. The cat cannot co-operate with the mouse; and if the cat does suggest co-operation and the mouse is fool enough to agree, in a very little while the mouse will be disappearing down the cat's throat. But it is always possible to co-operate so long as it is upon a basis of common interests. The people who have got to act together are all those who cringe to the boss and all those who shudder when they think of the rent. This means that the small-holder has got to ally himself with the factory-hand, the typist with the coal-miner, the schoolmaster with the garage mechanic. There is some hope of getting them to do so if they can be made to understand where their interest lies. But this will not happen if their social prejudices, which in some of them are at least as strong as any economic consideration, are needlessly irritated. There is, after all, a real difference of manners and traditions between a bank clerk and a dock labourer, and the bank clerk's feeling of superiority is very deeply rooted. Later on he will have to get rid of it, but this is not a good moment for asking him to do so. Therefore it would be a very great advantage if that rather meaningless and mechanical bourgeois-baiting, which is a part of nearly all Socialist propaganda, could be dropped for the time being. Throughout left-wing thought and writing – and the whole way through it, from the leading articles in the *Daily Worker* to the comic columns in the *News Chronicle* – there runs an anti-genteel tradition, a persistent and often very stupid gibing at genteel mannerisms and genteel loyalties (or, in Communist jargon, 'bourgeois values'). It is largely humbug, coming as it does from bourgeois-baiters who are bourgeois themselves, but it does great harm, because it allows a minor issue to block a major one. It directs attention away from the central fact that poverty is poverty, whether the tool you work with is a pick-axe or a fountain pen.

Once again, here am I, with my middle-class origins and my income of about three pounds a week from all sources. For what I am worth it would be better to get me in on the Socialist side than to turn me into a Fascist. But if you are constantly bullying me about my 'bourgeois ideology', if you give me to understand that in some subtle way I am an inferior person because I have never worked with my hands, you will only succeed in antagonizing me. For you are telling me either that I am inherently useless or that I ought to alter myself in some way that is beyond my power. I cannot proletarianize my accent or certain of my tastes and beliefs, and I would not if I could. Why should I? I don't ask anybody else to speak my dialect; why should anybody else ask me to speak his? It would be far better to take these miserable class-stigmata for granted and emphasize them as little as possible. They are comparable to a race-difference, and experience shows that one *can* co-operate with foreigners, even with foreigners whom one dislikes, when it is really necessary. Economically, I am in the same boat with the miner, the navvy and the farm-hand; remind me of that and I will fight at their side. But culturally I am different from the miner, the navvy and the farm-hand; lay the emphasis on that and you may arm me against them. If I were a solitary anomaly I should not matter, but what is true of myself is true of countless others. Every bank clerk dreaming of the sack, every shopkeeper teetering on the brink of bankruptcy, is in essentially the same position. These are the sinking middle class, and most of them are clinging to their gentility under the impression that it keeps them afloat. It is not good policy to *start* by telling them to throw away the life-belt. There is a quite obvious danger that in the next few years large sections of the middle class will make a sudden and violent swing to the Right. In doing so they may become formidable. The weakness of the middle class hitherto has lain in the fact that they have never learned to combine; but if you frighten them into combining *against* you, you may find that you have raised up a devil. We had a brief glimpse of this possibility in the General Strike.

To sum up: There is no chance of righting the conditions I described in the earlier chapters of this book, or of saving England from Fascism, unless we can bring an effective Socialist party into existence. It will have to be a party with genuinely revolutionary intentions, and it will have to be numerically strong enough to act. We can only get it if we offer an objective which fairly ordinary people will recognize as desirable. Beyond all else, therefore, we need intelligent propaganda. Less about 'class consciousness', 'expropriation of the expropriators', 'bourgeois ideology', and 'proletarian solidarity', not to mention the sacred sisters, thesis, antithesis and synthesis; and more about justice, liberty and the plight of the unemployed. And less about mechanical progress, tractors, the Dnieper dam and the latest salmon-canning factory in Moscow; that kind of thing is not an integral part of Socialist doctrine, and it drives away many people whom the Socialist cause needs, including most of those who can hold a pen. All that is needed is to hammer two facts home into the public consciousness. One, that the interests of all exploited people are the same; the other, that Socialism is compatible with common decency.

As for the terribly difficult issue of class-distinctions, the only possible policy for the moment is to go easy and not frighten more people than can be helped. And above all, no more of those muscular-curate efforts at class-breaking. If you belong to the bourgeoisie, don't be too eager to bound forward and embrace your proletarian brothers; they may not like it, and if they show that they don't like it you will probably find that your class-prejudices are not so dead as you imagined. And if you belong to the proletariat, by birth or in the sight of God, don't sneer too automatically at the Old School Tie; it covers loyalties which can be useful to you if you know how to handle them.

Yet I believe there is some hope that when Socialism is a living issue, a thing that large numbers of Englishmen genuinely care about, the class-difficulty may solve itself more rapidly than now seems thinkable. In the next few years we shall either get that effective Socialist party that we need, or we shall not get it. If we do not get it, then Fascism is coming; probably a slimy Anglicized form of Fascism, with cultured policemen instead of Nazi gorillas and the lion and the unicorn instead of the swastika. But if we do get it there will be a struggle, conceivably a physical one, for our plutocracy will not sit quiet under a genuinely revolutionary government. And when the widely separate classes who, necessarily, would form any real Socialist party have fought side by side, they may feel differently about one another. And then perhaps this misery of class-prejudice will fade away, and we of the sinking middle class – the private schoolmaster, the half-starved free-lance journalist, the colonel's spinster daughter with £75 a year, the jobless Cambridge graduate, the ship's officer without a ship, the clerks, the civil servants, the commercial travellers and the thrice-bankrupt drapers in the country towns – may sink without further struggles into the working class where we belong, and probably when we get there it will not be so dreadful as we feared, for, after all, we have nothing to lose but our aitches.

HOMAGE TO CATALONIA

Homage to Catalonia

Answer not a fool according to his folly, lest thou be like unto him.
Answer a fool according to his folly, lest he be wise in his own conceit.

Proverbs xxvi. 5–6

Chapter One

In the Lenin Barracks in Barcelona, the day before I joined the militia, I saw an Italian militiaman standing in front of the officers' table.

He was a tough-looking youth of twenty-five or six, with reddish-yellow hair and powerful shoulders. His peaked leather cap was pulled fiercely over one eye. He was standing in profile to me, his chin on his breast, gazing with a puzzled frown at a map which one of the officers had open on the table. Something in his face deeply moved me. It was the face of a man who would commit murder and throw away his life for a friend – the kind of face you would expect in an Anarchist, though as likely as not he was a Communist. There were both candour and ferocity in it; also the pathetic reverence that illiterate people have for their supposed superiors. Obviously he could not make head or tail of the map; obviously he regarded map-reading as a stupendous intellectual feat. I hardly know why, but I have seldom seen anyone – any man, I mean – to whom I have taken such an immediate liking. While they were talking round the table some remark brought it out that I was a foreigner. The Italian raised his head and said quickly:

'Italiano?'

I answered in my bad Spanish: 'No, Ingles. Y tu?'

'Italiano.'

As we went out he stepped across the room and gripped my hand very hard. Queer, the affection you can feel for a stranger! It was as though his spirit and mine had momentarily succeeded in bridging the gulf of language and tradition and meeting in utter intimacy. I hoped he liked me as well as I liked him. But I also knew that to retain my first impression of him I must not see him again; and needless to say I never did see him again. One was always making contacts of that kind in Spain.

I mention this Italian militiaman because he has stuck vividly in my memory. With his shabby uniform and fierce pathetic face he typifies for me the special atmosphere of that time. He is bound up with all my memories of that period of the war – the red flags in Barcelona, the gaunt trains full of shabby soldiers creeping to the front, the grey war-stricken towns farther up the line, the muddy, ice-cold trenches in the mountains.

This was in late December 1936, less than seven months ago as I write, and yet it is a period that has already receded into enormous distance. Later events have obliterated it much more completely than they have obliterated 1935, or 1905, for that matter. I had come to Spain with some notion of writing newspaper articles, but I had joined the militia almost immediately, because at that time and in that atmosphere it seemed the only conceivable thing to do. The Anarchists were still in virtual control of Catalonia and the revolution was still in full swing. To anyone who had been there since the beginning it probably seemed even in December or January that the revolutionary period was ending; but when one came straight from England the aspect of Barcelona was something startling and overwhelming. It was the first time that I had ever been in a town where the working class was in the saddle. Practically every building of any size had been seized by the workers and was draped with red flags or with the red and black flag of the Anarchists; every wall was scrawled with the hammer and sickle and with the initials of the revolutionary parties; almost every church had been gutted and its images burnt. Churches here and there were being systematically demolished by gangs of workmen. Every shop and café had an inscription saying that it had been collectivized; even the bootblacks had been collectivized and their boxes painted red and black. Waiters and shop-walkers looked you in the face and treated you as an equal. Servile and even ceremonial forms of speech had temporarily disappeared. Nobody said 'Señor' or 'Don' or even 'Usted'; everyone called everyone else 'Comrade' and 'Thou', and said 'Salud!' instead of 'Buenos dias'. Tipping was forbidden by law; almost my first experience was receiving a lecture from an hotel manager for trying to tip a lift-boy. There were no private motor cars, they had all been commandeered, and all the trams and taxis and much of the other transport were painted red and black. The revolutionary posters were everywhere, flaming from the walls in clean reds and blues that made the few remaining advertisements look like daubs of mud. Down the Ramblas, the wide central artery of the town where crowds of people streamed constantly to and fro, the loud-speakers were bellowing revolutionary songs all day and far into the night. And it was the aspect of the crowds that was the queerest thing of all. In outward appearance it was a town in which the wealthy classes had practically ceased to exist. Except for a small number of women and foreigners there were no 'well-dressed' people at all. Practically everyone wore rough working-class clothes, or blue overalls or some variant of the militia uniform. All this was queer and moving. There was much in it that I did not understand, in some ways I did not even like it, but I recognized it immediately as a state of affairs worth fighting for. Also I believed that things were as they appeared, that this was really a workers' State and that the entire bourgeoisie had either fled, been killed, or voluntarily come over to the workers' side; I did not realize that great numbers of well-to-do bourgeois were simply lying low and disguising themselves as proletarians for the time being.

Together with all this there was something of the evil atmosphere of war. The town had a gaunt untidy look, roads and buildings were in poor repair, the streets at night were dimly lit for fear of air-raids, the shops were mostly shabby and half-empty. Meat was scarce and milk practically unobtainable, there was a shortage of coal, sugar, and petrol, and a really serious shortage of bread. Even at this period the bread-queues were often hundreds of yards long. Yet so far as one could judge the people were contented and hopeful. There was no unemployment, and the price of living was still extremely low; you saw very few conspicuously destitute people, and no beggars except the gipsies. Above all, there was a belief in the revolution and the future, a feeling of having suddenly emerged into an era of equality and freedom. Human beings were trying to behave as human beings and not as cogs in the capitalist machine. In the barbers' shops were Anarchist notices (the barbers were mostly Anarchists) solemnly explaining that barbers were no longer slaves. In the streets were coloured posters appealing to prostitutes to stop being prostitutes. To anyone from the hard-boiled, sneering civilization of the English-speaking races there was something rather pathetic in the literalness with which these idealistic

Spaniards took the hackneyed phrases of revolution. At that time revolutionary ballads of the naïvest kind, all about proletarian brotherhood and the wickedness of Mussolini, were being sold on the streets for a few centimes each. I have often seen an illiterate militiaman buy one of these ballads, laboriously spell out the words, and then, when he had got the hang of it, begin singing it to an appropriate tune.

All this time I was at the Lenin Barracks, ostensibly in training for the front. When I joined the militia I had been told that I should be sent to the front the next day, but in fact I had to wait while a fresh *centuria* was got ready. The workers' militias, hurriedly raised by the trade unions at the beginning of the war, had not yet been organized on an ordinary army basis. The units of command were the 'section', of about thirty men, the *centuria*, of about a hundred men, and the 'column', which in practice meant any large number of men. The Lenin Barracks was a block of splendid stone buildings with a riding-school and enormous cobbled courtyards; it had been a cavalry barracks and had been captured during the July fighting. My *centuria* slept in one of the stables, under the stone mangers where the names of the cavalry chargers were still inscribed. All the horses had been seized and sent to the front, but the whole place still smelt of horse-piss and rotten oats. I was at the barracks about a week. Chiefly I remember the horsy smells, the quavering bugle-calls (all our buglers were amateurs – I first learned the Spanish bugle-calls by listening to them outside the Fascist lines), the tramp-tramp of hobnailed boots in the barrack yard, the long morning parades in the wintry sunshine, the wild games of football, fifty a side, in the gravelled riding-school. There were perhaps a thousand men at the barracks, and a score or so of women, apart from the militiamen's wives who did the cooking. There were still women serving in the militias, though not very many. In the early battles they had fought side by side with the men as a matter of course. It is a thing that seems natural in time of revolution. Ideas were changing already, however. The militiamen had to be kept out of the riding-school while the women were drilling there, because they laughed at the women and put them off. A few months earlier no one would have seen anything comic in a woman handling a gun.

The whole barracks was in the state of filth and chaos to which the militia reduced every building they occupied and which seems to be one of the by-products of revolution. In every corner you came upon piles of smashed furniture, broken saddles, brass cavalry-helmets, empty sabre-scabbards, and decaying food. There was frightful wastage of food, especially bread. From my barrack-room alone a basketful of bread was thrown away at every meal – a disgraceful thing when the civilian population was short of it. We ate at long trestle-tables out of permanently greasy tin pannikins, and drank out of a dreadful thing called a *puron*. A *puron* is a sort of glass bottle with a pointed spout from which a thin jet of wine spurts out whenever you tip it up; you can thus drink from a distance, without touching it with your lips, and it can be passed from hand to hand. I went on strike and demanded a drinking-cup as soon as I saw a *puron* in use. To my eye the things were altogether too like bed-bottles, especially when they were filled with white wine.

By degrees they were issuing the recruits with uniforms, and because this was Spain everything was issued piecemeal, so that it was never quite certain who had received what, and various of the things we most needed, such as belts and cartridge-boxes, were not issued till the last moment, when the train was actually waiting to take us to the front. I have spoken of the militia 'uniform', which probably gives a wrong impression. It was not exactly a uniform. Perhaps a 'multiform' would be the proper name for it. Everyone's clothes followed the same general plan, but they were never quite the same in any two cases. Practically everyone in the army wore corduroy knee-breeches, but there the uniformity ended. Some wore puttees, others corduroy gaiters, others leather leggings or high boots. Everyone wore a zipper jacket, but some of the jackets were of leather, others of wool and of every conceivable colour. The kinds of cap were about as numerous as their wearers. It was usual to adorn the front of your cap with a party badge, and in addition nearly every man wore a red or red and black handkerchief round his throat. A militia column at that time was an extraordinary-looking rabble. But the clothes had to be issued as this or that factory rushed them out, and they were not bad clothes considering the circumstances. The shirts and socks were wretched cotton things, however, quite useless against cold. I hate to think of what the militiamen must have gone through in the earlier months before anything was organized. I remember coming upon a newspaper of only about two months earlier in which one of the P.O.U.M. leaders, after a visit to the front, said that he would try to see to it that 'every militiaman had a blanket'. A phrase to make you shudder if you have ever slept in a trench.

On my second day at the barracks there began what was comically called 'instruction'. At the beginning there were frightful scenes of chaos. The recruits were mostly boys of sixteen or seventeen from the back streets of Barcelona, full of revolutionary ardour but completely ignorant of the meaning of war. It was impossible even to get them to stand in line. Discipline did not exist; if a man disliked an order he would step out of the ranks and argue fiercely with the officer. The lieutenant who instructed us was a stout, fresh-faced, pleasant young man who had previously been a Regular Army officer, and still looked like one, with his smart carriage and spick-and-span uniform. Curiously enough he was a sincere and ardent Socialist. Even more than the men themselves he insisted upon complete social equality between all ranks. I remember his pained surprise when an ignorant recruit addressed him as 'Señor'. 'What! Señor! Who is that calling me Señor? Are we not all comrades?' I doubt whether it made his job any easier. Meanwhile the raw recruits were getting no military training that could be of the slightest use to them. I had been told that foreigners were not obliged to attend 'instruction' (the Spaniards, I noticed, had a pathetic belief that all foreigners knew more of military matters than themselves), but naturally I turned out with the others. I was very anxious to learn how to use a machine-gun; it was a weapon I had never had a chance to handle. To my dismay I found that we were taught nothing about the use of weapons. The so-called instruction was simply parade-ground drill of the most antiquated, stupid kind; right turn, left turn, about turn, marching at attention in column of threes and all the rest of that useless nonsense which I had learned when I was fifteen years old. It was an extraordinary form for the training of a guerilla army to take. Obviously if you have only a few days in which to train a soldier, you must teach him the things he will most need; how to take cover, how to advance across open ground, how to mount guards and build a parapet – above all, how to use his weapons. Yet this mob of eager children, who were going to be thrown into the front line in a few days' time, were not even taught how to fire a rifle or pull the pin out of a bomb. At the time I did not grasp that this was because there were no weapons to be had. In the P.O.U.M. militia the shortage of rifles was so desperate that fresh troops reaching the front always had to take their rifles from the troops they relieved in the line. In the whole of the Lenin Barracks there were, I believe, no rifles except those used by the sentries.

After a few days, though still a complete rabble by any ordinary standard, we were considered fit to be seen in public, and in the mornings we were marched out to the public gardens on the hill beyond the Plaza de España. This was the common drill-ground of all the party militias, besides the Carabineros and the first contingents of the newly formed Popular Army. Up in the public gardens it was a strange and heartening sight. Down every path and alley-way, amid the formal flower-beds, squads and companies of men marched stiffly to and fro, throwing out their chests and trying desperately to look like soldiers. All of them were unarmed and none completely in uniform, though on most of them the militia uniform was breaking out in patches here and there. The procedure was always very much the same. For three hours we strutted to and fro (the Spanish marching step is very short and rapid), then we halted, broke the ranks and flocked thirstily to a little grocer's shop which was half-way down the hill and was doing a roaring trade in cheap wine. Everyone was very friendly to me. As an Englishman I was something of a curiosity, and the Carabinero officers made much of me and stood me drinks. Meanwhile, whenever I could get our lieutenant into a corner, I was clamouring to be instructed in the use of a machine-gun. I used to drag my Hugo's dictionary out of my pocket and start on him in my villainous Spanish:

'Yo se manejar fusil. No se manejar ametralladora. Quiero aprender ametralladora. Quando vamos aprender ametralladora?'

The answer was always a harassed smile and a promise that there should be machine-gun instruction *mañana*. Needless to say *mañana* never came. Several days passed and the recruits learned to march in step and spring to attention almost smartly, but if they knew which end of a rifle the bullet came out of, that was all they knew. One day an armed Carabinero strolled up to us when we were halting and allowed us to examine his rifle. It turned out that in the whole of my section no one except myself even knew how to load the rifle, much less how to take aim.

All this time I was having the usual struggles with the Spanish language. Apart from myself there was only one Englishman at the barracks, and nobody even among the officers spoke a word of French. Things were not made easier for me by the fact that when my companions spoke to one another they generally spoke in Catalan. The only way I could get along was to carry everywhere a small dictionary which I whipped out of my pocket in moments of crisis. But I would sooner be a foreigner in Spain than in most countries. How easy it is to make friends in Spain! Within a day or two there was a score of militiamen who called me by my Christian name, showed me the ropes and overwhelmed me with hospitality. I am not writing a book of propaganda and I do not want to idealize the P.O.U.M. militia. The whole militia-system had serious faults, and the men themselves were a mixed lot, for by this time voluntary recruitment was falling off and many of the best men were already at the front or dead. There was always among us a certain percentage who were completely useless. Boys of fifteen were being brought up for enlistment by their parents, quite openly for the sake of the ten pesetas a day which was the militiaman's wage; also for the sake of the bread which the militia received in plenty and could smuggle home to their parents. But I defy anyone to be thrown as I was among the Spanish working class – I ought perhaps to say the

Catalan working class, for apart from a few Aragonese and Andalusians I mixed only with Catalans – and not be struck by their essential decency; above all, their straightforwardness and generosity. A Spaniard's generosity, in the ordinary sense of the word, is at times almost embarrassing. If you ask him for a cigarette he will force the whole packet upon you. And beyond this there is generosity in a deeper sense, a real largeness of spirit, which I have met with again and again in the most unpromising circumstances. Some of the journalists and other foreigners who travelled in Spain during the war have declared that in secret the Spaniards were bitterly jealous of foreign aid. All I can say is that I never observed anything of the kind. I remember that a few days before I left the barracks a group of men returned on leave from the front. They were talking excitedly about their experiences and were full of enthusiasm for some French troops who had been next to them at Huesca. The French were very brave, they said; adding enthusiastically: 'Mas valientes que nosotros' – 'Braver than we are!' Of course I demurred, whereupon they explained that the French knew more of the art of war – were more expert with bombs, machine-guns, and so forth. Yet the remark was significant. An Englishman would cut his hand off sooner than say a thing like that.

Every foreigner who served in the militia spent his first few weeks in learning to love the Spaniards and in being exasperated by certain of their characteristics. In the front line my own exasperation sometimes reached the pitch of fury. The Spaniards are good at many things, but not at making war. All foreigners alike are appalled by their inefficiency, above all their maddening unpunctuality. The one Spanish word that no foreigner can avoid learning is *mañana* – 'tomorrow' (literally, 'the morning'). Whenever it is conceivably possible, the business of today is put off until *mañana*. This is so notorious that even the Spaniards themselves make jokes about it. In Spain nothing, from a meal to a battle, ever happens at the appointed time. As a general rule things happen too late, but just occasionally – just so that you shan't even be able to depend on their happening late – they happen too early. A train which is due to leave at eight will normally leave at any time between nine and ten, but perhaps once a week, thanks to some private whim of the engine-driver, it leaves at half-past seven. Such things can be a little trying. In theory I rather admire the Spaniards for not sharing our Northern time-neurosis; but unfortunately I share it myself.

After endless rumours, *mañanas*, and delays we were suddenly ordered to the front at two hours' notice, when much of our equipment was still unissued. There were terrible tumults in the quartermaster's store; in the end numbers of men had to leave without their full equipment. The barracks had promptly filled with women who seemed to have sprung up from the ground and were helping their men-folk to roll their blankets and pack their kit-bags. It was rather humiliating that I had to be shown how to put on my new leather cartridge-boxes by a Spanish girl, the wife of Williams, the other English militiaman. She was a gentle, dark-eyed, intensely feminine creature who looked as though her life-work was to rock a cradle, but who as a matter of fact had fought bravely in the street-battles of July. At this time she was carrying a baby which was born just ten months after the outbreak of war and had perhaps been begotten behind a barricade.

The train was due to leave at eight, and it was about ten past eight when the harassed, sweating officers managed to marshal us in the barrack square. I remember very vividly the torchlit scene – the uproar and excitement, the red flags flapping in the torchlight, the massed ranks of militiamen with their knapsacks on their backs and their rolled blankets worn bandolierwise across the shoulder; and the shouting and the clatter of boots and tin pannikins, and then a tremendous and finally successful hissing for silence; and then some political commissar standing beneath a huge rolling red banner and making us a speech in Catalan. Finally they marched us to the station, taking the longest route, three or four miles, so as to show us to the whole town. In the Ramblas they halted us while a borrowed band played some revolutionary tune or other. Once again the conquering-hero stuff – shouting and enthusiasm, red flags and red and black flags everywhere, friendly crowds thronging the pavement to have a look at us, women waving from the windows. How natural it all seemed then; how remote and improbable now! The train was packed so tight with men that there was barely room even on the floor, let alone on the seats. At the last moment Williams's wife came rushing down the platform and gave us a bottle of wine and a foot of that bright red sausage which tastes of soap and gives you diarrhoea. The train crawled out of Catalonia and onto the plateau of Aragon at the normal war-time speed of something under twenty kilometres an hour.

Chapter Two

Barbastro, though a long way from the front line, looked bleak and chipped. Swarms of militiamen in shabby uniforms wandered up and down the streets, trying to keep warm. On a ruinous wall I came upon a poster dating from the previous year and announcing that 'six handsome bulls' would be killed in the arena on such and such a date. How forlorn its faded colours looked! Where were the handsome bulls and the handsome bullfighters now? It appeared that even in Barcelona there were hardly any bullfights nowadays; for some reason all the best matadors were Fascists.

They sent my company by lorry to Sietamo, then westward to Alcubierre, which was just behind the line fronting Zaragoza. Sietamo had been fought over three times before the Anarchists finally took it in October, and parts of it were smashed to pieces by shell-fire and most of the houses pockmarked by rifle-bullets. We were 1,500 feet above sea-level now. It was beastly cold, with dense mists that came swirling up from nowhere. Between Sietamo and Alcubierre the lorry-driver lost his way (this was one of the regular features of the war) and we were wandering for hours in the mist. It was late at night when we reached Alcubierre. Somebody shepherded us through morasses of mud into a mule-stable where we dug ourselves down into the chaff and promptly fell asleep. Chaff is not bad to sleep in when it is clean, not so good as hay but better than straw. It was only in the morning light that I discovered that the chaff was full of breadcrusts, torn newspapers, bones, dead rats, and jagged milk tins.

We were near the front line now, near enough to smell the characteristic smell of war – in my experience a smell of excrement and decaying food. Alcubierre had never been shelled and was in a better state than most of the villages immediately behind the line. Yet I believe that even in peacetime you could not travel in that part of Spain without being struck by the peculiar squalid misery of the Aragonese villages. They are built like fortresses, a mass of mean little houses of mud and stone huddling round the church, and even in spring you see hardly a flower anywhere; the houses have no gardens, only back-yards where ragged fowls skate over the beds of mule-dung. It was vile weather, with alternate mist and rain. The narrow earth roads had been churned into a sea of mud, in places two feet deep, through which the lorries struggled with racing wheels and the peasants led their clumsy carts which were pulled by strings of mules, sometimes as many as six in a string, always pulling tandem. The constant come-and-go of troops had reduced the village to a state of unspeakable filth. It did not possess and never had possessed such a thing as a lavatory or a drain of any kind, and there was not a square yard anywhere where you could tread without watching your step. The church had long been used as a latrine; so had all the fields for a quarter of a mile round. I never think of my first two months at war without thinking of wintry stubble fields whose edges are crusted with dung.

Two days passed and no rifles were issued to us. When you had been to the Comite de Guerra and inspected the row of holes in the wall – holes made by rifle-volleys, various Fascists having been executed there – you had seen all the sights that Alcubierre contained. Up in the front line things were obviously quiet; very few wounded were coming in. The chief excitement was the arrival of Fascist deserters, who were brought under guard from the front line. Many of the troops opposite us on this part of the line were not Fascists at all, merely wretched conscripts who had been doing their military service at the time when war broke out and were only too anxious to escape. Occasionally small batches of them took the risk of slipping across to our lines. No doubt more would have done so if their relatives had not been in Fascist territory. These deserters were the first 'real' Fascists I had ever seen. It struck me that they were indistinguishable from ourselves, except that they wore khaki overalls. They were always ravenously hungry when they arrived – natural enough after a day or two of dodging about in no man's land, but it was always triumphantly pointed to as a proof that the Fascist troops were starving. I watched one of them being fed in a peasant's house. It was somehow rather a pitiful sight. A tall boy of twenty, deeply windburnt, with his clothes in rags, crouched over the fire shovelling a pannikinful of stew into himself at desperate speed; and all the while his eyes flitted nervously round the ring of militiamen who stood watching him. I think he still half-believed that we were bloodthirsty 'Reds' and were going to shoot him as soon as he had finished his meal; the armed man who guarded him kept stroking his shoulder and making reassuring noises. On one memorable day fifteen deserters arrived in a single batch. They were led through the village in triumph with a man riding in front of them on a white horse. I managed to take a rather blurry photograph which was stolen from me later.

On our third morning in Alcubierre the rifles arrived. A sergeant with a coarse dark-yellow face was handing them out in the mule-stable. I got a shock of dismay when I saw the thing they gave me. It was a German Mauser dated 1896 – more than forty years old! It was rusty, the bolt was stiff, the wooden barrel-guard was split; one glance down the muzzle showed that it was corroded and past praying for. Most of the rifles were equally bad, some of them even worse, and no attempt was made to give the best weapons to the men who knew how to use them. The best rifle of the lot, only ten years old, was given to a half-witted little beast of fifteen, known to everyone as the *maricon* (Nancy-boy). The sergeant gave us five minutes' 'instruction', which consisted in explaining how you loaded a rifle and how you took the bolt to pieces. Many of the militiamen had never had a gun in their hands before, and very few, I imagine, knew what the sights were for. Cartridges were handed out, fifty to a man, and then the ranks were formed and we strapped our kits on our backs and set out for the front line, about three miles away.

The *centuria*, eighty men and several dogs, wound raggedly up the road. Every militia column had at least one dog attached to it as a mascot. One wretched brute that marched with us had had P.O.U.M. branded on it in huge letters and slunk along as though conscious that there was something wrong with its appearance. At the head of the column, beside the red flag, Georges Kopp, the stout Belgian commandante, was riding a black horse; a little way ahead a youth from the brigand-like militia cavalry pranced to and fro, galloping up every piece of rising ground and posing himself in picturesque attitudes at the summit. The splendid horses of the Spanish cavalry had been captured in large numbers during the revolution and handed over to the militia, who, of course, were busy riding them to death.

The road wound between yellow infertile fields, untouched since last year's harvest. Ahead of us was the low sierra that lies between Alcubierre and Zaragoza. We were getting near the front line now, near the bombs, the machine-guns and the mud. In secret I was frightened. I knew the line was quiet at present, but unlike most of the men about me I was old enough to remember the Great War, though not old enough to have fought in it. War, to me, meant roaring projectiles and skipping shards of steel; above all it meant mud, lice, hunger, and cold. It is curious, but I dreaded the cold much more than I dreaded the enemy. The thought of it had been haunting me all the time I was in Barcelona; I had even lain awake at nights thinking of the cold in the trenches, the stand-to's in the grisly dawns, the long hours on sentry-go with a frosted rifle, the icy mud that would slop over my boot-tops. I admit, too, that I felt a kind of horror as I looked at the people I was marching among. You cannot possibly conceive what a rabble we looked. We straggled along with far less cohesion than a flock of sheep; before we had gone two miles the rear of the column was out of sight. And quite half of the so-called men were children – but I mean literally children, of sixteen years old at the very most. Yet they were happy and excited at the prospect of getting to the front at last. As we neared the line the boys round the red flag in front began to utter shouts of 'Visca P.O.U.M.!' 'Fascistas-maricones!' and so forth – shouts which were meant to be war-like and menacing, but which, from those childish throats, sounded as pathetic as the cries of kittens. It seemed dreadful that the defenders of the Republic should be this mob of ragged children carrying worn-out rifles which they did not know how to use. I remember wondering what would happen if a Fascist aeroplane passed our way – whether the airman would even bother to dive down and give us a burst from his machine-gun. Surely even from the air he could see that we were not real soldiers?

As the road struck into the sierra we branched off to the right and climbed a narrow mule-track that wound round the mountain-side. The hills in that part of Spain are of a queer formation, horseshoe-shaped with flattish tops and very steep sides running down into immense ravines. On the higher slopes nothing grows except stunted shrubs and heath, with the white bones of the limestone sticking out everywhere. The front line here was not a continuous line of trenches, which would have been impossible in such mountainous country; it was simply a chain of fortified posts, always known as 'positions', perched on each hill-top. In the distance you could see our 'position' at the crown of the horseshoe; a ragged barricade of sand-bags, a red flag fluttering, the smoke of dug-out fires. A little nearer, and you could smell a sickening sweetish stink that lived in my nostrils for weeks afterwards. Into the cleft immediately behind the position all the refuse of months had been tipped – a deep festering bed of breadcrusts, excrement, and rusty tins.

The company we were relieving were getting their kits together. They had been three months in the line; their uniforms were caked with mud, their boots falling to pieces, their faces mostly bearded. The captain commanding the position, Levinski by name, but known to everyone as Benjamin, and by birth a Polish Jew, but speaking French as his native language, crawled out of his dug-out and greeted us. He was a short youth of about twenty-five, with stiff black hair and a pale eager face which at this period of the war was always very dirty. A few stray bullets were cracking overhead. The position was a semi-circular enclosure about fifty yards across, with a parapet that was partly sand-bags and partly lumps of limestone. There were thirty or forty dug-outs running into the ground like rat-holes. Williams, myself, and Williams's Spanish brother-in-law made a swift dive for the nearest unoccupied dug-out that looked habitable. Somewhere in front an occasional rifle banged, making queer rolling echoes among the stony hills. We had just dumped our kits and were crawling out of the dug-out when there was another bang and one of the children of our company rushed back from the parapet with his face pouring blood. He had fired his rifle and had somehow managed to blow out the bolt; his scalp was torn to ribbons by the splinters of the burst cartridge-case. It was our first casualty, and, characteristically, self-inflicted.

In the afternoon we did our first guard and Benjamin showed us round the position. In front of the parapet there ran a system of narrow trenches hewn out of the rock, with extremely primitive loopholes made of piles of limestone. There were twelve sentries, placed at various points in the trench and behind the inner parapet. In front of the trench was the barbed wire, and then the hillside slid down into a seemingly bottomless ravine; opposite were naked hills, in places mere cliffs of rock, all grey and wintry, with no life anywhere, not even a bird. I peered cautiously through a loophole, trying to find the Fascist trench.

'Where are the enemy?'

Benjamin waved his hand expansively. 'Over zere.' (Benjamin spoke English – terrible English.)

'But *where*?'

According to my ideas of trench warfare the Fascists would be fifty or a hundred yards away. I could see nothing – seemingly their trenches were very well concealed. Then with a shock of dismay I saw where Benjamin was pointing; on the opposite hill-top, beyond the ravine, seven hundred metres away at the very least, the tiny outline of a parapet and a red-and-yellow flag – the Fascist position. I was indescribably disappointed. We were nowhere near them! At that range our rifles were completely useless. But at this moment there was a shout of excitement. Two Fascists, greyish figurines in the distance, were scrambling up the naked hill-side opposite. Benjamin grabbed the nearest man's rifle, took aim, and pulled the trigger. Click! A dud cartridge; I thought it a bad omen.

The new sentries were no sooner in the trench than they began firing a terrific fusillade at nothing in particular. I could see the Fascists, tiny as ants, dodging to and fro behind their parapet, and sometimes a black dot which was a head would pause for a moment, impudently exposed. It was obviously no use firing. But presently the sentry on my left, leaving his post in the typical Spanish fashion, sidled up to me and began urging me to fire. I tried to explain that at that range and with these rifles you could not hit a man except by accident. But he was only a child, and he kept motioning with his rifle towards one of the dots, grinning as eagerly as a dog that expects a pebble to be thrown. Finally I put my sights up to seven hundred and let fly. The dot disappeared. I hope it went near enough to make him jump. It was the first time in my life that I had fired a gun at a human being.

Now that I had seen the front I was profoundly disgusted. They called this war! And we were hardly even in touch with the enemy! I made no attempt to keep my head below the level of the trench. A little while later, however, a bullet shot past my ear with a vicious crack and banged into the parados behind. Alas! I ducked. All my life I had sworn that I would not duck the first time a bullet passed over me; but the movement appears to be instinctive, and almost everybody does it at least once.

Chapter Three

In trench warfare five things are important: firewood, food, tobacco, candles and the enemy. In winter on the Zaragoza front they were important in that order, with the enemy a bad last. Except at night, when a surprise-attack was always conceivable, nobody bothered about the enemy. They were simply remote black insects whom one occasionally saw hopping to and fro. The real preoccupation of both armies was trying to keep warm.

I ought to say in passing that all the time I was in Spain I saw very little fighting. I was on the Aragon front from January to May, and between January and late March little or nothing happened on that front, except at Teruel. In March there was heavy fighting round Huesca, but I personally played only a minor part in it. Later, in June, there was the disastrous attack on Huesca in which several thousand men were killed in a single day, but I had been wounded and disabled before that happened. The things that one normally thinks of as the horrors of war seldom happened to me. No aeroplane ever dropped a bomb anywhere near me, I do not think a shell ever exploded within fifty yards of me, and I was only in hand-to-hand fighting once (once is once too often, I may say). Of course I was often under heavy machine-gun fire, but usually at longish ranges. Even at Huesca you were generally safe enough if you took reasonable precautions.

Up here, in the hills round Zaragoza, it was simply the mingled boredom and discomfort of stationary warfare. A life as uneventful as a city clerk's, and almost as regular. Sentry-go, patrols, digging; digging, patrols, sentry-go. On every hill-top, Fascist or Loyalist, a knot of ragged, dirty men shivering round their flag and trying to keep warm. And all day and night the meaningless bullets wandering across the empty valleys and only by some rare improbable chance getting home on a human body.

Often I used to gaze round the wintry landscape and marvel at the futility of it all. The inconclusiveness of such a kind of war! Earlier, about October, there had been savage fighting for all these hills; then, because the lack of men and arms, especially artillery, made any large-scale operation impossible, each army had dug itself in and settled down on the hill-tops it had won. Over to our right there was a small outpost, also P.O.U.M., and on the spur to our left, at seven o'clock of us, a P.S.U.C. position faced a taller spur with several small Fascist posts dotted on its peaks. The so-called line zigzagged to and fro in a pattern that would have been quite unintelligible if every position had not flown a flag. The P.O.U.M. and P.S.U.C. flags were red, those of the Anarchists red and black; the Fascists generally flew the monarchist flag (red-yellow-red), but occasionally they flew the flag of the Republic (red-yellow-purple). The scenery was stupendous, if you could forget that every mountain-top was occupied by troops and was therefore littered with tin cans and crusted with dung. To the right of us the sierra bent south-eastwards and made way for the wide, veined valley that stretched across to Huesca. In the middle of the plain a few tiny cubes sprawled like a throw of dice; this was the town of Robres, which was in Loyalist possession. Often in the mornings the valley was hidden under seas of cloud, out of which the hills rose flat and blue, giving the landscape a strange resemblance to a photographic negative. Beyond Huesca there were more hills of the same formation as our own, streaked with a pattern of snow which altered day by day. In the far distance the monstrous peaks of the Pyrenees, where the snow never melts, seemed to float upon nothing. Even down in the plain everything looked dead and bare. The hills opposite us were grey and wrinkled like the skins of elephants. Almost always the sky was empty of birds. I do not think I have ever seen a country where there were so few birds. The only birds one saw at any time were a kind of magpie, and the coveys of partridges that startled one at night with their sudden whirring, and, very rarely, the flights of eagles that drifted slowly over, generally followed by rifleshots which they did not deign to notice.

At night and in misty weather patrols were sent out in the valley between ourselves and the Fascists. The job was not popular, it was too cold and too easy to get lost, and I soon found that I could get leave to go out on patrol as often as I wished. In the huge jagged ravines there were no paths or tracks of any kind; you could only find your way about by making successive journeys and noting fresh landmarks each time. As the bullet flies the nearest Fascist post was seven hundred metres from our own, but it was a mile and a half by the only practicable route. It was rather fun wandering about the dark valleys with the stray bullets flying high overhead like redshanks whistling. Better than night-time were the heavy mists, which often lasted all day and which had a habit of clinging round the hill-tops and leaving the valleys clear. When you were anywhere near the Fascist lines you had to creep at a snail's pace; it was very difficult to move quietly on those hill-sides, among the crackling shrubs and tinkling limestones. It was only at the third or fourth attempt that I managed to find my way to the Fascist lines. The mist was very thick, and I crept up to the barbed wire to listen. I could hear the Fascists talking and singing inside. Then to my alarm I heard several of them coming down the hill towards me. I cowered behind a bush that suddenly seemed very small, and tried to cock my rifle without noise. However, they branched off and did not come within sight of me. Behind the bush where I was hiding I came upon various relics of the earlier fighting – a pile of empty cartridge-cases, a leather cap with a bullet-hole in it, and a red flag, obviously one of our own. I took it back to the position, where it was unsentimentally torn up for cleaning-rags.

I had been made a corporal, or *cabo*, as it was called, as soon as we reached the front, and was in command of a guard of twelve men. It was no sinecure, especially at first. The *centuria* was an untrained mob composed mostly of boys in their teens. Here and there in the militia you came across children as young as eleven or twelve, usually refugees from Fascist territory who had been enlisted as militiamen as the easiest way of providing for them. As a rule they were employed on light work in the rear, but sometimes they managed to worm their way to the front line, where they were a public menace. I remember one little brute throwing a hand-grenade into the dug-out fire 'for a joke'. At Monte Pocero I do not think there was anyone younger than fifteen, but the average age must have been well under twenty. Boys of this age ought never to be used in the front line, because they cannot stand the lack of sleep which is inseparable from trench warfare. At the beginning it was almost impossible to keep our position properly guarded at night. The wretched children of my section could only be roused by dragging them out of their dug-outs feet foremost, and as soon as your back was turned they left their posts and slipped into shelter; or they would even, in spite of the frightful cold, lean up against the wall of the trench and fall fast asleep. Luckily the enemy were very unenterprising. There were nights when it seemed to me that our position could be stormed by twenty Boy Scouts armed with air-guns, or twenty Girl Guides armed with battledores, for that matter.

At this time and until much later the Catalan militias were still on the same basis as they had been at the beginning of the war. In the early days of Franco's revolt the militias had been hurriedly raised by the various trade unions and political parties; each was essentially a political organization, owing allegiance to its party as much as to the central Government. When the Popular Army, which was a 'non-political' army organized on more or less ordinary lines, was raised at the beginning of 1937, the party militias were theoretically incorporated in it. But for a long time the only changes that occurred were on paper; the new Popular Army troops did not reach the Aragon front in any numbers till June, and until that time the militia-system remained unchanged. The essential point of the system was social equality between officers and men. Everyone from general to private drew the same pay, ate the same food, wore the same clothes, and mingled on terms of complete equality. If you wanted to slap the general commanding the division on the back and ask him for a cigarette, you could do so, and no one thought it curious. In theory at any rate each militia was a democracy and not a hierarchy. It was understood that orders had to be obeyed, but it was also understood that when you gave an order you gave it as comrade to comrade and not as superior to inferior. There were officers and N.C.Os., but there was no military rank in the ordinary sense; no titles, no badges, no heel-clicking and saluting. They had attempted to produce within the militias a sort of temporary working model of the classless society. Of course there was not perfect equality, but there was a nearer approach to it than I had ever seen or than I would have thought conceivable in time of war.

But I admit that at first sight the state of affairs at the front horrified me. How on earth could the war be won by an army of this type? It was what everyone was saying at the time, and though it was true it was also unreasonable. For in the circumstances the militias could not have been much better than they were. A modern mechanized army does not spring up out of the ground, and if the Government had waited until it had trained troops at its disposal, Franco would never have been resisted. Later it became the fashion to decry the militias, and therefore to pretend that the faults which were due to lack of training and weapons were the result of the equalitarian system. Actually, a newly raised draft of militia was an undisciplined mob not because the officers called the privates 'Comrade' but because raw troops are *always* an undisciplined mob. In practice the democratic 'revolutionary' type of discipline is more reliable than might be expected. In a workers' army discipline is theoretically voluntary. It is based on class-loyalty, whereas the discipline of a bourgeois conscript army is based ultimately on fear. (The Popular Army that replaced the militias was midway between the two types.) In the militias the bullying and abuse that go on in an ordinary army would never have been tolerated for a moment. The normal military punishments existed, but they were only invoked for very serious offences. When a man refused to obey an order you did not immediately get him punished; you first appealed to him in the name of comradeship. Cynical people with no experience of handling men will say instantly that this would never 'work', but as a matter of fact it does 'work' in the long run. The discipline of even the worst drafts of militia visibly improved as time went on. In January the job of keeping a dozen raw recruits up to the mark almost turned my hair grey. In May for a short while I was acting-lieutenant in command of about thirty men, English and Spanish. We had all been under fire for months, and I never had the slightest difficulty in getting an order obeyed or in getting men to volunteer for a dangerous job. 'Revolutionary' discipline depends on political consciousness – on an understanding of *why* orders must be obeyed; it takes time to diffuse this, but it also takes time to drill a man into an automaton on the barrack-square. The journalists who sneered at the militia-system seldom remembered that the militias had to hold the line while the Popular Army was training in the rear. And it is a tribute to the strength of 'revolutionary' discipline that the militias stayed in the field at all. For until about June 1937 there was nothing to keep them there, except class loyalty. Individual deserters could be shot – were shot, occasionally – but if a thousand men had decided to walk out of the line together there was no force to stop them. A conscript army in the same circumstances – with its battle-police removed – would have melted away. Yet the militias held the line, though God knows they won very few victories, and even individual desertions were not common. In four or five months in the P.O.U.M. militia I only heard of four men deserting, and two of those were fairly certainly spies who had enlisted to obtain information. At the beginning the apparent chaos, the general lack of training, the fact that you often had to argue for five minutes before you could get an order obeyed, appalled and infuriated me. I had British Army ideas, and certainly the Spanish militias were very unlike the British Army. But considering the circumstances they were better troops than one had any right to expect.

Meanwhile, firewood – always firewood. Throughout that period there is probably no entry in my diary that does not mention firewood, or rather the lack of it. We were between two and three thousand feet above sea-level, it was mid-winter and the cold was unspeakable. The temperature was not exceptionally low, on many nights it did not even freeze, and the wintry sun often shone for an hour in the middle of the day; but even if it was not really cold, I assure you that it seemed so. Sometimes there were shrieking winds that tore your cap off and twisted your hair in all directions, sometimes there were mists that poured into the trench like a liquid and seemed to penetrate your bones; frequently it rained, and even a quarter of an hour's rain was enough to make conditions intolerable. The thin skin of earth over the limestone turned promptly into a slippery grease, and as you were always walking on a slope it was impossible to keep your footing. On dark nights I have often fallen half a dozen times in twenty yards; and this was dangerous, because it meant that the lock of one's rifle became jammed with mud. For days together clothes, boots, blankets, and rifles were more or less coated with mud. I had brought as many thick clothes as I could carry, but many of the men were terribly underclad. For the whole garrison, about a hundred men, there were only twelve great-coats, which had to be handed from sentry to sentry, and most of the men had only one blanket. One icy night I made a list in my diary of the clothes I was wearing. It is of some interest as showing the amount of clothes the human body can carry. I was wearing a thick vest and pants, a flannel shirt, two pull-overs, a woollen jacket, a pigskin jacket, corduroy breeches, puttees, thick socks, boots, a stout trench-coat, a muffler, lined leather gloves, and a woollen cap. Nevertheless I was shivering like a jelly. But I admit I am unusually sensitive to cold.

Firewood was the one thing that really mattered. The point about the firewood was that there was practically no firewood to be had. Our miserable mountain had not even at its best much vegetation, and for months it had been ranged over by freezing militiamen, with the result that everything thicker than one's finger had long since been burnt. When we were not eating, sleeping, on guard or on fatigue-duty we were in the valley behind the position, scrounging for fuel. All my memories of that time are memories of scrambling up and down the almost perpendicular slopes, over the jagged limestone that knocked one's boots to pieces, pouncing eagerly on tiny twigs of wood. Three people searching for a couple of hours could collect enough fuel to keep the dug-out fire alight for about an hour. The eagerness of our search for firewood turned us all into botanists. We classified according to their burning qualities every plant that grew on the mountain-side; the various heaths and grasses that were good to start a fire with but burnt out in a few minutes, the wild rosemary and the tiny whin bushes that would burn when the fire was well alight, the stunted oak tree, smaller than a gooseberry bush, that was practically unburnable. There was a kind of dried-up reed that was very good for starting fires with, but these grew only on the hill-top to the left of the position, and you had to go under fire to get them. If the Fascist machine-gunners saw you they gave you a drum of ammunition all to yourself. Generally their aim was high and the bullets sang overhead like birds, but sometimes they crackled and chipped the limestone uncomfortably close, whereupon you flung yourself on your face. You went on gathering reeds, however; nothing mattered in comparison with firewood.

Beside the cold the other discomforts seemed petty. Of course all of us were permanently dirty. Our water, like our food, came on mule-back from Alcubierre, and each man's share worked out at about a quart a day. It was beastly water, hardly more transparent than milk. Theoretically it was for drinking only, but I always stole a pannikinful for washing in the mornings. I used to wash one day and shave the next; there was never enough water for both. The position stank abominably, and outside the little enclosure of the barricade there was excrement everywhere. Some of the militiamen habitually defecated in the trench, a disgusting thing when one had to walk round it in the darkness. But the dirt never worried me. Dirt is a thing people make too much fuss about. It is astonishing how quickly you get used to doing without a handkerchief and to eating out of the tin pannikin in which you also wash. Nor was sleeping in one's clothes any hardship after a day or two. It was of course impossible to take one's clothes and especially one's boots off at night; one had to be ready to turn out instantly in case of an attack. In eighty nights I only took my clothes off three times, though I did occasionally manage to get them off in the daytime. It was too cold for lice as yet, but rats and mice abounded. It is often said that you don't find rats and mice in the same place, but you do when there is enough food for them.

In other ways we were not badly off. The food was good enough and there was plenty of wine. Cigarettes were still being issued at the rate of a packet a day, matches were issued every other day, and there was even an issue of candles. They were very thin candles, like those on a Christmas cake, and were popularly supposed to have been looted from churches. Every dug-out was issued daily with three inches of candle, which would burn for about twenty minutes. At that time it was still possible to buy candles, and I had brought several pounds of them with me. Later on the famine of matches and candles made life a misery. You do not realize the importance of these things until you lack them. In a night-alarm, for instance, when everyone in the dug-out is scrambling for his rifle and treading on everybody else's face, being able to strike a light may make the difference between life and death. Every militiaman possessed a tinder-lighter and several yards of yellow wick. Next to his rifle it was his most important possession. The tinder-lighters had the great advantage that they could be struck in a wind, but they would only smoulder, so that they were no use for lighting a fire. When the match famine was at its worst our only way of producing a flame was to pull the bullet out of a cartridge and touch the cordite off with a tinder-lighter.

It was an extraordinary life that we were living – an extraordinary way to be at war, if you could call it war. The whole militia chafed against the inaction and clamoured constantly to know why we were not allowed to attack. But it was perfectly obvious that there would be no battle for a long while yet, unless the enemy started it. Georges Kopp, on his periodical tours of inspection, was quite frank with us. 'This is not a war,' he used to say, 'it is a comic opera with an occasional death.' As a matter of fact the stagnation on the Aragon front had political causes of which I knew nothing at that time; but the purely military difficulties – quite apart from the lack of reserves of men – were obvious to anybody.

To begin with, there was the nature of the country. The front line, ours and the Fascists', lay in positions of immense natural strength, which as a rule could only be approached from one side. Provided a few trenches have been dug, such places cannot be taken by infantry, except in overwhelming numbers. In our own position or most of those round us a dozen men with two machine-guns could have held off a battalion. Perched on the hill-tops as we were, we should have made lovely marks for artillery; but there was no artillery. Sometimes I used to gaze round the landscape and long – oh, how passionately! – for a couple of batteries of guns. One could have destroyed the enemy positions one after another as easily as smashing nuts with a hammer. But on our side the guns simply did not exist. The Fascists did occasionally manage to bring a gun or two from Zaragoza and fire a very few shells, so few that they never even found the range and the shells plunged harmlessly into the empty ravines. Against machine-guns and without artillery there are only three things you can do: dig yourself in at a safe distance – four hundred yards, say – advance across the open and be massacred, or make small-scale night-attacks that will not alter the general situation. Practically the alternatives are stagnation or suicide.

And beyond this there was the complete lack of war materials of every description. It needs an effort to realize how badly the militias were armed at this time. Any public school O.T.C. in England is far more like a modern army than we were. The badness of our weapons was so astonishing that it is worth recording in detail.

For this sector of the front the entire artillery consisted of four trench-mortars with *fifteen rounds* for each gun. Of course they were far too precious to be fired and the mortars were kept in Alcubierre. There were machine-guns at the rate of approximately one to fifty men; they were oldish guns, but fairly accurate up to three or four hundred yards. Beyond this we had only rifles, and the majority of the rifles were scrap-iron. There were three types of rifle in use. The first was the long Mauser. These were seldom less than twenty years old, their sights were about as much use as a broken speedometer, and in most of them the rifling was hopelessly corroded; about one rifle in ten was not bad, however. Then there was the short Mauser, or *mousqueton*, really a cavalry weapon. These were more popular than the others because they were lighter to carry and less nuisance in a trench, also because they were comparatively new and looked efficient. Actually they were almost useless. They were made out of reassembled parts, no bolt belonged to its rifle, and three-quarters of them could be counted on to jam after five shots. There were also a few Winchester rifles. These were nice to shoot with, but they were wildly inaccurate, and as their cartridges had no clips they could only be fired one shot at a time. Ammunition was so scarce that each man entering the line was only issued with fifty rounds, and most of it was exceedingly bad. The Spanish-made cartridges were all refills and would jam even the best rifles. The Mexican cartridges were better and were therefore reserved for the machine-guns. Best of all was the German-made ammunition, but as this came only from prisoners and deserters there was not much of it. I always kept a clip of German or Mexican ammunition in my pocket for use in an emergency. But in practice when the emergency came I seldom fired my rifle; I was too frightened of the beastly thing jamming and too anxious to reserve at any rate one round that would go off.

We had no tin hats, no bayonets, hardly any revolvers or pistols, and not more than one bomb between five or ten men. The bomb in use at this time was a frightful object known as the 'F.A.I. bomb', it having been produced by the Anarchists in the early days of the war. It was on the principle of a Mills bomb, but the lever was held down not by a pin but a piece of tape. You broke the tape and then got rid of the bomb with the utmost possible speed. It was said of these bombs that they were 'impartial'; they killed the man they were thrown at and the man who threw them. There were several other types, even more primitive but probably a little less dangerous – to the thrower, I mean. It was not till late March that I saw a bomb worth throwing.

And apart from weapons there was a shortage of all the minor necessities of war. We had no maps or charts, for instance. Spain has never been fully surveyed, and the only detailed maps of this area were the old military ones, which were almost all in the possession of the Fascists. We had no rangefinders, no telescopes, no periscopes, no field-glasses except a few privately-owned pairs, no flares or Very lights, no wire-cutters, no armourers' tools, hardly even any cleaning materials. The Spaniards seemed never to have heard of a pull-through and looked on in surprise when I constructed one. When you wanted your rifle cleaned you took it to the sergeant, who possessed a long brass ramrod which was invariably bent and therefore scratched the rifling. There was not even any gun oil. You greased your rifle with olive oil, when you could get hold of it; at different times I have greased mine with vaseline, with cold cream, and even with bacon-fat. Moreover, there were no lanterns or electric torches – at this time there was not, I believe, such a thing as an electric torch throughout the whole of our sector of the front, and you could not buy one nearer than Barcelona, and only with difficulty even there.

As time went on, and the desultory rifle-fire rattled among the hills, I began to wonder with increasing scepticism whether anything would ever happen to bring a bit of life, or rather a bit of death, into this cock-eyed war. It was pneumonia that we were fighting against, not against men. When the trenches are more than five hundred yards apart no one gets hit except by accident. Of course there were casualties, but the majority of them were self-inflicted. If I remember rightly, the first five men I saw wounded in Spain were all wounded by our own weapons – I don't mean intentionally, but owing to accident or carelessness. Our worn-out rifles were a danger in themselves. Some of them had a nasty trick of going off if the butt was tapped on the ground; I saw a man shoot himself through the hand owing to this. And in the darkness the raw recruits were always firing at one another. One evening when it was barely even dusk a sentry let fly at me from a distance of twenty yards; but he missed me by a yard – goodness knows how many times the Spanish standard of marksmanship has saved my life. Another time I had gone out on patrol in the mist and had carefully warned the guard commander beforehand. But in coming back I stumbled against a bush, the startled sentry called out that the Fascists were coming, and I had the pleasure of hearing the guard commander order everyone to open rapid fire in my direction. Of course I lay down and the bullets went harmlessly over me. Nothing will convince a Spaniard, at least a young Spaniard, that fire-arms are dangerous. Once, rather later than this, I was photographing some machine-gunners with their gun, which was pointed directly towards me.

'Don't fire,' I said half-jokingly as I focused the camera.

'Oh no, we won't fire.'

The next moment there was a frightful roar and a stream of bullets tore past my face so close that my cheek was stung by grains of cordite. It was unintentional, but the machine-gunners considered it a great joke. Yet only a few days earlier they had seen a mule-driver accidentally shot by a political delegate who was playing the fool with an automatic pistol and had put five bullets in the mule-driver's lungs.

The difficult passwords which the army was using at this time were a minor source of danger. They were those tiresome double passwords in which one word has to be answered by another. Usually they were of an elevating and revolutionary nature, such as *Cultura – progreso*, or *Seremos – invencibles*, and it was often impossible to get illiterate sentries to remember these highfalutin' words. One night, I remember, the password was *Cataluña – eroica*, and a moon-faced peasant lad named Jaime Domenech approached me, greatly puzzled, and asked me to explain.

'Eroica – what does eroica mean?'

I told him that it meant the same as valiente. A little while later he was stumbling up the trench in the darkness, and the sentry challenged him:

'Alto! Cataluña!'

'Valiente!' yelled Jaime, certain that he was saying the right thing.

Bang!

However, the sentry missed him. In this war everyone always did miss everyone else, when it was humanly possible.

Chapter Four

When I had been about three weeks in the line a contingent of twenty or thirty men, sent out from England by the I.L.P., arrived at Alcubierre, and in order to keep the English on this front together Williams and I were sent to join them. Our new position was at Monte Oscuro, several miles farther west and within sight of Zaragoza.

The position was perched on a sort of razor-back of limestone with dug-outs driven horizontally into the cliff like sand-martins' nests. They went into the ground for prodigious distances, and inside they were pitch dark and so low that you could not even kneel in them, let alone stand. On the peaks to the left of us there were two more P.O.U.M. positions, one of them an object of fascination to every man in the line, because there were three militiawomen there who did the cooking. These women were not exactly beautiful, but it was found necessary to put the position out of bounds to men of other companies. Five hundred yards to our right there was a P.S.U.C. post at the bend of the Alcubierre road. It was just here that the road changed hands. At night you could watch the lamps of our supply-lorries winding out from Alcubierre and, simultaneously, those of the Fascists coming from Zaragoza. You could see Zaragoza itself, a thin string of lights like the lighted port-holes of a ship, twelve miles south-westward. The Government troops had gazed at it from that distance since August 1936, and they are gazing at it still.

There were about thirty of ourselves, including one Spaniard (Ramon, Williams's brother-in-law), and there were a dozen Spanish machine-gunners. Apart from the one or two inevitable nuisances – for, as everyone knows, war attracts riff-raff – the English were an exceptionally good crowd, both physically and mentally. Perhaps the best of the bunch was Bob Smillie – the grandson of the famous miners' leader – who afterwards died such an evil and meaningless death in Valencia. It says a lot for the Spanish character that the English and the Spaniards always got on well together, in spite of the language difficulty. All Spaniards, we discovered, knew two English expressions. One was 'O.K., baby,' the other was a word used by the Barcelona whores in their dealings with English sailors, and I am afraid the compositors would not print it.

Once again there was nothing happening all along the line: only the random crack of bullets and, very rarely, the crash of a Fascist mortar that sent everyone running to the top trench to see which hill the shells were bursting on. The enemy was somewhat closer to us here, perhaps three or four hundred yards away. Their nearest position was exactly opposite ours, with a machine-gun nest whose loopholes constantly tempted one to waste cartridges. The Fascists seldom bothered with rifle-shots, but sent bursts of accurate machine-gun fire at anyone who exposed himself. Nevertheless it was ten days or more before we had our first casualty. The troops opposite us were Spaniards, but according to the deserters there were a few German N.C.Os. among them. At some time in the past there had also been Moors there – poor devils, how they must have felt the cold! – for out in no man's land there was a dead Moor who was one of the sights of the locality. A mile or two to the left of us the line ceased to be continuous and there was a tract of country, lower-lying and thickly wooded, which belonged neither to the Fascists nor ourselves. Both we and they used to make daylight patrols there. It was not bad fun in a Boy Scoutish way, though I never saw a Fascist patrol nearer than several hundred yards. By a lot of crawling on your belly you could work your way partly through the Fascist lines and could even see the farm-house flying the monarchist flag, which was the local Fascist headquarters. Occasionally we gave it a rifle-volley and then slipped into cover before the machine-guns could locate us. I hope we broke a few windows, but it was a good eight hundred metres away, and with our rifles you could not make sure of hitting even a house at that range.

The weather was mostly clear and cold; sometimes sunny at midday, but always cold. Here and there in the soil of the hill-sides you found the green beaks of wild crocuses or irises poking through; evidently spring was coming, but coming very slowly. The nights were colder than ever. Coming off guard in the small hours we used to rake together what was left of the cook-house fire and then stand in the red-hot embers. It was bad for your boots, but it was very good for your feet. But there were mornings when the sight of the dawn among the mountain-tops made it almost worth while to be out of bed at godless hours. I hate mountains, even from a spectacular point of view. But sometimes the dawn breaking behind the hill-tops in our rear, the first narrow streaks of gold, like swords slitting the darkness, and then the growing light and the seas of carmine cloud stretching away into inconceivable distances, were worth watching even when you had been up all night, when your legs were numb from the knees down and you were sullenly reflecting that there was no hope of food for another three hours. I saw the dawn oftener during this campaign than during the rest of my life put together – or during the part that is to come, I hope.

We were short-handed here, which meant longer guards and more fatigues. I was beginning to suffer a little from the lack of sleep which is inevitable even in the quietest kind of war. Apart from guard-duties and patrols there were constant night-alarms and stand-to's, and in any case you can't sleep properly in a beastly hole in the ground with your feet aching with the cold. In my first three or four months in the line I do not suppose I had more than a dozen periods of twenty-four hours that were completely without sleep; on the other hand I certainly did not have a dozen nights of full sleep. Twenty or thirty hours' sleep in a week was quite a normal amount. The effects of this were not so bad as might be expected; one grew very stupid, and the job of climbing up and down the hills grew harder instead of easier, but one felt well and one was constantly hungry – heavens, how hungry! All food seemed good, even the eternal haricot beans which everyone in Spain finally learned to hate the sight of. Our water, what there was of it, came from miles away, on the backs of mules or little persecuted donkeys. For some reason the Aragon peasants treated their mules well but their donkeys abominably. If a donkey refused to go it was quite usual to kick him in the testicles. The issue of candles had ceased, and matches were running short. The Spaniards taught us how to make olive oil lamps out of a condensed milk tin, a cartridge-clip, and a bit of rag. When you had any olive oil, which was not often, these things would burn with a smoky flicker, about a quarter candle power, just enough to find your rifle by.

There seemed no hope of any real fighting. When we left Monte Pocero I had counted my cartridges and found that in nearly three weeks I had fired just three shots at the enemy. They say it takes a thousand bullets to kill a man, and at this rate it would be twenty years before I killed my first Fascist. At Monte Oscuro the lines were closer and one fired oftener, but I am reasonably certain that I never hit anyone. As a matter of fact, on this front and at this period of the war the real weapon was not the rifle but the megaphone. Being unable to kill your enemy you shouted at him instead. This method of warfare is so extraordinary that it needs explaining.

Wherever the lines were within hailing distance of one another there was always a good deal of shouting from trench to trench. From ourselves: 'Fascistas – maricones!' From the Fascists: 'Viva España! Viva Franco!' – or, when they knew that there were English opposite them: 'Go home, you English! We don't want foreigners here!' On the Government side, in the party militias, the shouting of propaganda to undermine the enemy morale had been developed into a regular technique. In every suitable position men, usually machine-gunners, were told off for shouting-duty and provided with megaphones. Generally they shouted a set-piece, full of revolutionary sentiments which explained to the Fascist soldiers that they were merely the hirelings of international capitalism, that they were fighting against their own class, etc., etc., and urged them to come over to our side. This was repeated over and over by relays of men; sometimes it continued almost the whole night. There is very little doubt that it had its effect; everyone agreed that the trickle of Fascist deserters was partly caused by it. If one comes to think of it, when some poor devil of a sentry – very likely a Socialist or Anarchist trade union member who has been conscripted against his will – is freezing at his post, the slogan, 'Don't fight against your own class!' ringing again and again through the darkness is bound to make an impression on him. It might make just the difference between deserting and not deserting. Of course such a proceeding does not fit in with the English conception of war. I admit I was amazed and scandalized when I first saw it done. The idea of trying to convert your enemy instead of shooting him! I now think that from any point of view it was a legitimate manoeuvre. In ordinary trench warfare, when there is no artillery, it is extremely difficult to inflict casualties on the enemy without receiving an equal number yourself. If you can immobilize a certain number of men by making them desert, so much the better; deserters are actually more useful to you than corpses, because they can give information. But at the beginning it dismayed all of us; it made us feel that the Spaniards were not taking this war of theirs sufficiently seriously. The man who did the shouting at the P.S.U.C. post down on our right was an artist at the job. Sometimes, instead of shouting revolutionary slogans he simply told the Fascists how much better we were fed than they were. His account of the Government rations was apt to be a little imaginative. 'Buttered toast!' – you could hear his voice echoing across the lonely valley – 'We're just sitting down to buttered toast over here! Lovely slices of buttered toast!' I do not doubt that, like the rest of us, he had not seen butter for weeks or months past, but in the icy night the news of buttered toast probably set many a Fascist mouth watering. It even made mine water, though I knew he was lying.

One day in February we saw a Fascist aeroplane approaching. As usual, a machine-gun was dragged into the open and its barrel cocked up, and everyone lay on his back to get a good aim. Our isolated positions were not worth bombing, and as a rule the few Fascist aeroplanes that passed our way circled round to avoid machine-gun fire. This time the aeroplane came straight over, too high up to be worth shooting at, and out of it came tumbling not bombs but white glittering things that turned over and over in the air. A few fluttered down into the position. They were copies of a Fascist newspaper, the *Heraldo de Aragon*, announcing the fall of Malaga.

That night the Fascists made a sort of abortive attack. I was just getting down into kip, half dead with sleep, when there was a heavy stream of bullets overhead and someone shouted into the dug-out: 'They're attacking!' I grabbed my rifle and slithered up to my post, which was at the top of the position, beside the machine-gun. There was utter darkness and diabolical noise. The fire of, I think, five machine-guns was pouring upon us, and there was a series of heavy crashes caused by the Fascists flinging bombs over their own parapet in the most idiotic manner. It was intensely dark. Down in the valley to the left of us I could see the greenish flash of rifles where a small party of Fascists, probably a patrol, were chipping in. The bullets were flying round us in the darkness, crack-zip-crack. A few shells came whistling over, but they fell nowhere near us and (as usual in this war) most of them failed to explode. I had a bad moment when yet another machine-gun opened fire from the hill-top in our rear – actually a gun that had been brought up to support us, but at the time it looked as though we were surrounded. Presently our own machine-gun jammed, as it always did jam with those vile cartridges, and the ramrod was lost in the impenetrable darkness. Apparently there was nothing that one could do except stand still and be shot at. The Spanish machine-gunners disdained to take cover, in fact exposed themselves deliberately, so I had to do likewise. Petty though it was, the whole experience was very interesting. It was the first time that I had been properly speaking under fire, and to my humiliation I found that I was horribly frightened. You always, I notice, feel the same when you are under heavy fire – not so much afraid of being hit as afraid because you don't know *where* you will be hit. You are wondering all the while just where the bullet will nip you, and it gives your whole body a most unpleasant sensitiveness.

After an hour or two the firing slowed down and died away. Meanwhile we had had only one casualty. The Fascists had advanced a couple of machine-guns into no man's land, but they had kept a safe distance and made no attempt to storm our parapet. They were in fact not attacking, merely wasting cartridges and making a cheerful noise to celebrate the fall of Malaga. The chief importance of the affair was that it taught me to read the war news in the papers with a more disbelieving eye. A day or two later the newspapers and the radio published reports of a tremendous attack with cavalry and tanks (up a perpendicular hill-side!) which had been beaten off by the heroic English.

When the Fascists told us that Malaga had fallen we set it down as a lie, but next day there were more convincing rumours, and it must have been a day or two later that it was admitted officially. By degrees the whole disgraceful story leaked out – how the town had been evacuated without firing a shot, and how the fury of the Italians had fallen not upon the troops, who were gone, but upon the wretched civilian population, some of whom were pursued and machine-gunned for a hundred miles. The news sent a sort of chill all along the line, for, whatever the truth may have been, every man in the militia believed that the loss of Malaga was due to treachery. It was the first talk I had heard of treachery or divided aims. It set up in my mind the first vague doubt about this war in which, hitherto, the rights and wrongs had seemed so beautifully simple.

In mid-February we left Monte Oscuro and were sent, together with all the P.O.U.M. troops in this sector, to make a part of the army besieging Huesca. It was a fifty-mile lorry journey across the wintry plain, where the clipped vines were not yet budding and the blades of the winter barley were just poking through the lumpy soil. Four kilometres from our new trenches Huesca glittered small and clear like a city of dolls' houses. Months earlier, when Sietamo was taken, the general commanding the Government troops had said gaily: 'To-morrow we'll have coffee in Huesca.' It turned out that he was mistaken. There had been bloody attacks, but the town did not fall, and 'Tomorrow we'll have coffee in Huesca' had become a standing joke throughout the army. If I ever go back to Spain I shall make a point of having a cup of coffee in Huesca.

Chapter Five

On the eastern side of Huesca, until late March, nothing happened – almost literally nothing. We were twelve hundred metres from the enemy. When the Fascists were driven back into Huesca the Republican Army troops who held this part of the line had not been over-zealous in their advance, so that the line formed a kind of pocket. Later it would have to be advanced – a ticklish job under fire – but for the present the enemy might as well have been non-existent; our sole preoccupation was keeping warm and getting enough to eat. As a matter of fact there were things in this period that interested me greatly, and I will describe some of them later. But I shall be keeping nearer to the order of events if I try here to give some account of the internal political situation on the Government side.

At the beginning I had ignored the political side of the war, and it was only about this time that it began to force itself upon my attention. If you are not interested in the horrors of party politics, please skip; I am trying to keep the political parts of this narrative in separate chapters for precisely that purpose. But at the same time it would be quite impossible to write about the Spanish war from a purely military angle. It was above all things a political war. No event in it, at any rate during the first year, is intelligible unless one has some grasp of the inter-party struggle that was going on behind the Government lines.

When I came to Spain, and for some time afterwards, I was not only uninterested in the political situation but unaware of it. I knew there was a war on, but I had no notion what kind of a war. If you had asked me why I had joined the militia I should have answered: 'To fight against Fascism,' and if you had asked me what I was fighting *for*, I should have answered: 'Common decency.' I had accepted the *News Chronicle-New Statesman* version of the war as the defence of civilization against a maniacal outbreak by an army of Colonel Blimps in the pay of Hitler. The revolutionary atmosphere of Barcelona had attracted me deeply, but I had made no attempt to understand it. As for the kaleidoscope of political parties and trade unions, with their tiresome names – P.S.U.C., P.O.U.M., F.A.I., C.N.T., U.G.T., J.C.I., J.S.U., A.I.T. – they merely exasperated me. It looked at first sight as though Spain were suffering from a plague of initials. I knew that I was serving in something called the P.O.U.M. (I had only joined the P.O.U.M. militia rather than any other because I happened to arrive in Barcelona with I.L.P. papers), but I did not realize that there were serious differences between the political parties. At Monte Pocero, when they pointed to the position on our left and said: 'Those are the Socialists' (meaning the P.S.U.C.), I was puzzled and said: 'Aren't we all Socialists?' I thought it idiotic that people fighting for their lives should *have* separate parties; my attitude always was, 'Why can't we drop all this political nonsense and get on with the war?' This of course was the correct 'anti-Fascist' attitude which had been carefully disseminated by the English newspapers, largely in order to prevent people from grasping the real nature of the struggle. But in Spain, especially in Catalonia, it was an attitude that no one could or did keep up indefinitely. Everyone, however unwillingly, took sides sooner or later. For even if one cared nothing for the political parties and their conflicting 'lines', it was too obvious that one's own destiny was involved. As a militiaman one was a soldier against Franco, but one was also a pawn in an enormous struggle that was being fought out between two political theories. When I scrounged for firewood on the mountain-side and wondered whether this was really a war or whether the *News Chronicle* had made it up, when I dodged the Communist machine-guns in the Barcelona riots, when I finally fled from Spain with the police one jump behind me – all these things happened to me in that particular way because I was serving in the P.O.U.M. militia and not in the P.S.U.C. So great is the difference between two sets of initials!

To understand the alignment on the Government side one has got to remember how the war started. When the fighting broke out on 18 July it is probable that every anti-Fascist in Europe felt a thrill of hope. For here at last, apparently, was democracy standing up to Fascism. For years past the so-called democratic countries had been surrendering to Fascism at every step. The Japanese had been allowed to do as they liked in Manchuria. Hitler had walked into power and proceeded to massacre political opponents of all shades. Mussolini had bombed the Abyssinians while fifty-three nations (I think it was fifty-three) made pious noises 'off'. But when Franco tried to overthrow a mildly Left-wing Government the Spanish people, against all expectation, had risen against him. It seemed – possibly it was – the turning of the tide.

But there were several points that escaped general notice. To begin with, Franco was not strictly comparable with Hitler or Mussolini. His rising was a military mutiny backed up by the aristocracy and the Church, and in the main, especially at the beginning, it was an attempt not so much to impose Fascism as to restore feudalism. This meant that Franco had against him not only the working class but also various sections of the liberal bourgeoisie – the very people who are the supporters of Fascism when it appears in a more modern form. More important than this was the fact that the Spanish working class did not, as we might conceivably do in England, resist Franco in the name of 'democracy' and the *status quo*; their resistance was accompanied by – one might almost say it consisted of – a definite revolutionary outbreak. Land was seized by the peasants; many factories and most of the transport were seized by the trade unions; churches were wrecked and the priests driven out or killed. The *Daily Mail*, amid the cheers of the Catholic clergy, was able to represent Franco as a patriot delivering his country from hordes of fiendish 'Reds'.

For the first few months of the war Franco's real opponent was not so much the Government as the trade unions. As soon as the rising broke out the organized town workers replied by calling a general strike and then by demanding – and, after a struggle, getting – arms from the public arsenals. If they had not acted spontaneously and more or less independently it is quite conceivable that Franco would never have been resisted. There can, of course, be no certainty about this, but there is at least reason for thinking it. The Government had made little or no attempt to forestall the rising, which had been foreseen for a long time past, and when the trouble started its attitude was weak and hesitant, so much so, indeed, that Spain had three premiers in a single day.[1] Moreover, the one step that could save the immediate situation, the arming of the workers, was only taken unwillingly and in response to violent popular clamour. However, the arms were distributed, and in the big towns of Eastern Spain the Fascists were defeated by a huge effort, mainly of the working class, aided by some of the armed forces (Assault Guards, etc.) who had remained loyal. It was the kind of effort that could probably only be made by people who were fighting with a revolutionary intention – i.e. believed that they were fighting for something better than the *status quo*. In the various centres of revolt it is thought that three thousand people died in the streets in a single day. Men and women armed only with sticks of dynamite rushed across the open squares and stormed stone buildings held by trained soldiers with machine-guns. Machine-gun nests that the Fascists had placed at strategic spots were smashed by rushing taxis at them at sixty miles an hour. Even if one had heard nothing of the seizure of the land by the peasants, the setting up of local soviets, etc., it would be hard to believe that the Anarchists and Socialists who were the backbone of the resistance were doing this kind of thing for the preservation of capitalist democracy, which especially in the Anarchist view was no more than a centralized swindling machine.

Meanwhile the workers had weapons in their hands, and at this stage they refrained from giving them up. (Even a year later it was computed that the Anarcho-Syndicalists in Catalonia possessed 30,000 rifles.) The estates of the big pro-Fascist landlords were in many places seized by the peasants. Along with the collectivization of industry and transport there was an attempt to set up the rough beginnings of a workers' government by means of local committees, workers' patrols to replace the old pro-capitalist police forces, workers' militias based on trade unions, and so forth. Of course the process was not uniform, and it went further in Catalonia than elsewhere. There were areas where the institutions of local government remained almost untouched, and others where they existed side by side with revolutionary committees. In a few places independent Anarchist communes were set up, and some of them remained in being till about a year later, when they were forcibly suppressed by the Government. In Catalonia, for the first few months, most of the actual power was in the hands of the Anarcho-Syndicalists, who controlled most of the key industries. The thing that had happened in Spain was, in fact,

[1] Quiroga, Barrios, and Giral. The first two refused to distribute arms to the trade unions.

not merely a civil war, but the beginning of a revolution. It is this fact that the anti-Fascist press outside Spain has made it its special business to obscure. The issue has been narrowed down to 'Fascism versus democracy' and the revolutionary aspect concealed as much as possible. In England, where the Press is more centralized and the public more easily deceived than elsewhere, only two versions of the Spanish war have had any publicity to speak of: the Right-wing version of Christian patriots versus Bolsheviks dripping with blood, and the Left-wing version of gentlemanly republicans quelling a military revolt. The central issue has been successfully covered up.

There were several reasons for this. To begin with, appalling lies about atrocities were being circulated by the pro-Fascist press, and well-meaning propagandists undoubtedly thought that they were aiding the Spanish Government by denying that Spain had 'gone Red'. But the main reason was this: that, except for the small revolutionary groups which exist in all countries, the whole world was determined upon preventing revolution in Spain. In particular the Communist Party, with Soviet Russia behind it, had thrown its whole weight against the revolution. It was the Communist thesis that revolution at this stage would be fatal and that what was to be aimed at in Spain was not workers' control, but bourgeois democracy. It hardly needs pointing out why 'liberal' capitalist opinion took the same line. Foreign capital was heavily invested in Spain. The Barcelona Traction Company, for instance, represented ten millions of British capital; and meanwhile the trade unions had seized all the transport in Catalonia. If the revolution went forward there would be no compensation, or very little; if the capitalist republic prevailed, foreign investments would be safe. And since the revolution had got to be crushed, it greatly simplified things to pretend that no revolution had happened. In this way the real significance of every event could be covered up; every shift of power from the trade unions to the central Government could be represented as a necessary step in military reorganization. The situation produced was curious in the extreme. Outside Spain few people grasped that there was a revolution; inside Spain nobody doubted it. Even the P.S.U.C. newspapers, Communist-controlled and more or less committed to an anti-revolutionary policy, talked about 'our glorious revolution'. And meanwhile the Communist press in foreign countries was shouting that there was no sign of revolution anywhere; the seizure of factories, setting up of workers' committees, etc., had not happened – or, alternatively, had happened, but 'had no political significance'. According to the *Daily Worker* (6 August 1936) those who said that the Spanish people were fighting for social revolution, or for anything other than bourgeois democracy, were 'downright lying scoundrels'. On the other hand, Juan Lopez, a member of the Valencia Government, declared in February 1937 that 'the Spanish people are shedding their blood, not for the democratic Republic and its paper Constitution, but for . . . a revolution.' So it would appear that the downright lying scoundrels included members of the Government for which we were bidden to fight. Some of the foreign anti-Fascist papers even descended to the pitiful lie of pretending that churches were only attacked when they were used as Fascist fortresses. Actually churches were pillaged everywhere and as a matter of course, because it was perfectly well understood that the Spanish Church was part of the capitalist racket. In six months in Spain I only saw two undamaged churches, and until about July 1937 no churches were allowed to reopen and hold services, except for one or two Protestant churches in Madrid.

But, after all, it was only the beginning of a revolution, not the complete thing. Even when the workers, certainly in Catalonia and possibly elsewhere, had the power to do so, they did not overthrow or completely replace the Government. Obviously they could not do so when Franco was hammering at the gate and sections of the middle class were on their side. The country was in a transitional state that was capable either of developing in the direction of Socialism or of reverting to an ordinary capitalist republic. The peasants had most of the land, and they were likely to keep it, unless Franco won; all large industries had been collectivized, but whether they remained collectivized, or whether capitalism was reintroduced, would depend finally upon which group gained control. At the beginning both the Central Government and the Generalite de Cataluña (the semi-autonomous Catalan Government) could definitely be said to represent the working class. The Government was headed by Caballero, a Left-wing Socialist, and contained ministers representing the U.G.T. (Socialist trade unions) and the C.N.T. (Syndicalist unions controlled by the Anarchists). The Catalan Generalite was for a while virtually superseded by an anti-Fascist Defence Committee[1] consisting mainly of delegates from the trade unions. Later the Defence Committee was dissolved and the Generalite was reconstituted so as to represent the unions and the various Left-wing parties. But every subsequent reshuffling of the Government was a move towards the Right. First the P.O.U.M. was expelled from the Generalite; six months later Caballero was replaced by the Right-wing Socialist Negrin; shortly afterwards the C.N.T. was eliminated from the Government; then the U.G.T.; then the C.N.T. was turned out of the Generalite; finally, a year after the outbreak of war and revolution, there remained a Government composed entirely of Right-wing Socialists, Liberals, and Communists.

The general swing to the Right dates from about October–November 1936, when the U.S.S.R. began to supply arms to the Government and power began to pass from the Anarchists to the Communists. Except Russia and Mexico no country had had the decency to come to the rescue of the Government, and Mexico, for obvious reasons, could not supply arms in large quantities. Consequently the Russians were in a position to dictate terms. There is very little doubt that these terms were, in substance, 'Prevent revolution or you get no weapons,' and that the first move against the revolutionary elements, the expulsion of the P.O.U.M. from the Catalan Generalite, was done under orders from the U.S.S.R. It has been denied that any direct pressure was exerted by the Russian Government, but the point is not of great importance, for the Communist parties of all countries can be taken as carrying out Russian policy, and it is not denied that the Communist Party was the chief mover first against the P.O.U.M., later against the Anarchists and against Caballero's section of the Socialists, and, in general, against a revolutionary policy. Once the U.S.S.R. had intervened the triumph of the Communist Party was assured. To begin with, gratitude to Russia for the arms and the fact that the Communist Party, especially since the arrival of the International Brigades, looked capable of winning the war, immensely raised the Communist prestige. Secondly, the Russian arms were supplied via the Communist Party and the

[1] Comite Central de Milicias Antifascistas. Delegates were chosen in proportion to the membership of their organizations. Nine delegates represented the trade unions, three the Catalan Liberal parties, and two the various Marxist parties (P.O.U.M., Communists, and others).

parties allied to them, who saw to it that as few as possible got to their political opponents.[1] Thirdly, by proclaiming a non-revolutionary policy the Communists were able to gather in all those whom the extremists had scared. It was easy, for instance, to rally the wealthier peasants against the collectivization policy of the Anarchists. There was an enormous growth in the membership of the party, and the influx was largely from the middle class – shopkeepers, officials, army officers, well-to-do peasants, etc., etc. The war was essentially a triangular struggle. The fight against Franco had to continue, but the simultaneous aim of the Government was to recover such power as remained in the hands of the trade unions. It was done by a series of small moves – a policy of pin-pricks, as somebody called it – and on the whole very cleverly. There was no general and obvious counter-revolutionary move, and until May 1937 it was scarcely necessary to use force. The workers could always be brought to heel by an argument that is almost too obvious to need stating: 'Unless you do this, that and the other we shall lose the war.' In every case, needless to say, it appeared that the thing demanded by military necessity was the surrender of something that the workers had won for themselves in 1936. But the argument could hardly fail, because to lose the war was the last thing that the revolutionary parties wanted; if the war was lost democracy and revolution, Socialism and Anarchism, became meaningless words. The Anarchists, the only revolutionary party that was big enough to matter, were obliged to give way on point after point. The process of collectivization was checked, the local committees were got rid of, the workers' patrols were abolished and the pre-war police forces, largely reinforced and very heavily armed, were restored, and various key industries which had been under the control of the trade unions were taken over by the Government (the seizure of the Barcelona Telephone Exchange, which led to the May fighting, was one incident in this process); finally, most important of all, the workers' militias, based on the trade unions, were gradually broken up and redistributed among the new Popular Army, a 'non-political' army on semi-bourgeois lines, with a differential pay rate, a privileged officer-caste, etc., etc. In the special circumstances this was the really decisive step; it happened later in Catalonia than elsewhere because it was there that the revolutionary parties were strongest. Obviously the only guarantee that the workers could have of retaining their winnings was to keep some of the armed forces under their own control. As usual, the breaking-up of the militias was done in the name of military efficiency; and no one denied that a thorough military reorganization was needed. It would, however, have been quite possible to reorganize the militias and make them more efficient while keeping them under direct control of the trade unions; the main purpose of the change was to make sure that the Anarchists did not possess an army of their own. Moreover, the democratic spirit of the militias made them breeding-grounds for revolutionary ideas. The Communists were well aware of this, and inveighed ceaselessly and bitterly against the P.O.U.M. and Anarchist principle of equal pay for all ranks. A general 'bourgeoisification', a deliberate destruction of the equalitarian spirit of the first few months of the revolution, was taking place. All happened so swiftly that people making successive visits

[1] This was why there were so few Russian arms on the Aragon front, where the troops were predominantly Anarchist. Until April 1937 the only Russian weapon I saw – with the exception of some aeroplanes which may or may not have been Russian – was a solitary sub-machine gun.

to Spain at intervals of a few months have declared that they seemed scarcely to be visiting the same country; what had seemed on the surface and for a brief instant to be a workers' State was changing before one's eyes into an ordinary bourgeois republic with the normal division into rich and poor. By the autumn of 1937 the 'Socialist' Negrin was declaring in public speeches that 'we respect private property', and members of the Cortes who at the beginning of the war had had to fly the country because of their suspected Fascist sympathies were returning to Spain.

The whole process is easy to understand if one remembers that it proceeds from the temporary alliance that Fascism, in certain forms, forces upon the bourgeois and the worker. This alliance, known as the Popular Front, is in essential an alliance of enemies, and it seems probable that it must always end by one partner swallowing the other. The only unexpected feature in the Spanish situation – and outside Spain it has caused an immense amount of misunderstanding – is that among the parties on the Government side the Communists stood not upon the extreme Left, but upon the extreme Right. In reality this should cause no surprise, because the tactics of the Communist Party elsewhere, especially in France, have made it clear that Official Communism must be regarded, at any rate for the time being, as an anti-revolutionary force. The whole of Comintern policy is now subordinated (excusably, considering the world situation) to the defence of U.S.S.R., which depends upon a system of military alliances. In particular, the U.S.S.R. is in alliance with France, a capitalist-imperialist country. The alliance is of little use to Russia unless French capitalism is strong, therefore Communist policy in France has got to be anti-revolutionary. This means not only that French Communists now march behind the tricolour and sing the Marseillaise, but, what is more important, that they have had to drop all effective agitation in the French colonies. It is less than three years since Thorez, the Secretary of the French Communist Party, was declaring that the French workers would never be bamboozled into fighting against their German comrades;[1] he is now one of the loudest-lunged patriots in France. The clue to the behaviour of the Communist Party in any country is the military relation of that country, actual or potential, towards the U.S.S.R. In England, for instance, the position is still uncertain, hence the English Communist Party is still hostile to the National Government, and, ostensibly, opposed to rearmament. If, however, Great Britain enters into an alliance or military understanding with the U.S.S.R., the English Communist, like the French Communist, will have no choice but to become a good patriot and imperialist; there are premonitory signs of this already. In Spain the Communist 'line' was undoubtedly influenced by the fact that France, Russia's ally, would strongly object to a revolutionary neighbour and would raise heaven and earth to prevent the liberation of Spanish Morocco. The *Daily Mail*, with its tales of red revolution financed by Moscow, was even more wildly wrong than usual. In reality it was the Communists above all others who prevented revolution in Spain. Later, when the Right-wing forces were in full control, the Communists showed themselves willing to go a great deal further than the Liberals in hunting down the revolutionary leaders.[2]

[1] In the Chamber of Deputies, March 1935.

[2] For the best account of the interplay between the parties on the Government side, see Franz Borkenau's *The Spanish Cockpit*. This is by a long way the ablest book that has yet appeared on the Spanish war.

I have tried to sketch the general course of the Spanish revolution during its first year, because this makes it easier to understand the situation at any given moment. But I do not want to suggest that in February I held all of the opinions that are implied in what I have said above. To begin with, the things that most enlightened me had not yet happened, and in any case my sympathies were in some ways different from what they are now. This was partly because the political side of the war bored me and I naturally reacted against the viewpoint of which I heard most – i.e. the P.O.U.M.-I.L.P. viewpoint. The Englishmen I was among were mostly I.L.P. members, with a few C.P. members among them, and most of them were much better educated politically than myself. For weeks on end, during the dull period when nothing was happening round Huesca, I found myself in the middle of a political discussion that practically never ended. In the draughty evil-smelling barn of the farm-house where we were billeted, in the stuffy blackness of dug-outs, behind the parapet in the freezing midnight hours, the conflicting party 'lines' were debated over and over. Among the Spaniards it was the same, and most of the newspapers we saw made the inter-party feud their chief feature. One would have had to be deaf or an imbecile not to pick up some idea of what the various parties stood for.

From the point of view of political theory there were only three parties that mattered, the P.S.U.C., the P.O.U.M., and the C.N.T.-F.A.I., loosely described as the Anarchists. I take the P.S.U.C. first, as being the most important; it was the party that finally triumphed, and even at this time it was visibly in the ascendant.

It is necessary to explain that when one speaks of the P.S.U.C. 'line' one really means the Communist Party 'line'. The P.S.U.C. (Partido Socialista Unificado de Catalunya) was the Socialist Party of Catalonia; it had been formed at the beginning of the war by the fusion of various Marxist parties, including the Catalan Communist Party, but it was now entirely under Communist control and was affiliated to the Third International. Elsewhere in Spain no formal unification between Socialists and Communists had taken place, but the Communist viewpoint and the Right-wing Socialist viewpoint could everywhere be regarded as identical. Roughly speaking, the P.S.U.C. was the political organ of the U.G.T. (Union General de Trabajadores), the Socialist trade unions. The membership of these unions throughout Spain now numbered about a million and a half. They contained many sections of the manual workers, but since the outbreak of war they had also been swollen by a large influx of middle-class members, for in the early 'revolutionary' days people of all kinds had found it useful to join either the U.G.T. or the C.N.T. The two blocks of unions overlapped, but of the two the C.N.T. was more definitely a working-class organization. The P.S.U.C. was therefore a party partly of the workers and partly of the small bourgeoisie – the shopkeepers, the officials, and the wealthier peasants.

The P.S.U.C. 'line', which was preached in the Communist and pro-Communist press throughout the world, was approximately this:

'At present nothing matters except winning the war; without victory in the war all else is meaningless. Therefore this is not the moment to talk of pressing forward with the revolution. We can't afford to alienate the peasants by forcing collectivization upon them, and we can't afford to frighten away the middle classes who were fighting on our side. Above all for the sake of efficiency we must do away with revolutionary chaos. We must have a strong central government in place of local committees, and we must have a properly trained and fully militarized army under a unified command. Clinging onto fragments of workers' control and parroting revolutionary phrases is worse than useless; it is not merely obstructive, but even counter-revolutionary, because it leads to divisions which can be used against us by the Fascists. At this stage we are not fighting for the dictatorship of the proletariat, we are fighting for parliamentary democracy. Whoever tries to turn the civil war into a social revolution is playing into the hands of the Fascists and is in effect, if not in intention, a traitor.'

The P.O.U.M. 'line' differed from this on every point except, of course, the importance of winning the war. The P.O.U.M. (Partido Obrero de Unificacion Marxista) was one of those dissident Communist parties which have appeared in many countries in the last few years as a result of the opposition to 'Stalinism'; i.e. to the change, real or apparent, in Communist policy. It was made up partly of ex-Communist and partly of an earlier party, the Workers' and Peasants' Bloc. Numerically it was a small party,[1] with not much influence outside Catalonia, and chiefly important because it contained an unusually high proportion of politically conscious members. In Catalonia its chief stronghold was Lerida. It did not represent any block of trade unions. The P.O.U.M. militiamen were mostly C.N.T. members, but the actual party-members generally belonged to the U.G.T. It was, however, only in the C.N.T. that the P.O.U.M. had any influence. The P.O.U.M. 'line' was approximately this:

'It is nonsense to talk of opposing Fascism by bourgeois "democracy", Bourgeois "democracy" is only another name for capitalism, and so is Fascism; to fight against Fascism on behalf of "democracy" is to fight against one form of capitalism on behalf of a second which is liable to turn into the first at any moment. The only real alternative to Fascism is workers' control. If you set up any less goal than this, you will either hand the victory to Franco, or, at best, let in Fascism by the back door. Meanwhile the workers must cling to every scrap of what they have won; if they yield anything to the semi-bourgeois Government they can depend upon being cheated. The workers' militias and police-forces must be preserved in their present form and every effort to "bourgeoisify" them must be resisted. If the workers do not control the armed forces, the armed forces will control the workers. The war and the revolution are inseparable.'

The Anarchist viewpoint is less easily defined. In any case the loose term 'Anarchists' is used to cover a multitude of people of very varying opinions. The huge block of unions making up the C.N.T. (Confederacion Nacional de Trabajadores), with round about two million members in all, had for its political organ the F.A.I. (Federacion Anarquista Iberica), an actual Anarchist organization. But even the members of the F.A.I., though always tinged, as perhaps most Spaniards are, with the Anarchist philosophy, were not necessarily Anarchists in the purest sense. Especially since the beginning of the war they had moved more in the direction of ordinary Socialism, because circumstances had forced them to take part in centralized administration and

[1] The figures for the P.O.U.M. membership are given as: July 1936, 10,000; December 1936, 70,000; June 1937, 40,000. But these are from P.O.U.M. sources; a hostile estimate would probably divide them by four. The only thing one can say with any certainty about the membership of the Spanish political parties is that every party over-estimates its own numbers.

even to break all their principles by entering the Government. Nevertheless they differed fundamentally from the Communists in so much that, like the P.O.U.M., they aimed at workers' control and not a parliamentary democracy. They accepted the P.O.U.M. slogan: 'The war and the revolution are inseparable,' though they were less dogmatic about it. Roughly speaking, the C.N.T.-F.A.I. stood for: (1) Direct control over industry by the workers engaged in each industry, e.g. transport, the textile factories, etc.; (2) Government by local committees and resistance to all forms of centralized authoritarianism; (3) Uncompromising hostility to the bourgeoisie and the Church. The last point, though the least precise, was the most important. The Anarchists were the opposite of the majority of so-called revolutionaries in so much that though their principles were rather vague their hatred of privilege and injustice was perfectly genuine. Philosophically, Communism and Anarchism are poles apart. Practically – i.e. in the form of society aimed at – the difference is mainly one of emphasis, but it is quite irreconcilable. The Communist's emphasis is always on centralism and efficiency, the Anarchist's on liberty and equality. Anarchism is deeply rooted in Spain and is likely to outlive Communism when the Russian influence is withdrawn. During the first two months of the war it was the Anarchists more than anyone else who had saved the situation, and much later than this the Anarchist militia, in spite of their indiscipline, were notoriously the best fighters among the purely Spanish forces. From about February 1937 onwards the Anarchists and the P.O.U.M. could to some extent be lumped together. If the Anarchists, the P.O.U.M. and the Left wing of the Socialists had had the sense to combine at the start and press a realistic policy, the history of the war might have been different. But in the early period, when the revolutionary parties seemed to have the game in their hands, this was impossible. Between the Anarchists and the Socialists there were ancient jealousies, the P.O.U.M., as Marxists, were sceptical of Anarchism, while from the pure Anarchist standpoint the 'Trotskyism' of the P.O.U.M. was not much preferable to the 'Stalinism' of the Communists. Nevertheless the Communist tactics tended to drive the two parties together. When the P.O.U.M. joined in the disastrous fighting in Barcelona in May, it was mainly from an instinct to stand by the C.N.T., and later, when the P.O.U.M. was suppressed, the Anarchists were the only people who dared to raise a voice in its defence.

So, roughly speaking, the alignment of forces was this. On the one side the C.N.T.-F.A.I., the P.O.U.M., and a section of the Socialists, standing for workers' control: on the other side the Right-wing Socialists, Liberals, and Communists, standing for centralized government and a militarized army.

It is easy to see why, at this time, I preferred the Communist viewpoint to that of the P.O.U.M. The Communists had a definite practical policy, an obviously better policy from the point of view of the common sense which looks only a few months ahead. And certainly the day-to-day policy of the P.O.U.M., their propaganda and so forth, was unspeakably bad; it must have been so, or they would have been able to attract a bigger mass-following. What clinched everything was that the Communists – so it seemed to me – were getting on with the war while we and the Anarchists were standing still. This was the general feeling at the time. The Communists had gained power and a vast increase of membership partly by appealing to the middle classes against the revolutionaries, but partly also because they were the only people who looked capable of winning the war. The Russian arms and the magnificent defence of

Madrid by troops mainly under Communist control had made the Communists the heroes of Spain. As someone put it, every Russian aeroplane that flew over our heads was Communist propaganda. The revolutionary purism of the P.O.U.M., though I saw its logic, seemed to me rather futile. After all, the one thing that mattered was to win the war.

Meanwhile there was the diabolical inter-party feud that was going on in the newspapers, in pamphlets, on posters, in books – everywhere. At this time the newspapers I saw most often were the P.O.U.M. papers *La Batalla* and *Adelante*, and their ceaseless carping against the 'counter-revolutionary' P.S.U.C. struck me as priggish and tiresome. Later, when I studied the P.S.U.C. and Communist press more closely, I realized that the P.O.U.M. were almost blameless compared with their adversaries. Apart from anything else, they had much smaller opportunities. Unlike the Communists, they had no footing in any press outside their own country, and inside Spain they were at an immense disadvantage because the press censorship was mainly under Communist control, which meant that the P.O.U.M. papers were liable to be suppressed or fined if they said anything damaging. It is also fair to the P.O.U.M. to say that though they might preach endless sermons on revolution and quote Lenin *ad nauseam*, they did not usually indulge in personal libel. Also they kept their polemics mainly to newspaper articles. Their large coloured posters, designed for a wider public (posters are important in Spain, with its large illiterate population), did not attack rival parties, but were simply anti-Fascist or abstractly revolutionary; so were the songs the militiamen sang. The Communist attacks were quite a different matter. I shall have to deal with some of these later in this book. Here I can only give a brief indication of the Communist line of attack.

On the surface the quarrel between the Communists and the P.O.U.M. was one of tactics. The P.O.U.M. was for immediate revolution, the Communists not. So far so good; there was much to be said on both sides. Further, the Communists contended that the P.O.U.M. propaganda divided and weakened the Government forces and thus endangered the war; again, though finally I do not agree, a good case could be made out for this. But here the peculiarity of Communist tactics came in. Tentatively at first, then more loudly, they began to assert that the P.O.U.M. was splitting the Government forces not by bad judgment but by deliberate design. The P.O.U.M. was declared to be no more than a gang of disguised Fascists, in the pay of Franco and Hitler, who were pressing a pseudo-revolutionary policy as a way of aiding the Fascist cause. The P.O.U.M. was a 'Trotskyist' organization and 'Franco's Fifth Column.' This implied that scores of thousands of working-class people, including eight or ten thousand soldiers who were freezing in the front-line trenches and hundreds of foreigners who had come to Spain to fight against Fascism, often sacrificing their livelihood and their nationality by doing so, were simply traitors in the pay of the enemy. And this story was spread all over Spain by means of posters, etc., and repeated over and over in the Communist and pro-Communist press of the whole world. I could fill half a dozen books with quotations if I chose to collect them.

This, then, was what they were saying about us: we were Trotskyists, Fascists, traitors, murderers, cowards, spies, and so forth. I admit it was not pleasant, especially when one thought of some of the people who were responsible for it. It is not a nice thing to see a Spanish boy of fifteen carried down the line on a stretcher, with a dazed white face looking out from among the blankets, and to think of the sleek persons in London and Paris who are writing pamphlets to prove that this boy is a Fascist in disguise. One of the most horrible features of war is that all the war-propaganda, all the screaming and lies and hatred, comes invariably from people who are not fighting. The P.S.U.C. militiamen whom I knew in the line, the Communists from the International Brigade whom I met from time to time, never called me a Trotskyist or a traitor; they left that kind of thing to the journalists in the rear. the people who wrote pamphlets against us and vilified us in the newspapers all remained safe at home, or at worst in the newspaper offices of Valencia, hundreds of miles from the bullets and the mud. And apart from the libels of the inter-party feud, all the usual war-stuff, the tub-thumping, the heroics, the vilification of the enemy – all these were done, as usual, by people who were not fighting and who in many cases would have run a hundred miles sooner than fight. One of the dreariest effects of this war has been to teach me that the Left-wing press is every bit as spurious and dishonest as that of the Right.[1] I do earnestly feel that on our side – the Government side – this war was different from ordinary, imperialistic wars; but from the nature of the war-propaganda you would never have guessed it. The fighting had barely started when the newspapers of the Right and Left divided simultaneously into the same cesspool of abuse. We all remember the *Daily Mail*'s poster: 'REDS CRUCIFY NUNS', while to the *Daily Worker* Franco's Foreign Legion was 'composed of murderers, white-slavers, dope-fiends and the offal of every European country'. As late as October 1937 the *New Statesman* was treating us to tales of Fascist barricades made of the bodies of living children (a most unhandy thing to make barricades with), and Mr Arthur Bryant was declaring that 'the sawing-off of a Conservative tradesman's legs' was 'a commonplace' in Loyalist Spain. The people who write that kind of stuff never fight; possibly they believe that to write it is a substitute for fighting. It is the same in all wars; the soldiers do the fighting, the journalists do the shouting, and no true patriot ever gets near a front-line trench, except on the briefest of propaganda-tours. Sometimes it is a comfort to me to think that the aeroplane is altering the conditions of war. Perhaps when the next great war comes we may see that sight unprecedented in all history, a jingo with a bullet-hole in him.

As far as the journalistic part of it went, this war was a racket like all other wars. But there was this difference, that whereas the journalists usually reserve their most murderous invective for the enemy, in this case, as time went on, the Communists and the P.O.U.M. came to write more bitterly about one another than about the Fascists. Nevertheless at the time I could not bring myself to take it very seriously. The inter-party feud was annoying and even disgusting, but it appeared to me as a domestic squabble. I did not believe that it would alter anything or that there was any really irreconcilable difference of policy. I grasped that the Communists and Liberals had set their faces against allowing the revolution to go forward; I did not grasp that they might be capable of swinging it *back*.

There was a good reason for this. All this time I was at the front, and at the front the social and political atmosphere did not change. I had left Barcelona in

[1] I should like to make an exception of the *Manchester Guardian*. In connection with this book I have had to go through the files of a good many English papers. Of our larger papers, the *Manchester Guardian* is the only one that leaves me with an increased respect for its honesty.

early January and I did not go on leave till late April; and all this time – indeed, till later – in the strip of Aragon controlled by Anarchist and P.O.U.M. troops, the same conditions persisted, at least outwardly. The revolutionary atmosphere remained as I had first known it. General and private, peasant and militiaman, still met as equals; everyone drew the same pay, wore the same clothes, ate the same food and called everyone else 'thou' and 'comrade'; there was no boss-class, no menial-class, no beggars, no prostitutes, no lawyers, no priests, no boot-licking, no cap-touching. I was breathing the air of equality, and I was simple enough to imagine that it existed all over Spain. I did not realize that more or less by chance I was isolated among the most revolutionary section of the Spanish working class.

So, when my more politically educated comrades told me that one could not take a purely military attitude towards the war, and that the choice lay between revolution and Fascism, I was inclined to laugh at them. On the whole I accepted the Communist viewpoint, which boiled down to saying: 'We can't talk of revolution till we've won the war,' and not the P.O.U.M. viewpoint, which boiled down to saying: 'We must go forward or we shall go back.' When later on I decided that the P.O.U.M. were right, or at any rate righter than the Communists, it was not altogether upon a point of theory. On paper the Communist case was a good one; the trouble was that their actual behaviour made it difficult to believe that they were advancing it in good faith. The often-repeated slogan: 'The war first and the revolution afterwards,' though devoutly believed in by the average P.S.U.C. militiaman, who honestly thought that the revolution could continue when the war had been won, was eyewash. The thing for which the Communists were working was not to postpone the Spanish revolution till a more suitable time, but to make sure that it never happened. This became more and more obvious as time went on, as power was twisted more and more out of working-class hands, and as more and more revolutionaries of every shade were flung into jail. Every move was made in the name of military necessity, because this pretext was, so to speak, ready-made, but the effect was to drive the workers back from an advantageous position and into a position in which, when the war was over, they would find it impossible to resist the reintroduction of capitalism. Please notice that I am saying nothing against the rank-and-file Communist, least of all against the thousands of Communists who died heroically round Madrid. But those were not the men who were directing party policy. As for the people higher up, it is inconceivable that they were not acting with their eyes open.

But, finally, the war was worth winning even if the revolution was lost. And in the end I came to doubt whether, in the long run, the Communist policy made for victory. Very few people seem to have reflected that a different policy might be appropriate at different periods of the war. The Anarchists probably saved the situation in the first two months, but they were incapable of organizing resistance beyond a certain point: the Communists probably saved the situation in October-December, but to win the war outright was a different matter. In England the Communist war-policy has been accepted without question, because very few criticisms of it have been allowed to get into print and because its general line – do away with revolutionary chaos, speed up production, militarize the army – sounds realistic and efficient. It is worth pointing out its inherent weakness.

In order to check every revolutionary tendency and make the war as much like an ordinary war as possible, it became necessary to throw away the strategic opportunities that actually existed. I have described how we were armed, or not armed, on the Aragon front. There is very little doubt that arms were deliberately withheld lest too many of them should get into the hands of the Anarchists, who would afterwards use them for a revolutionary purpose; consequently the big Aragon offensive which would have made Franco draw back from Bilbao, and possibly from Madrid, never happened. But this was comparatively a small matter. What was more important was that once the war had been narrowed down to a 'war for democracy' it became impossible to make any large-scale appeal for working-class aid abroad. If we face facts we must admit that the working class of the world has regarded the Spanish war with detachment. Tens of thousands of individuals came to fight, but the tens of millions behind them remained apathetic. During the first year of the war the entire British public is thought to have subscribed to various 'aid Spain' funds about a quarter of a million pounds – probably less than half of what they spend in a single week on going to the pictures. The way in which the working class in the democratic countries could really have helped her Spanish comrades was by industrial action – strikes and boycotts. No such thing ever even began to happen. The Labour and Communist leaders everywhere declared that it was unthinkable; and no doubt they were right, so long as they were also shouting at the tops of their voices that 'red' Spain was not 'red'. Since 1914–1918 'war for democracy' has had a sinister sound. For years past the Communists themselves had been teaching the militant workers in all countries that 'democracy' was a polite name for capitalism. To say first 'Democracy is a swindle,' and then 'Fight for democracy!' is not good tactics. If, with the huge prestige of Soviet Russia behind them, they had appealed to the workers of the world in the name not of 'democratic Spain', but of 'revolutionary Spain', it is hard to believe that they would not have got a response.

But what was most important of all, with a non-revolutionary policy it was difficult, if not impossible, to strike at Franco's rear. By the summer of 1937 Franco was controlling a larger population than the Government – much larger, if one counts in the colonies – with about the same number of troops. As everyone knows, with a hostile population at your back it is impossible to keep an army in the field without an equally large army to guard your communications, suppress sabotage, etc. Obviously, therefore, there was no real popular movement in Franco's rear. It was inconceivable that the people in his territory, at any rate the town-workers and the poorer peasants, liked or wanted Franco, but with every swing to the Right the Government's superiority became less apparent. What clinches everything is the case of Morocco. Why was there no rising in Morocco? Franco was trying to set up an infamous dictatorship, and the Moors actually preferred him to the Popular Front Government! The palpable truth is that no attempt was made to foment a rising in Morocco, because to do so would have meant putting a revolutionary construction on the war. The first necessity, to convince the Moors of the Government's good faith, would have been to proclaim Morocco liberated. And we can imagine how pleased the French would have been by that! The best strategic opportunity of the war was flung away in the vain hope of placating French and British capitalism. The whole tendency of the Communist policy was to reduce the war to an ordinary, non-revolutionary war in which the Government was heavily handicapped. For a war of that kind has got to be won by mechanical means, i.e. ultimately, by limitless supplies of weapons; and the Government's chief donor of weapons, the U.S.S.R., [illegible] a great disadvantage, geographically, compared with Italy and Germa[illegible] Perhaps the P.O.U.M. and Anarchist slogan: 'The war and the revolution are inseparable,' was less visionary than it sounds.

I have given my reasons for thinking that the Communist anti-revolutionary policy was mistaken, but so far as its effect upon the war goes I do not hope that my judgement is right. A thousand times I hope that it is wrong. I would wish to see this war won by any means whatever. And of course we cannot tell yet what may happen. The Government may swing to the Left again, the Moors may revolt of their own accord, England may decide to buy Italy out, the war may be won by straightforward military means – there is no knowing. I let the above opinions stand, and time will show how far I am right or wrong.

But in February 1937 I did not see things quite in this light. I was sick of the inaction of the Aragon front and chiefly conscious that I had not done my fair share of the fighting. I used to think of the recruiting poster in Barcelona which demanded accusingly of passers-by: 'What have *you* done for democracy?' and feel that I could only answer: 'I have drawn my rations.' When I joined the militia I had promised myself to kill one Fascist – after all, if each of us killed one they would soon be extinct – and I had killed nobody yet, had hardly had the chance to do so. And of course I wanted to go to Madrid. Everyone in the army, whatever his political opinions, always wanted to go to Madrid. This would probably mean exchanging into the International Column, for the P.O.U.M. had now very few troops at Madrid and the Anarchists not so many as formerly.

For the present, of course, one had to stay in the line, but I told everyone that when we went on leave I should, if possible, exchange into the International Column, which meant putting myself under Communist control. Various people tried to dissuade me, but no one attempted to interfere. It is fair to say that there was very little heresy-hunting in the P.O.U.M., perhaps not enough, considering their special circumstances; short of being a pro-Fascist no one was penalized for holding the wrong political opinions. I spent much of my time in the militia in bitterly criticizing the P.O.U.M. 'line', but I never got into trouble for it. There was not even any pressure upon one to become a political member of the party, though I think the majority of the militiamen did so. I myself never joined the party – for which afterwards, when the P.O.U.M. was suppressed, I was rather sorry.

Chapter Six

Meanwhile, the daily – more particularly nightly – round, the common task. Sentry-go, patrols, digging; mud, rain, shrieking winds, and occasional snow. It was not till well into April that the nights grew noticeably warmer. Up here on the plateau the March days were mostly like an English March, with bright blue skies and nagging winds. The winter barley was a foot high, crimson buds were forming on the cherry trees (the line here ran through deserted orchards and vegetable gardens), and if you searched the ditches you could find violets and a kind of wild hyacinth like a poor specimen of a bluebell. Immediately ere ran a wonderful, green, bubbling stream, the first ı had seen since coming to the front. One day I set my teeth he river to have my first bath in six weeks. It was what you bath, for the water was mainly snow-water and not much oint.

thing happened, nothing ever happened. The English had got into the saying that this wasn't a war, it was a bloody pantomime. We were hardly under direct fire from the Fascists. The only danger was from stray bullets, which, as the lines curved forward on either side, came from several directions. All the casualties at this time were from strays. Arthur Clinton got a mysterious bullet that smashed his left shoulder and disabled his arm, permanently, I am afraid. There was a little shell-fire, but it was extraordinarily ineffectual. The scream and crash of the shells was actually looked upon as a mild diversion. The Fascists never dropped their shells on our parapet. A few hundred yards behind us there was a country house, called La Granja, with big farm-buildings, which was used as a store, headquarters, and cook-house for this sector of the line. It was this that the Fascist gunners were trying for, but they were five or six kilometres away and they never aimed well enough to do more than smash the windows and chip the walls. You were only in danger if you happened to be coming up the road when the firing started, and the shells plunged into the fields on either side of you. One learned almost immediately the mysterious art of knowing by the sound of a shell how close it will fall. The shells the Fascists were firing at this period were wretchedly bad. Although they were 150 mm they only made a crater about six feet wide by four deep, and at least one in four failed to explode. There were the usual romantic tales of sabotage in the Fascist factories and unexploded shells in which, instead of the charge, there was found a scrap of paper saying 'Red Front', but I never saw one. The truth was that the shells were hopelessly old; someone picked up a brass fuse-cap stamped with the date, and it was 1917. The Fascist guns were of the same make and calibre as our own, and the unexploded shells were often reconditioned and fired back. There was said to be one old shell with a nickname of its own which travelled daily to and fro, never exploding.

At night small patrols used to be sent into no man's land to lie in ditches near the Fascist lines and listen for sounds (bugle-calls, motor-horns, and so forth) that indicated activity in Huesca. There was a constant come-and-go of Fascist troops, and the numbers could be checked to some extent from listeners' reports. We always had special orders to report the ringing of church bells. It seemed that the Fascists always heard mass before going into action. In among the fields and orchards there were deserted mud-walled huts which it was safe to explore with a lighted match when you had plugged up the windows. Sometimes you came on valuable pieces of loot such as a hatchet or a Fascist water-bottle (better than ours and greatly sought after). You could explore in the daytime as well, but mostly it had to be done crawling on all fours. It was queer to creep about in those empty, fertile fields where everything had been arrested just at the harvest-moment. Last year's crops had never been touched. The unpruned vines were snaking across the ground, the cobs on the standing maize had gone as hard as stone, the mangels and sugar-beets were hypertrophied into huge woody lumps. How the peasants must have cursed both armies! Sometimes parties of men went spud-gathering in no man's land. About a mile to the right of us, where the lines were closer together, there was a patch of potatoes that was frequented both by the Fascists and ourselves. We went there in the daytime, they only at night, as it was commanded by our machine-guns. One night to our annoyance they turned out *en masse* and cleared up the whole patch. We discovered another patch farther on, where there was practically no cover and you had to lift the potatoes lying on your belly – a fatiguing job. If their machine-gunners spotted you, you had to flatten yourself out like a rat when it squirms under a door, with the bullets cutting up the clods a few yards behind you. It seemed worth it at the time. Potatoes were getting very scarce. If you got a sackful you could take them down to the cook-house and swap them for a water-bottleful of coffee.

And still nothing happened, nothing ever looked like happening. 'When are we going to attack? Why don't we attack?' were the questions you heard night and day from Spaniard and Englishman alike. When you think what fighting means it is queer that soldiers want to fight, and yet undoubtedly they do. In stationary warfare there are three things that all soldiers long for: a battle, more cigarettes, and a week's leave. We were somewhat better armed now than before. Each man had a hundred and fifty rounds of ammunition instead of fifty, and by degrees we were being issued with bayonets, steel helmets, and a few bombs. There were constant rumours of forthcoming battles, which I have since thought were deliberately circulated to keep up the spirits of the troops. It did not need much military knowledge to see that there would be no major action on this side of Huesca, at any rate for the time being. The strategic point was the road to Jaca, over on the other side. Later, when the Anarchists made their attacks on the Jaca road, our job was to make 'holding attacks' and force the Fascists to divert troops from the other side.

During all this time, about six weeks, there was only one action on our part of the front. This was when our Shock Troopers attacked the Manicomio, a disused lunatic asylum which the Fascists had converted into a fortress. There were several hundred refugee Germans serving with the P.O.U.M. They were organized in a special battalion called the Batallon de Choque, and from a military point of view they were on quite a different level from the rest of the militia – indeed, were more like soldiers than anyone I saw in Spain, except the Assault Guards and some of the International Column. The attack was mucked up, as usual. How many operations in this war, on the Government side, were *not* mucked up, I wonder? The Shock Troops took the Manicomio by storm, but the troops, of I forget which militia, who were to support them by seizing the neighbouring hill that commanded the Manicomio, were badly let down. The captain who led them was one of those Regular Army officers of doubtful loyalty whom the Government persisted in employing. Either from fright or treachery he warned the Fascists by flinging a bomb when they were two hundred yards away. I am glad to say his men shot him dead on the spot. But the surprise-attack was no surprise, and the militiamen were mown down by heavy fire and driven off the hill, and at nightfall the Shock Troops had to abandon the Manicomio. Through the night the ambulances filed down the abominable road to Sietamo, killing the badly wounded with their joltings.

All of us were lousy by this time; though still cold it was warm enough for that. I have had a big experience of body vermin of various kinds, and for sheer beastliness the louse beats everything I have encountered. Other insects, mosquitoes for instance, make you suffer more, but at least they aren't *resident* vermin. The human louse somewhat resembles a tiny lobster, and he lives chiefly in your trousers. Short of burning all your clothes there is no known way of getting rid of him. Down the seams of your trousers he lays his glittering white eggs, like tiny grains of rice, which hatch out and breed families of their own at horrible speed. I think the pacifists might find it helpful to illustrate their pamphlets with enlarged photographs of lice. Glory of war, indeed! In war *all* soldiers are lousy, at least when it is warm enough. The men who fought at Verdun, at Waterloo, at Flodden, at Senlac, at Thermopylae – every one of them had lice crawling over his testicles. We kept the brutes down to some extent by burning out the eggs and by bathing as often as we could face it. Nothing short of lice could have driven me into that ice-cold river.

Everything was running short – boots, clothes, tobacco, soap, candles, matches, olive oil. Our uniforms were dropping to pieces, and many of the men had no boots, only rope-soled sandals. You came on piles of worn-out boots everywhere. Once we kept a dug-out fire burning for two days mainly with boots, which are not bad fuel. By this time my wife was in Barcelona and used to send me tea, chocolate, and even cigars when such things were procurable; but even in Barcelona everything was running short, especially tobacco. The tea was a godsend, though we had no milk and seldom any sugar. Parcels were constantly being sent from England to men in the contingent, but they never arrived; food, clothes, cigarettes – everything was either refused by the Post Office or seized in France. Curiously enough, the only firm that succeeded in sending packets of tea – even, on one memorable occasion, a tin of biscuits – to my wife was the Army and Navy Stores. Poor old Army and Navy! They did their duty nobly, but perhaps they might have felt happier if the stuff had been going to Franco's side of the barricade. The shortage of tobacco was the worst of all. At the beginning we had been issued with a packet of cigarettes a day, then it got down to eight cigarettes a day, then to five. Finally there were ten deadly days when there was no issue of tobacco at all. For the first time, in Spain, I saw something that you see every day in London – people picking up fag-ends.

Towards the end of March I got a poisoned hand that had to be lanced and put in a sling. I had to go into hospital, but it was not worth sending me to Sietamo for such a petty injury, so I stayed in the so-called hospital at Monflorite, which was merely a casualty clearing station. I was there ten days, part of the time in bed. The *practicantes* (hospital assistants) stole practically every valuable object I possessed, including my camera and all my photographs. At the front everyone stole, it was the inevitable effect of shortage, but the hospital people were always the worst. Later, in the hospital at Barcelona, an American who had come to join the International Column on a ship that was torpedoed by an Italian submarine, told me how he was carried ashore wounded, and how, even as they lifted him into the ambulance, the stretcher-bearers pinched his wrist-watch.

While my arm was in the sling I spent several blissful days wandering about the country-side. Monflorite was the usual huddle of mud and stone houses, with narrow tortuous alleys that had been churned by lorries till they looked like the craters of the moon. The church had been badly knocked about but was used as a military store. In the whole neighbourhood there were only two farm-houses of any size, Torre Lorenzo and Torre Fabian, and only two really large buildings, obviously the houses of the landowners who had once lorded it over the countryside; you could see their wealth reflected in the miserable huts of the peasants. Just behind the river, close to the front line, there was an enormous flour-mill with a country-house attached to it. It seemed shameful to see the huge costly machine rusting useless and the wooden flour-chutes torn down for firewood. Later on, to get firewood for the troops farther back, parties of men were sent in lorries to wreck the place systematically. They used to smash the floorboards of a room by bursting a hand-grenade in it. La Granja, our store and cook-house, had possibly at one time been a convent. It had huge courtyards and outhouses, covering an acre or more, with stabling for thirty or forty horses. The country-houses in that part of Spain are of no interest architecturally, but their farm-buildings, of lime-washed stone with round arches and magnificent roof-beams, are noble places, built on a plan that has probably not altered for centuries. Sometimes it gave you a sneaking sympathy with the Fascist ex-owners to see the way the militia treated the buildings they had seized. In La Granja every room that was not in use had been turned into a latrine – a frightful shambles of smashed furniture and excrement. The little church that adjoined it, its walls perforated by shell-holes, had its floor inches deep in dung. In the great courtyard where the cooks ladled out the rations the litter of rusty tins, mud, mule dung, and decaying food was revolting. It gave point to the old army song:

There are rats, rats,
Rats as big as cats,
In the quartermaster's store!

The ones at La Granja itself really were as big as cats, or nearly; great bloated brutes that waddled over the beds of muck, too impudent even to run away unless you shot at them.

Spring was really here at last. The blue in the sky was softer, the air grew suddenly balmy. The frogs were mating noisily in the ditches. Round the drinking-pool that served for the village mules I found exquisite green frogs the size of a penny, so brilliant that the young grass looked dull beside them. Peasant lads went out with buckets hunting for snails, which they roasted alive on sheets of tin. As soon as the weather improved the peasants had turned out for the spring ploughing. It is typical of the utter vagueness in which the Spanish agrarian revolution is wrapped that I could not even discover for certain whether the land here was collectivized or whether the peasants had simply divided it up among themselves. I fancy that in theory it was collectivized, this being P.O.U.M. and Anarchist territory. At any rate the landowners were gone, the fields were being cultivated, and people seemed satisfied. The friendliness of the peasants towards ourselves never ceased to astonish me. To some of the older ones the war must have seemed meaningless, visibly it produced a shortage of everything and a dismal dull life for everybody, and at the best of times peasants hate having troops quartered upon them. Yet they were invariably friendly – I suppose reflecting that, however intolerable we might be in other ways, we did stand between them and their one-time landlords. Civil war is a queer thing. Huesca was not five miles away, it was these people's market town, all of them had relatives there, every week of their lives they had gone there to sell their poultry and vegetables. And now for eight months an impenetrable barrier of barbed wire and machine-guns had lain between. Occasionally it slipped their memory. Once I was talking to an old woman who was carrying one of those tiny iron lamps in which the Spaniards burn olive oil. 'Where can I buy a lamp like that?' I said. 'In Huesca,' she said without thinking, and then we both laughed. The village girls were splendid vivid creatures with coal-black hair, a swinging walk, and a straightforward, man-to-man demeanour which was probably a by-product of the revolution.

Men in ragged blue shirts and black corduroy breeches, with broad-brimmed straw hats, were ploughing the fields behind teams of mules with rhythmically flopping ears. Their ploughs were wretched things, only stirring the soil, not cutting anything we should regard as a furrow. All the agricultural implements were pitifully antiquated, everything being governed by the expensiveness of metal. A broken ploughshare, for instance, was patched, and then patched again, till sometimes it was mainly patches. Rakes and pitchforks were made of wood. Spades, among a people who seldom possessed boots, were unknown; they did their digging with a clumsy hoe like those used in India. There was a kind of harrow that took one straight back to the later Stone Age. It was made of boards joined together, to about the size of a kitchen table; in the boards hundreds of holes were morticed, and into each hole was jammed a piece of flint which had been chipped into shape exactly as men used to chip them ten thousand years ago. I remember my feeling almost of horror when I first came upon one of these things in a derelict hut in no man's land. I had to puzzle over it for a long while before grasping that it was a harrow. It made me sick to think of the work that must go into the making of such a thing, and the poverty that was obliged to use flint in place of steel. I have felt more kindly towards industrialism ever since. But in the village there were two up-to-date farm tractors, no doubt seized from some big landowner's estate.

Once or twice I wandered out to the little walled graveyard that stood a mile or so from the village. The dead from the front were normally sent to Sietamo; these were the village dead. It was queerly different from an English graveyard. No reverence for the dead here! Everything overgrown with bushes and coarse grass, human bones littered everywhere. But the really surprising thing was the almost complete lack of religious inscriptions on the gravestones, though they all dated from before the revolution. Only once, I think, I saw the 'Pray for the soul of so-and-so' which is usual on Catholic graves. Most of the inscriptions were purely secular, with ludicrous poems about the virtues of the deceased. On perhaps one grave in four or five there was a small cross or a perfunctory reference to Heaven; this had usually been chipped off by some industrious atheist with a chisel.

It struck me that the people in this part of Spain must be genuinely without religious feeling – religious feeling, I mean, in the orthodox sense. It is curious that all the time I was in Spain I never once saw a person cross himself; yet you would think such a movement would become instinctive, revolution or no revolution. Obviously the Spanish Church will come back (as the saying goes, night and the Jesuits always return), but there is no doubt that at the outbreak of the revolution it collapsed and was smashed up to an extent that would be unthinkable even for the moribund C. of E. in like circumstances. To the Spanish people, at any rate in Catalonia and Aragon, the Church was a racket pure and simple. And possibly Christian belief was replaced to some extent by Anarchism, whose influence is widely spread and which undoubtedly has a religious tinge.

It was the day I came back from hospital that we advanced the line to what was really its proper position, about a thousand yards forward, along the little stream that lay a couple of hundred yards in front of the Fascist line. This operation ought to have been carried out months earlier. The point of doing it now was that the Anarchists were attacking on the Jaca road, and to advance on this side made them divert troops to face us.

We were sixty or seventy hours without sleep, and my memories go down into a sort of blur, or rather a series of pictures. Listening-duty in no man's land, a hundred yards from the Casa Francesa, a fortified farm-house which was part of the Fascist line. Seven hours lying in a horrible marsh, in reedy-smelling water into which one's body subsided gradually deeper and deeper: the reedy smell, the numbing cold, the stars immovable in the black sky, the harsh croaking of the frogs. Though this was April it was the coldest night that I remember in Spain. Only a hundred yards behind us the working-parties were hard at it, but there was utter silence except for the chorus of the frogs. Just once during the night I heard a sound – the familiar noise of a sand-bag being flattened with a spade. It is queer how, just now and again, Spaniards can carry out a brilliant feat of organization. The whole move was beautifully planned. In seven hours six hundred men constructed twelve hundred metres of trench and parapet, at distances of from a hundred and fifty to three hundred yards from the Fascist line, and all so silently that the Fascists heard nothing, and during the night there was only one casualty. There were more next day, of course. Every man had his job assigned to him, even to the cook-house orderlies who suddenly arrived when the work was done with buckets of wine laced with brandy.

And then the dawn coming up and the Fascists suddenly discovering that we were there. The square white block of the Casa Francesa, though it was two hundred yards away, seemed to tower over us, and the machine-guns in its sand-bagged upper windows seemed to be pointing straight down into the trench. We all stood gaping at it, wondering why the Fascists didn't see us. Then a vicious swirl of bullets, and everyone had flung himself on his knees and was frantically digging, deepening the trench and scooping out small shelters in the side. My arm was still in bandages, I could not dig, and I spent most of that day reading a detective story – *The Missing Money-lender* its name was. I don't remember the plot of it, but I remember very clearly the feeling of sitting there reading it; the dampish clay of the trench bottom underneath me, the constant shifting of my legs out of the way as men hurried stooping down the trench, the crack-crack-crack of bullets a foot or two overhead. Thomas Parker got a bullet through the top of his thigh, which, as he said, was nearer to being a D.S.O. than he cared about. Casualties were happening all along the line, but nothing to what there would have been if they had caught us on the move during the night. A deserter told us afterwards that five Fascist sentries were shot for negligence. Even now they could have massacred us if they had had the initiative to bring up a few mortars. It was an awkward job getting the wounded down the narrow, crowded trench. I saw one poor devil, his breeches dark with blood, flung out of his stretcher and gasping in agony. One had to carry wounded men a long distance, a mile or more, for even when a road existed the ambulances never came very near the front line. If they came too near the Fascists had a habit of shelling them – justifiably, for in modern war no one scruples to use an ambulance for carrying ammunition.

And then, next night, waiting at Torre Fabian for an attack that was called off at the last moment by wireless. In the barn where we waited the floor was a thin layer of chaff over deep beds of bones, human bones and cows' bones mixed up, and the place was alive with rats. The filthy brutes came swarming out of the ground on every side. If there is one thing I hate more than another it is a rat running over me in the darkness. However, I had the satisfaction of catching one of them a good punch that sent him flying.

And then waiting fifty or sixty yards from the Fascist parapet for the order to attack. A long line of men crouching in an irrigation ditch with their bayonets peeping over the edge and the whites of their eyes shining through the darkness. Kopp and Benjamin squatting behind us with a man who had a wireless receiving-box strapped to his shoulders. On the western horizon rosy gun-flashes followed at intervals of several seconds by enormous explosions. And then a pip-pip-pip noise from the wireless and the whispered order that we were to get out of it while the going was good. We did so, but not quickly enough. Twelve wretched children of the J.C.I. (the Youth League of the P.O.U.M., corresponding to the J.S.U. of the P.S.U.C.) who had been posted only about forty yards from the Fascist parapet, were caught by the dawn and unable to escape. All day they had to lie there, with only tufts of grass for cover, the Fascists shooting at them every time they moved. By nightfall seven were dead, then the other five managed to creep away in the darkness.

And then, for many mornings to follow, the sound of the Anarchist attacks on the other side of Huesca. Always the same sound. Suddenly, at some time in the small hours, the opening crash of several score bombs bursting simultaneously – even from miles away a diabolical, rending crash – and then the unbroken roar of massed rifles and machine-guns, a heavy rolling sound curiously similar to the roll of drums. By degrees the firing would spread all round the lines that encircled Huesca, and we would stumble out into the trench to lean sleepily against the parapet while a ragged meaningless fire swept overhead.

In the day-time the guns thundered fitfully. Torre Fabian, now our cook-house, was shelled and partially destroyed. It is curious that when you are watching artillery-fire from a safe distance you always want the gunner to hit his mark, even though the mark contains your dinner and some of your comrades. The Fascists were shooting well that morning; perhaps there were German gunners on the job. They bracketed neatly on Torre Fabian. One shell beyond it, one shell short of it, then whizz-BOOM! Burst rafters leaping upwards and a sheet of uralite skimming down the air like a flicked playing-card. The next shell took off the corner of a building as neatly as a giant might do it with a knife. But the cooks produced dinner on time – a memorable feat.

As the days went on the unseen but audible guns began each to assume a distinct personality. There were the two batteries of Russian 75-mm. guns which fired from close in our rear and which somehow evoked in my mind the picture of a fat man hitting a golf-ball. These were the first Russian guns I had seen – or heard, rather. They had a low trajectory and a very high velocity, so that you heard the cartridge explosion, the whizz and the shell-burst almost simultaneously. Behind Monflorite were two very heavy guns which fired a few times a day, with a deep, muffled roar that was like the baying of distant chained-up monsters. Up at Mount Aragon, the medieval fortress which the Government troops had stormed last year (the first time in its history, it was said), and which guarded one of the approaches to Huesca, there was a heavy gun which must have dated well back into the nineteenth century. Its great shells whistled over so slowly that you felt certain you could run beside them and keep up with them. A shell from this gun sounded like nothing so much as a man riding along on a bicycle and whistling. The trench-mortars, small though they were, made the most evil sound of all. Their shells are really a kind of winged torpedo, shaped like the darts thrown in public-houses and about the size of a quart bottle; they go off with a devilish metallic crash, as of some monstrous globe of brittle steel being shattered on an anvil. Sometimes our aeroplanes flew over and let loose the aerial torpedoes whose tremendous echoing roar makes the earth tremble even at two miles' distance. The shell-bursts from the Fascist anti-aircraft guns dotted the sky like cloudlets in a bad water-colour, but I never saw them get within a thousand yards of an aeroplane. When an aeroplane swoops down and uses its machine-gun the sound, from below, is like the fluttering of wings.

On our part of the line not much was happening. Two hundred yards to the right of us, where the Fascists were on higher ground, their snipers picked off a few of our comrades. Two hundred yards to the left, at the bridge over the stream, a sort of duel was going on between the Fascist mortars and the men who were building a concrete barricade across the bridge. The evil little shells whizzed over, zwing-crash! zwing-crash!, making a doubly diabolical noise when they landed on the asphalt road. A hundred yards away you could stand in perfect safety and watch the columns of earth and black smoke leaping into the air like magic trees. The poor devils round the bridge spent much of the day-time cowering in the little man-holes they had scooped in the side of the trench. But there were less casualties than might have been expected, and the barricade rose steadily, a wall of concrete two feet thick with embrasures for two machine-guns and a small field-gun. The concrete was being reinforced with old bedsteads, which apparently was the only iron that could be found for the purpose.

Chapter Seven

One afternoon Benjamin told us that he wanted fifteen volunteers. The attack on the Fascist redoubt which had been called off on the previous occasion was to be carried out to-night. I oiled my ten Mexican cartridges, dirtied my bayonet (the things give your position away if they flash too much), and packed up a hunk of bread, three inches of red sausage, and a cigar which my wife had sent from Barcelona and which I had been hoarding for a long time. Bombs were served out, three to a man. The Spanish Government had at last succeeded in producing a decent bomb. It was on the principle of a Mills bomb, but with two pins instead of one. After you had pulled the pins out there was an interval of seven seconds before the bomb exploded. Its chief disadvantage was that one pin was very stiff and the other very loose, so that you had the choice of leaving both pins in place and being unable to pull the stiff one out in a moment of emergency, or pulling out the stiff one beforehand and being in a constant stew lest the thing should explode in your pocket. But it was a handy little bomb to throw.

A little before midnight Benjamin led the fifteen of us down to Torre Fabian. Ever since evening the rain had been pelting down. The irrigation ditches were brimming over, and every time you stumbled into one you were in water up to your waist. In the pitch darkness and sheeting rain in the farm-yard a dim mass of men was waiting. Kopp addressed us, first in Spanish, then in English, and explained the plan of attack. The Fascist line here made an L-bend and the parapet we were to attack lay on rising ground at the corner of the L. About thirty of us, half English, and half Spanish, under the command of Jorge Roca, our battalion commander (a battalion in the militia was about four hundred men), and Benjamin, were to creep up and cut the Fascist wire. Jorge would fling the first bomb as a signal, then the rest of us were to send in a rain of bombs, drive the Fascists out of the parapet and seize it before they could rally. Simultaneously seventy Shock Troopers were to assault the next Fascist 'position', which lay two hundred yards to the right of the other, joined to it by a communication-trench. To prevent us from shooting each other in the darkness white armlets would be worn. At this moment a messenger arrived to say that there were no white armlets. Out of the darkness a plaintive voice suggested: 'Couldn't we arrange for the Fascists to wear white armlets instead?'

There was an hour or two to put in. The barn over the mule stable was so wrecked by shell-fire that you could not move about in it without a light. Half the floor had been torn away by a plunging shell and there was a twenty-foot drop onto the stones beneath. Someone found a pick and levered a burst plank out of the floor, and in a few minutes we had got a fire alight and our drenched clothes were steaming. Someone else produced a pack of cards. A rumour – one of those mysterious rumours that are endemic in war – flew round that hot coffee with brandy in it was about to be served out. We filed eagerly down the almost-collapsing staircase and wandered round the dark yard, enquiring where the coffee was to be found. Alas! there was no coffee. Instead, they called us together, ranged us into single file, and then Jorge and Benjamin set off rapidly into the darkness, the rest of us following.

It was still raining and intensely dark, but the wind had dropped. The mud was unspeakable. The paths through the beet-fields were simply a succession of lumps, as slippery as a greasy pole, with huge pools everywhere. Long before we got to the place where we were to leave our own parapet everyone had fallen several times and our rifles were coated with mud. At the parapet a small knot of men, our reserves, were waiting, and the doctor and a row of stretchers. We filed through the gap in the parapet and waded through another irrigation ditch. Splash-gurgle! Once again in water up to your waist, with the filthy, slimy mud oozing over your boot-tops. On the grass outside Jorge waited till we were all through. Then, bent almost double, he began creeping slowly forward. The Fascist parapet was about a hundred and fifty yards away. Our one chance of getting there was to move without noise.

I was in front with Jorge and Benjamin. Bent double, but with faces raised, we crept into the almost utter darkness at a pace that grew slower at every step. The rain beat lightly in our faces. When I glanced back I could see the men who were nearest to me, a bunch of humped shapes like huge black mushrooms gliding slowly forward. But every time I raised my head Benjamin, close beside me, whispered fiercely in my ear: 'To keep ze head down! To keep ze head down!' I could have told him that he needn't worry. I knew by experiment that on a dark night you can never see a man at twenty paces. It was far more important to go quietly. If they once heard us we were done for. They had only to spray the darkness with their machine-gun and there was nothing for it but to run or be massacred.

But on the sodden ground it was almost impossible to move quietly. Do what you would your feet stuck to the mud, and every step you took was slop-slop, slop-slop. And the devil of it was that the wind had dropped, and in spite of the rain it was a very quiet night. Sounds would carry a long way. There was a dreadful moment when I kicked against a tin and thought every Fascist within miles must have heard it. But no, not a sound, no answering shot, no movement in the Fascist lines. We crept onwards, always more slowly. I cannot convey to you the depth of my desire to get there. Just to get within bombing distance before they heard us! At such a time you have not even any fear, only a tremendous hopeless longing to get over the intervening ground. I have felt exactly the same thing when stalking a wild animal; the same agonized desire to get within range, the same dreamlike certainty that it is impossible. And how the distance stretched out! I knew the ground well, it was barely a hundred and fifty yards, and yet it seemed more like a mile. When you are creeping at that pace you are aware as an ant might be of the enormous variations in the ground; the splendid patch of smooth grass here, the evil patch of sticky mud there, the tall rustling reeds that have got to be avoided, the heap of stones that almost makes you give up hope because it seems impossible to get over it without noise.

We had been creeping forward for such an age that I began to think we had gone the wrong way. Then in the darkness thin parallel lines of something blacker were faintly visible. It was the outer wire (the Fascists had two lines of wire). Jorge knelt down, fumbled in his pocket. He had our only pair of wire-cutters. Snip, snip. The trailing stuff was lifted delicately aside. We waited for the men at the back to close up. They seemed to be making a frightful noise. It might be fifty yards to the Fascist parapet now. Still onwards, bent double. A stealthy step, lowering your foot as gently as a cat approaching a mousehole; then a pause to listen; then another step. Once I raised my head; in silence Benjamin put his hand behind my neck and pulled it violently down. I knew that the inner wire was barely twenty yards from the parapet. It seemed to me inconceivable that thirty men could get there unheard. Our breathing was enough to give us away. Yet somehow we did get there. The Fascist parapet was visible now, a dim black mound, looming high above us. Once again Jorge knelt and fumbled. Snip, snip. There was no way of cutting the stuff silently.

So that was the inner wire. We crawled through it on all fours and rather more rapidly. If we had time to deploy now all was well. Jorge and Benjamin crawled across to the right. But the men behind, who were spread out, had to form into single file to get through the narrow gap in the wire, and just at this moment there was a flash and a bang from the Fascist parapet. The sentry had heard us at last. Jorge poised himself on one knee and swung his arm like a bowler. Crash! His bomb burst somewhere over the parapet. At once, far more promptly than one would have thought possible, a roar of fire, ten or twenty rifles, burst out from the Fascist parapet. They had been waiting for us after all. Momentarily you could see every sand-bag in the lurid light. Men too far back were flinging their bombs and some of them were falling short of the parapet. Every loophole seemed to be spouting jets of flame. It is always hateful to be shot at in the dark – every rifle-flash seems to be pointed straight at yourself – but it was the bombs that were the worst. You cannot conceive the horror of these things till you have seen one burst close to you and in darkness; in the daytime there is only the crash of the explosion, in the darkness there is the blinding red glare as well. I had flung myself down at the first volley. All this while I was lying on my side in the greasy mud, wrestling savagely with the pin of a bomb. The damned thing *would* not come out. Finally I realized that I was twisting it in the wrong direction. I got the pin out, rose to my knees, hurled the bomb, and threw myself down again. The bomb burst over to the right, outside the parapet; fright had spoiled my aim. Just at this moment another bomb burst right in front of me, so close that I could feel the heat of the explosion. I flattened myself out and dug my face into the mud so hard that I hurt my neck and thought that I was wounded. Through the din I heard an English voice behind me say quietly: 'I'm hit.' The bomb had, in fact, wounded several people round about me without touching myself. I rose to my knees and flung my second bomb. I forget where that one went.

The Fascists were firing, our people behind were firing, and I was very conscious of being in the middle. I felt the blast of a shot and realized that a man was firing from immediately behind me. I stood up and shouted at him: 'Don't shoot at me, you bloody fool!' At this moment I saw that Benjamin, ten or fifteen yards to my right, was motioning to me with his arm. I ran across to him. It meant crossing the line of spouting loop-holes, and as I went I clapped my left hand over my cheek; an idiotic gesture – as though one's hand could stop a bullet! – but I had a horror of being hit in the face. Benjamin was kneeling on one knee with a pleased, devilish sort of expression on his face and firing carefully at the rifle-flashes with his automatic pistol. Jorge had dropped wounded at the first volley and was somewhere out of sight. I knelt beside Benjamin, pulled the pin out of my third bomb and flung it. Ah! No doubt about it that time. The bomb crashed inside the parapet, at the corner, just by the machine-gun nest.

The Fascist fire seemed to have slackened very suddenly. Benjamin leapt to his feet and shouted: 'Forward! Charge!' We dashed up the short steep slope on which the parapet stood. I say 'dashed'; 'lumbered' would be a better word; the fact is that you can't move fast when you are sodden and mudded from head to foot and weighted down with a heavy rifle and bayonet and a hundred and fifty cartridges. I took it for granted that there would be a Fascist waiting for me at the top. If he fired at that range he could not miss me, and yet somehow I never expected him to fire, only to try for me with his bayonet. I seemed to feel in advance the sensation of our bayonets crossing, and I wondered whether his arm would be stronger than mine. However, there was no Fascist waiting. With a vague feeling of relief I found that it was a low parapet and the sand-bags gave a good foothold. As a rule they are difficult to get over. Everything inside was smashed to pieces, beams flung all over the place, and great shards of uralite littered everywhere. Our bombs had wrecked all the huts and dug-outs. And still there was not a soul visible. I thought they would be lurking somewhere underground, and shouted in English (I could not think of any Spanish at the moment): 'Come on out of it! Surrender!' No answer. Then a man, a shadowy figure in the half-light, skipped over the roof of one of the ruined huts and dashed away to the left. I started after him, prodding my bayonet ineffectually into the darkness. As I rounded the corner of the hut I saw a man – I don't know whether or not it was the same man as I had seen before – fleeing up the communication-trench that led to the other Fascist position. I must have been very close to him, for I could see him clearly. He was bareheaded and seemed to have nothing on except a blanket which he was clutching round his shoulders. If I had fired I could have blown him to pieces. But for fear of shooting one another we had been ordered to use only bayonets once we were inside the parapet, and in any case I never even thought of firing. Instead, my mind leapt backwards twenty years, to our boxing instructor at school, showing me in vivid pantomime how he had bayoneted a

Turk at the Dardanelles. I gripped my rifle by the small of the butt and lunged at the man's back. He was just out of my reach. Another lunge: still out of reach. And for a little distance we proceeded like this, he rushing up the trench and I after him on the ground above, prodding at his shoulder-blades and never quite getting there – a comic memory for me to look back upon, though I suppose it seemed less comic to him.

Of course, he knew the ground better than I and had soon slipped away from me. When I came back the position was full of shouting men. The noise of firing had lessened somewhat. The Fascists were still pouring a heavy fire at us from three sides, but it was coming from a greater distance. We had driven them back for the time being. I remember saying in an oracular manner: 'We can hold this place for half an hour, not more.' I don't know why I picked on half an hour. Looking over the right-hand parapet you could see innumerable greenish rifle-flashes stabbing the darkness; but they were a long way back, a hundred or two hundred yards. Our job now was to search the position and loot anything that was worth looting. Benjamin and some others were already scrabbling among the ruins of a big hut or dug-out in the middle of the position. Benjamin staggered excitedly through the ruined roof, tugging at the rope handle of an ammunition box.

'Comrades! Ammunition! Plenty ammunition here!'

'We don't want ammunition,' said a voice, 'we want rifles.'

This was true. Half our rifles were jammed with mud and unusable. They could be cleaned, but it is dangerous to take the bolt out of a rifle in the darkness; you put it down somewhere and then you lose it. I had a tiny electric torch which my wife had managed to buy in Barcelona, otherwise we had no light of any description between us. A few men with good rifles began a desultory fire at the flashes in the distance. No one dared fire too rapidly; even the best of the rifles were liable to jam if they got too hot. There were about sixteen of us inside the parapet, including one or two who were wounded. A number of wounded, English and Spanish, were lying outside. Patrick O'Hara, a Belfast Irishman who had had some training in first-aid, went to and fro with packets of bandages, binding up the wounded men and, of course, being shot at every time he returned to the parapet, in spite of his indignant shouts of 'Poum!'

We began searching the position. There were several dead men lying about, but I did not stop to examine them. The thing I was after was the machine-gun. All the while when we were lying outside I had been wondering vaguely why the gun did not fire. I flashed my torch inside the machine-gun nest. A bitter disappointment! The gun was not there. Its tripod was there, and various boxes of ammunition and spare parts, but the gun was gone. They must have unscrewed it and carried it off at the first alarm. No doubt they were acting under orders, but it was a stupid and cowardly thing to do, for if they had kept the gun in place they could have slaughtered the whole lot of us. We were furious. We had set our hearts on capturing a machine-gun.

We poked here and there but did not find anything of much value. There were quantities of Fascist bombs lying about – a rather inferior type of bomb, which you touched off by pulling a string – and I put a couple of them in my pocket as souvenirs. It was impossible not to be struck by the bare misery of the Fascist dug-outs. The litter of spare clothes, books, food, petty personal belongings that you saw in our own dug-outs was completely absent; these poor unpaid conscripts seemed to own nothing except blankets and a few soggy hunks of bread. Up at the far end there was a small dug-out which was partly above ground and had a tiny window. We flashed the torch through the window and instantly raised a cheer. A cylindrical object in a leather case, four feet high and six inches in diameter, was leaning against the wall. Obviously the machine-gun barrel. We dashed round and got in at the doorway, to find that the thing in the leather case was not a machine-gun but something which, in our weapon-starved army, was even more precious. It was an enormous telescope, probably of at least sixty or seventy magnifications, with a folding tripod. Such telescopes simply did not exist on our side of the line and they were desperately needed. We brought it out in triumph and leaned it against the parapet, to be carried off later.

At this moment someone shouted that the Fascists were closing in. Certainly the din of firing had grown very much louder. But it was obvious that the Fascists would not counter-attack from the right, which meant crossing no man's land and assaulting their own parapet. If they had any sense at all they would come at us from inside the line. I went round to the other side of the dug-outs. The position was roughly horseshoe-shaped, with the dug-outs in the middle, so that we had another parapet covering us on the left. A heavy fire was coming from that direction, but it did not matter greatly. The danger-spot was straight in front, where there was no protection at all. A stream of bullets was passing just overhead. They must be coming from the other Fascist position farther up the line; evidently the Shock Troopers had not captured it after all. But this time the noise was deafening. It was the unbroken, drum-like roar of massed rifles which I was used to hearing from a little distance; this was the first time I had been in the middle of it. And by now, of course, the firing had spread along the line for miles around. Douglas Thompson, with a wounded arm dangling useless at his side, was leaning against the parapet and firing one-handed at the flashes. Someone whose rifle had jammed was loading for him.

There were four or five of us round this side. It was obvious what we must do. We must drag the sand-bags from the front parapet and make a barricade across the unprotected side. And we had got to be quick. The fire was high at present, but they might lower it at any moment; by the flashes all round I could see that we had a hundred or two hundred men against us. We began wrenching the sand-bags loose, carrying them twenty yards forward and dumping them into a rough heap. It was a vile job. They were big sand-bags, weighing a hundredweight each and it took every ounce of your strength to prise them loose; and then the rotten sacking split and the damp earth cascaded all over you, down your neck and up your sleeves. I remember feeling a deep horror at everything: the chaos, the darkness, the frightful din, the slithering to and fro in the mud, the struggles with the bursting sand-bags – all the time encumbered with my rifle, which I dared not put down for fear of losing it. I even shouted to someone as we staggered along with a bag between us: 'This is war! Isn't it bloody?' Suddenly a succession of tall figures came leaping over the front parapet. As they came nearer we saw that they wore the uniform of the Shock Troopers, and we cheered, thinking they were reinforcements. However, there were only four of them, three Germans and a Spaniard. We heard afterwards what had happened to the Shock Troopers. They did not know the ground and in the darkness had been led to the wrong place, where they were caught on the Fascist wire and numbers of them were shot down. These were four who had got lost, luckily for themselves. The Germans did not speak a word of English, French, or Spanish. With difficulty and much gesticulation we explained what we were doing and got them to help us in building the barricade.

The Fascists had brought up a machine-gun now. You could see it spitting like a squib a hundred or two hundred yards away; the bullets came over us with a steady, frosty crackle. Before long we had flung enough sand-bags into place to make a low breastwork behind which the few men who were on this side of the position could lie down and fire. I was kneeling behind them. A mortar-shell whizzed over and crashed somewhere in no man's land. That was another danger, but it would take them some minutes to find our range. Now that we had finished wrestling with those beastly sand-bags it was not bad fun in a way; the noise, the darkness, the flashes approaching, our own men blazing back at the flashes. One even had time to think a little. I remember wondering whether I was frightened, and deciding that I was not. Outside, where I was probably in less danger, I had been half sick with fright. Suddenly there was another shout that the Fascists were closing in. There was no doubt about it this time, the rifle-flashes were much nearer. I saw a flash hardly twenty yards away. Obviously they were working their way up the communication-trench. At twenty yards they were within easy bombing range; there were eight or nine of us bunched together and a single well-placed bomb would blow us all to fragments. Bob Smillie, the blood running down his face from a small wound, sprang to his knee and flung a bomb. We cowered, waiting for the crash. The fuse fizzled red as it sailed through the air, but the bomb failed to explode. (At least a quarter of these bombs were duds.) I had no bombs left except the Fascist ones and I was not certain how these worked. I shouted to the others to know if anyone had a bomb to spare. Douglas Moyle felt in his pocket and passed one across. I flung it and threw myself on my face. By one of those strokes of luck that happen about once in a year I had managed to drop the bomb almost exactly where the rifle had flashed. There was the roar of the explosion and then, instantly, a diabolical outcry of screams and groans. We had got one of them, anyway; I don't know whether he was killed, but certainly he was badly hurt. Poor wretch, poor wretch! I felt a vague sorrow as I heard him screaming. But at the same instant, in the dim light of the rifle-flashes, I saw or thought I saw a figure standing near the place where the rifle had flashed. I threw up my rifle and let fly. Another scream, but I think it was still the effect of the bomb. Several more bombs were thrown. The next rifle-flashes we saw were a long way off, a hundred yards or more. So we had driven them back, temporarily at least.

Everyone began cursing and saying why the hell didn't they send us some supports. With a sub-machine-gun or twenty men with clean rifles we could hold this place against a battalion. At this moment Paddy Donovan, who was second-in-command to Benjamin and had been sent back for orders, climbed over the front parapet.

'Hi! Come on out of it! All men to retire at once!'

'What?'

'Retire! Get out of it!'

'Why?'

'Orders. Back to our own lines double-quick.'

People were already climbing over the front parapet. Several of them were struggling with a heavy ammunition box. My mind flew to the telescope which I had left leaning against the parapet on the other side of the position. But at this moment I saw that the four Shock Troopers, acting I suppose on some mysterious orders they had received beforehand, had begun running up the communication-trench. It led to the other Fascist position and – if they got there – to certain death. They were disappearing into the darkness. I ran after them, trying to think of the Spanish for 'retire'; finally I shouted, 'Atras! Atras!', which perhaps conveyed the right meaning. The Spaniard understood it and brought the others back. Paddy was waiting at the parapet.

'Come on, hurry up.'

'But the telescope!'

'B—— the telescope! Benjamin's waiting outside.'

We climbed out. Paddy held the wire aside for me. As soon as we got away from the shelter of the Fascist parapet we were under a devilish fire that seemed to be coming at us from every direction. Part of it, I do not doubt, came from our own side, for everyone was firing all along the line. Whichever way we turned a fresh stream of bullets swept past; we were driven this way and that in the darkness like a flock of sheep. It did not make it any easier that we were dragging a captured box of ammunition – one of those boxes that hold 1750 rounds and weigh about a hundredweight – besides a box of bombs and several Fascist rifles. In a few minutes, although the distance from parapet to parapet was not two hundred yards and most of us knew the ground, we were completely lost. We found ourselves slithering about in a muddy field, knowing nothing except that bullets were coming from both sides. There was no moon to go by, but the sky was growing a little lighter. Our lines lay east of Huesca; I wanted to stay where we were till the first crack of dawn showed us which was east and which was west; but the others were against it. We slithered onwards, changing our direction several times and taking it in turns to haul at the ammunition-box. At last we saw the low flat line of a parapet looming in front of us. It might be ours or it might be the Fascists'; nobody had the dimmest idea which way we were going. Benjamin crawled on his belly through some tall whitish weed till he was about twenty yards from the parapet and tried a challenge. A shout of 'Poum!' answered him. We jumped to our feet, found our way along the parapet, slopped once more through the irrigation ditch – splash-gurgle! – and were in safety.

Kopp was waiting inside the parapet with a few Spaniards. The doctor and the stretchers were gone. It appeared that all the wounded had been got in except Jorge and one of our own men, Hiddlestone by name, who were missing. Kopp was pacing up and down, very pale. Even the fat folds at the back of his neck were pale; he was paying no attention to the bullets that streamed over the low parapet and cracked close to his head. Most of us were squatting behind the parapet for cover. Kopp was muttering. 'Jorge! Cogno! Jorge!' And then in English. 'If Jorge is gone it is terreeble, terreeble!' Jorge was his personal friend and one of his best officers. Suddenly he turned to us and asked for five volunteers, two English and three Spanish, to go and look for the missing men. Moyle and I volunteered with three Spaniards.

As we got outside the Spaniards murmured that it was getting dangerously light. This was true enough; the sky was dimly blue. There was a tremendous noise of excited voices coming from the Fascist redoubt. Evidently they had reoccupied the place in much greater force than before. We were sixty or seventy yards from the parapet when they must have seen or heard us, for they sent over a heavy burst of fire which made us drop on our faces. One of them flung a bomb over the parapet – a sure sign of panic. We were lying in the grass, waiting for an opportunity to move on, when we either heard or thought we heard – I have no doubt it was pure imagination, but it seemed real enough at the time – that the Fascist voices were much closer. They had left the parapet and were coming after us. 'Run!' I yelled to Moyle, and jumped to my feet. And heavens, how I ran! I had thought earlier in the night that you can't run when you are sodden from head to foot and weighted down with a rifle and cartridges; I learned now you can *always* run when you think you have fifty or a hundred armed men after you. But if I could run fast, others could run faster. In my flight something that might have been a shower of meteors sped past me. It was the three Spaniards, who had been in front. They were back to our own parapet before they stopped and I could catch up with them. The truth was that our nerves were all to pieces. I knew, however, that in a half light one man is invisible where five are clearly visible, so I went back alone. I managed to get to the outer wire and searched the ground as well as I could, which was not very well, for I had to lie on my belly. There was no sign of Jorge or Hiddlestone, so I crept back. We learned afterwards that both Jorge and Hiddlestone had been taken to the dressing-station earlier. Jorge was lightly wounded through the shoulder. Hiddlestone had received a dreadful wound – a bullet which travelled right up his left arm, breaking the bone in several places; as he lay helpless on the ground a bomb had burst near him and torn various other parts of his body. He recovered, I am glad to say. Later he told me that he had worked his way some distance lying on his back, then had clutched hold of a wounded Spaniard and they had helped one another in.

It was getting light now. Along the line for miles around a ragged meaningless fire was thundering, like the rain that goes on raining after a storm. I remember the desolate look of everything, the morasses of mud, the weeping poplar trees, the yellow water in the trench-bottoms; and men's exhausted faces, unshaven, streaked with mud and blackened to the eyes with smoke. When I got back to my dug-out the three men I shared it with were already fast asleep. They had flung themselves down with all their equipment on and their muddy rifles clutched against them. Everything was sodden, inside the dug-out as well as outside. By long searching I managed to collect enough chips of dry wood to make a tiny fire. Then I smoked the cigar which I had been hoarding and which, surprisingly enough, had not got broken during the night.

Afterwards we learned that the action had been a success, as such things go. It was merely a raid to make the Fascists divert troops from the other side of Huesca, where the Anarchists were attacking again. I had judged that the Fascists had thrown a hundred or two hundred men into the counter-attack, but a deserter told us later on that it was six hundred. I dare say he was lying – deserters, for obvious reasons, often try to curry favour. It was a great pity about the telescope. The thought of losing that beautiful bit of loot worries me even now.

Chapter Eight

The days grew hotter and even the nights grew tolerably warm. On a bullet-chipped tree in front of our parapet thick clusters of cherries were forming. Bathing in the river ceased to be an agony and became almost a pleasure. Wild roses with pink blooms the size of saucers straggled over the shell-holes round Torre Fabian. Behind the line you met peasants wearing wild roses over their ears. In the evenings they used to go out with green nets, hunting quails. You spread the net over the tops of the grasses and then lay down and made a noise like a female quail. Any male quail that was within hearing then came running towards you, and when he was underneath the net you threw a stone to scare him, whereupon he sprang into the air and was entangled in the net. Apparently only male quails were caught, which struck me as unfair.

There was a section of Andalusians next to us in the line now. I do not know quite how they got to this front. The current explanation was that they had run away from Malaga so fast that they had forgotten to stop at Valencia; but this, of course, came from the Catalans, who professed to look down on the Andalusians as a race of semi-savages. Certainly the Andalusians were very ignorant. Few if any of them could read, and they seemed not even to know the one thing that everybody knows in Spain – which political party they belonged to. They thought they were Anarchists, but were not quite certain; perhaps they were Communists. They were gnarled, rustic-looking men, shepherds or labourers from the olive groves, perhaps, with faces deeply stained by the ferocious suns of farther south. They were very useful to us, for they had an extraordinary dexterity at rolling the dried-up Spanish tobacco into cigarettes. The issue of cigarettes had ceased, but in Monflorite it was occasionally possible to buy packets of the cheapest kind of tobacco, which in appearance and texture was very like chopped chaff. Its flavour was not bad, but it was so dry that even when you had succeeded in making a cigarette the tobacco promptly fell out and left an empty cylinder. The Andalusians, however, could roll admirable cigarettes and had a special technique for tucking the ends in.

Two Englishmen were laid low by sunstroke. My salient memories of that time are the heat of the midday sun, and working half-naked with sand-bags punishing one's shoulders which were already flayed by the sun; and the lousiness of our clothes and boots, which were literally dropping to pieces; and the struggles with the mule which brought our rations and which did not mind rifle-fire but took to flight when shrapnel burst in the air; and the mosquitoes (just beginning to be active) and the rats, which were a public nuisance and would even devour leather belts and cartridge-pouches. Nothing was happening except an occasional casualty from a sniper's bullet and the sporadic artillery-fire and air-raids on Huesca. Now that the trees were in full leaf we had constructed snipers' platforms, like machans, in the poplar trees that fringed the line. On the other side of Huesca the attacks were petering out. The Anarchists had had heavy losses and had not succeeded in completely cutting the Jaca road. They had managed to establish themselves close enough on either side to bring the road itself under machine-gun fire and make it impassable for traffic; but the gap was a kilometre wide and the Fascists had constructed a sunken road, a sort of enormous trench, along which a certain number of lorries could come and go. Deserters reported that in Huesca there were plenty of munitions and very little food. But the town was evidently not going to fall. Probably it would have been impossible to take it with the fifteen thousand ill-armed men who were available. Later, in June, the Government brought troops from the Madrid front and concentrated thirty thousand men on Huesca, with an enormous quantity of aeroplanes, but still the town did not fall.

When we went on leave I had been a hundred and fifteen days in the line, and at the time this period seemed to me to have been one of the most futile of my whole life. I had joined the militia in order to fight against Fascism, and as yet I had scarcely fought at all, had merely existed as a sort of passive object, doing nothing in return for my rations except to suffer from cold and lack of sleep. Perhaps that is the fate of most soldiers in most wars. But now that I can see this period in perspective I do not altogether regret it. I wish, indeed, that I could have served the Spanish Government a little more effectively; but from a personal point of view – from the point of view of my own development – those first three or four months that I spent in the line were less futile than I then thought. They formed a kind of interregnum in my life, quite different from anything that had gone before and perhaps from anything that is to come, and they taught me things that I could not have learned in any other way.

The essential point is that all this time I had been isolated – for at the front one was almost completely isolated from the outside world: even of what was happening in Barcelona one had only a dim conception – among people who could roughly but not too inaccurately be described as revolutionaries. This was the result of the militia-system, which on the Aragon front was not radically altered till about June 1937. The workers' militias, based on the trade unions and each composed of people of approximately the same political opinions, had the effect of canalizing into one place all the most revolutionary sentiment in the country. I had dropped more or less by chance into the only community of any size in Western Europe where political consciousness and disbelief in capitalism were more normal than their opposites. Up here in Aragon one was among tens of thousands of people, mainly though not entirely of working-class origin, all living at the same level and mingling on terms of equality. In theory it was perfect equality, and even in practice it was not far from it. There is a sense in which it would be true to say that one was experiencing a foretaste of Socialism, by which I mean that the prevailing mental atmosphere was that of Socialism. Many of the normal motives of civilized life – snobbishness, money-grubbing, fear of the boss, etc. – had simply ceased to exist. The ordinary class-division of society had disappeared to an extent that is almost unthinkable in the money-tainted air of England; there was no one there except the peasants and ourselves, and no one owned anyone else as his master. Of course such a state of affairs could not last. It was simply a temporary and local phase in an enormous game that is being played over the whole surface of the earth. But it lasted long enough to have its effect upon anyone who experienced it. However much one cursed at the time, one realized afterwards that one had been in contact with something strange and valuable. One had been in a community where hope was more normal than apathy or cynicism, where the word 'comrade' stood for comradeship and not, as in most countries, for humbug. One had breathed the air of equality. I am well aware that it is now the fashion to deny that Socialism has anything to do with equality. In every country in the world a huge tribe of party-hacks and sleek little professors are busy 'proving' that Socialism means no more than a planned state-capitalism that the grab-motive left intact. But fortunately there also exists a vision of Socialism quite different from this. The thing that attracts ordinary men to Socialism and makes them willing to risk their skins for it, the 'mystique' of Socialism, is the idea of equality; to the vast majority of people Socialism means a classless society, or it means nothing at all. And it was here that those few months in the militia were valuable to me. For the Spanish militias, while they lasted, were a sort of microcosm of a classless society. In that community where no one was on the make, where there was a shortage of everything but no privilege and no boot-licking, one got, perhaps, a crude forecast of what the opening stages of Socialism might be like. And, after all, instead of disillusioning me it deeply attracted me. The effect was to make my desire to see Socialism established much more actual than it had been before. Partly, perhaps, this was due to the good luck of being among Spaniards, who, with their innate decency and their ever-present Anarchist tinge, would make even the opening stages of Socialism tolerable if they had the chance.

Of course at the time I was hardly conscious of the changes that were occurring in my own mind. Like everyone about me I was chiefly conscious of boredom, heat, cold, dirt, lice, privation, and occasional danger. It is quite different now. This period which then seemed so futile and eventless is now of great importance to me. It is so different from the rest of my life that already it has taken on the magic quality which, as a rule, belongs only to memories that are years old. It was beastly while it was happening, but it is a good patch for my mind to browse upon. I wish I could convey to you the atmosphere of that time. I hope I have done so, a little, in the earlier chapters of this book. It is all bound up in my mind with the winter cold, the ragged uniforms of militiamen, the oval Spanish faces, the morse-like tapping of machine-guns, the smells of urine and rotting bread, the tinny taste of bean-stews wolfed hurriedly out of unclean pannikins.

The whole period stays by me with curious vividness. In my memory I live over incidents that might seem too petty to be worth recalling. I am in the dug-out at Monte Pocero again, on the ledge of limestone that serves as a bed, and young Ramon is snoring with his nose flattened between my shoulder-blades. I am stumbling up the mucky trench, through the mist that swirls round me like cold steam. I am half-way up a crack in the mountain-side, struggling to keep my balance and to tug a root of wild rosemary out of the ground. High overhead some meaningless bullets are singing.

I am lying hidden among small fir-trees on the low ground west of Monte Oscuro, with Kopp and Bob Edwards and three Spaniards. Up the naked grey hill to the right of us a string of Fascists are climbing like ants. Close in front a bugle-call rings out from the Fascist lines. Kopp catches my eye and, with a schoolboy gesture, thumbs his nose at the sound.

I am in the mucky yard at La Granja, among the mob of men who are struggling with their tin pannikins round the cauldron of stew. The fat and harassed cook is warding them off with the ladle. At a table nearby a bearded man with a huge automatic pistol strapped to his belt is hewing loaves of bread into five pieces. Behind me a Cockney voice (Bill Chambers, with whom I quarrelled bitterly and who was afterwards killed outside Huesca) is singing:

There are rats, rats,
Rats as big as cats,
In the . . .

A shell comes screaming over. Children of fifteen fling themselves on their faces. The cook dodges behind the cauldron. Everyone rises with a sheepish expression as the shell plunges and booms a hundred yards away.

I am walking up and down the line of sentries, under the dark boughs of the poplars. In the flooded ditch outside the rats are paddling about, making as much noise as otters. As the yellow dawn comes up behind us, the Andalusian sentry, muffled in his cloak, begins singing. Across no man's land, a hundred or two hundred yards away, you can hear the Fascist sentry also singing.

On 25 April, after the usual *mañanas*, another section relieved us and we handed over our rifles, packed our kits and marched back to Monflorite. I was not sorry to leave the line. The lice were multiplying in my trousers far faster than I could massacre them, and for a month past I had had no socks and my boots had very little sole left, so that I was walking more or less barefoot. I wanted a hot bath, clean clothes and a night between sheets more passionately than it is possible to want anything when one has been living a normal civilized life. We slept a few hours in a barn in Monflorite, jumped a lorry in the small hours, caught the five o'clock train at Barbastro and – having the luck to connect with a fast train at Lerida – were in Barcelona by three o'clock in the afternoon of the 26th. And after that the trouble began.

Chapter Nine

From Mandalay, in Upper Burma, you can travel by train to Maymyo, the principal hill-station of the province, on the edge of the Shan plateau. It is rather a queer experience. You start off in the typical atmosphere of an eastern city – the scorching sunlight, the dusty palms, the smells of fish and spices and garlic, the squashy tropical fruits, the swarming dark-faced human beings – and because you are so used to it you carry this atmosphere intact, so to speak, in your railway carriage. Mentally you are still in Mandalay when the train stops at Maymyo, four thousand feet above sea-level. But in stepping out of the carriage you step into a different hemisphere. Suddenly you are breathing cool sweet air that might be that of England, and all round you are green grass, bracken, fir-trees, and hill-women with pink cheeks selling baskets of strawberries.

Getting back to Barcelona, after three and a half months at the front, reminded me of this. There was the same abrupt and startling change of atmosphere. In the train, all the way to Barcelona, the atmosphere of the front persisted; the dirt, the noise, the discomfort, the ragged clothes, the feeling of privation, comradeship and equality. The train, already full of militiamen when it left Barbastro, was invaded by more and more peasants at every station on the line; peasants with bundles of vegetables, with terrified fowls which they carried head-downwards, with sacks which looped and writhed all over the floor and were discovered to be full of live rabbits – finally with a quite considerable flock of sheep which were driven into the compartments and wedged into every empty space. The militiamen shouted revolutionary songs which drowned the rattle of the train and kissed their hands or waved red and black handkerchiefs to every pretty girl along the line. Bottles of wine and of anis, the filthy Aragonese liqueur, travelled from hand to hand. With the Spanish goat-skin water-bottles you can squirt a jet of wine right across a railway carriage into your friend's mouth, which saves a lot of trouble. Next to me a black-eyed boy of fifteen was recounting sensational and, I do not doubt, completely untrue stories of his own exploits at the front to two old leather-faced peasants who listened open-mouthed. Presently the peasants undid their bundles and gave us some sticky dark-red wine. Everyone was profoundly happy, more happy than I can convey. But when the train had rolled through Sabadell and into Barcelona, we stepped into an atmosphere that was scarcely less alien and hostile to us and our kind than if this had been Paris or London.

Everyone who has made two visits, at intervals of months, to Barcelona during the war has remarked upon the extraordinary changes that took place in it. And curiously enough, whether they went there first in August and again in January, or, like myself, first in December and again in April, the thing they said was always the same: that the revolutionary atmosphere had vanished. No doubt to anyone who had been there in August, when the blood was scarcely dry in the streets and militia were quartered in the smart hotels, Barcelona in December would have seemed bourgeois; to me, fresh from England, it was liker to a workers' city than anything I had conceived possible. Now the tide had rolled back. Once again it was an ordinary city, a little pinched and chipped by war, but with no outward sign of working-class predominance.

The change in the aspect of the crowds was startling. The militia uniform and the blue overalls had almost disappeared; everyone seemed to be wearing the smart summer suits in which Spanish tailors specialize. Fat prosperous men, elegant women, and sleek cars were everywhere. (It appeared that there were still no private cars; nevertheless, anyone who 'was anyone' seemed able to command a car.) The officers of the new Popular Army, a type that had scarcely existed when I left Barcelona, swarmed in surprising numbers. The Popular Army was officered at the rate of one officer to ten men. A certain number of these officers had served in the militia and been brought back from the front for technical instruction, but the majority were young men who had gone to the School of War in preference to joining the militia. Their relation to their men was not quite the same as in a bourgeois army, but there was a definite social difference, expressed by the difference of pay and uniform. The men wore a kind of coarse brown overalls, the officers wore an elegant khaki uniform with a tight waist, like a British Army officer's uniform, only a little more so. I do not suppose that more than one in twenty of them had yet been to the front, but all of them had automatic pistols strapped to their belts; we, at the front, could not get pistols for love or money. As we made our way up the street I noticed that people were staring at our dirty exteriors. Of course, like all men who have been several months in the line, we were a dreadful sight. I was conscious of looking like a scarecrow. My leather jacket was in tatters, my woollen cap had lost its shape and slid perpetually over one eye, my boots consisted of very little beyond splayed-out uppers. All of us were in more or less the same state, and in addition we were dirty and unshaven, so it was no wonder that the people stared. But it dismayed me a little, and brought it home to me that some queer things had been happening in the last three months.

During the next few days I discovered by innumerable signs that my first impression had not been wrong. A deep change had come over the town. There were two facts that were the keynote of all else. One was that the people – the civil population – had lost much of their interest in the war; the other was that the normal division of society into rich and poor, upper class and lower class, was reasserting itself.

The general indifference to the war was surprising and rather disgusting. It horrified people who came to Barcelona from Madrid or even from Valencia. Partly it was due to the remoteness of Barcelona from the actual fighting; I noticed the same thing a month later in Tarragona, where the ordinary life of a smart seaside town was continuing almost undisturbed. But it was significant that all over Spain voluntary enlistment had dwindled from about January onwards. In Catalonia, in February, there had been a wave of enthusiasm over the first big drive for the Popular Army, but it had not led to any great increase in recruiting. The war was only six months old or thereabouts when the Spanish Government had to resort to conscription, which would be natural in a foreign war, but seems anomalous in a civil war. Undoubtedly it was bound up with the disappointment of the revolutionary hopes with which the war had started. The trade union members who formed themselves into militias and chased the Fascists back to Zaragoza in the first few weeks of war had done so largely because they believed themselves to be fighting for working-class control; but it was becoming more and more obvious that working-class control was a lost cause, and the common people, especially the town proletariat, who have to fill the ranks in any war, civil or foreign, could not be blamed for a certain apathy. Nobody wanted to lose the war, but the majority were chiefly anxious for it to be over. You noticed this wherever you went. Everywhere you met with the same perfunctory remark: 'This war – terrible, isn't it? When is it going to end?' Politically conscious people were far more aware of the internecine struggle between Anarchist and Communist than of the fight against Franco. To the mass of the people the food-shortage was the most important thing. 'The front' had come to be thought of as a mythical far-off place to which young men disappeared and either did not return or returned after three or four months with vast sums of money in their pockets. (A militiaman usually received his back pay when he went on leave.) Wounded men, even when they were hopping about on crutches, did not receive any special consideration. To be in the militia was no longer fashionable. The shops, always the barometers of public taste, showed this clearly. When I first reached Barcelona the shops, poor and shabby though they were, had specialized in militiamen's equipment. Forage-caps, zipper jackets, Sam Browne belts, hunting-knives, water-bottles, revolver-holsters were displayed in every window. Now the shops were markedly smarter, but the war had been thrust into the background. As I discovered later, when buying my kit before going back to the front, certain things that one badly needed at the front were very difficult to procure.

Meanwhile there was going on a systematic propaganda against the party militias and in favour of the Popular Army. The position here was rather curious. Since February the entire armed forces had theoretically been incorporated in the Popular Army, and the militias were, on paper, reconstructed along Popular Army lines, with differential pay-rates, gazetted rank, etc., etc. The divisions were made up of 'mixed brigades', which were supposed to consist partly of Popular Army troops and partly of militia. But the only changes that had actually taken place were changes of name. The P.O.U.M. troops, for instance, previously called the Lenin Division, were now known as the 29th Division. Until June very few Popular Army troops reached the Aragon front, and in consequence the militias were able to retain their separate structure and their special character. But on every wall the Government agents had stencilled: 'We need a Popular Army,' and over the radio and in the Communist Press there was a ceaseless and sometimes very malignant jibing against the militias, who were described as ill-trained, undisciplined, etc., etc.; the Popular Army was always described as 'heroic'. From much of this propaganda you would have derived the impression that there was something disgraceful in having gone to the front voluntarily and something praiseworthy in waiting to be conscripted. For the time being, however, the militias were holding the line while the Popular Army was training in the rear, and this fact had to be advertised as little as possible. Drafts of militia returning to the front were no longer marched through the streets with drums beating and flags flying. They were smuggled away by train or lorry at five o'clock in the morning. A few drafts of the Popular Army were now beginning to leave for the front, and these, as before, were marched ceremoniously through the streets; but even they, owing to the general waning of interest in the war, met with comparatively little enthusiasm. The fact that the militia troops were also, on paper, Popular Army troops, was skilfully used in the Press propaganda. Any credit that happened to be going was automatically handed to the Popular Army, while all blame was reserved for the militias. It sometimes happened that the same troops were praised in one capacity and blamed in the other.

But besides all this there was the startling change in the social atmosphere – a thing difficult to conceive unless you have actually experienced it. When I first reached Barcelona I had thought it a town where class distinctions and great differences of wealth hardly existed. Certainly that was what it looked like. 'Smart' clothes were an abnormality, nobody cringed or took tips, waiters and flower-women and bootblacks looked you in the eye and called you 'comrade'. I had not grasped that this was mainly a mixture of hope and camouflage. The working class believed in a revolution that had been begun but never consolidated, and the bourgeoisie were scared and temporarily disguising themselves as workers. In the first months of revolution there must have been many thousands of people who deliberately put on overalls and shouted revolutionary slogans as a way of saving their skins. Now things were returning to normal. The smart restaurants and hotels were full of rich people wolfing expensive meals, while for the working-class population food-prices had jumped enormously without any corresponding rise in wages. Apart from the expensiveness of everything, there were recurrent shortages of this and that, which, of course, always hit the poor rather than the rich. The restaurants and hotels seemed to have little difficulty in getting whatever they wanted, but in the working-class quarters the queues for bread, olive oil, and other necessaries were hundreds of yards long. Previously in Barcelona I had been struck by the absence of beggars; now there were quantities of them. Outside the delicatessen shops at the top of the Ramblas gangs of barefooted children were always waiting to swarm round anyone who came out and clamour for scraps of food. The 'revolutionary' forms of speech were dropping out of use. Strangers seldom addressed you as *tu* and *camarada* nowadays; it was usually *señor* and *usted*. *Buenos dias* was beginning to replace *salud*. The waiters were back in their boiled shirts and the shop-walkers were cringing in the familiar manner. My wife and I went into a hosiery shop on the Ramblas to buy some stockings. The shopman bowed and rubbed his hands as they do not do even in England nowadays, though they used to do it twenty or thirty years ago. In a furtive indirect way the practice of tipping was coming back. The workers' patrols had been ordered to dissolve and the pre-war police forces were back on the streets. One result of this was that the cabaret show and high-class brothels, many of which had been closed by the workers' patrols, had promptly re-opened.[1] A small but significant instance of the way in which everything was now orientated in favour of the wealthier classes could be seen in the tobacco shortage. For the mass of the people the shortage of tobacco was so desperate that cigarettes filled with sliced liquorice-root were being sold in the streets. I tried some of these once. (A lot of people tried them once.) Franco held the Canaries, where all the Spanish tobacco is grown; consequently the only stocks of tobacco left on the Government side were those that had been in existence before the war. These were running so low that the tobacconists' shops only opened once a week; after waiting for a couple of hours in a queue you might, if you were lucky, get a three-quarter-ounce packet of tobacco. Theoretically the Government would not allow tobacco to be purchased from abroad, because this meant reducing the gold-reserves, which had got to be kept for arms and other necessities. Actually there was a steady supply of smuggled foreign cigarettes of the more expensive kinds, Lucky Strikes and so forth, which gave a grand opportunity for profiteering. You could buy the smuggled cigarettes openly in the smart hotels and hardly less openly in the streets, provided that you could pay ten pesetas (a militiaman's daily wage) for a packet. The smuggling was for the benefit of wealthy people, and was therefore connived at. If you had enough money there was nothing that you could not get in any quantity, with the possible exception of bread, which was rationed fairly strictly. This open contrast of wealth and poverty would have been impossible a few months earlier, when the working class still were or seemed to be in control. But it would not be fair to attribute it solely to the shift of political power. Partly it was a result of the safety of life in Barcelona, where there was little to remind one of the war except an occasional air-raid. Everyone who had been in Madrid said that it was completely different there. In Madrid the common danger forced people of almost all kinds into some sense of comradeship. A fat man eating quails while children are begging for bread is a disgusting sight, but you are less likely to see it when you are within sound of the guns.

A day or two after the street-fighting I remember passing through one of the fashionable streets and coming upon a confectioner's shop with a window full of pastries and bon-bons of the most elegant kinds, at staggering prices. It was the kind of shop you see in Bond Street or the Rue de la Paix. And I remember feeling a vague horror and amazement that money could still be wasted upon such things in a hungry war-stricken country. But God forbid that I should pretend to any personal superiority. After several months of discomfort I had a ravenous desire for decent food and wine, cocktails, American cigarettes, and so forth, and I admit to having wallowed in every luxury that I had money to buy. During that first week, before the street-fighting began, I had several preoccupations which interacted upon one another in a curious way. In the first place, as I have said, I was busy making myself as comfortable as I could. Secondly, thanks to over-eating and over-drinking, I was slightly out of health

[1] The workers' patrols are said to have closed 75 per cent of the brothels.

all that week. I would feel a little unwell, go to bed for half a day, get up and eat another excessive meal, and then feel ill again. At the same time I was making secret negotiations to buy a revolver. I badly wanted a revolver – in trench-fighting much more useful than a rifle – and they were very difficult to get hold of. The Government issued them to policemen and Popular Army officers, but refused to issue them to the militia; you had to buy them, illegally, from the secret stores of the Anarchists. After a lot of fuss and nuisance an Anarchist friend managed to procure me a tiny 26-mm automatic pistol, a wretched weapon, useless at more than five yards, but better than nothing. And besides all this I was making preliminary arrangements to leave the P.O.U.M. militia and enter some other unit that would ensure my being sent to the Madrid front.

I had told everyone for a long time past that I was going to leave the P.O.U.M. As far as my purely personal preferences went I would have liked to join the Anarchists. If one became a member of the C.N.T. it was possible to enter the F.A.I. militia, but I was told that the F.A.I. were likelier to send me to Teruel than to Madrid. If I wanted to go to Madrid I must join the International Column, which meant getting a recommendation from a member of the Communist Party. I sought out a Communist friend, attached to the Spanish Medical Aid, and explained my case to him. He seemed very anxious to recruit me and asked me, if possible, to persuade some of the other I.L.P. Englishmen to come with me. If I had been in better health I should probably have agreed there and then. It is hard to say now what difference this would have made. Quite possibly I should have been sent to Albacete before the Barcelona fighting started; in which case, not having seen the fighting at close quarters, I might have accepted the official version of it as truthful. On the other hand, if I had been in Barcelona during the fighting, under Communist orders but still with a sense of personal loyalty to my comrades in the P.O.U.M., my position would have been impossible. But I had another week's leave due to me and I was very anxious to get my health back before returning to the line. Also – the kind of detail that is always deciding one's destiny – I had to wait while the bootmakers made me a new pair of marching boots. (The entire Spanish army had failed to produce a pair of boots big enough to fit me.) I told my Communist friend that I would make definite arrangements later. Meanwhile I wanted a rest. I even had a notion that we – my wife and I – might go to the seaside for two or three days. What an idea! The political atmosphere ought to have warned me that that was not the kind of thing one could do nowadays.

For under the surface-aspect of the town, under the luxury and growing poverty, under the seeming gaiety of the streets, with their flower-stalls, their many-coloured flags, their propaganda-posters, and thronging crowds, there was an unmistakable and horrible feeling of political rivalry and hatred. People of all shades of opinion were saying forebodingly: 'There's going to be trouble before long.' The danger was quite simple and intelligible. It was the antagonism between those who wished the revolution to go forward and those who wished to check or prevent it – ultimately, between Anarchists and Communists. Politically there was now no power in Catalonia except the P.S.U.C. and their Liberal allies. But over against this there was the uncertain strength of the C.N.T., less well-armed and less sure of what they wanted than their adversaries, but powerful because of their numbers and their predominance in various key industries. Given this alignment of forces there was bound to be trouble. From the point of view of the P.S.U.C.-controlled Generalite, the first necessity, to make their position secure, was to get the weapons out of the C.N.T. workers' hands. As I have pointed out earlier, the move to break up the party militias was at bottom a manoeuvre towards this end. At the same time the pre-war armed police forces, Civil Guards, and so forth, had been brought back into use and were being heavily reinforced and armed. This could mean only one thing. The Civil Guards, in particular, were a gendarmerie of the ordinary continental type, who for nearly a century past had acted as the bodyguards of the possessing class. Meanwhile a decree had been issued that all arms held by private persons were to be surrendered. Naturally this order had not been obeyed; it was clear that the Anarchists' weapons could only be taken from them by force. Throughout this time there were rumours, always vague and contradictory owing to newspaper censorship, of minor clashes that were occurring all over Catalonia. In various places the armed police forces had made attacks on Anarchist strongholds. At Puigcerda, on the French frontier, a band of Carabineros were sent to seize the Customs Office, previously controlled by Anarchists, and Antonio Martin, a well-known Anarchist, was killed. Similar incidents had occurred at Figueras and, I think, at Tarragona. In Barcelona there had been a series of more or less unofficial brawls in the working-class suburbs. C.N.T. and U.G.T. members had been murdering one another for some time past; on several occasions the murders were followed by huge, provocative funerals which were quite deliberately intended to stir up political hatred. A short time earlier a C.N.T. member had been murdered, and the C.N.T. had turned out in hundreds of thousands to follow the cortège. At the end of April, just after I got to Barcelona, Roldan, a prominent member of the U.G.T., was murdered, presumably by someone in the C.N.T. The Government ordered all shops to close and staged an enormous funeral procession, largely of Popular Army troops, which took two hours to pass a given point. From the hotel window I watched it without enthusiasm. It was obvious that the so-called funeral was merely a display of strength; a little more of this kind of thing and there might be bloodshed. The same night my wife and I were woken by a fusillade of shots from the Plaza de Catalunya, a hundred or two hundred yards away. We learnt next day that it was a C.N.T. man being bumped off, presumably by someone in the U.G.T. It was of course distinctly possible that all these murders were committed by agents provocateurs. One can gauge the attitude of the foreign capitalist Press towards the Communist-Anarchist feud by the fact that Roldan's murder was given wide publicity, while the answering murder was carefully unmentioned.

The 1st of May was approaching, and there was talk of a monster demonstration in which both the C.N.T. and the U.G.T. were to take part. The C.N.T. leaders, more moderate than many of their followers, had long been working for a reconciliation with the U.G.T.; indeed the keynote of their policy was to try and form the two blocks of unions into one huge coalition. The idea was that the C.N.T. and the U.G.T. should march together and display their solidarity. But at the last moment the demonstration was called off. It was perfectly clear that it would only lead to rioting. So nothing happened on 1 May. It was a queer state of affairs. Barcelona, the so-called revolutionary city, was probably the only city in non-Fascist Europe that had no celebrations that day. But I admit I was rather relieved. The I.L.P. contingent was expected to march in the P.O.U.M. section of the procession, and everyone expected trouble. The last thing I wished for was to be mixed up in some meaningless street-fight. To be marching up the street behind red flags inscribed with elevating slogans, and then to be bumped off from an upper window by some total stranger with a sub-machine-gun – that is not my idea of a useful way to die.

Chapter Ten

About midday on 3 May a friend crossing the lounge of the hotel said casually: 'There's been some kind of trouble at the Telephone Exchange, I hear.' For some reason I paid no attention to it at the time.

That afternoon, between three and four, I was half-way down the Ramblas when I heard several rifle-shots behind me. I turned round and saw some youths, with rifles in their hands and the red and black handkerchiefs of the Anarchists round their throats, edging up a side-street that ran off the Ramblas northward. They were evidently exchanging shots with someone in a tall octagonal tower – a church, I think – that commanded the side-street. I thought instantly: 'It's started!' But I thought it without any very great feeling of surprise – for days past everyone had been expecting 'it' to start at any moment. I realized that I must get back to the hotel at once and see if my wife was all right. But the knot of Anarchists round the opening of the side-street were motioning the people back and shouting to them not to cross the line of fire. More shots rang out. The bullets from the tower were flying across the street and a crowd of panic-stricken people was rushing down the Ramblas, away from the firing; up and down the street you could hear snap – snap – snap as the shopkeepers slammed the steel shutters over their windows. I saw two Popular Army officers retreating cautiously from tree to tree with their hands on their revolvers. In front of me the crowd was surging into the Metro station in the middle of the Ramblas to take cover. I immediately decided not to follow them. It might mean being trapped underground for hours.

At this moment an American doctor who had been with us at the front ran up to me and grabbed me by the arm. He was greatly excited.

'Come on, we must get down to the Hotel Falcon.' (The Hotel Falcon was a sort of boarding-house maintained by the P.O.U.M. and used chiefly by militiamen on leave.) 'The P.O.U.M. chaps will be meeting there. The trouble's starting. We must hang together.'

'But what the devil is it all about?' I said.

The doctor was hauling me along by the arm. He was too excited to give a very clear statement. It appeared that he had been in the Plaza de Catalunya when several lorry-loads of armed Civil Guards had driven up to the Telephone Exchange, which was operated mainly by C.N.T. workers, and made a sudden assault upon it. Then some Anarchists had arrived and there had been a general affray. I gathered that the 'trouble' earlier in the day had been a demand by the Government to hand over the Telephone Exchange, which, of course, was refused.

As we moved down the street a lorry raced past us from the opposite direction. It was full of Anarchists with rifles in their hands. In front a ragged youth was lying on a pile of mattresses behind a light machine-gun. When we got to the Hotel Falcon, which was at the bottom of the Ramblas, a crowd of people was seething in the entrance-hall; there was a great confusion, nobody seemed to know what we were expected to do, and nobody was armed except the handful of Shock Troopers who usually acted as guards for the building. I went across to the Comite Local of the P.O.U.M., which was almost opposite. Upstairs, in the room where militiamen normally went to draw their pay, another crowd was seething. A tall, pale, rather handsome man of about thirty, in civilian clothes, was trying to restore order and handing out belts and cartridge-boxes from a pile in the corner. There seemed to be no rifles as yet. The doctor had disappeared – I believe there had already been casualties and a call for doctors – but another Englishman had arrived. Presently, from an inner office, the tall man and some others began bringing out armfuls of rifles and handing them round. The other Englishman and myself, as foreigners, were slightly under suspicion and at first nobody would give us a rifle. Then a militiaman whom I had known at the front arrived and recognized me, after which we were given rifles and a few clips of cartridges, somewhat grudgingly.

There was a sound of firing in the distance and the streets were completely empty of people. Everyone said that it was impossible to go up the Ramblas. The Civil Guards had seized buildings in commanding positions and were letting fly at everyone who passed. I would have risked it and gone back to the hotel, but there was a vague idea floating round that the Comite Local was likely to be attacked at any moment and we had better stand by. All over the building, on the stairs and on the pavement outside, small knots of people were standing and talking excitedly. No one seemed to have a very clear idea of what was happening. All I could gather was that the Civil Guards had attacked the Telephone Exchange and seized various strategic spots that commanded other buildings belonging to the workers. There was a general impression that the Civil Guards were 'after' the C.N.T. and the working class generally. It was noticeable that, at this stage, no one seemed to put the blame on the Government. The poorer classes in Barcelona looked upon the Civil Guards as something rather resembling the Black and Tans, and it seemed to be taken for granted that they had started this attack on their own initiative. Once I had heard how things stood I felt easier in my mind. The issue was clear enough. On one side the C.N.T., on the other side the police. I have no particular love for the idealized 'worker' as he appears in the bourgeois Communist's mind, but when I see an actual flesh-and-blood worker in conflict with his natural enemy, the policeman, I do not have to ask myself which side I am on.

A long time passed and nothing seemed to be happening at our end of the town. It did not occur to me that I could ring up the hotel and find out whether my wife was all right; I took it for granted that the Telephone Exchange would have stopped working – though, as a matter of fact, it was only out of action for a couple of hours. There seemed to be about three hundred people in the two buildings. Predominantly they were people of the poorest class, from the back-streets down by the quays; there was a number of women among them, some of them carrying babies, and a crowd of little ragged boys. I fancy that many of them had no notion what was happening and had simply fled into the P.O.U.M. buildings for protection. There was also a number of militiamen on leave, and a sprinkling of foreigners. As far as I could estimate, there were only about sixty rifles between the lot of us. The office upstairs was ceaselessly besieged by a crowd of people who were demanding rifles and being told that there were none left. The younger militia boys, who seemed to regard the whole affair as a kind of picnic, were prowling round and trying to wheedle or steal rifles from anyone who had them. It was not long before one of them got my rifle away from me by a clever dodge and immediately made himself scarce. So I was unarmed again, except for my tiny automatic pistol, for which I had only one clip of cartridges.

It grew dark, I was getting hungry, and seemingly there was no food in the 'Falcon'. My friend and I slipped out to his hotel, which was not far away, to get some dinner. The streets were utterly dark and silent, not a soul stirring, steel shutters drawn over all the shop windows, but no barricades built yet. There was a great fuss before they would let us into the hotel, which was locked and barred. When we got back I learned that the Telephone Exchange was working and went to the telephone in the office upstairs to ring up my wife. Characteristically, there was no telephone directory in the building, and I did not know the number of the Hotel Continental; after a searching from room to room for about an hour I came upon a guide-book which gave me the number. I could not make contact with my wife, but I managed to get hold of John McNair, the I.L.P. representative in Barcelona. He told me that all was well, nobody had been shot, and asked me if we were all right at the Comite Local. I said that we should be all right if we had some cigarettes. I only meant this as a joke; nevertheless half an hour later McNair appeared with two packets of Lucky Strike. He had braved the pitch-dark streets, roamed by Anarchist patrols who had twice stopped him at the pistol's point and examined his papers. I shall not forget this small act of heroism. We were very glad of the cigarettes.

They had placed armed guards at most of the windows, and in the street below a little group of Shock Troopers were stopping and questioning the few passers-by. An Anarchist patrol car drove up, bristling with weapons. Beside the driver a beautiful dark-haired girl of about eighteen was nursing a sub-machine-gun across her knees. I spent a long time wandering about the building, a great rambling place of which it was impossible to learn the geography. Everywhere was the usual litter, the broken furniture and torn paper that seem to be the inevitable products of revolution. All over the place people were sleeping; on a broken sofa in a passage two poor women from the quayside were peacefully snoring. The place had been a cabaret-theatre before the P.O.U.M. took it over. There were raised stages in several of the rooms; on one of them was a desolate grand piano. Finally I discovered what I was looking for – the armoury. I did not know how this affair was going to turn out, and I badly wanted a weapon. I had heard it said so often that all the rival parties, P.S.U.C., P.O.U.M., and C.N.T.-F.A.I. alike, were hoarding arms in Barcelona, that I could not believe that two of the principal P.O.U.M. buildings contained only the fifty or sixty rifles that I had seen. The room which acted as an armoury was unguarded and had a flimsy door; another Englishman and myself had no difficulty in prising it open. When we got inside we found that what they had told us was true – there *were* no more weapons. All we found there were about two dozen small-bore rifles of an obsolete pattern and a few shot-guns, with no cartridges for any of them. I went up to the office and asked if they had any spare pistol ammunition; they had none. There were a few boxes of bombs, however, which one of the Anarchist patrol cars had brought us. I put a couple in one of my cartridge-boxes. They were a crude type of bomb, ignited by rubbing a sort of match at the top and very liable to go off of their own accord.

People were sprawling asleep all over the floor. In one room a baby was crying, crying ceaselessly. Though this was May the night was getting cold. On one of the cabaret-stages the curtains were still up, so I ripped a curtain down with my knife, rolled myself up in it and had a few hours' sleep. My sleep was disturbed, I remember, by the thought of those beastly bombs, which might blow me into the air if I rolled on them too vigorously. At three in the morning the tall handsome man who seemed to be in command woke me up, gave me a rifle and put me on guard at one of the windows. He told me that Salas, the Chief of Police responsible for the attack on the Telephone Exchange, had been placed under arrest. (Actually, as we learned later, he had only been deprived of his post. Nevertheless the news confirmed the general impression that the Civil Guards had acted without orders.) As soon as it was dawn the people downstairs began building two barricades, one outside the Comite Local and the other outside the Hotel Falcon. The Barcelona streets are paved with square cobbles, easily built up into a wall, and under the cobbles is a kind of shingle that is good for filling sand-bags. The building of those barricades was a strange and wonderful sight; I would have given something to be able to photograph it. With the kind of passionate energy that Spaniards display when they have definitely decided to begin upon any job of work, long lines of men, women, and quite small children were tearing up the cobblestones, hauling them along in a hand-cart that had been found somewhere, and staggering to and fro under heavy sacks of sand. In the doorway of the Comite Local a German-Jewish girl, in a pair of militiaman's trousers whose knee-buttons just reached her ankles, was watching with a smile. In a couple of hours the barricades were head-high, with riflemen posted at the loopholes, and behind one barricade a fire was burning and men were frying eggs.

They had taken my rifle away again, and there seemed to be nothing that one could usefully do. Another Englishman and myself decided to go back to the Hotel Continental. There was a lot of firing in the distance, but seemingly none in the Ramblas. On the way up we looked in at the food-market. A very few stalls had opened; they were besieged by a crowd of people from the working-class quarters south of the Ramblas. Just as we got there, there was a heavy crash of rifle-fire outside, some panes of glass in the roof were shivered, and the crowd went flying for the back exits. A few stalls remained open, however; we managed to get a cup of coffee each and buy a wedge of goat's-milk cheese which I tucked in beside my bombs. A few days later I was very glad of that cheese.

At the street-corner where I had seen the Anarchists begin firing the day before a barricade was now standing. The man behind it (I was on the other side of the street) shouted to me to be careful. The Civil Guards in the church tower were firing indiscriminately at everyone who passed. I paused and then crossed the opening at a run: sure enough, a bullet cracked past me, uncomfortably close. When I neared the P.O.U.M. Executive Building, still on the other side of the road, there were fresh shouts of warning from some Shock Troopers standing in the doorway – shouts which, at the moment, I did not understand. There were trees and a newspaper kiosk between myself and the building (streets of this type in Spain have a broad walk running down the middle), and I could not see what they were pointing at. I went up to the 'Continental', made sure that all was well, washed my face and then went back to the P.O.U.M. Executive Building (it was about a hundred yards down the street) to ask for orders. By this time the roar of rifle and machine-gun fire from various directions was almost comparable to the din of a battle. I had just found Kopp and was asking him what we were supposed to do when there was a series of appalling crashes down below. The din was so loud that I made sure someone must be firing at us with a field-gun. Actually it was only hand-grenades, which make double their usual noise when they burst among stone buildings.

Kopp glanced out of the window, cocked his stick behind his back, said: 'Let us investigate,' and strolled down the stairs in his usual unconcerned manner, I following. Just inside the doorway a group of Shock Troopers were bowling bombs down the pavement as though playing skittles. The bombs were bursting twenty yards away with a frightful, ear-splitting crash which was mixed up with the banging of rifles. Half across the street, from behind the newspaper kiosk, a head – it was the head of an American militiaman whom I knew well – was sticking up, for all the world like a coconut at a fair. It was only afterwards that I grasped what was really happening. Next door to the P.O.U.M. building there was a café with an hotel above it, called the Café Moka. The day before twenty or thirty armed Civil Guards had entered the café and then, when the fighting started, had suddenly seized the building and barricaded themselves in. Presumably they had been ordered to seize the café as a preliminary to attacking the P.O.U.M. offices later. Early in the morning they had attempted to come out, shots had been exchanged and one Shock Trooper was badly wounded and a Civil Guard killed. The Civil Guards had fled back into the café, but when the American came down the street they had opened fire on him, though he was not armed. The American had flung himself behind the kiosk for cover, and the Shock Troopers were flinging bombs at the Civil Guards to drive them indoors again.

Kopp took in the scene at a glance, pushed his way forward and hauled back a red-haired German Shock Trooper who was just drawing the pin out of a bomb with his teeth. He shouted to everyone to stand back from the doorway, and told us in several languages that we had got to avoid bloodshed. Then he stepped out on to the pavement and, in sight of the Civil Guards, ostentatiously took off his pistol and laid it on the ground. Two Spanish militia officers did the same, and the three of them walked slowly up to the doorway where the Civil Guards were huddling. It was a thing I would not have done for twenty pounds. They were walking, unarmed, up to men who were frightened out of their wits and had loaded guns in their hands. A Civil Guard, in shirt-sleeves and livid with fright, came out of the door to parley with Kopp. He kept pointing in an agitated manner at two unexploded bombs that were lying on the pavement. Kopp came back and told us we had better touch the bombs off. Lying there, they were a danger to anyone who passed. A Shock Trooper fired his rifle at one of the bombs and burst it, then fired at the other and missed. I asked him to give me his rifle, knelt down and let fly at the second bomb. I also missed it, I am sorry to say. This was the only shot I fired during the disturbances. The pavement was covered with broken glass from the sign over the Café Moka, and two cars that were parked outside, one of them Kopp's official car, had been riddled with bullets and their windscreens smashed by bursting bombs.

Kopp took me upstairs again and explained the situation. We had got to defend the P.O.U.M. buildings if they were attacked, but the P.O.U.M.

leaders had sent instructions that we were to stand on the defensive and not open fire if we could possibly avoid it. Immediately opposite there was a cinematograph, called the Poliorama, with a museum above it, and at the top, high above the general level of the roofs, a small observatory with twin domes. The domes commanded the street, and a few men posted up there with rifles could prevent any attack on the P.O.U.M. buildings. The caretakers at the cinema were C.N.T. members and would let us come and go. As for the Civil Guards in the Café Moka, there would be no trouble with them; they did not want to fight and would be only too glad to live and let live. Kopp repeated that our orders were not to fire unless we were fired on ourselves or our buildings attacked. I gathered, though he did not say so, that the P.O.U.M. leaders were furious at being dragged into this affair, but felt that they had got to stand by the C.N.T.

They had already placed guards in the observatory. The next three days and nights I spent continuously on the roof of the Poliorama, except for brief intervals when I slipped across to the hotel for meals. I was in no danger, I suffered from nothing worse than hunger and boredom, yet it was one of the most unbearable periods of my whole life. I think few experiences could be more sickening, more disillusioning or, finally, more nerve-racking than those evil days of street warfare.

I used to sit on the roof marvelling at the folly of it all. From the little windows in the observatory you could see for miles around – vista after vista of tall slender buildings, glass domes and fantastic curly roofs with brilliant green and copper tiles; over to eastward the glittering pale blue sea – the first glimpse of the sea that I had had since coming to Spain. And the whole huge town of a million people was locked in a sort of violent inertia, a nightmare of noise without movement. The sunlit streets were quite empty. Nothing was happening except the streaming of bullets from barricades and sand-bagged windows. Not a vehicle was stirring in the streets; here and there along the Ramblas the trams stood motionless where their drivers had jumped out of them when the fighting started. And all the while the devilish noise, echoing from thousands of stone buildings, went on and on and on, like a tropical rainstorm. Crack-crack, rattle-rattle, roar – sometimes it died away to a few shots, sometimes it quickened to a deafening fusillade, but it never stopped while daylight lasted, and punctually next dawn it started again.

What the devil was happening, who was fighting whom and who was winning, was at first very difficult to discover. The people of Barcelona are so used to street-fighting and so familiar with the local geography that they know by a kind of instinct which political party will hold which streets and which buildings. A foreigner is at a hopeless disadvantage. Looking out from the observatory, I could grasp that the Ramblas, which is one of the principal streets of the town, formed a dividing line. To the right of the Ramblas the working-class quarters were solidly Anarchist; to the left a confused fight was going on among the tortuous by-streets, but on that side the P.S.U.C. and the Civil Guards were more or less in control. Up at our end of the Ramblas, round the Plaza de Catalunya, the position was so complicated that it would have been quite unintelligible if every building had not flown a party flag. The principal landmark here was the Hotel Colon, the headquarters of the P.S.U.C., dominating the Plaza de Catalunya. In a window near the last O but one in the huge 'Hotel Colon' that sprawled across its face they had a machine-gun that could sweep the square with deadly effect. A hundred yards to the right of us, down the Ramblas, the J.S.U., the youth league of the P.S.U.C. (corresponding to the Young Communist League in England), were holding a big department store whose sand-bagged side-windows fronted our observatory. They had hauled down their red flag and hoisted the Catalan national flag. On the Telephone Exchange, the starting-point of all the trouble, the Catalan national flag and the Anarchist flag were flying side by side. Some kind of temporary compromise had been arrived at there, the exchange was working uninterruptedly and there was no firing from the building.

In our position it was strangely peaceful. The Civil Guards in the Café Moka had drawn down the steel curtains and piled up the café furniture to make a barricade. Later half a dozen of them came on to the roof, opposite to ourselves, and built another barricade of mattresses, over which they hung a Catalan national flag. But it was obvious that they had no wish to start a fight. Kopp had made a definite agreement with them: if they did not fire at us we would not fire at them. He had grown quite friendly with the Civil Guards by this time, and had been to visit them several times in the Café Moka. Naturally they had looted everything drinkable the café possessed, and they made Kopp a present of fifteen bottles of beer. In return Kopp had actually given them one of our rifles to make up for one they had somehow lost on the previous day. Nevertheless, it was a queer feeling sitting on that roof. Sometimes I was merely bored with the whole affair, paid no attention to the hellish noise, and spent hours reading a succession of Penguin Library books which, luckily, I had bought a few days earlier; sometimes I was very conscious of the armed men watching me fifty yards away. It was a little like being in the trenches again; several times I caught myself, from force of habit, speaking of the Civil Guards as 'the Fascists'. There were generally about six of us up there. We placed a man on guard in each of the observatory towers, and the rest of us sat on the lead roof below, where there was no cover except a stone palisade. I was well aware that at any moment the Civil Guards might receive telephone orders to open fire. They had agreed to give us warning before doing so, but there was no certainty that they would keep to their agreement. Only once, however, did trouble look like starting. One of the Civil Guards opposite knelt down and began firing across the barricade. I was on guard in the observatory at the time. I trained my rifle on him and shouted across:

'Hi! Don't you shoot at us!'

'What?'

'Don't you fire at us or we'll fire back!'

'No, no! I wasn't firing at you. Look – down there!'

He motioned with his rifle towards the side street that ran past the bottom of our building. Sure enough, a youth in blue overalls, with a rifle in his hand, was dodging round the corner. Evidently he had just taken a shot at the Civil Guards on the roof.

'I was firing at him. He fired first.' (I believe this was true.) 'We don't want to shoot you. We're only workers, the same as you are.'

He made the anti-Fascist salute, which I returned. I shouted across:

'Have you got any more beer left?'

'No, it's all gone.'

The same day, for no apparent reason, a man in the J.S.U. building further down the street suddenly raised his rifle and let fly at me when I was leaning out of the window. Perhaps I made a tempting mark. I did not fire back. Though he was only a hundred yards away the bullet went so wide that it did not even hit the roof of the observatory. As usual, Spanish standards of marksmanship had saved me. I was fired at several times from this building.

The devilish racket of firing went on and on. But so far as I could see, and from all I heard, the fighting was defensive on both sides. People simply remained in their buildings or behind their barricades and blazed away at the people opposite. About half a mile away from us there was a street where some of the main offices of the C.N.T. and the U.G.T. were almost exactly facing one another; from that direction the volume of noise was terrific. I passed down that street the day after the fighting was over and the panes of the shop-windows were like sieves. (Most of the shop-keepers in Barcelona had their windows criss-crossed with strips of paper, so that when a bullet hit a pane it did not shiver to pieces.) Sometimes the rattle of rifle and machine-gun fire was punctuated by the crash of hand-grenades. And at long intervals, perhaps a dozen times in all, there were tremendously heavy explosions which at the time I could not account for; they sounded like aerial bombs, but that was impossible, for there were no aeroplanes about. I was told afterwards – quite possibly it was true – that agents provocateurs were touching off masses of explosive in order to increase the general noise and panic. There was, however, no artillery-fire. I was listening for this, for if the guns began to fire it would mean that the affair was becoming serious (artillery is the determining factor in street warfare). Afterwards there were wild tales in the newspapers about batteries of guns firing in the streets, but no one was able to point to a building that had been hit by a shell. In any case the sound of gunfire is unmistakable if one is used to it.

Almost from the start food was running short. With difficulty and under cover of darkness (for the Civil Guards were constantly sniping into the Ramblas) food was brought from the Hotel Falcon for the fifteen or twenty militiamen who were in the P.O.U.M. Executive Building, but there was barely enough to go round, and as many of us as possible went to the Hotel Continental for our meals. The 'Continental' had been 'collectivized' by the Generalite and not, like most of the hotels, by the C.N.T. or U.G.T., and it was regarded as neutral ground. No sooner had the fighting started than the hotel filled to the brim with a most extraordinary collection of people. There were foreign journalists, political suspects of every shade, an American airman in the service of the Government, various Communist agents, including a fat, sinister-looking Russian, said to be an agent of the Ogpu, who was nicknamed Charlie Chan and wore attached to his waist-band a revolver and a neat little bomb, some families of well-to-do Spaniards who looked like Fascist sympathizers, two or three wounded men from the International Column, a gang of lorry drivers from some huge French lorries which had been carrying a load of oranges back to France and had been held up by the fighting, and a number of Popular Army officers. The Popular Army, as a body, remained neutral throughout the fighting, though a few soldiers slipped away from the barracks and took part as individuals; on the Tuesday morning I had seen a couple of them at the P.O.U.M. barricades. At the beginning, before the food-shortage became acute and the newspapers began stirring up hatred, there was a tendency to regard the whole affair as a joke. This was the kind of thing that happened every year in Barcelona, people were saying. George Tioli, an Italian journalist, a great friend of ours, came in with his trousers drenched with blood. He had gone out to see what was happening and had been binding up a wounded man on the pavement when someone playfully tossed a hand-grenade at him, fortunately not wounding him seriously. I remember his remarking that the Barcelona paving-stones ought to be numbered; it would save such a lot of trouble in building and demolishing barricades. And I remember a couple of men from the International Column sitting in my room at the hotel when I came in tired, hungry, and dirty after a night on guard. Their attitude was completely neutral. If they had been good party-men they would, I suppose, have urged me to change sides, or even have pinioned me and taken away the bombs of which my pockets were full; instead they merely commiserated with me for having to spend my leave in doing guard-duty on a roof. The general attitude was: 'This is only a dust-up between the Anarchists and the police – it doesn't mean anything.' In spite of the extent of the fighting and the number of casualties I believe this was nearer the truth than the official version which represented the affair as a planned rising.

It was about Wednesday (5 May) that a change seemed to come over things. The shuttered streets looked ghastly. A very few pedestrians, forced abroad for one reason or another, crept to and fro, flourishing white handkerchiefs, and at a spot in the middle of the Ramblas that was safe from bullets some men were crying newspapers to the empty street. On Tuesday *Solidaridad Obrera*, the Anarchist paper, had described the attack on the Telephone Exchange as a 'monstrous provocation' (or words to that effect), but on Wednesday it changed its tune and began imploring everyone to go back to work. The Anarchist leaders were broadcasting the same message. The office of *La Batalla*, the P.O.U.M. paper, which was not defended, had been raided and seized by the Civil Guards at about the same time as the Telephone Exchange, but the paper was being printed, and a few copies distributed, from another address. It urged everyone to remain at the barricades. People were divided in their minds and wondering uneasily how the devil this was going to end. I doubt whether anyone left the barricades as yet, but everyone was sick of the meaningless fighting, which could obviously lead to no real decision, because no one wanted this to develop into a full-sized civil war which might mean losing the war against Franco. I heard this fear expressed on all sides. So far as one could gather from what people were saying at the time the C.N.T. rank and file wanted, and had wanted from the beginning, only two things: the handing back of the Telephone Exchange and the disarming of the hated Civil Guards. If the Generalite had promised to do these two things, and also promised to put an end to the food profiteering, there is little doubt that the barricades would have been down in two hours. But it was obvious that the Generalite was not going to give in. Ugly rumours were flying round. It was said that the Valencia Government was sending six thousand men to occupy Barcelona, and that five thousand Anarchist and P.O.U.M. troops had left the Aragon front to oppose them. Only the first of these rumours was true. Watching from the observatory tower we saw the low grey shapes of warships closing in upon the harbour. Douglas Moyle, who had been a sailor, said that they looked like British destroyers. As a matter of fact they *were* British destroyers, though we did not learn this till afterwards.

That evening we heard that on the Plaza de España four hundred Civil Guards had surrendered and handed their arms to the Anarchists; also the news was vaguely filtering through that in the suburbs (mainly working-class quarters) the C.N.T. were in control. It looked as though we were winning. But the same evening Kopp sent for me and, with a grave face, told me that according to information he had just received the Government was about to outlaw the P.O.U.M. and declare a state of war upon it. The news gave me a shock. It was the first glimpse I had had of the interpretation that was likely to be put upon this affair later on. I dimly foresaw that when the fighting ended the entire blame would be laid upon the P.O.U.M., which was the weakest party and therefore the most suitable scapegoat. And meanwhile our local neutrality was at an end. If the Government declared war upon us we had no choice but to defend ourselves, and here at the Executive building we could be certain that the Civil Guards next door would get orders to attack us. Our only chance was to attack them first. Kopp was waiting for orders on the telephone; if we heard definitely that the P.O.U.M. was outlawed we must make preparations at once to seize the Café Moka.

I remember the long, nightmarish evening that we spent in fortifying the building. We locked the steel curtains across the front entrance and behind them built a barricade of slabs of stone left behind by the workmen who had been making some alterations. We went over our stock of weapons. Counting the six rifles that were on the roof of the Poliorama opposite, we had twenty-one rifles, one of them defective, about fifty rounds of ammunition for each rifle, and a few dozen bombs; otherwise nothing except a few pistols and revolvers. About a dozen men, mostly Germans, had volunteered for the attack on the Café Moka, if it came off. We should attack from the roof, of course, some time in the small hours, and take them by surprise; they were more numerous, but our morale was better, and no doubt we could storm the place, though people were bound to be killed in doing so. We had no food in the building except a few slabs of chocolate, and the rumour had gone round that 'they' were going to cut off the water supply. (Nobody knew who 'they' were. It might be the Government that controlled the waterworks, or it might be the C.N.T. – nobody knew.) We spent a long time filling up every basin in the lavatories, every bucket we could lay hands on, and, finally, the fifteen beer bottles, now empty, which the Civil Guards had given to Kopp.

I was in a ghastly frame of mind and dog-tired after about sixty hours without much sleep. It was now late into the night. People were sleeping all over the floor behind the barricade downstairs. Upstairs there was a small room, with a sofa in it, which we intended to use as a dressing-station, though, needless to say, we discovered that there was neither iodine nor bandages in the building. My wife had come down from the hotel in case a nurse should be needed. I lay down on the sofa, feeling that I would like half an hour's rest before the attack on the 'Moka', in which I should presumably be killed. I remember the intolerable discomfort caused by my pistol, which was strapped to my belt and sticking into the small of my back. And the next thing I remember is waking up with a jerk to find my wife standing beside me. It was broad daylight, nothing had happened, the Government had not declared war on the P.O.U.M., the water had not been cut off, and except for the sporadic firing in the streets everything was normal. My wife said that she had not had the heart to wake me and had slept in an arm-chair in one of the front rooms.

That afternoon there was a kind of armistice. The firing died away and with surprising suddenness the streets filled with people. A few shops began to pull up their shutters, and the market was packed with a huge crowd clamouring for food, though the stalls were almost empty. It was noticeable, however, that the trams did not start running. The Civil Guards were still behind their barricades in the 'Moka'; on neither side were the fortified buildings evacuated. Everyone was rushing round and trying to buy food. And on every side you heard the same anxious questions: 'Do you think it's stopped? Do you think it's going to start again?' 'It' – the fighting – was now thought of as some kind of natural calamity, like a hurricane or an earthquake, which was happening to us all alike and which we had no power of stopping. And sure enough, almost immediately – I suppose there must really have been several hours' truce, but they seemed more like minutes than hours – a sudden crash of rifle-fire, like a June cloud-burst, sent everyone scurrying; the steel shutters snapped into place, the streets emptied like magic, the barricades were manned, and 'it' had started again.

I went back to my post on the roof with a feeling of concentrated disgust and fury. When you are taking part in events like these you are, I suppose, in a small way, making history, and you ought by rights to feel like an historical character. But you never do, because at such times the physical details always outweigh everything else. Throughout the fighting I never made the correct 'analysis' of the situation that was so glibly made by journalists hundreds of miles away. What I was chiefly thinking about was not the rights and wrongs of this miserable internecine scrap, but simply the discomfort and boredom of sitting day and night on that intolerable roof, and the hunger which was growing worse and worse – for none of us had had a proper meal since Monday. It was in my mind all the while that I should have to go back to the front as soon as this business was over. It was infuriating. I had been a hundred and fifteen days in the line and had come back to Barcelona ravenous for a bit of rest and comfort; and instead I had to spend my time sitting on a roof opposite Civil Guards as bored as myself, who periodically waved to me and assured me that they were 'workers' (meaning that they hoped I would not shoot them), but who would certainly open fire if they got the order to do so. If this was history it did not feel like it. It was more like a bad period at the front, when men were short and we had to do abnormal hours of guard-duty; instead of being heroic one just had to stay at one's post, bored, dropping with sleep and completely uninterested as to what it was all about.

Inside the hotel, among the heterogeneous mob who for the most part had not dared to put their noses out of doors, a horrible atmosphere of suspicion had grown up. Various people were infected with spy mania and were creeping round whispering that everyone else was a spy of the Communists, or the Trotskyists, or the Anarchists, or what-not. The fat Russian agent was cornering all the foreign refugees in turn and explaining plausibly that this whole affair was an Anarchist plot. I watched him with some interest, for it was the first time that I had seen a person whose profession was telling lies – unless one counts journalists. There was something repulsive in the parody of smart hotel life that was still going on behind shuttered windows amid the rattle of rifle-fire. The front dining-room had been abandoned after a bullet came through the window and chipped a pillar, and the guests were crowded into a darkish room at the back, where there were never quite enough tables to go round. The waiters were reduced in numbers – some of them were C.N.T. members and had joined in the general strike – and had dropped their boiled shirts for the time being, but meals were still being served with a pretence of ceremony. There was, however, practically nothing to eat. On that Thursday night the principal dish at dinner was *one* sardine each. The hotel had had no bread for days, and even the wine was running so low that we were drinking older and older wines at higher and higher prices. This shortage of food went on for several days after the fighting was over. Three days running, I remember, my wife and I breakfasted off a little piece of goat's-milk cheese with no bread and nothing to drink. The only thing that was plentiful was oranges. The French lorry drivers brought quantities of their oranges into the hotel. They were a tough-looking bunch; they had with them some flashy Spanish girls and a huge porter in a black blouse. At any other time the little snob of an hotel manager would have done his best to make them uncomfortable, in fact would have refused to have them on the premises, but at present they were popular because, unlike the rest of us, they had a private store of bread which everyone was trying to cadge from them.

I spent that final night on the roof, and the next day it did really look as though the fighting was come to an end. I do not think there was much firing that day – the Friday. No one seemed to know for certain whether the troops from Valencia were really coming; they arrived that evening, as a matter of fact. The Government was broadcasting half-soothing, half-threatening messages, asking everyone to go home and saying that after a certain hour anyone found carrying arms would be arrested. Not much attention was paid to the Government's broadcasts, but everywhere the people were fading away from the barricades. I have no doubt that it was mainly the food shortage that was responsible. From every side you heard the same remark: 'We have no more food, we must go back to work.' On the other hand the Civil Guards, who could count on getting their rations so long as there was any food in the town, were able to stay at their posts. By the afternoon the streets were almost normal, though the deserted barricades were still standing; the Ramblas were thronged with people, the shops nearly all open, and – most reassuring of all – the trams that had stood so long in frozen blocks jerked into motion and began running. The Civil Guards were still holding the Café Moka and had not taken down their barricades, but some of them brought chairs out and sat on the pavement with their rifles across their knees. I winked at one of them as I went past and got a not unfriendly grin; he recognized me, of course. Over the Telephone Exchange the Anarchist flag had been hauled down and only the Catalan flag was flying. That meant that the workers were definitely beaten; I realized – though, owing to my political ignorance, not so clearly as I ought to have done – that when the Government felt more sure of itself there would be reprisals. But at the time I was not interested in that aspect of things. All I felt was a profound relief that the devilish din of firing was over, and that one could buy some food and have a bit of rest and peace before going back to the front.

It must have been late that evening that the troops from Valencia first appeared in the streets. They were the Assault Guards, another formation similar to the Civil Guards and the Carabineros (i.e. a formation intended primarily for police work), and the picked troops of the Republic. Quite suddenly they seemed to spring up out of the ground; you saw them everywhere patrolling the streets in groups of ten – tall men in grey or blue uniforms, with long rifles slung over their shoulders, and a sub-machine-gun to each group. Meanwhile there was a delicate job to be done. The six rifles which we had used for the guard in the observatory towers were still lying there, and by hook or by crook we had got to get them back to the P.O.U.M. building. It was only a question of getting them across the street. They were part of the regular armoury of the building, but to bring them into the street was to contravene the Government's order, and if we were caught with them in our hands we should certainly be arrested – worse, the rifles would be confiscated. With only twenty-one rifles in the building we could not afford to lose six of them. After a lot of discussion as to the best method, a red-haired Spanish boy and myself began to smuggle them out. It was easy enough to dodge the Assault Guard patrols; the danger was the Civil Guards in the 'Moka', who were well aware that we had rifles in the observatory and might give the show away if they saw us carrying them across. Each of us partially undressed and slung a rifle over the left shoulder, the butt under the arm-pit, the barrel down the trouser-leg. It was unfortunate that they were long Mausers. Even a man as tall as I am cannot wear a long Mauser down his trouser-leg without discomfort. It was an intolerable job getting down the corkscrew staircase of the observatory with a completely rigid left leg. Once in the street, we found that the only way to move was with extreme slowness, so slowly that you did not have to bend your knees. Outside the picture-house I saw a group of people staring at me with great interest as I crept along at tortoise-speed. I have often wondered what they thought was the matter with me. Wounded in the war, perhaps. However, all the rifles were smuggled across without incident.

Next day the Assault Guards were everywhere, walking the streets like conquerors. There was no doubt that the Government was simply making a display of force in order to overawe a population which it already knew would not resist; if there had been any real fear of further outbreaks the Assault Guards would have been kept in barracks and not scattered through the streets in small bands. They were splendid troops, much the best I had seen in Spain, and, though I suppose they were in a sense 'the enemy', I could not help liking the look of them. But it was with a sort of amazement that I watched them strolling to and fro. I was used to the ragged, scarcely-armed militia on the Aragon front, and I had not known that the Republic possessed troops like these. It was not only that they were picked men physically, it was their weapons that most astonished me. All of them were armed with brand-new rifles of the type known as 'the Russian rifle' (these rifles were sent to Spain by the U.S.S.R., but were, I believe, manufactured in America). I examined one of them. It was a far from perfect rifle, but vastly better than the dreadful old blunderbusses we had at the front. The Assault Guards had one sub-machine-gun between ten men and an automatic pistol each; we at the front had approximately one machine-gun between fifty men, and as for pistols and revolvers, you could only procure them illegally. As a matter of fact, though I had not noticed it till now, it was the same everywhere. The Civil Guards and Carabineros, who were not intended for the front at all, were better armed and far better clad than ourselves. I suspect it is the same in all wars – always the same contrast between the sleek police in the rear and the ragged soldiers in the line. On the whole the Assault Guards got on very well with the population after the first day or two. On the first day there was a certain amount of trouble because some of the Assault Guards – acting on instructions, I suppose – began behaving in a provocative manner. Bands of them boarded trams, searched the passengers, and, if they had C.N.T. membership cards in their pockets, tore them up and stamped on them. This led to scuffles with armed Anarchists, and one or two people were killed. Very soon, however, the Assault Guards dropped their conquering air and relations became more friendly. It was noticeable that most of them had picked up a girl after a day or two.

The Barcelona fighting had given the Valencia Government the long-wanted excuse to assume fuller control of Catalonia. The workers' militias were to be broken up and redistributed among the Popular Army. The Spanish Republican flag was flying all over Barcelona – the first time I had seen it, I think, except over a Fascist trench. In the working-class quarters the barricades were being pulled down, rather fragmentarily, for it is a lot easier to build a barricade than to put the stones back. Outside the P.S.U.C. buildings the barricades were allowed to remain standing, and indeed many were standing as late as June. The Civil Guards were still occupying strategic points. Huge seizures of arms were being made from C.N.T. strongholds, though I have no doubt a good many escaped seizure. *La Batalla* was still appearing, but it was censored until the front page was almost completely blank. The P.S.U.C. papers were uncensored and were publishing inflammatory articles demanding the suppression of the P.O.U.M. The P.O.U.M. was declared to be a disguised Fascist organization, and a cartoon representing the P.O.U.M. as a figure slipping off a mask marked with the hammer and sickle and revealing a hideous, maniacal face marked with the swastika, was being circulated all over the town by P.S.U.C. agents. Evidently the official version of the Barcelona fighting was already fixed upon: it was to be represented as a 'fifth column' Fascist rising engineered solely by the P.O.U.M.

In the hotel the horrible atmosphere of suspicion and hostility had grown worse now that the fighting was over. In the face of the accusations that were being flung about it was impossible to remain neutral. The posts were working again, the foreign Communist papers were beginning to arrive, and their accounts of the fighting were not only violently partisan but, of course, wildly inaccurate as to facts. I think some of the Communists on the spot, who had seen what was actually happening, were dismayed by the interpretation that was being put upon events, but naturally they had to stick to their own side. Our Communist friend approached me once again and asked me whether I would not transfer into the International Column.

I was rather surprised. 'Your papers are saying I'm a Fascist,' I said. 'Surely I should be politically suspect, coming from the P.O.U.M.'

'Oh, that doesn't matter. After all, you were only acting under orders.'

I had to tell him that after this affair I could not join any Communist-controlled unit. Sooner or later it might mean being used against the Spanish working class. One could not tell when this kind of thing would break out again, and if I had to use my rifle at all in such an affair I would use it on the side of the working class and not against them. He was very decent about it. But from now on the whole atmosphere was changed. You could not, as before, 'agree to differ' and have drinks with a man who was supposedly your political opponent. There were some ugly wrangles in the hotel lounge. Meanwhile the jails were already full and overflowing. After the fighting was over the Anarchists had, of course, released their prisoners, but the Civil Guards had not released theirs, and most of them were thrown into prison and kept there without trial, in many cases for months on end. As usual, completely innocent people were being arrested owing to police bungling. I mentioned earlier that Douglas Thompson was wounded about the beginning of April. Afterwards we had lost touch with him, as usually happened when a man was wounded, for wounded men were frequently moved from one hospital to another. Actually he was at Tarragona hospital and was sent back to Barcelona about the time when the fighting started. On the Tuesday morning I met him in the street, considerably bewildered by the firing that was going on all round. He asked the question everyone was asking:

'What the devil is this all about?'

I explained as well as I could. Thompson said promptly:

'I'm going to keep out of this. My arm's still bad. I shall go back to my hotel and stay there.'

He went back to his hotel, but unfortunately (how important it is in street-fighting to understand the local geography!) it was an hotel in a part of the town controlled by the Civil Guards. The place was raided and Thompson was arrested, flung into jail, and kept for eight days in a cell so full of people that nobody had room to lie down. There were many similar cases. Numerous foreigners with doubtful political records were on the run, with the police on their track and in constant fear of denunciation. It was worst for the Italians and Germans, who had no passports and were generally wanted by the secret police in their own countries. If they were arrested they were liable to be deported to France, which might mean being sent back to Italy or Germany, where God knew what horrors were awaiting them. One or two foreign women hurriedly regularized their position by 'marrying' Spaniards. A German girl who had no papers at all dodged the police by posing for several days as a man's mistress. I remember the look of shame and misery on the poor girl's face when I accidentally bumped into her coming out of the man's bedroom. Of course she was not his mistress, but no doubt she thought I thought she was. You had all the while a hateful feeling that someone hitherto your friend might be denouncing you to the secret police. The long nightmare of the fighting, the noise, the lack of food and sleep, the mingled strain and boredom of sitting on the roof and wondering whether in another minute I should be shot myself or be obliged to shoot somebody else had put my nerves on edge. I had got to the point when every time a door banged I grabbed for my pistol. On the Saturday morning there was an uproar of shots outside and everyone cried out: 'It's starting again!' I ran into the street to find that it was only some Assault Guards shooting a mad dog. No one who was in Barcelona then, or for months later, will forget the horrible atmosphere produced by fear, suspicion, hatred, censored newspapers, crammed jails, enormous food queues and prowling gangs of armed men.

I have tried to give some idea of what it felt like to be in the middle of the Barcelona fighting; yet I do not suppose I have succeeded in conveying much of the strangeness of that time. One of the things that stick in my mind when I look back is the casual contacts one made at the time, the sudden glimpses of non-combatants to whom the whole thing was simply a meaningless uproar. I remember the fashionably-dressed woman I saw strolling down the Ramblas, with a shopping-basket over her arm and leading a white poodle, while the rifles cracked and roared a street or two away. It is conceivable that she was deaf. And the man I saw rushing across the completely empty Plaza de Catalunya, brandishing a white handkerchief in each hand. And the large party of people all dressed in black who kept trying for about an hour to cross the Plaza de Catalunya and always failing. Every time they emerged from the side-street at the corner the P.S.U.C. machine-gunners in the Hotel Colon opened fire and drove them back – I don't know why, for they were obviously unarmed. I have since thought that they may have been a funeral party. And the little man who acted as caretaker at the museum over the Poliorama and who seemed to regard the whole affair as a social occasion. He was so pleased to have the English visiting him – the English were so *simpatico*, he said. He hoped we would all come and see him again when the trouble was over; as a matter of fact I did go and see him. And the other little man, sheltering in a doorway, who jerked his head in a pleased manner towards the hell of firing on the Plaza de Catalunya and said (as though remarking that it was a fine morning): 'So we've got the nineteenth of July back again!' And the people in the shoe-shop who were making my marching-boots. I went there before the fighting, after it was over, and, for a very few minutes, during the brief armistice on 5 May. It was an expensive shop, and the shop-people were U.G.T. and may have been P.S.U.C. members – at any rate they were politically on the other side and they knew that I was serving with the P.O.U.M. Yet their attitude was completely indifferent. 'Such a pity, this kind of thing, isn't it? And so bad for business. What a pity it doesn't stop! As though there wasn't enough of that kind of thing at the front!' etc., etc. There must have been quantities of people, perhaps a majority of the inhabitants of Barcelona, who regarded the whole affair without a flicker of interest, or with no more interest than they would have felt in an air-raid.

In this chapter I have described only my personal experiences. In the next chapter I must discuss as best I can the larger issues – what actually happened and with what results, what were the rights and wrongs of the affair, and who if anyone was responsible. So much political capital has been made out of the Barcelona fighting that it is important to try and get a balanced view of it. An immense amount, enough to fill many books, has already been written on the subject, and I do not suppose I should exaggerate if I said that nine-tenths of it is untruthful. Nearly all the newspaper accounts published at the time were manufactured by journalists at a distance, and were not only inaccurate in their facts but intentionally misleading. As usual, only one side of the question has been allowed to get to the wider public. Like everyone who was in Barcelona at the time, I saw only what was happening in my immediate neighbourhood, but I saw and heard quite enough to be able to contradict many of the lies that have been circulated. As before, if you are not interested in political controversy and the mob of parties and sub-parties with their confusing names (rather like the names of the generals in a Chinese war), please skip. It is a horrible thing to have to enter into the details of inter-party polemics; it is like diving into a cesspool. But it is necessary to try and establish the truth, so far as it is possible. This squalid brawl in a distant city is more important than might appear at first sight.

Chapter Eleven

It will never be possible to get a completely accurate and unbiased account of the Barcelona fighting, because the necessary records do not exist. Future historians will have nothing to go upon except a mass of accusations and party propaganda. I myself have little data beyond what I saw with my own eyes and what I have learned from other eye-witnesses whom I believe to be reliable. I can, however, contradict some of the more flagrant lies and help to get the affair into some kind of perspective.

First of all, what actually happened?

For some time past there had been tension throughout Catalonia. In earlier chapters of this book I have given some account of the struggle between Communists and Anarchists. By May 1937 things had reached a point at which some kind of violent outbreak could be regarded as inevitable. The immediate cause of friction was the Government's order to surrender all private weapons, coinciding with the decision to build up a heavily-armed 'non-political' police-force from which trade union members were to be excluded. The meaning of this was obvious to everyone; and it was also obvious that the next move would be the taking over of some of the key industries controlled by the C.N.T. In addition there was a certain amount of resentment among the working classes because of the growing contrast of wealth and poverty and a general vague feeling that the revolution had been sabotaged. Many people were agreeably surprised when there was no rioting on 1 May. On 3 May the Government decided to take over the Telephone Exchange, which had been operated since the beginning of the war mainly by C.N.T. workers; it was alleged that it was badly run and that official calls were being tapped. Salas, the Chief of Police (who may or may not have been exceeding his orders), sent three lorry-loads of armed Civil Guards to seize the building, while the streets outside were cleared by armed police in civilian clothes. At about the same time bands of Civil Guards seized various other buildings in strategic spots. Whatever the real intention may have been, there was a widespread belief that this was the signal for a general attack on the C.N.T. by the Civil Guards and the P.S.U.C. (Communists and Socialists). The word flew round the town that the workers' buildings were being attacked, armed Anarchists appeared on the streets, work ceased, and fighting broke out immediately. That night and the next morning barricades were built all over the town, and there was no break in the fighting until the morning of 6 May. The fighting was, however, mainly defensive on both sides. Buildings were besieged, but, so far as I know, none were stormed, and there was no use of artillery. Roughly speaking, the C.N.T.-F.A.I.-P.O.U.M. forces held the working-class suburbs, and the armed police-forces and the P.S.U.C. held the central and official portion of the town. On 6 May there was an armistice, but fighting soon broke out again, probably because of premature attempts by Civil Guards to disarm C.N.T. workers. Next morning, however, the people began to leave the barricades of their own accord. Up till, roughly, the night of 5 May the C.N.T. had had the better of it, and large numbers of Civil Guards had surrendered. But there was no generally accepted leadership and no fixed plan – indeed, so far as one could judge, no plan at all except a vague determination to resist the Civil Guards. The official leaders of the C.N.T. had joined with those of the U.G.T. in imploring everyone to go back to work; above all, food was running short. In such circumstances nobody was sure enough of the issue to go on fighting. By the afternoon of 7 May conditions were almost normal. That evening six thousand Assault Guards, sent by sea from Valencia, arrived and took control of the town. The Government issued an order for the surrender of all arms except those held by the regular forces, and during the next few days large numbers of arms were seized. The casualties during the fighting were officially given out as four hundred killed and about a thousand wounded. Four hundred killed is possibly an exaggeration, but as there is no way of verifying this we must accept it as accurate.

Secondly, as to the after-effects of the fighting. Obviously it is impossible to say with any certainty what these were. There is no evidence that the outbreak had any direct effect upon the course of the war, though obviously it must have had if it had continued even a few days longer. It was made the excuse for bringing Catalonia under the direct control of Valencia, for hastening the break-up of the militias, and for the suppression of the P.O.U.M., and no doubt it also had its share in bringing down the Caballero Government. But we may take it as certain that these things would have happened in any case. The real question is whether the C.N.T. workers who came into the street gained or lost by showing fight on this occasion. It is pure guesswork, but my own opinion is that they gained more than they lost. The seizure of the Barcelona Telephone Exchange was simply one incident in a long process. Since the previous year direct power had been gradually manoeuvred out of the hands of the syndicates, and the general movement was away from working-class control and towards centralized control, leading on to State capitalism or, possibly, towards the reintroduction of private capitalism. The fact that at this point there was resistance probably slowed the process down. A year after the outbreak of war the Catalan workers had lost much of their power, but their position was still comparatively favourable. It might have been much less so if they had made it clear that they would lie down under no matter what provocation. There are occasions when it pays better to fight and be beaten than not to fight at all.

Thirdly, what purpose, if any, lay behind the outbreak? Was it any kind of *coup d'état* or revolutionary attempt? Did it definitely aim at overthrowing the Government? Was it preconcerted at all?

My own opinion is that the fighting was only preconcerted in the sense that everyone expected it. There were no signs of any very definite plan on either side. On the Anarchist side the action was almost certainly spontaneous, for it was an affair mainly of the rank and file. The people came into the streets and their political leaders followed reluctantly, or did not follow at all. The only people who even *talked* in a revolutionary strain were the Friends of Durruti, a small extremist group within the F.A.I., and the P.O.U.M. But once again they were following and not leading. The Friends of Durruti distributed some kind of revolutionary leaflet, but this did not appear until 5 May and cannot be said to have started the fighting, which had started of its own accord two days earlier. The official leaders of the C.N.T. disowned the whole affair from the start. There were a number of reasons for this. To begin with, the fact that the C.N.T. was still represented in the Government and the Generalite ensured that its leaders would be more conservative than their followers. Secondly, the main object of the C.N.T. leaders was to form an alliance with the U.G.T., and the fighting was bound to widen the split between C.N.T. and U.G.T., at any rate for the time being. Thirdly – though this was not generally known at the time – the Anarchist leaders feared that if things went beyond a certain point and the workers took possession of the town, as they were perhaps in a position to do on 5 May, there would be foreign intervention. A British cruiser and two British destroyers had closed in upon the harbour, and no doubt there were other warships not far away. The English newspapers gave it out that these ships were proceeding to Barcelona 'to protect British interests', but in fact they made no move to do so; that is, they did not land any men or take off any refugees. There can be no certainty about this, but it was at least inherently likely that the British Government, which had not raised a finger to save the Spanish Government from Franco, would intervene quickly enough to save it from its own working class.

The P.O.U.M. leaders did not disown the affair, in fact they encouraged their followers to remain at the barricades and even gave their approval (in *La Batalla*, 6 May) to the extremist leaflet issued by the Friends of Durruti. (There is great uncertainty about this leaflet, of which no one now seems able to produce a copy. In some of the foreign papers it was described as an 'inflammatory poster' which was 'plastered' all over the town. There was certainly no such poster. From comparison of various reports I should say that the leaflet called for (i) The formation of a revolutionary council (junta). (ii) The shooting of those responsible for the attack on the Telephone Exchange. (iii) The disarming of the Civil Guards. There is also some uncertainty as to how far *La Batalla* expressed agreement with the leaflet. I myself did not see the leaflet or *La Batalla* of that date. The only handbill I saw during the fighting was one issued by the tiny group of Trotskyists ('Bolshevik-Leninists') on 4 May. This merely said: 'Everyone to the barricades – general strike of all industries except war industries.' (In other words, it merely demanded what was happening already. (But in reality the attitude of the P.O.U.M leaders was hesitating. They had never been in favour of insurrection until the war against Franco was won; on the other hand the workers had come into the streets, and the P.O.U.M. leaders took the rather pedantic Marxist line that when the workers are on the streets it is the duty of the revolutionary parties to be with them. Hence, in spite of uttering revolutionary slogans about the 'reawakening of the spirit of 19 July', and so forth, they did their best to limit the workers' action to the defensive. They never, for instance, ordered an attack on any building; they merely ordered their followers to remain on guard and, as I mentioned in the last chapter, not to fire when it could be avoided. *La Batalla* also issued instructions that no troops were to leave the front.[1] As far as one can estimate it, I should say that the responsibility of the P.O.U.M. amounts to having urged everyone to remain at the barricades, and probably to having persuaded a certain number to remain there longer than they would otherwise have done. Those who were in personal touch with the P.O.U.M. leaders at the time (I myself was not) have told me that they were in reality dismayed by the whole business, but felt that they had got to associate themselves with it. Afterwards, of course, political capital was made out of it in the usual manner. Gorkin, one of the P.O.U.M. leaders, even spoke later of 'the glorious days of May'. From the propaganda point of view this may have been the right line; certainly the P.O.U.M. rose somewhat in numbers during the brief period before its suppression. Tactically it was probably a mistake to give countenance to the leaflet of the Friends of Durruti, which was a very small organization and normally hostile to the P.O.U.M. Considering the general excitement and the things that were being said on both sides, the leaflet did not in effect mean much more than 'Stay at the barricades', but by seeming to approve of it while *Solidaridad Obrera*, the Anarchist paper, repudiated it, the P.O.U.M. leaders made it easy for the Communist press to say afterwards that the fighting was a kind of insurrection engineered solely by the P.O.U.M. However, we may be certain that the Communist press would have said this in any case. It was nothing compared with the accusations that were made both before and afterwards on less evidence. The C.N.T. leaders did not gain much by their more cautious attitude; they were praised for their loyalty but were levered out of both the Government and the Generalite as soon as the opportunity arose.

So far as one could judge from what people were saying at the time, there

[1] A recent number of *Inprecor* states the exact opposite – that *La Batalla* ordered the P.O.U.M. troops to leave the front! The point can easily be settled by referring to *La Batalla* of the date named.

was no real revolutionary intention anywhere. The people behind the barricades were ordinary C.N.T. workers, probably with a sprinkling of U.G.T. workers among them, and what they were attempting was not to overthrow the Government but to resist what they regarded, rightly or wrongly, as an attack by the police. Their action was essentially defensive, and I doubt whether it should be described, as it was in nearly all the foreign newspapers, as a 'rising'. A rising implies aggressive action and a definite plan. More exactly it was a riot – a very bloody riot, because both sides had fire-arms in their hands and were willing to use them.

But what about the intentions on the other side? If it was not an Anarchist *coup d'état*, was it perhaps a Communist *coup d'état* – a planned effort to smash the power of the C.N.T. at one blow?

I do not believe it was, though certain things might lead one to suspect it. It is significant that something very similar (seizure of the Telephone Exchange by armed police acting under orders from Barcelona) happened in Tarragona two days later. And in Barcelona the raid on the Telephone Exchange was not an isolated act. In various parts of the town bands of Civil Guards and P.S.U.C. adherents seized buildings in strategic spots, if not actually before the fighting started, at any rate with surprising promptitude. But what one has got to remember is that these things were happening in Spain and not in England. Barcelona is a town with a long history of street-fighting. In such places things happen quickly, the factions are ready-made, everyone knows the local geography, and when the guns begin to shoot people take their places almost as in a fire-drill. Presumably those responsible for the seizure of the Telephone Exchange expected trouble – though not on the scale that actually happened – and had made ready to meet it. But it does not follow that they were planning a general attack on the C.N.T. There are two reasons why I do not believe that either side had made preparations for large-scale fighting:

(i) Neither side had brought troops to Barcelona beforehand. The fighting was only between those who were in Barcelona already, mainly civilians and police.

(ii) The food ran short almost immediately. Anyone who has served in Spain knows that the one operation of the war that Spaniards really perform really well is that of feeding their troops. It is most unlikely that if either side had contemplated a week or two of street-fighting and a general strike they would not have stored food beforehand.

Finally, as to the rights and wrongs of the affair.

A tremendous dust was kicked up in the foreign anti-Fascist press, but, as usual, only one side of the case has had anything like a hearing. As a result the Barcelona fighting has been represented as an insurrection by disloyal Anarchists and Trotskyists who were 'stabbing the Spanish Government in the back', and so forth. The issue was not quite so simple as that. Undoubtedly when you are at war with a deadly enemy it is better not to begin fighting among yourselves; but it is worth remembering that it takes two to make a quarrel and that people do not begin building barricades unless they have received something that they regard as a provocation.

The trouble sprang naturally out of the Government's order to the Anarchists to surrender their arms. In the English press this was translated into English terms and took this form: that arms were desperately needed on the Aragon front and could not be sent there because the unpatriotic Anarchists were holding them back. To put it like this is to ignore the conditions actually existing in Spain. Everyone knew that both the Anarchists and the P.S.U.C. were hoarding arms, and when the fighting broke out in Barcelona this was made clearer still; both sides produced arms in abundance. The Anarchists were well aware that even if they surrendered their arms, the P.S.U.C., politically the main power in Catalonia, would still retain theirs; and this in fact was what happened after the fighting was over. Meanwhile, actually visible on the streets, there were quantities of arms which would have been very welcome at the front, but which were being retained for the 'non-political' police forces in the rear. And underneath this there was the irreconcilable difference between Communists and Anarchists, which was bound to lead to some kind of struggle sooner or later. Since the beginning of the war the Spanish Communist Party had grown enormously in numbers and captured most of the political power, and there had come into Spain thousands of foreign Communists, many of whom were openly expressing their intention of 'liquidating' Anarchism as soon as the war against Franco was won. In the circumstances one could hardly expect the Anarchists to hand over the weapons which they had got possession of in the summer of 1936.

The seizure of the Telephone Exchange was simply the match that fired an already existing bomb. It is perhaps just conceivable that those responsible imagined that it would not lead to trouble. Companys, the Catalan President, is said to have declared laughingly a few days earlier that the Anarchists would put up with anything.[1] But certainly it was not a wise action. For months past there had been a long series of armed clashes between Communists and Anarchists in various parts of Spain. Catalonia and especially Barcelona was in a state of tension that had already led to street affrays, assassinations, and so forth. Suddenly the news ran round the city that armed men were attacking the buildings that the workers had captured in the July fighting and to which they attached great sentimental importance. One must remember that the Civil Guards were not loved by the working-class population. For generations past *la guardia* had been simply an appendage of the landlord and the boss, and the Civil Guards were doubly hated because they were suspected, quite justly, of being of very doubtful loyalty against the Fascists.[2] It is probable that the emotion that brought people into the streets in the first few hours was much the same emotion as had led them to resist the rebel generals at the beginning of the war. Of course it is arguable that the C.N.T. workers ought to have handed over the Telephone Exchange without protest. One's opinion here will be governed by one's attitude on the question of centralized government and working-class control. More relevantly it may be said: 'Yes, very likely the C.N.T. had a case. But, after all, there was a war on, and they had no business to start a fight behind the lines.' Here I agree entirely. Any internal disorder was likely to aid Franco. But what actually precipitated the fighting? The Government may or may not have had the right to seize the Telephone Exchange; the point is that in the actual circumstances it was bound to lead to a fight. It was a provocative action, a gesture which said in effect, and presumably was meant to say: 'Your power is at an end – we are taking over.' It was not common sense to expect anything but resistance. If one keeps a sense of

[1] *New Statesman* (14 May).

[2] At the outbreak of war the Civil Guards had everywhere sided with the stronger party. On several occasions later in the war, e.g. at Santander, the local Civil Guards went over to the Fascists in a body.

proportion one must realize that the fault was not – could not be, in a matter of this kind – entirely on one side. The reason why a one-sided version has been accepted is simply that the Spanish revolutionary parties have no footing in the foreign press. In the English press, in particular, you would have to search for a long time before finding any favourable reference, at any period of the war, to the Spanish Anarchists. They have been systematically denigrated, and, as I know by my own experience, it is almost impossible to get anyone to print anything in their defence.

I have tried to write objectively about the Barcelona fighting, though, obviously, no one can be completely objective on a question of this kind. One is practically obliged to take sides, and it must be clear enough which side I am on. Again, I must inevitably have made mistakes of fact, not only here but in other parts of this narrative. It is very difficult to write accurately about the Spanish war, because of the lack of non-propagandist documents. I warn everyone against my bias, and I warn everyone against my mistakes. Still, I have done my best to be honest. But it will be seen that the account I have given is completely different from that which appeared in the foreign and especially the Communist press. It is necessary to examine the Communist version, because it was published all over the world, has been supplemented at short intervals ever since, and is probably the most widely accepted one.

In the Communist and pro-Communist press the entire blame for the Barcelona fighting was laid upon the P.O.U.M. The affair was represented not as a spontaneous outbreak, but as a deliberate, planned insurrection against the Government, engineered solely by the P.O.U.M. with the aid of a few misguided 'uncontrollables'. More than this, it was definitely a Fascist plot, carried out under Fascist orders with the idea of starting civil war in the rear and thus paralysing the Government. The P.O.U.M. was 'Franco's Fifth Column' – a 'Trotskyist' organization working in league with the Fascists. According to the *Daily Worker* (11 May):

> 'The German and Italian agents, who poured into Barcelona ostensibly to "prepare" the notorious "Congress of the Fourth International", had one big task. It was this:
>
> 'They were – in co-operation with the local Trotskyists – to prepare a situation of disorder and bloodshed, in which it would be possible for the Germans and Italians to declare that they were "unable to exercise naval control of the Catalan coasts effectively because of the disorder prevailing in Barcelona" and were, therefore, "unable to do otherwise than land forces in Barcelona".
>
> 'In other words, what was being prepared was a situation in which the German and Italian Governments could land troops or marines quite openly on the Catalan coasts, declaring that they were doing so "in order to preserve order" . . .
>
> 'The instrument for all this lay ready to hand for the Germans and Italians in the shape of the Trotskyist organization known as the P.O.U.M.
>
> 'The P.O.U.M., acting in co-operation with well-known criminal elements, and with certain other deluded persons in the Anarchist organizations, planned, organized and led the attack in the rearguard, accurately timed to coincide with the attack on the front at Bilbao,' etc., etc.

Later in the article the Barcelona fighting becomes 'the P.O.U.M. attack', and in another article in the same issue it is stated that there is 'no doubt that it is at the door of the P.O.U.M. that the responsibility for the bloodshed in Catalonia must be laid'. *Inprecor* (29 May) states that those who erected the barricades in Barcelona were 'only members of the P.O.U.M. organized from that party for this purpose'.

I could quote a great deal more, but this is clear enough. The P.O.U.M. was wholly responsible and the P.O.U.M. was acting under Fascist orders. In a moment I will give some more extracts from the accounts that appeared in the Communist press; it will be seen that they are so self-contradictory as to be completely worthless. But before doing so it is worth pointing to several *a priori* reasons why this version of the May fighting as a Fascist rising engineered by the P.O.U.M. is next door to incredible.

(i) The P.O.U.M. had not the numbers or influence to provoke disorders of this magnitude. Still less had it the power to call a general strike. It was a political organization with no very definite footing in the trade unions, and it would have been hardly more capable of producing a strike throughout Barcelona than (say) the English Communist Party would be of producing a general strike throughout Glasgow. As I said earlier, the attitude of the P.O.U.M. leaders may have helped to prolong the fighting to some extent; but they could not have originated it even if they had wanted to.

(ii) The alleged Fascist plot rests on bare assertion and all the evidence points in the other direction. We are told that the plan was for the German and Italian Governments to land troops in Catalonia; but no German or Italian troopships approached the coast. As to the 'Congress of the Fourth International' and the 'German and Italian agents', they are pure myth. So far as I know there had not even been any talk of a Congress of the Fourth International. There were vague plans for a Congress of the P.O.U.M. and its brother-parties (English I.L.P., German S.A.P., etc., etc.); this had been tentatively fixed for some time in July – two months later – and not a single delegate had yet arrived. The 'German and Italian agents' have no existence outside the pages of the *Daily Worker*. Anyone who crossed the frontier at that time knows that it was not so easy to 'pour' into Spain, or out of it, for that matter.

(iii) Nothing happened either at Lerida, the chief stronghold of the P.O.U.M., or at the front. It is obvious that if the P.O.U.M. leaders had wanted to aid the Fascists they would have ordered their militia to walk out of the line and let the Fascists through. But nothing of the kind was done or suggested. Nor were any extra men brought out of the line beforehand, though it would have been easy enough to smuggle, say, a thousand or two thousand men back to Barcelona on various pretexts. And there was no attempt even at indirect sabotage of the front. The transport of food, munitions, and so forth continued as usual; I verified this by inquiry afterwards. Above all, a planned rising of the kind suggested would have needed months of preparation, subversive propaganda among the militia, and so forth. But there was no sign or rumour of any such thing. The fact that the militia at the front played no part in the 'rising' should be conclusive. If the P.O.U.M. were really planning a *coup d'état* it is inconceivable that they would not have used the ten thousand or so armed men who were the only striking force they had.

It will be clear enough from this that the Communist thesis of a P.O.U.M. 'rising' under Fascist orders rests on less than no evidence. I will add a few more extracts from the Communist press. The Communist accounts of the opening incident, the raid on the Telephone Exchange, are illuminating; they agree in nothing except in putting the blame on the other side. It is noticeable that in the English Communist papers the blame is put first upon the Anarchists and only later upon the P.O.U.M. There is a fairly obvious reason for this. Not everyone in England has heard of 'Trotskyism', whereas every English-speaking person shudders at the name of 'Anarchist'. Let it once be known that 'Anarchists' are implicated, and the right atmosphere of prejudice is established; after that the blame can safely be transferred to the 'Trotskyists'. The *Daily Worker* begins thus (6 May):

> 'A minority gang of Anarchists on Monday and Tuesday seized and attempted to hold the telephone and telegram buildings, and started firing into the street.'

There is nothing like starting off with a reversal of roles. The Civil Guards attack a building held by the C.N.T.; so the C.N.T. are represented as attacking their own building – attacking themselves, in fact. On the other hand, the *Daily Worker* of 11 May states:

> 'The Left Catalan Minister of Public Security, Aiguade, and the United Socialist General Commissar of Public Order, Rodrique Salas, sent the armed republican police into the Telefonica building to disarm the employees there, most of them members of C.N.T. unions.'

This does not seem to agree very well with the first statement; nevertheless the *Daily Worker* contains no admission that the first statement was wrong. The *Daily Worker* of 11 May states that the leaflets of the Friends of Durruti, which were disowned by the C.N.T., appeared on 4 May and 5 May, during the fighting. *Inprecor* (22 May) states that they appeared on 3 May, *before* the fighting, and adds that 'in view of these facts' (the appearance of various leaflets):

> 'The police, led by the Prefect of Police in person, occupied the central telephone exchange in the afternoon of May 3rd. The police were shot at while discharging their duty. This was the signal for the provocateurs to begin shooting affrays all over the city.'

And here is *Inprecor* for 29 May:

> 'At three o'clock in the afternoon the Commissar for Public Security, Comrade Sallas, went to the Telephone Exchange, which on the previous night had been occupied by 50 members of the P.O.U.M. and various uncontrollable elements.'

This seems rather curious. The occupation of the Telephone Exchange by 50 P.O.U.M. members is what one might call a picturesque circumstance, and one would have expected somebody to notice it at the time. Yet it appears that it was only discovered three or four weeks later. In another issue of *Inprecor* the 50 P.O.U.M. members become 50 P.O.U.M. militiamen. It would be difficult to pack together more contradictions than are contained in these few short passages. At one moment the C.N.T. are attacking the Telephone Exchange, the next they are being attacked there; a leaflet appears before the seizure of the Telephone Exchange and is the cause of it, or, alternatively, appears afterwards and is the result of it; the people in the Telephone Exchange are alternatively C.N.T. members and P.O.U.M. members – and so on. And in a still later issue of the *Daily Worker* (3 June) Mr J. R. Campbell informs us that the Government only seized the Telephone Exchange because the barricades were already erected!

For reasons of space I have taken only the reports of one incident, but the same discrepancies run all through the accounts in the Communist press. In addition there are various statements which are obviously pure fabrication. Here for instance is something quoted by the *Daily Worker* (7 May) and said to have been issued by the Spanish Embassy in Paris:

> 'A significant feature of the uprising has been that the old monarchist flag was flown from the balcony of various houses in Barcelona, doubtless in the belief that those who took part in the rising had become masters of the situation.'

The *Daily Worker* very probably reprinted this statement in good faith, but those responsible for it at the Spanish Embassy must have been quite deliberately lying. Any Spaniard would understand the internal situation better than that. A monarchist flag in Barcelona! It was the one thing that could have united the warring factions in a moment. Even the Communists on the spot were obliged to smile when they read about it. It is the same with the reports in the various Communist papers upon the arms supposed to have been used by the P.O.U.M. during the 'rising'. They would be credible only if one knew nothing whatever of the facts. In the *Daily Worker* of 17 May Mr Frank Pitcairn states:

> 'There were actually all sorts of arms used by them in the outrage. There were the arms which they have been stealing for months past, and hidden, and there were arms such as tanks, which they stole from the barracks just at the beginning of the rising. It is clear that scores of machine guns and several thousand rifles are still in their possession.'

Inprecor (29 May) also states:

> 'On May 3rd the P.O.U.M. had at its disposal some dozens of machine guns and several thousand rifles.... On the Plaza d'Espagna the Trotskyists brought into action batteries of "75" guns which were destined for the front in Aragon and which the militia had carefully concealed on their premises.'

Mr Pitcairn does not tell us how and when it became clear that the P.O.U.M. possessed scores of machine-guns and several thousand rifles. I have given an estimate of the arms which were at three of the principal P.O.U.M. buildings – about eighty rifles, a few bombs, and no machine-guns; i.e. about sufficient for the armed guards which, at that time, all the political parties placed on their buildings. It seems strange that afterwards, when the P.O.U.M. was suppressed and all its buildings seized, these thousands of weapons never came to light; especially the tanks and field guns, which are not the kind of thing that can be hidden up the chimney. But what is revealing in the two statements above is the complete ignorance they display of the local circumstances. According to Mr Pitcairn the P.O.U.M. stole tanks 'from the barracks'. He does not tell us which barracks. The P.O.U.M. militiamen who were in Barcelona (now comparatively few, as direct recruitment to the party militias had ceased) shared the Lenin Barracks with a considerably larger number of Popular Army troops. Mr Pitcairn is asking us to believe, therefore, that the P.O.U.M. stole tanks with the connivance of the Popular Army. It is the same with the 'premises' on which the 75-mm. guns were concealed. There is no mention of where these 'premises' were. Those batteries of guns, firing on the Plaza de España, appeared in many newspaper reports, but I think we can say with certainty that they never existed. As I mentioned earlier, I heard no artillery-fire during the fighting, though the Plaza de España was only a mile or so away. A few days later I examined the Plaza de España and could find no buildings that showed marks of shell-fire. And an eye-witness who was in that neighbourhood throughout the fighting declares that no guns ever appeared there. (Incidentally, the tale of the stolen guns may have originated with Antonov-Ovseenko, the Russian Consul-General. He, at any rate, communicated it to a well-known English journalist, who afterwards repeated it in good faith in a weekly paper. Antonov-Ovseenko has since been 'purged'. How this would affect his credibility I do not know.) The truth is, of course, that these tales about tanks, field-guns, and so forth have only been invented because otherwise it is difficult to reconcile the scale of the Barcelona fighting with the P.O.U.M.'s small numbers. It was necessary to claim that the P.O.U.M. was wholly responsible for the fighting; it was also necessary to claim that it was an insignificant party with no following and 'numbered only a few thousand members', according to *Inprecor*. The only hope of making both statements credible was to pretend that the P.O.U.M. had all the weapons of a modern mechanized army.

It is impossible to read through the reports in the Communist Press without realizing that they are consciously aimed at a public ignorant of the facts and have no other purpose than to work up prejudice. Hence, for instance, such statements as Mr Pitcairn's in the *Daily Worker* of 11 May that the 'rising' was suppressed by the Popular Army. The idea here is to give outsiders the impression that all Catalonia was solid against the 'Trotskyists'. But the Popular Army remained neutral throughout the fighting; everyone in Barcelona knew this, and it is difficult to believe that Mr Pitcairn did not know it too. Or again, the juggling in the Communist Press with the figures for killed and wounded, with the object of exaggerating the scale of the disorders. Diaz, General Secretary of the Spanish Communist Party, widely quoted in the Communist Press, gave the numbers as 900 dead and 2,500 wounded. The Catalan Minister of Propaganda, who was hardly likely to under-estimate, gave the numbers as 400 killed and 1,000 wounded. The Communist Party doubles the bid and adds a few more hundred for luck.

The foreign capitalist newspapers, in general, laid the blame for the fighting upon the Anarchists, but there were a few that followed the Communist line. One of these was the English *News Chronicle*, whose correspondent, Mr John Langdon-Davies, was in Barcelona at the time. I quote portions of his article here:

'A TROTSKYIST REVOLT

'... This has not been an Anarchist uprising. It is a frustrated *putsch* of the "Trotskyist" P.O.U.M., working through their controlled organizations, "Friends of Durruti" and Liberation Youth.... The tragedy began on Monday afternoon when the Government sent armed police into the Telephone Building, to disarm the workers there, mostly C.N.T. men. Grave irregularities in the service had been a scandal for some time. A large crowd gathered in the Plaza de Catalunya outside, while the C.N.T. men resisted, retreating floor by floor to the top of the building.... The incident was very obscure, but word went round that the Government was out against the Anarchists. The streets filled with armed men.... By nightfall every workers' centre and Government building was barricaded, and at ten o'clock the first volleys were fired and the first ambulances began ringing their way through the streets. By dawn all Barcelona was under fire.... As the day wore on and the dead mounted to over a hundred, one could make a guess at what was happening. The Anarchist C.N.T. and Socialist U.G.T. were not technically "out in the street". So long as they remained behind the barricades they were merely watchfully waiting, an attitude which included the right to shoot at anything armed in the open street ... (the) general bursts were invariably aggravated by *pacos* – hidden solitary men, usually Fascists, shooting from roof-tops at nothing in particular, but doing all they could to add to the general panic.... By Wednesday evening, however, it began to be clear who was behind the revolt. All the walls had been plastered with an inflammatory poster calling for an immediate revolution and for the shooting of Republican and Socialist leaders. It was signed by the "Friends of Durruti". On Thursday morning the Anarchist daily denied all knowledge or sympathy with it, but *La Batalla*, the P.O.U.M. paper, reprinted the document with the highest praise. Barcelona, the first city of Spain, was plunged into bloodshed by *agents provocateurs* using this subversive organization.'

This does not agree very completely with the Communist versions I have quoted above, but it will be seen that even as it stands it is self-contradictory. First the affair is described as 'a Trotskyist revolt', then it is shown to have resulted from a raid on the Telephone building and the general belief that the Government was 'out against' the Anarchists. The city is barricaded and both C.N.T. and U.G.T. are behind the barricades; two days afterwards the inflammatory poster (actually a leaflet) appears, and this is declared by implication to have started the whole business – effect preceding cause. But there is a piece of very serious misrepresentation here. Mr Langdon-Davies describes the Friends of Durruti and Libertarian Youth as 'controlled organizations' of the P.O.U.M. Both were Anarchist organizations and had no connection with the P.O.U.M. The Libertarian Youth was the youth league of the Anarchists, corresponding to the T.S.U. of the P.S.U.C., etc. The Friends of Durruti was a small organization within the F.A.I., and was in general bitterly hostile to the P.O.U.M. So far as I can discover, there was no one who was a member of both. It would be about equally true to say that the Socialist League is a 'controlled organization' of the English Liberal Party. Was Mr Langdon-Davies unaware of this? If he was, he should have written with more caution about this very complex subject.

I am not attacking Mr Langdon-Davies's good faith; but admittedly he left Barcelona as soon as the fighting was over, i.e. at the moment when he could have begun serious inquiries, and throughout his report there are clear signs that he has accepted the official version of a 'Trotskyist revolt' without sufficient verification. This is obvious even in the extract I have quoted. 'By nightfall' the barricades are built, and 'at ten o'clock' the first volleys are fired. These are not the words of an eye-witness. From this you would gather that it is usual to wait for your enemy to build a barricade before beginning to shoot at him. The impression given is that some hours elapsed between the building of the barricades and the firing of the first volleys; whereas – naturally – it was the other way about. I and many others saw the first volleys fired early in the afternoon. Again, there are the solitary men, 'usually Fascists', who are shooting from the roof-tops. Mr Langdon-Davies does not explain how he knew that these men were Fascists. Presumably he did not climb onto the roofs and ask them. He is simply repeating what he has been told and, as it fits in with the official version, is not questioning it. As a matter of fact, he indicates one probable source of much of his information by an incautious reference to the Minister of Propaganda at the beginning of his article. Foreign journalists in Spain were hopelessly at the mercy of the Ministry of Propaganda, though one would think that the very name of this ministry would be sufficient warning. The Minister of Propaganda was, of course, about as likely to give an objective account of the Barcelona trouble as (say) the late Lord Carson would have been to give an objective account of the Dublin rising of 1916.

I have given reasons for thinking that the Communist version of the Barcelona fighting cannot be taken seriously. In addition I must say something about the general charge that the P.O.U.M. was a secret Fascist organization in the pay of Franco and Hitler.

This charge was repeated over and over in the Communist Press, especially from the beginning of 1937 onwards. It was part of the world-wide drive of the official Communist Party against 'Trotskyism', of which the P.O.U.M. was supposed to be representative in Spain. 'Trotskyism', according to *Frente Rojo* (the Valencia Communist paper) 'is not a political doctrine. Trotskyism is an official capitalist organization, a Fascist terrorist band occupied in crime and sabotage against the people.' The P.O.U.M. was a 'Trotskyist' organization in league with the Fascists and part of 'Franco's Fifth Column'. What was noticeable from the start was that no evidence was produced in support of this accusation; the thing was simply asserted with an air of authority. And the attack was made with the maximum of personal libel and with complete irresponsibility as to any effects it might have upon the war. Compared with the job of libelling the P.O.U.M., many Communist writers appear to have considered the betrayal of military secrets unimportant. In a February number of the *Daily Worker*, for instance, a writer (Winifred Bates) is allowed to state that the P.O.U.M. had only half as many troops on its section of the front as it pretended. This was not true, but presumably the writer believed it to be true. She and the *Daily Worker* were perfectly willing, therefore, to hand to the enemy one of the most important pieces of information that can be handed through the columns of a newspaper. In the *New Republic* Mr Ralph Bates stated that the P.O.U.M. troops were 'playing football with the Fascists in no man's land' at a time when, as a matter of fact, the P.O.U.M. troops were suffering heavy casualties and a number of my personal friends were killed and wounded. Again, there was the malignant cartoon which was widely circulated, first in Madrid and later in Barcelona, representing the P.O.U.M. as slipping off a mask marked with the hammer and sickle and revealing a face marked with the swastika. Had the Government not been virtually under Communist control it would never have permitted a thing of this kind to be circulated in wartime. It was a deliberate blow at the morale not only of the P.O.U.M. militia, but of any others who happened to be near them; for it is not encouraging to be told that the troops next to you in the line are traitors. As a matter of fact, I doubt whether the abuse that was heaped upon them from the rear actually had the effect of demoralizing the P.O.U.M. militia. But certainly it was calculated to do so, and those responsible for it must be held to have put political spite before anti-Fascist unity.

The accusation against the P.O.U.M. amounted to this: that a body of some scores of thousands of people, almost entirely working class, besides numerous foreign helpers and sympathizers, mostly refugees from Fascist countries, and thousands of militia, was simply a vast spying organization in Fascist pay. The thing was opposed to common sense, and the past history of the P.O.U.M. was enough to make it incredible. All the P.O.U.M. leaders had revolutionary histories behind them. Some of them had been mixed up in the 1934 revolt, and most of them had been imprisoned for Socialist activities under the Lerroux Government or the monarchy. In 1936 its then leader, Joaquin Maurin, was one of the deputies who gave warning in the Cortes of Franco's impending revolt. Some time after the outbreak of war he was taken prisoner by the Fascists while trying to organize resistance in Franco's rear. When the revolt broke out the P.O.U.M. played a conspicuous part in resisting it, and in Madrid, in particular, many of its members were killed in the street-fighting. It was one of the first bodies to form columns of militia in Catalonia and Madrid. It seems almost impossible to explain these as the actions of a party in Fascist pay. A party in Fascist pay would simply have joined in on the other side.

Nor was there any sign of pro-Fascist activities during the war. It was arguable – though finally I do not agree – that by pressing for a more revolutionary policy the P.O.U.M. divided the Government forces and thus aided the Fascists; I think any Government of reformist type would be justified in regarding a party like the P.O.U.M. as a nuisance. But this is a very different matter from direct treachery. There is no way of explaining why, if the P.O.U.M. was really a Fascist body, its militia remained loyal. Here were eight or ten thousand men holding important parts of the line during the intolerable conditions of the winter of 1936–7. Many of them were in the trenches four or five months at a stretch. It is difficult to see why they did not simply walk out of the line or go over to the enemy. It was always in their power to do so, and at times the effect might have been decisive. Yet they continued to fight, and it was shortly after the P.O.U.M. was suppressed as a political party, when the event was fresh in everyone's mind, that the militia – not yet redistributed among the Popular Army – took part in the murderous attack to the east of Huesca when several thousand men were killed in one or two days. At the very least one would have expected fraternization with the enemy and a constant trickle of deserters. But, as I have pointed out earlier, the number of desertions was exceptionally small. Again, one would have expected pro-Fascist propaganda, 'defeatism' and so forth. Yet there was no sign of any such thing. Obviously there must have been Fascist spies and agents provocateurs in the P.O.U.M.; they exist in all Left-wing parties; but there is no evidence that there were more of them there than elsewhere.

It is true that some of the attacks in the Communist Press said, rather grudgingly, that only the P.O.U.M. leaders were in Fascist pay, and not the rank and file. But this was merely an attempt to detach the rank and file from their leaders. The nature of the accusations implied that ordinary members, militiamen, and so forth, were all in the plot together; for it was obvious that if Nin, Gorkin, and the others were really in Fascist pay, it was more likely to be known to their followers, who were in contact with them, than to journalists in London, Paris, and New York. And in any case, when the P.O.U.M. was suppressed the Communist-controlled secret police acted on the assumption that all were guilty alike and arrested everyone connected with the P.O.U.M. whom they could lay hands on, including even wounded men, hospital nurses, wives of P.O.U.M. members and in some cases, even children.

Finally, on 15–16 June, the P.O.U.M. was suppressed and declared an illegal organization. This was one of the first acts of the Negrin Government which came into office in May. When the Executive Committee of the P.O.U.M. had been thrown into jail, the Communist Press produced what purported to be the discovery of an enormous Fascist plot. For a while the Communist Press of the whole world was flaming with this kind of thing (*Daily Worker*, 21 June, summarizing various Spanish Communist papers):

> 'SPANISH TROTSKYISTS PLOT WITH FRANCO
>
> 'Following the arrest of a large number of leading Trotskyists in Barcelona and elsewhere ... there became known, over the week-end, details of one of the most ghastly pieces of espionage ever known in wartime, and the ugliest revelation of Trotskyist treachery to date.... Documents in the possession of the police, together with the full confession of no less than 200 persons under arrest, prove,' etc., etc.

What these revelations 'proved' was that the P.O.U.M. leaders were transmitting military secrets to General Franco by radio, were in touch with Berlin and were acting in collaboration with the secret Fascist organization in Madrid. In addition there were sensational details about secret messages in invisible ink, a mysterious document signed with the letter N. (standing for Nin), and so on and so forth.

But the final upshot was this: six months after the event, as I write, most of the P.O.U.M. leaders are still in jail, but they have never been brought to trial, and the charges of communicating with Franco by radio, etc., have never even been formulated. Had they really been guilty of espionage they would have been tried and shot in a week, as so many Fascist spies had been previously. But not a scrap of evidence was ever produced except the unsupported statements in the Communist Press. As for the two hundred 'full confessions', which, if they had existed, would have been enough to convict anybody, they have never been heard of again. They were, in fact, two hundred efforts of somebody's imagination.

More than this, most of the members of the Spanish Government have disclaimed all belief in the charges against the P.O.U.M. Recently the cabinet decided by five to two in favour of releasing anti-Fascist political prisoners; the two dissentients being the Communist ministers. In August an international delegation headed by James Maxton, M.P., went to Spain to inquire into the charges against the P.O.U.M. and the disappearance of Andres Nin. Prieto, the Minister of National Defence, Irujo, the Minister of Justice, Zugazagoitia,

Minister of the Interior, Ortega y Gasset, the Procureur-General, Prat Garcia, and others all repudiated any belief in the P.O.U.M. leaders being guilty of espionage. Irujo added that he had been through the dossier of the case, that none of the so-called pieces of evidence would bear examination, and that the document supposed to have been signed by Nin was 'valueless' – i.e. a forgery. Prieto considered the P.O.U.M. leaders to be responsible for the May fighting in Barcelona, but dismissed the idea of their being Fascist spies. 'What is most grave,' he added, is that the arrest of the P.O.U.M. leaders was not decided upon by the Government, and the police carried out these arrests on their own authority. Those responsible are not the heads of the police, but their entourage, which has been infiltrated by the Communists according to their usual custom.' He cited other cases of illegal arrests by the police. Irujo likewise declared that the police had become 'quasi-independent' and were in reality under the control of foreign Communist elements. Prieto hinted fairly broadly to the delegation that the Government could not afford to offend the Communist Party while the Russians were supplying arms. When another delegation, headed by John McGovern, M.P., went to Spain in December, they got much the same answers as before, and Zugazagoitia, the Minister of the Interior, repeated Prieto's hint in even plainer terms. 'We have received aid from Russia and have had to permit certain actions which we did not like.' As an illustration of the autonomy of the police, it is interesting to learn that even with a signed order from the Director of Prisons and the Minister of Justice, McGovern and the others could not obtain admission to one of the 'secret prisons' maintained by the Communist Party in Barcelona.[1]

I think this should be enough to make the matter clear. The accusation of espionage against the P.O.U.M. rested solely upon articles in the Communist press and the activities of the Communist-controlled secret police. The P.O.U.M. leaders, and hundreds or thousands of their followers, are still in prison, and for six months past the Communist press has continued to clamour for the execution of the 'traitors'. But Negrin and the others have kept their heads and refused to stage a wholesale massacre of 'Trotskyists'. Considering the pressure that has been put upon them, it is greatly to their credit that they have done so. Meanwhile, in the face of what I have quoted above, it becomes very difficult to believe that the P.O.U.M. was really a Fascist spying organization, unless one also believes that Maxton, McGovern, Prieto, Irujo, Zugazagoitia, and the rest are all in Fascist pay together.

Finally, as to the charge that the P.O.U.M. was 'Trotskyist'. This word is now flung about with greater and greater freedom, and it is used in a way that is extremely misleading and is often intended to mislead. It is worth stopping to define it. The word Trotskyist is used to mean three distinct things:

(i) One who, like Trotsky, advocates 'world revolution' as against 'Socialism in a single country'. More loosely, a revolutionary extremist.

(ii) A member of the actual organization of which Trotsky is head.

(iii) A disguised Fascist posing as a revolutionary who acts especially by sabotage in the U.S.S.R., but, in general, by splitting and undermining the Left-wing forces.

[1] For reports on the two delegations see *Le Populaire* (7 September), *La Flèche* (18 September), Report on the Maxton delegation published by *Independent News* (219 Rue Saint-Denis Paris), and McGovern's pamphlet *Terror in Spain*.

In sense (i) the P.O.U.M. could probably be described as Trotskyist. So can the English I.L.P., the German S.A.P., the Left Socialists in France, and so on. But the P.O.U.M. had no connection with Trotsky or the Trotskyist ('Bolshevik-Leninist') organization. When the war broke out the foreign Trotskyists who came to Spain (fifteen or twenty in number) worked at first for the P.O.U.M., as the party nearest to their own viewpoint, but without becoming party-members; later Trotsky ordered his followers to attack the P.O.U.M. policy, and the Trotskyists were purged from the party offices, though a few remained in the militia. Nin, the P.O.U.M. leader after Maurin's capture by the Fascists, was at one time Trotsky's secretary, but had left him some years earlier and formed the P.O.U.M. by the amalgamation of various Opposition Communists with an earlier party, the Workers' and Peasants' Bloc. Nin's one-time association with Trotsky had been used in the Communist press to show that the P.O.U.M. was really Trotskyist. By the same line of argument it could be shown that the English Communist Party is really a Fascist organization, because of Mr John Strachey's one-time association with Sir Oswald Mosley.

In sense (ii), the only exactly defined sense of the word, the P.O.U.M. was certainly not Trotskyist. It is important to make this distinction, because it is taken for granted by the majority of Communists that a Trotskyist in sense (ii) is invariably a Trotskyist in sense (iii) – i.e. that the whole Trotskyist organization is simply a Fascist spying-machine. 'Trotskyism' only came into public notice in the time of the Russian sabotage trials, and to call a man a Trotskyist is practically equivalent to calling him a murderer, agent provocateur, etc. But at the same time anyone who criticizes Communist policy from a Left-wing standpoint is liable to be denounced as a Trotskyist. Is it then asserted that everyone professing revolutionary extremism is in Fascist pay?

In practice it is or is not, according to local convenience. When Maxton went to Spain with the delegation I have mentioned above, *Verdad*, *Frente Rojo*, and other Spanish Communist papers instantly denounced him as a 'Trotsky-Fascist', spy of the Gestapo and so forth. Yet the English Communists were careful not to repeat this accusation. In the English Communist press Maxton becomes merely a 'reactionary enemy of the working class', which is conveniently vague. The reason, of course, is simply that several sharp lessons have given the English Communist press a wholesome dread of the law of libel. The fact that the accusation was not repeated in a country where it might have to be proved is sufficient confession that it is a lie.

It may seem that I have discussed the accusations against the P.O.U.M. at greater length that was necessary. Compared with the huge miseries of a civil war, this kind of internecine squabble between parties, with its inevitable injustices and false accusations, may appear trivial. It is not really so. I believe that libels and press-campaigns of this kind, and the habits of mind they indicate, are capable of doing the most deadly damage to the anti-Fascist cause.

Anyone who has given the subject a glance knows that the Communist tactic of dealing with political opponents by means of trumped-up accusations is nothing new. Today the key-word is 'Trotsky-Fascist'; yesterday it was 'Social-Fascist'. It is only six or seven years since the Russian State trials 'proved' that the leáders of the Second International, including, for instance, Léon Blum and prominent members of the British Labour Party, were hatching a huge plot for the military invasion of the U.S.S.R. Yet today the French Communists are glad enough to accept Blum as a leader, and the English Communists are raising heaven and earth to get inside the Labour Party. I doubt whether this kind of thing pays, even from a sectarian point of view. And meanwhile there is no possible doubt about the hatred and dissension that the 'Trotsky-Fascist' accusation is causing. Rank-and-file Communists everywhere are led away on a senseless witch-hunt after 'Trotskyists', and parties of the type of the P.O.U.M. are driven back into the terribly sterile position of being mere anti-Communist parties. There is already the beginning of a dangerous split in the world working-class movement. A few more libels against life-long Socialists, a few more frame-ups like the charges against the P.O.U.M., and the split may become irreconcilable. The only hope is to keep political controversy on a plane where exhaustive discussion is possible. Between the Communists and those who stand or claim to stand to the Left of them there is a real difference. The Communists hold that Fascism can be beaten by alliance with sections of the capitalist class (the Popular Front); their opponents hold that this manoeuvre simply gives Fascism new breeding-grounds. The question has got to be settled; to make the wrong decision may be to land ourselves in for centuries of semi-slavery. But so long as no argument is produced except a scream of 'Trotsky-Fascist!' the discussion cannot even begin. It would be impossible for me, for instance, to debate the rights and wrongs of the Barcelona fighting with a Communist Party member, because no Communist – that is to say, no 'good' Communist – could admit that I have given a truthful account of the facts. If he followed his party 'line' dutifully he would have to declare that I am lying or, at best, that I am hopelessly misled and that anyone who glanced at the *Daily Worker* headlines a thousand miles from the scene of events knows more of what was happening in Barcelona than I do. In such circumstances there can be no argument; the necessary minimum of agreement cannot be reached. What purpose is served by saying that men like Maxton are in Fascist pay? Only the purpose of making serious discussion impossible. It is as though in the middle of a chess tournament one competitor should suddenly begin screaming that the other is guilty of arson or bigamy. The point that is really at issue remains untouched. Libel settles nothing.

Chapter Twelve

It must have been three days after the Barcelona fighting ended that we returned to the front. After the fighting – more particularly after the slanging-match in the newspapers – it was difficult to think about this war in quite the same naïvely idealistic manner as before. I suppose there is no one who spent more than a few weeks in Spain without being in some degree disillusioned. My mind went back to the newspaper correspondent whom I had met my first day in Barcelona, and who said to me: 'This war is a racket the same as any other.' The remark had shocked me deeply, and at that time (December) I do not believe it was true; it was not true even now, in May; but it was becoming truer. The fact is that every war suffers a kind of progressive degradation with every month that it continues, because such things as individual liberty and a truthful press are simply not compatible with military efficiency.

One could begin now to make some kind of guess at what was likely to happen. It was easy to see that the Caballero Government would fall and be replaced by a more Right-wing Government with a stronger Communist influence (this happened a week or two later), which would set itself to break the power of the trade unions once and for all. And afterwards, when Franco was beaten – and putting aside the huge problems raised by the reorganization of Spain – the prospect was not rosy. As for the newspaper talk about this being a 'war for democracy', it was plain eyewash. No one in his senses supposed that there was any hope of democracy, even as we understand it in England or France, in a country so divided and exhausted as Spain would be when the war was over. It would have to be a dictatorship, and it was clear that the chance of a working-class dictatorship had passed. That meant that the general movement would be in the direction of some kind of Fascism. Fascism called, no doubt, by some politer name, and – because this was Spain – more human and less efficient than the German or Italian varieties. The only alternatives were an infinitely worse dictatorship by Franco, or (always a possibility) that the war would end with Spain divided up, either by actual frontiers or into economic zones.

Whichever way you took it it was a depressing outlook. But it did not follow that the Government was not worth fighting for as against the more naked and developed Fascism of Franco and Hitler. Whatever faults the post-war Government might have, Franco's régime would certainly be worse. To the workers – the town proletariat – it might in the end make very little difference who won, but Spain is primarily an agricultural country and the peasants would almost certainly benefit by a Government victory. Some at least of the seized lands would remain in their possession, in which case there would also be a distribution of land in the territory that had been Franco's, and the virtual serfdom that had existed in some parts of Spain was not likely to be restored. The Government in control at the end of the war would at any rate be anti-clerical and anti-feudal. It would keep the Church in check, at least for the time being, and would modernize the country – build roads, for instance, and promote education and public health; a certain amount had been done in this direction even during the war. Franco, on the other hand, in so far as he was not merely the puppet of Italy and Germany, was tied to the big feudal landlords and stood for a stuffy clerico-military reaction. The Popular Front might be a swindle, but Franco was an anachronism. Only millionaires or romantics could want him to win.

Moreover, there was the question of the international prestige of Fascism, which for a year or two past had been haunting me like a nightmare. Since 1930 the Fascists had won all the victories; it was time they got a beating, it hardly mattered from whom. If we could drive Franco and his foreign mercenaries into the sea it might make an immense improvement in the world situation, even if Spain itself emerged with a stifling dictatorship and all its best men in jail. For that alone the war would have been worth winning.

This was how I saw things at the time. I may say that I now think much more highly of the Negrin Government than I did when it came into office. It has kept up the difficult fight with splendid courage, and it has shown more political tolerance than anyone expected. But I still believe that – unless Spain splits up, with unpredictable consequences – the tendency of the post-war

Government is bound to be Fascistic. Once again I let this opinion stand, and take the chance that time will do to me what it does to most prophets.

We had just reached the front when we heard that Bob Smillie, on his way back to England, had been arrested at the frontier, taken down to Valencia and thrown into jail. Smillie had been in Spain since the previous October. He had worked for several months at the P.O.U.M. office and had then joined the militia when the other I.L.P. members arrived, on the understanding that he was to do three months at the front before going back to England to take part in a propaganda tour. It was some time before we could discover what he had been arrested for. He was being kept *incommunicado*, so that not even a lawyer could see him. In Spain there is – at any rate in practice – no habeas corpus, and you can be kept in jail for months at a stretch without even being charged, let alone tried. Finally we learned from a released prisoner that Smillie had been arrested for 'carrying arms'. The 'arms', as I happened to know, were two hand-grenades of the primitive type used at the beginning of the war, which he had been taking home to show off at his lectures, along with shell splinters and other souvenirs. The charges and fuses had been removed from them – they more mere cylinders of steel and completely harmless. It was obvious that this was only a pretext and that he had been arrested because of his known connection with the P.O.U.M. The Barcelona fighting had only just ended and the authorities were, at that moment, extremely anxious not to let anyone out of Spain who was in a position to contradict the official version. As a result people were liable to be arrested at the frontier on more or less frivolous pretexts. Very possibly the intention, at the beginning, was only to detain Smillie for a few days. But the trouble is that, in Spain, once you are in jail you generally stay there, with or without trial.

We were still at Huesca, but they had placed us further to the right, opposite the Fascist redoubt which we had temporarily captured a few weeks earlier. I was now acting as *teniente* – corresponding to second-lieutenant in the British Army, I suppose – in command of about thirty men, English and Spanish. They had sent my name in for a regular commission; whether I should get it was uncertain. Previously the militia officers had refused to accept regular commissions, which meant extra pay and conflicted with the equalitarian ideas of the militia, but they were now obliged to do so. Benjamin had already been gazetted captain and Kopp was in process of being gazetted major. The Government could not, of course, dispense with the militia officers, but it was not confirming any of them in a higher rank than major, presumably in order to keep the higher commands for Regular Army officers and the new officers from the School of War. As a result, in our division, the 29th, and no doubt in many others, you had the queer temporary situation of the divisional commander, the brigade commanders and the battalion commanders all being majors.

There was not much happening at the front. The battle round the Jaca road had died away and did not begin again till mid-June. In our position the chief trouble was the snipers. The Fascist trenches were more than a hundred and fifty yards away, but they were on higher ground and were on two sides of us, our line forming a right-angle salient. The corner of the salient was a dangerous spot; there had always been a toll of sniper casualties there. From time to time the Fascists let fly at us with a rifle-grenade or some similar weapon. It made a ghastly crash – unnerving, because you could not hear it coming in time to dodge – but was not really dangerous; the hole it blew in the ground was no bigger than a wash-tub. The nights were pleasantly warm, the days blazing hot, the mosquitoes were becoming a nuisance, and in spite of the clean clothes we had brought from Barcelona we were almost immediately lousy. Out in the deserted orchards in no man's land the cherries were whitening on the trees. For two days there were torrential rains, the dug-outs flooded and the parapet sank a foot; after that there were more days of digging out the sticky clay with the wretched Spanish spades which have no handles and bend like tin spoons.

They had promised us a trench-mortar for the company; I was looking forward to it greatly. At nights we patrolled as usual – more dangerous than it used to be, because the Fascist trenches were better manned and they had grown more alert; they had scattered tin cans just outside their wire and used to open up with the machine-guns when they heard a clank. In the daytime we sniped from no man's land. By crawling a hundred yards you could get to a ditch, hidden by tall grasses, which commanded a gap in the Fascist parapet. We had set up a rifle-rest in the ditch. If you waited long enough you generally saw a khaki-clad figure slip hurriedly across the gap. I had several shots. I don't know whether I hit anyone – it is most unlikely; I am a very poor shot with a rifle. But it was rather fun, the Fascists did not know where the shots were coming from, and I made sure I would get one of them sooner or later. However, the dog it was that died – a Fascist sniper got me instead. I had been about ten days at the front when it happened. The whole experience of being hit by a bullet is very interesting and I think it is worth describing in detail.

It was at the corner of the parapet, at five o'clock in the morning. This was always a dangerous time, because we had the dawn at our backs, and if you stuck your head above the parapet it was clearly outlined against the sky. I was talking to the sentries preparatory to changing the guard. Suddenly, in the very middle of saying something, I felt – it is very hard to describe what I felt, though I remember it with the utmost vividness.

Roughly speaking it was the sensation of being *at the centre* of an explosion. There seemed to be a loud bang and a blinding flash of light all round me, and I felt a tremendous shock – no pain, only a violent shock, such as you get from an electric terminal; with it a sense of utter weakness, a feeling of being stricken and shrivelled up to nothing. The sand-bags in front of me receded into immense distance. I fancy you would feel much the same if you were struck by lightning. I knew immediately that I was hit, but because of the seeming bang and flash I thought it was a rifle nearby that had gone off accidentally and shot me. All this happened in a space of time much less than a second. The next moment my knees crumpled up and I was falling, my head hitting the ground with a violent bang which, to my relief, did not hurt. I had a numb, dazed feeling, a consciousness of being very badly hurt, but no pain in the ordinary sense.

The American sentry I had been talking to had started forward. 'Gosh! Are you hit?' People gathered round. There was the usual fuss – 'Lift him up! Where's he hit? Get his shirt open!' etc., etc. The American called for a knife to cut my shirt open. I knew that there was one in my pocket and tried to get it out, but discovered that my right arm was paralysed. Not being in pain, I felt a vague satisfaction. This ought to please my wife, I thought; she had always wanted me to be wounded, which would save me from being killed when the great battle came. It was only now that it occurred to me to wonder where I was hit, and how badly; I could feel nothing, but I was conscious that the bullet had struck me somewhere in the front of the body. When I tried to speak I found that I had no voice, only a faint squeak, but at the second attempt I managed to ask where I was hit. In the throat, they said. Harry Webb, our stretcher-bearer, had brought a bandage and one of the little bottles of alcohol they gave us for field-dressings. As they lifted me up a lot of blood poured out of my mouth, and I heard a Spaniard behind me say that the bullet had gone clean through my neck. I felt the alcohol, which at ordinary times would sting like the devil, splash onto the wound as a pleasant coolness.

They laid me down again while somebody fetched a stretcher. As soon as I knew that the bullet had gone clean through my neck I took it for granted that I was done for. I had never heard of a man or an animal getting a bullet through the middle of the neck and surviving it. The blood was dribbling out of the corner of my mouth. 'The artery's gone,' I thought. I wondered how long you last when your carotid artery is cut; not many minutes, presumably. Everything was very blurry. There must have been about two minutes during which I assumed that I was killed. And that too was interesting – I mean it is interesting to know what your thoughts would be at such a time. My first thought, conventionally enough, was for my wife. My second was a violent resentment at having to leave this world which, when all is said and done, suits me so well. I had time to feel this very vividly. The stupid mischance infuriated me. The meaninglessness of it! To be bumped off, not even in battle, but in this stale corner of the trenches, thanks to a moment's carelessness! I thought, too, of the man who had shot me – wondered what he was like, whether he was a Spaniard or a foreigner, whether he knew he had got me, and so forth. I could not feel any resentment against him. I reflected that as he was a Fascist I would have killed him if I could, but that if he had been taken prisoner and brought before me at this moment I would merely have congratulated him on his good shooting. It may be, though, that if you were really dying your thoughts would be quite different.

They had just got me onto the stretcher when my paralysed right arm came to life and began hurting damnably. At the time I imagined that I must have broken it in falling; but the pain reassured me, for I knew that your sensations do not become more acute when you are dying. I began to feel more normal and to be sorry for the four poor devils who were sweating and slithering with the stretcher on their shoulders. It was a mile and a half to the ambulance, and vile going, over lumpy, slippery tracks. I knew what a sweat it was, having helped to carry a wounded man down a day or two earlier. The leaves of the silver poplars which, in places, fringed our trenches brushed against my face; I thought what a good thing it was to be alive in a world where silver poplars grow. But all the while the pain in my arm was diabolical, making me swear and then try not to swear, because every time I breathed too hard the blood bubbled out of my mouth.

The doctor re-bandaged the wound, gave me a shot of morphia, and sent me off to Sietamo. The hospitals at Sietamo were hurriedly constructed wooden huts where the wounded were, as a rule, only kept for a few hours before being sent on to Barbastro or Lerida. I was dopey from the morphia but still in great pain, practically unable to move and swallowing blood constantly. It was typical of Spanish hospital methods that while I was in this state the untrained nurse tried to force the regulation hospital meal – a huge meal of soup, eggs, greasy stew and so forth – down my throat and seemed surprised when I would not take it. I asked for a cigarette, but this was one of the periods of tobacco famine and there was not a cigarette in the place. Presently two comrades who had got permission to leave the line for a few hours appeared at my bedside.

'Hullo! You're alive, are you? Good. We want your watch and your revolver and your electric torch. And your knife, if you've got one.'

They made off with all my portable possessions. This always happened when a man was wounded – everything he possessed was promptly divided up; quite rightly, for watches, revolvers, and so forth were precious at the front and if they went down the line in a wounded man's kit they were certain to be stolen somewhere on the way.

By the evening enough sick and wounded had trickled in to make up a few ambulance-loads, and they sent us on to Barbastro. What a journey! It used to be said that in this war you got well if you were wounded in the extremities, but always died of a wound in the abdomen. I now realized why. No one who was liable to bleed internally could have survived those miles of jolting over metal roads that had been smashed to pieces by heavy lorries and never repaired since the war began. Bang, bump, wallop! It took me back to my early childhood and a dreadful thing called the Wiggle-Woggle at the White City Exhibition. They had forgotten to tie us into the stretchers. I had enough strength in my left arm to hang on, but one poor wretch was spilt onto the floor and suffered God knows what agonies. Another, a walking case who was sitting in the corner of the ambulance, vomited all over the place. The hospital in Barbastro was very crowded, the beds so close together that they were almost touching. Next morning they loaded a number of us onto the hospital train and sent us down to Lerida.

I was five or six days in Lerida. It was a big hospital, with sick, wounded, and ordinary civilian patients more or less jumbled up together. Some of the men in my ward had frightful wounds. In the next bed to me there was a youth with black hair who was suffering from some disease or other and was being given medicine that made his urine as green as emerald. His bed-bottle was one of the sights of the ward. An English-speaking Dutch Communist, having heard that there was an Englishman in the hospital, befriended me and brought me English newspapers. He had been terribly wounded in the October fighting, and had somehow managed to settle down at Lerida hospital and had married one of the nurses. Thanks to his wound, one of his legs had shrivelled till it was no thicker than my arm. Two militiamen on leave, whom I had met my first week at the front, came in to see a wounded friend and recognized me. They were kids of about eighteen. They stood awkwardly beside my bed, trying to think of something to say, and then, as a way of demonstrating that they were sorry I was wounded, suddenly took all the tobacco out of their pockets, gave it to me, and fled before I could give it back. How typically Spanish! I discovered afterwards that you could not buy tobacco anywhere in the town and what they had given me was a week's ration.

After a few days I was able to get up and walk about with my arm in a sling. For some reason it hurt much more when it hung down. I also had, for the time being, a good deal of internal pain from the damage I had done myself in falling, and my voice had disappeared almost completely, but I never had a moment's pain from the bullet wound itself. It seems this is usually the case. The tremendous shock of a bullet prevents sensation locally; a splinter of shell or bomb, which is jagged and usually hits you less hard, would probably hurt like the devil. There was a pleasant garden in the hospital grounds, and in it was a pool with gold-fishes and some small dark grey fish

– bleak, I think. I used to sit watching them for hours. The way things were done at Lerida gave me an insight into the hospital system on the Aragon front – whether it was the same on other fronts I do not know. In some ways the hospitals were very good. The doctors were able men and there seemed to be no shortage of drugs and equipment. But there were two bad faults on account of which, I have no doubt, hundreds or thousands of men have died who might have been saved.

One was the fact that all the hospitals anywhere near the front line were used more or less as casualty clearing-stations. The result was that you got no treatment there unless you were too badly wounded to be moved. In theory most of the wounded were sent straight to Barcelona or Tarragona, but owing to the lack of transport they were often a week or ten days in getting there. They were kept hanging about at Sietamo, Barbastro, Monzon, Lerida, and other places, and meanwhile they were getting no treatment except an occasional clean bandage, sometimes not even that. Men with dreadful shell wounds, smashed bones and so forth, were swathed in a sort of casing made of bandages and plaster of Paris; a description of the wound was written in pencil on the outside, and as a rule the casing was not removed till the man reached Barcelona or Tarragona ten days later. It was almost impossible to get one's wound examined on the way; the few doctors could not cope with the work, and they simply walked hurriedly past your bed, saying: 'Yes, yes, they'll attend to you at Barcelona.' There were always rumours that the hospital train was leaving for Barcelona *mañana*. The other fault was the lack of competent nurses. Apparently there was no supply of trained nurses in Spain, perhaps because before the war this work was done chiefly by nuns. I have no complaint against the Spanish nurses, they always treated me with the greatest kindness, but there is no doubt that they were terribly ignorant. All of them knew how to take a temperature, and some of them knew how to tie a bandage, but that was about all. The result was that men who were too ill to fend for themselves were often shamefully neglected. The nurses would let a man remain constipated for a week on end, and they seldom washed those who were too weak to wash themselves. I remember one poor devil with a smashed arm telling me that he had been three weeks without having his face washed. Even beds were left unmade for days together. The food in all the hospitals was very good – too good, indeed. Even more in Spain than elsewhere it seemed to be the tradition to stuff sick people with heavy food. At Lerida the meals were terrific. Breakfast, at about six in the morning, consisted of soup, an omelette, stew, bread, white wine, and coffee, and lunch was even larger – this at a time when most of the civil population was seriously underfed. Spaniards seem not to recognize such a thing as a light diet. They give the same food to sick people as to well ones – always the same rich, greasy cookery, with everything sodden in olive oil.

One morning it was announced that the men in my ward were to be sent down to Barcelona today. I managed to send a wire to my wife, telling her that I was coming, and presently they packed us into buses and took us down to the station. It was only when the train was actually starting that the hospital orderly who travelled with us casually let fall that we were not going to Barcelona after all, but to Tarragona. I suppose the engine-driver had changed his mind. 'Just like Spain!' I thought. But it was very Spanish, too, that they agreed to hold up the train while I sent another wire, and more Spanish still that the wire never got there.

They had put us into ordinary third-class carriages with wooden seats, and many of the men were badly wounded and had only got out of bed for the first time that morning. Before long, what with the heat and the jolting, half of them were in a state of collapse and several vomited on the floor. The hospital orderly threaded his way among the corpse-like forms that sprawled everywhere, carrying a large goat-skin bottle full of water which he squirted into this mouth or that. It was beastly water; I remember the taste of it still. We got into Tarragona as the sun was getting low. The line runs along the shore a stone's throw from the sea. As our train drew into the station a troop-train full of men from the International Column was drawing out, and a knot of people on the bridge were waving to them. It was a very long train, packed to bursting-point with men, with field-guns lashed on the open trucks and more men clustering round the guns. I remember with peculiar vividness the spectacle of that train passing in the yellow evening light; window after window full of dark, smiling faces, the long tilted barrels of the guns, the scarlet scarves fluttering – all this gliding slowly past us against a turquoise-coloured sea.

'Estranjeros – foreigners,' said someone. 'They're Italians.'

Obviously they were Italians. No other people could have grouped themselves so picturesquely or returned the salutes of the crowd with so much grace – a grace that was none the less because about half the men on the train were drinking out of up-ended wine bottles. We heard afterwards that these were some of the troops who won the great victory at Guadalajara in March; they had been on leave and were being transferred to the Aragon front. Most of them, I am afraid, were killed at Huesca only a few weeks later. The men who were well enough to stand had moved across the carriage to cheer the Italians as they went past. A crutch waved out of the window; bandaged forearms made the Red Salute. It was like an allegorical picture of war; the trainload of fresh men gliding proudly up the line, the maimed men sliding slowly down, and all the while the guns on the open trucks making one's heart leap as guns always do, and reviving that pernicious feeling, so difficult to get rid of, that war *is* glorious after all.

The hospital at Tarragona was a very big one and full of wounded from all fronts. What wounds one saw there! They had a way of treating certain wounds which I suppose was in accordance with the latest medical practice, but which was peculiarly horrible to look at. This was to leave the wound completely open and unbandaged, but protected from flies by a net of butter-muslin, stretched over wires. Under the muslin you would see the red jelly of a half-healed wound. There was one man wounded in the face and throat who had his head inside a sort of spherical helmet of butter-muslin; his mouth was closed up and he breathed through a little tube that was fixed between his lips. Poor devil, he looked so lonely, wandering to and fro, looking at you through his muslin cage and unable to speak. I was three or four days at Tarragona. My strength was coming back, and one day, by going slowly, I managed to walk down as far as the beach. It was queer to see the seaside life going on almost as usual; the smart cafés along the promenade and the plump local bourgeoisie bathing and sunning themselves in deck-chairs as though there had not been a war within a thousand miles. Nevertheless, as it happened, I saw a bather drowned, which one would have thought impossible in that shallow and tepid sea.

Finally, eight or nine days after leaving the front, I had my wound examined. In the surgery where newly-arrived cases were examined, doctors with huge pairs of shears were hacking away the breast-plates of plaster in which men with smashed ribs, collar-bones and so forth had been cased at the dressing-stations behind the line; out of the neck-hole of the huge clumsy breast-plate you would see protruding an anxious, dirty face, scrubby with a week's beard. The doctor, a brisk, handsome man of about thirty, sat me down in a chair, grasped my tongue with a piece of rough gauze, pulled it out as far as it would go, thrust a dentist's mirror down my throat and told me to say 'Eh'! After doing this till my tongue was bleeding and my eyes running with water, he told me that one vocal cord was paralysed.

'When shall I get my voice back?' I said.

'Your voice? Oh, you'll never get your voice back,' he said cheerfully.

However, he was wrong, as it turned out. For about two months I could not speak much above a whisper, but after that my voice became normal rather suddenly, the other vocal cord having 'compensated'. The pain in my arm was due to the bullet having pierced a bunch of nerves at the back of the neck. It was a shooting pain like neuralgia, and it went on hurting continuously for about a month, especially at night, so that I did not get much sleep. The fingers of my right hand were also semi-paralysed. Even now, five months afterwards, my forefinger is still numb – a queer effect for a neck wound to have.

The wound was a curiosity in a small way and various doctors examined it with much clicking of tongues and 'Que suerte! *Que* suerte!' One of them told me with an air of authority that the bullet had missed the artery by 'about a millimetre'. I don't know how he knew. No one I met at this time – doctors, nurses, *practicantes*, or fellow-patients – failed to assure me that a man who is hit through the neck and survives it is the luckiest creature alive. I could not help thinking that it would be even luckier not to be hit at all.

Chapter Thirteen

In Barcelona, during all those last weeks I spent there, there was a peculiar evil feeling in the air – an atmosphere of suspicion, fear, uncertainty, and veiled hatred. The May fighting had left ineradicable after-effects behind it. With the fall of the Caballero Government the Communists had come definitely into power, the charge of internal order had been handed over to Communist ministers, and no one doubted that they would smash their political rivals as soon as they got a quarter of a chance. Nothing was happening as yet, I myself had not even any mental picture of what was going to happen; and yet there was a perpetual vague sense of danger, a consciousness of some evil thing that was impending. However little you were actually conspiring, the atmosphere forced you to feel like a conspirator. You seemed to spend all your time holding whispered conversations in corners of cafés and wondering whether that person at the next table was a police spy.

Sinister rumours of all kinds were flying round, thanks to the press censorship. One was that the Negrin-Prieto Government was planning to compromise the war. At the time I was inclined to believe this, for the Fascists were closing in on Bilbao and the Government was visibly doing nothing to save it. Basque flags were displayed all over the town, girls rattled collecting-boxes in the cafés, and there were the usual broadcasts about 'heroic defenders', but the Basques were getting no real assistance. It was tempting to believe that the Government was playing a double game. Later events have proved that I was quite wrong here, but it seems probable that Bilbao could have been saved if a little more energy had been shown. An offensive on the Aragon front, even an unsuccessful one, would have forced Franco to divert part of his army; as it was the Government did not begin any offensive action till it was far too late – indeed, till about the time when Bilbao fell. The C.N.T. was distributing in huge numbers a leaflet saying: 'Be on your guard!' and hinting that 'a certain Party' (meaning the Communists) was plotting a *coup d'état*. There was also a widespread fear that Catalonia was going to be invaded. Earlier, when we went back to the front, I had seen the powerful defences that were being constructed scores of miles behind the front line, and fresh bomb-proof shelters were being dug all over Barcelona. There were frequent scares of air-raids and sea-raids; more often than not these were false alarms, but every time the sirens blew the lights all over the town blacked out for hours on end and timid people dived for the cellars. Police spies were everywhere. The jails were still crammed with prisoners left over from the May fighting, and others – always, of course, Anarchist and P.O.U.M. adherents – were disappearing into jail by ones and twos. So far as one could discover, no one was ever tried or even charged – not even charged with anything so definite as 'Trotskyism'; you were simply flung into jail and kept there, usually *incommunicado*. Bob Smillie was still in jail in Valencia. We could discover nothing except that neither the I.L.P. representative on the spot nor the lawyer who had been engaged, was permitted to see him. Foreigners from the International Column and other militias were getting into jail in larger and larger numbers. Usually they were arrested as deserters. It was typical of the general situation that nobody now knew for certain whether a militiaman was a volunteer or a regular soldier. A few months earlier anyone enlisting in the militia had been told that he was a volunteer and could, if he wished, get his discharge papers at any time when he was due for leave. Now it appeared that the Government had changed its mind, a militiaman was a regular soldier and counted as a deserter if he tried to go home. But even about this no one seemed certain. At some parts of the front the authorities were still issuing discharges. At the frontier these were sometimes recognized, sometimes not; if not, you were promptly thrown into jail. Later the number of foreign 'deserters' in jail swelled into hundreds, but most of them were repatriated when a fuss was made in their own countries.

Bands of armed Assault Guards roamed everywhere in the streets, the Civil Guards were still holding cafés and other buildings in strategic spots, and many of the P.S.U.C. buildings were still sandbagged and barricaded. At various points in the town there were posts manned by Civil Guards or Carabineros who stopped passers-by and demanded their papers. Everyone warned me not to show my P.O.U.M. militiaman's card but merely to show my passport and my hospital ticket. Even to be known to have served in the P.O.U.M. militia was vaguely dangerous. P.O.U.M. militiamen who were wounded or on leave were penalized in petty ways – it was made difficult for them to draw their pay, for instance. *La Batalla* was still appearing, but it was censored almost out of existence, and *Solidaridad* and the other Anarchist papers were also heavily censored. There was a new rule that censored portions of a newspaper must not be left blank but filled up with other matter; as a result it was often impossible to tell when something had been cut out.

The food shortage, which had fluctuated throughout the war, was in one of its bad stages. Bread was scarce and the cheaper sorts were being adulterated with rice; the bread the soldiers were getting in the barracks was dreadful stuff like putty. Milk and sugar were very scarce and tobacco almost non-existent, except for the expensive smuggled cigarettes. There was an acute shortage of olive oil, which Spaniards use for half a dozen different purposes. The queues of women waiting to buy olive oil were controlled by mounted Civil Guards who sometimes amused themselves by backing their horses into the queue and trying to make them tread on the women's toes. A minor annoyance of the time was the lack of small change. The silver had been withdrawn and as yet no new coinage had been issued, so that there was nothing between the ten-centime piece and the note for two and a half pesetas, and all notes below ten pesetas were very scarce.[1] For the poorest people this meant an aggravation of the food shortage. A woman with only a ten-peseta note in her possession might wait for hours in a queue outside the grocery and then be unable to buy anything after all because the grocer had no change and she could not afford to spend the whole note.

It is not easy to convey the nightmare atmosphere of that time – the peculiar uneasiness produced by rumours that were always changing, by censored newspapers and the constant presence of armed men. It is not easy to convey it because, at the moment, the thing essential to such an atmosphere does not exist in England. In England political intolerance is not yet taken for granted. There is political persecution in a petty way; if I were a coal-miner I would not care to be known to the boss as a Communist; but the 'good party man', the gangster-gramophone of continental politics, is still a rarity, and the notion of 'liquidating' or 'eliminating' everyone who happens to disagree with you does not yet seem natural. It seemed only too natural in Barcelona. The 'Stalinists' were in the saddle, and therefore it was a matter of course that every 'Trotskyist' was in danger. The thing everyone feared was a thing which, after all, did not happen – a fresh outbreak of street-fighting, which, as before, would be blamed on the P.O.U.M. and the Anarchists. There were times when I caught my ears listening for the first shots. It was as though some huge evil intelligence were brooding over the town. Everyone noticed it and remarked upon it. And it was queer how everyone expressed it in almost the same words: 'The atmosphere of this place – it's horrible. Like being in a lunatic asylum.' But perhaps I ought not to say *everyone*. Some of the English visitors who flitted briefly through Spain, from hotel to hotel, seem not to have noticed that there was anything wrong with the general atmosphere. The Duchess of Atholl writes, I notice (*Sunday Express*, 17 October 1937):

> 'I was in Valencia, Madrid, and Barcelona . . . perfect order prevailed in all three towns without any display of force. All the hotels in which I stayed were not only "normal" and "decent", but extremely comfortable, in spite of the shortage of butter and coffee.'

It is a peculiarity of English travellers that they do not really believe in the existence of anything outside the smart hotels. I hope they found some butter for the Duchess of Atholl.

[1] The purchasing value of the peseta was about fourpence.

I was at the Sanatorium Maurin, one of the sanatoria run by the P.O.U.M. It was in the suburbs near Tibidabo, the queer-shaped mountain that rises abruptly behind Barcelona and is traditionally supposed to have been the hill from which Satan showed Jesus the countries of the earth (hence its name). The house had previously belonged to some wealthy bourgeois and had been seized at the time of the revolution. Most of the men there had either been invalided out of the line or had some wound that had permanently disabled them – amputated limbs, and so forth. There were several other Englishmen there: Williams, with a damaged leg, and Stafford Cottman, a boy of eighteen, who had been sent back from the trenches with suspected tuberculosis, and Arthur Clinton, whose smashed left arm was still strapped on to one of those huge wire contraptions, nicknamed aeroplanes, which the Spanish hospitals were using. My wife was still staying at the Hotel Continental, and I generally came into Barcelona in the daytime. In the morning I used to attend the General Hospital for electrical treatment of my arm. It was a queer business – a series of prickly electric shocks that made the various sets of muscles jerk up and down – but it seemed to do some good; the use of my fingers came back and the pain grew somewhat less. Both of us had decided that the best thing we could do was to go back to England as soon as possible. I was extremely weak, my voice was gone, seemingly for good, and the doctors told me that at best it would be several months before I was fit to fight. I had got to start earning some money sooner or later, and there did not seem much sense in staying in Spain and eating food that was needed for other people. But my motives were mainly selfish. I had an overwhelming desire to get away from it all; away from the horrible atmosphere of political suspicion and hatred, from streets thronged by armed men, from air-raids, trenches, machine-guns, screaming trams, milkless tea, oil cookery, and shortage of cigarettes – from almost everything that I had learnt to associate with Spain.

The doctors at the General Hospital had certified me medically unfit, but to get my discharge I had to see a medical board at one of the hospitals near the front and then go to Sietamo to get my papers stamped at the P.O.U.M. militia headquarters. Kopp had just come back from the front, full of jubilation. He had just been in action and said that Huesca was going to be taken at last. The Government had brought troops from the Madrid front and were concentrating thirty thousand men, with aeroplanes in huge numbers. The Italians I had seen going up the line from Tarragona had attacked on the Jaca road but had had heavy casualties and lost two tanks. However, the town was bound to fall, Kopp said. (Alas! It didn't. The attack was a frightful mess-up and led to nothing except an orgy of lying in the newspapers.) Meanwhile Kopp had to go down to Valencia for an interview at the Ministry of War. He had a letter from General Pozas, now commanding the Army of the East – the usual letter, describing Kopp as a 'person of all confidence' and recommending him for a special appointment in the engineering section (Kopp had been an engineer in civil life). He left for Valencia the same day as I left for Sietamo – 15 June.

It was five days before I got back to Barcelona. A lorry-load of us reached Sietamo about midnight, and as soon as we got to the P.O.U.M. headquarters they lined us up and began handing out rifles and cartridges, before even taking our names. It seemed that the attack was beginning and they were likely to call for reserves at any moment. I had my hospital ticket in my pocket, but I could not very well refuse to go with the others. I kipped down on the ground, with a cartridge-box for a pillow, in a mood of deep dismay. Being wounded had spoiled my nerve for the time being – I believe this usually happens – and the prospect of being under fire frightened me horribly. However, there was a bit of *mañana*, as usual, we were not called out after all, and next morning I produced my hospital ticket and went in search of my discharge. It meant a series of confused, tiresome journeys. As usual they bandied one to and fro from hospital to hospital – Sietamo, Barbastro, Monzon, then back to Sietamo to get my discharge stamped, then down the line again via Barbastro and Lerida – and the convergence of troops on Huesca had monopolized all the transport and disorganized everything. I remember sleeping in queer places – once in a hospital bed, but once in a ditch, once on a very narrow bench which I fell off in the middle of the night, and once in a sort of municipal lodging-house in Barbastro. As soon as you got away from the railroad there was no way of travelling except by jumping chance lorries. You had to wait by the roadside for hours, sometimes three or four hours at a stretch, with knots of disconsolate peasants who carried bundles full of ducks and rabbits, waving to lorry after lorry. When finally you struck a lorry that was not chock full of men, loaves of bread or ammunition-boxes the bumping over the vile roads wallowed you to pulp. No horse has ever thrown me so high as those lorries used to throw me. The only way of travelling was to crowd all together and cling to one another. To my humiliation I found that I was still too weak to climb on to a lorry without being helped.

I slept a night at Monzon Hospital, where I went to see my medical board. In the next bed to me there was an Assault Guard, wounded over the left eye. He was friendly and gave me cigarettes. I said: 'In Barcelona we should have been shooting one another,' and we laughed over this. It was queer how the general spirit seemed to change when you got anywhere near the front line. All or nearly all of the vicious hatreds of the political parties evaporated. During all the time I was at the front I never once remember any P.S.U.C. adherent showing me hostility because I was P.O.U.M. That kind of thing belonged in Barcelona or in places even remoter from the war. There were a lot of Assault Guards in Sietamo. They had been sent on from Barcelona to take part in the attack on Huesca. The Assault Guards were a corps not intended primarily for the front, and many of them had not been under fire before. Down in Barcelona they were lords of the street, but up here they were *quintos* (rookies) and palled up with militia children of fifteen who had been in the line for months.

At Monzon Hospital the doctor did the usual tongue-pulling and mirror-thrusting business, assured me in the same cheerful manner as the others that I should never have a voice again, and signed my certificate. While I waited to be examined there was going on inside the surgery some dreadful operation without anaesthetics – why without anaesthetics I do not know. It went on and on, scream after scream, and when I went in there were chairs flung about and on the floor were pools of blood and urine.

The details of that final journey stand out in my mind with strange clarity. I was in a different mood, a more observing mood, than I had been in for months past. I had got my discharge, stamped with the seal of the 29th Division, and the doctor's certificate in which I was 'declared useless'. I was free to go back to England; consequently I felt able, almost for the first time, to look at Spain. I had a day to put in at Barbastro, for there was only one train a day. Previously I had seen Barbastro in brief glimpses, and it had seemed to me simply a part of the war – a grey, muddy, cold place, full of roaring lorries and shabby troops. It seemed queerly different now. Wandering through it I became aware of pleasant tortuous streets, old stone bridges, wine shops with great oozy barrels as tall as a man, and intriguing semi-subterranean shops where men were making cartwheels, daggers, wooden spoons and goatskin water-bottles. I watched a man making a skin bottle and discovered with great interest, what I had never known before, that they are made with the fur inside and the fur is not removed, so that you are really drinking distilled goat's hair. I had drunk out of them for months without knowing this. And at the back of the town there was a shallow jade-green river, and rising out of it a perpendicular cliff of rock, with houses built into the rock, so that from your bedroom window you could spit straight into the water a hundred feet below. Innumerable doves lived in the holes in the cliff. And in Lerida there were old crumbling buildings upon whose cornices thousands upon thousands of swallows had built their nests, so that at a little distance the crusted pattern of nests was like some florid moulding of the rococo period. It was queer how for nearly six months past I had had no eyes for such things. With my discharge papers in my pocket I felt like a human being again, and also a little like a tourist. For almost the first time I felt that I was really in Spain, in a country that I had longed all my life to visit. In the quiet back streets of Lerida and Barbastro I seemed to catch a momentary glimpse, a sort of far-off rumour of the Spain that dwells in everyone's imagination. White sierras, goatherds, dungeons of the Inquisition, Moorish palaces, black winding trains of mules, grey olive trees and groves of lemons, girls in black mantillas, the wines of Malaga and Alicante, cathedrals, cardinals, bullfights, gypsies, serenades – in short, Spain. Of all Europe it was the country that had had most hold upon my imagination. It seemed a pity that when at last I had managed to come here I had seen only this north-eastern corner, in the middle of a confused war and for the most part in winter.

It was late when I got back to Barcelona, and there were no taxis. It was no use trying to get to the Sanatorium Maurin, which was right outside the town, so I made for the Hotel Continental, stopping for dinner on the way. I remember the conversation I had with a very fatherly waiter about the oak jugs, bound with copper, in which they served the wine. I said I would like to buy a set of them to take back to England. The waiter was sympathetic. 'Yes, beautiful, were they not? But impossible to buy nowadays. Nobody was manufacturing them any longer – nobody was manufacturing anything. This war – such a pity!' We agreed that the war was a pity. Once again I felt like a tourist. The waiter asked me gently, had I liked Spain; would I come back to Spain? Oh, yes, I should come back to Spain. The peaceful quality of this conversation sticks in my memory, because of what happened immediately afterwards.

When I got to the hotel my wife was sitting in the lounge. She got up and came towards me in what struck me as a very unconcerned manner; then she put an arm round my neck and, with a sweet smile for the benefit of the other people in the lounge, hissed in my ear:

'*Get out!*'

'What?'

'Get out of here *at once*!'

'What?'

'Don't keep standing here! You must get outside quickly!'

'What? Why? What do you mean?'

She had me by the arm and was already leading me towards the stairs. Half-way down we met a Frenchman – I am not going to give his name, for though he had no connection with the P.O.U.M. he was a good friend to us all during the trouble. He looked at me with a concerned face.

'Listen! You mustn't come in here. Get out quickly and hide yourself before they ring up the police.'

And behold! at the bottom of the stairs one of the hotel staff, who was a P.O.U.M. member (unknown to the management, I fancy), slipped furtively out of the lift and told me in broken English to get out. Even now I did not grasp what had happened.

'What the devil is all this about?' I said as soon as we were on the pavement.

'Haven't you *heard*?'

'No. Heard what? I've heard nothing.'

'The P.O.U.M.'s been suppressed. They've seized all the buildings. Practically everyone's in prison. And they say they're shooting people already.'

So that was it. We had to have somewhere to talk. All the big cafés on the Ramblas were thronged with police, but we found a quiet café in a side street. My wife explained to me what had happened while I was away.

On 15 June the police had suddenly arrested Andres Nin in his office, and the same evening had raided the Hotel Falcon and arrested all the people in it, mostly militiamen on leave. The place was converted immediately into a prison, and in a very little while it was filled to the brim with prisoners of all kinds. Next day the P.O.U.M. was declared an illegal organization and all its offices, book-stalls, sanatoria, Red Aid centres and so forth were seized. Meanwhile the police were arresting everyone they could lay hands on who was known to have any connection with the P.O.U.M. Within a day or two all or almost all of the forty members of the Executive Committee were in prison. Possibly one or two had escaped into hiding, but the police were adopting the trick (extensively used on both sides in this war) of seizing a man's wife as a hostage if he disappeared. There was no way of discovering how many people had been arrested. My wife had heard that it was about four hundred in Barcelona alone. I have since thought that even at that time the number must have been greater. And the most fantastic people had been arrested. In some cases the police had even gone to the length of dragging wounded militiamen out of the hospitals.

It was all profoundly dismaying. What the devil was it all about? I could understand their suppressing the P.O.U.M., but what were they arresting people for? For nothing, so far as one could discover. Apparently the suppression of the P.O.U.M. had a retrospective effect; the P.O.U.M. was now illegal, and therefore one was breaking the law by having previously belonged to it. As usual, none of the arrested people had been charged. Meanwhile, however, the Valencia Communist papers were flaming with the story of a huge 'Fascist plot', radio communication with the enemy, documents signed in invisible ink, etc., etc. I have dealt with this story earlier. The significant thing was that it was appearing only in the Valencia papers; I think I am right in saying that there was not a single word about it, or about the suppression of the P.O.U.M., in any Barcelona papers, Communist, Anarchist, or Republican. We first learned the precise nature of the charges against the P.O.U.M. leaders not from any Spanish paper but from the English papers that reached Barcelona a day or two later. What we could not know at this time was that the Government was not responsible for the charge of treachery and espionage, and that members of the Government were later to repudiate it. We only vaguely knew that the P.O.U.M. leaders, and presumably all the rest of us, were accused of being in Fascist pay. And already the rumours were flying round that people were being secretly shot in jail. There was a lot of exaggeration about this, but it certainly happened in some cases, and there is not much doubt that it happened in the case of Nin. After his arrest Nin was transferred to Valencia and thence to Madrid, and as early as 21 June the rumour reached Barcelona that he had been shot. Later the rumour took a more definite shape: Nin had been shot in prison by the secret police and his body dumped into the street. This story came from several sources, including Federica Montsenys, an ex-member of the Government. From that day to this Nin has never been heard of alive again. When, later, the Government were questioned by delegates from various countries, they shilly-shallied and would say only that Nin had disappeared and they knew nothing of his whereabouts. Some of the newspapers produced a tale that he had escaped to Fascist territory. No evidence was given in support of it, and Irujo, the Minister of Justice, later declared that the Espagne news-agency had falsified his official *communiqué*.[1] In any case it is most unlikely that a political prisoner of Nin's importance would be allowed to escape. Unless at some future time he is produced alive, I think we must take it that he was murdered in prison.

The tale of arrests went on and on, extending over months, until the number of political prisoners, not counting Fascists, swelled into thousands. One noticeable thing was the autonomy of the lower ranks of the police. Many of the arrests were admittedly illegal, and various people whose release had been ordered by the Chief of Police were re-arrested at the jail gate and carried off to 'secret prisons'. A typical case is that of Kurt Landau and his wife. They were arrested about 17 June, and Landau immediately 'disappeared'. Five months later his wife was still in jail, untried and without news of her husband. She declared a hunger-strike, after which the Minister of Justice sent word to assure her that her husband was dead. Shortly afterwards she was released, to be almost immediately re-arrested and flung into prison again. And it was noticeable that the police, at any rate at first, seemed completely indifferent as to any effect their actions might have upon the war. They were quite ready to arrest military officers in important posts without getting permission beforehand. About the end of June Jose Rovira, the general commanding the 29th Division, was arrested somewhere near the front line by a party of police who had been sent from Barcelona. His men sent a delegation to protest at the Ministry of War. It was found that neither the Ministry of War, nor Ortega, the chief of Police, had even been informed of Rovira's arrest. In the whole business the detail that most sticks in my throat, though perhaps it is not of great importance, is that all news of what was happening was kept from the troops at the front. As you will have seen, neither I nor anyone else at the front had heard anything about the suppression of the P.O.U.M. All the P.O.U.M. militia headquarters, Red Aid centres and so forth were functioning as usual, and as late as 20 June and as far down the line as Lerida, only about 100 miles from Barcelona, no one had heard what was happening. All word of it was kept out of the Barcelona papers (the Valencia papers, which were running the spy stories, did not reach the Aragon front), and no doubt one reason for arresting all the P.O.U.M. militiamen on leave in Barcelona was to prevent them from getting back to the front with the news. The draft with which I had gone up the line on 15 June must have been about the last to go. I am still puzzled to know

[1] See the reports of the Maxton delegation which I referred to in Chapter Eleven.

how the thing was kept secret, for the supply lorries and so forth were still passing to and fro; but there is no doubt that it *was* kept secret, and, as I have since learned from a number of others, the men in the front line heard nothing till several days later. The motive for all this is clear enough. The attack on Huesca was beginning, the P.O.U.M. militia was still a separate unit, and it was probably feared that if the men knew what was happening they would refuse to fight. Actually nothing of the kind happened when the news arrived. In the intervening days there must have been numbers of men who were killed without ever learning that the newspapers in the rear were calling them Fascists. This kind of thing is a little difficult to forgive. I know it was the usual policy to keep bad news from the troops, and perhaps as a rule that is justified. But it is a different matter to send men into battle and not even tell them that behind their backs their party is being suppressed, their leaders accused of treachery, and their friends and relatives thrown into prison.

My wife began telling me what had happened to our various friends. Some of the English and other foreigners had got across the frontier. Williams and Stafford Cottman had not been arrested when the Sanatorium Maurin was raided, and were in hiding somewhere. So was John McNair, who had been in France and had re-entered Spain after the P.O.U.M. was declared illegal – a rash thing to do, but he had not cared to stay in safety while his comrades were in danger. For the rest it was simply a chronicle of 'They've got so and so' and 'They've got so and so.' They seemed to have 'got' nearly everyone. It took me aback to hear that they had also 'got' George Kopp.

'What! Kopp? I thought he was in Valencia.'

It appeared that Kopp had come back to Barcelona; he had a letter from the Ministry of War to the colonel commanding the engineering operations on the eastern front. He knew that the P.O.U.M. had been suppressed, of course, but probably it did not occur to him that the police could be such fools as to arrest him when he was on his way to the front on an urgent military mission. He had come round to the Hotel Continental to fetch his kit-bags; my wife had been out at the time, and the hotel people had managed to detain him with some lying story while they rang up the police. I admit I was angry when I heard of Kopp's arrest. He was my personal friend, I had served under him for months, I had been under fire with him, and I knew his history. He was a man who had sacrificed everything – family, nationality, livelihood – simply to come to Spain and fight against Fascism. By leaving Belgium without permission and joining a foreign army while he was on the Belgian Army reserve, and, earlier, by helping to manufacture munitions illegally for the Spanish Government, he had piled up years of imprisonment for himself if he should ever return to his own country. He had been in the line since October 1936, had worked his way up from militiaman to major, had been in action I do not know how many times, and had been wounded once. During the May trouble, as I had seen for myself, he had prevented fighting locally and probably saved ten or twenty lives. And all they could do in return was to fling him into jail. It is waste of time to be angry, but the stupid malignity of this kind of thing does try one's patience.

Meanwhile they had not 'got' my wife. Although she had remained at the 'Continental' the police had made no move to arrest her. It was fairly obvious that she was being used as a decoy duck. A couple of nights earlier, however, in the small hours of the morning, six of the plain-clothes police had invaded our room at the hotel and searched it. They had seized every scrap of paper we possessed, except, fortunately, our passports and cheque-book. They had taken my diaries, all our books, all the press-cuttings that had been piling up for months past (I have often wondered what use those press-cuttings were to them), all my war souvenirs, and all our letters. (Incidentally, they took away a number of letters I had received from readers. Some of them had not been answered, and of course I have not the addresses. If anyone who wrote to me about my last book, and who did not get an answer, happens to read these lines, will he please accept this as an apology?) I learned afterwards that the police had also seized various belongings that I had left at the Sanatorium Maurin. They even carried off a bundle of my dirty linen. Perhaps they thought it had messages written on it in invisible ink.

It was obvious that it would be safer for my wife to stay at the hotel, at any rate for the time being. If she tried to disappear they would be after her immediately. As for myself, I should have to go straight into hiding. The prospect revolted me. In spite of the innumerable arrests it was almost impossible for me to believe that I was in any danger. The whole thing seemed too meaningless. It was the same refusal to take this idiotic onslaught seriously that had led Kopp into jail. I kept saying, but why should anyone want to arrest me? What had I done? I was not even a party member of the P.O.U.M. Certainly I had carried arms during the May fighting, but so had (at a guess) forty or fifty thousand people. Besides, I was badly in need of a proper night's sleep. I wanted to risk it and go back to the hotel. My wife would not hear of it. Patiently she explained the state of affairs. It did not matter what I had done or not done. This was not a round-up of criminals; it was merely a reign of terror. I was not guilty of any definite act, but I was guilty of 'Trotskyism'. The fact that I had served in the P.O.U.M. militia was quite enough to get me into prison. It was no use hanging on to the English notion that you are safe so long as you keep the law. Practically the law was what the police chose to make it. The only thing to do was to lie low and conceal the fact that I had anything to do with the P.O.U.M. We went through the papers in my pockets. My wife made me tear up my militiaman's card, which had P.O.U.M. on it in big letters, also a photo of a group of militiamen with a P.O.U.M. flag in the background; that was the kind of thing that got you arrested nowadays. I had to keep my discharge papers, however. Even these were a danger, for they bore the seal of the 29th Division, and the police would probably know that the 29th Division was the P.O.U.M.; but without them I could be arrested as a deserter.

The thing we had got to think of now was getting out of Spain. There was no sense in staying here with the certainty of imprisonment sooner or later. As a matter of fact both of us would greatly have liked to stay, just to see what happened. But I foresaw that Spanish prisons would be lousy places (actually they were a lot worse than I imagined), once in prison you never knew when you would get out, and I was in wretched health, apart from the pain in my arm. We arranged to meet next day at the British Consulate, where Cottman and McNair were also coming. It would probably take a couple of days to get our passports in order. Before leaving Spain you had to have your passport stamped in three separate places – by the Chief of Police, by the French Consul and by the Catalan immigration authorities. The Chief of Police was the danger, of course. But perhaps the British Consul could fix things up without letting it be known that we had anything to do with the P.O.U.M. Obviously there must be a list of foreign 'Trotskyist' suspects, and very likely our names were on it, but with luck we might get to the frontier before the list. There was sure to be a lot of muddle and *mañana*. Fortunately this was Spain and not Germany. The Spanish secret police had some of the spirit of the Gestapo, but not much of its competence.

So we parted. My wife went back to the hotel and I wandered off into the darkness to find somewhere to sleep. I remember feeling sulky and bored. I had so wanted a night in bed! There was nowhere I could go, no house where I could take refuge. The P.O.U.M. had practically no underground organization. No doubt the leaders had always realized that the party was likely to be suppressed, but they had never expected a wholesale witch-hunt of this description. They had expected it so little, indeed, that they were actually continuing the alterations to the P.O.U.M. buildings (among other things they were constructing a cinema in the Executive Building, which had previously been a bank) up to the very day when the P.O.U.M. was suppressed. Consequently the rendezvous and hiding-places which every revolutionary party ought to possess as a matter of course did not exist. Goodness knows how many people – people whose homes had been raided by the police – were sleeping in the streets that night. I had had five days of tiresome journeys, sleeping in impossible places, my arm was hurting damnably, and now these fools were chasing me to and fro and I had got to sleep on the ground again. That was about as far as my thoughts went. I did not make any of the correct political reflections. I never do when things are happening. It seems to be always the case when I get mixed up in war or politics – I am conscious of nothing save physical discomfort and a deep desire for this damned nonsense to be over. Afterwards I can see the significance of events, but while they are happening I merely want to be out of them – an ignoble trait, perhaps.

I walked a long way and fetched up somewhere near the General Hospital. I wanted a place where I could lie down without some nosing policeman finding me and demanding my papers. I tried an air-raid shelter, but it was newly dug and dripping with damp. Then I came upon the ruins of a church that had been gutted and burnt in the revolution. It was a mere shell, four roofless walls surrounding piles of rubble. In the half-darkness I poked around and found a kind of hollow where I could lie down. Lumps of broken masonry are not good to lie on, but fortunately it was a warm night and I managed to get several hours' sleep.

Chapter Fourteen

The worst of being wanted by the police in a town like Barcelona is that everything opens so late. When you sleep out of doors you always wake about dawn, and none of the Barcelona cafés opens much before nine. It was hours before I could get a cup of coffee or a shave. It seemed queer, in the barber's shop, to see the Anarchist notice still on the wall, explaining that tips were prohibited. 'The Revolution has struck off our chains', the notice said. I felt like telling the barbers that their chains would soon be back again if they didn't look out.

I wandered back to the centre of the town. Over the P.O.U.M. buildings the red flags had been torn down, Republican flags were floating in their place, and knots of armed Civil Guards were lounging in the doorways. At the Red Aid centre on the corner of the Plaza de Catalunya the police had amused themselves by smashing most of the windows. The P.O.U.M. bookstalls had been emptied of books and the notice-board farther down the Ramblas had been plastered with an anti-P.O.U.M. cartoon – the one representing the mask and the Fascist face beneath. Down at the bottom of the Ramblas, near the quay, I came upon a queer sight; a row of militiamen, still ragged and muddy from the front, sprawling exhaustedly on the chairs placed there for the bootblacks. I knew who they were – indeed, I recognized one of them. They were P.O.U.M. militiamen who had come down the line on the previous day to find that the P.O.U.M. had been suppressed, and had had to spend the night in the streets because their homes had been raided. Any P.O.U.M. militiaman who returned to Barcelona at this time had the choice of going straight into hiding or into jail – not a pleasant reception after three or four months in the line.

It was a queer situation that we were in. At night one was a hunted fugitive, but in the daytime one could live an almost normal life. Every house known to harbour P.O.U.M. supporters was – or at any rate was likely to be – under observation, and it was impossible to go to a hotel or boarding-house, because it had been decreed that on the arrival of a stranger the hotel-keeper must inform the police immediately. Practically this meant spending the night out of doors. In the daytime, on the other hand, in a town the size of Barcelona, you were fairly safe. The streets were thronged by Civil Guards, Assault Guards, Carabineros and ordinary police, besides God knows how many spies in plain clothes; still, they could not stop everyone who passed, and if you looked normal you might escape notice. The thing to do was to avoid hanging round P.O.U.M. buildings and going to cafés and restaurants where the waiters knew you by sight. I spent a long time that day, and the next, in having a bath at one of the public baths. This struck me as a good way of putting in the time and keeping out of sight. Unfortunately the same idea occurred to a lot of people, and a few days later – after I left Barcelona – the police raided one of the public baths and arrested a number of 'Trotskyists' in a state of nature.

Half-way up the Ramblas I ran into one of the wounded men from the Sanatorium Maurin. We exchanged the sort of invisible wink that people were exchanging at that time, and managed in an unobtrusive way to meet in a café farther up the street. He had escaped arrest when the Maurin was raided, but, like the others, had been driven into the street. He was in shirt-sleeves – had had to flee without his jacket – and had no money. He described to me how one of the Civil Guards had torn the large coloured portrait of Maurin from the wall and kicked it to pieces. Maurin (one of the founders of the P.O.U.M.) was a prisoner in the hands of the Fascists and at that time was believed to have been shot by them.

I met my wife at the British Consulate at ten o'clock. McNair and Cottman turned up shortly afterwards. The first thing they told me was that Bob Smillie was dead. He had died in prison at Valencia – of what, nobody knew for certain. He had been buried immediately, and the I.L.P. representative on the spot, David Murray, had been refused permission to see his body.

Of course I assumed at once that Smillie had been shot. It was what everyone believed at the time, but I have since thought that I may have been wrong. Later the cause of his death was given out as appendicitis, and we heard afterwards from another prisoner who had been released that Smillie had certainly been ill in prison. So perhaps the appendicitis story was true. The refusal to let Murray see his body may have been due to pure spite. I must say this, however. Bob Smillie was only twenty-two years old and physically he was one of the toughest people I have met. He was, I think, the only person I knew, English or Spanish, who went three months in the trenches without a day's illness. People so tough as that do not usually die of appendicitis if they are properly looked after. But when you saw what the Spanish jails were like – the makeshift jails used for political prisoners – you realized how much chance there was of a sick man getting proper attention. The jails were places that could only be described as dungeons. In England you would have to go back to the eighteenth century to find anything comparable. People were penned together in small rooms where there was barely space for them to lie down, and often they were kept in cellars and other dark places. This was not as a temporary measure – there were cases of people being kept four and five months almost without sight of daylight. And they were fed on a filthy and insufficient diet of two plates of soup and two pieces of bread a day. (Some months later, however, the food seems to have improved a little.) I am not exaggerating; ask any political suspect who was imprisoned in Spain. I have had accounts of the Spanish jails from a number of separate sources, and they agree with one another too well to be disbelieved; besides, I had a few glimpses into one Spanish jail myself. Another English friend who was imprisoned later writes that his experiences in jail 'make Smillie's case easier to understand'. Smillie's death is not a thing I can easily forgive. Here was this brave and gifted boy, who had thrown up his career at Glasgow University in order to come and fight against Fascism, and who, as I saw for myself, had done his job at the front with faultless courage and willingness; and all they could find to do with him was to fling him into jail and let him die like a neglected animal. I know that in the middle of a huge and bloody war it is no use making too much fuss over an individual death. One aeroplane bomb in a crowded street causes more suffering than quite a lot of political persecution. But what angers one about a death like this is its utter pointlessness. To be killed in battle – yes, that is what one expects; but to be flung into jail, not even for any imaginary offence, but simply owing to dull blind spite, and then left to die in solitude – that is a different matter. I fail to see how this kind of thing – and it is not as though Smillie's case were exceptional – brought victory any nearer.

My wife and I visited Kopp that afternoon. You were allowed to visit prisoners who were not *incommunicado*, though it was not safe to do so more than once or twice. The police watched the people who came and went, and if you visited the jails too often you stamped yourself as a friend of 'Trotskyists' and probably ended in jail yourself. This had already happened to a number of people.

Kopp was not *incommunicado* and we got a permit to see him without difficulty. As they led us through the steel doors into the jail, a Spanish militiaman whom I had known at the front was being led out between two Civil Guards. His eye met mine; again the ghostly wink. And the first person we saw inside was an American militiaman who had left for home a few days earlier; his papers were in good order, but they had arrested him at the frontier all the same, probably because he was still wearing corduroy breeches and was therefore identifiable as a militiaman. We walked past one another as though we had been total strangers. That was dreadful. I had known him for months, had shared a dug-out with him, he had helped to carry me down the line when

I was wounded; but it was the only thing one could do. The blue-clad guards were snooping everywhere. It would be fatal to recognize too many people.

The so-called jail was really the ground floor of a shop. Into two rooms each measuring about twenty feet square, close on a hundred people were penned. The place had the real eighteenth-century Newgate Calendar appearance, with its frowsy dirt, its huddle of human bodies, its lack of furniture – just the bare stone floor, one bench and a few ragged blankets – and its murky light, for the corrugated steel shutters had been drawn over the windows. On the grimy walls revolutionary slogans – 'Visca P.O.U.M.!' 'Viva la Revolucion!' and so forth – had been scrawled. The place had been used as a dump for political prisoners for months past. There was a deafening racket of voices. This was the visiting hour, and the place was so packed with people that it was difficult to move. Nearly all of them were of the poorest of the working-class population. You saw women undoing pitiful packets of food which they had brought for their imprisoned men-folk. There were several of the wounded men from the Sanatorium Maurin among the prisoners. Two of them had amputated legs; one of them had been brought to prison without his crutch and was hopping about on one foot. There was also a boy of not more than twelve; they were even arresting children, apparently. The place had the beastly stench that you always get when crowds of people are penned together without proper sanitary arrangements.

Kopp elbowed his way through the crowd to meet us. His plump flesh-coloured face looked much as usual, and in that filthy place he had kept his uniform neat and had even contrived to shave. There was another officer in the uniform of the Popular Army among the prisoners. He and Kopp saluted as they struggled past one another; the gesture was pathetic, somehow. Kopp seemed in excellent spirits. 'Well, I suppose we shall all be shot,' he said cheerfully. The word 'shot' gave me a sort of inward shudder. A bullet had entered my own body recently and the feeling of it was fresh in my memory; it is not nice to think of that happening to anyone you know well. At that time I took it for granted that all the principal people in the P.O.U.M., and Kopp among them, *would* be shot. The first rumour of Nin's death had just filtered through, and we knew that the P.O.U.M. were being accused of treachery and espionage. Everything pointed to a huge frame-up trial followed by a massacre of leading 'Trotskyists'. It is a terrible thing to see your friend in jail and to know yourself impotent to help him. For there was nothing that one could do; useless even to appeal to the Belgian authorities, for Kopp had broken the law of his own country by coming here. I had to leave most of the talking to my wife; with my squeaking voice I could not make myself heard in the din. Kopp was telling us about the friends he had made among the other prisoners, about the guards, some of whom were good fellows, but some of whom abused and beat the more timid prisoners, and about the food, which was 'pig-wash'. Fortunately we had thought to bring a packet of food, also cigarettes. Then Kopp began telling us about the papers that had been taken from him when he was arrested. Among them was his letter from the Ministry of War, addressed to the colonel commanding engineering operations in the Army of the East. The police had seized it and refused to give it back; it was said to be lying in the Chief of Police's office. It might make a very great difference if it were recovered.

I saw instantly how important this might be. An official letter of that kind, bearing the recommendation of the Ministry of War and of General Pozas, would establish Kopp's bona fides. But the trouble was to prove that the letter existed; if it were opened in the Chief of Police's office one could be sure that some nark or other would destroy it. There was only one person who might possibly be able to get it back, and that was the officer to whom it was addressed. Kopp had already thought of this, and he had written a letter which he wanted me to smuggle out of the jail and post. But it was obviously quicker and surer to go in person. I left my wife with Kopp, rushed out and, after a long search, found a taxi. I knew that time was everything. It was now about half-past five, the colonel would probably leave his office at six, and by tomorrow the letter might be God knew where – destroyed, perhaps, or lost somewhere in the chaos of documents that was presumably piling up as suspect after suspect was arrested. The colonel's office was at the War Department down by the quay. As I hurried up the steps the Assault Guard on duty at the door barred the way with his long bayonet and demanded 'papers'. I waved my discharge ticket at him; evidently he could not read, and he let me pass, impressed by the vague mystery of 'papers'. Inside, the place was a huge complicated warren running round a central courtyard, with hundreds of offices on each floor; and, as this was Spain, nobody had the vaguest idea where the office I was looking for was. I kept repeating: 'El colonel ——, jefe de ingenieros, Ejercito de Este!' People smiled and shrugged their shoulders gracefully. Every one who had an opinion sent me in a different direction; up these stairs, down those, along interminable passages which turned out to be blind alleys. And time was slipping away. I had the strangest sensation of being in a nightmare: the rushing up and down flights of stairs, the mysterious people coming and going, the glimpses through open doors of chaotic offices with papers strewn everywhere and typewriters clicking; and time slipping away and a life perhaps in the balance.

However, I got there in time, and slightly to my surprise I was granted a hearing. I did not see Colonel ——, but his aide-de-camp or secretary, a little slip of an officer in smart uniform, with large and squinting eyes, came out to interview me in the ante-room. I began to pour forth my story. I had come on behalf of my superior officer, Major Jorge Kopp, who was on an urgent mission to the front and had been arrested by mistake. The letter to Colonel —— was of a confidential nature and should be recovered without delay. I had served with Kopp for months, he was an officer of the highest character, obviously his arrest was a mistake, the police had confused him with someone else, etc., etc., etc. I kept piling it on about the urgency of Kopp's mission to the front, knowing that this was the strongest point. But it must have sounded a strange tale, in my villainous Spanish which elapsed into French at every crisis. The worst was that my voice gave out almost at once and it was only by violent straining that I could produce a sort of croak. I was in dread that it would disappear altogether and the little officer would grow tired of trying to listen to me. I have often wondered what he thought was wrong with my voice – whether he thought I was drunk or merely suffering from a guilty conscience.

However, he heard me patiently, nodded his head a great number of times and gave a guarded assent to what I said. Yes, it sounded as though there might have been a mistake. Clearly the matter should be looked into. *Mañana*——. I protested. Not *mañana*! The matter was urgent; Kopp was due at the front already. Again the officer seemed to agree. Then came the question I was dreading:

'This Major Kopp – what force was he serving in?'

The terrible word had to come out: 'In the P.O.U.M. militia.'

'P.O.U.M.!'

I wish I could convey to you the shocked alarm in his voice. You have got to remember how the P.O.U.M. was regarded at that moment. The spy-scare was at its height; probably all good Republicans did believe for a day or two that the P.O.U.M. was a huge spying organization in German pay. To have to say such a thing to an officer in the Popular Army was like going into the Cavalry Club immediately after the Red Letter scare and announcing yourself a Communist. His dark eyes moved obliquely across my face. Another long pause, then he said slowly:

'And you say you were with him at the front. Then you were serving in the P.O.U.M. militia yourself?'

'Yes.'

He turned and dived into the colonel's room. I could hear an agitated conversation. 'It's all up,' I thought. We should never get Kopp's letter back. Moreover I had had to confess that I was in the P.O.U.M. myself, and no doubt they would ring up the police and get me arrested, just to add another Trotskyist to the bag. Presently, however, the officer reappeared, fitting on his cap, and sternly signed to me to follow. We were going to the Chief of Police's office. It was a long way, twenty minutes' walk. The little officer marched stiffly in front with a military step. We did not exchange a single word the whole way. When we got to the Chief of Police's office a crowd of the most dreadful-looking scoundrels, obviously police narks, informers, and spies of every kind, were hanging about outside the door. The little officer went in; there was a long, heated conversation. You could hear voices furiously raised; you pictured violent gestures, shruggings of the shoulders, bangings on the table. Evidently the police were refusing to give the letter up. At last, however, the officer emerged, flushed, but carrying a large official envelope. It was Kopp's letter. We had won a tiny victory – which, as it turned out, made not the slightest difference. The letter was duly delivered, but Kopp's military superiors were quite unable to get him out of jail.

The officer promised me that the letter should be delivered. But what about Kopp? I said. Could we not get him released? He shrugged his shoulders. That was another matter. They did not know what Kopp had been arrested for. He would only tell me that the proper inquiries would be made. There was no more to be said; it was time to part. Both of us bowed slightly. And then there happened a strange and moving thing. The little officer hesitated a moment, then stepped across and shook hands with me.

I do not know if I can bring home to you how deeply that action touched me. It sounds a small thing, but it was not. You have got to realize what was the feeling of the time – the horrible atmosphere of suspicion and hatred, the lies and rumours circulating everywhere, the posters screaming from the hoardings that I and everyone like me was a Fascist spy. And you have got to remember that we were standing outside the Chief of Police's office, in front of that filthy gang of tale-bearers and agents provocateurs, any one of whom might know that I was 'wanted' by the police. It was like publicly shaking hands with a German during the Great War. I suppose he had decided in some way that I was not really a Fascist spy; still, it was good of him to shake hands.

I record this, trivial though it may sound, because it is somehow typical of Spain – of the flashes of magnanimity that you get from Spaniards in the worst of circumstances. I have the most evil memories of Spain, but I have very few bad memories of Spaniards. I only twice remember even being seriously angry with a Spaniard, and on each occasion, when I look back, I believe I was in the wrong myself. They have, there is no doubt, a generosity, a species of nobility, that do not really belong to the twentieth century. It is this that makes one hope that in Spain even Fascism may take a comparatively loose and bearable form. Few Spaniards possess the damnable efficiency and consistency that a modern totalitarian state needs. There had been a queer little illustration of this fact a few nights earlier, when the police had searched my wife's room. As a matter of fact that search was a very interesting business, and I wish I had seen it, though perhaps it is as well that I did not, for I might not have kept my temper.

The police conducted the search in the recognized Ogpu or Gestapo style. In the small hours of the morning there was a pounding on the door, and six men marched in, switched on the light and immediately took up various positions about the room, obviously agreed upon beforehand. They then searched both rooms (there was a bathroom attached) with inconceivable thoroughness. They sounded the walls, took up the mats, examined the floor, felt the curtains, probed under the bath and the radiator, emptied every drawer and suitcase and felt every garment and held it up to the light. They impounded all papers, including the contents of the waste-paper basket, and all our books into the bargain. They were thrown into ecstasies of suspicion by finding that we possessed a French translation of Hitler's *Mein Kampf*. If that had been the only book they found our doom would have been sealed. It is obvious that a person who reads *Mein Kampf* must be a Fascist. The next moment, however, they came upon a copy of Stalin's pamphlet, *Ways of Liquidating Trotskyists and other Double Dealers*, which reassured them somewhat. In one drawer there was a number of packets of cigarette papers. They picked each packet to pieces and examined each paper separately, in case there should be messages written on them. Altogether they were on the job for nearly two hours. Yet all this time they *never searched the bed*. My wife was lying in bed all the while; obviously there might have been half a dozen sub-machine-guns under the mattress, not to mention a library of Trotskyist documents under the pillow. Yet the detectives made no move to touch the bed, never even looked underneath it. I cannot believe that this is a regular feature of the Ogpu routine. One must remember that the police were almost entirely under Communist control, and these men were probably Communist Party members themselves. But they were also Spaniards, and to turn a woman out of bed was a little too much for them. This part of the job was silently dropped, making the whole search meaningless.

That night McNair, Cottman, and I slept in some long grass at the edge of a derelict building-lot. It was a cold night for the time of year and no one slept much. I remember the long dismal hours of loitering about before one could get a cup of coffee. For the first time since I had been in Barcelona I went to have a look at the cathedral – a modern cathedral, and one of the most hideous buildings in the world. It had four crenellated spires exactly the shape of hock bottles. Unlike most of the churches in Barcelona it was not damaged during the revolution – it was spared because of its 'artistic value', people said. I think the Anarchists showed bad taste in not blowing it up when they had the chance, though they did hang a red and black banner between its spires. That afternoon my wife and I went to see Kopp for the last time. There was nothing that we could do for him, absolutely nothing, except to say good-bye and leave money with Spanish friends who would take him food and cigarettes. A little while later, however, after we had left Barcelona, he was placed *incommunicado* and not even food could be sent to him. That night, walking down the Ramblas, we passed the Café Moka, which the Civil Guards were still holding in force. On an impulse I went in and spoke to two of them who were leaning against the counter with their rifles slung over their shoulders. I asked them if they knew which of their comrades had been on duty here at the time of the May fighting. They did not know, and, with the usual Spanish vagueness, did not know how one could find out. I said that my friend Jorge Kopp was in prison and would perhaps be put on trial for something in connection with the May fighting; that the men who were on duty here would know that he had stopped the fighting and saved some of their lives; they ought to come forward and give evidence to that effect. One of the men I was talking to was a dull, heavy-looking man who kept shaking his head because he could not hear my voice in the din of the traffic. But the other was different. He said he had heard of Kopp's action from some of his comrades; Kopp was *buen chico* (a good fellow). But even at the time I knew that it was all useless. If Kopp were ever tried, it would be, as in all such trials, with faked evidence. If he has been shot (and I am afraid it is quite likely), that will be his epitaph: the *buen chico* of the poor Civil Guard who was part of a dirty system but had remained enough of a human being to know a decent action when he saw one.

It was an extraordinary, insane existence that we were leading. By night we were criminals, but by day we were prosperous English visitors – that was our pose, anyway. Even after a night in the open, a shave, a bath and a shoe-shine do wonders with your appearance. The safest thing at present was to look as bourgeois as possible. We frequented the fashionable residential quarter of the town, where our faces were not known, went to expensive restaurants and were very English with the waiters. For the first time in my life I took to writing things on walls. The passage-ways of several smart restaurants had 'Visca P.O.U.M.!' scrawled on them as large as I could write it. All the while, though I was technically in hiding, I could not feel myself in danger. The whole thing seemed too absurd. I had the ineradicable English belief that 'they' cannot arrest you unless you have broken the law. It is a most dangerous belief to have during a political pogrom. There was a warrant out for McNair's arrest, and the chances were that the rest of us were on the list as well. The arrests, raids, searchings were continuing without pause; practically everyone we knew, except those who were still at the front, was in jail by this time. The police were even boarding the French ships that periodically took off refugees and seizing suspected 'Trotskyists'.

Thanks to the kindness of the British consul, who must have had a very trying time during that week, we had managed to get our passports into order. The sooner we left the better. There was a train that was due to leave for Port Bou at half-past seven in the evening and might normally be expected to leave at about half-past eight. We arranged that my wife should order a taxi beforehand and then pack her bags, pay her bill and leave the hotel at the last possible moment. If she gave the hotel-people too much notice they would be sure to send for the police. I got down to the station at about seven to find that the train had already gone – it had left at ten to seven. The engine-driver had changed his mind, as usual. Fortunately we managed to warn my wife in time. There was another train early the following morning. McNair, Cottman, and I had dinner at a little restaurant near the station and by cautious questioning discovered that the restaurant-keeper was a C.N.T. member and friendly. He let us a three-bedded room and forgot to warn the police. It was the first time in five nights that I had been able to sleep with my clothes off.

Next morning my wife slipped out of the hotel successfully. The train was about an hour late in starting. I filled in the time by writing a long letter to the Ministry of War, telling them about Kopp's case – that without a doubt he had been arrested by mistake, that he was urgently needed at the front, that countless people would testify that he was innocent of any offence, etc., etc., etc. I wonder if anyone read that letter, written on pages torn out of a note-book in wobbly handwriting (my fingers were still partly paralysed) and still more wobbly Spanish. At any rate, neither this letter nor anything else took effect. As I write, six months after the event, Kopp (if he has not been shot) is still in jail, untried and uncharged. At the beginning we had two or three letters from him, smuggled out by released prisoners and posted in France. They all told the same story – imprisonment in filthy dark dens, bad and insufficient food, serious illness due to the conditions of imprisonment, and refusal of medical attention. I have had all this confirmed from several other sources, English and French. More recently he disappeared into one of the 'secret prisons' with which it seems impossible to make any kind of communication. His case is the case of scores or hundreds of foreigners and no one knows how many thousands of Spaniards.

In the end we crossed the frontier without incident. The train had a first class and a dining-car, the first I had seen in Spain. Until recently there had been only one class on the trains in Catalonia. Two detectives came round the train taking the names of foreigners, but when they saw us in the dining-car they seemed satisfied that we were respectable. It was queer how everything had changed. Only six months ago, when the Anarchists still reigned, it was looking like a proletarian that made you respectable. On the way down from Perpignan to Cerbères a French commercial traveller in my carriage had said to me in all solemnity: 'You mustn't go into Spain looking like that. Take off that collar and tie. They'll tear them off you in Barcelona.' He was exaggerating, but it showed how Catalonia was regarded. And at the frontier the Anarchist guards had turned back a smartly dressed Frenchman and his wife, solely – I think – because they looked too bourgeois. Now it was the other way about; to look bourgeois was the one salvation. At the passport office they looked us up in the card-index of suspects, but thanks to the inefficiency of the police our names were not listed, not even McNair's. We were searched from head to foot, but we possessed nothing incriminating, except my discharge-papers, and the carabineros who searched me did not know that the 29th Division was the P.O.U.M. So we slipped through the barrier, and after just six months I was on French soil again. My only souvenirs of Spain were a goatskin waterbottle and one of those tiny iron lamps in which the Aragon peasants burn olive-oil – lamps almost exactly the shape of the terra-cotta lamps that the Romans used two thousand years ago – which I had picked up in some ruined hut, and which had somehow got stuck in my luggage.

After all, it turned out that we had come away none too soon. The very first newspaper we saw announced McNair's arrest for espionage. The Spanish authorities had been a little premature in announcing this. Fortunately, 'Trotskyism' is not extraditable.

I wonder what is the appropriate first action when you come from a country at war and set foot on peaceful soil. Mine was to rush to the tobacco-kiosk and buy as many cigars and cigarettes as I could stuff into my pockets. Then we all went to the buffet and had a cup of tea, the first tea with fresh milk in it that we had had for many months. It was several days before I could get used to the idea that you could buy cigarettes whenever you wanted them. I always half-expected to see the tobacconists' doors barred and the forbidding notice 'No hay tobaco' in the window.

McNair and Cottman were going on to Paris. My wife and I got off the train at Banyuls, the first station up the line, feeling that we would like a rest. We were not too well received in Banyuls when they discovered that we had come from Barcelona. Quite a number of times I was involved in the same conversation: 'You come from Spain? Which side were you fighting on? The Government? Oh!' – and then a marked coolness. The little town seemed solidly pro-Franco, no doubt because of the various Spanish Fascist refugees who had arrived there from time to time. The waiter at the café I frequented was a pro-Franco Spaniard and used to give me glowering glances as he served me with an aperitif. It was otherwise in Perpignan, which was stiff with Government partisans and where all the different factions were caballing against one another almost as in Barcelona. There was one café where the word 'P.O.U.M.' immediately procured you French friends and smiles from the waiter.

I think we stayed three days in Banyuls. It was a strangely restless time. In this quiet fishing-town, remote from bombs, machine-guns, food-queues, propaganda, and intrigue, we ought to have felt profoundly relieved and thankful. We felt nothing of the kind. The things we had seen in Spain did not recede and fall into proportion now that we were away from them; instead they rushed back upon us and were far more vivid than before. We thought, talked, dreamed incessantly of Spain. For months past we had been telling ourselves that 'when we get out of Spain' we would go somewhere beside the Mediterranean and be quiet for a little while and perhaps do a little fishing; but now that we were here it was merely a bore and a disappointment. It was chilly weather, a persistent wind blew off the sea, the water was dull and choppy, round the harbour's edge a scum of ashes, corks, and fish-guts bobbed against the stones. It sounds like lunacy, but the thing that both of us wanted was to be back in Spain. Though it could have done no good to anybody, might indeed have done serious harm, both of us wished that we had stayed to be imprisoned along with the others. I suppose I have failed to convey more than a little of what those months in Spain mean to me. I have recorded some of the outward events, but I cannot record the feeling they have left me with. It is all mixed up with sights, smells, and sounds that cannot be conveyed in writing: the smell of the trenches, the mountain dawns stretching away into inconceivable distances, the frosty crackle of bullets, the roar and glare of bombs; the clear cold light of the Barcelona mornings, and the stamp of boots in the barrack yard, back in December when people still believed in the revolution; and the food-queues and the red and black flags and the faces of Spanish militiamen; above all the faces of militiamen – men whom I knew in the line and who are now scattered Lord knows where, some killed in battle, some maimed, some in prison – most of them, I hope, still safe and sound. Good luck to them all; I hope they win their war and drive all the foreigners out of Spain, Germans, Russians and Italians alike. This war, in which I played so ineffectual a part, has left me with memories that are mostly evil, and yet I do not wish that I had missed it. When you have had a glimpse of such a disaster as this – and however it ends the Spanish war will turn out to have been an appalling disaster, quite apart from the slaughter and physical suffering – the result is not necessarily disillusionment and cynicism. Curiously enough the whole experience has left me with not less but more belief in the decency of human beings. And I hope the account I have given is not too misleading. I believe that on such an issue as this no one is or can be completely truthful. It is difficult to be certain about anything except what you have seen with your own eyes, and consciously or unconsciously everyone writes as a partisan. In case I have not said this somewhere earlier in the book I will say it now: beware of my partisanship, my mistakes of fact and the distortion inevitably caused by my having seen only one corner of events. And beware of exactly the same things when you read any other book on this period of the Spanish war.

Because of the feeling that we ought to be doing something, though actually there was nothing we could do, we left Banyuls earlier than we had intended. With every mile that you went northward France grew greener and softer. Away from the mountain and the vine, back to the meadow and the elm. When I had passed through Paris on my way to Spain it had seemed to be decayed and gloomy, very different from the Paris I had known eight years earlier, when living was cheap and Hitler was not heard of. Half the cafés I used to know were shut for lack of custom, and everyone was obsessed with the high cost of living and the fear of war. Now, after poor Spain, even Paris seemed gay and prosperous. And the Exhibition was in full swing, though we managed to avoid visiting it.

And then England – southern England, probably the sleekest landscape in the world. It is difficult when you pass that way, especially when you are peacefully recovering from sea-sickness with the plush cushions of a boat-train carriage under your bum, to believe that anything is really happening anywhere. Earthquakes in Japan, famines in China, revolutions in Mexico? Don't worry, the milk will be on the doorstep tomorrow morning, the *New Statesman* will come out on Friday. The industrial towns were far away, a smudge of smoke and misery hidden by the curve of the earth's surface. Down here it was still the England I had known in my childhood: the railway-cuttings smothered in wild flowers, the deep meadows where the great shining horses browse and meditate, the slow-moving streams bordered by willows, the green bosoms of the elms, the larkspurs in the cottage gardens; and then the huge peaceful wilderness of outer London, the barges on the miry river, the familiar streets, the posters telling of cricket matches and Royal weddings, the men in bowler hats, the pigeons in Trafalgar Square, the red buses, the blue policemen – all sleeping the deep, deep sleep of England, from which I sometimes fear that we shall never wake till we are jerked out of it by the roar of bombs.

ESSAYS AND JOURNALISM 1931-1940

A Hanging

It was in Burma, a sodden morning of the rains. A sickly light, like yellow tinfoil, was slanting over the high walls into the jail yard. We were waiting outside the condemned cells, a row of sheds fronted with double bars, like small animal cages. Each cell measured about ten feet by ten and was quite bare within except for a plank bed and a pot of drinking water. In some of them brown silent men were squatting at the inner bars, with their blankets draped round them. These were the condemned men, due to be hanged within the next week or two.

One prisoner had been brought out of his cell. He was a Hindu, a puny wisp of a man, with a shaven head and vague liquid eyes. He had a thick, sprouting moustache, absurdly too big for his body, rather like the moustache of a comic man on the films. Six tall Indian warders were guarding him and getting him ready for the gallows. Two of them stood by with rifles and fixed bayonets, while the others handcuffed him, passed a chain through his handcuffs and fixed it to their belts, and lashed his arms tight to his sides. They crowded very close about him, with their hands always on him in a careful, caressing grip, as though all the while feeling him to make sure he was there. It was like men handling a fish which is still alive and may jump back into the water. But he stood quite unresisting, yielding his arms limply to the ropes, as though he hardly noticed what was happening.

Eight o'clock struck and a bugle call, desolately thin in the wet air, floated from the distant barracks. The superintendent of the jail, who was standing apart from the rest of us, moodily prodding the gravel with his stick, raised his head at the sound. He was an army doctor, with a grey toothbrush moustache and a gruff voice. 'For God's sake hurry up, Francis,' he said irritably. 'The man ought to have been dead by this time. Aren't you ready yet?'

Francis, the head jailer, a fat Dravidian in a white drill suit and gold spectacles, waved his black hand. 'Yes sir, yes sir,' he bubbled. 'All iss satisfactorily prepared. The hangman iss waiting. We shall proceed.'

'Well, quick march, then. The prisoners can't get their breakfast till this job's over.'

We set out for the gallows. Two warders marched on either side of the prisoner, with their rifles at the slope; two others marched close against him, gripping him by arm and shoulder, as though at once pushing and supporting him. The rest of us, magistrates and the like, followed behind. Suddenly, when we had gone ten yards, the procession stopped short without any order or warning. A dreadful thing had happened – a dog, come goodness knows whence, had appeared in the yard. It came bounding among us with a loud volley of barks, and leapt round us wagging its whole body, wild with glee at finding so many human beings together. It was a large woolly dog, half Airedale, half pariah. For a moment it pranced round us, and then, before anyone could stop it, it had made a dash for the prisoner, and jumping up tried to lick his face. Everyone stood aghast, too taken aback even to grab at the dog.

'Who let that bloody brute in here?' said the superintendent angrily. 'Catch it, someone!'

A warder, detached from the escort, charged clumsily after the dog, but it danced and gambolled just out of his reach, taking everything as part of the game. A young Eurasian jailer picked up a handful of gravel and tried to stone the dog away, but it dodged the stones and came after us again. Its yaps echoed from the jail walls. The prisoner, in the grasp of the two warders, looked on incuriously, as though this was another formality of the hanging. It was several minutes before someone managed to catch the dog. Then we put my handkerchief through its collar and moved off once more, with the dog still straining and whimpering.

It was about forty yards to the gallows. I watched the bare brown back of the prisoner marching in front of me. He walked clumsily with his bound arms, but quite steadily, with that bobbing gait of the Indian who never straightens his knees. At each step his muscles slid neatly into place, the lock of hair on his scalp danced up and down, his feet printed themselves on the wet gravel. And once, in spite of the men who gripped him by each shoulder, he stepped slightly aside to avoid a puddle on the path.

It is curious, but till that moment I had never realized what it means to destroy a healthy, conscious man. When I saw the prisoner step aside to avoid the puddle, I saw the mystery, the unspeakable wrongness, of cutting a life short when it is in full tide. This man was not dying, he was alive just as we were alive. All the organs of his body were working – bowels digesting food, skin renewing itself, nails growing, tissues forming – all toiling away in solemn foolery. His nails would still be growing when he stood on the drop, when he was falling through the air with a tenth of a second to live. His eyes saw the yellow gravel and the grey walls, and his brain still remembered, foresaw, reasoned – reasoned even about puddles. He and we were a party of men walking together, seeing, hearing, feeling, understanding the same world; and in two minutes, with a sudden snap, one of us would be gone – one mind less, one world less.

The gallows stood in a small yard, separate from the main grounds of the prison, and overgrown with tall prickly weeds. It was a brick erection like three sides of a shed, with planking on top, and above that two beams and a crossbar with the rope dangling. The hangman, a grey-haired convict in the white uniform of the prison, was waiting beside his machine. He greeted us with a servile crouch as we entered. At a word from Francis the two warders, gripping the prisoner more closely than ever, half led, half pushed him to the gallows and helped him clumsily up the ladder. Then the hangman climbed up and fixed the rope round the prisoner's neck.

We stood waiting, five yards away. The warders had formed in a rough circle round the gallows. And then, when the noose was fixed, the prisoner began crying out on his god. It was a high, reiterated cry of 'Ram! Ram! Ram! Ram!', not urgent and fearful like a prayer or a cry for help but steady, rhythmical, almost like the tolling of a bell. The dog answered the sound with a whine. The hangman, still standing on the gallows, produced a small cotton bag like a flour bag and drew it down over the prisoner's face. But the sound, muffled by the cloth, still persisted, over and over again: 'Ram! Ram! Ram! Ram! Ram!'

The hangman climbed down and stood ready, holding the lever. Minutes seemed to pass. The steady, muffled crying from the prisoner went on and on,

'Ram! Ram! Ram!' never faltering for an instant. The superintendent, his head on his chest, was slowly poking the ground with his stick; perhaps he was counting the cries, allowing the prisoner a fixed number – fifty, perhaps, or a hundred. Everyone had changed colour. The Indians had gone grey like bad coffee, and one or two of the bayonets were wavering. We looked at the lashed, hooded man on the drop, and listened to his cries – each cry another second of life; the same thought was in all our minds: oh, kill him quickly, get it over, stop that abominable noise!

Suddenly the superintendent made up his mind. Throwing up his head he made a swift motion with his stick. 'Chalo!' he shouted almost fiercely.

There was a clanking noise, and then dead silence. The prisoner had vanished, and the rope was twisting on itself. I let go of the dog, and it galloped immediately to the back of the gallows; but when it got there it stopped short, barked, and then retreated into a corner of the yard, where it stood among the weeds, looking timorously out at us. We went round the gallows to inspect the prisoner's body. He was dangling with his toes pointed straight downwards, very slowly revolving, as dead as a stone.

The superintendent reached out with his stick and poked the bare body; it oscillated, slightly. '*He's* all right,' said the superintendent. He backed out from under the gallows, and blew out a deep breath. The moody look had gone out of his face quite suddenly. He glanced at his wrist-watch. 'Eight minutes past eight. Well, that's all for this morning, thank God.'

The warders unfixed bayonets and marched away. The dog, sobered and conscious of having misbehaved itself, slipped after them. We walked out of the gallows yard, past the condemned cells with their waiting prisoners, into the big central yard of the prison. The convicts, under the command of warders armed with lathis, were already receiving their breakfast. They squatted in long rows, each man holding a tin pannikin, while two warders with buckets marched round ladling out rice; it seemed quite a homely, jolly scene, after the hanging. An enormous relief had come upon us now that the job was done. One felt an impulse to sing, to break into a run, to snigger. All at once everyone began chattering gaily.

The Eurasian boy walking beside me nodded towards the way we had come, with a knowing smile: 'Do you know, sir, our friend (he meant the dead man), when he heard his appeal had been dismissed, he pissed on the floor of his cell. From fright. – Kindly take one of my cigarettes, sir. Do you not admire my new silver case, sir? From the boxwallah, two rupees eight annas. Classy European style.'

Several people laughed – at what, nobody seemed certain.

Francis was walking by the superintendent, talking garrulously: 'Well, sir, all hass passed off with the utmost satisfactoriness. It wass all finished – flick! like that. It iss not always so – oah, no! I have known cases where the doctor wass obliged to go beneath the gallows and pull the prisoner's legs to ensure decease. Most disagreeable!'

'Wriggling about, eh? That's bad,' said the superintendent.

'Ach, sir, it iss worse when they become refractory! One man, I recall, clung to the bars of hiss cage when we went to take him out. You will scarcely credit, sir, that it took six warders to dislodge him, three pulling at each leg. We reasoned with him. "My dear fellow," we said, "think of all the pain and trouble you are causing to us!" But no, he would not listen! Ach, he wass very troublesome!'

I found that I was laughing quite loudly. Everyone was laughing. Even the superintendent grinned in a tolerant way. 'You'd better all come out and have a drink,' he said quite genially. 'I've got a bottle of whisky in the car. We could do with it.'

We went through the big double gates of the prison, into the road. 'Pulling at his legs!' exclaimed a Burmese magistrate suddenly, and burst into a loud chuckling. We all began laughing again. At that moment Francis's anecdote seemed extraordinarily funny. We all had a drink together, native and European alike, quite amicably. The dead man was a hundred yards away.

Eric A. Blair

Adelphi, August 1931

Hop-Picking

25 August 1931

On the night of the 25th I started off from Chelsea with about 14/– in hand, and went to Lew Levy's kip in Westminster Bridge Road. It is much the same as it was three years ago, except that nearly all the beds are now a shilling instead of ninepence. This is owing to interference by the LCC[1] who have enacted (in the interests of hygiene, as usual) that beds in lodging houses must be further apart. There is a whole string of laws of this type relating to lodging-houses,[2] but there is not and never will be a law to say that the beds must be reasonably comfortable. The net result of this law is that one's bed is now three feet from the next instead of two feet, and threepence dearer.

26 August

The next day I went to Trafalgar Square and camped by the north wall, which is one of the recognized rendezvous of down and out people in London. At this time of year the square has a floating population of 100 to 200 people (about ten per cent of them women), some of whom actually look on it as their home. They get their food by regular begging rounds (Covent Garden at 4 a.m. for damaged fruit, various convents during the morning, restaurants and dustbins late at night, etc.) and they manage to 'tap' likely-looking passers-by for enough to keep them in tea. Tea is going on the square at all hours, one person supplying a 'drum', another sugar and so on. The milk is condensed milk at 2½d a tin. You jab two holes in the tin with a knife, apply your mouth to one of them and blow, whereupon a sticky greyish stream dribbles from the other. The holes are then plugged with chewed paper, and the tin is kept for days, becoming coated with dust and filth. Hot water is cadged at coffee shops, or at night boiled over watchmen's fires, but this has to be done on the sly, as the police won't allow it. Some of the people I met on the square had been there without a break for six weeks, and did not seem much the worse, except that they are all fantastically dirty. As always among the destitute, a large

[1] London County Council.

[2] For instance, Dick's Café in Billingsgate. Dick's was one of the very few places where you could get a cup of tea for 1d, and there were fires there, so that anyone who had a penny could warm himself for hours in the early mornings. Only this last week the LCC closed it on the ground that it was unhygienic. [Author's footnote.]

proportion of them are Irishmen. From time to time these men go home on visits, and it appears that they never think of paying their passage, but always stow away on small cargo boats, the crews conniving.

I had meant to sleep in St Martin's Church, but from what the others said it appeared that when you go in you are asked searching questions by some woman known as the Madonna, so I decided to stay the night in the square. It was not so bad as I expected, but between the cold and the police it was impossible to get a wink of sleep, and no one except a few hardened old tramps even tried to do so. There are seats enough for about fifty people, and the rest have to sit on the ground, which of course is forbidden by law. Every few minutes there would be a shout of 'Look out, boys, here comes the flattie!' and a policeman would come round and shake those who were asleep, and make the people on the ground get up. We used to kip down again the instant he had passed, and this went on like a kind of game from eight at night till three or four in the morning. After midnight it was so cold that I had to go for long walks to keep warm. The streets are somehow rather horrible at that hour; all silent and deserted, and yet lighted almost as bright as day with those garish lamps, which give everything a deathly air, as though London were the corpse of a town. About three o'clock another man and I went down to the patch of grass behind the Guards' parade ground, and saw prostitutes and men lying in couples there in the bitter cold mist and dew. There are always a number of prostitutes in the square; they are the unsuccessful ones, who can't earn enough for their night's kip. Overnight one of these women had been lying on the ground crying bitterly, because a man had gone off without paying her fee, which was sixpence. Towards morning they do not even get sixpence, but only a cup of tea or a cigarette. About four somebody got hold of a number of newspaper posters, and we sat down six or eight on a bench and packed ourselves in enormous paper parcels, which kept us fairly warm till Stewart's café in St Martin's Lane opened. At Stewart's you can sit from five till nine for a cup of tea (or sometimes three or four people even share a cup between them) and you are allowed to sleep with your head on the table till seven; after that the proprietor wakes you. One meets a very mixed crowd there – tramps, Covent Garden porters, early business people, prostitutes – and there are constant quarrels and fights. On this occasion an old, very ugly woman, wife of a porter, was violently abusing two prostitutes, because they could afford a better breakfast than she could. As each dish was brought to them she would point at it and shout accusingly, 'There goes the price of another fuck! *We* don't get kippers for breakfast, do we girls? 'Ow do you think she paid for them doughnuts? That's that there Negro that 'as 'er for a tanner,' etc., etc., but the prostitutes did not mind much.

27 August

At about eight in the morning we all had a shave in the Trafalgar Square fountains, and I spent most of the day reading *Eugénie Grandet*, which was the only book I had brought with me. The sight of a French book produced the usual remarks – 'Ah, French? That'll be something pretty warm, eh?', etc. Evidently most English people have no idea that there are French books which are not pornographic. Down and out people seem to read exclusively books of the Buffalo Bill type. Every tramp carries one of these, and they have a kind of circulating library, all swapping books when they get to the spike.

That night, as we were starting for Kent the next morning, I decided to sleep in bed and went to a lodging house in the Southwark Bridge Road. This is a sevenpenny kip, one of the few in London, and looks it. The beds are five feet long, with no pillows (you use your coat rolled up), and infested by fleas, besides a few bugs. The kitchen is a small, stinking cellar where the deputy sits with a table of flyblown jam tarts, etc., for sale a few feet from the door of the lavatory. The rats are so bad that several cats have to be kept exclusively to deal with them. The lodgers were dock workers, I think, and they did not seem a bad crowd. There was a youth among them, pale and consumptive-looking but evidently a labourer, who was devoted to poetry. He repeated

> A voice so thrilling ne'er was 'eard
> In Ipril from the cuckoo bird,
> Briking the silence of the seas
> Beyond the furthest 'Ebrides

with genuine feeling. The others did not laugh at him much.

28 August

The next day in the afternoon four of us started out for the hop-fields. The most interesting of the men with me was a youth named Ginger, who is still my mate when I write this. He is a strong, athletic youth of twenty-six, almost illiterate and quite brainless, but daring enough for anything. Except when in prison, he has probably broken the law every day for the last five years. As a boy he did three years in Borstal, came out, married at eighteen on the strength of a successful burglary, and shortly afterwards enlisted in the artillery. His wife died, and a little while afterwards he had an accident to his left eye and was invalided out of the service. They offered him a pension or a lump sum, and of course he chose the lump sum and blued it in about a week. After that he took to burglary again, and has been in prison six times, but never for a long sentence, as they have only caught him for small jobs; he has done one or two jobs which brought him over £500. He has always been perfectly honest towards me, as his partner, but in a general way he will steal anything that is not tied down. I doubt his ever being a successful burglar, though, for he is too stupid to be able to foresee risks. It is all a great pity, for he could earn a decent living if he chose. He has a gift for street selling, and has had a lot of jobs selling on commission, but when he has had a good day he bolts instantly with the takings. He is a marvellous hand at picking up bargains and can always, for instance, persuade the butcher to give him a pound of eatable meat for twopence, yet at the same time he is an absolute fool about money, and never saves a halfpenny. He is given to singing songs of the Little Grey Home in the West type, and he speaks of his dead wife and mother in terms of the most viscid sentimentality. I should think he is a fairly typical petty criminal.

Of the other two, one was a boy of twenty named Young Ginger, who seemed rather a likely lad, but he was an orphan and had had no kind of upbringing, and had lived the last year chiefly on Trafalgar Square. The other was a little Liverpool Jew of eighteen, a thorough guttersnipe. I do not know when I have seen anyone who disgusted me so much as this boy. He was as greedy as a pig about food, perpetually scrounging round dustbins, and he had a face that recalled some low-down carrion-eating beast. His manner of talking about women, and the expression of his face when he did so, were so loathsomely obscene as to make me feel almost sick. We could never persuade him to wash more of himself than his nose and a small circle round it, and he mentioned quite casually that he had several different kinds of louse on him. He too was an orphan, and had been 'on the toby' almost from infancy.

I had now about 6/–, and before starting we bought a so-called blanket for 1/6d and cadged several tins for 'drums'. The only reliable tin for a drum is a two-pound snuff tin, which is not very easy to come by. We had also a supply of bread and margarine and tea, and a number of knives and forks, etc., all stolen at different times from Woolworth's. We took the twopenny tram as far as Bromley, and there 'drummed up' on a rubbish dump, waiting for two others who were to have joined us, but who never turned up. It was dark when we finally stopped waiting for them, so we had no chance to look for a good camping place, and had to spend the night in long wet grass at the edge of a recreation ground. The cold was bitter. We had only two thin blankets between the four of us, and it was not safe to light a fire, as there were houses all round; we were also lying on a slope, so that one rolled into the ditch from time to time. It was rather humiliating to see the others, all younger than I, sleeping quite soundly in these conditions, whereas I did not close my eyes all night. To avoid being caught we had to be on the road before dawn, and it was several hours before we managed to get hot water and have our breakfast.

29 August

When we had gone a mile or two we came to an orchard, and the others at once went in and began stealing apples. I had not been prepared for this when we started out, but I saw that I must either do as the others did or leave them, so I shared the apples; I did not however take any part in the thefts for the first day, except to keep guard. We were going more or less in the direction of Sevenoaks, and by dinner time we had stolen about a dozen apples and plums and fifteen pounds of potatoes. The others also went in and tapped whenever we passed a baker's or a teashop, and we got quite a quantity of broken bread and meat. When we stopped to light a fire for dinner we fell in with two Scotch tramps who had been stealing apples from an orchard nearby, and stayed talking with them for a long time. The others all talked about sexual subjects, in a revolting manner. Tramps are disgusting when on this subject, because their poverty cuts them off entirely from women, and their minds consequently fester with obscenity. Merely lecherous people are all right, but people who would like to be lecherous, but don't get the chance, are horribly degraded by it. They remind me of the dogs that hang enviously round while two other dogs are copulating. During the conversation Young Ginger related how he and some others on Trafalgar Square had discovered one of their number to be a 'Poof', or Nancy Boy. Whereupon they had instantly fallen upon him, robbed him of 12/6d, which was all he had, and spent it on themselves. Evidently they thought it quite fair to rob him, as he was a Nancy Boy.

We had been making very poor progress, chiefly because Young Ginger and the Jew were not used to walking and wanted to stop and search for scraps of food all the time. On one occasion the Jew even picked up some chipped potatoes that had been trodden on, and ate them. As it was getting on in the afternoon we decided to make not for Sevenoaks but for Ide Hill spike, which the Scotchmen had told us was better than it is usually represented. We halted about a mile from the spike for tea, and I remember that a gentleman in a car nearby helped us in the kindest manner to find wood for our fire, and gave us a cigarette each. Then we went on to the spike, and on the way picked a bunch of honeysuckle to give to the Tramp Major. We thought this might put him in a good temper and induce him to let us out next morning, for it is not usual to let tramps out of the spike on Sundays. When we got there however the Tramp Major said that he would have to keep us in till Tuesday morning. It appeared that the Workhouse Master was very keen on making every casual do a day's work, and at the same time would not hear of their working on Sunday; so we should have to be idle all Sunday and work on Monday. Young Ginger and the Jew elected to stay till Tuesday, but Ginger and I went and kipped on the edge of a park near the church. It was beastly cold, but a little better than the night before, for we had plenty of wood and could make a fire. For our supper, Ginger tapped the local butcher, who gave us the best part of two pounds of sausages. Butchers are always very generous on Saturday nights.

30 August

Next morning the clergyman coming to early service caught us and turned us out, though not very disagreeably. We went on through Sevenoaks to Seal, and a man we met advised us to try for a job at Mitchell's farm, about three miles further on. We went there, but the farmer told us that he could not give us a job, as he had nowhere where we could live, and the Government inspectors had been scouting round to see that all hop-pickers had 'proper accommodation'. (These inspectors,[1] by the way, managed to prevent some hundreds of unemployed from getting jobs in the hop-fields this year. Not having 'proper accommodation' to offer to pickers, the farmers could only employ local people, who lived in their own houses.) We stole about a pound of raspberries from one of Mitchell's fields, and then went and applied to another farmer called Kronk, who gave us the same answer; we had five or ten pounds of potatoes from his fields, however. We were starting off in the direction of Maidstone when we fell in with an old Irishwoman, who had been given a job by Mitchell on the understanding that she had a lodging in Seal, which she had not. (Actually she was sleeping in a toolshed in somebody's garden. She used to slip in after dark and out before daylight.) We got some hot water from a cottage and the Irishwoman had tea with us, and gave us a lot of food that she had begged and did not want; we were glad of this, for we had now only 2½d left, and none too much food. It had now come on to rain, so we went to a farmhouse beside the church and asked leave to shelter in one of their cowsheds. The farmer and family were just starting out for evening service, and they said in a scandalized manner that of course they could not give us shelter. We sheltered instead in the lych-gate of the church, hoping that by looking draggled and tired we might get a few coppers from the congregation as they went in. We did not get anything, but after the service Ginger managed to tap a fairly good pair of flannel trousers from the clergyman. It was very uncomfortable in the lych-gate, and we were wet through and out of tobacco, and Ginger and I had walked twelve miles; yet I remember that we were quite happy and laughing all the time. The Irishwoman (she was sixty, and had been on the road all her life, evidently) was an extraordinarily cheerful old girl, and full of stories. Talking of places to 'skipper' in, she told us that one cold night she had crept into a pigsty and snuggled up to an old sow, for warmth.

When night came on it was still raining, so we decided to find an empty house to sleep in, but we went first to buy half a pound of sugar and two candles

[1] Appointed by the Labour Government. [Author's footnote.]

at the grocer's. While I was buying them Ginger stole three apples off the counter, and the Irishwoman a packet of cigarettes. They had plotted this beforehand, deliberately not telling me, so as to use my innocent appearance as a shield. After a good deal of searching we found an unfinished house and slipped in by a window the builders had left open. The bare floor was beastly hard, but it was warmer than outside, and I managed to get two or three hours' sleep.

1 September

We got out before dawn, and by appointment met the Irishwoman in a wood nearby. It was raining, but Ginger could get a fire going in almost any circumstances, and we managed to make tea and roast some potatoes. When it was light the Irishwoman went off to work, and Ginger and I went down to Chambers's farm, a mile or two away, to ask for work. When we got to the farm they had just been hanging a cat, a thing I never heard of anyone doing before. The bailiff said that he thought he could give us a job, and told us to wait; we waited from eight in the morning till one, when the bailiff said that he had no work for us after all. We made off, stealing a large quantity of apples and damsons, and started along the Maidstone road. At about three we halted to have our dinner and make some jam out of the raspberries we had stolen the day before. Near here, I remember, they refused at two houses to give me cold water, because 'the mistress doesn't allow us to give anything to tramps'. Ginger saw a gentleman in a car picknicking nearby, and went up to tap him for matches, for he said that it always pays to tap from picnickers, who usually have some food left over when they are going home. Sure enough the gentleman presently came across with some butter he had not used, and began talking to us. His manner was so friendly that I forgot to put on my cockney accent, and he looked closely at me, and said how painful it must be for a man of my stamp, etc. Then he said, 'I say, you won't be offended, will you? Do you mind taking this?' 'This' was a shilling, with which we bought some tobacco and had our first smoke that day. This was the only time in the whole journey when we managed to tap money.

We went on in the direction of Maidstone, but when we had gone a few miles it began to pour with rain, and my left boot was pinching me badly. I had not had my boots off for three days and had only had about eight hours' sleep in the last five nights, and I did not feel equal to another night in the open. We decided to make for West Malling spike, which was about eight miles distant, and if possible to get a lift part of the way. I think we hailed forty lorries before we got a lift. The lorry drivers will not give lifts nowadays, because they are not insured for third party risks and they get the sack if they have an accident. Finally we did get a lift, and were set down about two miles from the spike, getting there at eight in the evening. Outside the gates we met an old deaf tramp who was going to skipper in the pouring rain, as he had been in the spike the night before, and they would confine him for a week if he came again. He told us that Blest's farm nearby would probably give us a job, and that they would let us out of the spike early in the morning if we told them we had already got a job. Otherwise we should be confined all day, unless we went out 'over the wall' – i.e. bolted when the Tramp Major was not looking. Tramps often do this, but you have to cache your possessions outside, which we could not in the heavy rain. We went in, and I found that (if West Malling is typical) spikes have improved a lot since I was last in.[1] The bathroom was clean and decent, and we were actually given a clean towel each. The food was the same old bread and marg, though, and the Tramp Major got angry when we asked in good faith whether the stuff they gave us to drink was tea or cocoa.[2] We had beds with straw palliasses and plenty of blankets, and both slept like logs.

In the morning they told us we must work till eleven, and set us to scrubbing out one of the dormitories. As usual, the work was a mere formality. (I have never done a stroke of real work in the spike, and I have never met anybody who has.) The dormitory was a room of fifty beds, close together, with that warm, faecal stink that you never seem to get away from in the workhouse. There was an imbecile pauper there, a great lump of about sixteen stone, with a tiny, snouty face and a sidelong grin. He was at work very slowly emptying chamberpots. These workhouses seem all alike, and there is something intensely disgusting in the atmosphere of them. The thought of all those grey-faced, ageing men living a very quiet, withdrawn life in a smell of WCs, and practising homosexuality, makes me feel sick. But it is not easy to convey what I mean, because it is all bound up with the smell of the workhouse.

At eleven they let us out with the usual hunk of bread and cheese, and we went on to Blest's farm, about three miles away; but we did not get there till one, because we stopped on the way and got a big haul of damsons. When we arrived at the farm the foreman told us that he wanted pickers and sent us up to the field at once. We had now only about 3d left, and that evening I wrote home asking them to send me 10/–; it came two days later, and in the meantime we should have had practically nothing to eat if the other pickers had not fed us. For nearly three weeks after this we were at work hop-picking, and I had better describe the different aspects of this individually.

2 to 19 September

Hops are trained up poles or over wires about 10 feet high, and grown in rows a yard to two apart. All the pickers have to do is to tear them down and strip the hops into a bin, keeping them as clean as possible of leaves. In practice, of course, it is impossible to keep all the leaves out, and the experienced pickers swell the bulk of their hops by putting in just as many leaves as the farmer will stand for. One soon gets the knack of the work, and the only hardships are the standing (we were generally on our feet ten hours a day), the plagues of plant lice, and the damage to one's hands. One's hands get stained as black as a Negro's with the hop-juice, which only mud will remove,[3] and after a day or two they crack and are cut to bits by the stems of the vines, which are spiny. In the mornings, before the cuts had reopened, my hands used to give me perfect agony, and even at the time of typing this (10 October) they show the marks. Most of the people who go down hopping have done it every year since they were children, and they pick like lightning and know all the tricks, such as shaking the hops up to make them lie loose in the bin, etc. The most successful pickers are families, who have two or three adults to strip the vines, and a couple of children to pick up the fallen hops and clear the odd strands. The laws about child labour are disregarded utterly, and some of the people drive their children pretty hard. The woman in the next bin to us, a regular old-fashioned East Ender, kept her grandchildren at it like slaves – 'Go on, Rose, you lazy

[1] No: a bit worse if anything. [Author's footnote.]
[2] To this day I don't know which it was. [Author's footnote.]
[3] Or hop-juice, funnily enough. [Author's footnote.]

little cat, pick them 'ops up. I'll warm your arse if I get up to you,' etc., until the children, aged from 6 to 10, used to drop down and fall asleep on the ground. But they liked the work, and I don't suppose it did them more harm than school.

As to what one can earn, the system of payment is this. Two or three times a day the hops are measured, and you are due a certain sum (in our case twopence) for each bushel you have picked. A good vine yields about half a bushel of hops, and a good picker can strip a vine in about ten minutes, so that theoretically one *might* earn about 30/– by a sixty-hour week. But in practice this is quite impossible. To begin with, the hops vary enormously. On some vines they are as large as small pears, and on others hardly bigger than peas; the bad vines take rather longer to strip than the good ones – they are generally more tangled – and sometimes it needs five or six of them to make a bushel. Then there are all kinds of delays, and the pickers get no compensation for lost time. Sometimes it rains (if it rains hard the hops get too slippery to pick), and one is always kept waiting when changing from field to field, so that an hour or two is wasted every day. And above all there is the question of measurement. Hops are soft things like sponges, and it is quite easy for the measurer to crush a bushel of them into a quart if he chooses. Some days he merely scoops the hops out, but on other days he has orders from the farmer to 'take them heavy', and then he crams them tight into the basket, so that instead of getting 20 bushels for a full bin one gets only 12 or 14, i.e. a shilling or so less. There was a song about this, which the old East End woman and her grandchildren were always singing:

Our lousy hops!
Our lousy hops!
When the measurer he comes round.
Pick 'em up, pick 'em up off the ground!
When he comes to measure
He never knows where to stop;
Ay, ay, get in the bin
And take the fucking lot!

From the bin the hops are put into 10-bushel pokes which are supposed to weigh a hundredweight and are normally carried by one man. It used to take two men to hoist a full poke when the measurer had been taking them heavy.

With all these difficulties one can't earn 30/– a week or anything near it. It is a curious fact, though, that very few of the pickers were aware how little they really earned, because the piece-work system disguises the low rate of payment. The best pickers in our gang were a family of gypsies, five adults and a child, all of whom, of course, had picked hops every year since they could walk. In a little under three weeks these people earned exactly £10 between them – i.e. leaving out the child, about 14/– a week each. Ginger and I earned about 9/– a week each, and I doubt if any individual picker made over 15/– a week. A family working together can make their keep and their fare back to London at these rates, but a single picker can hardly do even that. On some of the farms nearby the tally, instead of being 6 bushels to the shilling, was 8 or 9, at which one would have a hard job to earn 10/– a week.

When one starts work the farm gives one a printed copy of rules, which are designed to reduce a picker more or less to a slave. According to these rules the farmer can sack a picker without notice and on any pretext whatever, and pay him off at 8 bushels a shilling instead of six – i.e. confiscate a quarter of his earnings. If a picker leaves his job before the picking is finished his earnings are docked the same amount. You cannot draw what you have earned and then clear off, because the farm will never pay you more than two-thirds of your earnings in advance, and so are in your debt till the last day. The binmen (i.e. foremen of gangs) get wages instead of being paid on the piece-work system, and these wages cease if there is a strike, so naturally they will raise heaven and earth to prevent one. Altogether the farmers have the hop-pickers in a cleft stick, and always will have until there is a pickers' union. It is not much use to try and form a union, though, for about half the pickers are women and gypsies, and are too stupid to see the advantages of it.

As to our living accommodation, the best quarters on the farm, ironically enough, were disused stables. Most of us slept in round tin huts about 10 feet across, with no glass in the windows, and all kinds of holes to let in the wind and rain. The furniture of these huts consisted of a heap of straw and hop-vines, and nothing else. There were four of us in our hut, but in some of them there were seven or eight – rather an advantage really, for it kept the hut warm. Straw is rotten stuff to sleep in (it is much more draughty than hay) and Ginger and I had only a blanket each, so we suffered agonies of cold for the first week; after that we stole enough pokes to keep us warm. The farm gave us free firewood, though not as much as we needed.The water tap was 200 yards away, and the latrine the same distance, but it was so filthy that one would have walked a mile sooner than use it. There was a stream where one could do some laundering, but getting a bath in the village would have been about as easy as buying a tame whale.

The hop-pickers seemed to be of three types: East Enders (mostly costermongers), gypsies, and itinerant agricultural labourers with a sprinkling of tramps. The fact that Ginger and I were tramps got us a great deal of sympathy, especially among the fairly well-to-do people. There was one couple, a coster and his wife, who were like a father and mother to us. They were the kind of people who are generally drunk on Saturday nights and who tack a 'fucking' on to every noun, yet I have never seen anything that exceeded their kindness and delicacy. They gave us food over and over again. A child would come to the hut with a saucepan: 'Eric, mother was going to throw this stew away, but she said it was a pity to waste it. Would you like it?' Of course they were not really going to have thrown it away, but said this to avoid the suggestion of charity. One day they gave us a whole pig's head, ready cooked. These people had been on the road several years themselves, and it made them sympathetic – 'Ah, I know what it's like. Skippering in the fucking wet grass, and then got to tap the milkman in the morning before you can get a cup of tea. Two of my boys were born on the road,' etc. Another man who was very decent to us was an employee in a paper factory. Before this he had been vermin man to ——, and he told me that the dirt and vermin in —— passed belief. When he worked at ——, the rats were so numerous that it was not safe to go into the kitchens at night unarmed; you had to carry a revolver. After I had mixed with these people for a few days it was too much fag to go on putting on my cockney accent, and they noticed that I talked 'different'. As usual, this made them still more friendly, for these people seem to think that it is especially dreadful to 'come down in the world'.

Out of 200 pickers at Blest's farm, 50 or 60 were gypsies. They are curiously like oriental peasants – the same heavy faces, at once dull and sly, and the same sharpness in their own line and startling ignorance outside it. Most of them could not read even a word, and none of their children seemed ever to have gone to school. One gypsy, aged about 40, used to ask me such questions as, 'How far is Paris from France?' 'How many days' journey by caravan to Paris?', etc. A youth, aged twenty, used to ask this riddle half a dozen times a day – 'I'll tell you something you can't do?' – 'What?' – 'Tickle a gnat's arse with a telegraph pole.' (At this, never-failing yells of laughter.) The gypsies seem to be quite rich, owning caravans, horses, etc. yet they go on all the year round working as itinerant labourers and saving money. They used to say that our way of life (living in houses, etc.) seemed disgusting to them, and to explain how clever they had been in dodging the army during the war. Talking to them, you had the feeling of talking to people from another century. I often heard a gypsy say, 'If I knew where so and so was, I'd ride my horse till it hadn't a shoe left to catch him' – not a twentieth-century metaphor at all. One day some gypsies were talking about a noted horse-thief called George Bigland, and one man, defending him, said; 'I don't think George is as bad as you make out. I've known him to steal Gorgias' (Gentiles') horses, but he wouldn't go so far as to steal from one of us.'

The gypsies call us Gorgias and themselves Romanies, but they are nicknamed Didecais (not certain of spelling). They all knew Romany, and occasionally used a word or two when they didn't want to be understood. A curious thing I noticed about the gypsies – I don't know whether it is the same everywhere – was that you would often see a whole family who were totally unlike one another. It almost seems to countenance the stories about gypsies stealing children; more likely, though, it is because it's a wise child, etc.

One of the men in our hut was the old deaf tramp we had met outside West Malling spike – Deafie, he was always called. He was rather a Mr F's aunt in conversation, and he looked just like a drawing by George Belcher, but he was an intelligent, decently educated man, and no doubt would not have been on the road if he could hear. He was not strong enough for heavy work, and he had done nothing for years past except odd jobs like hopping. He calculated that he had been in over 400 different spikes. The other man, named Barrett, and a man in our gang named George, were good specimens of the itinerant agricultural labourer. For years past they had worked on a regular round: lambing in early spring, then pea-picking, strawberries, various other fruits, hops, 'spud-grabbing', turnips and sugar beet. They were seldom out of work for more than a week or two, yet even this was enough to swallow up anything they could earn. They were both penniless when they arrived at Blest's farm, and I saw Barrett work certainly one day without a bite to eat. The proceeds of all their work were the clothes they stood up in, straw to sleep on all the year round, meals of bread and cheese and bacon, and I suppose one or two good drunks a year. George was a dismal devil, and took a sort of worm-like pride in being underfed and overworked, and always tobying from job to job. His line was, 'It doesn't do for people like us to have fine ideas'. (He could not read or write, and seemed to think even literacy a kind of extravagance.) I know this philosophy well, having often met it among the dishwashers in Paris. Barrett, who was 63, used to complain a lot about the badness of food nowadays, compared with what you could get when he was a boy – 'In them days we didn't live on this fucking bread and marg, we 'ad good solid tommy. Bullock's 'eart. Bacon dumpling. Black pudden. Pig's 'ead.' The glutinous, reminiscent tone in which he said 'pig's 'ead' suggested decades of underfeeding.

Besides all these regular pickers there were what are called 'home-dwellers', i.e. local people who pick at odd times, chiefly for the fun of it. They are mostly farmers' wives and the like, and as a rule they and the regular pickers loathe one another. One of them, however, was a very decent woman, who gave Ginger a pair of shoes and me an excellent coat and waistcoat and two shirts. Most of the local people seemed to look on us as dirt, and the shopkeepers were very insolent, though between us we must have spent several hundred pounds in the village.

One day at hop-picking was very much like another. At about a quarter to six in the morning we crawled out of the straw, put on our coats and boots (we slept in everything else) and went out to get a fire going – rather a job this September, when it rained all the time. By half past six we had made tea and fried some bread for breakfast, and then we started off for work, with bacon sandwiches and a drum of cold tea for our dinner. If it didn't rain we were working pretty steadily till about one, and then we would start a fire between the vines, heat up our tea and knock off for half an hour. After that we were at it again till half past five, and by the time we had got home, cleaned the hop-juice off our hands and had tea, it was already dark and we were dropping with sleep. A good many nights, though, we used to go out and steal apples. There was a big orchard nearby, and three or four of us used to rob it systematically, carrying a sack and getting half a hundred-weight of apples at a time, besides several pounds of cobnuts. On Sundays we used to wash our shirts and socks in the stream, and sleep the rest of the day. As far as I remember I never undressed completely all the time we were down there, nor washed my teeth, and I only shaved twice a week. Between working and getting meals (and that meant fetching everlasting cans of water, struggling with wet faggots, frying in tin-lids, etc.) one seemed to have not an instant to spare. I only read one book all the time I was down there, and that was a Buffalo Bill. Counting up what we spent I find that Ginger and I fed ourselves on about 5/– a week each, so it is not surprising that we were constantly short of tobacco and constantly hungry, in spite of the apples and what the others gave us. We seemed to be forever doing sums in farthings to find out whether we could afford another half ounce of shag or another two-pennorth of bacon. It wasn't a bad life, but what with standing all day, sleeping rough and getting my hands cut to bits, I felt a wreck at the end of it. It was humiliating to see that most of the people there looked on it as a holiday – in fact, it is because hopping is regarded as a holiday that the pickers will take such starvation wages. It gives one an insight into the lives of farm labourers, too, to realize that according to their standards hop-picking is hardly work at all.

One night a youth knocked at our door and said that he was a new picker and had been told to sleep in our hut. We let him in and fed him in the morning, after which he vanished. It appeared that he was not a picker at all, but a tramp, and that tramps often work this dodge in the hopping season, in order to get a kip under shelter. Another night a woman who was going home asked to to help her get her luggage to Wateringbury station. As she was leaving early they had paid her off at eight bushels a shilling, and her total earnings were only just enough to get herself and family home. I had to push a perambulator, with one eccentric wheel and loaded with huge packages, two and a half miles through the dark, followed by a retinue of yelling children. When we got to the station the last train was just coming in, and in rushing the pram across the level crossing I upset it. I shall never forget that moment – the train bearing down on us, and the porter and I chasing a tin chamberpot that was rolling up the track. On several nights Ginger tried to persuade me to come and rob the church with him, and he would have done it alone if I had not managed to get it into his head that suspicion was bound to fall on him, as a known criminal. He had robbed churches before, and he said, what surprised me, that there is generally something worth having in the Poorbox. We had one or two jolly nights, on Saturdays, sitting round a huge fire till midnight and roasting apples. One night, I remember, it came out that, of about fifteen people round the fire, everyone except myself had been in prison. There were uproarious scenes in the village on Saturdays, for the people who had money used to get well drunk, and it needed the police to get them out of the pub. I have no doubt the residents thought us a nasty vulgar lot, but I could not help feeling that it was rather good for a dull village to have this invasion of cockneys once a year.

19 September
On the last morning, when we had picked the last field, there was a queer game of catching the women and putting them in the bins. Very likely there will be something about this in the Golden Bough. It is evidently an old custom, and all harvests have some custom of this kind attached to them. The people who were illiterate or thereabouts brought their tally books to me and other 'scholars' to have them reckoned up, and some of them paid a copper or two to have it done. I found that in quite a number of cases the farm cashiers had made a mistake in the addition, and invariably the mistake was in favour of the farm. Of course the pickers got the sum due when they complained, but they would not have if they had accepted the farm cashier's reckoning. Moreover, the farm had a mean little rule that anyone who was going to complain about his tally book had to wait till all the other pickers had been paid off. This meant waiting till the afternoon, so that some people who had buses to catch had to go home without claiming the sum due to them. (Of course it was only a few coppers in most cases. One woman's book, however, was added up over £1 wrong.)

Ginger and I packed our things and walked over to Wateringbury to catch the hop-pickers' train. On the way we stopped to buy tobacco, and as a sort of farewell to Kent, Ginger cheated the tobacconist's girl of fourpence, by a very cunning dodge. When we got to Wateringbury station about fifty hoppers were waiting for the train, and the first person we saw was old Deafie, sitting on the grass with a newspaper in front of him. He lifted it aside, and we saw that he had his trousers undone and was exhibiting his penis to the women and children as they passed. I was surprised – such a decent old man, really; but there is hardly a tramp who has not some sexual abnormality. The Hoppers' train was ninepence cheaper than the ordinary fare, and it took nearly five hours to get us to London – 30 miles. At about 10 at night the hop-pickers poured out at London Bridge station, a number of them drunk and all carrying bunches of hops; people in the street readily bought these bunches of hops, I don't know why. Deafie, who had travelled in our carriage, asked us into the nearest pub and stood us each a pint, the first beer I had had in three weeks. Then he went off to Hammersmith, and no doubt he will be on the bum till next year's fruit-picking begins.

On adding up our tally book, Ginger and I found that we had made just 26/–

each by eighteen days' work. We had drawn 8/– each in advances (or 'subs' as they are called), and we had made another 6/– between us by selling stolen apples. After paying our fares we got to London with about 16/– each. So we had, after all, kept ourselves while we were in Kent and come back with a little in pocket; but we had only done it by living on the very minimum of everything.

19 September to 8 October
Ginger and I went to a kip in Tooley Street, owned by Lew Levy who owns the one in Westminster Bridge Road. It is only sevenpence a night, and it is probably the best sevenpenny one in London. There are bugs in the beds, but not many, and the kitchens, though dark and dirty, are convenient, with abundant fires and hot water. The lodgers are a pretty low lot – mostly Irish unskilled labourers, and out of work at that. We met some queer types among them. There was one man, aged 68, who worked carrying crates of fish (they weigh a hundredweight each) in Billingsgate Market. He was interested in politics, and he told me that on Bloody Sunday in '88 he had taken part in the rioting and been sworn in as a special constable on the same day. Another old man, a flower seller, was mad. Most of the time he behaved quite normally, but when his fits were on he would walk up and down the kitchen uttering dreadful beast-like yells, with an expression of agony on his face. Curiously enough, the fits only came on in wet weather. Another man was a thief. He stole from shop counters and vacant motor cars, especially commercial travellers' cars, and sold the stuff to a Jew in Lambeth Cut. Every evening you would see him smartening himself up to go 'up West'. He told me that he could count on £2 a week, with a big haul from time to time. He managed to swoop the till of a public house almost every Christmas, generally getting £40 or £50 by this. He had been stealing for years and only been caught once, and then was bound over. As always seems the case with thieves, his work brought him no good, for when he got a large sum he blued it instantly. He had one of the ignoblest faces I ever saw, just like a hyena's; yet he was likeable, and decent about sharing food and paying debts.

Several mornings Ginger and I worked helping the porters at Billingsgate. You go there at about five and stand at the corner of one of the streets which lead up from Billingsgate to Eastcheap. When a porter is having trouble to get his barrow up, he shouts 'Up the 'ill!' and you spring forward (there is fierce competition for the jobs, of course) and shove the barrow behind. The payment is 'twopence an up'. They take on about one shover-up for four hundredweight, and the work knocks it out of your thighs and elbows, but you don't get enough jobs to tire you out. Standing there from five till nearly midday, I never made more than 1/6d. If you are very lucky a porter takes you on as his regular assistant, and then you make about 4/6d a morning. The porters themselves seem to make about £4 or £5 a week. There are several things worth noticing about Billingsgate. One is that vast quantities of the work done there are quite unnecessary, being due to the complete lack of any centralized transport system. What with porters, barrowmen, shovers-up, etc., it now costs round about £1 to get a ton of fish from Billingsgate to one of the London railway termini. If it were done in an orderly manner, by lorries, I suppose it would cost a few shillings. Another thing is that the pubs in Billingsgate are open at the hours when other pubs are shut. And another is that the barrowmen in Billingsgate do a regular traffic in stolen fish, and you can get fish dirt cheap if you know one of them.

After about a fortnight in the lodging-house I found that I was writing nothing, and the place itself was beginning to get on my nerves, with its noise and lack of privacy, and the stifling heat of the kitchen, and above all the dirt. The kitchen had a permanent sweetish reek of fish, and all the sinks were blocked with rotting fish guts which stank horribly. You had to store your food in dark corners which were infested by black beetles and cockroaches, and there were clouds of horrible languid flies everywhere. The dormitory was also disgusting, with the perpetual din of coughing and spitting – everyone in a lodging-house has a chronic cough, no doubt from the foul air. I had got to write some articles, which could not be done in such surroundings, so I wrote home for money and took a room in Windsor Street near the Harrow Road. Ginger has gone off on the road again. Most of this narrative was written in the Bermondsey public library, which has a good reading room and was convenient for the lodging-house.

NOTES:

New Words (i.e. words new to me) discovered this time.

Shackles: broth or gravy.
Drum, a: a billy can. (With verb to drum up meaning to light a fire.)
Toby, on the: on the tramp. (Also to toby, and a toby, meaning a tramp. Slang Dictionary gives the toby as the highroad.)
Chat, a: a louse. (Also chatty, lousy. SD gives this but not a chat.)
Get, a: ? (Word of abuse, meaning unknown.)
Didecai, a: a gypsy.
Sprowsie, a: a sixpence.
Hard-up: tobacco made from fag ends. (SD gives a hard-up as a man who collects fag ends.)
Skipper, to: to sleep out. (SD gives a skipper as a barn.)
Scrump, to: to steal.
Knock off, to: to arrest.
Jack off, to: to go away.
Jack, on his: on his own.
Clods: coppers.

Burglar's Slang

A stick, or a cane: a jemmy. (SD gives stick.)
Peter, a: a safe. (In SD.)
Bly, a: an oxy-acetylene blowlamp.[1]

Use of the word 'tart' among East Enders. This word now seems absolutely interchangeable with 'girl', with no implication of 'prostitute'. People will speak of their daughter or sister as a tart.

Rhyming slang. I thought this was extinct, but it is far from it. The hop-pickers used these expressions freely: a dig in the grave, meaning a shave. The hot cross bun, meaning the sun. Greengages, meaning wages. They also used the

[1] I forgot to mention that these lamps are hired out to burglars. Ginger said that he had paid £3.10.0 a night for the use of one. So also with other burglars' tools of the more elaborate kinds. When opening a puzzle lock, clever safe-breakers use a stethoscope to listen for the click of the tumblers. [Author's footnote.]

abbreviated rhyming slang, e.g. 'Use your twopenny' for 'Use your head'. This is arrived at like this: Head, loaf of bread, loaf, twopenny loaf, twopenny.

Homosexual vice in London. It appears that one of the great rendezvous is Charing Cross underground station. It appeared to be taken for granted by the people on Trafalgar Square that youths could earn a bit this way, and several said to me, 'I need never sleep out if I choose to go down to Charing Cross.' They added that the usual fee is a shilling.

Written October 1931

Clink

This trip was a failure, as the object of it was to get into prison, and I did not, in fact, get more than forty-eight hours in custody; however, I am recording it, as the procedure in the police court, etc., was fairly interesting. I am writing this eight months after it happened, so am not certain of any dates, but it all happened a week or ten days before Xmas 1931.

I started out on Saturday afternoon with four or five shillings, and went out to the Mile End Road, because my plan was to get drunk and incapable, and I thought they would be less lenient towards drunkards in the East End. I bought some tobacco and a 'Yank Mag' against my forthcoming imprisonment, and then, as soon as the pubs opened, went and had four or five pints, topping up with a quarter bottle of whisky, which left me with twopence in hand. By the time the whisky was low in the bottle I was tolerably drunk – more drunk than I had intended, for it happened that I had eaten nothing all day, and the alcohol acted quickly on my empty stomach. It was all I could do to stand upright, though my brain was quite clear – with me, when I am drunk, my brain remains clear long after my legs and speech have gone. I began staggering along the pavement in a westward direction, and for a long time did not meet any policemen, though the streets were crowded and all the people pointed and laughed at me. Finally I saw two policemen coming. I pulled the whisky bottle out of my pocket and, in their sight, drank what was left, which nearly knocked me out, so that I clutched a lamp-post and fell down. The two policemen ran towards me, turned me over and took the bottle out of my hand.

They: ''Ere, what you bin drinking?' (For a moment they may have thought it was a case of suicide.)

I: 'Thass my boll whisky. You lea' me alone.'

They: 'Coo, 'e's fair bin bathing in it! – What you bin doing of, eh?'

I: 'Bin in boozer, 'avin' bit o' fun. Christmas, ain't it?'

They: 'No, not by a week it ain't. You got mixed up in the dates, you 'ave. You better come along with us. We'll look after yer.'

I: 'Why sh'd I come along you?'

They: 'Jest so's we'll look after you and make you comfortable. You'll get run over, rolling about like that.'

I: 'Look. Boozer over there. Less go in 'ave drink.'

They: 'You've 'ad enough for one night, ole chap. You best come with us.'

I: 'Where you takin' me?'

They: 'Jest somewhere as you'll get a nice quiet kip with a clean sheet and two blankets and all.'

I: 'Shall I get drink there?'

They: 'Course you will. Got a boozer on the premises, we 'ave.'

All this while they were leading me gently along the pavement. They had my arms in the grip (I forget what it is called) by which you can break a man's arm with one twist, but they were as gentle with me as though I had been a child. I was internally quite sober, and it amused me very much to see the cunning way in which they persuaded me along, never once disclosing the fact that we were making for the police station. This is, I suppose, the usual procedure with drunks.

When we got to the station (it was Bethnal Green, but I did not learn this till Monday) they dumped me in a chair and began emptying my pockets while the sergeant questioned me. I pretended, however, to be too drunk to give sensible answers, and he told them in disgust to take me off to the cells, which they did. The cell was about the same size as a Casual Ward cell (about 10 ft by 5 ft by 10 ft high), but much cleaner and better appointed. It was made of white porcelain bricks, and was furnished with a WC, a hot water pipe, a plank bed, a horsehair pillow and two blankets. There was a tiny barred window high up near the roof, and an electric bulb behind a guard of thick glass was kept burning all night. The door was steel, with the usual spy-hole and aperture for serving food through. The constables in searching me had taken away my money, matches, razor, and also my scarf – this, I learned afterwards, because prisoners have been known to hang themselves on their scarves.

There is very little to say about the next day and night, which were unutterably boring. I was horribly sick, sicker than I have ever been from a bout of drunkenness, no doubt from having an empty stomach. During Sunday I was given two meals of bread and marg and tea (spike quality), and one of meat and potatoes – this, I believe, owing to the kindness of the sergeant's wife, for I think only bread and marg is provided for prisoners in the lock-up. I was not allowed to shave, and there was only a little cold water to wash in. When the charge sheet was filled up I told the story I always tell, viz. my name was Edward Burton, and my parents kept a cake-shop in Blythburgh, where I had been employed as a clerk in a draper's shop; that I had had the sack for drunkenness, and my parents, finally getting sick of my drunken habits, had turned me adrift. I added that I had been working as an outside porter at Billingsgate, and having unexpectedly 'knocked up' six shillings on Saturday, had gone on the razzle. The police were quite kind, and read me lectures on drunkenness, with the usual stuff about seeing that I still had some good in me, etc., etc. They offered to let me out on bail on my own recognizance, but I had no money and nowhere to go, so I elected to stay in custody. It was very dull, but I had my 'Yank Mag', and could get a smoke if I asked the constable on duty in the passage for a light – prisoners are not allowed matches, of course.

The next morning very early they turned me out of my cell to wash, gave me back my scarf, and took me out into the yard and put me in the Black Maria. Inside, the Black Maria was just like a French public lavatory, with a row of tiny locked compartments on either side, each just large enough to sit down in. People had scrawled their names, offences and the lengths of their sentences all over the walls of my compartment; also, several times, variants on this couplet:

Detective Smith knows how to gee;
Tell him he's a cunt from me.

('Gee' in this context means to act as an *agent provocateur.*) We drove round to various stations picking up about ten prisoners in all, until the Black Maria was quite full. They were quite a jolly crowd inside. The compartment doors were open at the top, for ventilation, so that you could reach across, and somebody had managed to smuggle matches in, and we all had a smoke. Presently we began singing, and, as it was near Christmas, sang several carols. We drove up to Old Street Police Court singing:

Adeste, fideles, laeti, triumphantes,
Adeste, adeste ad Bethlehem etc.

which seemed to me rather inappropriate.

At the police court they took me off and put me in a cell identical with the one at Bethnal Green, even to having the same number of bricks in it – I counted in each case. There were three men in the cell besides myself. One was a smartly dressed, florid, well-set-up man of about thirty-five, whom I would have taken for a commercial traveller or perhaps a bookie, and another a middle-aged Jew, also quite decently dressed. The other man was evidently a habitual burglar. He was a short rough-looking man with grey hair and a worn face, and at this moment in such a state of agitation over his approaching trial that he could not keep still an instant. He kept pacing up and down the cell like a wild beast, brushing against our knees as we sat on the plank bed, and exclaiming that he was innocent – he was charged, apparently, with loitering with intent to commit burglary. He said that he had nine previous convictions against him, and that in these cases, which are mainly of suspicion, old offenders are nearly always convicted. From time to time he would shake his fist towards the door and exclain 'Fucking toe-rag! Fucking toe-rag!', meaning the 'split' who had arrested him.

Presently two more prisoners were put into the cell, an ugly Belgian youth charged with obstructing traffic with a barrow, and an extraordinary hairy creature who was either deaf and dumb or spoke no English. Except this last all the prisoners talked about their cases with the utmost freedom. The florid, smart man, it appeared, was a public house 'guv'nor' (it is a sign of how utterly the London publicans are in the claws of the brewers that they are always referred to as 'governors', not 'landlords'; being, in fact, no better than employees), and had embezzled the Christmas Club money. As usual, he was head over ears in debt to the brewers, and no doubt had taken some of the money in hopes of backing a winner. Two of the subscribers had discovered this a few days before the money was due to be paid out, and laid an information. The 'guv'nor' immediately paid back all save £12, which was also refunded before his case came up for trial. Nevertheless, he was certain to be sentenced, as the magistrates are hard on these cases – he did, in fact, get four months later in the day. He was ruined for life, of course. The brewers would file bankruptcy proceedings and sell up all his stock and furniture, and he would never be given a pub licence again. He was trying to brazen it out in front of the rest of us, and smoking cigarettes incessantly from a stock of Gold Flake packets he had laid in – the last time in his life, I dare say, that he would have quite enough cigarettes. There was a staring, abstracted look in his eyes all the time while he talked. I think the fact that his life was at an end, as far as any decent position in society went, was gradually sinking into him.

The Jew had been a buyer at Smithfields for a Kosher butcher. After working seven years for the same employer he suddenly misappropriated £28, went up to Edinburgh – I don't know why Edinburgh – and had a 'good time' with tarts, and came back and surrendered himself when the money was gone. £16 of the money had been repaid, and the rest was to be repaid by monthly instalments. He had a wife and a number of children. He told us, what interested me, that his employer would probably get into trouble at the synagogue for prosecuting him. It appears that the Jews have arbitration courts of their own, and a Jew is not supposed to prosecute another Jew, at least in a breach of trust case like this, without first submitting it to the arbitration court.

One remark made by these men struck me – I heard it from almost every prisoner who was up for a serious offence. It was, 'It's not the prison I mind, it's losing my job.' This is, I believe, symptomatic of the dwindling power of the law compared with that of the capitalist.

The kept us waiting several hours. It was very uncomfortable in the cell, for there was not room for all of us to sit down on the plank bed, and it was beastly cold in spite of the number of us. Several of the men used the WC, which was disgusting in so small a cell, especially as the plug did not work. The publican distributed his cigarettes generously, the constable in the passage supplying lights. From time to time an extraordinary clanking noise came from the cell next door, where a youth who had stabbed his 'tart' in the stomach – she was likely to recover, we heard – was locked up alone. Goodness knows what was happening, but it sounded as though he were chained to the wall. At about ten they gave us each a mug of tea – this, it appeared, not provided by the authorities but by the police court missionaries – and shortly afterwards shepherded us along to a sort of large waiting room where the prisoners awaited trial.

There were perhaps fifty prisoners here, men of every type, but on the whole much more smartly dressed than one would expect. They were strolling up and down with their hats on, shivering with the cold. I saw here a thing which interested me greatly. When I was being taken to my cell I had seen two dirty-looking ruffians, much dirtier than myself and presumably drunks or obstruction cases, being put into another cell in the row. Here, in the waiting room these two were at work with note-books in their hands, interrogating prisoners. It appeared that they were 'splits', and were put into the cells disguised as prisoners, to pick up any information that was going – for there is complete freemasonry between prisoners, and they talk without reserve in front of one another. It was a dingy trick, I thought.

All the while the prisoners were being taken by ones and twos along a corridor to the court. Presently a sergeant shouted 'Come on the drunks!' and four or five of us filed along the corridor and stood waiting at the entrance of the court. A young constable on duty there advised me:

'Take your cap off when you go in, plead guilty and don't give back any answers. Got any previous convictions?'

'No.'

'Six bob you'll get. Going to pay it?'

'I can't. I've only twopence.'

'Ah well, it don't matter. Lucky for you Mr Brown isn't on the bench this morning. Teetotaller he is. He don't half give it to the drunks. Coo!'

The drunk cases were dealt with so rapidly that I had not even time to notice what the court was like. I only had a vague impression of a raised platform with a coat of arms over it, clerks sitting at tables below, and a railing. We filed past the railing like people passing through a turnstile, and the proceedings in each case sounded like this:

'Edward-Burton-drunk-and-incapable-Drunk?-Yes-Six-shillings-move-on-NEXT!'

All this in the space of about five seconds. At the other side of the court we reached a room where a sergeant was sitting at a desk with a ledger.

'Six shillings?' he said.

'Yes.'

'Going to pay it?'

'I can't.'

'All right, back you go to your cell.'

And they took me back and locked me in the cell from which I had come, about ten minutes after I had left it.

The publican had also been brought back, his case having been postponed, and the Belgian youth, who, like me, could not pay his fine. The Jew was gone, whether released or sentenced we did not know. Throughout the day prisoners were coming and going, some waiting trial, some until the Black Maria was available to take them to prison. It was cold, and the nasty faecal stench in the cell became unbearable. They gave us our dinner at about two o'clock – it consisted of a mug of tea and two slices of bread and marg for each man. Apparently this was the regulation meal. One could, if one had friends outside, get food sent in, but it struck me as damnably unfair that a penniless man must face his trial with only bread and marg in his belly; also unshaven – I, at this time, had had no chance of shaving for over forty-eight hours – which is likely to prejudice the magistrates against him.

Among the prisoners who were put temporarily in the cell were two friends or partners named apparently Snouter and Charlie, who had been arrested for some street offence – obstruction with a barrow, I dare say. Snouter was a thin, red-faced, malignant-looking man, and Charlie a short, powerful, jolly man. Their conversation was rather interesting.

Charlie: 'Cripes, it ain't 'alf fucking cold in 'ere. Lucky for us ole Brown ain't on today. Give you a month as soon as look at yer.'

Snouter: (bored, and singing)

> *'Tap, tap, tapetty tap,*
> *I'm a perfect devil at that;*
> *Tapping 'em 'ere, tapping 'em there,*
> *I bin tapping 'em everywhere –'*

Charlie: 'Oh, fuck off with yer tapping! Scrumping's what yer want at this time of year. All them rows of turkeys in the winders, like rows of fucking soldiers with no clo'es on – don't it make yer fucking mouth water to look at 'em. Bet yer a tanner I 'ave one of 'em afore tonight.'

Snouter: 'What's 'a good? Can't cook the bugger over the kip-'ouse fire, can you?'

Charlie: 'Oo wants to cook it? I know where I can flog (sell) it for a bob or two, though.'

Snouter: ''S no good. Chanting's the game this time of year. Carols. Fair twist their 'earts round, I can, when I get on the mournful. Old tarts weep their fucking eyes out when they 'ear me. I won't 'alf give them a doing this Christmas. I'll kip indoors if I 'ave to cut it out of their bowels.'

Charlie: 'Ah, *I* can slign you a bit of a carol. 'Ymns, too.' (He begins singing in a good bass voice)

'Jesu, lover of my soul,
Let me to thy bosom fly –'

The Constable on duty: (looking through the grille) 'Nah then, in 'ere, nah then! What yer think this is? Baptist prayer meeting?'

Charlie: (in a low voice as the constable disappears) 'Fuck off, pisspot.' (He hums)

'While the gathering waters roll,
While the tempest still is 'igh!

You won't find many in the 'ymnal as I can't sling you. Sung bass in the choir my last two years in Dartmoor, I did.'

Snouter: 'Ah? Wassit like in Dartmoor now? D'you get jam now?'

Charlie: 'Not jam. Gets cheese, though, twice a week.'

Snouter: 'Ah? 'Ow long was you doing?'

Charlie: 'Four year.'

Snouter: 'Four years without cunt – Cripes! Fellers inside'd go 'alf mad if they saw a pair of legs (a woman), eh?'

Charlie: 'Ah well, in Dartmoor we used to fuck old women down on the allotments. Take 'em under the 'edge in the mist. Spudgrabbers they was – ole trots seventy years old. Forty of us was caught and went through 'ell for it. Bread and water, chains – everythink. I took my Bible oath as I wouldn't get no more stretches after that.'

Snouter: 'Yes, you! 'Ow come you got in the stir lars' time, then?'

Charlie: 'You wouldn't 'ardly believe it, boy. I was narked – narked by my own sister! Yes, my own fucking sister. My sister's a cow if ever there was one. She got married to a religious maniac, and 'e's so fucking religious that she's got fifteen kids now. Well, it was 'im put 'er up to narking me. But I got it back on 'em, *I* can tell you. What do you think I done first thing, when I come out of the stir? I bought a 'ammer, and I went round to my sister's 'ouse and smashed 'er piano to fucking matchwood. I did. "There," I says, "that's what you get for narking me! You mare!" I says.' etc., etc.

This kind of conversation went on more or less all day between these two, who were only in for some petty offence and were quite pleased with themselves. Those who were going to prison were silent and restless, and the look on some of the men's faces – respectable men under arrest for the first time – was dreadful. They took the publican out at about three in the afternoon, to be sent off to prison. He had cheered up a little on learning from the constable on duty that he was going to the same prison as Lord Kylsant.[1] He thought that by sucking up to Lord K in jail he might get a job from him when he came out.

I had no idea how long I was gong to be incarcerated, and supposed that it would be several days at least. However, between four and five o'clock they took me out of the cell, gave back the things which had been confiscated, and

[1] Lord Kylsant (1863–1937), Conservative MP and Chairman of The Royal Mail Steam Package Company was sentenced to twelve months' imprisonment in 1931 for circulating a false prospectus, but his personal guilt was never entirely established in the public mind.

shot me into the street forthwith. Evidently the day in custody served instead of the fine. I had only twopence and had had nothing to eat all day except bread and marg and was damnably hungry; however, as always happens when it is a choice between tobacco and food, I bought tobacco with my twopence. Then I went down to the Church Army shelter in the Waterloo Road, where you get a kip, two meals of bread and corned beef and tea and a prayer meeting, for four hours' work at sawing wood.

The next morning I went home, got some money, and went out to Edmonton. I turned up at the Casual Ward about nine at night, not downright drunk but more or less under the influence, thinking this would lead to prison – for it is an offence under the Vagrancy Act for a tramp to come drunk to the Casual Ward. The porter, however, treated me with great consideration, evidently feeling that a tramp with money enough to buy drink ought to be respected. During the next few days I made several more attempts to get into trouble by begging under the noses of the police, but I seemed to bear a charmed life – no one took any notice of me. So, as I did not want to do anything serious which might lead to investigations about my identity, etc., I gave it up. The trip, therefore, was more or less a failure, but I have recorded it as a fairly interesting experience.

Written August 1932

The Road to Wigan Pier Diary

31 January–25 March 1936

[This is a typescript diary found among Orwell's papers which, with other notes, formed the basis for *The Road to Wigan Pier*.]

31 January
To Coventry by train as arranged, arriving about 4 p.m. Bed and Breakfast house, very lousy, 3/6d. Framed certificate in hall setting forth that (John Smith) has been elected to the rank of Primo Buffo. Two beds in room – charge for room to yourself 5/–. Smell as in common lodging-houses. Half-witted servant girl with huge body, tiny head and rolls of fat at back of neck curiously recalling ham-fat.

1 February
Lousy breakfast with Yorkshire commercial traveller. Walked 12 miles to outskirts of Birmingham, took bus to Bull Ring (very like Norwich Market) and arrived 1 p.m. Lunch in Birmingham and bus to Stourbridge. Walked 4–5 miles to Clent Youth Hostel. Red soil everywhere. Birds courting a little, cock chaffinches and bullfinches very bright and cock partridge making mating call. Except for village of Meriden, hardly a decent house between Coventry and Birmingham. West of Birmingham the usual villa-civilization creeping out over the hills. Raining all day, on and off.

Distance walked, 16 miles. Spent on conveyances, 1/4d. On food, 2/3d.

2 February
Comfortable night in hostel, which I had to myself. One-storey wooden building with huge coke stove which kept it very hot. You pay 1/– for bed, 2d for the stove and put pennies in the gas for cooking. Bread, milk, etc. on sale at hostel. You have to have your own sleeping bag but get blankets, mattress and pillows. Tiring evening because the warden's son, I suppose out of kindness, came across and played ping-pong with me till I could hardly stand on my feet. In the morning long talk with the warden who keeps poultry and collects glass and pewter. He told me how in France in 1918, on the heels of the retreating Germans, he looted some priceless glass which was discovered and looted from him in turn by his divisional general. Also showed me some nice pieces of pewter and some very curious Japanese pictures, showing clear traces of European influence, looted by his father in some naval expedition about 1860.

Left 10 a.m., walked to Stourbridge, took bus to Wolverhampton, wandered about slummy parts of Wolverhampton for a while, then had lunch and walked 10 miles to Penkridge. Wolverhampton seems frightful place. Everywhere vistas of mean little houses still enveloped in drifting smoke, though this was Sunday, and along the railway line huge banks of clay and conical chimneys ('pot-banks'). Walk from W'ton to Penkridge very dull and raining all the way. Villa-civilization stretches almost unbroken between the two towns. In Penkridge about 4.30 halted for cup of tea. A tiny frowzy parlour with a nice fire, a little wizened oldish man and an enormous woman about 45, with tow-coloured bobbed hair and no front teeth. Both of them thought me a hero to be walking on such a day. Had tea with them en famille. About 5.15 left and walked another couple of miles, then caught bus the remaining 4 miles to Stafford. Went to Temperance Hotel thinking this would be cheap, but bed and breakfast 5/–. The usual dreadful room and twill sheets greyish and smelly as usual. Went to bathroom and found commercial traveller developing snapshots in bath. Persuaded him to remove them and had bath, after which I find myself very footsore.

Distance walked, about 16 miles. Spent on conveyances, 1/5d. On food, 2/8½d.

3 February
Left 9 a.m. and took bus to Hanley. Walked round Hanley and part of Burslem. Frightfully cold, bitter wind, and it had been snowing in the night; blackened snow lying about everywhere. Hanley and Burslem about the most dreadful places I have seen. Labyrinths of tiny blackened houses and among them the pot-banks like monstrous burgundy bottles half buried in the soil, belching forth smoke. Signs of poverty everywhere and very poor shops. In places enormous chasms delved out, one of them about 200 yards wide and about as deep, with rusty iron trucks on a chain railway crawling up one side, and here and there on the almost perpendicular face of the other, a few workmen hanging like samphire-gatherers, cutting into the face with their picks apparently aimlessly, but I suppose digging out clay. Walked on to Endon and lunch at pub there. Frightfully cold. Hilly country, splendid views, especially when one gets further east and hedges give way to stone walls. Lambs here seem much more backward than down south. Walked on to Rudyard Lake.

Rudyard Lake (really a reservoir, supplying the pottery towns) very depressing. In the summer it is a pleasure resort. Cafés, house-boats and pleasure-boats every ten yards, all deserted and flyblown, this being the off-season. Notices relating to fishing, but I examined the water and it did not look to me as though it had any fish in it. Not a soul anywhere and bitter wind blowing. All the broken ice had been blown up to the south end, and the waves were rocking it up and down, making a clank-clank, clank-clank – the most melancholy noise I ever heard. (Mem. to use in novel some time and to have an empty Craven A packet bobbing up and down among the ice.)

Found hostel, about 1 mile further on, with difficulty. Alone again. A most peculiar place this time. A great draughty barrack of a house, built in the sham-castle style – somebody's Folly – about 1860. All but three or four of the rooms quite empty. Miles of echoing stone passages, no lighting except candles and only smoky little oilstoves to cook on. Terribly cold.

Only 2/8d left, so tomorrow must go into Manchester (walk to Macclesfield, then bus) and cash cheque.

Distance walked, 12 miles. Spent on conveyances 1/8d. On food, 2/8½d.

4 February

Got out of bed so cold that I could not do up any buttons and had to [go] down and thaw my hands before I could dress. Left about 10.30 a.m. A marvellous morning. Earth frozen hard as iron, not a breath of wind and the sun shining brightly. Not a soul stirring. Rudyard Lake (about 1½ miles long) had frozen over during the night. Wild ducks walking about disconsolately on the ice. The sun coming up and the light slanting along the ice the most wonderful red-gold colour I have ever seen. Spent a long time throwing stones over the ice. A jagged stone skimming across ice makes exactly the same sound as a redshank whistling.

Walked to Macclesfield, 10 or 11 miles, then bus to Manchester. Went and collected letters, then to bank to cash cheque but found they were shut – they shut at 3 p.m. here. Very awkward as I had only 3d in hand. Went to Youth Hostel headquarters and asked them to cash cheque, but they refused, then to Police Station to ask them to introduce me to a solicitor who would cash a cheque, but they also refused. Frightfully cold. Streets encrusted with mounds of dreadful black stuff which was really snow frozen hard and blackened by smoke. Did not want to spend night in streets. Found my way to poor quarter (Chester Street), went to pawnshop and tried to pawn raincoat but they said they did not take them any longer. Then it occurred to me my scarf was pawnable, and they gave me 1/11d on it. Went to common lodging-house, of which there were three close together in Chester Street.

Long letter from Rees advising me about people to go and see, one of them, luckily, in Manchester.

Distance walked, about 13 miles. Spent on conveyances, 2/–. On food, 10d.

5 February

Went and tried to see Meade but he was out. Spent day in common lodging-house. Much as in London. 11d for bed, cubicles not dormitories. The 'deputy' a cripple as they seem so often to be. Dreadful method here of making tea in tin bowls. Cashed cheque in morning but shall stay tonight in lodging-house and go and see Meade tomorrow.

6–10 February
Staying with the Meades at 49 Brynton Rd, Longsight, Manchester. Brynton Rd is in one of the new building estates. Very decent houses with bathrooms and electric light, rent I suppose about 12/– or 14/–. Meade is some kind of Trade Union Official and has something to do with the editing of *Labour's Northern Voice* – these are the people who do the publishing side of the *Adelphi*. The Ms have been very decent to me. Both are working-class people, speak with Lancashire accents and have worn the clogs in their childhood, but the atmosphere in a place like this is entirely middle-class. Both the Ms were faintly scandalized to hear I had been in the common lodging-house in Manchester. I am struck again by the fact that as soon as a working man gets an official post in the Trade Union or goes into Labour politics, he become middle-class whether he will or no, i.e. by fighting against the bourgeoisie he becomes bourgeois. The fact is that you *cannot help* living in the manner appropriate and developing the ideology appropriate to your income (in M's case I suppose about £4 a week). The only quarrel I have with the Ms is that they call me 'comrade'. Mrs M, as usual, does not understand much about politics but has adopted her husband's views as a wife ought to; she pronounces the word 'comrade' with manifest discomfort. Am struck by the difference of manners even as far north as this. Mrs M is surprised and not altogether approving when I get up when she enters the room, offer to help with the washing-up, etc. She says, 'Lads up here expect to be waited on.'

M sent me across to Wigan to see Joe Kennan, an electrician who takes a prominent part in the Socialist movement. Kennan also lives in a decent Corporation house (Beech Hill Building Estate) but is more definitely a working man. A very short, stout, powerful man with an extraordinarily gentle, hospitable manner and very anxious to help. His elder child was upstairs in bed (scarlet fever suspected), the younger on the floor playing with soldiers and a toy cannon. Kennan smiles and says, 'You see – and I'm supposed to be a pacifist.' He sent me to the NUWM shelter with a letter to the secretary asking him to find me a lodging in Wigan. The shelter is a dreadful ramshackle little place but a godsend to these unemployed men as it is warm and there are newspapers, etc. there. The secretary, Paddy Grady, an unemployed miner. A tall lean man about 35, intelligent and well-informed and very anxious to help. He is a single man getting 17/– a week and is in a dreadful state physically from years of underfeeding and idleness. His front teeth are almost entirely rotted away. All the men at the NUWM very friendly and anxious to supply me with information as soon as they heard I was a writer and collecting facts about working-class conditions. I cannot get them to treat me precisely as an equal, however. They call me either 'Sir' or 'Comrade'.

11 February
Staying at Warrington Lane, Wigan. Board and lodging 25/– a week. Share room with another lodger (unemployed railwayman), meals in kitchen and wash at scullery sink. Food all right but indigestible and in monstrous quantities. Lancashire method of eating tripe (cold with vinegar) horrible.

The family. Mr H, aged 39, has worked in the pit since he was 13. Now out of work for nine months. A largish, fair, slow-moving, very mild and nice-mannered man who considers carefully before he answers when you ask him a question, and begins, 'In my estimation'. Has not much accent. Ten years ago he got a spurt of coal dust in his left eye and practically lost the sight of it. Was put to work 'on top' for a while but went back to the pit as he could earn more there. Nine months ago his other eye went wrong (there is something called 'nyastygmus' or some such name that miners suffer from) and he can only see a few yards. Is on 'compensation' of 29/– a week, but they are talking of putting him on 'partial compensation' of 14/– a week. It all depends whether the doctor passes him as fit for work, though of course there would not be any work, except perhaps a job 'on top', but there are very few of these. If he is put on partial compensation he can draw the dole until his stamps are exhausted.

Mrs H. Four years older than her husband. Less than 5 feet tall. Toby-jug figure. Merry disposition. Very ignorant – adds up 27 and 10 and makes it 31. Very broad accent. There seem to be 2 ways of dealing with the 'the' here. Before consonants it is often omitted altogether ('Put joog on table', etc.); before vowels it is often incorporated with the word, e.g. 'My sister's in thospital' – th as in thin.

The son 'our Joe', just turned 15 and has been working in the pit a year. At present is on night shift. Goes to work about 9 p.m. returns between 7 and 8 a.m., has breakfast and promptly goes to bed in bed vacated by another lodger. Usually sleeps till 5 or 6 p.m. He started work on 2/8d a day, was raised to 3/4d, i.e. £1 a week. Out of this 1/8d a week comes off for stoppages (insurance, etc.) and 4d a day for his tram fares to and from the pit. So his net wage, working full time, is 16/4d a week. In summer, however, he will only be working short-time. A tallish, frail, deadly pale youth, obviously much exhausted by his work, but seems fairly happy.

Tom, Mrs H's cousin, unmarried and lodging there – paying 25/– a week. A very hairy man with a hare-lip, mild disposition and very simple, Also on night shift.

Joe, another lodger, single. Unemployed on 17/–[1] a week. Pays 6/– a week for his room and sees to his own food. Gets up about 8 to give his bed up to 'our Joe' and remains out of doors, in Public Library, etc. most of day. A bit of an ass but has some education and enjoys a resounding phrase. Explaining why he never married, he says portentously, 'Matrimonial chains is a big item.' Repeated this sentence a number of times, evidently having an affection for it. Has been totally unemployed for 7 years. Drinks when he gets the chance, which of course he never does nowadays.

The house has two rooms and scullery downstairs, 3 rooms upstairs, tiny back yard and outside lavatory. No hot water laid on. Is in bad repair – front wall is bulging. Rent 12/– and with rates 15/–. The total income of the Hs is:

Mr H's compensation	29/– a week.
Joe's wages	16/4d ,,
Tom's weekly payment	25/– ,,
Joe's ditto	6/– ,,
Total	£3–16–4d.

Payment of rent and rates leaves £3–2–4d. This has to feed 4 people and clothe and otherwise provide for 3.[2] Of course at present there is my own contribution

[1] 15/–? [Author's footnote.]
[2] The Hs are well off by local standards. [Author's footnote.]

as well but that is an abnormality.

Wigan in the centre does not seem as bad as it has been represented – distinctly less depressing than Manchester. Wigan Pier said to have been demolished. Clogs commonly worn here and general in the smaller places outside such as Hindley. Shawl over head commonly worn by older women, but girls evidently only do it under pressure of dire poverty. Nearly everyone one sees very badly dressed and youths on the corners markedly less smart and rowdy than in London, but no very obvious signs of poverty except the number of empty shops. One in three of registered workers said to be unemployed.

Last night to Co-op hall with various people from the NUWM to hear Wal Hannington speak. A poor speaker, using all the padding and clichés of the Socialist orator, and with the wrong kind of cockney accent (once again, though a Communist entirely a bourgeois), but he got the people well worked up. Was surprised by the amount of Communist feeling here. Loud cheers when Hannington announced that if England and USSR went to war USSR would win. Audience very rough and all obviously unemployed (about 1 in 10 of them women) but very attentive. After the address a collection taken for expenses – hire of hall and H's train-fare from London. £1–6–0d raised – not bad from about 200 unemployed people.

You can always tell a miner by the blue tattooing of coal dust on the bridge of his nose. Some of the older men have their foreheads veined with it like Roquefort cheese.

12 February

Terribly cold. Long walk along the canal (one-time site of Wigan Pier) towards some slag-heaps in the distance. Frightful landscape of slag-heaps and belching chimneys. Some of the slag-heaps almost like mountains – one just like Stromboli. Bitter wind. They have had to send a steamer to break the ice in front of the coal barges on the canal. The bargemen were muffled to the eyes in sacks. All the 'flashes' (stagnant pools made by the subsidence of disused pits) covered with ice the colour of raw umber. Beards of ice on the lock gates. A few rats running slowly through the snow, very tame, presumably weak with hunger.

13 February

Housing conditions in Wigan terrible. Mrs H tells me that at her brother's house (he is only 25, so I think he must be her half brother, but he has already a child of 8), 11 people, 5 of them adults, belonging to 3 different families, live in 4 rooms, '2 up 2 down'.

All the miners I meet have either had serious accidents themselves or have friends or relatives who have. Mrs H's cousin had his back broken by a fall of rock – 'And he lingered seven year afore he died and it were a-punishing of him all the while' – and her brother-in-law fell 1,200 feet down the shaft of a new pit. Apparently he bounced from side to side, so was presumably dead before he got to the bottom. Mrs H adds: 'They wouldn't never have collected t'pieces only he were wearing a new suit of oilskins.'

15 February

Went with NUWM collectors on their rounds with a view to collecting facts about housing conditions, especially in the caravans. Have made notes on these, q.v. What chiefly struck me was the expression on some of the women's faces, especially those in the more crowded caravans. One woman had a face like a death's head. She had a look of absolutely intolerable misery and degradation. I gathered that she felt as I would feel if I were coated all over with dung. All the people however seemed to take these conditions quite for granted. They have been promised houses over and over again but nothing has come of it and they have got into the way of thinking that a livable house is something absolutely unattainable.

Passing up a horrible squalid side-alley, saw a woman, youngish but very pale and with the usual draggled exhausted look, kneeling by the gutter outside a house and poking a stick up the leaden waste-pipe, which was blocked. I thought how dreadful a destiny it was to be kneeling in the gutter in a back-alley in Wigan, in the bitter cold, prodding a stick up a blocked drain. At that moment she looked up and caught my eye, and her expression was as desolate as I have ever seen; it struck me that she was thinking just the same thing as I was.

Changing lodgings as Mrs H is ill with some mysterious malady and ordered into hospital. They have found lodgings for me at Darlington Rd, over a tripe shop where they take in lodgers. The husband an ex-miner (age 58), the wife ill with a weak heart, in bed on sofa in kitchen. Social atmosphere much as at the Hs but house appreciably dirtier and very smelly. A number of other lodgers. An old ex-miner, age about 75, on old age pension plus half a crown weekly from parish (12/6d in all). Another, said to be of superior type and 'come down in the world', more or less bedridden. An Irish ex-miner who had [a] shoulder blade and several ribs crushed by a fall of stone a few years ago and lives on disability pension of about 25/– a week. Of distinctly superior type and started off as a clerk but went 'down pit' because he was big and strong and could earn more as a miner (this was before the war). Also some newspaper canvassers. Two for *John Bull*, [1] distinctly motheaten, ages about 40 and 55, one quite young and was for four years in rubber firm in Calcutta. Cannot quite make this lad out. He puts on [a] Lancashire accent when talking to the others (he belongs locally) but to me talks in the usual 'educated' accent. The family apart from the Fs themselves consists of a fat son who is at work somewhere and lives nearby, his wife Maggie who is in the shop nearly all day, their two kids, and Annie, fiancée of the other son who is in London. Also a daughter in Canada (Mrs F says 'at Canada'). Maggie and Annie do practically the whole work of the house and shop. Annie very thin, overworked (she also works in a dress-sewing place) and obviously unhappy. I gather that the marriage is by no means certain to take place but that Mrs F treats Annie as a relative all the same and that Annie groans under her tyranny. Number of rooms in the house exclusive of shop premises, 5 or 6 and a bathroom–WC. Nine people sleeping here. Three in my room besides myself.

Struck by the astonishing ignorance about and wastefulness of food among the working class people here – more even than in the south, I think. One morning when washing in the Hs' scullery made an inventory of the following food: A piece of bacon about 5 pounds. About 2 pounds of shin beef. About a pound and a half of liver (all of these uncooked). The wreck of a monstrous meat pie (Mrs H when making a pie always made it in an enamelled *basin* such as is used for washing up in. Ditto with puddings). A dish containing 15 or 20 eggs. A number of small cakes. A flat fruit pie and a 'cake-a-pie' (pastry with

[1] A popular weekly paper containing topical articles of a sensational nature and with competitions offering large prizes.

currants in it). Various fragments of earlier pies. 6 large loaves and 12 small ones (I had seen Mrs H cook these the night before). Various odds and ends of butter, tomatoes, opened tins of milk, etc. There was also more food keeping warm in the oven in the kitchen. Everything except bread habitually left about uncovered and shelves filthy. Food here consists almost entirely of bread and starch. A typical day's meals at the Hs. Breakfast (about 8 a.m.): two fried eggs and bacon, bread (no butter) and tea. Dinner (about 12.30 p.m.): a monstrous plate of stewed beef, dumplings and boiled potatoes (equal to about 3 Lyons portions) and a big helping of rice pudding or suet pudding. Tea (about 5 p.m.): plate of cold meat, bread and butter, sweet pastries and tea. Supper (about 11 p.m.): fish and chips, bread and butter and tea.

16 February

Great excitement because a couple who stayed here for a month about Xmas have been arrested (at Preston) as coiners and it is believed they were making their false coins while here. The police inspector here for about an hour asking questions. Mrs F tells of snooping round their room while they were out and finding a lump of something like solder under the mattress and some little pots like egg-cups only larger. Mrs F agreed instantly to everything the police inspector suggested, and when he was upstairs searching the room I made two suggestions and she agreed to those too. I could see she had made up her mind they were guilty on hearing they were unmarried. When the inspector had written out her statement it came out that she could not read or write (except her signature), though her husband can read a little.

One of the canvassers' beds is jammed across the foot of mine. Impossible to stretch my legs out straight as if I do so my feet are in the small of his back. It seems a long time since I slept between linen sheets. Twill sheets even at the Ms. Theirs (the Ms') was the only house I have been in since leaving London that did not smell.

17 February

The newspaper-canvassers are rather pathetic. Of course it is a quite desperate job. I fancy what *John Bull* do is to take on people who make frantic efforts and work up a little more or less spurious business for a while, then sack them and take on more, and so on. I should judge these men each make £2 or £3 a week. Both have families and one is a grandfather. They are so hard up that they cannot pay for full board but pay something for their rooms and have a squalid little cupboard of food in the kitchen, from which they take out bread, packets of marg, etc. and cook themselves meals in a shamefaced manner. They are allocated so many houses each day and have to knock at every door and book a minimum number of orders. They are at present working some swindle on behalf of *John Bull* by which you get a 'free' tea set by sending two shillings worth of stamps and twenty four coupons. As soon as they have had their food they start filling up blank forms for the next day, and presently the older one falls asleep in his chair and begins snoring loudly.

Am struck, though, by their knowledge of working-class conditions. They can tell you all about housing, rents, rates, state of trade, etc. in every town in the north of England.

18 February

In the early morning the mill girls clumping down the cobbled street, all in clogs, make a curiously formidable sound, like an army hurrying into battle. I suppose this is the typical sound of Lancashire. And the typical imprint in the mud the outline of a clog-iron, like one half of a cow's hoof. Clogs are very cheap. They cost about 5/– a pair and need not wear out for years because all they need is new irons costing a few pence.

As always and everywhere, the dress peculiar to the locality is considered plebeian. A very down in the mouth respectable woman, at one of the houses I visited with the NUWM collectors, said: 'I've always kept myself decent-like. I've never worn a shawl over my head – I wouldn't be seen in such a thing. I've worn a hat since I was a girl. But it don't do you much good. At Christmas time we was that hard put to it that I thought I'd go up and try for a well-wisher. (Hamper given away by some charitable organization.) When I got up there the clergyman says to me, "*You* don't want no well-wisher," he says. "There's plenty worse than you. We knows many a one that's living on bread and jam," he says. "And how do you know what *we're* living on?' I says. He says, "You can't be so bad if you can dress as well as that," he says – meaning my hat. I didn't get no well-wisher. If I'd ha' gone up with a shawl over my head I'd ha' got it. That's what you get for keeping yourself respectable.'

19 February

When a 'dirt-heap' sinks, as it does ultimately, it leaves a hummocky surface which is made more so by the fact that in times of strikes the miners dig into some of these places in search of small coals. One which is used as a playground looks like a choppy sea suddenly frozen. It is called locally 'the flock mattress'. The soil over them is grey and cindery and only an evil-looking brownish grass grows on them.

This evening to a social the NUWM had got up in aid of Thaelmann's[1] defence-fund. Admission and refreshments (cup of tea and meat pie) 6d. About 200 people, preponderantly women, largely members of the Co-op, in one of whose rooms it was held, and I suppose for the most part living directly or indirectly on the dole. Round the back a few aged miners sitting looking on benevolently, a lot of very young girls in front. Some dancing to the concertina (many of the girls confessed that they could not dance, which struck me as rather pathetic) and some excruciating singing. I suppose these people represented a fair cross-section of the more revolutionary element in Wigan. If so, God help us. Exactly the same sheeplike crowd – gaping girls and shapeless middle-aged women dozing over their knitting – that you see everywhere else. There is no *turbulence* left in England. One good song, however, by an old woman, I think a cockney, who draws the old age pension and makes a bit by singing at pubs, with the refrain:

For you can't do that there 'ere,
No, you can't do that there 'ere;
Anywhere else you can do that there,
But you can't do that there 'ere.

20 February

This afternoon with Paddy Grady to see the unemployed miners robbing the

[1] Ernst Thaelmann (1886–1944), a transport worker who became Chairman of the German Communist Party from 1925 onwards. A member of the Reichstag 1924–33, he ran for Presidency in 1932 against Hindenburg and polled five million votes. Arrested in 1933, the date for his trial was postponed several times and in October 1936 Berlin announced that he would be detained for life without one. Officially reported killed in an air raid, he was shot by the Nazis in August 1944 at Buchenwald.

'dirt-train', or, as they call it, 'scrambling for the coal'. A most astonishing sight. We went by the usual frightful routes along the colliery railway line to Fir Tree Sidings, on our way meeting various men and women with sacks of stolen coal which they had slung over bicycles. I would like to know where they got these bicycles – perhaps made of odd parts picked off rubbish dumps. None had mudguards, few had saddles and some had not even tyres. When we got to the big dirt-heap where the trainloads of shale from that pit are discharged, we found about 50 men picking over the dirt, and they directed us to the place further up the line where the men board the train. When we got there we found not less than 100 men, a few boys, waiting, each with a sack and coal hammer strapped under his coat tails. Presently the train hove in sight, coming round the bend at about 20 mph. 50 or 70 men rushed for it, seized hold of the bumpers, etc. and hoisted themselves onto the the trucks. It appears that each truck is regarded as the property of the men who have succeeded in getting onto it while it is moving. The engine ran the trucks up onto the dirt-heap, uncoupled them and came back for the remaining trucks. There was the same wild rush and the second train was boarded in the same manner, only a few men failing to get onto it. As soon as the trucks had been uncoupled the men on top began shovelling the stuff out to their women and other supporters below, who rapidly sorted out the dirt and put all the coal (a considerable amount but all small, in lumps about the size of eggs) into their sacks. Further down the 'broo' were the people who had failed to get onto either train and were collecting the tiny fragments of coal that came sliding down from above. You do not, of course, when you are boarding the train, know whether you are getting onto a good truck or not, and what kind of truck you get is entirely luck. Thus some of the trucks, instead of being loaded with the dirt from the floor of the mine, which of course contains a fair quantity of coal, were loaded entirely with shale. But it appears, what I had never heard of before, that among the shale, at any rate in some mines, there occurs an inflammable rock called 'cannel' (not certain of spelling) which makes fairly good fuel. It is not commercially valuable because it is hard to work and burns too fast, but for ordinary purposes is good enough. Those who were on the shale trucks were picking out the 'cannel', which is almost exactly like the shale except that it is a little darker and is known by splitting horizontally, almost like slate. I watched the people working until they had almost emptied the trucks. There were twenty trucks and something over 100 people were at work on them. Each, so far as I could judge, got about ½ cwt of either coal or 'cannel'. This performance sometimes happens more than once a day when several dirt-trains are sent out, so it is evident that several tons of fuel are stolen every day.

The economics and ethics of the whole business are rather interesting. In the first place, robbing the dirt-train is of course illegal, and one is technically trespassing by being on the dirt-heap at all. Periodically people are prosecuted – in fact in this morning's *Examiner* there was a report of 3 men being fined for it. But no notice is taken of the prosecutions, and in fact one of the men fined was there this afternoon. But at the same time the coal company have no intention of using the coal, etc. that is thrown out among the dirt, because it would not repay the cost of sorting. If not stolen, therefore, it would be wasted. Moreover, this business saves the company the expense of emptying the trucks, because by the time the coal-pickers have done with them they are empty. Therefore they connive at the raiding of the train – I noticed that the engine-driver took no notice of the men clambering onto the trucks. The reason for the periodical prosecutions is said to be that there are so many accidents. Only recently a man slipped under the train and had both legs cut off. Considering the speed the train goes at, it is remarkable that accidents do not happen oftener.

The most curious vehicle I saw used for carrying away coal was a cart made of a packing case and the wheels from two kitchen mangles.

Some of this coal that is stolen is said to be on sale in the town at 1/6d a bag.

21 February

The squalor of this house is beginning to get on my nerves. Nothing is ever cleaned or dusted, the rooms not done out till 5 in the afternoon, and the cloth never even removed from the kitchen table. At supper you still see the crumbs from breakfast. The most revolting feature is Mrs F being always in bed on the kitchen sofa. She has a terrible habit of tearing off strips of newspaper, wiping her mouth with them and then throwing them onto the floor. Unemptied chamberpot under the table at breakfast this morning. The food is dreadful, too. We are given those little twopenny ready-made steak and kidney pies out of stock. I hear horrible stories, too, about the cellars where the tripe is kept and which are said to swarm with black beetles. Apparently they only get in fresh supplies of tripe at long intervals. Mrs F dates events by this. 'Let me see, now. I've had in three lots of froze (frozen tripe) since then,' etc. I judge they get in a consignment of 'froze' about once in a fortnight. Also it is very tiring being unable to stretch my legs straight out at night.

24 February

Yesterday went down Crippen's mine with Jerry Kennan, another electrician friend of his, two small sons of the latter, two other electricians and an engineer belonging to the pit, who showed us round. The depth to the cage bottom was 300 yards. We went down at 10.30 and came up at 1.30, having covered, according to the engineer who showed us round, about 2 miles.

As the cage goes down you have the usual momentary qualm in your belly, then a curious stuffed-up feeling in your ears. In the middle of its run the cage works up a tremendous speed (in some of the deeper mines they are said to touch 60 mph or more) then slows down so abruptly that it is difficult to believe you are not going upwards again. The cages are tiny – about 8 feet long by 3½ wide by 6 high. They are supposed to hold 10 men or (I think) about a ton and a half of coal. There were only six of us and two boys, but we had difficulty in packing in and it is important to face in the direction you are going to get out the other end.

Down below it was lighter than I expected, because apart from the lamps we all carried there were electric lights in the main roads. But what I had not expected, and what for me was the most important feature all through, was the lowness of the roof. I had vaguely imagined wandering about in places rather like the tunnels of the Underground; but as a matter of fact there were very few places where you could stand upright. In general the roof was about 4 ft or 4 ft 6 ins high, sometimes much lower, with every now and again a beam larger than the others under which you had to duck especially low. In places the walls were quite neatly built up, almost like the stone walls in Derbyshire, with slabs of shale. There were pit-props, almost all of wood, every yard or so overhead. They are made of small larch trees sawn to the appropriate length (from the quantity used I see now why people laying down plantations almost always plant larch) and are simply laid on the ends of the upright props, which are laid on slabs of wood, and not fixed in any way. The bottom slabs gradually sink into the floor, or, as the miners put it, 'the floor comes up', but the weight overhead keeps the whole thing in place. By the way the steel girders used here and there instead of wooden props had buckled, you got an idea of the weight of the roof. Underfoot is thick stone dust and the rails, about 2½ ft wide, for the trolleys. When the path is downhill miners often slide down these on their clogs, which, being hollow underneath, more or less fit onto the rails.

After a few hundred yards of walking doubled up and once or twice having to crawl, I began to feel the effects in a violent pain all down my thighs. One also gets a bad crick in the neck, because though stooping one has to look up for fear of knocking into the beams, but the pain in the thighs is the worst. Of course as we got nearer the coal face the roads tended to get lower. Once we crawled through a temporary tunnel which was like an enlarged rat hole, with no props, and in one place there had been a fall of stone during the night – 3 or 4 tons[1] of the stuff, I should judge. It had blocked up the entire road except for a tiny aperture near the roof which we had to crawl through without touching any timber. Presently I had to stop for a minute to rest my knees, which were giving way, and then after a few hundred yards more we came to the first working. This was only a small working with a machine worked by two men, much like an enlarged version of the electric drills used for street mending. Nearby was the dynamo (or whatever it is called) which supplied the power through cables to this and the other machines; also the comparatively small drills (but they weigh 50 lbs each and have to be hoisted onto the shoulder) for drilling holes for blasting charges; also bundles of miners' tools locked together on wires like bundles of keys, which is always done for fear of losing them.

We went a few hundred yards further and came to one of the main workings. The men were not actually working here, but a shift was just coming down to start work about 250 yards further on. Here there was one of the larger machines which have a crew of 5 men to work them. This machine has a revolving wheel on which there are teeth about a couple of inches long set at various angles; in principle it is rather like an immensely thickened circular saw with the teeth much further apart, and running horizontally instead of vertically. The machine is dragged into position by the crew and the front part of it can be swivelled round in any direction and pressed against the coal face by the man working it. Two men called 'scufters' shovel the coal onto a rubber-belt conveyor which carries it through a tunnel to the tubs on the main road, where it is hauled by steam haulage to the cages. I had not realized before that the men operating the coal-cutter are working in a place rather less than a yard high. When we crawled in under the roof to the coal face we could at best kneel, and then not kneel upright, and I fancy the men must do most of their work lying on their bellies. The heat also was frightful – round about 100 degrees F so far as I could judge. The crew keep burrowing into the coal face, cutting a semi-circular track, periodically hauling the machine forward and propping as they go. I was puzzled to know how that monstrous machine – flat in shape, of course, but 6 or 8 feet long and weighing several tons, and only fitted with skids, not wheels – could have

[1] Jerry Kennan said 20 or 30. I don't know which of us would be best judge. [Author's footnote.]

been got into position through that mile or so of passages. Even to drag the thing forward as the seam advances must be a frightful labour, seeing that the men have to do it practically lying down. Up near the coal face we saw a number of mice, which are said to abound there. They are said to be commonest in pits where there are or have been horses. I don't know how they get down into the mine in the first place. Probably in the cages, but possibly by falling down the shaft, as it is said that a mouse (owing to its surface area being large relative to its weight) can drop any distance uninjured.

On the way back my exhaustion grew so great that I could hardly keep going at all, and towards the end I had to stop and rest every fifty yards. The periodical effort of bending and raising oneself at each successive beam was fearful, and the relief when one could stand upright, usually owing to a hole in the roof, was enormous. At times my knees simply refused to lift me after I had knelt down. It was made worse by the fact that at the lowest parts the roof is usually on a slope, so that besides bending you have to walk more or less sideways. We were all pretty distressed except the engineer taking us round, who was used to it, and the two small boys, who did not have to bend to any extent; but I was by a good deal the worst, being the tallest. I would like to know whether any miners are as tall as I am, and if so, whether they suffer for it. The few miners whom we met down the pit could move with extraordinary agility, running about on all fours among the props almost like dogs.

After we had at last emerged and washed off the more obtrusive dirt and had some beer, I went home and had dinner and then soaked myself for a long time in a hot bath. I was surprised at the quantity of dirt and the difficulty of getting it off. It had penetrated to every inch of my body in spite of my overalls and my clothes underneath those. Of course very few miners have baths in their homes – only a tub of water in front of the kitchen fire. I should say it would be quite impossible to keep clean without a proper bathtub.

In the room where we changed our clothes there were several cages of canaries. These have to be kept there by law, to test the air in cases of explosion. They are sent down in the cage, and, if they do not faint, the air is all right.

The Davy lamps give out a fair amount of light. There is an air intake at the top but the flame is cut off from this by a fine gauze. Flame cannot pass through holes of less than a certain diameter. The gauze therefore lets the air in to sustain the flame but will not let the flame out to explode dangerous gases. Each lamp when full will burn for 8–12 hours, and they are locked, so that if they go out down the pit they cannot be relighted. Miners are searched for matches before going down the pit.

27 February

On Wednesday (25th) went over to Liverpool to see the Deiners and Garrett. I was to have come back the same night, but almost as soon as I got to Liverpool I felt unwell and was ignominiously sick, so the Deiners insisted on putting me to bed and then on my staying the night. I came back yesterday evening.

I was very greatly impressed by Garrett. Had I known before that it is he who writes under the pseudonym of Matt Low in the *Adelphi* and one or two other places, I would have taken steps to meet him earlier. He is a biggish hefty chap of about 36, Liverpool-Irish, brought up as a Catholic but now a Communist. He says he has had about 9 months' work in (I think) about the last 6 years. He went to sea as a lad and was at sea about 10 years, then worked as a docker. During the war he was torpedoed on a ship that sank in 7 minutes, but they had expected to be torpedoed and had got their boats ready, and were all saved except the wireless operator, who refused to leave his post until he had got an answer. He also worked in an illicit brewery in Chicago during Prohibition, saw various hold-ups, saw Battling Siki immediately after he had been shot in a street brawl, etc., etc. All this however interests him much less than Communist politics. I urged him to write his autobiography, but as usual, living in about 2 rooms on the dole with a wife (who I gather objects to his writing) and a number of kids, he finds it impossible to settle to any long work and can only do short stories. Apart from the enormous unemployment in Liverpool it is almost impossible for him to get work because he is blacklisted everywhere as a Communist.

He took me down to the docks to see dockers being taken on for an unloading job. When we got there we found about 200 men waiting in a ring and police holding them back. It appeared that there was a fruit ship which needed unloading and, on the news that there were jobs going, there had been a fight between the dockers which the police had to intervene to stop. After a while the agent of the company (known as the stevedore, I think) emerged from a shed and began calling out the names or rather numbers of gangs whom he had engaged earlier in the day. Then he needed about 10 men more, and walked round the ring picking out a man here and there. He would pause, select a man, take him by the shoulder and haul him forward, exactly as at a sale of cattle. Presently he announced that that was all. A sort of groan went up from the remaining dockers, and they trailed off, about 50 men having been engaged out of 200. It appears that unemployed dockers have to sign on twice a day, otherwise they are presumed to have been working (as their work is mainly casual labour, by the day) and their dole docked for that day.

I was impressed by the fact that Liverpool is doing much more in the way of slum-clearance than most towns. The slums are still very bad but there are great quantities of Corporation houses and flats at low rents. Just outside Liverpool there are quite considerable towns consisting entirely of Corporation houses, which are really quite livable and decent to look at, but having as usual the objection that they take people a long way from their work. In the centre of the town there are huge blocks of workers' flats imitated from those in Vienna. They are built in the form of an immense ring, five storeys high, round a central courtyard about 60 yards across, which forms a playground for children. Round the inner side run balconies, and there are wide windows on each side so that everyone gets some sunlight. I was not able to get inside any of these flats, but I gather each has either 2 or 3 rooms,[1] kitchenette and bathroom with hot water. The rents vary from about 7/– at the top to 10/– at the bottom. (No lifts, of course.) It is noteworthy that the people in Liverpool have got used to the idea of flats (or tenements, as they call them) whereas in a place like Wigan the people, though realizing that flats solve the problem of letting people live near their work, all say they would rather have a house of their own, however bad it was.

There are one or two interesting points here. The re-housing is almost entirely the work of the Corporation, which is said to be entirely ruthless towards private ownership and to be even too ready to condemn slum houses

[1] Presumably 3 – living room and 2 bedrooms. [Author's footnote.]

without compensation. Here therefore you have what is in effect Socialist legislation, though it is done by a local authority. But the Corporation of Liverpool is almost entirely Conservative. Moreover, though the re-housing from the public funds is, as I say, in effect a Socialist measure, the actual work is done by private contractors, and one may assume that here as elsewhere the contractors tend to be the friends, brothers, nephews, etc. of those on the Corporation. Beyond a certain point therefore Socialism and Capitalism are not easy to distinguish, the State and the capitalist tending to merge into one. On the other side of the river, the Birkenhead side (we went through the Mersey tunnel) you have Port Sunlight, a city within a city, all built and owned by the Leverhulme soap works. Here again are excellent houses at fairly low rents, but, as with publicly-owned property, burdened by restrictions. Looking at the Corporation buildings on the one side, and Lord Leverhulme's buildings on the other, you would find it hard to say which was which.

Another point is this. Liverpool is practically governed by Roman Catholics. The Roman Catholic ideal, at any rate as put forward by the Chesterton-Beachcomber[1] type of writer, is always in favour of private ownership and against Socialist legislation and 'progress' generally. The Chesterton type of writer wants to see a free peasant or other small-owner living in his own privately owned and probably insanitary cottage; not a wage-slave living in an excellently appointed Corporation flat and tied down by restrictions as to sanitation, etc. The RCs in Liverpool, therefore, are going against the supposed implications of their own religion. But I suppose that if the Chestertons *et hoc genus* grasped that it is possible for the RCs to capture the machinery of local and other government, even when it is called Socialist, they would change their tune.

No clogs or shawl over head in Liverpool. Returning by car, notices how abruptly this custom stops a little west of Wigan.[2]

Am trying to arrange to return to London by sea if G can get me a passage on a cargo boat.

Bought two brass candlesticks and a ship in a bottle. Paid 9/– for the candlesticks. G considered I was swindled but they are quite nice brass.

2 March

At Wallace Road, Sheffield. Thick snow everywhere on the hills as I came along. Stone boundaries between the fields running across the snow like black piping across a white dress. Warm and sunny, however. For the first time in my life saw rooks copulating. On the ground, not in a tree. The manner of courtship was peculiar. The female stood with her beak open and the male walked round her and it appeared as though he was feeding her.

Memories of Wigan: slag-heaps like mountains, smoke, rows of blackened houses, sticky mud criss-crossed by imprints of clogs, heavy-set young women standing at street corners with their babies wrapped in their shawls, immense piles of broken chocolate in cut-price confectioners' windows.

[1] 'Beachcomber', a column in the *Daily Express*, started in 1924 by J. B. Morton, a Roman Catholic. Throughout his journalism Orwell makes pejorative references to it.

[2] It is said by everyone in Wigan that clogs are going out. Yet in the poorer quarters 1 person in 2 seems to me to wear clogs, and there are (I think) 10 shops which sell nothing else. [Author's footnote.]

3 March

This house: two up two down, living-room about 14′ by 12′, parlour rather smaller. Sink and copper in living-room, no gas fire, outside WC. Rent with rates about 8/6d. 2 cellars as well. Husband is out of work (P.A.C.[1] – was previously store-keeper at a factory which closed down and discharged its whole staff), wife works as a char at 6d an hour. One kid aged 5.

B: age 45 but looks less. Has malformed right hand, also one foot. This was inherited and he fears it is transmissible, so will not marry. Owing to this has never had much in the way of regular work. Was with a circus for some years as groom, clown and 'Wild West' rider – he could apparently handle the bridle with his damaged hand. Now lives alone and for some reason gets no dole, only something from the parish and help from his brother. Has a single room with only an open fireplace – no oven – to cook on. Is terribly embittered and declares that feeling of actual hatred for the bourgeoisie, even personal hatred of individuals, is necessary to any genuine Socialist. Is nevertheless a good fellow and very anxious to help. Mixed up with his political feelings is the usual local patriotism of the Yorkshireman and much of his conversation consists of comparison between London and Sheffield to the detriment of the former. Sheffield is held to lead London in everything, e.g. on the one hand the new housing schemes in Sheffield are immensely superior, and on the other hand the Sheffield slums are more squalid than anything London can show. I notice that apart from the usual hatred between the Northerner and the Southerner, there is also hatred between the Yorkshireman and the Lancashireman, and also internecine hatred between the various Yorkshire towns. No one up here seems to have heard of any place in the south of England except London. If you come from the south you are assumed to be a cockney however often you deny it. At the same time as the Northerner despises the Southerner he has an uneasy feeling that the latter knows more of the arts of life and is very anxious to impress him.

Had a very long and exhausting day (I am now continuing this March 4th) being shown every quarter of Sheffield on foot and by tram. I have now traversed almost the whole city. It seems to me, by daylight, one of the most appalling places I have ever seen. In whichever direction you look you see the same landscape of monstrous chimneys pouring forth smoke which is sometimes black and sometimes of a rosy tint said to be due to sulphur. You can smell the sulphur in the air all the while. All buildings are blackened within a year or two of being put up. Halting at one place I counted the factory chimneys I could see and there were 33. But it was very misty as well as smoky – there would have been many more visible on a clear day. I doubt whether there are any architecturally decent buildings in the town. The town is very hilly (said to be built on seven hills, like Rome) and everywhere streets of mean little houses blackened by smoke run up at sharp angles, paved with cobbles which are purposely set unevenly to give horses, etc. a grip. At night the hilliness creates fine effects because you look across from one hillside to the other and see the lamps twinkling like stars. Huge jets of flame shoot periodically out of the roofs of the foundries (many working night shifts at present) and show a splendid rosy colour through the smoke and steam. When you get a glimpse inside you see enormous fiery serpents of red-hot and white-

[1] Drawing the dole from the Public Assistance Committee of the local authority.

hot (really lemon-coloured) iron being rolled out into rails. In the central slummy part of the town are the small workshops of the 'little bosses', i.e. smaller employers who are making chiefly cutlery. I don't think I ever in my life saw so many broken windows. Some of these workshops have hardly a pane of glass in their windows and you would not believe they were inhabitable if you did not see the employees, mostly girls, at work inside.

The town is being torn down and rebuilt at an immense speed. Everywhere among the slums are gaps with squalid mounds of bricks where condemned houses have been demolished and on all the outskirts of the town new estates of Corporation houses are going up. These are much inferior, at any rate in appearance, to those at Liverpool. They are in terribly bleak situations, too. One estate just behind where I am living now, at the very summit of a hill, on horrible sticky clay soil and swept by icy winds. Notice that the people going into these new houses from the slums will always be paying higher rents, and also will have to spend much more on fuel to keep themselves warm. Also, in many cases, will be further from their work and therefore spend more on conveyances.

In the evening was taken to a Methodist Church where some kind of men's association (they call it a Brotherhood) meet once a week to listen to a lecture and have discussions. Next week a Communist is speaking, to the evident dismay of the clergyman who made the announcements. This week a clergyman who spoke on 'Clean and Dirty Water'. His lecture consisted of incredibly silly and disconnected ramblings about Shaw's *Adventures of a Black Girl*, etc. Most of the audience did not understand a word of it and in fact hardly listened, and the talk and the questions afterwards were so unbearable that B and I slipped out with his friend Binns to see the latter's back to back house, on which I took notes. B says that most of the members of this Brotherhood are unemployed men who will put up with almost anything in order to have a warm place where they can sit for a few hours.

Accent in Sheffield not so broad as in Lancashire. A very few people, mostly miners I think, wear clogs.

5 March

At 21 Estcourt Avenue, Headingley, Leeds.[1] I left Sheffield at 10.30 this morning, and in spite of its being such a frightful place and of the relief of getting back into a comfortable house, I was quite sorry to leave the Searles. I have seldom met people with more natural decency. They were as kind to me as anyone could possibly be, and I hope and trust they liked me. Of course I got their whole life-history from them by degrees. Searle is 33 and was an only child. When a youth he joined the Army and was in the Ordnance Corps (or whatever it is called) with the army of occupation in Palestine and in Egypt. He has vivid memories of Egypt and wishes he was back there. Since then he has only had short-lived jobs, e.g. as store-keeper and check-weighman at various works, also as railway (outside) porter. Mrs S comes from a somewhat more prosperous family, as her father till only a few weeks ago[2] was in a good job at £5 a week and also made something on the side by making fishing rods. But it was a very large family (11) and she went

[1] The home of Orwell's elder sister, Marjorie, and her husband, Humphrey Dakin.
[2] He died very suddenly and his wife has now no resources except the old age pension. [Author's footnote.]

into service. She married S when he was on the dole, against the opposition of her family. At first they could not get a house, and lived in a single room, in which two children were born and one died. They told me they had only one bed for the family and had to 'lay out' the dead baby in the perambulator. Finally, after frightful difficulty (one reason for this is that private landlords are not too keen on letting to people on the dole and there is a certain amount of bribery of agents) they got this house, of which the rent is about 8/6d. Mrs S earns about 9/– a week from her charing. Exactly what deduction is made for this from S's dole I don't know, but their total income is 32/6d. In spite of which I had great difficulty in getting them to accept enough for my keep while there – they wanted to charge only 6/– for full board and lodging from Monday night to Thursday morning. They keep the house very clean and decent, have a bit of garden, though they can't do much with it, as it has factory chimneys on one side and the gas works on the other, besides being poor soil, and are very fond of one another. I was surprised by Mrs S's grasp of the economic situation and also of abstract ideas – quite unlike most working-class women in this, though she is I think not far from illiterate. She does not seem resentful against the people who employ her – indeed she says they are kind to her – but sees quite clearly the essential facts about domestic service. She told me how the other day as she waited at the lunch table she calculated the price of the food on the table (for 5 persons for one meal) and it came to 6/3d – as much as the P.A.C. allows her child for a fortnight.

B was very good and took my request to 'show me over Sheffield' even too seriously, so that from morning to night I was being rushed from place to place, largely on foot, to see public buildings, slums, housing estates, etc. But he is a tiresome person to be with, being definitely disgruntled and too conscious of his Communist convictions. In Rotherham we had to have lunch at a slightly expensive restaurant because there didn't seem to be any others except pubs (B is TT), and when in there he was sweating and groaning about the 'bourgeois atmosphere' and saying he could not eat this kind of food. As he declares that it is necessary to literally hate the bourgeoisie, I wondered what he thought of me, because he told me at the very start I was a bourgeois and remarked on my 'public school twang'. However, I think he was disposed to treat me as a sort of honorary proletarian, partly because I had no objection to washing in the sink, etc. but more because I seemed interested in Sheffield. He was very generous and though I had told him at the start that I was going to pay for his meals, etc. while we were together he would always go out of his way to spare me expense. It seems that he lives on 10/– a week – I had this from Searle: exactly where B's 10/– comes from I don't know – and the rent of his room is 6/–. Of course it would not be possible to subsist on the remainder, allowing for fuel. You could only keep alive on 4/– a week[1] if you spent nothing on fuel and nothing on tobacco or clothes. I gather B gets meals from time to time from the Ss and other friends, also from his brother who is in comparatively good employ. His room is decent and even cultured-looking, as it has bits of 'antique' furniture which he has made himself, and some crude but not disagreeable pictures, mostly of circuses, which he has painted. Much of his bitterness obviously comes from sexual starvation. His deformity handicaps him with women, his fear of trans-

[1] See next page.

mitting it has stopped him from marrying (he says he would only marry a woman past the childbearing age), and his inability to earn money makes it more impossible still. However, at one of the *Adelphi* summer schools he picked up with some school-mistress (aged 43) who I gather is his mistress when opportunities permit and who is willing to marry him, only her parents oppose it. The Searles say he has improved greatly since taking up with this woman – before that he used to have fits occasionally.

We had an argument one evening in the Searles' house because I helped Mrs S with the washing-up. Both of the men disapproved of this, of course. Mrs S seemed doubtful. She said that in the North working-class men never offered any courtesies to women (women are allowed to do all the house-work unaided, even when the man is unemployed, and it is always the man who sits in the comfortable chair), and she took this state of things for granted, but did not see why it should not be changed. She said that she thought the women now-a-days, especially the younger women, would like it if men opened doors for them, etc. The position now-a-days is anomalous. The man is practically always out of work, whereas the woman occasionally is working. Yet the woman continues to do all the housework and the man not a hand's-turn, except carpentering and gardening. Yet I think it is instinctively felt by both sexes that the man would lose his manhood if, merely because he was out of work, he became a 'Mary Ann'.

LIVING ON 4s A WEEK: MAN'S DESCRIPTION OF HOW HE DOES IT. Following the disclosures in the *News of the World* of parents who have to bring up big families on tiny incomes, a correspondent draws our attention to the case of a man who spend less than 4s a week on food.

His week's supply and its cost is as follows:

	s.	d.
3 Wholemeal loaves	1	0
½lb. Margarine		2½
½lb. Dripping		3
1 lb. Cheese		7
1 lb. Onions		1½
1lb. Carrots		1½
1lb. Broken biscuits		4
2lb. Dates		6
1 Tin evaporated milk		5
10 Oranges		5
Total cost	3	11½

The man, Mr W. Leach, of Lilford Road, London, S.E., adds that he would prefer to boil the carrots to eating them raw 'but, of course, to boil the water would cost too much.' *News of the World*, 1 March 1936. Also in *New Statesman and Nation*. [Newspaper cutting kept by Orwell among his notes.]

One particular picture of Sheffield stays by me. A frightful piece of waste ground (somehow, up here a piece of waste ground attains a squalor that would be impossible even in London), trampled quite bare of grass and littered with newspaper, old saucepans, etc. To the right, an isolated row of gaunt four-room houses, dark red, blackened by smoke. To the left an interminable vista of factory chimneys, chimney behind chimney, fading away into a dim blackish haze. Behind me a railway embankment made from the slag of furnaces. In front, across the piece of waste ground, a cubical building of dingy red and yellow brick, with the sign, 'John Grocock, Haulage Contractor'.

Other memories of Sheffield: stone walls blackened by smoke, a shallow river yellow with chemicals, serrated flames, like circular saws, coming out from the cowls of the foundry chimneys, thump and scream of steam hammers (the iron seems to scream under the blow), smell of sulphur, yellow clay, backsides of women wagging laboriously from side to side as they shove their perambulators up the hills. . . .

7 March

Staying till next Wed. with M[arjorie] and H[umphrey] at 21 Estcourt Avenue, Headingley. Conscious all the while of difference in atmosphere between middle-class home even of this kind and working-class home. The essential difference is that here there is *elbow-room*, in spite of there being 5 adults and 3 children, besides animals, at present in the house. The children make peace and quiet difficult, but if you definitely want to be alone you can be so – in a working-class house *never*, either by night or day.

One of the kinds of discomfort inseparable from a working man's life is *waiting about*. If you receive a salary it is paid into your bank and you draw it out when you want it. If you receive *wages*, you have to go and get them in somebody else's time and are probably kept hanging about and probably expected to behave as though being paid your wages at all was a favour. When Mr H at Wigan went to the mine to draw his compensation, he had to go, for some reason I did not understand, on two separate days each week, and was kept waiting in the cold for about an hour before he was paid. In addition the four tram journeys to and from the mine cost him 1/–, reducing his compensation from 29/– weekly to 28/–. He took this for granted, of course. The result of long training in this kind of thing is that whereas the bourgeois goes through life expecting to get what he wants, within limits, the working man always feels himself the slave of a more or less mysterious authority. I was impressed by the fact that when I went to Sheffield Town Hall to ask for certain statistics, both B and Searle – both of them people of much more forcible character than myself – were nervous, would not come into the office with me, and assumed that the Town Clerk would refuse information. They said, 'He might give it to *you*, but he wouldn't to *us*.' Actually the Town Clerk was snooty and I did not get all the information I asked for. But the point was that I assumed my questions would be answered, and the other two assumed the contrary.

It is for this reasons that in countries where the class hierarchy exists, people of the higher class always tend to come to the front in times of stress, though not really more gifted than the others. That they will do so seems to be taken for granted always and everywhere. NB. to look up the passage in Lissagaray's *History of the Commune* describing the shootings after the Commune had been suppressed. They were shooting the ringleaders without trial, and as they did not know who the ringleaders were, they were picking them out on the principle that those of better class than the others would be the ringleaders. One man was shot because he was wearing a watch, another because he 'had an intelligent face'. NB. to look up this passage.

Yesterday with H and M to Haworth Parsonage, home of the Brontës and now a museum. Was chiefly impressed by a pair of Charlotte Brontë's cloth-topped boots, very small, with square toes and lacing up at the sides.

9 March

Yesterday with H and M to their cottage at Middlesmoor, high up on the edge of the moors. Perhaps it is only the time of year, but even up there, miles from any industrial towns, the smoky look peculiar to this part of the country seems to hang about anything. Grass dull-coloured, streams muddy, houses all blackened as though by smoke. There was snow everywhere, but thawing and slushy. Sheep very dirty – no lambs, apparently. The palm was out and primroses putting out new shoots; otherwise nothing moving.

11 March

On the last two evenings to 'discussion groups' – societies of people who meet once a week, listen-in to some talk on the radio and then discuss it. Those at the one on Monday were chiefly unemployed men and I believe these 'discussion groups' were started or at any rate suggested by the Social Welfare people who run the unemployed occupational centres. That on Monday was decorous and rather dull. Thirteen people including ourselves (one woman besides M) and we met in a room adjoining a public library. The talk was on Galsworthy's play *The Skin Game* and the discussion kept to the subject until most of us adjourned to a pub for bread and cheese and beer afterwards. Two people dominated the assembly, one a huge bull-headed man named Rowe who contradicted whatever the last speaker had said and involved himself in the most appalling contradictions, the other a youngish, very intelligent and extremely well-informed man named Creed. From his refined accent, quiet voice and apparent omniscience, I took him for a librarian. I find he keeps a tobacconist's shop and was previously a commercial traveller. During the war he was imprisoned as a conscientious objector. The other meeting was at a pub and the people were of higher standing. The other arrangement is that M and H go there taking the portable radio, and the publican, who is a member of the group, lets them have a room for the evening. On this occasion the talk was called 'If Plato lived Today', but actually no one listened-in except M and myself – H has gone to Bedford. When the talk was over the publican, a Canadian with a very bald head, a market gardener who was already the worse for drink, and another man rolled in and there began an orgy of drinking from which we escaped with difficulty about an hour later. Much of the talk on both nights about the European situation and most people saying (some of them with ill-dissembled hope) that war is certain. With two exceptions all pro-German.

Today to Barnsley to fix up about a place to stay. Wilde, secretary of the South Yorkshire Branch of the Working Men's Club & Institute Union, has fixed it all up for me. The address is Agnes Avenue. The usual 2 up 2 down house, with sink in living-room, as at Sheffield. The husband is a miner and was away at work when we got there. House very disorganized as it was washing day, but seemed clean. Wilde, though kind and helpful, was a very vague person. He was a working miner till 1924 but as usual has been bourgeois-ified. Smartly dressed with gloves and umbrella and very little accent – I would have taken him for a solicitor from his appearance.

Barnsley is slightly smaller than Wigan – about 70,000 inhabitants – but distinctly less poverty-stricken, at any rate in appearance. Much better shops and more appearance of business being done. Many miners coming home from the morning shift. Mostly wearing clogs but of a square-toed pattern different from the Lancashire ones.

13 March

At Agnes Terrace, Barnsley.

This house is bigger than I had imagined. Two rooms and tiny larder under the stairs downstairs, 3 or 4[1] rooms upstairs. Eight people in the house – 5 adults and 3 children. Front room which should be parlour is used as bedroom. Living-room, about 14′ by 12′, has the usual kitchener, sink and copper. No gas stove. Electric light in all rooms save one. Outside WC.

The Family. Mr G, a short powerful man, age about 45, with coarse features, enlarged nose and a very fatigued, pale look. He is rather bald, has his own teeth (unusual in a working-class person of that age) but they are very discoloured. A bit deaf, but very ready to talk, especially about technicalities of mining. Has worked in the pit ever since a small boy. On one occasion was buried by a fall of earth or stone – no bones broken, but it took ten minutes to dig him out and two hours to drag him to the cage. He tells me no machinery (stretchers, etc.) exists for conveying injured men away from the scene of accidents. Obviously some kind of stretcher running on the trolley rails could be contrived, but this would involve stopping all the haulage of coal while it was being done. So injured men have to be carried to the cage by helpers who are themselves bending double and can only get them along very slowly. Mr G works at removing the coal onto the trucks after it is cut – 'scufting' I think it is called. He and his mate are paid piece-work 2/2d per ton – 1/1d each. On full time his wages average £2–10–0d a week. His stoppages amount to 6/11d. He works at Darton, about 4 miles away and goes there by bus. Journeys cost 6d a day. So his net wages on full time are about £2–0–0d a week.

Mrs G is about 10 years younger,[2] motherly type, always cooking and cleaning, accent less broad than her husband's. Two little girls, Doreen and Ireen (spelling?) aged 11 and 10. The other lodgers are a widowed joiner, employed on the woodwork at the new dog-track, and his son aged about 11, and a professional singer who is going to sing at one of the pubs. All the larger pubs in Barnsley employ singers and dancers (some of these very immoral according to Mrs G) more or less constantly.

The house is very clean and decent and my room the best I have had in lodgings up here. Flannelette sheets this time.

14 March

Much talk last night with Mr G about his war experiences. Especially about the malingering he saw going on when he was invalided with some injury to his leg, and the astute ways the doctors had of detecting it. One man feigned complete deafness and successfully kept it up during tests lasting two hours. Finally he was told by signs that he would be discharged and could go, and just as he was passing through the door the doctor said casually, 'Shut that door after you, would you?' The man turned and shut it, and was passed for active service. Another man feigned insanity and got away with it. For days he was going round with a bent pin on a bit of string, pretending to

[1] 3. [Author's footnote.]
[2] Actually their ages are 50 and 38. [Author's footnote.]

be catching fish. Finally he was discharged, and on a parting with G he held up his discharge papers and said, 'This is what I was fishing for.' I was reminded of the malingering I saw in the Hôpital Cochin in Paris, where unemployed men used to remain for months together on pretence of being ill.[1]

Beastly cold again. Sleet this morning. But yesterday as I came on the train they were ploughing and the earth looked much more spring-like; especially in one field where the earth was very black, not like the usual clay soil hereabouts, and as the ploughshare turned it over it looked like chocolate fudge being sliced up with a knife.

I am very comfortable in this house but do not think I shall pick up much of interest in Barnsley. I know no one here except Wilde, who is thoroughly vague. Cannot discover whether there is a branch of the NUWM here. The public library is no good. There is no proper reference library and it seems no separate directory of Barnsley is published.

15 March

Last night with Wilde and others to the general meeting of the South Yorkshire Branch of the Working Men's Club & Institute Union, held at one of the clubs in Barnsley. About 200 people there, all busily tucking into beer and sandwiches, though it was only 4.30 p.m. – they had got an extension for the day. The club was a big building, really an enlarged pub with one big hall which could be used for concerts, etc. and in which the meeting was held. It was a bit stormy in parts, but Wilde and the chairman had them pretty well in hand and were complete masters of all the usual platform phraseology and procedure. I notice from the balance sheet that W's salary is £260 per annum. Before this I had never realized the number and importance of these working men's clubs, especially in the North and especially in Yorkshire. Those at this meeting consisted of pairs of delegates sent by all the clubs in South Yorkshire. There would have been I should say 150 delegates, representing therefore 75 clubs and probably about 10,000 members. That is in South Yorkshire alone. After the meeting I was taken to have tea in the committee room with about 30 of what were, I gathered, some of the more important delegates. We had cold ham, bread and butter, cakes and whisky which everyone poured into their tea. After that with W and the others went down to the Radical and Liberal Club in the middle of the town, where I have been before. There was a sort of smoking concert going on, as these clubs, like the pubs, all engage singers, etc. for the week-ends. There was quite a good knockabout comedian whose jokes were of the usual twins-mother-in-law-kippers type, and pretty steady boozing. Wilde's accent becomes much broader when he is in these surroundings. It appears that these clubs were first started as a kind of charitable concern in the mid-nineteenth century, and were, of course, Temperance. But they escaped by becoming financially self-supporting and have developed, as I say, into sort of glorified co-operative pubs. G, who belongs to the Radical and Liberal Club, tells me his subscription is 1/6d a quarter and all drinks are 1d or 2d a pint cheaper than at the pubs. Youths under 21 are not admitted and (I think) women cannot be members but can go there with their husbands. Most of the clubs are avowedly non-political, and in this and in the fact that the members are mostly of the more prosperous working-class type – comparatively few unemployed – one can

[1] See *How the Poor Die.*

foresee the germs of a danger that they will be politically mobilized for anti-Socialist purposes.

Talking with a man who was previously a miner but now works as a labourer for the Corporation. He was telling me about the housing conditions in Barnsley in his childhood. He grew up in a back to back house in which there were 11 people (two bedrooms, I suppose) and you not only had to walk 200 yards to get to the lavatory, but shared it with, in all, 36 people.

Have arranged to go down the Grimethorpe pit next Saturday. This is a very up-to-date pit and possesses certain machinery that does not exist anywhere else in England. Also to go down a 'day hole' pit on Thursday afternoon. The man I spoke to told me it was a mile to the coal face, so if the 'travelling' is bad I shan't go the whole way – I only want to see what a 'day hole' is like and am not going to incapacitate myself like last time.

When G comes back from the pit he washes before having his food. I don't know whether this is usual, but I have often seen miners sitting down to eat with Christy Minstrel faces – completely black except very red lips which become clean by eating. When G arrives he is as black as ink, especially his scalp – for this reason miners usually wear their hair short. He pours out a large basin of hot water, strips to the waist and washes himself very methodically, first his hands, then his upper arms, then his forearms, then his chest and shoulders, then his face and head. Then he dries himself and his wife washes his back. His navel is still a nest of coal-dust. I suppose from the waist down he must normally be quite black. There are public baths and the miners go to them but as a rule nor more than once a week – one cannot be surprised at this, as a miner has not much time between working and sleeping. Miners' houses with bathrooms, other than the new Corporation ones, are practically unknown. Only a few colliery companies have baths at the pit-heads.

I notice that G does not eat very much. At present, working on the afternoon shift, he has the same breakfast as I have (an egg and bacon, bread – no butter – and tea) and has a light lunch, such as bread and cheese, about half past twelve. He says he cannot do his work if he has eaten too much. All he takes with him to the pit is some bread and dripping and cold tea. This is the usual thing. The men do not want much in the stifling air down there, and besides, they are not allowed any time off for eating. He gets home between 10 and 11 p.m. and it is then that he has his only heavy meal of the day.

16 March

Last night to hear Mosley speak at the Public Hall, which is in structure a theatre. It was quite full – about 700 people I should say. About 100 Blackshirts on duty, with two or three exceptions weedy-looking specimens, and girls selling *Action*[1], etc. Mosley spoke for an hour and a half and to my dismay seemed to have the meeting mainly with him. He was booed at the start but loudly clapped at the end. Several men who tried at the beginning to interject questions were thrown out, one of them – who as far as I could see was only trying to get a question answered – with quite unnecessary violence, several Blackshirts throwing themselves upon him and raining blows on him while he was still sitting down and had not attempted any violence. M is a very good speaker. His speech was the usual claptrap – Empire free trade, down

[1] The journal of the British Union of Fascists.

with the Jew and the foreigner, higher wages and shorter hours all round, etc., etc. After the preliminary booing the (mainly) working-class audience was easily bamboozled by M speaking from as it were a Socialist angle, condemning the treachery of successive governments towards the workers. The blame for everything was put upon mysterious international gangs of Jews who are said to be financing, among other things, the British Labour Party and the Soviet. M's statement re the international situation: 'We fought Germany before in a British quarrel; we are not going to fight them now in a Jewish one' was received with loud applause. Afterwards there were questions as usual, and it struck me how easy it is to bamboozle an uneducated audience if you have prepared beforehand a set of repartees with which to evade awkward questions, e.g. M kept extolling Italy and Germany, but when questioned about concentration camps, etc. always replied, 'We have no foreign models; what happens in Germany need not happen here.' To the question, 'How do you know that your own money is not used to finance cheap foreign labour?' (M having denounced the Jewish financiers who are supposed to do this), M replied, 'All my money is invested in England,' and I suppose comparatively few of the audience realized that this means nothing.

At the beginning M said that anyone ejected would be charged under the Public Meetings Act. I don't know whether this was actually done, but presumably the power to do so exists. In connection with this the fact that there are no police on duty *inside the building* is of great importance. Anyone who interrupts can be assaulted and thrown out and then charged into the bargain, and of course the stewards, i.e. M himself, are the judges of what constitutes an interruption. Therefore one is liable to get both a hammering and a fine for asking a question which M finds it difficult to answer.

At the end of the meeting a great crowd collected outside, as there was some public indignation about the men who had been thrown out. I waited for a long time in the crowd to see what would happen, but M and party did not emerge. Then the police managed to split the crowd and I found myself at the front, whereupon a policeman ordered me away, but quite civilly. I went round to the back of the crowd and waited again, but still M did not appear and I concluded he had been sneaked out by a back door, so went home. In the morning at the *Chronicle* office, however, I was told that there had been some stone-throwing and two men had been arrested and remanded.

G changed this morning onto the early morning shift. He gets up at 3.45 a.m. and has to be at work, i.e. at the coal face, at 6. He gets home about 2.30 p.m. His wife does not get up to get his breakfast and he says few miners will allow their wives to do so. Also that there are still some miners who if they meet a woman on their way to work will turn back and go home. It is considered bad luck to see a woman before going to work. I presume this only applies to the early morning shift.

18 March

The Barnsley public baths are very bad. Old-fashioned bathtubs, none too clean, and not nearly enough of them. I judged by the appearance of the place there were at most 50 baths[1] – this in a town of 70–80 thousand inhabitants, largely miners, not one of whom has a bath in his own house, except in the new Corporation houses.

[1] Actually 19! [Author's footnote.]

Some curious coincidences. When I went to see Len Kaye he recommended me to see Tommy Degnan, to whom I had also been recommended by Paddy Grady at Wigan. But what was more curious still, D was one of the men who were thrown out at Mosley's meeting, though not the one I actually saw thrown out. I went round to see D last night and had some difficulty in finding him. He lives in a dreadful barn of a place called Garden House, which is an old almost ruinous house which half a dozen unemployed men have taken and made a sort of lodging-house of. D himself is not unemployed, though at the moment 'playing' because a few days before the hammering he got at M's meeting he was slightly crushed by a fall of stone in the mine. We went out to look for the man whom I actually saw thrown out, as I want to get particulars and see his bruises before writing to the papers about it, but couldn't find him, and I am to see him today. Then in the street we ran across another man whom I saw thrown out. The latter's ejection was an interesting instance of the way any upset can be misrepresented and turned to advantage by a demagogue of the type of Mosley. At the time of the uproar at the back of the hall, this last man – name Hennessey,[1] I think – was seen to rush onto the stage, and everyone thought he had gone there to shout something out and interrupt M's speech. It struck me at the time as curious that though on the stage he didn't shout anything out, and the next moment, of course, the Blackshirts on the platform seized him and bundled him out. M shouted out, 'A typical example of Red tactics!' It now appears what happened was this. Hennessey saw the Blackshirts at the back of the hall bashing D, and couldn't get to him to help him because there is no aisle up the middle; but there was an aisle up the right hand side, and the only way he could get to this was over the stage. D after being thrown out was charged under the Public Meetings Act, but H not. I don't know yet whether the other man, Marshall, was. The woman who was thrown out – this was somewhere at the back and I didn't see it – was hit on the head with a trumpet and was a day in hospital. D and H were in the Army together and H was wounded in the leg and D taken prisoner when the Vth Army was defeated in 1918. D, being a miner, was sent to work in the Polish mines. He said all of them had pit-head baths. H says the French ones have them too.

G told me a dreadful story of how a friend of his, a 'dataller', was buried alive. He was buried under a fall of small stone, and they rushed to him and, though they could not get him out completely, they got his head and shoulders free so that he could breathe. He was alive and spoke to them. At this moment they saw that the roof was coming down again and had to take to flight themselves. Once again he was buried, and once again they managed to get to him and uncover his head, and again he was alive and spoke to them. Then the roof came down again, and this time they did not get him out for some hours, after which, of course, he was dead. But the real point of the story, from G's point of view, was that this man had known beforehand that this part of the mine was unsafe and likely to bury him: 'And it worked on his mind to that extent that he kissed his wife before he went to work. And she told me afterwards that it was the first time in years he'd kissed her.'

There is a very old woman – a Lancashire woman – living near here who in her day has worked down the pit, dragging tubs of coal with a harness and chain. She is 83, so I suppose this would be in the 'seventies.

[1] His name is Firth. I got it as Hennessey because he was introduced to me as Hellis Firth. (*E*llis Firth – people here very capricious about their H's.) [Author's footnote.]

19 March
In frightful exhaustion after going down the 'day hole', as, of course, when the time came I had not the strength of mind to say I did not want to go as far as the coal face.

I went down with the 'deputy' (Mr Lawson) about 3 p.m. and came up about 6.15 p.m. L said we had covered not quite 2 miles. I must say that I got on perceptibly better than at Wigan, either because the going was a little better, as I think it was – probably one could stand upright about one third of the way – or because L, who is an old man, moderated his pace to mine. The chief feature of this pit, apart from its being a 'day hole', is that it is infernally wet in most places. There were quite considerable streams running here and there, and two enormous pumps have to be kept running all day and most of the night. The water is pumped up to ground level and has made a considerable pool, but curiously enough it is clear, clean water – even drinkable, L said – and the pool was quite ornamental with water-hens swimming about on it. We went down when the morning shift came up, and there are comparatively few men on the afternoon shift for some reason I did not understand. When we got to the coal face the men were there with the coal-cutter, which was not running at the moment, but they set it running to show me. The teeth on a revolving chain – in principle it is an enormously tough and powerful bandsaw – cut in underneath the coal face, after which huge boulders of coal can be easily tumbled out and broken up with picks before being loaded onto the tubs. Some of these boulders of coal, not yet broken up, were about 8 feet long by two thick by four high – the seam is four feet six, I think – and must have weighed many tons.[1] As it cuts the machine travels backwards or forwards, as desired, along the coal face, on its own power. The place where these men, and those loading the broken coal onto the tubs, were working was like hell. I had never thought of it before but of course as the machine works it sends forth clouds of coal dust which almost stifle one and make it impossible to see more than a few feet. No lamps except Davy lamps of an old-fashioned pattern, not more than two or three candle-power, and it puzzled one to see how these men can see to work, except when there are a number of them together. To get from one part of the coal face to another you had to crawl along awful tunnels cut through the coal, a yard high by two feet wide, and then to work yourself on your bottom over mountainous boulders of coal. Of course in doing this I dropped my lamp and it went out. L called to one of the men working and he gave me his lamp. Then L said, 'You'd better cut yourself a bit of coal as a memento' (visitors always do this), and while I was cutting out a piece of coal with the pick, I knocked my second lamp over and put that out too. We had to go about a quarter of a mile with only one lamp between the two of us, which was disconcerting and brought it home to me how easily you could lose yourself down there if you didn't happen to know the roads.

We passed tubs, carrying props etc, going to and fro on the endless belt, which is worked by electricity. The tubs only move at 1½ miles an hour. All the miners at this pit seem to carry sticks, and they gave me one which was a great help. They are about two foot six long and hollowed out just below the knob. At moderate heights (4 ft to 5 ft) you keep your hand on the knob, and when you have to bend really low you grip the stick by the hollow. The

[1] A cubic yard of coal is said to weigh 27 cwt. [Author's footnote]

ground underfoot was as mucky as a farmyard in many places. They say the best way to go is to keep one foot on the trolley-rail and the other on the sleepers, if you can find them. The miners going down the roads *run*, bent double of course, in places where I could barely stagger. They say it is easier to run than walk when you have the hang of it. It was rather humiliating that coming back, which we did by the most direct route, took me three quarters of an hour and only takes the miners a quarter of an hour. But we had gone to the nearest working, only about half way to the end. Those who work at the furthest working take nearly an hour to get to their work. This time I was given one of the new crash helmets which many, though not all, miners now wear. To look at they are very like a French or Italian tin hat, and I had always imagined they were made of metal. Actually they are of a kind of compressed fibre and very light. Mine was a bore because it was too small and fell off when I bent very low. But how glad of it I was! Coming back when I was tired and could not bend much I must have bashed my head twenty times – once hard enough to bring down a huge chunk of stone – but felt absolutely nothing.

Walked home with L to Dodworth as I could get the bus more easily there. He has a two-mile walk with some pretty stiff hills going to and from work, in addition to the walk inside the mine when he gets there. But I suppose as 'deputy' he doesn't do much manual work. He has worked in this mine 22 years and says he knows it so well that he never needs to look up to see when there is a beam coming.

Birds all singing. Tiny pink buds on the elms that I had never noticed before. Many female flowers on the hazels. But I suppose as usual the old maids will be cutting them all off for Easter decorations.

When I sit typing the family, especially Mrs G and the kids, all gather round to watch absorbedly, and appear to admire my prowess almost as much as I admire that of the miners.

20 March

Talking with Firth. He gets 32/– a week from the UAB.[1] Mrs F is a Derbyshire woman. Two kids, ages 2 years 5 months and 10 months. They are fairly sturdy as yet and it is evidently the case that these kids do much better in infancy than later, as for about their first three years they get help from the Infants' Welfare Clinic. Mrs F gets three packets of baby's food (dried milk) a week and also a little Nestle's milk. On one occasion she got an allowance of 2/– a week for a month to buy eggs for the elder child. While there we sent out for some beer. I noted both the Fs let the children drink a little beer out of their glasses. Another kid was in and out of the house mothering the F baby. Her father was murdered four years ago. The widowed mother gets an allowance of 22/– a week, I do not know from what source, on which she has to keep herself and 4 children.

I did not know before, what F told me, that when the mines have baths at the pit-head these are built not by the company but by the miners themselves, out of the Welfare Fund to which every miner subscribes. This is the case at any rate round here – must try and find out if it is so everywhere. It is by the way another argument against the statement that miners do not want or appreciate baths. One reason why not all pits have baths is that when a pit is anywhere near being worked out it is not considered worth while to build baths.

[1] Unemployment Assistance Board.

I forgot to mention that in the 'day hole' at Wentworth the pit props, owing to the damp, had strange fungi exactly like cotton wool growing on them. If you touched them they went all to nothing, leaving a nasty smell. It appears that a Lancashire miner, instead of slinging his lamp round his neck, has a band above the elbow and hangs the lamp from that.

Today G earned little or nothing. The coal-cutter had broken down so there was no coal for him to fill into the tubs. When this happens those on piece-work get no compensation, except a shilling or two for odd jobs called bye-work.

I see the *Manchester Guardian* has not printed my letter re Mosley and I suppose they never will. I hardly expected *The Times* to print it, but I think the *MG* might, considering their reputation.

21 March

This morning went down the Grimethorpe pit. Not exhausting this time, because in order not to clash with the visit of some students from the Technical College we went to the nearest working, only about ¼ mile and little bending.

The depth of the mine, at least at the part we went to, is a little over 400 yards. The young engineer who took me thought the cages *average* 60 mph when going down, in which case they must touch 80 or more at their fastest. I think this must be an exaggeration, but they certainly travel faster than the average railway train. The especial feature of this pit is the 'skip wagon', by which the coal is sent straight up in special cages instead of being sent up, much more laboriously, in tubs. The full tubs come slowly along an inclined rail and are controlled by men at the sides with brakes. Each tub halts for a moment on a weighing machine and its weight is entered up, then the tubs move on and move two at a time into a kind of container which grips them underneath. The container then turns right over, spilling the coal down a chute into the cage below. When the cage has got 8 tons, i.e. about 16 tubs, in it, it goes out and the coal is spilt down a similar chute on the surface. Then it goes along conveyor belts and over screens which automatically sort it, and it washed as well. The coal which is being sold to factories, etc., is shot straight into goods trucks on the railway line below and then weighed truck and all, the weight of the truck being known. This is the only pit in England which works this system – all others send the coal up in the tubs, which takes much more time and needs more tubs. The system has been worked for a long time in Germany and USA. The Grimethorpe pit turns out about 500 tons of coal a day.

This time I saw the fillers actually working at the coal face, and now having seen the different operations of coal-getting, except blasting, in progress separately, I understand more or less how it is done. The coal-cutter travels along the face cutting into the bottom of the ledge of coal to the depth of 5 feet. Then the coal can be tumbled out in boulders with picks, or – as here, the Grimethorpe coal being very hard – is first loosened with blasting charges and then extracted. Then the fillers (who have also extracted it) load it onto the conveyor belt which runs behind them and carries it to a chute from which it runs into the tubs. As far as possible the three operations are done in three separate shifts. The coal cutter works on the afternoon shift, the blasting is done on the night shift (when the minimum number of people are in the pit), and the fillers extract the coal on the morning shift. Each man has to clear a space 4 or 5 yards wide. So, as the seam of coal is about a yard high and the cutter has undermined it to a depth of 5 feet, each man has to extract and load onto the belt (say) 14 × 5 × 3 cubic feet of coal, equals 210 cubic feet, equals nearly 8 cubic yards of coal. If it is really the case that a cubic yard of coal weighs 27 cwt, this would be well over 10 tons – i.e. each man has to shift nearly a ton and a half an hour. When the job is done the coal face has advanced 5 feet, so during the next shift the conveyor belt is taken to pieces, moved 5 feet forward and reassembled, and fresh props are put in.

The place where the fillers were working was fearful beyond description. The only thing one could say was that, as conditions underground go, it was not particularly hot. But as the seam of coal is only a yard high or a bit more, the men can only kneel or crawl to their work, never stand up. The effort of constantly shovelling coal over your left shoulder and flinging it a yard or two beyond, while in a kneeling position, must be very great even to men who are used to it. Added to this there are the clouds of coal dust which are flying down your throat all the time and which make it difficult to see any distance. The men were all naked except for trousers and knee-pads. It was difficult to get through the conveyor belt to the coal face. You had to pick your moment and wriggle through quickly when the belt stopped for a moment. Coming back we crawled onto the belt while it was moving; I had not been warned of the difficulty of doing this and immediately fell down and had to be hauled off before the belt dashed me against the props, etc. which were littered about further down. Added to the other discomforts of the men working there, there is the fearful din of the belt which never stops for more than a minute or so.

Electric lights this time – no Davy lamps used in the pit except for testing for gas. They can detect the presence of gas by the flame turning blue. By the height to which the flame can be turned while still remaining blue, they have a rough test of the percentage of gas in the atmosphere. All the roads we went through, except one or two galleries used for short cuts, were high and well-built and even paved underfoot in places. I have at last grasped the reason for the doors one passes through from time to time. The air is sucked out of one entry by fans and goes in of its own accord to another entry. But if not prevented it will come back by the shortest route instead of going all round the mine. Hence the doors, which stop it from taking short cuts.

Excellent baths at the pit. They have no less than 1,000 h & c shower baths. Each miner has two lockers, one for his pit clothes and one for his ordinary clothes (so that the pit clothes shall not dirty the others). Thus he can come and go clean and decent. According to the engineer, the baths were built partly by the Miners' Welfare, partly by the royalty owners, and the company also contributed.

During this week G has had two narrow escapes from falls of stone, one of which actually grazed him on its way down. These men would not last long if it were not that they are used to the conditions and know when to stand from under. I am struck by the difference between the miners when you see them underground and when you see them in the street, etc. Above ground, in their thick ill-fitting clothes, they are ordinary-looking men, usually small and not at all impressive and indeed not distinguishable from other people except by their distinctive walk (clumping tread, shoulders very square) and the blue scars on their noses. Below, when you see them stripped, all, old and young, have splendid bodies, with every muscle defined and wonderfully small waists. I saw some miners going into their baths. As I thought, they are quite black from head to foot. So the ordinary miner, who has not access to a bath, must be black from the waist down six days a week at least.

I have been wondering about what people like the Firths have to eat. Their total income is 32/– a week. Rent 9/0½d. Gas say 1/3d. Coal (say 3 cwt @ 9d) 2/3d. Other minor expenses (e.g. F keeps up his Union payments) say 1/–. That leaves 18/6d. But Mrs F gets a certain amount of baby-food free from the Clinic, so say the baby only costs 1/– a week beyond this. That leaves 17/6d. F smokes at any rate some cigarettes, say 1/– (6 packets of Woodbines a week).That leaves 16/6d a week to feed 2 adults and a girl aged 2 years, or about 5/6d per week per head. And this takes no account of clothes, soap, matches, etc., etc. Mrs F said they fed chiefly on bread and jam. If I can do so delicately I must ask F to give me a fairly exact account of their meals for one day.

22 March

Kaye says his father, a collier (now too old for work), always washed the top half his body and his feet and legs to above the knees. The rest of his body was only washed at very long intervals, the old man believing that washing all over led to lumbago.

Communist meeting in the Market Place disappointing. The trouble with all these Communist speakers is that instead of using the popular idiom they employ immensely long sentences full of 'despite' and 'notwithstanding' and 'be that as it may', etc. in the Garvin[1] strain – and this in spite of always speaking with broad provincial or cockney accents – Yorkshire in this case. I suppose they are given set speeches which they learn by heart. After the visiting speaker Degnan got up to speak and was a much more effective speaker – he speaks very broad Lancashire and though he can talk like a leading article if he wants to he doesn't choose. The usual crowd of men of all ages gaping with entirely expressionless faces and the usual handful of women a little more animated than the men – I suppose because no woman would go to a political meeting unless exceptionally interested in politics. About 150 people. Collection taken for the defence of the young men arrested in the Mosley affair and realized 6/–.

Wandering round Barnsley Main Colliery and the glassworks along the canal with F and another man whose name I did not get. The latter's mother had just died and was lying dead at home. She was 89 and had been a midwife for 50 years. I noted the lack of hypocrisy with which he was laughing and joking and came into the pub to have a drink, etc. The monstrous slag-heaps round Barnsley Main are all more or less on fire under the surface. In the darkness you can see long serpentine fires creeping all over them, not only red but very sinister blue flames (from sulphur) which always seem on the point of going out and then flicker up again.

I notice that the word 'spink' (for a great tit, I think, but at any rate some small bird) is in use here as well as in Suffolk.

23 March

At Mapplewell. Houses about the worst I have seen, though we did not manage to get into the very worst ones, which were one-roomed or two-roomed cabins of stone, about 20′ by 15′ by 15′ high, or even less, and practically ruinous.

[1] J. L. Garvin (1868–1947), right-wing editor of the *Observer*, 1908 to 1942.

Rent of these, some of which are property of colliery, said to be about 3/–. In the row called Spring Gardens we found public indignation because the landlords have served about half the row with notices to quit for arrears of, in some cases, only a few shillings. (Firth, in Barnsley, has a notice to quit though only about 5/– in arrear and paying this off at 3d per week.) The people took us in and insisted on our seeing their houses. Frightful interiors. In the first one old father, out of work of course, obviously horribly bewildered by his notice to quit after 22 years tenancy and turning anxiously to F and me with some idea that we could help him. The mother rather more self-possessed. Two sons aged about 24, fine big men with powerful well-shaped bodies, narrow faces and red hair, but thin and listless from obvious under-nourishment and with dull brutalized expressions. Their sister, a little older and very like them, with prematurely lined face, glancing from F to me, again with the idea that perhaps we might help. One of the sons, taking no notice of our presence, all the while slowly peeling off his socks in front of the fire; his feet almost black with sticky dirt. The other son was at work. The house terribly bare – no bedclothes except overcoats, etc. – but fairly clean and tidy. At the back children playing about in the muck, some of them, aged 5 or 6, barefoot and naked except for a sort of shift. F told the tenants if the notice to quit was persisted with to come into Barnsley and see him and Degnan. I told them the landlord was only bluffing and to hold their ground and if he threatened taking it to court to threaten in return to sue him for lack of repairs. Hope I did the right thing.

I have glanced at B's novel. It is b——s.

25 March

Men along the private line leading to Gauber pit unloading trucks of slack. They say the mine 'can't get shut o' t'slack' and are laying it by. This is regarded as a sinister sign. If the pits are storing slack already they will soon be running short time. The men get 4d a ton for unloading the slack. A truck holds about 10 tons, so they had to unload 3 trucks to make a day's wage.

I think in the dirtiest interiors I see, more than any of the various kinds of squalor – the piles of unwashed crocks, the scraps of miscellaneous food all over the lino-topped table, the dreadful rag mats with the crumbs of years trodden into them – the things that oppress me most are the scraps of newspaper that are scattered all over the floor.

G is quite badly ill with bronchitis. He stayed away from work yesterday, then this morning, when still obviously ill, insisted on going to work.

Returning to Leeds tomorrow, then on to London on Monday.

Shooting an Elephant

In Moulmein, in Lower Burma, I was hated by large numbers of people – the only time in my life that I have been important enough for this to happen to me. I was sub-divisional police officer of the town, and in an aimless, petty kind of way anti-European feeling was very bitter. No one had the guts to raise a riot, but if a European woman went through the bazaars alone somebody would probably spit betel juice over her dress. As a police officer I was an obvious target and was baited whenever it seemed safe to do so. When a nimble Burman tripped me up on the football field and the referee (another Burman) looked the other way, the crowd yelled with hideous laughter. This happened more than once. In the end the sneering yellow faces of young men that met me everywhere, the insults hooted after me when I was at a safe distance, got badly on my nerves. The young Buddhist priests were the worst of all. There were several thousands of them in the town and none of them seemed to have anything to do except stand on street corners and jeer at Europeans.

All this was perplexing and upsetting. For at that time I had already made up my mind that imperialism was an evil thing and the sooner I chucked up my job and got out of it the better. Theoretically – and secretly, of course – I was all for the Burmese and all against their oppressors, the British. As for the job I was doing, I hated it more bitterly than I can perhaps make clear. In a job like that you see the dirty work of Empire at close quarters. The wretched prisoners huddling in the stinking cages of the lock-ups, the grey, cowed faces of the long-term convicts, the scarred buttocks of the men who had been flogged with bamboos – all these oppressed me with an intolerable sense of guilt. But I could get nothing into perspective. I was young and ill-educated and I had had to think out my problems in the utter silence that is imposed on every Englishman in the East. I did not even know that the British Empire is dying, still less did I know that it is a great deal better than the younger empires that are going to supplant it. All I knew was that I was stuck between my hatred of the empire I served and my rage against the evil-spirited little beasts who tried to make my job impossible. With one part of my mind I thought of the British Raj as an unbreakable tyranny, as something clamped down, *in saecula saeculorum*, upon the will of prostrate peoples; with another part I thought that the greatest joy in the world would be to drive a bayonet into a Buddhist priest's guts. Feelings like these are the normal by-products of imperialism; ask any Anglo-Indian official, if you can catch him off duty.

One day something happened which in a roundabout way was enlightening. It was a tiny incident in itself, but it gave me a better glimpse than I had had before of the real nature of imperialism – the real motives for which despotic governments act. Early one morning the sub-inspector at a police station the other end of the town rang me up on the phone and said that an elephant was ravaging the bazaar. Would I please come and do something about it? I did not know what I could do, but I wanted to see what was happening and I got on to a pony and started out. I took my rifle, an old ·44 Winchester and much too small to kill an elephant, but I thought the noise might be useful *in terrorem*. Various Burmans stopped me on the way and told me about the elephant's doings. It was not, of course, a wild elephant, but a tame one which had gone 'must'. It had been chained up as tame elephants always are when their attack of 'must' is due, but on the previous night it had broken its chain and escaped. Its mahout, the only person who could manage it when it was in that state, had set out in pursuit, but he had taken the wrong direction and was now twelve hours' journey away, and in the morning the elephant had suddenly reappeared in the town. The Burmese population had no weapons and were quite helpless against it. It had already destroyed somebody's bamboo hut, killed a cow and raided some fruit-stalls and devoured the stock; also it had met the municipal rubbish van, and, when the driver jumped out and took to his heels, had turned the van over and inflicted violence upon it.

The Burmese sub-inspector and some Indian constables were waiting for me in the quarter where the elephant had been seen. It was a very poor quarter, a labyrinth of squalid bamboo huts, thatched with palm-leaf, winding all over a steep hillside. I remember that it was a cloudy stuffy morning at the beginning of the rains. We began questioning the people as to where the elephant had gone, and, as usual, failed to get any definite information. That is invariably the case in the East; a story always sounds clear enough at a distance, but the nearer you get to the scene of events the vaguer it becomes. Some of the people said that the elephant had gone in one direction, some said that he had gone in another, some professed not even to have heard of any elephant. I had almost made up my mind that the whole story was a pack of lies, when we heard yells a little distance away. There was a loud, scandalized cry of 'Go away, child! Go away this instant!' and an old woman with a switch in her hand came round the corner of a hut, violently shooing away a crowd of naked children. Some more women followed, clicking their tongues and exclaiming; evidently there was something there that the children ought not to have seen. I rounded the hut and saw a man's dead body sprawling in the mud. He was an Indian, a black Dravidian coolie, almost naked, and he could not have been dead many minutes. The people said that the elephant had come suddenly upon him round the corner of the hut, caught him with its trunk, put its foot on his back and ground him into the earth. This was the rainy season and the ground was soft, and his face had scored a trench a foot deep and a couple of yards long. He was lying on his belly with arms crucified and head sharply twisted to one side. His face was coated with mud, the eyes wide open, the teeth bared and grinning with an expression of unendurable agony. (Never tell me, by the way, that the dead look peaceful. Most of the corpses I have seen looked devilish.) The friction of the great beast's foot had stripped the skin from his back as neatly as one skins a rabbit. As soon as I saw the dead man I sent an orderly to a friend's house nearby to borrow an elephant rifle. I had already sent back the pony, not wanting it to go mad with fright and throw me if it smelled the elephant.

The orderly came back in a few minutes with a rifle and five cartridges, and meanwhile some Burmans had arrived and told us that the elephant was in the paddy fields below, only a few hundred yards away. As I started forward practically the whole population of the quarter flocked out of their houses and followed me. They had seen the rifle and were all shouting excitedly that I was going to shoot the elephant. They had not shown much interest in the elephant when he was merely ravaging their homes, but it was different now that he was going to be shot. It was a bit of fun to them, as it would be to an English crowd; besides, they wanted the meat. It made me vaguely uneasy. I had no intention of shooting the elephant – I had merely sent for the rifle to defend myself if necessary – and it is always unnerving to have a crowd following you. I marched down the hill, looking and feeling a fool, with the rifle over my shoulder and an ever-growing army of people jostling at my heels. At the bottom, when you got away from the huts, there was a metalled road and beyond that a miry waste of paddy fields a thousand yards across, not yet ploughed but soggy from the first rains and dotted with coarse grass. The elephant was standing eighty yards from the road, his left side towards us. He took not the slightest notice of the crowd's approach. He was tearing up bunches of grass, beating them against his knees to clean them and stuffing them into his mouth.

I had halted on the road. As soon as I saw the elephant I knew with perfect certainty that I ought not to shoot him. It is a serious matter to shoot a working elephant – it is comparable to destroying a huge and costly piece of machinery – and obviously one ought not to do it if it can possibly be avoided. And at that distance, peacefully eating, the elephant looked no more dangerous than a cow. I thought then and I think now that his attack of 'must' was already passing off; in which case he would merely wander harmlessly about until the mahout came back and caught him. Moreover, I did not in the least want to shoot him. I decided that I would watch him for a little while to make sure that he did not turn savage again, and then go home.

But at that moment I glanced round at the crowd that had followed me. It was an immense crowd, two thousand at the least and growing every minute. It blocked the road for a long distance on either side. I looked at the sea of yellow faces above the garish clothes – faces all happy and excited over this bit of fun, all certain that the elephant was going to be shot. They were watching me as they would watch a conjuror about to perform a trick. They did not like me, but with the magical rifle in my hands I was momentarily worth watching. And suddenly I realized that I should have to shoot the elephant after all. The people expected it of me and I had got to do it; I could feel their two thousand wills pressing me forward, irresistibly. And it was at this moment, as I stood there with the rifle in my hands, that I first grasped the hollowness, the futility of the white man's dominion in the East. Here was I, the white man with his gun, standing in front of the unarmed native crowd – seemingly the leading actor of the piece; but in reality I was only an absurd puppet pushed to and fro by the will of those yellow faces behind. I perceived in this moment that when the white man turns tyrant it is his own freedom that he destroys. He becomes a sort of hollow, posing dummy, the conventionalized figure of a sahib. For it is the condition of his rule that he shall spend his life in trying to impress the 'natives' and so in every crisis he has got to do what the 'natives' expect of him. He wears a mask, and his face grows to fit it. I had got to shoot the elephant. I had committed myself to doing it when I sent for the rifle. A sahib has got to act like a sahib; he has got to appear resolute, to know his own mind and do definite things. To come all that way, rifle in hand, with two thousand people marching at my heels, and then to trail feebly away, having done nothing – no, that was impossible. The crowd would laugh at me. And my whole life, every white man's life in the East, was one long struggle not to be laughed at.

But I did not want to shoot the elephant. I watched him beating his bunch of grass against his knees, with that preoccupied grandmotherly air that elephants have. It seemed to me that it would be murder to shoot him. At that age I was not squeamish about killing animals, but I had never shot an elephant and never wanted to. (Somehow it always seems worse to kill a *large* animal.) Besides, there was the beast's owner to be considered. Alive, the elephant was worth at least a hundred pounds; dead, he would only be worth the value of his tusks – five pounds, possibly. But I had got to act quickly. I turned to some experienced-looking Burmans who had been there when we arrived, and asked them how the elephant had been behaving. They all said the same thing: he took no notice of you if you left him alone, but he might charge if you went too close to him.

It was perfectly clear to me what I ought to do. I ought to walk up to within. say, twenty-five yards of the elephant and test his behaviour. If he charged I could shoot, if he took no notice of me it would be safe to leave him until the mahout came back. But also I knew that I was going to do no such thing. I was a poor shot with a rifle and the ground was soft mud into which one would sink at every step. If the elephant charged and I missed him, I should have about as much chance as a toad under a steam-roller. But even then I was not thinking particularly of my own skin, only the watchful yellow faces behind. For at that moment, with the crowd watching me, I was not afraid in the ordinary sense, as I would have been if I had been alone. A white man mustn't be frightened in front of 'natives'; and so, in general, he isn't frightened. The sole thought in my mind was that if anything went wrong those two thousand Burmans would see me pursued, caught, trampled on and reduced to a grinning corpse like that Indian up the hill. And if that happened it was quite probable that some of them would laugh. That would never do. There was only one alternative. I shoved the cartridges into the magazine and lay down on the road to get a better aim.

The crowd grew very still, and a deep, low, happy sigh, as of people who see the theatre curtain go up at last, breathed from innumerable throats. They were going to have their bit of fun after all. The rifle was a beautiful German thing with cross-hair sights. I did not then know that in shooting an elephant one should shoot to cut an imaginary bar running from ear-hole to ear-hole. I ought therefore, as the elephant was sideways on, to have aimed straight at his ear-hole; actually I aimed several inches in front of this, thinking the brain would be further forward.

When I pulled the trigger I did not hear the bang or feel the kick – one never does when a shot goes home – but I heard the devilish roar of glee that went up from the crowd. In that instant, in too short a time, one would have thought, even for the bullet to get there, a mysterious, terrible change had come over the elephant. He neither stirred nor fell, but every line of his body had altered. He looked suddenly stricken, shrunken, immensely old, as though the frightful impact of the bullet had paralysed him without knocking him down. At last, after what seemed a long time – it might have been five seconds, I dare say – he sagged flabbily to his knees. His mouth slobbered. An enormous senility settled upon him. One could have imagined him thousands of years old. I fired again into the same spot. At the second shot he did not collapse but climbed with desperate slowness to his feet and stood weakly upright, with legs sagging and head drooping. I fired a third time. That was the shot that did for him. You could see the agony of it jolt his whole body and knock the last remnant of strength from his legs. But in falling he seemed for a moment to rise, for as his hind legs collapsed beneath him he seemed to tower upwards like a huge rock toppling, his trunk reaching skyward like a tree. He trumpeted, for the first and only time. And then down he came, his belly towards me, with a crash that seemed to shake the ground even where I lay.

I got up. The Burmans were already racing past me across the mud. It was obvious that the elephant would never rise again, but he was not dead. He was breathing very rhythmically with long rattling gasps, his great mound of a side painfully rising and falling. His mouth was wide open – I could see far down into caverns of pale pink throat. I waited a long time for him to die, but his breathing did not weaken. Finally I fired my two remaining shots into the spot where I thought his heart must be. The thick blood welled out of him like red velvet, but still he did not die. His body did not even jerk when the shots hit him, the tortured breathing continued without a pause. He was dying, very slowly and in great agony, but in some world remote from me where not even a bullet could damage him further. I felt that I had got to put an end to that dreadful noise. It seemed dreadful to see the great beast lying there, powerless to move and yet powerless to die, and not even to be able to finish him. I sent back for my small rifle and poured shot after shot into his heart and down his throat. They seemed to make no impression. The tortured gasps continued as steadily as the ticking of a clock.

In the end I could not stand it any longer and went away. I heard later that it took him half an hour to die. Burmans were arriving with dahs and baskets even before I left, and I was told they had stripped his body almost to the bones by the afternoon.

Afterwards, of course, there were endless discussions about the shooting of the elephant. The owner was furious, but he was only an Indian and could do nothing. Besides, legally I had done the right thing, for a mad elephant has to be killed, like a mad dog, if its owner fails to control it. Among the Europeans opinion was divided. The older men said I was right, the younger men said it was a damn shame to shoot an elephant for killing a coolie, because an elephant was worth more than any damn Coringhee coolie. And afterwards I was very glad that the coolie had been killed; it put me legally in the right and it gave me a sufficient pretext for shooting the elephant. I often wondered whether any of the others grasped that I had done it solely to avoid looking a fool.

New Writing, Autumn 1936

Bookshop Memories

When I worked in a second-hand bookshop – so easily pictured, if you don't work in one, as a kind of paradise where charming old gentlemen browse eternally among calf-bound folios – the thing that chiefly struck me was the rarity of really bookish people. Our shop had an exceptionally interesting stock, yet I doubt whether ten per cent of our customers knew a good book from a bad one. First edition snobs were much commoner than lovers of literature, but oriental students haggling over cheap textbooks were commoner still, and vague-minded women looking for birthday presents for their nephews were commonest of all.

Many of the people who came to us were of the kind who would be a nuisance anywhere but have special opportunities in a bookshop. For example, the dear old lady who 'wants a book for an invalid' (a very common demand, that), and the other dear old lady who read such a nice book in 1897 and wonders whether you can find her a copy. Unfortunately she doesn't remember the title or the author's name or what the book was about, but she does remember that it had a red cover. But apart from these there are two well-known types of pest by whom every second-hand bookshop is haunted. One is the decayed person smelling of old breadcrusts who comes every day, sometimes several times a day, and tries to sell you worthless books. The other is the person who orders large quantities of books for which he has not the smallest intention of paying. In our shop we sold nothing on credit, but we would put books aside, or order them if necessary, for people who arranged to fetch them away later. Scarcely half the people who ordered books from us ever came back. It used to puzzle me at first. What made them do it? They would come in and demand some rare and expensive book, would make us promise over and over again to keep it for them, and then would vanish never to return. But many of them, of course, were unmistakable paranoiacs. They used to talk in a grandiose manner about themselves and tell the most ingenious stories to explain how they had happened to come out of doors without any money – stories which, in many cases, I am sure they themselves believed. In a town like London there are always plenty of not quite certifiable lunatics walking the streets, and they tend to gravitate towards bookshops, because a bookshop is one of the few places where you can hang about for a long time without spending any money. In the end one gets to know these people almost at a glance. For all their big talk there is something moth-eaten and aimless about them. Very often, when we were dealing with an obvious paranoiac, we would put aside the books he asked for and then put them back on the shelves the moment he had gone. None of them, I noticed, ever attempted to take books away without paying for them; merely to order them was enough – it gave them, I suppose, the illusion that they were spending real money.

Like most second-hand bookshops we had various sidelines. We sold second-hand typewriters, for instance, and also stamps – used stamps, I mean. Stamp-collectors are a strange, silent, fish-like breed, of all ages, but only of the male sex; women, apparently, fail to see the peculiar charm of gumming bits of coloured paper into albums. We also sold sixpenny horoscopes compiled by somebody who claimed to have foretold the Japanese earthquake. They were in sealed envelopes and I never opened one of them myself, but the people who bought them often came back and told us how 'true' their horoscopes had been. (Doubtless any horoscope seems 'true' if it tells you that you are highly attractive to the opposite sex and your worst fault is generosity.) We did a good deal of business in children's books, chiefly 'remainders'. Modern books for children are rather horrible things, especially when you see them in the mass. Personally I would sooner give a child a copy of Petronius Arbiter than *Peter Pan*, but even Barrie seems manly and wholesome compared with some of his later imitators. At Christmas time we spent a feverish ten days struggling with Christmas cards and calendars, which are tiresome things to sell but good business while the season lasts. It used to interest me to see the brutal cynicism with which Christian sentiment is exploited. The touts from the Christmas card firms used to come round with their catalogues as early as June. A phrase from one of their invoices sticks in my memory. It was: '2 doz. Infant Jesus with rabbits'.

But our principal sideline was a lending library – the usual 'twopenny no-deposit' library of five or six hundred volumes, all fiction. How the book thieves must love those libraries! It is the easiest crime in the world to borrow a book at one shop for twopence, remove the label and sell it at another shop for a shilling. Nevertheless booksellers generally find that it pays them better to have a certain number of books stolen (we used to lose about a dozen a month) than to frighten customers away by demanding a deposit.

Our shop stood exactly on the frontier between Hampstead and Camden Town, and we were frequented by all types from baronets to bus-conductors. Probably our library subscribers were a fair cross-section of London's reading public. It is therefore worth noting that of all the authors in our library the one who 'went out' the best was – Priestley? Hemingway? Walpole? Wodehouse? No, Ethel M. Dell, with Warwick Deeping a good second and Jeffrey Farnol, I should say, third. Dell's novels, of course, are read solely by women, but by women of all kinds and ages and not, as one might expect, merely by wistful spinsters and the fat wives of tobacconists. It is not true that men don't read novels, but it is true that there are whole branches of fiction that they avoid. Roughly speaking, what one might call the *average* novel – the ordinary, good-bad, Galsworthy-and-water stuff which is the norm of the English novel – seems to exist only for women. Men read either the novels it is possible to respect, or detective stories. But their consumption of detective stories is terrific. One of our subscribers to my knowledge read four or five detective stories every week for over a year, besides others which he got from another library. What chiefly surprised me was that he never read the same book twice. Apparently the whole of that frightful torrent of trash (the pages read every year would, I calculated, cover nearly three-quarters of an acre) was stored for ever in his memory. He took no notice of titles or author's names, but he could tell by merely glancing into a book whether he had 'had it already'.

In a lending library you see people's real tastes, not their pretended ones, and one thing that strikes you is how completely the 'classical' English novelists have dropped out of favour. It is simply useless to put Dickens, Thackeray, Jane Austen, Trollope. etc. into the ordinary lending library; nobody takes them out. At the mere sight of a nineteenth-century novel people say 'Oh, but that's *old*!' and shy away immediately. Yet it is always fairly easy to *sell* Dickens, just as it is always easy to sell Shakespeare. Dickens is one of those authors whom people are 'always meaning to' read, and, like the Bible, he is widely known at second hand. People know by hearsay that Bill Sikes was a burglar and that Mr Micawber had a bald head, just as they know by hearsay that Moses was found in a basket of bulrushes and saw the 'back parts' of the Lord. Another thing that is very noticeable is the growing unpopularity of American books. And another – the publishers get into a stew about this every two or three years – is the unpopularity of short stories. The kind of person who asks the librarian to choose a book for him nearly always starts by saying 'I don't want short stories', or 'I do not desire little stories', as a German customer of ours used to put it. If you ask them why, they sometimes explain that it is too much fag to get used to a new set of characters with every story; they like to 'get into' a novel which demands no further thought after the first chapter. I believe, though, that the writers are more to blame here than the readers. Most modern short stories, English and American, are utterly lifeless and worthless, far more so than most novels. The short stories which *are* stories are popular enough, *vide* D. H. Lawrence, whose short stories are as popular as his novels.

Would I like to be a bookseller *de métier*? On the whole – in spite of my employer's kindness to me, and some happy days I spent in the shop – no.

Given a good pitch and the right amount of capital, any educated person ought to be able to make a small secure living out of a bookshop. Unless one goes in for 'rare' books it is not a difficult trade to learn, and you start at a great advantage if you know anything about the insides of books. (Most booksellers don't. You can get their measure by having a look at the trade papers where they advertise their wants. If you don't see an ad for Boswell's *Decline and Fall* you are pretty sure to see one for *The Mill on the Floss* by T. S. Eliot.) Also it is a humane trade which is not capable of being vulgarized beyond a certain point. The combines can never squeeze the small independent bookseller out of existence as they have squeezed the grocer and the milkman. But the hours of work are very long – I was only a part-time employee, but my employer put in a 70-hour week, apart from constant expeditions out of hours to buy books – and it is an unhealthy life. As a rule a bookshop is horribly cold in winter, because if it is too warm the windows get misted over, and a bookseller lives on his windows. And books give off more and nastier dust than any other class of objects yet invented, and the top of a book is the place where every bluebottle prefers to die.

But the real reason why I should not like to be in the book trade for life is that while I was in it I lost my love of books. A bookseller has to tell lies about books, and that gives him a distaste for them; still worse is the fact that he is constantly dusting them and hauling them to and fro. There was a time when I really did love books – loved the sight and smell and feel of them, I mean, at least if they were fifty or more years old. Nothing pleased me quite so much as to buy a job lot of them for a shilling at a country auction. There is a peculiar flavour about the battered unexpected books you pick up in that kind of collection: minor eighteenth-century poets, out of date gazetteers, odd volumes of forgotten novels, bound numbers of ladies' magazines of the 'sixties. For casual reading – in your bath, for instance, or late at night when you are too tired to go to bed, or in the odd quarter of an hour before lunch – there is nothing to touch a back number of the *Girl's Own Paper*. But as soon as I went to work in the bookshop I stopped buying books. Seen in the mass, five or ten thousand at a time, books were boring and even slightly sickening. Nowadays I do buy one occasionally, but only if it is a book that I want to read and can't borrow, and I never buy junk. The sweet smell of decaying paper appeals to me no longer. It is too closely associated in my mind with paranoiac customers and dead bluebottles.

Fortnightly, November 1936

Spilling the Spanish Beans

The Spanish war has probably produced a richer crop of lies than any event since the Great War of 1914–18, but I honestly doubt, in spite of all those hecatombs of nuns who have been raped and crucified before the eyes of *Daily Mail* reporters, whether it is the pro-Fascist newspapers that have done the most harm. It is the left-wing papers, the *News Chronicle* and the *Daily Worker*, with their far subtler methods of distortion, that have prevented the British public from grasping the real nature of the struggle.

The fact which these papers have so carefully obscured is that the Spanish Government (including the semi-autonomous Catalan Government) is far more afraid of the revolution than of the Fascists. It is now almost certain that the war will end with some kind of compromise, and there is even reason to doubt whether the Government, which let Bilbao fall without raising a finger, wishes to be too victorious; but there is no doubt whatever about the thoroughness with which it is crushing its own revolutionaries. For some time past a reign of terror – forcible suppression of political parties, a stifling censorship of the press, ceaseless espionage and mass imprisonment without trial – has been in progress. When I left Barcelona in late June the jails were bulging; indeed, the regular jails had long since overflowed and the prisoners were being huddled into empty shops and any other temporary dump that could be found for them. But the point to notice is that the people who are in prison now are not Fascists but revolutionaries; they are there not because their opinions are too much to the Right, but because they are too much to the Left. And the people responsible for putting them there are those dreadful revolutionaries at whose very name Garvin quakes in his galoshes – the Communists.

Meanwhile the war against Franco continues, but, except for the poor devils in the front-line trenches, nobody in Government Spain thinks of it as the real war. The real struggle is between revolution and counter-revolution; between the workers who are vainly trying to hold onto a little of what they won in 1936, and the Liberal-Communist bloc who are so successfully taking it away from them. It is unfortunate that so few people in England have yet caught up with the fact that Communism is now a counter-revolutionary force; that Communists everywhere are in alliance with bourgeois reformism and using the whole of their powerful machinery to crush or discredit any party that shows signs of revolutionary tendencies. Hence the grotesque spectacle of Communists assailed as wicked 'Reds' by right-wing intellectuals who are in essential agreement with them. Mr Wyndham Lewis, for instance, ought to love the Communists, at least temporarily. In Spain the Communist-Liberal alliance has been almost completely victorious. Of all that the Spanish workers won for themselves in 1936 nothing solid remains, except for a few collective farms and a certain amount of land seized by the peasants last year; and presumably even the peasants will be sacrificed later, when there is no longer any need to placate them. To see how the present situation arose, one has got to look back to the origins of the civil war.

Franco's bid for power differed from those of Hitler and Mussolini in that it was a military insurrection, comparable to a foreign invasion, and therefore had not much mass backing, though Franco has since been trying to acquire one. Its chief supporters, apart from certain sections of Big Business, were the land-owning aristocracy and the huge, parasitic Church. Obviously a rising of this kind will array against it various forces which are not in agreement on any other point. The peasant and the worker hate feudalism and clericalism; but so does the 'liberal' bourgeois, who is not in the least opposed to a more modern version of Fascism, at least so long as it isn't called Fascism. The 'liberal' bourgeois is genuinely liberal up to the point where his own interests stop. He stands for the degree of progress implied in the phrase 'la carrière ouverte aux talents'. For clearly he has no chance to develop in feudal society where the worker and the peasant are too poor to buy goods, where industry is burdened with huge taxes to pay for bishops' vestments, and where every lucrative job is given as a matter of course to the friend of the catamite of the duke's illegitimate son. Hence, in the face of such a blatant reactionary as Franco, you get for a while a situation in which the worker and the bourgeois, in reality deadly enemies, are fighting side by side. This uneasy alliance is known as the Popular Front (or, in the Communist press, to give it a spuriously democratic appeal, People's Front). It is a combination with about as much vitality, and about as much right to exist, as a pig with two heads or some other Barnum and Bailey monstrosity.

In any serious emergency the contradiction implied in the Popular Front is bound to make itself felt. For even when the worker and the bourgeois are both fighting against Fascism, they are not fighting for the same things; the bourgeois is fighting for bourgeois democracy, i.e. capitalism, the worker, in so far as he understands the issue, for Socialism. And in the early days of the revolution the Spanish workers understood the issue very well. In the areas where Fascism was defeated they did not content themselves with driving the rebellious troops out of the towns; they also took the opportunity of seizing land and factories and setting up the rough beginnings of a workers' government by means of local committees, workers' militias, police forces, and so forth. They made the mistake, however (possibly because most of the active revolutionaries were Anarchists with a mistrust of all parliaments), of leaving the Republican Government in nominal control. And, in spite of various changes in personnel, every subsequent Government had been of approximately the same bourgeois-reformist character. At the beginning this seemed not to matter, because the Government, especially in Catalonia, was almost powerless and the bourgeoisie had to lie low or even (this was still happening when I reached Spain in December) to disguise themselves as workers. Later, as power slipped from the hands of the Anarchists into the hands of the Communists and right-wing Socialists, the Government was able to reassert itself, the bourgeoisie came out of hiding and the old division of society into rich and poor reappeared, not much modified. Henceforward every move, except a few dictated by military emergency, was directed towards undoing the work of the first few months of revolution. Out of the many illustrations I could choose, I will cite only one, the breaking-up of the old workers' militias, which were organized on a genuinely democratic system, with officers and men receiving the same pay and mingling on terms of complete equality, and the substitution of the Popular Army (once again, in Communist jargon, 'People's Army'), modelled as far as possible on an ordinary bourgeois army, with a privileged officer-caste, immense differences of pay, etc., etc. Needless to say, this is given out as a military necessity, and almost certainly it does make for military efficiency, at least for a short period. But the undoubted purpose of the change was to strike a blow at equalitarianism. In every department the same policy has been followed, with the result that only a year after the outbreak of war and revolution you get what is in effect an ordinary bourgeois State, with, in addition, a reign of terror to preserve the *status quo*.

This process would probably have gone less far if the struggle could have taken place without foreign interference. But the military weakness of the Government made this impossible. In the face of Franco's foreign mercenaries they were obliged to turn to Russia for help, and though the quantity of arms supplied by Russia has been greatly exaggerated (in my first three months in Spain I saw only one Russian weapon, a solitary machine-gun), the mere fact of their arrival brought the Communists into power. To begin with, the Russian aeroplanes and guns, and the good military qualities of the International Brigades (not necessarily Communist but under Communist control), immensely raised the Communist prestige. But, more important, since Russia and Mexico were the only countries openly supplying arms, the Russians were able not only to get money for their weapons, but to extort terms as well. Put in their crudest form, the terms were: 'Crush the revolution or you get no more arms.' The reason usually given for the Russian attitude is that if Russia appeared to be abetting the revolution, the Franco-Soviet pact (and the hoped-for alliance with Great Britain) would be imperilled; it may be, also, that the spectacle of a genuine revolution in Spain would rouse unwanted echoes in Russia. The Communists, of course, deny that any direct pressure has been exerted by the Russian Government. But this, even if true, is hardly relevant, for the Communist Parties of all countries can be taken as carrying out Russian policy; and it is certain that the Spanish Communist Party, plus the right-wing Socialists whom they control, plus the Communist press of the whole world, have used all their immense and ever-increasing influence upon the side of counter-revolution.

In the first half of this article I suggested that the real struggle in Spain, on the Government side, has been between revolution and counter-revolution; that the Government, though anxious enough to avoid being beaten by Franco, has been even more anxious to undo the revolutionary changes with which the outbreak of war was accompanied.

Any Communist would reject this suggestion as mistaken or wilfully dishonest. He would tell you that it is nonsense to talk of the Spanish Government crushing the revolution, because the revolution never happened; and that our job at present is to defeat Fascism and defend democracy. And in this connection it is most important to see just how the Communist anti-revolutionary propaganda works. It is a mistake to think that this has no relevance in England, where the Communist Party is small and comparatively weak. We shall see its relevance quickly enough if England enters into an alliance with the USSR; or perhaps even earlier, for the influence of the Communist Party is bound to increase – visibly is increasing – as more and more of the capitalist class realize that latter-day Communism is playing their game.

Broadly speaking, Communist propaganda depends upon terrifying people with the (quite real) horrors of Fascism. It also involves pretending – not in so many words, but by implication – that Fascism has nothing to do with capitalism. Fascism is just a kind of meaningless wickedness, an aberration, 'mass sadism', the sort of thing that would happen if you suddenly let loose an asylumful of homicidal maniacs. Present Fascism in this form, and you can mobilize public opinion against it, at any rate for a while, without provoking any revolutionary movement. You can oppose Fascism by bourgeois 'democracy', meaning capitalism. But meanwhile you have got to get rid of the troublesome person who points out that Fascism and bourgeois 'democracy' are Tweedledum and Tweedledee. You do it at the beginning by calling him an impracticable visionary. You tell him that he is confusing the issue, that he is splitting the anti-Fascist forces, that this is not the moment for revolutionary phrase-mongering, that for the moment we have got to fight against Fascism without enquiring too closely what we are fighting *for*. Later, if he still refuses to shut up, you change your tune and call him a traitor. More exactly, you call him a Trotskyist.

And what is a Trotskyist? This terrible word – in Spain at this moment you can be thrown into jail and kept there indefinitely, without trial, on the mere rumour that you are a Trotskyist – is only beginning to be bandied to and fro in England. We shall be hearing more of it later. The word 'Trotskyist' (or 'Trotsky-Fascist') is generally used to mean a disguised Fascist who poses as an ultra-revolutionary in order to split the left-wing forces. But it derives its peculiar power from the fact that it means three separate things. It can mean one who, like Trotsky, wished for world revolution; or a member of the actual organization of which Trotsky is head (the only legitimate use of the word); or the disguised Fascist already mentioned. The three meanings can be telescoped one into the other at will. Meaning No 1 may or may not carry with it meaning No 2, and meaning No 2 almost invariably carries with it meaning No 3. Thus: 'XY has been heard to speak favourably of world revolution; therefore he is a Trotskyist; therefore he is a Fascist.' In Spain, to some extent even in England, *anyone* professing revolutionary Socialism (i.e. professing the things the Communist Party professed until a few years ago) is under suspicion of being a Trotskyist in the pay of Franco or Hitler.

The accusation is a very subtle one, because in any given case, unless one happened to know the contrary, it might be true. A Fascist spy probably *would* disguise himself as a revolutionary. In Spain, everyone whose opinions are to the Left of those of the Communist Party is sooner or later discovered to be a Trotskyist, or at least, a traitor. At the beginning of the war the POUM, an opposition Communist party roughly corresponding to the English ILP, was an accepted party and supplied a minister to the Catalan Government; later it was expelled from the Government; then it was denounced as Trotskyist; then it was suppressed, every member that the police could lay their hands on being flung into jail.

Until a few months ago the Anarcho-Syndicalists were described as 'working loyally' beside the Communists. Then the Anarcho-Syndicalists were levered out of the Government; then it appeared that they were not working so loyally; now they are in the process of becoming traitors. After that will come the turn of the left-wing Socialists. Caballero, the left-wing Socialist ex-premier, until May 1937 the idol of the Communist press, is already in outer darkness, a Trotskyist and 'enemy of the people'. And so the game continues. The logical end is a régime in which every opposition party and newspaper is suppressed and every dissentient of any importance is in jail. Of course, such a régime will be Fascism. It will not be the same as the Fascism Franco would impose, it will even be better than Franco's Fascism to the extent of being worth fighting for, but it will be Fascism. Only, being operated by Communists and Liberals, it will be called something different.

Meanwhile, can the war be won? The Communist influence has been against revolutionary chaos and has therefore, apart from the Russian aid, tended to produce greater military efficiency. If the Anarchists saved the Government from August to October 1936, the Communists have saved it from October onwards. But in organizing the defence they have succeeded in killing enthusiasm (inside Spain, not outside). They made a militarized conscript army possible, but they also made it necessary. It is significant that as early as January of this year voluntary recruiting had practically ceased. A revolutionary army can sometimes win by enthusiasm, but a conscript army has got to win with weapons, and it is unlikely that the Government will ever have a large preponderance of arms unless France intervenes or unless Germany and Italy decide to make off with the Spanish colonies and leave Franco in the lurch. On the whole, a deadlock seems the likeliest thing.

And does the Government seriously intend to win? It does not intend to lose, that is certain. On the other hand, an outright victory, with Franco in flight and the Germans and Italians driven into the sea, would raise difficult problems, some of them too obvious to need mentioning. There is no real evidence and one can only judge by the event, but I suspect that what the Government is playing for is a compromise that would leave the war situation essentially in being. All prophecies are wrong, therefore this one will be wrong, but I will take a chance and say that though the war may end quite soon or may drag on for years, it will end with Spain divided up, either by actual frontiers or into economic zones. Of course, such a compromise might be claimed as a victory by either side, or by both.

All that I have said in this article would seem entirely commonplace in Spain, or even in France. Yet in England, in spite of the intense interest the Spanish war has aroused, there are very few people who have even heard of the enormous struggle that is going on behind the Government lines. Of course, this is no accident. There has been a quite deliberate conspiracy (I could give detailed instances) to prevent the Spanish situation from being understood. People who ought to know better have lent themselves to the deception on the ground that if you tell the truth about Spain it will be used as Fascist propaganda.

It is easy to see where such cowardice leads. if the British public had been given a truthful account of the Spanish war they would have had an opportunity of learning what Fascism is and how it can be combated. As it is, the *News Chronicle* version of Fascism as a kind of homicidal mania peculiar to Colonel Blimps bombinating in the economic void has been established more firmly than ever. And thus we are one step nearer to the great war 'against Fascism' (cf 1914, 'against militarism') which will allow Fascism, British variety, to be slipped over our necks during the first week.

New English Weekly, 29 July and 2 September 1937

Notes[1] on the Spanish Militias[2]

[These notes were found among Orwell's papers after his death. He had never mentioned them and it is extremely difficult to know when they were written, although it is clear they were written after he had left Spain. It is likely they were not written until some time in 1939 when he was in Morocco but they are placed here as they could well serve as an appendix to *Homage to Catalonia*.]

I joined the POUM militia at the end of 1936. The circumstances of my joining this militia rather than any other were the following. I had intended going to Spain to gather materials for newspaper articles, etc., and had also some

[1] NB. that these notes refer only to the POUM militia, exceptional because of the internal political struggle, but in actual composition, etc, probably not very dissimilar from the other militias in Catalonia in the first year of war. [Author's footnote.]

[2] . . . 'From the point of view of political theory there were only three parties that mattered, the PSUC, the POUM and the CNT [Confederacion Nacional de Trabajadores] – FAI [Federacion Anarquista Iberica], loosely described as the Anarchists.

vague idea of fighting if it seemed worth while, but was doubtful about this owing to my poor health and comparatively small military experience. Just before I started someone told me I should not be able to cross the frontier unless I had papers from some left-wing organization (this was untrue at that time although party cards, etc. undoubtedly made it easier). I applied to John Strachey who took me to see Pollitt. P after questioning me evidently decided that I was politically unreliable and refused to help me, also tried to frighten me out of going by talking a lot about Anarchist terrorism. Finally he asked

I take the PSUC first, as being the most important; it was the party that finally triumphed....

It is necessary to explain that when one speaks of the PSUC "line" one really means the Communist Party "line". The PSUC (Partido Socialista Unificado de Catalunya) was the Socialist Party of Catalonia; it had been formed at the beginning of the war by the fusion of various Marxist parties, including the Catalan Communist Party, but it was now entirely under Communist control and was affiliated to the Third International. Elsewhere in Spain no formal unification between Socialists and Communists had taken place, but the Communist viewpoint and the right-wing Socialist viewpoint could everywhere be regarded as identical. Roughly speaking, the PSUC was the political organ of the UGT (Unión General de Trabajadores), the Socialist trade unions.... They contained many sections of the manual workers, but since the outbreak of war they had also been swollen by a large influx of middle-class members....

The PSUC "line" which was preached in the Communist and pro-Communist press throughout the world, was approximately this: "At present nothing matters except winning the war; without victory in the war all else is meaningless. Therefore this is not the moment to talk of pressing forward with the revolution.... At this stage we are not fighting for the dictatorship of the proletariat, we are fighting for parliamentary democracy. Whoever tries to turn the civil war into a social revolution is playing into the hands of the Fascists and is in effect, if not in intention, a traitor."

The POUM "line" differed from this on every point except, of course, the importance of winning the war. The POUM was one of those dissident Communist parties which have appeared in many countries in the last few years as a result of the opposition to "Stalinism".... It was made up partly of ex-Communists and partly of an earlier party, the Workers' and Peasants' Bloc. Numerically it was a small party, with not much influence outside Catalonia, and chiefly important because it contained an unusually high proportion of politically conscious members.... It did not represent any block of trade unions. The POUM militiamen were mostly CNT members, but the actual party-members generally belonged to the UGT. It was, however, only in the CNT that the POUM had any influence. The POUM "line" was approximately this: "It is nonsense to talk of opposing Fascism by bourgeois 'democracy'. Bourgeois 'democracy' is only another name for capitalism, and so is Fascism; to fight against Fascism on behalf of 'democracy' is to fight against one form of capitalism on behalf of a second which is liable to turn into the first at any moment. The only real alternative to Fascism is workers' control. If you set up any less goal than this, you will either hand the victory to Franco, or, at best, let in Fascism by the back door.... The war and the revolution are inseparable."' From *Homage to Catalonia*, Chapter Five, (pp 30, 31).

Professor Hugh Thomas, author of *The Spanish Civil War* (Eyre & Spottiswoode 1961), in a letter to the editors, comments: '... first, that the CNT and FAI were actually different organisations of which the latter was, broadly speaking, the leadership of the former, having been set up in the 'twenties to keep the CNT from revisionism. Secondly, where George Orwell said in *Homage to Catalonia* that the Communists' viewpoint and the right-wing Socialists' viewpoint could everywhere be regarded as identical, this was only the case for quite a short time, since Prieto, the leading right-wing Socialist, moved over into a very strong anti-Communist position quite soon. Thirdly, it is only very "roughly speaking" that the PSUC was the political organ of the UGT. Indeed, this is nearer a mistake than any of the other points, because the UGT was the nationwide labour organisation, admittedly led by Socialists, whereas the PSUC was simply confined to Catalonia.'

whether I would undertake to join the International Brigade. I said I could not undertake to join anything until I had seen what was happening. He then refused to help me but advised me to get a safe-conduct from the Spanish Embassy in Paris, which I did. Just before leaving England I also rang up the ILP, with which I had some slight connections, mainly personal, and asked them to give me some kind of recommendation. They sent me a letter to Paris addressed to John McNair at Barcelona. When I crossed the frontier the passport people and others, at that time Anarchists, did not pay much attention to my safe-conduct but seemed impressed by the letter with ILP heading, which they evidently knew by sight. It was this that made me decide to produce my letter to McNair (whom I did not know) and through this that I joined the POUM militia. After one glimpse of the troops in Spain I saw that I had relatively a lot of training as a soldier and decided to join the militia. At that time I was only rather dimly aware of the differences between the political parties, which had been covered up in the English left-wing press. Had I had a complete understanding of the situation I should probably have joined the CNT militia.

At this time the militias, though theoretically being re-cast on an ordinary army basis, were still organized in column, centuria, secion, the centuria of about 100 men more or less centring round some individual and often being called 'So-and-so's bandera'. The commander of the centuria ranked more or less as captain, but below that there was no well-defined rank except corporal and private. People wore stripes, etc., of rank in Barcelona but it was 'not done' to wear them at the front. Theoretically promotion was by election, but actually the officers and NCOs were appointed from above. As I shall point out later this does not in practice make much difference. One peculiar feature however was that a man could choose which section he should belong to and as a rule could also change to another bandera if he wanted to. At that time men were being sent into the line with only a few days' training and that of a parade-ground kind, and in many cases without ever having fired a rifle. I had brought with me ordinary British army ideas and was appalled by the lack of discipline. It is of course always difficult to get recruits to obey orders and becomes much more so when they find themselves thrust into trenches and having to put up with cold, etc., which they are not accustomed to. If they have not had a chance to familiarize themselves with firearms they are often much more afraid of bullets than they need be and this is an added source of indiscipline. (Incidentally a lot of harm was done by the lies published in the left-wing papers to the effect that the Fascists were using explosive bullets. So far as I know there is no such thing as an explosive bullet, and certainly the Fascists weren't using them.) At the beginning one had to get orders obeyed (a) by appealing to party loyalty and (b) by force of personality, and for the first week or two I made myself thoroughly unpopular. After about a week a man flatly refused to go to a certain place which he declared was exposed to fire, and I made him do so by force – always a mistake, of course, and doubly so with a Spaniard. I was immediately surrounded by a ring of men calling me a Fascist. There was a tremendous argument; however most of the men took my side and I found that people rather competed to join my section. After this, for some weeks or months, both among the Spaniards and the few English who were on this front, this kind of argument recurred over and over again, i.e. indiscipline, arguments as to what was justifiable and what was 'revolutionary', but in general a consensus of opinion that one must have strict discipline combined with social equality. There was always a lot of argument as to whether it was justifiable to shoot men for desertion and disobedience and in general people agreed that it was, though some would never do so. Much later, about March, near Huesca, some 200 CNT troops suddenly decided to walk out of the line. One could hardly blame them as they had been there about five months, but obviously such a thing could not be allowed and there was a call for some POUM troops to go and stop them. I volunteered though not feeling very happy about it. Fortunately they were persuaded to go back by their political delegates or somebody, so it never came to violence. There was a lot of argument about this, but again the majority agreed that it would be justifiable to use one's rifle against men doing this if necessary. Throughout this period, i.e. January–April 1937, the gradual improvement in discipline was brought about almost entirely by 'diffusion of revolutionary consciousness', i.e. endless arguments and explanations as to *why* such and such a thing was necessary. Everyone was fanatically keen on keeping social equality between officers and men, no military titles and no differences of food, etc. and this was often carried to lengths that were rather ridiculous, though they seemed less ridiculous in the line where minute differences of comfort were very appreciable. When the militias were theoretically incorporated in the Popular Army[1] all officers were expected to pay their extra pay, i.e. anything over 10 pesetas a day, into the Party funds, and everyone agreed to do so, though whether this actually happened I don't know, because I am not certain whether anyone actually began drawing extra pay before the POUM militia was redistributed. Punishments for disobedience were, however, being used even at the time when I first reached the front. It is extremely difficult to punish men who are already in the front line, because short of killing them it is hard to make them more uncomfortable than they are already. The usual punishment was double hours of sentry-go – very unsatisfactory because everyone is already short of sleep. Occasionally men were shot. One man who attempted to cross to the Fascist lines and was clearly a spy was shot. Another caught stealing from other militiamen was sent back supposedly to be shot, though I don't think he actually was. Courts Martial were supposed to consist of one officer, one NCO and one militiaman, though I never saw one in action.

Periodically political delegates used to be sent round by the Party to visit the men in the line and, when possible, deliver [some] sort of political discourses. In addition every centuria had one or more men in its own ranks who were called its political delegates. I never grasped what the function of these men had originally been – they had evidently at the beginning had some function for which there was afterwards no need. When with the ILP English I was appointed their political delegate, but this time the political delegate was simply a go-between who was sent to headquarters to complain about rations, etc. and therefore so far as the English were concerned it was simply a question of choosing among the few men who spoke Spanish. The English were stricter than the Spaniards about electing officers and in one or two cases changed an NCO by election. They also appointed a committee

[1] Popular Army: ... 'Since February [1937] the entire armed forces had theoretically been incorporated in the Popular Army [by the Government], and the militias were, on paper, reconstructed along Popular Army lines ...' From *Homage to Catalonia*, Chapter Nine.

of 5 men who were supposed to regulate all the affairs of the section. Although I was voted onto the committee myself I opposed its formation on the ground that we were now part of an army being commanded from above in more or less the ordinary way, and therefore such a committee had no function. Actually it had no important function but was occasionally useful for regulating very small matters. Contrary to what is generally believed the political leaders of the POUM were very hostile to this committee idea and were anxious to prevent the idea spreading from the English to the Spaniards.

Before joining the English I was some weeks in a Spanish bandera, and of about 80 men in it some 60 were completely raw recruits. In these weeks the discipline improved a good deal, and from then on till the end of April there was a slow but fairly steady improvement in discipline throughout the militia. By April a militia unit when it had to march anywhere still *looked* like a retreat from Moscow, but this was partly because the men had been experienced solely in trench warfare. But by this time there was no difficulty in getting an order obeyed and no fear that it would be disobeyed as soon as your back was turned. Outwardly the special 'revolutionary' characteristics remained the same till the end of May, but in fact certain differences were showing themselves by this time. In May when I was commanding a seccion (which now meant a platoon) the younger Spaniards called me 'usted'. I pulled them up about it but the word was evidently coming back, and no doubt the universal use of 'tu' in the early months of the war was an affectation and would seem most unnatural to a Latin people. One thing that seemed to stop abruptly about March was the shouting of revolutionary slogans to the Fascists. This was not practised at Huesca, though in many cases the trenches were very close together. On the Zaragoza front it had been practised regularly and probably had its share in bringing in the deserters who were very numerous there (at one time about 15 a week on a section of front held by about 1,000 men). But the universal use of 'camarada' and the notion that we were all supposed to be equals persisted until the militia was redistributed.[1] It was noticeable that the first drafts of the Popular Army who came up to the line conformed with this. Between the POUM and PSUC militias, up to the time when I last saw the latter at the beginning of March, there was no perceptible difference in state of discipline and social atmosphere.

The general organization was in some ways very good but in others quite unnecessarily incompetent. One striking feature about this war was the good food organization. Up till May 1937 when certain things began to give out the food was always good, and it was always regular, a thing not easy to arrange even in a very stationary war. The cooks were very devoted, sometimes bringing food up under heavy fire. I was impressed by the food-organization behind the lines and the way in which the peasants had been got to co-operate. The men's clothes were laundered from time to time, but it was not done very well or very regularly. The postal arrangements were good and letters which had started from Barcelona always got to the front promptly, though an extraordinary number of letters sent into Spain went astray somewhere on the way to Barcelona. Ideas of sanitation practically did not exist and no doubt only the dry climate prevented epidemics. There was no medical service worth mentioning till one got about 10 miles behind the lines. This

[1] My medical discharge-ticket, signed by a doctor at Monzon (a long way behind the line) about 18 June refers to me as 'Comrade Blair'. [Author's footnote.]

did not matter so long as there was only a small trickle of casualties, but even so many lives were lost unnecessarily. Trenches were at the beginning extremely primitive but about March a labour battalion was organized. This was very efficient and able to construct long sections of trench very rapidly and without noise. Nevertheless up to about May there was not much idea of communication-trenches, even where the front line was near the enemy, and it was not possible, e.g. to get wounded men away without carrying them under fire. No effort was made to keep the roads behind the line in repair, although, no doubt, the labour to do so was available. The POUM Red Aid, to which it was voluntary-compulsory to subscribe, were very good about looking after wounded men in hospital, etc. In regard to stores, there was probably some peculation and favouritism, but I think extremely little. When cigarettes began to run short the little English section received rather more than their fair share, a tribute to the Spanish character. The grand and inexcusable mistake made in this war, at any rate on the Aragon front, was to keep the men in the line for unnecessarily long periods. By Xmas 1936 the war was almost entirely stationary and for long periods during the next six months there was little fighting. It should therefore have been perfectly possible to organize the four days in four days out, or even four days in two days out, system. On this arrangement men do not actually get more hours of rest but they do periodically get a few nights in bed or at any rate with the chance to take their clothes off. As it was men were sometimes kept as long as five months in the line continuously. It sometimes happened that trenches were a long way from the enemy, say 1,000 yards, but this is more boring and therefore worse for morale than being at 50–100 yards. Meanwhile they were sleeping in trenches in intolerable discomfort, usually lousy and up till April almost always cold. Moreover even when one is 1,000 yards from the enemy one is under rifle and occasional shell fire, causing a trickle of casualties and therefore fear which is cumulative. In these circumstances it is difficult to do more than keep on keeping on. During February–March, the period when there was little fighting round Huesca, attempts were made to train the men in various things, use of the machine-gun, signalling, open-order work (advancing by rushes), etc. These were mainly a failure because everyone was suffering from lack of sleep and too exhausted to learn. I myself at this time tried to master the mechanism of the Hotchkiss machine-gun and found that lack of sleep had simply deprived me of the power to learn. In addition it would no doubt have been feasible to grant leave at shorter intervals, but the failure to do so probably had reasons other than incompetence. But it would have been quite easy to take the men in and out of trenches as I have indicated, and to provide some kind of amenities for the troops not in the line. Even as far back as Barbastro the life of the troops was much drearier than it need have been. With a little organization it would have been possible to arrange immediately behind the lines for hot baths, delousing, entertainments of some kind, cafés (actually there were some very feeble attempts at these) and also women. The very few women who were in or near the line and were get-atable were simply a source of jealousy. There was a certain amount of sodomy among the younger Spaniards. I doubt whether troops can simultaneously engage in trench warfare and be trained for mobile warfare, but more training would certainly have been possible if more care had been devoted to resting the men. As it was they were exhausted for nothing at a period when the war was stagnant. Looking back I see that they stood it extremely well, and even at the time it was the fact that they did *not* disintegrage or show mutinous tendencies under these intolerable conditions that converted me (to some extent) to the notion of 'revolutionary discipline'. Nevertheless the strain that was put upon them was partly unnecessary.

As to jealousies between the different militias, so far as the rank and file were concerned I myself did not see serious signs of these till May 1937. To what extent the Aragon front was sabotaged from political motives I suppose we shall learn sooner or later. I do not know how important the capture of Huesca would have been, but there is little doubt that it could have been taken in February or March with adequate artillery. As it was it was surrounded except for one gap about a km wide, and this with so little artillery that preliminary bombardments were an impossibility, as they would only have served as a warning. This meant that attacks could only be surprise attacks delivered by a few hundred men at most. By the beginning of April Huesca appeared to be doomed, but the gap was never closed, the attacks petered out and a little later it became clear that the Fascist trenches were more strongly held and that they had improved their defences. At the end of June the big attack on Huesca was staged, clearly from political motives, to provide the Popular Army with a victory and discredit the CNT militia. The result was what could have been foreseen – heavy losses and an actual worsening of the position. But as far as the rank and file were concerned party-feeling did not usually get beyond vague rumours that 'they', usually meaning the PSUC, had stolen guns, etc. meant for ourselves. On the Zaragoza front where POUM and PSUC militia were distributed more or less alternately relations were good. When the POUM took over a sector from the PSUC at Huesca there were signs of jealousy, but this I think was purely military, the PSUC troops having failed to take Huesca and the POUM boasting that they were going to do so. The Guadalajara victory in February could be regarded as, and in fact was, a Communist victory, but everyone was unaffectedly glad and in fact enthusiastic. A little later than this one of our aeroplanes, presumably Russian, dropped a bomb in the wrong place and killed a number of POUM militiamen. Later, no doubt, it would have been said that this was 'done on purpose', but at the time this did not occur to anybody. About May, perhaps following on the Barcelona trouble, relations worsened. In Lerida, where large numbers of the new Popular Army formations were in training, when detachments of Popular Army marched past, I saw militiamen of I do not know what militia giving them raspberries and bleating in imitation of sheep. As to victimization of men known to have served with the POUM, I doubt whether it began until after the alleged espionage discoveries. Immediately after these there appear to have been one or two serious incidents. About the end of June it seems that a detachment of PSUC militia were sent or came of their own accord to attack one of the POUM positions outside Huesca, and the men at the latter had to defend themselves with their machine-guns. I have not either the exact date or more than general facts of this, but the source from which I had it leaves me in no doubt that it happened. It was no doubt the result of irresponsible statements in the press about espionage, desertion, etc. which had caused or almost caused trouble on earlier occasions.

The fact that the militias were organized by and owed loyalty to different parties had bad effects after a certain date. At the beginning, when everyone was full of enthusiasm, inter-party rivalry was perhaps not a bad thing – this impression at least I derived from those who were in the earlier fighting when Sietamo, etc. were taken. But when the militias were dwindling as against the Popular Army the effect was to make every party anxious to keep its strength up at no matter what cost. I believe that this was one reason for the fact, noted above, that leave was not granted as often as it might have been. Up till about June there was in reality no way of making a man who had gone on leave rejoin his unit, and conscription into the Popular Army, [when] passed into law (I forget when exactly it was passed) was completely ineffective. Therefore a militiaman once on leave could simply go home, and he had the more motive to do so as he had just drawn a big wad of back-pay, or he could join another organization, which was often done at that time. In practice most men returned from leave, but some did not, so that every spell of leave meant a dwindling of numbers. In addition, I am certain that anxiety to keep up numbers made local commanders over-anxious not to incur casualties when they could not gain *éclat* by incurring them. On the Zaragoza front valuable minor opportunities – the kind of thing that would not have got into the papers but would have made a certain difference – were lost owing to this, while such casualties as did occur were completely pointless. Also the useless riff-raff, amounting to five or ten per cent, who are to be found in all bodies of troops and who should be got rid of ruthlessly, were seldom or never got rid of. In January when I complained about the state of discipline a higher-up officer gave me his opinion that all the militias competed in slackness of discipline in order to detach recruits from the others. I don't know whether this was true or said owing to momentary fed-upness.

As to the personnel of the POUM militia, I doubt whether it was much different from the others. In standard of physique, which is a rough test, they were about equal to the PSUC. The POUM did not ask party affiliation from their militiamen, doubtless because being a minority party they found it hard to attract recruits. When the men were in the line efforts were made to get them to join the party, but it is fair to say that there was not kind of pressure. There was the usual proportion of riff-raff, and in addition a certain number of very ignorant peasants and people of no particular political alignment who had probably joined the POUM militia more or less by accident. In addition there was a certain number of people who had simply joined for the sake of a job. The fact that in December 1936 there was already a serious bread shortage in Barcelona and militiamen got bread in plenty had a lot to do with this. Nevertheless some of these nondescripts afterwards turned into quite good soldiers. Apart from a rather large number of refugee Germans there was a sprinkling of foreigners of many races, even including a few Portuguese. Putting aside the Germans, the best soldiers were usually the machine-gunners, who were organized in crews of six and kept rather apart from the others. The fetichistic attitude which men in this position develop towards their gun, rather as towards a household god, is interesting and should be studied. A few of the machine-gunners were old soldiers who had done their service over and over again owing to the Spanish substitute system, but most of them were 'good party men', some of them men of extremely high character and intelligence. I came to the conclusion, somewhat against my will, that in the long run 'good party men' make the best soldiers. The detachment of in all about 30 English and Americans sent out by the ILP were divided rather sharply between old soldiers of no particular political affiliations and 'good party men' with no military experience. As I am nearer to the first type myself I am probably not prejudiced in saying that I believe the second to be superior. Old soldiers are of course more useful at the beginning of a campaign, and they are all right when there is any fighting, but they have more tendency to go to pieces under inaction and physical exhaustion. A man who has fully identified with some political party is reliable in *all* circumstances. One would get into trouble in left-wing circles for saying so, but the feeling of many Socialists towards their party is very similar to that of the thicker-headed type of public-school man towards his old school. There are individuals who have no particular political feelings and are completely reliable, but they are usually of bourgeois origin. In the POUM militia there was a slight but perceptible tendency for people of bourgeois origin to be chosen as officers. Given the existing class-structure of society I regard this as inevitable. Middle-class and upper-class people have usually more self-confidence in unfamiliar circumstances, and in countries where conscription is not in force they usually have more military tradition than the working class. This is notably the case in England. As to age, 20 to 35 seems to be the proper age for front-line soldiers. Above 35 I would not trust anybody in the line as a common soldier or junior officer unless he is of known political reliability. As for the younger limit, boys as young as 14 are often very brave and reliable, but they simply cannot stand the lack of sleep. They will even fall asleep standing up.

As to treachery, fraternization, etc. there were just enough rumours about this to suggest that such things happened occasionally, and in fact they are inevitable in civil war. There were vague rumours that at some time pre-arranged truces had been held in no man's land for exchange of newspapers. I do not know of an instance of this but once saw some Fascist papers which might have been procured in this manner. The stories circulated in the Communist press about non-aggression pacts and people coming and going freely between our lines and the Fascists were lies. There was undoubtedly treachery among the peasants. The reason why no attack on this front ever came off at the time scheduled was no doubt partly incompetence, but it was also said that if the time was fixed more than a few hours ahead it was invariably known to the Fascists. The Fascists always appeared to know what troops they had opposite them, whereas we only knew what we could infer from patrols, etc. I do not know what method was used by spies for getting messages into Huesca, but the method of sending messages out was flash-lamp signalling. There were morse code signals at a certain hour every night. These were always recorded, but except for slogans such as 'Viva Franco' they were always in cipher. I don't know whether they were successfully deciphered. The spies behind the lines were never caught in spite of many attempts. Desertions were very rare, though up to May 1937 it would have been easy to walk out of the line, or with a little risk, across to the Fascists. I knew of a few desertions among our men and a few among the PSUC, but the whole number would have been tiny. It is noticeable that men in a force of this type retain political feeling against the enemy as they would not in an ordinary army. When I first reached the front it was taken for granted that officer-prisoners taken by us must be shot, and the Fascists were said to shoot all prisoners – a lie, no doubt, but the significant thing was that people believed it. As late as March 1937 I heard credibly of an officer-prisoner taken by us being shot – again the significant thing is that no one seemed to think this wrong.

As to the actual performance of the POUM militia, I know of this chiefly from others, as I was at the front during the most inactive period of the war.

They took part in the taking of Sietamo and the advance on Huesca, and after this the division was split up, some at Huesca, some on the Zaragoza front and a few at Teruel. I believe there was also a handful on the Madrid front. In late February the whole division was concentrated on the eastern side of Huesca. Tactically this was the less important side, and during March–April the part played by the POUM was only raids and holding attacks, affairs involving at most two hundred men and a few score casualties. In some of these they did well, especially the refugee Germans. In the attack on Huesca at the end of June the division lost heavily, 4–600 killed. I was not in this show but heard from others who were that the POUM troops behaved well. By this time the campaigns in the press had begun to produce a certain amount of disaffection. By April even the politically uninterested had grasped that except in their own press and that of the Anarchists no good would be reported of them, whatever their actual performance might be. At the time this produced only a certain irritation, but I know that later, when the division was redistributed, some men who were able to dodge the conscription did so and got civilian jobs on the ground that they were tired of being libelled. A number of men who were in the Huesca attack assured me that General Pozas deliberately withheld the artillery to get as many POUM troops killed as possible – doubtless untrue, but showing the effect of campaigns like that conducted by the Communist press. I do not know what happened to the division after being redistributed, but believe they mostly went to the 26th division. Considering the circumstances and their opportunities, I should say that the performance of the POUM militia was respectable though in no way brilliant.

Marrakech

As the corpse went past the flies left the restaurant table in a cloud and rushed after it, but they came back a few minutes later.

The little crowd of mourners – all men and boys, no women – threaded their way across the market-place between the piles of pomegranates and the taxis and the camels, wailing a short chant over and over again. What really appeals to the flies is that the corpses here are never put into coffins, they are merely wrapped in a piece of rag and carried on a rough wooden bier on the shoulders of four friends. When the friends get to the burying-ground they hack an oblong hole a foot or two deep, dump the body in it and fling over it a little of the dried-up, lumpy earth, which is like broken brick. No gravestone, no name, no identifying mark of any kind. The burying-ground is merely a huge waste of hummocky earth, like a derelict building-lot. After a month or two no one can even be certain where his own relatives are buried.

When you walk through a town like this – two hundred thousand inhabitants, of whom at least twenty thousand own literally nothing except the rags they stand up in – when you see how the people live, and still more how easily they die, it is always difficult to believe that you are walking among human beings. All colonial empires are in reality founded upon that fact. The people have brown faces – besides, there are so many of them! Are they really the same flesh as yourself? Do they even have names? Or are they merely a kind of undifferentiated brown stuff, about as individual as bees or coral insects? They rise out of the earth, they sweat and starve for a few years, and then they sink back into the nameless mounds of the graveyard and nobody notices that they are gone. And even the graves themselves soon fade back into the soil. Sometimes, out for a walk, as you break your way through the prickly pear, you notice that it is rather bumpy underfoot, and only a certain regularity in the bumps tells you that you are walking over skeletons.

I was feeding one of the gazelles in the public gardens.

Gazelles are almost the only animals that look good to eat when they are still alive, in fact, one can hardly look at their hindquarters without thinking of mint sauce. The gazelle I was feeding seemed to know that this thought was in my mind, for though it took the piece of bread I was holding out it obviously did not like me. It nibbled rapidly at the bread, then lowered its head and tried to butt me, then took another nibble and then butted again. Probably its idea was that if it could drive me away the bread would somehow remain hanging in mid-air.

An Arab navvy working on the path nearby lowered his heavy hoe and sidled towards us. He looked from the gazelle to the bread and from the bread to the gazelle, with a sort of quiet amazement, as though he had never seen anything quite like this before. Finally he said shyly in French:

'*I* could eat some of that bread.'

I tore off a piece and he stowed it gratefully in some secret place under his rags. This man is an employee of the Municipality.

When you go through the Jewish quarters you gather some idea of what the medieval ghettoes were probably like. Under their Moorish rulers the Jews were only allowed to own land in certain restricted areas, and after centuries of this kind of treatment they have ceased to bother about overcrowding. Many of the streets are a good deal less than six feet wide, the houses are completely windowless, and sore-eyed children cluster everywhere in unbelievable numbers, like clouds of flies. Down the centre of the street there is generally running a little river of urine.

In the bazaar huge families of Jews, all dressed in the long black robe and little black skull-cap, are working in dark fly-infested booths that look like caves. A carpenter sits cross-legged at a prehistoric lathe, turning chair-legs at lightning speed. He works the lathe with a bow in his right hand and guides the chisel with his left foot, and thanks to a lifetime of sitting in this position his left leg is warped out of shape. At his side his grandson, aged six, is already starting on the simpler parts of the job.

I was just passing the coppersmiths' booths when somebody noticed that I was lighting a cigarette. Instantly, from the dark holes all round, there was a frenzied rush of Jews, many of them old grandfathers with flowing grey beards, all clamouring for a cigarette. Even a blind man somewhere at the back of one of the booths heard a rumour of cigarettes and came crawling out, groping in the air with his hand. In about a minute I had used up the whole packet. None of these people, I suppose, works less than twelve hours a day, and every one of them looks on a cigarette as a more or less impossible luxury.

As the Jews live in self-contained communities they follow the same trades as the Arabs, except for agriculture. Fruit-sellers, potters, silversmiths, blacksmiths, butchers, leather-workers, tailors, water-carriers, beggars, porters – whichever way you look you see nothing but Jews. As a matter of fact there are thirteen thousand of them, all living in the space of a few acres. A good job Hitler isn't here. Perhaps he is on his way, however. You hear the usual dark rumours about the Jews, not only from the Arabs but from the poorer Europeans.

'Yes, *mon vieux*, they took my job away from me and gave it to a Jew. The Jews! They're the real rulers of this country, you know. They've got all the money. They control the banks, finance – everything.'

'But,' I said, 'isn't it a fact that the average Jew is a labourer working for about a penny an hour?'

'Ah, that's only for show! They're all moneylenders really. They're cunning, the Jews.'

In just the same way, a couple of hundred years ago, poor old women used to be burned for witchcraft when they could not even work enough magic to get themselves a square meal.

All people who work with their hands are partly invisible, and the more important the work they do, the less visible they are. Still, a white skin is always fairly conspicuous. In northern Europe, when you see a labourer ploughing a field, you probably give him a second glance. In a hot country, anywhere south of Gibraltar or east of Suez, the chances are that you don't even see him. I have noticed this again and again. In a tropical landscape one's eye takes in everything except the human beings. It takes in the dried-up soil, the prickly pear, the palm-tree and the distant mountain, but it always misses the peasant hoeing at his patch. He is the same colour as the earth, and a great deal less interesting to look at.

It is only because of this that the starved countries of Asia and Africa are accepted as tourist resorts. No one would think of running cheap trips to the Distressed Areas. But where the human beings have brown skins their poverty is simply not noticed. What does Morocco mean to a Frenchman? An orange-grove or a job in government service. Or to an Englishman? Camels, castles, palm-trees, Foreign Legionnaires, brass trays and bandits. One could probably live here for years without noticing that for nine-tenths of the people the reality of life is an endless, back-breaking struggle to wring a little food out of an eroded soil.

Most of Morocco is so desolate that no wild animal bigger than a hare can live on it. Huge areas which were once covered with forest have turned into a treeless waste where the soil is exactly like broken-up brick. Nevertheless a good deal of it is cultivated, with frightful labour. Everything is done by hand. Long lines of women, bent double like inverted capital Ls, work their way slowly across the fields, tearing up the prickly weeds with their hands, and the peasant gathering lucerne for fodder pulls it up stalk by stalk instead of reaping it, thus saving an inch or two on each stalk. The plough is a wretched wooden thing, so frail that one can easily carry it on one's shoulder, and fitted underneath with a rough iron spike which stirs the soil to a depth of about four inches. This is as much as the strength of the animals is equal to. It is usual to plough with a cow and a donkey yoked together. Two donkeys would not be quite strong enough, but on the other hand two cows would cost a little more to feed. The peasants possess no harrows, they merely plough the soil several times over in different directions, finally leaving it in rough furrows, after which the whole field has to be shaped with hoes into small oblong patches, to conserve water. Except for a day or two after the rare rainstorms there is never enough water. Along the edges of the fields channels are hacked out to a depth of thirty or forty feet to get at the tiny trickles which run through the subsoil.

Every afternoon a file of very old women passes down the road outside my house, each carrying a load of firewood. All of them are mummified with age and the sun, and all of them are tiny. It seems to be generally the case in primitive communities that the women, when they get beyond a certain age, shrink to the size of children. One day a poor old creature who could not have been more than four feet tall crept past me under a vast load of wood. I stopped her and put a five-sou piece (a little more than a farthing) into her hand. She answered with a shrill wail, almost a scream, which was partly gratitude but mainly surprise. I suppose that from her point of view, by taking any notice of her, I seemed almost to be violating a law of nature. She accepted her status as an old woman, that is to say as a beast of burden. When a family is travelling it is quite usual to see a father and a grown-up son riding ahead on donkeys, and an old woman following on foot, carrying the baggage.

But what is strange about these people is their invisibility. For several weeks, always at about the same time of day, the file of old women had hobbled past the house with their firewood, and though they had registered themselves on my eyeballs I cannot truly say that I had seen them. Firewood was passing – that was how I saw it. It was only that one day I happened to be walking behind them, and the curious up-and-down motion of a load of wood drew my attention to the human being underneath it. Then for the first time I noticed the poor old earth-coloured bodies, bodies reduced to bones and leathery skin, bent double under the crushing weight. Yet I suppose I had not been five minutes on Moroccan soil before I noticed the overloading of the donkeys and was infuriated by it. There is no question that the donkeys are damnably treated. The Moroccan donkey is hardly bigger than a St Bernard dog, it carries a load which in the British army would be considered too much for a fifteen-hands mule, and very often its pack-saddle is not taken off its back for weeks together. But what is peculiarly pitiful is that it is the most willing creature on earth, it follows its master like a dog and does not need either bridle or halter. After a dozen years of devoted work it suddenly drops dead, whereupon its master tips it into the ditch and the village dogs have torn its guts out before it is cold.

This kind of thing makes one's blood boil, whereas – on the whole – the plight of the human beings does not. I am not commenting, merely pointing to a fact. People with brown skins are next door to invisible. Anyone can be sorry for the donkey with its galled back, but it is generally owing to some kind of accident if one even notices the old woman under her load of sticks.

As the storks flew northward the Negroes were marching southward – a long, dusty column, infantry, screw-gun batteries and then more infantry, four or five thousand men in all, winding up the road with a clumping of boots and a clatter of iron wheels.

They were Senegalese, the blackest Negroes in Africa, so black that sometimes it is difficult to see whereabouts on their necks the hair begins. Their splendid bodies were hidden in reach-me-down khaki uniforms, their feet squashed into boots that looked like blocks of wood, and every tin hat seemed to be a couple of sizes too small. It was very hot and the men had marched a long way. They slumped under the weight of their packs and the curiously sensitive black faces were glistening with sweat.

As they went past a tall, very young Negro turned and caught my eye. But the look he gave me was not in the least the kind of look you might expect. Not hostile, not contemptuous, not sullen, not even inquisitive. It was the shy, wide-eyed Negro look, which actually is a look of profound respect. I saw how it was. This wretched boy, who is a French citizen and has therefore been dragged from the forest to scrub floors and catch syphilis in garrison towns, actually has feelings of reverence before a white skin. He has been taught that the white race are his masters, and he still believes it.

But there is one thought which every white man (and in this connection it doesn't matter twopence if he called himself a Socialist) thinks when he sees a black army marching past. 'How much longer can we go on kidding these people? How long before they turn their guns in the other direction?'

It was curious, really. Every white man there has this thought stowed somewhere or other in his mind. I had it, so had the other onlookers, so had the officers on their sweating chargers and the white NCOs marching in the ranks. It was a kind of secret which we all knew and were too clever to tell; only the Negroes didn't know it. And really it was almost like watching a flock of cattle to see the long column, a mile or two miles of armed men, flowing peacefully up the road, while the great white birds drifted over them in the opposite direction, glittering like scraps of paper.

Written [Spring] 1939

Charles Dickens

One

Dickens is one of those writers who are well worth stealing. Even the burial of his body in Westminster Abbey was a species of theft, if you come to think of it.

When Chesterton wrote his Introductions to the Everyman Edition of Dickens's works, it seemed quite natural to him to credit Dickens with his own highly individual brand of medievalism, and more recently a Marxist writer, Mr T. A. Jackson,[1] has made spirited efforts to turn Dickens into a bloodthirsty revolutionary. The Marxist claims him as 'almost' a Marxist, the Catholic claims him as 'almost' a Catholic, and both claim him as a champion of the proletariat (or 'the poor', as Chesterton would have put it). On the other hand, Nadezhda Krupskaya, in her little book on Lenin, relates

[1] *Charles Dickens: The Progress of a Radical* by T. A. Jackson, 1937.

that towards the end of his life Lenin went to see a dramatized version of *The Cricket on the Hearth*, and found Dickens's 'middle-class sentimentality' so intolerable that he walked out in the middle of a scene.

Taking 'middle-class' to mean what Krupskaya might be expected to mean by it, this was probably a truer judgement than those of Chesterton and Jackson. But it is worth noticing that the dislike of Dickens implied in this remark is something unusual. Plenty of people have found him unreadable, but very few seem to have felt any hostility towards the general spirit of his work. Some years ago Mr Bechhofer Roberts published a full-length attack on Dickens in the form of a novel (*This Side Idolatry*), but it was a merely personal attack, concerned for the most part with Dickens's treatment of his wife. It dealt with incidents which not one in a thousand of Dickens's readers would ever hear about, and which no more invalidate his work than the second-best bed invalidates *Hamlet*. All that the book really demonstrated was that a writer's literary personality has little or nothing to do with his private character. It is quite possible that in private life Dickens was just the kind of insensitive egoist that Mr Bechhofer Roberts makes him appear. But in his published work there is implied a personality quite different from this, a personality which has won him far more friends than enemies. It might well have been otherwise, for even if Dickens was a bourgeois, he was certainly a subversive writer, a radical, one might truthfully say a rebel. Everyone who has read widely in his work has felt this. Gissing, for instance, the best of the writers on Dickens, was anything but a radical himself, and he disapproved of this strain in Dickens and wished it were not there, but it never occurred to him to deny it. In *Oliver Twist*, *Hard Times*, *Bleak House*, *Little Dorrit*, Dickens attacked English institutions with a ferocity that has never since been approached. Yet he managed to do it without making himself hated, and, more than this, the very people he attacked have swallowed him so completely that he has become a national institution himself. In its attitude towards Dickens the English public has always been a little like the elephant which feels a blow with a walking-stick as a delightful tickling. Before I was ten years old I was having Dickens ladled down my throat by schoolmasters in whom even at that age I could see a strong resemblance to Mr Creakle, and one knows without needing to be told that lawyers delight in Serjeant Buzfuz and that *Little Dorrit* is a favourite in the Home Office. Dickens seems to have succeeded in attacking everybody and antagonizing nobody. Naturally this makes one wonder whether after all there was something unreal in his attack upon society. Where exactly does he stand, socially, morally and politically? As usual, one can define his position more easily if one starts by deciding what he was *not*.

In the first place he was *not*, as Messrs Chesterton and Jackson seem to imply, a 'proletarian' writer. To begin with, he does not write about the proletariat, in which he merely resembles the overwhelming majority of novelists, past and present. If you look for the working classes in fiction, and especially English fiction, all you find is a hole. This statement needs qualifying, perhaps. For reasons that are easy enough to see, the agricultural labourer (in England a proletarian) gets a fairly good showing in fiction, and a great deal has been written about criminals, derelicts and, more recently, the working-class intelligentsia. But the ordinary town proletariat, the people who make the wheels go round, have always been ignored by novelists. When they do find their way between the covers of a book, it is nearly always as objects of pity or as comic relief. The central action of Dickens's stories almost invariably takes place in middle-class surroundings. If one examines his novels in detail one finds that his real subject-matter is the London commercial bourgeoisie and their hangers-on – lawyers, clerks, tradesmen, innkeepers, small craftsmen and servants. He has no portrait of an agricultural worker, and only one (Stephen Blackpool in *Hard Times*) of an industrial worker. The Plornishes in *Little Dorrit* are probably his best picture of a working-class family – the Peggottys, for instance, hardly belong to the working class – but on the whole he is not successful with this type of character. If you ask any ordinary reader which of Dickens's proletarian characters he can remember, the three he is almost certain to mention are Bill Sikes, Sam Weller and Mrs Gamp. A burglar, a valet and a drunken midwife – not exactly a representative cross-section of the English working class.

Secondly, in the ordinarily accepted sense of the word, Dickens is not a 'revolutionary' writer. but his position here needs some defining.

Whatever else Dickens may have been, he was not a hole-and-corner soul-saver, the kind of well-meaning idiot who thinks that the world will be perfect if you amend a few by-laws and abolish a few anomalies. It is worth comparing him with Charles Reade, for instance. Reade was a much better informed man than Dickens and in some ways more public-spirited. He really hated the abuses he could understand, he showed them up in a series of novels which for all their absurdity are extremely readable, and he probably helped to alter public opinion on a few minor but important points. But it was quite beyond him to grasp that, given the existing form of society, certain evils *cannot* be remedied. Fasten upon this or that minor abuse, expose it, drag it into the open, bring it before a British jury, and all will be well – that is how he sees it. Dickens at any rate never imagined that you can cure pimples by cutting them off. In every page of his work one can see a consciousness that society is wrong somewhere at the root. It is when one asks 'Which root?' that one begins to grasp his position.

The truth is that Dickens's criticism of society is almost exclusively moral. Hence the utter lack of any constructive suggestion anywhere in his work. He attacks the law, parliamentary government, the educational system and so forth, without ever clearly suggesting what he would put in their places. Of course it is not necessarily the business of a novelist, or a satirist, to make constructive suggestions, but the point is that Dickens's attitude is at bottom not even *de*structive. There is no clear sign that he wants the existing order to be overthrown, or that he believes it would make very much difference if it *were* overthrown. For in reality his target is not so much society as 'human nature'. It would be difficult to point anywhere in his books to a passage suggesting that the economic system is wrong *as a system*. Nowhere, for instance, does he make any attack on private enterprise or private property. Even in a book like *Our Mutual Friend*, which turns on the power of corpses to interfere with living people by means of idiotic wills, it does not occur to him to suggest that individuals ought not to have this irresponsible power. Of course one can draw this inference for oneself, and one can draw it again from the remarks about Bounderby's will at the end of *Hard Times*, and indeed from the whole of Dickens's work one can infer the evil of *laissez-faire* capitalism; but Dickens makes no such inference himself. It is said that Macaulay refused to review *Hard Times* because he disapproved of its 'sullen Socialism'. Obviously Macaulay is here using the word 'Socialism' in the same sense in which, twenty years ago, a vegetarian meal or a Cubist picture used to be referred to as

'Bolshevism'. There is not a line in the book that can properly be called Socialistic; indeed, its tendency if anything is pro-capitalist, because its whole moral is that capitalists ought to be kind, not that workers ought to be rebellious. Bounderby is a bullying windbag and Gradgrind has been morally blinded, but if they were better men, the system would work well enough – that, all through, is the implication. And so far as social criticism goes, one can never extract much more from Dickens than this, unless one deliberately reads meanings into him. His whole 'message' is one that at first glance looks like an enormous platitude: If men would behave decently the world would be decent.

Naturally this calls for a few characters who are in positions of authority and who *do* behave decently. Hence that recurrent Dickens figure, the Good Rich Man. This character belongs especially to Dickens's early optimistic period. He is usually a 'merchant' (we are not necessarily told what merchandise he deals in), and he is always a superhumanly kind-hearted old gentleman who 'trots' to and fro, raising his employees' wages, patting children on the head, getting debtors out of jail and, in general, acting the fairy godmother. Of course he is a pure dream figure, much further from real life than, say, Squeers or Micawber. Even Dickens must have reflected occasionally that anyone who was so anxious to give his money away would never have acquired it in the first place. Mr Pickwick, for instance, had 'been in the city', but it is difficult to imagine him making a fortune there. Nevertheless this character runs like a connecting thread through most of the earlier books. Pickwick, the Cheerybles, old Chuzzlewit, Scrooge – it is the same figure over and over again, the good rich man, handing out guineas. Dickens does however show signs of development here. In the books of the middle period the good rich man fades out to some extent. There is no one who plays this part in *A Tale of Two Cities*, nor in *Great Expectations* – *Great Expectations* is, in fact, definitely an attack on patronage – and in *Hard Times* it is only very doubtfully played by Gradgrind after his reformation. The character reappears in a rather different form as Meagles in *Little Dorrit* and John Jarndyce in *Bleak House* – one might perhaps add Betsy Trotwood in *David Copperfield*. But in these books the good rich man has dwindled from a 'merchant' to a *rentier*. This is significant. A *rentier* is part of the possessing class, he can and, almost without knowing it, does make other people work for him, but he has very little direct power. Unlike Scrooge or the Cheerybles, he cannot put everything right by raising everybody's wages. The seeming inference from the rather despondent books that Dickens wrote in the 'fifties is that by that time he had grasped the helplessness of well-meaning individuals in a corrupt society. Nevertheless in the last completed novel, *Our Mutual Friend* (published 1864–5), the good rich man comes back in full glory in the person of Boffin. Boffin is a proletarian by origin and only rich by inheritance, but he is the usual *deus ex machina*, solving everybody's problems by showering money in all directions. He even 'trots' like the Cheerybles. In several ways *Our Mutual Friend* is a return to the earlier manner, and not an unsuccessful return either. Dickens's thoughts seem to have come full circle. Once again, individual kindliness is the remedy for everything.

One crying evil of his time that Dickens says very little about is child labour. There are plenty of pictures of suffering children in his books, but usually they are suffering in schools rather than in factories. The one detailed account of child labour that he gives is the description in *David Copperfield* of little

David washing bottles in Murdstone & Grinby's warehouse. This, of course, is autobiography. Dickens himself, at the age of ten, had worked in Warren's blacking factory in the Strand, very much as he describes it here. It was a terribly bitter memory to him, partly because he felt the whole incident to be discreditable to his parents, and he even concealed it from his wife till long after they were married. Looking back on this period, he says in *David Copperfield*:

> It is a matter of some surprise to me, even now, that I can have been so easily thrown away at such an age. A child of excellent abilities and with strong powers of observation, quick, eager, delicate, and soon hurt bodily or mentally, it seems wonderful to me that nobody should have made any sign in my behalf. But none was made; and I became, at ten years old, a little labouring hind in the service of Murdstone & Grinby.

And again, having described the rough boys among whom he worked:

> No words can express the secret agony of my soul as I sunk into this companionship ... and felt my hopes of growing up to be a learned and distinguished man crushed in my bosom.

Obviously it is not David Copperfield who is speaking, it is Dickens himself. He uses almost the same words in his autobiography that he began and abandoned a few months earlier. Of course Dickens is right in saying that a gifted child ought not to work ten hours a day pasting labels on bottles, but what he does not say is that *no* child ought to be condemned to such a fate, and there is no reason for inferring that he thinks it. David escapes from the warehouse, but Mick Walker and Mealy Potatoes and the others are still there, and there is no sign that this troubles Dickens particularly. As usual, he displays no consciousness that the *structure* of society can be changed. He despises politics, does not believe that any good can come out of Parliament – he had been a parliamentary shorthand writer, which was no doubt a disillusioning experience – and he is slightly hostile to the most hopeful movement of his day, trade unionism. In *Hard Times* trade unionism is represented as something not much better than a racket, something that happens because employers are not sufficiently paternal. Stephen Blackpool's refusal to join the union is rather a virtue in Dicken's eyes. Also, as Mr Jackson has pointed out, the apprentices' association in *Barnaby Rudge*, to which Sim Tappertit belongs, is probably a hit at the illegal or barely legal unions of Dickens's own day, with their secret assemblies, passwords and so forth. Obviously he wants the workers to be decently treated, but there is no sign that he wants them to take their destiny into their own hands, least of all by open violence.

As it happens, Dickens deals with revolution in the narrower sense in two novels, *Barnaby Rudge* and *A Tale of Two Cities*. In *Barnaby Rudge* it is a case of rioting rather than revolution. The Gordon Riots of 1780, though they had religious bigotry as a pretext, seem to have been little more than a pointless outburst of looting. Dickens's attitude to this kind of thing is sufficiently indicated by the fact that his first idea was to make the ringleaders of the riots three lunatics escaped from an asylum. He was dissuaded from this, but the principal figure of the book is in fact a village idiot. In the chapters dealing with the riots Dickens shows a most profound horror of mob violence. He delights in describing scenes in which the 'dregs' of the population behave with atrocious bestiality. These chapters are of great psychological interest, because they show how deeply he had brooded on this subject. The things he describes can only have come out of his imagination, for no riots on anything like the same scale had happened in his lifetime. Here is one of his descriptions, for instance:

> If Bedlam gates had been flung open wide, there would not have issued forth such maniacs as the frenzy of that night had made. There were men there who danced and trampled on the beds of flowers as though they trod down human enemies, and wrenched them from their stalks, like savages who twisted human necks. There were men who cast their lighted torches in the air, and suffered them to fall upon their heads and faces, blistering the skin with deep unseemly burns. There were men who rushed up to the fire, and paddled in it with their hands as if in water; and others who were restrained by force from plunging in, to gratify their deadly longing. On the skull of one drunken lad – not twenty, by his looks – who lay upon the ground with a bottle to his mouth, the lead from the roof came streaming down in a shower of liquid fire, white hot, melting his head like wax ... But of all the howling throng not one learnt mercy from, or sickened at, these sights; nor was the fierce, besotted, senseless rage of one man glutted.

You might almost think you were reading a description of 'red' Spain by a partisan of General Franco. One ought, of course, to remember that when Dickens was writing, the London 'mob' still existed. (Nowadays there is no mob, only a flock.) Low wages and the growth and shift of population had brought into existence a huge, dangerous slum-proletariat, and until the early middle of the nineteenth century there was hardly such a thing as a police force. When the brickbats began to fly there was nothing between shuttering your windows and ordering the troops to open fire. In *A Tale of Two Cities* he is dealing with a revolution which was really *about* something, and Dickens's attitude is different, but not entirely different. As a matter of fact, *A Tale of Two Cities* is a book which tends to leave a false impression behind, especially after a lapse of time.

The one thing that everyone who has read *A Tale of Two Cities* remembers is the Reign of Terror. The whole book is dominated by the guillotine – tumbrils thundering to and fro, bloody knives, heads bouncing into the basket, and sinister old women knitting as they watch. Actually these scenes only occupy a few chapters, but they are written with terrible intensity, and the rest of the book is rather slow going. But *A Tale of Two Cities* is not a companion volume to *The Scarlet Pimpernel*. Dickens sees clearly enough that the French Revolution was bound to happen and that many of the people who were executed deserved what they got. If, he says, you behave as the French aristocracy had behaved, vengeance will follow. He repeats this over and over again. We are constantly being reminded that while 'my lord' is lolling in bed, with four liveried footmen serving his chocolate and the peasants starving outside, somewhere in the forest a tree is growing while will presently be sawn into planks for the platform of the guillotine, etc., etc., etc. The inevitability of the Terror, given its causes, is insisted upon in the clearest terms:

> It was too much the way ... to talk of this terrible Revolution as if it were the only harvest ever known under the skies that had not been sown – as if nothing had ever been done, or omitted to be done, that had led to it – as if observers of the wretched millions in France, and of the misused and perverted resources that should have made them prosperous, had not seen it inevitably coming, years before, and had not in plain terms recorded what they saw.

And again:

> All the devouring and insatiate monsters imagined since imagination could record itself, are fused in the one realization, Guillotine. And yet there is not in France, with its rich variety of soil and climate, a blade, a leaf, a root, a sprig, a peppercorn, which will grow to maturity under conditions more certain than those that have produced this horror. Crush humanity out of shape once more, under similar hammers, and it will twist itself into the same tortured forms.

In other words, the French aristocracy had dug their own graves. But there is no perception here of what is now called historic necessity. Dickens sees that the results are inevitable, given the causes, but he thinks that the causes might have been avoided. The Revolution is something that happens because centuries of oppression have made the French peasantry sub-human. If the wicked nobleman could somehow have turned over a new leaf, like Scrooge, there would have been no Revolution, no *jacquerie*, no guillotine – and so much the better. This is the opposite of the 'revolutionary' attitude. From the 'revolutionary' point of view the class-struggle is the main source of progress, and therefore the nobleman who robs the peasant and goads him to revolt is playing a necessary part, just as much as the Jacobin who guillotines the nobleman. Dickens never writes anywhere a line that can be interpreted as meaning this. Revolution as he sees it is merely a monster that is begotten by tyranny and always ends by devouring its own instruments. In Sydney Carton's vision at the foot of the guillotine, he foresees Defarge and the other leading spirits of the Terror all perishing under the same knife – which, in fact, was approximately what happened.

And Dickens is very sure that revolution *is* a monster. That is why everyone remembers the revolutionary scenes in *A Tale of Two Cities*; they have the quality of nightmare, and it is Dickens's own nightmare. Again and again he insists upon the meaningless horrors of revolution – the mass-butcheries, the injustice, the ever-present terror of spies, the frightful blood-lust of the mob. The descriptions of the Paris mob – the description, for instance, of the crowd of murderers struggling round the grindstone to sharpen their weapons before butchering the prisoners in the September massacres – outdo anything in *Barnaby Rudge*. The revolutionaries appear to him simply as degraded savages – in fact, as lunatics. He broods over their frenzies with a curious imaginative intensity. He describes them dancing the 'Carmagnole', for instance:

> There could not be fewer than five hundred people, and they were dancing like five thousand demons.... They danced to the popular Revolution song, keeping a ferocious time that was like a gnashing of

> teeth in unison ... They advanced, retreated, struck at one another's heads, spun round alone, caught one another, and spun round in pairs, until many of them dropped ... Suddenly they stopped again, paused, struck out the time afresh, forming into lines the width of the public way, and, with their heads low down and their hands high up, swooped screaming off. No fight could have been half so terrible as this dance. It was so emphatically a fallen sport – a something, once innocent, delivered over to all devilry.

He even credits some of these wretches with a taste for guillotining children. The passage I have abridged above ought to be read in full. It and others like it show how deep was Dickens's horror of revolutionary hysteria. Notice, for instance, that touch, 'with their heads low down and their hands high up', etc., and the evil vision it conveys. Madame Defarge is a truly dreadful figure, certainly Dickens's most successful attempt at a *malignant* character. Defarge and others are simply 'the new oppressors who have risen on the destruction of the old', the revolutionary courts are presided over by 'the lowest, cruellest and worst populace', and so on and so forth. All the way through Dickens insists upon the nightmare insecurity of a revolutionary period, and in this he shows a great deal of prescience. 'A law of the suspected, which struck away all security for liberty or life, and delivered over any good and innocent person to any bad and guilty one; prisons gorged with people who had committed no offence, and could obtain no hearing' – it would apply pretty accurately to several countries today.

The apologists of any revolution generally try to minimize its horrors; Dickens's impulse is to exaggerate them – and from a historical point of view he has certainly exaggerated. Even the Reign of Terror was a much smaller thing than he makes it appear. Though he quotes no figures, he gives the impression of a frenzied massacre lasting for years, whereas in reality the whole of the Terror, so far as the number of deaths goes, was a joke compared with one of Napoleon's battles. But the bloody knives and the tumbrils rolling to and fro create in his mind a special, sinister vision which he has succeeded in passing on to generations of readers. Thanks to Dickens, the very word 'tumbril' has a murderous sound; one forgets that a tumbril is only a sort of farm-cart. To this day, to the average Englishman, the French Revolution means no more than a pyramid of severed heads. It is a strange thing that Dickens, much more in sympathy with the ideas of the Revolution than most Englishmen of his time, should have played a part in creating this impression.

If you hate violence and don't believe in politics, the only major remedy remaining is education. Perhaps society is past praying for, but there is always hope for the individual human being, if you can catch him young enough. This belief partly accounts for Dickens's preoccupation with childhood.

No one, at any rate no English writer, has written better about childhood than Dickens. In spite of all the knowledge that has accumulated since, in spite of the fact that children are now comparatively sanely treated, no novelist has shown the same power of entering into the child's point of view. I must have been about nine years old when I first read *David Copperfield*. The mental atmosphere of the opening chapters was so immediately intelligible to me that I vaguely imagined they had been written *by a child*. And yet when one re-reads the book as an adult and seen the Murdstones, for instance, dwindle from gigantic figures of doom into semi-comic monsters, these passages lose nothing.

Dickens has been able to stand both inside and outside the child's mind, in such a way that the same scene can be wild burlesque or sinister reality, according to the age at which one reads it. Look, for instance, at the scene in which David Copperfield is unjustly suspected of eating the mutton chops; or the scene in which Pip, in *Great Expectations*, coming back from Miss Havisham's house and finding himself completely unable to describe what he has seen, takes refuge in a series of outrageous lies – which, of course, are eagerly believed. All the isolation of the childhood is there. And how accurately he has recorded the mechanisms of the child's mind, its visualizing tendency, its sensitiveness to certain kinds of impression. Pip relates how in his childhood his ideas about his dead parents were derived from their tombstones:

> The shape of the letters on my father's, gave me an odd idea that he was a square, stout, dark man, with curly black hair. From the character and turn of the inscription, 'ALSO GEORGIANA, WIFE OF THE ABOVE', I drew a childish conclusion that my mother was freckled and sickly. To five little stone lozenges, each about a foot and a half long, which were arranged in a neat row beside their grave, and were sacred to the memory of five little brothers of mine ... I am indebted for a belief I religiously entertained that they had all been born on their backs with their hands in their trouser-pockets, and had never taken them out in this state of existence.

There is a similar passage in *David Copperfield*. After biting Mr Murdstone's hand, David is sent away to school and obliged to wear on his back a placard saying, 'Take care of him. He bites'. He looks at the door in the playground where the boys have carved their names, and from the appearance of each name he seems to know in just what tone of voice the boy will read out the placard:

> There was one boy – a certain J. Steerforth – who cut his name very deep and very often, who, I conceived, would read it in a rather strong voice, and afterwards pull my hair. There was another boy, one Tommy Traddles, who I dreaded would make game of it, and pretend to be dreadfully frightened of me. There was a third, George Demple, who I fancied would sing it.

When I read this passage as a child, it seemed to me that those were exactly the pictures that those particular names would call up. The reason, of course, is the sound-associations of the words (Demple – 'temple'; Traddles – probably 'skedaddle'). But how many people, before Dickens, had ever noticed such things? A sympathetic attitude towards children was a much rarer thing in Dickens's day than it is now. The early nineteenth century was not a good time to be a child. In Dickens's youth children were still being 'solemnly tried at a criminal bar, where they were held up to be seen', and it was not so long since boys of thirteen had been hanged for petty theft. The doctrine of 'breaking the child's spirit' was in full vigour, and *The Fairchild Family*[1]

[1] *The History of the Fairchild Family* by May M. Sherwood, 3 parts, 1818–47.

was a standard book for children till late into the century. This evil book is now issued in pretty-pretty expurgated editions, but it is well worth reading in the original version. It gives one some idea of the lengths to which child-discipline was sometimes carried. Mr Fairchild, for instance, when he catches his children quarrelling, first thrashes them, reciting Doctor Watts's 'Let dogs delight to bark and bite' between blows of the cane, and then takes them to spend the afternoon beneath a gibbet where the rotting corpse of a murderer is hanging. In the earlier part of the century scores of thousands of children, aged sometimes as young as six, were literally worked to death in the mines or cotton mills, and even at the fashionable public schools boys were flogged till they ran with blood for a mistake in their Latin verses. One thing which Dickens seems to have recognized, and which most of his contemporaries did not, is the sadistic sexual element in flogging. I think this can be inferred from *David Copperfield* and *Nicholas Nickleby*. But mental cruelty to a child infuriates him as much as physical, and though there is a fair number of exceptions, his schoolmasters are generally scoundrels.

Except for the universities and the big public schools, every kind of education then existing in England gets a mauling at Dickens's hands. There is Doctor Blimber's Academy, where little boys are blown up with Greek until they burst, and the revolting charity schools of the period, which produced specimens like Noah Claypole and Uriah Heep, and Salem House, and Dotheboys Hall, and the disgraceful little dame-school kept by Mr Wopsle's great-aunt. Some of what Dickens says remains true even today. Salem House is the ancestor of the modern 'prep school', which still has a good deal of resemblance to it; and as for Mr Wopsle's great-aunt, some old fraud of much the same stamp is carrying on at this moment in nearly every small town in England. But, as usual, Dickens's criticism is neither creative nor destructive. He sees the idiocy of an educational system founded on the Greek lexicon and the wax-ended cane; on the other hand, he has no use for the new kind of school that is coming up in the 'fifties and 'sixties, the 'modern' school, with its gritty insistence on 'facts'. What, then, *does* he want? As always, what he appears to want is a moralized version of the existing thing – the old type of school, but with no caning, no bullying or underfeeding, and not quite so much Greek. Doctor Strong's school, to which David Copperfield goes after he escapes from Murdstone & Grinby's, is simply Salem House with the vices left out and a good deal of 'old grey stones' atmosphere thrown in:

> Doctor Strong's was an excellent school, as different from Mr Creakle's as good is from evil. It was very gravely and decorously ordered, and on a sound system; with an appeal, in everything, to the honour and good faith of the boys ... which worked wonders. We all felt that we had a part in the management of the place, and in sustaining its character and dignity. Hence, we soon became warmly attached to it – I am sure I did for one, and I never knew, in all my time, of any boy being otherwise – and learnt with a good will, desiring to do it credit. We had noble games out of hours, and plenty of liberty; but even then, as I remember, we were well spoken of in the town, and rarely did any disgrace, by our appearance or manner, to the reputation of Doctor Strong and Doctor Strong's boys.

In the woolly vagueness of this passage one can see Dickens's utter lack of any educational theory. He can imagine the *moral* atmosphere of a good school, but nothing further. The boys 'learnt with a good will', but what did they learn? No doubt it was Doctor Blimber's curriculum, a little watered down. Considering the attitude to society that is everywhere implied in Dickens's novels, it comes as rather a shock to learn that he sent his eldest son to Eton and sent all his children through the ordinary educational mill. Gissing seems to think that he may have done this because he was painfully conscious of being under-educated himself. Here perhaps Gissing is influenced by his own love of classical learning. Dickens had had little or no formal education, but he lost nothing by missing it, and on the whole he seems to have been aware of this. If he was unable to imagine a better school than Doctor Strong's, or, in real life, than Eton, it was probably due to an intellectual deficiency rather different from the one Gissing suggests.

It seems that in every attack Dickens makes upon society he is always pointing to a change of spirit rather than a change of structure. It is hopeless to try and pin him down to any definite remedy, still more to any political doctrine. His approach is always along the moral plane, and his attitude is sufficiently summed up in that remark about Strong's school being as different from Creakle's 'as good is from evil'. Two things can be very much alike and yet abysmally different. Heaven and Hell are in the same place. Useless to change institutions without a 'change of heart' – that, essentially, is what he is always saying.

If that were all, he might be no more than a cheer-up writer, a reactionary humbug. A 'change of heart' is in fact *the* alibi of people who do not wish to endanger the *status quo*. But Dickens is not a humbug, except in minor matters, and the strongest single impression one carries away from his books is that of a hatred of tyranny. I said earlier that Dickens is not *in the accepted sense* a revolutionary writer. but it is not at all certain that a merely moral criticism of society may not be just as 'revolutionary' – and revolution, after all, means turning things upside down – as the politico-economic criticism which is fashionable at this moment. Blake was not a politician, but there is more understanding of the nature of capitalist society in a poem like 'I wander through each charter'd street' than in three-quarters of Socialist literature. Progress is not an illusion, it happens, but it is slow and invariably disappointing. There is always a new tyrant waiting to take over from the old – generally not quite so bad, but still a tyrant. Consequently two viewpoints are always tenable. The one, how can you improve human nature until you have changed the system? The other, what is the use of changing the system before you have improved human nature? They appeal to different individuals, and they probably show a tendency to alternate in point of time. The moralist and the revolutionary are constantly undermining one another. Marx exploded a hundred tons of dynamite beneath the moralist position, and we are still living in the echo of that tremendous crash. But already, somewhere or other, the sappers are at work and fresh dynamite is being stamped in place to blow Marx at the moon. Then Marx, or somebody like him, will come back with yet more dynamite, and so the process continues, to an end we cannot yet foresee. The central problem – how to prevent power from being abused – remains unsolved. Dickens, who had not the vision to see that private property is an obstructive nuisance, had the vision to see that. 'If men would behave decently the world would be decent' is not such a platitude as it sounds.

Two

More completely than most writers, perhaps, Dickens can be explained in terms of his social origin, though actually his family history was not quite what one would infer from his novels. His father was a clerk in government service, and through his mother's family he had connections with both the army and the navy. But from the age of nine onwards he was brought up in London in commercial surroundings, and generally in an atmosphere of struggling poverty. Mentally he belongs to the small urban bourgeoisie, and he happens to be an exceptionally fine specimen of this class, with all the 'points', as it were, very highly developed. That is partly what makes him so interesting. If one wants a modern equivalent, the nearest would be H. G. Wells, who has had a rather similar history and who obviously owes something to Dickens as a novelist. Arnold Bennett was essentially of the same type, but, unlike the other two, he was a midlander, with an industrial and Noncomformist rather than commercial and Anglican background.

The great disadvantage, and advantage, of the small urban bourgeois is his limited outlook. He sees the world as a middle-class world, and everything outside these limits is either laughable or slightly wicked. On the one hand, he has no contact with industry or the soil; on the other, no contact with the governing classes. Anyone who has studied Wells's novels in detail will have noticed that though he hates the aristocrat like poison, he has no particular objection to the plutocrat, and no enthusiasm for the proletarian. His most hated types, the people he believes to be responsible for all human ills, are kings, landowners, priests, nationalists, soldiers, scholars and peasants. At first sight a list beginning with kings and ending with peasants looks like a mere omnium gatherum, but in reality all these people have a common factor. All of them are archaic types, people who are governed by tradition and whose eyes are turned towards the past – the opposite, therefore, of the rising bourgeois who has put his money on the future and sees the past simply as a dead hand.

Actually, although Dickens lived in a period when the bourgeoisie was really a rising class, he displays this characteristic less strongly than Wells. He is almost unconscious of the future and has a rather sloppy love of the picturesque (the 'quaint old church', etc.). Nevertheless his list of most hated types is like enough to Wells's for the similarity to be striking. He is vaguely on the side of the working class – has a sort of generalized sympathy with them because they are oppressed – but he does not in reality know much about them; they come into his books chiefly as servants, and comic servants at that. At the other end of the scale he loathes the aristocrat and – going one better than Wells in this – loathes the big bourgeois as well. His real sympathies are bounded by Mr Pickwick on the upper side and Mr Barkis on the lower. But the term 'aristocrat', for the type Dickens hates, is vague and needs defining.

Actually Dickens's target is not so much the great aristocracy, who hardly enter into his books, as their petty offshoots, the cadging dowagers who live up mews in Mayfair, and the bureaucrats and professional soldiers. All through his books there are countless hostile sketches of these people, and hardly any that are friendly. There are practically no friendly pictures of the land-owning class, for instance. One might make a doubtful exception of Sir Leicester Dedlock; otherwise there is only Mr Wardle (who is a stock figure – the 'good old squire') and Haredale in *Barnaby Rudge*, who has Dickens's sympathy because he is a persecuted Catholic. There are no friendly pictures of soldiers (i.e. officers), and none at all of naval men. As for his bureaucrats, judges and magistrates, most of them would feel quite at home in the Circumlocution Office. The only officials whom Dickens handles with any kind of friendliness are, significantly enough, policemen.

Dickens's attitude is easily intelligible to an Englishman, because it is part of the English puritan tradition, which is not dead even at this day. The class Dickens belonged to, at least by adoption, was growing suddenly rich after a couple of centuries of obscurity. It had grown up mainly in the big towns, out of contact with agriculture, and politically impotent; government, in its experience, was something which either interfered or persecuted. Consequently it was a class with no tradition of public service and not much tradition of usefulness. What now strikes us as remarkable about the new moneyed class of the nineteenth century is their complete irresponsibility; they see everything in terms of individual success, with hardly any consciousness that the community exists. On the other hand, a Tite Barnacle, even when he was neglecting his duties, would have some vague notion of what duties he was neglecting. Dickens's attitude is never irresponsible, still less does he take the money-grubbing Smilesian line; but at the back of his mind there is usually a half-belief that the whole apparatus of government is unnecessary. Parliament is simply Lord Coodle and Sir Thomas Doodle, the Empire is simply Major Bagstock and his Indian servant, the army is simply Colonel Chowser and Doctor Slammer, the public services are simply Bumble and the Circumlocution Office – and so on and so forth. What he does not see, or only intermittently sees, is that Coodle and Doodle and all the other corpses left over from the eighteenth century *are* performing a function which neither Pickwick nor Boffin would ever bother about.

And of course this narrowness of vision is in one way a great advantage to him, because it is fatal for a caricaturist to see too much. From Dickens's point of view 'good' society is simply a collection of village idiots. What a crew! Lady Tippins! Mrs Gowan! Lord Verisopht! The Honourable Bob Stables! Mrs Sparsit (whose husband was a Powler)! The Tite Barnacles! Nupkins! It is practically a case-book in lunacy. But at the same time his remoteness from the landowning-military-bureaucratic class incapacitates him for full-length satire. He only succeeds with this class when he depicts them as mental defectives. The accusation which used to be made against Dickens in his lifetime, that he 'could not paint a gentleman', was an absurdity, but it is true in this sense, that what he says against the 'gentleman' class is seldom very damaging. Sir Mulberry Hawk, for instance, is a wretched attempt at the wicked-baronet type. Harthouse in *Hard Times* is better, but he would be only an ordinary achievement for Trollope or Thackeray. Trollope's thoughts hardly move outside the 'gentleman' class, but Thackeray has the great advantage of having a foot in two moral camps. In some ways his outlook is very similar to Dickens's. Like Dickens, he identifies with the puritanical moneyed class against the card-playing, debt-bilking aristocracy. The eighteenth century, as he sees it, is sticking out into the nineteenth in the person of the wicked Lord Steyne. *Vanity Fair* is a full-length version of what Dickens did for a few chapters in *Little Dorrit*. But by origins and upbringing Thackeray happens to be somewhat nearer to the class he is satirizing. Consequently he can produce such comparatively subtle types as, for instance, Major Pendennis and Rawdon Crawley. Major Pendennis is a shallow old snob, and Rawdon Crawley is a thick-headed ruffian who sees nothing wrong in living for years by swindling tradesmen; but what Thackeray realizes is that according to their tortuous code they are neither of them bad men. Major Pendennis would not sign a dud cheque, for instance. Rawdon certainly would, but on the other hand he would not desert a friend in a tight corner. Both of them would behave well on the field of battle – a thing that would not particularly appeal to Dickens. The result is that at the end one is left with a kind of amused tolerance for Major Pendennis and with something approaching respect for Rawdon; and yet one sees, better than any diatribe could make one, the utter rottenness of that kind of cadging, toadying life on the fringes of smart society. Dickens would be quite incapable of this. In his hands both Rawdon and the Major would dwindle to traditional caricatures. And, on the whole, his attacks on 'good' society are rather perfunctory. The aristocracy and the big bourgeoisie exist in his books chiefly as a kind of 'noises off', a haw-hawing chorus somewhere in the wings, like Podsnap's dinner-parties. When he produces a really subtle and damaging portrait, like John Dorrit or Harold Skimpole, it is generally of some rather middling, unimportant person.

One very striking thing about Dickens, especially considering the time he lived in, is his lack of vulgar nationalism. All peoples who have reached the point of becoming nations tend to despise foreigners, but there is not much doubt that the English-speaking races are the worst offenders. One can see this from the fact that as soon as they become fully aware of any foreign race, they invent an insulting nickname for it. Wop, Dago, Froggy, Squarehead, Kike, Sheeny, Nigger, Wog, Chink, Greaser, Yellowbelly – these are merely a selection. Any time before 1870 the list would have been shorter, because the map of the world was different from what it is now, and there were only three or four foreign races that had fully entered into the English consciousness. But towards these, and especially towards France, the nearest and best-hated nation, the English attitude of patronage was so intolerable that English 'arrogance' and 'xenophobia' are still a legend. And of course they are not a completely untrue legend even now. Till very recently nearly all English children were brought up to despise the southern European races, and history as taught in schools was mainly a list of battles won by England. But one has got to read, say, the *Quarterly Review* of the 'thirties to know what boasting really is. Those were the days when the English built up their legend of themselves as 'sturdy islanders' and 'stubborn hearts of oak' and when it was accepted as a kind of scientific fact that one Englishman was the equal of three foreigners. All through nineteenth-century novels and comic papers there runs the traditional figure of the 'Froggy' – a small ridiculous man with a tiny beard and a pointed top-hat, always jabbering and gesticulating, vain, frivolous and fond of boasting of his martial exploits, but generally taking to flight when real danger appears. Over against him was John Bull, the 'sturdy English yeoman', or (a more public-school version) the 'strong, silent Englishman' of Charles Kingsley, Tom Hughes and others.

Thackeray, for instance, has this outlook very strongly, though there are moments when he sees through it and laughs at it. The one historical fact that is firmly fixed in his mind is that the English won the battle of Waterloo. One never reads far in his books without coming upon some reference to it. The English, as he sees it, are invincible because of their tremendous physical strength, due mainly to living on beef. Like most Englishmen of his time, he has the curious illusion that the English are larger than other people (Thackeray, as it happened, *was* larger than most people), and therefore he is capable of writing passages like this:

> I say to you that you are better than a Frenchman. I would lay even money that you who are reading this are more than five feet seven in height, and weigh eleven stone; while a Frenchman is five feet four and does not weigh nine. The Frenchman has after his soup a dish of vegetables, where you have one of meat. You are a different and superior animal – a French-beating animal (the history of hundreds of years has shown you to be so), etc., etc.

There are similar passages scattered all through Thackeray's works. Dickens would never be guilty of anything of the kind. It would be an exaggeration to say that he nowhere pokes fun at foreigners, and of course, like nearly all nineteenth-century Englishmen, he is untouched by European culture. But never anywhere does he indulge in the typical English boasting, the 'island race', 'bulldog breed', 'right little, tight little island' style of talk. In the whole of *A Tale of Two Cities* there is not a line that could be taken as meaning, 'Look how these wicked Frenchmen behave!' The one place where he seems to display a normal hatred of foreigners is in the American chapters of *Martin Chuzzlewit*. This, however, is simply the reaction of a generous mind against cant. If Dickens were alive today he would make a trip to Soviet Russia and come back with a book rather like Gide's *Retour de l'URSS*. But he is remarkably free from the idiocy of regarding nations as individuals. He seldom even makes jokes turning on nationality. He does not exploit the comic Irishman and the comic Welshman, for instance, and not because he objects to stock characters and ready-made jokes, which obviously he does not. It is perhaps more significant that he shows no prejudice against Jews. It is true that he takes it for granted (*Oliver Twist* and *Great Expectations*) that a receiver of stolen goods will be a Jew, which at the time was probably justified. But the 'Jew joke', endemic in English literature until the rise of Hitler, does not appear in his books, and in *Our Mutual Friend* he makes a pious though not very convincing attempt to stand up for the Jews.

Dickens's lack of vulgar nationalism is in part the mark of a real largeness of mind, and in part results from his negative, rather unhelpful political attitude. He is very much an Englishman, but he is hardly aware of it – certainly the thought of being an Englishman does not thrill him. He has no imperialist feeling, no discernible views on foreign politics, and is untouched by the military tradition. Temperamentally he is much nearer to the small Nonconformist tradesman who looks down on the 'red-coats' and thinks that war is wicked – a one-eyed view, but, after all, war *is* wicked. It is noticeable that Dickens hardly writes of war, even to denounce it. With all his marvellous powers of description, and of describing things he had never seen, he never describes a battle, unless one counts the attack on the Bastille in *A Tale of Two Cities*. Probably the subject would not strike him as interesting, and in any case he would not regard a battlefield as a place where anything worth settling could be settled. It is one up to the lower-middle-class, puritan mentality.

Three

Dickens had grown up near enough to poverty to be terrified of it, and in spite of his generosity of mind, he is not free from the special prejudices of the shabby-genteel. It is usual to claim him as a 'popular' writer, a champion of the 'oppressed masses'. So he is, so long as he thinks of them as oppressed; but there are two things that condition his attitude. In the first place, he is a south of England man, and a cockney at that, and therefore out of touch with the bulk of the real oppressed masses, the industrial and agricultural labourers. It is interesting to see how Chesterton, another cockney, always presents Dickens as the spokesman of 'the poor', without showing much awareness of who 'the poor' really are. To Chesterton 'the poor' means small shopkeepers and servants. Sam Weller, he says, 'is the great symbol in English literature of the populace peculiar to England'; and Sam Weller is a valet! The other point is that Dickens's early experiences have given him a horror of proletarian roughness. He shows this unmistakably whenever he writes of the very poorest of the poor, the slum-dwellers. His descriptions of the London slums are always full of undisguised repulsion:

> The ways were foul and narrow; the shops and houses wretched; and people half naked, drunken, slipshod and ugly. Alleys and archways, like so many cesspools, disgorged their offences of smell, and dirt, and life, upon the straggling streets; and the whole quarter reeked with crime, and filth, and misery, etc., etc.

There are many similar passages in Dickens. From them one gets the impression of whole submerged populations whom he regards as being beyond the pale. In rather the same way the modern doctrinaire Socialist contemptuously writes off a large block of the population as 'lumpenproletariat'. Dickens also shows less understanding of criminals than one would expect of him. Although he is well aware of the social and economic causes of crime, he often seems to feel that when a man has once broken the law he has put himself outside human society. There is a chapter at the end of *David Copperfield* in which David visits the prison where Littimer and Uriah Heep are serving their sentences. Dickens actually seems to regard the horrible 'model' prisons, against which Charles Reade delivered his memorable attack in *It Is Never Too Late to Mend*, as too humane. He complains that the food is too good! As soon as he comes up against crime or the worst depths of poverty, he shows traces of the 'I've always kept myself respectable' habit of mind. The attitude of Pip (obviously the attitude of Dickens himself) towards Magwitch in *Great Expectations* is extremely interesting. Pip is conscious all along of his ingratitude towards Joe, but far less so of his ingratitude towards Magwitch. When he discovers that the person who has loaded him with benefits for years is actually a transported convict, he falls into frenzies of disgust. 'The abhorrence in which I held the man, the dread I had of him, the repugnance with which I shrank from him, could not have been exceeded if he had been some terrible beast', etc., etc. So far as one can discover from the text, this is not because when Pip was a child he had been terrorized by Magwitch in the churchyard; it is because Magwitch is a criminal and a convict. There is an even more 'kept-myself-respectable' touch in the fact that Pip feels as a matter of course that he cannot take Magwitch's money. The money is not the product of a crime, it has been honestly acquired; but it is an ex-convict's money and therefore 'tainted'. There is nothing psychologically false in this, either. Psychologically the latter part of *Great Expectations* is about the best thing Dickens ever did; throughout this part of the book one feels 'Yes, that is just how Pip would have behaved.' But the point is that in the matter of Magwitch, Dickens identifies with Pip, and his attitude is at bottom snobbish. The result is that Magwitch belongs to the same queer class of characters as Falstaff and, probably, Don Quixote – characters who are more pathetic than the author intended.

When it is a question of the non-criminal poor, the ordinary, decent, labouring poor, there is of course nothing contemptuous in Dickens's attitude. He has the sincerest admiration for people like the Peggottys and the Plornishes. But it is questionable whether he really regards them as equals. It is of the greatest interest to read Chapter XI of *David Copperfield* and side by side with it the autobiographical fragment (parts of this are given in Forster's *Life*), in which Dickens expresses his feelings about the blacking-factory episode a great deal more strongly than in the novel. For more than twenty years afterwards the memory was so painful to him that he would go out of his way to avoid that part of the Strand. He says that to pass that way 'made me cry, after my eldest child could speak.' The text makes it quite clear that what hurt him most of all then and in retrospect, was the enforced contact with 'low' associates:

> No words can express the secret agony of my soul as I sunk into this companionship; compared these everyday associates with those of my happier childhood ... But I held some station at the blacking warehouse too ... I soon became at least as expeditious and as skilful with my hands as either of the other boys. Though perfectly familiar with them, my conduct and manners were different enough from theirs to place a space between us. They, and the men, always spoke of me as 'the young gentleman'. A certain man ... used to call me 'Charles' sometimes in speaking to me; but I think it was mostly when we were very confidential ... Poll Green uprose once, and rebelled against the 'young-gentleman' usage; but Bob Fagin settled him speedily.

It was as well that there should be 'a space between us', you see. However much Dickens may admire the working classes, he does not wish to resemble them. Given his origins, and the time he lived in, it could hardly be otherwise. In the early nineteenth century class-animosities may have been no sharper than they are now, but the surface differences between class and class were enormously greater. The 'gentleman' and the 'common man' must have seemed like different species of animal. Dickens is quite genuinely on the side of the poor against the rich, but it would be next door to impossible for him not to think of a working-class exterior as a stigma. In one of Tolstoy's fables the peasants of a certain village judge every stranger who arrives from the state of his hands. If his palms are hard from work, they let him in; if his palms are soft, out he goes. This would be hardly intelligible to Dickens; all his heroes have soft hands. His younger heroes – Nicholas Nickleby, Martin Chuzzlewit, Edward Chester, David Copperfield, John Harmon – are usually of the type known as 'walking gentlemen'. He likes a bourgeois exterior and a bourgeois (not aristocratic) accent. One curious symptom of this is that he will not allow anyone who is to play a heroic part to speak like a working man. A comic hero like Sam Weller, or a merely pathetic figure like Stephen Blackpool, can speak with a broad accent, but the *jeune premier* always speaks the then equivalent of BBC. This is so, even when it involves absurdities. Little Pip, for instance, is brought up by people speaking broad Essex, but talks upper-class English from his earliest childhood; actually he would have talked the same dialect as Joe, or at least as Mrs Gargery. So also with Biddy Wopsle, Lizzie Hexam, Sissie Jupe, Oliver Twist – one ought perhaps to add Little Dorrit. Even Rachel in *Hard Times* has barely a trace of Lancashire accent, an impossibility in her case.

One thing that often gives the clue to a novelist's real feelings on the class question is the attitude he takes up when class collides with sex. This is a thing too painful to be lied about, and consequently it is one of the points at which the 'I'm-not-a-snob' pose tends to break down.

One sees that at its most obvious where a class-distinction is also a colour-distinction. And something resembling the colonial attitude ('native' women are fair game, white women are sacrosanct) exists in a veiled form in all-white communities, causing bitter resentment on both sides. When this issue arises, novelists often revert to crude class-feelings which they might disclaim at other times. A good example of 'class-conscious' reaction is a rather forgotten novel, *The People of Clopton*, by Andrew Barton. The author's moral code is quite clearly mixed up with class-hatred. He feels the seduction of a poor girl by a rich man to be something atrocious, a kind of defilement, something quite different from her seduction by a man in her own walk of life. Trollope deals with this theme twice (*The Three Clerks* and *The Small House at Allington*) and, as one might expect, entirely from the upper-class angle. As he sees it, an affair with a barmaid or a landlady's daughter is simply an 'entanglement' to be escaped from. Trollope's moral standards are strict, and he does not allow the seduction actually to happen, but the implication is always that a working-class girl's feelings do not greatly matter. In *The Three Clerks* he even gives the typical class-reaction by noting that the girl 'smells'. Meredith (*Rhoda Fleming*) takes the more 'class-conscious' viewpoint. Thackeray, as often, seems to hesitate. In *Pendennis* (Fanny Bolton) his attitude is much the same as Trollope's; in *A Shabby Genteel Story* it is nearer to Meredith's.

One could divine a good deal about Trollope's social origin, or Meredith's, or Barton's, merely from their handling of the class-sex theme. So one can with Dickens, but what emerges, as usual, is that he is more inclined to identify himself with the middle class than with the proletariat. The one incident that seems to contradict this is the tale of the young peasant-girl in Doctor Manette's manuscript in *A Tale of Two Cities*. This, however, is merely a costume-piece put in to explain the implacable hatred of Madame Defarge, which Dickens does not pretend to approve of. In *David Copperfield*, where he is dealing with a typical nineteenth-century seduction, the class-issue does not seem to strike him as paramount. It is a law of Victorian novels that sexual misdeeds must not go unpunished, and so Steerforth is drowned on Yarmouth sands, but neither Dickens, nor old Peggotty, nor even Ham, seems to feel that Steerforth has added to his offence by being the son of rich parents. The Steerforths are moved by class-motives, but the Peggottys are not – not even in the scene between Mrs Steerforth and old Peggotty; if they were, of course, they would probably turn against David as well as against Steerforth.

In *Our Mutual Friend* Dickens treats the episode of Eugene Wrayburn and

Lizzie Hexam very realistically and with no appearance of class bias. According to the 'unhand me, monster' tradition, Lizzie ought either to 'spurn' Eugene or to be ruined by him and throw herself off Waterloo Bridge; Eugene ought to be either a heartless betrayer or a hero resolved upon defying society. Neither behaves in the least like this. Lizzie is frightened by Eugene's advances and actually runs away from them, but hardly pretends to dislike them; Eugene is attracted by her, has too much decency to attempt seducing her and dare not marry her because of his family. Finally they are married and no one is any the worse, except perhaps Mr Twemlow, who will lose a few dinner engagements. It is all very much as it might have happened in real life. But a 'class-conscious' novelist would have given her to Bradley Headstone.

But when it is the other way about – when it is a case of a poor man aspiring to some woman who is 'above' him – Dickens instantly retreats into the middle-class attitude. He is rather fond of the Victorian notion of a woman (woman with a capital W) being 'above' a man. Pip feels that Estella is 'above' him, Esther Summerson is 'above' Guppy, Little Dorrit is 'above' John Chivery, Lucy Manette is 'above' Sydney Carton. In some of these the 'above'-ness is merely moral, but in others it is social. There is a scarcely mistakable class-reaction when David Copperfield discovers that Uriah Heep is plotting to marry Agnes Wickfield. The disgusting Uriah suddenly announces that he is in love with her:

> 'Oh, Master Copperfield, with what a pure affection do I love the ground my Agnes walks on.'
>
> I believe I had the delirious idea of seizing the red-hot poker out of the fire, and running him through with it. It went from me with a shock, like a ball fired from a rifle: but the image of Agnes, outraged by so much as a thought of this red-headed animal's, remained in my mind (when I looked at him, sitting all awry as if his mean soul griped his body) and made me giddy ... 'I believe Agnes Wickfield to be as far above *you* (David says later on), and as far removed from all *your* aspirations, as that moon herself.'

Considering how Heep's general lowness – his servile manners, dropped aitches and so forth – has been rubbed in throughout the book, there is not much doubt about the nature of Dickens's feelings. Heep, of course, is playing a villainous part, but even villains have sexual lives; it is the thought of the 'pure' Agnes in bed with a man who drops his aitches that really revolts Dickens. But his usual tendency is to treat a man in love with a woman who is 'above' him as a joke. It is one of the stock jokes of English literature, from Malvolio onwards. Guppy in *Bleak House* is an example, John Chivery is another, and there is a rather ill-natured treatment of this theme in the 'swarry' in *Pickwick Papers*. Here Dickens describes the Bath footmen as living a kind of fantasy-life, holding dinner-parties in imitation of their 'betters' and deluding themselves that their young mistresses are in love with them. This evidently strikes him as very comic. So it is, in a way, though one might question whether it is not better for a footman even to have delusions of this kind than simply to accept his status in the spirit of the catechism.

In his attitude towards servants Dickens is not ahead of his age. In the nineteenth century the revolt against domestic service was just beginning, to the great annoyance of everyone with over £500 a year. An enormous number of the jokes in nineteenth-century comic papers deal with the uppishness of servants. For years *Punch* ran a series of jokes called 'Servant Gal-isms', all turning on the then astonishing fact that a servant is a human being. Dickens is sometimes guilty of this kind of thing himself. His books abound with the ordinary comic servants; they are dishonest (*Great Expectations*), incompetent (*David Copperfield*), turn up their noses at good food (*Pickwick Papers*), etc., etc. – all rather in the spirit of the suburban housewife with one down-trodden cook-general. But what is curious, in a nineteenth-century radical, is that when he wants to draw a sympathetic picture of a servant, he creates what is recognizably a feudal type. Sam Weller, Mark Tapley, Clara Peggotty are all of them feudal figures. They belong to the genre of the 'old family retainer'; they identify themselves with their master's family and are at once doggishly faithful and completely familiar. No doubt Mark Tapley and Sam Weller are derived to some extent from Smollett, and hence from Cervantes; but it is interesting that Dickens should have been attracted by such a type. Sam Weller's attitude is definitely medieval. He gets himself arrested in order to follow Mr Pickwick into the Fleet, and afterwards refuses to get married because he feels that Mr Pickwick still needs his services. There is a characteristic scene between them:

> 'Vages or no vages, board or no board, lodgin' or no lodgin', Sam Veller, as you took from the old inn in the Borough, sticks by you, come what may . . .'
>
> 'My good fellow,' said Mr Pickwick, when Mr Weller had sat down again, rather abashed at his own enthusiasm, 'you are bound to consider the young woman also.'
>
> 'I do consider the young 'ooman, sir,' said Sam. 'I have considered the young 'ooman. I've spoke to her. I've told her how I'm sitivated; she's ready to vait till I'm ready, and I believe she vill. If she don't, she's not the young 'ooman I take her for, and I give her up with readiness.'

It is easy to imagine what the young woman would have said to this in real life. But notice the feudal atmosphere. Sam Weller is ready as a matter of course to sacrifice years of life to his master, and he can also sit down in his master's presence. A modern manservant would never think of doing either. Dickens's views on the servant question do not get much beyond wishing that master and servant would love one another. Sloppy in *Our Mutual Friend*, though a wretched failure as a character, represents the same kind of loyalty as Sam Weller. Such loyalty, of course, is natural, human and likeable; but so was feudalism.

What Dickens seems to be doing, as usual, is to reach out for an idealized version of the existing thing. He was writing at a time when domestic service must have seemed a completely inevitable evil. There were no labour-saving devices, and there was huge inequality of wealth. It was an age of enormous families, pretentious meals and inconvenient houses, when the slavey drudging fourteen hours a day in the basement kitchen was something too normal to be noticed. And given the *fact* of servitude, the feudal relationship is the only tolerable one. Sam Weller and Mark Tapley are dream figures, no less than the Cheerybles. If there have got to be masters and servants, how much better that the master should be Mr Pickwick and the servant should be Sam Weller. Better still, of course, if servants did not exist at all – but this Dickens is probably unable to imagine. Without a high level of mechanical development, human equality is not practically possible; Dickens goes to show that it is not imaginable either.

Four

It is not merely a coincidence that Dickens never writes about agriculture and writes endlessly about food. He was a cockney, and London is the centre of the earth in rather the same sense that the belly is the centre of the body. It is a city of consumers, of people who are deeply civilized but not primarily useful. A thing that strikes one when one looks below the surface of Dickens's books is that, as nineteenth-century novelists go, he is rather ignorant. He knows very little about the way things really happen. At first sight this statement looks flatly untrue, and it needs some qualification.

Dickens had had vivid glimpses of 'low life' – life in a debtor's prison, for example – and he was also a popular novelist and able to write about ordinary people. So were all the characteristic English novelists of the nineteenth century. They felt at home in the world they lived in, whereas a writer nowadays is so hopelessly isolated that the typical modern novel is a novel about a novelist. Even when Joyce, for instance, spends a decade or so in patient efforts to make contact with the 'common man', his 'common man' finally turns out to be a Jew, and a bit of a highbrow at that. Dickens at least does not suffer from this kind of thing. He has no difficulty in introducing the common motives, love, ambition, avarice, vengeance and so forth. What he does not noticeably write about, however, is *work*.

In Dickens's novels anything in the nature of work happens off-stage. The only one of his heroes who has a plausible profession is David Copperfield, who is first a shorthand writer and then a novelist, like Dickens himself. With most of the others, the way they earn their living is very much in the background. Pip, for instance, 'goes into business' in Egypt; we are not told what business, and Pip's working life occupies about half a page of the book. Clennam has been in some unspecified business in China, and later goes into another barely specified business with Doyce. Martin Chuzzlewit is an architect, but does not seem to get much time for practising. In no case do their adventures spring directly out of their work. Here the contrast between Dickens and, say, Trollope is startling. And one reason for this is undoubtedly that Dickens knows very little about the professions his characters are supposed to follow. What exactly went on in Gradgrind's factories? How did Podsnap make his money? How did Merdle work his swindles? One knows that Dickens could never follow up the details of parliamentary elections and Stock Exchange rackets as Trollope could. As soon as he has to deal with trade, finance, industry or politics he takes refuge in vagueness, or in satire. This is the case even with legal processes, about which actually he must have known a good deal. Compare any lawsuit in Dickens with the lawsuit in *Orley Farm*, for instance.

And this partly accounts for the needless ramifications of Dickens's novels, the awful Victorian 'plot'. It is true that not all his novels are alike in this. *A Tale of Two Cities* is a very good and fairly simple story, and so in its different way is *Hard Times*; but these are just the two which are always rejected as 'not like Dickens' – and incidentally they were not published in monthly numbers'[1] The two first-person novels are also good stories, apart from their sub-plots. But the typical Dickens novel, *Nicholas Nickleby, Oliver Twist, Martin Chuzzlewit, Our Mutual Friend,* always exists round a framework of melodrama. The last thing anyone every remembers about these books is their central story. On the other hand, I suppose no one has ever read them without carrying the memory of individual pages to the day of his death. Dickens sees human beings with the most intense vividness, but he sees them always in private life, as 'characters', not as functional members of society; that is to say, he sees them statically. Consequently his greatest success is *The Pickwick Papers,* which is not a story at all, merely a series of sketches; there is little attempt at development – the characters simply go on and on, behaving like idiots, in a kind of eternity. As soon as he tries to bring his characters into action, the melodrama begins. He cannot make the action revolve round their ordinary occupations; hence the crossword puzzle of coincidences, intrigues, murders, disguises, buried wills, long-lost brothers, etc., etc. In the end even people like Squeers and Micawber get sucked into the machinery.

Of course it would be absurd to say that Dickens is a vague or merely melodramatic writer. Much that he wrote is extremely factual, and in the power of evoking visual images he has probably never been equalled. When Dickens has once described something you see it for the rest of your life. But in a way the concreteness of his vision is a sign of what he is missing. For, after all, that is what the merely casual onlooker always sees – the outward appearance, the non-functional, the surfaces of things. No one who is really involved in the landscape ever sees the landscape. Wonderfully as he can describe an *appearance,* Dickens does not often describe a *process.* The vivid pictures that he succeeds in leaving in one's memory are nearly always the pictures of things seen in leisure moments, in the coffee-rooms of country inns or through the windows of a stage-coach; the kind of things he notices are inn-signs, brass door-knockers, painted jugs, the interiors of shops and private houses, clothes, faces and, above all, food. Everything is seen from the consumer-angle. When he writes about Coketown he manages to evoke, in just a few paragraphs, the atmosphere of a Lancashire town as a slightly disgusted southern visitor would see it. 'It had a black canal in it, and a river that ran purple with evil-smelling dye, and vast piles of buildings full of windows where there was a rattling and a trembling all day long, and where the piston of the steam-engine worked monotonously up and down, like the head of an elephant in a state of melancholy madness.' That is as near as Dickens ever gets to the machinery of the mills. An engineer or a cotton-broker would see it differently; but then neither of them would be capable of that impressionistic touch about the heads of the elephants.

In a rather different sense his attitude to life is extremely unphysical. He is a man who lives through his eyes and ears rather than through his hands and muscles. Actually his habits were not so sedentary as this seems to imply. In spite of rather poor health and physique, he was active to the point of restlessness; throughout his life he was a remarkable walker, and he could at

[1] *Hard Times* was published as a serial in *Household Words* and *Great Expectations* and *A Tale of Two Cities* in *All the Year Round.* Forster says that the shortness of the weekly instalments made it 'much more difficult to get sufficient interest into each'. Dickens himself complained of the lack of 'elbow-room'. In other words, he had to stick more closely to the story. [Author's footnote.]

any rate carpenter well enough to put up stage scenery. But he was not one of those people who feel a need to use their hands. It is difficult to imagine him digging at a cabbage-patch, for instance. He gives no evidence of knowing anything about agriculture, and obviously knows nothing about any kind of game or sport. He has no interest in pugilism, for instance. Considering the age in which he was writing, it is astonishing how little physical brutality there is in Dickens's novels. Martin Chuzzlewit and Mark Tapley, for instance, behave with the most remarkable mildness towards the Americans who are constantly menacing them with revolvers and bowie-knives. The average English or American novelist would have had them handing out socks on the jaw and exchanging pistol-shots in all directions. Dickens is too decent for that; he sees the stupidity of violence, and also he belongs to a cautious urban class which does not deal in socks on the jaw, even in theory. And his attitude towards sport is mixed up with social feelings. In England, for mainly geographical reasons, sport, especially field-sports, and snobbery are inextricably mingled. English Socialists are often flatly incredulous when told that Lenin, for instance, was devoted to shooting. In their eyes shooting, hunting, etc. are simply snobbish observances of the landed gentry; they forget that these things might appear differently in a huge virgin country like Russia. From Dickens's point of view almost any kind of sport is at best a subject for satire. Consequently one side of nineteenth-century life – the boxing, racing, cock-fighting, badger-digging, poaching, rat-catching side of life, so wonderfully embalmed in Leech's illustrations to Surtees – is outside his scope.

What is more striking, in a seemingly 'progressive' radical, is that he is not mechanically minded. He shows no interest either in the details of machinery or in the things machinery can do. As Gissing remarks, Dickens nowhere describes a railway journey with anything like the enthusiasm he shows in describing journeys by stage-coach. In nearly all of his books one has a curious feeling that one is living in the first quarter of the nineteenth century, and in fact, he does tend to return to this period. *Little Dorrit*, written in the middle 'fifties, deals with the late 'twenties; *Great Expectations* (1861) is not dated, but evidently deals with the 'twenties and 'thirties. Several of the inventions and discoveries which have made the modern world possible (the electric telegraph, the breech-loading gun, india-rubber, coal gas, wood-pulp paper) first appeared in Dickens's lifetime, but he scarcely notes them in his books. Nothing is queerer than the vagueness with which he speaks of Doyce's 'invention' in *Little Dorrit.* It is represented as something extremely ingenious and revolutionary, 'of great importance to his country and his fellow-creatures', and it is also an important minor link in the book; yet we are never told what the 'invention' is! On the other hand, Doyce's physical appearance is hit off with the typical Dickens touch; he has a peculiar way of moving his thumb, a way characteristic of engineers. After that, Doyce is firmly anchored in one's memory; but, as usual, Dickens has done it by fastening on something external.

There are people (Tennyson is an example) who lack the mechanical faculty but can see the social possibilities of machinery. Dickens has not this stamp of mind. He shows very little consciousness of the future. When he speaks of human progress it is usually in terms of *moral* progress – men growing better; probably he would never admit that men are only as good as their technical development allows them to be. At this point the gap between Dickens and his modern analogue, H. G. Wells, is at its widest. Wells wears the future round his neck like a millstone, but Dickens's unscientific cast of mind is just as damaging in a different way. What it does is to make any *positive* attitude more difficult for him. He is hostile to the feudal, agricultural past and not in real touch with the industrial present. Well, then, all that remains is the future (meaning science, 'progress' and so forth), which hardly enters into his thoughts. Therefore, while attacking everything in sight, he has no definable standard of comparison. As I have pointed out already, he attacks the current educational system with perfect justice, and yet, after all, he has no remedy to offer except kindlier schoolmasters. Why did he not indicate what a school *might* have been? Why did he not have his own sons educated according to some plan of his own, instead of sending them to public schools to be stuffed with Greek? Because he lacked that kind of imagination. He has an infallible moral sense, but very little intellectual curiosity. And here one comes upon something which really is an enormous deficiency in Dickens, something that really does make the nineteenth century seem remote from us – that he has no ideal of *work*.

With the doubtful exception of David Copperfield (merely Dickens himself), one cannot point to a single one of his central characters who is primarily interested in his job. His heroes work in order to make a living and to marry the heroine, not because they feel a passionate interest in one particular subject. Martin Chuzzlewit, for instance, is not burning with zeal to be an architect; he might just as well be a doctor or a barrister. In any case, in the typical Dickens novel, the *deus ex machina* enters with a bag of gold in the last chapter and the hero is absolved from further struggle. The feeling, 'This is what I came into the world to do. Everything else is uninteresting. I will do this even if it means starvation', which turns men of differing temperaments into scientists, inventors, artists, priests, explorers and revolutionaries – this motif is almost entirely absent from Dickens's books. He himself, as is well known, worked like a slave and believed in his work as few novelists have ever done. But there seems to be no calling except novel-writing (and perhaps acting) towards which he can imagine this kind of devotion. And, after all, it is natural enough, considering his rather negative attitude towards society. In the last resort there is nothing he admires except common decency. Science is uninteresting and machinery is cruel and ugly (the heads of the elephants). Business is only for ruffians like Bounderby. As for politics – leave that to the Tite Barnacles. Really there is no objective except to marry the heroine, settle down, live solvently and be kind. And you can do that much better in private life.

Here, perhaps, one gets a glimpse of Dickens's secret imaginative background. What did he think of as the most desirable way to live? When Martin Chuzzlewit had made it up with his uncle, when Nicholas Nickleby had married money, when John Harmon had been enriched by Boffin – what did they *do*?

The answer evidently is that they did nothing. Nicholas Nickleby invested his wife's money with the Cheerybles and 'became a rich and prosperous merchant', but as he immediately retired into Devonshire, we can assume that he did not work very hard. Mr and Mrs Snodgrass 'purchased and cultivated a small farm, more for occupation than profit'. That is the spirit in which most of Dickens's books end – a sort of radiant idleness. Where he appears to disapprove of young men who do not work (Harthouse, Harry Gowan, Richard Carstone, Wrayburn before his reformation), it is because they are cynical and immoral or because they are a burden on somebody else; if you are 'good', and also self-supporting, there is no reason why you should not spend fifty years in simply drawing your dividends. Home life is always enough. And, after all, it was the general assumption of his age. The 'genteel sufficiency', the 'competence', the 'gentleman of independent means' (or 'in easy circumstances') – the very phrases tell one all about the strange, empty dream of the eighteenth- and nineteenth-century middle bourgeoisie. It was a dream of *complete idleness*. Charles Reade conveys its spirit perfectly in the ending of *Hard Cash*. Alfred Hardie, hero of *Hard Cash*, is the typical nineteenth-century novel hero (public-school style), with gifts which Reade describes as amounting to 'genius'. He is an old Etonian and a scholar of Oxford, he knows most of the Greek and Latin classics by heart, he can box with prize-fighters and win the Diamond Sculls at Henley. He goes through incredible adventures in which, of course, he behaves with faultless heroism, and then, at the age of twenty-five, he inherits a fortune, marries his Julia Dodd and settles down in the suburbs of Liverpool, in the same house as his parents-in-law:

> They all lived together at Albion Villa, thanks to Alfred ... Oh, you happy little villa! You were as like Paradise as any mortal dwelling can be. A day came, however, when your walls could no longer hold all the happy inmates. Julia presented Alfred with a lovely boy; enter two nurses and the villa showed symptoms of bursting. Two months more, and Alfred and his wife overflowed into the next villa. It was but twenty yards off; and there was a double reason for the migration. As often happens after a long separation, Heaven bestowed on Captain and Mrs Dodd another infant to play about their knees, etc., etc., etc.

This is the type of the Victorian happy ending – a vision of a huge, loving family of three or four generations, all crammed together in the same house and constantly multiplying, like a bed of oysters. What is striking about it is the utterly soft, sheltered, effortless life that it implies. It is not even a violent idleness, like Squire Western's. That is the significance of Dickens's urban background and his non-interest in the blackguardly-sporting-military side of life. His heroes, once they had come into money and 'settled down', would not only do no work; they would not even ride, hunt, shoot, fight duels, elope with actresses or lose money at the races. They would simply live at home in feather-bed respectability, and preferably next door to a blood-relation living exactly the same life:

> The first act of Nicholas, when he became a rich and prosperous merchant, was to buy his father's old house. As time crept on, and there came gradually about him a group of lovely children, it was altered and enlarged; but none of the old rooms were ever pulled down, no old tree was ever rooted up, nothing with which there was any association of bygone times was ever removed or changed.
>
> Within a stone's-throw was another retreat enlivened by children's pleasant voices too; and here was Kate ... the same true, gentle creature, the same fond sister, the same in the love of all about her, as in her girlish days.

It is the same incestuous atmosphere as in the passage quoted from Reade.

And evidently this is Dickens's ideal ending. It is perfectly attained in *Nicholas Nickleby*, *Martin Chuzzlewit* and *Pickwick*, and it is approximated to in varying degrees in almost all the others. The exceptions are *Hard Times* and *Great Expectations* – the latter actually has a 'happy ending', but it contradicts the general tendency of the book, and it was put in at the request of Bulwer Lytton.

The ideal to be striven after, then, appears to be something like this: a hundred thousand pounds, a quaint old house with plenty of ivy on it, a sweetly womanly wife, a horde of children, and no work. Everything is safe, soft, peaceful and, above all, domestic. In the moss-grown churchyard down the road are the graves of the loved ones who passed away before the happy ending happened. The servants are comic and feudal, the children prattle round your feet, the old friends sit at your fireside, talking of past days, there is the endless succession of enormous meals, the cold punch and sherry negus, the feather beds and warming-pans, the Christmas parties with charades and blind man's buff; but nothing ever happens, except the yearly childbirth. The curious thing is that it is a genuinely happy picture, or so Dickens is able to make it appear. The thought of that kind of existence is satisfying to him. This alone would be enough to tell one that more than a hundred years have passed since Dickens's first book was written. No modern man could combine such purposelessness with so much vitality.

Five

By this time anyone who is a lover of Dickens, and who has read as far as this, will probably be angry with me.

I have been discussing Dickens simply in terms of his 'message', and almost ignoring his literary qualities. But every writer, especially every novelist, *has* a 'message', whether he admits it or not, and the minutest details of his work are influenced by it. All art is propaganda. Neither Dickens himself nor the majority of Victorian novelists would have thought of denying this. On the other hand, not all propaganda is art. As I said earlier, Dickens is one of those writers who are felt to be worth stealing. He has been stolen by Marxists, by Catholics and, above all, by Conservatives. The question is, What is there to steal? Why does anyone care about Dickens? Why do *I* care about Dickens?

That kind of question is never easy to answer. As a rule, an aesthetic preference is either something inexplicable or it is so corrupted by non-aesthetic motives as to make one wonder whether the whole of literary criticism is not a huge network of humbug. In Dickens's case the complicating factor is his familiarity. He happens to be one of those 'great authors' who are ladled down everyone's throat in childhood. At the time this causes rebellion and vomiting, but it may have different after-effects in later life. For instance, nearly everyone feels a sneaking affection for the patriotic poems that he learned by heart as a child, 'Ye Mariners of England', 'The Charge of the Light Brigade' and so forth. What one enjoys is not so much the poems themselves as the memories they call up. And with Dickens the same forces of association are at work. Probably there are copies of one or two of his books lying about in an actual majority of English homes. Many children begin to know his characters by sight before they can even read, for on the whole Dickens was lucky in his illustrators. A thing that is absorbed as early as that does not come up against any critical judgement. And when one thinks of this, one thinks of all that is bad and silly in Dickens – the cast-iron 'plots', the characters who don't come off, the *longueurs*, the paragraphs in blank verse, the awful pages of 'pathos'. And then the thought arises, when I say I like Dickens, do I simply mean that I like thinking about my childhood? Is Dickens merely an institution?

If so, he is an institution that there is no getting away from. How often one really thinks about any writer, even a writer one cares for, is a difficult thing to decide; but I should doubt whether anyone who has actually read Dickens can go a week without remembering him in one context or another. Whether you approve of him or not, he is *there*, like the Nelson Column. At any moment some scene or character, which may come from some book you cannot even remember the name of, is liable to drop into your mind. Micawber's letters! Winkle in the witness box! Mrs Gamp! Mrs Wititterly and Sir Tumley Snuffim! Todgers's! (George Gissing said that when he passed the Monument it was never of the Fire of London that he thought, always of Todgers's.) Mrs Leo Hunter! Squeers! Silas Wegg and the Decline and Fall-off of the Russian Empire! Miss Mills and the Desert of Sahara! Wopsle acting Hamlet! Mrs Jellyby! Mantalini! Jerry Cruncher! Barkis! Pumblechook! Tracy Tupman! Skimpole! Joe Gargery! Pecksniff! – and so it goes on and on. It is not so much a series of books, it is more like a world. And not a purely comic world either, for part of what one remembers in Dickens is his Victorian morbidness and necrophilia and the blood-and-thunder scenes – the death of Sikes, Krook's spontaneous combustion, Fagin in the condemned cell, the women knitting round the guillotine. To a surprising extent all this has entered even into the minds of people who do not care about it. A music-hall comedian can (or at any rate could quite recently) go on the stage and impersonate Micawber or Mrs Gamp with a fair certainty of being understood, although not one in twenty of the audience had ever read a book of Dickens's right through. Even people who affect to despise him quote him unconsciously.

Dickens is a writer who can be imitated, up to a certain point. In genuinely popular literature – for instance, the Elephant and Castle version of *Sweeney Todd* – he has been plagiariazed quite shamelessly. What has been imitated, however, is simply a tradition that Dickens himself took from earlier novelists and developed, the cult of 'character', i.e. eccentricity. The thing that cannot be imitated is his fertility of invention, which is invention not so much of characters, still less of 'situations', as of turns of phrase and concrete details. The outstanding, unmistakable mark of Dickens's writing is the *unnecessary detail*. Here is an example of what I mean. The story given below is not particularly funny, but there is one phrase in it that is as individual as a fingerprint. Mr Jack Hopkins, at Bob Sawyer's party, is telling the story of the child who swallowed its sister's necklace:

> Next day, child swallowed two beads; the day after that, he treated himself to three, and so on, till in a week's time he had got through the necklace – five-and-twenty beads in all. The sister, who was an industrious girl and seldom treated herself to a bit of finery, cried her eyes out at the loss of the necklace; looked high and low for it; but I needn't say, didn't find it. A few days afterwards, the family were at dinner – baked shoulder of mutton and potatoes under it – the child, who wasn't hungry, was playing about the room, when suddenly there was heard

> the devil of a noise, like a small hailstorm. 'Don't do that, my boy,' says the father. 'I ain't a-doin' nothing,' said the child. 'Well, don't do it again,' said the father. There was a short silence, and then the noise began again, worse than ever. 'If you don't mind what I say, my boy,' said the father, 'you'll find yourself in bed, in something less than a pig's whisper.' He gave the child a shake to make him obedient, and such a rattling ensued as nobody ever heard before. 'Why, dam' me, it's *in* the child,' said the father; 'he's got the croup in the wrong place!' 'No, I haven't, father,' said the child, beginning to cry, 'it's the necklace; I swallowed it, father.' The father caught the child up, and ran with him to the hospital, the beads in the boy's stomach rattling all the way with the jolting; and the people looking up in the air, and down in the cellars, to see where the unusual sound came from. 'He's in the hospital now,' said Jack Hopkins, 'and he makes such a devil of a noise when he walks about, that they're obliged to muffle him in a watchman's coat, for fear he should wake the patients.'

As a whole, this story might come out of any nineteenth-century comic paper. But the unmistakable Dickens touch, the thing nobody else would have though of, is the baked shoulder of mutton and potatoes under it. How does this advance the story? The answer is that it doesn't. It is something totally unnecessary, a florid little squiggle on the edge of the page; only, it is by just these squiggles that the special Dickens atmosphere is created. The other thing one would notice here is that Dickens's way of telling a story takes a long time. An interesting example, too long to quote, is Sam Weller's story of the obstinate patient in Chapter XLIV of *The Pickwick Papers*. As it happens, we have a standard of comparison here, because Dickens is plagiarizing, consciously or unconsciously. The story is also told by some ancient Greek writer. I cannot now find the passage, but I read it years ago as a boy at school, and it runs more or less like this:

> A certain Thracian, renowned for his obstinacy, was warned by his physician that if he drank a flagon of wine it would kill him. The Thracian thereupon drank the flagon of wine and immediately jumped off the house-top and perished. 'For,' said he, 'in this way I shall prove that the wine did not kill me.'

As the Greek tells it, that is the whole story – about six lines. As Sam Weller tells it, it takes round about a thousand words. Long before getting to the point we have been told all about the patient's clothes, his meals, his manners, even the newspapers he reads, and about the peculiar construction of the doctor's carriage, which conceals the fact that the coachman's trousers do not match his coat. Then there is the dialogue between the doctor and the patient. '"Crumpets is wholesome, sir," said the patient. "Crumpets is *not* wholesome, sir," says the doctor, very fierce,' etc., etc. In the end the original story has been buried under the details. And in all of Dickens's most characteristic passages it is the same. His imagination overwhelms everything, like a kind of weed. Squeers stands up to address his boys, and immediately we are hearing about Bolder's father who was two pounds ten short, and Mobbs's stepmother who took to her bed on hearing that Mobbs wouldn't eat fat and hoped Mr Squeers would flog him into a happier state of mind. Mrs Leo

Hunter writes a poem, 'Expiring Frog'; two full stanzas are given. Boffin takes a fancy to pose as a miser, and instantly we are down among the squalid biographies of eighteenth-century misers, with names like Vulture Hopkins and the Rev. Blewberry Jones, and chapter headings like 'The Story of the Mutton Pies' and 'The Treasures of a Dunghill'. Mrs Harris, who does not even exist, has more detail piled onto her than any three characters in an ordinary novel. Merely in the middle of a sentence we learn, for instance, that her infant nephew has been seen in a bottle at Greenwich Fair, along with the pink-eyed lady, the Prussian dwarf and the living skeleton. Joe Gargery describes how the robbers broke into the house of Pumblechook, the corn and seed merchant – 'and they took his till, and they took his cashbox, and they drinked his wine, and they partook of his wittles, and they slapped his face, and they pulled his nose, and they tied him up to his bedpust, and they give him a dozen, and they stuffed his mouth full of flowering annuals to perwent his crying out.' Once again the unmistakable Dickens touch, the flowering annuals; but any other novelist would only have mentioned about half of these outrages. Everything is piled up and up, detail on detail, embroidery on embroidery. It is futile to object that this kind of thing is rococo – one might as well make the same objection to a wedding-cake. Either you like it or you do not like it. Other nineteenth-century writers, Surtees, Barham, Thackeray, even Marryat, have something of Dickens's profuse, overflowing quality, but none of them on anything like the same scale. The appeal of all these writers now depends partly on period-flavour, and though Marryat is still officially a 'boys' writer' and Surtees has a sort of legendary fame among hunting men, it is probable that they are read mostly by bookish people.

Significantly, Dickens's most successful books (not his *best* books) are *The Pickwick Papers*, which is not a novel, and *Hard Times* and *A Tale of Two Cities*, which are not funny. As a novelist his natural fertility greatly hampers him, because the burlesque which he is never able to resist is constantly breaking into what ought to be serious situations. There is a good example of this in the opening chapter of *Great Expectations*. The escaped convict, Magwitch, has just captured the six-year-old Pip in the churchyard. The scene starts terrifyingly enough, from Pip's point of view. The convict, smothered in mud and with his chain trailing from his leg, suddenly starts up among the tombs, grabs the child, turns him upside down and robs his pockets. Then he begins terrorizing him into bringing food and a file:

> He held me by the arms in an upright position on the top of the stone, and went on in these fearful terms:
>
> 'You bring me, tomorrow morning early, that file and them wittles. You bring the lot to me, at that old Battery over yonder. You do it, and you never dare to say a word or dare to make a sign concerning your having seen such a person as me, or any person sumever, and you shall be let to live. You fail, or you go from my words in any partickler, no matter how small it is, and your heart and liver shall be tore out, roasted and ate. Now, I ain't alone, as you may think I am. There's a young man hid with me, in comparison with which young man I am a Angel. That young man hears the words I speak. That young man has a secret way pecooliar to himself, of getting at a boy, and at his heart, and at his liver. It is in wain for a boy to attempt to hide himself from that young man. A boy may lock his door, may be warm in bed,

may tuck himself up, may draw the clothes over his head, may think himself comfortable and safe, but that young man will softly creep and creep his way to him and tear him open. I am keeping that young man from harming you at the present moment, but with great difficulty. I find it wery hard to hold that young man off of your inside. Now, what do you say?'

Here Dickens has simply yielded to temptation. To begin with, no starving and hunted man would speak in the least like that. Moreover, although the speech shows a remarkable knowledge of the way in which a child's mind works, its actual words are quite out of tune with what is to follow. It turns Magwitch into a sort of pantomime wicked uncle, or, if one sees him through the child's eyes, into an appalling monster. Later in the book he is to be represented as neither, and his exaggerated gratitude, on which the plot turns, is to be incredible because of just this speech. As usual, Dickens's imagination has overwhelmed him. The picturesque details were too good to be left out. Even with characters who are more of a piece than Magwitch he is liable to be tripped up by some seductive phrase. Mr Murdstone, for instance, is in the habit of ending David Copperfield's lessons every morning with a dreadful sum in arithmetic. 'If I go into a cheesemonger's shop, and buy five thousand double-Gloucester cheeses at fourpence halfpenny each, present payment,' it always begins. Once again the typical Dickens detail, the double-Gloucester cheeses. But it is far too human a touch for Murdstone; he would have made it five thousand cashboxes. Every time this note is struck, the unity of the novel suffers. Not that it matters very much, because Dickens is obviously a writer whose parts are greater than his wholes. He is all fragments, all details – rotten architecture, but wonderful gargoyles – and never better than when he is building up some character who will later on be forced to act inconsistently.

Of course it is not usual to urge against Dickens that he makes his characters behave inconsistently. Generally he is accused of doing just the opposite. His characters are supposed to be mere 'types', each crudely representing some single trait and fitted with a kind of label by which you recognize him. Dickens is 'only a caricaturist' – that is the usual accusation, and it does him both more and less than justice. To begin with, he did not think of himself as a caricaturist, and was constantly setting into action characters who ought to have been purely static. Squeers, Micawber, Miss Mowcher,[1] Wegg, Skimpole, Pecksniff and many others are finally involved in 'plots' where they are out of place and where they behave quite incredibly. They start off as magic-lantern slides and they end by getting mixed up in a third-rate movie. Sometimes one can put one's finger on a single sentence in which the original illusion is destroyed. There is such a sentence in *David Copperfield*. After the famous dinner-party (the one where the leg of mutton was underdone), David is showing his guests out. He stops Traddles at the top of the stairs:

'Traddles,' said I, 'Mr Micawber don't mean any harm, poor fellow: but if I were you I wouldn't lend him anything.'

[1] Dickens turned Miss Mowcher into a sort of heroine because the real woman whom he had caricatured had read the earlier chapters and was bitterly hurt. He had previously meant her to play a villainous part. But *any* action by such a character would seem incongruous. [Author's footnote.]

'My dear Copperfield,' returned Traddles smiling, 'I haven't got anything to lend.'

'You have got a name, you know,' I said.

At the place where one reads it this remark jars a little, though something of the kind was inevitable sooner or later. The story is a fairly realistic one, and David is growing up; ultimately he is bound to see Mr Micawber for what he is, a cadging scoundrel. Afterwards, of course, Dickens's sentimentality overcomes him and Micawber is made to turn over a new leaf. But from then on the original Micawber is never quite recaptured, in spite of desperate efforts. As a rule, the 'plot' in which Dickens's characters get entangled is not particularly credible, but at least it makes some pretence at reality, whereas the world to which they belong is a never-never land, a kind of eternity. But just here one sees that 'only a caricaturist' is not really a condemnation. The fact that Dickens is always thought of as a caricaturist, although he was constantly trying to be something else, is perhaps the surest mark of his genius. The monstrosities that he created are still remembered as monstrosities, in spite of getting mixed up in would-be probable melodramas. Their first impact is so vivid that nothing that comes afterwards effaces it. As with the people one knew in childhood, one seems always to remember them in one particular attitude, doing one particular thing. Mrs Squeers is always ladling out brimstone and treacle, Mrs Gummidge is always weeping, Mrs Gargery is always banging her husband's head against the wall, Mrs Jellyby is always scribbling tracts while her children fall into the area – and there they all are, fixed for ever like little twinkling miniatures painted on snuff-box lids, completely fantastic and incredible, and yet somehow more solid and infinitely more memorable than the efforts of serious novelists. Even by the standards of his time Dickens was an exceptionally artificial writer. As Ruskin said, he 'chose to work in a circle of stage fire.' His characters are even more distorted and simplified than Smollett's. But there are no rules in novel writing, and for any work of art there is only one test worth bothering about – survival. By this test Dickens's characters have succeeded, even if the people who remember them hardly think of them as human beings. They are monsters, but at any rate they *exist.*

But all the same there is a disadvantage in writing about monsters. It amounts to this, that it is only certain moods that Dickens can speak to. There are large areas of the human mind that he never touches. There is no poetic feeling anywhere in his books, and no genuine tragedy, and even sexual love is almost outside his scope. Actually his books are not so sexless as they are sometimes declared to be, and considering the time in which he was writing, he is reasonably frank. But there is not a trace in him of the feeling that one finds in *Manon Lescaut*, *Salammbô*, *Carmen*, *Wuthering Heights*. According to Aldous Huxley, D. H. Lawrence once said that Balzac was 'a gigantic dwarf', and in a sense the same is true of Dickens. There are whole worlds which he either knows nothing about or does not wish to mention. Except in a rather roundabout way, one cannot *learn* very much from Dickens. And to say this is to think almost immediately of the great Russian novelists of the nineteenth century. Why is it that Tolstoy's grasp seems to be so much larger than Dickens's – why is it that he seems able to tell you so much more *about yourself*? It is not that he is more gifted, or even, in the last analysis, more intelligent. It is because he is writing about people who are growing. His characters are struggling to make their souls, whereas Dickens's are already finished and perfect. In my own mind Dickens's people are present far more often and far more vividly than Tolstoy's, but always in a single unchangeable attitude, like pictures or pieces of furniture. You cannot hold an imaginary conversation with a Dickens character as you can with, say, Pierre Bezukov. And this is not merely because of Tolstoy's greater seriousness, for there are also comic characters that you can imagine yourself talking to – Bloom, for instance, or Pécuchet, or even Wells's Mr Polly. It is because Dickens's characters have no mental life. They say perfectly the thing that they have to say, but they cannot be conceived as talking about anything else. They never learn, never speculate. Perhaps the most meditative of his characters is Paul Dombey, and his thoughts are mush. Does this mean that Tolstoy's novels are 'better' than Dickens's? The truth is that it is absurd to make such comparisons in terms of 'better' and 'worse'. If I were forced to compare Tolstoy with Dickens, I should say that Tolstoy's appeal will probably be wider in the long run, because Dickens is scarcely intelligible outside the English-speaking culture; on the other hand, Dickens is able to reach simple people, which Tolstoy is not. Tolstoy's characters can cross a frontier, Dickens's can be portrayed on a cigarette-card.[1] But one is no more obliged to choose between them than between a sausage and a rose. Their purposes barely intersect.

Six

If Dickens had been *merely* a comic writer, the chances are that no one would now remember his name. Or at best a few of his books would survive in rather the same way as books like *Frank Fairlegh*, *Mr Verdant Green* and *Mrs Caudle's Curtain Lectures*,[2] as a sort of hangover of the Victorian atmosphere, a pleasant little whiff of oysters and brown stout. Who has not felt sometimes that it was 'a pity' that Dickens ever deserted the vein of *Pickwick* for things like *Little Dorrit* and *Hard Times*? What people always demand of a popular novelist is that he shall write the same book over and over again, forgetting that a man who would write the same book twice could not even write it once. Any writer who is not utterly lifeless moves upon a kind of parabola, and the downward curve is implied in the upward one. Joyce has to start with the frigid competence of *Dubliners* and end with the dream-language of *Finnegans Wake*, but *Ulysses* and *Portrait of the Artist* are part of the trajectory. The thing that drove Dickens forward into a form of art for which he was not really suited, and at the same time caused us to remember him, was simply the fact that he was a moralist, the consciousness of 'having something to say'. He is always preaching a sermon, and that is the final secret of his inventiveness. For you can only create if you can *care*. Types like Squeers and Micawber could not have been produced by a hack writer looking for something to be funny about. A joke worth laughing at always has an idea behind it, and usually a subversive idea. Dickens is able to go on being funny because he

[1] Messrs John Player and Sons issued two series of cigarette cards entitled 'Characters from Dickens' in 1913; they reissued them as a single series in 1923.
[2] *Frank Fairlegh* by F. E. Smedley, 1850; *The Adventures of Mr Verdant Green* by Cuthbert Bede (pseud. of Edward Bradley), 1953; *Mrs Caudle's Curtain Lectures* by Douglas Jerrold (reprinted from *Punch*, 1846).

is in revolt against authority, and authority is always there to be laughed at. There is always room for one more custard pie.

His radicalism is of the vaguest kind, and yet one always knows that it is there. That is the difference between being a moralist and a politician. He has no constructive suggestions, not even a clear grasp of the nature of the society he is attacking, only an emotional perception that something is wrong. All he can finally say is, 'Behave decently,' which, as I suggested earlier, is not necessarily so shallow as it sounds. Most revolutionaries are potential Tories, because they imagine that everything can be put right by altering the *shape* of society; once that change is effected, as it sometimes is, they see no need for any other. Dickens has not this kind of mental coarseness. The vagueness of his discontent is the mark of its permanence. What he is out against is not this or that institution, but, as Chesterton put it, 'an expression on the human face'. Roughly speaking, his morality is the Christian morality, but in spite of his Anglican upbringing he was essentially a Bible-Christian, as he took care to make plain when writing his will. In any case he cannot properly be described as a religious man. He 'believed', undoubtedly, but religion in the devotional sense does not seem to have entered much into his thoughts.[1] Where he is Christian is in his quasi-instinctive siding with the oppressed against the oppressors. As a matter of course he is on the side of the underdog, always and everywhere. To carry this to its logical conclusion one has got to change sides when the underdog becomes an upperdog, and in fact Dickens does tend to do so. He loathes the Catholic Church, for instance, but as soon as the Catholics are persecuted (*Barnaby Rudge*) he is on their side. He loathes the aristocratic class even more, but as soon as they are really overthrown (the revolutionary chapters in *A Tale of Two Cities*) his sympathies swing round. Whenever he departs from this emotional attitude he goes astray. A well-known example is at the ending of *David Copperfield*, in which everyone who reads it feels that something has gone wrong. What is wrong is that the closing chapters are pervaded, faintly but noticeably, by the cult of success. It is the gospel according to Smiles, instead of the gospel according to Dickens. The attractive, out-at-elbow characters are got rid of, Micawber makes a fortune, Heep gets into prison – both of these events are flagrantly impossible – and even Dora is killed off to make way for Agnes. If you like, you can read Dora as Dickens's wife and Agnes as his sister-in-law, but the essential point is that Dickens has 'turned respectable' and done violence to his own nature. Perhaps that is why Agnes is the most disagreeable of his heroines, the real legless angel of Victorian romance, almost as bad as Thackeray's Laura.

No grown-up person can read Dickens without feeling his limitations, and yet there does remain his native generosity of mind, which acts as a kind of anchor and nearly always keeps him where he belongs. It is probably the central secret of his popularity. A good-tempered antinomianism rather of Dickens's type is one of the marks of western popular culture. One sees it in

[1] From a letter to his youngest son (in 1868): 'You will remember that you have never at home been harassed about religious observances, or mere formalities. I have always been anxious not to weary my children with such things, before they are old enough to form opinions respecting them. You will therefore understand the better that I now most solemnly impress upon you the truth and beauty of the Christian Religion, as it came from Christ Himself, and the impossibility of your going far wrong if you humbly but heartily respect it.... Never abandon the wholesome practice of saying your own private prayers, night and morning. I have never abandoned it myself, and I know the comfort of it.' [Author's footnote.]

folk-stories and comic songs, in dream-figures like Mickey Mouse and Popeye the Sailor (both of them variants of Jack the Giant-Killer), in the history of working-class Socialism, in the popular protests (always ineffective but not always a sham) against imperialism, in the impulse that makes a jury award excessive damages when a rich man's car runs over a poor man; it is the feeling that one is always on the side of the underdog, on the side of the weak against the strong. In one sense it is a feeling that is fifty years out of date. The common man is still living in the mental world of Dickens, but nearly every modern intellectual has gone over to some or other form of totalitarianism. From the Marxist or Fascist point of view, nearly all that Dickens stands for can be written off as 'bourgeois morality'. But in moral outlook no one could be more 'bourgeois' than the English working classes. The ordinary people in the western countries have never entered, mentally, into the world of 'realism' and power politics. They may do so before long, in which case Dickens will be as out of date as the cab-horse. But in his own age and ours he has been popular chiefly because he was able to express in a comic, simplified and therefore memorable form the native decency of the common man. And it is important that from this point of view people of very different types can be described as 'common'. In a country like England, in spite of its class-structure there does exist a certain cultural unity. All through the Christian ages, and especially since the French Revolution, the western world has been haunted by the idea of freedom and equality; it is only an *idea*, but it has penetrated to all ranks of society. The most atrocious injustices, cruelties, lies, snobberies exist everywhere, but there are not many people who can regard these things with the same indifference as, say, a Roman slave-owner. Even the millionaire suffers from a vague sense of guilt, like a dog eating a stolen leg of mutton. Nearly everyone, whatever his actual conduct may be, responds emotionally to the idea of human brotherhood. Dickens voiced a code which was and on the whole still is believed in, even by people who violate it. It is difficult otherwise to explain why he could be both read by working people (a thing that has happened to no other novelist of his stature) and buried in Westminster Abbey.

When one reads any strongly individual piece of writing, one has the impression of seeing a face somewhere behind the page. It is not necessarily the actual face of the writer. I feel this very strongly with Swift, with Defoe, with Fielding, Stendhal, Thackeray, Flaubert, though in several cases I do not know what these people looked like and do not want to know. What one sees is the face that the writer *ought* to have. Well, in the case of Dickens I see a face that is not quite the face of Dickens's photographs, though it resembles it. It is the face of a man of about forty, with a small beard and a high colour. He is laughing, with a touch of anger in his laughter, but no triumph, no malignity. It is the face of a man who is always fighting against something, but who fights in the open and is not frightened, the face of a man who is *generously angry* – in other words, of a nineteenth-century liberal, a free intelligence, a type hated with equal hatred by all the smelly little orthodoxies which are now contending for our souls.

Written 1939

Boys' Weeklies

You never walk far through any poor quarter in any big town without coming upon a small newsagent's shop. The general appearance of these shops is always very much the same: a few posters for the *Daily Mail* and the *News of the World* outside, a poky little window with sweet-bottles and packets of Players, and a dark interior smelling of liquorice allsorts and festooned from floor to ceiling with vilely printed twopenny papers, most of them with lurid cover illustrations in three colours.

Except for the daily and evening papers, the stock of these shops hardly overlaps at all with that of the big newsagents. Their main selling line is the twopenny weekly, and the number and variety of these are almost unbelievable. Every hobby and pastime – cagebirds, fretwork, carpentering, bees, carrier-pigeons, home conjuring, philately, chess – has at least one paper devoted to it, and generally several. Gardening and livestock-keeping must have at least a score between them. Then there are the sporting papers, the radio papers, the children's comics, the various snippet papers such as *Tit-Bits*, the large range of papers devoted to the movies and all more or less exploiting women's legs, the various trade papers, the women's story-papers (the *Oracle*, *Secrets*, *Peg's Paper*, etc., etc.), the needlework papers – these so numerous that a display of them alone will often fill an entire window – and in addition the long series of 'Yank Mags' (*Fight Stories*, *Action Stories*, *Western Short Stories*, etc.), which are imported shop-soiled from America and sold at twopence-halfpenny or threepence. And the periodical proper shades off into the fourpenny novelette, the *Aldine Boxing Novels*, the *Boys' Friend Library*, the *Schoolgirls' Own Library* and many others.

Probably the contents of these shops is the best available indication of what the mass of the English people really feels and thinks. Certainly nothing half so revealing exists in documentary form. Bestseller novels, for instance, tell one a great deal, but the novel is aimed almost exclusively at people above the £4-a-week level. The movies are probably a very unsafe guide to popular taste, because the film industry is virtually a monopoly, which means that it is not obliged to study its public at all closely. The same applies to some extent to the daily papers, and most of all to the radio. But it does not apply to the weekly paper with a smallish circulation and specialized subject-matter. Papers like the *Exchange and Mart*, for instance, or *Cage-Birds*, or the *Oracle*, or *Prediction*, or the *Matrimonial Times*, only exist because there is a definite demand for them, and they reflect the minds of their readers as a great national daily with a circulation of millions cannot possibly do.

Here I am only dealing with a single series of papers, the boys' twopenny weeklies, often inaccurately described as 'penny dreadfuls'. Falling strictly within this class there are at present ten papers, the *Gem*, *Magnet*, *Modern Boy*, *Triumph* and *Champion*, all owned by the Amalgamated Press, and the *Wizard*, *Rover*, *Skipper*, *Hotspur* and *Adventure*, all owned by D. C. Thomson & Co. What the circulations of these papers are, I do not know. The editors and proprietors refuse to name any figures, and in any case the circulation of a paper carrying serial stories is bound to fluctuate widely. But there is no question that the combined public of the ten papers is a very large one. They are on sale in every town in England, and nearly every boy who reads at all goes through a phase of reading one or more of them. The *Gem* and *Magnet*, which are much the oldest of these papers, are of rather different type from the rest, and they have evidently lost some of their popularity during the past few years. A good many boys now regard them as old-fashioned and 'slow'. Nevertheless I want to discuss them first, because they are more interesting psychologically than the others, and also because the mere survival of such papers into the nineteen-thirties is a rather startling phenomenon.

The *Gem* and *Magnet* are sister-papers (characters out of one paper frequently appear in the other), and were both started more than thirty years ago. At that time, together with *Chums* and the old *B[oy's] O[wn] P[aper]*, they were the leading papers for boys, and they remained dominant till quite recently. Each of them carries every week a fifteen- or twenty-thousand word school story, complete in itself, but usually more or less connected with the story of the week before. The *Gem* in addition to its school story carries one or more adventure serials. Otherwise the two papers are so much alike that they can be treated as one, though the *Magnet* has always been the better known of the two, probably because it possesses a really first-rate character in the fat boy, Billy Bunter.

The stories are stories of what purports to be public-school life, and the schools (Greyfriars in the *Magnet* and St Jim's in the *Gem*) are represented as ancient and fashionable foundations of the type of Eton or Winchester. All the leading characters are fourth-form boys aged fourteen or fifteen, older or younger boys only appearing in very minor parts. Like Sexton Blake and Nelson Lee, these boys continue week after week and year after year, never growing any older. Very occasionally a new boy arrives or a minor character drops out, but in at any rate the last twenty-five years the personnel has barely altered. All the principal characters in both papers – Bob Cherry, Tom Merry, Harry Wharton, Johnny Bull, Billy Bunter and the rest of them – were at Greyfriars or St Jim's long before the Great War, exactly the same age as at present, having much the same kind of adventures and talking almost exactly the same dialect. And not only the characters but the whole atmosphere of both the *Gem* and *Magnet* has been preserved unchanged, partly by means of very elaborate stylization. The stories in the *Magnet* are signed 'Frank Richards' and those in the *Gem* 'Martin Clifford', but a series lasting thirty years could hardly be the work of the same person every week.[1] Consequently they have to be written in a style that is easily imitated – an extraordinary, artificial, repetitive style, quite different from anything else now existing in English literature. A couple of extracts will do as illustrations. Here is one from the *Magnet*:

> Groan!
> 'Shut up, Bunter!'
> Groan!
> Shutting up was not really in Billy Bunter's line. He seldom shut up,

[1] This is quite incorrect. These stories have been written throughout the whole period by 'Frank Richards' and 'Martin Clifford', who are one and the same person! See articles in *Horizon*, May 1940, and *Summer Pie*, summer 1944. [Author's footnote 1945.]

though often requested to do so. On the present awful occasion the fat Owl of Greyfriars was less inclined than ever to shut up. And he did not shut up! He groaned, and groaned, and went on groaning.

Even groaning did not fully express Bunter's feeling. His feelings, in fact, were inexpressible.

There were six of them in the soup! Only one of the six uttered sounds of woe and lamentation. But that one, William George Bunter, uttered enough for the whole party and a little over.

Harry Wharton & Co stood in a wrathy and worried group. They were landed and stranded, diddled, dished and done! etc., etc., etc.

Here is one from the *Gem*:

'Oh cwumbs!'

'Oh gum!'

'Oooogh!'

'Urrggh!'

Arthur Augustus sat up dizzily. He grabbed his handkerchief and pressed it to his damaged nose. Tom Merry sat up, gasping for breath. They looked at one another.

'Bai Jove! This is a go, deah boy!' gurgled Arthur Augustus.

'I have been thwown into quite a fluttah! Oogh! The wottahs! The wuffians! The feahful outsidahs! Wow!' etc., etc., etc.

Both of these extracts are entirely typical; you would find something like them in almost every chapter of every number, today or twenty-five years ago. The first thing that anyone would notice is the extraordinary amount of tautology (the first of these two passages contains a hundred and twenty-five words and could be compressed into about thirty), seemingly designed to spin out the story, but actually playing its part in creating the atmosphere. For the same reason various facetious expressions are repeated over and over again; 'wrathy', for instance, is a great favourite, and so is 'diddled, dished and done'. 'Oooogh!', 'Grooo!' and 'Yaroo!' (stylized cries of pain) recur constantly, and so does 'Ha! ha! ha!', always given a line to itself, so that sometimes a quarter of a column or thereabouts consists of 'Ha! ha! ha!' The slang ('Go and eat coke!' 'What the thump!', 'You frabjous ass!', etc., etc.) has never been altered, so that the boys are now using slang which is at least thirty years out of date. In addition, the various nicknames are rubbed in on every possible occasion. Every few lines we are reminded that Harry Wharton & Co are 'the Famous Five', Bunter is always 'the fat Owl' or 'the Owl of the Remove', Vernon-Smith is always 'the Bounder of Greyfriars', Gussy (the Honourable Arthur Augustus D'Arcy) is always 'the swell of St Jim's', and so on and so forth. There is a constant, untiring effort to keep the atmosphere intact and to make sure that every new reader learns immediately who is who. The result has been to make Greyfriars and St Jim's into an extraordinary little world of their own, a world which cannot be taken seriously by anyone over fifteen, but which at any rate is not easily forgotten. By a debasement of the Dickens technique a series of stereotyped 'characters' has been built up, in several cases very successfully. Billy Bunter, for instance, must be one of the best-known figures in English fiction; for the mere number of people who know him he ranks with Sexton Blake, Tarzan, Sherlock Holmes and a handful of characters in Dickens.

Needless to say, these stories are fantastically unlike life at a real public school. They run in cycles of rather differing types, but in general they are the clean-fun, knockabout type of story, with interest centring round horseplay, practical jokes, ragging masters, fights, canings, football, cricket and food. A constantly recurring story is one in which a boy is accused of some misdeed committed by another and is too much of a sportsman to reveal the truth. The 'good' boys are 'good' in the clean-living Englishman tradition – they keep in hard training, wash behind their ears, never hit below the belt, etc., etc. – and by way of contrast there is a series of 'bad' boys, Racke, Crooke, Loder and others, whose badness consists in betting, smoking cigarettes and frequenting public houses. All these boys are constantly on the verge of expulsion, but as it would mean a change of personnel if any boy were actually expelled, no one is ever caught out in any really serious offence. Stealing, for instance, barely enters as a motif. Sex is completely taboo, especially in the form in which it actually arises at public schools. Occasionally girls enter into the stories, and very rarely there is something approaching a mild flirtation, but it is always entirely in the spirit of clean fun. A boy and a girl enjoy going for bicycle rides together – that is all it ever amounts to. Kissing, for instance, would be regarded as 'soppy'. Even the bad boys are presumed to be completely sexless. When the *Gem* and *Magnet* were started, it is probable that there was a deliberate intention to get away from the guilty sex-ridden atmosphere that pervaded so much of the earlier literature for boys. In the 'nineties the *Boy's Own Paper*, for instance, used to have its correspondence columns full of terrifying warnings against masturbation, and books like *St Winifred's* and *Tom Brown's Schooldays* were heavy with homosexual feeling, though no doubt the authors were not fully aware of it. In the *Gem* and *Magnet* sex simply does not exist as a problem. Religion is also taboo; in the whole thirty years' issue of the two papers the word 'God' probably does not occur, except in 'God save the King'. On the other hand, there has always been a very strong 'temperance' strain. Drinking and, by association, smoking are regarded as rather disgraceful even in an adult ('shady' is the usual word), but at the same time as something irresistibly fascinating, a sort of substitute for sex. In their moral atmosphere the *Gem* and *Magnet* have a great deal in common with the Boy Scout movement, which started at about the same time.

All literature of this kind is partly plagiarism. Sexton Blake, for instance, started off quite frankly as an imitation of Sherlock Holmes, and still resembles him fairly strongly; he has hawk-like features, lives in Baker Street, smokes enormously and puts on a dressing-gown when he wants to think. The *Gem* and *Magnet* probably owe something to the school story writers who were flourishing when they began, Gunby Hadath, Desmond Coke and the rest, but they owe more to nineteenth-century models. In so far as Greyfriars and St Jim's are like real schools at all, they are much more like Tom Brown's Rugby than a modern public school. Neither school has an OTC for instance, games are not compulsory, and the boys are even allowed to wear what clothes they like. But without doubt the main origin of these papers is *Stalky & Co*. This book has had an immense influence on boys' literature, and it is one of those books which have a sort of traditional reputation among people who have never even seen a copy of it. More than once in boys' weekly papers I have come across a reference to *Stalky & Co* in which the word was spelt 'Storky'. Even the name of the chief comic among the Greyfriars masters, Mr Prout, is taken from *Stalky & Co* and so is much of the slang: 'jape', 'merry', 'giddy', 'bizney' (business), 'frabjous', 'don't' for 'doesn't' – all of them out of date even when *Gem* and *Magnet* started. There are also traces of earlier origins. The name 'Greyfriars' is probably taken from Thackeray, and Gosling, the school porter in the *Magnet*, talks in an imitation of Dickens's dialect.

With all this, the supposed 'glamour' of public-school life is played for all it is worth. There is all the usual paraphernalia – lock-up, roll-call, house matches, fagging, prefects, cosy teas round the study fire, etc., etc. – and constant reference to the 'old school', the 'old grey stones' (both schools were founded in the early sixteenth century), the 'team spirit' of the 'Greyfriars men'. As for the snob-appeal, it is completely shameless. Each school has a titled boy or two whose titles are constantly thrust in the reader's face; other boys have the names of well-known aristocratic families, Talbot, Manners, Lowther. We are for ever being reminded that Gussy is the Honourable Arthur A. D'Arcy, son of Lord Eastwood, that Jack Blake is heir to 'broad acres', that Hurree Jamset Ram Singh (nicknamed Inky) is the nabob of Bhanipur, that Vernon-Smith's father is a millionaire. Till recently the illustrations in both papers always depicted the boys in clothes imitated from those of Eton; in the last few years Greyfriars has changed over to blazers and flannel trousers, but St Jim's still sticks to the Eton jacket, and Gussy sticks to his tophat. In the school magazine which appears every week as part of the *Magnet*, Harry Wharton writes an article discussing the pocket-money received by the 'fellows in the Remove', and reveals that some of them get as much as five pounds a week! This kind of thing is a perfectly deliberate incitement to wealth-fantasy. And here it is worth noticing a rather curious fact, and that is that the school story is a thing peculiar to England. So far as I know, there are extremely few school stories in foreign languages. The reason, obviously, is that in England education is mainly a matter of status. The most definite dividing-line between the petite bourgeoisie and the working class is that the former pay for their education, and within the bourgeoisie there is another unbridgeable gulf between the 'public' school and the 'private' school. It is quite clear that there are tens and scores of thousands of people to whom every detail of life at a 'posh' public school is wildly thrilling and romantic. They happen to be outside that mystic world of quadrangles and house-colours, but they yearn after it, day-dream about it, live mentally in it for hours at a stretch. The question is, Who are these people? Who reads the *Gem* and *Magnet*?

Obviously one can never be quite certain about this kind of thing. All I can say from my own observation is this. Boys who are likely to go to public schools themselves generally read the *Gem* and *Magnet*, but they nearly always stop reading them when they are about twelve; they may continue for another year from force of habit, but by that time they have ceased to take them seriously. On the other hand, the boys at very cheap private schools, the schools that are designed for people who can't afford a public school but consider the Council schools 'common', continue reading the *Gem* and *Magnet* for several years longer. A few years ago I was a teacher at two of these schools myself. I found that not only did virtually all the boys read the *Gem* and *Magnet*, but that they were still taking them fairly seriously when they were fifteen or even sixteen. These boys were the sons of shopkeepers, office employees and small business and professional men, and obviously it is this class that the *Gem* and *Magnet* are aimed at. But they are certainly read by working-class boys as well. They are generally on sale in the poorest quarters of big towns, and I have known them to be read by boys whom one might expect to be completely immune from public school 'glamour'. I have seen a young coal miner, for instance, a lad who had already worked a year or two underground, eagerly reading the *Gem*. Recently I offered a batch of English papers to some British legionairies of the French Foreign Legion in North Africa; they picked out the *Gem* and *Magnet* first. Both papers are much read by girls,[1] and the Pen Pals' department of the *Gem* shows that it is read in every corner of the British Empire, by Australians, Canadians, Palestine Jews, Malays, Arabs, Straits Chinese, etc., etc. The editors evidently expect their readers to be aged round about fourteen, and the advertisements (milk chocolate, postage stamps, water pistols, blushing cured, home conjuring tricks, itching-powder, the Phine Phun Ring which runs a needle into your friend's hand, etc., etc.) indicate roughly the same age; there are also the Admiralty advertisements, however, which call for youths between seventeen and twenty-two. And there is no question that these papers are also read by adults. It is quite common for people to write to the editor and say that they have read every number of the *Gem* or *Magnet* for the past thirty years. Here, for instance, is a letter from a lady in Salisbury:

> I can say of your splendid yarns of Harry Wharton & Co of Greyfriars, that they never fail to reach a high standard. Without doubt they are the finest stories of their type on the market today, which is saying a good deal. They seem to bring you face to face with Nature. I have taken the *Magnet* from the start, and have followed the adventures of Harry Wharton & Co with rapt interest. I have no sons, but two daughters, and there's always a rush to be the first to read the grand old paper. My husband, too, was a staunch reader of the *Magnet* until he was suddenly taken away from us.

It is well worth getting hold of some copies of the *Gem* and *Magnet*, especially the *Gem*, simply to have a look at the correspondence columns. What is truly startling is the intense interest with which the pettiest details of life at Greyfriars and St Jim's are followed up. Here, for instance, are a few of the questions sent in by readers:

> 'What age is Dick Roylance?' 'How old is St Jim's?' 'Can you give me a list of the Shell and their studies?' 'How much did D'Arcy's monocle cost?' 'How is it fellows like Crooke are in the Shell and decent fellows like yourself are only in the Fourth?' 'What are the Form captain's three chief duties?' 'Who is the chemistry master at St Jim's?' (From a girl) 'Where is St Jim's situated? *Could* you tell me how to get there, as I would love to see the building? Are you boys just "phoneys", as I think you are?'

It is clear that many of the boys and girls who write these letters are living a complete fantasy-life. Sometimes a boy will write, for instance, giving his age, height, weight, chest and biceps measurements and asking which member

[1] There are several corresponding girls' papers. The *Schoolgirl* is companion-paper to the *Magnet* and has stories by 'Hilda Richards'. The characters are interchangeable to some extent. Bessie Bunter, Billy Bunter's sister, figures in the *Schoolgirl*. [Author's footnote.]

of the Shell or Fourth Form he most exactly resembles. The demand for a list of the studies on the Shell passage, with an exact account of who lives in each, is a very common one. The editors, of course, do everything in their power to keep up the illusion. In the *Gem* Jack Blake is supposed to write the answers to correspondents, and in the *Magnet* a couple of pages is always given up to the school magazine (the *Greyfriars Herald*, edited by Harry Wharton), and there is another page in which one or other character is written up each week. The stories run in cycles, two or three characters being kept in the foreground for several weeks at a time. First there will be a series of rollicking adventure stories, featuring the Famous Five and Billy Bunter; then a run of stories turning on mistaken identity, with Wibley (the make-up wizard) in the star part; then a run of more serious stories in which Vernon-Smith is trembling on the verge of expulsion. And here one comes upon the real secret of the *Gem* and *Magnet* and the probable reason why they continue to be read in spite of their obvious out-of-dateness.

It is that the characters are so carefully graded as to give almost every type of reader a character he can identify himself with. Most boys' papers aim at doing this, hence the boy-assistant (Sexton Blake's Tinker, Nelson Lee's Nipper, etc.) who usually accompanies the explorer, detective or what not on his adventures. But in these cases there is only one boy, and usually it is much the same type of boy. In the *Gem* and *Magnet* there is a model for very nearly everybody. There is the normal, athletic, high-spirited boy (Tom Merry, Jack Blake, Frank Nugent), a slightly rowdier version of this type (Bob Cherry), a more aristocratic version (Talbot, Manners), a quieter, more serious version (Harry Wharton), and a stolid, 'bulldog' version (Johnny Bull). Then there is the reckless, dare-devil type of boy (Vernon-Smith), the definitely 'clever', studious boy (Mark Linley, Dick Penfold), and the eccentric boy who is not good at games but possesses some special talent (Skinner, Wibley). And there is the scholarship-boy (Tom Redwing), an important figure in this class of story because he makes it possible for boys from very poor homes to project themselves into the public-school atmosphere. In addition there are Australian, Irish, Welsh, Manx, Yorkshire and Lancashire boys to play upon local patriotism. But the subtlety of characterization goes deeper than this. If one studies the correspondence columns one sees that there is probably *no* character in the *Gem* and *Magnet* whom some or other reader does not identify with, except the out-and-out comics, Coker, Billy Bunter, Fisher T. Fish (the money-grubbing American boy) and, of course, the masters. Bunter, though in his origin he probably owed something to the fat boy in *Pickwick*, is a real creation. His tight trousers against which boots and canes are constantly thudding, his astuteness in search of food, his postal order which never turns up, have made him famous wherever the Union Jack waves. But he is not a subject for day-dreams. On the other hand, another seeming figure of fun, Gussy (the Honourable Arthur A. D'Arcy, 'the swell of St Jim's'), is evidently much admired. Like everything else in the *Gem* and *Magnet*, Gussy is at least thirty years out of date. He is the 'knut' of the early twentieth century or even the 'masher' of the 'nineties ('Bai Jove, deah boy!' and 'Weally, I shall be obliged to give you a feahful thwashin'!'), the monocled idiot who made good on the fields of Mons and Le Cateau. And his evident popularity goes to show how deep the snob-appeal of this type is. English people are extremely fond of the titled ass (cf Lord Peter Wimsey) who always turns up trumps in the moment of emergency. Here is a letter from one of Gussy's girl admirers:

I think your're too hard on Gussy. I wonder he's still in existence, the way you treat him. He's my hero. Did you know I write lyrics? How's this – to the tune of 'Goody Goody'?

Gonna get my gas-mask, join the ARP
'Cos I'm wise to all those bombs you drop on me.
Gonna dig myself a trench
Inside the garden fence;
Gonna seal my windows up with tin
So that the tear gas can't get in;
Gonna park my cannon right outside the kerb
With a note to Adolf Hitler: 'Don't disturb!'
And if I never fall in Nazi hands
That's soon enough for me
Gonna get my gas-mask, join the ARP.

P.S. – Do you get on well with girls?

I quote this in full because (dated April 1939) it is interesting as being probably the earliest mention of Hitler in the *Gem*. In the *Gem* there is also a heroic fat boy, Fatty Wynn, as a set-off against Bunter. Vernon-Smith, 'the Bounder of the Remove', a Byronic character, always on the verge of the sack, is another great favourite. And even some of the cads probably have their following. Loder, for instance, 'the rotter of the Sixth', is a cad, but he is also a highbrow and given to saying sarcastic things about football and the team spirit. The boys of the Remove only think him all the more of a cad for this, but a certain type of boy would probably identify with him. Even Racke, Crooke and Co. are probably admired by small boys who think it diabolically wicked to smoke cigarettes. (A frequent question in the correspondence column: 'What brand of cigarettes does Racke smoke?')

Naturally the politics of the *Gem* and *Magnet* are Conservative, but in a completely pre-1914 style, with no Fascist tinge. In reality their basic political assumptions are two: nothing ever changes, and foreigners are funny. In the *Gem* of 1939 Frenchmen are still Froggies and Italians are still Dagoes. Mossoo, the French master at Greyfriars, is the usual comic-paper Frog, with pointed beard, pegtop trousers, etc. Inky, the Indian boy, though a rajah, and therefore possessing snob-appeal, is also the comic babu of the *Punch* tradition. ('"The rowfulness is not the proper caper, my esteemed Bob," said Inky. "Let dogs delight in the barkfulness and bitefulness, but the soft answer is the cracked pitcher that goes longest to a bird in the bush, as the English proverb remarks."')? Fisher T. Fish is the old-style stage Yankee ('"Waal, I guess,"' etc.) dating from a period of Anglo-American jealousy. Wun Lung, the Chinese boy (he has rather faded out of late, no doubt because some of the *Magnet*'s readers are Straits Chinese), is the nineteenth-century pantomime Chinaman, with saucer-shaped hat, pigtail and pidgin-English. The assumption all along is not only that foreigners are comics who are put there for us to laugh at, but that they can be classified in much the same way as insects. That is why in all boys' papers, not only the *Gem* and *Magnet*, a Chinese is invariably portrayed with a pigtail. It is the thing you recognize him by, like the Frenchman's beard or the Italian's barrel-organ. In papers of this kind it occasionally happens that when the setting of a story is in a foreign country some attempt is made to describe the natives as individual human beings, but as a rule it is assumed that foreigners of any one race are all alike and will conform more or less exactly to the following patterns:

FRENCHMAN: Excitable. Wears beard, gesticulates wildly.
SPANIARD, MEXICAN, etc.: Sinister, treacherous.
ARAB, AFGHAN, etc.: Sinister, treacherous.
CHINESE: Sinister, treacherous. Wears pigtail.
ITALIAN: Excitable. Grinds barrel-organ or carries stiletto.
SWEDE, DANE, etc.: Kind hearted, stupid.
NEGRO: Comic, very faithful.

The working classes only enter into the *Gem* and *Magnet* as comics or semi-villains (race-course touts etc.). As for class-friction, trade unionism, strikes, slumps, unemployment, Fascism and civil war – not a mention. Somewhere or other in the thirty years' issue of the two papers you might perhaps find the word 'Socialism', but you would have to look a long time for it. If the Russian Revolution is anywhere referred to, it will be indirectly, in the word 'Bolshy' (meaning a person of violent disagreeable habits). Hitler and the Nazis are just beginning to make their appearance, in the sort of reference I quoted above. The war crisis of September 1938 made just enough impression to produce a story in which Mr Vernon-Smith, the Bounder's millionaire father, cashed in on the general panic by buying up country houses in order to sell them to 'crisis scuttlers'. But that is probably as near to noticing the European situation as the *Gem* and *Magnet* will come, until the war actually starts.[1] That does not mean that these papers are unpatriotic – quite the contrary! Throughout the Great War the *Gem* and *Magnet* were perhaps the most consistently and cheerfully patriotic papers in England. Almost every week the boys caught a spy or pushed a conchy into the army, and during the rationing period 'EAT LESS BREAD' was printed in large type on every page. But their patriotism has nothing whatever to do with power politics or 'ideological' warfare. It is more akin to family loyalty, and actually it gives one a valuable clue to the attitude of ordinary people, especially the huge untouchable block of the middle class and the better-off working class. These people are patriotic to the middle of their bones, but they do not feel that what happens in foreign countries is any of their business. When England is in danger they rally to its defence as a matter of course, but in between times they are not interested. After all, England is always in the right and England always wins, so why worry? It is an attitude that has been shaken during the past twenty years, but not so deeply as is sometimes supposed. Failure to understand it is one of the reasons why left-wing political parties are seldom able to produce an acceptable foreign policy.

The mental world of the *Gem* and *Magnet*, therefore, is something like this:

The year is 1910 – or 1940, but it is all the same. You are at Greyfriars, a rosy-cheeked boy of fourteen in posh, tailor-made clothes, sitting down to tea in your study on the Remove passage after an exciting game of football which was won by an odd goal in the last half-minute. There is a cosy fire in the study, and outside the wind is whistling. The ivy clusters thickly round

[1] This was written some months before the outbreak of war. Up to the end of September 1939 no mention of the war has appeared in either paper. [Author's footnote.]

the old grey stones. The King is on his throne and the pound is worth a pound. Over in Europe the comic foreigners are jabbering and gesticulating, but the grim grey battleships of the British Fleet are steaming up the Channel and at the outposts of Empire the monocled Englishmen are holding the niggers at bay. Lord Mauleverer has just got another fiver and we are all settling down to a tremendous tea of sausages, sardines, crumpets, potted meat, jam and doughbuts. After tea we shall sit round the study fire having a good laugh at Billy Bunter and discussing the team for next week's match against Rookwood. Everything is safe, solid and unquestionable. Everything will be the same for ever and ever. That approximately is the atmosphere.

But now turn from the *Gem* and *Magnet* to the more up-to-date papers which have appeared since the Great War. The truly significant thing is that they have more points of resemblance to the *Gem* and *Magnet* than points of difference. But it is better to consider the differences first.

There are eight of these newer papers, the *Modern Boy*, *Triumph*, *Champion*, *Wizard*, *Rover*, *Skipper*, *Hotspur* and *Adventure*. All of these have appeared since the Great War, but except for the *Modern Boy* none of them is less than five years old. Two papers which ought also to be mentioned briefly here, though they are not strictly in the same class as the rest, are the *Detective Weekly* and the *Thriller*, both owned by the Amalgamated Press. The *Detective Weekly* has taken over Sexton Blake. Both of these papers admit a certain amount of sex-interest into their stories, and though certainly read by boys, they are not aimed at them exclusively. All the others are boys' papers pure and simple, and they are sufficiently alike to be considered together. There does not seem to be any notable difference between Thomson's publications and those of the Amalgamated Press.

As soon as one looks at these papers one sees their technical superiority to the *Gem* and *Magnet*. To begin with, they have the great advantage of not being written entirely by one person. Instead of one long complete story, a number of the *Wizard* or *Hotspur* consists of half a dozen or more serials, none of which goes on for ever. Consequently there is far more variety and far less padding, and none of the tiresome stylization and facetiousness of the *Gem* and *Magnet*. Look at these two extracts, for example:

> Billy Bunter groaned.
>
> A quarter of an hour had elapsed out of the two hours that Bunter was booked for extra French.
>
> In a quarter of an hour there were only fifteen minutes! But every one of those minutes seemed inordinately long to Bunter. They seemed to crawl by like tired snails.
>
> Looking at the clock in Class-room No. 10 the fat Owl could hardly believe that only fifteen minutes had passed. It seemed more like fifteen hours, if not fifteen days!
>
> Other fellows were in extra French as well as Bunter. They did not matter. Bunter did! (*Magnet.*)

> After a terrible climb, hacking out handholds in the smooth ice every step of the way up, Sergeant Lionheart Logan of the Mounties was now clinging like a human fly to the face of an icy cliff, as smooth and treacherous as a giant pane of glass.
>
> An Arctic blizzard, in all its fury, was buffeting his body, driving the

blinding snow into his face, seeking to tear his fingers loose from their handholds and dash him to death on the jagged boulders which lay at the foot of the cliff a hundred feet below.

Crouching among those boulders were eleven villainous trappers who had done their best to shoot down Lionheart and his companion, Constable Jim Rogers – until the blizzard had blotted the two Mounties out of sight from below. (*Wizard*.)

The second extract gets you some distance with the story, the first takes a hundred words to tell you that Bunter is in the detention class. Moreover, by not concentrating on school stories (in point of numbers the school story slightly predominates in all these papers, except the *Thriller* and *Detective Weekly*), the *Wizard*, *Hotspur*, etc. have far greater opportunities for sensationalism. Merely looking at the cover illustrations of the papers which I have on the table in front of me, here are some of the things I see. On one a cowboy is clinging by his toes to the wing of an aeroplane in mid-air and shooting down another aeroplane with his revolver. On another a Chinese is swimming for his life down a sewer with a swarm of ravenous-looking rats swimming after him. On another an engineer is lighting a stick of dynamite while a steel robot feels for him with its claws. On another a man in airman's costume is fighting bare-handed against a rat somewhat larger than a donkey. On another a nearly naked man of terrific muscular development has just seized a lion by the tail and flung it thirty yards over the wall of an arena, with the words, 'Take back your blooming lion!' Clearly no school story can compete with this kind of thing. From time to time the school buildings may catch fire or the French master may turn out to be the head of an international anarchist gang, but in a general way the interest must centre round cricket, school rivalries, practical jokes, etc. There is not much room for bombs, death-rays, sub-machine-guns, aeroplanes, mustangs, octopuses, grizzly bears or gangsters.

Examination of a large number of these papers shows that, putting aside school stories, the favourite subjects are Wild West, Frozen North, Foreign Legion, crime (always from the detective's angle), the Great War (Air Force or Secret Service, not the infantry), the Tarzan motif in varying forms, professional football, tropical exploration, historical romance (Robin Hood, Cavaliers and Roundheads, etc.) and scientific invention. The Wild West still leads, at any rate as a setting, though the Red Indian seems to be fading out. The one theme that is really new is the scientific one. Death-rays, Martians, invisible men, robots, helicopters and interplanetary rockets figure largely; here and there there are even far-off rumours of psychotherapy and ductless glands. Whereas the *Gem* and *Magnet* derive from Dickens and Kipling, the *Wizard*, *Champion*, *Modern Boy*, etc. owe a great deal to H. G. Wells, who, rather than Jules Verne, is the father of 'Scientifiction'. Naturally it is the magical, Martian aspect of science that is most exploited, but one or two papers include serious articles on scientific subjects, besides quantities of informative snippets. (Examples: 'A Kauri tree in Queensland, Australia, is over 12,000 years old'; 'Nearly 50,000 thunderstorms occur every day'; 'Helium gas costs £1 per 1,000 cubic feet'; 'There are over 500 varieties of spiders in Great Britain'; 'London firemen use 14,000,000 gallons of water annually', etc., etc.) There is a marked advance in intellectual curiosity and, on the whole, in the demand made on the reader's attention. In practice the *Gem* and *Magnet* and the post-war papers are read by much the same public, but the mental age aimed at seems to have risen by a year or two years – an improvement probably corresponding to the improvement in elementary education since 1909.

The other thing that has emerged in the post-war boys' papers, though not to anything like the extent one would expect, is bully-worship and the cult of violence.

If one compares the *Gem* and *Magnet* with a genuinely modern paper, the thing that immediately strikes one is the absence of the leader-principle. There is no central dominating character; instead there are fifteen or twenty characters, all more or less on an equality, with whom readers of different types can identify. In the more modern papers this is not usually the case. Instead of identifying with a schoolboy of more or less his own age, the reader of the *Skipper*, *Hotspur*, etc. is led to identify with a G-man, with a Foreign Legionary, with some variant of Tarzan, with an air ace, a master spy, an explorer, a pugilist – at any rate with some single all-powerful character who dominates everyone about him and whose usual method of solving any problem is a sock on the jaw. This character is intended as a superman, and as physical strength is the form of power that boys can best understand, he is usually a sort of human gorilla; in the Tarzan type of story he is sometimes actually a giant, eight or ten feet high. At the same time the scenes of violence in nearly all these stories are remarkably harmless and unconvincing. There is a great difference in tone between even the most bloodthirsty English paper and the threepenny Yank Mags, *Fight Stories*, *Action Stories*, etc. (not strictly boys' papers, but largely read by boys). In the Yank Mags you get real blood-lust, really gory descriptions of the all-in, jump-on-his-testicles style of fighting, written in a jargon that has been perfected by people who brood endlessly on violence. A paper like *Fight Stories*, for instance, would have very little appeal except to sadists and masochists. You can see the comparative gentleness of the English civilization by the amateurish way in which prize-fighting is always described in the boys' weeklies. There is no specialized vocabulary. Look at these four extracts, two English, two American:

> When the gong sounded, both men were breathing heavily, and each had great red marks on his chest, Bill's chin was bleeding, and Ben had a cut over his right eye.
>
> Into their corners they sank, but when the gong clanged again they were up swiftly, and they went like tigers at each other. (*Rover.*)

> He walked in stolidly and smashed a clublike right to my face. Blood spattered and I went back on my heels, but surged in and ripped my right under his heart. Another right smashed full on Sven's already battered mouth, and, spitting out the fragments of a tooth, he crashed a flailing left to my body. (*Fight Stories.*)

> It was amazing to watch the Black Panther at work. His muscles rippled and slid under his dark skin. There was all the power and grace of a giant cat in his swift and terrible onslaught.
>
> He volleyed blows with a bewildering speed for so huge a fellow. In a moment Ben was simply blocking with his gloves as well as he could. Ben was really a past-master of defence. He had many fine victories behind him. But the Negro's rights and lefts crashed through openings that hardly any other fighter could have found. (*Wizard.*)

> Haymakers which packed the bludgeoning weight of forest monarchs crashing down under the ax hurled into the bodies of the two heavies as they swapped punches. (*Fight Stories*.)

Notice how much more knowledgeable the American extracts sound. They are written for devotees of the prize-ring, the others are not. Also, it ought to be emphasized that on its level the moral code of the English boys' papers is a decent one. Crime and dishonesty are never held up to admiration, there is none of the cynicism and corruption of the American gangster story. The huge sale of the Yank Mags in England shows that there is a demand for that kind of thing, but very few English writers seem able to produce it. When hatred of Hitler became a major emotion in America, it was interesting to see how promptly 'anti-Fascism' was adapted to pornographic purposes by the editors of the Yank Mags. One magazine which I have in front of me is given up to a long, complete story, 'When Hell Came to America', in which the agents of a 'blood-maddened European dictator' are trying to conquer the USA with death-rays and invisible aeroplanes. There is the frankest appeal to sadism, scenes in which the Nazis tie bombs to women's backs and fling them off heights to watch them blown to pieces in mid-air, others in which they tie naked girls together by their hair and prod them with knives to make them dance, etc., etc. The editor comments solemnly on all this, and uses it as a plea for tightening up restrictions against immigrants. On another page of the same paper: 'LIVES OF THE HOTCHA CHORUS GIRLS. Reveals all the intimate secrets and fascinating pastimes of the famous Broadway Hotcha girls. NOTHING IS OMITTED. Price 10c.' 'HOW TO LOVE. 10c.' 'FRENCH PHOTO RING, 25c.' 'NAUGHTY NUDIES TRANSFERS. From the outside of the glass you see a beautiful girl, innocently dressed. Turn it around and look through the glass and oh! what a difference! Set of 3 transfers 25c.' etc., etc., etc. There is nothing at all like this in any English paper likely to be read by boys. But the process of Americanization is going on all the same. The American ideal, the 'he-man', the 'tough guy', the gorilla who puts everything right by socking everybody else on the jaw, now figures in probably a majority of boys' papers. In one serial now running in the *Skipper* he is always portrayed, ominously enough, swinging a rubber truncheon.

The development of the *Wizard*, *Hotspur*, etc., as against the earlier boys' papers, boils down to this: better technique, more scientific interest, more bloodshed, more leader-worship. But, after all, it is the *lack* of development that is the really striking thing.

To begin with, there is no political development whatever. The world of the *Skipper* and the *Champion* is still the pre-1914 world of the *Magnet* and the *Gem*. The Wild West story, for instance, with its cattle-rustlers, lynch-law and other paraphernalia belonging to the 'eighties, is a curiously archaic thing. It is worth noticing that in papers of this type it is always taken for granted that adventures only happen at the ends of the earth, in tropical forests, in Arctic wastes, in African deserts, on Western prairies, in Chinese opium dens – everywhere, in fact, except the places where things really *do* happen. That is a belief dating from thirty or forty years ago, when the new continents were in process of being opened up. Nowadays, of course, if you really want adventure, the place to look for it is in Europe. But apart from the picturesque side of the Great War, contemporary history is carefully excluded. And except that Americans are now admired instead of being laughed at, foreigners are exactly the same figures of fun that they always were. If a Chinese character appears, he is still the sinister pigtailed opium-smuggler of Sax Rohmer; no indication that things have been happening in China since 1912 – no indication that a war is going on there, for instance. If a Spaniard appears, he is still a 'dago' or 'greaser' who rolls cigarettes and stabs people in the back; no indication that things have been happening in Spain. Hitler and the Nazis have not yet appeared, or are barely making their appearance. There will be plenty about them in a little while, but it will be from a strictly patriotic angle (Britain versus Germany), with the real meaning of the struggle kept out of sight as much as possible. As for the Russian Revolution, it is extremely difficult to find any reference to it in any of these papers. When Russia is mentioned at all it is usually in an information snippet (example: 'There are 29,000 centenarians in the USSR'), and any reference to the Revolution is indirect and twenty years out of date. In one story in the *Rover*, for instance, somebody has a tame bear, and as it is a Russian bear, it is nicknamed Trotsky – obviously an echo of the 1917–23 period and not of recent controversies. The clock has stopped at 1910. Britannia rules the waves, and no one has heard of slumps, booms, unemployment, dictatorships, purges or concentration camps.

And in social outlook there is hardly any advance. The snobbishness is somewhat less open than in the *Gem* and *Magnet* – that is the most one can possibly say. To begin with, the school story, always partly dependent on snob-appeal, is by no means eliminated. Every number of a boys' paper includes at least one school story, these stories slightly outnumbering the Wild Westerns. The very elaborate fantasy-life of the *Gem* and *Magnet* is not imitated and there is more emphasis on extraneous adventure, but the social atmosphere (old grey stones) is much the same. When a new school is introduced at the beginning of a story we are often told in just about those words that 'it was a very posh school'. From time to time a story appears which is ostensibly directed *against* snobbery. The scholarship-boy (cf. Tom Redwing in the *Magnet*) makes fairly frequent appearances, and what is essentially the same theme is sometimes presented in this form; there is great rivalry between two schools, one of which considers itself more 'posh' than the other, and there are fights, practical jokes, football matches, etc. always ending in the discomfiture of the snobs. If one glances very superfically at some of these stories it is possible to imagine that a democratic spirit has crept into the boys' weeklies, but when one looks more closely one sees that they merely reflect the bitter jealousies that exist within the white-collar class. Their real function is to allow the boy who goes to a cheap private school (*not* a Council school) to feel that his school is just as 'posh' in the sight of God as Winchester or Eton. The sentiment of school loyalty ('We're better than the fellows down the road'), a thing almost unknown to the real working class, is still kept up. As these stories are written by many different hands, they do, of course, vary a good deal in tone. Some are reasonably free from snobbishness, in others money and pedigree are exploited even more shamelessly than in the *Gem* and *Magnet*. In one that I came across an actual *majority* of the boys mentioned were titled.

Where working-class characters appear, it is usually either as comics (jokes about tramps, convicts, etc.) or as prize-fighters, acrobats, cowboys, professional footballers and Foreign Legionaries – in other words, as adventurers. There is no facing of the facts about working-class life, or, indeed, about *working* life of any description. Very occasionally one may come across a realistic description of, say, work in a coal mine, but in all probability it will only be there as the background of some lurid adventure. In any case the central character is not likely to be a coal miner. Nearly all the time the boy who reads these papers – in nine cases out of ten a boy who is going to spend his life working in a shop, in a factory or in some subordinate job in an office – is led to identify with people in positions of command, above all with people who are never troubled by shortage of money. The Lord Peter Wimsey figure, the seeming idiot who drawls and wears a monocle but is always to the fore in moments of danger, turns up over and over again. (This character is a great favourite in Secret Service stories.) And, as usual, the heroic characters all have to talk BBC; they may talk Scottish or Irish or American, but no one in a star part is ever permitted to drop an aitch. Here it is worth comparing the social atmosphere of the boys' weeklies with that of the women's weeklies, the *Oracle*, the *Family Star*, *Peg's Paper*, etc.

The women's papers are aimed at an older public and are read for the most part by girls who are working for a living. Consequently they are on the surface much more realistic. It is taken for granted, for example, that nearly everyone has to live in a big town and work at a more or less dull job. Sex, so far from being taboo, is *the* subject. The short, complete stories, the special feature of these papers, are generally of the 'came the dawn' type: the heroine narrowly escapes losing her 'boy' to a designing rival, or the 'boy' loses his job and has to postpone marriage, but presently gets a better job. The changeling-fantasy (a girl brought up in a poor home is 'really' the child of rich parents) is another favourite. Where sensationalism comes in, usually in the serials, it arises out of the more domestic type of crime, such as bigamy, forgery or sometimes murder; no Martians, death-rays or international anarchist gangs. These papers are at any rate aiming at credibility, and they have a link with real life in their correspondence columns, where genuine problems are being discussed. Ruby M. Ayres's column of advice in the *Oracle*, for instance, is extremely sensible and well written. And yet the world of the *Oracle* and *Peg's Paper* is a pure fantasy-world. It is the same fantasy all the time, pretending to be richer than you are. The chief impression that one carries away from almost every story in these papers is of frightful, overwhelming 'refinement'. Ostensibly the characters are working-class people, but their habits, the interiors of their houses, their clothes, their outlook and, above all, their speech are entirely middle class. They are all living at several pounds a week above their income. And needless to say, that is just the impression that is intended. The idea is to give the bored factory-girl or worn-out mother of five a dream-life in which she pictures herself – not actually as a duchess (that convention has gone out) but as, say, the wife of a bank-manager. Not only is a five-to-six-pound-a-week standard of life set up as the ideal, but it is tacitly assumed that that is how working-class people really *do* live. The major facts are simply not faced. It is admitted, for instance, that people sometimes lose their jobs; but then the dark clouds roll away and they get better jobs instead. No mention of unemployment as something permanent and inevitable, no mention of the dole, no mention of trade unionism. No suggestion anywhere that there can be anything wrong with the system *as a system*; there are only individual misfortunes, which are generally due to somebody's wickedness and can in any case be put right in the last chapter. Always the dark clouds roll away, the kind employer raises Alfred's wages, and there are jobs for everybody except the drunks. It is still the world of the *Wizard* and the *Gem*, except that there are orange-blossoms instead of machine-guns.

The outlook inculcated by all these papers is that of a rather exceptionally stupid member of the Navy League in the year 1910. Yes, it may be said, but what does it matter? And in any case, what else do you expect?

Of course no one in his senses would want to turn the so-called penny dreadful into a realistic novel or a Socialist tract. An adventure story must of its nature be more or less remote from real life. But, as I have tried to make clear, the unreality of the *Wizard* and the *Gem* is not so artless as it looks. These papers exist because of a specialized demand, because boys at certain ages find it necessary to read about Martians, death-rays, grizzly bears and gangsters. They get what they are looking for, but they get it wrapped up in the illusions which their future employers think suitable for them. To what extent people draw their ideas from fiction is disputable. Personally I believe that most people are influenced far more than they would care to admit by novels, serial stories, films and so forth, and that from this point of view the worst books are often the most important, because they are usually the ones that are read earliest in life. It is probable that many people who could consider themselves extremely sophisticated and 'advanced' are actually carrying through life an imaginative background which they acquired in childhood from (for instance) Sapper and Ian Hay. If that is so, the boys' twopenny weeklies are of the deepest importance. Here is the stuff that is read somewhere between the ages of twelve and eighteen by a very large proportion, perhaps an actual majority, of English boys, including many who will never read anything else except newspapers; and along with it they are absorbing a set of beliefs which would be regarded as hopelessly out of date in the Central Office of the Conservative Party. All the better because it is done indirectly, there is being pumped into them the conviction that the major problems of our time do not exist, that there is nothing wrong with *laissez-faire* capitalism, that foreigners are unimportant comics and that the British Empire is a sort of charity-concern which will last for ever. Considering who owns these papers, it is difficult to believe that this is unintentional. Of the twelve papers I have been discussing (i.e. twelve including the *Thriller* and *Detective Weekly*) seven are the property of the Amalgamated Press, which is one of the biggest press-combines in the world and controls more than a hundred different papers. The *Gem* and *Magnet*, therefore, are closely linked up with the *Daily Telegraph* and the *Financial Times*. This in itself would be enough to rouse certain suspicions, even if it were not obvious that the stories in the boys' weeklies are politically vetted. So it appears that if you feel the need of a fantasy-life in which you travel to Mars and fight lions bare-handed (and what boy doesn't?) you can only have it by delivering yourself over, mentally, to people like Lord Camrose. For there is no competition. Throughout the whole of this run of papers the differences are negligible, and on this level no others exist. This raises the question, why is there no such thing as a left-wing boys' paper?

At first glance such an idea merely makes one slightly sick. It is so horribly easy to imagine what a left-wing boys' paper would be like, if it existed. I remember in 1920 or 1921 some optimistic person handing round Communist tracts among a crowd of public-school boys. The tract I received was of the question-and-answer kind:

Q. 'Can a Boy Communist be a Boy Scout, Comrade?'

A. 'No, Comrade.'
Q. 'Why, Comrade?'
A. 'Because, Comrade, a Boy Scout must salute the Union Jack, which is the symbol of tyranny and oppression,' etc., etc.

Now, suppose that at this moment somebody started a left-wing paper deliberately aimed at boys of twelve or fourteen. I do not suggest that the whole of its contents would be exactly like the tract I have quoted above, but does anyone doubt that they would be *something* like it? Inevitably such a paper would either consist of dreary uplift or it would be under Communist influence and given over to adulation of Soviet Russia; in either case no normal boy would ever look at it. Highbrow literature apart, the whole of the existing left-wing press, in so far as it is at all vigorously 'left', is one long tract. The one Socialist paper in England which could live a week on its merits *as a paper* is the *Daily Herald*, and how much Socialism is there in the *Daily Herald*? At this moment, therefore, a paper with a 'left' slant and at the same time likely to have an appeal to ordinary boys in their teens is something almost beyond hoping for.

But it does not follow that it is impossible. There is no clear reason why every adventure story should necessarily be mixed up with snobbishness and gutter patriotism. For, after all, the stories in the *Hotspur* and the *Modern Boy* are not Conservative tracts; they are merely adventure stories with a Conservative bias. It is fairly easy to imagine the process being reversed. It is possible, for instance, to imagine a paper as thrilling and lively as the *Hotspur*, but with subject-matter and 'ideology' a little more up to date. It is even possible (though this raises other difficulties) to imagine a women's paper at the same literary level as the *Oracle*, dealing in approximately the same kind of story, but taking rather more account of the realities of working-class life. Such things have been done before, though not in England. In the last years of the Spanish monarchy there was a large output in Spain of left-wing novelettes, some of them evidently of Anarchist origin. Unfortunately at the time when they were appearing I did not see their social significance, and I lost the collection of them that I had, but no doubt copies would still be procurable. In get-up and style of story they were very similar to the English fourpenny novelette, except that their inspiration was 'left'. If, for instance, a story described police pursuing Anarchists through the mountains, it would be from the point of view of the Anarchists and not of the police. An example nearer to hand is the Soviet film *Chapaiev*, which has been shown a number of times in London. Technically, by the standards of the time when it was made, *Chapaiev* is a first-rate film, but mentally, in spite of the unfamiliar Russian background, it is not so very remote from Hollywood. The one thing that lifts it out of the ordinary is the remarkable performance by the actor who takes the part of the White officer (the fat one) – a performance which looks very like an inspired piece of gagging. Otherwise the atmosphere is familiar. All the usual paraphernalia is there – heroic fight against odds, escape at the last moment, shots of galloping horses, love interest, comic relief. The film is in fact a fairly ordinary one, except that its tendency is 'left'. In a Hollywood film of the Russian civil war the Whites would probably be angels and the Reds demons. In the Russian version the Reds are angels and the Whites demons. That also is a lie, but, taking the long view, it is a less pernicious lie than the other.

Here several difficult problems present themselves. Their general nature is obvious enough. and I do not want to discuss them. I am merely pointing to the fact that, in England, popular imaginative literature is a field that left-wing thought has never begun to enter. *All* fiction from the novels in the mushroom libraries downwards is censored in the interests of the ruling class. And boys' fiction above all, the blood-and-thunder stuff which nearly every boy devours at some time or other, is sodden in the worst illusions of 1910. The fact is only unimportant if one believes that what is read in childhood leaves no impression behind. Lord Camrose and his colleagues evidently believe nothing of the kind, and, after all, Lord Camrose ought to know.

Written 1939

Inside the Whale

One

When Henry Miller's novel, *Tropic of Cancer*, appeared in 1935, it was greeted with rather cautious praise, obviously conditioned in some cases by a fear of seeming to enjoy pornography. Among the people who praised it were T. S. Eliot, Herbert Read, Aldous Huxley, John dos Passos, Ezra Pound – on the whole, not the writers who are in fashion at this moment. And in fact the subject-matter of the book, and to a certain extent its mental atmosphere, belong to the 'twenties rather than to the 'thirties.

Tropic of Cancer is a novel in the first person, or autobiography in the form of a novel, whichever way you like to look at it. Miller himself insists that it is straight autobiography, but the tempo and method of telling the story are those of a novel. It is a story of the American Paris, but not along quite the usual lines, because the Americans who figure in it happen to be people without money. During the boom years, when dollars were plentiful and the exchange-value of the franc was low, Paris was invaded by such a swarm of artists, writers, students, dilettanti, sight-seers, debauchees and plain idlers as the world has probably never seen. In some quarters of the town the so-called artists must actually have outnumbered the working population – indeed, it has been reckoned that in the late 'twenties there were as many as 30,000 painters in Paris, most of them impostors. The populace had grown so hardened to artists that gruff-voiced lesbians in corduroy breeches and young men in Grecian or medieval costume could walk the streets without attracting a glance, and along the Seine banks by Notre Dame it was almost impossible to pick one's way between the sketching-stools. It was the age of dark horses and neglected genii; the phrase on everybody's lips was 'Quand je serai lancé'. As it turned out, nobody was 'lancé', the slump descended like another Ice Age, the cosmopolitan mob of artists vanished, and the huge Montparnasse cafés which only ten years ago were filled till the small hours by hordes of shrieking poseurs have turned into darkened tombs in which there are not even any ghosts. It is this world – described in, among other novels, Wyndham Lewis's *Tarr* – that Miller is writing about, but he is dealing only with the under side of it, the lumpenproletarian fringe which has been able to survive the slump because it is composed partly of genuine artists and partly of genuine scoundrels. The neglected genii, the paranoiacs who are always 'going to' write the novel that will knock Proust into a cocked hat, are there, but they are only genii in the rather rare moments when they are not scouting about for the next meal. For the most part it is a story of bug-ridden rooms in working-men's hotels, of fights, drinking bouts, cheap brothels, Russian refugees, cadging, swindling and temporary jobs. And the whole atmosphere of the poor quarters of Paris as a foreigner sees them – the cobbled alleys, the sour reek of refuse, the bistros with their greasy zinc counters and worn brick floors, the green waters of the Seine, the blue cloaks of the Republican Guard, the crumbling iron urinals, the peculiar sweetish smell of the Métro stations, the cigarettes that come to pieces, the pigeons in the Luxembourg Gardens – it is all there, or at any rate the feeling of it is there.

On the face of it no material could be less promising. When *Tropic of Cancer* was published the Italians were marching into Abyssinia and Hitler's concentration camps were already bulging. The intellectual foci of the world were Rome, Moscow and Berlin. It did not seem to be a moment at which a novel of outstanding value was likely to be written about American dead-beats cadging drinks in the Latin Quarter. Of course a novelist is not obliged to write directly about contemporary history, but a novelist who simply disregards the major public events of the moment is generally either a footler or a plain idiot. From a mere account of the subject-matter of *Tropic of Cancer* most people would probably assume it to be no more than a bit of naughty-naughty left over from the 'twenties. Actually, nearly everyone who read it saw at once that it was nothing of the kind, but a very remarkable book. How or why remarkable? That question is never easy to answer. It is better to begin by describing the impression that *Tropic of Cancer* has left on my own mind.

When I first opened *Tropic of Cancer* and saw that it was full of unprintable words, my immediate reaction was a refusal to be impressed. Most people's would be the same, I believe. Nevertheless, after a lapse of time the atmosphere of the book, besides innumerable details, seemed to linger in my memory in a peculiar way. A year later Miller's second book, *Black Spring*, was published. By this time *Tropic of Cancer* was much more vividly present in my mind than it had been when I first read it. My first feeling about *Black Spring* was that it showed a falling-off, and it is a fact that it has not the same unity as the other book. Yet after another year there were many passages in *Black Spring* that had also rooted themselves in my memory. Evidently these books are of the sort to leave a flavour behind them – books that 'create a world of their own', as the saying goes. The books that do this are not necessarily good books, they may be good bad books like *Raffles* or the *Sherlock Holmes* stories, or perverse and morbid books like *Wuthering Heights* or *The House with the Green Shutters*. But now and again there appears a novel which opens up a new world not by revealing what is strange, but by revealing what is familiar. The truly remarkable thing about *Ulysses*, for instance, is the commonplaceness of its material. Of course there is much more in *Ulysses* than this, because Joyce is a kind of poet and also an elephantine pedant, but his real achievement has been to get the familiar onto paper. He dared – for it is a matter of *daring* just as much as of technique – to expose the imbecilities of the inner mind, and in doing so he discovered an America which was under everybody's nose. Here is a whole world of stuff which you have lived with since childhood, stuff which you supposed to be of its nature incommunicable, and somebody has managed to communicate it. The effect is to break down, at any rate momentarily, the solitude in which the human being lives. When you read certain passages in *Ulysses* you feel that Joyce's mind and your mind are one, that he knows all about you though he has never heard your name, that there exists some world outside time and space in which you and he are together. And though he does not resemble Joyce in other ways, there is a touch of this quality in Henry Miller. Not everywhere, because his work is very uneven, and sometimes, especially in *Black Spring*, tends to slide away into mere verbiage or into the squashy universe of the surrealists. But read him for five pages, ten pages, and you feel the peculiar relief that comes not so much from understanding as from *being understood*. 'He knows all about me,' you feel; 'he wrote this specially for me.' It is as though you could hear a voice speaking to you, a friendly American voice, with no humbug in it, no moral purpose, merely an implicit assumption that we are all alike. For the moment you have got away from the lies and simplifications, the stylized, marionette-like quality of ordinary fiction, even quite good fiction, and are dealing with the recognizable experiences of human beings.

But what kind of experience? What kind of human beings? Miller is writing about the man in the street, and it is incidentally rather a pity that it should be a street full of brothels. That is the penalty of leaving your native land. It means transferring your roots into shallower soil. Exile is probably more damaging to a novelist than to a painter or even a poet, because its effect is to take him out of contact with working life, and narrow down his range to the street, the café, the church, the brothel and the studio. On the whole, in Miller's books you are reading about people living the expatriate life, people drinking, talking, meditating and fornicating, not about people working, marrying and bringing up children; a pity, because he would have described the one set of activities as well as the other. In *Black Spring* there is a wonderful flashback of New York, the swarming Irish-infested New York of the O. Henry period, but the Paris scenes are the best, and, granted their utter worthlessness as social types, the drunks and dead-beats of the cafés are handled with a feeling for character and a mastery of technique that are unapproached in any at all recent novel. All of them are not only credible but completely familiar; you have the feeling that all their adventures have happened to yourself. Not that they are anything very startling in the way of adventures. Henry gets a job with a melancholy Indian student, gets another job at a dreadful French school during a cold snap when the lavatories are frozen solid, goes on drinking bouts in Le Havre with his friend Collins, the sea captain, goes to brothels where there are wonderful negresses, talks with his friend Van Norden, the novelist, who has got the great novel of the world in his head but can never bring himself to begin writing it. His friend Karl, on the verge of starvation, is picked up by a wealthy widow who wishes to marry him. There are interminable, Hamlet-like conversations in which Karl tries to decide which is worse, being hungry or sleeping with an old woman. In great detail he describes his visits to the widow, how he went to the hotel dressed in his best, how before going in he neglected to urinate, so that the whole evening was one long crescendo of torment, etc., etc. And after all, none of it is true, the widow doesn't even exist – Karl has simply invented her in order to make himself seem important. The whole book is in this vein, more or less. Why is it that these monstrous trivialities are so engrossing? Simply because the whole atmosphere is deeply familiar, because you have all the while the feeling that these things are happening to *you*. And you have this feeling because somebody has chosen to drop the Geneva language of the ordinary novel and drag the *real-politik* of the inner mind into the open. In Miller's case it is not so much a questions of exploring the mechanisms of the mind as of owning up to everyday facts and everyday emotions. For the truth is that many ordinary people, perhaps an actual majority, do speak and behave in just the way that is recorded here. The callous coarseness with which the characters in *Tropic of Cancer* talk is very rare in fiction, but it is extremely common in real life; again and again I have heard just such conversations from people who were not even aware that they were talking coarsely. It is worth noticing that *Tropic of Cancer* is not a young man's book. Miller was in his forties when it was published, and though since then he has produced three or four others, it is obvious that this first book had been lived with for years. It is one of those books that are slowly matured in poverty and obscurity, by people who know what they have got to do and therefore are able to wait. The prose is astonishing, and in parts of *Black Spring* it is even better. Unfortunately I cannot quote; unprintable words occur almost everywhere. But get hold of *Tropic of Cancer*, get hold of *Black Spring* and read especially the first hundred pages. They give you an idea of what can still be done, even at this late date, with English prose. In them, English is treated as a spoken language, but spoken *without fear*, i.e. without fear of rhetoric or of the unusual or poetical word. The adjective has come back, after its ten years' exile. It is a flowing, swelling prose, a prose with rhythms in it, something quite different from the flat, cautious statements and snack-bar dialects that are now in fashion.

When a book like *Tropic of Cancer* appears, it is only natural that the first thing people notice should be its obscenity. Given our current notions of literary decency, it is not at all easy to approach an unprintable book with detachment. Either one is shocked and disgusted, or one is morbidly thrilled, or one is determined above all else not to be impressed. The last is probably the commonest reaction, with the result that unprintable books often get less attention than they deserve. It is rather the fashion to say that nothing is easier than to write an obscene book, that people only do it in order to get themselves talked about and make money, etc., etc. What makes it obvious that this is *not* the case is that books which are obscene in the police-court sense are distinctly uncommon. If there were easy money to be made out of dirty words, a lot more people would be making it. But, because 'obscene' books do not appear very frequently, there is a tendency to lump them together, as a rule quite unjustifiably. *Tropic of Cancer* has been vaguely associated with two other books, *Ulysses* and *Voyage au Bout de la Nuit*, but in neither case is there much resemblance. What Miller has in common with Joyce is a willingness to mention the inane squalid facts of everyday life. Putting aside differences of technique, the funeral scene in *Ulysses*, for instance, would fit into *Tropic of Cancer*; the whole chapter is a sort of confession, an *exposé* of the frightful inner callousness of the human being. But there the resemblance ends. As a novel, *Tropic of Cancer* is far inferior to *Ulysses*. Joyce is an artist, in a sense in which Miller is not and probably would not wish to be, and in any case he is attempting much more. He is exploring different states of consciousness, dream, reverie (the 'bronze-by-gold' chapter), drunkenness, etc., and dovetailing them all into a huge complex pattern, almost like a Victorian 'plot'. Miller is simply a hardboiled person talking about life, an ordinary American businessman with intellectual courage and a gift for words. It is perhaps significant that he *looks* exactly like everyone's idea of an American businessman. As for the comparison with *Voyage au Bout de la Nuit*, it is even further from the point. Both books use unprintable words, both are in some sense autobiographical, but that is all. *Voyage au Bout de la Nuit* is a book-with-a-purpose, and its purpose is to protest against the horror and meaninglessness of modern life – actually, indeed, of *life*. It is a cry of unbearable disgust, a voice from the cesspool. *Tropic of Cancer* is almost exactly the opposite. The thing has become so unusual as to seem almost anomalous, but it is the book of a man who is happy. So is *Black Spring*, though slightly less so, because tinged in places with nostalgia. With years of lumpenproletarian life behind him, hunger, vagabondage, dirt, failure, nights in the open, battles with immigration officers, endless struggles for a bit of cash, Miller finds that he is enjoying himself. Exactly the aspects of life that fill Céline with horror are the ones that appeal to him. So far from protesting, he is *accepting*. And the very word 'acceptance' calls up his real affinity, another American, Walt Whitman.

But there is something rather curious in being Whitman in the nineteen-thirties. It is not certain that if Whitman himself were alive at this moment he would write anything in the least degree resembling *Leaves of Grass*. For what he is saying, after all, is 'I accept', and there is a radical difference between acceptance now and acceptance then. Whitman was writing in a time of unexampled prosperity, but more than that, he was writing in a country where freedom was something more than a word. The democracy, equality and comradeship that he is always talking about are not remote ideals, but something that existed in front of his eyes. In mid-nineteenth-century America men felt themselves free and equal, *were* free and equal, so far as that is possible outside a society of pure Communism. There was poverty and there were even class-distinctions, but except for the Negroes there was no permanently submerged class. Everyone had inside him, like a kind of core, the knowledge that he could earn a decent living, and earn it without boot-licking. When you read about Mark Twain's Mississippi raftsmen and pilots, or Bret Harte's Western gold miners, they seem more remote than the cannibals of the Stone Age. The reason is simply that they are free human beings. But it is the same even with the peaceful domesticated America of the Eastern states, the America of *Little Women*, *Helen's Babies* and 'Riding Down from Bangor'. Life has a buoyant, carefree quality that you can feel as you read, like a physical sensation in your belly. It is this that Whitman is celebrating, though actually he does it very badly, because he is one of those writers who tell you what you ought to feel instead of making you feel it. Luckily for his beliefs, perhaps, he died too early to see the deterioration in American life that came with the rise of large-scale industry and the exploiting of cheap immigrant labour.

Miller's outlook is deeply akin to that of Whitman, and nearly everyone who has read him has remarked on this. *Tropic of Cancer* ends with an especially Whitmanesque passage, in which, after the lecheries, the swindles, the fights, the drinking bouts and the imbecilities, he simply sits down and watches the Seine flowing past, in a sort of mystical acceptance of the thing-as-it-is. Only, what is he accepting? In the first place, not America, but the ancient bone-heap of Europe, where every grain of soil has passed through innumerable human bodies. Secondly, not an epoch of expansion and liberty, but an epoch of fear, tyranny and regimentation. To say 'I accept' in an age like your own is to say that you accept concentration camps, rubber truncheons, Hitler, Stalin, bombs, aeroplanes, tinned food, machine-guns, putsches, purges, slogans, Bedaux belts, gas-masks, submarines, spies, *provocateurs*, press censorship, secret prisons, aspirins, Hollywood films and political murders. Not *only* those things, of course, but those things among others. And on the whole this is Henry Miller's attitude. Not quite always, because at moments he shows signs of a fairly ordinary kind of literary nostalgia. There is a long passage in the earlier part of *Black Spring*, in praise of the Middle Ages, which as prose must be one of the most remarkable pieces of writing in recent years, but which displays an attitude not very different from that of Chesterton. In *Max and the White Phagocytes* there is an attack on modern American civilization (breakfast cereals, cellophane, etc.) from the usual angle of the literary man who hates industrialism. But in general the attitude is 'Let's swallow it whole'. And hence the seeming preoccupation with indecency and with the dirty-handkerchief side of life. It is only seeming, for the truth is that life, ordinary everyday life, consists far more largely of horrors than writers of fiction usually care to admit. Whitman himself 'accepted' a great deal that his contemporaries found unmentionable. For he is not only writing of the prairie, he also wanders through the city and notes the shattered skull of the suicide, the 'grey sick faces of onanists', etc., etc. But unquestionably our own age, at any rate in western Europe, is less healthy and less hopeful than the age in which Whitman was writing. Unlike Whitman, we live in a *shrinking* world. The 'democratic vistas' have ended in barbed wire. There is less feeling of creation and growth, less and less emphasis on the cradle, endlessly rocking, more and more emphasis on the teapot, endlessly stewing. To accept civilization *as it is* practically means accepting decay. It has ceased to be a strenuous attitude and become a passive attitude – even 'decadent', if that word means anything.

But precisely because, in one sense, he is passive to experience, Miller is able to get nearer to the ordinary man than is possible to more purposive writers. For the ordinary man is also passive. Within a narrow circle (home life, and perhaps the trade union or local politics) he feels himself master of his fate, but against major events he is as helpless as against the elements. So far from endeavouring to influence the future, he simply lies down and lets things happen to him. During the past ten years literature has involved itself more and more deeply in politics, with the result that there is now less room in it for the ordinary man than at any time during the past two centuries. One can see the change in the prevailing literary attitude by comparing the books written about the Spanish civil war with those written about the war of 1914–18. The immediately striking thing about the Spanish war books, at any rate those written in English, is their shocking dullness and badness. But what is more significant is that almost all of them, right-wing or left-wing, are written from a political angle, by cocksure partisans telling you what to think, whereas the books about the Great War were written by common soldiers or junior officers who did not even pretend to understand what the whole thing was about. Books like *All Quiet on the Western Front*, *Le Feu*, *A Farewell to Arms*, *Death of a Hero*, *Good-Bye to All That*, *Memoirs of an Infantry Officer* and *A Subaltern on the Somme* were written not by propagandists but by *victims*. They are saying in effect, 'What the hell is all this about? God knows. All we can do is to endure.' And though he is not writing about war, nor, on the whole, about unhappiness, this is nearer to Miller's attitude than the omniscience which is now fashionable. The *Booster*, a short-lived periodical of which he was part-editor, used to describe itself in its advertisements as 'non-political, non-educational, non-progressive, non-cooperative, non-ethical, non-literary, non-consistent, non-contemporary', and Miller's own work could be described in nearly the same terms. It is a voice from the crowd, from the underling, from the third-class carriage, from the ordinary, non-political, non-moral, passive man.

I have been using the phrase 'ordinary man' rather loosely, and I have taken it for granted that the 'ordinary man' exists, a thing now denied by some people. I do not mean that the people Miller is writing about constitute a majority, still less that he is writing about proletarians. No English or American novelist has as yet seriously attempted that. And again, the people in *Tropic of Cancer* fall short of being ordinary to the extent that they are idle, disreputable and more or less 'artistic'. As I have said already, this is a pity, but it is the necessary result of expatriation. Miller's 'ordinary man' is neither the manual worker nor the suburban householder, but the derelict, the *déclassé*, the adventurer, the American intellectual without roots and without money. Still, the experiences even of this type overlap fairly widely with those of more normal people. Miller has been able to get the most out of his rather limited material because he has had the courage to identify with it. The ordinary man, the 'average sensual man', has been given the power of speech, like Balaam's ass.

It will be seen that this is something out of date, or at any rate out of fashion. The average sensual man is out of fashion. The passive, non-political attitude is out of fashion. Preoccupation with sex and truthfulness about the inner life are out of fashion. American Paris is out of fashion. A book like *Tropic of Cancer*, published at such a time, must be either a tedious preciosity or something unusual, and I think a majority of the people who have read it would agree that it is not the first. It is worth trying to discover just what this escape from the current literary fashion means. But to do that one has got to see it against its background – that is, against the general development of English literature in the twenty years since the Great War.

Two

When one says that a writer is fashionable one practically always means that he is admired by people under thirty. At the beginning of the period I am speaking of, the years during and immediately after the war, the writer who had the deepest hold upon the thinking young was almost certainly Housman. Among people who were adolescent in the years 1910–25, Housman had an influence which was enormous and is not not at all easy to understand. In 1920, when I was about seventeen, I probably knew the whole of *A Shropshire Lad* by heart. I wonder how much impression *A Shropshire Lad* makes at this moment on a boy of the same age and more or less the same cast of mind? No doubt he has heard of it and even glanced into it; it might strike him as rather cheaply clever – probably that would be about all. Yet these are the poems that I and my contemporaries used to recite to ourselves, over and over, in a kind of ecstasy, just as earlier generations had recited Meredith's 'Love in a Valley', Swinburne's 'Garden of Proserpine', etc., etc.

With rue my heart is laden
For golden friends I had,
For many a rose-lipt maiden
And many a lightfoot lad.

By brooks too broad for leaping
The lightfoot boys are laid;
The rose-lipt girls are sleeping
In fields where roses fade.

It just tinkles. But it did not seem to tinkle in 1920. Why does the bubble always burst? To answer that question one has to take account of the *external* conditions that make certain writers popular at certain times. Housman's poems had not attracted much notice when they were first published. What was there in them that appealed so deeply to a single generation, the generation born round about 1900?

In the first place, Housman is a 'country' poet. His poems are full of the charm of buried villages, the nostalgia of place-names, Clunton and Clunbury, Knighton, Ludlow, 'on Wenlock Edge', 'in summer time on Bredon', thatched roofs and the jingle of smithies, the wild jonquils in the pastures, the 'blue, remembered hills'. War poems apart, English verse of the 1910–25 period is mostly 'country'. The reason no doubt was that the *rentier*-professional class was ceasing once and for all to have any real relationship with the soil; but at any rate there prevailed then, far more than now, a kind of snobbism of belonging to the country and despising the town. England at that time was hardly more an agricultural country than it is now, but before the light industries began to spread themselves it was easier to think of it as one. Most middle-class boys grew up within sight of a farm, and naturally it was the picturesque side of farm life that appealed to them – the ploughing, harvesting, stack-thrashing and so forth. Unless he has to do it himself a boy is not likely to notice the horrible drudgery of hoeing turnips, milking cows with chapped teats at four o'clock in the morning, etc., etc. Just before, just after and, for that matter, during the war was the great age of the 'nature poet', the heyday of Richard Jefferies and W. H. Hudson. Rupert Brooke's 'Grantchester', the star poem of 1913, is nothing but an enormous gush of 'country' sentiment, a sort of accumulated vomit from a stomach stuffed with place-names. Considered as a poem 'Grantchester' is something worse than worthless but as an illustration of what the thinking middle-class young of that period *felt* it is a valuable document.

Housman, however, did not enthuse over the rambler roses in the week-ending spirit of Brooke and the others. The 'country' motif is there all the time, but mainly as a background. Most of the poems have a quasi-human subject, a kind of idealized rustic, in reality Strephon or Corydon brought up to date. This in itself had a deep appeal. Experience shows that over-civilized people enjoy reading about rustics (key-phrase, 'close to the soil') because they imagine them to be more primitive and passionate than themselves. Hence the 'dark earth' novels of Sheila Kaye-Smith, etc. And at that time a middle-class boy, with his 'country' bias, would identify with an agricultural worker as he would never have thought of doing with a town worker. Most boys had in their minds a vision of an idealized ploughman, gypsy, poacher, or gamekeeper, always pictured as a wild, free, roving blade, living a life of rabbit-snaring, cock-fighting, horses, beer and women. Masefield's *Everlasting Mercy*, another valuable period piece, immensely popular with boys round about the war years, gives you this vision in a very crude form. But Housman's Maurices and Terences could be taken seriously where Masefield's Saul Kane could not; on this side of him, Housman was Masefield with a dash of Theocritus. Moreover all his themes are adolescent – murder, suicide, unhappy love, early death. They deal with the simple, intelligible disasters that give you the feeling of being up against the 'bedrock facts' of life:

The sun burns on the half-mown hill,
By now the blood is dried;
And Maurice amongst the hay lies still
And my knife is in his side.

And again:

They hang us now in Shrewsbury jail:
The whistles blow forlorn,
And trains all night groan on the rail
To men that die at morn.

It is all more or less in the same tune. Everything comes unstuck. 'Dick lies long in the churchyard, and Ned lies long in jail.' And notice also the exquisite self-pity – the 'nobody loves me' feeling:

The diamond tears adorning
Thy low mound on the lea,
Those are the tears of morning,
That weeps, but not for thee.

Hard cheese, old chap! Such poems might have been written expressly for adolescents. And the unvarying sexual pessimism (the girl always dies or marries somebody else) seemed like wisdom to boys who were herded together together in public schools and were half-inclined to think of women as something unattainable. Whether Housman ever had the same appeal for girls I doubt. In his poems the women's point of view is not considered, she is merely the nymph, the siren, the treacherous half-human creature who leads you a little distance and then gives you the slip.

But Housman would not have appealed so deeply to the people who were young in 1920 if it had not been for another strain in him, and that was his blasphemous, antinomian, 'cynical' strain. The fight that always occurs between the generations was exceptionally bitter at the end of the Great War; this was partly due to the war itself, and partly it was an indirect result of the Russian Revolution, but an intellectual struggle was in any case due at about that date. Owing probably to the ease and security of life in England, which even the war hardly disturbed, many people whose ideas were formed in the 'eighties or earlier had carried them quite unmodified into the nineteen-twenties. Meanwhile, so far as the younger generation was concerned, the official beliefs were dissolving like sand-castles. The slump in religious belief, for instance, was spectacular. For several years the old-young antagonism took on a quality of real hatred. What was left of the war generation had crept out of the massacre to find their elders still bellowing the slogans of 1914, and a slightly younger generation of boys were writhing under dirty-minded celibate schoolmasters. It was to these that Housman appealed, with his implied sexual revolt and his personal grievance against God. He was patriotic, it was true, but in a harmless old-fashioned way, to the tune of red coats and 'God save the Queen' rather than steel helmets and 'Hang the Kaiser'. And he was satisfyingly anti-Christian – he stood for a kind of bitter, defiant paganism, a conviction that life is short and the gods are against you, which exactly fitted the prevailing mood of the young; and all in charming fragile verse that was composed almost entirely of words of one syllable.

It will be seen that I have discussed Housman as though he were merely a propagandist, an utterer of maxims and quotable 'bits'. Obviously he was more than that. There is no need to under-rate him now because he was over-rated a few years ago. Although one gets into trouble nowadays for saying so, there is a number of his poems ('Into my heart an air that kills', for instance, and 'Is my team ploughing?') that are not likely to remain long out of favour. But at bottom it is always a writer's tendency, his 'purpose', his 'message', that makes him liked or disliked. The proof of this is the extreme difficulty of seeing any literary merit in a book that seriously damages your deepest beliefs. And no book is ever truly neutral. Some tendency or other is always discernible, in verse as much as in prose, even if it does not more than determine the form and the choice of imagery. But poets who attain wide popularity, like Housman, are as a rule definitely gnomic writers.

After the war, after Housman and the Nature poets, there appears a group of writers of completely different tendency – Joyce, Eliot, Pound, Lawrence, Wyndham Lewis, Aldous Huxley, Lytton Strachey. So far as the middle and late 'twenties go, these are 'the movement', as surely as the Auden–Spender group have been 'the movement' during the past few years. It is true that not all of the gifted writers of the period can be fitted into the pattern. E. M. Forster, for instance, though he wrote his best book in 1923 or thereabouts, was essentially pre-war, and Yeats does not seem in either of his phases to belong to the 'twenties. Others who were still living, Moore, Conrad, Bennett, Wells, Norman Douglas, had shot their bolt before the war ever happened. On the other hand, a writer who should be added to the group, though in the narrowly literary sense he hardly 'belongs', is Somerset Maugham. Of course the dates do not fit exactly; most of these writers had already published books before the war, but they can be classified as post-war in the same sense that the younger men now writing are post-slump. Equally of course, you could read through most of the literary papers of the time without grasping that these people *are* 'the movement'. Even more then than at most times the big shots of literary journalism were busy pretending that the age-before-last had not come to an end. Squire ruled the *London Mercury*, Gibbs and Walpole were the gods of the lending libraries, there was a cult of cheeriness and manliness, beer and cricket, briar pipes and monogamy, and it was at all times possible to earn a few guineas by writing an article denouncing 'highbrows'. But all the same it was the despised highbrows who had captured the young. The wind was blowing from Europe, and long before 1930 it had blown the beer-and-cricket school naked, except for their knighthoods.

But the first thing one would notice about the group of writers I have named above is that they do not look like a group. Moreover several of them would strongly object to being coupled with several of the others. Lawrence and Eliot were in reality antipathetic, Huxley worshipped Lawrence but was repelled by Joyce, most of the others would have looked down on Huxley, Strachey and Maugham, and Lewis attacked everyone in turn; indeed, his reputation as a writer rests largely on these attacks. And yet there is a certain temperamental similarity, evident enough now, though it would not have been so a dozen years ago. What it amounts to is *pessimism of outlook*. But it is necessary to make clear what is meant by pessimism.

If the keynote of the Georgian poets was 'beauty of Nature', the keynote of the post-war writers would be 'tragic sense of life'. The spirit behind Housman's poems, for instance, is not tragic, merely querulous; it is hedonism disappointed. The same is true of Hardy, though one ought to make an exception of *The Dynasts*. But the Joyce-Eliot group come later in time, puritanism is not their main adversary, they are able from the start to 'see through' most of the things that their predecessors had fought for. All of them are temperamentally hostile to the notion of 'progress'; it is felt that progress not only doesn't happen, but *ought not* to happen. Given this general similarity, there are, of course, differences of approach between the writers I have named as well as very different degrees of talent. Eliot's pessimism is partly the Christian pessimism, which implies a certain indifference to human misery, partly a lament over the decadence of western civilization ('We are the hollow men, we are the stuffed men', etc., etc.), a sort of twilight-of-the-gods feeling which finally leads him, in 'Sweeney Agonistes' for instance, to achieve the difficult feat of making modern life out to be worse than it is. With Strachey it is merely a polite eighteenth-century scepticism mixed up with a taste for debunking. With Maugham it is a kind of stoical resignation, the stiff upper lip of the pukka sahib somewhere East of Suez, carrying on with his job without believing in it, like an Antonine Emperor. Lawrence at first sight does not seem to be a pessimistic writer, because, like Dickens, he is a 'change-of-heart' man and constantly insisting that life here and now would be all right if only you looked at it a little differently. But what he is demanding is a movement away from our mechanized civilization, which is not going to happen, and which he knows is not going to happen. Therefore his exasperation with the present turns once more into idealization of the past, this time a safely mythical past, the Bronze Age. When Lawrence prefers the Etruscans (*his* Etruscans) to ourselves it is difficult not to agree with him, and yet, after all, it is a species of defeatism, because that is not the direction in which the world is moving. The kind of life that he is always pointing to, a life centring round the simple mysteries – sex, earth, fire, water, blood – is merely a lost cause. All he has been able to produce, therefore, is a wish that things would happen in a way in which they are manifestly not going to happen. 'A wave of generosity or a wave of death', he says, but it is obvious that there are no waves of generosity this side of the horizon. So he flees to Mexico, and then dies at forty-five, a few years before the wave of death gets going. It will be seen that once again I am speaking of these people as though they were not artists, as though they were merely propagandists putting a 'message' across. And once again it is obvious that all of them are more than that. It would be absurd, for instance, to look on *Ulysses* as *merely* a show-up of the horror of modern life, the 'dirty *Daily Mail* era', as Pound put it. Joyce actually is more of a 'pure artist' than most writers. But *Ulysses* could not have been written by someone who was merely dabbling with word-patterns; it is the product of a special vision of life, the vision of a Catholic who has lost his faith. What Joyce is saying is 'Here is life without God. Just look at it!' and his technical innovations, important though they are, are there primarily to serve this purpose.

But what is noticeable about all these writers is that what 'purpose' they have is very much up in the air. There is no attention to the urgent problems of the moment, above all no politics in the narrower sense. Our eyes are directed to Rome, to Byzantium, to Montparnasse, to Mexico, to the Etruscans, to the subconscious, to the solar plexus – to everywhere except the places where things are actually happening. When one looks back at the 'twenties, nothing is queerer than the way in which every important event in Europe escaped the notice of the English intelligentsia. The Russian Revolution, for instance, all but vanishes from the English consciousness between the death of Lenin and the Ukraine famine – about ten years. Throughout those years Russia means Tolstoy, Dostoievski and exiled counts driving taxi-cabs. Italy means picture-galleries, ruins, churches and museums – but not Blackshirts. Germany means films, nudism and psychoanalysis – but not Hitler, of whom hardly anyone had heard till 1931. In 'cultured' circles art-for-art's-saking extended practically to a worship of the meaningless. Literature was supposed to consist solely in the manipulation of words. To judge a book by its subject-matter was the unforgivable sin, and even to be aware of its subject-matter was looked on as a lapse of taste. About 1928, in one of the three genuinely funny jokes that *Punch* has produced since the Great War, an intolerable youth is pictured informing his aunt that he intends to 'write'. 'And what are you going to write about, dear?' asks the aunt. 'My dear aunt,' says the youth crushingly, 'one doesn't write *about* anything, one just *writes*.' The best writers of the 'twenties did not subscribe to this doctrine, their 'purpose' is in most cases fairly overt, but it is usually a 'purpose' along moral-religious-cultural lines. Also, when translatable into political terms, it is in no case 'left'. In one way or another the tendency of all the writers in this group is conservative. Lewis, for instance, spent years in frenzied witch-smellings after 'Bolshevism', which he was able to detect in very unlikely places. Recently he has cnanged some of his views, perhaps influenced by Hitler's treatment of artists, but it is safe to bet that he will not go very far leftward. Pound seems to have plumped definitely for Fascism, at any rate the Italian variety. Eliot has remained aloof, but if forced at the pistol's point to choose between Fascism and some more democratic form of Socialism, would probably choose Fascism. Huxley starts off with the usual despair-of-life, then, under the influence of Lawrence's 'dark abdomen', tries something called Life-Worship, and finally arrives at pacifism – a tenable position, and at this moment an honourable one, but probably in the long run involving rejection of Socialism. It is also noticeable that most of the writers in this group have a certain tenderness for the Catholic Church, though not usually of a kind that an orthodox Catholic would accept.

The mental connection between pessimism and a reactionary outlook is no doubt obvious enough. What is perhaps less obvious is just *why* the leading writers of the 'twenties were predominantly pessimistic. Why always the sense of decadence, the skulls and cactuses, the yearning after lost faith and impossible civilizations? Was it not, after all, *because* these people were writing in an exceptionally comfortable epoch? It is just in such times that 'cosmic despair' can flourish. People with empty bellies never despair of the universe, nor even think about the universe, for that matter. The whole period 1910–30 was a prosperous one, and even the war years were physically tolerable if one happened to be a non-combatant in one of the Allied countries. As for the 'twenties, they were the golden age of the *rentier*-intellectual, a period of irresponsibility such as the world had never before seen. The war was over, the new totalitarian states had not arisen, moral and religious taboos of all descriptions had vanished, and the cash was rolling in. 'Disillusionment' was all the fashion. Everyone with a safe £500 a year turned highbrow and began training himself in *taedium vitae*. It was an age of eagles and of crumpets, facile despairs, backyard Hamlets, cheap return tickets to the end of the night. In some of the minor characteristic novels of the period, books like *Told by an Idiot*, the despair-of-life reaches a Turkish-bath atmosphere of self-pity. And even the best writers of the time can be convicted of a too Olympian attitude, a too great readiness to wash their hands of the immediate practical problem. They see life very comprehensively, much more so than those who come immediately before or after them, but they see it through the wrong end of the telescope. Not that that invalidates their books, as books. The first test of any work of art is survival, and it is a fact that a great deal that was written in the period 1910–30 has survived and looks like continuing to survive. One has only to think of *Ulysees*, *Of Human Bondage*, most of Lawrence's early work, especially his short stories, and virtually the whole of Eliot's poems up to about 1930, to wonder what is now being written that will wear so well.

But quite suddenly, in the years 1930–5, something happens. The literary climate changes. A new group of writers, Auden and Spender and the rest of them, has made its appearance, and although technically these writers owe something to their predecessors, their 'tendency' is entirely different. Suddenly we have got out of the twilight of the gods into a sort of Boy Scout atmosphere of bare knees and community singing. The typical literary man ceases to be a cultured expatriate with a leaning towards the Church, and becomes an eager-minded schoolboy with a leaning towards Communism. If the keynote of the writers of the 'twenties is 'tragic sense of life', the keynote of the new writers is 'serious purpose'.

The differences between the two schools are discussed at some length in Mr Louis MacNeice's book *Modern Poetry*. This book is, of course, written entirely from the angle of the younger group and takes the superiority of their standards for granted. According to Mr MacNeice:

> The poets of *New Signatures*,[1] unlike Yeats and Eliot, are emotionally partisan. Yeats proposed to turn his back on desire and hatred; Eliot sat back and watched other people's emotions with ennui and an ironical self-pity.... The whole poetry, on the other hand, of Auden, Spender and Day-Lewis implies that they have desires and hatreds of their own and, further, that they think some things *ought* to be desired and others hated.

And again:

> The poets of *New Signatures* have swung back ... to the Greek preference for information or statement. The first requirement is to have something to say, and after that you must say it as well as you can.

[1] Published in 1932. [Author's footnote.]

In other words, 'purpose' has come back, the younger writers have 'gone into politics'. As I have pointed out already, Eliot & Co. are not really so non-partisan as Mr MacNeice seems to suggest. Still, it is broadly true that in the 'twenties the literary emphasis was more on technique and less on subject-matter than it is now.

The leading figures in this group are Auden, Spender, Day-Lewis, MacNeice, and there is a long string of writers of more or less the same tendency, Isherwood, John Lehmann, Arthur Calder-Marshall, Edward Upward, Alec Brown, Philip Henderson, and many others. As before, I am lumping them together simply according to tendency. Obviously there are very great variations in talent. But when one compares these writers with the Joyce-Eliot generation, the immediately striking thing is how much easier it is to form them into a group. Technically they are closer together, politically they are almost indistinguishable, and their criticisms of one another's work have always been (to put it mildly) good-natured. The outstanding writers of the 'twenties were of very varied origins, few of them had passed through the ordinary English educational mill (incidentally, the best of them, barring Lawrence, were not Englishmen), and most of them had had at some time to struggle against poverty, neglect, and even downright persecution. On the other hand, nearly all the younger writers fit easily into the public-school–university–Bloomsbury pattern. The few who are of proletarian origin are of the kind that is declassed early in life, first by means of scholarships and then by the bleaching-tub of London 'culture'. It is significant that several of the writers in this group have been not only boys but, subsequently, masters at public schools. Some years ago I described Auden as 'a sort of gutless Kipling'. As criticism this was quite unworthy, indeed it was merely a spiteful remark, but it is a fact that in Auden's work, especially his earlier work, an atmosphere of uplift – something rather like Kipling's 'If' or Newbolt's 'Play Up, Play Up, and Play the Game!' – never seems to be very far away. Take, for instance, a poem like 'You're leaving now, and it's up to you boys.'[1] It is pure scoutmaster, the exact note of the ten-minutes' straight talk on the dangers of self-abuse. No doubt there is an element of parody that he intends, but there is also a deeper resemblance that he does not intend. And of course the rather priggish note that is common to most of these writers is a symptom of release. By throwing 'pure art' overboard they have freed themselves from the fear of being laughed at and vastly enlarged their scope. The prophetic side of Marxism, for example, is new material for poetry and has great possibilities:

We are nothing.
We have fallen
Into the dark and shall be destroyed.
Think though, that in this darkness
We hold the secret hub of an idea
Whose living sunlit wheel revolves in future years outside.

(Spender, *Trial of a Judge.*)

But at the same time, by being Marxized literature has moved no nearer to the masses. Even allowing for the time-lag, Auden and Spender are somewhat farther from being popular writers than Joyce and Eliot, let alone

[1] This is in fact the first line of Poem No. 10 in Cecil Day-Lewis's early volume of poetry *The Magnetic Mountain.*

Lawrence. As before, there are many contemporary writers who are outside the current, but there is not much doubt about what *is* the current. For the middle and late 'thirties, Auden, Spender & Co. *are* 'the movement', just as Joyce, Eliot & Co. were for the 'twenties. And the movement is in the direction of some rather ill-defined thing called Communism. As early as 1934 or 1935 it was considered eccentric in literary circles not to be more or less 'left', and in another year or two there had grown up a leftwing orthodoxy that made a certain set of opinions absolutely *de rigueur* on certain subjects. The idea had begun to gain ground (*vide* Edward Upward and others) that a writer must either be actively 'left' or write badly. Between 1935 and 1939 the Communist Party had an almost irresistible fascination for any writer under forty. It became as normal to hear that so-and-so had 'joined' as it had been a few years earlier, when Roman Catholicism was fashionable, to hear that so-and-so had 'been received'. For about three years, in fact, the central stream of English literature was more or less directly under Communist control. How was it possible for such a thing to happen? And at the same time, what is meant by 'Communism'? It is better to answer the second question first.

The Communist movement in western Europe began as a movement for the violent overthrow of capitalism, and degenerated within a few years into an instrument of Russian foreign policy. This was probably inevitable when the revolutionary ferment that followed the Great War had died down. So far as I know, the only comprehensive history of this subject in English is Franz Borkenau's book, *The Communist International*. What Borkenau's facts even more than his deductions make clear is that Communism could never have developed along its present lines if any real revolutionary feeling had existed in the industrialized countries. In England, for instance, it is obvious that no such feeling has existed for years past. The pathetic membership figures of all extremist parties show this clearly. It is only natural, therefore, that the English Communist movement should be controlled by people who are mentally subservient to Russia and have no real aim except to manipulate British foreign policy in the Russian interest. Of course such an aim cannot be openly admitted, and it is this fact that gives the Communist Party its very peculiar character. The more vocal kind of Communist is in effect a Russian publicity agent posing as an international Socialist. It is a pose that is easily kept up at normal times, but becomes difficult in moment of crisis, because of the fact that the USSR is no more scrupulous in its foreign policy than the rest of the Great Powers. Alliances, changes of front, etc. which only make sense as part of the game of power politics have to be explained and justified in terms of international Socialism. Every time Stalin swaps partners, 'Marxism' has to be hammered into a new shape. This entails sudden and violent changes of 'line', purges, denunciations, systematic destruction of party literature, etc., etc. Every Communist is in fact liable at any moment to have to alter his most fundamental convictions, or leave the party. The unquestionable dogma of Monday may become the damnable heresy of Tuesday, and so on. This has happened at least three times during the past ten years. It follows that in any western country a Communist Party is always unstable and usually very small. Its long-term membership really consists of an inner ring of intellectuals who have identified with the Russian bureaucracy, and a slightly larger body of working-class people who feel a loyalty towards Soviet Russia without necessarily understanding its policies. Otherwise there is only a shifting membership, one lot coming and another going with each change of 'line'.

In 1930 the English Communist Party was a tiny, barely legal organization whose main activity was libelling the Labour Party. But by 1935 the face of Europe had changed, and left-wing politics changed with it. Hitler had risen to power and begun to re-arm, the Russian Five-Year plans had succeeded, Russia had reappeared as a great military power. As Hitler's three targets of attack were, to all appearances, Great Britain, France and the USSR, the three countries were forced into a sort of uneasy *rapprochement*. This meant that the English or French Communist was obliged to become a good patriot and imperialist – that is, to defend the very things he had been attacking for the past fifteen years. The Comintern slogans suddenly faded from red to pink. 'World revolution' and 'Social-Fascism' gave way to 'Defence of democracy' and 'Stop Hitler!' The years 1935–9 were the period of anti-Fascism and the Popular Front, the heyday of the Left Book Club, when red duchesses and 'broadminded' deans toured the battlefields of the Spanish war and Winston Churchill was the blue-eyed boy of the *Daily Worker*. Since then, of course, there has been yet another change of 'line'. But what is important for my purpose is that it was during the 'anti-Fascist' phase that the younger English writers gravitated towards Communism.

The Fascism-democracy dogfight was no doubt an attraction in itself, but in any case their conversion was due at about that date. It was obvious that *laissez-faire* capitalism was finished and that there had got to be some kind of reconstruction; in the world of 1935 it was hardly possible to remain politically indifferent. But why did these young men turn towards anything so alien as Russian Communism? Why should *writers* be attracted by a form of Socialism that makes mental honesty impossible? The explanation really lies in something that had already made itself felt before the slump and before Hitler: middle-class unemployment.

Unemployment is not merely a matter of not having a job. Most people can *get* a job of sorts, even at the worst of times. The trouble was that by 1930 there was no activity, except perhaps scientific research, the arts and left-wing politics, that a thinking person could believe in. The debunking of western civilization had reached its climax and 'disillusionment' was immensely widespread. Who now could take it for granted to go through life in the ordinary middle-class way, as a soldier, a clergyman, a stockbroker, an Indian Civil Servant or what not? And how many of the values by which our grandfathers lived could now be taken seriously? Patriotism, religion, the Empire, the family, the sanctity of marriage, the Old School Tie, birth, breeding, honour, discipline – anyone of ordinary education could turn the whole lot of them inside out in three minutes. But what do you achieve, after all, by getting rid of such primal things as patriotism and religion? You have not necessarily got rid of the need for *something to believe in*. There had been a sort of false dawn a few years earlier when numbers of young intellectuals, including several quite gifted writers (Evelyn Waugh, Christopher Hollis and others), had fled into the Catholic Church. It is significant that these people went almost invariably to the Roman Church and not, for instance, to the C of E, the Greek Church or the Protestant sects. They went, that is, to the Church with a world-wide organization, the one with a rigid discipline, the one with power and prestige behind it. Perhaps it is even worth noticing that the only latter-day convert of really first-rate gifts, Eliot, has embraced not Romanism but Anglo-Catholicism, the ecclesiastical equivalent of Trotskyism. But I do not think one need look farther than this for the reason why the young writers of the 'thirties flocked into or towards the Communist Party. It was simply something to believe in. Here was a church, an army, an orthodoxy, a discipline. Here was a Fatherland and – at any rate since 1935 or thereabouts – a Fuehrer. All the loyalties and superstitions that the intellect had seemingly banished could come rushing back under the thinnest of disguises. Patriotism, religion, empire, military glory – all in one word, Russia. Father, king, leader, hero, saviour – all in one word, Stalin. God – Stalin. The devil – Hitler. Heaven – Moscow. Hell – Berlin. All the gaps were filled up. So, after all, the 'Communism' of the English intellectual is something explicable enough. It is the patriotism of the deracinated.

But there is one thing that undoubtedly contributed to the cult of Russia among the English intelligentsia during these years, and that is the softness and security of life in England itself. With all its injustices, England is still the land of habeas corpus, and the overwhelming majority of English people have no experience of violence or illegality. If you have grown up in that sort of atmosphere it is not at all easy to imagine what a despotic régime is like. Nearly all the dominant writers of the 'thirties belonged to the soft-boiled emancipated middle class and were too young to have effective memories of the Great War. To people of that kind such things as purges, secret police, summary executions, imprisonment without trial, etc., etc. are too remote to be terrifying. They can swallow totalitarianism *because* they have no experience of anything except liberalism. Look, for instance, at this extract from Mr Auden's poem 'Spain' (incidentally this poem is one of the few decent things that have been written about the Spanish war):

Tomorrow for the young, the poets exploding like bombs,
The walks by the lake, the weeks of perfect communion;
Tomorrow the bicycle races
Through the suburbs on summer evenings. But today the struggle.

Today the deliberate increase in the chances of death,
The conscious acceptance of guilt in the necessary murder;
Today the expending of powers
On the flat ephemeral pamphlet and the boring meeting.

The second stanza is intended as a sort of thumbnail sketch of a day in the life of a 'good party man'. In the morning a couple of political murders, a ten-minutes' interlude to stifle 'bourgeois' remorse, and then a hurried luncheon and a busy afternoon and evening chalking walls and distributing leaflets. All very edifying. But notice the phrase 'necessary murder'. It could only be written by a person to whom murder is at most a *word*. Personally I would not speak so lightly of murder. It so happens that I have seen the bodies of numbers of murdered men – I don't mean killed in battle, I mean murdered. Therefore I have some conception of what murder means – the terror, the hatred, the howling relatives, the post-mortems, the blood, the smells. To me, murder is something to be avoided. So it is to any ordinary person. The Hitlers and Stalins find murder necessary, but they don't advertise their callousness, and they don't speak of it as murder; it is 'liquidation', 'elimination' or some other soothing phrase. Mr Auden's brand of amoralism is only possible if you are the kind of person who is always somewhere else when the trigger is pulled. So much of left-wing thought is a kind of playing with fire by people who don't even know that fire is hot. The war-mongering to which the English intelligentsia gave themselves up in the period 1935–9 was largely based on a sense of personal immunity. The attitude was very different in France, where the military service is hard to dodge and even literary men know the weight of a pack.

Towards the end of Mr Cyril Connolly's recent book, *Enemies of Promise*, there occurs an interesting and revealing passage. The first part of the book is, more or less, an evaluation of present-day literature. Mr Connolly belongs exactly to the generation of the writers of 'the movement', and with not many reservations their values are his values. It is interesting to notice that among prose writers he admires chiefly those specializing in violence – the would-be tough American school, Hemingway, etc. The latter part of the book, however, is autobiographical and consists of an account, fascinatingly accurate, of life at a preparatory school and Eton in the years 1910–20. Mr Connolly ends by remarking:

> Were I to deduce anything from my feelings on leaving Eton, it might be called *The Theory of Permanent Adolescence*. It is the theory that the experiences undergone by boys at the great public schools are so intense as to dominate their lives and to arrest their development.

When you read the second sentence in this passage, your natural impulse is to look for the misprint. Presumably there is a 'not' left out, or something. But no, not a bit of it! He means it! And what is more, he is merely speaking the truth, in an inverted fashion. 'Cultured' middle-class life has reached a depth of softness at which a public-school education – five years in a lukewarm bath of snobbery – can actually be looked back upon as an eventful period. To nearly all the writers who have counted during the 'thirties, what more has ever happened than Mr Connolly records in *Enemies of Promise*? It is the same pattern all the time; public school, university, a few trips abroad, then London. Hunger, hardship, solitude, exile, war, prison, persecution, manual labour – hardly even words. No wonder that the huge tribe known as 'the right left people' found it so easy to condone the purge-and-Ogpu side of the Russian régime and the horrors of the First Five Year Plan. They were so gloriously incapable of understanding what it all meant.

By 1937 the whole of the intelligentsia was mentally at war. Left-wing thought had narrowed down to 'anti-Fascism', i.e. to a negative, and a torrent of hate-literature directed against Germany and the politicians supposedly friendly to Germany was pouring from the press. The thing that, to me, was truly frightening about the war in Spain was not such violence as I witnessed, nor even the party feuds behind the lines, but the immediate reappearance in left-wing circles of the mental atmosphere of the Great War. The very people who for twenty years had sniggered over their own superiority to war hysteria were the ones who rushed straight back into the mental slum of 1915. All the familiar war-time idiocies, spy-hunting, orthodoxy-sniffing (Sniff, sniff. Are you a good anti-Fascist?), the retailing of incredible atrocity stories, came back into vogue as though the intervening years had never happened. Before the end of the Spanish war, and even before Munich, some of the better of the left-wing writers were beginning to squirm. Neither Auden nor, on the whole, Spender wrote about the Spanish war in quite the vein that was expected of them. Since then there has been a change of feeling and much dismay and confusion, because the actual course of events has made nonsense of the left-wing orthodoxy of the last few years. But then it did not need very great acuteness to see that much of it was nonsense from the start. There is no certainty, therefore, that the next orthodoxy to emerge will be any better than the last.

On the whole the literary history of the 'thirties seems to justify the opinion that a writer does well to keep out of politics. For any writer who accepts or partially accepts the discipline of a political party is sooner or later faced with the alternative: toe the line, or shut up. It is, of course, possible to toe the line and go on writing – after a fashion. Any Marxist can demonstrate with the greatest of ease that 'bourgeois' liberty of thought is an illusion. But when he has finished his demonstration there remains the psychological *fact* that without this 'bourgeois' liberty the creative powers wither away. In the future a totalitarian literature may arise, but it will be quite different from anything we can now imagine. Literature as we know it is an individual thing, demanding mental honesty and a minimum of censorship. And this is even truer of prose than of verse. It is probably not a coincidence that the best writers of the 'thirties have been poets. The atmosphere of orthodoxy is always damaging to prose, and above all it is completely ruinous to the novel, the most anarchical of all forms of literature. How many Roman Catholics have been good novelists? Even the handful one could name have usually been bad Catholics. The novel is practically a Protestant form of art; it is a product of the free mind, of the autonomous individual. No decade in the past hundred and fifty years has been so barren of imaginative prose as the nineteen-thirties. There have been good poems, good sociological works, brilliant pamphlets, but practically no fiction of any value at all. From 1933 onwards the mental climate was increasingly against it. Anyone sensitive enough to be touched by the *zeitgeist* was also involved in politics. Not everyone, of course, was definitely *in* the political racket, but practically everyone was on its periphery and more or less mixed up in propaganda campaigns and squalid controversies. Communists and near-Communists had a disproportionately large influence in the literary reviews. It was a time of labels, slogans and evasions. At the worst moments you were expected to lock yourself up in a constipating little cage of lies; at the best a sort of voluntary censorship ('Ought I to say this? Is it pro-Fascist?') was at work in nearly everyone's mind. It is almost inconceivable that good novels should be written in such an atmosphere. Good novels are not written by orthodoxy-sniffers, nor by people who are conscience-stricken about their own unorthodoxy. Good novels are written by people who are *not frightened*. This brings me back to Henry Miller.

Three

If this were a likely moment for the launching of 'schools' of literature, Henry Miller might be the starting-point of a new 'school'. He does at any rate mark an unexpected swing of the pendulum. In his books one gets right away from the 'political animal' and back to a viewpoint not only individualistic but completely passive – the viewpoint of a man who believes the world-process to be outside his control and who in any case hardly wishes to control it.

I first met Miller at the end of 1936, when I was passing through Paris on my way to Spain. What most intrigued me about him was to find that he felt no interest in the Spanish war whatever. He merely told me in forcible terms that to go to Spain at that moment was the act of an idiot. He could understand anyone going there from purely selfish motives, out of curiosity, for instance, but to mix oneself up in such things *from a sense of obligation* was sheer stupidity. In any case my ideas about combating Fascism, defending democracy, etc., etc. were all boloney. Our civilization was destined to be swept away and replaced by something so different that we should scarcely regard it as human – a prospect that did not bother him, he said. And some such outlook is implicit throughout his work. Everywhere there is the sense of the approaching cataclysm, and almost everywhere the implied belief that it doesn't matter. The only political declaration which, so far as I know, he has ever made in print is a purely negative one. A year or so ago an American magazine, the *Marxist Quarterly*, sent out a questionnaire to various American writers asking them to define their attitude on the subject of war. Miller replied in terms of extreme pacifism, but a merely personal pacifism, an individual refusal to fight, with no apparent wish to convert others to the same opinion – practically, in fact, a declaration of irresponsibility.

However, there is more than one kind of irresponsibility. As a rule, writers who do not wish to identify themselves with the historical process of the moment either ignore it or fight against it. If they can ignore it, they are probably fools. If they can understand it well enough to want to fight against it, they probably have enough vision to realize that they cannot win. Look, for instance, at a poem like 'The Scholar Gypsy', with its railing against the 'strange disease of modern life' and its magnificent defeatist simile in the final stanza. It expresses one of the normal literary attitudes, perhaps actually the prevailing attitude during the last hundred years. And on the other hand there are the 'progressives', the yea-sayers, the Shaw-Wells type, always leaping forward to embrace the ego-projections which they mistake for the future. On the whole the writers of the 'twenties took the first line and the writers of the 'thirties the second. And at any given moment, of course, there is a huge tribe of Barries and Deepings and Dells who simply don't notice what is happening. Where Miller's work is symptomatically important is in its avoidance of any of these attitudes. He is neither pushing the world-process forward nor trying to drag it back, but on the other hand he is by no means ignoring it. I should say that he believes in the impending ruin of western civilization much more firmly than the majority of 'revolutionary' writers; only he does not feel called upon to do anything about it. He is fiddling while Rome is burning, and, unlike the enormous majority of people who do this, fiddling with his face towards the flames.

In *Max and the White Phagocytes* there is one of those revealing passages in which a writer tells you a great deal about himself while talking about somebody else. The book includes a long essay on the diaries of Anais Nin, which I have never read, except for a few fragments, and which I believe have not been published. Miller claims that they are the only truly feminine writing that has ever appeared, whatever that may mean. But the interesting passage is one in which he compares Anais Nin – evidently a completely subjective, introverted writer – to Jonah in the whale's belly. In passing he refers to an essay that Aldous Huxley wrote some years ago about El Greco's picture 'The Dream of Philip the Second'. Huxley remarks that the people in El Greco's pictures always look as though they were in the bellies of whales, and professes to find something peculiarly horrible in the idea of being in a 'visceral prison'. Miller retorts that, on the contrary, there are many worse things than being swallowed by whales, and the passage makes it clear that he himself finds the idea rather attractive. Here he is touching upon what is probably a very widespread fantasy. It is perhaps worth noticing that everyone, at least every English-speaking person, invariably speaks of Jonah and the *whale*. Of course the creature that swallowed Jonah was a fish, and is so described in the Bible (Jonah 1:17), but children naturally confuse it with a whale, and this fragment of baby-talk is habitually carried into later life – a sign, perhaps, of the hold that the Jonah myth has upon our imaginations. For the fact is that being inside a whale is a very comfortable, cosy, homelike thought. The historical Jonah, if he can be so called, was glad enough to escape, but in imagination, in day-dream, countless people have envied him. It is, of course, quite obvious why. The whale's belly is simply a womb big enough for an adult. There you are, in the dark, cushioned space that exactly fits you, with yards of blubber between yourself and reality, able to keep up an attitude of the completest indifference, no matter *what* happens. A storm that would sink all the battleships in the world would hardly reach you as an echo. Even the whale's own movements would probably be imperceptible to you. He might be wallowing among the surface waves or shooting down into the blackness of the middle seas (a mile deep, according to Herman Melville), but you would never notice the difference. Short of being dead, it is the final, unsurpassable stage of irresponsibility. And however it may be with Anais Nin, there is no question that Miller himself is inside the whale. All his best and most characteristic passages are written from the angle of Jonah, a willing Jonah. Not that he is especially introverted – quite the contrary. In his case the whale happens to be transparent. Only he feels no impulse to alter or control the process that he is undergoing. He has performed the essential Jonah act of allowing himself to be swallowed, remaining passive, *accepting*.

It will be seen what this amounts to. It is a species of quietism, implying either complete unbelief or else a degree of belief amounting to mysticism. The attitude is 'Je m'en fous' or 'Though He slay me, yet will I trust in Him', whichever way you like to look at it; for practical purposes both are identical, the moral in either case being 'Sit on your bum'. But in a time like ours, is this a defensible attitude? Notice that it is almost impossible to refrain from asking this question. At the moment of writing we are still in a period in which it is taken for granted that books ought always to be positive, serious and 'constructive'. A dozen years ago this idea would have been greeted with titters. ('My dear aunt, one doesn't write *about* anything, one just *writes*.') Then the pendulum swung away from the frivolous notion that art is merely technique, but it swung a very long distance, to the point of asserting that a book can only be 'good' if it is founded on a 'true' vision of life. Naturally the people who believe this also believe that they are in possession of the truth themselves. Catholic critics, for instance, tend to claim that books are only 'good' when they are of Catholic tendency. Marxist critics make the same claim more boldly for Marxist books. For instance, Mr Edward Upward ('A Marxist Interpretation of Literature', in *The Mind in Chains*):

> Literary criticism which aims at being Marxist must ... proclaim that no book written *at the present time* can be 'good' unless it is written from a Marxist or near-Marxist viewpoint.

Various other writers have made similar or comparable statements. Mr Upward italicizes 'at the present time' because he realizes that you cannot, for instance, dismiss *Hamlet* on the ground that Shakespeare was not a Marxist. Nevertheless his interesting essay only glances very shortly at this difficulty. Much of the literature that comes to us out of the past is permeated by and in fact founded on beliefs (the belief in the immortality of the soul, for example) which now seem to us false and in some cases contemptibly silly. Yet it is 'good' literature, if survival is any test. Mr Upward would no doubt answer that a belief which was appropriate several centuries ago might be inappropriate and therefore stultifying now. But this does not get one much farther, because it assumes that in any age there will be *one* body of belief which is the current approximation to truth, and that the best literature of the time will be more or less in harmony with it. Actually no such uniformity has ever existed. In seventeenth-century England, for instance, there was a religious and political cleavage which distinctly resembled the left–right antagonism of today. Looking back, most modern people would feel that the bourgeois–Puritan viewpoint was a better approximation to truth than the Catholic–feudal one. But it is certainly not the case that all or even a majority of the best writers of the time were Puritans. And more than this, there exist 'good' writers whose world-view would in *any* age be recognized as false and silly. Edgar Allan Poe is an example. Poe's outlook is at best a wild romanticism and at worst is not far from being insane in the literal clinical sense. Why is it, then, that stories like 'The Black Cat', 'The Tell-tale Heart', 'The Fall of the House of Usher' and so forth, which might very nearly have been written by a lunatic, do not convey a feeling of falsity? Because they are true within a certain framework, they keep the rules of their own peculiar world, like a Japanese picture. But it appears that to write successfully about such a world you have got to believe in it. One sees the difference immediately if one compares Poe's *Tales* with what is, in my opinion, an insincere attempt to work up a similar atmosphere, Julian Green's *Minuit*. The thing that immediately strikes one about *Minuit* is that there is no reason why any of the events in it should happen. Everything is completely arbitrary; there is no emotional sequence. But this is exactly what one does *not* feel with Poe's stories. Their maniacal logic, in its own setting, is quite convincing. When, for instance, the drunkard seizes the black cat and cuts its eye out with his penknife, one knows exactly *why* he did it, even to the point of feeling that one would have done the same oneself. It seems therefore that for a creative writer possession of the 'truth' is less important than emotional sincerity. Even Mr Upward would not claim that a writer needs nothing beyond a Marxist training. He also needs talent. But talent, apparently, is a matter of being able to *care*, of really *believing* in your beliefs, whether they are true or false. The difference between, for instance, Céline and Evelyn Waugh is a difference of emotional intensity. It is the difference between genuine despair and a despair that is at least partly a pretence. And with this there goes another consideration which is perhaps less obvious: that there are occasions when an 'untrue' belief is more likely to be sincerely held than a 'true' one.

If one looks at the books of personal reminiscence written about the war of 1914–18, one notices that nearly all that have remained readable after a lapse of time are written from a passive, negative angle. They are the records of something completely meaningless, a nightmare happening in a void. That was not actually the truth about the war, but it was the truth about the individual reaction. The soldier advancing into a machine-gun barrage or standing waist-deep in a flooded trench knew only that here was an appalling experience in which he was all but helpless. He was likelier to make a good book out of his helplessness and his ignorance than out of a pretended power to see the whole thing in perspective. As for the books that were written during the war itself, the best of them were nearly all the work of people who simply turned their backs and tried not to notice that the war was happening. Mr E. M. Forster has described how in 1917 he read 'Prufrock' and others of Eliot's early poems, and how it heartened him at such a time to get hold of poems that were 'innocent of public-spiritedness':

> They sang of private disgust and diffidence, and of people who seemed genuine because they were unattractive or weak.... Here was a protest, and a feeble one, and the more congenial for being feeble.... He who could turn aside to complain of ladies and drawing-rooms preserved a tiny drop of our self-respect, he carried on the human heritage.

That is very well said. Mr MacNeice, in the book I have referred to already, quotes this passage and somewhat smugly adds:

> Ten years later less feeble protests were to be made by poets and the human heritage carried on rather differently.... The contemplation of a world of fragments becomes boring and Eliot's successors are more interested in tidying it up.

Similar remarks are scattered throughout Mr MacNeice's book. What he wishes us to believe is that Eliot's 'successors' (meaning Mr MacNeice and his friends) have in some way 'protested' more effectively than Eliot did by publishing 'Prufrock' at the moment when the Allied armies were assaulting the Hindenburg Line. Just where these 'protests' are to be found I do not know. But in the contrast between Mr Forster's comment and Mr MacNeice's lies all the difference between a man who knows what the 1914–18 war was like and a man who barely remembers it. The truth is that in 1917 there was nothing that a thinking and sensitive person could do, except to remain human, if possible. And a gesture of helplessness, even of frivolity, might be the best way of doing that. If I had been a soldier fighting in the Great War, I would sooner have got hold of 'Prufrock' than *The First Hundred Thousand* or Horatio Bottomley's *Letters to the Boys in the Trenches*. I should have felt, like Mr Forster, that by simply standing aloof and keeping touch with pre-war emotions, Eliot was carrying on the human heritage. What a relief it would have been at such a time, to read about the hesitations of a middle-aged highbrow with a bald spot! So different from bayonet drill! After the bombs and the food queues and the recruiting posters, a human voice! What a relief!

But, after all, the war of 1914–18 was only a heightened moment in an almost continuous crisis. At this date it hardly even needs a war to bring home to us the disintegration of our society and the increasing helplessness of all decent people. It is for this reason that I think that the passive, non-cooperative attitude implied in Henry Miller's work is justified. Whether or not it is an expression of what people *ought* to feel, it probably comes somewhere near to expressing what they *do* feel. Once again it is the human voice among the bomb-explosions, a friendly American voice, 'innocent of public-spiritedness'. No sermons, merely the subjective truth. And along those lines, apparently, it is still possible for a good novel to be written. Not necessarily an edifying novel, but a novel worth reading and likely to be remembered after it is read.

While I have been writing this book[1] another European war has broken out. It will either last several years and tear western civilization to pieces, or it will end inconclusively and prepare the way for yet another war which will do the job once and for all. But war is only 'peace intensified'. What is quite obviously happening, war or no war, is the break-up of *laissez-faire* capitalism and of the liberal-Christian culture. Until recently the full implications of this were not foreseen, because it was generally imagined that Socialism could preserve and even enlarge the atmosphere of liberalism. It is now beginning to be realized how false this idea was. Almost certainly we are moving into an age of totalitarian dictatorships – an age in which freedom of thought will be at first a deadly sin and later on a meaningless abstraction. The autonomous individual is going to be stamped out of existence. But this means that literature, in the form in which we know it, must suffer at least a temporary death. The literature of liberalism is coming to an end and the literature of totalitarianism has not yet appeared and is barely imaginable. As for the writer, he is sitting on a melting iceberg; he is merely an anachronism, a hangover from the bourgeois age, as surely doomed as the hippopotamus. Miller seems to me a man out of the common because he saw and proclaimed this fact a long while before most of his contemporaries – at a time, indeed, when many of them were actually burbling about a renaissance of literature. Wyndham Lewis had said years earlier that the major history of the English language was finished, but he was basing this on different and rather trivial reasons. But from now onwards the all-important fact for the creative writer is going to be that this is not a writer's world. That does not mean that he cannot help to bring the new society into being, but he can take no part in the process *as a writer*. For *as a writer* he is a liberal, and what is happening is the destruction of liberalism. It seems likely, therefore, that in the remaining years of free speech any novel worth reading will follow more or less along the lines that Miller has followed – I do not mean in technique or subject-matter, but in implied outlook. The passive attitude will come back, and it will be more consciously passive than before. Progress and reaction have both turned out to be swindles. Seemingly there is nothing left but quietism – robbing reality of its terrors by simply submitting to it. Get inside the whale – or rather, admit that you are inside the whale (for you *are*, of course). Give yourself over to the world-process, stop fighting against it or pretending that you control it; simply accept it, endure it, record it. That seems to be the formula that any sensitive novelist is now likely to adopt. A novel on more positive, 'constructive' lines, and not emotionally spurious, is at present very difficult to imagine.

But do I mean by this that Miller is a 'great author', a new hope for English prose? Nothing of the kind. Miller himself would be the last to claim or want any such thing. No doubt he will go on writing – anybody who has once started always goes on writing – and associated with him there is a number of writers of approximately the same tendency, Lawrence Durrell, Michael Fraenkel and others, almost amounting to a 'school'. But he himself seems to

[1] *Inside the Whale.*

me essentially a man of one book. Sooner or later I should expect him to descend into unintelligibility, or into charlatanism; there are signs of both in his later work. His last book, *Tropic of Capricorn*, I have not even read. This was not because I did not want to read it, but because the police and customs authorities have so far managed to prevent me from getting hold of it. But it would surprise me if it came anywhere near *Tropic of Cancer* or the opening chapters of *Black Spring*. Like certain other autobiographical novelists, he had it in him to do just one thing perfectly, and he did it. Considering what the fiction of the nineteen-thirties has been like, that is something.

Miller's books are published by the Obelisk Press in Paris. What will happen to the Obelisk Press, now that war has broken out and Jack Kahane, the publisher, is dead, I do not know, but at any rate the books are still procurable. I earnestly counsel anyone who has not done so to read at least *Tropic of Cancer*. With a little ingenuity, or by paying a little over the published price, you can get hold of it, and even if parts of it disgust you, it will stick in your memory. It is also an 'important' book, in a sense different from the sense in which that word is generally used. As a rule novels are spoken of as 'important' when they are either a 'terrible indictment' of something or other or when they introduce some technical innovation. Neither of these applies to *Tropic of Cancer*. Its importance is merely symptomatic. Here in my opinion is the only imaginative prose writer of the slightest value who has appeared among the English-speaking races for some years past. Even if that is objected to as an overstatement, it will probably be admitted that Miller is a writer out of the ordinary, worth more than a single glance; and, after all, he is a completely negative, unconstructive, amoral writer, a mere Jonah, a passive accepter of evil, a sort of Whitman among the corpses. Symptomatically, that is more significant than the mere fact that five thousand novels are published in England every year and four thousand nine hundred of them are tripe. It is a demonstration of the *impossibility* of any major literature until the world has shaken itself into its new shape.

Published 1940

ESSAYS AND JOURNALISM 1940-1943

Review

Mein Kampf by Adolf Hitler (unabridged translation)

It is a sign of the speed at which events are moving that Hurst and Blackett's unexpurgated edition of *Mein Kampf*, published only a year ago, is edited from a pro-Hitler angle. The obvious intention of the translator's preface and notes is to tone down the book's ferocity and present Hitler in as kindly a light as possible. For at that date Hitler was still respectable. He had crushed the German labour movement, and for that the property-owning classes were willing to forgive him almost anything. Both Left and Right concurred in the very shallow notion that National Socialism was merely a version of Conservatism.

Then suddenly it turned out that Hitler was not respectable after all. As one result of this, Hurst and Blackett's edition was reissued in a new jacket explaining that all profits would be devoted to the Red Cross. Nevertheless, simply on the internal evidence of *Mein Kampf*, it is difficult to believe that any real change has taken place in Hitler's aims and opinions. When one compares his utterances of a year or so ago with those made fifteen years earlier, a thing that strikes one is the rigidity of his mind, the way in which his world-view *doesn't* develop. It is the fixed vision of a monomaniac and not likely to be much affected by the temporary manoeuvres of power politics. Probably, in Hitler's own mind, the Russo-German Pact represents no more than an alteration of time-table. The plan laid down in *Mein Kampf* was to smash Russia first, with the implied intention of smashing England afterwards. Now, as it has turned out, England has got to be dealt with first, because Russia was the the more easily bribed of the two. But Russia's turn will come when England is out of the picture – that, no doubt, is how Hitler sees it. Whether it will turn out that way is of course a different question.

Suppose that Hitler's programme could be put into effect. What he envisages, a hundred years hence, is a continuous state of 250 million Germans with plenty of 'living room' (i.e. stretching to Afghanistan or thereabouts), a horrible brainless empire in which, essentially, nothing ever happens except the training of young men for war and the endless breeding of fresh cannon-fodder. How was it that he was able to put this monstrous vision across? It is easy to say that at one stage of his career he was financed by the heavy industrialists, who saw in him the man who would smash the Socialists and Communists. They would not have backed him, however, if he had not talked a great movement into existence already. Again, the situation in Germany, with its seven million unemployed, was obviously favourable for demagogues. But Hitler could not have succeeded against his many rivals if it had not been for the attraction of his own personality, which one can feel even in the clumsy writing of *Mein Kampf*, and which is no doubt overwhelming when one hears his speeches. I should like to put it on record that I have never been able to dislike Hitler. Ever since he came to power – till then, like nearly everyone,

I had been deceived into thinking that he did not matter – I have reflected that I would certainly kill him if I could get within reach of him, but that I could feel no personal animosity. The fact is that there is something deeply appealing about him. One feels it again when one sees his photographs – and I recommend especially the photograph at the beginning of Hurst and Blackett's edition, which shows Hitler in his early Brownshirt days. It is a pathetic, dog-like face, the face of a man suffering under intolerable wrongs. In a rather more manly way it reproduces the expression of innumerable pictures of Christ crucified, and there is little doubt that that is how Hitler sees himself. The initial, personal cause of his grievance against the universe can only be guessed at; but at any rate the grievance is there. He is the martyr, the victim, Prometheus chained to the rock, the self-sacrificing hero who fights single-handed against impossible odds. If he were killing a mouse he would know how to make it seem like a dragon. One feels, as with Napoleon, that he is fighting against destiny, that he *can't* win, and yet that he somehow deserves to. The attraction of such a pose is of course enormous; half the films that one sees turn upon some such theme.

Also he has grasped the falsity of the hedonistic attitude to life. Nearly all western thought since the last war, certainly all 'progressive' thought, has assumed tacitly that human beings desire nothing beyond ease, security and avoidance of pain. In such a view of life there is no room, for instance, for patriotism and the military virtues. The Socialist who finds his children playing with soldiers is usually upset, but he is never able to think of a substitute for the tin soldiers; tin pacifists somehow won't do. Hitler, because in his own joyless mind he feels it with exceptional strength, knows that human beings *don't* only want comfort, safety, short working-hours, hygiene, birth-control and, in general, common sense; they also, at least intermittently, want struggle and self-sacrifice, not to mention drums, flags and loyalty-parades. However they may be as economic theories, Fascism and Nazism are psychologically far sounder than any hedonistic conception of life. The same is probably true of Stalin's militarized version of Socialism. All three of the great dictators have enhanced their power by imposing intolerable burdens on their peoples. Whereas Socialism, and even capitalism in a more grudging way, have said to people 'I offer you a good time,' Hitler has said to them 'I offer you struggle, danger and death,' and as a result a whole nation flings itself at his feet. Perhaps later on they will get sick of it and change their minds, as at the end of the last war. After a few years of slaughter and starvation 'Greatest happiness of the greatest number' is a good slogan, but at this moment 'Better an end with horror than a horror without end' is a winner. Now that we are fighting against the man who coined it, we ought not to underrate its emotional appeal.

New English Weekly, 21 March 1940

Charles Reade

Since Charles Reade's books are published in cheap editions one can assume that he still has his following, but it is unusual to meet anyone who has voluntarily read him. In most people his name seems to evoke, at most, a vague memory of 'doing' *The Cloister and the Hearth* as a school holiday task. It is his bad luck to be remembered by this particular book, rather as Mark Twain, thanks to the films, is chiefly remembered by *A Connecticut Yankee in King Arthur's Court*. Reade wrote several dull books, and *The Cloister and the Hearth* is one of them. But he also wrote three novels which I personally would back to outlive the entire works of Meredith and George Eliot, besides some brilliant long-short stories such as *A Jack of All Trades* and *The Autobiography of a Thief*.

What is the attraction of Reade? At bottom it is the same charm as one finds in R. Austin Freeman's detective stories or Lieutenant-Commander Gould's collections of curiosities – the charm of useless knowledge. Reade was a man of what one might call penny-encyclopaedic learning. He possessed vast stocks of disconnected information which a lively narrative gift allowed him to cram into books which would at any rate pass as novels. If you have the sort of mind that takes a pleasure in dates, lists, catalogues, concrete details, descriptions of processes, junk-shop windows and back numbers of the *Exchange and Mart*, the sort of mind that likes knowing exactly how a medieval catapult worked or just what objects a prison cell of the eighteen-forties contained, then you can hardly help enjoying Reade. He himself, of course, did not see his work in quite this light. He prided himself on his accuracy and compiled his books largely from newspaper cuttings, but the strange facts which he collected were subsidiary to what he would have regarded as his 'purpose'. For he was a social reformer in a fragmentary way, and made vigorous attacks on such diverse evils as blood-letting, the treadmill, private lunatic asylums, clerical celibacy and tight-lacing.

My own favourite has always been *Foul Play*, which as it happens is not an attack on anything in particular. Like most nineteenth-century novels *Foul Play* is too complicated to be summarized, but its central story is that of a young clergyman, Robert Penfold, who is unjustly convicted of forgery, is transported to Australia, absconds in disguise, and is wrecked on a desert island together with the heroine. Here, of course, Reade is in his element. Of all men who ever lived, he was the best fitted to write a desert-island story. Some desert-island stories, of course, are worse than others, but none is altogether bad when it sticks to the actual concrete details of the struggle to keep alive. A list of the objects in a shipwrecked man's possession is probably the surest winner in fiction, surer even that a trial scene. Nearly thirty years after reading the book I can still remember more or less exactly what things the three heroes of Ballantyne's *Coral Island* possessed between them. (A telescope, six yards of whipcord, a penknife, a brass ring and a piece of hoop iron.) Even a dismal book like *Robinson Crusoe*, so unreadable as a whole that few people even know that the second part exists, becomes interesting when it describes Crusoe's efforts to make a table, glaze earthenware and grow a patch of wheat. Reade, however, was an expert on desert islands, or at any rate he was very well up in the geography textbooks of the time. Moreover he was the kind of man who would have been at home on a desert island himself. He would never, like Crusoe, have been stumped by such an easy problem as that of leavening bread and, unlike Ballantyne, he knew that civilized men cannot make fire by rubbing sticks together.

The hero of *Foul Play*, like most of Reade's heroes, is a kind of superman. He is hero, saint, scholar, gentleman, athlete, pugilist, navigator, physiologist, botanist, blacksmith and carpenter all rolled into one, the sort of compendium of all the talents that Reade honestly imaged to be the normal product of an English university. Needless to say, it is only a month or two before this wonderful clergyman has got the desert island running like a West End hotel. Even before reaching the island, when the last survivors of the wrecked ship are dying of thirst in an open boat, he has shown his ingenuity by constructing a distilling apparatus with a jar, a hot-water bottle and a piece of tubing. But his best stroke of all is the way in which he contrives to leave the island. He himself, with a price on his head, would be glad enough to remain, but the heroine, Helen Rollestone, who has no idea that he is a convict, is naturally anxious to escape. She asks Robert to turn his 'great mind' to this problem. The first difficulty, of course, is to discover exactly where the island is. Luckily, however, Helen is still wearing her watch, which is still keeping Sydney time. By fixing a stick in the ground and watching its shadow Robert notes the exact moment of noon, after which it is a simple matter to work out the longitude – for naturally a man of his calibre would know the longitude of Sydney. It is equally natural that he can determine the latitude within a degree or two by the nature of the vegetation. But the next difficulty is to send a message to the outside world. After some thought Robert writes a series of messages on pieces of parchment made from seals' bladders, with ink obtained from cochineal insects. He has noticed that migrant birds often use the island as a stopping-place, and he fixes on ducks as the likeliest messengers, because every duck is liable to be shot sooner or later. By a stratagem often used in India he captures a number of ducks, ties a message to each of their legs and lets them go. Finally, of course, one of the ducks takes refuge on a ship, and the couple are rescued, but even then the story is barely half finished. There follow enormous ramifications, plots and counterplots, intrigues, triumphs and disasters, ending with the vindication of Robert, and wedding bells.

In any of Reade's three best books, *Foul Play*, *Hard Cash* and *It Is Never Too Late to Mend*, it is not fair to say that the sole interest is in the technical detail. His power of descriptive writing, especially of describing violent action, is also very striking, and on a serial-story level he is a wonderful contriver of plots. Simply as a novelist it is impossible to take him seriously, because he has no sense whatever of character or of probability, but he himself had the advantage of believing in even the absurdest details of his own stories. He wrote of life as he saw it, and many Victorians saw it in the same way: that is, as a series of tremendous melodramas, with virtue triumphant every time. Of all the nineteenth-century novelists who have remained readable, he is perhaps the only one who is completely in tune with his own age. For all his unconventionality, his 'purpose', his eagerness to expose abuses, he never makes a fundamental criticism. Save for a few surface evils he sees nothing wrong in an acquisitive society, with its equation of money and virtue, its pious millionaires and erastian clergymen. Perhaps nothing gives one his measure better than the fact that in introducing Robert Penfold, at the beginning of *Foul Play*, he mentions that he is a scholar and a cricketer and only thirdly and almost casually adds that he is a priest.

That is not to say that Reade's social conscience was not sound so far as it went, and in several minor ways he probably helped to educate public opinion. His attack on the prison system in *It Is Never Too Late to Mend* is relevant to this day, or was so till very recently, and in his medical theories he is said to have been a long way ahead of his time. What he lacked was any notion that the early railway age, with the special scheme of values appropriate to it, was not going to last for ever. This is a little surprising when one remembers that he was the brother of Winwood Reade. However hasty and unbalanced Winwood Reade's *Martyrdom of Man* may seem now, it is a book that shows an astonishing width of vision, and it is probably the unacknowledged grandparent of the 'outlines' so popular today. Charles Reade might have written an 'outline' of phrenology, cabinet-making or the habits of whales, but not of human history. He was simply a middle-class gentleman with a little more conscience than most, a scholar who happened to prefer popular science to the classics. Just for that reason he is one of the best 'escape' novelists we have. *Foul Play* and *Hard Cash* would be good books to send to a soldier enduring the miseries of trench warfare, for instance. There are no problems in them, no genuine 'message', merely the fascination of a gifted mind functioning within very narrow limits, and offering as complete a detachment from real life as a game of chess or a jigsaw puzzle.

New Statesman and Nation, 17 August 1940

The Lion and the Unicorn: Socialism and the English Genius

Part I: England Your England

ONE

As I write, highly civilized human beings are flying overhead, trying to kill me.

They do not feel any enmity against me as an individual, nor I against them. They are 'only doing their duty', as the saying goes. Most of them, I have no doubt, are kind-hearted law-abiding men who would never dream of committing murder in private life. On the other hand, if one of them succeeds in blowing me to pieces with a well-placed bomb, he will never sleep any the worse for it. He is serving his country, which has the power to absolve him from evil.

One cannot see the modern world as it is unless one recognizes the overwhelming strength of patriotism, national loyalty. In certain circumstances it can break down, at certain levels of civilization it does not exist, but as a *positive* force there is nothing to set beside it. Christianity and international Socialism are as weak as straw in comparison with it. Hitler and Mussolini rose to power in their own countries very largely because they could grasp this fact and their opponents could not.

Also, one must admit that the divisions between nation and nation are founded on real differences of outlook. Till recently it was thought proper to pretend that all human beings are very much alike, but in fact anyone able to use his eyes knows that the average of human behaviour differs enormously from country to country. Things that could happen in one country could not happen in another. Hitler's June Purge, for instance, could not have happened in England. And, as western peoples go, the English are very highly differentiated. There is a sort of backhanded admission of this in the dislike which nearly all foreigners feel for our national way of life. Few Europeans can endure living in England, and even Americans often feel more at home in Europe.

When you come back to England from any foreign country, you have immediately the sensation of breathing a different air. Even in the first few minutes dozens of small things conspire to give you this feeling. The beer is bitterer, the coins are heavier, the grass is greener, the advertisements are more blatant. The crowds in the big towns, with their mild knobby faces, their bad teeth and gentle manners, are different from a European crowd. Then the vastness of England swallows you up, and you lose for a while your feeling that the whole nation has a single identifiable character. Are there really such things as nations? Are we not 46 million individuals, all different? And the diversity of it, the chaos! The clatter of clogs in the Lancashire mill towns, the to-and-fro of the lorries on the Great North Road, the queues outside the Labour Exchanges, the rattle of pin-tables in the Soho pubs, the old maids biking to Holy Communion through the mists of the autumn mornings – all these are not only fragments, but *characteristic* fragments, of the English scene. How can one make a pattern out of this muddle?

But talk to foreigners, read foreign books or newspapers, and you are brought back to the same thought. Yes, there *is* something distinctive and recognizable in English civilization. It is a culture as individual as that of Spain. It is somehow bound up with solid breakfasts and gloomy Sundays, smoky towns and winding roads, green fields and red pillar-boxes. It has a flavour of its own. Moreover it is continuous, it stretches into the future and the past, there is something in it that persists, as in a living creature. What can the England of 1940 have in common with the England of 1840? But then, what have you in common with the child of five whose photograph your mother keeps on the mantelpiece? Nothing, except that you happen to be the same person.

And above all, it is *your* civilization, it is *you*. However much you hate it or laugh at it, you will never be happy away from it for any length of time. The suet puddings and the red pillar-boxes have entered into your soul. Good or evil, it is yours, you belong to it, and this side the grave you will never get away from the marks that it has given you.

Meanwhile England, together with the rest of the world, is changing. And like everything else it can change only in certain directions, which up to a point can be foreseen. That is not to say that the future is fixed, merely that certain alternatives are possible and others not. A seed may grow or not grow, but at any rate a turnip seed never grows into a parsnip. It is therefore of the deepest importance to try and determine what England *is*, before guessing what part England *can play* in the huge events that are happening.

TWO

National characteristics are not easy to pin down, and when pinned down they often turn out to be trivialities or seem to have no connection with one another. Spaniards are cruel to animals, Italians can do nothing without making a deafening noise, the Chinese are addicted to gambling. Obviously such things don't matter in themselves. Nevertheless, nothing is causeless, and even the fact that Englishmen have bad teeth can tell one something about the realities of English life.

Here are a couple of generalizations about England that would be accepted by almost all observers. One is that the English are not gifted artistically. They are not as musical as the Germans or Italians, painting and sculpture have never flourished in England as they have in France. Another is that, as Europeans go, the English are not intellectual. They have a horror of abstract thought, they feel no need for any philosophy or systematic 'world-view'. Nor is this because they are 'practical', as they are so fond of claiming for themselves. One has only to look at their methods of town planning and water supply, their obstinate clinging to everything that is out of date and a nuisance, a spelling system that defies analysis and a system of weights and measures that is intelligible only to the compilers of arithmetic books, to see how little they care about mere efficiency. But they have a certain power of acting without taking thought. Their world-famed hypocrisy – their double-faced attitude towards the Empire, for instance – is bound up with this. Also, in moments of supreme crisis the whole nation can suddenly draw together and act upon a species of instinct, really a code of conduct which is understood by almost everyone, though never formulated. The phrase that Hitler coined for the Germans, 'a sleep-walking people', would have been better applied to the English. Not that there is anything to be proud of in being called a sleep-walker.

But here it is worth noting a minor English trait which is extremely well marked though not often commented on, and that is a love of flowers. This is one of the first things that one notices when one reaches England from abroad, especially if one is coming from southern Europe. Does it not contradict the English indifference to the arts? Not really, because it is found in people who have no aesthetic feelings whatever. What it does link up with, however, is another English characteristic which is so much a part of us that we barely notice it, and that is the addiction to hobbies and spare-time occupations, the *privateness* of English life. We are a nation of flower-lovers, but also a nation of stamp-collectors, pigeon-fanciers, amateur carpenters, coupon-snippers, darts-players, crossword-puzzle fans. All the culture that is most truly native centres round things which even when they are communal are not official – the pub, the football match, the back garden, the fireside and the 'nice cup of tea'. The liberty of the individual is still believed in, almost as in the nineteenth century. But this has nothing to do with economic liberty, the right to exploit others for profit. It is the liberty to have a home of your own, to do what you like in your spare time, to choose your own amusements instead of having them chosen for you from above. The most hateful of all names in an English ear is Nosey Parker. It is obvious, of course, that even this purely private liberty is a lost cause. Like all other modern peoples, the English are in process of being numbered, labelled, conscripted, 'co-ordinated'. But the pull of their impulses is in the other direction, and the kind of regimentation that can be imposed on them will be modified in consequence. No party rallies, no Youth Movements, no coloured shirts, no Jew-baiting or 'spontaneous' demonstrations. No Gestapo either, in all probability.

But in all societies the common people must live to some extent *against* the existing order. The genuinely popular culture of England is something that goes on beneath the surface, unofficially and more or less frowned on by the authorities. One thing one notices if one looks directly at the common people, especially in the big towns, is that they are not puritanical. They are inveterate gamblers, drink as much beer as their wages will permit, are devoted to bawdy jokes, and use probably the foulest language in the world. They have to satisfy these tastes in the face of astonishing, hypocritical laws (licensing laws, lottery acts, etc., etc.) which are designed to interfere with everybody but in practice allow everything to happen. Also, the common people are without definite religious belief, and have been so for centuries. The Anglican Church never had a real hold on them, it was simply a preserve of the landed gentry, and the Nonconformist sects only influenced minorities. And yet they have retained a deep tinge of Christian feeling, while almost forgetting the name of Christ. The power-worship which is the new religion of Europe, and which has infected the English intelligentsia, has never touched the common people. They have never caught up with power politics. The 'realism' which is preached in Japanese and Italian newspapers would horrify them. One can learn a good deal about the spirit of England from the comic coloured postcards that you see in the windows of cheap stationers' shops. These things are a sort of diary upon which the English people have unconsciously recorded themselves. Their old-fashioned outlook, their graded snobberies, their mixture of bawdiness and hypocrisy, their extreme gentleness, their deeply moral attitude to life, are all mirrored there.

The gentleness of the English civilization is perhaps its most marked characteristic. You notice it the instant you set foot on English soil. It is a land where the bus conductors are good-tempered and the policemen carry no revolvers. In no country inhabited by white men is it easier to shove people off the pavement. And with this goes something that is always written off by European observers as 'decadence' or hypocrisy, the English hatred of war and militarism. It is rooted deep in history, and it is strong in the lower-middle class as well as the working class. Successive wars have shaken it but not destroyed it. Well within living memory it was common for 'the redcoats' to be booed at in the streets and for the landlords of respectable public houses to refuse to allow soldiers on the premises. In peace time, even when there are two million unemployed, it is difficult to fill the ranks of the tiny standing army, which is officered by the country gentry and a specialized stratum of the middle class, and manned by farm labourers and slum proletarians. The mass of the people are without military knowledge or tradition, and their attitude towards war is invariably defensive. No politician could rise to power by promising them conquests or military 'glory', no Hymn of Hate has ever made any appeal to them. In the last war the songs which the soldiers made up and sang of their own accord were not vengeful but humorous and mock-defeatist.[1] The only enemy they ever named was the sergeant-major.

In England all the boasting and flag-wagging, the 'Rule Britannia' stuff, is done by small minorities. The patriotism of the common people is not vocal or even conscious. They do not retain among their historical memories the name of a single military victory. English literature, like other literatures, is full of battle-poems, but it is worth noticing that the ones that have won for themselves a kind of popularity are always a tale of disasters and retreats. There is no popular poem about Trafalgar or Waterloo, for instance. Sir John Moore's army at Corunna, fighting a desperate rearguard action before escaping overseas (just like Dunkirk!) has more appeal than a brilliant victory. The most stirring battle-poem in English is about a brigade of cavalry which charged in the wrong direction. And of the last war, the four names which have really engraved themselves on the popular memory are Mons, Ypres, Gallipoli and Passchendaele, every time a disaster. The names of the great battles that finally broke the German armies are simply unknown to the general public.

The reason why the English anti-militarism disgusts foreign observers is that it ignores the existence of the British Empire. It looks like sheer hypocrisy. After all, the English have absorbed a quarter of the earth and held onto it by means of a huge navy. How dare they then turn round and say that war is wicked?

It is quite true that the English are hypocritical about their Empire. In the working class this hypocrisy takes the form of not knowing that the Empire exists. But their dislike of standing armies is a perfect sound instinct. A navy employs comparatively few people, and it is an external weapon which cannot affect home politics directly. Military dictatorships exist everywhere, but there is no such thing as a naval dictatorship. What English people of nearly all classes loathe from the bottom of their hearts is the swaggering officer type, the jingle of spurs and the crash of boots. Decades before Hitler was ever heard of, the word 'Prussian' had much the same significance in England as 'Nazi' has today. So deep does this feeling go that for a hundred years past the officers of the British army, in peace time, have always worn civilian clothes when off duty.

One rapid but fairly sure guide to the social atmosphere of a country is the parade-step of its army. A military parade is really a kind of ritual dance, something like a ballet, expressing a certain philosophy of life. The goose-step, for instance, is one of the most horrible sights in the world, far more terrifying than a dive-bomber. It is simply an affirmation of naked power; contained in it, quite consciously and intentionally, is the vision of a boot crashing down on a face. Its ugliness is part of its essence, for what it is saying is 'Yes, I *am* ugly, and you daren't laugh at me', like the bully who makes faces at his victim. Why is the goose-step not used in England? There are, heaven knows, plenty of army officers who would be only too glad to introduce some such thing. It is not used because the people in the street would laugh. Beyond a certain point, military display is only possible in countries where the common

---

[1] For example:

I don't want to join the bloody Army,
I don't want to go unto the war;
I want no more to roam,
I'd rather stay at home,
Living on the earnings of a whore.

But it was not in that spirit that they fought. [Author's footnote.]

people dare not laugh at the army. The Italians adopted the goose-step at about the time when Italy passed definitely under German control, and, as one would expect, they do it less well than the Germans. The Vichy government, if it survives, is bound to introduce a stiffer parade-ground discipline into what is left of the French army. In the British army the drill is rigid and complicated, full of memories of the eighteenth century, but without definite swagger; the march is merely a formalized walk. It belongs to a society which is ruled by the sword, no doubt, but a sword which must never be taken out of the scabbard.

And yet the gentleness of English civilization is mixed up with barbarities and anachronisms. Our criminal law is as out-of-date as the muskets in the Tower. Over against the Nazi Storm Trooper you have got to set that typically English figure, the hanging judge, some gouty old bully with his mind rooted in the nineteenth century, handing out savage sentences. In England people are still hanged by the neck and flogged with the cat o' nine tails. Both of these punishments are obscene as well as cruel, but there has never been any genuinely popular outcry against them. People accept them (and Dartmoor, and Borstal) almost as they accept the weather. They are part of 'the law', which is assumed to be unalterable.

Here one comes upon an all-important English trait: the respect for constitutionalism and legality, the belief in 'the law' as something above the State and above the individual, something which is cruel and stupid, of course, but at any rate *incorruptible*.

It is not that anyone imagines the law to be just. Everyone knows that there is one law for the rich and another for the poor. But no one accepts the implications of this, everyone takes it for granted that the law, such as it is, will be respected, and feels a sense of outrage when it is not. Remarks like 'They can't run me in; I haven't done anything wrong', or 'They can't do that; it's against the law', are part of the atmosphere of England. The professed enemies of society have this feeling as strongly as anyone else. One sees it in prison-books like Wilfred Macartney's *Walls Have Mouths* or Jim Phelan's *Jail Journey*, in the solemn idiocies that take place at the trials of conscientious objectors, in letters to the papers from eminent Marxist professors, pointing out that this or that is a 'miscarriage of British justice'. Everyone believes in his heart that the law can be, ought to be, and, on the whole, will be impartially administered. The totalitarian idea that there is no such thing as law, there is only power, has never taken root. Even the intelligentsia have only accepted it in theory.

An illusion can become a half-truth, a mask can alter the expression of a face. The familiar arguments to the effect that democracy is 'just the same as' or 'just as bad as' totalitarianism never take account of this fact. All such arguments boil down to saying that half a loaf is the same as no bread. In England such concepts as justice, liberty and objective truth are still believed in. They may be illusions, but they are very powerful illusions. The belief in them influences conduct, national life is different because of them. In proof of which, look about you. Where are the rubber truncheons, where is the castor oil? The sword is still in the scabbard, and while it stays there corruption cannot go beyond a certain point. The English electoral system, for instance, is an all but open fraud. In a dozen obvious ways it is gerrymandered in the interest of the moneyed class. But until some deep change has occurred in the public mind, it cannot become *completely* corrupt. You do not arrive at the polling booth to find men with revolvers telling you which way to vote. nor are the votes miscounted, nor is there any direct bribery. Even hypocrisy is a powerful safeguard. The hanging judge, that evil old man in scarlet robe and horse-hair wig, whom nothing short of dynamite will ever teach what century he is living in, but who will at any rate interpret the law according to the books and will in no circumstances take a money bribe, is one of the symbolic figures of England. He is a symbol of the strange mixture of reality and illusion, democracy and privilege, humbug and decency, the subtle network of compromises, by which the nation keeps itself in its familiar shape.

THREE

I have spoke all the while of 'the nation, 'England', 'Britain', as though 45 million souls could somehow be treated as a unit. But is not England notoriously two nations, the rich and the poor? Dare one pretend that there is anything in common between people with £100,000 a year and people with £1 a week? And even Welsh and Scottish readers are likely to have been offended because I have used the word 'England' oftener than 'Britain', as though the whole population dwelt in London and the Home Counties and neither north nor west possessed a culture of its own.

One gets a better view of this question if one considers the minor point first. It is quite true that the so-called races of Britain feel themselves to be very different from one another. A Scotsman, for instance, does not thank you if you call him an Englishman. You can see the hesitation we feel on this point by the fact that we call our islands by no less than six different names, England, Britain, Great Britain, the British Isles, the United Kingdom and, in very exalted moments, Albion. Even the differences between north and south England loom large in our own eyes. But somehow these differences fade away the moment that any two Britons are confronted by a European. It is very rare to meet a foreigner, other than an American, who can distinguish between English and Scots or even English and Irish. To a Frenchman, the Breton and the Auvergnat seem very different beings, and the accent of Marseilles is a stock joke in Paris. Yet we speak of 'France' and 'the French', recognizing France as an entity, a single civilization, which in fact it is. So also with ourselves. Looked at from the outside, even the cockney and the Yorkshireman have a strong family resemblance.

And even the distinction between rich and poor dwindles somewhat when one regards the nation from the outside. There is no question about the inequality of wealth in England. It is grosser than in any European country, and you have only to look down the nearest street to see it. Economically, England is certainly two nations, if not three or four. But at the same time the vast majority of the people *feel* themselves to be a single nation and are conscious of resembling one another more than they resemble foreigners. Patriotism is usually stronger than class-hatred, and always stronger than any kind of internationalism. Except for a brief moment in 1920 (the 'Hands off Russia' movement) the British working class have never thought or acted internationally. For two and a half years they watched their comrades in Spain slowly strangled, and never aided them by even a single strike.[1] But when their own country (the country of Lord Nuffield and Mr Montagu

[1] It is true that they aided them to a certain extent with money. Still, the sums raised for the various aid-Spain funds would not equal five per cent of the turnover of the Football Pools during the same period. [Author's footnote.]

Norman) was in danger, their attitude was very different. At the moment when it seemed likely that England might be invaded, Anthony Eden appealed over the radio for Local Defence Volunteers. He got a quarter of a million men in the first twenty-four hours, and another million in the subsequent month. One has only to compare these figures with, for instance, the number of conscientious objectors to see how vast is the strength of traditional loyalties compared with new ones.

In England patriotism takes different forms in different classes, but it runs like a connecting thread through nearly all of them. Only the Europeanized intelligentsia are really immune to it. As a positive emotion it is stronger in the middle class than in the upper class – the cheap public schools, for instance, are more given to patriotic demonstrations than the expensive ones – but the number of definitely treacherous rich men, the Laval-Quisling type, is probably very small. In the working class patriotism is profound, but it is unconscious. The working man's heart does not leap when he sees a Union Jack. But the famous 'insularity' and 'xenophobia' of the English is far stronger in the working class than in the bourgeoisie. In all countries the poor are more national than the rich, but the English working class are outstanding in their abhorrence of foreign habits. Even when they are obliged to live abroad for years they refuse either to accustom themselves to foreign food or to learn foreign languages. Nearly every Englishman of working-class origin considers it effeminate to pronounce a foreign word correctly. During the war of 1914–18 the English working class were in contact with foreigners to an extent that is rarely possible. The sole result was that they brought back a hatred of all Europeans, except the Germans, whose courage they admired. In four years on French soil they did not even acquire a liking for wine. The insularity of the English, their refusal to take foreigners seriously, is a folly that has to be paid for very heavily from time to time. But it plays its part in the English mystique, and the intellectuals who have tried to break it down have generally done more harm than good. At bottom it is the same quality in the English character that repels the tourist and keeps out the invader.

Here one comes back to two English characteristics that I pointed out, seemingly rather at random, at the beginning of the last chapter. One is the lack of artistic ability. This is perhaps another way of saying that the English are outside the European culture. For there is one art in which they have shown plenty of talent, namely literature. But this is also the only art that cannot cross frontiers. Literature, especially poetry, and lyric poetry most of all, is a kind of family joke, with little or no value outside its own language-group. Except for Shakespeare, the best English poets are barely known in Europe, even as names. The only poets who are widely read are Byron, who is admired for the wrong reasons, and Oscar Wilde, who is pitied as a victim of English hypocrisy. And linked up with this, though not very obviously, is the lack of philosophical faculty, the absence in nearly all Englishmen of any need for an ordered system of thought or even for the use of logic.

Up to a point, the sense of national unity is a substitute for a 'world-view'. Just because patriotism is all but universal and not even the rich are uninfluenced by it, there can be moments when the whole nation suddenly swings together and does the same thing, like a herd of cattle facing a wolf. There was such a moment, unmistakably, at the time of the disaster in France. After eight months of vaguely wondering what the war was about, the people suddenly knew what they had got to do: first, to get the army away from

Dunkirk, and secondly to prevent invasion. It was like the awakening of a giant. Quick! Danger! The Philistines be upon thee, Samson! And then the swift unanimous action – and then, alas, the prompt relapse into sleep. In a divided nation that would have been exactly the moment for a big peace movement to arise. But does this mean that the instinct of the English will always tell them to do the right thing? Not at all, merely that it will tell them to do the same thing. In the 1931 General Election, for instance, we all did the wrong thing in perfect unison. We were as single-minded as the Gadarene swine. But I honestly doubt whether we can say that we were shoved down the slope against our will.

It follows that British democracy is less of a fraud than it sometimes appears. A foreign observer sees only the huge inequality of wealth, the unfair electoral system, the governing-class control over the press, the radio and education, and concludes that democracy is simply a polite name for dictatorship. But this ignores the considerable agreement that does unfortunately exist between the leaders and the led. However much one may hate to admit it, it is almost certain that between 1931 and 1940 the National Government represented the will of the mass of the people. It tolerated slums, unemployment and a cowardly foreign policy. Yes, but so did public opinion. It was a stagnant period, and its natural leaders were mediocrities.

In spite of the campaigns of a few thousand left-wingers, it is fairly certain that the bulk of the English people were behind Chamberlain's foreign policy. More, it is fairly certain that the same struggle was going on in Chamberlain's mind as in the minds of ordinary people. His opponents professed to see in him a dark and wily schemer, plotting to sell England to Hitler, but it is far likelier that he was merely a stupid old man doing his best according to his very dim lights. It is difficult otherwise to explain the contradictions of his policy, his failure to grasp any of the courses that were open to him. Like the mass of the people, he did not want to pay the price either of peace or of war. And public opinion was behind him all the while, in policies that were completely incompatible with one another. It was behind him when he went to Munich, when he tried to come to an understanding with Russia, when he gave the guarantee to Poland, when he honoured it, and when he prosecuted the war half-heartedly. Only when the results of his policy became apparent did it turn against him; which is to say that it turned against its own lethargy of the past seven years. Thereupon the people picked a leader nearer to their mood, Churchill, who was at any rate able to grasp that wars are not won without fighting. Later, perhaps, they will pick another leader who can grasp that only Socialist nations can fight effectively.

Do I mean by all this that England is a genuine democracy? No, not even a reader of the *Daily Telegraph* could quite swallow that.

England is the most class-ridden country under the sun. It is a land of snobbery and privilege, ruled largely by the old and silly. But in any calculation about it one has got to take into account its emotional unity, the tendency of nearly all its inhabitants to feel alike and act together in moments of supreme crisis. It is the only great country in Europe that is not obliged to drive hundreds of thousands of its nationals into exile or the concentration camp. At this moment, after a year of war, newspapers and pamphlets abusing the Government, praising the enemy and clamouring for surrender are being sold on the streets, almost without interference. And this is less from a respect for freedom of speech than from a simple perception that these things don't matter. It is safe to let a paper like *Peace News* be sold, because it is certain that ninety-five per cent of the population will never want to read it. The nation is bound together by an invisible chain. At any normal time the ruling class will rob, mismanage, sabotage, lead us into the muck; but let popular opinion really make itself heard, let them get a tug from below that they cannot avoid feeling, and it is difficult for them not to respond. The left-wing writers who denounce the whole of the ruling class as 'pro-Fascist' are grossly over-simplifying. Even among the inner clique of politicians who brought us to our present pass, it is doubtful whether there were any *conscious* traitors. The corruption that happens in England is seldom of that kind. Nearly always it is more in the nature of self-deception, of the right hand not knowing what the left hand doeth. And being unconscious, it is limited. One sees this at its most obvious in the English press. Is the English press honest or dishonest? At normal times it is deeply dishonest. All the papers that matter live off their advertisements, and the advertisers exercise an indirect censorship over news. Yet I do not suppose there is one paper in England that can be straightforwardly bribed with hard cash. In the France of the Third Republic all but a very few of the newspapers could notoriously be bought over the counter like so many pounds of cheese. Public life in England has never been *openly* scandalous. It has not reached the pitch of disintegration at which humbug can be dropped.

England is not the jewelled isle of Shakespeare's much-quoted passage, nor is it the inferno depicted by Dr Goebbels. More than either it resembles a family, a rather stuffy Victorian family, with not many black sheep in it but with all its cupboards bursting with skeletons. It has rich relations who have to be kow-towed to and poor relations who are horribly sat upon, and there is a deep conspiracy of silence about the source of the family income. It is a family in which the young are generally thwarted and most of the power is in the hands of irresponsible uncles and bedridden aunts. Still, it is a family. It has its private language and its common memories, and at the approach of an enemy it closes its ranks. A family with the wrong members in control – that, perhaps, is as near as one can come to describing England in a phrase.

FOUR

Probably the battle of Waterloo *was* won on the playing-fields of Eton, but the opening battles of all subsequent wars have been lost there. One of the dominant facts in English life during the past three-quarters of a century has been the decay of ability in the ruling class.

In the years between 1920 and 1940 it was happening with the speed of a chemical reaction. Yet at the moment of writing it is still possible to speak of a ruling class. Like the knife which has had two new blades and three new handles, the upper fringe of English society is still almost what it was in the mid-nineteenth century. After 1832 the old land-owning aristocracy steadily lost power, but instead of disappearing or becoming a fossil they simply intermarried with the merchants, manufacturers and financiers who had replaced them, and soon turned them into accurate copies of themselves. The wealthy ship-owner or cotton-miller set up for himself an alibi as a country gentleman, while his sons learned the right mannerisms at public schools which had been designed for just that purpose. England was ruled by an aristocracy constantly recruited from parvenus. And considering what energy the self-made men possessed, and considering that they were buying their way into a class which at any rate had a tradition of public service, one might have expected that able rulers could be produced in some such way.

And yet somehow the ruling class decayed, lost its ability, its daring, finally even its ruthlessness, until a time came when stuffed shirts like Eden or Halifax could stand out as men of exceptional talent. As for Baldwin, one could not even dignify him with the name of stuffed shirt. He was simply a hole in the air. The mishandling of England's domestic problems during the nineteen-twenties had been bad enough, but British foreign policy between 1931 and 1939 is one of the wonders of the world. Why? What had happened? What was it that at every decisive moment made every British statesman do the wrong thing with so unerring an instinct?

The underlying fact was that the whole position of the moneyed class had long ceased to be justifiable. There they sat, at the centre of a vast empire and a world-wide financial network, drawing interest and profits and spending them – on what? It was fair to say that life within the British Empire was in many ways better than life outside it. Still, the Empire was undeveloped, India slept in the Middle Ages, the Dominions lay empty, with foreigners jealously barred out, and even England was full of slums and unemployment. Only half a million people, the people in the country houses, definitely benefited from the existing system. Moreover, the tendency of small businesses to merge together into large ones robbed more and more of the moneyed class of their function and turned them into mere *owners*, their work being done for them by salaried managers and technicians. For long past there had been in England an entirely functionless class, living on money that was invested they hardly knew where, the 'idle rich', the people whose photographs you can look at in the *Tatler* and the *Bystander*, always supposing that you want to. The existence of these people was by any standard unjustifiable. They were simply parasites, less useful to society than his fleas are to a dog.

By 1920 there were many people who were aware of all this. By 1930 millions were aware of it. But the British ruling class obviously could not admit to themselves that their usefulness was at an end. Had they done that they would have had to abdicate. For it was not possible for them to turn themselves into mere bandits, like the American millionaires, consciously clinging to unjust privileges and beating down opposition by bribery and tear-gas bombs. After all, they belonged to a class with a certain tradition, they had been to public schools where the duty of dying for you country, if necessary, is laid down as the first and greatest of the Commandments. They had to *feel* themselves true patriots, even while they plundered their countrymen. Clearly there was only one escape for them – into stupidity. They could keep society in its existing shape only by being *unable* to grasp that any improvement was possible. Difficult though this was, they achieved it, largely by fixing their eyes on the past and refusing to notice the changes that were going on round them.

There is much in England that this explains. It explains the decay of country life, due to the keeping-up of a sham feudalism which drives the more spirited workers off the land. It explains the immobility of the public schools, which have barely altered since the 'eighties of the last century. It explains the military incompetence which has again and again startled the world. Since the 'fifties every war in which England has engaged has started off with a series of disasters, after which the situation has been saved by people comparatively low in the social scale. The higher commanders, drawn from the aristocracy, could never prepare for modern war, because in order to do so they would have had to admit to themselves that the world was changing. They have always clung to obsolete methods and weapons, because they inevitably saw each war as a repetition of the last. Before the Boer War they prepared for the Zulu War, before the 1914 for the Boer War, and before the present war for 1914. Even at this moment hundreds of thousands of men in England are being trained with the bayonet, a weapon entirely useless except for opening tins. It is worth noticing that the navy and, latterly, the air force, have always been more efficient than the regular army. But the navy is only partially, and the air force hardly at all, within the ruling-class orbit.

It must be admitted that so long as things were peaceful the methods of the British ruling class served them well enough. Their own people manifestly tolerated them. However unjustly England might be organized, it was at any rate not torn by class warfare or haunted by secret police. The Empire was peaceful as no area of comparable size has ever been. Throughout its vast extent, nearly a quarter of the earth, there were fewer armed men than would be found necessary by a minor Balkan state. As people to live under, and looking at them merely from a liberal, *negative* standpoint, the British ruling class had their points. They were preferable to the truly modern men, the Nazis and Fascists. But it had long been obvious that they would be helpless against any serious attack from the outside.

They could not struggle against Nazism or Fascism, because they could not understand them. Neither could they have struggled against Communism, if Communism had been a serious force in western Europe. To understand Fascism they would have had to study the theory of Socialism, which would have forced them to realize that the economic system by which they lived was unjust, inefficient and out-of-date. But it was exactly this fact that they had trained themselves never to face. They dealt with Fascism as the cavalry generals of 1914 dealt with the machine-gun – by ignoring it. After years of aggression and massacres, they had grasped only one fact, that Hitler and Mussolini were hostile to Communism. Therefore, it was argued, they *must* be friendly to the British dividend-drawer. Hence the truly frightening spectacle of Conservative MPs wildly cheering the news that British ships, bringing food to the Spanish Republican government, had been bombed by Italian aeroplanes. Even when they had begun to grasp that Fascism was dangerous, its essentially revolutionary nature, the huge military effort it was capable of making, the sort of tactics it would use, were quite beyond their comprehension. At the time of the Spanish civil war, anyone with as much political knowledge as can be acquired from a sixpenny pamphlet on Socialism knew that, if Franco won, the result would be strategically disastrous for England; and yet generals and admirals who had given their lives to the study of war were unable to grasp this fact. This vein of political ignorance runs right through English official life, through Cabinet ministers, ambassadors, consuls, judges, magistrates, policemen. The policeman who arrests the 'red' does not understand the theories the 'red' is preaching; if he did, his own position as bodyguard of the moneyed class might seem less pleasant to him. There is reason to think that even military espionage is hopelessly hampered by ignorance of the new economic doctrines and the ramifications of the underground parties.

The British ruling class were not altogether wrong in thinking that Fascism was on their side. It is a fact that any rich man, unless he is a Jew, has less to fear from Fascism than from either Communism or democratic Socialism. One ought never to forget this, for nearly the whole of German and Italian propaganda is designed to cover it up. The natural instinct of men like Simon, Hoare, Chamberlain, etc. was to come to an agreement with Hitler. But – and here the peculiar feature of English life that I have spoken of, the deep sense of national solidarity, comes in – they could only do so by breaking up the Empire and selling their own people into semi-slavery. A truly corrupt class would have done this without hesitation, as in France. But things had not gone that distance in England. Politicians who would make cringing speeches about 'the duty of loyalty to our conquerors' are hardly to be found in English public life. Tossed to and fro between their incomes and their principles, it was impossible that men like Chamberlain should do anything but make the worst of both worlds.

One thing that has always shown that the English ruling class are *morally* fairly sound, is that in time of war they are ready enough to get themselves killed. Several dukes, earls and what nots were killed in the recent campaign in Flanders. That could not happen if these people were the cynical scoundrels that they are sometimes declared to be. It is important not to misunderstand their motives, or one cannot predict their actions. What is to be expected of them is not treachery or physical cowardice, but stupidity, unconscious sabotage, an infallible instinct for doing the wrong thing. They are not wicked, or not altogether wicked; they are merely unteachable. Only when their money and power are gone will the younger among them begin to grasp what century they are living in.

FIVE

The stagnation of the Empire in the between-war years affected everyone in England, but it had an especially direct effect upon two important sub-sections of the middle class. One was the military and imperialist middle class, generally nicknamed the Blimps, and the other the left-wing intelligentsia. These two seemingly hostile types, symbolic opposites – the half-pay colonel with his bull neck and diminutive brain, like a dinosaur, the highbrow with his domed forehead and stalk-like neck – are mentally linked together and constantly interact upon one another; in any case they are born to a considerable extent into the same families.

Thirty years ago the Blimp class was already losing its vitality. The middle-class families celebrated by Kipling, the prolific lowbrow families whose sons officered the army and navy and swarmed over all the waste places of the earth from the Yukon to the Irrawaddy, were dwindling before 1914. The thing that had killed them was the telegraph. In a narrowing world, more and more governed from Whitehall, there was every year less room for individual initiative. Men like Clive, Nelson, Nicholson, Gordon would find no place for themselves in the modern British Empire. By 1920 nearly every inch of the colonial empire was in the grip of Whitehall. Well-meaning, over-civilized men, in dark suits and black felt hats, with neatly-rolled umbrellas crooked over the left forearm, were imposing their constipated view of life on Malaya and Nigeria, Mombasa and Mandalay. The one-time empire builders were reduced to the status of clerks, buried deeper and deeper under mounds of paper and red tape. In the early 'twenties one could see, all over the Empire, the older officials, who had known more spacious days, writhing impotently under the changes that were happening. From that time onwards it has been next door to impossible to induce young men of spirit to take any part in imperial administration. And what was true of the official world was true also of the commercial. The great monopoly companies swallowed up hosts of petty traders. Instead of going out to trade adventurously in the Indies one went to an office stool in Bombay or Singapore. And life in Bombay or Singapore was actually duller and safer than life in London. Imperialist sentiment remained strong in the middle class, chiefly owing to family tradition, but the job of administering the Empire had ceased to appeal. Few able men went east of Suez if there was any way of avoiding it.

But the general weakening of imperialism, and to some extent of the whole British morale, that took place during the nineteen-thirties, was partly the work of the left-wing intelligentsia, itself a kind of growth that had sprouted from the stagnation of the Empire.

It should be noted that there is now no intelligentsia that is not in some sense 'left'. Perhaps the last right-wing intellectual was T. E. Lawrence. Since about 1930 everyone describable as an 'intellectual' has lived in a state of chronic discontent with the existing order. Necessarily so, because society as it was constituted had no room for him. In an Empire that was simply stagnant, neither being developed nor falling to pieces, and in an England ruled by people whose chief asset was their stupidity, to be 'clever' was to be suspect. If you had the kind of brain that could understand the poems of T. S. Eliot or the theories of Karl Marx, the higher-ups would see to it that you were kept out of any important job. The intellectuals could find a function for themselves only in the literary reviews and the left-wing political parties.

The mentality of the English left-wing intelligentsia can be studied in half a dozen weekly and monthly papers. The immediately striking thing about all these papers is their generally negative, querulous attitude, their complete lack at all times of any constructive suggestion. There is little in them except the irresponsible carping of people who have never been and never expect to be in a position of power. Another marked characteristic is the emotional shallowness of people who live in a world of ideas and have little contact with physical reality. Many intellectuals of the Left were flabbily pacifist up to 1935, shrieked for war against Germany in the years 1935–9, and then promptly cooled off when the war started. It is broadly though not precisely true that the people who were most 'anti-Fascist' during the Spanish civil war are most defeatist now. And underlying this is the really important fact about so many of the English intelligentsia – their severance from the common culture of the country.

In intention, at any rate, the English intelligentsia are Europeanized. They take their cookery from Paris and their opinions from Moscow. In the general patriotism of the country they form a sort of island of dissident thought. England is perhaps the only great country whose intellectuals are ashamed of their own nationality. In left-wing circles it is always felt that there is something slightly disgraceful in being an Englishman and that it is a duty to snigger at every English institution, from horse racing to suet puddings. It is a strange fact, but it is unquestionably true, that almost any English intellectual would feel more ashamed of standing to attention during 'God save the King' than of stealing from a poor box. All through the critical years many left-wingers were chipping away at English morale, trying to spread an outlook that was sometimes squashily pacifist, sometimes violently pro-Russian, but always anti-British. It is questionable how much effect this had, but it certainly had some. If the English people suffered for several years a real weakening of morale, so that the Fascist nations judged that they were 'decadent' and that it was safe to plunge into war, the intellectual sabotage from the Left was partly responsible. Both the *New Statesman* and the *News Chronicle* cried out against the Munich settlement, but even they had done something to make it possible. Ten years of systematic Blimp-baiting affected even the Blimps themselves and made it harder than it had been before to get intelligent young men to enter the armed forces. Given the stagnation of the Empire the military middle class must have decayed in any case, but the spread of a shallow Leftism hastened the process.

It is clear that the special position of the English intellectuals during the past ten years, as purely *negative* creatures, mere anti-Blimps, was a by-product of ruling-class stupidity. Society could not use them, and they had not got it in them to see that devotion to one's country implies 'for better, for worse'. Both Blimps and highbrows took for granted, as though it were a law of nature, the divorce between patriotism and intelligence. If you were a patriot you read *Blackwood's Magazine* and publicly thanked God that you were 'not brainy'. If you were an intellectual you sniggered at the Union Jack and regarded physical courage as barbarous. It is obvious that this preposterous convention cannot continue. The Bloomsbury highbrow, with his mechanical snigger, is as out-of-date as the cavalry colonel. A modern nation cannot afford either of them. Patriotism and intelligence will have to come together again. It is the fact that we are fighting a war, and a very peculiar kind of war, that may make this possible.

SIX

One of the most important developments in England during the past twenty years has been the upward and downward extension of the middle class. It has happened on such a scale as to make the old classification of society into capitalists, proletarians and petit-bourgeois (small property-owners) almost obsolete.

England is a country in which property and financial power are concentrated in very few hands. Few people in modern England *own* anything at all, except clothes, furniture and possibly a house. The peasantry have long since disappeared, the independent shop-keeper is being destroyed, the small businessman is diminishing in numbers. But at the same time modern industry is so complicated that it cannot get along without great numbers of managers, salesmen, engineers, chemists and technicians of all kinds, drawing fairly large salaries. And these in turn call into being a professional class of doctors, lawyers, teachers, artists, etc., etc. The tendency of advanced capitalism has therefore been to enlarge the middle class and not to wipe it out as it once seemed likely to do.

But much more important than this is the spread of middle-class ideas and habits among the working class. The British working class are now better off in almost all ways than they were thirty years ago. This is partly due to the efforts of the trade unions, but partly to the mere advance of physical science. It is not always realized that within rather narrow limits the standard of life of a country can rise without a corresponding rise in real-wages. Up to a point, civilization can lift itself up by its boot-tags. However unjustly society is organized, certain technical advances are bound to benefit the whole community, because certain kinds of goods are necessarily held in common. A millionaire cannot, for example, light the streets for himself while darkening them for other people. Nearly all citizens of civilized countries now enjoy the use of good roads, germ-free water, police protection, free libraries and probably free education of a kind. Public education in England has been meanly starved of money, but it has nevertheless improved, largely owing to the devoted efforts of the teachers, and the habit of reading has become enormously more widespread. To an increasing extent the rich and the poor read the same books, and they also see the same films and listen to the same radio programmes. And the differences in their way of life have been diminished by the mass-production of cheap clothes and improvements in housing. So far as outward appearance goes, the clothes of rich and poor, especially in the case of women, differ far less than they did thirty or even fifty years ago. As to housing, England still has slums which are a blot on civilization, but much building has been done during the past ten years, largely by the local authorities. The modern council house, with its bathroom and electric light, is smaller than the stockbroker's villa, but it is recognizably the same kind of house, which the farm labourer's cottage is not. A person who has grown up in a council housing estate is likely to be – indeed, visibly *is* – more middle class in outlook than a person who has grown up in a slum.

The effect of all this is a general softening of manners. It is enhanced by the fact that modern industrial methods tend always to demand less muscular effort and therefore to leave people with more energy when their day's work is done. Many workers in the light industries are less truly manual labourers than is a doctor or a grocer. In tastes, habits, manners and outlook the working class and the middle class are drawing together. The unjust distinctions remain, but the real differences diminish. The old-style 'proletarian' – collarless, unshaven and with muscles warped by heavy labour – still exists, but he is constantly decreasing in numbers; he only predominates in the heavy-industry areas of the north of England.

After 1918 there began to appear something that had never existed in England before: people of indeterminate social class. In 1910 every human being in these islands could be 'placed' in an instant by his clothes, manners and accent. That is no longer the case. Above all, it is not the case in the new townships that have developed as a result of cheap motor cars and the southward shift of industry. The place to look for the germs of the future England is in light-industry areas and along the arterial roads. In Slough, Dagenham, Barnet, Letchworth, Hayes – everywhere, indeed, on the outskirts of great towns – the old pattern is gradually changing into something new. In those vast new wildernesses of glass and brick the sharp distinctions of the older kind of town, with its slums and mansions, or of the country, with its manor-houses and squalid cottages, no longer exist. There are wide gradations of income, but it is the same kind of life that is being lived at different levels, in labour-saving flats or council houses, along the concrete roads and in the naked democracy of the swimming-pools. It is a rather restless, cultureless life, centring round tinned food, *Picture Post*, the radio and the internal combustion engine. It is a civilization in which children grow up with an intimate knowledge of magnetoes and in complete ignorance of the Bible. To that civilization belong the people who are most at home in and most definitely *of* the modern world, the technicians and the higher-paid skilled workers, the airmen and their mechanics, the radio experts, film producers, popular journalists and industrial chemists. They are the indeterminate stratum at which the older class distinctions are beginning to break down.

This war, unless we are defeated, will wipe out most of the existing class privileges. There are every day fewer people who wish them to continue. Nor need we fear that as the pattern changes life in England will lose its peculiar flavour. The new red cities of Greater London are crude enough, but these things are only the rash that accompanies a change. In whatever shape England emerges from the war, it will be deeply tinged with the characteristics that I have spoken of earlier. The intellectuals who hope to see it Russianized or Germanized will be disappointed. The gentleness, the hypocrisy, the thoughtlessness, the reverence for law and the hatred of uniforms will remain, along with the suet puddings and the misty skies. It needs some very great disaster, such as prolonged subjugation by a foreign enemy, to destroy a national culture. The Stock Exchange will be pulled down, the horse plough will give way to the tractor, the country houses will be turned into children's holiday camps, the Eton and Harrow match will be forgotten, but England will still be England, an everlasting animal stretching into the future and the past, and, like all living things, having the power to change out of recognition and yet remain the same.

Part II: Shopkeepers at War

ONE

I began this book to the tune of German bombs, and I begin this second chapter in the added racket of the barrage. The yellow gunflashes are lighting the sky, the splinters are rattling on the housetops, and London Bridge is falling down, falling down, falling down. Anyone able to read a map knows that we are in deadly danger. I do not mean that we are beaten or need be beaten. Almost certainly the outcome depends on our own will. But at this moment we are in the soup, full fathom five, and we have been brought there by follies which we are still committing and which will drown us altogether if we do not mend our ways quickly.

What this war has demonstrated is that private capitalism – that is, an economic system in which land, factories, mines and transport are owned privately and operated solely for profit – *does not work*. It cannot deliver the goods. This fact had been known to millions of people for years past, but nothing ever came of it, because there was no real urge from below to alter the system, and those at the top had trained themselves to be impenetrably stupid on just this point. Argument and propaganda got one nowhere. The lords of property simply sat on their bottoms and proclaimed that all was for the best. Hitler's conquest of Europe, however, was a *physical* debunking of capitalism. War, for all its evil, is at any rate an unanswerable test of strength, like a try-your-grip machine. Great strength returns the penny, and there is no way of faking the result.

When the nautical screw was first invented, there was a controversy that lasted for years as to whether screw-steamers or paddle-steamers were better. The paddle-steamers, like all obsolete things, had their champions, who supported them by ingenious arguments. Finally, however, a distinguished admiral tied a screw-steamer and a paddle-steamer of equal horse-power stern to stern and set their engines running. That settled the question once and for all. And it was something similar that happened on the fields of Norway and of Flanders. Once and for all it was proved that a planned economy is stronger than a planless one. But it is necessary here to give some kind of definition to those much-abused words, Socialism and Facism.

Socialism is usually defined as 'common ownership of the means of production'. Crudely: the State, representing the whole nation, owns everything, and everyone is a State employee. This does *not* mean that people are stripped of private possessions such as clothes and furniture, but it *does* mean that all productive goods, such as land, mines, ships and machinery, are the property of the State. The State is the sole large-scale producer. It is not certain that Socialism is in all ways superior to capitalism, but it is certain that, unlike capitalism, it can solve the problems of production and consumption. At normal times a capitalist economy can never consume all that it produces, so that there is always a wasted surplus (wheat burned in furnaces, herrings dumped back into the sea, etc., etc.) and always unemployment. In time of war, on the other hand, it has difficulty in producing all that it needs, because nothing is produced unless someone sees his way to making a profit out of it.

In a Socialist economy these problems do not exist. The State simply calculates what goods will be needed and does its best to produce them. Production is only limited by the amount of labour and raw materials. Money, for internal purposes, ceases to be a mysterious all-powerful thing and becomes a sort of coupon or ration-ticket, issued in sufficient quantities to buy up such consumption goods as may be available at the moment.

However, it has become clear in the last few years that 'common ownership of the means of production' is not in itself a sufficient definition of Socialism. One must also add the following: approximate equality of incomes (it need be no more than approximate), political democracy, and abolition of all hereditary privilege, especially in education. These are simply the necessary safeguards against the reappearance of a class-system. Centralized ownership has very little meaning unless the mass of the people are living roughly upon an equal level, and have some kind of control over the government. 'The State' may come to mean no more than a self-elected political party, and oligarchy and privilege can return, based on power rather than on money.

But what then is Fascism?

Fascism, at any rate the German version, is a form of capitalism that borrows from Socialism just such features as will make it efficent for war purposes. Internally, Germany has a good deal in common with a Socialist state. Ownership has never been abolished, there are still capitalists and workers, and – this is the important point, and the real reason why rich men all over the world tend to sympathize with Fascism – generally speaking the same people are capitalists and the same people workers as before the Nazi revolution. But at the same time the State, which is simply the Nazi Party, is in control of everything. It controls investment, raw materials, rates of interest, working hours, wages. The factory owner still owns his factory, but he is for practical purposes reduced to the status of a manager. Everyone is in effect a State employee, though the salaries vary very greatly. The mere *efficiency* of such a system, the elimination of waste and obstruction, is obvious. In seven years it has built up the most powerful war machine the world has ever seen.

But the idea underlying Fascism is irreconcilably different from that which underlies Socialism. Socialism aims, ultimately, at a world-state of free and equal human beings. It takes the equality of human rights for granted. Nazism assumes just the opposite. The driving force behind the Nazi movement is the belief in human *inequality*, the superiority of Germans to all other races, the right of Germany to rule the world. Outside the German Reich it does not recognize any obligations. Eminent Nazi professors have 'proved' over and over again that only nordic man is fully human, have even mooted the idea that non-nordic peoples (such as ourselves) can interbreed with gorillas! Therefore, while a species of war-Socialism exists within the German state, its attitude towards conquered nations is frankly that of an exploiter. The function of the Czechs, Poles, French, etc. is simply to produce such goods as Germany may need, and get in return just as little as will keep them from open rebellion. If we are conquered, our job will probably be to manufacture weapons for Hitler's forthcoming wars with Russia and America. The Nazis aim, in effect, at setting up a kind of caste system, with four main castes corresponding rather closely to those of the Hindu religion. At the top comes the Nazi Party, second come the mass of the German people, third come the conquered European populations. Fourth and last are to come the coloured peoples, the 'semi-apes' as Hitler calls them, who are to be reduced quite openly to slavery.

However horrible this system may seem to us, *it works*. It works because it is a planned system geared to a definite purpose, world-conquest, and not allowing any private interest, either of capitalist or worker, to stand in its way. British capitalism does not work, because it is a competitive system in which private profit is and must be the main objective. It is a system in which all the forces are pulling in opposite directions and the interests of the individual are as often as not totally opposed to those of the State.

All through the critical years British capitalism, with its immense industrial plant and its unrivalled supply of skilled labour, was unequal to the strain of preparing for war. To prepare for war on the modern scale you have got to divert the greater part of your national income to armaments, which means cutting down on consumption goods. A bombing plane, for instance, is equivalent in price to fifty small motor cars, or eighty thousand pairs of silk stockings, or a million loaves of bread. Clearly you can't have *many* bombing planes without lowering the national standard of life. It is guns or butter, as Marshal Goering remarked. But in Chamberlain's England the transition could not be made. The rich would not face the necessary taxation, and while the rich are still visibly rich it is not possible to tax the poor very heavily either. Moreover, so long as *profit* was the main object the manufacturer had no incentive to change over from consumption goods to armaments. A businessman's first duty is to his shareholders. Perhaps England needs tanks, but perhaps it pays better to manufacture motor cars. To prevent war material from reaching the enemy is common sense, but to sell in the highest market is a business duty. Right at the end of August 1939 the British dealers were tumbling over one another in their eagerness to sell Germany tin, rubber, copper and shellac – and this in the clear, certain knowledge that war was going to break out in a week or two. It was about as sensible as selling somebody a razor to cut your throat with. But it was 'good business'.

And now look at the results. After 1934 it was known that Germany was rearming. After 1936 everyone with eyes in his head knew that war was coming. After Munich it was merely a question of how soon the war would begin. In September 1939 war broke out. *Eight months later* it was discovered that, so far as equipment went, the British army was barely beyond the standard of 1918. We saw our soldiers fighting their way desperately to the coast, with one aeroplane against three, with rifles against tanks, with bayonets against tommy-guns. There were not even enough revolvers to supply all the officers. After a year of war the regular army was still short of 300,000 tin hats. There had even, previously, been a shortage of uniforms – this in one of the greatest woollen-goods producing countries in the world!

What had happened was that the whole moneyed class, unwilling to face a change in their way of life, had shut their eyes to the nature of Fascism and modern war. And false optimism was fed to the general public by the gutter press, which lives on its advertisements and is therefore interested in keeping trade conditions normal. Year after year the Beaverbrook press assured us in huge headlines that THERE WILL BE NO WAR, and as late as the beginning of 1939 Lord Rothermere was describing Hitler as 'a great gentleman'. And while England in the moment of disaster proved to be short of every war material except ships, it is not recorded that there was any shortage of motor cars, fur coats, gramophones, lipstick, chocolates or silk stockings. And dare anyone pretend that the same tug-of-war between private profit and public necessity is not still continuing? England fights for her life, but business must fight for profits. You can hardly open a newspaper without seeing the two contradictory processes happening side by side. On the very same page you will find the Government urging you to save and the seller of some useless luxury urging you to spend. Lend to Defend, but Guinness is Good for You. Buy a Spitfire, but also buy Haig and Haig, Pond's Face Cream and Black Magic Chocolates.

But one thing gives hope – the visible swing in public opinion. If we can survive this war, the defeat in Flanders will turn out to have been one of the great turning-points in English history. In that spectacular disaster the working class, the middle class and even a section of the business community could see the utter rottenness of private capitalism. Before that the case against capitalism had never been *proved*. Russia, the only definitely Socialist country, was backward and far away. All criticism broke itself against the rat-trap faces of bankers and the brassy laughter of stockbrokers. Socialism? Ha! ha! ha! Where's the money to come from? Ha! ha! ha! The lords of property were firm in their seats, and they knew it. But after the French collapse there came something that could not be laughed away, something that neither cheque-books nor policemen were any use against – the bombing. Zweee – BOOM! What's that? Oh, only a bomb on the Stock Exchange. Zwee – BOOM! Another acre of somebody's valuable slum-property gone west. Hitler will at any rate go down in history as the man who made the City of London laugh on the wrong side of its face. For the first time in their lives the comfortable were uncomfortable, the professional optimists had to admit that there was something wrong. It was a great step forward. From that time onwards the ghastly job of trying to convince artificially stupefied people that a planned economy might be better than a free-for-all in which the worst man wins – that job will never be quite so ghastly again.

TWO

The difference between Socialism and capitalism is not primarily a difference of technique. One cannot simply change from one system to the other as one might install a new piece of machinery in a factory, and then carry on as before, with the same people in positions of control. Obviously there is also needed a complete shift of power. New blood, new men, new ideas – in the true sense of the word, a revolution.

I have spoken earlier of the soundness and homogeneity of England, the patriotism that runs like a connecting thread through almost all classes. After Dunkirk anyone who had eyes in his head could see this. But it is absurd to pretend that the promise of that moment has been fulfilled. Almost certainly the mass of the people are now ready for the vast changes that are necessary; but those changes have not even begun to happen.

England is a family with the wrong members in control. Almost entirely we are governed by the rich, and by people who step into positions of command by right of birth. Few if any of these people are consciously treacherous, some of them are not even fools, but as a class they are quite incapable of leading us to victory. They could not do it, even if their material interests did not constantly trip them up. As I pointed out earlier, they have been artificially stupefied. Quite apart from anything else, the rule of money sees to it that we shall be governed largely by the old – that is, by people utterly unable to grasp what age they are living in or what enemy they are fighting. Nothing was more desolating at the beginning of this war than the way in which the whole of the older generation conspired to pretend that it was the war of 1914–18 over again. All the old duds were back on the job, twenty years older, with the skull plainer in their faces. Ian Hay was cheering up the troops, Belloc was writing articles on strategy, Maurois doing broadcasts, Bairnsfather drawing cartoons. It was like a tea-party of ghosts. And that state of affairs has barely altered. The shock of disaster brought a few able men like Bevin to the front, but in general we are still commanded by people who managed to live through the years 1931–9 without even discovering that Hitler was dangerous. A generation of the unteachable is hanging upon us like a necklace of corpses.

As soon as one considers any problem of this war – and it does not matter whether it is the widest aspect of strategy or the tiniest detail of home organization – one sees that the necessary moves cannot be made while the social structure of England remains what it is. Inevitably, because of their position and upbringing, the ruling class are fighting for their own privileges, which cannot possibly be reconciled with the public interest. It is a mistake to imagine that war aims, strategy, propaganda and industrial organization exist in watertight compartments. All are interconnected. Every strategic plan, every tactical method, even every weapon will bear the stamp of the social system that produced it. The British ruling class are fighting against Hitler, whom they have always regarded and whom some of them still regard as their protector against Bolshevism. That does not mean that they will deliberately sell out; but it does mean that at every decisive moment they are likely to falter, pull their punches, do the wrong thing.

Until the Churchill Government called some sort of halt to the process, they have done the wrong thing with an unerring instinct ever since 1931. They helped Franco to overthrow the Spanish Government, although anyone not an imbecile could have told them that a Fascist Spain would be hostile to England. They fed Italy with war materials all through the winter of 1939–40, although it was obvious to the whole world that the Italians were going to attack us in the spring. For the sake of a few hundred thousand dividend-drawers they are turning India from an ally into an enemy. Moreover, so long as the moneyed classes remain in control, we cannot develop any but a *defensive* strategy. Every victory means a change in the *status quo*. How can we drive the Italians out of Abyssinia without rousing echoes among the coloured peoples of our own Empire? How can we even smash Hitler without the risk of bringing the German Socialists and Communists into power? The left-wingers who wail that 'this is a capitalist war' and that 'British Imperialism' is fighting for loot have got their heads screwed on backwards. The last thing the British moneyed class wish for is to acquire fresh territory. It would simply be an embarrassment. Their war aim (both unattainable and unmentionable) is simply to hang on to what they have got.

Internally, England is still the rich man's Paradise. All talk of 'equality of sacrifice' is nonsense. At the same time as factory-workers are asked to put up with longer hours, advertisements for 'Butler. One in family, eight in staff' are appearing in the press. The bombed-out populations of the East End go hungry and homeless while wealthier victims simply step into their cars and flee to comfortable country houses. The Home Guard swells to a million men in a few weeks, and is deliberately organized from above in such a way that only people with private incomes can hold positions of command. Even the rationing system is so arranged that it hits the poor all the time, while people with over £2,000 a year are practically unaffected by it. Everywhere privilege is squandering good will. In such circumstances even propaganda becomes almost impossible. As attempts to stir up patriotic feeling, the red posters issued by the Chamberlain Government at the beginning of the war broke all depth-records. Yet they could not have been much other than they were, for how could Chamberlain and his followers take the risk of rousing strong popular feeling *against Fascism*? Anyone who was genuinely hostile to Fascism must also be opposed to Chamberlain himself and to all the others who had helped Hitler into power. So also with external propaganda. In all Lord Halifax's speeches there is not one concrete proposal for which a single inhabitant of Europe would risk the top joint of his little finger. For what war-aim can Halifax, or anyone like him, conceivably have, except to put the clock back to 1933?

It is only by revolution that the native genius of the English people can be set free. Revolution does not mean red flags and street fighting, it means a fundamental shift of power. Whether it happens with or without bloodshed is largely an accident of time and place. Nor does it mean the dictatorship of a single class. The people in England who grasp what changes are needed and are capable of carrying them through are not confined to any one class, though it is true that very few people with over £2,000 a year are among them. What is wanted is a conscious open revolt by ordinary people against inefficiency, class privilege and the rule of the old. It is not primarily a question of a change of government. British governments do, broadly speaking, represent the will of the people, and if we alter our structure from below we shall get the government we need. Ambassadors, generals, officials and colonial admistrators who are senile or pro-Fascist are more dangerous than Cabinet ministers whose follies have to be committed in public. Right through our national life we have got to fight against privilege, against the notion that a half-witted public-schoolboy is better fitted for command than an intelligent mechanic. Although there are gifted and honest *individuals* among them, we have got to break the grip of the moneyed class as a whole. England has got to assume its real shape. The England that is only just beneath the surface, in the factories and the newspaper offices, in the aeroplanes and the submarines, has got to take charge of its own destiny.

In the short run, equality of sacrifice, 'war-Communism', is even more important than radical economic changes. It is very necessary that industry should be nationalized, but it is more urgently necessary that such monstrosities as butlers and 'private incomes' should disappear forthwith. Almost certainly the main reason why the Spanish Republic could keep up the fight for two and a half years against impossible odds was that there were no gross contrasts of wealth. The people suffered horribly, but they all suffered alike. When the private soldier had not a cigarette, the general had not one either. Given equality of sacrifice, the morale of a country like England would probably be unbreakable. But at present we have nothing to appeal to except traditional patriotism, which is deeper here than elsewhere, but is not necessarily bottomless. At some point or another you have got to deal with the man who says 'I should be no worse off under Hitler'. But what answer can you give him – that is, what answer that you can expect him to listen to – while common soldiers risk their lives for two and sixpence a day, and fat women ride about in Rolls-Royce cars, nursing pekineses?

It is quite likely that this war will last three years. It will mean cruel overwork, cold dull winters, uninteresting food, lack of amusements, prolonged bombing. It cannot but lower the general standard of living, because the essential act of war is to manufacture armaments instead of consumable goods. The working class will have to suffer terrible things. And they *will* suffer them, almost indefinitely, provided that they know what they are fighting for. They are not cowards, and they are not even internationally minded. They can stand all that the Spanish workers stood, and more. But they will want some kind of proof that a better life is ahead for themselves and their children. The one sure earnest of that is that when they are taxed and overworked they shall see that the rich are being hit even harder. And if the rich squeal audibly, so much the better.

We can bring these things about, if we really want to. It is not true that public opinion has no power in England. It never makes itself heard without achieving something; it has been responsible for most of the changes for the better during the past six months. But we have moved with glacier-like slowness, and we have learned only from disasters. It took the fall of Paris to get rid of Chamberlain and the unnecessary suffering of scores of thousands of people in the East End to get rid or partially rid of Sir John Anderson. It is not worth losing a battle in order to bury a corpse. For we are fighting against swift evil intelligences, and time presses, and

history to the defeated
May say Alas! but cannot alter or pardon.

THREE

During the last six months there has been much talk of 'the Fifth Column'. From time to time obscure lunatics have been jailed for making speeches in favour of Hitler, and large numbers of German refugees have been interned, a thing which has almost certainly done us great harm in Europe. It is of course obvious that the idea of a large, organized army of Fifth Columnists suddenly appearing on the streets with weapons in their hands, as in Holland and Belgium, is ridiculous. Nevertheless a Fifth Column danger does exist.

One can only consider it if one also considers in what way England might be defeated.

It does not seem probable that air bombing can settle a major war. England might well be invaded and conquered, but the invasion would be a dangerous gamble, and if it happened and failed it would probably leave us more united and less Blimp-ridden than before. Moreover, if England were overrun by foreign troops the English people would know that they had been beaten and would continue the struggle. It is doubtful whether they could be held down permanently, or whether Hitler wishes to keep an army of a million men stationed in these islands. A government of——, —— and —— (you can fill in the names) would suit him better. The English can probably not be bullied into surrender, but they might quite easily be bored, cajoled or cheated into it, provided that, as at Munich, they did not know that they were surrendering. It could happen most easily when the war seemed to be going well rather than badly. The threatening tone of so much of the German and Italian propaganda is a psychological mistake. It only gets home on intellectuals. With the general public the proper approach would be 'Let's call it a draw'. It is when a peace-offer along *those* lines is made that the pro-Fascists will raise their voices.

But who are the pro-Fascists? The idea of a Hitler victory appeals to the very rich, to the Communists, to Mosley's followers, to the pacifists, and to certain sections among the Catholics. Also, if things went badly enough on the Home Front, the whole of the poorer section of the working class might swing round to a position that was defeatist though not actively pro-Hitler.

In this motley list one can see the daring of German propaganda, its willingness to offer everything to everybody. But the various pro-Fascist forces are not consciously acting together, and they operate in different ways.

The Communists must certainly be regarded as pro-Hitler, and are bound to remain so unless Russian policy changes, but they have not very much influence. Mosley's Blackshirts, though now lying very low, are a more serious danger, because of the footing they probably possess in the armed forces. Still, even in its palmiest days Mosley's following can hardly have numbered 50,000. Pacifism is a psychological curiosity rather than a political movement. Some of the extremer pacifists, starting out with a complete renunciation of violence, have ended by warmly championing Hitler and even toying with antisemitism. This is interesting, but it is not important. 'Pure' pacifism, which is a by-product of naval power, can only appeal to people in very sheltered positions. Moreover, being negative and irresponsible, it does not inspire much devotion. Of the membership of the Peace Pledge Union, less than 15 per cent even pay their annual subscriptions. None of these bodies of people, pacifists, Communists or Blackshirts, could bring a large-scale stop-the-war movement into being by their own efforts. But they might help to make things very much easier for a treacherous government negotiating surrender. Like the French Communists, they might become the half-conscious agents of millionaires.

The real danger is from above. One ought not to pay any attention to Hitler's recent line of talk about being the friend of the poor man, the enemy of plutocracy, etc., etc. Hitler's real self is in *Mein Kampf*, and in his actions. He has never persecuted the rich, except when they were Jews or when they tried actively to oppose him. He stands for a centralized economy which robs the capitalist of most of his power but leaves the structure of society much as before. The State controls industry, but there are still rich and poor, masters and men. Therefore, as against genuine Socialism, the moneyed class have always been on his side. This was crystal clear at the time of the Spanish civil war, and clear again at the time when France surrendered. Hitler's puppet government are not working men, but a gang of bankers, gaga generals and corrupt right-wing politicians.

That kind of spectacular, *conscious* treachery is less likely to succeed in England, indeed is far less likely even to be tried. Nevertheless, to many payers of supertax this war is simply an insane family squabble which ought to be stopped at all costs. One need not doubt that a 'peace' movement is on foot somewhere in high places; probably a shadow Cabinet has already been formed. These people will get their chance not in the moment of defeat but in some stagnant period when boredom is reinforced by discontent. They will not talk about surrender, only about peace; and doubtless they will persuade themselves, and perhaps other people, that they are acting for the best. An army of unemployed led by millionaires quoting the Sermon on the Mount – that is our danger. But it cannot arise when we have once introduced a reasonable degree of social justice. The lady in the Rolls-Royce car is more damaging to morale than a fleet of Goering's bombing planes.

Part III: The English Revolution

ONE

The English revolution started several years ago, and it began to gather momentum when the troops came back from Dunkirk. Like all else in England, it happens in a sleepy, unwilling way, but it is happening. The war has speeded it up, but it has also increased, and desperately, the necessity for speed.

Progress and reaction are ceasing to have anything to do with party labels. If one wishes to name a particular moment, one can say that the old distinction between Right and Left broke down when *Picture Post* was first published. What are the politics of *Picture Post*? Or of *Cavalcade*, or Priestley's broadcasts, or the leading articles in the *Evening Standard*? None of the old classifications will fit them. They merely point to the existence of multitudes of unlabelled people who have grasped within the last year or two that something is wrong. But since a classless, ownerless society is generally spoken of as 'Socialism', we can give that name to the society towards which we are now moving. The war and the revolution are inseparable. We cannot establish anything that a western nation would regard as Socialism without defeating Hitler; on the other hand we cannot defeat Hitler while we remain economically and socially in the nineteenth century. The past is fighting the future and we have two years, a year, possibly only a few months, to see to it that the future wins.

We cannot look to this or to any similar government to put through the necessary changes of its own accord. The initiative will have to come from below. That means that there will have to arise something that has never existed in England, a Socialist movement that actually has the mass of the people behind it. But one must start by recognizing why it is that English Socialism has failed.

In England there is only one Socialist party that has ever seriously mattered, the Labour Party. It has never been able to achieve any major change, because except in purely domestic matters it has never possessed a genuinely independent policy. It was and is primarily a party of the trade unions, devoted to raising wages and improving working conditions. This meant that all through the critical years it was directly interested in the prosperity of British capitalism. In particular it was interested in the maintenance of the British Empire, for the wealth of England was drawn largely from Asia and Africa. The standard of living of the trade union workers, whom the Labour Party represented, depended indirectly on the sweating of Indian coolies. At the same time the Labour Party was a Socialist party, using Socialist phraseology, thinking in terms of an old-fashioned anti-imperialism and more or less pledged to make restitution to the coloured races. It had to stand for the 'independence' of India, just as it had to stand for disarmament and 'progress' generally. Nevertheless everyone was aware that this was nonsense. In the age of the tank and the bombing plane, backward agricultural countries like India and the African colonies can no more be independent than can a cat or a dog. Had any Labour government come into office with a clear majority and then proceeded to grant India anything that could truly be called independence, India would simply have been absorbed by Japan, or divided between Japan and Russia.

To a Labour government in power, three imperial policies would have been open. One was to continue administering the empire exactly as before, which meant dropping all pretensions to Socialism. Another was to set the subject peoples 'free', which meant in practice handing them over to Japan, Italy and other predatory powers, and incidentally causing a catastrophic drop in the British standard of living. The third was to develop a *positive* imperial policy, and aim at transforming the Empire into a federation of Socialist states, like a looser and freer version of the Union of Soviet Republics. But the Labour Party's history and background made this impossible. It was a party of the trade unions, hopelessly parochial in outlook, with little interest in imperial affairs and no contacts among the men who actually held the Empire together. It would have had to hand the administration of India and Africa and the whole job of imperial defence to men drawn from a different class and traditionally hostile to Socialism. Overshadowing everything was the doubt whether a Labour government which meant business could make itself obeyed. For all the size of its following, the Labour Party had no footing in the navy, little or none in the army or air force, none whatever in the Colonial Services, and not even a sure footing in the Home Civil Service. In England its position was strong but not unchallengeable, and outside England all the key points were in the hands of its enemies. Once in power, the same dilemma would always have faced it: carry out your promises, and risk revolt, or continue with the same policy as the Conservatives, and stop talking about Socialism. The Labour leaders never found a solution, and from 1935 onwards it was very doubtful whether they had any wish to take office. They had degenerated into a Permanent Opposition.

Outside the Labour Party there existed several extremist parties, of whom the Communists were the strongest. The Communists had considerable influence in the Labour Party in the years 1920–6 and 1935–9. Their chief importance, and that of the whole left wing of the Labour movement, was the part they played in alienating the middle classes from Socialism.

The history of the past seven years has made it perfectly clear that Communism has no chance in western Europe. The appeal of Fascism is enormously greater. In one country after another the Communists have been rooted out by their more up-to-date enemies, the Nazis. In the English-speaking countries they never had a serious footing. The creed they were spreading could appeal only to a rather rare type of person, found chiefly in the middle-class intelligentsia, the type who has ceased to love his own country but still feels the need of patriotism, and therefore develops patriotic sentiments towards Russia. By 1940, after working for twenty years and spending a great deal of money, the British Communists had barely 20,000 members, actually a smaller number than they had started out with in 1920. The other Marxist parties were of even less importance. They had not the Russian money and prestige behind them, and even more than the Communists they were tied to the nineteenth-century doctrine of the class war. They continued year after year to preach this out-of-date gospel, and never drew any inference from the fact that it got them no followers.

Nor did any strong native Fascist movement grow up. Material conditions were not bad enough, and no leader who could be taken seriously was forthcoming. One would have had to look a long time to find a man more barren of ideas than Sir Oswald Mosley. He was as hollow as a jug. Even the elementary fact that Fascism must not offend national sentiment had escaped him. His entire movement was imitated slavishly from abroad, the uniform and the party programme from Italy and the salute from Germany, with the Jew-baiting tacked on as an afterthought, Mosley having actually started his movement with Jews among his most prominent followers. A man of the stamp of Bottomley or Lloyd George could perhaps have brought a real British Fascist movement into existence. But such leaders only appear when the psychological need for them exists.

After twenty years of stagnation and unemployment, the entire English Socialist movement was unable to produce a version of Socialism which the mass of the people could even find desirable. The Labour Party stood for a timid reformism, the Marxists were looking at the modern world through nineteenth-century spectacles. Both ignored agriculture and imperial problems, and both antagonized the middle classes. The suffocating stupidity of left-wing propaganda had frightened away whole classes of necessary people, factory managers, airmen, naval officers, farmers, white-collar workers, shopkeepers, policemen. All of these people had been taught to think of Socialism as something which menaced their livelihood, or as something seditious, alien, 'anti-British' as they would have called it. Only the intellectuals, the least useful section of the middle class, gravitated towards the movement.

A Socialist Party which genuinely wished to achieve anything would have started by facing several facts which to this day are considered unmentionable in left-wing circles. It would have recognized that England is more united than most countries, that the British workers have a great deal to lose besides their chains, and that the differences in outlook and habits between class and class are rapidly diminishing. In general, it would have recognized that the old-fashioned 'proletarian revolution' is an impossibility. But all through the between-war years no Socialist programme that was both revolutionary and workable ever appeared; basically, no doubt, because no one genuinely wanted any major change to happen. The Labour leaders wanted to go on and on, drawing their salaries and periodically swapping jobs with the Conservatives. The Communists wanted to go on and on, suffering a comfortable martyrdom, meeting with endless defeats and afterwards putting the blame on other people.

The left-wing intelligentsia wanted to go on and on, sniggering at the Blimps, sapping away at middle-class morale, but still keeping their favoured position as hangers-on of the dividend-drawers. Labour Party politics had become a variant of Conservatism, 'revolutionary' politics had become a game of make-believe.

Now, however, the circumstances have changed, the drowsy years have ended. Being a Socialist no longer means kicking theoretically against a system which in practice you are fairly well satisfied with. This time our predicament is real. It is 'the Philistines be upon thee, Samson'. We have got to make our words take physical shape, or perish. We know very well that with its present social structure England cannot survive, and we have got to make other people see that fact and act upon it. We cannot win the war without introducing Socialism, nor establish Socialism without winning the war. At such a time it is possible, as it was not in the peaceful years, to be both revolutionary and realistic. A Socialist movement which can swing the mass of the people behind it, drive the pro-Fascists out of positions of control, wipe out the grosser injustices and let the working class see that they have something to fight for, win over the middle classes instead on antagonizing them, produce a workable imperial policy instead of a mixture of humbug and Utopianism, bring patriotism and intelligence into partnership – for the first time, a movement of such a kind becomes possible.

TWO

The fact that we are at war has turned Socialism from a textbook word into a realizable policy.

The inefficiency of private capitalism has been proved all over Europe. Its injustice has been proved in the East End of London. Patriotism, against which the Socialists fought so long, has become a tremendous lever in their hands. People who at any other time would cling like glue to their miserable scraps of privilege, will surrender them fast enough when their country is in danger. War is the greatest of all agents of change. It speeds up all processes, wipes out minor distinctions, brings realities to the surface. Above all, war brings it home to the individual that he is *not* altogether an individual. It is only because they are aware of this that men will die on the field of battle. At this moment it is not so much a question of surrendering life as of surrendering leisure, comfort, economic liberty, social prestige. There are very few people in England who really want to see their country conquered by Germany. If it can be made clear that defeating Hitler means wiping out class privilege, the great mass of middling people, the £6 a week to £2,000 a year class, will probably be on our side. These people are quite indispensable, because they include most of the technical experts. Obviously the snobbishness and political ignorance of people like airmen and naval officers will be a very great difficulty. But without those airmen, destroyer commanders, etc., etc. we could not survive for a week. The only approach to them is through their patriotism. An intelligent Socialist movement will *use* their patriotism, instead of merely insulting it, as hitherto.

But do I mean that there will be no opposition? Of course not. It would be childish to expect anything of the kind.

There will be a bitter political struggle, and there will be unconscious and half-conscious sabotage everywhere. At some point or other it may be necessary to use violence. It is easy to imagine a pro-Fascist rebellion breaking out in, for instance, India. We shall have to fight abainst bribery, ignorance and snobbery. The bankers and the larger businessmen, the landowners and dividend-drawers, the officials with their prehensile bottoms, will obstruct for all they are worth. Even the middle classes will writhe when their accustomed way of life is menaced. But just because the English sense of national unity has never disintegrated, because patriotism is finally stronger than class-hatred, the chances are that the will of the majority will prevail. It is no use imagining that one can make fundamental changes without causing a split in the nation; but the treacherous minority will be far smaller in time of war than it would be at any other time.

The swing of opinion is visibly happening, but it cannot be counted on to happen fast enough of its own accord. This war is a race between the consolidation of Hitler's empire and the growth of democratic consciousness. Everywhere in England you can see a ding-dong battle ranging to and fro – in Parliament and in the Government, in the factories and the armed forces, in the pubs and the air-raid shelters, in the newspapers and on the radio. Every day there are tiny defeats, tiny victories. Morrison for Home Security – a few yards forward. Priestley shoved off the air – a few yards back. It is a struggle between the groping and the unteachable, between the young and the old, between the living and the dead. But it is very necessary that the discontent which undoubtedly exists should take a purposeful and not merely obstructive form. It is time for *the people* to define their war-aims. What is wanted is a simple, concrete programme of action, which can be given all possible publicity, and round which public opinion can group itself.

I suggest that the following six-point programme is the kind of thing we need. The first three points deal with England's internal policy, the other three with the Empire and the world:

1. Nationalization of land, mines, railways, banks and major industries.

2. Limitation of incomes, on such a scale that the highest tax-free income in Britain does not exceed the lowest by more than ten to one.

3. Reform of the educational system along democratic lines.

4. Immediate Dominion status for India, with power to secede when the war is over.

5. Formation of an Imperial General Council, in which the coloured peoples are to be represented.

6. Declaration of formal alliance with China, Abyssinia and all other victims of the Fascist powers.

The general tendency of this programe is unmistakable. It aims quite frankly at turning this war into a revolutionary war and England into a Socialist democracy. I have deliberately included in it nothing that the simplest person could not understand and see the reason for. In the form in which I have put it, it could be printed on the front page of the *Daily Mirror*. But for the purposes of this book a certain amount of amplification is needed.

1. *Nationalization*. One can 'nationalize' industry by the stroke of a pen, but the actual process is slow and complicated. What is needed is that the ownership of all major industry shall be formally vested in the State, representing the common people. Once that is done it becomes possible to eliminate the class of mere *owners* who live not by virtue of anything they produce but by the possession of title-deeds and share certificates. State-ownership implies, therefore, that nobody shall live without working. How sudden a change in the conduct of industry it implies is less certain. In a

country like England we cannot rip down the whole structure and build again from the bottom, least of all in time of war. Inevitably the majority of industrial concerns will continue with much the same personnel as before, the one-time owners or managing directors carrying on with their jobs as State employees. There is reason to think that many of the smaller capitalists would actually welcome some such arrangement. The resistance will come from the big capitalists, the bankers, the landlords and the idle rich, roughly speaking the class with over £2,000 a year – and even if one counts in all their dependants there are not more than half a million of these people in England. Nationalization of agricultural land implies cutting out the landlord and the tithe drawer, but not necessarily interfering with the farmer. It is difficult to imagine any reorganization of English agriculture that would not retain most of the existing farms as units, at any rate at the beginning. The farmer, when he is competent, will continue as a salaried manager. He is virtually that already, with the added disadvantage of having to make a profit and being permanently in debt to the bank. With certain kinds of petty trading, and even the small-scale ownership of land, the State will probably not interfere at all. It would be a great mistake to start by victimizing the smallholder class, for instance. These people are necessary, on the whole they are competent, and the amount of work they do depends on the feeling that they are 'their own masters'. But the State will certainly impose an upward limit to the ownership of land (probably fifteen acres at the very most), and will never permit any ownership of land in town areas.

From the moment that all productive goods have been declared the property of the State, the common people will feel, as they cannot feel now, that the State *is themselves*. They will be ready then to endure the sacrifices that are ahead of us, war or no war. And even if the face of England hardly seems to change, on the day that our main industries are formally nationalized the dominance of a single class will have been broken. From then onwards the emphasis will be shifted from ownership to management, from privilege to competence. It is quite possible that State-ownership will in itself bring about less social change than will be forced upon us by the common hardships of war. But it is the necessary first step without which any *real* reconstruction is impossible.

2. *Incomes*. Limitation of incomes implies the fixing of a minimum wage, which implies a managed internal currency based simply on the amount of consumption goods available. And this again implies a stricter rationing scheme than is now in operation. It is no use at this stage of the world's history to suggest that all human beings should have *exactly* equal incomes. It has been shown over and over again that without some kind of money reward there is no incentive to undertake certain jobs. On the other hand the money reward need not be very large. In practice it is impossible that earnings should be limited quite as rigidly as I have suggested. There will always be anomalies and evasions. But there is no reason why ten to one should not be the maximum normal variation. And within those limits some sense of equality is possible. A man with £3 a week and a man with £1,500 a year can feel themselves fellow creatures, which the Duke of Westminster and the sleepers on the Embankment benches cannot.

3. *Education*. In wartime, educational reform must necessarily be promise rather than performance. At the moment we are not in a position to raise the school-leaving age or increase the teaching staffs of the elementary schools.

But there are certain immediate steps that we could take towards a democratic educational system. We could start by abolishing the autonomy of the public schools and the older universities and flooding them with State-aided pupils chosen simply on grounds of ability. At present, public-school education is partly a training in class prejudice and partly a sort of tax that the middle classes pay to the upper class in return for the right to enter certain professions. It is true that that state of affairs is altering. The middle classes have begun to rebel against the expensiveness of education, and the war will bankrupt the majority of the public schools if it continues for another year or two. The evacuation is also producing certain minor changes. But there is a danger that some of the older schools, which will be able to weather the financial storm longest, will survive in some form or another as festering centres of snobbery. As for the 10,000 'private' schools that England possesses, the vast majority of them deserve nothing except suppression. They are simply commercial undertakings, and in many cases their educational level is actually lower than that of the elementary schools. They merely exist because of a widespread idea that there is something disgraceful in being educated by the public authorities. The State could quell this idea by declaring itself responsible for *all* education, even if at the start this were no more than a gesture. We need gestures as well as actions. It is all too obvious that our talk of 'defending democracy' is nonsense while it is a mere accident of birth that decides whether a gifted child shall or shall not get the education it deserves.

4. *India*. What we must offer India is not 'freedom', which, as I have said earlier, is impossible, but alliance, partnership – in a word, equality. But we must also tell the Indians that they are free to secede, if they want to. Without that there can be no equality of partnership, and our claim to be defending the coloured peoples against Fascism will never be believed. But it is a mistake to imagine that if the Indians were free to cut themselves adrift they would immediately do so. When a British government *offers* them unconditional independence, they will refuse it. For as soon as they have the power to secede the chief reasons for doing so will have disappeared.

A complete severance of the two countries would be a disaster for India, no less than for England. Intelligent Indians know this. As things are at present, India not only cannot defend itself, it is hardly even capable of feeding itself. The whole administration of the country depends on a framework of experts (engineers, forest officers, railwaymen, soldiers, doctors) who are predominantly English and could not be replaced within five or ten years. Moreover, English is the chief lingua franca and nearly the whole of the Indian intelligentsia is deeply anglicized. Any transference to foreign rule – for if the British marched out of India the Japanese and other powers would immediately march in – would mean an immense dislocation. Neither the Japanese, the Russians, the Germans nor the Italians would be capable of administering India even at the low level of efficiency that is attained by the British. They do not possess the necessary supplies of technical experts or the knowledge of languages and local conditions, and they probably could not win the confidence of indispensable go-betweens such as the Eurasians. If India were simply 'liberated', i.e. deprived of British military protection, the first result would be a fresh foreign conquest, and the second a series of enormous famines which would kill millions of people within a few years.

What India needs is the power to work out its own constitution without

British interference, but in some kind of partnership that ensures its protection and technical advice. This is unthinkable until there is a Socialist government in England. For at least eighty years England has artificially prevented the development of India, partly from fear of trade competition if Indian industries were too highly developed, partly because backward peoples are more easily governed than civilized ones. It is a commonplace that the average Indian suffers far more from his own countrymen than from the British. The petty Indian capitalist exploits the town worker with the utmost ruthlessness, the peasant lives from birth to death in the grip of the money-lender. But all this is an indirect result of the British rule, which aims half-consciously at keeping India as backward as possible. The classes most loyal to Britain are the princes, the landowners and the business community – in general, the reactionary classes who are doing fairly well out of the *status quo*. The moment that England ceased to stand towards India in the relation of an exploiter, the balance of forces would be altered. No need then for the British to flatter the ridiculous Indian princes, with their gilded elephants and cardboard armies, to prevent the growth of the Indian trade unions, to play off Moslem against Hindu, to protect the worthless life of the money-lender, to receive the salaams of toadying minor officials, to prefer the half-barbarous Gurkha to the educated Bengali. Once check that stream of dividends that flows from the bodies of Indian coolies to the banking accounts of old ladies in Cheltenham, and the whole sahib-native nexus, with its haughty ignorance on one side and envy and servility on the other, can come to an end. Englishmen and Indians can work side by side for the development of India, and for the training of Indians in all the arts which, so far, they have been systematically prevented from learning. How many of the existing British personnel in India, commercial or official, would fall in with such an arrangement – which would mean ceasing once and for all to be 'sahibs' – is a different question. But, broadly speaking, more is to be hoped from the younger men and from those officials (civil engineers, forestry and agricultural experts, doctors, educationists) who have been scientifically educated. The higher officials, the provincial governors, commissioners, judges, etc. are hopeless; but they are also the most easily replaceable.

That, roughly, is what would be meant by Dominion status if it were offered to India by a Socialist government. It is an offer of partnership on equal terms until such time as the world has ceased to be ruled by bombing planes. But we must add to it the unconditional right to secede. It is the only way of proving that we mean what we say. And what applies to India applies, *mutatis mutandis*, to Burma, Malaya and most of our African possessions.

5 and 6 explain themselves. They are the necessary preliminary to any claim that we are fighting this war for the protection of peaceful peoples against Fascist aggression.

Is it impossibly hopeful to think that such a policy as this could get a following in England? A year ago, even six months ago, it would have been, but not now. Moreover – and this is the peculiar opportunity of this moment – it could be given the necessary publicity. There is now a considerable weekly press, with a circulation of millions, which would be ready to popularize – if not *exactly* the programme I have sketched above, at any rate *some* policy along those lines. There are even three or four daily papers which would be prepared to give it a sympathetic hearing. That is the distance we have travelled in the last six months.

But is such a policy realizable? That depends entirely on ourselves.

Some of the points I have suggested are of the kind that could be carried out immediately, others would take years or decades and even then would not be perfectly achieved. No political programme is ever carried out in its entirety. But what matters is that that or something like it should be our declared policy. It is always the *direction* that counts. It is of course quite hopeless to expect the present Government to pledge itself to any policy that implies turning this war into a revolutionary war. It is at best a government of compromise, with Churchill riding two horses like a circus acrobat. Before such measures as limitation of incomes become even thinkable, there will have to be a complete shift of power away from the old ruling class. If during this winter the war settles into another stagnant period, we ought in my opinion to agitate for a General Election, a thing which the Tory Party machine will make frantic efforts to prevent. But even without an election we can get the government we want, provided that we want it urgently enough. A real shove from below will accomplish it. As to who will be in that government when it comes, I make no guess. I only know that the right men will be there when the people really want them, for it is movements that make leaders and not leaders movements.

Within a year, perhaps even within six months, if we are still unconquered, we shall see the rise of something that has never existed before, a specifically *English* Socialist movement. Hitherto there has been only the Labour Party, which was the creation of the working class but did not aim at any fundamental change, and Marxism, which was a German theory interpreted by Russians and unsuccessfully transplanted to England. There was nothing that really touched the heart of the English people. Throughout its entire history the English Socialist movement has never produced a song with a catchy tune – nothing like *La Marseillaise* or *La Cucuracha*, for instance. When a Socialist movement native to England appears, the Marxists, like all others with a vested interest in the past, will be its bitter enemies. Inevitably they will denounce it as 'Fascism'. Already it is customary among the more soft-boiled intellectuals of the Left to declare that if we fight against the Nazis we shall 'go Nazi' ourselves. They might equally well say that if we fight against Negroes we shall turn black. To 'go Nazi' we should have to have the history of Germany behind us. Nations do not escape from their past merely by making a revolution. An English Socialist government will transform the nation from top to bottom, but it will still bear all over it the unmistakable marks of our own civilization, the peculiar civilization which I discussed earlier in this book.

It will not be doctrinaire, nor even logical. It will abolish the House of Lords, but quite probably will not abolish the Monarchy. It will leave anachronisms and loose ends everywhere, the judge in his ridiculous horsehair wig and the lion and the unicorn on the soldier's cap-buttons. It will not set up any explicit class dictatorship. It will group itself round the old Labour Party and its mass following will be in the trade unions, but it will draw into it most of the middle class and many of the younger sons of the bourgeoisie. Most of its directing brains will come from the new indeterminate class of skilled workers, technical experts, airmen, scientists, architects and journalists, the people who feel at home in the radio and ferro-concrete age. But it will never lose touch with the tradition of compromise and the belief in a law that is above the State. It will shoot traitors, but it will give them a solemn trial beforehand and occasionally it will acquit them. It will crush any open revolt promptly and cruelly, but it will interfere very little with the spoken and written word. Political parties with different names will still exist, revolutionary sects will still be publishing their newspapers and making as little impression as ever. It will disestablish the Church, but will not persecute religion. It will retain a vague reverence for the Christain moral code, and from time to time will refer to England as 'a Christian country'. The Catholic Church will war against it, but the Nonconformist sects and the bulk of the Anglican Church will be able to come to terms with it. It will show a power of assimilating the past which will shock foreign observers and sometimes make them doubt whether any revolution has happened.

But all the same it will have done the essential thing. It will have nationalized industry, scaled down incomes, set up a classless educational system. Its real nature will be apparent from the hatred which the surviving rich men of the world will feel for it. It will aim not at disintegrating the Empire but at turning it into a federation of Socialist states, freed not so much from the British flag as from the money-lender, the dividend-drawer and the wooden-headed British official. Its war strategy will be totally different from that of any property-ruled state, because it will not be afraid of the revolutionary after-effects when any existing régime is brought down. It will not have the smallest scruple about attacking hostile neutrals or stirring up native rebellion in enemy colonies. It will fight in such a way that even if it is beaten its memory will be dangerous to the victor, as the memory of the French Revolution was dangerous to Metternich's Europe. The dictators will fear it as they could not fear the existing British régime, even if its military strength were ten times what it is.

But at this moment, when the drowsy life of England has barely altered, and the offensive contrast of wealth and poverty still exists everywhere, even amid the bombs, why do I dare to say that all these things 'will' happen?

Because the time has come when one can predict the future in terms of 'either – or'. Either we turn this war into a revolutionary war (I do not say that our policy will be *exactly* what I have indicated above – merely that it will be along those general lines) or we lose it, and much more besides. Quite soon it will be possible to say definitely that our feet are set upon one path or the other. But at any rate it is certain that with our present social structure we cannot win. Our real forces, physical, moral or intellectual, cannot be mobilized.

THREE

Patriotism has nothing to do with Conservatism. It is actually the opposite of Conservatism, since it is a devotion to something that is always changing and yet is felt to be mystically the same. It is the bridge between the future and the past. No real revolutionary has ever been an internationalist.

During the past twenty years the negative, *fainéant* outlook which has been fashionable among English left-wingers, the sniggering of the intellectuals at patriotism and physical courage, the persistent effort to chip away English morale and spread a hedonistic, what-do-I-get-out-of-it attitude to life, has done nothing but harm. It would have been harmful even if we had been living in the squashy League of Nations universe that these people imagined. In an age of Fuehrers and bombing planes it was a disaster. However little we may like it, toughness is the price of survival. A nation trained to think hedonistically cannot survive amid peoples who work like slaves and breed like rabbits, and whose chief national industry is war. English Socialists of nearly all colours have wanted to make a stand against Fascism, but at the same time they have aimed at making their own countrymen unwarlike. They have failed, because in England traditional loyalties are stronger than new ones. But in spite of all the 'anti-Fascist' heroics of the left-wing press, what chance should we have stood when the real struggle with Fascism came, if the average Englishman had been the kind of creature that the *New Statesman*, the *Daily Worker* or even the *News Chronicle* wished to make him?

Up to 1935 virtually all English left-wingers were vaguely pacifist. After 1935 the more vocal of them flung themselves eagerly into the Popular Front movement, which was simply an evasion of the whole problem posed by Fascism. It set out to be 'anti-Fascist' in a purely negative way – 'against' Fascism without being 'for' any discoverable policy – and underneath it lay the flabby idea that when the time came the Russians would do our fighting for us. It is astonishing how this illusion fails to die. Every week sees its spate of letters to the press, pointing out that if we had a government with no Tories in it the Russians could hardly avoid coming round to our side. Or we are to publish high-sounding war-aims (*vide* books like *Unser Kampf*, *A Hundred Million Allies – If We Choose*, etc.), whereupon the European populations will infallibly rise on our behalf. It is the same idea all the time – look abroad for your inspiration, get someone else to do your fighting for you. Underneath it lies the frightful inferiority complex of the English intellectual, the belief that the English are no longer a martial race, no longer capable of enduring.

In truth there is no reason to think that anyone will do our fighting for us yet awhile, except the Chinese, who have been doing it for three years already.[1] The Russians may be driven to fight on our side by the fact of a direct attack, but they have made it clear enough that they will not stand up to the German army if there is any way of avoiding it. In any case they are not likely to be attracted by the spectacle of a left-wing government in England. The present Russian régime must almost certainly be hostile to any revolution in the West. The subject peoples of Europe will rebel when Hitler begins to totter, but not earlier. Our potential allies are not the Europeans but on the one hand the Americans, who will need a year to mobilize their resources even if Big Business can be brought to heel, and on the other hand the coloured peoples, who cannot be even sentimentally on our side till our own revolution has started. For a long time, a year, two years, possibly three years, England has got to be the shock-absorber of the world. We have got to face bombing, hunger, overwork, influenza, boredom and treacherous peace offers. Manifestly it is a time to stiffen morale, not to weaken it. Instead of taking the mechanically anti-British attitude which is usual on the Left, it is better to consider what the world would really be like if the English-speaking culture perished. For it is childish to suppose that the other English-speaking countries, even the USA, will be unaffected if Britain is conquered.

Lord Halifax, and all his tribe, believe that when the war is over things will be exactly as they were before. Back to the crazy pavement of Versailles, back to 'democracy', i.e. capitalism, back to dole queues and the Rolls-Royce

[1] Written before the outbreak of the war in Greece. [Author's footnote.]

cars, back to the grey top hats and the sponge-bag trousers, *in saecula saeculorum*. It is of course obvious that nothing of the kind is going to happen. A feeble imitation of it might just possibly happen in the case of a negotiated peace, but only for a short while. *Laissez-faire* capitalism is dead.[1] The choice lies between the kind of collective society that Hitler will set up and the kind that can arise if he is defeated.

If Hitler wins this war he will consolidate his rule over Europe, Africa and the Middle East, and if his armies have not been too greatly exhausted beforehand, he will wrench vast territories from Soviet Russia. He will set up a graded caste-society in which the German *Herrenvolk* ('master race' or 'aristocratic race') will rule over Slavs and other lesser peoples whose job it will be to produce low-priced agricultural products. He will reduce the coloured peoples once and for all to outright slavery. The real quarrel of the Fascist powers with British imperialism is that they know that it is disintegrating. Another twenty years along the present line of development, and India will be a peasant republic linked with England only by voluntary alliance. The 'semi-apes' of whom Hitler speaks with such loathing will be flying aeroplanes and manufacturing machine-guns. The Fascist dream of a slave empire will be at an end. On the other hand, if we are defeated we simply hand over our own victims to new masters who come fresh to the job and have not developed any scruples.

But more is involved than the fate of the coloured peoples. Two incompatible visions of life are fighting one another. 'Between democracy and totalitarianism,' says Mussolini, 'there can be no compromise.' The two creeds cannot even, for any length of time, live side by side. So long as democracy exists, even in its very imperfect English form, totalitarianism is in deadly danger. The whole English-speaking world is haunted by the idea of human equality, and though it would be simply a lie to say that either we or the Americans have ever acted up to our professions, still, the *idea* is there, and it is capable of one day becoming a reality. From the English-speaking culture, if it does not perish, a society of free and equal human beings will ultimately arise. But it is precisely the idea of human equality – the 'Jewish' or 'Judaeo-Christian' idea of equality – that Hitler came into the world to destroy. He has, heaven knows, said so often enough. The thought of a world in which black men would be as good as white men and Jews treated as human beings brings him the same horror and despair as the thought of endless slavery brings to us.

It is important to keep in mind how irreconcilable these two viewpoints are. Some time within the next year a pro-Hitler reaction within the left-wing intelligentsia is likely enough. There are premonitory signs of it already. Hitler's positive achievement appeals to the emptiness of these people, and, in the case of those with pacifist leanings, to their masochism. One knows in advance more or less what they will say. They will start by refusing to admit that British capitalism is evolving into something different, or that the defeat of Hitler can mean any more than a victory for the British and American millionaires. And from that they will proceed to argue that, after all, democracy is 'just the same as' or 'just as bad as' totalitarianism. There is *not much* freedom of speech in England; therefore there is *no more* than exists

[1] It is interesting to notice that Mr Kennedy, USA Ambassador in London, remarked on his return to New York in October 1940 that as a result of the war 'democracy is finished'. By 'democracy', of course, he meant private capitalism. [Author's footnote.]

in Germany. To be on the dole is a horrible experience; therefore it is *no worse* to be in the torture-chambers of the Gestapo. In general, two blacks make a white, half a loaf is the same as no bread.

But in reality, whatever may be true about democracy and totalitarianism, it is not true that they are the same. It would not be true, even if British democracy were incapable of evolving beyond its present stage. The whole conception of the militarized continental state, with its secret police, its censored literature and its conscript labour, is utterly different from that of the loose maritime democracy, with its slums and unemployment, its strikes and party politics. It is the difference between land power and sea power, between cruelty and inefficiency, between lying and self-deception, between the SS man and the rent-collector. And in choosing between them one chooses not so much on the strength of what they now are as of what they are capable of becoming. But in a sense it is irrelevant whether democracy, at its higher or at its lowest, is 'better' than totalitarianism. To decide that one would have to have access to absolute standards. The only question that matters is where one's real sympathies will lie when the pinch comes. The intellectuals who are so fond of balancing democracy against totalitarianism and 'proving' that one is as bad as the other are simply frivolous people who have never been shoved up against realities. They show the same shallow misunderstanding of Fascism now, when they are beginning to flirt with it, as a year or two ago, when they were squealing against it. The question is not, 'Can you make out a debating-society "case" in favour of Hitler?' The question is, 'Do you genuinely accept that case? Are you willing to submit to Hitler's rule? Do you want to see England conquered, or don't you?' It would be better to be sure on that point before frivolously siding with the enemy. For there is no such thing as neutrality in war; in practice one must help one side or the other.

When the pinch comes, no one bred in the western tradition can accept the Fascist vision of life. It is important to realize that *now*, and to grasp what it entails. With all its sloth, hypocrisy and injustice, the English-speaking civilization is the only large obstacle in Hitler's path. It is a living contradiction of all the 'infallible' dogmas of Fascism. That is why all Fascist writers for years past have agreed that England's power must be destroyed. England must be 'exterminated', must be 'annihilated', must 'cease to exist'. Strategically it would be possible for this war to end with Hitler in secure possession of Europe, and with the British Empire intact and British sea-power barely affected. But ideologically it is not possible; were Hitler to make an offer along those lines, it could only be treacherously, with a view to conquering England indirectly or renewing the attack at some more favourable moment. England cannot possibly be allowed to remain as a sort of funnel through which deadly ideas from beyond the Atlantic flow into the police states of Europe. And turning it round to our own point of view, we see the vastness of the issue before us, the all-importance of preserving our democracy more or less as we have known it. But to *preserve* is always to *extend*. The choice before us is not so much between victory and defeat as between revolution and apathy. If the thing we are fighting for is altogether destroyed, it will have been destroyed partly by our own act.

It could happen that England could introduce the beginnings of Socialism, turn this war into a revolutionary war, and still be defeated. That is at any rate thinkable. But, terrible as it would be for anyone who is now adult, it would be far less deadly than the 'compromise peace' which a few rich men and their hired liars are hoping for. The final ruin of England could only be accomplished by an English government acting under orders from Berlin. But that cannot happen if England has awakened beforehand. For in that case the defeat would be unmistakable, the struggle would continue, the *idea* would survive. The difference between going down fighting, and surrendering without a fight, is by no means a questions of 'honour' and schoolboy heroics. Hitler said once that to *accept* defeat destroys the soul of a nation. This sounds like a piece of claptrap, but it is strictly true. The defeat of 1870 did not lessen the world-influence of France. The Third Republic had more influence, intellectually, than the France of Napolean III. But the sort of peace that Pétain, Laval and Co have accepted can only be purchased by deliberately wiping out the national culture. The Vichy Government will enjoy a spurious independence only on condition that it destroys the distinctive marks of French culture: republicanism, secularism, respect for the intellect, absence of colour prejudice. We cannot be *utterly* defeated if we have made our revolution beforehand. We may see German troops marching down Whitehall, but another process, ultimately deadly to the German power-dream, will have been started. The Spanish people were defeated, but the things they learned during those two and a half memorable years will one day come back upon the Spanish Fascists like a boomerang.

A piece of Shakespearean bombast was much quoted at the beginning of the war. Even Mr Chamberlain quoted it once, if my memory does not deceive me:

Come the four corners of the world in arms
And we shall shock them: naught shall make us rue
If England to herself do rest but true.

It is right enough, if you interpret it rightly. But England has got to be true to herself. She is not being true to herself while the refugees who have sought our shores are penned up in concentration camps, and company directors work out subtle schemes to dodge their Excess Profits Tax. It is goodbye to the *Tatler* and the *Bystander*, and farewell to the lady in the Rolls-Royce car. The heirs of Nelson and of Cromwell are not in the House of Lords. They are in the fields and the streets, in the factories and the armed forces, in the four-ale bar and the suburban back garden; and at present they are still kept under by a generation of ghosts. Compared with the task of bringing the real England to the surface, even the winning of the war, necessary though it is, is secondary. By revolution we become more ourselves, not less. There is no question of stopping short, striking a compromise, salvaging 'democracy', standing still. Nothing ever stands still. We must add to our heritage or lose it, we must grow greater or grow less, we must go forward or backward. I believe in England, and I believe that we shall go forward.

Published 19 February 1941

Literature and Totalitarianism

I said at the beginning of my first talk that this is not a critical age. It is an age of partisanship and not of detachment, an age in which it is especially difficult to see literary merit in a book with whose conclusions you disagree. Politics – politics in the most general sense – have invaded literature, to an extent that does not normally happen, and this has brought to the surface of our consciousness the struggle that always goes on between the individual and the community. It is when one considers the difficulty of writing honest unbiased criticism in a time like ours that one begins to grasp the nature of the threat that hangs over the whole of literature in the coming age.

We live in an age in which the autonomous individual is ceasing to exist – or perhaps one ought to say, in which the individual is ceasing to have the illusion of being autonomous. Now, in all that we say about literature, and (above all) in all that we say about criticism, we instinctively take the autonomous individual for granted. The whole of modern European literature – I am speaking of the literature of the past four hundred years – is built on the concept of intellectual honesty, or, if you like to put it that way, on Shakespeare's maxim, 'To thine own self be true'. The first thing that we ask of a writer is that he shall not tell lies, that he shall say what he really thinks, what he really feels. The worst thing we can say about a work of art is that it is insincere. And this is even truer of criticism than of creative literature, in which a certain amount of posing and mannerism, and even a certain amount of downright humbug, doesn't matter so long as the writer is fundamentally sincere. Modern literature is essentially an individual thing. It is either the truthful expression of what one man thinks and feels, or it is nothing.

As I say, we take this notion for granted, and yet as soon as one puts it into words one realizes how literature is menaced. For this is the age of the totalitarian state, which does not and probably cannot allow the individual any freedom whatever. When one mentions totalitarianism one thinks immediately of Germany, Russia, Italy, but I think one must face the risk that this phenomenon is going to be world-wide. It is obvious that the period of free capitalism is coming to an end and that one country after another is adopting a centralized economy that one can call Socialism or state capitalism according as one prefers. With that the economic liberty of the individual, and to a great extent his liberty to do what he likes, to choose his own work, to move to and fro across the surface of the earth, comes to an end. Now, till recently the implications of this were not foreseen. It was never fully realized that the disappearance of economic liberty would have any effect on intellectual liberty. Socialism was usually thought of as a sort of moralized liberalism. The state would take charge of your economic life and set you free from the fear of poverty, unemployment and so forth, but it would have no need to interfere with your private intellectual life. Art could flourish just as it had done in the liberal-capitalist age, only a little more so, because the artist would not any longer be under economic compulsions.

Now, on the existing evidence, one must admit that these ideas have been falsified. Totalitarianism has abolished freedom of thought to an extent unheard of in any previous age. And it is important to realize that its control of thought is not only negative, but positive. It not only forbids you to express – even to think – certain thoughts, but it dictates what you *shall* think, it creates an ideology for you, it tries to govern your emotional life as well as setting up a code of conduct. And as far as possible it isolates you from the outside world, it shuts you up in an artificial universe in which you have no standards of comparison. The totalitarian state tries, at any rate, to control the thoughts and emotions of its subjects at least as completely as it controls their actions.

The question that is important for us is: can literature survive in such an atmosphere? I think one must answer shortly that it cannot. If totalitarianism becomes world-wide and permanent, what we have known as literature must come to an end. And it will not do – as may appear plausible at first – to say that what will come to an end is merely the literature of post-Renaissance Europe.

There are several vital differences between totalitarianism and all the orthodoxies of the past, either in Europe or in the East. The most important is that the orthodoxies of the past did not change, or at least did not change rapidly. In medieval Europe the Church dictated what you should believe, but at least it allowed you to retain the same beliefs from birth to death. It did not tell you to believe one thing on Monday and another on Tuesday. And the same is more or less true of any orthodox Christian, Hindu, Buddhist or Muslim today. In a sense his thoughts are circumscribed, but he passes his whole life within the same framework of thought. His emotions are not tampered with.

Now, with totalitarianism, exactly the opposite is true. The peculiarity of the totalitarian state is that though it controls thought, it does not fix it. It sets up unquestionable dogmas, and it alters them from day to day. It needs the dogmas, because it needs absolute obedience from its subjects, but it cannot avoid the changes, which are dictated by the needs of power politics. It declares itself infallible, and at the same time it attacks the very concept of objective truth. To take a crude, obvious example, every German up to September 1939, had to regard Russian Bolshevism with horror and aversion, and since September 1939, he has had to regard it with admiration and affection. If Russia and Germany go to war, as they may well do within the next few years, another equally violent change will have to take place. The German's emotional life, his loves and hatreds, are expected, when necessary, to reverse themselves overnight. I hardly need to point out the effect of this kind of thing upon literature. For writing is largely a matter of feeling, which cannot always be controlled from outside. It is easy to pay lip-service to the orthodoxy of the moment, but writing of any consequence can only be produced when a man *feels* the truth of what he is saying; without that, the creative impulse is lacking. All the evidence we have suggests that the sudden emotional changes which totalitarianism demands of its followers are psychologically impossible. And that is the chief reason why I suggest that if totalitarianism triumphs throughout the world, literature, as we have known it, is at an end. And, in fact, totalitarianism does seem to have had that effect so far. In Italy literature has been crippled, and in Germany it seems almost to have ceased. The most characteristic activity of the Nazis is burning books. And even in Russia the literary renaissance we once expected has not happened, and the most promising Russian writers show a marked tendency to commit suicide or disappear into prison.

I said earlier that liberal capitalism is obviously coming to an end, and therefore I may have seemed to suggest that freedom of thought is also inevitably doomed. But I do not believe this to be so, and I will simply say in conclusion that I believe the hope of literature's survival lies in those countries in which liberalism has struck its deepest roots, the non-military countries, western Europe and the Americas, India and China. I believe – it may be no more than a pious hope – that though a collectivized economy is bound to come, those countries will know how to evolve a form of Socialism which is not totalitarian, in which freedom of thought can survive the disappearance of economic individualism. That, at any rate, is the only hope to which anyone who cares for literature can cling. Whoever feels the value of literature, whoever sees the central part it plays in the development of human history, must also see the life and death necessity of resisting totalitarianism, whether it is imposed on us from without or from within.

Listener, 19 June 1941

Wells, Hitler and the World State

> 'In March or April, say the wiseacres, there is to be a stupendous knockout blow at Britain ... What Hitler has to do it with, I cannot imagine. His ebbing and dispersed military resources are now probably not so very much greater than the Italians' before they were put to the test in Greece and Africa.'
>
> 'The German air power has been largely spent. It is behind the times and its first-rate men are mostly dead or disheartened or worn out.'
>
> 'In 1914 the Hohenzollern army was the best in the world. Behind that screaming little defective in Berlin there is nothing of the sort ... Yet our military "experts" discuss the waiting phantom. In their imaginations it is perfect in its equipment and invincible in discipline. Sometimes it is to strike a decisive "blow" through Spain and North Africa and on, or march through the Balkans, march from the Danube to Ankara, to Persia, to India, or "crush Russia", or "pour" over the Brenner into Italy. The weeks pass and the phantom does none of these things – for one excellent reason. It does not exist to that extent. Most of such inadequate guns and munitions as it possessed must have been taken away from it and fooled away in Hitler's silly feints to invade Britain. And its raw jerry-built discipline is wilting under the creeping realization that the Blitzkrieg is spent, and the war is coming home to roost.'

These quotations are not taken from the *Cavalry Quarterly* but from a series of newspaper articles by Mr H. G. Wells, written at the beginning of this year and now reprinted in a book entitled *Guide to the New World*. Since they were written, the German army has overrun the Balkans and reconquered Cyrenaica, it can march through Turkey or Spain at such time as may suit it, and it has undertaken the invasion of Russia. How that campaign will turn out I do not know, but it is worth noticing that the German general staff, whose opinion is probably worth something, would not have begun it if they had not felt fairly certain of finishing it within three months. So much for the idea that the German army is a bogey, its equipment inadequate, its morale breaking down, etc., etc.

What has Wells to set against the 'screaming little defective in Berlin'? The usual rigmarole about a World State, plus the Sankey Declaration, which is an attempted definition of fundamental human rights, of anti-totalitarian tendency. Except that he is now especially concerned with federal world control of air power, it is the same gospel as he has been preaching almost without interruption for the past forty years, always with an air of angry surprise at the human beings who can fail to grasp anything so obvious.

What is the use of saying that we need federal world control of the air? The whole question is how we are to get it. What is the use of pointing out that a World State is desirable? What matters is that not one of the five great military powers would think of submitting to such a thing. All sensible men for decades past have been substantially in agreement with what Mr Wells says; but the sensible men have no power and, in too many cases, no disposition to sacrifice themselves. Hitler is a criminal lunatic, and Hitler has an army of millions of men, aeroplanes in thousands, tanks in tens of thousands. For his sake a great nation has been willing to overwork itself for six years and then to fight for two years more, whereas for the common-sense, essentially hedonistic world-view which Mr Wells puts forward, hardly a human creature is willing to shed a pint of blood. Before you can even talk of world reconstruction, or even of peace, you have got to eliminate Hitler, which means bringing into being a dynamic not necessarily the same as that of the Nazis, but probably quite as unacceptable to 'enlightened' and hedonistic people. What has kept England on its feet during the past year? In part, no doubt, some vague idea about a better future, but chiefly the atavistic emotion of patriotism, the ingrained feeling of the English-speaking peoples that they are superior to foreigners. For the last twenty years the main object of English left-wing intellectuals has been to break this feeling down, and if they had succeeded, we might be watching the SS men patrolling the London streets at this moment. Similarly, why are the Russians fighting like tigers against the German invasion? In part, perhaps, for some half-remembered ideal of Utopian Socialism, but chiefly in defence of Holy Russia (the 'sacred soil of the Fatherland', etc., etc.), which Stalin has revived in an only slightly altered form. The energy that actually shapes the world springs from emotions – racial pride, leader-worship, religious belief, love of war – which liberal intellectuals mechanically write off as anachronisms, and which they have usually destroyed so completely in themselves as to have lost all power of action.

The people who say that Hitler is Antichrist, or alternatively, the Holy Ghost, are nearer an understanding of the truth than the intellectuals who for ten dreadful years have kept it up that he is merely a figure out of comic opera, not worth taking seriously. All that this idea really reflects is the sheltered conditions of English life. The Left Book Club was at bottom a product of Scotland Yard, just as the Peace Pledge Union is a product of the navy. One development of the last ten years has been the appearance of the 'political book', a sort of enlarged pamphlet combining history with political criticism, as an important literary form. But the best writers in this line – Trotsky, Rauschning, Rosenberg, Silone, Borkenau, Koestler and others – have none of them been Englishmen, and nearly all of them have been renegades from one or other extremist party, who have seen totalitarianism at close quarters and known the meaning of exile and persecution. Only in the English-speaking countries was it fashionable to believe, right up to the outbreak of war, that Hitler was an unimportant lunatic and the German tanks made of cardboard. Mr Wells, it will be seen from the quotations I have given above, believes something of the kind still. I do not suppose that either the bombs or the German campaign in Greece have altered his opinion. A lifelong habit of thought stands between him and an understanding of Hitler's power.

Mr Wells, like Dickens, belongs to the non-military middle class. The thunder of guns, the jingle of spurs, the catch in the throat when the old flag goes by, leave him manifestly cold. He has an invincible hatred of the fighting, hunting, swashbuckling side of life, symbolized in all his early books by a violent propaganda against horses. The principal villain of his *Outline of History* is the military adventurer, Napoleon. If one looks through nearly any book that he has written in the last forty years one finds the same idea constantly recurring: the supposed antithesis between the man of science who is working towards a planned World State and the reactionary who is trying to restore a disorderly past. In novels, Utopias, essays, films, pamphlets, the antithesis crops up, always more or less the same. On the one side science, order, progress, internationalism, aeroplanes, steel, concrete, hygiene: on the other side war, nationalism, religion, monarchy, peasants, Greek professors, poets, horses. History as he sees it is a series of victories won by the scientific man over the romantic man. Now, he is probably right in assuming that a 'reasonable', planned form of society, with scientists rather than witch-doctors in control, will prevail sooner or later, but that is a different matter from assuming that it is just round the corner. There survives somewhere or other an interesting controversy which took place between Wells and Churchill at the time of the Russian Revolution. Wells accuses Churchill of not really believing his own propaganda about the Bolsheviks being monsters dripping with blood, etc., but of merely fearing that they were going to introduce an era of common sense and scientific control, in which flag-wavers like Churchill himself would have no place. Churchill's estimate of the Bolsheviks, however, was nearer the mark than Wells's. The early Bolsheviks may have been angels or demons, according as one chooses to regard them, but at any rate they were not sensible men. They were not introducing a Wellsian Utopia but a Rule of the Saints, which, like the English Rule of the Saints, was a military despotism enlivened by witchcraft trials. The same misconception reappears in an inverted form in Wells's attitude to the Nazis. Hitler is all the war-lords and witch-doctors in history rolled into one. Therefore, argues Wells, he is an absurdity, a ghost from the past, a creature doomed to disappear almost immediately. But unfortunately the equation of science with common sense does not really hold good. The aeroplane, which was looked forward to as a civilizing influence but in practice has hardly been used except for dropping bombs, is the symbol of the fact. Modern Germany is far more scientific than England, and far more barbarous. Much of what Wells has imagined and worked for is physically there in Nazi Germany. The order, the planning, the State encouragement of science, the steel, the concrete, the aeroplanes, are all there, but all in the service of ideas appropriate to the Stone Age.

Science is fighting on the side of superstition. But obviously it is impossible for Wells to accept this. It would contradict the world-view on which his own works are based. The war-lords and the witch-doctors *must* fail, the common-sense World State, as seen by a nineteenth-century liberal whose heart does not leap at the sound of bugles, *must* triumph. Treachery and defeatism apart, Hitler *cannot* be a danger. That he should finally win would be an impossible reversal of history, like a Jacobite restoration.

But is it not a sort of parricide for a person of my age (thirty-eight) to find fault with H. G. Wells? Thinking people who were born about the beginning of this century are in some sense Wells's own creation. How much influence any mere writer has, and especially a 'popular' writer whose work takes effect quickly, is unquestionable, but I doubt whether anyone who was writing books between 1900 and 1920, at any rate in the English language, influenced the young so much. The minds of all of us, and therefore the physical world, would be perceptibly different if Wells had never existed. Only, just the singleness of mind, the one-sided imagination that made him seem like an inspired prophet in the Edwardian age, make him a shallow, inadequate thinker now. When Wells was young, the antithesis between science and reaction was not false. Society was ruled by narrow-minded, profoundly incurious people, predatory businessmen, dull squires, bishops, politicians who could quote Horace but had never heard of algebra. Science was faintly disreputable and religious belief obligatory. Traditionalism, stupidity, snobbishness, patriotism, superstition and love of war seemed to be all on the same side; there was need of someone who could state the opposite point of view. Back in the nineteen-hundreds it was a wonderful experience for a boy to discover H. G. Wells. There you were, in a world of pedants, clergymen and golfers, with your future employers exhorting you to 'get on or get out', your parents systematically warping your sexual life, and your dull-witted schoolmasters sniggering over their Latin tags; and here was this wonderful man who could tell you about the inhabitants of the planets and the bottom of the sea, and who *knew* that the future was not going to be what respectable people imagined. A decade or so before aeroplanes were technically feasible Wells knew that within a little while men would be able to fly. He knew that because he himself *wanted* to be able to fly, and therefore felt sure that research in that direction would continue. On the other hand, even when I was a little boy, at a time when the Wright brothers had actually lifted their machine off the ground for fifty-nine seconds, the generally accepted opinion was that if God had meant us to fly He would have given us wings. Up to 1914 Wells was in the main a true prophet. In physical details his vision of the new world has been fulfilled to a surprising extent.

But because he belonged to the nineteenth century and to a non-military nation and class, he could not grasp the tremendous strength of the old world which was symbolized in his mind by foxhunting Tories. He was, and still is, quite incapable of understanding that nationalism, religious bigotry and feudal loyalty are far more powerful forces than what he himself would describe as sanity. Creatures out of the Dark Ages have come marching into the present, and if they are ghosts they are at any rate ghosts which need a strong magic to lay them. The people who have shown the best understanding of Fascism are either those who have suffered under it or those who have a Fascist streak in themselves. A crude book like *The Iron Heel*, written nearly thirty years ago, is a truer prophecy of the future than either *Brave New World* or *The*

Shape of Things to Come. If one had to choose among Wells's own contemporaries a writer who could stand towards him as a corrective, one might choose Kipling, who was not deaf to the evil voices of power and military 'glory'. Kipling would have understood the appeal of Hitler, or for that matter of Stalin, whatever his attitude towards them might be. Wells is too sane to understand the modern world. The succession of lower-middle-class novels which are his greatest achievement stopped short at the other war and never really began again, and since 1920 he has squandered his talents in slaying paper dragons. But how much it is, after all, to have any talents to squander.

Horizon, August 1941

The Art of Donald McGill

Who does not know the 'comics' of the cheap stationers' windows, the penny or twopenny coloured postcards with their endless succession of fat women in tight bathing-dresses and their crude drawing and unbearable colours, chiefly hedge-sparrow's egg tint and Post Office red?

This question ought to be rhetorical, but it is a curious fact that many people seem to be unaware of the existence of these things, or else to have a vague notion that they are something to be found only at the seaside, like nigger minstrels or peppermint rock. Actually they are on sale everywhere – they can be bought at nearly any Woolworth's, for example – and they are evidently produced in enormous numbers, new series constantly appearing. They are not to be confused with the various other types of comic illustrated postcard, such as the sentimental ones dealing with puppies and kittens or the Wendyish, sub-pornographic ones which exploit the love-affairs of children. They are a genre of their own, specializing in very 'low' humour, the mother-in-law, baby's nappy, policemen's boots type of joke, and distinguishable from all other kinds by having no artistic pretensions. Some half-dozen publishing houses issue them, though the people who draw them seem not to be numerous at any one time.

I have associated them especially with the name of Donald McGill because he is not only the most prolific and by far the best of contemporary postcard artists, but also the most representative, the most perfect in the tradition. Who Donald McGill is, I do not know. He is apparently a trade name, for at least one series of postcards is issued simply as 'The Donald McGill Comics', but he is also unquestionably a real person with a style of drawing which is recognizable at a glance. Anyone who examines his postcards in bulk will notice that many of them are not despicable even as drawings, but it would be mere dilettantism to pretend that they have any direct aesthetic value. A comic postcard is simply an illustration to a joke, invariably a 'low' joke, and it stands or falls by its ability to raise a laugh. Beyond that it has only 'ideological' interest. McGill is a clever draughtsman with a real caricaturist's touch in the drawing of faces, but the special value of his postcards is that they are so completely typical. They represent, as it were, the norm of the comic postcard. Without being in the least imitative, they are exactly what comic postcards have been any time these last forty years, and from them the meaning and purpose of the whole genre can be inferred.

Get hold of a dozen of these things, preferably McGill's – if you pick out from a pile the ones that seem to you funniest, you will probably find that most of them are McGill's – and spread them out on a table. What do you see?

Your first impression is of overpowering vulgarity. This is quite apart from the ever-present obscenity, and apart also from the hideousness of the colours. They have an utter lowness of mental atmosphere which comes out not only in the nature of the jokes but, even more, in the grotesque, staring, blatant quality of the drawings. The designs, like those of a child, are full of heavy lines and empty spaces, and all the figures in them, every gesture and attitude, are deliberately ugly, the faces grinning and vacuous, the women monstrously parodied, with bottoms like Hottentots. Your second impression, however, is of indefinable familiarity. What do these things remind you of? What are they so like? In the first place, of course, they remind you of the barely different postcards which you probably gazed at in your childhood. But more than this, what you are really looking at is something as traditional as Greek tragedy, a sort of sub-world of smacked bottoms and scrawny mothers-in-law which is a part of western European consciousness. Not that the jokes, taken one by one, are necessarily stale. Not being debarred from smuttiness, comic postcards repeat themselves less often than the joke columns in reputable magazines, but their basic subject-matter, the *kind* of joke they are aiming at, never varies. A few are genuinely witty, in a Max Millerish style. Examples:

> 'I like seeing experienced girls home.'
> 'But I'm not experienced!'
> 'You're not home yet!'
>
> 'I've been struggling for years to get a fur coat. How did you get yours?'
> 'I left off struggling.'
>
> Judge: 'You are prevaricating, sir. Did you or did you not sleep with this woman?'
> Co-respondent: 'Not a wink, my lord!'

In general, however, they are not witty but humorous, and it must be said for McGill's postcards, in particular, that the drawing is often a good deal funnier than the joke beneath it. Obviously the outstanding characteristic of comic postcards is their obscenity, and I must discuss that more fully later. But I give here a rough analysis of their habitual subject-matter, with such explanatory remarks as seem to be needed:

Sex. More than half, perhaps three-quarters, of the jokes are sex jokes, ranging from the harmless to the all but unprintable. First favourite is probably the illegitimate baby. Typical captions: 'Could you exchange this lucky charm for a baby's feeding-bottle?' 'She didn't ask me to the christening, so I'm not going to the wedding.' Also newlyweds, old maids, nude statues and women in bathing-dresses. All of these are *ipso facto* funny, mere mention of them being enough to raise a laugh. The cuckoldry joke is very seldom exploited, and there are no references to homosexuality.

Conventions of the sex joke:

a. Marriage only benefits the woman. Every man is plotting seduction and every woman is plotting marriage. No woman ever remains unmarried voluntarily.
b. Sex-appeal vanishes at about the age of twenty-five. Well-preserved and good-looking people beyond their first youth are never represented. The amorous honeymooning couple reappear as the grim-visaged wife and shapeless, mustachioed, red-nosed husband, no intermediate stage being allowed for.

Home life. Next to sex, the henpecked husband is the favourite joke. Typical caption: 'Did they get an X-ray of your wife's jaw at the hospital?' – 'No, they got a moving picture instead.'

Conventions:

a. There is no such thing as a happy marriage.
b. No man ever gets the better of a woman in argument.

Drunkenness. Both drunkenness and teetotalism are *ipso facto* funny.

Conventions:

a. All drunken men have optical illusions.
b. Drunkenness is something peculiar to middle-aged men. Drunken youths or women are never represented.

WC jokes. There is not a large number of these. Chamber-pots are *ipso facto* funny, and so are public lavatories. A typical postcard, captioned 'A Friend in Need', shows a man's hat blown off his head and disappearing down the steps of a ladies' lavatory.

Inter-working-class snobbery. Much in these postcards suggests that they are aimed at the better-off working class and poorer middle class. There are many jokes turning on malaproprisms, illiteracy, dropped aitches and the rough manners of slum-dwellers. Countless postcards show draggled hags of the stage-charwoman type exchanging 'unladylike' abuse. Typical repartee: 'I wish you were a statue and I was a pigeon!' A certain number produced since the war treat evacuation from the anti-evacuee angle. There are the usual jokes about tramps, beggars and criminals, and the comic maidservant appears fairly frequently. Also the comic navvy, bargee, etc.; but there are no anti-trade-union jokes. Broadly speaking, everyone with much over or much under £5 a week is regarded as laughable. The 'swell' is almost as automatically a figure of fun as the slum-dweller.

Stock figures. Foreigners seldom or never appear. The chief locality joke is the Scotsman, who is almost inexhaustible. The lawyer is always a swindler, the clergyman always a nervous idiot who says the wrong thing. The 'knut' or 'masher' still appears, almost as in Edwardian days, in out-of-date-looking evening clothes and an opera hat, or even with spats and a knobby cane. Another survival is the Suffragette, one of the big jokes of the pre-1914 period and too valuable to be relinquished. She has reappeared, unchanged in physical appearance, as the Feminist lecturer or Temperance fanatic. A feature of the last few years is the complete absence of anti-Jew postcards. The 'Jew joke', always somewhat more ill-natured than the 'Scotch joke', disappeared abruptly soon after the rise of Hitler.

Politics. Any contemporary event, cult or activity which has comic possibilities (for example, 'free love', feminism, ARP, nudism) rapidly finds its way into the picture postcards, but their general atmosphere is extremely old-fashioned. The implied political outlook is a radicalism appropriate to about the year 1900. At normal times they are not only not patriotic, but go in for a mild guying of patriotism, with jokes about 'God save the King', the Union Jack, etc. The European situation only began to reflect iself in them at some time in 1939, and first did so through the comic aspects of ARP. Even at this date few postcards mention the war except in ARP jokes (fat woman stuck in the mouth of Anderson shelter: wardens neglecting their duty while young woman undresses at window she had forgotten to black out, etc., etc.). A few express anti-Hitler sentiments of a not very vindictive kind. One, not McGill's, shows Hitler, with the usual hypertrophied backside, bending down to pick a flower. Caption: 'What would *you* do, chums?' This is about as high a flight of patriotism as any postcard is likely to attain. Unlike the twopenny weekly papers, comic postcards are not the product of any great monopoly company, and evidently they are not regarded as having any importance in forming public opinion. There is no sign in them of any attempt to induce an outlook acceptable to the ruling class.

Here one comes back to the outstanding, all-important feature of comic postcards – their obscenity. It is by this that everyone remembers them, and it is also central to their purpose, though not in a way that is immediately obvious.

A recurrent, almost dominant motif in comic postcards is the woman with the stuck-out behind. In perhaps half of them, or more than half, even when the point of the joke has nothing to do with sex, the same female figure appears, a plump 'voluptuous' figure with the dress clinging to it as tightly as another skin and with breasts or buttocks grossly over-emphasized, according to which way it is turned. There can be no doubt that these pictures lift the lid off a very widespread repression, natural enough in a country whose women when young tend to be slim to the point of skimpiness. But at the same time the McGill postcard – and this applies to all other postcards in this genre – is not intended as pornography but, a subtler thing, as a skit on pornography. The Hottentot figures of the women are caricatures of the Englishman's secret ideal, not portraits of it. When one examines McGill's postcards more closely, one notices that his brand of humour only has meaning in relation to a fairly strict moral code. Whereas in papers like *Esquire*, for instance, or *La Vie Parisienne*, the imaginary background of the jokes is always promiscuity, the utter breakdown of all standards, the background of the McGill postcard is marriage. The four leading jokes are nakedness, illegitimate babies, old maids and newly married couples, none of which would seem funny in a really dissolute or even 'sophisticated' society. The postcards dealing with honeymoon couples always have the enthusiastic indecency of those village weddings where it is still considered screamingly funny to sew bells to the bridal bed. In one, for example, a young bridegroom is shown getting out of bed the morning after his wedding night. 'The first morning in our own little home, darling!' he is saying; 'I'll go and get the milk and paper and bring you a cup of tea.' Inset is a picture of the front doorstep; on it are four newspapers and four bottles of milk. This is obscene, if you like, but it is not immoral. Its implication – and this is just the implication that *Esquire* or the *New Yorker* would avoid at all costs – is that marriage is something profoundly exciting and important, the biggest event in the average human being's life. So also with jokes about nagging wives and tyrannous mothers-in-law. They do at least imply a stable society in which marriage is indissoluble and family loyalty taken for granted. And bound up with this is something I noted earlier, the fact that there are no pictures, or hardly any, of good-looking people beyond their first youth. There is the 'spooning' couple and the middle-aged, cat-and-dog couple, but nothing in between. The liaison, the illicit but more or less decorous love-affair which used to be the stock joke of French comic papers, is not a postcard subject. And this reflects, on a comic level, the working-class outlook which takes it as a matter of course that youth and adventure – almost, indeed, individual life – end with marriage. One of the few authentic class-differences, as opposed to class-distinctions, still existing in England is that the working classes age very much earlier. They do not live less long, provided that they survive their childhood, nor do they lose their physical activity earlier, but they do lose very early their youthful appearance. This fact is observable everywhere, but can be most easily verified by watching one of the higher age groups registering for military service; the middle- and upper-class members look, on average, ten years younger than the others. It is usual to attribute this to the harder lives that the working classes have to live, but it is doubtful whether any such difference now exists as would account for it. More probably the truth is that the working classes reach middle age earlier because they accept it earlier. For to look young after, say, thirty is largely a matter of wanting to do so. This generalization is less true of the better-paid workers, especially those who live in council houses and labour-saving flats, but it is true enough even of them to point to a difference of outlook. And in this, as usual, they are more traditional, more in accord with the Christian past than the well-to-do women who try to stay young at forty by means of physical jerks, cosmetics and avoidance of child-bearing. The impulse to cling to youth at all costs, to attempt to preserve your sexual attraction, to see even in middle age a future for yourself and not merely for your children, is a thing of recent growth and has only precariously established itself. It will probably disappear again when our standard of living drops and our birth-rate rises. 'Youth's a stuff will not endure' expresses the normal, traditional attitude. It is this ancient wisdom that McGill and his colleagues are reflecting, no doubt unconsciously, when they allow for no transition stage between the honeymoon couple and those glamourless figures, Mum and Dad.

I have said that at least half McGill's postcards are sex jokes, and a proportion, perhaps ten per cent, are far more obscene than anything else that is now printed in England. Newsagents are occasionally prosecuted for selling them, and there would be many more prosecutions if the broadest jokes were not invariably protected by double meanings. A single example will be enough to show how this is done. In one postcard, captioned 'They didn't believe her', a young woman is demonstrating, with her hands held apart, something about two feet long to a couple of open-mouthed acquaintances. Behind her on the wall is a stuffed fish in a glass case, and beside that is a photograph of a nearly naked athlete. Obviously it is not the fish that she is referring to, but this could never be proved. Now, it is doubtful whether there is any paper in England that would print a joke of this kind, and certainly there is no paper that does so habitually. There is an immense amount of pornography of a mild sort, countless illustrated papers cashing in on women's legs, but there is no popular literature specializing in the 'vulgar', farcical aspect of sex. On the other hand, jokes exactly like McGill's are the ordinary small change of the revue and music-hall stage, and are also to be heard on the radio, at moments when the censor happens to be nodding. In England the gap between what can be said and what can be printed is rather exceptionally wide. Remarks and gestures which hardly anyone objects to on the stage would raise a public outcry if any attempt were made to reproduce them on paper. (Compare Max Miller's[1] stage patter with his weekly column in the *Sunday Dispatch*.) The comic postcards are the only existing exception to this rule, the only medium in which really 'low' humour is considered to be printable. Only in postcards and on the variety stage can the stuck-out behind, dog and lamp-post, baby's nappy type of joke be freely exploited. Remembering that, one sees what function these postcards, in their humble way, are performing.

What they are doing is to give expression to the Sancho Panza view of life, the attitude to life that Miss Rebecca West once summed up as 'extracting as much fun as possible from smacking behinds in basement kitchens'. The Don Quixote-Sancho Panza combination, which of course is simply the ancient dualism of body and soul in fiction form, recurs more frequently in the literature of the last four hundred years than can be explained by mere imitation. It comes up again and again, in endless variations, Bouvard and Pécuchet, Jeeves and Wooster, Bloom and Dedalus, Holmes and Watson (the Holmes-Watson variant is an exceptionally subtle one, because the usual physical characteristics of two partners have been transposed). Evidently it

[1] Reviewing *Applesauce*, a variety show, in *Time and Tide*, 7 September 1940, Orwell wrote: 'Anyone wanting to see something really vulgar should visit the Holborn Empire, where you can get quite a good matinée seat for three shillings. Max Miller, of course, is the main attraction.

'Max Miller, who looks more like a Middlesex Street hawker than ever when he is wearing a tail coat and a shiny top hat, is one of a long line of English comedians who have specialized in the Sancho Panza side of life, in real *lowness*. To do this probably needs more talent than to express nobility. Little Tich was a master at it. There was a music-hall farce which Little Tich used to act in, in which he was supposed to be factotum to a crook solicitor. The solicitor is giving him his instructions:

"Now, our client who's coming this morning is a widow with a good figure. Are you following me?"

Little Tich: "I'm ahead of you."

'As it happens, I have seen this farce acted several times with other people in the same part, but I have never seen anyone who could approach the utter baseness that Little Tich could get into these simple words. There is a touch of the same quality in Max Miller. Quite apart from the laughs they give one, it is important that such comedians should exist. They express something which is valuable in our civilization and which might drop out of it in certain circumstances. To begin with, their genius is entirely masculine. A woman cannot be low without being disgusting, whereas a good male comedian can give the impression of something irredeemable and yet innocent, like a sparrow. Again, they are intensely national. They remind one how closely-knit the civilization of England is, and how much it resembles a family, in spite of its out-of-date class distinctions. The startling obscenities which occur in *Applesauce* are only possible because they are expressed in *doubles entendres* which imply a common background in the audience. Anyone who has not been brought up on the *Pink 'Un* would miss the point of them. So long as comedians like Max Miller are on the stage and the comic coloured postcards which express approximately the same view of life are in the stationers' windows, one knows that the popular culture of England is surviving ...'

corresponds to something enduring in our civilization, not in the sense that either character is to be found in a 'pure' state in real life, but in the sense that the two principles, noble folly and base wisdom, exist side by side in nearly every human being. If you look into your own mind, which are you, Don Quixote or Sancho Panza? Almost certainly you are both. There is one part of you that wishes to be a hero or a saint, but another part of you is a little fat man who sees very clearly the advantages of staying alive with a whole skin. He is your unofficial self, the voice of the belly protesting against the soul. His tastes lie towards safety, soft beds, no work, pots of beer and women with 'voluptuous' figures. He it is who punctures your fine attitudes and urges you to look after Number One, to be unfaithful to your wife, to bilk your debts, and so on and so forth. Whether you allow yourself to be influenced by him is a different question. But it is simply a lie to say that he is not part of you, just as it is a lie to say that Don Quixote is not part of you either, though most of what is said and written consists of one lie or the other, usually the first.

But though in varying forms he is one of the stock figures of literature, in real life, especially in the way society is ordered, his point of view never gets a fair hearing. There is a constant world-wide conspiracy to pretend that he is not there, or at least that he doesn't matter. Codes of law and morals, or religious systems, never have much room in them for a humorous view of life. Whatever is funny is subversive, every joke is ultimately a custard pie, and the reason why so large a proportion of jokes centre round obscenity is simply that all societies, as the price of survival, have to insist on a fairly high standard of sexual morality. A dirty joke is not, of course, a serious attack upon morality, but it is a sort of mental rebellion, a momentary wish that things were otherwise. So also with all other jokes, which always centre round cowardice, laziness, dishonesty or some other quality which society cannot afford to encourage. Society has always to demand a little more from human beings than it will get in practice. It has to demand faultless discipline and self-sacrifice, it must expect it subjects to work hard, pay their taxes, and be faithful to their wives, it must assume that men think it glorious to die on the battlefield and women want to wear themselves out with child-bearing. The whole of what one may call official literature is founded on such assumptions. I never read the proclamations of generals before battle, the speeches of Fuehrers and prime ministers, the solidarity songs of public schools and left-wing political parties, national anthems, Temperance tracts, Papal encyclicals and sermons against gambling and contraception, without seeming to hear in the background a chorus of raspberries from all the millions of common men to whom these high sentiments make no appeal. Nevertheless the high sentiments always win in the end, leaders who offer blood, toil, tears and sweat always get more out of their followers than those who offer safety and a good time. When it comes to the pinch, human beings are heroic. Women face childbed and the scrubbing brush, revolutionaries keep their mouths shut in the torture chamber, battleships go down with their guns still firing when their decks are awash. It is only that the other element in man, the lazy, cowardly, debt-bilking adulterer who is inside all of us, can never be suppressed altogether and needs a hearing occasionally.

The comic postcards are one expression of his point of view, a humble one, less important than the music halls, but still worthy of attention. In a society which is still basically Christian they naturally concentrate on sex jokes; in a totalitarian society, if they had any freedom of expression at all, they would probably concentrate on laziness or cowardice, but at any rate on the unheroic in one form or another. It will not do to condemn them on the ground that they are vulgar and ugly. That is exactly what they are meant to be. Their whole meaning and virtue is in their unredeemed lowness, not only in the sense of obscenity, but lowness of outlook in every direction whatever. The slightest hint of 'higher' influences would ruin them utterly. They stand for the worm's-eye view of life, for the music-hall world where marriage is a dirty joke or a comic disaster, where the rent is always behind and the clothes are always up the spout, where the lawyer is always a crook and the Scotsman always a miser, where the newlyweds make fools of themselves on the hideous beds of seaside lodging houses and the drunken, red-nosed husbands roll home at four in the morning to meet the linen-nightgowned wives who wait for them behind the front door, poker in hand. Their existence, the fact that people want them, is symptomatically important. Like the music halls, they are a sort of saturnalia, a harmless rebellion against virtue. They express only one tendency in the human mind, but a tendency which is always there and will find its own outlet, like water. On the whole, human beings want to be good, but not too good, and not quite all the time. For:

> there is a just man that perishes in his righteousness, and there is a wicked man that prolongeth his life in his wickedness. Be not righteous over much; neither make thyself over wise; why shouldst thou destroy theyself? Be not overmuch wicked, neither be thou foolish: why shouldst thou die before thy time?

In the past the mood of the comic postcard could enter into the central stream of literature, and jokes barely different from McGill's could casually be uttered between the murders in Shakespeare's tragedies. That is no longer possible, and a whole category of humour, integral to our literature till 1800 or thereabouts, has dwindled down to these ill-drawn postcards, leading a barely legal existence in cheap stationers' windows. The corner of the human heart that they speak for might easily manifest itself in worse forms, and I for one should be sorry to see them vanish.

Horizon, September 1941

Rudyard Kipling

It was a pity that Mr Eliot should be so much on the defensive in the long essay with which he prefaces this selection of Kipling's poetry,[1] but it was not to be avoided, because before one can even speak about Kipling one has to clear away a legend that has been created by two sets of people who have not read his works. Kipling is in the peculiar position of having been a byword for fifty years. During five literary generations every enlightened person

[1] *A Choice of Kipling's Verse* made by T. S. Eliot.

has despised him, and at the end of that time nine-tenths of those enlightened persons are forgotten and Kipling is in some sense still there. Mr Eliot never satisfactorily explains this fact, because in answering the shallow and familiar charge that Kipling is a 'Fascist', he falls into the opposite error of defending him where he is not defensible. It is no use pretending that Kipling's view of life, as a whole, can be accepted or even forgiven by any civilized person. It is no use claiming, for instance, that when Kipling describes a British soldier beating a 'nigger' with a cleaning rod in order to get money out of him, he is acting merely as a reporter and does not necessarily approve what he describes. There is not the slightest sign anywhere in Kipling's work that he disapproves of that kind of conduct – on the contrary, there is a definite strain of sadism in him, over and above the brutality which a writer of that type has to have. Kipling *is* a jingo imperialist, he *is* morally insensitive and aesthetically disgusting. It is better to start by admitting that, and then to try to find out why it is that he survives while the refined people who have sniggered at him seem to wear so badly.

And yet the 'Fascist' charge has to be answered, because the first clue to any understanding of Kipling, morally or politically, is the fact that he was *not* a Fascist. He was further from being one than the most humane or the most 'progressive' person is able to be nowadays. An interesting instance of the way in which quotations are parroted to and fro without any attempt to look up their context or discover their meaning is the line from 'Recessional', 'Lesser breeds without the Law'. This line is always good for a snigger in pansy-left circles. It is assumed as a matter of course that the 'lesser breeds' are 'natives', and a mental picture is called up of some pukka sahib in a pith helmet kicking a coolie. In its context the sense of the line is almost the exact opposite of this. The phrase 'lesser breeds' refers almost certainly to the Germans, and especially the pan-German writers, who are 'without the Law' in the sense of being lawless, not in the sense of being powerless. The whole poem, conveniently thought of as an orgy of boasting, is a denunciation of power politics, British as well as German. Two stanzas are worth quoting (I am quoting this as politics, not as poetry):

If, drunk with sight of power, we loose
Wild tongues that have not Thee in awe,
Such boastings as the Gentiles use,
Or lesser breeds without the Law –
Lord God of hosts, be with us yet,
Lest we forget – lest we forget!

For heathen heart that puts her trust
In reeking tube and iron shard,
All valiant dust that builds on dust,
And guarding, calls not Thee to guard,
For frantic boast and foolish word –
Thy mercy on Thy People, Lord!

Much of Kipling's phraseology is taken from the Bible, and no doubt in the second stanza he had in mind the text from Psalm 127: 'Except the Lord build the house, they labour in vain that build it; except the Lord keep the city, the watchman waketh but in vain.' It is not a text that makes much impression on the post-Hitler mind. No one, in our time, believes in any sanction greater than military power; no one believes that it is possible to overcome force except by greater force. There is no 'law', there is only power. I am not saying that that is a true belief, merely that it is the belief which all modern men do actually hold. Those who pretend otherwise are either intellectual cowards, or power-worshippers under a thin disguise, or have simply not caught up with the age they are living in. Kipling's outlook is pre-Fascist. He still believes that pride comes before a fall and that the gods punish *hubris*. He does not foresee the tank, the bombing plane, the radio and the secret police, or their psychological results.

But in saying this, does not one unsay what I said above about Kipling's jingoism and brutality? No, one is merely saying that the nineteenth-century imperialist outlook and the modern gangster outlook are two different things. Kipling belongs very definitely to the period 1885–1902. The Great War and its aftermath embittered him, but he shows little sign of having learned anything from any event later than the Boer War. He was the prophet of British imperialism in its expansionist phase (even more than his poems, his solitary novel, *The Light that Failed*, gives you the atmosphere of that time) and also the unofficial historian of the British army, the old mercenary army which began to change its shape in 1914. All his confidence, his bouncing vulgar vitality, sprang out of limitations which no Fascist or near-Fascist shares.

Kipling spent the later part of his life in sulking, and no doubt it was political disappointment rather than literary vanity that accounted for this. Somehow history had not gone according to plan. After the greatest victory she had ever known, Britain was a lesser world power than before, and Kipling was quite acute enough to see this. The virtue had gone out of the classes he idealized, the young were hedonistic or disaffected, the desire to paint the map red had evaporated. He could not understand what was happening, because he had never had any grasp of the economic forces underlying imperial expansion. It is notable that Kipling does not seem to realize, any more than the average soldier or colonial administrator, that an empire is primarily a money-making concern. Imperialism as he sees it is a sort of forcible evangelizing. You turn a Gatling gun on a mob of unarmed 'natives', and then you establish 'the Law', which includes roads, railways and a court-house. He could not foresee, therefore, that the same motives which brought the Empire into existence would end by destroying it. It was the same motive, for example, that caused the Malayan jungles to be cleared for rubber estates, and which now causes those estates to be handed over to the Japanese. The modern totalitarians know what they are doing, and the nineteenth-century English did not know what they were doing. Both attitudes have their advantages, but Kipling was never able to move forward from one into the other. His outlook, allowing for the fact that after all he was an artist, was that of the salaried bureaucrat who despises the 'box-wallah' and often lives a lifetime without realizing that the 'box-wallah' calls the tune.

But because he identifies himself with the official class, he does possess one thing which 'enlightened' people seldom or never possess, and that is a sense of responsibility. The middle-class Left hate him for this quite as much as for his cruelty and vulgarity. All left-wing parties in the highly industrialized countries are at bottom a sham, because they make it their business to fight against something which they do not really wish to destroy. They have internationalist aims, and at the same time they struggle to keep up a standard of life with which those aims are incompatible. We all live by robbing Asiatic coolies, and those of us who are 'enlightened' all maintain that those coolies ought to be set free; but our standard of living, and hence our 'enlightenment', demands that the robbery shall continue. A humanitarian is always a hypocrite, and Kipling's understanding of this is perhaps the central secret of his power to create telling phrases. It would be difficult to hit off the one-eyed pacifism of the English in fewer words than in the phrase, 'making mock of uniforms that guard you while you sleep'. It is true that Kipling does not understand the economic aspect of the relationship between the highbrow and the Blimp. He does not see that the map is painted red chiefly in order that the coolie may be exploited. Instead of the coolie he sees the Indian Civil Servant; but even on that plane his grasp of function, of who protects whom, is very sound. He sees clearly that men can only be highly civilized while other men, inevitably less civilized, are there to guard and feed them.

How far does Kipling really identify himself with the administrators, soldiers and engineers whose praises he sings? Not so completely as is sometimes assumed. He had travelled very widely while he was still a young man, he had grown up with a brilliant mind in mainly philistine surroundings, and some streak in him that may have been partly neurotic led him to prefer the active man to the sensitive man. The nineteenth-century Anglo-Indians, to name the least sympathetic of his idols, were at any rate people who did things. It may be that all that they did was evil, but they changed the face of the earth (it is instructive to look at a map of Asia and compare the railway system of India with that of the surrounding countries), whereas they could have achieved nothing, could not have maintained themselves in power for a single week, if the normal Anglo-Indian outlook had been that of, say, E. M. Forster. Tawdry and shallow though it is, Kipling's is the only literary picture that we possess of nineteenth-century Anglo-India, and he could only make it because he was just coarse enough to be able to exist and keep his mouth shut in clubs and regimental messes. But he did not greatly resemble the people he admired. I know from several private sources that many of the Anglo-Indians who were Kipling's contemporaries did not like or approve of him. They said, no doubt truly, that he knew nothing about India, and on the other hand, he was from their point of view too much of a highbrow. While in India he tended to mix with 'the wrong' people, and because of his dark complexion he was wrongly suspected of having a streak of Asiatic blood. Much in his development is traceable to his having been born in India and having left school early. With a slightly different background he might have been a good novelist or a superlative writer of music-hall songs. But how true is it that he was a vulgar flag-waver, a sort of publicity agent for Cecil Rhodes? It is true, but it is not true that he was a yes-man or a time-server. After his early days, if then, he never courted public opinion. Mr Eliot says that what is held against him is that he expressed unpopular views in a popular style. This narrows the issue by assuming that 'unpopular' means unpopular with the intelligentsia, but it is a fact the Kipling's 'message' was one that the big public did not want, and, indeed, has never accepted. The mass of the people, in the 'nineties as now, were anti-militarist, bored by the Empire, and only unconsciously patriotic. Kipling's official admirers are and were the 'service' middle class, the people who read *Blackwood's*. In the stupid early years of this century, the Blimps, having at last discovered someone who could be called a poet and who was on their side, set Kipling on a pedestal, and some of his more sententious poems, such as 'If', were given almost Biblical status. But it is doubtful whether the Blimps have ever read him with attention, any more than they have read the Bible. Much of what he says they could not possibly approve. Few people who have criticized England from the inside have said bitterer things about her than this gutter patriot. As a rule it is the British working class that he is attacking, but not always. That phrase about 'the flannelled fools at the wicket and the muddied oafs at the goal' sticks like an arrow to this day, and it is aimed at the Eton and Harrow match as well as the Cup-Tie Final. Some of the verses he wrote about the Boer War have a curiously modern ring, so far as their subject-matter goes. 'Stellenbosch', which must have been written about 1902, sums up what every intelligent infantry officer was saying in 1918, or is saying now, for that matter.

Kipling's romantic ideas about England and the Empire might not have mattered if he could have held them without having the class prejudices which at that time went with them. If one examines his best and most representative work, his soldier poems, especially *Barrack-Room Ballads*, one notices that what more than anything else spoils them is an underlying air of patronage. Kipling idealizes the army officer, especially the junior officer, and that to an idiotic extent, but the private soldier, though lovable and romantic, has to be a comic. He is always made to speak in a sort of stylized cockney, not very broad but with all the aitches and final 'g's' carefully omitted. Very often the result is as embarrassing as the humorous recitation at a church social. And this accounts for the curious fact that one can often improve Kipling's poems, make them less facetious and less blatant, by simply going through them and transplanting them from cockney into standard speech. This is especially true of his refrains, which often have a truly lyrical quality. Two examples will do (one is about a funeral and the other about a wedding):

So it's knock out your pipes and follow me!
And it's finish up your swipes and follow me!
Oh, hark to the big drum calling.
Follow me – follow me home!

and again

Cheer for the Sergeant's wedding –
Give them one cheer more!
Grey gun-horses in the lando,
And a rogue is married to a whore!

Here I have restored the aitches, etc. Kipling ought to have known better. He ought to have seen that the two closing lines of the first of these stanzas are very beautiful lines, and that ought to have overridden his impulse to make fun of a working-man's accent. In the ancient ballads the lord and the peasant speak the same language. This is impossible to Kipling, who is looking down a distorting class perspective, and by a piece of poetic justice one of his best lines is spoiled – for 'follow me 'ome' is much uglier than 'follow me home'. But even where it makes no difference musically the facetiousness of his stage cockney dialect is irritating. However, he is more often quoted aloud than read on the printed page, and most people instinctively make the necessary alterations when they quote him.

Can one imagine any private soldier, in the 'nineties or now, reading *Barrack-Room Ballads* and feeling that here was a writer who spoke for him? It is very hard to do so. Any soldier capable of reading a book of verse would notice at once that Kipling is almost unconscious of the class war that goes on in an army as much as elsewhere. It is not only that he thinks the soldier comic, but that he thinks him patriotic, feudal, a ready admirer of his officers and proud to be a soldier of the Queen. Of course that is partly true, or battles could not be fought, but 'What have I done for thee, England, my England?' is essentially a middle-class query. Almost any working man would follow it up immediately with 'What has England done for me?' In so far as Kipling grasps this, he simply sets it down to 'the intense selfishness of the lower classes' (his own phrase). When he is writing not of British but of 'loyal' Indians he carries the 'Salaam, sahib' motif to sometimes disgusting lengths. Yet it remains true that he has far more interest in the common soldier, far more anxiety that he shall get a fair deal, than most of the 'liberals' of his day or our own. He sees that the soldier is neglected, meanly underpaid and hypocritically despised by the people whose incomes he safeguards. 'I came to realize,' he says in his posthumous memoirs, 'the bare horrors of the private's life, and the unnecessary torments he endured.' He is accused of glorifying war, and perhaps he does so, but not in the usual manner, by pretending that war is a sort of football match. Like most people capable of writing battle poetry, Kipling had never been in battle, but his vision of war is realistic. He knows that bullets hurt, that under fire everyone is terrified, that the ordinary soldier never knows what the war is about or what is happening except in his own corner of the battlefield, and that British troops, like other troops, frequently run away:

I 'eard the knives be'ind me, but I dursn't face my man,
Nor I don't know where I went to, 'cause I didn't stop to see,
Till I 'eard a beggar squealin' out for quarter as 'e ran,
An' I thought I knew the voice an' – it was me!

Modernize the style of this, and it might have come out of one of the debunking war books of the nineteen-twenties. Or again:

An' now the hugly bullets come peckin' through the dust,
An' no one wants to face 'em, but every beggar must;
So, like a man in irons, which isn't glad to go,
They moves 'em off by companies uncommon stiff an' slow.

Compare this with:

'Forward the Light Brigade!'
Was there a man dismayed?
No! though the soldier knew
Someone had blundered.

If anything, Kipling overdoes the horrors, for the wars of his youth were hardly wars at all by our standards. Perhaps that is due to the neurotic strain in him, the hunger for cruelty. But at least he knows that men ordered to attack impossible objectives *are* dismayed, and also that fourpence a day is not a generous pension.

How complete or truthful a picture has Kipling left us of the long-service, mercenary army of the late nineteenth century? One must say of this, as of what Kipling wrote about nineteenth-century Anglo-India, that it is not only the best but almost the only literary picture we have. He has put on record an immense amount of stuff that one could otherwise only gather from verbal tradition or from unreadable regimental histories. Perhaps his picture of army life seems fuller and more accurate than it is because any middle-class English person is likely to know enough to fill up the gaps. At any rate, reading the essay on Kipling that Mr Edmund Wilson has just published or is just about to publish,[1] I was struck by the number of things that are boringly familiar to us and seem to be barely intelligible to an American. But from the body of Kipling's early work there does seem to emerge a vivid and not seriously misleading picture of the old pre-machine-gun army – the sweltering barracks in Gibraltar or Lucknow, the red coats, the pipeclayed belts and the pillbox hats, the beer, the fights, the floggings, hangings and crucifixions, the bugle-calls, the smell of oats and horse-piss, the bellowing sergeants with foot-long moustaches, the bloody skirmishes, invariably mismanaged, the crowded troopships, the cholera-stricken camps, the 'native' concubines, the ultimate death in the workhouse. It is a crude, vulgar picture, in which a patriotic music-hall turn seems to have got mixed up with one of Zola's gorier passages, but from it future generations will be able to gather some idea of what a long-term volunteer army was like. On about the same level they will be able to learn something of British India in the days when motor cars and refrigerators were unheard of. It is an error to imagine that we might have had better books on these subjects if, for example, George Moore, or Gissing, or Thomas Hardy, had had Kipling's opportunities. That is the kind of accident that cannot happen. It was not possible that nineteenth-century England should produce a book like *War and Peace*, or like Tolstoy's minor stories of army life, such as *Sebastopol* or *The Cossacks*, not because the talent was necessarily lacking but because no one with sufficient sensitiveness to write such books would ever have made the appropriate contacts. Tolstoy lived in a great military empire in which it seemed natural for almost any young man of family to spend a few years in the army, whereas the British Empire was and still is demilitarized to a degree which continental observers find almost incredible. Civilized men do not readily move away from the centres of civilization, and in most languages there is a great dearth of what one might call colonial literature. It took a very improbable combination of circumstances to produce Kipling's gaudy tableau, in which Private Ortheris and Mrs Hauksbee pose against a background of palm trees to the sound of temple bells, and one necessary circumstance was that Kipling himself was only half civilized.

Kipling is the only English writer of our time who has added phrases to the language. The phrases and neologisms which we take over and use without remembering their origin do not always come from writers we admire. It is strange, for instance, to hear the Nazi broadcasters referring to the Russian soldiers as 'robots', thus unconsciously borrowing a word from a Czech

[1] Published in a volume of collected essays, *The Wound and the Bow*. [Author's footnote 1945]

democrat whom they would have killed if they could have laid hands on him. Here are half a dozen phrases coined by Kipling which one sees quoted in leaderettes in the gutter press or overhears in saloon bars from people who have barely heard his name. it will be seen that they all have a certain characteristic in common:

East is East, and West is West.
The white man's burden.
What do they know of England who only England know?
The female of the species is more deadly than the male.
Somewhere East of Suez.
Paying the Dane-gold.

There are various others, including some that have outlived their context by many years. The phrase 'killing Kruger with your mouth', for instance, was current till very recently. It is also possible that it was Kipling who first let loose the use of the word 'Huns' for Germans; at any rate he began using it as soon as the guns opened fire in 1914. But what the phrases I have listed above have in common is that they are all of them phrases which one utters semi-derisively (as it might be 'For I'm to be Queen o' the May, mother, I'm to be Queen o' the May'), but which one is bound to make use of sooner or later. Nothing could exceed the contempt of the *New Statesman*, for instance, for Kipling, but how many times during the Munich period did the *New Statesman* find itself quoting that phrase about paying the Dane-geld?[1] The fact is that Kipling, apart from his snack-bar wisdom and his gift for packing much cheap picturesqueness into a few words ('Palm and Pine' – 'East of Suez' – 'The Road to Mandalay'), is generally talking about things that are of urgent interest. It does not matter, from this point of view, that thinking and decent people generally find themselves on the other side of the fence from him. 'White man's burden' instantly conjures up a real problem, even if one feels that it ought to be altered to 'black man's burden'. One may disagree to the middle of one's bones with the political attitude implied in 'The Islanders', but one cannot say that it is a frivolous attitude. Kipling deals in thoughts which are both vulgar and permanent. This raises the question of his special status as a poet, or verse-writer.

Mr Eliot describes Kipling's metrical work as 'verse' and not 'poetry', but adds that it is '*great* verse', and further qualifies this by saying that a writer can only be described as a 'great verse-writer' if there is some of his work 'of which we cannot say whether it is verse or poetry'. Apparently Kipling was a versifier who occasionally wrote poems, in which case it was a pity that Mr Eliot did not specify these poems by name. The trouble is that

[1] On the first page of his recent book, *Adam and Eve*, Mr Middleton Murry quotes the well-known lines:

There are nine and sixty ways
Of constructing tribal lays,
And every single one of them is right.

He attributes these lines to Thackeray. This is probably what is known as a 'Freudian error'. A civilized person would prefer not to quote Kipling – i.e. would prefer not to feel that it was Kipling who had expressed his thought for him. [Author's footnote 1945.]

whenever an aesthetic judgement on Kipling's work seems to be called for, Mr Eliot is too much on the defensive to be able to speak plainly. What he does not say, and what I think one ought to start by saying in any discussion of Kipling, is that most of Kipling's verse is so horribly vulgar that it gives one the same sensation as one gets from watching a third-rate music-hall performer recite 'The Pigtail of Wu Fang Fu' with the purple limelight on his face, *and yet* there is much of it that is capable of giving pleasure to people who know what poetry means. At his worst, and also his most vital, in poems like 'Gunga Din' or 'Danny Deever', Kipling is almost a shameful pleasure, like the taste for cheap sweets that some people secretly carry into middle life. But even with his best passages one has the same sense of being seduced by something spurious, and yet unquestionably seduced. Unless one is merely a snob and a liar it is impossible to say that no one who cares for poetry could not get any pleasure out of such lines as:

For the wind is in the palm trees, and the temple bells they say,
'Come you back, you British soldier, come you back to Mandalay!'

and yet those lines are not poetry in the same sense as 'Felix Randal' or 'When icicles hang by the wall' are poetry. One can, perhaps, place Kipling more satisfactorily than by juggling with the words 'verse' and 'poetry', if one describes him simply as a good bad poet. He is as a poet what Harriet Beecher Stowe was as a novelist. And the mere existence of work of this kind, which is perceived by generation after generation to be vulgar and yet goes on being read, tells one something about the age we live in.

There is a great deal of good bad poetry in English, all of it, I should say, subsequent to 1790. Examples of good bad poems – I am deliberately choosing diverse ones – are 'The Bridge of Sighs', 'When all the World is Young, Lad', 'The Charge of the Light Brigade', Bret Harte's 'Dickens in Camp', 'The Burial of Sir John Moore', 'Jenny Kissed Me', 'Keith of Ravelston', 'Casabianca'. All of these reek of sentimentality, and yet – not these particular poems, perhaps, but poems of this kind, are capable of giving true pleasure to people who can see clearly what is wrong with them. One could fill a fair-sized anthology with good bad poems, if it were not for the significant fact that good bad poetry is usually too well known to be worth reprinting. It is no use pretending that in an age like our own, 'good' poetry can have any genuine popularity. It is, and must be, the cult of a very few people, the least tolerated of the arts. Perhaps that statement needs a certain amount of qualification. True poetry can sometimes be acceptable to the mass of the people when it disguises itself as something else. One can see an example of this in the folk-poetry that England still possesses, certain nursery rhymes and mnemonic rhymes, for instance, and the songs that soldiers make up, including the words that go to some of the bugle-calls. But in general ours is a civilization in which the very word 'poetry' evokes a hostile snigger or, at best, the sort of frozen disgust that most people feel when they hear the word 'God'. If you are good at playing the concertina you could probably go into the nearest public bar and get yourself an appreciative audience within five minutes. But what would be the attitude of that same audience if you suggested reading them Shakespeare's sonnets, for instance? Good bad poetry, however, can get across to the most unpromising audiences if the right atmosphere has been worked up beforehand. Some months back Churchill produced a great effect by quoting Clough's 'Endeavour' in one of his broadcast speeches. I listened to this speech among people who could certainly not be accused of caring for poetry, and I am convinced that the lapse into verse impressed them and did not embarrass them. But not even Churchill could have got away with it if he had quoted anything much better than this.

In so far as a writer of verse can be popular, Kipling has been and probably still is popular. In his own lifetime some of his poems travelled far beyond the bounds of the reading public, beyond the world of school prize-days, Boy Scout sing-songs, limp-leather editions, poker-work and calendars, and out into the yet vaster world of the music halls. Nevertheless, Mr Eliot thinks it worth while to edit him, thus confessing to a taste which others share but are not always honest enough to mention. The fact that such a thing as good bad poetry can exist is a sign of the emotional overlap between the intellectual and the ordinary man. The intellectual *is* different from the ordinary man, but only in certain sections of his personality, and even then not all the time. But what is the peculiarity of a good bad poem? A good bad poem is a graceful monument to the obvious. It records in memorable form – for verse is a mnemonic device, among other things – some emotion which very nearly every human being can share. The merit of a poem like 'When all the World is Young, Lad' is that, however sentimental it may be, its sentiment is 'true' sentiment in the sense that you are bound to find yourself thinking the thought it expresses sooner or later; and then, if you happen to know the poem, it will come back into your mind and seem better than it did before. Such poems are a kind of rhyming proverb, and it is a fact that definitely popular poetry is usually gnomic or sententious. One example from Kipling will do:

White hands cling to the bridle rein,
Slipping the spur from the booted heel;
Tenderest voices cry 'Turn again!'
Red lips tarnish the scabbarded steel:
Down to Gehenna or up to the Throne,
He travels the fastest who travels alone.

There is a vulgar thought vigorously expressed. It may not be true, but at any rate it is a thought that everyone thinks. Sooner or later you will have occasion to feel that he travels the fastest who travels alone, and there the thought is, ready made and, as it were, waiting for you. So the chances are that, having once heard this line, you will remember it.

One reason for Kipling's power as a good bad poet I have already suggested – his sense of responsibility, which made it possible for him to have a world-view, even though it happened to be a false one. Although he had no direct connection with any political party, Kipling was a Conservative, a thing that does not exist nowadays. Those who now call themselves Conservatives are either Liberals, Fascists or the accomplices of Fascists. He identified himself with the ruling power and not with the opposition. In a gifted writer this seems to us strange and even disgusting, but it did have the advantage of giving Kipling a certain grip on reality. The ruling power is always faced with the question, 'In such and such circumstances, what would you *do*?', whereas the opposition is not obliged to take responsibility or make any real decisions. Where it is a permanent and pensioned opposition, as in England, the quality of its thought deteriorates accordingly. Moreover, anyone who starts out with a pessimistic, reactionary view of life tends to be justified by events, for Utopia never arrives and 'the gods of the copybook headings', as Kipling himself put it, always return. Kipling sold out to the British governing class, not financially but emotionally. This warped his political judgement, for the British ruling class were not what he imagined, and it led him into abysses of folly and snobbery, but he gained a corresponding advantage from having at least tried to imagine what action and responsibility are like. It is a great thing in his favour that he is not witty, not 'daring', has no wish to *épater les bourgeois*. He dealt largely in platitudes, and since we live in a world of platitudes, much of what he said sticks. Even his worst follies seem less shallow and less irritating that the 'enlightened' utterances of the same period, such as Wilde's epigrams or the collection of cracker-mottoes at the end of *Man and Superman*.

Horizon, February 1942

The Rediscovery of Europe

When I was a small boy and was taught history – very badly, of course, as nearly everyone in England is – I used to think of history as a sort of long scroll with thick black lines ruled across it at intervals. Each of these lines marked the end of what was called a 'period', and you were given to understand that what came afterwards was completely different from what had gone before. It was almost like a clock striking. For instance, in 1499 you were still in the Middle Ages, with knights in plate armour riding at one another with long lances, and then suddenly the clock struck 1500, and you were in something called the Renaissance, and everyone wore ruffs and doublets and was busy robbing treasure ships on the Spanish Main. There was another very thick black line drawn at the year 1700. After that it was the Eighteenth Century, and people suddenly stopped being Cavaliers and Roundheads and became extraordinarily elegant gentlemen in knee breeches and three-cornered hats. They all powdered their hair, took snuff and talked in exactly balanced sentences, which seemed all the more stilted because for some reason I didn't understand they pronounced most of their S's as F's. The whole of history was like that in my mind – a series of completely different periods changing abruptly at the end of a century, or at any rate at some sharply defined date.

Now in fact these abrupt transitions don't happen, either in politics, manners or literature. Each age lives on into the next – it must do so, because there are innumerable human lives spanning every gap. And yet there are such things as periods. We feel our own age to be deeply different from, for instance, the early Victorian period, and an eighteenth-century sceptic like Gibbon would have felt himself to be among savages if you had suddenly thrust him into the Middle Ages. Every now and again something happens – no doubt it's ultimately traceable to changes in industrial technique, though the connection isn't always obvious – and the whole spirit and tempo of life changes, and people acquire a new outlook which reflects itself in their political behaviour, their manners, their architecture, their literature and everything else. No one could write a poem like Gray's 'Elegy in a Country Churchyard' today, for instance, and no one could have written Shakespeare's lyrics in the age of Gray. These things belong in different periods. And though, of course, those black lines across the page of history are an illusion, there are times when the transition is quite rapid, sometimes rapid enough for it to be possible to give it a fairly accurate date. One can say without grossly over-simplifying, 'About such and such a year, such and such a style of literature began'. If I were asked for the starting point of modern literature – and the fact that we still call it 'modern' shows that this particular period isn't finished yet – I should put it at 1917, the year in which T. S. Eliot published his poem 'Prufrock'. At any rate that date isn't more than five years out. It is certain that about the end of the last war the literary climate changed, the typical writer came to be quite a different person, and the best books of the subsequent period seemed to exist in a different world from the best books of only four or five years before.

To illustrate what I mean, I ask you to compare in your mind two poems which haven't any connection with one another, but which will do for purposes of comparison because each is entirely typical of its period. Compare, for instance, one of Eliot's characteristic earlier poems with a poem of Rupert Brooke, who was, I should say, the most admired English poet in the years before 1914. Perhaps the most representative of Brooke's poems are his patriotic ones, written in the early days of the war. A good one is the sonnet beginning 'If I should die, think only this of me: That there's some corner of a foreign field That is for ever England'. Now read side by side with this one of Eliot's Sweeney poems; for example, 'Sweeney among the nightingales' – you know, 'The circles of the stormy moon Slide westward toward the River Plate'. As I say, these poems have no connection in theme or anything else, but it's possible in a way to compare them, because each is representative of its own time and each seemed a good poem when it was written. The second still seems a good poem now.

Not only the technique but the whole spirit, the implied outlook on life, the intellectual paraphernalia of these poems are abysmally different. Between the young Englishman with a public-school and university background, going out enthusiastically to die for his country with his head full of English lanes, wild roses and what not, and the rather jaded cosmopolitan American, getting glimpses of eternity in some slightly squalid restaurant in the Latin Quarter of Paris, there is a huge gulf. That might be only an individual difference, but the point is that you come upon rather the same kind of difference, a difference that raises the same comparisons, if you read side by side almost any two characteristic writers of the two periods. It's the same with the novelists as with the poets – Joyce, Lawrence, Huxley and Wyndham Lewis on the one side, and Wells, Bennett and Galsworthy on the other, for instance. The new writers are immensely less prolific than the older ones, more scrupulous, more interested in technique, less optimistic and, in general, less confident in their attitude to life. But more than that, you have all the time the feeling that their intellectual and aesthetic background is different, rather as you do when you compare a nineteenth-century French writer such as, say, Flaubert with a nineteenth-century English writer like Dickens. The Frenchman seems enormously more sophisticated than the Englishman, though he isn't necessarily a better writer because of that. But let me go back a bit and consider what English literature was like in the days before 1914.

The giants of that time were Thomas Hardy – who, however, had stopped writing novels some time earlier – Shaw, Wells, Kipling, Bennett, Galsworthy and, somewhat different from the others – not an Englishman, remember, but a Pole who chose to write in English – Joseph Conrad. There were also A. E. Housman (*A Shropshire Lad*), and the various Georgian poets, Rupert Brooke and the others. There were also the innumerable comic writers, Sir James Barrie, W. W. Jacobs, Barry Pain and many others. If you read all those writers I've just mentioned, you would get a not misleading picture of the English mind before 1914. There were other literary tendencies at work, there were various Irish writers, for instance, and in a quite different vein, much nearer to our own time, there was the American novelist Henry James, but the main stream was the one I've indicated. But what is the common denominator between writers who are individually as far apart as Bernard Shaw and A. E. Housman, or Thomas Hardy and H. G. Wells? I think the basic fact about nearly all English writers of that time is their complete unawareness of anything outside the contemporary English scene. Some are better writers than others, some are politically conscious and some aren't, but they are all alike in being untouched by any European influence. This is true even of novelists like Bennett and Galsworthy, who derived in a very superficial sense from French and perhaps Russian models. All of these writers have a background of ordinary, respectable, middle-class English life, and a half-conscious belief that this kind of life will go on for ever, getting more humane and more enlightened all the time. Some of them, like Hardy and Housman, are pessimistic in outlook, but they all at least believe that what is called progress would be desirable if it were possible. Also – a thing that generally goes with lack of aesthetic sensibility – they are all uninterested in the past, at any rate the remote past. It is very rare to find in a writer of that time anything we should now regard as a sense of history. Even Thomas Hardy, when he attempts a huge poetic drama based on the Napoleonic wars – *The Dynasts*, it's called – sees it all from the angle of a patriotic school textbook. Still more, they're all aesthetically uninterested in the past. Arnold Bennett, for instance, wrote a great deal of literary criticism, and it's clear that he is almost unable to see any merit in any book earlier than the nineteenth century, and indeed hasn't much interest in any writer other than his contemporaries. To Bernard Shaw most of the past is simply a mess which ought to be swept away in the name of progress, hygiene, efficiency and what not. H. G. Wells, though later on he was to write a history of the world, looks at the past with the same sort of surprised disgust as a civilized man contemplating a tribe of cannibals. All of these people, whether they liked their own age or not, at least thought it was better than what had gone before, and took the literary standards of their own time for granted. The basis of all Bernard Shaw's attacks on Shakespeare is really the charge – quite true, of course – that Shakespeare wasn't an enlightened member of the Fabian Society. If any of these writers had been told that the writers immediately subsequent to them would hark back to the English poets of the sixteenth and seventeenth centuries, to the French poets of the mid-nineteenth century and to the philosophers of the Middle Ages, they would have thought it a kind of dilettantism.

But now look at the writers who begin to attract notice – some of them had begun writing rather earlier, of course – immediately after the last war:

Joyce, Eliot, Pound, Huxley, Lawrence, Wyndham Lewis. Your first impression of them, compared with the others – this is true even of Lawrence – is that something has been punctured. To begin with, the notion of progress has gone by the board. They don't any longer believe that men are getting better and better by having lower mortality rates, more effective birth control, better plumbing, more aeroplanes and faster motor cars. Nearly all of them are homesick for the remote past, or some period of the past, from D. H. Lawrence's ancient Etruscans onwards. All of them are politically reactionary, or at best are uninterested in politics. None of them cares twopence about the various hole-and-corner reforms which had seemed important to their predecessors, such as female suffrage, temperance reform, birth control or prevention of cruelty to animals. All of them are more friendly, or at least less hostile, towards the Christian churches than the previous generation had been. And nearly all of them seem to be aesthetically alive in a way that hardly any English writer since the Romantic Revival had been.

Now, one can best illustrate what I have been saying by means of individual examples, that is, by comparing outstanding books of more or less comparable type in the two periods. As a first example, compare H. G. Wells's short stories – there's a large number of them collected together under the title of *The Country of the Blind* – with D. H. Lawrence's short stories, such as those in *England, my England* and *The Prussian Officer*.

This isn't an unfair comparison, since each of these writers was at his best, or somewhere near his best, in the short story, and each of them was expressing a new vision of life which had a great effect on the young of his generation. The ultimate subject-matter of H. G. Wells's stories is, first of all, scientific discovery, and beyond that the petty snobberies and tragi-comedies of contemporary English life, especially lower-middle-class life. His basic 'message', to use an expression I don't like, is that Science can solve all the ills that humanity is heir to, but that man is at present too blind to see the possibility of his own powers. The alternation between ambitious Utopian themes and light comedy, almost in the W. W. Jacobs vein, is very marked in Wells's work. He writes about journeys to the moon and to the bottom of the sea, and also he writes about small shopkeepers dodging bankruptcy and fighting to keep their end up in the frightful snobbery of provincial towns. The connecting link is Wells's belief in Science. He is saying all the time, if only that small shopkeeper could acquire a scientific outlook, his troubles would be ended. And of course he believes that this is going to happen, probably in the quite near future. A few more million pounds for scientific research, a few more generations scientifically educated, a few more superstitions shovelled into the dustbin, and the job is done. Now, if you turn to Lawrence's stories, you don't find this belief in Science – rather a hostility towards it, if anything – and you don't find any marked interest in the future, certainly not in a rationalized hedonistic future of the kind that Wells deals in. You don't even find the notion that the small shopkeeper, or any of the other victims of our society, would be better off if he were better educated. What you do find is a persistent implication that man has thrown away his birthright by becoming civilized. The ultimate subject-matter of nearly all Lawrence's books is the failure of contemporary men, especially in the English-speaking countries, to live their lives intensely enough. Naturally he fixes first on their sexual lives, and it is a fact that most of Lawrence's books centre round sex. But he isn't, as is sometimes supposed, demanding more of what people call sexual liberty. He is completely disillusioned about that, and he hates the so-called sophistication of bohemian intellectuals just as much as he hates the puritanism of the middle class. What he is saying is simply that modern men aren't fully alive, whether they fail through having too narrow standards or through not having any. Granted that they can be fully alive, he doesn't much care what social or political or economic system they live under. He takes the structure of existing society, with its class distinctions and so on, almost for granted in his stories, and doesn't show any very urgent wish to change it. All he asks is that men shall live more simply, nearer to the earth, with more sense of the magic of things like vegetation, fire, water, sex, blood, than they can in a world of celluloid and concrete where the gramophones never stop playing. He imagines – quite likely he is wrong – that savages or primitive peoples live more intensely than civilized men, and he builds up a mythical figure who is not far from being the Noble Savage over again. Finally, he projects these virtues onto the Etruscans, an ancient pre-Roman people who lived in northern Italy and about whom we don't, in fact, know anything. From the point of view of H. G. Wells all this abandonment of Science and Progress, this actual wish to revert to the primitive, is simply heresy and nonsense. And yet one must admit that whether Lawrence's view of life is true or whether it is perverted, it is at least an advance on the Science worship of H. G. Wells or the shallow Fabian progressivism of writers like Bernard Shaw. It is an advance in the sense that it results from seeing through the other attitude and not from falling short of it. Partly that was the effect of the war of 1914–18, which succeeded in debunking both Science, Progress and civilized man. Progress had finally ended in the biggest massacre in history, Science was something that created bombing planes and poison gas, civilized man, as it turned out, was ready to behave worse than any savage when the pinch came. But Lawrence's discontent with modern machine civilization would have been the same, no doubt, if the war of 1914–18 had never happened.

Now I want to make another comparison, between James Joyce's great novel *Ulysses*, and John Galsworthy's at any rate very large novel sequence *The Forsyte Saga*. This time it isn't a fair comparison, in effect it's a comparison between a good book and a bad one, and it also isn't quite correct chronologically, because the later parts of *The Forsyte Saga* were written in the nineteen-twenties. But the parts of it that anyone is likely to remember were written about 1910, and for my purpose the comparison is relevant, because both Joyce and Galsworthy are making efforts to cover an enormous canvas and get the spirit and social history of a whole epoch between the covers of a single book. *The Man of Property* may not seem to us *now* a very profound criticism of society, but it seemed so to its contemporaries, as you can see by what they wrote about it.

Joyce wrote *Ulysses* in the seven years between 1914 and 1921, working away all through the war, to which he probably paid little or no attention, and earning a miserable living as a teacher of languages in Italy and Switzerland. He was quite ready to work seven years in poverty and complete obscurity so as to get his great book onto paper. But what is it that it was so urgently important for him to express? Parts of *Ulysses* aren't very easily intelligible, but from the book as a whole you get two main impressions. The first is that Joyce is interested to the point of obsession with technique. This has been one of the main characteristics of modern literature, though more recently it has been a diminishing one. You get a parallel development in the plastic arts, painters, and even sculptors, being more and more interested in the material they work in, in the brush-marks of a picture, for instance, as against its design, let alone its subject-matter. Joyce is interested in mere words, the sounds and associations of words, even the pattern of words on the paper, in a way that wasn't the case with any of the preceding generation of writers, except to some extent the Polish-English writer, Joseph Conrad. With Joyce you are back to the conception of style, of fine writing, or poetic writing, perhaps even to purple passages. A writer like Bernard Shaw, on the other hand, would have said as a matter of course that the sole use of words is to express exact meanings as shortly as possible. And apart from this technical obsession, the other main theme of *Ulysses* is the squalor, even the meaninglessness of modern life after the triumph of the machine and the collapse of religious belief. Joyce – an Irishman, remember, and it's worth noting that the best English writers during the nineteen-twenties were in many cases not Englishmen – is writing as a Catholic who has lost his faith but has retained the mental framework which he acquired in his Catholic childhood and boyhood. *Ulysses*, which is a very long novel, is a description of the events of a single day, as seen mostly through the eyes of an out-at-elbow Jewish commercial traveller. At the time when the book came out there was a great outcry and Joyce was accused of deliberately exploiting the sordid, but as a matter of fact, considering what everyday human life is like when you contemplate it in detail, it doesn't seem that he overdid either the squalor or the silliness of the day's events. What you do feel all through, however, is the conviction from which Joyce can't escape, that the whole of this modern world which he is describing has no meaning in it now that the teachings of the Church are no longer credible. He is yearning after the religious faith which the two or three generations preceding him had had to fight against in the name of religious liberty. But finally the main interest of the book is technical. Quite a considerable proportion of it consists of pastiche or parody – parodies of everything from the Irish legends of the Bronze Age down to contemporary newspaper reports. And one can see there that, like all the characteristic writers of his time, Joyce doesn't derive from the English nineteenth-century writers but from Europe and from the remoter past. Part of his mind is in the Bronze Age, another part in the Middle Ages, another part in the England of Elizabeth. The twentieth century, with its hygiene and its motor-cars, doesn't particularly appeal to him.

Now look again at Galsworthy's book, *The Forsyte Saga*, and you see how comparatively narrow its range is. I have said already that this isn't a fair comparison, and indeed from a strictly literary point of view it's a ridiculous one, but it will do as an illustration in the sense that both books are intended to give a comprehensive picture of existing society. Well, the thing that strikes one about Galsworthy is that though he's trying to be iconoclastic, he has been utterly unable to move his mind outside the wealthy bourgeois society he is attacking. With only slight modifications he takes all its values for granted. All he conceives to be wrong is that human beings are a little too inhumane, a little too fond of money, and aesthetically not quite sensitive enough. When he sets out to depict what he conceives as the desirable type of human being, it turns out to be simply a cultivated, humanitarian version of the upper-middle-class *rentier*, the sort of person who in those days used to haunt picture galleries in Italy and subscribe heavily to the Society for the Prevention of Cruelty to Animals. And this fact – the fact that Galsworthy hasn't any really deep aversion to the social types he thinks he is attacking – gives you the clue to his weakness. It is, that he has no contact with anything outside contemporary English society. He may think he doesn't like it, but he is part of it. Its money and security, the ring of battleships that separated it from Europe, have been too much for him. At the bottom of his heart he despises foreigners, just as much as any illiterate businessman in Manchester. The feeling you have with Joyce or Eliot, or even Lawrence, that they have got the whole of human history inside their heads and can look outwards from their own place and time towards Europe and the past, isn't to be found in Galsworthy or in any characteristic English writer in the period before 1914.

Finally, one more brief comparison. Compare almost any of H. G. Wells's Utopia books, for instance *A Modern Utopia*, or *The Dream*, or *Men Like Gods*, with Aldous Huxley's *Brave New World*. Again it's rather the same contrast, the contrast between the over-confident and the deflated, between the man who believes innocently in Progress and the man who happens to have been born later and has therefore lived to see that Progress, as it was conceived in the early days of the aeroplane, is just as much of a swindle as reaction.

The obvious explanation of this sharp difference between the dominant writers before and after the war of 1914–18 is the war itself. Some such development would have happened in any case as the insufficiency of modern materialistic civilization revealed itself, but the war speeded the process, partly by showing how very shallow the veneer of civilization is, partly by making England less prosperous and therefore less isolated. After 1918 you couldn't live in such a narrow and padded world as you did when Britannia ruled not only the waves but also the markets. One effect of the ghastly history of the last twenty years has been to make a great deal of ancient literature seem much more modern. A lot that has happened in Germany since the rise of Hitler might have come straight out of the later volumes of Gibbon's *Decline and Fall of the Roman Empire*. Recently I saw Shakespeare's *King John* acted – the first time I had seen it, because it is a play which isn't acted very often. When I had read it as a boy it seemed to me archaic, something dug out of a history book and not having anything to do with our own time. Well, when I saw it acted, what with its intrigues and doublecrossings, non-aggression pacts, quislings, people changing sides in the middle of a battle, and what not, it seemed to me extraordinarily up to date. And it was rather the same thing that happened in the literary development between 1910 and 1920. The prevailing temper of the time gave a new reality to all sorts of themes which had seemed out of date and puerile when Bernard Shaw and his Fabians were – so they thought – turning the world into a sort of super garden city. Themes like revenge, patriotism, exile, persecution, race hatred, religious faith, loyalty, leader worship, suddenly seemed real again. Tamerlane and Genghis Khan seem credible figures now, and Machiavelli seems a serious thinker, as they didn't in 1910. We have got out of a backwater and back into history. I haven't an unqualified admiration for the writers of the early nineteen-twenties, the writers among whom Eliot and Joyce are chief names. Those who followed them have had to undo a great deal of what they did. Their revulsion from a shallow conception of progress drove them politically in the wrong direction, and it isn't an accident that Ezra Pound, for instance, is now shouting antisemitism on the Rome radio. But one must concede that their writings are more grown-up, and have a wider scope, than what went immediately before them. They broke the cultural circle in which England had existed for something like a century. They re-established contact with Europe, and they brought back the sense of history and the possibility of tragedy. On that basis all subsequent English literature that matters twopence has rested, and the development that Eliot and the others started, back in the closing years of the last war, has not yet run its course.

Listener, 19 March 1942

Looking Back on the Spanish War

ONE

First of all the physical memories, the sounds, the smells and the surfaces of things.

It is curious that more vividly than anything that came afterwards in the Spanish war I remember the week of so-called training that we received before being sent to the front – the huge cavalry barracks in Barcelona with its draughty stables and cobbled yards, the icy cold of the pump where one washed, the filthy meals made tolerable by pannikans of wine, the trousered militia-women chopping firewood, and the roll-call in the early mornings where my prosaic English name made a sort of comic interlude among the resounding Spanish ones, Manuel Gonzalez, Pedro Aguilar, Ramon Fenellosa, Roque Ballaster, Jaime Domenech, Sebastian Viltron, Ramon Nuvo Bosch. I name those particular men because I remember the faces of all of them. Except for two who were mere riff-raff and have doubtless become good Falangists by this time, it is probable that all of them are dead. Two of them I know to be dead. The eldest would have been about twenty-five, the youngest sixteen.

One of the essential experiences of war is never being able to escape from disgusting smells of human origin. Latrines are an overworked subject in war literature, and I would not mention them if it were not that the latrine in our barracks did its necessary bit towards puncturing my own illusions about the Spanish civil war. The Latin type of latrine, at which you have to squat, is bad enough at its best, but these were made of some kind of polished stone so slippery that it was all you could do to keep on your feet. In addition they were always blocked. Now I have plenty of other disgusting things in my memory, but I believe it was these latrines that first brought home to me the thought, so often to recur: 'Here we are, soldiers of a revolutionary army, defending democracy against Fascism, fighting a war which is *about* something, and the detail of our lives is just as sordid and degrading as it could be in prison, let alone in a bourgeois army.' Many other things reinforced this impression later; for instance, the boredom and animal hunger of trench life, the squalid intrigues over scraps of food, the mean, nagging quarrels which people exhausted by lack of sleep indulge in.

The essential horror of army life (whoever has been a soldier will know what I mean by the essential horror of army life) is barely affected by the nature of the war you happen to be fighting in. Discipline, for instance, is ultimately the same in all armies. Orders have to be obeyed and enforced by punishment if necessary, the relationship of officer and man has to be the relationship of superior and inferior. The picture of war set forth in books like *All Quiet on the Western Front* is substantially true. Bullets hurt, corpses stink, men under fire are often so frightened that they wet their trousers. It is true that the social background from which an army springs will colour its training, tactics and general efficiency, and also that the consciousness of being in the right can bolster up morale, though this affects the civilian population more than the troops. (People forget that a soldier anywhere near the front line is usually too hungry, or frightened, or cold, or, above all, too tired to bother about the political origins of the war.) But the laws of nature are not suspended for a 'red' army any more than for a 'white' one. A louse is a louse and a bomb is a bomb, even though the cause you are fighting for happens to be just.

Why is it worth while to point out anything so obvious? Because the bulk of the British and American intelligentsia were manifestly unaware of it then, and are now. Our memories are short nowadays, but look back a bit, dig out the files of *New Masses* or the *Daily Worker*, and just have a look at the romantic warmongering muck that our left-wingers were spilling at that time. All the stale old phrases! And the unimaginative callousness of it! The sang-froid with which London faced the bombing of Madrid! Here I am not bothering about the counter-propagandists of the Right, the Lunns, Garvins *et hoc genus*; they go without saying. But here were the very people who for twenty years had hooted and jeered at the 'glory' of war, at atrocity stories, at patriotism, even at physical courage, coming out with stuff that with the alteration of a few names would have fitted into the *Daily Mail* of 1918. If there was one thing that the British intelligentsia were committed to, it was the debunking version of war, the theory that war is all corpses and latrines and never leads to any good result. Well, the same people who in 1933 sniggered pityingly if you said that in certain circumstances you would fight for your country, in 1937 were denouncing you as a Trotsky-Fascist if you suggested that the stories in *New Masses* about freshly wounded men clamouring to get back into the fighting might be exaggerated. And the Left intelligentsia made their swing-over from 'War is hell' to 'War is glorious' not only with no sense of incongruity but almost without any intervening stage. Later the bulk of them were to make other transitions equally violent. There must be a quite large number of people, a sort of central core of the intelligentsia, who approved the 'King and Country' declaration in 1935, shouted for a 'firm line' against Germany in 1937, supported the People's Convention in 1940, and are demanding a Second Front now.

As far as the mass of the people go, the extraordinary swings of opinion which occur nowadays, the emotions which can be turned on and off like a tap, are the result of newspaper and radio hypnosis. In the intelligentsia I should say they result rather from money and mere physical safety. At a given moment they may be 'pro-war' or 'anti-war', but in either case they have no realistic picture of war in their minds. When they enthused over the Spanish war they knew, of course, that people were being killed and that to be killed is unpleasant, but they did feel that for a soldier in the Spanish Republican army the experience of war was somehow not degrading. Somehow the latrines stank less, discipline was less irksome. You have only to glance at the *New Statesman* to see that they believed that; exactly similar blah is being written about the Red army at this moment. We have become too civilized to grasp the obvious. For the truth is very simple. To survive you often have to fight, and to fight you have to dirty yourself. War is evil, and it is often the lesser evil. Those who take the sword perish by the sword, and those who don't take the sword perish by smelly diseases. The fact that such a platitude is worth writing down shows what the years of *rentier* capitalism have done to us.

TWO

In connection with what I have just said, a footnote on atrocities.

I have little direct evidence about the atrocities in the Spanish civil war. I know that some were committed by the Republicans, and far more (they are still continuing) by the Fascists. But what impressed me then, and has impressed me ever since, is that atrocities are believed in or disbelieved in solely on grounds of political predilection. Everyone believes in the atrocities of the enemy and disbelieves in those of his own side, without ever bothering to examine the evidence. Recently I drew up a table of atrocities during the period 1918 and the present; there was never a year when atrocities were not occurring somewhere or other, and there was hardly a single case when the Left and the Right believed in the same stories simultaneously. And stranger yet, at any moment the situation can suddenly reverse itself and yesterday's proved-to-the-hilt atrocity story can become a ridiculous lie, merely because the political landscape has changed.

In the present war we are in the curious situation that our 'atrocity campaign' was done largely before the war had started, and done mostly by the Left, the people who normally pride themselves on their incredulity. In the same period the Right, the atrocity-mongers of 1914–18, were gazing at Nazi Germany and flatly refusing to see any evil in it. Then as soon as war broke out it was the pro-Nazis of yesterday who were repeating horror stories, while the anti-Nazis suddenly found themselves doubting whether the Gestapo really existed. Nor was this solely the result of the Russo-German Pact. It was partly because before the war the Left had wrongly believed that Britain and Germany would never fight and were therefore able to be anti-German and anti-British simultaneously; partly also because official war propaganda, with its disgusting hypocrisy and self-righteousness, always tends to make thinking people sympathize with the enemy. Part of the price we paid for the systematic lying of 1914–18 was the exaggerated pro-German reaction which followed. During the years 1918–33 you were hooted at in left-wing circles if you suggested that Germany bore even a fraction of responsibility for the war. In all the denunciations of Versailles I listened to during those years I don't think I ever once heard the question, 'What would have happened if Germany had won?' even mentioned, let alone discussed. So also with atrocities. The truth, it is felt, becomes untruth when your enemy utters it. Recently I noticed that the very people who swallowed any and every horror story about the Japanese in Nanking in 1937 refused to believe exactly the same stories about Hong Kong in 1942. There was even a tendency to feel that the Nanking atrocities had become, as it were, retrospectively untrue because the British Government now drew attention to them.

But unfortunately the truth about atrocities is far worse than that they are lied about and made into propaganda. The truth is that they happen. The fact often adduced as a reason for scepticism – that the same horror stories come up in war after war – merely makes it rather more likely that these stories are true. Evidently they are widespread fantasies, and war provides an opportunity of putting them into practice. Also, although it has ceased to be fashionable to say so, there is little question that what one may roughly call the 'whites' commit far more and worse atrocities than the 'reds'. There is not the slightest doubt, for instance, about the behaviour of the Japanese in China. Nor is there much doubt about the long tale of Fascist outrages during the last ten years in Europe. The volume of testimony is enormous, and a respectable proportion of it comes from the German press and radio. These things really happened, that is the thing to keep one's eye on. They happened even though Lord Halifax said they happened. The raping and butchering in Chinese cities, the tortures in the cellars of the Gestapo, the elderly Jewish professors flung into cesspools, the machine-gunning of refugees along the Spanish roads – they all happened, and they did not happen any the less because the *Daily Telegraph* has suddenly found out about them when it is five years too late.

THREE

Two memories, the first not proving anything in particular, the second, I think, giving one a certain insight into the atmosphere of a revolutionary period.

Early one morning another man and I had gone out to snipe at the Fascists in the trenches outside Huesca. Their line and ours here lay three hundred yards apart, at which range our aged rifles would not shoot accurately, but by sneaking out to a spot about a hundred yards from the Fascist trench you might, if you were lucky, get a shot at someone through a gap in the parapet. Unfortunately the ground between was a flat beetfield with no cover except a few ditches, and it was necessary to go out while it was still dark and return soon after dawn, before the light became too good. This time no Fascists appeared, and we stayed too long and were caught by the dawn. We were in a ditch, but behind us were two hundred yards of flat ground with hardly enough cover for a rabbit. We were still trying to nerve ourselves to make a dash for it when there was an uproar and a blowing of whistles in the Fascist trench. Some of our aeroplanes were coming over. At this moment a man, presumably carrying a message to an officer, jumped out of the trench and ran along the top of the parapet in full view. He was half-dressed and was holding up his trousers with both hands as he ran. I refrained from shooting at him. It is true that I am a poor shot and unlikely to hit a running man at a hundred yards, and also that I was thinking chiefly about getting back to our trench while the Fascists had their attention fixed on the aeroplanes. Still, I did not shoot partly because of that detail about the trousers. I had come here to shoot at 'Fascists'; but a man who is holding up his trousers isn't a 'Fascist', he is visibly a fellow creature, similar to yourself, and you don't feel like shooting at him.

What does this incident demonstrate? Nothing very much, because it is the kind of thing that happens all the time in all wars. The other is different. I don't suppose that in telling it I can make it moving to you who read it, but I ask you to believe that it is moving to me, as an incident characteristic of the moral atmosphere of a particular moment in time.

One of the recruits who joined us while I was at the barracks was a wild-looking boy from the back streets of Barcelona. He was ragged and barefooted. He was also extremely dark (Arab blood, I dare say), and made gestures you do not usually see a European make; one in particular – the arm outstretched, the palm vertical – was a gesture characteristic of Indians. One day a bundle of cigars, which you could still buy dirt cheap at that time, was stolen out of my bunk. Rather foolishly I reported this to the officer, and one of the scallywags I have already mentioned promptly came forward and said quite untruly that twenty-five pesetas had been stolen from his bunk. For some reason the officer instantly decided that the brown-skinned boy must be the thief. They were very hard on stealing in the militia, and in theory people could be shot for it. The wretched boy allowed himself to be led off to the guardroom to be searched. What most struck me was that he barely attempted to protest his innocence. In the fatalism of his attitude you could see the desperate poverty in which he had been bred. The officer ordered him to take his clothes off. With a humility which was horrible to me he stripped himself naked, and his clothes were searched. Of course neither the cigars nor the money were there; in fact he had not stolen them. What was most painful of all was that he seemed no less ashamed after his innocence had been established. That night I took him to the pictures and gave him brandy and chocolate. But that too was horrible – I mean the attempt to wipe out an injury with money. For a few minutes I had half believed him to be a thief, and that could not be wiped out.

Well, a few weeks later at the front I had trouble with one of the men in my section. By this time I was a 'cabo', or corporal, in command of twelve men. It was static warfare, horribly cold, and the chief job was getting sentries to stay awake at their posts. One day a man suddenly refused to go to a certain post, which he said quite truly was exposed to enemy fire. He was a feeble creature, and I seized hold of him and began to drag him towards his post. This roused the feelings of the others against me, for Spaniards, I think, resent being touched more than we do. Instantly I was surrounded by a ring of shouting men: 'Fascist! Fascist! Let that man go! This isn't a bourgeois army. Fascist!" etc., etc. As best I could in my bad Spanish I shouted back that orders had got to be obeyed, and the row developed into one of those enormous arguments by means of which discipline is gradually hammered out in revolutionary armies. Some said I was right, others said I was wrong. But the point is that the one who took my side the most warmly of all was the brown-faced boy. As soon as he saw what was happening he sprang into the ring and began passionately defending me. With his strange, wild, Indian gesture he kept exclaiming, 'He's the best corporal we've got!' (*¡No hay cabo come el!*) Later on he applied for leave to exchange into my section.

Why is this incident touching to me? Because in any normal circumstances it would have been impossible for good feelings ever to be re-established between this boy and myself. The implied accusation of theft would not have been made any better, probably somewhat worse, by my efforts to make amends. One of the effects of safe and civilized life is an immense over-sensitiveness which makes all the primary emotions seem somewhat disgusting. Generosity is as painful as meanness, gratitude as hateful as ingratitude. But in Spain in 1936 we were not living in a normal time. It was a time when generous feelings and gestures were easier than they ordinarily are. I could relate a dozen similar incidents, not really communicable but bound up in my own mind with the special atmosphere of the time, the shabby clothes and the gay-coloured revolutionary posters, the universal use of the word 'comrade', the anti-Fascist ballads printed on flimsy paper and sold for a penny, the phrases like 'international proletarian solidarity', pathetically repeated by ignorant men who believed them to mean something. Could you feel friendly towards somebody, and stick up for him in a quarrel, after you had been ignominiously searched in his presence for property you were supposed to have stolen from him? No, you couldn't; but you might if you had both been through some emotionally widening experience. That is one of the by-products of revolution, though in this case it was only the beginnings of a revolution, and obviously foredoomed to failure.

FOUR

The struggle for power between the Spanish Republican parties is an unhappy, far-off thing which I have no wish to revive at this date. I only mention it in order to say: believe nothing, or next to nothing, of what you read about internal affairs on the Government side. It is all, from whatever source, party propaganda – that is to say, lies. The broad truth about the war is simple enough. The Spanish bourgeoisie saw their chance of crushing the labour movement, and took it, aided by the Nazis and by the forces of reaction all over the world. It is doubtful whether more than that will ever be established.

I remember saying once to Arthur Koestler, 'history stopped in 1936,' at which he nodded in immediate understanding. We were both thinking of totalitarianism in general, but more particularly of the Spanish civil war. Early in life I had noticed that no event is ever correctly reported in a newspaper, but in Spain, for the first time, I saw newspaper reports which did not bear any relation to the facts, not even the relationship which is implied in an ordinary lie. I saw great battles reported where there had been no fighting, and complete silence where hundreds of men had been killed. I saw troops who had fought bravely denounced as cowards and traitors, and others who had never seen a shot fired hailed as the heroes of imaginary victories; and I saw newspapers in London retailing these lies and eager intellectuals building emotional superstructures over events that had never happened. I saw, in fact, history being written not in terms of what happened but of what ought to have happened according to various 'party lines'. Yet in a way, horrible as all this was, it was unimportant. It concerned secondary issues – namely, the struggle for power between the Comintern and the Spanish left-wing parties, and the efforts of the Russian Government to prevent revolution in Spain. But the broad picture of the war which the Spanish Government presented to the world was not untruthful. The main issues were what it said they were. But as for the Fascists and their backers, how could they come even as near to the truth as that? How could they possibly mention their real aims? Their version of the war was pure fantasy, and in the circumstances it could not have been otherwise.

The only propaganda line open to the Nazis and Fascists was to represent themselves as Christian patriots saving Spain from a Russian dictatorship. This involved pretending that life in Government Spain was just one long massacre (*vide* the *Catholic Herald* or the *Daily Mail* – but these were child's play compared with the continental Fascist press), and it involved immensely exaggerating the scale of Russian intervention. Out of the huge pyramid of lies which the Catholic and reactionary press all over the world built up, let me take just one point – the presence in Spain of a Russian army. Devout

Franco partisans all believed in this; estimates of its strength went as high as half a million. Now, there was no Russian army in Spain. There may have been a handful of airmen and other technicians, a few hundred at the most, but an army there was not. Some thousands of foreigners who fought in Spain, not to mention millions of Spaniards, were witnesses of this. Well, their testimony made no impression at all upon the Franco propagandists, not one of whom had set foot in Government Spain. Simultaneously these people refused utterly to admit the fact of German or Italian intervention, at the same time as the German and Italian press were openly boasting about the exploits of their 'legionaries'. I have chosen to mention only one point, but in fact the whole of Fascist propaganda about the war was on this level.

This kind of thing is frightening to me, because it often gives me the feeling that the very concept of objective truth is fading out of the world. After all, the chances are that those lies, or at any rate similar lies, will pass into history. How will the history of the Spanish war be written? If Franco remains in power his nominees will write the history books, and (to stick to my chosen point) the Russian army which never existed will become historical fact, and schoolchildren will learn about it generations hence. But suppose Fascism is finally defeated and some kind of democratic government restored in Spain in the fairly near future; even then, how is the history of the war to be written? What kind of records will Franco have left behind him? Suppose even that the records kept on the Government side are recoverable – even so, how is a true history of the war to be written? For, as I have pointed out already, the Government also dealt extensively in lies. From the anti-Fascist angle one could write a broadly truthful history of the war, but it would be a partisan history, unreliable on every minor point. Yet, after all, *some* kind of history will be written, and after those who actually remember the war are dead, it will be universally accepted. So for all practical purposes the lie will have become truth.

I know it is the fashion to say that most of recorded history is lies anyway. I am willing to believe that history is for the most part inaccurate and biased, but what is peculiar to our own age is the abandonment of the idea that history *could* be truthfully written. In the past people deliberately lied, or they unconsciously coloured what they wrote, or they struggled after the truth, well knowing that they must make many mistakes; but in each case they believed that 'the facts' existed and were more or less discoverable. And in practice there was always a considerable body of fact which would have been agreed to by almost everyone. If you look up the history of the last war in, for instance, the *Encyclopaedia Britannica*, you will find that a respectable amount of the material is drawn from German sources. A British and a German historian would disagree deeply on many things, even on fundamentals, but there would still be that body of, as it were, neutral fact on which neither would seriously challenge the other. It is just this common basis of agreement, with its implication that human beings are all one species of animal, that totalitarianism destroys. Nazi theory indeed specifically denies that such a thing as 'the truth' exists. There is, for instance, no such thing as 'science'. There is only 'German science', 'Jewish science', etc. The implied objective of this line of thought is a nightmare world in which the Leader, or some ruling clique, controls not only the future but *the past*. If the Leader says of such and such an event, 'It never happened' – well, it never happened. If he says that two and two are five – well, two and two are five. This prospect frightens me much more than bombs – and after our experiences of the last few years that is not a frivolous statement.

But is it perhaps childish or morbid to terrify oneself with visions of a totalitarian future? Before writing off the totalitarian world as a nightmare that can't come true, just remember that in 1925 the world of today would have seemed a nightmare that couldn't come true. Against that shifting phantasmagoric world in which black may be white tomorrow and yesterday's weather can be changed by decree, there are in reality only two safeguards. One is that however much you deny the truth, the truth goes on existing, as it were, behind your back, and you consequently can't violate it in ways that impair military efficiency. The other is that so long as some parts of the earth remain unconquered, the liberal tradition can be kept alive. Let Fascism, or possibly even a combination of several Fascisms, conquer the whole world, and those two conditions no longer exist. We in England underrate the danger of this kind of thing, because our traditions and our past security have given us a sentimental belief that it all comes right in the end and the thing you most fear never really happens. Nourished for hundreds of years on a literature in which Right invariably triumphs in the last chapter, we believe half-instinctively that evil always defeats itself in the long run. Pacifism, for instance, is founded largely on this belief. Don't resist evil, and it will somehow destroy itself. But why should it? What evidence is there that it does? And what instance is there of a modern industrialized state collapsing unless conquered from the outside by military force?

Consider for instance the re-institution of slavery. Who could have imagined twenty years ago that slavery would return to Europe? Well, slavery has been restored under our noses. The forced-labour camps all over Europe and North Africa where Poles, Russians, Jews and political prisoners of every race toil at road-making or swamp-draining for their bare rations, are simple chattel slavery. The most one can say is that the buying and selling of slaves by individuals is not yet permitted. In other ways – the breaking-up of families, for instance – the conditions are probably worse than they were on the American cotton plantations. There is no reason for thinking that this state of affairs will change while any totalitarian domination endures. We don't grasp its full implications, because in our mystical way we feel that a régime founded on slavery *must* collapse. But it is worth comparing the duration of the slave empires of antiquity with that of any modern state. Civilizations founded on slavery have lasted for such periods as four thousand years.

When I think of antiquity, the detail that frightens me is that those hundreds of millions of slaves on whose backs civilization rested generation after generation have left behind them no record whatever. We do not even know their names. In the whole of Greek and Roman history, how many slaves' names are known to you? I can think of two, or possibly three. One is Spartacus and the other is Epictetus. Also, in the Roman room at the British Museum there is a glass jar with the maker's name inscribed on the bottom, '*Felix fecit*'. I have a vivid mental picture of poor Felix (a Gaul with red hair and a metal collar round his neck), but in fact he may not have been a slave; so there are only two slaves whose names I definitely know, and probably few people can remember more. The rest have gone down into utter silence.

FIVE

The backbone of the resistance against Franco was the Spanish working class, especially the urban trade union members. In the long run – it is important to remember that it is only in the long run – the working class remains the most reliable enemy of Fascism, simply because the working class stands to gain most by a decent reconstruction of society. Unlike other classes or categories, it can't be permanently bribed.

To say this is not to idealize the working class. In the long struggle that has followed the Russian Revolution it is the manual workers who have been defeated, and it is impossible not to feel that it was their own fault. Time after time, in country after country, the organized working-class movements have been crushed by open, illegal violence and their comrades abroad, linked to them in theoretical solidarity, have simply looked on and done nothing; and underneath this, secret cause of many betrayals, has lain the fact that between white and coloured workers there is not even lip-service to solidarity. Who can believe in the class-conscious international proletariat after the events of the past ten years? To the British working class the massacre of their comrades in Vienna, Berlin, Madrid, or wherever it might be, seemed less interesting and less important than yesterday's football match. Yet this does not alter the fact that the working class will go on struggling against Fascism after the others have caved in. One feature of the Nazi conquest of France was the astonishing defections among the intelligentsia, including some of the left-wing political intelligentsia. The intelligentsia are the people who squeal loudest against Fascism, and yet a respectable proportion of them collapse into defeatism when the pinch comes. They are far-sighted enough to see the odds against them, and moreover they can be bribed – for it is evident that the Nazis think it worth while to bribe intellectuals. With the working class it is the other way about. Too ignorant to see through the trick that is being played on them, they easily swallow the promises of Fascism, yet sooner or later they always take up the struggle again. They must do so, because in their own bodies they always discover that the promises of Fascism cannot be fulfilled. To win over the working class permanently, the Fascists would have to raise the general standard of living, which they are unable and probably unwilling to do. The struggle of the working class is like the growth of a plant. The plant is blind and stupid, but it knows enough to keep pushing upwards towards the light, and it will do this in the face of endless discouragements. What are the workers struggling for? Simply for the decent life which they are more and more aware is now technically possible. Their consciousness of this aim ebbs and flows. In Spain, for a while, people were acting consciously, moving towards a goal which they wanted to reach and believed they could reach. It accounted for the curiously buoyant feeling that life in Government Spain had during the early months of the war. The common people knew in their bones that the Republic was their friend and Franco was their enemy. They knew that they were in the right, because they were fighting for something which the world owed them and was able to give them.

One has to remember this to see the Spanish war in its true perspective. When one thinks of the cruelty, squalor, and futility of war – and in this particular case of the intrigues, the persecutions, the lies and the misunderstandings – there is always the temptation to say: 'One side is as bad as the other. I am neutral.' In practice, however, one cannot be neutral, and there is hardly such a thing as a war in which it makes no difference who wins. Nearly always one side stands more or less for progress, the other side more or less for reaction. The hatred which the Spanish Republic excited in millionaires, dukes, cardinals, play-boys, Blimps and what not would in itself be enough to show one how the land lay. In essence it was a class war. If it had been won, the cause of the common people everywhere would have been strengthened. It was lost, and the dividend-drawers all over the world rubbed their hands. That was the real issue; all else was froth on its surface.

SIX

The outcome of the Spanish war was settled in London, Paris, Rome, Berlin – at any rate not in Spain. After the summer of 1937 those with eyes in their heads realized that the Government could not win the war unless there was some profound change in the international set-up, and in deciding to fight on Negrin and the others may have been partly influenced by the expectation that the world war which actually broke out in 1939 was coming in 1938. The much-publicized disunity on the Government side was not a main cause of defeat. The Government militias were hurriedly raised, ill-armed and unimaginative in their military outlook, but they would have been the same if complete political agreement had existed from the start. At the outbreak of war the average Spanish factory-worker did not even know how to fire a rifle (there had never been universal conscription in Spain), and the traditional pacifism of the Left was a great handicap. The thousands of foreigners who served in Spain made good infantry, but there were very few experts of any kind among them. The Trotskyist thesis that the war could have been won if the revolution had not been sabotaged was probably false. To nationalize factories, demolish churches, and issue revolutionary manifestos would not have made the armies more efficient. The Fascists won because they were the stronger; they had modern arms and the others hadn't. No political strategy could offset that.

The most baffling thing in the Spanish war was the behaviour of the great powers. The war was actually won for Franco by the Germans and Italians, whose motives were obvious enough. The motives of France and Britain are less easy to understand. In 1936 it was clear to everyone that if Britain would only help the Spanish Government, even to the extent of a few million pounds' worth of arms, Franco would collapse and German strategy would be severely dislocated. By that time one did not need to be a clairvoyant to foresee that war between Britain and Germany was coming; one could even foretell within a year or two when it would come. Yet in the most mean, cowardly, hypocritical way the British ruling class did all they could to hand Spain over to Franco and the Nazis. Why? Because they were pro-Fascist, was the obvious answer. Undoubtedly they were, and yet when it came to the final showdown they chose to stand up to Germany. It is still very uncertain what plan they acted on in backing Franco, and they may have had no clear plan at all. Whether the British ruling class are wicked or merely stupid is one of the most difficult questions of our time, and at certain moments a very important question. As to the Russians, their motives in the Spanish war are completely inscrutable. Did they, as the pinks believed, intervene in Spain in order to defend democracy and thwart the Nazis? Then why did they intervene on such a niggardly scale and finally leave Spain in the lurch? Or did they, as the Catholics maintained, intervene in order to foster revolution in Spain? Then why did they do all in their power to crush the Spanish revolutionary movements, defend private property and hand power to the middle class as against the working class? Or did they, as the Trotskyists suggested, intervene simply in order to *prevent* a Spanish revolution? Then why not have backed Franco? Indeed, their actions are most easily explained if one assumes that they were acting on several contradictory motives. I believe that in the future we shall come to feel that Stalin's foreign policy, instead of being so diabolically clever as it is claimed to be, has been merely opportunistic and stupid. But at any rate, the Spanish civil war demonstrated that the Nazis knew what they were doing and their opponents did not. The war was fought at a low technical level and its major strategy was very simple. That side which had arms would win. The Nazis and the Italians gave arms to their Spanish Fascist friends, and the western democracies and the Russians didn't give arms to those who should have been their friends. So the Spanish Republic perished, having 'gained what no republic missed'.

Whether it was right, as all left-wingers in other countries undoubtedly did, to encourage the Spaniards to go on fighting when they could not win is a question hard to answer. I myself think it was right, because I believe that it is better even from the point of view of survival to fight and be conquered than to surrender without fighting. The effects on the grand strategy of the struggle against Fascism cannot be assessed yet. The ragged, weaponless armies of the Republic held out for two and a half years, which was undoubtedly longer than their enemies expected. But whether that dislocated the Fascist time-table, or whether, on the other hand, it merely postponed the major war and gave the Nazis extra time to get their war machine into trim, is still uncertain.

SEVEN

I never think of the Spanish war without two memories coming into my mind. One is of the hospital ward at Lerida and the rather sad voices of the wounded militiamen singing some song with a refrain that ended:

Una resolucion,
Luchar hast' al fin!

Well, they fought to the end all right. For the last eighteen months of the war the Republican armies must have been fighting almost without cigarettes, and with precious little food. Even when I left Spain in the middle of 1937, meat and bread were scarce, tobacco a rarity, coffee and sugar almost unobtainable.

The other memory is of the Italian militiaman who shook my hand in the guardroom, the day I joined the militia. I wrote about this man at the beginning of my book on the Spanish war,[1] and do not want to repeat what I said there. When I remember – oh, how vividly! – his shabby uniform and fierce, pathetic, innocent face, the complex side-issues of the war seem to fade away and I see clearly that there was at any rate no doubt as to who was in the right. In spite of power politics and journalistic lying, the central issue of the war was the attempt of people like this to win the decent life which they knew to be their birthright. It is difficult to think of this particular man's probable end without several kinds of bitterness. Since I met him in the Lenin Barracks he was probably a Trotskyist or an Anarchist, and in the peculiar conditions of our time, when people of that sort are not killed by the Gestapo

[1] *Homage to Catalonia.*

they are usually killed by the GPU. But that does not affect the long-term issues. This man's face, which I saw only for a minute or two, remains with me as a sort of visual reminder of what the war was really about. He symbolizes for me the flower of the European working class, harried by the police of all countries, the people who fill the mass graves of the Spanish battlefields and are now, to the tune of several millions, rotting in forced-labour camps.

When one thinks of all the people who support or have supported Fascism, one stands amazed at their diversity. What a crew! Think of a programme which at any rate for a while could bring Hitler, Pétain, Montagu Norman, Pavelitch, William Randolph Hearst, Streicher, Buchman, Ezra Pound, Juan March, Cocteau, Thyssen, Father Coughlin, the Mufti of Jerusalem, Arnold Lunn, Antonescu, Spengler, Beverley Nichols, Lady Houston, and Marinetti all into the same boat! But the clue is really very simple. They are all people with something to lose, or people who long for a hierarchical society and dread the prospect of a world of free and equal human beings. Behind all the ballyhoo that is talked about 'godless' Russia and the 'materialism' of the working class lies the simple intention of those with money or privileges to cling to them. Ditto, though it contains a partial truth, with all the talk about the worthlessness of social reconstruction not accompanied by a 'change of heart'. The pious ones, from the Pope to the yogis of California, are great on the 'change of heart', much more reassuring from their point of view than a change in the economic system. Pétain attributes the fall of France to the common people's 'love of pleasure'. One sees this in its right perspective if one stops to wonder how much pleasure the ordinary French peasant's or working-man's life would contain compared with Pétain's own. The damned impertinence of these politicians, priests, literary men, and what not who lecture the working-class Socialist for his 'materialism'! All that the working man demands is what these others would consider the indispensable minimum without which human life cannot be lived at all. Enough to eat, freedom from the haunting terror of unemployment, the knowledge that your children will get a fair chance, a bath once a day, clean linen reasonably often, a roof that doesn't leak, and short enough working hours to leave you with a little energy when the day is done. Not one of those who preach against 'materialism' would consider life livable without these things. And how easily that minimum could be attained if we chose to set our minds to it for only twenty years! To raise the standard of living of the whole world to that of Britain would not be a greater undertaking than the war we are now fighting. I don't claim, and I don't know who does, that that would solve anything in itself. It is merely that privation and brute labour have to be abolished before the real problems of humanity can be tackled. The major problem of our time is the decay of the belief in personal immortality, and it cannot be dealt with while the average human being is either drudging like an ox or shivering in fear of the secret police. How right the working classes are in their 'materialism'! How right they are to realize that the belly comes before the soul, not in the scale of values but in point of time! Understand that, and the long horror that we are enduring becomes at least intelligible. All the considerations that are likely to make one falter – the siren voices of a Pétain or of a Gandhi, the inescapable fact that in order to fight one has to degrade oneself, the equivocal moral position of Britain, with its democratic phrases and its coolie empire, the sinister development of Soviet Russia, the squalid farce of left-wing politics – all this fades away and one sees only the struggle of the gradually awakening common people against the lords of property and their hired liars and bumsuckers. The question is very simple. Shall people like that Italian soldier be allowed to live the decent, fully human life which is now technically achievable, or shan't they? Shall the common man be pushed back into the mud, or shall he not? I myself believe, perhaps on insufficient grounds, that the common man will win his fight sooner or later, but I want it to be sooner and not later – some time within the next hundred years, say, and not some time within the next ten thousand years. That was the real issue of the Spanish war, and of the present war, and perhaps of other wars yet to come.

I never saw the Italian militiaman again, nor did I ever learn his name. It can be taken as quite certain that he is dead. Nearly two years later, when the war was visibly lost, I wrote these verses in his memory:

The Italian soldier shook my hand
Beside the guard-room table;
The strong hand and the subtle hand
Whose palms are only able

To meet within the sound of guns,
But oh! What peace I knew then
In gazing on his battered face
Purer than any woman's!

For the flyblown words that make me spew
Still in his ears were holy,
And he was born knowing what I had learned
Out of books and slowly.

The treacherous guns had told their tale
And we both had bought it,
But my gold brick was made of gold –
Oh! who ever would have thought it?

Good luck go with you, Italian soldier!
But luck is not for the brave;
What would the world give back to you?
Always less than you gave.

Between the shadow and the ghost,
Between the white and the red,
Between the bullet and the lie,
Where would hide your head?

For where is Manuel Gonzalez,
And where is Pedro Aguilar,
And where is Ramon Fenellosa?
The earthworms know where they are.

Your name and your deeds were forgotten
Before your bones were dry,
And the lie that slew you is buried
Under a deeper lie;

But the thing that I saw in your face
No power can disinherit:
No bomb that ever burst
Shatters the crystal spirit.

Written [Autumn] 1942

W. B. Yeats

One thing that Marxist criticism has not succeeded in doing is to trace the connection between 'tendency' and literary style. The subject-matter and imagery of a book can be explained in sociological terms, but its texture seemingly cannot. Yet some such connection there must be. One knows, for instance, that a Socialist would not write like Chesterton or a Tory imperialist like Bernard Shaw, though *how* one knows it is not easy to say. In the case of Yeats, there must be some kind of connection between his wayward, even tortured style of writing and his rather sinister vision of life. Mr Menon[1] is chiefly concerned with the esoteric philosophy underlying Yeats's work, but the quotations which are scattered all through his interesting book serve to remind one how artificial Yeats's manner of writing was. As a rule, this artificiality is accepted as Irishism, or Yeats is even credited with simplicity because he uses short words, but in fact one seldom comes on six consecutive lines of his verse in which there is not an archaism or an affected turn of speech. To take the nearest example:

Grant me an old man's Frenzy,
My self must I remake
Till I am Timon and Lear
Or that William Blake
Who beat upon the wall
Till Truth obeyed his call.

The unnecessary 'that' imports a feeling of affectation, and the same tendency is present in all but Yeats's best passages. One is seldom long away from a suspicion of 'quaintness', something that links up not only with the 'nineties, the Ivory Tower and the 'calf covers of pissed-on green', but also with Rackham's drawings, Liberty art-fabrics and the *Peter Pan* never-never land, of which, after all, 'The Happy Townland' is merely a more appetizing example. This does not matter, because, on the whole, Yeats gets away with it, and if his straining after effect is often irritating, it can also produce phrases ('the chill, footless years', 'the mackerel-crowded seas') which suddenly overwhelm one like a girl's face seen across a room. He is an exception to the rule that poets do not use poetical language.

[1] *The Development of William Butler Yeats* by V. K. Narayana Menon.

How many centuries spent
The sedentary soul
In toils of measurement
Beyond eagle or mole,
Beyond hearing or seeing,
Or Archimedes' guess,
To raise into being
That loveliness?

Here he does not flinch from a squashy vulgar word like 'loveliness', and after all it does not seriously spoil this wonderful passage. But the same tendencies, together with a sort of raggedness which is no doubt intentional, weaken his epigrams and polemical poems. For instance (I am quoting from memory) the epigram against the critics who damned *The Playboy of the Western World*:

Once when midnight smote the air
Eunuchs ran through Hell and met
On every crowded street to stare
Upon great Juan riding by;
Even like these to rail and sweat,
Staring upon his sinewy thigh.

The power which Yeats has within himself gives him the analogy ready made and produces the tremendous scorn of the last line, but even in this short poem there are six or seven unnecessary words. It would probably have been deadlier if it had been neater.

Mr Menon's book is incidentally a short biography of Yeats, but he is above all interested in Yeats's philosophical 'system', which in his opinion supplies the subject-matter of more of Yeats's poems than is generally recognized. This system is set forth fragmentarily in various places, and at full length in *A Vision*, a privately printed book which I have never read but which Mr Menon quotes from extensively. Yeats gave conflicting accounts of its origin, and Mr Menon hints pretty broadly that the 'documents' on which it was ostensibly founded were imaginary. Yeats's philosophical system, says Mr Menon, 'was at the back of his intellectual life almost from the beginning. His poetry is full of it. Without it his later poetry becomes almost completely unintelligible.' As soon as we begin to read about the so-called system we are in the middle of a hocus-pocus of Great Wheels, gyres, cycles of the moon, reincarnation, disembodied spirits, astrology and what not. Yeats hedges as to the literalness with which he believed in all this, but he certainly dabbled in spiritualism and astrology, and in earlier life had made experiments in alchemy. Although almost buried under explanations, very difficult to understand, about the phases of the moon, the central idea of his philosophical system seems to be our old friend, the cyclical universe, in which everything happens over and over again. One has not, perhaps, the right to laugh at Yeats for his mystical beliefs – for I believe it could be shown that *some* degree of belief in magic is almost universal – but neither ought one to write such things off as mere unimportant eccentricities. It is Mr Menon's perception of this that gives his book its deepest interest. 'In the first flush of admiration and enthusiasm,' he says, 'most people dismissed the fantastical philosophy as the price we have to pay for a great and curious intellect. One did not quite realize where he was heading. And those who did, like Pound and perhaps Eliot, approved the stand that he finally took. The first reaction to this did not come, as one might have expected, from the politically-minded young English poets. They were puzzled because a less rigid or artificial system than that of *A Vision* might not have produced the great poetry of Yeats's last days.' It might not, and yet Yeats's philosophy has some very sinister implications, as Mr Menon points out.

Translated into political terms, Yeats's tendency is Fascist. Throughout most of his life, and long before Fascism was ever heard of, he had had the outlook of those who reach Fascism by the aristocratic route. He is a great hater of democracy, of the modern world, science, machinery, the concept of progress – above all, of the idea of human equality. Much of the imagery of his work is feudal, and it is clear that he was not altogether free from ordinary snobbishness. Later these tendencies took clearer shape and led him to 'the exultant acceptance of authoritarianism as the only solution. Even violence and tyranny are not necessarily evil because the people, knowing not evil and good, would become perfectly acquiescent to tyranny . . . Everything must come from the top. Nothing can come from the masses.' Not much interested in politics, and no doubt disgusted by his brief incursions into public life, Yeats nevertheless makes political pronouncements. He is too big a man to share the illusions of Liberalism, and as early as 1920 he foretells in a justly famous passage ('The Second Coming') the kind of world that we have actually moved into. But he appears to welcome the coming age, which is to be 'hierarchical, masculine, harsh, surgical', and is influenced both by Ezra Pound and by various Italian Fascist writers. He describes the new civilization which he hopes and believes will arrive: 'an aristocratic civilization in its most completed form, every detail of life hierarchical, every great man's door crowded at dawn by petitioners, great wealth everywhere in a few men's hands, all dependent upon a few, up to the Emperor himself, who is a God dependent on a greater God, and everywhere, in Court, in the family, an inequality made law.' The innocence of this statement is as interesting as its snobbishness. To begin with, in a single phrase, 'great wealth in a few men's hands', Yeats lays bare the central reality of Fascism, which the whole of its propaganda is designed to cover up. The merely political Fascist claims always to be fighting for justice: Yeats, the poet, sees at a glance that Fascism means injustice, and acclaims it for that very reason. But at the same time he fails to see that the new authoritarian civilization, if it arrives, will not be aristocratic, or what he means by aristocratic. It will not be ruled by noblemen with Van Dyck faces, but by anonymous millionaires, shiny-bottomed bureaucrats and murdering gangsters. Others who have made the same mistake have afterwards changed their views, and one ought not to assume that Yeats, if he had lived longer, would necessarily have followed his friend Pound, even in sympathy. But the tendency of the passage I have quoted above is obvious, and its complete throwing overboard of whatever good the past two thousand years have achieved is a disquieting symptom.

How do Yeats's political ideas link up with his leaning towards occultism? It is not clear at first glance why hatred of democracy and a tendency to believe in crystal-gazing should go together. Mr Menon only discusses this rather shortly, but it is possible to make two guesses. To begin with, the theory that civilization moves in recurring cycles is one way out for people who hate the concept of human equality. If it is true that 'all this', or something like it, 'has happened before', then science and the modern world are debunked at one stroke and progress becomes for ever impossible. It does not much matter if the lower orders are getting above themselves, for, after all, we shall soon be returning to an age of tyranny. Yeats is by no means alone in this outlook. If the universe is moving round on a wheel, the future must be foreseeable, perhaps even in some detail. It is merely a question of discovering the laws of its motion, as the early astronomers discovered the solar year. Believe that, and it becomes difficult not to believe in astrology or some similar system. A year before the war, examining a copy of *Gringoire*, the French Fascist weekly, much read by army officers, I found in it no less than thirty-eight advertisements of clairvoyants. Secondly, the very concept of occultism carries with it the idea that knowledge must be a secret thing, limited to a small circle of initiates. But the same idea is integral to Fascism. Those who dread the prospect of universal suffrage, popular education, freedom of thought, emancipation of women, will start off with a predilection towards secret cults. There is another link between Fascism and magic in the profound hostility of both to the Christian ethical code.

No doubt Yeats wavered in his beliefs and held at different times many different opinions, some enlightened, some not. Mr Menon repeats for him Eliot's claim that he had the longest period of development of any poet who has ever lived. But there is one thing that seems constant, at least in all of his work that I can remember, and that is his hatred of modern western civilization and desire to return to the Bronze Age, or perhaps to the Middle Ages. Like all such thinkers, he tends to write in praise of ignorance. The Fool in his remarkable play, *The Hour-Glass*, is a Chestertonian figure, 'God's fool', the 'natural born innocent', who is always wiser than the wise man. The philosopher in the play dies on the knowledge that all his lifetime of thought has been wasted (I am quoting from memory again):

The stream of the world has changed its course,
And with the stream my thoughts have run
Into some cloudly, thunderous spring
That is its mountain-source;
Ay, to a frenzy of the mind,
That all that we have done's undone
Our speculation but as the wind.[1]

Beautiful words, but by implication profoundly obscurantist and reactionary; for if it is really true that a village idiot, as such, is wiser than a philosopher, then it would be better if the alphabet had never been invented. Of course, all praise of the past is partly sentimental, because we do not live in the past. The poor do not praise poverty. Before you can despise the machine, the machine must set you free from brute labour. But that is not to say that Yeats's yearning for a more primitive and more hierarchical age was not sincere. How

[1] The last three lines actually read:

Aye, to some frenzy of the mind
For all that we have done's undone
Our speculation but as the wind.

much of all this is traceable to mere snobbishness, product of Yeats's own position as an impoverished offshoot of the aristocracy, is a different question. And the connection between his obscurantist opinions and his tendency towards 'quaintness' of language remains to be worked out; Mr Menon hardly touches upon it.

This is a very short book, and I would greatly like to see Mr Menon go ahead and write another book on Yeats, starting where this one leaves off. 'If the greatest poet of our times is exultantly ringing in an era of Fascism, it seems a somewhat disturbing symptom,' he says on the last page, and leaves it at that. It is a disturbing symptom, because it is not an isolated one. By and large the best writers of our time have been reactionary in tendency, and though Fascism does not offer any real return to the past, those who yearn for the past will accept Fascism sooner than its probable alternatives. But there are other lines of approach, as we have seen during the past two or three years. The relationship between Fascism and the literary intelligentsia badly needs investigating, and Yeats might well be the starting-point. He is best studied by someone like Mr Menon, who can approach a poet primarily as a poet, but who also knows that a writer's political and religious beliefs are not excrescences to be laughed away, but something that will leave their mark even on the smallest detail of his work.

Horizon, January 1943

Literature and the Left

'When a man of true Genius appears in the World, you may know him by this infallible Sign, that all the Dunces are in Conspiracy against him.' So wrote Jonathan Swift, 200 years before the publication of *Ulysses*.

If you consult any sporting manual or yearbook you will find many pages devoted to the hunting of the fox and the hare, but not a word about the hunting of the highbrow. Yet this, more than any other, is the characteristic British sport, in season all the year round and enjoyed by rich and poor alike, with no complications from either class-feeling or political alignment.

For it should be noted that in its attitude towards 'highbrows' – that is, towards any writer or artist who makes experiments in technique – the Left is no friendlier than the Right. Not only is 'highbrow' almost as much a word of abuse in the *Daily Worker* as in *Punch*, but it is exactly those writers whose work shows both originality and the power to endure that Marxist doctrinaires single out for attack. I could name a long list of examples, but I am thinking expecially of Joyce, Yeats, Lawrence and Eliot. Eliot, in particular, is damned in the left-wing press almost as automatically and perfunctorily as Kipling – and that by critics who only a few years back were going into raptures over the already forgotten masterpieces of the Left Book Club.

If you ask a 'good party man' (and this goes for almost any party of the Left) what he objects to in Eliot, you get an answer that ultimately reduces to this. Eliot is a reactionary (he has declared himself a royalist, an Anglo-Catholic, etc.), and he is also a 'bourgeois intellectual', out of touch with the common man: therefore he is a bad writer. Contained in this statement is a half-conscious confusion of ideas which vitiates nearly all politico-literary criticism.

To dislike a writer's politics is one thing. To dislike him because he forces you to think is another, not necessarily incompatible with the first. But as soon as you start talking about 'good' and 'bad' writers you are tacitly appealing to literary tradition and thus dragging in a totally different set of values. For what is a 'good' writer? Was Shakespeare 'good'? Most people would agree that he was. Yet Shakespeare is, and perhaps was even by the standards of his own time, reactionary in tendency; and he is also a difficult writer, only doubtfully accessible to the common man. What, then, becomes of the notion that Eliot is disqualified, as it were, by being an Anglo-Catholic royalist who is given to quoting Latin?

Left-wing literary criticism has not been wrong in insisting on the importance of subject-matter. It may not even have been wrong, considering the age we live in, in demanding that literature shall be first and foremost propaganda. Where it has been wrong is in making what are ostensibly literary judgements for political ends. To take a crude example, what Communist would dare to admit in public that Trotsky is a better writer than Stalin – as he is, of course? To say 'X is a gifted writer, but he is a political enemy and I shall do my best to silence him' is harmless enough. Even if you end by silencing him with a tommy-gun you are not really sinning against the intellect. The deadly sin is to say 'X is a political enemy: therefore he is a bad writer.' And if anyone says that this kind of thing doesn't happen, I answer merely: look up the literary pages of the left-wing press, from the *News Chronicle* to the *Labour Monthly*, and see what you find.

There is no knowing just how much the Socialist movement has lost by alienating the literary intelligentsia. But it has alienated them, partly by confusing tracts with literature, and partly by having no room in it for a humanistic culture. A writer can vote Labour as easily as anyone else, but it is very difficult for him to take part in the Socialist movement *as a writer*. Both the book-trained doctrinaire and the practical politician will despise him as a 'bourgeois intellectual', and will lose no opportunity of telling him so. They will have much the same attitude towards his work as a golfing stock-broker would have. The illiteracy of politicians is a special feature of our age – as G. M. Trevelyan put it, 'In the seventeenth century Members of Parliament quoted the Bible, in the eighteenth and nineteenth centuries, the classics, and in the twentieth century nothing' – and its corollary is the [political] impotence of writers. In the years following the last war the best English writers were reactionary in tendency, though most of them took no direct part in politics. After them, about 1930, there came a generation of writers who tried very hard to be actively useful in the left-wing movement. Numbers of them joined the Communist Party, and got there exactly the same reception as they would have got in the Conservative Party. That is, they were first regarded with patronage and suspicion, and then, when it was found that they would not or could not turn themselves into gramophone records, they were thrown out on their ears. Most of them retreated into individualism. No doubt they still vote Labour, but their talents are lost to the movement; and – a more sinister development – after them there comes a new generation of writers who, without being strictly non-political, are outside the Socialist movement from the start. Of the very young writers who are now beginning their careers, the most gifted are pacifists; a few may even have a leaning towards Fascism. There is hardly one to whom the mystique of the Socialist movement appears to mean anything. The ten-year-long struggle against Fascism seems to them meaningless and uninteresting, and they say so frankly. One could explain this in a number of ways, but the contemptuous attitude of the Left towards 'bourgeois intellectuals' is likely to be part of the reason.

Gilbert Murray relates somewhere or other that he once lectured on Shakespeare to a Socialist debating society. At the end he called for questions in the usual way, to receive as the sole question asked: 'Was Shakespeare a capitalist?' The depressing thing about this story is that it might well be true. Follow up its implications, and you perhaps get a glimpse of the reason why Céline wrote *Mea Culpa* and Auden is watching his navel in America.

Tribune, 4 June 1943

Review

Beggar My Neighbour by Lionel Fielden

If you compare commercial advertising with political propaganda, one thing that strikes you is its relative intellectual honesty. The advertiser at least knows what he is aiming at – that is, money – whereas the propagandist, when he is not a lifeless hack, is often a neurotic working off some private grudge and actually desirous of the exact opposite of the thing he advocates. The ostensible purpose of Mr Fielden's book is to further the cause of Indian independence. It will not have that effect, and I do not see much reason for thinking that he himself wishes for anything of the kind. For if someone is genuinely working for Indian independence, what is he likely to do? Obviously he will start by deciding what forces are potentially on his side, and then, as cold-bloodedly as any toothpaste advertiser, he will think out the best method of appealing to them. This is not Mr Fielden's manner of approach. A number of motives are discernible in this book, but the immediately obvious one is a desire to work off various quarrels with the Indian Government, All India Radio and various sections of the British press. He does indeed marshal a number of facts about India, and towards the end he even produces a couple of pages of constructive suggestions, but for the most part his book is simply a nagging, irrelevant attack on British rule, mixed up with tourist-like gush about the superiority of Indian civilization. On the fly-leaf, just to induce that matey atmosphere which all propagandists aim at, he signs his dedicatory letter 'among the European barbarians', and then a few pages later introduces an imaginary Indian who denounces western civilization with all the shrillness of a spinster of thirty-nine denouncing the male sex:

> ... an Indian who is intensely proud of his own traditions, and regards Europeans as barbarians who are continually fighting, who use force to dominate other peaceful peoples, who think chiefly in terms of big business, whisky, and bridge; as people of comparatively recent growth,

> who, while they put an exaggerated value on plumbing, have managed to spread tuberculosis and venereal disease all over the world ... he will say that to sit in the water in which you have washed, instead of bathing yourself in running water, is not clean, but dirty and disgusting; he will show, and I shall agree with him absolutely, that the English are a dirty and even a smelly nation compared with the Indians; he will assert, and I am not at all sure that he is wrong, that the use of half-washed forks, spoons and knives by different people for food is revoltingly barbaric when compared with the exquisite manipulation of food by Indian fingers; he will be confident that the Indian room, with its bare walls and beautiful carpets, is infinitely superior to the European clutter of uncomfortable chairs and tables, etc., etc., etc.

The whole book is written in this vein, more or less. The same nagging, hysterical note crops up every few pages, and where a comparison can be dragged in it is dragged in, the upshot always being that the East is Good and the West is Bad. Now before stopping to inquire what service this kind of thing really does to the cause of Indian freedom, it is worth trying an experiment. Let me rewrite this passage as it might be uttered by an Englishman speaking up for his own civilization as shrilly as Mr Fielden's Indian. It is important to notice that what he says is not more dishonest or more irrelevant than what I have quoted above:

> ... an Englishman who is intensely proud of his own traditions, and regards Indians as an unmanly race who gesticulate like monkeys, are cruel to women and talk incessantly about money; as a people who take it upon them to despise western science and consequently are rotten with malaria and hookworm ... he will say that in a hot climate washing in running water has its points, but that in cold climates all Orientals either wash as we do or as in the case of many Indian hill tribes – not at all; he will show, and I shall agree with him absolutely, that no western European can walk through an Indian village without wishing that his smell organs had been removed beforehand; he will assert, and I am not at all sure that he is wrong, that eating with your fingers is a barbarous habit since it cannot be done without making disgusting noises; he will be confident that the English room, with its comfortable armchairs and friendly bookshelves, is infinitely superior to the bare Indian interior where the mere effort of sitting with no support to your back makes for vacuity of mind, etc., etc., etc.

Two points emerge here. To begin with, no English person would now write like that. No doubt many people think such thoughts, and even utter them behind closed doors, but to find anything of the kind in print you would have to go back ten years or so. Secondly, it is worth asking, what would be the effect of this passage on an Indian who happened to take it seriously? He would be offended, and very rightly. Well then, isn't it just possible that passages like the one I quoted from Mr Fielden might have the same effect on a British reader? No one likes hearing his own habits and customs abused. This is not a trivial consideration, because at this moment books about India have, or could have, a special importance. There is no political solution in sight, the Indians cannot win their freedom and the British Government will not give it, and all one can for the moment do is to push public opinion in this country and America in the right direction. But that will not be done by any propaganda that is merely anti-European. A year ago, soon after the Cripps mission had failed, I saw a well-known Indian nationalist address a small meeting at which he was to explain why the Cripps offer had been refused. It was a valuable opportunity, because there were present a number of American newspaper correspondents who, if handled tactfully, might cable to America a sympathetic account of the Congress Party's case. They had come there with fairly open minds. Within about ten minutes the Indian had converted all of them into ardent supporters of the British Government, because instead of sticking to his subject he launched into an anti-British tirade quite obviously founded on spite and inferiority complex. That is just the mistake that a toothpaste advertiser would not make. But then the toothpaste advertiser is trying to sell toothpaste and not to get his own back on that Blimp who turned him out of a first-class carriage fifteen years ago.

However, Mr Fielden's book raises wider issues than the immediate political problem. He upholds the East against the West on the ground that the East is religious, artistic and indifferent to 'progress', while the West is materialistic, scientific, vulgar and warlike. The great crime of Britain is to have forced industrialization on India. (Actually, the real crime of Britain during the last thirty years has been to do the opposite.) The West looks on work as an end in itself, but at the same time is obsessed with a 'high standard of living' (it is worth noticing that Mr Fielden is anti-Socialist, russophobe and somewhat contemptuous of the English working class), while India wants only to live in ancestral simplicity in a world freed from the machine. India must be independent, and at the same time must be de-industrialized. It is also suggested a number of times, though not in very clear terms, that India ought to be neutral in the present war. Needless to say, Mr Fielden's hero is Gandhi, about whose financial background he says nothing. 'I have a notion that the legend of Gandhi may yet be a flaming inspiration to the millions of the East, and perhaps to those of the West. But it is, for the time being, the East which provides the fruitful soil, because the East has not yet fallen prone before the Golden Calf. And it may be for the East, once again, to show mankind that human happiness does not depend on that particular form of worship, and that the conquest of materialism is also the conquest of war.' Gandhi makes many appearances in the book, playing rather the same part as 'Frank' in the literature of the Buchmanites.

Now, I do not know whether or not Gandhi will be a 'flaming inspiration' in years to come. When one thinks of the creatures who *are* venerated by humanity it does not seem particularly unlikely. But the statement that India 'ought' to be independent, *and* de-industrialized, *and* neutral in the present war, is an absurdity. If one forgets the details of the political struggle and looks at the strategic realities, one sees two facts which are in seeming conflict. The first is that whatever the 'ought' of the question may be, India is very unlikely ever to be independent in the sense in which Britain or Germany is now independent. The second is that India's *desire* for independence is a reality and cannot be talked out of existence.

In a world in which national sovereignty exists, India cannot be a sovereign state, because she is unable to defend herself. And the more she is the cow and spinning-wheel paradise imagined by Mr Fielden, the more this is true. What is now called independence means the power to manufacture aeroplanes in large numbers. Already there are only five genuinely independent states in the world, and if present trends continue there will in the end be only three. On a long-term view it is clear that India has little chance in a world of power politics, while on a short-term view it is clear that the necessary first step towards Indian freedom is an Allied victory. Even that would only be a short and uncertain step, but the alternatives must lead to India's continued subjection. If we are defeated, Japan or Germany takes over India and that is the end of the story. If there is a compromise peace (Mr Fielden seems to hint at times that this is desirable), India's chances are no better, because in such circumstances we should inevitably cling to any territories we had captured or not lost. A compromise peace is always a peace of 'grab what you can'. Mr Fielden brings forward his imaginary Indian to suggest that if India were neutral Japan might leave her alone; I doubt whether any responsible Indian nationalist has said anything quite so stupid as that. The other idea, more popular in left-wing circles, that India could defend herself better on her own than with our help, is a sentimentality. If the Indians were militarily superior to ourselves they would have driven us out long ago. The much-quoted example of China is very misleading here. India is a far easier country to conquer than China, if only because of its better communications, and in any case Chinese resistance depends on help from the highly industrialized states and would collapse without it. One must conclude that for the next few years India's destiny is linked with that of Britain and the USA. It might be different if the Russians could get their hands free in the West or if China were a great military power; but that again implies a complete defeat of the Axis, and points away from the neutrality which Mr Fielden seems to think desirable. The idea put forward by Gandhi himself, that if the Japanese came they could be dealt with by sabotage and 'non-co-operation', is a delusion, nor does Gandhi show any very strong signs of believing in it. Those methods have never seriously embarrassed the British and would make no impression on the Japanese. After all, where is the Korean Gandhi?

But against this is the *fact* of Indian nationalism, which is not to be exorcized by the humbug of White Papers or by a few phrases out of Marx. And it is nationalism of an emotional, romantic, even chauvinistic kind. Phrases like 'the sacred soil of the Motherland', which now seem merely ludicrous in Britain, come naturally enough to an Indian intellectual. When the Japanese appeared to be on the point of invading India, Nehru actually used the phrase, 'Who dies if India live?' So the wheel comes full circle and the Indian rebel quotes Kipling. And nationalism at this level works indirectly in favour of Fascism. Extremely few Indians are at all attracted by the idea of a federated world, the only kind of world in which India could actually be free. Even those who pay lip-service to federalism usually want only an eastern federation, thought of as a military alliance against the West. The idea of the class struggle has little appeal anywhere in Asia, nor do Russia and China evoke much loyalty in India. As for the Nazi domination of Europe, only a handful of Indians are able to see that it affects their own destiny in any way. In some of the smaller Asiatic countries the 'my country right or wrong' nationalists were exactly the ones who went over to the Japanese – a step which may not have been wholly due to ignorance.

But here there arises a point which Mr Fielden hardly touches on, and that is: we don't know to what extent Asiatic nationalism is simply the product of our own oppression. For a century all the major oriental nations except

Japan have been more or less in subjection, and the hysteria and short-sightedness of the various nationalist movements may be the result simply of that. To realize that national sovereignty is the enemy of national freedom may be a great deal easier when you are not being ruled by foreigners. It is not certain that this is so, since the most nationalist of the oriental nations, Japan, is also the one that has never been conquered, but at least one can say that if the solution is not along these lines, then there *is* no solution. Either power politics must yield to common decency, or the world must go spiralling down into a nightmare of which we can already catch some dim glimpses. And the necessary first step, before we can make our talk about world federation sound even credible, is that Britain shall get off India's back. This is the only large-scale decent action that is possible in the world at this moment. The immediate preliminaries would be: abolish the Viceroyalty and the India Office, release the Congress prisoners, and declare India formally independent. The rest is detail.[1]

But how are we to bring any such thing about? If it is done at this time, it can only be a voluntary act. Indian independence has no asset except public opinion in Britain and America, which is only a potential asset. Japan, Germany and the British Government are all on the other side, and India's possible friends, China and the USSR, are fighting for their lives and have little bargaining power. There remain the peoples of Britain and America, who are in a position to put pressure on their own governments if they see a reason for doing so. At the time of the Cripps mission, for instance, it would have been quite easy for public opinion in this country to force the Government into making a proper offer, and similar opportunities may recur. Mr Fielden, by the way, does his best to throw doubt on Cripps's personal honesty, and also lets it appear that the Congress Working Committee were unanimously against accepting the Cripps proposals, which was not the case. In fact, Cripps extorted the best terms he could get from the Government; to get better ones he would have had to have public opinion actively and intelligently behind him. Therefore the first job is – win over the ordinary people of this country. Make them see that India matters, and that India has been shamefully treated and deserves restitution. But you are not going to do that by insulting them. Indians, on the whole, grasp this better than their English apologists. After all, what is the probable effect of a book which irrelevantly abuses every English institution, rapturizes over the 'wisdom of the East' like an American schoolmarm on a conducted tour, and mixes up pleas for Indian freedom with pleas for surrender to Hitler? At best it can only convert the converted, and it may deconvert a few of those. The net effect must be to strengthen British imperialism, though its motives are probably more complex than this may seem to imply.

On the surface, Mr Fielden's book is primarily a plea for 'spirituality' as against 'materialism'. On the one hand an uncritical reverence for everything oriental; on the other a hatred of the West generally, and of Britain in particular, hatred of science and the machine, suspicion of Russia, contempt for the working-class conception of Socialism. The whole adds up to Parlour Anarchism – a plea for the simple life, based on dividends. Rejection of the machine is, of course, always founded on tacit acceptance of the machine,

[1] Of course the necessary corollary would be a military alliance for the duration of the war. But it is not likely that there would be any difficulty in securing this. Extremely few Indians really want to be ruled by Japan or Germany. [Author's footnote.]

a fact symbolized by Gandhi as he plays with his spinning-wheel in the mansion of some cotton millionaire. But Gandhi also comes into the picture in another way. It is noticeable that both Gandhi and Mr Fielden have an exceedingly equivocal attitude towards the present war. Although variously credited in this country with being a 'pure' pacifist and a Japanese agent, Gandhi has, in fact, made so many conflicting pronouncements on the war that it is difficult to keep track of them. At one moment his 'moral support' is with the Allies, at another it is withdrawn, at one moment he thinks it best to come to terms with the Japanese, at another he wishes to oppose them by non-violent means – at the cost, he thinks, of several million lives – at another he urges Britain to give battle in the West and leave India to be invaded, at another he 'has no wish to harm the Allied cause' and declares that he does not want the Allied troops to leave India. Mr Fielden's views on the war are less complicated, but equally ambiguous. In no place does he state whether or not he wishes the Axis to be defeated. Over and over again he urges that an Allied victory can lead to no possible good result, but at the same time he disclaims 'defeatism' and even argues that Indian neutrality would be useful to us in a *military* sense, i.e. that we could fight better if India were not a liability. Now, if this means anything, it means that he wants a compromise, a negotiated peace; and though he fails to say so, I do not doubt that that is what he does want. But curiously enough, this is the *imperialist* solution. The appeasers have always wanted neither defeat nor victory but a compromise with the other imperialist powers; and they too have known how to use the manifest folly of war as an argument.

For years past the more intelligent imperialists have been in favour of compromising with the Fascists, even if they had to give away a good deal in order to do so, because they have seen that only thus could imperialism be salvaged. Some of them are not afraid to hint this fairly broadly even now. If we carry the war to a destructive conclusion, the British Empire will either be lost, or democratized, or pawned to America. On the other hand it could and probably would survive in something like its present form if there were other sated imperialist powers which had an interest in preserving the existing world system. If we came to an understanding with Germany and Japan we might diminish our possessions (even that isn't certain: it is a little-noticed fact that *in territory* Britain and the USA have gained more than they have lost in this war), but we should at least be confirmed in what we had already. The world would be split up between three or four great imperial powers who, for the time being, would have no motive for quarrelling. Germany would be there to neutralize Russia, Japan would be there to prevent the development of China. Given such a world system, India could be kept in subjection almost indefinitely. And more than this, it is doubtful whether a compromise peace *could* follow any other lines. So it would seem that Parlour Anarchism is [not] something very innocuous after all. Objectively it only demands what the worst of the appeasers want, subjectively it is of a kind to irritate the possible friends of India in this country. And does not this bear a sort of resemblance to the career of Gandhi, who has alienated the British public by his extremism and aided the British Government by his moderation? Impossibilism and reaction are usually in alliance, though not, of course, conscious alliance.

Hypocrisy is a very rare thing, true villainy is perhaps as difficult as virtue. We live in a lunatic world in which opposites are constantly changing into one another, in which pacifists find themselves worshipping Hitler, Socialists become nationalists, patriots become quislings, Buddhists pray for the success of the Japanese army, and the Stock Market takes an upward turn when the Russians stage an offensive. But though these people's motives are often obvious enough when seen from the outside, they are not obvious to themselves. The scenes imagined by Marxists, in which wicked rich men sit in little secret rooms and hatch schemes for robbing the workers, don't happen in real life. The robbery takes place, but it is committed by sleepwalkers. Now, one of the finest weapons that the rich have ever evolved for use against the poor is 'spirituality'. If you can induce the working man to believe that his desire for a decent standard of living is 'materialism', you have got him where you want him. Also, if you can induce the Indian to remain 'spiritual' instead of taking up with vulgar things like trade unions, you can ensure that he will always remain a coolie. Mr Fielden is indignant with the 'materialism' of the western working class, whom he accuses of being even worse in this respect than the rich and of wanting not only radios but even motor cars and fur coats. The obvious answer is that these sentiments don't come well from someone who is in a comfortable and privileged position himself. But that is only an answer, not a diagnosis, for the problem of the disaffected intelligentsia would be hardly a problem at all if ordinary dishonesty were involved.

In the last twenty years western civilization has given the intellectual security without responsibility, and in England, in particular, it has educated him in scepticism while anchoring him almost immovably in the privileged class. He has been in the position of a young man living on an allowance from a father whom he hates. The result is a deep feeling of guilt and resentment, not combined with any genuine desire to escape. But some psychological escape, some form of self-justification there must be, and one of the most satisfactory is transferred nationalism. During the nineteen-thirties the normal transference was to Soviet Russia, but there are other alternatives, and it is noticeable that pacifism and anarchism, rather than Stalinism, are now gaining ground among the young. These creeds have the advantage that they aim at the impossible and therefore in effect demand very little. If you throw in a touch of oriental mysticism and Buchmanite raptures over Gandhi, you have everything that a disaffected intellectual needs. The life of an English gentleman and the moral attitudes of a saint can be enjoyed simultaneously. By merely transferring your allegiance from England to India (it used to be Russia), you can indulge to the full in all the chauvinistic sentiments which would be totally impossible if you recognized them for what they were. In the name of pacifism you can compromise with Hitler, and in the name of 'spirituality' you can keep your money. It is no accident that those who wish for an inconclusive ending to the war tend to extol the East as against the West. The actual facts don't matter very much. The fact that the eastern nations have shown themselves at least as warlike and bloodthirsty as the western ones, that so far from rejecting industrialism, the East is adopting it as swiftly as it can – this is irrelevant, since what is wanted is the mythos of the peaceful, religious and patriarchal East to set against the greedy materialistic West. As soon as you have 'rejected' industrialism, and hence Socialism, you are in that strange no man's land where the Fascist and the pacifist join forces. There is indeed a sort of apocalyptic truth in the statement of the German radio that the teachings of Hitler and Gandhi are the same. One realizes this when one sees Middleton Murry praising the Japanese invasion of China and Gerald Heard proposing to institute the Hindu caste system in Europe at the same time as the Hindus themselves are abandoning it. We shall be hearing a lot about the superiority of eastern civilization in the next few years. Meanwhile this is a mischievous book, which will be acclaimed in the left-wing press and welcomed for quite different reasons by the more intelligent Right.

Horizon, September 1943

Who Are the War Criminals?

On the face of it, Mussolini's collapse was a story straight out of Victorian melodrama. At long last Righteousness had triumphed, the wicked man was discomfited, the mills of God were doing their stuff. On second thoughts, however, this moral tale is less simple and less edifying. To begin with, what crime, if any, has Mussolini committed? In power politics there are no crimes, because there are no laws. And, on the other hand, is there any feature in Mussolini's *internal* régime that could be seriously objected to by any body of people likely to sit in judgement on him? For, as the author of this book[1] abundantly shows – and this in fact is the main purpose of the book – there is not one scoundrelism committed by Mussolini between 1922 and 1940 that has not been lauded to the skies by the very people who are now promising to bring him to trial.

For the purposes of his allegory 'Cassius' imagines Mussolini indicted before a British court, with the Attorney General as prosecutor. The list of charges is an impressive one, and the main facts – from the murder of Matteotti to the invasion of Greece, and from the destruction of the peasants' co-operatives to the bombing of Addis Ababa – are not denied. Concentration camps, broken treaties, rubber truncheons, castor oil – everything is admitted. The only troublesome question is: How can something that was praiseworthy at the time when you did it – ten years ago, say – suddenly become reprehensible now? Mussolini is allowed to call witnesses, both living and dead, and to show by their own printed words that from the very first the responsible leaders of British opinion have encouraged him in everything that he did. For instance, here is Lord Rothermere in 1928:

> In his own country [Mussolini] was the antidote to a deadly poison. For the rest of Europe he has been a tonic which has done to all incalculable good. I can claim with sincere satisfaction to have been the first man in a position of public influence to put Mussolini's splendid achievement in its right light.
> ... He is the greatest figure of our age.

Here is Winston Churchill in 1927:

> If I had been an Italian I am sure I should have been wholeheartedly with you in your triumphant struggle against the bestial appetites and

[1] *The Trial of Mussolini* by 'Cassius'.

> passions of Leninism ... [Italy] has provided the necessary antidote to the Russian poison. Hereafter no great nation will be unprovided with an ultimate means of protection against the cancerous growth of Bolshevism.

Here is Lord Mottistone in 1935:

> I did not oppose [the Italian action in Abyssinia]. I wanted to dispel the ridiculous illusion that it was a nice thing to sympathize with the underdog ... I said it was a wicked thing to send arms or connive to send arms to these cruel, brutal Abyssinians and still to deny them to others who are playing an honourable part.

Here is Mr Duff Cooper in 1938:

> Concerning the Abyssinian episode, the less said now the better. When old friends are reconciled after a quarrel it is always dangerous for them to discuss its original causes.

Here is Mr Ward Price, of the *Daily Mail*, in 1932:

> Ignorant and prejudiced people talk of Italian affairs as if that nation were subject to some tyranny which it would willingly throw off. With that rather morbid commiseration for fanatical minorities which is the rule with certain imperfectly informed sections of British public opinion, this country long shut its eyes to the magnificent work that the Fascist régime was doing. I have several times heard Mussolini himself express his gratitude to the *Daily Mail* as having been the first British newspaper to put his aims fairly before the world.

And so on, and so on, and so on. Hoare, Simon, Halifax, Neville Chamberlain, Austen Chamberlain, Hore-Belisha, Amery, Lord Lloyd and various others enter the witness-box, all of them ready to testify that, whether Mussolini was crushing the Italian trade unions, non-intervening in Spain, pouring mustard gas on the Abyssinians, throwing Arabs out of aeroplanes or building up a navy for use against Britain, the British Government and its official spokesmen supported him through thick and thin. We are shown Lady (Austen) Chamberlain shaking hands with Mussolini in 1924, Chamberlain and Halifax banqueting with him and toasting 'the Emperor of Abyssinia' in 1939, Lord Lloyd buttering up the Fascist régime in an official pamphlet as late as 1940. The net impression left by this part of the trial is quite simply that Mussolini is not guilty. Only later, when an Abyssinian, a Spaniard and an Italian anti-Fascist give their evidence, does the real case against him begin to appear.

Now, the book is a fanciful one, but this conclusion is realistic. It is immensely unlikely that the British Tories will ever put Mussolini on trial. There is nothing that they could accuse him of except his declaration of war in 1940. If the 'trial of war criminals' that some people enjoy dreaming about ever happens, it can only happen after revolutions in the Allied countries. But the whole notion of finding scapegoats, of blaming individuals, or parties, or nations for the calamities that have happened to us, raises other trains of thought, some of them rather disconcerting.

The history of British relations with Mussolini illustrates the structural weakness of a capitalist state. Granting that power politics are not moral, to attempt to buy Italy out of the Axis – and clearly this idea underlay British policy from 1934 onwards – was a natural strategic move. But it was not a move which Baldwin, Chamberlain and the rest of them were capable of carrying out. It could only have been done by being so strong that Mussolini would not dare to side with Hitler. This was impossible, because an economy ruled by the profit motive is simply not equal to rearming on a modern scale. Britain only began to arm when the Germans were in Calais. Before that, fairly large sums had, indeed, been voted for armaments, but they slid peaceably into the pockets of the shareholders and the weapons did not appear. Since they had no real intention of curtailing their own privileges, it was inevitable that the British ruling class should carry out every policy half-heartedly and blind themselves to the coming danger. But the moral collapse which this entailed was something new in British politics. In the nineteenth and early twentieth centuries, British politicians might be hypocritical, but hypocrisy implies a moral code. It was something new when Tory MPs cheered the news that British ships had been bombed by Italian aeroplanes, or when members of the House of Lords lent themselves to organized libel campaigns against the Basque children who had been brought here as refugees.

When one thinks of the lies and betrayals of those years, the cynical abandonment of one ally after another, the imbecile optimism of the Tory press, the flat refusal to believe that the dictators meant war, even when they shouted it from the housetops, the inability of the moneyed class to see anything wrong whatever in concentration camps, ghettos, massacres and undeclared wars, one is driven to feel that moral decadence played its part as well as mere stupidity. By 1937 or thereabouts it was not possible to be in doubt about the nature of the Fascist régimes. But the lords of property had decided that Fascism was on their side and they were willing to swallow the most stinking evils so long as their property remained secure. In their clumsy way they were playing the game of Machiavelli, of 'political realism', of 'anything is right which advances the cause of the Party' – the Party in this case, of course, being the Conservative Party.

All this 'Cassius' brings out, but he does shirk its corollary. Throughout his book it is implied that only Tories are immoral. 'Yet there is still another England,' he says. 'This other England detested Fascism from the day of its birth ... This was the England of the Left, the England of Labour.' True, but only part of the truth. The actual behaviour of the Left has been more honourable than its theories. It has fought against Fascism, but its representative thinkers have entered just as deeply as their opponents into the evil world of 'realism' and power politics.

'Realism' (it used to be called dishonesty) is part of the general political atmosphere of our time. It is a sign of the weakness of 'Cassius's' position that one could compile a quite similar book entitled *The Trial of Winston Churchill*, or *The Trial of Chiang Kai-Shek*, or even *The Trial of Ramsay MacDonald.* In each case you would find the leaders of the Left contradicting themselves almost as grossly as the Tory leaders quoted by 'Cassius'. For the Left has also been willing to shut its eyes to a great deal and to accept some very doubtful allies. We laugh now to hear the Tories abusing Mussolini when they were flattering him five years ago, but who would have foretold in 1927 that the Left would one day take Chiang Kai-Shek to its bosom? Who would have foretold just after the General Strike that ten years later Winston Churchill would be the darling of the *Daily Worker*? In the years 1935–9, when almost any ally against Fascism seemed acceptable, left-wingers found themselves praising Mustapha Kemal and then developing a tenderness for Carol of Rumania.

Although it was in every way more pardonable, the attitude of the Left towards the Russian régime has been distinctly similar to the attitude of the Tories towards Fascism. There has been the same tendency to excuse almost anything 'because they're on our side'. It is all very well to talk about Lady Chamberlain photographed shaking hands with Mussolini; the photograph of Stalin shaking hands with Ribbentrop is much more recent. On the whole, the intellectuals of the Left defended the Russo-German Pact. It was 'realist', like Chamberlain's appeasement policy, and with similar consequences. If there is a way out of the moral pigsty we are living in, the first step towards it is probably to grasp that 'realism' does *not* pay, and that to sell out your friends and sit rubbing your hands while they are destroyed is not the last word in political wisdom.

This fact is demonstrable in any city between Cardiff and Stalingrad, but not many people can see it. Meanwhile it is a pamphleteer's duty to attack the Right, but not to flatter the Left. It is partly because the Left have been too easily satisfied with themselves that they are where they are now.

Mussolini, in 'Cassius's' book, after calling his witnesses, enters the box himself. He sticks to his Machiavellian creed: Might is Right, *vae victis!* He is guilty of the only crime that matters, the crime of failure, and he admits that his adversaries have a right to kill him – but not, he insists, a right to blame him. Their conduct has been similar to his own, and their moral condemnations are all hypocrisy. But thereafter come the other three witnesses, the Abyssinian, the Spaniard and the Italian, who are morally upon a different plane, since they have never temporized with Fascism nor had a chance to play at power politics; and all three of them demand the death penalty.

Would they demand it in real life? Will any such thing ever happen? It is not very likely, even if the people who have a real right to try Mussolini should somehow get him into their hands. The Tories, of course, though they would shrink from a real inquest into the origins of the war, are not sorry to have the chance of pushing the whole blame onto a few notorious individuals like Mussolini and Hitler. In this way the Darlan-Badoglio manoeuvre is made easier. Mussolini is a good scapegoat while he is at large, though he would be an awkward one in captivity. But how about the common people? Would they kill their tyrants, in cold blood and with the forms of law, if they had the chance?

It is a fact that there have been very few such executions in history. At the end of the last war an election was won partly on the slogan 'Hang the Kaiser', and yet if any such thing had been attempted the conscience of the nation would probably have revolted. When tyrants are put to death, it should be by their own subjects; those who are punished by a foreign authority, like Napoleon, are simply made into martyrs and legends.

What is important is not that these political gangsters should be made to suffer, but that they should be made to discredit themselves. Fortunately they do do so in many cases, for to a surprising extent the war-lords in shining armour, the apostles of the martial virtues, tend not to die fighting when the time comes. History is full of ignominious getaways by the great and famous.

Napoleon surrendered to the English in order to get protection from the Prussians, the Empress Eugénie fled in a hansom cab with an American dentist, Ludendorff resorted to blue spectacles, one of the more unprintable Roman emperors tried to escape assassination by locking himself in the lavatory, and during the early days of the Spanish civil war one leading Fascist made his escape from Barcelona, with exquisite fitness, through a sewer.

It is some such exit that one would wish for Mussolini, and if he is left to himself perhaps he will achieve it. Possibly Hitler also. It used to be said of Hitler that when his time came he would never fly or surrender, but would perish in some operatic manner, by suicide at the very least. But that was when Hitler was successful; during the last year, since things began to go wrong, it is difficult to feel that he has behaved with dignity or courage. 'Cassius' ends his book with the judge's summing-up, and leaves the verdict open, seeming to invite a decision from his readers. Well, if it were left to me, my verdict on both Hitler and Mussolini would be: not death, unless it is inflicted in some hurried unspectacular way. If the Germans and Italians feel like giving them a summary court-martial and then a firing-squad, let them do it. Or better still, let the pair of them escape with a suitcaseful of bearer securities and settle down as the accredited bores of some Swiss *pension*. But no martyrizing, no St Helena business. And, above all, no solemn hypocritical 'trial of war criminals', with all the slow cruel pageantry of the law, which after a lapse of time has so strange a way of focusing a romantic light on the accused and turning a scoundrel into a hero.

Tribune, 22 October 1943

ESSAYS AND JOURNALISM 1944-1945

As I Please

When Sir Walter Raleigh was imprisoned in the Tower of London, he occupied himself with writing a history of the world. He had finished the first volume and was at work on the second when there was a scuffle between some workmen beneath the window of his cell, and one of the men was killed. In spite of diligent enquiries, and in spite of the fact that he had actually seen the thing happen, Sir Walter was never able to discover what the quarrel was about: whereupon, so it is said – and if the story is not true it certainly ought to be – he burned what he had written and abandoned his project.

This story has come into my head I do not know how many times during the past ten years, but always with the reflection that Raleigh was probably wrong. Allowing for all the difficulties of research at that date, and the special difficulty of conducting research in prison, he could probably have produced a world history which had some resemblance to the real course of events. Up to a fairly recent date, the major events recorded in the history books probably happened. It is probably true that the battle of Hastings was fought in 1066, that Columbus discovered America, that Henry VIII had six wives, and so on. A certain degree of truthfulness was possible so long as it was admitted that a fact may be true even if you don't like it. Even as late as the last war it was possible for the *Encyclopaedia Britannica*, for instance, to compile its articles on the various campaigns partly from German sources. Some of the facts – the casualty figures, for instance – were regarded as neutral and in substance accepted by everybody. No such thing would be possible now. A Nazi and a non-Nazi version of the present war would have no resemblance to one another, and which of them finally gets into the history books will be decided not by evidential methods but on the battlefield.

During the Spanish civil war I found myself feeling very strongly that a true history of this war never would or could be written. Accurate figures, objective accounts of what was happening, simply did not exist. And if I felt that even in 1937, when the Spanish Government was still in being, and the lies which the various Republican factions were telling about each other and about the enemy were relatively small ones, how does the case stand now? Even if Franco is overthrown, what kind of records will the future historian have to go upon? And if Franco or anyone at all resembling him remains in power, the history of the war will consist quite largely of 'facts' which millions of people now living know to be lies. One of these 'facts', for instance, is that there was a considerable Russian army in Spain. There exists the most abundant evidence that there was no such army. Yet if Franco remains in power, and if Fascism in general survives, that Russian army will go into the history books and future schoolchildren will believe in it. So for practical purposes the lie will have become truth.

This kind of thing is happening all the time. Out of the millions of instances which must be available, I will choose one which happens to be verifiable. During part of 1941 and 1942, when the Luftwaffe was busy in Russia, the German radio regaled its home audience with stories of devastating air raids on

London. Now, we are aware that those raids did not happen. But what use would our knowledge be if the Germans conquered Britian? For the purposes of a future historian, did those raids happen, or didn't they? The answer is: If Hitler survives, they happened, and if he falls they didn't happen. So with innumerable other events of the past ten or twenty years. Is the Protocols of the Elders of Zion a genuine document? Did Trotsky plot with the Nazis? How many German aeroplanes were shot down in the Battle of Britain? Does Europe welcome the New Order? In no case do you get one answer which is universally accepted because it is true: in each case you get a number of totally incompatible answers, one of which is finally adopted as the result of a physical struggle. History is written by the winners.

In the last analysis our only claim to victory is that if we win the war we shall tell less lies about it than our adversaries. The really frightening thing about totalitarianism is not that it commits 'atrocities' but that it attacks the concept of objective truth: it claims to control the past as well as the future. In spite of all the lying and self-righteousness that war encourages, I do not honestly think it can be said that that habit of mind is growing in Britain. Taking one thing with another, I should say that the press is slightly freer than it was before the war. I know out of my own experience that you can print things now which you couldn't print ten years ago. War resisters have probably been less maltreated in this war than in the last one, and the expression of unpopular opinions in public is certainly safer. There is some hope, therefore, that the liberal habit of mind, which thinks of truth as something outside yourself, something to be discovered, and not as something you can make up as you go along, will survive. But I still don't envy the future historian's job. Is it not a strange commentary on our time that even the casualties in the present war cannot be estimated within several millions?

Tribune, 4 February 1944

A Hundred Up

It is now a hundred years since the final numbers of *Martin Chuzzlewit* were published, and though it came thus early in Dickens's career (it was his fourth novel, if one counts *Pickwick* as a novel), it has more the air of being a pot-boiler than any of his books except the *Sketches*. There cannot be many people living who could outline its plot from memory. Whereas books like *Oliver Twist*, or *Bleak House*, or *Great Expectations*, have a central theme which can in some cases be reduced to a single word, the various parts of *Martin Chuzzlewit* have not much more relationship to one another than the sounds produced by a cat walking across the piano. The best characters are 'supers'.

What do people remember when they think of *Martin Chuzzelwit*? The American interlude, Mrs Gamp, and Todgers's (especially Bailey). Martin Chuzzlewit himself is a stick, Mark Tapley a tedious paradox on two legs, Pecksniff a partial failure. It is ironical that Dickens should have tried, more or less unsuccessfully, to make Pecksniff into a monumental figure of a hypocrite, and at the same time, almost incidentally, should have painted such a devastating picture of hypocrisy in the American chapters. Dickens's comic genius is dependent on his moral sense. He is funniest when he is discovering new sins. To denounce Pecksniff did not call into play his special powers, because, after all, no one supposes that hypocrisy is desirable. But to see through the pretensions of American democracy, or even, at that date, to see that Mrs Gamp was a luxury that society might well do without, did need the eye of a Dickens. The book's lack of any real central theme can be seen in its fearful ending. It is as though Dickens were dissolving into lukewarm treacle, and – as so often when he says something that he does not really feel – whole paragraphs of the final chapter will go straight into blank verse:

Thy life is tranquil, calm, and happy, Tom.
In the soft strain which ever and again
Comes stealing back upon the ear, the memory
Of thine old love may find a voice perhaps;
But it is a pleasant, softened, whispering memory,
Like that in which we sometimes hold the dead,
And does not pain or grieve thee, God be thanked!

Yet the man who could write this stuff could also record the conversations of Bailey, and could not only create Mrs Gamp but could throw in, just for good measure, the metaphysical puzzle, Mrs Harris.

The American chapters are a good example of Dickens's habit of telling small lies in order to emphasize what he regards as a big truth. No doubt many of the things he reports actually happened (other travellers of the time confirm him on some details) but his picture of American society as a whole cannot possibly be true; not only because no community is wholly bad, but because the chaos of real life has been deliberately left out. Every incident, every character, is simply an illustration of Dickens's thesis. Moreover, the strongest charge that he makes against the Americans, that they boast of being democratic while actually living on slave labour, is obviously unfair. It implies that American opinion as a whole acquiesced in slavery, whereas a bloody civil war was to be fought mainly on this issue only twenty years later. But Dickens says these things in order to hit at what he feels to be the real fault of the Americans, their ignorant contempt for Europe and unjustified belief in their own superiority. Perhaps there *were* a few Americans who did not edit libellous newspapers or emit sentences like 'the libation of freedom must sometimes be quaffed in blood'; but to lay too much stress upon them would have been to spoil the picture. After all, the business of a caricaturist is to make his point, and these chapters have worn very much better than *American Notes*.

The mental atmosphere of the American interlude is one that has since become familiar to us in the books written by British travellers to Soviet Russia. Some of these report that everything is good, others that everything is bad, but nearly all share the same propagandist outlook. A hundred years ago America, 'the land of the free', had rather the same place in the European imagination that Soviet Russia has now, and *Martin Chuzzlewit* is the 1844 equivalent of André Gide's *Retour de l'URSS*. But it is a sign of the changing temper of the world that Dickens's attack, so much more violent and unfair than Gide's, could be so quickly forgiven.

Martin Chuzzlewit stands somewhere near the turning-point of Dickens's literary development, when he was becoming less of a picaresque writer and more of a novelist. The times were changing with the rise of the new cautious middle class, and Dickens was too much alive not to be affected by the atmosphere he lived in. *Martin Chuzzlewit* is his last completely disorderly book. In spite of its frequent flashes of genius, it is difficult to feel that by following up this vein in himself Dickens could have given us anything to compensate for the loss of *Hard Times* and *Great Expectations*.

Observer, 13 February 1944

As I Please

Some weeks ago a Catholic reader of *Tribune* wrote to protest against a review by Mr Charles Hamblett. She objected to his remarks about St Teresa and about St Joseph of Copertino, the saint who once flew round a cathedral carrying a bishop on his back. I answered, defending Mr Hamblett, and got a still more indignant letter in return. This letter raises a number of very important points, and at least one of them seems to me to deserve discussion. The relevance of flying saints to the Socialist movement may not at first sight be very clear, but I think I can show that the present nebulous state of Christian doctrine has serious implications which neither Christians nor Socialists have faced.

The substance of my correspondent's letter is that it doesn't matter whether St Teresa and the rest of them flew through the air or not: what matters is that St Teresa's 'vision of the world changed the course of history'. I would concede this. Having lived in an oriental country I have developed a certain indifference to miracles, and I well know that having delusions, or even being an outright lunatic, is quite compatible with what is loosely called genius. William Blake, for instance, was a lunatic in my opinion. Joan of Arc was probably a lunatic. Newton believed in astrology, Strindberg believed in magic. However, the miracles of the saints are a minor matter. It also appears from my correspondent's letter that even the most central doctrines of the Christian religion don't have to be accepted in a literal sense. It doesn't matter, for instance, whether Jesus Christ ever existed. 'The figure of Christ (myth, or man, or god, it does not matter) so transcends all the rest that I only wish that everyone would look, before rejecting that version of life.' Christ, therefore, may be a myth, or he may have been merely a human being, or the account given of him in the Creeds may be true. So we arrive at this position: *Tribune* must not poke fun at the Christian religion, but the existence of Christ, which innumerable people have been burnt for denying, is a matter of indifference.

Now, is this orthodox Catholic doctrine? My impression is that it is not. I can think of passages in the writing of popular Catholic apologists such as Father Woodlock and Father Ronald Knox in which it is stated in the clearest terms that Christian doctrine means what it appears to mean, and is not to be accepted in some wishy-washy metaphorical sense. Father Knox refers specifically to the idea that it doesn't matter whether Christ actually existed as a 'horrible' idea. But what my correspondent says would be echoed by many Catholic intellectuals. If you talk to a thoughtful Christian, Catholic or Anglican, you often find yourself laughed at for being so ignorant as to suppose that anyone ever took the doctrines of the Church literally. These doctrines have, you are told, a quite other meaning which you are too crude to understand. Immortality of the soul doesn't 'mean' that you, John Smith, will remain conscious after you are dead. Resurrection of the body doesn't mean that John Smith's body will actually be resurrected – and so on and so on. Thus the Catholic intellectual is able, for controversial purposes, to play a sort of handy-pandy game, repeating the articles of the Creed in exactly the same terms as his forefathers, while defending himself from the charge of superstition by explaining that he is speaking in parables. Substantially his claim is that though he himself doesn't believe in any very definite way of life after death, there has been no change in Christian belief, since our ancestors didn't really believe in it either. Meanwhile a vitally important fact – that one of the props of western civilization has been knocked away – is obscured.

I do not know whether, officially, there has been any alteration in Christian doctrine. Father Knox and my correspondent would seem to be in disagreement about this. But what I do know is that belief in survival after death – the individual survival of John Smith, still conscious of himself as John Smith – is enormously less widespread than it was. Even among professing Christians it is probably decaying: other people, as a rule, don't even entertain the possibility that it might be true. But our forefathers, so far as we know, did believe in it. Unless all that they wrote about it was intended to mislead us, they believed it in an exceedingly literal, concrete way. Life on earth, as they saw it, was simply a short period of preparation for an infinitely more important life beyond the grave. But that notion has disappeared, or is disappearing, and the consequences have not really been faced.

Western civilization, unlike some oriental civilizations, was founded partly on the belief in individual immortality. If one looks at the Christian religion from the outside, this belief appears far more important than the belief in God. The western conception of good and evil is very difficult to separate from it. There is little doubt that the modern cult of power worship is bound up with the modern man's feeling that life here and now is the only life there is. If death ends everything, it becomes much harder to believe that you can be in the right even if you are defeated. Statesmen, nations, theories, causes are judged almost inevitably by the test of material success. Supposing that one can separate the two phenomena, I would say that the decay of the belief in personal immortality has been as important as the rise of machine civilization. Machine civilization has terrible possibilities, as you probably reflected the other night when the ack-ack guns started up: but the other thing has terrible possibilities too, and it cannot be said that the Socialist movement has given much thought to them.

I do not want the belief in life after death to return, and in any case it is not likely to return. What I do point out is that its disappearance has left a big hole, and that we ought to take notice of that fact. Reared for thousands of years on the notion that the individual survives, man has got to make a considerable psychological effort to get used to the notion that the individual perishes. He is not likely to salvage civilization unless he can evolve a system of good and evil which is independent of heaven and hell. Marxism, indeed, does supply this, but it has never really been popularized. Most Socialists are content to point out that once Socialism has been established we shall be happier in a material sense, and to assume that all problems lapse when one's belly is full. But the truth is the opposite: when one's belly is empty, one's only problem is an empty belly. It is when we have got away from drudgery and exploitation that we shall really start wondering about man's destiny and the reason for his existence. One cannot have any worth-while picture of the future unless one realizes how much we have lost by the decay of Christianity. Few Socialists seem to be aware of this. And the Catholic intellectuals who cling to the letter of the Creeds while reading into them meanings they were never meant to have, and who snigger at anyone simple enough to suppose that the Fathers of the Church meant what they said, are simply raising smoke-screens to conceal their own disbelief from themselves.

Tribune, 3 March 1944

Propaganda and Demotic Speech

... When you examine Government leaflets and White Papers, or leading articles in the newspapers, or the speeches and broadcasts of politicians, or the pamphlets and manifestos of any political party whatever, the thing that nearly always strikes you is their remoteness from the average man. It is not merely that they assume non-existent knowledge: often it is right and necessary to do that. It is also that clear, popular, everyday language seems to be instinctively avoided. The bloodless dialect of government spokesmen (characteristic phrases are: in due course, no stone unturned, take the earliest opportunity, the answer is in the affirmative) is too well known to be worth dwelling on. Newspaper leaders are written either in this same dialect or in an inflated bombastic style with a tendency to fall back on archaic words (peril, valour, might, foe, succour, vengeance, dastardly, rampart, bulwark, bastion) which no normal person would ever think of using. Left-wing political parties specialize in a bastard vocabulary made up of Russian and German phrases translated with the maximum of clumsiness. And even posters, leaflets and broadcasts which are intended to give instructions, to tell people what to do in certain circumstances, often fail in their effect. For example, during the first air raids on London, it was found that innumerable people did not know which siren meant the Alert and which the All Clear. This was after months or years of gazing at ARP posters. These posters had described the Alert as a 'warbling note': a phrase which made no impression, since air-raid sirens don't warble, and few people attach any definite meaning to the word.

When Sir Richard Acland, in the early months of the war, was drawing up a manifesto to be presented to the Government, he engaged a squad of Mass Observers to find out what meaning, if any, the ordinary man attaches to the high-sounding abstract words which are flung to and fro in politics. The most fantastic misunderstandings came to light. It was found, for instance, that most people don't know that 'immorality' means anything besides sexual immorality.[1] One man thought that 'movement' had something to do with constipation. And it is a nightly experience in any pub to see broadcast speeches and news bulletins make no impression on the average listener, because they are uttered in stilted bookish language and, incidentally, in an upper-class accent. At the time of Dunkirk I watched a gang of navvies eating their bread and cheese in a pub while the one o'clock news came over. Nothing registered: they just went on stolidly eating. Then, just for an instant, reporting the words of some soldier who had been hauled aboard a boat, the announcer dropped into spoken English, with the phrase, 'Well, I've learned to swim this trip, anyway!' Promptly you could see ears being pricked up: it was ordinary language, and so it got across. A few weeks later, the day after Italy entered the war, Duff Cooper announced that Mussolini's rash act would 'add to the ruins for which Italy has been famous'. It was neat enough, and a true prophecy, but how much impression does that kind of language make on nine people out of ten? The colloquial version of it would have been: 'Italy has always been famous for ruins. Well, there are going to be a damn' sight more of them now.' But that is not how Cabinet Ministers speak, at any rate in public.

Examples of futile slogans, obviously incapable of stirring strong feelings or being circulated by word of mouth, are: 'Deserve Victory', 'Freedom is in Peril. Defend it with all your Might', 'Socialism the only Solution', 'Expropriate the Expropriators', 'Austerity', 'Evolution not Revolution', 'Peace is Indivisible'. Examples of slogans phrased in spoken English are: 'Hands off Russia', 'Make Germany Pay', 'Stop Hitler', 'No Stomach Taxes', 'Buy a Spitfire', 'Votes for Women'. Examples about mid-way between these two classes are: 'Go to it', 'Dig for Victory', 'It all depends on ME', and some of Churchill's phrases, such as 'the end of the beginning', 'soft underbelly', 'blood, toil, tears and sweat' and 'never was so much owed by so many to so few'. (Significantly, in so far as this last saying has been repeated by word of mouth, the bookish phrase *in the field of human conflict* has dropped out of it.) One has to take into account the fact that nearly all English people dislike anything that sounds high-flown and boastful. Slogans like 'They shall not pass', or 'Better to die on your feet than live on your knees', which have thrilled continental nations, seem slightly embarrassing to an Englishman, especially a workingman. But the main weakness of propagandists and popularizers is their failure to notice that spoken and written English are two different things.

When recently I protested in print against the Marxist dialect which makes use of phrases like 'objectively counter-revolutionary left-deviationism' or 'drastic liquidation of petty-bourgeois elements', I received indignant letters from lifelong Socialists who told me that I was 'insulting the language of the proletariat'. In rather the same spirit, Professor Harold Laski devotes a long passage in his last book, *Faith, Reason and Civilisation*, to an attack on Mr T. S. Eliot, whom he accuses of 'writing only for the few'. Now Eliot, as it happens, is one of the few writers of our time who have tried seriously to write English as it is spoken. Lines like:

And nobody came, and nobody went,
But he took in the milk and he paid the rent

[1] In spite of this, Common Wealth has adopted the astonishingly feeble slogan: 'What is morally wrong cannot be politically right'. [Author's footnote.]

are about as near to spoken English as print can come. On the other hand, here is an entirely typical sentence from Laski's own writing:

> As a whole, our system was a compromise between democracy in the political realm – itself a very recent development in our history – and an economic power oligarchically organized which was in its turn related to a certain aristocratic vestigia still able to influence profoundly the habits of our society.

This sentence, incidentally, comes from a reprinted lecture; so one must assume that Professor Laski actually stood up on a platform and spouted it forth, parenthesis and all. It is clear that people capable of speaking or writing in such a way have simply forgotten what everyday language is like. But this is nothing to some of the other passages I could dig out of Professor Laski's writings, or better still, from Communist literature, or best of all, from Trotskyist pamphlets. Indeed, from reading the left-wing press you get the impression that the louder people yap about the proletariat, the more they despise its language.

I have said already that spoken English and written English are two different things. This variation exists in all languages, but is probably greater in English than in most. Spoken English is full of slang, it is abbreviated wherever possible, and people of all social classes treat its grammar and syntax in a slovenly way. Extremely few English people ever button up a sentence if they are speaking extempore. Above all, the vast English vocabulary contains thousands of words which everyone uses when writing, but which have no real currency in speech: and it also contains thousands more which are really obsolete but which are dragged forth by anyone who wants to sound clever or uplifting. If one keeps this in mind, one can think of ways of ensuring that propaganda, spoken or written, shall reach the audience it is aimed at.

So far as writing goes, all one can attempt is a process of simplification. The first step – and any social survey organization could do this for a few hundreds or thousands of pounds – is to find out which of the abstract words habitually used by politicians are really understood by large numbers of people. If phrases like 'unprincipled violation of declared pledges' or 'insidious threat to the basic principles of democracy' don't mean anything to the average man, then it is stupid to use them. Secondly, in writing one can keep the spoken word constantly in mind. To get genuine spoken English on to paper is a complicated matter, as I shall show in a moment. But if you habitually say to yourself, 'Could I simplify this? Could I make it more like speech?' you are not likely to produce sentences like the one quoted from Professor Laski above: nor are you likely to say 'eliminate' when you mean kill, or 'static water' when you mean fire tank.

Spoken propaganda, however, offers greater possibilities of improvement. It is here that the problem of writing in spoken English really arises.

Speeches, broadcasts, lectures and even sermons are normally written down beforehand. The most effective orators, like Hitler or Lloyd George, usually speak extempore, but they are very great rarities. As a rule – you can test this by listening at Hyde Park Corner – the so-called extempore speaker only keeps going by endlessly tacking one cliché on to another. In any case, he is probably delivering a speech which he has delivered dozens of times before. Only a few exceptionally gifted speakers can achieve the simplicity and intelligibility which even the most tongue-tied person achieves in ordinary conversation. On the air extempore speaking is seldom even attempted. Except for a few programmes, like the Brains Trust, which in any case are carefully rehearsed beforehand, every word that comes from the BBC has been written down, and is delivered exactly as written. This is not only for censorship reasons: it is also because many speakers are liable to dry up at the microphone if they have no script to follow. The result is the heavy, dull, bookish lingo which causes most radio users to switch off as soon as a talk is announced. It might be thought that one could get nearer to colloquial speech by dictating than by writing; but actually, it is the other way about. Dictating, at any rate to a human being, is always slightly embarrassing. One's impulse is to avoid long pauses, and one necessarily does so by clutching at the ready-made phrases and the dead and stinking metaphors (ring the changes on, ride rough-shod over, cross swords with, take up the cudgels for) with which the English language is littered. A dictated script is usually less life-like than a written one. What is wanted, evidently, is some way of getting ordinary, slipshod, colloquial English on to paper.

But is this possible? I think it is, and by a quite simple method which so far as I know has never been tried. It is this: Set a fairly ready speaker down at the microphone and let him just talk, either continuously or intermittently, on any subject he chooses. Do this with a dozen different speakers, recording it every time. Vary it with a few dialogues or conversations between three or four people. Then play your recordings back and let a stenographer reduce them to writing: not in the shortened, rationalized version that stenographers usually produce, but word for word, with such punctuation as seems appropriate. You would then – for the first time, I believe – have on paper some authentic specimens of spoken English. Probably they would not be readable as a book or a newspaper article is readable, but then spoken English is not meant to be read, it is meant to be listened to. From these specimens you could, I believe, formulate the rules of spoken English and find out how it differs from the written language. And when writing in spoken English had become practicable, the average speaker or lecturer who has to write his material down beforehand could bring it far closer to his natural diction, make it more essentially speakable, than he can at present.

Of course, demotic speech is not solely a matter of being colloquial and avoiding ill-understood words. There is also the question of accent. It seems certain that in modern England the 'educated', upper-class accent is deadly to any speaker who is aiming at a large audience. All effective speakers in recent times have had either cockney or provincial accents. The success of Priestley's broadcasts in 1940 was largely due to his Yorkshire accent, which he probably broadened a little for the occasion. Churchill is only a seeming exception to this rule. Too old to have acquired the modern 'educated' accent he speaks with the Edwardian upper-class twang which to the average man's ear sounds like cockney. The 'educated' accent, of which the accent of the BBC announcers is a sort of parody, has no asset except its intelligibility to English-speaking foreigners. In England the minority to whom it is natural don't particularly like it, while in the other three-quarters of the population it arouses an immediate class antagonism. It is also noticeable that where there is doubt about the pronunciation of a name, successful speakers will stick to the working-class pronunciation even if they know it to be wrong. Churchill, for instance, mispronounced 'Nazi' and 'Gestapo' as long as the common people continued to do so. Lloyd George during the last war rendered 'Kaiser' as 'Kayser', which was the popular version of the word.

In the early days of the war the Government had the greatest difficulty in inducing people to bother to collect their ration books. At parliamentary elections, even when there is an up-to-date register, it often happens that less than half of the electorate use their votes. Things like these are symptoms of the intellectual gulf between the rulers and the ruled. But the same gulf lies always between the intelligentsia and the common man. Journalists, as we can see by their election forecasts, never know what the public is thinking. Revolutionary propaganda is incredibly ineffective. Churches are empty all over the country. The whole idea of trying to find out what the average man thinks, instead of assuming that he thinks what he ought to think, is novel and unwelcome. Social surveys are viciously attacked from Left and Right alike. Yet some mechanism for testing public opinion is an obvious necessity of modern government, and more so in a democratic country than in a totalitarian one. Its complement is the ability to speak to the ordinary man in words that he will understand and respond to.

At present propaganda only seems to succeed when it coincides with what people are inclined to do in any case. During the present war, for instance, the Government has done extraordinarily little to preserve morale: it has merely drawn on the existing reserves of goodwill. And all political parties alike have failed to interest the public in vitally important questions – in the problem of India, to name only one. But some day we may have a genuinely democratic government, a government which will want to tell people what is happening, and what must be done next, and what sacrifices are necessary, and why. It will need the mechanisms for doing so, of which the first are the right words, the right tone of voice. The fact that when you suggest finding out what the common man is like, and approaching him accordingly, you are either accused of being an intellectual snob who wants to 'talk down to' the masses, or else suspected of plotting to establish an English Gestapo, shows how sluggishly nineteenth-century our notion of democracy has remained.

Written [late April 1944]

Benefit of Clergy: Some Notes on Salvador Dali

Autobiography is only to be trusted when it reveals something disgraceful. A man who gives a good account of himself is probably lying, since any life when viewed from the inside is simply a series of defeats. However, even the most flagrantly dishonest book (Frank Harris's autobiographical writings are an example) can without intending it give a true picture of its author. Dali's recently published *Life*[1] comes under this heading. Some of the incidents in it are flatly incredible, others have been rearranged and romanticized, and not

[1] *The Secret Life of Salvador Dali*, Dial Press, New York.

merely the humiliation but the persistent *ordinariness* of everyday life has been cut out. Dali is even by his own diagnosis narcissistic, and his autobiography is simply a strip-tease act conducted in pink limelight. But as a record of fantasy, of the perversion of instinct that has been made possible by the machine age, it has great value.

Here, then, are some of the episodes in Dali's life, from his earliest years onward. Which of them are true and which are imaginary hardly matters: the point is that this is the kind of thing that Dali would have *liked* to do.

When he is six years old there is some excitement over the appearance of Halley's comet:

> Suddenly one of my father's office clerks appeared in the drawing-room doorway and announced that the comet could be seen from the terrace ... While crossing the hall I caught sight of my little three-year-old sister crawling unobtrusively through a doorway. I stopped, hesitated a second, then gave her a terrible kick in the head as though it had been a ball, and continued running, carried away with a 'delirious joy' induced by this savage act. But my father, who was behind me, caught me and led me down into his office, where I remained as a punishment till dinner-time.

A year earlier than this Dali had 'suddenly, as most of my ideas occur' flung another little boy off a suspension bridge. Several other incidents of the same kind are recorded, including (*this was when he was twenty-nine years old*) knocking down and trampling on a girl 'until they had to tear her, bleeding, out of my reach'.

When he is about five he gets hold of a wounded bat which he puts into a tin pail. Next morning he finds that the bat is almost dead and is covered with ants which are devouring it. He puts it in his mouth, ants and all, and bites it almost in half.

When he is adolescent a girl falls desperately in love with him. He kisses and caresses her so as to excite her as much as possible, but refuses to go further. He resolves to keep this up for five years (he calls it his 'five-year plan'), enjoying her humiliation and the sense of power it gives him. He frequently tells her that at the end of five years he will desert her, and when time comes he does so.

Till well into adult life he keeps up the practice of masturbation, and likes to do this, apparently, in front of a looking-glass. For ordinary purposes he is impotent, it appears, till the age of thirty or so. When he first meets his future wife, Gala, he is greatly tempted to push her off a precipice. He is aware that there is something that she wants him to do to her, and after their first kiss the confession is made:

> I threw back Gala's head, pulling it by the hair, and trembling with complete hysteria, I commanded:
>
> 'Now tell me what you want me to do with you! But tell me slowly, looking me in the eye, with the crudest, the most ferociously erotic words that can make both of us feel the greatest shame!'
>
> ... Then Gala, transforming the last glimmer of her expression of pleasure into the hard light of her own tyranny, answered:
>
> 'I want you to kill me!'

He is somewhat disappointed by this demand, since it is merely what he wanted to do already. He contemplates throwing her off the bell-tower of the cathedral of Toledo, but refrains from doing so.

During the Spanish civil war he astutely avoids taking sides, and makes a trip to Italy. He feels himself more and more drawn towards the aristocracy, frequents smart *salons*, finds himself wealthy patrons, and is photographed with the plump Vicomte de Noailles, whom he describes as his 'Maecenas'. When the European war approaches he has one preoccupation only: how to find a place which has good cookery and from which he can make a quick bolt if danger comes too near. He fixes on Bordeaux, and duly flees to Spain during the Battle of France. He stays in Spain long enough to pick up a few anti-red atrocity stories, then makes for America. The story ends in a blaze of respectability. Dali, at thirty-seven, has become a devoted husband, is cured of his aberrations, or some of them, and is completely reconciled to the Catholic Church. He is also, one gathers, making a good deal of money.

However, he has by no means ceased to take pride in the pictures of his Surrealist period, with titles like 'The Great Masturbator', 'Sodomy of a Skull with a Grand Piano', etc. There are reproductions of these all the way through the book. Many of Dali's drawings are simply representational and have a characteristic to be noted later. But from his Surrealist paintings and photographs the two things that stand out are sexual perversity and necrophilia. Sexual objects and symbols – some of them well known, like our old friend the high-heeled slipper, others, like the crutch and the cup of warm milk, patented by Dali himself – recur over and over again, and there is a fairly well-marked excretory motif as well. Of his painting, 'Le Jeu Lugubre', he says, 'the drawers bespattered with excrement were painted with such minute and realistic complacency that the whole little Surrealist group was anguished by the question: Is he coprophagic or not?' Dali adds firmly that he is *not*, and that he regards this aberration as 'repulsive', but it seems to be only at that point that his interest in excrement stops. Even when he recounts the experience of watching a woman urinate standing up, he has to add the detail that she misses her aim and dirties her shoes. It is not given to any one person to have all the vices, and Dali also boasts that he is not homosexual, but otherwise he seems to have as good an outfit of perversions as anyone could wish for.

However, his most notable characteristic is his necrophilia. He himself freely admits to this, and claims to have been cured of it. Dead faces, skulls, corpses of animals occur fairly frequently in his pictures, and the ants which devoured the dying bat make countless reappearances. One photograph shows an exhumed corpse, far gone in decomposition. Another shows the dead donkeys putrefying on top of grand pianos which formed part of the Surrealist film, 'Le Chien Andalou'. Dali still looks back on these donkeys with great enthusiasm.

> I 'made up' the putrefaction of the donkeys with great pots of sticky glue which I poured over them. Also I emptied their eye-sockets and made them larger by hacking them out with scissors. In the same way I furiously cut their mouths open to make the rows of their teeth show to better advantage, and I added several jaws to each mouth, so that it would appear that although the donkeys were already rotting they were vomiting up a little more of their own death, above those other rows of teeth formed by the keys of the black pianos.

And finally there is the picture – apparently some kind of faked photograph – of 'Mannequin rotting in a taxi-cab'. Over the already somewhat bloated face and breast of an apparently dead girl, huge snails are crawling. In the caption below the picture Dali notes that these are Burgundy snails – that is, the edible kind.

Of course, in this long book of 400 quarto pages there is more than I have indicated, but I do not think that I have given an unfair account of its moral atmosphere and mental scenery. It is a book that stinks. If it were possible for a book to a give a physical stink off its pages, this one would – a thought that might please Dali, who before wooing his future wife for the first time rubbed himself all over with an ointment made of goat's dung boiled up in fish glue. But against this has to be set the fact that Dali is a draughtsman of very exceptional gifts. He is also, to judge by the minuteness and the sureness of his drawings, a very hard worker. He is an exhibitionist and a careerist, but he is not a fraud. He has fifty times more talent than most of the people who would denounce his morals and jeer at his painting. And these two sets of facts, taken together, raise a question which for lack of any basis of agreement seldom gets a real discussion.

The point is that you have here a direct, unmistakable assault on sanity and decency; and even – since some of Dali's pictures would tend to poison the imagination like a pornographic postcard – on life itself. What Dali has done and what he has imagined is debatable, but in his outlook, his character, the bedrock decency of a human being does not exist. He is as antisocial as a flea. Clearly, such people are undesirable, and a society in which they can flourish has something wrong with it.

Now, if you showed this book, with its illustrations, to Lord Elton, to Mr Alfred Noyes, to *The Times* leader-writers who exult over the 'eclipse of the highbrow' – in fact, to any 'sensible' art-hating English person – it is easy to imagine what kind of response you would get. They would flatly refuse to see any merit in Dali whatever. Such people are not only unable to admit that what is morally degraded can be aesthetically right, but their real demand of every artist is that he shall pat them on the back and tell them that thought is unnecessary. And they can be especially dangerous at a time like the present, when the Ministry of Information and the British Council put power into their hands. For their impulse is not not only to crush every new talent as it appears, but to castrate the past as well. Witness the renewed highbrow-baiting that is now going on in this country and America, with its outcry not only against Joyce, Proust and Lawrence, but even against T. S. Eliot.

But if you talk to the kind of person who *can* see Dali's merits, the response that you get is not as a rule very much better. If you say that Dali, though a brilliant draughtsman, is a dirty little scoundrel, you are looked upon as a savage. If you say that you don't like rotting corpses, and that people who do like rotting corpses are mentally diseased, it is assumed that you lack the aesthetic sense. Since 'Mannequin rotting in a taxi-cab' is a good composition (as it undoubtedly is), it cannot be a disgusting, degrading picture; whereas Noyes, Elton, etc would tell you that because it is disgusting it cannot be a good composition. And between these two fallacies there is no middle position; or, rather, there is a middle position, but we seldom hear much about it. On the one side *Kulturbolschewismus*: on the other (though the phrase itself is out of fashion) 'Art for Art's sake'. Obscenity is a very difficult question to discuss honestly. People are too frightened either of seeming to be shocked or of seeming not to be shocked, to be able to define the relationship between art and morals.

It will be seen that what the defenders of Dali are claiming is a kind of *benefit of clergy*. The artist is to be exempt from the moral laws that are binding on ordinary people. Just pronounce the magic word 'art', and everything is OK. Rotting corpses with snails crawling over them are OK; kicking little girls on the head is OK; even a film like 'L'Age d'Or' is OK.[1] It is also OK that Dali should batten on France for years and then scuttle off like a rat as soon as France is in danger. So long as you can paint well enough to pass the test, all shall be forgiven you.

One can see how false this is if one extends it to cover ordinary crime. In an age like our own, when the artist is an altogether exceptional person, he must be allowed a certain amount of irresponsibility, just as a pregnant woman is. Still, no one would say that a pregnant woman should be allowed to commit murder, nor would anyone make such a claim for the artist, however gifted. If Shakespeare returned to the earth tomorrow, and if it were found that his favourite recreation was raping little girls in railway carriages, we should not tell him to go ahead with it on the ground that he might write another *King Lear*. And, after all, the worst crimes are not always the punishable ones. By encouraging necrophilic reveries one probably does quite as much harm as by, say, picking pockets at the races. One ought to be able to hold in one's head simultaneously the two facts the Dali is a good draughtsman and a disgusting human being. The one does not invalidate or, in a sense, affect the other. The first thing that we demand of a wall is that it shall stand up. If it stands up, it is a good wall, and the question of what purpose it serves is separable from that. And yet even the best wall in the world deserves to be pulled down if it surrounds a concentration camp. In the same way it should be possible to say, 'This is a good book or a good picture, and it ought to be burned by the public hangman.' Unless one can say that, at least in imagination, one is shirking the implications of the fact that an artist is also a citizen and a human being.

Not, of course, that Dali's autobiography, or his pictures, ought to be suppressed. Short of the dirty postcards that used to be sold in Mediterranean seaport towns, it is doubtful policy to suppress anything, and Dali's fantasies probably cast useful light on the decay of capitalist civilization. But what he clearly needs is diagnosis. The question is not so much *what* he is, as *why* he is like that. It ought not to be in doubt that he is a diseased intelligence, probably not much altered by his alleged conversion, since genuine penitents, or people who have returned to sanity, do not flaunt their past vices in that complacent way. He is a symptom of the world's illness. The important thing is not to denounce him as a cad who ought to be horse-whipped or to defend him as a genius who ought not to be questioned, but to find out *why* he exhibits that particular set of aberrations.

The answer is probably discoverable in his pictures, and those I myself am not competent to examine. But I can point to one clue which perhaps takes one part of the distance. This is the old-fashioned, over-ornate, Edwardian style of drawing to which Dali tends to revert when he is not being Surrealist. Some of Dali's drawings are reminiscent of Dürer, one (p. 113) seems to show the influence of Beardsley, another (p. 269) seems to borrow something from Blake. But the most persistent strain is the Edwardian one. When I opened the book for the first time and looked at its innumerable marginal illustrations, I was

[1] Dali mentions 'L'Age d'Or' and adds that its first public showing was broken up by hooligans, but he does not say in detail what it was about. According to Henry Miller's account of it, it showed among other things some fairly detailed shots of a woman defecating. [Author's footnote.]

haunted by a resemblance which I could not immediately pin down. I fetched up at the ornamental candlestick at the beginning of Part I (p. 7). What did this remind me of? Finally I tracked it down. It reminded me of a large, vulgar, expensively got-up edition of Anatole France (in translation) which must have been published about 1914. That had ornamental chapter headings and tailpieces after this style. Dali's candlestick displays at one end a curly fish-like creature that looks curiously familiar (it seems to be based on the conventional dolphin), and at the other is the burning candle. This candle, which recurs in one picture after another, is a very old friend. You will find it, with the same picturesque gouts of wax arranged on its sides, in those phony electric lights done up as candlesticks which are popular in sham-Tudor country hotels. This candle, and the design beneath it, convey at once an intense feeling of sentimentality. As though to counteract this, Dali has spattered a quill-full of ink all over the page, but without avail. The same impression keeps popping up on page after page. The design at the bottom of page 62, for instance, would nearly go into *Peter Pan*. The figure on page 224, in spite of having her cranium elongated into an immense sausage-like shape, is the witch of the fairy-tale books. The horse on page 234 and the unicorn on page 218 might be illustrations to James Branch Cabell. The rather pansified drawings of youths on page 97, 100 and elsewhere convey the same impression. Picturesqueness keeps breaking in. Take away the skulls, ants, lobsters, telephones and other paraphernalia, and every now and again you are back in the world of Barrie, Rackham, Dunsany and *Where the Rainbow Ends*.

Curiously enough, some of the naughty-naughty touches in Dali's autobiography tie up with the same period. When I read the passage I quoted at the beginning, about the kicking of the little sister's head, I was aware of another phantom resemblance. What was it? Of course! *Ruthless Rhymes for Heartless Homes* by Harry Graham. Such rhymes were very popular round about 1912, and one that ran:

Poor little Willy is crying so sore,
A sad little boy is he,
For he's broken his little sister's neck
And he'll have no jam for tea.

might almost have been founded on Dali's anecdote. Dali, of course, is aware of his Edwardian leanings, and makes capital out of them, more or less in a spirit of pastiche. He professes an especial affection for the year 1900, and claims that every ornamental object of 1900 is full of mystery, poetry, eroticism, madness, perversity, etc. Pastiche, however, usually implies a real affection for the thing parodied. It seems to be, if not the rule, at any rate distinctly common for an intellectual bent to be accompanied by a non-rational, even childish urge in the same direction. A sculptor, for instance, is interested in planes and curves, but he is also a person who enjoys the physical act of mucking about with clay or stone. An engineer is a person who enjoys the feel of tools, the noise of dynamos and the smell of oil. A psychiatrist usually has a leaning towards some sexual aberration himself. Darwin became a biologist partly because he was a country gentleman and fond of animals. It may be, therefore, that Dali's seemingly perverse cult of Edwardian things (for example, his 'discovery' of the 1900 subway-entrances) is merely the symptom of a much deeper, less conscious affection. The innumerable, beautifully executed copies of text-book illustrations, solemnly labelled *le rossignol, une montre* and so on, which he scatters all over his margins, may be meant partly as a joke. The little boy in knickerbockers playing with a diabolo on page 103 is a perfect period piece. But perhaps these things are also there because Dali can't help drawing that kind of thing, because it is to that period and that style of drawing that he really belongs.

If so, his aberrations are partly explicable. Perhaps they are a way of assuring himself that he is not commonplace. The two qualities that Dali unquestionably possesses are a gift for drawing and an atrocious egoism. 'At seven,' he says in the first paragraph of his book, 'I wanted to be Napoleon. And my ambition has been growing steadily ever since.' This is worded in a deliberately startling way, but no doubt it is substantially true. Such feelings are common enough. 'I knew I was a genius,' somebody once said to me, 'long before I knew what I was going to be a genius *about*.' And suppose that you have nothing in you except your egoism and a dexterity that goes no higher than the elbow; suppose that your real gift is for a detailed, academic, representational style of drawing, your real *métier* to be an illustrator of scientific textbooks. How then do you become Napoleon?

There is always one escape: *into wickedness*. Always do the thing that will shock and wound people. At five, throw a little boy off a bridge, strike an old doctor across the face with a whip and break his spectacles – or, at any rate, dream about doing such things. Twenty years later, gouge the eyes out of dead donkeys with a pair of scissors. Along those lines you can always feel yourself original. And after all, it pays! It is much less dangerous than crime. Making all allowance for the probable suppressions in Dali's autobiography, it is clear that he has not had to suffer for his eccentricities as he would have done in an earlier age. He grew up in the corrupt world of the nineteen-twenties, when sophistication was immensely widespread and every European capital swarmed with aristocrats and *rentiers* who had given up sport and politics and taken to patronizing the arts. If you threw dead donkeys at people, they threw money back. A phobia for grasshoppers – which a few decades back would merely have provoked a snigger – was now an interesting 'complex' which could be profitably exploited. And when that particular world collapsed before the German army, America was waiting. You could even top it all up with religious conversion, moving at one hop and without a shadow of repentance from the fashionable *salons* of Paris to Abraham's bosom.

That, perhaps, is the essential outline of Dali's history. But why his aberrations should be the particular ones they were, and why it should be so easy to 'sell' such horrors as rotting corpses to a sophisticated public – those are questions for the psychologist and the sociological critic. Marxist criticism has a short way with such phenomena as Surrealism. They are 'bourgeois decadence' (much play is made with the phrases 'corpse poisons' and 'decaying *rentier* class'), and that is that. But though this probably states a fact, it does not establish a connection. One would still like to know *why* Dali's leaning was towards necrophilia (and not, say, homosexuality), and *why* the *rentiers* and the aristocrats should buy his pictures instead of hunting and making love like their grandfathers. Mere moral disapproval does not get one any further. But neither ought one to pretend, in the name of 'detachment', that such pictures as 'Mannequin rotting in a taxi-cab' are morally neutral. They are diseased and disgusting, and any investigation ought to start out from that fact.

Written [June] 1944

Raffles and Miss Blandish

Nearly half a century after his first appearance, Raffles, 'the amateur cracksman', is still one of the best-known characters in English fiction. Very few people would need telling that he played cricket for England, had bachelor chambers in Albany and burgled the Mayfair houses which he also entered as a guest. Just for that reason he and his exploits make a suitable background against which to examine a more modern crime story such as *No Orchids for Miss Blandish.* Any such choice is necessarily arbitrary – I might equally well have chosen *Arsène Lupin*, for instance – but at any rate *No Orchids* and the Raffles books[1] have the common quality of being crime stories which play the limelight on the criminal rather than the policeman. For sociological purposes they can be compared. *No Orchids* is the 1939 version of glamorized crime, *Raffles* the 1900 version. What I am concerned with here is the immense difference in moral atmosphere between the two books, and the change in popular attitude that this probably implies.

At this date, the charm of *Raffles* is partly in the period atmosphere and partly in the technical excellence of the stories. Hornung was a very conscientious and on his level a very able writer. Anyone who cares for sheer efficiency must admire his work. However, the truly dramatic thing about Raffles, the thing that makes him a sort of by-word even to this day (only a few weeks ago, in a burglary case, a magistrate referred to the prisoner as 'a Raffles in real life'), is the fact that he is a *gentleman.* Raffles is presented to us – and this is rubbed home in countless scraps of dialogue and casual remarks – not as an honest man who has gone astray, but as a public-school man who has gone astray. His remorse, when he feels any, is almost purely social; he has disgraced 'the old school', he has lost his right to enter 'decent society', he has forfeited his amateur status and become a cad. Neither Raffles nor Bunny appears to feel at all strongly that stealing is wrong in itself, though Raffles does once justify himself by the casual remark that 'the distribution of property is all wrong anyway'. They think of themselves not as sinners but as renegades, or simply as outcasts. And the moral code of most of us is still so close to Raffles's own that we do feel his situation to be an especially ironical one. A West End club man who is really a burglar! That is almost a story in itself, is it not? But how if it were a plumber or a greengrocer who was really a burglar? Would there be anything inherently dramatic in that? No – although the theme of the 'double life', of respectability covering crime, is still there. Even Charles Peace in his clergyman's dog-collar seems somewhat less of a hypocrite than Raffles in his I Zingari blazer.

Raffles, of course, is good at all games, but it is peculiarly fitting that his chosen game should be cricket. This allows not only of endless analogies between his cunning as a slow bowler and his cunning as a burglar, but also

[1] *Raffles*, *A Thief in the Night* and *Mr Justice Raffles* by E. W. Hornung. The third of these is definitely a failure, and only the first has the true Raffles atmosphere. Hornung wrote a number of crime stories, usually with a tendency to take the side of the criminal. A successful book in rather the same vein as *Raffles* is *Stingaree*. [Author's footnote.]

helps to define the exact nature of his crime. Cricket is not in reality a very popular game in England – it is nowhere near so popular as football, for instance – but it gives expression to a well-marked trait in the English character, the tendency to value 'form' or 'style' more highly than success. In the eyes of any true cricket-lover it is possible for an innings of ten runs to be 'better' (i.e. more elegant) than an innings of a hundred runs: cricket is also one of the very few games in which the amateur can excel the professional. It is a game full of forlorn hopes and sudden dramatic changes of fortune, and its rules are so ill-defined that their interpretation is partly an ethical business. When Larwood, for instance, practised body-line bowling in Australia he was not actually breaking any rule: he was merely doing something that was 'not cricket'. Since cricket takes up a lot of time and is rather an expensive game to play, it is predominantly an upper-class game, but for the whole nation it is bound up with such concepts as 'good form', 'playing the game', etc, and it has declined in popularity just as the tradition of 'don't hit a man when he's down' has declined. It is not a twentieth-century game, and nearly all modern-minded people dislike it. The Nazis, for instance, were at pains to discourage cricket, which had gained a certain footing in Germany before and after the last war. In making Raffles a cricketer as well as a burglar, Hornung was not merely providing him with a plausible disguise; he was also drawing the sharpest moral contrast that he was able to imagine.

Raffles, no less than *Great Expectations* or *Le Rouge et le Noir,* is a story of snobbery, and it gains a great deal from the precariousness of Raffles's social position. A cruder writer would have made the 'gentleman burglar' a member of the peerage, or at least a baronet. Raffles, however, is of upper-middle-class origin and is only accepted by the aristocracy because of his personal charm. 'We were in Society but not of it,' he says to Bunny towards the end of the book; and 'I was asked about for my cricket.' Both he and Bunny accept the values of 'society' unquestioningly, and would settle down in it for good if only they could get away with a big enough haul. The ruin that constantly threatens them is all the blacker because they only doubtfully 'belong'. A duke who has served a prison sentence is still a duke, whereas a mere man about town, if once disgraced, ceases to be 'about town' for evermore. The closing chapters of the book, when Raffles has been exposed and is living under an assumed name, have a 'twilight of the gods' feeling, a mental atmosphere rather similar to that of Kipling's poem, 'Gentleman Rankers':

Yes, a trooper of the forces –
Who has run his own six horses! etc

Raffles now belongs irrevocably to the 'cohorts of the damned'. He can still commit successful burglaries, but there is no way back into Paradise, which means Piccadilly and the MCC[1]. According to the public-school code there is only one means of rehabilitation: death in battle. Raffles dies fighting against the Boers (a practised reader would foresee this from the start), and in the eyes of both Bunny and his creator this cancels his crimes.

Both Raffles and Bunny, of course, are devoid of religious belief, and they have no real ethical code, merely certain rules of behaviour which they observe semi-instinctively. But it is just here that the deep moral difference between

[1] Marylebone Cricket Club.

Raffles and *No Orchids* becomes apparent. Raffles and Bunny, after all, are gentleman, and such standards as they do have are not to be violated. Certain things are 'not done', and the idea of doing them hardly arises. Raffles will not, for example, abuse hospitality. He will commit a burglary in a house where he is staying as a guest, but the victim must be a fellow guest and not the host. He will not commit murder,[1] and he avoids violence wherever possible and prefers to carry out his robberies unarmed. He regards friendship as sacred, and is chivalrous though not moral in his relations with women. He will take extra risks in the name of 'sportsmanship', and sometimes even for aesthetic reasons. And above all, he is intensely patriotic. He celebrates the Diamond Jubilee ('For sixty years, Bunny, we've been ruled over by absolutely the finest sovereign the world has ever seen') by despatching to the Queen through the post, an antique gold cup which he has stolen from the British Museum. He steals, from partly political motives, a pearl which the German Emperor is sending to one of the enemies of Britain, and when the Boer war begins to go badly his one thought is to find his way into the fighting line. At the front he unmasks a spy at the cost of revealing his own identity, and then dies gloriously by a Boer bullet. In this combination of crime and patriotism he resembles his near-contemporary Arsène Lupin, who also scores off the German Emperor and wipes out his very dirty past by enlisting in the Foreign Legion.

It is important to note that by modern standards Raffles's crimes are very petty ones. Four hundred pounds' worth of jewellery seems to him an excellent haul. And though the stories are convincing in their physical detail, they contain very little sensationalism – very few corpses, hardly any blood, no sex crimes, no sadism, no perversions of any kind. It seems to be the case that the crime story, at any rate on its higher levels, has greatly increased in bloodthirstiness during the past twenty years. Some of the early detective stories do not even contain a murder. The Sherlock Holmes stories, for instance, are not all murders, and some of them do not even deal with an indictable crime. So also with the John Thorndyke stories, while of the Max Carrados stories only a minority are murders. Since 1918, however, a detective story not containing a murder has been a great rarity, and the most disgusting details of dismemberment and exhumation are commonly exploited. Some of the Peter Wimsey stories, for instance, display an extremely morbid interest in corpses. The Raffles stories, written from the angle of the criminal, are much less antisocial than many modern stories written from the angle of the detective. The main impression that they leave behind is of boyishness. They belong to a time when people had standards, though they happened to be foolish standards. Their key-phrase is 'not done'. The line that they draw between good and evil is as senseless as a Polynesian taboo, but at least, like the taboo, it has the advantage that everyone accepts it.

So much for *Raffles*. Now for a header into the cesspool. *No Orchids for Miss Blandish*, by James Hadley Chase, was published in 1939, but seems to have enjoyed its greatest popularity in 1940, during the Battle of Britain and the blitz. In its main outlines its story is this:

Miss Blandish, the daughter of a millionaire, is kidnapped by some gangsters

[1] Actually Raffles does kill one man and is more or less consciously responsible for the death of two others. But all three of them are foreigners and have behaved in a very reprehensible manner. He also, on one occasion, contemplates murdering a blackmailer. It is, however, a fairly well-established convention in crime stories that murdering a blackmailer 'doesn't count'. [Author's footnote, 1945.]

who are almost immediately surprised and killed off by a larger and better organized gang. They hold her to ransom and extract half a million dollars from her father. Their original plan had been to kill her as soon as the ransom-money was received, but a chance keeps her alive. One of the gang is a young man named Slim, whose sole pleasure in life consists in driving knives into other people's bellies. In childhood he had graduated by cutting up living animals with a pair of rusty scissors. Slim is sexually impotent, but takes a kind of fancy to Miss Blandish. Slim's mother, who is the real brains of the gang, sees in this the chance of curing Slim's impotence, and decides to keep Miss Blandish in custody till Slim shall have succeeded in raping her. After many efforts and much persuasion, including the flogging of Miss Blandish with a length of rubber hosepipe, the rape is achieved. Meanwhile Miss Blandish's father has hired a private detective, and by means of bribery and torture the detective and the police manage to round up and exterminate the whole gang. Slim escapes with Miss Blandish and is killed after a final rape, and the detective prepares to restore Miss Blandish to her family. By this time, however, she has developed such a taste for Slim's caresses[1] that she feels unable to live without him, and she jumps out of the window of a sky-scraper.

Several other points need noticing before one can grasp the full implications of this book. To begin with, its central story bears a very marked resemblance to William Faulkner's novel *Sanctuary*. Secondly, it is not, as one might expect, the product of an illiterate hack, but a brilliant piece of writing, with hardly a wasted word or a jarring note anywhere. Thirdly, the whole book, *récit* as well as dialogue, is written in the American language; the author, an Englishman who has (I believe) never been in the United States, seems to have made a complete mental transference to the American underworld. Fourthly, the book sold, according to its publishers, no less than half a million copies.

I have already outlined the plot, but the subject-matter is much more sordid and brutal than this suggests. The book contains eight full-dress murders, an unassessable number of casual killings and woundings, an exhumation (with a careful reminder of the stench), the flogging of Miss Blandish, the torture of another woman with red-hot cigarette-ends, a strip-tease act, a third-degree scene of unheard-of cruelty and much else of the same kind. It assumes great sexual sophistication in its readers (there is a scene, for instance, in which a gangster, presumably of masochistic tendency, has an orgasm in the moment of being knifed), and it takes for granted the most complete corruption and self-seeking as the norm of human behaviour. The detective, for instance, is almost as great a rogue as the gangsters, and actuated by nearly the same motives. Like them, he is in pursuit of 'five hundred grand'. It is necessary to the machinery of the story that Mr Blandish should be anxious to get his daughter back, but apart from this, such things as affection, friendship, good nature or even ordinary politeness simply do not enter. Nor, to any great extent, does normal sexuality. Ultimately only one motive is at work throughout the whole story: the pursuit of power.

It should be noticed that the book is not in the ordinary sense pornography. Unlike most books that deal in sexual sadism, it lays the emphasis on the cruelty and not on the pleasure. Slim, the ravisher of Miss Blandish, has 'wet, slobbering lips': this is disgusting, and it is meant to be disgusting. But the

[1] Another reading of the final episode is possible. It may mean merely that Miss Blandish is pregnant. But the interpretation I have given above seems more in keeping with the general brutality of the book. [Author's footnote, 1945.]

scenes describing cruelty to women are comparatively perfunctory. The real highspots of the book are cruelties committed by men upon other men: above all, the third-degreeing of the gangster, Eddie Schultz, who is lashed into a chair and flogged on the windpipe with truncheons, his arms broken by fresh blows as he breaks loose. In another of Mr Chase's books, *He Won't Need It Now*, the hero, who is intended to be a sympathetic and perhaps even noble character, is described as stamping on somebody's face, and then, having crushed the man's mouth in, grinding his heel round and round in it. Even when physical incidents of this kind are not occurring, the mental atmosphere of these books is always the same. Their whole theme is the struggle for power and the triumph of the strong over the weak. The big gangsters wipe out the little ones as mercilessly as a pike gobbling up the little fish in a pond; the police kill off the criminals as cruelly as the angler kills the pike. If ultimately one sides with the police against the gangsters, it is merely because they are better organized and more powerful, because, in fact, the law is a bigger racket than crime. Might is right: *vae victis*.

As I have mentioned already, *No Orchids* enjoyed its greatest vogue in 1940, though it was successfully running as a play till some time later. It was, in fact, one of the things that helped to console people for the boredom of being bombed. Early in the war the *New Yorker* had a picture of a little man approaching a news-stall littered with papers with such headlines as 'Great Tank Battles in Northern France', 'Big Naval Battle in the North Sea', 'Huge Air Battles over the Channel', etc etc. The little man is saying '*Action Stories*, please'. That little man stood for all the drugged millions to whom the world of the gangsters and the prize-ring is more 'real', more 'tough', than such things as wars, revolutions, earthquakes, famines and pestilences. From the point of view of a reader of *Action Stories*, a description of the London blitz, or of the struggles of the European underground parties, would be 'sissy stuff'. On the other hand, some puny gun-battle in Chicago, resulting in perhaps half a dozen deaths, would seem genuinely 'tough'. This habit of mind is now extremely widespread. A soldier sprawls in a muddy trench, with the machine-gun bullets crackling a foot or two overhead, and whiles away his intolerable boredom by reading an American gangster story. And what it is that makes that story so exciting? Precisely the fact that people are shooting at each other with machine-guns! Neither the soldier nor anyone else sees anything curious in this. It is taken for granted that an imaginary bullet is more thrilling than a real one.

The obvious explanation is that in real life one is usually a passive victim, whereas in the adventure story one can think of oneself as being at the centre of events. But there is more to it than that. Here it is necessary to refer again to the curious fact of *No Orchids* being written – with technical errors, perhaps, but certainly with considerable skill – in the American language.

There exists in America an enormous literature of more or less the same stamp as *No Orchids*. Quite apart from books, there is the huge array of 'pulp magazines', graded so as to cater for different kinds of fantasy, but nearly all having much the same mental atmosphere. A few of them go in for straight pornography, but the great majority are quite plainly aimed at sadists and masochists. Sold at threepence a copy under the title of Yank Mags,[1] these things used to enjoy considerable popularity in England, but when the supply

[1] They are said to have been imported into this country as ballast, which accounted for their low price and crumpled appearance. Since the war the ships have been ballasted with something more useful, probably gravel. [Author's footnote.]

dried up owing to the war, no satisfactory substitute was forthcoming. English imitations of the 'pulp magazine' do now exist, but they are poor things compared with the original. English crook films, again, never approach the American crook film in brutality. And yet the career of Mr Chase shows how deep the American influence has already gone. Not only is he himself living a continuous fantasy-life in the Chicago underworld, but he can count on hundreds of thousands of readers who know what is meant by a 'clipshop' or the 'hotsquat', do not have to do mental arithmetic when confronted by 'fifty grand', and understand at sight a sentence like 'Johnnie was a rummy and only two jumps ahead of the nut-factory.' Evidently there are great numbers of English people who are partly Americanized in language and, one ought to add, in moral outlook. For there was no popular protest against *No Orchids*. In the end it was withdrawn, but only retrospectively, when a later work, *Miss Callaghan Comes to Grief*, brought Mr Chase's books to the attention of the authorities. Judging by casual conversations at the time, ordinary readers got a mild thrill out of the obscenities of *No Orchids*, but saw nothing undesirable in the book as a whole. Many people, incidentally, were under the impression that it was an American book reissued in England.

The thing that the ordinary reader *ought* to have objected to – almost certainly would have objected to, a few decades earlier – was the equivocal attitude towards crime. It is implied throughout *No Orchids* that being a criminal is only reprehensible in the sense that it does not pay. Being a policeman pays better, but there is no moral difference, since the police use essentially criminal methods. In a book like *He Won't Need It Now* the distinction between crime and crime prevention practically disappears. This is a new departure for English sensational fiction, in which till recently there has always been a sharp distinction between right and wrong and a general agreement that virtue must triumph in the last chapter. English books glorifying crime (modern crime, that is – pirates and highwaymen are different) are very rare. Even a book like *Raffles*, as I have pointed out, is governed by powerful taboos, and it is clearly understood that Raffles's crimes must be expiated sooner or later. In America, both in life and fiction, the tendency to tolerate crime, even to admire the criminal so long as he is successful, is very much more marked. It is, indeed, ultimately this attitude that has made it possible for crime to flourish upon so huge a scale. Books have been written about Al Capone that are hardly different in tone from the books written about Henry Ford, Stalin, Lord Northcliffe and all the rest of the 'log cabin to White House' brigade. And switching back eighty years, one finds Mark Twain adopting much the same attitude towards the disgusting bandit Slade, hero of twenty-eight murders, and towards the Western desperadoes generally. They were successful, they 'made good', therefore he admired them.

In a book like *No Orchids* one is not, as in the old-style crime story, simply escaping from dull reality into an imaginary world of action. One's escape is essentially into cruelty and sexual perversion. *No Orchids* is aimed at the power instinct, which *Raffles* or the Sherlock Holmes stories are not. At the same time the English attitude towards crime is not so superior to the American as I may have seemed to imply. It too is mixed up with power worship, and has become more noticeably so in the last twenty years. A writer who is worth examining is Edgar Wallace, especially in such typical books as *The Orator* and the Mr J. G. Reeder stories. Wallace was one of the first crime-story writers to break away from the old tradition of the private detective and make his central figure a

Scotland Yard official. Sherlock Holmes is an amateur, solving his problems without the help and even, in the earlier stories, against the opposition of the police. Moreover, like Lupin, he is essentially an intellectual, even a scientist. He reasons logically from observed fact, and his intellectuality is constantly contrasted with the routine methods of the police. Wallace objected strongly to this slur, as he considered it, on Scotland Yard, and in several newspaper articles he went out of his way to denounce Holmes by name. His own ideal was the detective inspector who catches criminals not because he is intellectually brilliant but because he is part of an all-powerful organization. Hence the curious fact that in Wallace's most characteristic stories the 'clue' and the 'deduction' play no part. The criminal is always defeated either by an incredible coincidence, or because in some unexplained manner the police know all about the crime beforehand. The tone of the stories makes it quite clear that Wallace's admiration for the police is pure bully-worship. A Scotland Yard detective is the most powerful kind of being that he can imagine, while the criminal figures in his mind as an outlaw against whom anything is permissible, like the condemned slaves in the Roman arena. His policemen behave much more brutally than British policemen do in real life – they hit people without provocation, fire revolvers past their ears to terrify them and so on – and some of the stories exhibit a fearful intellectual sadism. (For instance, Wallace likes to arrange things so that the villain is hanged on the same day as the heroine is married.) But it is sadism after the English fashion: that is to say, it is unconscious, there is not overtly any sex in it, and it keeps within the bounds of the law. The British public tolerates a harsh criminal law and gets a kick out of monstrously unfair murder trials: but still that is better, on any count, than tolerating or admiring crime. If one must worship a bully, it is better that he should be policeman than a gangster. Wallace is still governed to some extent by the concept of 'not done'. In *No Orchids* anything is 'done' so long as it leads on to power. All the barriers are down, all the motives are out in the open. Chase is a worse symptom than Wallace, to the extent that all-in wrestling is worse than boxing, or Fascism is worse than capitalist democracy.

In borrowing from William Faulkner's *Sanctuary*, Chase only took the plot; the mental atmosphere of the two books is not similar. Chase really derives from other sources, and this particular bit of borrowing is only symbolic. What it symbolizes is the vulgarization of ideas which is constantly happening, and which probably happens faster in an age of print. Chase has been described as 'Faulkner for the masses', but it would be more accurate to describe him as Carlyle for the masses. He is a popular writer – there are many such in America, but they are still rarities in England – who has caught up with what it is now fashionable to call 'realism', meaning the doctrine that might is right. The growth of 'realism' has been the great feature of the intellectual history of our own age. Why this should be so is a complicated question. The interconnection between sadism, masochism, success worship, power worship, nationalism and totalitarianism is a huge subject whose edges have barely been scratched, and even to mention it is considered somewhat indelicate. To take merely the first example that comes to mind, I believe no one has ever pointed out the sadistic element in Bernard Shaw's work, still less suggested that this probably has some connection with Shaw's admiration for dictators. Fascism is often loosely equated with sadism, but nearly always by people who see nothing wrong in the most slavish worship of Stalin. The truth is, of course, that the countless English intellectuals who kiss the arse of Stalin are not different from the minority who give their allegiance to Hitler or Mussolini, nor from the efficiency experts who preached 'punch', 'drive', 'personality' and 'learn to be a Tiger man' in the nineteen-twenties, nor from the older generation of intellectuals, Carlyle, Creasy and the rest of them, who bowed down before German militarism. All of them are worshipping power and successful cruelty. It is important to notice that the cult of power tends to be mixed up with a love of cruelty and wickedness *for their own sakes*. A tyrant is all the more admired if he happens to be a blood-stained crook as well, and 'the end justifies the means' often becomes, in effect, 'the means justify themselves provided they are dirty enough'. This idea colours the outlook of all sympathizers with totalitarianism, and accounts, for instance, for the positive delight with which many English intellectuals greeted the Nazi-Soviet Pact. It was a step only doubtfully useful to the USSR, but it was entirely unmoral, and for that reason to be admired; the explanations of it, which were numerous and self-contradictory, could come afterwards.

Until recently the characteristic adventure stories of the English-speaking peoples have been stories in which the hero fights *against odds*. This is true all the way from Robin Hood to Popeye the Sailor. Perhaps the basic myth of the western world is Jack the Giant-Killer, but to be brought up to date this should be renamed Jack the Dwarf-Killer, and there already exists a considerable literature which teaches, either overtly or implicitly, that one should side with the big man against the little man. Most of what is now written about foreign policy is simply embroidery on this theme, and for several decades such phrases as 'Play the game', 'Don't hit a man when he's down' and 'It's not cricket' have never failed to draw a snigger from anyone of intellectual pretensions. What is comparatively new is to find the accepted pattern according to which (a) right is right and wrong is wrong, whoever wins, and (b) weakness must be respected, disappearing from popular literature as well. When I first read D. H. Lawrence's novels, at the age of about twenty, I was puzzled by the fact that there did not seem to be any classification of the characters into 'good' and 'bad'. Lawrence seemed to sympathize with all of them about equally, and this was so unusual as to give me the feeling of having lost my bearings. Today no one would think of looking for heroes and villains in a serious novel, but in lowbrow fiction one still expects to find a sharp distinction between right and wrong and between legality and illegality. The common people, on the whole, are still living in the world of absolute good and evil from which the intellectuals have long since escaped. But the popularity of *No Orchids* and the American books and magazines to which it is akin shows how rapidly the doctrine of 'realism' is gaining ground.

Several people, after reading *No Orchids*, have remarked to me, 'It's pure Fascism'. This is a correct description, although the book has not the smallest connection with politics and very little with social or economic problems. It has merely the same relation to Fascism as, say, Trollope's novels have to nineteenth-century capitalism. It is a day-dream appropriate to a totalitarian age. In his imagined world of gangsters Chase is presenting, as it were, a distilled version of the modern political scene, in which such things as mass bombing of civilians, the use of hostages, torture to obtain confessions, secret prisons, execution without trial, floggings with rubber truncheons, drownings in cesspools, systematic falsification of records and statistics, treachery, bribery and quislingism are normal and morally neutral, even admirable when they are done in a large and bold way. The average man is not directly interested in politics and, when he reads, he wants the current struggles of the world to be translated into a simple story about individuals. He can take an interest in Slim and Fenner as he could not in the GPU and the Gestapo. People worship power in the form in which they are able to understand it. A twelve-year-old boy worships Jack Dempsey. An adolescent in a Glasgow slum worships Al Capone. An aspiring pupil at a business college worships Lord Nuffield. A *New Statesman* reader worships Stalin. There is a difference in intellectual maturity, but none in moral outlook. Thirty years ago the heroes of popular fiction had nothing in common with Mr Chase's gangsters and detectives, and the idols of the English liberal intelligentsia were also comparatively sympathetic figures. Between Holmes and Fenner on the one hand, and between Abraham Lincoln and Stalin on the other, there is a similar gulf.

One ought not to infer too much from the success of Mr Chase's books. It is possible that it is an isolated phenomenon, brought about by the mingled boredom and brutality of war. But if such books should definitely acclimatize themselves in England, instead of being merely a half-understood import from America, there would be good grounds for dismay. In choosing *Raffles* as a background for *No Orchids* I deliberately chose a book which by the standards of its time was morally equivocal. Raffles, as I have pointed out, has no real moral code, no religion, certainly no social consciousness. All he has is a set of reflexes – the nervous system, as it were, of a gentleman. Give him a sharp tap on this reflex or that (they are called 'sport', 'pal', 'woman', 'king and country' and so forth), and you get a predictable reaction. In Mr Chase's books there are no gentlemen and no taboos. Emancipation is complete, Freud and Machiavelli have reached the outer suburbs. Comparing the schoolboy atmosphere of the one book with the cruelty and corruption of the other, one is driven to feel that snobbishness, like hypocrisy, is a check upon behaviour whose value from a social point of view has been underrated.

Horizon, October 1944

As I Please

It is not my primary job to discuss the details of contemporary politics, but this week there is something that cries out to be said. Since, it seems, nobody else will do so, I want to protest against the mean and cowardly attitude adopted by the British press towards the recent rising in Warsaw.

As soon as the news of the rising broke, the *News Chronicle* and kindred papers adopted a markedly disapproving attitude. One was left with the general impression that the Poles deserved to have their bottoms smacked for doing what all the Allied wirelesses had been urging them to do for years past, and that they would not be given and did not deserve to be given any help from outside. A few papers tentatively suggested that arms and supplies might be dropped by the Anglo-Americans, a thousand miles away: no one, so far as I know, suggested that this might be done by the Russians, perhaps twenty miles away. The *New Statesman*, in its issue of August 18, even went so far as to doubt whether appreciable help could be given from the air in such circumstances. All or nearly all the papers of the Left were full of blame for the *émigré* London Government which had 'prematurely' ordered its followers to rise when the Red Army was at the gates. This line of thought is adequately set forth in a letter to last week's *Tribune* from Mr G. Barraclough. He makes the following specific charges:

1. The Warsaw rising was 'not a spontaneous popular rising', but was 'begun on orders from the *soi-disant* Polish Government in London'.

2. The order to rise was given 'without consultation with either the British or Soviet Governments', and 'no attempt was made to co-ordinate the rising with Allied action'.

3. The Polish resistance movement is no more united round the London Government than the Greek resistance movement is united round King George of the Hellenes. (This is further emphasized by frequent use of the words *émigré, soi-disant*, etc applied to the London Government.)

4. The London Government precipitated the rising in order to be in possession of Warsaw when the Russians arrived, because in that case 'the bargaining position of the *émigré* Government would be improved'. The London Government, we are told, 'is ready to betray the Polish people's cause to bolster up its own tenure of precarious office', with much more to the same effect.

No shadow of proof is offered for any of these charges, though 1 and 2 are of the kind that could be verified and may well be true. My own guess is that 2 is true and 1 partly true. The third charge makes nonsense of the first two. If the London Government is not accepted by the mass of the people in Warsaw, why should they raise a desperate insurrection on its orders? By blaming Sosnkowski and the rest for the rising, you are automatically assuming that it is to them that the Polish people looks for guidance. This obvious contradiction has been repeated in paper after paper, without, so far as I know, a single person having the honesty to point it out. As for the use of such expressions as *émigré*, it is simply a rhetorical trick. If the London Poles are *émigrés*, so are the Polish National Committee of Liberation, besides the 'free' Governments of all the occupied countries. Why does one become an *émigré* by emigrating to London and not by emigrating to Moscow?

Charge No. 4 is morally on a par with the *Osservatore Romano*'s suggestion that the Russians held up their attack on Warsaw in order to get as many Polish resisters as possible killed off. It is the unproved and unprovable assertion of a mere propagandist who has no wish to establish the truth, but is simply out to do as much dirt on his opponent as possible. And all that I have read about this matter in the press – except for some very obscure papers and some remarks in *Tribune*, the *Economist* and the *Evening Standard* – is on the same level as Mr Barraclough's letter.

Now, I know nothing of Polish affairs, and even if I had the power to do so I would not intervene in the struggle between the London Polish Government and the Moscow National Committee of Liberation. What I am concerned with is the attitude of the British intelligentsia, who cannot raise between them one single voice to question what they believe to be Russian policy, no matter what turn it takes, and in this case have had the unheard-of meanness to hint that our bombers ought not to be sent to the aid of our comrades fighting in Warsaw. The enormous majority of left-wingers who swallow the policy put out by the *News Chronicle* etc know no more about Poland than I do. All they know is that the Russians object to the London Government and have set up a rival organization, and so far as they are concerned that settles the matter. If tomorrow Stalin were to drop the Committee of Liberation and recognize the London Government, the whole British intelligentsia would flock after him like a troop of parrots. Their attitude towards Russian foreign policy is not 'Is this policy right or wrong?' but 'This is Russian policy: how can we make it appear right?' And this attitude is defended, if at all, solely on grounds of power. The Russians are powerful in eastern Europe, we are not: therefore we must not oppose them. This involves the principle, of its nature alien to Socialism, that you must not protest against any evil which you cannot prevent.

I cannot discuss here why it is that the British intelligentsia, with few exceptions, have developed a nationalistic loyalty towards the USSR and are dishonestly uncritical of its policies. In any case, I have discussed it elsewhere. But I would like to close with two considerations which are worth thinking over.

First of all, a message to English left-wing journalists and intellectuals generally: 'Do remember that dishonesty and cowardice always have to be paid for. Don't imagine that for years on end you can make yourself the boot-licking propagandist of the Soviet régime, or any other régime, and then suddenly return to mental decency. Once a whore, always a whore.'

Secondly, a wider consideration. Nothing is more important in the world today than Anglo-Russian friendship and co-operation, and that will not be attained without plain speaking. The best way to come to an agreement with a foreign nation is *not* to refrain from criticizing its policies, even to the extent of leaving your own people in the dark about them. At present, so slavish is the attitude of nearly the whole British press that ordinary people have very little idea of what is happening, and may well be committed to policies which they will repudiate in five years' time. In a shadowy sort of way we have been told that the Russian peace terms are a super-Versailles, with partition of Germany, astronomical reparations, and forced labour on a huge scale. These proposals go practically uncriticized, while in much of the left-wing press hack writers are even hired to extol them. The result is that the average man has no notion of the enormity of what is proposed. I don't know whether, when the time comes, the Russians will really want to put such terms into operation. My guess is that they won't. But what I do know is that if any such thing were done, the British and probably the American public would never support it when the passion of war had died down. Any flagrantly unjust peace settlement will simply have the result, as it did last time, of making the British people unreasonably sympathetic with the victims. Anglo-Russian friendship depends upon there being a policy which both countries can agree upon, and this is impossible without free discussion and genuine criticism *now*. There can be no real alliance on the basis of 'Stalin is always right'. The first step towards a real alliance is the dropping of illusions.

Tribune, 1 September 1944

Arthur Koestler

One striking fact about English literature during the present century is the extent to which it has been dominated by foreigners – for example, Conrad, Henry James, Shaw, Joyce, Yeats, Pound and Eliot. Still, if you chose to make this a matter of national prestige and examine our achievement in the various branches of literature, you would find that England made a fairly good showing until you came to what may be roughly described as political writing, or pamphleteering. I mean by this the special class of literature that has arisen out of the European political struggle since the rise of Fascism. Under this heading novels, autobiographies, books of 'reportage', sociological treatises and plain pamphlets can all be lumped together, all of them having a common origin and to a great extent the same emotional atmosphere.

Some out of the outstanding figures in this school of writers are Silone, Malraux, Salvemini, Borkenau, Victor Serge, and Koestler himself. Some of these are imaginative writers, some not, but they are all alike in that they are trying to write contemporary history, but *unofficial* history, the kind that is ignored in the text-books and lied about in the newspapers. Also they are all alike in being continental Europeans. It may be an exaggeration, but it cannot be a very great one, to say that whenever a book dealing with totalitarianism appears in this country, and still seems worth reading six months after publication, it is a book translated from some foreign language. English writers, over the past dozen years, have poured forth an enormous spate of political literature but they have produced almost nothing of aesthetic value, and very little of historical value either. The Left Book Club, for instance, has been running ever since 1936. How many of its chosen volumes can you even remember the names of? Nazi Germany, Soviet Russia, Spain, Abyssinia, Austria, Czechoslovakia – all that these and kindred subjects have produced, in English, are slick books of reportage, dishonest pamphlets in which propaganda is swallowed whole and then spewed up again, half digested, and a very few reliable guide books and text-books. There has been nothing resembling, for instance, *Fontamara* or *Darkness at Noon*, because there is almost no English writer to whom it has happened to see totalitarianism from the inside. In Europe, during the past decade and more, things have been happening to middle-class people which in England do not even happen to the working class. Most of the European writers I mentioned above, and scores of others like them, have been obliged to break the law in order to engage in politics at all; some of them have thrown bombs and fought in street battles, many have been in prison or the concentration camp, or fled across frontiers with false names and forged passports. One cannot imagine, say, Professor Laski indulging in activities of that kind. England is lacking, therefore, in what one might call concentration-camp literature. The special world created by secret-police forces, censorship of opinion, torture and frame-up trials is, of course, known about and to some extent disapproved of, but it has made very little emotional impact. One result of this is that there exists in England almost no literature of disillusionment about the Soviet Union. There is the attitude of ignorant disapproval, and there is the attitude of uncritical admiration, but very little in between. Opinion on the Moscow sabotage trials, for instance, was divided, but divided chiefly on the question of whether the accused were guilty. Few people were able to see that, whether justified or not, the trials were an unspeakable horror. And English disapproval of the Nazi outrages has also been an unreal thing, turned on and off like a tap according to political expediency. To understand such things one has to be able to imagine oneself as the victim, and for an Englishman to write *Darkness at Noon* would be as unlikely an accident as for a slave-trader to write *Uncle Tom's Cabin.*

Koestler's published work really centres about the Moscow trials. His main theme is the decadence of revolutions owing to the corrupting effects of power, but the special nature of the Stalin dictatorship has driven him back into a position not far removed from pessimistic Conservatism. I do not know how many books he has written in all. He is a Hungarian whose earlier books were written in German, and five books have been published in England: *Spanish Testament, The Gladiators, Darkness at Noon, Scum of the Earth,* and *Arrival and Departure.* The subject-matter of all of them is similar, and none of them ever escapes for more than a few pages from the atmosphere of nightmare. Of the five books, the action of three takes place entirely or almost entirely in prison.

In the opening months of the Spanish civil war Koestler was the *News Chronicle*'s correspondent in Spain, and early in 1937 he was taken prisoner when the Fascists captured Malaga. He was nearly shot out of hand, then spent some months imprisoned in a fortress, listening every night to the roar of rifle fire as batch after batch of Republicans was executed, and being most of the time in acute danger of execution himself. This was not a chance adventure which 'might have happened to anybody', but was in accordance with Koestler's life-style. A politically indifferent person would not have been in Spain at that date, a more cautious observer would have got out of Malaga before the Fascists arrived, and a British or American newspaper man would have been treated with more consideration. The book that Koestler wrote about this, *Spanish Testament,* has remarkable passages, but apart from the scrappiness that is usual in a book of reportage, it is definitely false in places. In the prison scenes Koestler successfully establishes the nightmare atmosphere which is, so to speak, his patent, but the rest of the book is too much coloured by the Popular Front orthodoxy of the time. One or two passages even look as though they had been doctored for the purposes of the Left Book Club. At that time Koestler still was, or recently had been, a member of the Communist Party, and the complex politics of the civil war made it impossible for any Communist to write honestly about the internal struggle on the Government side. The sin of nearly all left-wingers from 1933 onwards is that they have wanted to be anti-Fascist without being anti-totalitarian. In 1937 Koestler already knew this, but did not feel free to say so. He came much nearer to saying it – indeed, he did say it, though he put on a mask to do so – in his next book, *The Gladiators,* which was published about a year before the war and for some reason attracted very little attention.

The Gladiators is in some ways an unsatisfactory book. It is about Spartacus, the Thracian gladiator who raised a slaves' rebellion in Italy round about 65 BC, and any book on such a subject is handicapped by challenging comparison with *Salammbô.* In our own age it would not be possible to write a book like *Salammbô*, even if one had the talent. The great thing about *Salammbô*, even more important than its physical detail, is its utter mercilessness. Flaubert could think himself into the stony cruelty of antiquity, because in the mid-nineteeth century one still had peace of mind. One had time to travel in the past. Nowadays the present and the future are too terrifying to be escaped from, and if one bothers with history it is in order to find modern meanings there. Koestler makes Spartacus into an allegorical figure, a primitive version of the proletarian dictator. Whereas Flaubert has been able, by a prolonged effort of the imagination, to make his mercenaries truly pre-Christian, Spartacus is a modern man dressed up. But this might not matter if Koestler were fully aware of what his allegory means. Revolutions always go wrong – that is the main theme. It is on the question of *why* they go wrong that he falters, and his uncertainty enters into the story and makes the central figures enigmatic and unreal.

For several years the rebellious slaves are uniformly successful. Their numbers swell to a hundred thousand, they overrun great areas of Southern Italy, they defeat one punitive expedition after another, they ally themselves with the pirates who at that time were the masters of the Mediterranean, and finally they set to work to build a city of their own, to be named the City of the Sun. In this city human beings are to be free and equal, and above all, they are to be happy: no slavery, no hunger, no injustice, no floggings, no executions. It is the dream of a just society which seems to haunt the human imagination ineradicably and in all ages, whether it is called the Kingdom of Heaven or the classless society, or whether it is thought of as a Golden Age which once existed in the past and from which we have degenerated. Needless to say, the slaves fail to achieve it. No sooner have they formed themselves into a community than their way of life turns out to be as unjust, laborious and fear-ridden as any other. Even the cross, symbol of slavery, has to be revived for the punishment of malefactors. The turning-point comes when Spartacus finds himself obliged to crucify twenty of his oldest and most faithful followers. After that the City of the Sun is doomed, the slaves split up and are defeated in detail, the last fifteen thousand of them being captured and crucified in one batch.

The serious weakness of this story is that the motives of Spartacus himself are never made clear. The Roman lawyer Fulvius, who joins the rebellion and acts as its chronicler, sets forth the familiar dilemma of ends and means. You can achieve nothing unless you are willing to use force and cunning, but in using them you pervert your original aims. Spartacus, however, is not represented as power hungry, nor, on the other hand, as a visionary. He is driven onwards by some obscure force which he does not understand, and he is frequently in two minds as to whether it would not be better to throw up the whole adventure and flee to Alexandria while the going is good. The slaves' republic is in any case wrecked rather by hedonism than by the struggle for power. The slaves are discontented with their liberty because they still have to work, and the final break-up happens because the more turbulent and less civilized slaves, chiefly Gauls and Germans, continue to behave like bandits after the republic has been established. This may be a true account of events – naturally we know very little about the slave rebellions of antiquity – but by allowing the Sun City to be destroyed because Crixus the Gaul cannot be prevented from looting and raping, Koestler has faltered between allegory and history. If Spartacus is the prototype of the modern revolutionary – and obviously he is intended as that – he should have gone astray because of the impossibility of combining power with righteousness. As it is, he is an almost passive figure, acted upon rather than acting, and at times not convincing. The story partly fails because the central problem of revolution has been avoided or, at least, has not been solved.

It is again avoided in a subtler way in the next book, Koestler's masterpiece, *Darkness at Noon*. Here, however, the story is not spoiled, because it deals with individuals and its interest is psychological. It is an episode picked out from a background that does not have to be questioned. *Darkness at Noon* describes the imprisonment and death of an Old Bolshevik, Rubashov, who first denies and ultimately confesses to crimes which he is well aware he has not committed. The grown-upness, the lack of surprise or denunciation, the pity and irony with which the story is told, show the advantage, when one is handling a theme of this kind, of being a European. The book reaches the stature of tragedy, whereas an English or American writer could at most have made it into a polemical tract. Koestler has digested his material and can treat it on the aesthetic level. At the same time his handling of it has a political implication, not important in this case but likely to be damaging in later books.

Naturally the whole book centres round one question: Why did Rubashov confess? He is not guilty – that is, not guilty of anything except the essential crime of disliking the Stalin régime. The concrete acts of treason in which he is supposed to have engaged are all imaginary. He has not even been tortured, or not very severely. He is worn down by solitude, toothache, lack of tobacco, bright lights glaring in his eyes, and continuous questioning, but these in themselves would not be enough to overcome a hardened revolutionary. The Nazis have previously done worse to him without breaking his spirit. The confessions obtained in the Russian state trials are capable of three explanations:

1. That the accused were guilty.
2. That they were tortured, and perhaps blackmailed by threats to relatives and friends.
3. That they were actuated by despair, mental bankruptcy and the habit of loyalty to the Party.

For Koestler's purpose in *Darkness at Noon* 1 is ruled out, and though this is not the place to discuss the Russian purges, I must add that what little verifiable evidence there is suggests that the trials of the Bolsheviks were frame-ups. If one assumes that the accused were not guilty – at any rate, not guilty of the particular things they confessed to – then 2 is the common-sense explanation. Koestler, however, plumps for 3, which is also accepted by the Trotskyist Boris Souvarine, in his pamphlet *Cauchemar en URSS*. Rubashov ultimately confesses because he cannot find in his own mind any reason for not doing so. Justice and objective truth have long ceased to have any meaning for him. For decades he has been simply the creature of the Party, and what the Party now demands is that he shall confess to non-existent crimes. In the end, though he had to be bullied and weakened first, he is somewhat proud of his decision to confess. He feels superior to the poor Czarist officer who inhabits the next cell and who talks to Rubashov by tapping on the wall. The Czarist officer is shocked when he learns that Rubashov intends to capitulate. As he sees it from his 'bourgeois' angle, everyone ought to stick to his guns, even a Bolshevik. Honour, he says, consists in doing what you think right. 'Honour is to be useful without fuss,' Rubashov taps back; and he reflects with a certain satisfaction that he is tapping with his pince-nez while the other, the relic of the past, is tapping with a monocle. Like Bukharin, Rubashov is 'looking out upon black darkness'. What is there, what code, what loyalty, what notion of good and evil, for the sake of which he can defy the Party and endure further torment? He is not only alone, he is also hollow. He has himself committed worse crimes than the one that is now being perpetrated against him. For example, as a secret envoy of the Party of Nazi Germany, he has got rid of disobedient followers by betraying them to the Gestapo. Curiously enough, if he has any inner strength to draw upon, it is the memories of his boyhood when he was the son of a landowner. The last thing he remembers, when he is shot from behind, is the leaves of poplar trees on his father's estate. Rubashov belongs to the older generation of Bolsheviks that was largely wiped out in the purges. He is aware of art and literature, and of the world outside Russia. He contrasts sharply with Gletkin, the young GPU man who conducts his interrogation, and who is the typical 'good party man', completely without scruples or curiosity, a thinking gramophone. Rubashov, unlike Gletkin, does not have the Revolution as his starting-point. His mind was not a blank sheet when the Party got hold of it. His superiority to the other is finally traceable to his bourgeois origin.

One cannot, I think, argue that *Darkness at Noon* is simply a story dealing with the adventures of an imaginary individual. Clearly it is a political book, founded on history and offering an interpretation of disputed events. Rubashov might be called Trotsky, Bukharin, Rakovsky or some other relatively civilized figure among the Old Bolsheviks. If one writes about the Moscow trials one must answer the question, 'Why did the accused confess?' and which answer one makes is a political decision. Koestler answers, in effect, 'Because these people had been rotted by the Revolution which they served', and in doing so he comes near to claiming that revolutions are of their nature bad. If one assumes that the accused in the Moscow trials were made to confess by means of some kind of terrorism, one is only saying that one particular set of revolutionary leaders has gone astray. Individuals, and not the situation, are to blame. The implication of Koestler's book, however, is that Rubashov in power would be no better than Gletkin; or rather, only better in that his outlook is still partly pre-revolutionary. Revolution, Koestler seems to say, is a corrupting process. Really enter into the Revolution and you must end up as either Rubashov or Gletkin. It is not merely that 'power corrupts': so also do the ways of attaining power. Therefore, all efforts to regenerate *by violent means* lead to the cellars of the OGPU, Lenin leads to Stalin, and would have come to resemble Stalin if he had happened to survive.

Of course, Koestler does not say this quite explicitly, and perhaps is not altogether conscious of it. He is writing about darkness, but it is darkness at what ought to be noon. Part of the time he feels that things might have turned out differently. The notion that so-and-so has 'betrayed', that things have only gone wrong because of individual wickedness, is ever present in left-wing thought. Later, in *Arrival and Departure,* Koestler swings over much further towards the anti-revolutionary position, but in between these two books there is another, *Scum of the Earth*, which is straight autobiography and has only an indirect bearing upon the problems raised by *Darkness at Noon.* True to his life-style, Koestler was caught in France by the outbreak of war and, as a foreigner and a known anti-Fasçist, was prompty arrested and interned by the Daladier Government. He spent the first nine months of war mostly in a prison camp, then, during the collapse of France, escaped and travelled by devious routes to England, where he was once again thrown into prison as an enemy alien. This time he was soon released, however. The book is a valuable piece of reportage, and together with a few other scraps of honest writing that happened to be produced at the time of the débâcle, it is a reminder of the depths that bourgeois democracy can descend to. At this moment, with France newly liberated and the witch-hunt after collaborators in full swing, we are apt to forget that in 1940 various observers on the spot considered that about forty per cent of the French population was either actively pro-German or completely apathetic. Truthful war books are never acceptable to non-combatants, and Koestler's book did not have a very good reception. Nobody came well out of it – neither the bourgeois politicians, whose idea of conducting an anti-Fascist war was to jail every left-winger they could lay their hands on, nor the French Communists, who were effectively pro-Nazi and did their best to sabotage the French war effort, nor the common people, who were just as likely to follow mountebanks like Doriot as responsible leaders. Koestler records some fantastic conversations with fellow victims in the concentration camp, and adds that till then, like most middle-class Socialists and Communists, he had never made contact with real proletarians, only with the educated minority. He draws the pessimistic conclusion: 'Without education of the masses, no social progress; without social progress, no education of the masses.' In *Scum of the Earth* Koestler ceases to idealize the common people. He has abandoned Stalinism, but he is not a Trotskyist either. This is the book's real link with *Arrival and Departure*, in which what is normally called a revolutionary outlook is dropped, perhaps for good.

Arrival and Departure is not a satisfactory book. The pretence that it is a novel is very thin; in effect it is a tract purporting to show that revolutionary creeds are rationalizations of neurotic impulses. With all too neat a symmetry, the book begins and ends with the same action – a leap into a foreign country. A young ex-Communist who has made his escape from Hungary jumps ashore in Portugal, where he hopes to enter the service of Britain, at that time the only power fighting against Germany. His enthusiasm is somewhat cooled by the fact that the British Consulate is uninterested in him and almost ignores him for a period of several months, during which his money runs out and other astuter refugees escape to America. He is successively tempted by the World in the form of a Nazi propagandist, the Flesh in the form of a French girl, and – after a nervous breakdown – the Devil in the form of a psychoanalyst. The psychoanalyst drags out of him the fact that his revolutionary enthusiasm is not founded on any real belief in historical necessity, but on a morbid guilt complex arising from an attempt in early childhood to blind his baby brother. By the time that he gets an opportunity of serving the Allies he has lost all reason for wanting to do so, and he is on the point of leaving for America when his irrational impulses seize hold of him again. In practice he cannot abandon the struggle. When the book ends, he is floating down in a parachute over the dark landscape of his native country, where he will be employed as a secret agent of Britain.

As a political statement (and the book is not much more), this is insufficient. Of course it is true in many cases, and it may be true in all cases, that revolutionary activity is the result of personal maladjustment. Those who struggle against society are, on the whole, those who have reason to dislike it, and normal healthy people are no more attracted by violence and illegality than they are by war. The young Nazi in *Arrival and Departure* makes the penetrating remark that one can see what is wrong with the left-wing movement by the ugliness of its women. But after all, this does not invalidate the Socialist case. Actions have results, irrespective of their motives. Marx's ultimate motives may well have been envy and spite, but this does not prove that his conclusions were false. In making the hero of *Arrival and Departure* take his final decision from a mere instinct not to shirk action and danger, Koestler is making him suffer a sudden loss of intelligence. With such a history as he has behind him, he would be able to see that certain things have to be done, whether our reasons for doing them are 'good' or 'bad'. History has to move in a certain direction, even if it has to be pushed that way by neurotics. In *Arrival and Departure* Peter's idols are overthrown one after the other. The Russian Revolution has degenerated, Britain, symbolized by the aged consul with gouty fingers, is no better, the international class-conscious proletariat is a myth. But the conclusion (since, after all, Koestler and his hero 'support' the war) ought to be that getting rid of Hitler is still a worth-while objective, a necessary bit of scavenging in which motives are almost irrelevant.

To take a rational political decision one must have a picture of the future. At present Koestler seems to have none, or rather to have two which cancel out. As an ultimate objective he believes in the Earthly Paradise, the Sun State which the gladiators set out to establish, and which has haunted the imagination of Socialists, Anarchists and religious heretics for hundreds of years. But his intelligence tells him that the Earthly Paradise is receding into the far distance and that what is actually ahead of us is bloodshed, tyranny and privation. Recently he described himself as a 'short-term pessimist'. Every kind of horror is blowing up over the horizon, but somehow it will all come right in the end. This outlook is probably gaining ground among thinking people: it results from the very great difficulty, once one has abandoned orthodox religious belief, of accepting life on earth as inherently miserable, and on the other hand, from the realization that to make life liveable is a much bigger problem than it recently seemed. Since about 1930 the world has given no reason for optimism whatever. Nothing is in sight except a welter of lies, hatred, cruelty and ignorance, and beyond our present troubles loom vaster ones which are only now entering into the European consciousness. It is quite possible that man's major problems will *never* be solved. But it is also unthinkable! Who is there who dares to look at the world of today and say to himself, 'It will always be like this: even in a million years it cannot get appreciably better'? So you get the quasi-mystical belief that for the present there is no remedy, all political action is useless, but that somewhere in space and time human life will cease to be the miserable brutish thing it now is.

The only easy way out is that of the religious believer, who regards this life merely as a preparation for the next. But few thinking people now believe in life after death, and the number of those who do is probably diminishing. The Christian churches would probably not survive on their own merits if their economic basis were destroyed. The real problem is how to restore the religious attitude while accepting death as final. Men can only be happy when they do not assume that the object of life is happiness. It is most unlikely, however, that Koestler would accept this. There is a well-marked hedonistic strain in his writings, and his failure to find a political position after breaking with Stalinism is a result of this.

The Russian Revolution, the central event in Koestler's life, started out with high hopes. We forget these things now, but a quarter of a century ago it was confidently expected that the Russian Revolution would lead to Utopia. Obviously this has not happened. Koestler is too acute not to see this, and too sensitive not to remember the original objective. Moreover, from his European angle he can see such things as purges and mass deportations for what they are; he is not, like Shaw or Laski, looking at them through the wrong end of the telescope. Therefore he draws the conclusion: This is what revolutions lead to. There is nothing for it except to be a 'short-term pessimist', i.e. to keep out of politics, make a sort of oasis within which you and your friends can remain sane, and hope that somehow things will be better in a hundred years. At the basis of this lies his hedonism, which leads him to think of the Earthly Paradise as desirable. Perhaps, however, whether desirable or not, it isn't possible. Perhaps some degree of suffering is ineradicable from human life, perhaps the choice before man is always a choice of evils, perhaps even the aim of Socialism is not to make the world perfect but to make it better. All revolutions are failures, but they are not all the same failure. It is unwillingness to admit this that has led Koestler's mind temporarily into a blind alley and that makes *Arrival and Departure* seem shallow compared with the earlier books.

Written [September] 1944

Tobias Smollett: Scotland's Best Novelist

'Realism', a much abused word, has at least four current meanings, but when applied to novels it normally means a photographic imitation of everyday life. A 'realistic' novel is one in which the dialogue is colloquial and physical objects are described in such a way that you can visualize them. In this sense almost all modern novels are more 'realistic' than those of the past, because the describing of everyday scenes and the construction of natural-sounding dialogue are largely a matter of technical tricks which are passed on from one generation to another, gradually improving in the process. But there is another sense in which the stilted, artificial novelists of the eighteenth century are more 'realistic' than almost any of their successors, and that is in their attitude towards human motives. They may be weak at describing scenery, but they are extraordinarily good at describing scoundrelism. This is true even of Fielding, who in *Tom Jones* and *Amelia* already shows the moralizing tendency which was to mark English novels for a hundred and fifty years. But it is much truer of Smollett, whose outstanding intellectual honesty may have been connected with the fact that he was not an Englishman.

Smollett is a picaresque novelist, a writer of long, formless tales full of farcical and improbable adventures. He derives to some extent from Cervantes who he translated into English and who he also plagiarized in *Sir Lancelot Greaves*. Inevitably a great deal that he wrote is no longer worth reading, even including, perhaps, his most-praised book, *Humphrey Clinker*, which is written in the form of letters and was considered comparatively respectable in the nineteenth century, because most of its obscenities are hidden under puns. But Smollett's real masterpieces are *Roderick Random* and *Peregrine Pickle*, which are frankly pornographic in a harmless way and which contain some of the best passages of sheer farce in the English language.

Dickens, in *David Copperfield*, names these two books among his childhood favourites, but the resemblance sometimes claimed as existing between Smollett and Dickens is very superficial. In *Pickwick Papers*, and in several others of Dickens's early books, you have the picaresque form, the endless travelling to and fro, the fantastic adventures, the willingness to sacrifice no matter what amount of probability for the sake of a joke; but the moral atmosphere has greatly altered. Between Smollett's day and Dickens's there had happened not only the French Revolution, but the rise of a new industrial middle class, Low Church in its theology and puritanical in its outlook. Smollett writes of the middle class, but the mercantile and professional middle class, the kind of people who are cousins to a landowner and take their manners from the aristocracy.

Duelling, gambling and fornication seem almost morally neutral to him. It so happens that in private life he was a better man than the majority of writers. He was a faithful husband who shortened his life by overworking for the sake of his family, a sturdy republican who hated France as the country of the Grand Monarchy, and a patriotic Scotsman at a time when – the 1745 rebellion being a fairly recent memory – it was far from fashionable to be a Scotsman. But he has very little sense of sin. His heroes do things, and do them on almost every page, which in any nineteenth-century English novel would instantly call forth vengeance from the skies. He accepts as a law of nature the viciousness, the nepotism and the disorder of eighteenth-century society, and therein lies his charm. Many of his best passages would be ruined by any intrusion of the moral sense.

Both *Peregrine Pickle* and *Roderick Random* follow roughly the same course. Both heroes go through great vicissitudes of fortune, travel widely, seduce numerous women, suffer imprisonment for debt, and end up prosperous and happily married. Of the two, Peregrine is somewhat the greater blackguard, because he has no profession – Roderick is a naval surgeon, as Smollett himself had been for a while – and can consequently devote more time to seductions and practical jokes. But neither is ever shown acting from an unselfish motive, nor is it admitted that such things as religious belief, political conviction or even ordinary honesty are serious factors in human affairs.

In the world of Smollett's novels there are only three virtues. One is feudal loyalty (Roderick and Peregrine each have a retainer who is faithful through thick and thin), another is masculine 'honour', i.e. willingness to fight on any provocation, and another is female 'chastity', which is inextricably mixed up with the idea of capturing a husband. Otherwise anything goes. It is nothing out of the way to cheat at cards, for instance. It seems quite natural to Roderick, when he has got hold of £1,000 from somewhere, to buy himself a smart outfit of clothes and go to Bath posing as a rich man, in hopes of entrapping an heiress. When he is in France and out of a job, he decides to join the army, and as the French army happens to be the nearest one, he joins that, and fights against the British at the battle of Dettingen: he is nevertheless ready soon afterwards to fight a duel with a Frenchman who has insulted Britain.

Peregrine devotes himself for months at a time to the elaborate and horribly cruel practical jokes in which the eighteenth century delighted. When, for instance, an unfortunate English painter is thrown into the Bastille for some trifling offence and is about to be released, Peregrine and his friends, playing on his ignorance of the language, let him think that he has been sentenced to be broken on a wheel. A little later they tell him that this punishment has been commuted to castration, and then extract a last bit of fun out of his terrors by letting him think that he is escaping in disguise when he is merely being released from the prison in the normal way.

Why are these petty rogueries worth reading about? In the first place because they are funny. In the continental writers from whom Smollett derived there may be better things than the description of Peregrine Pickle's adventures on the Grand Tour, but there is nothing better of that particular kind in English. Secondly, by simply ruling out 'good' motives and showing no respect whatever for human dignity, Smollett often attains a truthfulness that more serious novelists have missed. He is willing to mention things which do happen in real life but are almost invariably kept out of fiction. Roderick Random, for instance, at one stage of his career, catches a venereal disease – the only English novel hero, I believe, to whom this has happened. And the fact that Smollett, in spite of his fairly enlightened views, takes patronage, official jobbery and general corruption for granted gives great historical interest to certain passages in his books.

Smollett had been for a while in the navy, and in *Roderick Random* we are given not only an unvarnished account of the Cartagena expedition, but an extraordinarily vivid and disgusting description of the inside of a warship, in those days a sort of floating compendium of disease, discomfort, tyranny and incompetence. The command of Roderick's ship is for a while given to a young man of family, a scented homosexual fop who has hardly seen a ship in his life, and who spends the whole voyage in his cabin to avoid contact with the vulgar sailormen, almost fainting when he smells tobacco. The scenes in the debtors' prison are even better. In the prisons of those days, a debtor who had no resources might actually starve to death unless he could keep alive by begging from more fortunate prisoners. One of Roderick's fellow prisoners is so reduced that he has no clothes at all and preserves decency as best he can by wearing a very long beard. Some of the prisoners, needless to say, are poets, and the book includes a self-contained story, 'Mr Melopoyn's Tragedy', which should make anyone who thinks aristocratic patronage a good basis for literature think twice.

Smollett's influence on subsequent English writers has not been as great as that of his contemporary, Fielding. Fielding deals in the same kind of boisterous adventure, but his sense of sin never quite leaves him. It is interesting, in *Joseph Andrews*, to watch Fielding start out with the intention of writing a pure farce, and then, in spite of himself as it were, begin punishing vice and rewarding virtue in the way that was to be customary in English novels until almost yesterday. Tom Jones would fit into a novel by Meredith, or for that matter by Ian Hay, whereas Peregrine Pickle seems to belong to a more European background. The writers nearest to Smollett are perhaps Surtees and Marryat, but when sexual frankness ceased to be possible, picaresque literature was robbed of perhaps half of its subject-matter. The eighteenth-century inn where it was almost abnormal to go into the right bedroom was a lost dominion.

In our own day various English writers – Evelyn Waugh, for instance, and Aldous Huxley in his early novels – drawing on other sources, have tried to revive the picaresque tradition. One has only to watch their eager efforts to be shocking, and their readiness to be shocked themselves – whereas Smollett was merely trying to be funny in what seemed to him the natural way – to see what an accumulation of pity, decency and public spirit lies between that age and ours.

Tribune, 22 September 1944

Review

The Vicar of Wakefield by Oliver Goldsmith

When Mark Twain said of *The Vicar of Wakefield*, 'Nothing could be funnier than its pathos, and nothing could be sadder than its humour', he was probably not exaggerating his own feelings very greatly. To a man of Mark Twain's generation it was natural that the elegance of the eighteenth century should seem frigid and ridiculous, just as it was natural that Dr Johnson should see nothing to admire in the Robin Hood ballads. *The Vicar of Wakefield*, now reprinted in Penguin Books in the English Classics series, is essentially a period piece, and its charm is about equalled by its absurdity. It is impossible to be moved by its story, which has none of the psychological realism that can be found in some eighteenth-century novels – for instance, *Amelia*. Its characters are sticks and its plot is somewhat less probable than those of the serial stories in *Peg's Paper*. But it remains extremely readable, and it has never been quite out of print in the 177 years since its first appearance. Like a Japanese woodcut, it is something perfectly executed after its own fashion, and at this date there is an historical interest in the remoteness of the standards of conduct which it is trying to uphold.

The Vicar of Wakefield is intended as a 'moral tale', a sermon in fiction form. Its theme is the familiar one, preached without much success by hundreds of writers from Horace to Thackeray, of the vanity of worldly ambitions and the pleasures of the simple life. Its hero, Dr Primrose (he tells his own story in the first person), is a clergyman in what used to be called 'easy circumstances', who temporarily loses his fortune and has to remove to another parish, where he supports himself by farming his own land. Here a whole series of disasters fall upon the family, traceable in every case to their having ambitions 'above their station' and trying to associate with the nobility instead of with the neighbouring farmers. The eldest daughter is seduced by a heartless rascal, the farm-house is burnt to the ground, the eldest son is arrested for manslaughter, Primrose himself is thrown into a debtors' prison, and various other calamities happen. In the end, of course, everything is put right in an outrageously improbable way, one detail after another clicking into place like the teeth of a zip-fastener. Primrose's fortune is restored, the seemingly seduced daughter turns out to be an 'honest woman' after all, the suitor of the second daughter, who has been posing as a poor man in order to try her affections, is discovered to be a wealthy nobleman, and so on and so forth. Virtue is rewarded and vice punished with relentless thoroughness. But the confusion in Goldsmith's mind between simple goodness and financial prudence gives the book, at this date, a strange moral atmosphere.

The main incidents are the various marriages, and the cold-blooded eighteenth-century attitude towards marriage is indicated on the first page when Dr Primrose remarks (Goldsmith probably does not intend this ironically): 'I had scarcely taken orders a year, before I began to think seriously of matrimony, and chose my wife, as she did her wedding gown, not for a fine glossy surface, but such qualities as would wear well.' But quite apart from this notion of choosing a wife as one might choose a length of cloth, there is the fact that getting married is inextricably mixed up with the idea of making a good financial bargain. A thumping dowry or a secure settlement is the first consideration, and the most passionate love match is promptly called off if the expected cash is not forthcoming. But together with this mercenary outlook there goes a superstitious regard for the sanctity of marriage which makes the most dramatic episode in the book ridiculous and even slightly disgusting.

Olivia is seduced by a Mr Thornhill, a wealthy young squire who has dazzled the Primrose family with his fashionable clothes and London manners. He is represented as a complete scoundrel, the 'betrayer', as it was called, of innumerable women, and with every possible vice, even including physical cowardice. To entrap Olivia he uses the favourite eighteenth-century device of a false marriage. A marriage licence is forged, somebody impersonates a priest, and the girl can then be 'ruined' under the delusion that she is married. Today it seems almost incredible that anyone should go to such lengths, but stratagems like this are inevitable in a society where technical chastity is highly valued and a woman has in effect no profession except marriage. In such a society there is an endless struggle between the sexes – a struggle which from the woman's point of view resembles an egg-and-spoon race, and from the man's a game of ninepins. Having been deceived in this manner, Olivia is now finished for life. She herself is made to express the current outlook by singing the justly famous lyric which Goldsmith throws into the tale:

When lovely woman stoops to folly,
And finds too late that men betray,
What charm can soothe her melancholy?
What art can wash her guilt away?

The only art her guilt to cover,
To hide her shame from every eye,
To give repentance to her lover,
And wring his bosom, is – to die.

Olivia indeed ought to die, and does actually begin to die – of sheer grief, after the manner of novel heroines. But here comes the *dénouement*, the great stroke of fortune that puts everything right. It turns out that Olivia was *not* seduced; she was legally married! Mr Thornhill has been in the habit of 'marrying' women with a false priest and a false licence, but on this occasion a confederate of his, for purposes of his own, has deceived him by bringing a genuine licence and a real priest in holy orders. So the marriage was valid after all! And at this glorious news 'a burst of pleasure seemed to fill the whole apartment ... Happiness was expanded upon every face, and even Olivia's cheeks seemed flushed with pleasure. To be thus restored to reputation and fortune at once was a rapture sufficient to stop the progress of decay and restore former health and vivacity.'

When Olivia was believed to have 'lost her virtue' she had lost all reason for living, but when it is discovered that she is tied for life to a worthless scoundrel all is well. Goldsmith does not make the ending quite so ridiculous as he might, for it is explained that Olivia continues to live apart from her husband. But she has the all-important wedding-ring, and a comfortable settlement into the bargain. Thornhill's rich uncle punishes him by depriving him of his fortune and bestowing part of it on Olivia. We are never indeed allowed quite to forget the connection between cash and virtue. Olivia sees herself 'restored to reputation *and fortune at once*', while Thornhill sees 'a gulf of infamy *and want*' opening before him.

Except for a scene or two in the debtors' prison and a few minor adventures at horse fairs and on muddy country roads, there is no realistic detail in *The Vicar of Wakefield*. The dialogue is quite exceptionally improbable. But the main theme – the hollowness of fashionable life and the superiority of country pleasures and family affection – is not so false as the absurd incidents which are meant to illustrate it make it appear. In inveighing against social ambition, against absentee landlords, against fine clothes, gambling, duelling, cosmetics and urban raffishness generally, Goldsmith is attacking a real tendency of his time, which Swift and Fielding had also denounced after their own fashion.

A phenomenon he is very much aware of is the growth of a new moneyed class with no sense of responsibility. Thanks to the expansion of foreign trade and wealth accumulated in the capital, the aristocracy were ceasing to be rustics. England was becoming more and more of an oligarchy, and the life of the countryside was broken up by the enclosure of the common lands and the magnetic pull of London. The peasants were proletarianized, the petty gentry were corrupted. Goldsmith himself described the process in the often-quoted lines from 'The Deserted Village':

Ill fares the land, to hastening ills a prey,
Where wealth accumulates and men decay;
Princes and lords may flourish or may fade,
A breath can make them, as a breath has made;
But a bold peasantry, their country's pride,
When once destroyed, can never be supplied.

Thornhill stands for the new kind of rich man, the Whig aristocrat; the Primroses, who make their own gooseberry wine and even in the days of their wealth have hardly been ten miles from home, stand for the old type of yeoman farmer or small landlord.

In praising country life, Goldsmith was probably praising something that he did not know much about. His descriptions of country scenes have an unreal, idyllic atmosphere, and the Primroses are not shown as doing much work on their farm. More often they are sitting under some shady tree, reciting ballads and listening to the blackbirds – pastimes that a practical farmer would seldom have time for. Nor do we hear much of Dr Primrose's ministrations as a clergyman: indeed, he only seems to remember at intervals that he is in orders. But the general moral of the book is clear enough, and thrust rather irrelevantly into one chapter there is a long political discourse against oligarchy and the accumulation of capital. Goldsmith's conclusion – no doubt it was a common Tory theory at the time – is that the only defence against oligarchy is a strong monarchy. Dr Primrose's son George, returning from travels in Europe, is made to come to the same conclusion: 'I found that monarchy was the best government for the poor to live in, and commonwealths for the rich.' Dictatorship is defended on the same grounds in our own day, and it is an instance of the way in which the same political ideas come up again and again in slightly different forms that George continues: 'I found that riches in general were in every country another name for freedom; and that no man is so fond of liberty himself as not to be desirous of subjecting the will of some individuals in society to his own.'

But though there is some serious social criticism buried under its artificialities, it is not there that the enduring charm of *The Vicar of Wakefield* lies. The charm is in its manner – in the story, which for all its absurdity is beautifully put together, in the simple and yet elegant language, in the poems that are thrown in here and there, and in certain minor incidents, such as the well-known story of Moses and the green spectacles. Most people who read at all have read this book once, and it repays a second reading. It is one of those books which you can enjoy in one way as a child and in another as an adult, and which do not seem any the worse because you are frequently inclined to laugh in the wrong places.

Tribune, 10 November 1944

Funny, But Not Vulgar

The great age of English humorous writing – not witty and not satirical, but simply humorous – was the first three-quarters of the nineteenth century.

Within that period lie Dickens's enormous output of comic writings, Thackeray's brilliant burlesques and short stories, such as 'The Fatal Boots' and 'A Little Dinner at Timmins's', Surtees's *Handley Cross*, Lewis Carroll's *Alice in Wonderland*, Douglas Jerrold's *Mrs Caudle's Curtain Lectures*, and a considerable body of humorous verse by R. H. Barham, Thomas Hood, Edward Lear, Arthur Hugh Clough, Charles Stuart Calverley and others. Two other comic masterpieces, F. Anstey's *Vice Versa* and the two Grossmiths' *Diary of a Nobody*, lie only just outside the period I have named. And, at any rate until 1860 or thereabouts, there was still such a thing as comic draughtsmanship, witness Cruikshank's illustrations to Dickens, Leech's illustrations to Surtees, and even Thackeray's illustrations of his own work.

I do not want to exaggerate by suggesting that, within our own century, England has produced no humorous writing of any value. There have been, for instance, Barry Pain, W. W. Jacobs, Stephen Leacock, P. G. Wodehouse, H. G. Wells in his lighter moments, Evelyn Waugh, and – a satirist rather than a humorist – Hilaire Belloc. Still, we have not only produced no laugh-getter of anything like the stature of *Pickwick Papers*, but, what is probably more significant, there is not and has not been for decades past, any such thing as a first-rate humorous periodical. The usual charge against *Punch*, that it 'isn't what it was', is perhaps unjustified at this moment, since *Punch* is somewhat funnier than it was ten years ago: but it is also very much *less* funny than it was ninety years ago.

And comic verse has lost all its vitality – there has been no English light verse of any value within this century, except Mr Belloc's, and a poem or two by Chesterton – while a drawing that is funny in its own right, and not merely because of the joke it illustrates, is a great rarity.

All this is generally admitted. If you want a laugh you are likelier to go to a music hall or a Disney film, or switch on Tommy Handley, or buy a few of Donald McGill's postcards, than to resort to a book or a periodical. It is generally recognized, too, that American comic writers and illustrators are superior to our own. At present we have nobody to set against either James Thurber or Damon Runyon.

We do not know with certainty how laughter originated or what biological purpose it serves, but we do know, in broad terms, what causes laughter.

A thing is funny when – in some way that is not actually offensive or frightening – it upsets the established order. Every joke is a tiny revolution. If you had to define humour in a single phrase, you might define it as dignity sitting on a tin-tack. Whatever destroys dignity, and brings down the mighty from their seats, preferably with a bump, is funny. And the bigger the fall, the bigger the joke. It would be better fun to throw a custard pie at a bishop than at a curate. With this general principle in mind, one can, I think, begin to see what has been wrong with English comic writing during the present century.

Nearly all English humorists today are too genteel, too kind-hearted and too consciously lowbrow. P. G. Wodehouse's novels, or A. P. Herbert's verses, seem always to be aimed at prosperous stockbrokers whiling away an odd half hour in the lounge of some suburban golf course. They and all their kind are dominated by an anxiety not to stir up mud, either moral, religious, political or intellectual. It is no accident that most of the best comic writers of our time – Belloc, Chesterton, 'Timothy Shy' and the recent 'Beachcomber' – have been Catholic apologists; that is, people with a serious purpose and a noticeable willingness to hit below the belt. The silly-ass tradition in modern English humour, the avoidance of brutality and horror of intelligence, is summed up in the phrase *funny without being vulgar*. 'Vulgar' in this context usually means 'obscene', and it can be admitted at once that the best jokes are not necessarily dirty ones. Edward Lear and Lewis Carroll, for instance, never made jokes of that description, and Dickens and Thackeray very rarely.

On the whole, the early Victorian writers avoided sex jokes, though a few, for instance Surtees, Marryat and Barham, retained traces of eighteenth-century coarseness. But the point is that the modern emphasis on what is called 'clean fun' is really the symptom of a general unwillingness to touch upon any serious or controversial subject. Obscenity is, after all, a kind of subversiveness. Chaucer's 'Miller's Tale' is a rebellion in the moral sphere, as *Gulliver's Travels* is a rebellion in the political sphere. The truth is that you cannot be memorably funny without *at some point* raising topics which the rich, the powerful and the complacent would prefer to see left alone.

I named above some of the best comic writers of the nineteenth century, but the case becomes much stronger if one draws in the English humorists of earlier ages – for instance, Chaucer, Shakespeare, Swift and the picaresque novelists, Smollett, Fielding and Sterne. It becomes stronger again if one considers foreign writers, both ancient and modern – for example, Aristophanes, Voltaire, Rabelais, Boccaccio and Cervantes. All of these writers are remarkable for their brutality and coarseness. People are tossed in blankets, they fall through cucumber frames, they are hidden in washing baskets, they rob, lie, swindle, and are caught out in every conceivable humiliating situation. And all great humorous writers show a willingness to attack the beliefs and the virtues on which society necessarily rests. Boccaccio treats Hell and Purgatory as a ridiculous fable, Swift jeers at the very conception of human dignity, Shakespeare makes Falstaff deliver a speech in favour of cowardice in the middle of a battle. As for the sanctity of marriage, it was the principal subject of humour in Christian society for the better part of a thousand years.

All this is not to say that humour is, of its nature, immoral or antisocial. A joke is at most a temporary rebellion against virtue, and its aim is not to degrade the human being but to remind him that he is already degraded. A willingness to make extremely obscene jokes can co-exist with very strict moral standards, as in Shakespeare. Some comic writers, like Dickens, have a direct political purpose, others, like Chaucer or Rabelais, accept the corruption of society as something inevitable; but no comic writer of any stature has ever suggested that society is *good.*

Humour is the debunking of humanity, and nothing is funny except in relation to human beings. Animals, for instance, are only funny because they are caricatures of ourselves. A lump of stone could not of itself be funny; but it can become funny if it hits a human being in the eye, or if it is carved into human likeness.

However, there are subtler methods of debunking than throwing custard pies. There is also the humour of pure fantasy, which assaults man's notion of himself as not only a dignified but a rational being. Lewis Carroll's humour consists essentially in making fun of logic, and Edward Lear's in a sort of poltergeist interference with common sense. When the Red Queen remarks, '*I've* seen hills compared with which you'd call that one a valley', she is in her way attacking the bases of society as violently as Swift or Voltaire. Comic verse, as in Lear's poem 'The Courtship of the Yonghy-Bonghy-Bò', often depends on building up a fantastic universe which is just similar enough to the real universe to rob it of its dignity. But more often it depends on anticlimax – that is, on starting out with a high-flown language and then suddenly coming down with a bump. For instance, Calverley's lines:

Once, a happy child, I carolled
On green lawns the whole day through,
Not unpleasingly apparelled
In a tightish suit of blue,

in which the first two lines would give the impression that this is going to be a sentimental poem about the beauties of childhood. Or Mr Belloc's various invocations to Africa in *The Modern Traveller*:

O Africa, mysterious land,
Surrounded by a lot of sand,
And full of grass and trees . . .
Far land of Ophir, mined for gold
By lordly Solomon of old
Who, sailing northward to Perim,
Took all the gold away with him
And left a lot of holes, etc.

Bret Harte's sequel to 'Maud Muller', with such couplets as:

But the very day that they were mated
Maud's brother Bob was intoxicated

plays essentially the same trick, and so in a different way do Voltaire's mock epic, *La Pucelle*, and many passages in Byron.

English light verse in the present century – witness the work of Owen Seaman, Harry Graham, A. P. Herbert, A. A. Milne and others – has mostly been poor stuff, lacking not only in fancifulness but in intellectuality. Its authors are too anxious not to be highbrows – even, though they are writing in verse, not to be poets. Early-Victorian light verse is generally haunted by the ghost of poetry; it is often extremely skilful as verse, and it is sometimes allusive and 'difficult'. When Barham wrote:

The Callipyge's injured behind,
Bloudie Jack!
The de Medici's injured before;
And the Anadyomene's injured in so many
Places, I think there's a score,
If not more,
Of her fingers and toes on the floor.

he was performing a feat of sheer virtuosity which the most serious poet would respect. Or, to quote Calverley again, in his 'Ode to Tobacco':

Thou, who when fears attack,
Bidst them avaunt, and Black
Care, at the horseman's back
Perching, unseatest;
Sweet when the morn is grey,
Sweet when they've cleared away
Lunch, and at close of day
Possibly sweetest!

Calverley is not afraid, it will be seen, to put a tax on his reader's attention and to drag in a recondite Latin allusion. He is not writing for lowbrows, and – particularly in his 'Ode to Beer' – he can achieve magnificent anticlimaxes because he is willing to sail close to true poetry and to assume considerable knowledge in his readers.

It would seem that you *cannot* be funny without being vulgar – that is, vulgar by the standards of the people at whom English humorous writing in our own day seems mostly to be aimed. For it is not only sex that is 'vulgar'. So are death, childbirth and poverty, the other three subjects upon which the best music-hall humour turns. And respect for the intellect and strong political feeling, if not actually vulgar, are looked upon as being in doubtful taste. You cannot be really funny if your main aim is to flatter the comfortable classes: it means leaving out too much. To be funny, indeed, you have got to be serious. *Punch*, for at least forty years past, has given the impression of trying not so much to amuse as to reassure. Its implied message is that all is for the best and nothing will ever really change.

It was by no means with that creed that it started out.

Written [December 1944]

Oysters and Brown Stout

G. K. Chesterton said once that every novelist writes one book whose title seems to be a summing-up of his attitude to life. He instances, for Dickens, *Great Expectations*, and for Scott, *Tales of a Grandfather*.

What title would one choose as especially representative of Thackeray? The obvious one is *Vanity Fair*, but I believe that if one looked more closely one would choose either *Christmas Books, Burlesques*, or *A Book of Snobs* – at any rate, one would choose the title of one of the collections of scraps which Thackeray had previously contributed to *Punch* and other magazines. Not only was he by nature a burlesque writer, but he was primarily a journalist, a writer of fragments, and his most characteristic work is not fully separable from the illustrations. Some of the best of these are by Cruikshank, but Thackeray was also a brilliant comic draughtsman himself, and in some of his very short sketches the picture and the letter-press belong organically together. All that is best in his full-length novels seems to have grown out of his contributions to *Punch*, and even *Vanity Fair* has a fragmentary quality that makes it possible to begin reading in it at almost any place, without looking back to see what has happened earlier.

At this date some of his major works – for instance, *Esmond* or *The Virginians* – are barely readable, and only once, in a rather short book, *A Shabby Genteel Story*, did he write what we should now regard as a serious novel. Thackeray's two main themes are snobbishness and extravagance, but he is at his best when he handles them in the comic vein, because – unlike Dickens, for instance – he has very little social insight and not even a very clear moral code. *Vanity Fair*, it is true, is a valuable social document as well as being an extremely readable and amusing book. It records, with remarkable fidelity so far as physical detail goes, the ghastly social competition of the early nineteenth century, when an aristocracy which could no longer pay its way was still the arbiter of fashion and of behaviour. In *Vanity Fair*, and indeed throughout Thackeray's writings, it is almost exceptional to find anyone living inside his income.

To live in a house which is too big for you, to engage servants whom you cannot pay, to ruin yourself by giving pretentious dinner parties with hired footmen, to bilk your tradesmen, to overdraw your banking account, to live permanently in the clutches of money-lenders – this is almost the norm of human behaviour. It is taken for granted that anyone who is not halfway to being a saint will ape the aristocracy if possible. The desire for expensive clothes, gilded carriages and hordes of liveried servants is assumed to be a natural instinct, like the desire for food and drink. And the people Thackeray is best able to describe are those who are living the fashionable life upon no income whatever – people like Becky Sharp and Rawdon Crawley in *Vanity Fair*, or the innumerable seedy adventurers, Major Loder, Captain Rook, Captain Costigan, Mr Deuceace, whose life is an endless to-and-fro between the card-table and the sponging-house.

So far as it goes, Thackeray's picture of society is probably true. The types he depicts, the mortgage-ridden aristocrats, the brandy-drinking army officers, the elderly bucks with their stays and their dyed whiskers, the match-making mothers, the vulgar City magnates, did exist. But he is observing chiefly externals. In spite of endless musings on the French Revolution, a subject that fascinated him, he does not see that the structure of society is altering: he sees the nation-wide phenomenon of snobbery and extravagance, without seeing its deeper causes. Moreover, unlike Dickens, he does not see that the social struggle is three-sided: his sympathies hardly extend to the working class, whom he is conscious of chiefly as servants. Nor is he ever certain where he himself stands. He cannot make up his mind whether the raffish upper class or the money-grubbing middle class is more objectionable. Not having any definite social, political or, probably, religious convictions, he can hardly imagine any virtues except simplicity, courage and, in the case of women, 'purity'. (Thackeray's 'good' women, incidentally, are completely intolerable.) The implied moral of both *Vanity Fair* and *Pendennis* is the rather empty one: 'Don't be selfish, don't be worldly, don't live outside your income.' And *A Shabby Genteel Story* says the same thing in a more delicate way.

But Thackeray's narrow intellectual range is actually an advantage to him when he abandons the attempt to portray real human beings. A thing that is very striking is the vitality of his *minor* writings, even of things that he himself must have thought of as purely ephemeral. If you dip almost anywhere in his collected works – even in his book reviews, for instance – you come upon the characteristic flavour. Partly it is the atmosphere of surfeit which belongs to the early nineteenth century, an atmosphere compounded of oysters, brown stout, brandy and water, turtle soup, roast sirloin, haunch of venison, Madeira and cigar smoke, which Thackeray is well able to convey because he has a good grip on physical detail and is extremely interested in food.

He writes about food perhaps more often even than Dickens, and more accurately. His account of his dinners in Paris – not expensive dinners, either – in 'Memorials of Gormandizing' is fascinating reading. 'The Ballad of the Bouillabaisse' is one of the best poems of that kind in English. But the characteristic flavour of Thackeray is the flavour of burlesque, of a world where no one is good and nothing is serious. It pervades all the best passages in his novels, and it reaches its perfection in short sketches and stories like 'Dr Birch and his Young Friends', *The Rose and the Ring*, 'The Fatal Boots' and 'A Little Dinner at Timmins's'.

The Rose and the Ring is a sort of charade, similar in spirit to *The Ingoldsby Legends*, 'A Little Dinner at Timmins's' is a relatively naturalistic story, and 'The Fatal Boots' is about midway between the two. But in all these and similar pieces Thackeray has got away from the difficulty that besets most novelists and has never been solved by any characteristically English novelist – the difficulty of combining characters who are meant to be real and exist 'in the round' with mere figures of fun.

English writers from Chaucer onwards have found it very difficult to resist burlesque, but as soon as burlesque enters the reality of the story suffers. Fielding, Dickens, Trollope, Wells, even Joyce, have all stumbled over this problem. Thackeray, in the best of his short pieces, solves it by making *all* his characters into caricatures. There is no question of the hero of 'The Fatal Boots' existing 'in the round'. He is as flat as an ikon. In 'A Little Dinner at Timmins's' – one of the best comic short stories ever written, though it is seldom reprinted – Thackeray is really doing the same thing as he did in *Vanity Fair*, but without the complicating factor of having to simulate real life and introduce disinterested motives. It is a simple little story, exquisitely told and rising gradually to a sort of crescendo which stops at exactly the right moment. A lawyer who has received an unusually large fee decides to celebrate it by giving a dinner party. He is at once led into much greater expense than he can afford, and there follows a series of disasters which leave him heavily in debt, with his friends alienated and his mother-in-law permanently installed in his home. From start to finish no one has had anything from the dinner party except misery. And when, at the end, Thackeray remarks, 'Why, in fact, did the Timminses give that party at all?' one feels the folly of social ambition has been more conclusively demonstrated than it is by *Vanity Fair*. This is the kind of thing that Thackeray could do perfectly, and it is the recurrence of farcical incidents like this, rather than their central story, that makes the longer novels worth reading.

Tribune, 22 December 1944

Antisemitism in Britain

There are about 400,000 known Jews in Britain, and in addition some thousands or, at most, scores of thousands of Jewish refugees who have entered the country from 1934 onwards. The Jewish population is almost entirely concentrated in half a dozen big towns and is mostly employed in the food, clothing and furniture trades. A few of the big monopolies, such as the ICI, one or two leading newspapers and at least one big chain of department stores are Jewish-owned or partly Jewish-owned, but it would be very far from the truth to say that British business life is dominated by Jews. The Jews seem, on the contrary, to have failed to keep up with the modern tendency towards big amalgamations and to have remained fixed in those trades which are necessarily carried out on a small scale and by old-fashioned methods.

I start off with these background facts, which are already known to any well-informed person, in order to emphasize that there is no real Jewish 'problem' in England. The Jews are not numerous or powerful enough, and it is only in what are loosely called 'intellectual circles' that they have any noticeable influence. Yet it is generally admitted that antisemitism is on the increase, that it has been greatly exacerbated by the war, and that humane and enlightened people are not immune to it. It does not take violent forms (English people are almost invariably gentle and law-abiding), but it is ill-natured enough, and in favourable circumstances it could have political results. Here are some samples of antisemitic remarks that have been made to me during the past year or two:

> Middle-aged office employee: 'I generally come to work by bus. It takes longer, but I don't care about using the Underground from Golders Green nowadays. There's too many of the Chosen Race travelling on that line.'

> Tobacconist (woman): 'No, I've got no matches for you. I should try the lady down the street. *She's* always got matches. One of the Chosen Race, you see.'

Young intellectual, Communist or near-Communist: 'No, I do *not* like Jews. I've never made any secret of that. I can't stick them. Mind you, I'm not antisemitic, of course.'

Middle-class woman: 'Well, no one could call me antisemitic, but I do think the way these Jews behave is too absolutely stinking. The way they push their way to the head of queues, and so on. They're so abominably selfish. I think they're responsible for a lot of what happens to them.'

Milk roundsman: 'A Jew don't do no work, not the same as what an Englishman does. 'E's too clever. We work with this 'ere' (flexes his biceps). 'They work with that there' (taps his forehead).

Chartered accountant, intelligent, left-wing in an undirected way: 'These bloody Yids are all pro-German. They'd change sides tomorrow if the Nazis got here. I see a lot of them in my business. They admire Hitler at the bottom of their hearts. They'll always suck up to anyone who kicks them.'

Intelligent woman, on being offered a book dealing with antisemitism and German atrocities: 'Don't show it me, *please* don't show it to me. It'll only make me hate the Jews more than ever.'

I could fill pages with similar remarks, but these will do to go on with. Two facts emerge from them. One – which is very important and which I must return to in a moment – is that above a certain intellectual level people are ashamed of being antisemitic and are careful to draw a distinction between 'antisemitism' and 'disliking Jews'. The other is that antisemitism is an irrational thing. The Jews are accused of specific offences (for instance, bad behaviour in food queues) which the person speaking feels strongly about, but it is obvious that these accusations merely rationalize some deep-rooted prejudice. To attempt to counter them with facts and statistics is useless, and may sometimes be worse than useless. As the last of the above-quoted remarks shows, people can remain antisemitic, or at least anti-Jewish, while being fully aware that their outlook is indefensible. If you dislike somebody, you dislike him and there is an end of it: your feelings are not made any better by a recital of his virtues.

It so happens that the war has encouraged the growth of antisemitism and even, in the eyes of many ordinary people, given some justification for it. To begin with, the Jews are one people of whom it can be said with complete certainty that they will benefit by an Allied victory. Consequently the theory that 'this is a Jewish war' has a certain plausibility, all the more so because the Jewish war effort seldom gets its fair share of recognition. The British Empire is a huge heterogeneous organization held together largely by mutual consent, and it is often necessary to flatter the less reliable elements at the expense of the more loyal ones. To publicize the exploits of Jewish soldiers, or even to admit the existence of a considerable Jewish army in the Middle East, rouses hostility in South Africa, the Arab countries and elsewhere: it is easier to ignore the whole subject and allow the man in the street to go on thinking that Jews are exceptionally clever at dodging military service. Then again, Jews are to be found in exactly those trades which are bound to incur unpopularity with the civilian public in war-time. Jews are mostly concerned with selling food, clothes, furniture and tobacco – exactly the commodities of which there is a chronic shortage, with consequent overcharging, black-marketing and favouritism. And again, the common charge that Jews behave in an exceptionally cowardly way during air raids was given a certain amount of colour by the big raids of 1940. As it happened, the Jewish quarter of Whitechapel was one of the first areas to be heavily blitzed, with the natural result that swarms of Jewish refugees distributed themselves all over London. If one judged merely from these war-time phenomena, it would be easy to imagine that antisemitism is a quasi-rational thing, founded on mistaken premises. And naturally the antisemite thinks of himself as a reasonable being. Whenever I have touched on this subject in a newspaper article, I have always had a considerable 'come-back', and invariably some of the letters are from well-balanced, middling people – doctors, for example – with no apparent economic grievance. These people always say (as Hitler says in *Mein Kampf*) that they started out with no anti-Jewish prejudice but were driven into their present position by mere observation of the facts. Yet one of the marks of antisemitism is an ability to believe stories that could not possibly be true. One could see a good example of this in the strange accident that occurred in London in 1942, when a crowd, frightened by a bomb-burst nearby, fled into the mouth of an Underground station, with the result that something over a hundred people were crushed to death. The very same day it was repeated all over London that 'the Jews were responsible'. Clearly, if people will believe this kind of thing, one will not get much further by arguing with them. The only useful approach is to discover *why* they can swallow absurdities on one particular subject while remaining sane on others.

But now let me come back to that point I mentioned earlier – that there is widespread awareness of the prevalence of antisemitic feeling, and unwillingness to admit sharing it. Among educated people, antisemitism is held to be an unforgivable sin and in a quite different category from other kinds of racial prejudice. People will go to remarkable lengths to demonstrate that they are *not* antisemitic. Thus, in 1943 an intercession service on behalf of the Polish Jews was held in a synagogue in St John's Wood. The local authorities declared themselves anxious to participate in it, and the service was attended by the mayor of the borough in his robes and chain, by representatives of all the churches, and by detachments of RAF, Home Guards, nurses, Boy Scouts and what not. On the surface it was a touching demonstration of solidarity with the suffering Jews. But it was essentially a *conscious* effort to behave decently by people whose subjective feelings must in many cases have been very different. That quarter of London is partly Jewish, antisemitism is rife there, and, as I well knew, some of the men sitting round me in the synagogue were tinged by it. Indeed, the commander of my own platoon of Home Guards, who had been especially keen beforehand that we should 'make a good show' at the intercession service, was an ex-member of Mosley's Blackshirts. While this division of feeling exists, tolerance of mass violence against Jews, or, what is more important, antisemitic legislation, are not possible in England. It is not at present possible, indeed, that antisemitism should *become respectable*. But this is less of an advantage than it might appear.

One effect of the persecutions in Germany has been to prevent antisemitism from being seriously studied. In England a brief inadequate survey was made by Mass Observation a year or two ago, but if there has been any other investigation of the subject, then its findings have been kept strictly secret. At the same time there has been conscious suppression, by all thoughtful people, of anything likely to wound Jewish susceptibilities. After 1934 the 'Jew joke' disappeared as though by magic from postcards, periodicals and the music-hall stage, and to put an unsympathetic Jewish character into a novel or short story came to be regarded as antisemitism. On the Palestine issue, too, it was *de rigueur* among enlightened people to accept the Jewish case as proved and avoid examining the claims of the Arabs – a decision which might be correct on its own merits, but which was adopted primarily because the Jews were in trouble and it was felt that one must not criticize them. Thanks to Hitler, therefore, you had a situation in which the press was in effect censored in favour of the Jews while in private antisemitism was on the up-grade, even, to some extent, among sensitive and intelligent people. This was particularly noticeable in 1940 at the time of the internment of the refugees. Naturally, every thinking person felt that it was his duty to protest against the wholesale locking-up of unfortunate foreigners who for the most part were only in England because they were opponents of Hitler. Privately, however, one heard very different sentiments expressed. A minority of the refugees behaved in an exceedingly tactless way, and the feeling against them necessarily had an antisemitic undercurrent, since they were largely Jews. A very eminent figure in the Labour Party – I won't name him, but he is one of the most respected people in England – said to me quite violently: 'We never asked these people to come to this country. If they choose to come here, let them take the consequences.' Yet this man would as a matter of course have associated himself with any kind of petition or manifesto against the internment of aliens. This feeling that antisemitism is something sinful and disgraceful, something that a civilized person does not suffer from, is unfavourable to a scientific approach, and indeed many people will admit that they are frightened of probing too deeply into the subject. They are frightened, that is to say, of discovering not only that antisemitism is spreading, but that they themselves are infected by it.

To see this in perspective one must look back a few decades, to the days when Hitler was an out-of-work house-painter whom nobody had heard of. One would then find that though antisemitism is sufficiently in evidence now, it is probably *less* prevalent in England than it was thirty years ago. It is true that antisemitism as a fully thought-out racial or religious doctrine has never flourished in England. There has never been much feeling against intermarriage, or against Jews taking a prominent part in public life. Nevertheless, thirty years ago it was accepted more or less as a law of nature that a Jew was a figure of fun and – though superior in intelligence – slightly deficient in 'character'. In theory a Jew suffered from no legal disabilities, but in effect he was debarred from certain professions. He would probably not have been accepted as an officer in the navy, for instance, nor in what is called a 'smart' regiment in the army. A Jewish boy at a public school almost invariably had a bad time. He could, of course, live down his Jewishness if he was exceptionally charming or athletic, but it was an initial disability comparable to a stammer or a birthmark. Wealthy Jews tended to disguise themselves under aristocratic English or Scottish names, and to the average person it seemed quite natural that they should do this, just as it seems natural for a criminal to change his identity if possible. About twenty years ago, in Rangoon, I was getting into a taxi with a friend when a small ragged boy of fair complexion rushed up to us and began a complicated story about having arrived from Colombo on a ship and wanting money to get back. His manner and appearance were difficult to 'place', and I said to him:

'You speak very good English. What nationality are you?'

He answered eagerly in his chi-chi accent: 'I am a *Joo*, sir!'

And I remember turning to my companion and saying, only partly in joke, 'He admits it openly.' All the Jews I had known till then were people who were ashamed of being Jews, or at any rate preferred not to talk about their ancestry, and if forced to do so tended to use the word 'Hebrew'.

The working-class attitude was no better. The Jew who grew up in Whitechapel took it for granted that he would be assaulted, or at least hooted at, if he ventured into one of the Christian slums nearby, and the 'Jew joke' of the music halls and the comic papers was almost consistently ill-natured.[1] There was also literary Jew-baiting, which in the hands of Belloc, Chesterton and their followers reached an almost continental level of scurrility. Non-Catholic writers were sometimes guilty of the same thing in a milder form. There has been a perceptible antisemitic strain in English literature from Chaucer onwards, and without even getting up from this table to consult a book I can think of passages which *if written now* would be stigmatized as antisemitism, in the works of Shakespeare, Smollett, Thackeray, Bernard Shaw, H. G. Wells, T. S. Eliot, Aldous Huxley and various others. Offhand, the only English writers I can think of who, before the days of Hitler, made a definite effort to stick up for Jews are Dickens and Charles Reade. And however little the average intellectual may have agreed with the opinions of Belloc and Chesterton, he did not acutely disapprove of them. Chesterton's endless tirades against Jews, which he thrust into stories and essays upon the flimsiest pretexts, never got him into trouble – indeed Chesterton was one of the most generally respected figures in English literary life. Anyone who wrote in that strain *now* would bring down a storm of abuse upon himself, or more probably would find it impossible to get his writings published.

If, as I suggest, prejudice against Jews has always been pretty widespread in England, there is no reason to think that Hitler has genuinely diminished it. He has merely caused a sharp division between the politically conscious person who realizes that this is not a time to throw stones at the Jews, and the unconscious person whose native antisemitism is increased by the nervous strain of the war. One can assume, therefore, that many people who would perish rather than admit to antisemitic feelings are secretly prone to them. I have already indicated that I believe antisemitism to be essentially a neurosis, but of course it has its rationalizations, which are sincerely believed in and are partly true. The rationalization put forward by the common man is that the

[1] It is interesting to compare the 'Jew joke' with that other stand-by of the music halls, the 'Scotch joke', which superficially it resembles. Occasionally a story is told (e.g. the Jew and the Scotsman who went into a pub together and both died of thirst) which puts both races on an equality, but in general the Jew is credited *merely* with cunning and avarice while the Scotsman is credited with physical hardihood as well. This is seen, for example, in the story of the Jew and the Scotsman who go together to a meeting which has been advertised as free. Unexpectedly there is a collection, and to avoid this the Jew faints and the Scotsman carries him out. Here the Scotsman performs the athletic feat of carrying the other. It would seem vaguely wrong if it were the other way about. [Author's footnote.]

Jew is an exploiter. The partial justification for this is that the Jew, in England, is generally a small businessman – that is to say a person whose depredations are more obvious and intelligible than those of, say, a bank or an insurance company. Higher up the intellectual scale, antisemitism is rationalized by saying that the Jew is a person who spreads disaffection and weakens national morale. Again there is some superficial justification for this. During the past twenty-five years the activities of what are called 'intellectuals' have been largely mischievous. I do not think it an exaggeration to say that if the 'intellectuals' had done their work a little more thoroughly, Britain would have surrendered in 1940. But the disaffected intelligentsia inevitably included a large number of Jews. With some plausibility it can be said that the Jews are the enemies of our native culture and our national morale. Carefully examined, the claim is seen to be nonsense, but there are always a few prominent individuals who can be cited in support of it. During the past few years there has been what amounts to a counter-attack against the rather shallow Leftism which was fashionable in the previous decade and which was exemplified by such organizations as the Left Book Club. This counter-attack (see for instance such books as Arnold Lunn's *The Good Gorilla* or Evelyn Waugh's *Put Out More Flags*) has an antisemitic strain, and it would probably be more marked if the subject were not so obviously dangerous. It so happens that for some decades past Britain has had no intelligentsia worth bothering about. But British nationalism, i.e. nationalism of an intellectual kind, may revive, and probably will revive if Britain comes out of the present war greatly weakened. The young intellectuals of 1950 may be as naively patriotic as those of 1914. In that case the kind of antisemitism which flourished among the anti-Dreyfusards in France, and which Chesterton and Belloc tried to import into this country, might get a foothold.

I have no hard-and-fast theory about the origins of antisemitism. The two current explanations, that it is due to economic causes, or on the other hand, that it is a legacy from the Middle Ages, seem to me unsatisfactory, though I admit that if one combines them they can be made to cover the facts. All I would say with confidence is that antisemitism is part of the larger problem of nationalism, which has not yet been seriously examined, and that the Jew is evidently a scapegoat, though *for what* he is a scapegoat we do not yet know. In this essay I have relied almost entirely on my own limited experience, and perhaps every one of my conclusions would be negatived by other observers. The fact is that there are almost no data on this subject. But for what they are worth I will summarize my opinions. Boiled down, they amount to this:

There is more antisemitism in England than we care to admit, and the war has accentuated it, but it is not certain that it is on the increase if one thinks in terms of decades rather than years.

It does not at present lead to open persecution, but it has the effect of making people callous to the sufferings of Jews in other countries.

It is at bottom quite irrational and will not yield to argument.

The persecutions in Germany have caused much concealment of antisemitic feeling and thus obscured the whole picture.

The subject needs serious investigation.

Only the last point is worth expanding. To study any subject scientifically one needs a detached attitude, which is obviously harder when one's own interests or emotions are involved. Plenty of people who are quite capable of being objective about sea urchins, say, or the square root of 2, become schizophrenic if they have to think about the sources of their own income. What vitiates nearly all that is written about antisemitism is the assumption in the writer's mind that *he himself* is immune to it. 'Since I know that antisemitism is irrational,' he argues, 'it follows that I do not share it.' He thus fails to start his investigation in the one place where he could get hold of some reliable evidence – that is, in his own mind.

It seems to me a safe assumption that the disease loosely called nationalism is now almost universal. Antisemitism is only one manifestation of nationalism, and not everyone will have the disease in that particular form. A Jew, for example, would not be antisemitic: but then many Zionist Jews seem to me to be merely antisemites turned upside-down, just as many Indians and Negroes display the normal colour prejudices in an inverted form. The point is that something, some psychological vitamin, is lacking in modern civilization, and as a result we are all more or less subject to this lunacy of believing that whole races or nations are mysteriously good or mysteriously evil. I defy any modern intellectual to look closely and honestly into his own mind without coming upon nationalist loyalties and hatreds of one kind or another. It is the fact that he can feel the emotional tug of such things, and yet see them dispassionately for what they are, that gives him his status as an intellectual. It will be seen, therefore, that the starting point for any investigation of antisemitism should not be 'Why does this obviously irrational belief appeal to other people?' but 'Why does antisemitism appeal to *me*? What is there about it that I feel to be true?' If one asks this question one at least discovers one's own rationalizations, and it may be possible to find out what lies beneath them. Antisemitism should be investigated – and I will not say by antisemites, but at any rate by people who know that they are not immune to that kind of emotion. When Hitler has disappeared a real enquiry into this subject will be possible, and it would probably be best to start not by debunking antisemitism, but by marshalling all the justifications for it that can be found, in one's own mind or anybody else's. In that way one might get some clues that would lead to its psychological roots. But that antisemitism will be definitely *cured*, without curing the larger disease of nationalism, I do not believe.

Written [early February 1945]

In Defence of P. G. Wodehouse

When the Germans made their rapid advance through Belgium in the early summer of 1940, they captured, among other things, Mr P. G. Wodehouse, who had been living throughout the early part of the war in his villa at Le Touquet, and seems not to have realized until the last moment that he was in any danger. As he was led away into captivity, he is said to have remarked, 'Perhaps after this I shall write a serious book.' He was placed for the time being under house arrest, and from his subsequent statements it appears that he was treated in a fairly friendly way, German officers in the neighbourhood frequently 'dropping in for a bath or a party'.

Over a year later, on 25 June 1941, the news came that Wodehouse had been released from internment and was living at the Adlon Hotel in Berlin. On the following day the public was astonished to learn that he had agreed to do some broadcasts of a 'non-political' nature over the German radio. The full texts of these broadcasts are not easy to obtain at this date, but Wodehouse seems to have done five of them between 26 June and 2 July, when the Germans took him off the air again. The first broadcast, on 26 June, was not made on the Nazi radio but took the form of an interview with Harry Flannery, the representative of the Columbia Broadcasting System, which still had its correspondents in Berlin. Wodehouse also published in the *Saturday Evening Post* an article which he had written while still in the internment camp.

The article and the broadcasts dealt mainly with Wodehouse's experiences in internment, but they did include a very few comments on the war. The following are fair samples:

> I never was interested in politics, I'm quite unable to work up any kind of belligerent feeling. Just as I'm about to feel belligerent about some country I meet a decent sort of chap. We go out together and lose any fighting thoughts or feelings.

> A short time ago they had a look at us on parade and got the right idea; at least they sent us to the local lunatic asylum. And I have been there forty-two weeks. There is a good deal to be said for internment. It keeps you out of the saloon and helps you to keep up with your reading. The chief trouble is that it means you are away from home for a long time. When I join my wife I had better take along a letter of introduction to be on the safe side.

> In the days before the war I had always been modestly proud of being an Englishman, but now that I have been some months resident in this bin or repository of Englishmen I am not so sure . . . The only concession I want from Germany is that she gives me a loaf of bread, tells the gentlemen with muskets at the main gate to look the other way, and leaves the rest to me. In return I am prepared to hand over India, an autographed set of my books, and to reveal the secret process of cooking sliced potatoes on a radiator. This offer holds good till Wednesday week.

The first extract quoted above caused great offence. Wodehouse was also censured for using (in the interview with Flannery) the phrase 'whether Britain wins the war or not', and he did not make things better by describing in another broadcast the filthy habits of some Belgian prisoners among whom he was interned. The Germans recorded this broadcast and repeated it a number of times. They seem to have supervised his talks very lightly, and they allowed him not only to be funny about the discomforts of internment but to remark that 'the internees at Trost camp all fervently believe that Britain will eventually win'. The general upshot of the talks, however, was that he had not been ill treated and bore no malice.

These broadcasts caused an immediate uproar in England. There were questions in Parliament, angry editorial comments in the press, and a stream of letters from fellow authors, nearly all of them disapproving, though one or two suggested that it would be better to suspend judgement, and several pleaded that Wodehouse probably did not realize what he was doing. On 15th July, the Home Service of the BBC carried an extremely violent Postscript by

'Cassandra' of the *Daily Mirror*, accusing Wodehouse of 'selling his country'. This postscript made free use of such expressions as 'quisling' and 'worshipping the Fuehrer'. The main charge was that Wodehouse had agreed to do German propaganda as a way of buying himself out of the internment camp.

'Cassandra's' Postscript caused a certain amount of protest, but on the whole it seems to have intensified popular feeling against Wodehouse. One result of it was that numerous lending libraries withdrew Wodehouse's books from circulation. Here is a typical news item:

> Within twenty-four hours of listening to the broadcast of Cassandra, the *Daily Mirror* columnist, Portadown (North Ireland) Urban District Council banned P. G. Wodehouse's books from their public library. Mr Edward McCann said that Cassandra's broadcast had clinched the matter. Wodehouse was funny no longer. (*Daily Mirror.*)

In addition the BBC banned Wodehouse's lyrics from the air and was still doing so a couple of years later. As late as December 1944 there were demands in Parliament that Wodehouse should be put on trial as a traitor.

There is an old saying that if you throw enough mud some of it will stick, and the mud has stuck to Wodehouse in a rather peculiar way. An impression has been left behind that Wodehouse's talks (not that anyone remembers what he said in them) showed him up not merely as a traitor but as an ideological sympathizer with Fascism. Even at the time several letters to the press claimed that 'Fascist tendencies' could be detected in his books, and the charge has been repeated since. I shall try to analyse the mental atmosphere of those books in a moment, but it is important to realize that the events of 1941 do not convict Wodehouse of anything worse than stupidity. The really interesting question is how and why he could be so stupid. When Flannery met Wodehouse (released, but still under guard) at the Adlon Hotel in June 1941, he saw at once that he was dealing with a political innocent, and when preparing him for their broadcast interview he had to warn him against making some exceedingly unfortunate remarks, one of which was by implication slightly anti-Russian. As it was, the phrase 'whether England wins or not' did get through. Soon after the interview Wodehouse told him that he was also going to broadcast on the Nazi radio, apparently not realizing that this action had any special significance. Flannery comments:[1]

> By this time the Wodehouse plot was evident. It was one of the best Nazi publicity stunts of the war, the first with a human angle . . . Plack (Goebbels's assistant) had gone to the camp near Gleiwitz to see Wodehouse, found that the author was completely without political sense, and had an idea. He suggested to Wodehouse that in return for being released from the prison camp he write a series of broadcasts about his experiences; there would be no censorship and he would put them on the air himself. In making that proposal Plack showed that he knew his man. He knew that Wodehouse made fun of the English in all his stories and that he seldom wrote in any other way, that he was still living in the period about which he wrote and had no conception of Nazism and all it meant. Wodehouse was his own Bertie Wooster.

[1]*Assignment to Berlin* by Harry W. Flannery. [Author's footnote.]

The striking of an actual bargain between Wodehouse and Plack seems to be merely Flannery's own interpretation. The arrangement may have been of a much less definite kind, and to judge from the broadcasts themselves, Wodehouse's main idea in making them was to keep in touch with his public and – the comedian's ruling passion – to get a laugh. Obviously they are not the utterances of a quisling of the type of Ezra Pound or John Amery,[1] nor, probably, of a person capable of understanding the nature of quislingism. Flannery seems to have warned Wodehouse that it would be unwise to broadcast, but not very forcibly. He adds that Wodehouse (though in one broadcast he refers to himself as an Englishman) seemed to regard himself as an American citizen. He had contemplated naturalization, but had never filled in the necessary papers. He even used, to Flannery, the phrase, 'We're not at war with Germany.'

I have before me a bibliography of P. G. Wodehouse's works. It names round about fifty books, but is certainly incomplete. It is as well to be honest, and I ought to start by admitting that there are many books by Wodehouse – perhaps a quarter or a third of the total – which I have not read. It is not, indeed, easy to read the whole output of a popular writer who is normally published in cheap editions. But I have followed his work fairly closely since 1911, when I was eight years old, and am well acquainted with its peculiar mental atmosphere – an atmosphere which has not, of course, remained completely unchanged, but shows little alteration since about 1925. In the passage from Flannery's book which I quoted above there are two remarks which would immediately strike any attentive reader of Wodehouse. One is to the effect that Wodehouse 'was still living in the period about which he wrote', and the other that the Nazi Propaganda Ministry made use of him because he 'made fun of the English'. The second statement is based on a misconception to which I will return presently. But Flannery's other comment is quite true and contains in it part of the clue to Wodehouse's behaviour.

A thing that people often forget about P. G. Wodehouse's novels is how long ago the better-known of them were written. We think of him as in some sense typifying the silliness of the nineteen-twenties and nineteen-thirties, but in fact the scenes and characters by which he is best remembered had all made their appearance before 1925. Psmith first appeared in 1909, having been foreshadowed by other characters in early school stories. Blandings Castle, with Baxter and the Earl of Emsworth both in residence, was introduced in 1915. The Jeeves-Wooster cycle began in 1919, both Jeeves and Wooster having made brief appearances earlier. Ukridge appeared in 1924. When one looks through the list of Wodehouse's books from 1902 onwards, one can observe three fairly well-marked periods. The first is the school-story period. It includes such books as *The Gold Bat*, *The Pothunters*, etc. and has its high-spot in *Mike* (1909). *Psmith in the City*, published in the following year, belongs in this category, though it is not directly concerned with school life. The next is the American period. Wodehouse seems to have lived in the United States from about 1913 to 1920, and for a while showed signs of becoming americanized in

[1]John Amery (1912–1945), right-wing politician and son of Leo Amery, who was a Conservative and patriotic MP and Secretary of State for India 1940–45. John Amery was an ardent admirer of Hitler, and had broadcast from Germany during the war urging British subjects in captivity to fight for Germany against England and Russia, and also made public speeches throughout occupied Europe on behalf of the German régime. He was executed for treason by the British in December 1945.

idiom and outlook. Some of the stories in *The Man with Two Left Feet* (1917) appear to have been influenced by O. Henry, and other books written about this time contain Americanisms (e.g. 'highball' for 'whisky and soda') which an Englishman would not normally use *in propria persona*. Nevertheless, almost all the books of this period – *Psmith, Journalist; The Little Nugget; The Indiscretions of Archie; Piccadilly Jim* and various others – depend for their effect on the *contrast* between English and American manners. English characters appear in an American setting, or vice versa: there is a certain number of purely English stories, but hardly any purely American ones. The third period might fitly be called the country-house period. By the early nineteen-twenties Wodehouse must have been making a very large income, and the social status of his characters moved upwards accordingly, though the Ukridge stories form a partial exception. The typical setting is now a country mansion, a luxurious bachelor flat or an expensive golf club. The schoolboy athleticism of the earlier books fades out, cricket and football giving way to golf, and the element of farce and burlesque becomes more marked. No doubt many of the later books, such as *Summer Lightning*, are light comedy rather than pure farce, but the occasional attempts at moral earnestness which can be found in *Psmith, Journalist; The Little Nugget; The Coming of Bill; The Man with Two Left Feet* and some of the school stories, no longer appear. Mike Jackson has turned into Bertie Wooster. That, however, is not a very startling metamorphosis, and one of the most noticeable things about Wodehouse is his *lack* of development. Books like *The Gold Bat* and *Tales of St Austin's*, written in the opening years of this century, already have the familiar atmosphere. How much of a formula the writing of his later books had become one can see from the fact that he continued to write stories of English life although throughout the sixteen years before his internment he was living at Hollywood and Le Touquet.

Mike, which is now a difficult book to obtain in an unabridged form, must be one of the best 'light' school stories in English. But though its incidents are largely farcical, it is by no means a satire on the public-school system, and *The Gold Bat, The Pothunters*, etc. are even less so. Wodehouse was educated at Dulwich, and then worked in a bank and graduated into novel writing by way of very cheap journalism. It is clear that for many years he remained 'fixated' on his old school and loathed the unromantic job and the lower-middle-class surroundings in which he found himself. In the early stories the 'glamour' of public-school life (house matches, fagging, teas round the study fire, etc.) is laid on fairly thick, and the 'play the game' code of morals is accepted with not many reservations. Wrykyn, Wodehouse's imaginary public school, is a school of a more fashionable type than Dulwich, and one gets the impression that between *The Gold Bat* (1904) and *Mike* (1908) Wrykyn itself has become more expensive and moved farther from London. Psychologically the most revealing book of Wodehouse's early period is *Psmith in the City*. Mike Jackson's father has suddenly lost his money, and Mike, like Wodehouse himself, is thrust at the age of about eighteen into an ill-paid subordinate job in a bank. Psmith is similarly employed, though not from financial necessity. Both this book and *Psmith, Journalist* (1915) are unusual in that they display a certain amount of political consciousness. Psmith at this stage chooses to call himself a Socialist – in his mind, and no doubt in Wodehouse's, this means no more than ignoring class distinctions – and on one occasion the two boys attend an open-air meeting on Clapham Common and go home to tea with an elderly Socialist orator, whose shabby-genteel home is described with some accuracy. But the most striking feature of the book is Mike's inability to wean himself from the atmosphere of school. He enters upon his job without any pretence of enthusiasm, and his main desire is not, as one might expect, to find a more interesting and useful job, but simply to be playing cricket. When he has to find himself lodgings he chooses to settle at Dulwich, because there he will be near a school and will be able to hear the agreeable sound of the ball striking against the bat. The climax of the book comes when Mike gets the chance to play in a county match and simply walks out of his job in order to do so. The point is that Wodehouse here sympathizes with Mike: indeed he identified himself with him, for it is clear enough that Mike bears the same relation to Wodehouse as Julien Sorel to Stendhal. But he created many other heroes essentially similar. Through the books of this and the next period there passes a whole series of young men to whom playing games and 'keeping fit' are a sufficient life-work. Wodehouse is almost incapable of imagining a desirable job. The great thing is to have money of your own, or, failing that, to find a sinecure. The hero of *Something Fresh* (1915) escapes from low-class journalism by becoming physical-training instructor to a dyspeptic millionaire: this is regarded as a step up, morally as well as financially.

In the books of the third period there is no narcissism and no serious interludes, but the implied moral and social background has changed much less than might appear at first sight. If one compares Bertie Wooster with Mike, or even with the rugger-playing prefects of the earliest school stories, one sees that the only real difference between them is that Bertie is richer and lazier. His ideals would be almost the same as theirs, but he fails to live up to them. Archie Moffam, in *The Indiscretions of Archie* (1921), is a type intermediate between Bertie and the earlier heroes: he is an ass, but he is also honest, kind-hearted, athletic and courageous. From first to last Wodehouse takes the public-school code of behaviour for granted, with the difference that in his later, more sophisticated period he prefers to show his characters violating it or living up to it against their will:

> 'Bertie! You wouldn't let down a pal?'
> 'Yes, I would.'
> 'But we were at school together, Bertie.'
> 'I don't care.'
> 'The old school, Bertie, the old school!'
> 'Oh, well – dash it!'

Bertie, a sluggish Don Quixote, has no wish to tilt at windmills, but he would hardly think of refusing to do so when honour calls. Most of the people whom Wodehouse intends as sympathetic characters are parasites, and some of them are plain imbeciles, but very few of them could be described as immoral. Even Ukridge is a visionary rather than a plain crook. The most immoral, or rather un-moral, of Wodehouse's characters is Jeeves, who acts as a foil to Bertie Wooster's comparative high-mindedness and perhaps symbolizes the widespread English belief that intelligence and unscrupulousness are much the same thing. How closely Wodehouse sticks to conventional morality can be seen from the fact that nowhere in his books is there anything in the nature of a sex joke. This is an enormous sacrifice for a farcical writer to make. Not only are there no dirty jokes, but there are hardly any compromising situations: the horns-on-the-forehead motif is almost completely avoided. Most of the full-length books, of course, contain a 'love interest', but it is always at the light-comedy level: the love affair, with its complications and its idyllic scenes, goes on and on, but, as the saying goes 'nothing happens'. It is significant that Wodehouse, by nature a writer of farces, was able to collaborate more than once with Ian Hay, a serio-comic writer and an exponent (*vide Pip*, etc.) of the 'clean-living Englishman' tradition at its silliest.

In *Something Fresh* Wodehouse had discovered the comic possibilities of the English aristocracy, and a succession of ridiculous but, save in a very few instances, not actually contemptible barons, earls and what not followed accordingly. This had the rather curious effect of causing Wodehouse to be regarded, outside England, as a penetrating satirist of English society. Hence Flannery's statement that Wodehouse 'made fun of the English', which is the impression he would probably make on a German or even an American reader. Some time after the broadcasts from Berlin I was discussing them with a young Indian Nationalist who defended Wodehouse warmly. He took it for granted that Wodehouse *had* gone over to the enemy, which from his own point of view was the right thing to do. But what interested me was to find that he regarded Wodehouse as an anti-British writer who had done useful work by showing up the British aristocracy in their true colours. This is a mistake that it would be very difficult for an English person to make, and is a good instance of the way in which books, especially humorous books, lose their finer nuances when they reach a foreign audience. For it is clear enough that Wodehouse is not anti-British, and not anti-upper-class either. On the contrary, a harmless old-fashioned snobbishness is perceptible all through his work. Just as an intelligent Catholic is able to see that the blasphemies of Baudelaire or James Joyce are not seriously damaging to the Catholic faith, so an English reader can see that in creating such characters as Hildebrand Spencer Poyns de Burgh John Hanneyside Coombe-Crombie, 12th Earl of Dreever, Wodehouse is not really attacking the social hierarchy. Indeed, no one who genuinely despised titles would write of them so much. Wodehouse's attitude towards the English social system is the same as his attitude towards the public-school moral code – a mild facetiousness covering an unthinking acceptance. The Earl of Emsworth is funny because an earl ought to have more dignity, and Bertie Wooster's helpless dependence on Jeeves is funny partly because the servant ought not to be superior to the master. An American reader can mistake these two, and others like them, for hostile caricatures because he is inclined to be anglophobe already and they correspond to his preconceived ideas about a decadent aristocracy. Bertie Wooster, with his spats and his cane, is the traditional stage Englishman. But, as any English reader would see, Wodehouse intends him as a sympathetic figure, and Wodehouse's real sin has been to present the English upper classes as much nicer people than they are. All through his books certain problems are consistently avoided. Almost without exception his moneyed young men are unassuming, good mixers, not avaricious; their tone is set for them by Psmith, who retains his own upper-class exterior but bridges the social gap by addressing everyone as 'Comrade'.

But there is another important point about Bertie Wooster: his out-of-dateness. Conceived in 1917 or thereabouts, Bertie really belongs to an epoch earlier than that. He is the 'knut' of the pre-1914 period, celebrated in such songs as 'Gilbert the Filbert' or 'Reckless Reggie of the Regent's Palace'. The kind of life that Wodehouse writes about by preference, the life of the 'clubman' or 'man about town', the elegant young man who lounges all the morning in

Piccadilly with a cane under his arm and a carnation in his buttonhole, barely survived into the nineteen-twenties. It is significant that Wodehouse could publish in 1936 a book entitled *Young Men in Spats*. For who was wearing spats at that date? They had gone out of fashion quite ten years earlier. But the traditional 'knut', the 'Piccadilly Johnny', *ought* to wear spats, just as the pantomime Chinese ought to wear a pigtail. A humorous writer is not obliged to keep up to date, and having struck one or two good veins, Wodehouse continued to exploit them with a regularity that was no doubt all the easier because he did not set foot in England during the sixteen years that preceded his internment. His picture of English society had been formed before 1914, and it was a naive, traditional and, at bottom, admiring picture. Nor did he ever become genuinely americanized. As I have pointed out, spontaneous Americanisms do occur in the books of the middle period, but Wodehouse remained English enough to find American slang an amusing and slightly shocking novelty. He loves to thrust a slang phrase or a crude fact in among Wardour Street English ('With a hollow groan Ukridge borrowed five shillings from me and went out into the night'), and expressions like 'a piece of cheese' or 'bust him on the noggin' lend themselves to this purpose. But the trick had been developed before he made any American contacts, and his use of garbled quotations is a common device of English writers running back to Fielding. As Mr John Hayward has pointed out,[1] Wodehouse owes a good deal to his knowledge of English literature and especially of Shakespeare. His books are aimed, not, obviously, at a highbrow audience, but at an audience educated along traditional lines. When, for instance, he describes somebody as heaving 'the kind of sigh that Prometheus might have heaved when the vulture dropped in for its lunch', he is assuming that his readers will know something of Greek mythology. In his early days the writers he admired were probably Barry Pain, Jerome K. Jerome, W. W. Jacobs, Kipling and F. Anstey, and he has remained closer to them than to the quick-moving American comic writers such as Ring Lardner or Damon Runyon. In his radio interview with Flannery, Wodehouse wondered whether 'the kind of people and the kind of England I write about will live after the war', not realizing that they were ghosts already. 'He was still living in the period about which he wrote,' says Flannery, meaning, probably, the nineteen-twenties. But the period was really the Edwardian age, and Bertie Wooster, if he ever existed, was killed round about 1915.

If my analysis of Wodehouse's mentality is accepted, the idea that in 1941 he consciously aided the Nazi propaganda machine becomes untenable and even ridiculous. He *may* have been induced to broadcast by the promise of an earlier release (he was due for release a few months later, on reaching his sixtieth birthday), but he cannot have realized that what he did would be damaging to British interests. As I have tried to show, his moral outlook has remained that of a public-school boy, and according to the public-school code, treachery in time of war is the most unforgivable of all the sins. But how could he fail to grasp that what he did would be a big propaganda score for the Germans and would bring down a torrent of disapproval on his own head? To answer this one must take two things into consideration. First, Wodehouse's complete lack – so far as one can judge from his printed works – of political awareness. It is nonsense to talk of 'Fascist tendencies' in his books. There are no post-1918 tendencies at

[1] 'P. G. Wodehouse' by John Hayward. (*The Saturday Book*, 1942.) I believe this is the only full-length critical essay on Wodehouse. [Author's footnote.]

all. Throughout his work there is a certain uneasy awareness of the problem of class distinctions, and scattered through it at various dates there are ignorant though not unfriendly references to Socialism. In *The Heart of a Goof* (1926) there is a rather silly story about a Russian novelist, which seems to have been inspired by the factional struggle then raging in the USSR. But the references in it to the Soviet system are entirely frivolous and, considering the date, not markedly hostile. That is about the extent of Wodehouse's political consciousness, so far as it is discoverable from his writings. Nowhere, so far as I know, does he so much as use the word 'Fascism' or 'Nazism'. In left-wing circles, indeed in 'enlightened' circles of any kind, to broadcast on the Nazi radio, to have any truck with Nazis whatever, would have seemed just as shocking an action before the war as during it. But that is a habit of mind that had been developed during nearly a decade of ideological struggle against Fascism. The bulk of the British people, one ought to remember, remained anaesthetic to that struggle until late into 1940. Abyssinia, Spain, China, Austria, Czechoslovakia – the long series of crimes and aggressions had simply slid past their consciousness or were dimly noted as quarrels occurring among foreigners and 'not our business'. One can gauge the general ignorance from the fact that the ordinary Englishman thought of 'Fascism' as an exclusively Italian thing and was bewildered when the same word was applied to Germany. And there is nothing in Wodehouse's writings to suggest that he was better informed, or more interested in politics, than the general run of his readers.

The other thing one must remember is that Wodehouse happened to be taken prisoner at just the moment when the war reached its desperate phase. We forget these things now, but until that time feelings about the war had been noticeably tepid. There was hardly any fighting, the Chamberlain Government was unpopular, eminent publicists were hinting that we should make a compromise peace as quickly as possible, trade union and Labour Party branches all over the country were passing anti-war resolutions. Afterwards, of course, things changed. The army was with difficulty extricated from Dunkirk, France collapsed, Britain was alone, the bombs rained on London, Goebbels announced that Britain was to be 'reduced to degradation and poverty'. By the middle of 1941 the British people knew what they were up against and feelings against the enemy were far fiercer than before. But Wodehouse had spent the intervening year in internment, and his captors seem to have treated him reasonably well. He had missed the turning-point of the war, and in 1941 he was still reacting in terms of 1939. He was not alone in this. On several occasions about this time the Germans brought captured British soldiers to the microphone, and some of them made remarks at least as tactless as Wodehouse's. They attracted no attention, however. And even an outright quisling like John Amery was afterwards to arouse much less indignation than Wodehouse had done.

But why? Why should a few rather silly but harmless remarks by an elderly novelist have provoked such an outcry? One has to look for the probable answer amid the dirty requirements of propaganda warfare.

There is one point about the Wodehouse broadcasts that is almost certainly significant – the date. Wodehouse was released two or three days before the invasion of the USSR, and at a time when the higher ranks of the Nazi party must have known that the invasion was imminent. It was vitally necessary to keep America out of the war as long as possible, and in fact, about this time, the German attitude towards the USA did become more conciliatory than it had been before. The Germans could hardly hope to defeat Russia, Britain and the USA in combination, but if they could polish off Russia quickly – and presumably they expected to do so – the Americans might never intervene. The release of Wodehouse was only a minor move, but it was not a bad sop to throw to the American isolationists. He was well known in the United States, and he was – or so the Germans calculated – popular with the anglophobe public as a caricaturist who made fun of the silly-ass Englishman with his spats and his monocle. At the microphone he could be trusted to damage British prestige in one way or another, while his release would demonstrate that the Germans were good fellows and knew how to treat their enemies chivalrously. That presumably was the calculation, though the fact that Wodehouse was only broadcasting for about a week suggests that he did not come up to expectations.

But on the British side similar though opposite calculations were at work. For the two years following Dunkirk, British morale depended largely upon the feeling that this was not only a war for democracy but a war which the common people had to win by their own efforts. The upper classes were discredited by their appeasement policy and by the disasters of 1940, and a social-levelling process appeared to be taking place. Patriotism and left-wing sentiments were associated in the popular mind, and numerous able journalists were at work to tie the association tighter. Priestley's 1940 broadcasts and 'Cassandra's' articles in the *Daily Mirror* were good examples of the demagogic propaganda flourishing at that time. In this atmosphere, Wodehouse made an ideal whipping-boy. For it was generally felt that the rich were treacherous, and Wodehouse – as 'Cassandra' vigorously pointed out in his broadcast – was a rich man. But he was the kind of rich man who could be attacked with impunity and without risking any damage to the structure of society. To denounce Wodehouse was not like denouncing, say, Beaverbrook. A mere novelist, however large his earnings may happen to be, is not *of* the possessing class. Even if his income touches £50,000 a year he has only the outward semblance of a millionaire. He is a lucky outsider who has fluked into a fortune – usually a very temporary fortune – like the winner of the Calcutta Derby Sweep. Consequently, Wodehouse's indiscretion gave a good propaganda opening. It was a chance to 'expose' a wealthy parasite without drawing attention to any of the parasites who really mattered.

In the desperate circumstances of the time, it was excusable to be angry at what Wodehouse did, but to go on denouncing him three or four years later – and more, to let an impression remain that he acted with conscious treachery – is not excusable. Few things in this war have been more morally disgusting than the present hunt after traitors and quislings. At best it is largely the punishment of the guilty by the guilty. In France, all kinds of petty rats – police officials, penny-a-lining journalists, women who have slept with German soldiers – are hunted down while almost without exception the big rats escape. In England the fiercest tirades against quislings are uttered by Conservatives who were practising appeasement in 1938 and Communists who were advocating it in 1940. I have striven to show how the wretched Wodehouse – just because success and expatriation had allowed him to remain mentally in the Edwardian age – became the *corpus vile* in a propaganda experiment, and I suggest that it is now time to regard the incident as closed. If Ezra Pound is caught and shot by the American authorities, it will have the effect of establishing his reputation as a poet for hundreds of years; and even in the case of Wodehouse, if we drive him to retire to the United States and renounce his

British citizenship, we shall end by being horribly ashamed of ourselves. Meanwhile, if we really want to punish the people who weakened national morale at critical moments, there are other culprits who are nearer home and better worth chasing.

Written [February] 1945

Notes on Nationalism

Somewhere or other Byron makes use of the French word *longueur*, and remarks in passing that though in England we happen not to have the *word*, we have the *thing* in considerable profusion. In the same way, there is a habit of mind which is now so widespread that it affects our thinking on nearly every subject, but which has not yet been given a name. As the nearest existing equivalent I have chosen the word 'nationalism', but it will be seen in a moment that I am not using it in quite the ordinary sense, if only because the emotion I am speaking about does not always attach itself to what is called a nation – that is, a single race or a geographical area. It can attach itself to a church or a class, or it may work in a merely negative sense, *against* something or other and without the need for any positive object of loyalty.

By 'nationalism' I mean first of all the habit of assuming that human beings can be classified like insects and that whole blocks of millions or tens of millions of people can be confidently labelled 'good' or 'bad'.[1] But secondly – and this is much more important – I mean the habit of identifying oneself with a single nation or other unit, placing it beyond good and evil and recognizing no other duty than that of advancing its interests. Nationalism is not to be confused with patriotism. Both words are normally used in so vague a way that any definition is liable to be challenged, but one must draw a distinction between them, since two different and even opposing ideas are involved. By 'patriotism' I mean devotion to a particular place and a particular way of life, which one believes to be the best in the world but has no wish to force upon other people. Patriotism is of its nature defensive, both militarily and culturally. Nationalism, on the other hand, is inseparable from the desire for power. The abiding purpose of every nationalist is to secure more power and more prestige, *not* for himself but for the nation or other unit in which he has chosen to sink his own individuality.

So long as it is applied merely to the more notorious and identifiable nationalist movements in Germany, Japan and other countries, all this is obvious enough. Confronted with a phenomenon like Nazism, which we can

[1] Nations, and even vaguer entities such as the Catholic Church or the proletariat, are commonly thought of as individuals and often referred to as 'she'. Patently absurd remarks such as 'Germany is naturally treacherous' are to be found in any newspaper one opens, and reckless generalizations about national character ('The Spaniard is a natural aristocrat' or 'Every Englishman is a hypocrite') are uttered by almost everyone. Intermittently these generalizations are seen to be unfounded, but the habit of making them persists, and people of professedly international outlook, e.g. Tolstoy or Bernard Shaw, are often guilty of them. [Author's footnote.]

observe from the outside, nearly all of us would say much the same things about it. But here I must repeat what I said above, that I am only using the word 'nationalism' for lack of a better. Nationalism, in the extended sense in which I am using the word, includes such movements and tendencies as Communism, political Catholicism, Zionism, Antisemitism, Trotskyism and Pacifism. It does not necessarily mean loyalty to a government or a country, still less to *one's own* country, and it is not even strictly necessary that the units in which it deals should actually exist. To name a few obvious examples, Jewry, Islam, Christendom, the Proletariat and the White Race are all of them the objects of passionate nationalistic feeling: but their existence can be seriously questioned, and there is no definition of any one of them that would be universally accepted.

It is also worth emphasizing once again that nationalist feeling can be purely negative. There are, for example, Trotskyists who have become simply the enemies of the USSR without developing a corresponding loyalty to any other unit. When one grasps the implications of this, the nature of what I mean by nationalism becomes a good deal clearer. A nationalist is one who thinks solely, or mainly, in terms of competitive prestige. He may be a positive or a negative nationalist – that is, he may use his mental energy either in boosting or in denigrating – but at any rate his thoughts always turn on victories, defeats, triumphs and humiliations. He sees history, especially contemporary history, as the endless rise and decline of great power units, and every event that happens seems to him a demonstration that his own side is on the up-grade and some hated rival on the down-grade. But finally, it is important not to confuse nationalism with mere worship of success. The nationalist does not go on the principle of simply ganging up with the strongest side. On the contrary, having picked his side, he persuades himself that it *is* the strongest, and is able to stick to his belief even when the facts are overwhelmingly against him. Nationalism is power hunger tempered by self-deception. Every nationalist is capable of the most flagrant dishonesty, but he is also – since he is conscious of serving something bigger than himself – unshakeably certain of being in the right.

Now that I have given this lengthy definition, I think it will be admitted that the habit of mind I am talking about is widespread among the English intelligentsia, and more widespread there than among the mass of the people. For those who feel deeply about contemporary politics, certain topics have become so infected by considerations of prestige that a genuinely rational approach to them is almost impossible. Out of the hundreds of examples that one might choose, take this question: Which of the three great allies, the USSR, Britain and the USA, has contributed most to the defeat of Germany? In theory it should be possible to give a reasoned and perhaps even a conclusive answer to this question. In practice, however, the necessary calculations cannot be made, because any one likely to bother his head about such a question would inevitably see it in terms of competitive prestige. He would therefore *start* by deciding in favour of Russia, Britain or America as the case might be, and only *after* this would begin searching for arguments that seemed to support his case. And there are whole strings of kindred questions to which you can only get an honest answer from someone who is indifferent to the whole subject involved, and whose opinion on it is probably worthless in any case. Hence, partly, the remarkable failure in our time of political and military prediction. It is curious to reflect that out of all the 'experts' of all the schools, there was not a single one who was able to foresee so likely an event as the Russo-German Pact of 1939.[1] And when the news of the Pact broke, the most wildly divergent explanations of it were given, and predictions were made which were falsified almost immediately, being based in nearly every case not on a study of probabilities but on a desire to make the USSR seem good or bad, strong or weak. Political or military commentators, like astrologers, can survive almost any mistake, because their more devoted followers do not look to them for an appraisal of the facts but for the stimulation of nationalistic loyalties.[2] And aesthetic judgements, especially literary judgements, are often corrupted in the same way as political ones. It would be difficult for an Indian Nationalist to enjoy reading Kipling or for a Conservative to see merit in Mayakovsky, and there is always a temptation to claim that any book whose tendency one disagrees with must be a bad book from a *literary* point of view. People of strongly nationalistic outlook often perform this sleight of hand without being conscious of dishonesty.

In England, if one simply considers the number of people involved, it is probable that the dominant form of nationalism is old-fashioned British jingoism. It is certain that this is still widespread, and much more so than most observers would have believed a dozen years ago. However, in this essay I am concerned chiefly with the reactions of the intelligentsia, among whom jingoism and even patriotism of the old kind are almost dead, though they now seem to be reviving among a minority. Among the intelligentsia, it hardly needs saying that the dominant form of nationalism is Communism – using this word in a very loose sense, to include not merely Communist Party members but 'fellow-travellers' and russophiles generally. A Communist, for my purpose here, is one who looks upon the USSR as his Fatherland and feels it is his duty to justify Russian policy and advance Russian interests at all costs. Obviously such people abound in England today, and their direct and indirect influence is very great. But many other forms of nationalism also flourish, and it is by noticing the points of resemblance between different and even seemingly opposed currents of thought that one can best get the matter into perspective.

Ten or twenty years ago, the form of nationalism most closely corresponding to Communism today was political Catholicism. Its most outstanding exponent – though he was perhaps an extreme case rather than a typical one – was G. K. Chesterton. Chesterton was a writer of considerable talent who chose to suppress both his sensibilities and his intellectual honesty in the cause of Roman Catholic propaganda. During the last twenty years or so of his life,

[1] A few writers of conservative tendency, such as Peter Drucker, foretold an agreement between Germany and Russia, but they expected an actual alliance or amalgamation which would be permanent. No Marxist or other left-wing writer, of whatever colour, came anywhere near foretelling the Pact. [Author's footnote.]

[2] The military commentators of the popular press can mostly be classified as pro-Russian or anti-Russian, pro-Blimp or anti-Blimp. Such errors as believing the Maginot Line impregnable, or predicting that Russia would conquer Germany in three months, have failed to shake their reputation, because they were always saying what their own particular audience wanted to hear. The two military critics most favoured by the intelligentsia are Captain Liddell Hart and Major-General Fuller, the first of whom teaches that the defence is stronger than the attack, and the second that the attack is stronger than the defence. This contradiction has not prevented both of them from being accepted as authorities by the same public. The secret reason for their vogue in left-wing circles is that both of them are at odds with the War Office. [Author's footnote.]

his entire output was in reality an endless repetition of the same thing, under its laboured cleverness as simple and boring as 'Great is Diana of the Ephesians'. Every book that he wrote, every paragraph, every sentence, every incident in every story, every scrap of dialogue, had to demonstrate beyond possibility of mistake the superiority of the Catholic over the Protestant or the Pagan. But Chesterton was not content to think of this superiority as merely intellectual or spiritual: it had to be translated into terms of national prestige and military power, which entailed an ignorant idealization of the Latin countries, especially France. Chesterton had not lived long in France, and his picture of it – as a land of Catholic peasants incessantly singing the *Marseillaise* over glasses of red wine – had about as much relation to reality as *Chu Chin Chow* has to everyday life in Baghdad. And with this went not only an enormous overestimation of French military power (both before and after 1914–18 he maintained that France, by itself, was stronger than Germany), but a silly and vulgar glorification of the actual process of war. Chesterton's battle poems, such as 'Lepanto' or 'The Ballad of Saint Barbara', make 'The Charge of the Light Brigade' read like a pacifist tract: they are perhaps the most tawdry bits of bombast to be found in our language. The interesting thing is that had the romantic rubbish which he habitually wrote about France and the French army been written by somebody else about Britian and the British army, he would have been the first to jeer. In home politics he was a Little Englander, a true hater of jingoism and imperialism, and according to his lights a true friend of democracy. Yet when he looked outwards into the international field, he could forsake his principles without even noticing that he was doing so. Thus, his almost mystical belief in the virtues of democracy did not prevent him from admiring Mussolini. Mussolini had destroyed the representative government and the freedom of the press for which Chesterton had struggled so hard at home, but Mussolini was an Italian and had made Italy strong, and that settled the matter. Nor did Chesterton ever find a word to say against imperialism and the conquest of coloured races when they were practised by Italians or Frenchmen. His hold on reality, his literary taste, and even to some extent his moral sense, were dislocated as soon as his nationalistic loyalties were involved.

Obviously there are considerable resemblances between political Catholicism, as exemplified by Chesterton, and Communism. So there are between either of these and, for instance, Scottish nationalism, Zionism, Antisemitism or Trotskyism. It would be an oversimplication to say that all forms of nationalism are the same, even in their mental atmosphere, but there are certain rules that hold good in all cases. The following are the principal characteristics of nationalist thought:

OBSESSION. As nearly as possible, no nationalist ever thinks, talks or writes about anything except the superiority of his own power unit. It is difficult if not impossible for any nationalist to conceal his allegiance. The smallest slur upon his own unit, or any implied praise of a rival organization, fills him with uneasiness which he can only relieve by making some sharp retort. If the chosen unit is an actual country, such as Ireland or India, he will generally claim superiority for it not only in military power and political virtue, but in art, literature, sport, the structure of the language, the physical beauty of the inhabitants, and perhaps even in climate, scenery and cooking. He will show great sensitiveness about such things as the correct display of flags, relative size of headlines and the order in which different countries are named.[1] Nomenclature plays a very important part in nationalist thought. Countries which have won their independence or gone through a nationalist revolution usually change their names, and any country or other unit round which strong feelings revolve is likely to have several names, each of them carrying a different implication. The two sides in the Spanish civil war had between them nine or ten names expressing different degrees of love and hatred. Some of these names (e.g., 'Patriots' for Franco-supporters, or 'Loyalists' for Government-supporters) were frankly question-begging, and there was no single one of them which the two rival factions could have agreed to use. All nationalists consider it a duty to spread their own language to the detriment of rival languages, and among English-speakers this struggle reappears in subtler form as a struggle between dialects. Anglophobe Americans will refuse to use a slang phrase if they know it to be of British origin, and the conflict between Latinizers and Germanizers often has nationalist motives behind it. Scottish nationalists insist on the superiority of Lowland Scots, and Socialists whose nationalism takes the form of class hatred tirade against the BBC accent and even the broad A. One could multiply instances. Nationalist thought often gives the impression of being tinged by belief in sympathetic magic – a belief which probably comes out in the widespread custom of burning political enemies in effigy, or using pictures of them as targets in shooting galleries.

INSTABILITY. The intensity with which they are held does not prevent nationalist loyalties from being transferable. To begin with, as I have pointed out already, they can be and often are fastened upon some foreign country. One quite commonly finds that great national leaders, or the founders of nationalist movements, do not even belong to the country they have glorified. Sometimes they are outright foreigners, or more often they come from peripheral areas where nationality is doubtful. Examples are Stalin, Hitler, Napoleon, de Valera, Disraeli, Poincaré, Beaverbrook. The Pan-German movement was in part the creation of an Englishman, Houston Chamberlain. For the past fifty or a hundred years, transferred nationalism has been a common phenomenon among literary intellectuals. With Lafcadio Hearne the transference was to Japan, with Carlyle and many others of his time to Germany, and in our own age it is usually to Russia. But the peculiarly interesting fact is that *re*-transference is also possible. A country or other unit which has been worshipped for years may suddenly become detestable, and some other object of affection may take its place with almost no interval. In the first version of H. G. Wells's *Outline of History*, and others of his writings about that time, one finds the United States praised almost as extravagantly as Russia is praised by Communists today: yet within a few years this uncritical admiration had turned into hostility. The bigoted Communist who changes in a space of weeks, or even of days, into an equally bigoted Trotskyist is a common spectacle. In continental Europe Fascist movements were largely recruited from among Communists, and the opposite process may well happen within the next few years. What remains constant in the nationalist is his own state of mind: the object of his feelings is changeable, and may be imaginary.

But for an intellectual, transference has an important function which I have

[1] Certain Americans have expressed dissatisfaction because 'Anglo-American' is the normal form of combination of these two words. It has been proposed to substitute 'Americo-British'. [Author's footnote.]

already mentioned shortly in connection with Chesterton. It makes it possible for him to be much *more* nationalistic – more vulgar, more silly, more malignant, more dishonest – than he could ever be on behalf of his native country, or any unit of which he had real knowledge. When one sees the slavish or boastful rubbish that is written about Stalin, the Red army, etc. by fairly intelligent and sensitive people, one realizes that this is only possible because some kind of dislocation has taken place. In societies such as ours, it is unusual for anyone describable as an intellectual to feel a very deep attachment to his own country. Public opinion – that is, the section of public opinion of which he as an intellectual is aware – will not allow him to do so. Most of the people surrounding him are sceptical and disaffected, and he may adopt the same attitude from imitativeness or sheer cowardice: in that case he will have abandoned the form of nationalism that lies nearest to hand without getting any closer to a genuinely internationalist outlook. He still feels the need for a Fatherland, and it is natural to look for one somewhere abroad. Having found it, he can wallow unrestrainedly in exactly those emotions from which he believes that he has emancipated himself. God, the King, the Empire, the Union Jack – all the overthrown idols can reappear under different names, and because they are not recognized for what they are they can be worshipped with a good conscience. Transferred nationalism, like the use of scapegoats, is a way of attaining salvation without altering one's conduct.

INDIFFERENCE TO REALITY. All nationalists have the power of not seeing resemblances between similar sets of facts. A British Tory will defend self-determination in Europe and oppose it in India with no feeling of inconsistency. Actions are held to be good or bad, not on their own merits but according to who does them, and there is almost no kind of outrage – torture, the use of hostages, forced labour, mass deportations, imprisonment without trial, forgery, assassination, the bombing of civilians – which does not change its moral colour when it is committed by 'our' side. The Liberal *News Chronicle* published, as an example of shocking barbarity, photographs of Russians hanged by the Germans, and then a year or two later published with warm approval almost exactly similar photographs of Germans hanged by the Russians.[1] It is the same with historical events. History is thought of largely in nationalist terms, and such things as the Inquisition, the tortures of the Star Chamber, the exploits of the English buccaneers (Sir Francis Drake, for instance, who was given to sinking Spanish prisoners alive), the Reign of Terror, the heroes of the Mutiny blowing hundreds of Indians from the guns, or Cromwell's soldiers slashing Irishwomen's faces with razors, become morally neutral or even meritorious when it is felt that they were done in the 'right' cause. If one looks back over the past quarter of a century, one finds that there was hardly a single year when atrocity stories were not being reported from some part of the world: and yet in not one single case were these atrocities – in Spain, Russia, China, Hungary, Mexico, Amritsar, Smyrna – believed in and disapproved of by the English intelligentsia as a whole. Whether such deeds

[1] The *News Chronicle* advised its readers to visit the news film at which the entire execution could be witnessed, with close-ups. The *Star* published with seeming approval photographs of nearly naked female collaborationists being baited by the Paris mob. These photographs had a marked resemblance to the Nazi photographs of Jews being baited by the Berlin mob. [Author's footnote.]

were reprehensible, or even whether they happened, was always decided according to political predilection.

The nationalist not only does not disapprove of atrocities committed by his own side, but he has a remarkable capacity for not even hearing about them. For quite six years the English admirers of Hitler contrived not to learn of the existence of Dachau and Buchenwald. And those who are loudest in denouncing the German concentration camps are often quite unaware, or only very dimly aware, that there are also concentration camps in Russia. Huge events like the Ukraine famine of 1933, involving the deaths of millions of people, have actually escaped the attention of the majority of English russophiles. Many English people have heard almost nothing about the extermination of German and Polish Jews during the present war. Their own antisemitism has caused this vast crime to bounce off their consciousness. In nationalist thought there are facts which are both true and untrue, known and unknown. A known fact may be so unbearable that it is habitually pushed aside and not allowed to enter into logical processes, or on the other hand it may enter into every calculation and yet never be admitted as a fact, even in one's own mind.

Every nationalist is haunted by the belief that the past can be altered. He spends part of his time in a fantasy world in which things happen as they should – in which, for example, the Spanish Armada was a success or the Russian Revolution was crushed in 1918 – and he will transfer fragments of this world to the history books whenever possible. Much of the propagandist writing of our time amounts to plain forgery. Material facts are suppressed, dates altered, quotations removed from their context and doctored so as to change their meaning. Events which, it is felt, ought not to have happened are left unmentioned and ultimately denied.[1] In 1927 Chiang Kai-Shek boiled hundreds of Communists alive, and yet within ten years he had become one of the heroes of the Left. The re-alignment of world politics had brought him into the anti-Fascist camp, and so it was felt that the boiling of the Communists 'didn't count', or perhaps had not happened. The primary aim of propaganda is, of course, to influence contemporary opinion, but those who rewrite history do probably believe with part of their minds that they are actually thrusting facts into the past. When one considers the elaborate forgeries that have been committed in order to show that Trotsky did not play a valuable part in the Russian civil war, it is difficult to feel that the people responsible are merely lying. More probably they feel that their own version *was* what happened in the sight of God, and that one is justified in rearranging the records accordingly.

Indifference to objective truth is encouraged by the sealing-off of one part of the world from another, which makes it harder and harder to discover what is actually happening. There can often be a genuine doubt about the most enormous events. For example, it is impossible to calculate within millions, perhaps even tens of millions, the number of deaths caused by the present war. The calamities that are constantly being reported – battles, massacres, famines, revolutions – tend to inspire in the average person a feeling of unreality. One has no way of verifying the facts, one is not even fully certain that they have happened, and one is always presented with totally different interpretations

[1] An example is the Russo-German Pact, which is being effaced as quickly as possible from public memory. A Russian correspondent informs me that mention of the Pact is already being omitted from Russian year-books which table recent political events. [Author's footnote.]

from different sources. What were the rights and wrongs of the Warsaw rising of August 1944? Is it true about the German gas ovens in Poland? Who was really to blame for the Bengal famine? Probably the truth is discoverable, but the facts will be so dishonestly set forth in almost any newspaper that the ordinary reader can be forgiven either for swallowing lies or for failing to form an opinion. The general uncertainty as to what is really happening makes it easier to cling to lunatic beliefs. Since nothing is ever quite proved or disproved, the most unmistakable fact can be impudently denied. Moreover, although endlessly brooding on power, victory, defeat, revenge, the nationalist is often somewhat uninterested in what happens in the real world. What he wants is to *feel* that his own unit is getting the better of some other unit, and he can more easily do this by scoring off an adversary than by examining the facts to see whether they support him. All nationalist controversy is at the debating-society level. It is always entirely inconclusive, since each contestant invariably believes himself to have won the victory. Some nationalists are not far from schizophrenia, living quite happily amid dreams of power and conquest which have no connection with the physical world.

I have examined as best I can the mental habits which are common to all forms of nationalism. The next thing is to classify those forms, but obviously this cannot be done comprehensively. Nationalism is an enormous subject. The world is tormented by innumerable delusions and hatreds which cut across one another in an extremely complex way, and some of the most sinister of them have not yet even impinged on the European consciousness. In this essay I am concerned with nationalism as it occurs among the English intelligentsia. In them, much more often than in ordinary English people, it is unmixed with patriotism and can therefore be studied pure. Below are listed the varieties of nationalism now flourishing among English intellectuals, with such comments as seem to be needed. It is convenient to use three headings, Positive, Transferred and Negative, though some varieties will fit into more than one category:

POSITIVE NATIONALISM

1. NEO-TORYISM. Exemplified by such people as Lord Elton, A. P. Herbert, G. M. Young, Professor Pickthorn, by the literature of the Tory Reform Committee, and by such magazines as the *New English Review* and the *Nineteenth Century and After*. The real motive force of neo-Toryism, giving it its nationalistic character and differentiating it from ordinary Conservatism, is the desire not to recognize that British power and influence have declined. Even those who are realistic enough to see that Britain's military position is not what it was, tend to claim that 'English ideas' (usually left undefined) must dominate the world. All neo-Tories are anti-Russian, but sometimes the main emphasis is anti-American. The significant thing is that this school of thought seems to be gaining ground among youngish intellectuals, sometimes ex-Communists, who have passed through the usual process of disillusionment and become disillusioned with that. The anglophobe who suddenly becomes violently pro-British is a fairly common figure. Writers who illustrate this tendency are F. A. Voigt, Malcolm Muggeridge, Evelyn Waugh, Hugh Kingsmill, and a psychologically similar development can be observed in T. S. Eliot, Wyndham Lewis and various of their followers.

2. CELTIC NATIONALISM. Welsh, Irish and Scottish nationalism have points of difference but are alike in their anti-English orientation. Members of all three movements have opposed the war while continuing to describe themselves as pro-Russian, and the lunatic fringe has even contrived to be simultaneously pro-Russian and pro-Nazi. But Celtic nationalism is not the same thing as anglophobia. Its motive force is a belief in the past and future greatness of the Celtic peoples, and it has a strong tinge of racialism. The Celt is supposed to be spiritually superior to the Saxon – simpler, more creative, less vulgar, less snobbish, etc – but the usual power hunger is there under the surface. One symptom of it is the delusion that Eire, Scotland or even Wales could preserve its independence unaided and owes nothing to British protection. Among writers, good examples of this school of thought are Hugh MacDiarmid and Sean O'Casey. No modern Irish writer, even of the stature of Yeats or Joyce, is completely free from traces of nationalism.

3. ZIONISM. This has the usual characteristics of a nationalist movement, but the American variant of it seems to be more violent and malignant than the British. I classify it under Direct and not Transferred nationalism because it flourishes almost exclusively among the Jews themselves. In England, for several rather incongruous reasons, the intelligentsia are mostly pro-Jew on the Palestine issue, but they do not feel strongly about it. All English people of goodwill are also pro-Jew in the sense of disapproving of Nazi persecution. But any actual nationalistic loyalty, or belief in the innate superiority of Jews, is hardly to be found among Gentiles.

TRANSFERRED NATIONALISM

1. COMMUNISM.

2. POLITICAL CATHOLICISM.

3. COLOUR FEELING. The old-style contemptuous attitude towards 'natives' has been much weakened in England, and various pseudo-scientific theories emphasizing the superiority of the white race have been abandoned.[1] Among the intelligentsia, colour feeling only occurs in the transposed form, that is, as a belief in the innate superiority of the coloured races. This is now increasingly common among English intellectuals, probably resulting more often from masochism and sexual frustration than from contact with the Oriental and Negro nationalist movements. Even among those who do not feel strongly on the colour question, snobbery and imitation have a powerful influence. Almost any English intellectual would be scandalized by the claim that the white races are superior to the coloured, whereas the opposite claim would seem to him unexceptionable even if he disagreed with it. Nationalistic attachment to the coloured races is usually mixed up with the belief that their sex lives are

[1] A good example is the sunstroke superstition. Until recently it was believed that the white races were much more liable to sunstroke than the coloured, and that a white man could not safely walk about in tropical sunshine without a pith helmet. There was no evidence whatever for this theory, but it served the purpose of accentuating the difference between 'natives' and Europeans. During the present war the theory has been quietly dropped and whole armies manoeuvre in the tropics without pith helmets. So long as the sunstroke superstition survived, English doctors in India appear to have believed in it as firmly as laymen. [Author's footnote.]

superior, and there is a large underground mythology about the sexual prowess of Negroes.

4. CLASS FEELING. Among upper-class and middle-class intellectuals, only in the transposed form – i.e. as a belief in the superiority of the proletariat. Here again, inside the intelligentsia, the pressure of public opinion is overwhelming. Nationalistic loyalty towards the proletariat, and most vicious theoretical hatred of the bourgeoisie, can and often do co-exist with ordinary snobbishness in everyday life.

5. PACIFISM. The majority of pacifists either belong to obscure religious sects or are simply humanitarians who object to taking life and prefer not to follow their thoughts beyond that point. But there is a minority of intellectual pacifists whose real though unadmitted motive appears to be hatred of western democracy and admiration for totalitarianism. Pacifist propaganda usually boils down to saying that one side is as bad as the other, but if one looks closely at the writings of the younger intellectual pacifists, one finds that they do not by any means express impartial disapproval but are directed almost entirely against Britain and the United States. Moreover they do not as a rule condemn violence as such, but only violence used in defence of the western countries. The Russians, unlike the British, are not blamed for defending themselves by warlike means, and indeed all pacifist propaganda of this type avoids mention of Russia or China. It is not claimed, again, that the Indians should abjure violence in their struggle against the British. Pacifist literature abounds with equivocal remarks which, if they mean anything, appear to mean that statesmen of the type of Hitler are preferable to those of the type of Churchill, and that violence is perhaps excusable if it is violent enough. After the fall of France, the French pacifists, faced by a real choice which their English colleagues have not had to make, mostly went over to the Nazis, and in England there appears to have been some small overlap of membership between the Peace Pledge Union and the Blackshirts. Pacifist writers have written in praise of Carlyle, one of the intellectual fathers of Fascism. All in all it is difficult not to feel that pacifism, as it appears among a section of the intelligentsia, is secretly inspired by an admiration for power and successful cruelty. The mistake was made of pinning this emotion to Hitler, but it could easily be retransferred.

NEGATIVE NATIONALISM

1. ANGLOPHOBIA. Within the intelligentsia, a derisive and mildly hostile attitude towards Britain is more or less compulsory, but it is an unfaked emotion in many cases. During the war it was manifested in the defeatism of the intelligentsia, which persisted long after it had become clear that the Axis power could not win. Many people were undisguisedly pleased when Singapore fell or when the British were driven out of Greece, and there was a remarkable unwillingness to believe in good news, e.g. el Alamein, or the number of German planes shot down in the Battle of Britain. English left-wing intellectuals did not, of course, actually want the Germans or Japanese to win the war, but many of them could not help getting a certain kick out of seeing their own country humiliated, and wanted to feel that the final victory would be due to Russia, or perhaps America, and not to Britain. In foreign politics many intellectuals follow the principle that any faction backed by Britain must

be in the wrong. As a result, 'enlightened' opinion is quite largely a mirror-image of Conservative policy. Anglophobia is always liable to reversal, hence that fairly common spectacle, the pacifist of one war who a bellicist in the next.

2. ANTISEMITISM. There is little evidence about this at present, because the Nazi persecutions have made it necessary for any thinking person to side with the Jews against their oppressors. Anyone educated enough to have heard the word 'antisemitism' claims as a matter of course to be free of it, and anti-Jewish remarks are carefully eliminated from all classes of literature. Actually antisemitism appears to be widespread, even among intellectuals, and the general conspiracy of silence probably helps to exacerbate it. People of Left opinions are not immune to it, and their attitude is sometimes affected by the fact that Trotskyists and Anarchists tend to be Jews. But antisemitism comes more naturally to people of Conservative tendency, who suspect the Jews of weakening national morale and diluting the national culture. Neo-Tories and political Catholics are always liable to succumb to antisemitism, at least intermittently.

3. TROTSKYISM. This word is used so loosely as to include Anarchists, democratic Socialists and even Liberals. I use it here to mean a doctrinaire Marxist whose main motive is hostility to the Stalin régime. Trotskyism can be better studied in obscure pamphlets or in papers like the *Socialist Appeal* than in the works of Trotsky himself, who was by no means a man of one idea. Although in some places, for instance in the United States, Trotskyism is able to attract a fairly large number of adherents and develop into an organized movement with a petty fuehrer of its own, its inspiration is essentially negative. The Trotskyist is *against* Stalin just as the Communist is *for* him, and, like the majority of Communists, he wants not so much to alter the external world as to feel that the battle for prestige is going in his own favour. In each case there is the same obsessive fixation on a single subject, the same inability to form a genuinely rational opinion based on probabilities. The fact that Trotskyists are everywhere a persecuted minority, and that the accusation usually made against them, i.e. of collaborating with the Fascists, is obviously false, creates an impression that Trotskyism is intellectually and morally superior to Communism; but it is doubtful whether there is much difference. The most typical Trotskyists, in any case, are ex-Communists, and no one arrives at Trotskyism except via one of the left-wing movements. No Communist, unless tethered to his party by years of habit, is secure against a sudden lapse into Trotskyism. The opposite process does not seem to happen equally often, though there is no clear reason why it should not.

In the classification I have attempted above, it will seem that I have often exaggerated, oversimplified, made unwarranted assumptions and have left out of account the existence of ordinarily decent motives. This was inevitable, because in this essay I am trying to isolate and identify tendencies which exist in all our minds and pervert our thinking, without necessarily occurring in a pure state or operating continuously. It is important at this point to correct the over-simplified picture which I have been obliged to make. To begin with, one has no right to assume that *everyone*, or even every intellectual, is infected by nationalism. Secondly, nationalism can be intermittent and limited. An intelligent man may half-succumb to a belief which attracts him but which he knows to be absurd, and he may keep it out of his mind for long periods, only reverting to it in moments of anger or sentimentality, or when he is certain that no important issue is involved. Thirdly, a nationalistic creed may be adopted in good faith from non-nationalist motives. Fourthly, several kinds of nationalism, even kinds that cancel out, can co-exist in the same person.

All the way through I have said 'the nationalist does this' or 'the nationalist does that', using for purposes of illustration the extreme, barely sane type of nationalist who has no neutral areas in his mind and no interest in anything except the struggle for power. Actually such people are fairly common, but they are not worth powder and shot. In real life Lord Elton, D. N. Pritt, Lady Houston, Ezra Pound, Lord Vansittart, Father Coughlin and all the rest of their dreary tribe have to be fought against, but their intellectual deficiencies hardly need pointing out. Monomania is not interesting, and the fact that no nationalist of the more bigoted kind can write a book which still seems worth reading after a lapse of years has a certain deodorizing effect. But when one has admitted that nationalism has not triumphed everywhere, that there are still people whose judgements are not at the mercy of their desires, the fact does remain that the pressing problems – India, Poland, Palestine, the Spanish civil war, the Moscow trials, the American Negroes, the Russo-German Pact or what have you – cannot be, or at least never are, discussed upon a reasonable level. The Eltons and Pritts and Coughlins, each of them simply an enormous mouth bellowing the same lie over and over again, are obviously extreme cases, but we deceive ourselves if we do not realize that we can all resemble them in unguarded moments. Let a certain note be struck, let this or that corn be trodden on – and it may be a corn whose very existence has been unsuspected hitherto – and the most fair-minded and sweet-tempered person may suddenly be transformed into a vicious partisan, anxious only to 'score' over his adversary and indifferent as to how many lies he tells or how many logical errors he commits in doing so. When Lloyd George, who was an opponent of the Boer war, announced in the House of Commons that the British communiqués, if one added them together, claimed the killing of more Boers than the whole Boer nation contained, it is recorded that Arthur Balfour rose to his feet and shouted 'Cad!' Very few people are proof against lapses of this type. The Negro snubbed by a white woman, the Englishman who hears England ignorantly criticized by an American, the Catholic apologist reminded of the Spanish Armarda, will all react in much the same way. One prod to the nerve of nationalism, and the intellectual decencies can vanish, the past can be altered, and the plainest facts can be denied.

If one harbours anywhere in one's mind a nationalistic loyalty or hatred, certain facts, although in a sense known to be true, are inadmissible. Here are just a few examples. I list below five types of nationalist, and against each I append a fact which it is impossible for that type of nationalist to accept, even in his secret thoughts:

BRITISH TORY. Britain will come out of this war with reduced power and prestige.

COMMUNIST. If she had not been aided by Britain and America, Russia would have been defeated by Germany.

IRISH NATIONALIST. Eire can only remain independent because of British protection.

TROTSKYIST. The Stalin régime is accepted by the Russian masses.

PACIFIST. Those who 'abjure' violence can only do so because others are committing violence on their behalf.

All of these facts are grossly obvious if one's emotions do not happen to be involved: but to the kind of person named in each case they are also *intolerable*, and so they have to be denied, and false theories constructed upon their denial. I come back to the astonishing failure of military prediction in the present war. It is, I think, true to say that the intelligentsia have been more wrong about the progress of the war than the common people, and that they were more swayed by partisan feelings. The average intellectual of the Left believed, for instance, that the war was lost in 1940, that the Germans were bound to overrun Egypt in 1942, that the Japanese would never be driven out of the lands they had conquered, and that the Anglo-American bombing offensive was making no impression on Germany. He could believe these things because his hatred of the British ruling class forbade him to admit that British plans could succeed. There is no limit to the follies that can be swallowed if one is under the influence of feelings of this kind. I have heard it confidently stated, for instance, that the American troops had been brought to Europe not to fight the Germans but to crush an English revolution. One has to belong to the intelligentsia to believe things like that: no ordinary man could be such a fool. When Hitler invaded Russia, the officials of the MOI issued 'as background' a warning that Russia might be expected to collapse in six weeks. On the other hand the Communists regarded every phase of the war as a Russian victory, even when the Russians were driven back almost to the Caspian Sea and had lost several million prisoners. There is no need to multiply instances. The point is that as soon as fear, hatred, jealousy and power worship are involved, the sense of reality becomes unhinged. And, as I have pointed out already, the sense of right and wrong becomes unhinged also. There is no crime, absolutely none, that cannot be condoned when 'our' side commits it. Even if one does not deny that the crime has happened, even if one knows that it is exactly the same crime as one had condemned in some other case, even if one admits in an intellectual sense that it is unjustified – still one cannot *feel* that it is wrong. Loyalty is involved, and so pity ceases to function.

The reason for the rise and spread of nationalism is far too big a question to be raised here. It is enough to say that, in the forms in which it appears among English intellectuals, it is a distorted reflection of the frightful battles actually happening in the external world, and that its worst follies have been made possible by the break-down of patriotism and religious belief. If one follows up this train of thought, one is in danger of being led into a species of Conservatism, or into political quietism. It can be plausibly argued, for instance – it is even probably true – that patriotism is an inoculation against nationalism, that monarchy is a guard against dictatorship, and that organized religion is a guard against superstition. Or again it can be argued that *no* unbiassed outlook is possible, that *all* creeds and causes involve the same lies, follies and barbarities; and this is often advanced as a reason for keeping out of politics altogether. I do not accept this argument, if only because in the modern world no one describable as an intellectual *can* keep out of politics in the sense of not caring about them. I think one must engage in politics – using the word in a wide sense – and that one must have preferences: that is, one must recognize that some causes are objectively better than others, even if they are advanced by equally bad means. As for the nationalistic loves and hatreds that I have spoken of, they are part of the make-up of most of us, whether we like it or not. Whether it is possible to get rid of them I do not know, but I do believe that it is possible to struggle against them, and that this is essentially a *moral* effort. It is a question first of all of discovering what one really is, what one's own feelings really are, and then making allowance for the inevitable bias. If you hate and fear Russia, if you are jealous of the wealth and power of America, if you despise Jews, if you have a sentiment of inferiority towards the British ruling class, you cannot get rid of those feelings simply by taking thought. But you can at least recognize that you have them, and prevent them from contaminating your mental processes. The emotional urges which are inescapable, and are perhaps even necessary to political action, should be able to exist side by side with an acceptance of reality. But this, I repeat, needs a *moral* effort, and contemporary English literature, so far as it is alive at all to the major issues of our time, shows how few of us are prepared to make it.

Written [May 1945]

ESSAYS AND JOURNALISM 1945-1949

Revenge Is Sour

Whenever I read phrases like 'war guilt trials', 'punishment of war criminals', and so forth, there comes back into my mind the memory of something I saw in a prisoner-of-war camp in South Germany, earlier this year.

Another correspondent and myself were being shown round the camp by a little Viennese Jew who had been enlisted in the branch of the American army which deals with the interrogation of prisoners. He was an alert, fair-headed, rather good-looking youth of about twenty-five, and politically so much more knowledgeable than the average American officer that it was a pleasure to be with him. The camp was on an airfield, and, after we had been round the cages, our guide led us to a hangar where various prisoners who were in a different category from the others were being 'screened'.

Up at one end of the hangar about a dozen men were lying in a row on the concrete floor. These, it was explained, were SS officers who had been segregated from the other prisoners. Among them was a man in dingy civilian clothes who was lying with his arms across his face and apparently asleep. He had strangely and horribly deformed feet. The two of them were quite symmetrical, but they were clubbed out into an extraordinary globular shape which made them more like a horse's hoof than anything human. As we approached the group the little Jew seemed to be working himself up into a state of excitement.

'That's the real swine!' he said, and suddenly he lashed out with his heavy army boot and caught the prostrate man a fearful kick right on the bulge of one of his deformed feet.

'Get up, you swine!' he shouted as the man started out of sleep, and then repeated something of the kind in German. The prisoner scrambled to his feet and stood clumsily to attention. With the same air of working himself up into a fury – indeed he was almost dancing up and down as he spoke – the Jew told us the prisoner's history. He was a 'real' Nazi: his party number indicated that he had been a member since the very early days, and he had held a post corresponding to a General in the political branch of the SS. It could be taken as quite certain that he had had charge of concentration camps and had presided over tortures and hangings. In short, he represented everything that we had been fighting against during the past five years.

Meanwhile, I was studying his appearance. Quite apart from the scrubby, unfed, unshaven look that a newly captured man generally has, he was a disgusting specimen. But he did not look brutal or in any way frightening: merely neurotic and, in a low way, intellectual. His pale, shifty eyes were deformed by powerful spectacles. He could have been an unfrocked clergyman, an actor ruined by drink, or a spiritualist medium. I have seen very similar people in London common lodging-houses, and also in the Reading Room of the British Museum. Quite obviously he was mentally unbalanced – indeed, only doubtfully sane, though at this moment sufficiently in his right mind to be frightened of getting another kick. And yet everything that the Jew was telling me of his history could have been true, and probably was true! So the Nazi torturer of one's imagination, the monstrous figure against whom one had struggled for so many years, dwindled to this pitiful wretch, whose obvious need was not for punishment, but for some kind of psychological treatment.

Later, there were further humiliations. Another SS officer, a large, brawny man, was ordered to strip to the waist and show the blood-group number tattooed on his under-arm; another was forced to explain to us how he had lied about being a member of the SS and attempted to pass himself off as an ordinary soldier of the Wehrmacht. I wondered whether the Jew was getting any real kick out of this new-found power that he was exercising. I concluded that he wasn't really enjoying it, and that he was merely – like a man in a brothel, or a boy smoking his first cigar, or a tourist traipsing round a picture gallery – *telling* himself that he was enjoying it, and behaving as he had planned to behave in the days when he was helpless.

It is absurd to blame any German or Austrian Jew for getting his own back on the Nazis. Heaven knows what scores this particular man may have had to wipe out; very likely his whole family had been murdered; and, after all, even a wanton kick to a prisoner is a very tiny thing compared with the outrages committed by the Hitler régime. But what this scene, and much else that I saw in Germany, brought home to me was that the whole idea of revenge and punishment is a childish day-dream. Properly speaking, there is no such thing as revenge. Revenge is an act which you want to commit when you are powerless and because you are powerless: as soon as the sense of impotence is removed, the desire evaporates also.

Who would not have jumped for joy, in 1940, at the thought of seeing SS officers kicked and humiliated? But when the thing becomes possible, it is merely pathetic and disgusting. It is said that when Mussolini's corpse was exhibited in public, an old woman drew a revolver and fired shots into it, exclaiming, 'Those are for my five sons!' It is the kind of story that the newspapers make up, but it might be true. I wonder how much satisfaction she got out of those five shots, which, doubtless, she had dreamed years earlier of firing. The condition of her being able to get near enough to Mussolini to shoot at him was that he should be a corpse.

In so far as the big public in this country is responsible for the monstrous peace settlement now being forced on Germany, it is because of a failure to see in advance that punishing an enemy brings no satisfaction. We acquiesced in crimes like the expulsion of all Germans from East Prussia – crimes which in some cases we could not prevent but might at least have protested against – because the Germans had angered and frightened us, and therefore we were certain that when they were down we should feel no pity for them. We persist in these policies, or let others persist in them on our behalf, because of a vague feeling that, having set out to punish Germany, we ought to go ahead and do it. Actually there is little acute hatred of Germany left in this country, and even less, I should expect to find, in the army of occupation. Only the minority of sadists, who must have their 'atrocities' from one source or another, take a keen interest in the hunting-down of war criminals and quislings. If you ask the average man what crime Goering, Ribbentrop and the rest are to be charged with at their trial, he cannot tell you. Somehow the punishment of these monsters ceases to seem attractive when it becomes possible: indeed, once under lock and key, they almost cease to be monsters.

Unfortunately, there is often need of some concrete incident before one can discover the real state of one's feelings. Here is another memory from Germany.

A few hours after Stuttgart was captured by the French army, a Belgian journalist and myself entered the town, which was still in some disorder. The Belgian had been broadcasting throughout the war for the European Service of the BBC, and, like nearly all Frenchmen or Belgians, he had a very much tougher attitude towards 'the Boche' than an Englishman or an American would have. All the main bridges into the town had been blown up, and we had to enter by a small footbridge which the Germans had evidently made efforts to defend. A dead German soldier was lying supine at the foot of the steps. His face was a waxy yellow. On his breast someone had laid a bunch of the lilac which was blossoming everywhere.

The Belgian averted his face as we went past. When we were well over the bridge he confided to me that this was the first time he had seen a dead man. I suppose he was thirty-five years old, and for four years he had been doing war propaganda over the radio. For several days after this, his attitude was quite different from what it had been earlier. He looked with disgust at the bomb-wrecked town and the humiliations the Germans were undergoing, and even on one occasion intervened to prevent a particularly bad bit of looting. When he left, he gave the residue of the coffee we had brought with us to the Germans on whom we were billeted. A week earlier he would probably have been scandalized at the idea of giving coffee to a 'Boche'. But his feelings, he told me, had undergone a change at the sight of 'ce pauvre mort' beside the bridge: it had suddenly brought home to him the meaning of war. And yet, if we had happened to enter the town by another route, he might have been spared the experience of seeing even one corpse out of the – perhaps – twenty million that the war has produced.

Tribune, 9 November 1945

You and the Atom Bomb

Considering how likely we all are to be blown to pieces by it within the next five years, the atomic bomb has not roused so much discussion as might have been expected. The newspapers have published numerous diagrams, not very helpful to the average man, of protons and neutrons doing their stuff, and there has been much reiteration of the useless statements that the bomb 'ought to be put under international control'. But curiously little has been said, at any rate in print, about the question that is of most urgent interest to all of us, namely: 'How difficult are these things to manufacture?'

Such information as we – that is, the big public – possess on this subject has come to us in a rather indirect way, apropos of President Truman's decision not to hand over certain secrets to the USSR. Some months ago, when the bomb was still only a rumour, there was widespread belief that splitting the atom was merely a problem for the physicists, and that when they had solved it a new and devastating weapon would be within reach of almost everybody. (At any moment, so the rumour went, some lonely lunatic in a laboratory might blow civilization to smithereens, as easily as touching off a firework.)

Had that been true, the whole trend of history would have been abruptly altered. The distinction between great states and small states would have been wiped out, and the power of the State over the individual would have been greatly weakened. However, it appears from President Truman's remarks, and various comments that have been made on them, that the bomb is fantastically expensive and that its manufacture demands an enormous industrial effort, such as only three or four countries in the world are capable of making. This point is of cardinal importance, because it may mean that the discovery of the atomic bomb, so far from reversing history, will simply intensify the trends which have been apparent for a dozen years past.

It is a commonplace that the history of civilization is largely the history of weapons. In particular, the connection between the discovery of gunpowder and the overthrow of feudalism by the bourgeoisie has been pointed out over and over again. And though I have no doubt exceptions can be brought forward, I think the following rule would be found generally true: that ages in which the dominant weapon is expensive or difficult to make will tend to be ages of despotism, whereas when the dominant weapon is cheap and simple, the common people have a chance. Thus, for example, tanks, battleships and bombing planes are inherently tyrannical weapons, while rifles, muskets, long-bows and hand-grenades are inherently democratic weapons. A complex weapon makes the strong stronger, while a simple weapon – so long as there is no answer to it – gives claws to the weak.

The great age of democracy and of national self-determination was the age of the musket and the rifle. After the invention of the flint-lock, and before the invention of the percussion cap, the musket was a fairly efficient weapon, and at the same time so simple that it could be produced almost anywhere. Its combination of qualities made possible the success of the American and French revolutions, and made a popular insurrection a more serious business than it could be in our own day. After the musket came the breech-loading rifle. This was a comparatively complex thing, but it could still be produced in scores of countries, and it was cheap, easily smuggled and economical of ammunition. Even the most backward nation could always get hold of rifles from one source or another, so that Boers, Bulgars, Abyssinians, Moroccans – even Tibetans – could put up a fight for their independence, sometimes with success. But thereafter every development in military technique has favoured the State as against the individual, and the industrialized country as against the backward one. There are fewer and fewer foci of power. Already, in 1939, there were only five states capable of waging war on the grand scale, and now there are only three – ultimately, perhaps, only two. This trend has been obvious for years, and was pointed out by a few observers even before 1914. The one thing that might reverse it is the discovery of a weapon – or, to put it more broadly, of a method of fighting – not dependent on huge concentrations of industrial plant.

From various symptoms one can infer that the Russians do not yet possess the secret of making the atomic bomb; on the other hand, the consensus of opinion seems to be that they will possess it within a few years. So we have before us the prospect of two or three monstrous super-states, each possessed of a weapon by which millions of people can be wiped out in a few seconds, dividing the world between them. It has been rather hastily assumed that this means bigger and bloodier wars, and perhaps an actual end to the machine civilization. But suppose – and really this is the likeliest development – that the surviving great nations make a tacit agreement never to use the atomic bomb against one another? Suppose they only use it, or the threat of it, against people who are unable to retaliate? In that case we are back where we were before, the only difference being that power is concentrated in still fewer hands and that the outlook for subject peoples and oppressed classes is still more hopeless.

When James Burnham wrote *The Managerial Revolution* it seemed probable to many Americans that the Germans would win the European end of the war, and it was therefore natural to assume that Germany and not Russia would dominate the Eurasian land mass, while Japan would remain master of East Asia. This was a miscalculation, but it does not affect the main argument. For Burnham's geographical picture of the new world has turned out to be correct. More and more obviously the surface of the earth is being parcelled off into three great empires, each self-contained and cut off from contact with the outer world, and each ruled, under one disguise or another, by a self-elected oligarchy. The haggling as to where the frontiers are to be drawn is still going on, and will continue for some years, and the third of the three super-states – East Asia, dominated by China – is still potential rather than actual. But the general drift is unmistakable, and every scientific discovery of recent years has accelerated it.

We were once told that the aeroplane had 'abolished frontiers'; actually it is only since the aeroplane became a serious weapon that frontiers have become definitely impassable. The radio was once expected to promote international understanding and co-operation; it has turned out to be a means of insulating one nation from another. The atomic bomb may complete the process by robbing the exploited classes and peoples of all power to revolt, and at the same time putting the possessors of the bomb on a basis of military equality. Unable to conquer one another, they are likely to continue ruling the world between them, and it is difficult to see how the balance can be upset except by slow and unpredictable demographic changes.

For forty or fifty years past, Mr H. G. Wells and others have been warning us that man is in danger of destroying himself with his own weapons, leaving the ants or some other gregarious species to take over. Anyone who has seen the ruined cities of Germany will find this notion at least thinkable. Nevertheless, looking at the world as a whole, the drift for many decades has been not towards anarchy but towards the reimposition of slavery. We may be heading not for general breakdown but for an epoch as horribly stable as the slave empires of antiquity. James Burnham's theory has been much discussed, but few people have yet considered its ideological implications – that is, the kind of world-view, the kind of beliefs, and the social structure that would probably prevail in a state which was at once *unconquerable* and in a permanent state of 'cold war' with its neighbours.

Had the atomic bomb turned out to be something as cheap and easily manufactured as a bicycle or an alarm clock, it might well have plunged us back into barbarism, but it might, on the other hand, have meant the end of national sovereignty and of the highly-centralized police state. If, as seems to be the case, it is a rare and costly object as difficult to produce as a battleship, it is likelier to put an end to large-scale wars at the cost of prolonging indefinitely a 'peace that is no peace'.

Tribune, 19 October 1945

Introduction to *Love of Life and Other Stories* by Jack London

In her little book, *Memories of Lenin*, Nadezhda Krupskaya relates that when Lenin was in his last illness she used to read aloud to him in the evenings:

> Two days before his death I read to him in the evening a tale by Jack London, 'Love of Life' – it is still lying on the table in his room. It was a very fine story. In a wilderness of ice, where no human being had set foot, a sick man, dying of hunger, is making for the harbour of a big river. His strength is giving out, he cannot walk but keeps slipping, and beside him there slides a wolf – also dying of hunger. There is a fight between them: the man wins. Half dead, half demented, he reaches his goal. That tale greatly pleased Ilyich (Lenin). Next day he asked me to read him more Jack London.

However, Krupskaya goes on, the next tale turned out to be 'saturated with bourgeois morals', and 'Ilyich smiled and dismissed it with a wave of his hand.' These two pieces by Jack London were the last things that she read to him.

The story, 'Love of Life', is even grimmer than Krupskaya suggests in her short summary of it, for it actually ends with the man eating the wolf, or at any rate biting into its throat hard enough to draw blood. That is the sort of theme towards which Jack London was irresistibly drawn, and this episode of Lenin's death bed readings is of itself not a bad criticism of London's work. He was a writer who excelled in describing cruelty, whose main theme, indeed, was the cruelty of Nature, or at any rate of contemporary life; he was also an extremely variable writer, much of whose work was produced hurriedly and at low pressure; and he had in him a strain of feeling which Krupskaya is probably right in calling 'bourgeois' – at any rate, a strain which did not accord with his democratic and Socialist convictions.

During the last twenty years Jack London's short stories have been rather unaccountably forgotten – how thoroughly forgotten, one could gauge by the completeness with which they were out of print. So far as the big public went, he was remembered by various animal books, particularly *White Fang* and *The Call of the Wild* – books which appealed to the Anglo-Saxon sentimentality about animals – and after 1933 his reputation took an upward bound because of *The Iron Heel*, which had been written in 1907, and is in some sense a prophecy of Fascism. *The Iron Heel* is not a good book, and on the whole its predictions have not been borne out. Its dates and its geography are ridiculous, and London makes the mistake, which was usual at that time, of assuming that revolution would break out first in the highly industrialized countries. But on several points London was right where nearly all other prophets were wrong, and he was right because of just that strain in his nature that made him a good short-story writer and a doubtfully reliable Socialist.

London imagines a proletarian revolution breaking out in the United States and being crushed, or partially crushed, by a counter-offensive of the capitalist class; and, following on this, a long period during which society is ruled over by a small group of tyrants known as the Oligarchs, who are served by a kind of SS known as the Mercenaries. An underground struggle against dictatorship was the kind of thing that London could imagine, and he foresaw certain of the details with surprising accuracy; he foresaw, for instance, that peculiar horror of totalitarian society, the way in which suspected enemies of the régime *simply disappear*. But the book is chiefly notable for maintaining that capitalist society would not perish of its 'contradictions', but that the possessing class would be able to form itself into a vast corporation and even evolve a sort of perverted Socialism, sacrificing many of its privileges in order to preserve its superior status. The passages in which London analyses the mentality of the Oligarchs are of great interest:

> They, as a class (writes the imaginary author of the book), believed that they alone maintained civilization. It was their belief that, if they ever weakened, the great beast would engulf them and everything of beauty and joy and wonder and good in its cavernous and slime-dripping maw. Without them, anarchy would reign and humanity would drop backward into the primitive night out of which it had so painfully emerged... In short, they alone, by their unremitting toil and self-sacrifice, stood between weak humanity and the all-devouring beast: and they believed it, firmly believed it.
>
> I cannot lay too great stress upon this high ethical righteousness of the whole Oligarch class. This has been the strength of the Iron Heel, and too many of the comrades have been slow or loath to realize it. Many of them have ascribed the strength of the Iron Heel to its system of reward and punishment. This is a mistake. Heaven and hell may be the prime factors of zeal in the religion of a fanatic; but for the great majority of the religious, heaven and hell are incidental to right and wrong. Love of the right, desire for the right, unhappiness with anything less than the right – in short, right conduct, is the prime factor of religion. And so with the Oligarchy... The great driving force of the Oligarchs is the belief that they are doing right.

From these and similar passages it can be seen that London's understanding of the nature of a ruling class – that is, the characteristics which a ruling class must have if it is to survive – went very deep. According to the conventional left-wing view, the 'capitalist' is simply a cynical scoundrel, without honour or courage, and intent only on filling his own pockets. London knew that that view is false. But why, one might justly ask, should this hurried, sensational, in some ways childish writer have understood that particular thing so much better than the majority of his fellow Socialists?

The answer is surely that London could foresee Fascism because he had a Fascist streak in himself: or at any rate a marked strain of brutality and an almost unconquerable preference for the strong man as against the weak man. He knew instinctively that the American businessmen would fight when their possessions were menaced, because in their place he would have fought himself. He was an adventurer and a man of action as few writers have ever been. Born into dire poverty, he had already escaped from it at sixteen, thanks to his commanding character and powerful physique: his early years were spent among oyster pirates, gold prospectors, tramps and prize-fighters, and he was ready to admire toughness wherever he found it. On the other hand he never forgot the sordid miseries of his childhood, and he never faltered in his loyalty to the exploited classes. Much of his time was spent in working and lecturing for the Socialist movement, and when he was already a successful and famous man he could explore the worst depths of poverty in the London slums, passing himself off as an American sailor, and compile a book (*The People of the Abyss*) which still has sociological value. His outlook was democratic in the sense that he hated exploitation and hereditary privilege, and that he felt most at home in the company of people who worked with their hands: but his instinct lay towards acceptance of a 'natural aristocracy' of strength, beauty and talent. Intellectually he knew, as one can see from various remarks in *The Iron Heel*, that Socialism ought to mean the meek inheriting the earth, but that was not what his temperament demanded. In much of his work one strain in his character simply kills the other off: he is at his best where they interact, as they do in certain of his short stories.

Jack London's great theme is the cruelty of Nature. Life is a savage struggle, and victory has nothing to do with justice. In the best of his short stories there is a startling lack of comment, a suspension of judgement arising out of the fact that he both delights in the struggle and perceives its cruelty. Perhaps the best thing he ever wrote is 'Just Meat'. Two burglars have got away with a big haul of jewellery: each is intent on swindling the other out of his share, and they poison one another simultaneously with strychnine, the story ending with the two men dead on the floor. There is almost no comment, and certainly no 'moral'. As Jack London sees it, it is simply a fragment of life, the kind of thing that happens in the present-day world: nevertheless it is doubtful whether such a plot would occur to any writer who was not fascinated by cruelty. Or take a story like 'The *Francis Spaight*'. The starving crew of a waterlogged ship have decided to resort to cannibalism, and have just nerved themselves to begin when another ship heaves in sight. It is characteristic of Jack London that the second ship should appear after and not before the cabin boy's throat has been cut. A still more typical story is 'A Piece of Steak'. London's love of boxing and admiration for sheer physical strength, his perception of the meanness and cruelty of a competitive society, and at the same time his instinctive tendency to accept *vae victis* as a law of Nature, are all expressed here. An old prize-fighter is fighting his last battle: his opponent is a beginner, young and full of vigour, but without experience. The old man nearly wins, but in the end his ring-craft is no match for the youthful resilience of the other. Even when he has him at his mercy he is unable to strike the blow that would finish him, because he has been underfed for weeks before the fight and his muscles cannot make the necessary effort. He is left bitterly reflecting that if only he had had a good piece of steak on the day of the fight he would have won.

The old man's thoughts all run upon the theme: 'Youth will be served.' First you are young and strong, and you knock out older men and make money which you squander: then your strength wanes and in turn you are knocked out by younger men, and then you sink into poverty. This does in fact tell the story of the average boxer's life, and it would be a gross exaggeration to say that Jack London *approves* of the way in which men are used up like gladiators by a society which cannot even bother to feed them. The detail of the piece of steak – not strictly necessary, since the main point of the story is that the younger man is bound to win by virtue of his youth – rubs in the economic implication. And yet there is something in London that takes a kind of pleasure in the whole cruel process. It is not so much an approval of the harshness of Nature, as a mystical belief that Nature *is* like that. Nature is 'red in tooth and claw'. Perhaps fierceness is bad, but fierceness is the price of survival. The young slay the old, the strong slay the weak, by an inexorable law. Man fights against the elements or against his fellow man, and there is nothing except his own toughness to help him through. London would have said that he was merely describing life as it is actually lived, and in his best stories he does so: still, the constant recurrence of the same theme – struggle, toughness, survival – shows which way his inclinations pointed.

London has been deeply influenced by the theory of the Survival of the Fittest. His book, *Before Adam* – an inaccurate but very readable story of prehistory, in which ape-man and early and late Palaeolithic men are all shown as existing simultaneously – is an attempt to popularize Darwin. Although Darwin's main thesis has not been shaken, there has been, during the past twenty or thirty years, a change in the interpretation put upon it by the average thinking man. In the late nineteenth century Darwinism was used as a justification for *laissez-faire* capitalism, for power politics and for the exploiting of subject peoples. Life was a free-for-all in which the fact of survival was proof of fitness to survive: this was a comforting thought for successful businessmen, and it also led naturally, though not very logically, to the notion of 'superior' and 'inferior' races. In our day we are less willing to apply biology to politics, partly because we have watched the Nazis do just that thing, with great thoroughness and with horrible results. But when London was writing, a crude version of Darwinism was widespread and must have been difficult to escape. He himself was even capable at times of succumbing to racial mysticism. He toyed for a while with a race theory similar to that of the Nazis, and throughout his work the cult of the 'nordic' is fairly well marked. It ties up on the one hand with his admiration for prize-fighters, and on the other with his anthropomorphic view of animals: for there seems to be good reason for thinking that an exaggerated love of animals generally goes with a rather brutal attitude towards human beings. London was a Socialist with the instincts of a buccaneer and the education of a nineteenth-century materialist. In general the background of his stories is not industrial, nor even civilized. Most of them take place – and much of his own life was lived – on ranches or South Sea islands, in ships, in prison or in the wastes of the Arctic; places where a man is either alone and dependent on his own strength and cunning, or where life is naturally patriarchal.

Nevertheless, London did write from time to time about contemporary industrial society, and on the whole he was at his best when he did so. Apart from his short stories, there are *The People of the Abyss*, *The Road* (a brilliant little book describing London's youthful experiences as a tramp), and certain passages in *The Valley of the Moon*, which have the tumultuous history of American trade unionism as their background. Although the tug of his impulses was away from civilization, London had read deeply in the literature of the Socialist movement, and his early life had taught him all he needed to know about urban poverty. He himself was working in a factory at the age of eleven, and without that experience behind him he could hardly have written such a story as 'The Apostate'. In this story, as in all his best work, London does not comment, but he does unquestionably aim at rousing pity and indignation.

It is generally when he writes of more primitive scenes that his moral attitude becomes equivocal. Take, for instance, a story like 'Make Westing'. With whom do London's sympathies lie – with Captain Cullen or with George Dorety? One has the impression that if he were forced to make a choice he would side with the Captain, who commits two murders but does succeed in getting his ship round Cape Horn. On the other hand, in a story like 'The Chinago', although it is told in the usual pitiless style, the 'moral' is plain enough for anyone who wants to find it. London's better angel is his Socialist convictions, which come into play when he deals with such subjects as coloured exploitation, child labour or the treatment of criminals, but are hardly involved when he is writing about explorers or animals. It is probably for this reason that a high proportion of his better writings deal with urban life. In stories like 'The Apostate', 'Just Meat', 'A Piece of Steak' and 'Semper Idem', however cruel and sordid they may seem, something is keeping him on the rails and checking his natural urge towards the glorification of brutality. That 'something is his knowledge, theoretical as well as practical, of what industrial capitalism means in terms of human suffering.

Jack London is a very uneven writer. In his short and restless life he poured forth an immense quantity of work, setting himself to produce 1,000 words every day and generally achieving it. Even his best stories have the curious quality of being well told and yet not well written: they are told with admirable economy, with just the right incidents in just the right place, but the texture of the writing is poor, the phrases are worn and obvious,. and the dialogue is erratic. His reputation has had its ups and downs, and for a long period he seems to have been much more admired in France and Germany than in the English-speaking countries. Even before the triumph of Hitler, which brought *The Iron Heel* out of its obscurity, he had a certain renown as a left-wing and 'proletarian' writer – rather the same kind of renown as attaches to Robert Tressell, W. B. Traven or Upton Sinclair. He has also been attacked by Marxist writers for his 'Fascist tendencies'. These tendencies unquestionably existed in him, so much so that if one imagines him as living on into our own day, instead of dying in 1915, it is very hard to be sure where his political allegiance would have lain. One can imagine him in the Communist Party, one can imagine him falling a victim to Nazi racial theory, and one can imagine him the quixotic champion of some Trotskyist or Anarchist sect. But, as I have tried to make clear, if he had been a politically reliable person he would probably have left behind nothing of interest. Meanwhile his reputation rests mainly on *The Iron Heel*, and the excellence of his short stories has been almost forgotten. A dozen of the best of them are collected in this volume, and a few more are worth rescuing from the museum shelves and the second-hand boxes. It is to be hoped, too, that new editions of *The Road, The Jacket, Before Adam* and *The Valley of the Moon* will appear when paper becomes more plentiful. Much of Jack London's work is scamped and unconvincing, but he produced at least six volumes which deserve to stay in print, and that is not a bad achievement from a life of only forty-one years.

Written [November 1945]

The Prevention of Literature

About a year ago I attended a meeting of the PEN Club, the occasion being the tercentenary of Milton's *Areopagitica* – a pamphlet, it may be remembered, in defence of freedom of the press. Milton's famous phrase about the sin of 'killing' a book was printed on the leaflets, advertising the meeting, which had been circulated beforehand.

There were four speakers on the platform. One of them delivered a speech which did deal with the freedom of the press, but only in relation to India; another said, hesitantly, and in very general terms, that liberty was a good thing; a third delivered an attack on the laws relating to obscenity in literature. The fourth devoted most of his speech to a defence of the Russian purges. Of the speeches from the body of the hall, some reverted to the question of obscenity and the laws that deal with it, others were simply eulogies of Soviet Russia. Moral liberty – the liberty to discuss sex questions frankly in print – seemed to be generally approved, but political liberty was not mentioned. Out of this concourse of several hundred people, perhaps half of whom were directly connected with the writing trade, there was not a single one who could point out that freedom of the press, if it means anything at all, means the freedom to criticise and oppose. Significantly, no speaker quoted from the pamphlet which was ostensibly being commemorated. Nor was there any mention of the various books that have been 'killed' in this country and the United States during the war. In its net effect the meeting was a demonstration in favour of censorship.[1]

There was nothing particularly surprising in this. In our age, the idea of intellectual liberty is under attack from two directions. On the one side are its theoretical enemies, the apologists of totalitarianism, and on the other its immediate, practical enemies, monopoly and bureaucracy. Any writer or journalist who wants to retain his integrity finds himself thwarted by the general drift of society rather than by active persecution. The sort of things that are working against him are the concentration of the press in the hands of a few rich men, the grip of monopoly on radio and the films, the unwillingness of the public to spend money on books, making it necessary for nearly every writer to earn part of his living by hack work, the encroachment of official bodies like the MOI[2] and the British Council, which help the writer to keep alive but also waste his time and dictate his opinions, and the continuous war atmosphere of the past ten years, whose distorting effects no one has been able to escape. Everything in our age conspires to turn the writer, and every other kind of artist as well, into a minor official, working on themes handed to him from above and never telling what seems to him the whole of the truth. But in

[1] It is fair to say that the PEN Club celebrations, which lasted a week or more, did not always stick at quite the same level. I happened to strike a bad day. But an examination of the speeches (printed under the title *Freedom of Expression*) shows that almost nobody in our own day is able to speak out as roundly in favour of intellectual liberty as Milton could do 300 years ago – and this in spite of the fact Milton was writing in a period of civil war. [Author's footnote.]

[2] Ministry of Information.

struggling against this fate he gets no help from his own side: that is, there is no large body of opinion which will assure him that he is in the right. In the past, at any rate throughout the Protestant centuries, the idea of rebellion and the idea of intellectual integrity were mixed up. A heretic – political, moral, religious, or aesthetic – was one who refused to outrage his own conscience. His outlook was summed up in the words of the Revivalist hymn:

Dare to be a Daniel,
Dare to stand alone;
Dare to have a purpose firm,
Dare to make it known.

To bring this hymn up to date one would have to add a 'Don't' at the beginning of each line. For it is the peculiarity of our age that the rebels against the existing order, at any rate the most numerous and characteristic of them, are also rebelling against the idea of individual integrity. 'Daring to stand alone' is ideologically criminal as well as practically dangerous. The independence of the writer and the artist is eaten away by vague economic forces, and at the same time it is undermined by those who should be its defenders. It is with the second process that I am concerned here.

Freedom of thought and of the press are usually attacked by arguments which are not worth bothering about. Anyone who has experience of lecturing and debating knows them off backwards. Here I am not trying to deal with the familiar claim that freedom is an illusion, or with the claim that there is more freedom in totalitarian countries than in democratic ones, but with the much more tenable and dangerous proposition that freedom is undesirable and that intellectual honesty is a form of antisocial selfishness. Although other aspects of the question are usually in the foreground, the controversy over freedom of speech and of the press is at the bottom a controversy over the desirability, or otherwise, of telling lies. What is really at issue is the right to report contemporary events truthfully, or as truthfully as is consistent with the ignorance, bias and self-deception from which every observer necessarily suffers. In saying this I may seem to be saying that straightforward 'reportage' is the only branch of literature that matters: but I will try to show later that at every literary level, and probably in every one of the arts, the same issue arises in more or less subtilized forms. Meanwhile, it is necessary to strip away the irrelevancies in which this controversy is usually wrapped up.

The enemies of intellectual liberty always try to present their case as a plea for discipline versus individualism. The issue truth-versus-untruth is as far as possible kept in the background. Although the point of emphasis may vary, the writer who refuses to sell his opinions is always branded as a mere egoist. He is accused, that is, either of wanting to shut himself up in an ivory tower, or of making an exhibitionist display of his own personality, or of resisting the inevitable current of history in an attempt to cling to unjustified privileges. The Catholic and the Communist are alike in assuming that an opponent cannot be both honest and intelligent. Each of them tacitly claims that 'the truth' has already been revealed, and that the heretic, if he is not simply a fool, is secretly aware of 'the truth' and merely resists it out of selfish motives. In Communist literature the attack on intellectual liberty is usually masked by oratory about 'petty-bourgeois individualism', 'the illusions of nineteenth-century liberalism', etc., and backed up by words of abuse such as 'romantic' and 'sentimental', which, since they do not have any agreed meaning, are difficult to answer. In this way the controversy is manoeuvred away from its real issue. One can accept, and most enlightened people would accept, the Communist thesis that pure freedom will only exist in a classless society, and that one is most nearly free when one is working to bring such a society about. But slipped in with this is the quite unfounded claim that the Communist Party is itself aiming at the establishment of the classless society, and that in the USSR this aim is actually on the way to being realized. If the first claim is allowed to entail the second, there is almost no assault on common sense and common decency that cannot be justified. But meanwhile, the real point has been dodged. Freedom of the intellect means the freedom to report what one has seen, heard, and felt, and not to be obliged to fabricate imaginary facts and feelings. The familiar tirades against 'escapism', 'individualism', 'romanticism' and so forth, are merely a forensic device, the aim of which is to make the perversion of history seem respectable.

Fifteen years ago, when one defended the freedom of the intellect, one had to defend it against Conservatives, against Catholics, and to some extent – for they were not of great importance in England – against Fascists. Today one has to defend it against Communists and 'fellow-travellers'. One ought not to exaggerate the direct influence of the small English Communist Party, but there can be no question about the poisonous effect of the Russian *mythos* on English intellectual life. Because of it, known facts are suppressed and distorted to such an extent as to make it doubtful whether a true history of our times can ever be written. Let me give just one instance out of the hundreds that could be cited. When Germany collapsed, it was found that very large numbers of Soviet Russians – mostly, no doubt, from non-political motives – had changed sides and were fighting for the Germans. Also, a small but not negligible proportion of the Russian prisoners and Displaced Persons refused to go back to the USSR, and some of them, at least, were repatriated against their will. These facts, known to many journalists on the spot, went almost unmentioned in the British press, while at the same time russophile publicists in England continued to justify the purges and deportations of 1936–8 by claiming that the USSR 'had no quislings'. The fog of lies and misinformation that surrounds such subjects as the Ukraine famine, the Spanish civil war, Russian policy in Poland, and so forth, is not due entirely to conscious dishonesty, but any writer or journalist who is fully sympathetic to the USSR – sympathetic, that is, in the way the Russians themselves would want him to be – does have to acquiesce in deliberate falsification on important issues. I have before me what must be a very rare pamphlet, written by Maxim Litvinov in 1918 and outlining the recent events in the Russian Revolution. It makes no mention of Stalin, but gives high praise to Trotsky, and also to Zinoviev, Kamenev and others. What could be the attitude of even the most intellectually scrupulous Communist towards such a pamphlet? At best, the obscurantist attitude of saying that it is an undesirable document and better suppressed. And if for some reason it were decided to issue a garbled version of the pamphlet, denigrating Trotsky and inserting references to Stalin, no Communist who remained faithful to his Party could protest. Forgeries almost as gross as this have been committed in recent years. But the significant thing is not that they happen, but that even when they are known about they provoke no reaction from the left-wing intelligentsia as a whole. The argument that to tell the truth would be 'inopportune' or would 'play into the hands of' somebody or other is felt to be unanswerable, and few people are bothered by the prospect of the lies which they condone getting out of the newspapers and into the history books.

The organized lying practised by totalitarian states is not, as is sometimes claimed, a temporary expedient of the same nature as military deception. It is something integral to totalitarianism, something that would still continue even if concentration camps and secret police forces had ceased to be necessary. Among intelligent Communists there is an underground legend to the effect that although the Russian Government is obliged now to deal in lying propaganda, frame-up trials, and so forth, it is secretly recording the true facts and will publish them at some future time. We can, I believe, be quite certain that this is not the case, because the mentality implied by such an action is that of a liberal historian who believes that the past cannot be altered and that a correct knowledge of history is valuable as a matter of course. From the totalitarian point of view history is something to be created rather than learned. A totalitarian state is in effect a theocracy, and its ruling caste, in order to keep its position, has to be thought of as infallible. But since, in practice, no one is infallible, it is frequently necessary to rearrange past events in order to show that this or that mistake was not made, or that this or that imaginary triumph actually happened. Then, again, every major change in policy demands a corresponding change of doctrine and a revaluation of prominent historical figures. This kind of thing happens everywhere, but is clearly likelier to lead to outright falsification in societies where only one opinion is permissible at any given moment. Totalitarianism demands, in fact, the continuous alteration of the past, and in the long run probably demands a disbelief in the very existence of objective truth. The friends of totalitarianism in this country usually tend to argue that since absolute truth is not attainable, a big lie is no worse than a little lie. It is pointed out that all historical records are biassed and inaccurate, or, on the other hand, that modern physics has proved that what seems to us the real world is an illusion, so that to believe in the evidence of one's senses is simply vulgar philistinism. A totalitarian society which succeeded in perpetuating itself would probably set up a schizophrenic system of thought, in which the laws of common sense held good in everyday life and in certain exact sciences, but could be disregarded by the politician, the historian, and the sociologist. Already there are countless people who would think it scandalous to falsify a scientific text-book, but would see nothing wrong in falsifying an historical fact. It is at the point where literature and politics cross that totalitarianism exerts its greatest pressure on the intellectual. The exact sciences are not, at this date, menaced to anything like the same extent. This partly accounts for the fact that in all countries it is easier for the scientists than for the writers to line up behind their respective governments.

To keep the matter in perspective, let me repeat what I said at the beginning of this essay: that in England the immediate enemies of truthfulness, and hence of freedom of thought, are the press lords, the film magnates, and the bureaucrats, but that on a long view the weakening of the desire for liberty among the intellectuals themselves is the most serious symptom of all. It may seem that all this time I have been talking about the effects of censorship, not on literature as a whole, but merely on one department of political journalism. Granted that Soviet Russia constitutes a sort of forbidden area in the British press, granted that issues like Poland, the Spanish civil war, the Russo-German Pact, and so forth, are debarred from serious discussion, and that if you possess information that conflicts with the prevailing orthodoxy you are expected to distort it or to keep quiet about it – granted all this, why should literature in the wider sense be affected? Is every writer a politician, and is every book necessarily a work of straightforward 'reportage'? Even under the tightest dictatorship, cannot the individual writer remain free inside his own mind and distil or disguise his unorthodox ideas in such a way that the authorities will be too stupid to recognize them? And in any case, if the writer himself is in agreement with the prevailing orthodoxy, why should it have a cramping effect on him? Is not literature, or any of the arts, likeliest to flourish in societies in which there are no major conflicts of opinion and no sharp distinction between the artist and his audience? Does one have to assume that every writer is a rebel, or even that a writer as such is an exceptional person?

Whenever one attempts to defend intellectual liberty against the claims of totalitarianism, one meets with these arguments in one form or another. They are based on a complete misunderstanding of what literature is, and how – one should perhaps rather say why – it comes into being. They assume that a writer is either a mere entertainer or else a venal hack who can switch from one line of propaganda to another as easily as an organ-grinder changing tunes. But after all, how is it that books ever come to be written? Above a quite low level, literature is an attempt to influence the viewpoint of one's contemporaries by recording experience. And so far as freedom of expression is concerned, there is not much difference between a mere journalist and the most 'unpolitical' imaginative writer. The journalist is unfree, and is conscious of unfreedom, when he is forced to write lies or suppress what seems to him important news: the imaginative writer is unfree when he has to falsify his subjective feelings, which from his point of view are facts. He may distort and caricature reality in order to make his meaning clearer, but he cannot misrepresent the scenery of his own mind: he cannot say with any conviction that he likes what he dislikes, or believes what he disbelieves. If he is forced to do so, the only result is that his creative faculties dry up. Nor can he solve the problem by keeping away from controversial topics. There is no such thing as genuinely non-political literature, and least of all in an age like our own, when fears, hatreds, and loyalties of a directly political kind are near to the surface of everyone's consciousness. Even a single taboo can have an all-round crippling effect upon the mind, because there is always the danger that any thought which is freely followed up may lead to the forbidden thought. It follows that the atmosphere of totalitarianism is deadly to any kind of prose writer, though a poet, at any rate a lyric poet, might possibly find it breathable. And in any totalitarian society that survives for more than a couple of generations, it is probable that prose literature, of the kind that has existed during the past four hundred years, must actually come to an end.

Literature has sometimes flourished under despotic régimes, but, as has often been pointed out, the despotisms of the past were not totalitarian. Their repressive apparatus was always inefficient, their ruling classes were usually either corrupt or apathetic or half-liberal in outlook, and the prevailing religious doctrines usually worked against perfectionism and the notion of human infallibility. Even so it is broadly true that prose literature has reached its highest levels in periods of democracy and free speculation. What is new in totalitarianism is that its doctrines are not only unchallengeable but also unstable. They have to be accepted on pain of damnation, but on the other hand they are always liable to be altered at a moment's notice. Consider, for example, the various attitudes, completely incompatible with one another, which an English Communist or 'fellow-traveller' has had to adopt towards the war between Britain and Germany. For years before September 1939 he was expected to be in a continuous stew about 'the horrors of Nazism' and to twist everything he wrote into a denunciation of Hitler: after September 1939, for twenty months, he had to believe that Germany was more sinned against than sinning, and the word 'Nazi', at least so far as print went, had to drop right out of his vocabulary. Immediately after hearing the 8 o'clock news bulletin on the morning of June 22, 1941, he had to start believing once again that Nazism was the most hideous evil the world had ever seen. Now, it is easy for a politician to make such changes: for a writer the case is somewhat different. If he is to switch his allegiance at exactly the right moment, he must either tell lies about his subjective feelings, or else suppress them altogether. In either case he has destroyed his dynamo. Not only will ideas refuse to come to him, but the very words he uses will seem to stiffen under his touch. Political writing in our time consists almost entirely of prefabricated phrases bolted together like the pieces of a child's Meccano set. It is the unavoidable result of self-censorship. To write in plain, vigorous language one has to think fearlessly, and if one thinks fearlessly one cannot be politically orthodox. It might be otherwise in an 'age of faith', when the prevailing orthodoxy has been long established and is not taken too seriously. In that case it would be possible, or might be possible, for large areas of one's mind to remain unaffected by what one oficially believed. Even so, it is worth noticing that prose literature almost disappeared during the only age of faith that Europe has ever enjoyed. Throughout the whole of the Middle Ages there was almost no imaginative prose literature and very little in the way of historical writing: and the intellectual leaders of society expressed their most serious thoughts in a dead language which barely altered during a thousand years.

Totalitarianism, however, does not so much promise an age of faith as an age of schizophrenia. A society becomes totalitarian when its structure becomes flagrantly artificial: that is, when its ruling class has lost its function but succeeds in clinging to power by force or fraud. Such a society, no matter how long it persists, can never afford to become either tolerant or intellectually stable. It can never permit either the truthful recording of facts, or the emotional sincerity, that literary creation demands. But to be corrupted by totalitarianism one does not have to live in a totalitarian country. The mere prevalence of certain ideas can spread a kind of poison that makes one subject after another impossible for literary purposes. Wherever there is an enforced orthodoxy – or even two orthodoxies, as often happens – good writing stops. This was well illustrated by the Spanish civil war. To many English intellectuals the war was a deeply moving experience, but not an experience about which they could write sincerely. There were only two things that you were allowed to say, and both of them were palpable lies; as a result, the war produced acres of print but almost nothing worth reading.

It is not certain whether the effects of totalitarianism upon verse need be so deadly as its effects on prose. There is a whole series of converging reasons why it is somewhat easier for a poet than for a prose writer to feel at home in an authoritarian society. To begin with, bureaucrats and other 'practical' men usually despise the poet too deeply to be much interested in what he is saying. Secondly, what the poet is saying – that is, what his poem 'means' if translated into prose – is relatively unimportant even to himself. The thought contained in a poem is always simple, and is no more the primary purpose of the poem than the anecdote is the primary purpose of a picture. A poem is an arrangement of sounds and associations, as a painting is an arrangement of brush-marks. For short snatches, indeed, as in the refrain of a song, poetry can even dispense with meaning altogether. It is therefore fairly easy for a poet to keep away from dangerous subjects and avoid uttering heresies: and even when he does utter them, they may escape notice. But above all, good verse, unlike good prose, is not necessarily an individual product. Certain kinds of poems, such as ballads, or, on the other hand, very artificial verse forms, can be composed co-operatively by groups of people. Whether the ancient English and Scottish ballads were originally produced by individuals, or by the people at large, is disputed; but at any rate they are non-individual in the sense that they constantly change in passing from mouth to mouth. Even in print no two versions of a ballad are ever quite the same. Many primitive peoples compose verse communally. Someone begins to improvise, probably accompanying himself on a musical instrument, somebody else chips in with a line or a rhyme when the first singer breaks down, and so the process continues until there exists a whole song or ballad which has no identifiable author.

In prose, this kind of intimate collaboration is quite impossible. Serious prose, in any case, has to be composed in solitude, whereas the excitement of being part of a group is actually an aid to certain kinds of versification. Verse – and perhaps good verse of its kind, though it would not be the highest kind – might survive under even the most inquisitorial régime. Even in a society where liberty and individuality had been extinguished, there would still be need either for patriotic songs and heroic ballads celebrating victories, or for elaborate exercises in flattery: and these are the kinds of poem that can be written to order, or composed communally, without necessarily lacking artistic value. Prose is a different matter, since the prose writer cannot narrow the range of his thoughts without killing his inventiveness. But the history of totalitarian societies, or of groups of people who have adopted the totalitarian outlook, suggests that loss of liberty is inimical to all forms of literature. German literature almost disappeared during the Hitler régime, and the case was not much better in Italy. Russian literature, so far as one can judge by translations, has deteriorated markedly since the early days of the Revolution, though some of the verse appears to be better than the prose. Few if any Russian novels that it is possible to take seriously have been translated for about fifteen years. In western Europe and America large sections of the literary intelligentsia have either passed through the Communist Party or been warmly sympathetic to it, but this whole leftward movement has produced extraordinarily few books worth reading. Orthodox Catholicism, again, seems to have a crushing effect upon certain literary forms, especially the novel. During a period of three hundred years, how many people have been at once good novelists and good Catholics? The fact is that certain themes cannot be celebrated in words, and tyranny is one of them. No one ever wrote a good book in praise of the Inquisition. Poetry might survive, in a totalitarian age, and certain arts or half-arts, such as architecture, might even find tyranny beneficial, but the prose writer would have no choice between silence and death. Prose literature as we know it is the product of rationalism, of the Protestant centuries, of the autonomous individual. And the destruction of intellectual liberty cripples the journalist, the sociological writer, the historian, the novelist, the critic and the poet, in that order. In the future it is possible that a new kind of literature, not involving individual feeling or truthful observation, may arise, but no such thing is at present imaginable. It seems much likelier that if the liberal culture that we have lived in since the Renaissance actually comes to an end, the literary art will perish with it.

Of course, print will continue to be used, and it is interesting to speculate what kinds of reading matter would survive in a rigidly totalitarian society. Newspapers will presumably continue until television technique reaches a higher level, but apart from newspapers it is doubtful even now whether the great mass of people in the industrialized countries feel the need for any kind of literature. They are unwilling, at any rate, to spend anywhere near as much on reading matter as they spend on several other recreations. Probably novels and stories will be completely superseded by film and radio productions. Or perhaps some kind of low-grade sensational fiction will survive, produced by a sort of conveyor-belt process that reduces human initiative to the mimimum.

It would probably not be beyond human ingenuity to write books by machinery. But a sort of mechanizing process can already be seen at work in the film and radio, in publicity and propaganda, and in the lower reaches of journalism. The Disney films, for instance, are produced by what is essentially a factory process, the work being done partly mechanically and partly by teams of artists who have to subordinate their individual style. Radio features are commonly written by tired hacks to whom the subject and the manner of treatment are dictated beforehand: even so, what they write is merely a kind of raw material to be chopped into shape by producers and censors. So also with the innumerable books and pamphlets commissioned by government departments. Even more machine-like is the production of short stories, serials, and poems for the very cheap magazines. Papers such as the *Writer* abound with advertisements of Literary Schools, all of them offering you ready-made plots at a few shillings a time. Some, together with the plot, supply the opening and closing sentences of each chapter. Others furnish you with a sort of algebraical formula by the use of which you can construct your plots for yourself. Others offer packs of cards marked with characters and situations, which have only to be shuffled and dealt in order to produce ingenious stories automatically. It is probably in some such way that the literature of a totalitarian society would be produced, if literature were still felt to be necessary. Imagination – even consciousness, so far as possible – would be eliminated from the process of writing. Books would be planned in their broad lines by bureaucrats, and would pass through so many hands that when finished they would be no more an individual product than a Ford car at the end of the assembly line. It goes without saying that anything so produced would be rubbish; but anything that was not rubbish would endanger the structure of the State. As for the surviving literature of the past, it would have to be suppressed or at least elaborately rewritten.

Meanwhile totalitarianism has not fully triumphed everywhere. Our own society is still, broadly speaking, liberal. To exercise your right of free speech you have to fight against economic pressure and against strong sections of public opinion, but not, as yet, against a secret police force. You can say or print almost anything so long as you are willing to do it in a hole-and-corner way. But what is sinister, as I said at the beginning of this essay, is that the conscious enemies of liberty are those to whom liberty ought to mean most. The big public do not care about the matter one way or the other. They are not in favour of persecuting the heretic, and they will not exert themselves to defend him. They are at once too sane and too stupid to acquire the totalitarian outlook. The direct, conscious attack on intellectual decency comes from the intellectuals themselves.

It is possible that the russophile intelligentsia, if they had not succumbed to that particular myth, would have succumbed to another of much the same kind. But at any rate the Russian myth is there, and the corruption it causes stinks. When one sees highly educated men looking on indifferently at oppression and persecution, one wonders which to despise more, their cynicism or their shortsightedness. Many scientists, for example, are the uncritical admirers of the USSR. They appear to think that the destruction of liberty is of no importance so long as their own line of work is for the moment unaffected. The USSR is a large, rapidly developing country which has acute need of scientific workers and, consequently, treats them generously. Provided that they steer clear of dangerous subjects such as psychology, scientists are privileged persons. Writers, on the other hand, are viciously persecuted. It is true that literary prostitutes like Ilya Ehrenburg or Alexei Tolstoy are paid huge sums of money, but the only thing which is of any value to the writer as such – his freedom of expression – is taken away from him. Some, at least, of the English scientists who speak so enthusiastically of the opportunities enjoyed by scientists in Russia are capable of understanding this. But their reflection appears to be: 'Writers are persecuted in Russia. So what? I am not a writer.' They do not see that any attack on intellectual liberty, and on the concept of objective truth, threatens in the long run every department of thought.

For the moment the totalitarian state tolerates the scientist because it needs him. Even in Nazi Germany, scientists, other than Jews, were relatively well treated, and the German scientific community, as a whole, offered no resistance to Hitler. At this stage of history, even the most autocratic ruler is forced to take account of physical reality, partly because of the lingering-on liberal habits of thought, partly because of the need to prepare for war. So long as physical reality cannot be altogether ignored, so long as two and two have to make four when you are, for example, drawing the blue-print of an aeroplane, the scientist has his function, and can even be allowed a measure of liberty. His awakening will come later, when the totalitarian state is firmly established. Meanwhile, if he wants to safeguard the integrity of science, it is his job to develop some kind of solidarity with his literary colleagues and not regard it as a matter of indifference when writers are silenced or driven to suicide, and newspapers systematically falsified.

But however it may be with the physical sciences, or with music, painting, and architecture, it is – as I have tried to show – certain that literature is doomed if liberty of thought perishes. Not only is it doomed in any country which retains a totalitarian structure; but any writer who adopts the totalitarian outlook, who finds excuses for persecution and the falsification of reality, thereby destroys himself as a writer. There is no way out of this. No tirades against 'individualism' and 'the ivory tower', no pious platitudes to the effect that 'true individuality is only attained through identification with the community', can get over the fact that a bought mind is a spoiled mind. Unless spontaneity enters at some point or another, literary creation is impossible, and language itself becomes ossified. At some time in the future, if the human mind becomes something totally different from what it now is, we may learn to separate literary creation from intellectual honesty. At present we know only that the imagination, like certain wild animals, will not breed in captivity. Any writer or journalist who denies that fact – and nearly all the current praise of the Soviet Union contains or implies such a denial – is, in effect, demanding his own destruction.

Polemic, No. 2, January 1946

Pleasure Spots

Some months ago I cut out of a shiny magazine some paragraphs written by a female journalist and describing the pleasure resort of the future. She had recently been spending some time at Honolulu, where the rigours of war do not seem to have been very noticeable. However, 'a transport pilot . . . told me that with all the inventiveness packed into this war, it was a pity someone hadn't found out how a tired and life-hungry man could relax, rest, play poker, drink, and make love, all at once, and round the clock, and come out of it feeling good and fresh and ready for the job again'. This reminded her of an entrepreneur she had met recently who was planning a 'pleasure spot which he thinks will catch on tomorrow as dog racing and dance halls did yesterday'. The entrepreneur's dream is described in some detail:

> His blue-prints pictured a space covering several acres, under a series of sliding roofs – for the British weather is unreliable – and with a central space spread over with an immense dance floor made of translucent plastic which can be illuminated from beneath. Around it are grouped other functional spaces, at different levels. Balcony bars and restaurants commanding high views of the city roofs, and ground-level replicas. A battery of skittle alleys. Two blue lagoons: one, periodically agitated by waves, for strong swimmers, and another, a smooth and summery pool, for playtime bathers. Sunlight lamps over the pools to simulate high summer on days when the roofs don't slide back to disclose a hot sun in a cloudless sky. Rows of bunks on which people wearing sun-glasses and slips can lie and start a tan or deepen an existing one under a sunray lamp.
>
> Music seeping through hundreds of grills connected with a central distributing stage, where dance or symphonic orchestras play or the radio programme can be caught, amplified, and disseminated. Outside, two 1,000-car parks. One, free. The other, an open-air cinema drive-in, cars queueing to move through turnstiles, and the film thrown on a giant screen facing a row of assembled cars. Uniformed male attendants check the cars, provide free aid and water, sell petrol and oil. Girls in white satin slacks take orders for buffet dishes and drinks, and bring them on trays.

Whenever one hears such phrases as 'pleasure spot', 'pleasure resort', 'pleasure city', it is difficult not to remember the often-quoted opening of Coleridge's 'Kubla Khan'.

> *In Xanadu did Kubla Khan*
> *A stately pleasure-dome decree:*

Where Alph, the sacred river, ran
Through caverns measureless to man
Down to a sunless sea.
So twice five miles of fertile ground
With walls and towers were girdled round:
And there were gardens bright with sinuous rills
Where blossomed many an incense-bearing tree;
And here were forests ancient as the hills,
Enfolding sunny spots of greenery.

But it will be seen that Coleridge has got it all wrong. He strikes a false note straight off with that talk about 'sacred' rivers and 'measureless' caverns. In the hands of the above-mentioned entrepreneur, Kubla Khan's project would have become something quite different. The caverns, air-conditioned, discreetly lighted and with their original rocky interior buried under layers of tastefully-coloured plastics, would be turned into a series of tea-grottoes in the Moorish, Caucasian or Hawaiian styles. Alph, the sacred river, would be dammed up to make an artificially-warmed bathing pool, while the sunless sea would be illuminated from below with pink electric lights, and one would cruise over it in real Venetian gondolas each equipped with its own radio set. The forests and 'spots of greenery' referred to by Coleridge would be cleaned up to make way for glass-covered tennis courts, a bandstand, a roller-skating rink and perhaps a nine-hole golf course. In short, there would be everything that a 'life-hungry' man could desire.

I have no doubt that, all over the world, hundreds of pleasure resorts similar to the one described above are now being planned, and perhaps are even being built. It is unlikely that they will be finished – world events will see to that – but they represent faithfully enough the modern civilized man's idea of pleasure. Something of the kind is already partially attained in the more magnificent dance halls, movie palaces, hotels, restaurants and luxury liners. On a pleasure cruise or in a Lyons Corner House one already gets something more than a glimpse of this future paradise. Analysed, its main characteristics are these:

1. One is never alone.
2. One never does anything for oneself.
3. One is never within sight of wild vegetation or natural objects of any kind.
4. Light and temperature are always artificially regulated.
5. One is never out of the sound of music.

The music – and if possible it should be the same music for everybody – is the most important ingredient. Its function is to prevent thought and conversation, and to shut out any natural sound, such as the song of birds or the whistling of the wind, that might otherwise intrude. The radio is already consciously used for this purpose by innumerable people. In very many English homes the radio is literally never turned off, though it is manipulated from time to time so as to make sure that only light music will come out of it. I know people who will keep the radio playing all through a meal and at the same time continue talking just loudly enough for the voices and the music to cancel out. This is done with a definite purpose. The music prevents the conversation from becoming serious or even coherent, while the chatter of voices stops one from listening attentively to the music and thus prevents the onset of that dreaded thing, thought. For

The lights must never go out.
The music must always play,
Lest we should see where we are;
Lost in a haunted wood,
Children afraid of the dark
Who have never been happy or good.

It is difficult not to feel that the unconscious aim in the most typical modern pleasure resorts is a return to the womb. For there, too, one was never alone, one never saw daylight, the temperature was always regulated, one did not have to worry about work or food, and one's thoughts, if any, were drowned by a continuous rhythmic throbbing.

When one looks at Coleridge's very different conception of a 'pleasure dome', one sees that it revolves partly round gardens and partly round caverns, rivers, forests and mountains with 'deep romantic chasms' – in short, round what is called Nature. But the whole notion of admiring Nature, and feeling a sort of religious awe in the presence of glaciers, deserts or waterfalls, is bound up with the sense of man's littleness and weakness against the power of the universe. The moon is beautiful partly because we cannot reach it, the sea is impressive because one can never be sure of crossing it safely. Even the pleasure one takes in a flower – and this is true even of a botanist who knows all there is to be known about the flower – is dependent partly on the sense of mystery. But meanwhile man's power over Nature is steadily increasing. With the aid of the atomic bomb we could literally move mountains: we could even, so it is said, alter the climate of the earth by melting the polar ice-caps and irrigating the Sahara. Isn't there, therefore, something sentimental and obscurantist in prefering bird-song to swing music and in wanting to leave a few patches of wildness here and there instead of covering the whole surface of the earth with a network of *Autobahnen* flooded by artificial sunlight?

The question only arises because in exploring the physical universe man has made no attempt to explore himself. Much of what goes by the name of pleasure is simply an effort to destroy consciousness. If one started by asking, what is man? what are his needs? how can he best express himself? one would discover that merely having the power to avoid work and live one's life from birth to death in electric light and to the tune of tinned music is not a reason for doing so. Man needs warmth, society, leisure, comfort and security: he also needs solitude, creative work and the sense of wonder. If he recognized this he could use the products of science and industrialism eclectically, applying always the same test: does this make me more human or less human? He would then learn that the highest happiness does *not* lie in relaxing, resting, playing poker, drinking and making love simultaneously. And the instinctive horror which all sensitive people feel at the progressive mechanization of life would be seen not to be a mere sentimental archaism, but to be fully justified. For man only stays human by preserving large patches of simplicity in his life, while the tendency of many modern inventions – in particular the film, the radio and the aeroplane – is to weaken his consciousness, dull his curiosity, and, in general, drive him nearer to the animals.

Tribune, 11 January 1946

Decline of the English Murder

It is Sunday afternoon, preferably before the war. The wife is already asleep in the armchair, and the children have been sent out for a nice long walk. You put your feet up on the sofa, settle your spectacles on your nose, and open the *News of the World*. Roast beef and Yorkshire, or roast pork and apple sauce, followed up by suet pudding and driven home, as it were, by a cup of mahogany-brown tea, have put you in just the right mood. Your pipe is drawing sweetly, the sofa cushions are soft underneath you, the fire is well alight, the air is warm and stagnant. In these blissful circumstances, what is it that you want to read about?

Naturally, about a murder. But what kind of murder? If one examines the murders which have given the greatest amount of pleasure to the British public, the murders whose story is known in its general outline to almost everyone and which have been made into novels and rehashed over and over again by the Sunday papers, one finds a fairly strong family resemblance running through the greater number of them. Our great period in murder, our Elizabethan period, so to speak, seems to have been between roughly 1850 and 1925, and the murderers whose reputation has stood the test of time are the following: Dr Palmer of Rugeley, Jack the Ripper, Neill Cream, Mrs Maybrick, Dr Crippen, Seddon, Joseph Smith, Armstrong, and Bywaters and Thompson. In addition, in 1919 or thereabouts, there was another very celebrated case which fits into the general pattern but which I had better not mention by name, because the accused man was acquitted.

Of the above-mentioned nine cases, at least four have had successful novels based on them, one has been made into a popular melodrama, and the amount of literature surrounding them, in the form of newspaper write-ups, criminological treatises and reminiscences by lawyers and police officers, would make a considerable library. It is difficult to believe that any recent English crime will be remembered so long and so intimately, and not only because the violence of external events has made murder seem unimportant, but because the prevalent type of crime seems to be changing. The principle *cause célèbre* of the war years was the so-called Cleft Chin Murder, which has now been written up in a popular booklet;[1] the verbatim account of the trial was published some time last year by Messrs Jarrolds with an introduction by Mr Bechhofer-Roberts. Before returning to this pitiful and sordid case, which is only interesting from a sociological and perhaps a legal point of view, let me try to define what it is that the readers of Sunday papers mean when they say fretfully that 'you never seem to get a good murder nowadays'.

In considering the nine murders I named above, one can start by excluding the Jack the Ripper case, which is in a class by itself. Of the other eight, six were poisoning cases, and eight of the ten criminals belonged to the middle class. In one way or another, sex was a powerful motive in all but two cases, and in at least four cases respectability – the desire to gain a secure position in life, or not

[1] *The Cleft Chin Murder* by R. Alwyn Raymond.

to forfeit one's social position by some scandal such as a divorce – was one of the main reasons for committing murder. In more than half the cases, the object was to get hold of a certain known sum of money such as a legacy or an insurance policy, but the amount involved was nearly always small. In most of the cases the crime only came to light slowly, as the result of careful investigation which started off with the suspicions of neighbours or relatives; and in nearly every case there was some dramatic coincidence, in which the finger of Providence could be clearly seen, or one of those episodes that no novelist would dare to make up, such as Crippen's flight across the Atlantic with his mistress dressed as a boy, or Joseph Smith playing 'Nearer, my God, to Thee' on the harmonium while one of his wives was drowning in the next room. The background of all these crimes, except Neill Cream's, was essentially domestic; of twelve victims, seven were either wife or husband of the murderer.

With all this in mind one can construct what would be, from a *News of the World* reader's point of view, the 'perfect' murder. The murderer should be a little man of the professional class – a dentist or a solicitor, say – living an intensely respectable life somewhere in the suburbs, and preferably in a semi-detached house, which will allow the neighbours to hear suspicious sounds through the wall. He should be either chairman of the local Conservative Party branch, or a leading Nonconformist and strong Temperance advocate. He should go astray through cherishing a guilty passion for his secretary or the wife of a rival professional man, and should only bring himself to the point of murder after long and terrible wrestles with his conscience. Having decided on murder, he should plan it all with the utmost cunning, and only slip up over some tiny, unforeseeable detail. The means chosen should, of course, be poison. In the last analysis he should commit murder because this seems to him less disgraceful, and less damaging to his career, than being detected in adultery. With this kind of background, a crime can have dramatic and even tragic qualities which make it memorable and excite pity for both victim and murderer. Most of the crimes mentioned above have a touch of this atmosphere, and in three cases, including the one I referred to but did not name, the story approximates to the one I have outlined.

Now compare the Cleft Chin Murder. There is no depth of feeling in it. It was almost chance that the two people committed that particular murder, and it was only by good luck that they did not commit several others. The background was not domesticity, but the anonymous life of the dance halls and the false values of the American film. The two culprits were an eighteen-year-old ex-waitress named Elizabeth Jones, and an American army deserter, posing as an officer, named Karl Hulten. They were only together for six days, and it seems doubtful whether, until they were arrested, they even learned one another's true names. They met casually in a teashop, and that night went out for a ride in a stolen army truck. Jones described herself as a strip-tease artist, which was not strictly true (she had given one unsuccessful performance in this line), and declared that she wanted to do something dangerous, 'like being a gun-moll'. Hulten described himself as a big-time Chicago gangster, which was also untrue. They met a girl bicycling along the road, and to show how tough he was Hulten ran over her with his truck, after which the pair robbed her of the few shillings that were on her. On another occasion they knocked out a girl to whom they had offered a lift, took her coat and handbag and threw her into a river. Finally, in the most wanton way, they murdered a taxi-driver who happened to have £8 in his pocket. Soon afterwards they parted. Hulten was caught because he had foolishly kept the dead man's car, and Jones made spontaneous confessions to the police. In court each prisoner incriminated the other. In between crimes, both of them seem to have behaved with the utmost callousness: they spent the dead taxi-driver's £8 at the dog races.

Judging from her letters, the girl's case has a certain amount of psychological interest, but this murder probably captured the headlines because it provided distraction amid the doodlebugs and the anxieties of the Battle of France. Jones and Hulten committed their murder to the tune of V1,[1] and were convicted to the tune of V2.[2] There was also considerable excitement because – as has become usual in England – the man was sentenced to death and the girl to imprisonment. According to Mr Raymond, the reprieving of Jones caused widespread indignation and streams of telegrams to the Home Secretary: in her native town, 'She should hang' was chalked on the walls beside pictures of a figure dangling from a gallows. Considering that only ten women have been hanged in Britain in this century, and that the practice has gone out largely because of popular feeling against it, it is difficult not to feel that this clamour to hang an eighteen-year-old girl was due partly to the brutalizing effects of war. Indeed, the whole meaningless story, with its atmosphere of dance-halls, movie palaces, cheap perfume, false names and stolen cars, belongs essentially to a war period.

Perhaps it is significant that the most talked-of English murder of recent years should have been committed by an American and an English girl who had become partly americanized. But it is difficult to believe that this case will be so long remembered as the old domestic poisoning dramas, product of a stable society where the all-prevailing hypocrisy did at least ensure that crimes as serious as murder should have strong emotions behind them.

Tribune, 15 February 1946

Politics and the English Language

Most people who bother with the matter at all would admit that the English language is in a bad way, but it is generally assumed that we cannot by conscious action do anything about it. Our civilization is decadent, and our language – so the argument runs – must inevitably share in the general collapse. It follows that any struggle against the abuse of language is a sentimental archaism, like preferring candles to electric light or hansom cabs to aeroplanes. Underneath this lies the half-conscious belief that language is a natural growth and not an instrument which we shape for our own purposes.

Now, it is clear that the decline of a language must ultimately have political and economic causes: it is not due simply to the bad influence of this or that

[1]The V1, an unmanned aircraft developed by the Germans and used by them to bomb London from June 1944; they were nicknamed 'doodlebugs' by the Londoners.
[2]The V2, a rocket bomb used by the Germans on London from September 1944.

individual writer. But an effect can become a cause, reinforcing the original cause and producing the same effect in an intensified form, and so on indefinitely. A man may take to drink because he feels himself to be a failure, and then fail all the more completely because he drinks. It is rather the same thing that is happening to the English language. It becomes ugly and inaccurate because our thoughts are foolish, but the slovenliness of our language makes it easier for us to have foolish thoughts. The point is that the process is reversible. Modern English, especially written English, is full of bad habits which spread by imitation and which can be avoided if one is willing to take the necessary trouble. If one gets rid of these habits one can think more clearly, and to think clearly is a necessary first step towards political regeneration: so that the fight against bad English is not frivolous and is not the exclusive concern of professional writers. I will come back to this presently, and I hope that by that time the meaning of what I have said here will have become clearer. Meanwhile, here are five specimens of the English language as it is now habitually written.

These five passages have not been picked out because they are especially bad – I could have quoted far worse if I had chosen – but because they illustrate various of the mental vices from which we now suffer. They are a little below the average, but are fairly representative samples. I number them so that I can refer back to them when necessary:

> 1. I am not, indeed, sure whether it is not true to say that the Milton who once seemed not unlike a seventeenth-century Shelley had not become, out of experience ever more bitter in each year, more alien (sic) to the founder of that Jesuit sect which nothing could induce him to tolerate.
>
> Professor Harold Laski (Essay in *Freedom of Expression*).

> 2. Above all, we cannot play ducks and drakes with a native battery of idioms which prescribes such egregious collocations of vocables as the Basic *put up with* for *tolerate* or *put at a loss* for *bewilder.*
>
> Professor Lancelot Hogben (*Interglossa*).

> 3. On the one side we have the free personality: by definition it is not neurotic, for it has neither conflict nor dream. Its desires, such as they are, are transparent, for they are just what institutional approval keeps in the forefront of consciousness; another institutional pattern would alter their number and intensity; there is little in them that is natural, irreducible, or culturally dangerous. But *on the other side*, the social bond itself is nothing but the mutual reflection of these self-secure integrities. Recall the definition of love. Is not this the very picture of a small academic? Where is there a place in this hall of mirrors for either personality or fraternity?
>
> Essay on psychology in *Politics* (New York).

> 4. All the 'best people' from the gentlemen's clubs, and all the frantic Fascist captains, united in common hatred of Socialism and bestial horror of the rising tide of the mass revolutionary movement, have turned to acts of provocation, to foul incendiarism, to medieval legends of poisoned wells, to legalize their own destruction to proletarian organizations, and arouse the agitated petty-bourgeoisie to chauvinistic fervour on behalf of the fight against the revolutionary way out of the crisis.
>
> Communist pamphlet.

5. If a new spirit *is* to be infused into this country, there is one thorny and contentious reform which must be tackled, and that is the humanization and galvanization of the BBC. Timidity here will bespeak canker and atrophy of the soul. The heart of Britain may be sound and of strong beat, for instance, but the British lion's roar at present is like that of Bottom in Shakespeare's *Midsummer Night's Dream* – as gentle as any sucking dove. A virile new Britain cannot continue indefinitely to be traduced in the eyes, or rather ears, of the world by the effete languors of Langham Place, brazenly masquerading as 'standard English'. When the Voice of Britain is heard at nine o'clock, better far and infinitely less ludicrous to hear aitches honestly dropped than the present priggish, inflated, inhibited, school-ma'amish arch braying of blameless bashful mewing maidens!

Letter in *Tribune*.

Each of these passages has faults of its own, but, quite apart from avoidable ugliness, two qualities are common to all of them. The first is staleness of imagery: the other is lack of precision. The writer either has a meaning and cannot express it, or he inadvertently says something else, or he is almost indifferent as to whether his words mean anything or not. This mixture of vagueness and sheer incompetence is the most marked characteristic of modern English prose, and especially of any kind of political writing. As soon as certain topics are raised, the concrete melts into the abstract and no one seems able to think of turns of speech that are not hackneyed: prose consists less and less of *words* chosen for the sake of their meaning, and more of *phrases* tacked together like the sections of a prefabricated hen-house. I list below, with notes and examples, various of the tricks by means of which the work of prose construction is habitually dodged:

Dying metaphors. A newly invented metaphor assists thought by evoking a visual image, while on the other hand a metaphor which is technically 'dead' (e.g. *iron resolution*) has in effect reverted to being an ordinary word and can generally be used without loss of vividness. But in between these two classes there is a huge dump of worn-out metaphors which have lost all evocative power and are merely used because they save people the trouble of inventing phrases for themselves. Examples are: *Ring the changes on, take up the cudgels for, toe the line, ride roughshod over, stand shoulder to shoulder with, play into the hands of, no axe to grind, grist to the mill, fishing in troubled waters, rift within the lute, on the order of the day, Achilles' heel, swan song, hotbed.* Many of these are used without knowledge of their meaning (what is a 'rift', for instance?), and incompatible metaphors are frequently mixed, a sure sign that the writer is not interested in what he is saying. Some metaphors now current have been twisted out of their original meaning without those who use them even being aware of the fact. For example, *toe the line* is sometimes written *tow the line*. Another example is *the hammer and the anvil,* now always used with the implication that the anvil gets the worst of it. In real life it is always the anvil that breaks the hammer, never the other way about: a writer who stopped to think what he was saying would be aware of this, and would avoid perverting the original phrase.

Operators, or *verbal false limbs*. These save the trouble of picking out appropriate verbs and nouns, and at the same time pad each sentence with extra syllables which give it an appearance of symmetry. Characteristic phrases are: *render inoperative, militate against, prove unacceptable, make contact with, be subjected to, give rise to, give grounds for, have the effect of, play a leading part (rôle) in, make itself felt, take effect, exhibit a tendency to, serve the purpose of,* etc etc. The keynote is the elimination of simple verbs. Instead of being a single word, such as *break, stop, spoil, mend, kill,* a verb becomes a *phrase,* made up of a noun or adjective tacked on to some general-purposes verb such as *prove, serve, form, play, render.* In addition, the passive voice is wherever possible used in preference to the active, and noun constructions are used instead of gerunds (*by examination of* instead of *by examining*). The range of verbs is further cut down by means of the *-ize* and *de-* formations, and banal statements are given an appearance of profundity by means of the *not un-* formation. Simple conjunctions and prepositions are replaced by such phrases as *with respect to, having regard to, the fact that, by dint of, in view of, in the interests of, on the hypothesis that*; and the ends of sentences are saved from anticlimax by such resounding commonplaces as *greatly to be desired, cannot be left out of account, a development to be expected in the near future, deserving of serious consideration, brought to a satisfactory conclusion*, and so on and so forth.

Pretentious diction. Words like *phenomenon, element, individual* (as noun), *objective, categorical, effective, virtual, basic, primary, promote, constitute, exhibit, exploit, utilize, eliminate, liquidate,* are used to dress up simple statements and give an air of scientific impartiality to biassed judgements. Adjectives like *epoch-making, epic, historic, unforgettable, triumphant, age-old, inevitable, inexorable, veritable,* are used to dignify the sordid processes of international politics, while writing that aims at glorifying war usually takes on an archaic colour, its characteristic words being: *realm, throne, chariot, mailed fist, trident, sword, shield, buckler, banner, jackboot, clarion.* Foreign words and expressions such as *cul de sac, ancien régime, deus ex machina, mutatis mutandis, status quo, Gleichschaltung, Weltanschauung,* are used to give an air of culture and elegance. Except for the useful abbreviations *i.e., e.g.,* and *etc,* there is no real need for any of the hundreds of foreign phrases now current in English. Bad writers, and especially scientific, political and sociological writers, are nearly always haunted by the notion that Latin or Greek words are grander than Saxon ones, and unnecessary words like *expedite, ameliorate, predict, extraneous, deracinated, clandestine, sub-aqueous* and hundreds of others constantly gain ground from the Anglo-Saxon opposite numbers.[1] The jargon peculiar to Marxist writing (*hyena, hangman, cannibal, petty bourgeois, these gentry, lackey, flunkey, mad dog, White Guard,* etc) consists largely of words and phrases translated from Russian, German or French; but the normal way of coining a new word is to use a Latin or Greek root with the appropriate affix and, where necessary, the *-ize* formation. It is often easier to make up words of this kind (*deregionalize, impermissible, extramarital, non-fragmentatory* and so forth) than to think up the English words that will cover one's meaning. The result, in general, is an increase in slovenliness and vagueness.

Meaningless words. In certain kinds of writing, particularly in art criticism and literary criticism, it is normal to come across long passages which are almost

[1] An interesting illustration of this is the way in which the English flower names which were in use till very recently are being ousted by Greek ones, *snapdragon* becoming *antirrhinum, forget-me-not* becoming *myosotis,* etc. It is hard to see any practical reason for this change of fashion: it is probably due to an instinctive turning-away from the more homely word and a vague feeling that the Greek word is scientific. [Author's footnote.]

completely lacking in meaning.[1] Words like *romantic, plastic, values, human, dead, sentimental, natural, vitality,* as used in art criticism, are strictly meaningless, in the sense that they not only do not point to any discoverable object, but are hardly even expected to do so by the reader. When one critic writes, 'The outstanding features of Mr X's work is its living quality', while another writes, 'The immediately striking thing about Mr X's work is its peculiar deadness', the reader accepts this as a simple difference of opinion. If words like *black* and *white* were involved, instead of the jargon words *dead* and *living,* he would see at once that language was being used in an improper way. Many political words are similarly abused. The word *Fascism* has now no meaning except in so far as it signifies 'something not desirable'. The words *democracy, socialism, freedom, patriotic, realistic, justice,* have each of them several different meanings which cannot be reconciled with one another. In the case of a word like *democracy,* not only is there no agreed definition, but the attempt to make one is resisted from all sides. It is almost universally felt that when we call a country democratic we are praising it: consequently the defenders of every kind of régime claim that it is a democracy, and fear that they might have to stop using the word if it were tied down to any one meaning. Words of this kind are often used in a consciously dishonest way. That is, the person who uses them has his own private definition, but allows his hearer to think he means something quite different. Statements like *Marshal Pétain was a true patriot, The Soviet press is the freest in the world, The Catholic Church is opposed to persecution,* are almost always made with intent to deceive. Other words used in variable meanings, in most cases more or less dishonestly, are: *class, totalitarian, science, progressive, reactionary, bourgeois, equality.*

Now that I have made this catalogue of swindles and perversions, let me give another example of the kind of writing that they lead to. This time it must of its nature be an imaginary one. I am going to translate a passage of good English into modern English of the worst sort. Here is a well-known verse from *Ecclesiastes*:

> I returned, and saw under the sun, that the race is not to the swift, nor the battle to the strong, neither yet bread to the wise, nor yet riches to men of understanding, nor yet favour to men of skill; but time and chance happeneth to them all.

Here it is in modern English:

> Objective consideration of contemporary phenomena compels the conclusion that success or failure in competitive activities exhibits no tendency to be commensurate with innate capacity, but that a considerable element of the unpredictable must invariably be taken into account.

This is a parody, but not a very gross one. Exhibit 3, above, for instance, contains several patches of the same kind of English. It will be seen that I have

[1] Example: 'Comfort's catholicity of perception and image, strangely Whitmanesque in range, almost the exact opposite in aesthetic compulsion, continues to evoke that trembling atmospheric accumulative hinting at a cruel, an inexorably serene timelessness . . . Wrey Gardiner scores by aiming at simple bullseyes with precision. Only they are not so simple, and through this contented sadness runs more than the surface bitter-sweet of resignation'. (*Poetry Quarterly.*) [Author's footnote.]

not made a full translation. The beginning and ending of the sentence follow the original meaning fairly closely, but in the middle the concrete illustrations – race, battle, bread – dissolve into the vague phrase 'success or failure in competitive activities'. This had to be so, because no modern writer of the kind I am discussing – no one capable of using phrases like 'objective consideration of contemporary phenomena' – would ever tabulate his thoughts in that precise and detailed way. The whole tendency of modern prose is away from concreteness. Now analyse these two sentences a little more closely. The first contains 49 words but only 60 syllables, and all its words are those of everyday life. The second contains 38 words of 90 syllables: 18 of its words are from Latin roots, and one from Greek. The first sentence contains six vivid images, and only one phrase ('time and chance') that could be called vague. The second contains not a single fresh, arresting phrase, and in spite of its 90 syllables it gives only a shortened version of the meaning contained in the first. Yet without a doubt it is the second kind of sentence that is gaining ground in modern English. I do not want to exaggerate. This kind of writing is not yet universal, and outcrops of simplicity will occur here and there in the worst-written page. Still, if you or I were told to write a few lines on the uncertainty of human fortunes, we should probably come much nearer to my imaginary sentence than to the one from *Ecclesiastes.*

As I have tried to show, modern writing at its worst does not consist in picking out words for the sake of their meaning and inventing images in order to make the meaning clearer. It consists in gumming together long strips of words which have already been set in order by someone else, and making the results presentable by sheer humbug. The attraction of this way of writing is that it is easy. It is easier – even quicker, once you have the habit – to say *In my opinion it is a not unjustifiable assumption that* than to say *I think.* If you use ready-made phrases, you not only don't have to hunt about for words; you also don't have to bother with the rhythms of your sentences, since these phrases are generally so arranged as to be more or less euphonious. When you are composing in a hurry – when you are dictating to a stenographer, for instance, or making a public speech – it is natural to fall into a pretentious, latinized style. Tags like *a consideration which we should do well to bear in mind* or *a conclusion to which all of us would readily assent* will save many a sentence from coming down with a bump. By using stale metaphors, similes and idioms, you save much mental effort, at the cost of leaving your meaning vague, not only for your reader but for yourself. This is the significance of mixed metaphors. The sole aim of a metaphor is to call up a visual image. When these images clash – as in *The Fascist octopus has sung its swan song, the jackboot is thrown into the melting pot* – it can be taken as certain that the writer is not seeing a mental image of the objects he is naming; in other words he is not really thinking. Look again at the examples I gave at the beginning of this essay. Professor Laski (1) uses five negatives in 53 words. One of these is superfluous, making nonsense of the whole passage, and in addition there is the slip *alien* for akin, making further nonsense, and several avoidable pieces of clumsiness which increase the general vagueness. Professor Hogben (2) plays ducks and drakes with a battery which is able to write prescriptions, and, while disapproving of the everyday phrase *put up with,* is unwilling to look *egregious* up in the dictionary and see what it means. (3), if one takes an uncharitable attitude towards it, is simply meaningless: probably one could work out its intended meaning by reading the whole of the article in which it occurs. In (4) the writer knows more or less what he wants to say, but an accumulation of stale phrases chokes him like tea-leaves blocking a sink. In (5) words and meaning have almost parted company. People who write in this manner usually have a general emotional meaning – they dislike one thing and want to express solidarity with another – but they are not interested in the detail of what they are saying. A scrupulous writer, in every sentence that he writes, will ask himself at least four questions, thus: What am I trying to say? What words will express it? What image or idiom will make it clearer? Is this image fresh enough to have an effect? And he will probably ask himself two more: Could I put it more shortly? Have I said anything that is avoidably ugly? But you are not obliged to go to all this trouble. You can shirk it by simply throwing your mind open and letting the ready-made phrases come crowding in. They will construct your sentences for you – even think your thoughts for you, to a certain extent – and at need they will perform the important service of partially concealing your meaning even from yourself. It is at this point that the special connection between politics and the debasement of language becomes clear.

In our time it is broadly true that political writing is bad writing. Where it is not true, it will generally be found that the writer is some kind of rebel, expressing his private opinions, and not a 'party line'. Orthodoxy, of whatever colour, seems to demand a lifeless, imitative style. The political dialects to be found in pamphlets, leading articles, manifestos, White Papers and the speeches of Under-Secretaries do, of course, vary from party to party, but they are all alike in that one almost never finds in them a fresh, vivid, home-made turn of speech. When one watches some tired hack on the platform mechanically repeating the familiar phrases – *bestial atrocities, iron heel, blood-stained tyranny, free peoples of the world, stand shoulder to shoulder* – one often has a curious feeling that one is not watching a live human being but some kind of dummy: a feeling which suddenly becomes stronger at moments when the light catches the speaker's spectacles and turns them into blank discs which seem to have no eyes behind them. And this is not altogether fanciful. A speaker who uses that kind of phraseology has gone some distance towards turning himself into a machine. The appropriate noises are coming out of his larynx, but his brain is not involved as it would be if he were choosing his words for himself. If the speech he is making is one that he is accustomed to make over and over again, he may be almost unconscious of what he is saying, as one is when one utters the responses in church. And this reduced state of consciousness, if not indispensable, is at any rate favourable to political conformity.

In our time, political speech and writing are largely the defence of the indefensible. Things like the continuance of British rule in India, the Russian purges and deportations, the dropping of the atom bombs on Japan, can indeed be defended, but only by arguments which are too brutal for most people to face, and which do not square with the professed aims of political parties. Thus political language has to consist largely of euphemism, question-begging and sheer cloudy vagueness. Defenceless villages are bombarded from the air, the inhabitants driven out into the countryside, the cattle machine-gunned, the huts set on fire with incendiary bullets: this is called *pacification*. Millions of peasants are robbed of their farms and sent trudging along the roads with no more than they can carry: this is called *transfer of population* or *rectification of frontiers*. People are imprisoned for years without trial, or shot in the back of the neck or sent to die of scurvy in Arctic lumber camps: this is called *elimination of unreliable elements*. Such phraseology is needed if one wants to name things without calling up mental pictures of them. Consider for instance some comfortable English professor defending Russian totalitarianism. He cannot say outright, 'I believe in killing off your opponents when you can get good results by doing so.' Probably, therefore, he will say something like this:

> While freely conceding that the Soviet régime exhibits certain features which the humanitarian may be inclined to deplore, we must, I think, agree that a certain curtailment of the right to political opposition is an unavoidable concomitant of transitional periods, and that the rigours which the Russian people have been called upon to undergo have been amply justified in the sphere of concrete achievement.

The inflated style is itself a kind of euphemism. A mass of Latin words falls upon the facts like soft snow, blurring the outlines and covering up all the details. The great enemy of clear language is insincerity. When there is a gap between one's real and one's declared aims, one turns as it were instinctively to long words and exhausted idioms, like a cuttlefish squirting out ink. In our age there is no such thing as 'keeping out of politics'. All issues are political issues, and politics itself is a mass of lies, evasions, folly, hatred and schizophrenia. When the general atmosphere is bad, language must suffer. I should expect to find – this is a guess which I have not sufficient knowledge to verify – that the German, Russian and Italian languages have all deteriorated in the last ten or fifteen years, as a result of dictatorship.

But if thought corrupts language, language can also corrupt thought. A bad usage can spread by tradition and imitation, even among people who should and do know better. The debased language that I have been discussing is in some ways very convenient. Phrases like *a not unjustifiable assumption, leaves much to be desired, would serve no good purpose, a consideration which we should do well to bear in mind,* are a continuous temptation, a packet of aspirins always at one's elbow. Look back through this essay, and for certain you will find that I have again and again committed the very faults I am protesting against. By this morning's post I have received a pamphlet dealing with conditions in Germany. The author tells me that he 'felt impelled' to write it. I open it at random, and here is almost the first sentence that I see: '(The Allies) have an opportunity not only of achieving a radical transformation of Germany's social and political structure in such a way as to avoid a nationalistic reaction in Germany itself, but at the same time of laying the foundations of a co-operative and unified Europe'. You see, he 'feels impelled' to write – feels, presumably, that he has something new to say – and yet his words, like cavalry horses answering the bugle, group themselves automatically into the familiar dreary pattern. This invasion of one's mind by ready-made phrases (*lay the foundations, achieve a radical transformation*) can only be prevented if one is constantly on guard against them, and every such phrase anaesthetizes a portion of one's brain.

I said earlier that the decadence of our language is probably curable. Those who deny this would argue, if they produced an argument at all, that language merely reflects existing social conditions, and that we cannot influence its development by any direct tinkering with words and constructions. So far as the general tone or spirit of a language goes, this may be true, but it is not true in detail. Silly words and expressions have often disappeared, not through any evolutionary process but owing to the conscious action of a minority. Two recent examples were *explore every avenue* and *leave no stone unturned,* which were killed by the jeers of a few journalists. There is a long list of fly-blown metaphors which could similarly be got rid of if enough people would interest themselves in the job; and it should also be possible to laugh the *not un-* formation out of existence,[1] to reduce the amount of Latin and Greek in the average sentence, to drive out foreign phrases and strayed scientific words, and, in general, to make pretentiousness unfashionable. But all these are minor points. The defence of the English language implies more than this, and perhaps it is best to start by saying what it does *not* imply.

To begin with, it has nothing to do with archaism, with the salvaging of obsolete words and turns of speech, or with the setting-up of a 'standard English' which must never be departed from. On the contrary, it is especially concerned with the scrapping of every word or idiom which has outworn its usefulness. It has nothing to do with correct grammar and syntax, which are of no importance so long as one makes one's meaning clear, or with the avoidance of Americanisms, or with having what is called a 'good prose style'. On the other hand it is not concerned with fake simplicity and the attempt to make written English colloquial. Nor does it even imply in every case preferring the Saxon word to the Latin one, though it does imply using the fewest and shortest words that will cover one's meaning. What is above all needed is to let the meaning choose the word, and not the other way about. In prose, the worst thing one can do with words is to surrender to them. When you think of a concrete object, you think wordlessly, and then, if you want to describe the thing you have been visualizing, you probably hunt about till you find the exact words that seem to fit it. When you think of something abstract you are more inclined to use words from the start, and unless you make a conscious effort to prevent it, the existing dialect will come rushing out and do the job for you, at the expense of blurring or even changing your meaning. Probably it is better to put off using words as long as possible and get one's meaning as clear as one can through pictures or sensations. Afterwards one can choose – not simply *accept* – the phrases that will best cover the meaning, and then switch round and decide what impression one's words are likely to make on another person. This last effort of the mind cuts out all stale or mixed images, all prefabricated phrases, needless repetitions, and humbug and vagueness generally. But one can often be in doubt about the effect of a word or a phrase, and one needs rules that one can rely on when instinct fails. I think the following rules will cover most cases:

i. Never use a metaphor, simile or other figure of speech which you are used to seeing in print.

ii. Never use a long word where a short one will do.

iii. If it is possible to cut a word out, always cut it out.

iv. Never use the passive where you can use the active.

v. Never use a foreign phrase, a scientific word or a jargon word if you can think of an everyday English equivalent.

vi. Break any of these rules sooner than say anything outright barbarous.

These rules sound elementary, and so they are, but they demand a deep change of attitude in anyone who has grown used to writing in the style now fashionable. One could keep all of them and still write bad English, but one could not write the kind of stuff that I quoted in those five specimens at the beginning of this article.

[1] One can cure oneself of the *not un-* formation by memorizing this sentence: *A not unblack dog was chasing a not unsmall rabbit across a not ungreen field.* [Author's footnote.]

I have not here been considering the literary use of language, but merely language as an instrument for expressing and not for concealing or preventing thought. Stuart Chase and others have come near to claiming that all abstract words are meaningless, and have used this as a pretext for advocating a kind of political quietism. Since you don't know what Fascism is, how can you struggle against Fascism? One need not swallow such absurdities as this, but one ought to recognize that the present political chaos is connected with the decay of language, and that one can probably bring about some improvement by starting at the verbal end. If you simplify your English, you are freed from the worst follies of orthodoxy. You cannot speak any of the necessary dialects, and when you make a stupid remark its stupidity will be obvious, even to yourself. Political language – and with variations this is true of all political parties, from Conservatives to Anarchists – is designed to make lies sound truthful and murder respectable, and to give an appearance of solidity to pure wind. One cannot change this all in a moment, but one can at least change one's own habits, and from time to time one can even, if one jeers loudly enough, send some worn-out and useless phrase – some *jackboot, Achilles' heel, hotbed, melting pot, acid test, veritable inferno* or other lump of verbal refuse – into the dustbin where it belongs.

Horizon, April 1946

Some Thoughts on the Common Toad

Before the swallow, before the daffodil, and not much later than the snowdrop, the common toad salutes the coming of spring after his own fashion, which is to emerge from a hole in the ground, where he has lain buried since the previous autumn, and crawl as rapidly as possible towards the nearest suitable patch of water. Something – some kind of shudder in the earth, or perhaps merely a rise of a few degrees in the temperature – has told him that it is time to wake up: though a few toads appear to sleep the clock round and miss out a year from time to time – at any rate, I have more than once dug them up, alive and apparently well, in the middle of the summer.

At this period, after his long fast, the toad has a very spiritual look, like a strict Anglo-Catholic towards the end of Lent. His movements are languid but purposeful, his body is shrunken, and by contrast his eyes look abnormally large. This allows one to notice, what one might not at another time, that a toad has about the most beautiful eye of any living creature. It is like gold, or more exactly it is like the golden-coloured semi-precious stone which one sometimes sees in signet-rings, and which I think is called a chrysoberyl.

For a few days after getting into the water the toad concentrates on building up his strength by eating small insects. Presently he has swollen to his normal size again, and then he goes through a phase of intense sexiness. All he knows, at least if he is a male toad, is that he wants to get his arms round something, and if you offer him a stick, or even your finger, he will cling to it with surprising strength and take a long time to discover that it is not a female toad. Frequently one comes upon shapeless masses of ten or twenty toads rolling over and over in the water, one clinging to another without distinction of sex. By degrees, however, they sort themselves out into couples, with the male duly sitting on the female's back. You can now distinguish males from females, because the male is smaller, darker and sits on top, with his arms tightly clasped round the female's neck. After a day or two the spawn is laid in long strings which wind themselves in and out of the reeds and soon become invisible. A few more weeks, and the water is alive with masses of tiny tadpoles which rapidly grow larger, sprout hind-legs, then forelegs, then shed their tails: and finally, about the middle of the summer, the new generation of toads, smaller than one's thumb-nail but perfect in every particular, crawl out of the water to begin the game anew.

I mention the spawning of the toads because it is one of the phenomena of spring which most deeply appeal to me, and because the toad, unlike the skylark and the primrose, has never had much of a boost from the poets. But I am aware that many people do not like reptiles or amphibians, and I am not suggesting that in order to enjoy the spring you have to take an interest in toads. There are also the crocus, the missel-thrush, the cuckoo, the blackthorn, etc. The point is that the pleasures of spring are available to everybody, and cost nothing. Even in the most sordid street the coming of spring will register itself by some sign or other, if it is only a brighter blue between the chimney pots or the vivid green of an elder sprouting on a blitzed site. Indeed it is remarkable how Nature goes on existing unofficially, as it were, in the very heart of London. I have seen a kestrel flying over the Deptford gasworks, and I have heard a first-rate performance by a blackbird in the Euston Road. There must be some hundreds of thousands, if not millions, of birds living inside the four-mile radius, and it is rather a pleasing thought that none of them pays a halfpenny of rent.

As for spring, not even the narrow and gloomy streets round the Bank of England are quite able to exclude it. It comes seeping in everywhere, like one of those new poison gases which pass through all filters. The spring is commonly referred to as 'a miracle', and during the past five or six years this worn-out figure of speech has taken on a new lease of life. After the sort of winters we have had to endure recently, the spring does seem miraculous, because it has become gradually harder and harder to believe that it is actually going to happen. Every February since 1940 I have found myself thinking that this time winter is going to be permanent. But Persephone, like the toads, always rises from the dead at about the same moment. Suddenly, towards the end of March, the miracle happens and the decaying slum in which I live is transfigured. Down in the square the sooty privets have turned bright green, the leaves are thickening on the chestnut trees, the daffodils are out, the wallflowers are budding, the policeman's tunic looks positively a pleasant shade of blue, the fishmonger greets his customers with a smile, and even the sparrows are quite a different colour, having felt the balminess of the air and nerved themselves to take a bath, their first since last September.

Is it wicked to take a pleasure in spring and other seasonal changes? To put it more precisely, is it politically reprehensible, while we are all groaning, or at any rate ought to be groaning, under the shackles of the capitalist system, to point out that life is frequently more worth living because of a blackbird's song, a yellow elm tree in October, or some other natural phenomenon which does not cost money and does not have what the editors of left-wing newspapers call a class angle? There is no doubt that many people think so. I know by experience that a favourable reference to 'Nature' in one of my articles is liable to bring me abusive letters, and though the key-word in these letters is usually 'sentimental', two ideas seem to be mixed up in them. One is that any pleasure in the actual process of life encourages a sort of political quietism. People, so the thought runs, ought to be discontented, and it is our job to multiply our wants and not simply to increase our enjoyment of the things we have already. The other idea is that this is the age of machines and that to dislike the machine, or even to want to limit its domination, is backward-looking, reactionary and slightly ridiculous. This is often backed up by the statement that a love of Nature is a foible of urbanized people who have no notion what Nature is really like. Those who really have to deal with the soil, so it is argued, do not love the soil, and do not take the faintest interest in birds or flowers, except from a strictly utilitarian point of view. To love the country one must live in the town, merely taking an occasional week-end ramble at the warmer times of year.

This last idea is demonstrably false. Medieval literature, for instance, including the popular ballads, is full of an almost Georgian enthusiasm for Nature, and the art of agricultural peoples such as the Chinese and Japanese centres always round trees, birds, flowers, rivers, mountains. The other idea seems to me to be wrong in a subtler way. Certainly we ought to be discontented, we ought not simply to find out ways of making the best of a bad job, and yet if we kill all pleasure in the actual process of life, what sort of future are we preparing for ourselves? If a man cannot enjoy the return of spring, why should he be happy in a labour-saving Utopia? What will he do with the leisure that the machine will give him? I have always suspected that if our economic and political problems are ever really solved, life will become simpler instead of more complex, and that the sort of pleasure one gets from finding the first primrose will loom larger than the sort of pleasure one gets from eating an ice to the tune of a Wurlitzer. I think that by retaining one's childhood love of such things as trees, fishes, butterflies and – to return to my first instance – toads, one makes a peaceful and decent future a little more probable, and that by preaching the doctrine that nothing is to be admired except steel and concrete, one merely makes it a little surer that human beings will have no outlet for their surplus energy except in hatred and leader worship.

At any rate, spring is here, even in London N.1, and they can't stop you enjoying it. This is a satisfying reflection. How many a time have I stood watching the toads mating, or a pair of hares having a boxing match in the young corn, and thought of all the important persons who would stop me enjoying this if they could. But luckily they can't. So long as you are not actually ill, hungry, frightened or immured in a prison or a holiday camp, spring is still spring. The atom bombs are piling up in the factories, the police are prowling through the cities, the lies are streaming from the loudspeakers, but the earth is still going round the sun, and neither the dictators nor the bureaucrats, deeply as they disapprove of the process, are able to prevent it.

Tribune, 12 April 1946

A Good Word for the Vicar of Bray

Some years ago a friend took me to the little Berkshire church of which the celebrated Vicar of Bray was once the incumbent. (Actually it is a few miles from Bray, but perhaps at that time the two livings were one.) In the churchyard there stands a magnificent yew tree which, according to a notice at its foot, was planted by no less a person than the Vicar of Bray himself. And it struck me at the time as curious that such a man should have left such a relic behind him.

The Vicar of Bray, though he was well equipped to be a leader-writer on *The Times,* could hardly be described as an admirable character. Yet, after this lapse of time, all that is left of him is a comic song and a beautiful tree, which has rested the eyes of generation after generation and must surely have outweighed any bad effects which he produced by his political quislingism.

Thibaw, the last King of Burma, was also far from being a good man. He was a drunkard, he had five hundred wives – he seems to have kept them chiefly for show, however – and when he came to the throne his first act was to decapitate seventy or eighty of his brothers. Yet he did posterity a good turn by planting the dusty streets of Mandalay with tamarind trees which cast a pleasant shade until the Japanese incendiary bombs burned them down in 1942.

The poet, James Shirley, seems to have generalized too freely when he said that 'Only the actions of the just Smell sweet and blossom in their dust.' Sometimes the actions of the unjust make quite a good showing after the appropriate lapse of time. When I saw the Vicar of Bray's yew tree it reminded me of something, and afterwards I got hold of a book of selections from the writings of John Aubrey and reread a pastoral poem which must have been written some time in the first half of the seventeenth century, and which was inspired by a certain Mrs Overall.

Mrs Overall was the wife of a Dean and was extensively unfaithful to him. According to Aubrey she 'could scarcely denie any one', and she had 'the loveliest Eies that were ever seen, but wondrous wanton'. The poem (the 'shepherd swaine' seems to have been somebody called Sir John Selby) starts off:

Downe lay the Shepherd Swaine
So sober and demure
Wishing for his wench againe
So bonny and so pure
With his head on hillock lowe
And his arms akimboe
And all was for the losse of his
Hye nonny nonny noe . . .

Sweet she was, as kind a love
As ever fetter'd Swaine;
Never such a daynty one
Shall man enjoy again.
Sett a thousand on a rowe
I forbid that any showe
Ever the like of her
Hye nonny nonny noe.

As the poem proceeds through another six verses, the refrain 'Hye nonny nonny noe' takes on an unmistakably obscene meaning, but it ends with the exquisite stanza:

But gone she is the prettiest lasse
That ever trod on plaine.
What ever hath betide of her
Blame not the Shepherd Swaine.
For why? She was her owne Foe,
And gave herself the overthrowe
By being so franke of her
Hye nonny nonny noe.

Mrs Overall was no more an exemplary character than the Vicar of Bray, though a more attractive one. Yet in the end all that remains of her is a poem which still gives pleasure to many people, though for some reason it never gets into the anthologies. The suffering which she presumably caused, and the misery and futility in which her own life must have ended, have been transformed into a sort of lingering fragrance like the smell of tobacco-plants on a summer evening.

But to come back to trees. The planting of a tree, especially one of the long-living hardwood trees, is a gift which you can make to posterity at almost no cost and with almost no trouble, and if the tree takes root it will far outlive the visible effect of any of your other actions, good or evil. A year or two ago I wrote a few paragraphs in *Tribune* about some sixpenny rambler roses from Woolworth's which I had planted before the war. This brought me an indignant letter from a reader who said that roses are bourgeois, but I still think that my sixpence was better spent than if it had gone on cigarettes or even on one of the excellent Fabian Research Pamphlets.

Recently, I spent a day at the cottage where I used to live, and noted with a pleased surprise – to be exact, it was a feeling of having done good unconsciously – the progress of the things I had planted nearly ten years ago. I think it is worth recording what some of them cost, just to show what you can do with a few shillings if you invest them in something that grows.

First of all there were the two ramblers from Woolworth's, and three polyantha roses, all at sixpence each. Then there were two bush roses which were part of a job lot from a nursery garden. This job lot consisted of six fruit trees, three rose bushes and two gooseberry bushes, all for ten shillings. One of the fruit trees and one of the rose bushes died, but the rest are all flourishing. The sum total is five fruit trees, seven roses and two gooseberry bushes, all for twelve and sixpence. These plants have not entailed much work, and have had nothing spent on them beyond the original amount. They never even received any manure, except what I occasionally collected in a bucket when one of the farm horses happened to have halted outside the gate.

Between them, in nine years, those seven rose bushes will have given what would add up to a hundred or a hundred and fifty months of bloom. The fruit trees, which were mere saplings when I put them in, are now just about getting in their stride. Last week one of them, a plum, was a mass of blossom, and the apples looked as if they were going to do fairly well. What had originally been the weakling of the family, a Cox's Orange Pippin – it would hardly have been included in the job lot if it had been a good plant – had grown into a sturdy tree with plenty of fruit spurs on it. I maintain that it was a public-spirited action to plant that Cox, for these trees do not fruit quickly and I did not expect to stay there long. I never had an apple off it myself, but it looks as if someone else will have quite a lot. By their fruits ye shall know them, and the Cox's Orange Pippin is a good fruit to be known by. Yet I did not plant it with the conscious intention of doing anybody a good turn. I just saw the job lot going cheap and stuck the things into the ground without much preparation.

A thing which I regret, and which I will try to remedy some time, is that I have never in my life planted a walnut. Nobody does plant them nowadays – when you see a walnut it is almost invariably an old tree. If you plant a walnut you are planting it for your grandchildren, and who cares a damn for his grandchildren? Nor does anybody plant a quince, a mulberry or a medlar. But these are garden trees which you can only be expected to plant if you have a patch of ground of your own. On the other hand, in any hedge or in any piece of waste ground you happen to be walking through, you can do something to remedy the appalling massacre of trees, especially oaks, ashes, elms and beeches, which has happened during the war years.

Even an apple tree is liable to live for about 100 years, so that the Cox I planted in 1936 may still be bearing fruit well into the twenty-first century. An oak or a beech may live for hundreds of years and be a pleasure to thousands or tens of thousands of people before it is finally sawn up into timber. I am not suggesting that one can discharge all one's obligations towards society by means of a private re-afforestation scheme. Still, it might not be a bad idea, every time you commit an antisocial act, to make a note of it in your diary, and then, at the appropriate season, push an acorn into the ground.

And, if even one in twenty of them came to maturity, you might do quite a lot of harm in your lifetime, and still, like the Vicar of Bray, end up as a public benefactor after all.

Tribune, 26 April 1946

Why I Write

From a very early age, perhaps the age of five or six, I knew that when I grew up I should be a writer. Between the ages of about seventeen and twenty-four I tried to abandon this idea, but I did so with the consciousness that I was outraging my true nature and that sooner or later I should have to settle down and write books.

I was the middle child of three, but there was a gap of five years on either side, and I barely saw my father before I was eight. For this and other reasons I was somewhat lonely, and I soon developed disagreeable mannerisms which made me unpopular throughout my schooldays. I had the lonely child's habit of making up stories and holding conversations with imaginary persons, and I think from the very start my literary ambitions were mixed up with the feeling of being isolated and undervalued. I knew that I had a facility with words and a power of facing unpleasant facts, and I felt that this created a sort of private world in which I could get my own back for my failure in everyday life. Nevertheless the volume of serious – i.e. seriously intended – writing which I produced all through my childhood and boyhood would not amount to half a dozen pages. I wrote my first poem at the age of four or five, my mother taking it down to dictation. I cannot remember anything about it except that it was about a tiger and the tiger had 'chair-like teeth' – a good enough phrase, but I fancy the poem was a plagiarism of Blake's 'Tiger, Tiger'. At eleven, when the war of 1914–18 broke out, I wrote a patriotic poem which was printed in the local newspaper, as was another, two years later, on the death of Kitchener. From time to time, when I was a bit older, I wrote bad and usually unfinished 'nature poems' in the Georgian style. I also, about twice, attempted a short story which was a ghastly failure. That was the total of the would-be serious work that I actually set down on paper during all those years.

However, throughout this time I did in a sense engage in literary activities. To begin with there was the made-to-order stuff which I produced quickly, easily and without much pleasure to myself. Apart from school work, I wrote *vers d'occasion*, semi-comic poems which I could turn out at what now seems to me astonishing speed – at fourteen I wrote a whole rhyming play, in imitation of Aristophanes, in about a week – and helped to edit school magazines, both printed and in a manuscript. These magazines were the most pitiful burlesque stuff that you could imagine, and I took far less trouble with them than I now would with the cheapest journalism. But side by side with all this, for fifteen years or more, I was carrying out a literary exercise of a quite different kind: this was the making up of a continuous 'story' about myself, a sort of diary existing only in the mind. I believe this is a common habit of children and adolescents. As a very small child I used to imagine that I was, say, Robin Hood, and picture myself as the hero of thrilling adventures, but quite soon my 'story' ceased to be narcissistic in a crude way and became more and more a mere description of what I was doing and the things I saw. For minutes at a time this kind of thing would be running through my head: 'He pushed the door open and entered the room. A yellow beam of sunlight, filtering through the muslin curtains, slanted on to the table, where a matchbox, half open, lay beside the inkpot. With his right hand in his pocket he moved across to the window. Down in the street a tortoiseshell cat was chasing a dead leaf,' etc, etc. This habit continued till I was about twenty-five, right through my non-literary years. Although I had to search, and did search, for the right words, I seemed to be making this descriptive effort almost against my will, under a kind of compulsion from outside. The 'story' must, I suppose, have reflected the styles of the various writers I admired at different ages, but so far as I remember it always had the same meticulous descriptive quality.

When I was about sixteen I suddenly discovered the joy of mere words, i.e. the sounds and associations of words. The lines from *Paradise Lost*,

So hee with difficulty and labour hard
Moved on: with difficulty and labour hee,

which do not now seem to me so very wonderful, sent shivers down my backbone; and the spelling 'hee' for 'he' was an added pleasure. As for the need to describe things, I knew all about it already. So it is clear what kind of books I wanted to write, in so far as I could be said to want to write books at that time. I wanted to write enormous naturalistic novels with unhappy endings, full of detailed descriptions and arresting similes, and also full of purple passages in which words were used partly for the sake of their sound. And in fact my first completed novel, *Burmese Days*, which I wrote when I was thirty but projected much earlier, is rather that kind of book.

I give all this background information because I do not think one can assess a writer's motives without knowing something of his early development. His subject matter will be determined by the age he lives in – at least this is true in tumultuous, revolutionary ages like our own – but before he ever begins to write he will have acquired an emotional attitude from which he will never completely escape. It is his job, no doubt, to discipline his temperament and avoid getting stuck at some immature stage, or in some perverse mood: but if he escapes from his early influences altogether, he will have killed his impulse to write. Putting aside the need to earn a living, I think there are four great motives for writing, at any rate for writing prose. They exist in different degrees in every writer, and in any one writer the proportions will vary from time to time, according to the atmosphere in which he is living. They are:

1. Sheer egoism. Desire to seem clever, to be talked about, to be remembered after death, to get your own back on grown-ups who snubbed you in childhood, etc etc. It is humbug to pretend that this is not a motive, and a strong one. Writers share this characteristic with scientists, artists, politicians, lawyers, soldiers, successful businessmen – in short, with the whole top crust of humanity. The great mass of human beings are not acutely selfish. After the age of about thirty they abandon individual ambition – in many cases, indeed, they almost abandon the sense of being individuals at all – and live chiefly for others, or are simply smothered under drudgery. But there is also the minority of gifted, wilful people who are determined to live their own lives to the end, and writers belong in this class. Serious writers, I should say, are on the whole more vain and self-centred than journalists, though less interested in money.

2. Aesthetic enthusiasm. Perception of beauty in the external world, or, on the other hand, in words and their right arrangement. Pleasure in the impact of one sound on another, in the firmness of good prose or the rhythm of a good story. Desire to share an experience which one feels is valuable and ought not to be missed. The aesthetic motive is very feeble in a lot of writers, but even a pamphleteer or a writer of textbooks will have pet words and phrases which appeal to him for non-utilitarian reasons; or he may feel strongly about typography, width of margins, etc. Above the level of a railway guide, no book is quite free from aesthetic considerations.

3. Historical impulse. Desire to see things as they are, to find out true facts and store them up for the use of posterity.

4. Political purpose – using the word 'political' in the widest possible sense. Desire to push the world in a certain direction, to alter other people's idea of the kind of society that they should strive after. Once again, no book is genuinely free from political bias. The opinion that art should have nothing to do with politics is itself a political attitude.

It can be seen how these various impulses must war against one another, and how they must fluctuate from person to person and from time to time. By nature – taking your 'nature' to be the state you have attained when you are first adult – I am a person in whom the first three motives would outweigh the fourth. In a peaceful age I might have written ornate or merely descriptive books, and might have remained almost unaware of my political loyalties. As it is I have been forced into becoming a sort of pamphleteer. First I spent five years in an unsuitable profession (the Indian Imperial Police, in Burma), and then I underwent poverty and the sense of failure. This increased my natural hatred of authority and made me for the first time fully aware of the existence of the working classes, and the job in Burma had given me some understanding of the nature of imperialism: but these experiences were not enough to give me an accurate political orientation. Then came Hitler, the Spanish civil war, etc. By the end of 1935 I had still failed to reach a firm decision. I remember a little poem that I wrote at that date, expressing my dilemma:

A happy vicar I might have been
Two hundred years ago,
To preach upon eternal doom
And watch my walnuts grow;

But born, alas, in an evil time,
I missed that pleasant haven,
For the hair has grown on my upper lip
And the clergy are all clean-shaven.

And later still the times were good,
We were so easy to please,
We rocked our troubled thoughts to sleep
On the bosoms of the trees.

All ignorant we dared to own
The joys we now dissemble;
The greenfinch on the apple bough
Could make my enemies tremble.

But girls' bellies and apricots,
Roach in a shaded stream,
Horses, ducks in flight at dawn,
All these are a dream.

It is forbidden to dream again;
We maim our joys or hide them;
Horses are made of chromium steel
And little fat men shall ride them.

I am the worm who never turned,
The eunuch without a harem;
Between the priest and the commissar
I walk like Eugene Aram;

And the commissar is telling my fortune
While the radio plays,
But the priest has promised an Austin Seven,
For Duggie always pays.

I dreamed I dwelt in marble halls,
And woke to find it true;
I wasn't born for an age like this;
Was Smith? Was Jones? Were you?[1]

The Spanish war and other events in 1936–37 turned the scale and thereafter I knew where I stood. Every line of serious work that I have written since 1936 has been written, directly or indirectly, *against* totalitarianism and *for* democratic Socialism, as I understand it. It seems to me nonsense, in a period like our own, to think that one can avoid writing of such subjects. Everyone writes of them in one guise or another. It is simply a question of which side one takes and what approach one follows. And the more one is conscious of one's political bias, the more chance one has of acting politically without sacrificing one's aesthetic and intellectual integrity.

What I have most wanted to do throughout the past ten years is to make political writing into an art. My starting point is always a feeling of partisanship, a sense of injustice. When I sit down to write a book, I do not say to myself, 'I am going to produce a work of art.' I write it because there is some lie that I want to expose, some fact to which I want to draw attention, and my initial concern is to get a hearing. But I could not do the work of writing a book, or even a long magazine article, if it were not also an aesthetic experience. Anyone who cares to examine my work will see that even when it is downright propaganda it contains much that a full-time politician would consider irrelevant. I am not able, and I do not want, completely to abandon the world-view that I acquired in childhood. So long as I remain alive and well I shall continue to feel strongly about prose style, to love the surface of the earth, and to take pleasure in solid objects and scraps of useless information. It is no use trying to suppress that side of myself. The job is to reconcile my ingrained likes and dislikes with the essentially public, non-individual activities that this age forces on all of us.

It is not easy. It raises problems of construction and of language, and it raises in a new way the problem of truthfulness. Let me give just one example of the cruder kind of difficulty that arises. My book about the Spanish civil war, *Homage to Catalonia*, is, of course, a frankly political book, but in the main it is written with a certain detachment and regard for form. I did try very hard in it to tell the whole truth without violating my literary instincts. But among other things it contains a long chapter, full of newspaper quotations and the like, defending the Trotskyists who were accused of plotting with Franco. Clearly such a chapter, which after a year or two would lose its interest for any ordinary reader, must ruin the book. A critic whom I respect read me a lecture about it. 'Why did you put in all that stuff?' he said. 'You've turned what might have been a good book into journalism.' What he said was true, but I could not have done otherwise. I happened to know, what very few people in England had been allowed to know, that innocent men were being falsely accused. If I had not been angry about that I should never have written the book.

In one form or another this problem comes up again. The problem of language is subtler and would take too long to discuss. I will only say that of late years I have tried to write less picturesquely and more exactly. In any case I find that by the time you have perfected any style of writing, you have always

[1] This poem first appeared in the *Adelphi*, December 1936.

outgrown it. *Animal Farm* was the first book in which I tried, with full consciousness of what I was doing, to fuse political purpose and artistic purpose into one whole. I have not written a novel for seven years, but I hope to write another fairly soon. It is bound to be a failure, every book is a failure, but I know with some clarity what kind of book I want to write.

Looking back through the last page or two, I see that I have made it appear as though my motives in writing were wholly public-spirited. I don't want to leave that as the final impression. All writers are vain, selfish and lazy, and at the very bottom of their motives there lies a mystery. Writing a book is a horrible, exhausting struggle, like a long bout of some painful illness. One would never undertake such a thing if one were not driven on by some demon whom one can neither resist nor understand. For all one knows that demon is simply the same instinct that makes a baby squall for attention. And yet it is also true that one can write nothing readable unless one constantly struggles to efface one's own personality. Good prose is like a window pane. I cannot say with certainty which of my motives are the strongest, but I know which of them deserve to be followed. And looking back through my work, I see that it is invariably where I lacked a *political* purpose that I wrote lifeless books and was betrayed into purple passages, sentences without meaning, decorative adjectives and humbug generally.

Gangrel, Summer 1946

James Burnham and the Managerial Revolution[1]

James Burnham's book, *The Managerial Revolution*, made a considerable stir both in the United States and in this country at the time when it was published, and its main thesis has been so much discussed that a detailed exposition of it is hardly necessary. As shortly as I can summarize it, the thesis is this:

Capitalism is disappearing, but Socialism is not replacing it. What is now arising is a new kind of planned, centralized society which will be neither capitalist nor, in any accepted sense of the word, democratic. The rulers of this new society will be the people who effectively control the means of production: that is, business executives, technicians, bureaucrats and soldiers, lumped together by Burnham under the name of 'managers'. These people will eliminate the old capitalist class, crush the working class, and so organize society that all power and economic privilege remain in their own hands. Private property rights will be abolished, but common ownership will not be established. The new 'managerial' societies will not consist of a patchwork of small, independent states, but of great super-states grouped round the main industrial centres in Europe, Asia, and America. These super-states will fight among themselves for possession of the remaining uncaptured portions of the earth, but will probably be unable to conquer one another completely.

[1] This essay was originally printed in *Polemic* under the title 'Second Thoughts on James Burnham', and later reprinted as a pamphlet with the present title.

Internally, each society will be hierarchical, with an aristocracy of talent at the top and a mass of semi-slaves at the bottom.

In his next published book, *The Machiavellians,* Burnham elaborates and also modifies his original statement. The greater part of the book is an exposition of the theories of Machiavelli and of his modern disciples, Mosca, Michels, and Pareto: with doubtful justification, Burnham adds to these the syndicalist writer, Georges Sorel. What Burnham is mainly concerned to show is that a democratic society has never existed and, so far as we can see, never will exist. Society is of its nature oligarchical, and the power of the oligarchy always rests upon force and fraud. Burnham does not deny that 'good' motives may operate in private life, but he maintains that politics consists of the struggle for power, and nothing else. All historical changes finally boil down to the replacement of one ruling class by another. All talk about democracy, liberty, equality, fraternity, all revolutionary movements, all visions of Utopia, or 'the classless society', or 'the Kingdom of Heaven on earth', are humbug (not necessarily conscious humbug) covering the ambitions of some new class which is elbowing its way into power. The English Puritans, the Jacobins, the Bolsheviks, were in each case simply power seekers using the hopes of the masses in order to win a privileged position for themselves. Power can sometimes be won or maintained without violence, but never without fraud, because it is necessary to make use of the masses, and the masses would not co-operate if they knew that they were simply serving the purposes of a minority. In each great revolutionary struggle the masses are led on by vague dreams of human brotherhood, and then, when the new ruling class is well established in power, they are thrust back into servitude. This is practically the whole of political history, as Burnham sees it.

Where the second book departs from the earlier one is in asserting that the whole process could be somewhat moralized if the facts were faced more honestly. *The Machiavellians* is sub-titled *Defenders of Freedom.* Machiavelli and his followers taught that in politics decency simply does not exist, and, by doing so, Burnham claims, made it possible to conduct political affairs more intelligently and less oppressively. A ruling class which recognized that its real aim was to stay in power would also recognize that it would be more likely to succeed if it served the common good, and might avoid stiffening into a hereditary aristocracy. Burnham lays much stress on Pareto's theory of the 'circulation of the élites'. If it is to stay in power a ruling class must constantly admit suitable recruits from below, so that the ablest men may always be at the top and a new class of power-hungry malcontents cannot come into being. This is likeliest to happen, Burnham considers, in a society which retains democratic habits – that is, where opposition is permitted and certain bodies such as the press and the trade unions can keep their autonomy. Here Burnham undoubtedly contradicts his earlier opinion. In *The Managerial Revolution*, which was written in 1940, it is taken as a matter of course that 'managerial' Germany is in all ways more efficient than a capitalist democracy such as France or Britain. In the second book, written in 1942, Burnham admits that the Germans might have avoided some of their more serious errors if they had permitted freedom of speech. However, the main thesis is not abandoned. Capitalism is doomed, and Socialism is a dream. If we grasp what is at issue we may guide the course of the managerial revolution to some extent, but that revolution is *happening*, whether we like it or not. In both books, but especially the earlier one, there is a note of unmistakable relish over the cruelty and wickedness of the processes that are being discussed. Although he reiterates that he is merely setting forth the facts and not stating his own preferences, it is clear that Burnham is fascinated by the spectacle of power, and that his sympathies were with Germany so long as Germany appeared to be winning the war. A more recent essay, 'Lenin's Heir', published in the *Partisan Review* about the beginning of 1945, suggests that this sympathy has since been transferred to the USSR. 'Lenin's Heir', which provoked violent controversy in the American left-wing press, has not yet been reprinted in England, and I must return to it later.

It will be seen that Burnham's theory is not, strictly speaking, a new one. Many earlier writers have foreseen the emergence of a new kind of society, neither capitalist nor Socialist, and probably based upon slavery: though most of them have differed from Burnham in not assuming this development to be *inevitable*. A good example is Hilaire Belloc's book, *The Servile State*, published in 1911. *The Servile State* is written in a tiresome style, and the remedy it suggests (a return to small-scale peasant ownership) is for many reasons impossible: still, it does foretell with remarkable insight the kind of things that have been happening from about 1930 onwards. Chesterton, in a less methodical way, predicted the disappearance of democracy and private property, and the rise of a slave society which might be called either capitalist or Communist. Jack London, in *The Iron Heel* (1909), foretold some of the essential features of Fascism, and such books as Wells's *The Sleeper Awakes* (1900), Zamyatin's *We* (1923), and Aldous Huxley's *Brave New World* (1930), all described imaginary worlds in which the special problems of capitalism had been solved without bringing liberty, equality, or true happiness any nearer. More recently, writers like Peter Drucker and F. A. Voigt have argued that Fascism and Communism are substantially the same thing. And indeed, it has always been obvious that a planned and centralized society is liable to develop into an oligarchy or a dictatorship. Orthodox Conservatives were unable to see this, because it comforted them to assume that Socialism 'wouldn't work', and that the disappearance of capitalism would mean chaos and anarchy. Orthodox Socialists could not see it, because they wished to think that they themselves would soon be in power, and therefore assumed that when capitalism disappears, Socialism takes its place. As a result they were unable to foresee the rise of Fascism, or to make correct predictions about it after it had appeared. Later, the need to justify the Russian dictatorship and to explain away the obvious resemblances between Communism and Nazism clouded the issue still more. But the notion that industrialism must end in monopoly, and that monopoly must imply tyranny, is not a startling one.

Where Burnham differs from most other thinkers is in trying to plot the course of the 'managerial revolution' accurately on a world scale, and in assuming that the drift towards totalitarianism is irresistible and must not be fought against, though it may be guided. According to Burnham, writing in 1940, 'managerialism' has reached its fullest development in the USSR, but is almost equally well developed in Germany, and has made its appearance in the United States. He describes the New Deal as 'primitive managerialism'. But the trend is the same everywhere, or almost everywhere. Always *laissez-faire* capitalism gives way to planning and state interference, the mere *owner* loses power as against the technician and the bureaucrat, but Socialism – that is to say, what used to be called Socialism – shows no sign of emerging:

> Some apologists try to excuse Marxism by saying that it has 'never had a chance'. This is far from the truth. Marxism and the Marxist parties have had dozens of chances. In Russia, a Marxist party took power. Within a short time it abandoned Socialism; if not in words, at any rate in the effect of its actions. In most European nations there were during the last months of the first world war and the years immediately thereafter, social crises which left a wide-open door for the Marxist parties: without exception they proved unable to take and hold power. In a large number of countries – Germany, Denmark, Norway, Sweden, Austria, England, Australia, New Zealand, Spain, France – the reformist Marxist parties have administered the governments, and have uniformly failed to introduce Socialism or make any genuine step towards Socialism . . . These parties have, in practice, at every historical test – and there have been many – either failed Socialism or abandoned it. This is the fact which neither the bitterest foe nor the most ardent friend of Socialism can erase. This fact does not, as some think, prove anything about the moral quality of the Socialist ideal. But it does constitute unblinkable evidence that, whatever its moral quality, Socialism is not going to come.

Burnham does not, of course, deny that the new 'managerial' régimes, like the régimes of Russia and Nazi Germany, may be *called* Socialist. He means merely that they will not *be* Socialist in any sense of the word which would have been accepted by Marx, or Lenin, or Keir Hardie, or William Morris, or indeed, by any representative Socialist prior to about 1930. Socialism, until recently, was supposed to connote political democracy, social equality and internationalism. There is not the smallest sign that any of these things is in a way to being established anywhere, and the one great country in which something described as a proletarian revolution once happened, i.e. the USSR, has moved steadily away from the old concept of a free and equal society aiming at universal human brotherhood. In an almost unbroken progress since the early days of the Revolution, liberty has been chipped away and representative institutions smothered, while inequalities have increased and nationalism and militarism have grown stronger. But at the same time, Burnham insists, there has been no tendency to return to capitalism. What is happening is simply the growth of 'managerialism', which, according to Burnham, is in progress everywhere, though the manner in which it comes about may vary from country to country.

Now, as an interpretation of what is *happening*, Burnham's theory is extremely plausible, to put it at the lowest. The events of, at any rate, the last fifteen years in the USSR can be far more easily explained by this theory than by any other. Evidently the USSR is not Socialist, and can only be called Socialist if one gives the word a meaning different from what it would have in any other context. On the other hand, prophecies that the Russian régime would revert to capitalism have always been falsified, and now seem further than ever from being fulfilled. In claiming that the process had gone almost equally far in Nazi Germany, Burnham probably exaggerates, but it seems certain that the drift was away from old-style capitalism and towards a planned economy with an adoptive oligarchy in control. In Russia the capitalists were destroyed first and the workers were crushed later. In Germany the workers were crushed first, but the elimination of the capitalists had at any rate begun, and calculations based on the assumption that Nazism was 'simply capitalism' were always contradicted by events. Where Burnham seems to go most astray is in believing 'managerialism' to be on the up-grade in the United States, the one great country where free capitalism is still vigorous. But if one considers the world movement as a whole, his conclusions are difficult to resist; and even in the United States the all-prevailing faith in *laissez-faire* may not survive the next great economic crisis. It has been urged against Burnham that he assigns far too much importance to the 'managers', in the narrow sense of the word – that is, factory bosses, planners and technicians – and seems to assume that even in Soviet Russia it is these people, and not the Communist Party chiefs, who are the real holders of power. However, this is a secondary error, and it is partially corrected in *The Machiavellians*. The real question is not whether the people who wipe their boots on us during the next fifty years are to be called managers, bureaucrats, or politicians: the question is whether capitalism, now obviously doomed, is to give way to oligarchy or to true democracy.

But curiously enough, when one examines the predictions which Burnham has based on his general theory, one finds that in so far as they are verifiable, they have been falsified. Numbers of people have pointed this out already. However, it is worth following up Burnham's predictions in detail, because they form a sort of pattern which is related to contemporary events, and which reveals, I believe, a very important weakness in present-day political thought.

To begin with, writing in 1940, Burnham takes a German victory more or less for granted. Britain is described as 'dissolving', and as displaying 'all the characteristics which have distinguished decadent cultures in past historical transitions', while the conquest and integration of Europe which Germany achieved in 1940 is described as 'irreversible'. 'England,' writes Burnham, 'no matter with what non-European allies, cannot conceivably hope to conquer the European continent.' Even if Germany should somehow manage to lose the war, she could not be dismembered or reduced to the status of the Weimar Republic, but is bound to remain as the nucleus of a unified Europe. The future map of the world, with its three great super-states is, in any case, already settled in its main outlines: and 'the nuclei of the three super-states are, whatever may be their future names, the previously existing nations, Japan, Germany, and the United States.'

Burnham also commits himself to the opinion that Germany will not attack the USSR until after Britain has been defeated. In a condensation of his book published in the *Partisan Review* of May-June 1941, and presumably written later than the book itself, he says:

> As in the case of Russia, so with Germany, the third part of the managerial problem – the contest for dominance with other sections of managerial society – remains for the future. First had to come the death-blow that assured the toppling of the capitalist world order, which meant above all the destruction of the foundations of the British Empire (the keystone of the capitalist world order) both directly and through the smashing of the European political structure, which was a necessary prop of the Empire. This is the basic explanation of the Nazi-Soviet Pact, which is not intelligible on other grounds. The future conflict between Germany and Russia will be a managerial conflict proper; prior to the great world-managerial battles, the end of the capitalist order must be assured. The belief that Nazism is 'decadent capitalism' ... makes it impossible to

> explain reasonably the Nazi-Soviet Pact. From this belief followed the always expected war between Germany and Russia, not the actual war to the death between Germany and the British Empire. The war between Germany and Russia is one of the managerial wars of the future, not of the anti-capitalist wars of yesterday and today.

However, the attack on Russia will come later, and Russia is certain, or almost certain, to be defeated. 'There is every reason to believe ... that Russia will split apart, with the western half gravitating towards the European base and the eastern towards the Asiatic.' This quotation comes from *The Managerial Revolution*. In the above-quoted article, written probably about six months later, it is put more forcibly: 'the Russian weaknesses indicate that Russia will not be able to endure, that it will crack apart, and fall towards east and west.' And in a supplementary note which was added to the English (Pelican) edition, and which appears to have been written at the end of 1941, Burnham speaks as though the 'cracking apart' process were already happening. The war, he says, 'is part of the means whereby the western half of Russia is being integrated into the European super-state'.

Sorting these various statements out, we have the following prophecies:

1. Germany is bound to win the war.
2. Germany and Japan are bound to survive as great states, and to remain the nuclei of power in their respective areas.
3. Germany will not attack the USSR until after the defeat of Britain.
4. The USSR is bound to be defeated.

However, Burnham has made other predictions besides these. In a short article in the *Partisan Review*, in the summer of 1944, he gives his opinion that the USSR will gang up with Japan in order to prevent the total defeat of the latter, while the American Communists will be set to work to sabotage the eastern end of the war. And finally, in an article in the same magazine in the winter of 1944–5, he claims that Russia, destined so short a while ago to 'crack apart', is within sight of conquering the whole of Eurasia. This article which was the cause of violent controversies among the American intelligentsia, has not been reprinted in England. I must give some account of it here, because its manner of approach and its emotional tone are of a peculiar kind, and by studying them one can get nearer to the real roots of Burnham's theory.

The article is entitled 'Lenin's Heir', and it sets out to show that Stalin is the true and legitimate guardian of the Russian Revolution, which he has not in any sense 'betrayed' but has merely carried forward on lines that were implicit in it from the start. In itself, this is an easier opinion to swallow than the usual Trotskyist claim that Stalin is a mere crook who has perverted the Revolution to his own ends, and that things would somehow have been different if Lenin had lived or Trotsky had remained in power. Actually there is no strong reason for thinking that the main lines of development would have been very different. Well before 1923 the seeds of a totalitarian society were quite plainly there. Lenin, indeed, is one of those politicians who win an undeserved reputation by dying prematurely.[1] Had he lived, it is probable that he would either have

[1] It is difficult to think of any politician who has lived to be eighty and still been regarded as a success. What we call a 'great' statesman normally means one who dies before his

been thrown out, like Trotsky, or would have kept himself in power by methods as barbarous, or nearly as barbarous, as those of Stalin. The *title* of Burnham's essay, therefore, sets forth a reasonable thesis, and one would expect him to support it by an appeal to the facts.

However, the essay barely touches upon its ostensible subject-matter. It is obvious that anyone genuinely concerned to show that there has been continuity of policy as between Lenin and Stalin would start by outlining Lenin's policy and then explain in what way Stalin's has resembled it. Burnham does not do this. Except for one or two cursory sentences he says nothing about Lenin's policy, and Lenin's name only occurs five times in an essay of twelve pages: in the first seven pages, apart from the title, it does not occur at all. The real aim of the essay is to present Stalin as a towering, superhuman figure, indeed a species of demigod, and Bolshevism as an irresistible force which is flowing over the earth and cannot be halted until it reaches the outermost borders of Eurasia. In so far as he makes any attempt to prove his case, Burnham does so by repeating over and over again that Stalin is 'a great man' – which is probably true, but is almost completely irrelevant. Moreover, though he does advance some solid arguments for believing in Stalin's genius, it is clear that in his mind the idea of 'greatness' is inextricably mixed up with the idea of cruelty and dishonesty. There are curious passages in which it seems to be suggested that Stalin is to be admired *because of* the limitless suffering that he has caused:

> Stalin proves himself a 'great man', in the grand style. The accounts of the banquets, staged in Moscow for the visiting dignitaries, set the symbolic tone. With their enormous menus of sturgeon, and roasts, and fowl, and sweets; their streams of liquor; the scores of toasts with which they end; the silent, unmoving secret police behind each guest; all against the winter background of the starving multitudes of besieged Leningrad; the dying millions at the front; the jammed concentration camps; the city crowds kept by their minute rations just at the edge of life; there is little trace of dull mediocrity or the hand of Babbitt. We recognize, rather, the tradition of the most spectacular of the Tsars, of the Great Kings of the Medes and Persians, of the Khanate of the Golden Horde, of the banquet we assign to the gods of the Heroic Ages in tribute to the insight that insolence, and indifference, and brutality on such a scale remove beings from the human level ... Stalin's political techniques shows a freedom from conventional restrictions that is incompatible with mediocrity: the mediocre man is custom-bound. Often it is the scale of the operations that sets them apart. It is usual, for example, for men active in practical life to engineer an occasional frame-up. But to carry out a frame-up against tens of thousands of persons, important percentages of whole strata of society, including most of one's own comrades, is so far out of the ordinary that the long-run mass conclusion is either that the frame-up must be true – at least 'have some truth in it' – or that power so immense must be submitted to –

policy has had time to take effect. If Cromwell had lived a few years longer he would probably have fallen from power, in which case we should now regard him as a failure. If Pétain had died in 1930, France would have venerated him as a hero and patriot. Napoleon remarked once that if only a cannon-ball had happened to hit him when he was riding into Moscow, he would have gone down to history as the greatest man who ever lived. [Author's footnote.]

> is a 'historical necessity', as intellectuals put it ... There is nothing unexpected in letting a few individuals starve for reasons of state; but to starve by deliberate decision, several millions, is a type of action attributed ordinarily only to gods.

In these and other similar passages there may be a tinge of irony, but it is difficult not to feel that there is also a sort of fascinated admiration. Towards the end of the essay Burnham compares Stalin with those semi-mythical heroes, like Moses or Asoka, who embody in themselves a whole epoch, and can justly be credited with feats that they did not actually perform. In writing of Soviet foreign policy and its supposed objectives, he touches an even more mystical note:

> Starting from the magnetic core of the Eurasian heartland, the Soviet power, like the reality of the One of Neo-Platonism overflowing in the descending series of the emanative progression, flows outward, west into Europe, south into the Near East, east into China, already lapping the shores of the Atlantic, the Yellow and China Seas, the Mediterranean, and the Persian Gulf. As the undifferentiated One, in its progression, descends through the stages of Mind, Soul, and Matter, and then through its fatal Return back to itself; so does the Soviet power, emanating from the integrally totalitarian centre, proceed outwards by Absorption (the Baltics, Bessarabia, Bukovina, East Poland), Domination (Finland, the Balkans, Mongolia, North China and, tomorrow, Germany), Orienting Influence (Italy, France, Turkey, Iran, Central and south China ...), until it is dissipated in *MH ON*, the outer material sphere, beyond the Eurasian boundaries, of momentary Appeasement and Infiltration (England, the United States).

I do not think it is fanciful to suggest that the unnecessary capital letters with which this passage is loaded are intended to have a hypnotic effect on the reader. Burnham is trying to build up a picture of terrifying, irresistible power, and to turn a normal political manoeuvre like infiltration into Infiltration adds to the general portentousness. The essay should be read in full. Although it is not the kind of tribute that the average russophile would consider acceptable, and although Burnham himself would probably claim that he is being strictly objective, he is in effect performing an act of homage, and even of self-abasement. Meanwhile, this essay gives us another prophecy to add to the list: i.e. that the USSR will conquer the whole of Eurasia, and probably a great deal more. And one must remember that Burnham's basic theory contains, in itself, a prediction which still has to be tested – that is, that whatever else happens, the 'managerial' form of society is bound to prevail.

Burnham's earlier prophecy, of a German victory in the war and the integration of Europe round the German nucleus, was falsified, not only in its main outlines, but in some important details. Burnham insists all the way through that 'managerialism' is not only more efficient than capitalist democracy or Marxist Socialism, but also more acceptable to the masses. The slogans of democracy and national self-determination, he says, no longer have any mass appeal: 'managerialism', on the other hand, can rouse enthusiasm, produce intelligible war aims, establish fifth columns everywhere, and inspire its soldiers with a fanatical morale. The 'fanaticism' of the Germans, as against the 'apathy' or 'indifference' of the British, French, etc, is much emphasized, and Nazism is represented as a revolutionary force sweeping across Europe and spreading its philosophy 'by contagion'. The Nazi fifth columns 'cannot be wiped out', and the democratic nations are quite incapable of projecting any settlement which the German or other European masses would prefer to the New Order. In any case, the democracies can only defeat Germany if they go 'still further along the managerial road than Germany has yet gone'.

The germ of truth in all this is that the smaller European states, demoralized by the chaos and stagnation of the pre-war years, collapsed rather more quickly than they need have done, and might conceivably have accepted the New Order if the Germans had kept some of their promises. But the actual experience of German rule aroused almost at once such a fury of hatred and vindictiveness as the world has seldom seen. After about the beginning of 1941 there was hardly any need of a positive war aim, since getting rid of the Germans was a sufficient objective. The question of morale, and its relation to national solidarity, is a nebulous one, and the evidence can be so manipulated as to prove almost anything. But if one goes by the proportion of prisoners to other casualties, and the amount of quislingism, the totalitarian states come out of the comparison worse than the democracies. Hundreds of thousands of Russians appear to have gone over to the Germans during the course of the war, while comparable numbers of Germans and Italians had gone over to the Allies before the war started: the corresponding number of American or British renegades would have amounted to a few scores. As an example of the inability of 'capitalist ideologies' to enlist support, Burnham cites 'the complete failure of voluntary military recruiting in England (as well as the entire British Empire) and in the United States'. One would gather from this that the armies of the totalitarian states were manned by volunteers. Actually, no totalitarian state has ever so much as considered voluntary recruitment for any purpose, nor, throughout history, has a large army ever been raised by voluntary means.[1] It is not worth listing the many similar arguments that Burnham puts forward. The point is that he assumes that the Germans must win the propaganda war as well as the military one, and that, at any rate in Europe, this estimate was not borne out by events.

It will be seen that Burnham's predictions have not merely, when they were verifiable, turned out to be wrong, but that they have sometimes contradicted one another in a sensational way. It is this last fact that is significant. Political predictions are usually wrong, because they are usually based on wish-thinking, but they can have symptomatic value, especially when they change abruptly. Often the revealing factor is the date at which they are made. Dating Burnham's various writings as accurately as can be done from internal evidence, and then noting what events they coincided with, we find the following relationships:

In *The Managerial Revolution* Burnham prophesies a German victory, postponement of the Russo-German war until after Britain is defeated, and, subsequently, the defeat of Russia. The book, or much of it, was written in the

[1] Great Britain raised a million volunteers in the earlier part of the 1914–18 war. This must be a world's record, but the pressures applied were such that it is doubtful whether the recruitment ought to be described as voluntary. Even the most 'ideological' wars have been fought largely by pressed men. In the English civil war, the Napoleonic wars, the American civil war, the Spanish civil war, etc, both sides resorted to conscription or the press gang. [Author's footnote.]

second half of 1940 – i.e. at a time when the Germans had overrun western Europe and were bombing Britain, and the Russians were collaborating with them fairly closely, and in what appeared, at any rate, to be a spirit of appeasement.

In the supplementary note added to the English edition of the book, Burnham appears to assume that the USSR is already beaten and the splitting-up process is about to begin. This was published in the spring of 1942 and presumably written at the end of 1941; i.e. when the Germans were in the suburbs of Moscow.

The prediction that Russia would gang up with Japan against the USA was written early in 1944, soon after the conclusion of a new Russo-Japanese treaty.

The prophecy of Russian world conquest was written in the winter of 1944, when the Russians were advancing rapidly in eastern Europe while the Western Allies were still held up in Italy and northern France.

It will be seen that at each point Burnham is predicting *a continuation of the thing that is happening*. Now the tendency to do this is not simply a bad habit, like inaccuracy of exaggeration, which one can correct by taking thought. It is a major mental disease, and its roots lie partly in cowardice and partly in the worship of power, which is not fully separable from cowardice.

Suppose in 1940 you had taken a Gallup poll, in England, on the question 'Will Germany win the war?' You would have found, curiously enough, that the group answering 'Yes' contained a far higher percentage of intelligent people – people with IQ of over 120, shall we say – than the group answering 'No'. The same would have held good in the middle of 1942. In this case the figures would not have been so striking, but if you had made the question 'Will the Germans capture Alexandria?' or 'Will the Japanese be able to hold on to the territories they have captured?', then once again there would have been a very marked tendency for intelligence to concentrate in the 'Yes' group. In every case the less-gifted person would have been likelier to give a right answer.

If one went simply by these instances, one might assume that high intelligence and bad military judgement always go together. However, it is not so simple as that. The English intelligentsia, on the whole, were more defeatist than the mass of the people – and some of them went on being defeatist at a time when the war was quite plainly won – partly because they were better able to visualize the dreary years of warfare that lay ahead. Their morale was worse because their imaginations were stronger. The quickest way of ending a war is to lose it, and if one finds the prospect of a long war intolerable, it is natural to disbelieve in the possibility of victory. But there was more to it than that. There was also the disaffection of large numbers of intellectuals, which made it difficult for them not to side with any country hostile to Britain. And deepest of all, there was admiration – though only in a very few cases conscious admiration – for the power, energy, and cruelty of the Nazi régime. It would be a useful though tedious labour to go through the left-wing press and enumerate all the hostile references to Nazism during the years 1935–45. One would find, I have little doubt, that they reached their high-water mark in 1937–8 and 1944–5, and dropped off noticeably in the years 1939–42 – that is, during the period when Germany seemed to be winning. One would find, also, the same people advocating a compromise peace in 1940 and approving the dismemberment of Germany in 1945. And if one studied the reactions of the English intelligentsia towards the USSR, there, too, one would find genuinely progressive impulses mixed up with admiration for power and cruelty. It would be grossly unfair to suggest that power worship is the only motive for russophile feeling, but it is one motive, and among intellectuals it is probably the strongest one.

Power worship blurs political judgement because it leads, almost unavoidably, to the belief that present trends will continue. Whoever is winning at the moment will always seem to be invincible. If the Japanese have conquered south Asia, then they will keep south Asia for ever, if the Germans have captured Tobruk, they will infallibly capture Cairo; if the Russians are in Berlin, it will not be long before they are in London: and so on. This habit of mind leads also to the belief that things will happen more quickly, completely, and catastrophically than they ever do in practice. The rise and fall of empires, the disappearance of cultures and religions, are expected to happen with earthquake suddenness, and processes which have barely started are talked about as though they were already at an end. Burnham's writings are full of apocalyptic visions. Nations, governments, classes and social systems are constantly described as expanding, contracting, decaying, dissolving, toppling, crashing, crumbling, crystallizing, and, in general, behaving in an unstable and melodramatic way. The slowness of historical change, the fact that any epoch always contains a great deal of the last epoch, is never sufficiently allowed for. Such a manner of thinking is bound to lead to mistaken prophecies, because, even when it gauges the direction of events rightly, it will miscalculate their tempo. Within the space of five years Burnham foretold the domination of Russia by Germany and of Germany by Russia. In each case he was obeying the same instinct: the instinct to bow down before the conqueror of the moment, to accept the existing trend as irreversible. With this in mind one can criticize his theory in a broader way.

The mistakes I have pointed out do not disprove Burnham's theory, but they do cast light on his probable reasons for holding it. In this connection one cannot leave out of account the fact that Burnham is an American. Every political theory has a certain regional tinge about it, and every nation, every culture, has its own characteristic prejudices and patches of ignorance. There are certain problems that must almost inevitably be seen in a different perspective according to the geographical situation from which one is looking at them. Now, the attitude that Burnham adopts, of classifying Communism and Fascism as much the same thing, and at the same time accepting both of them – or, at any rate, not assuming that either must be violently struggled against – is essentially an American attitude, and would be almost impossible for an Englishman or any other western European. English writers who consider Communism and Fascism to be the *the same thing* invariably hold that both are monstrous evils which must be fought to the death: on the other hand, any Englishman who believes Communism and Fascism to be opposites will feel that he ought to side with one or the other.[1] The reason for this difference of outlook is simple enough and, as usual, is bound up with wish-thinking. If totalitarian triumphs and the dreams of the geopoliticians come true, Britain will disappear as a world power and the whole of western Europe will be swallowed by some single great state. This is not a prospect that it is easy for an

[1] The only exception I am able to think of is Bernard Shaw, who, for some years at any rate, declared Communism and Fascism to be much the same thing, and was in favour of both of them. But Shaw, after all, is not an Englishman, and probably does not feel his fate to be bound up with that of Britain. [Author's footnote.]

Englishman to contemplate with detachment. Either he does not want Britain to disappear – in which case he will tend to construct theories proving the thing that he wants – or, like a minority of intellectuals, he will decide that his country is finished and transfer his allegiance to some foreign power. An American does not have to make the same choice. Whatever happens, the United States will survive as a great power, and from the American point of view it does not make much difference whether Europe is dominated by Russia or by Germany. Most Americans who think of the matter at all would prefer to see the world divided between two or three monster states which had reached their natural boundaries and could bargain with one another on economic issues without being troubled by ideological differences. Such a world-picture fits in with the American tendency to admire size for its own sake and to feel that success constitutes justification, and it fits in with the all-prevailing anti-British sentiment. In practice, Britain and the United States have twice been forced into alliance against Germany, and will probably, before long, be forced into alliance against Russia: but, subjectively, a majority of Americans would prefer Russia or Germany to Britain, and, as between Russia and Germany, would prefer whichever seemed stronger at the moment.[1] It is, therefore, not surprising that Burnham's world-view should often be noticeably close to that of the American imperialists on the one side, or to that of the isolationists on the other. It is a 'tough' or 'realistic' world-view which fits in with the American form of wish-thinking. The almost open admiration for Nazi methods which Burnham shows in the earlier of his two books, and which would seem shocking to almost any English reader, depends ultimately on the fact that the Atlantic is wider than the Channel.

As I have said earlier, Burnham has probably been more right than wrong about the present and immediate past. For quite fifty years past the general drift has almost certainly been towards oligarchy. The ever-increasing concentration of industrial and financial power: the diminishing importance of the individual capitalist or shareholder, and the growth of the new 'managerial' class of scientists, technicians, and bureaucrats; the weakness of the proletariat against the centralized state; the increasing helplessness of small countries against big ones; the decay of representative institutions and the appearance of one-party régimes based on police terrorism, faked plebiscites, etc: all these things seem to point in the same direction. Burnham sees the trend and assumes that it is irresistible, rather as a rabbit fascinated by a boa constrictor might assume that a boa constrictor is the strongest thing in the world. When one looks a little deeper, one sees that all his ideas rest upon two axioms which are taken for granted in the earlier book and made partly explicit in the second one. They are:

1. Politics is essentially the same in all ages.
2. Political behaviour is different from other kinds of behaviour.

To take the second point first. In *The Machiavellians*, Burnham insists that politics is simply the struggle for power. Every great social movement, every war, every revolution, every political programme, however edifying and

[1] As late as the autumn of 1945, a Gallup poll taken among the American troops in Germany showed that 51 per cent 'thought Hitler did much good before 1939'. This was after five years of anti-Hitler propaganda.

The verdict, as quoted, is not very strongly favourable to Germany, but it is hard to believe that a verdict equally favourable to Britain would be given by anywhere near 51 per cent of the American army. [Author's footnote.]

Utopian, really has behind it the ambitions of some sectional group which is out to grab power for itself. Power can never be restrained by any ethical or religious code, but only by other power. The nearest possible approach to altruistic behaviour is the perception by a ruling group that it will probably stay in power longer if it behaves decently. But curiously enough, these generalizations only apply to political behaviour, not to any other kind of behaviour. In everyday life, as Burnham sees and admits, one cannot explain every human action by applying the principle of *cui bono*? Obviously, human beings have impulses which are not selfish. Man, therefore, is an animal that can act morally when he acts as an individual, but becomes unmoral when he acts collectively. But even this generalization only holds good for the higher groups. The masses, it seems, have vague aspirations towards liberty and human brotherhood, which are easily played upon by power-hungry individuals or minorities. So that history consists of a series of swindles, in which the masses are first lured into revolt by the promise of Utopia, and then, when they have done their job, enslaved over again by new masters.

Political activity, therefore, is a special kind of behaviour, characterized by its complete unscrupulousness, and occurring only among small groups of the population, especially among dissatisfied groups whose talents do not get free play under the existing form of society. The great mass of the people – and this is where (2) ties up with (1) – will always be unpolitical. In effect, therefore, humanity is divided into two classes: the self-seeking, hypocritical minority, and the brainless mob whose destiny is always to be led or driven, as one gets a pig back to the sty by kicking it on the bottom or by rattling a stick inside a swill-bucket, according to the needs of the moment. And this beautiful pattern is to continue for ever. Individuals may pass from one category to another, whole classes may destroy other classes and rise to the dominant position, but the division of humanity into rulers and ruled is unalterable. In their capabilities, as in their desires and needs, men are not equal. There is an 'iron law of oligarchy', which would operate even if democracy were not impossible for mechanical reasons.

It is curious that in all his talk about the struggle for power, Burnham never stops to ask *why* people want power. He seems to assume that power hunger, although only dominant in comparatively few people, is a natural instinct that does not have to be explained, like the desire for food. He also assumes that the division of society into classes serves the same purpose in all ages. This is practically to ignore the history of hundreds of years. When Burnham's master, Machiavelli, was writing, class divisions were not only unavoidable, but desirable. So long as methods of production were primitive, the great mass of the people were necessarily tied down to dreary, exhausting manual labour: and a few people had to be set free from such labour, otherwise civilization could not maintain itself, let alone make any progress. But since the arrival of the machine the whole pattern has altered. The justification for class distinctions, if there is a justification, is no longer the same, because there is no mechanical reason why the average human being should continue to be a drudge. True, drudgery persists; class distinctions are probably re-establishing themselves in a new form, and individual liberty is on the down-grade: but as these developments are now technically avoidable, they must have some psychological cause which Burnham makes no attempt to discover. The question that he ought to ask, and never does ask, is: Why does the lust for naked power become a major human motive exactly *now*, when the dominion of man over man is ceasing to be necessary? As for the claim that 'human nature', or 'inexorable laws' of this and that, make Socialism impossible, it is simply a projection of the past into the future. In effect, Burnham argues that because a society of free and equal human beings has never existed, it never can exist. By the same argument one could have demonstrated the impossibility of aeroplanes in 1900, or of motor cars in 1850.

The notion that the machine has altered human relationships, and that in consequence Machiavelli is out of date, is a very obvious one. If Burnham fails to deal with it, it can, I think, only be because his own power instinct leads him to brush aside any suggestion that the Machiavellian world of force, fraud, and tyranny may somehow come to an end. It is important to bear in mind what I said above: that Burnham's theory is only a variant – an American variant, and interesting because of its comprehensiveness – of the power worship now so prevalent among intellectuals. A more normal variant, at any rate in England, is Communism. If one examines the people who, having some idea of what the Russian régime is like, are strongly russophile, one finds that, on the whole, they belong to the 'managerial' class of which Burnham writes. That is, they are not managers in the narrow sense, but scientists, technicians, teachers, journalists, broadcasters, bureaucrats, professional politicians: in general, middling people who feel themselves cramped by a system that is still partly aristocratic, and are hungry for more power and more prestige. These people look towards the USSR and see in it, or think they see, a system which eliminates the upper class, keeps the working class in its place, and hands unlimited power to people very similar to themselves. It was only *after* the Soviet régime became unmistakably totalitarian that English intellectuals, in large numbers, began to show an interest in it. Burnham, although the English russophile intelligentsia would repudiate him, is really voicing their secret wish: the wish to destroy the old, equalitarian version of Socialism and usher in a hierarchical society where the intellectual can at last get his hands on the whip. Burnham at least has the honesty to say that Socialism isn't coming; the others merely say that Socialism *is* coming, and then give the word 'Socialism' a new meaning which makes nonsense of the old one. But his theory, for all its appearance of objectivity, is the rationalization of a wish. There is no strong reason for thinking that it tells us anything about the future, except perhaps the immediate future. It merely tells us what kind of world the 'managerial' class themselves, or at least the more conscious and ambitious members of the class, would like to live in.

Fortunately the 'managers' are not so invincible as Burnham believes. It is curious how persistently, in *The Managerial Revolution*, he ignores the advantages, military as well as social, enjoyed by a democratic country. At every point the evidence is squeezed in order to show the strength, vitality, and durability of Hitler's crazy régime. Germany is expanding rapidly, and 'rapid territorial expansion has always been a sign, not of decadence ... but of renewal'. Germany makes war successfully, and 'the ability to make war well is never a sign of decadence but of its opposite'. Germany also 'inspires in millions of persons a fanatical loyalty. This, too, never accompanies decadence.' Even the cruelty and dishonesty of the Nazi régime are cited in its favour, since 'the young, new, rising social order is, as against the old, more likely to resort on a large scale to lies, terror, persecution'. Yet, within only five years this young, new, rising social order had smashed itself to pieces and become, in Burnham's usage of the word, decadent. And this had happened quite largely because of the 'managerial' (i.e. undemocratic) structure which Burnham admires. The immediate cause of the German defeat was the unheard-of folly of attacking the USSR while Britain was still undefeated and America was manifestly getting ready to fight. Mistakes of this magnitude can only be made, or at any rate they are most likely to be made, in countries where public opinion has no power. So long as the common man can get a hearing, such elementary rules as not fighting all your enemies simultaneously are less likely to be violated.

But, in any case, one should have been able to see from the start that such a movement as Nazism could not produce any good or stable result. Actually, so long as they were winning, Burnham seems to have seen nothing wrong with the methods of the Nazis. Such methods, he says, only appear wicked because they are new:

> There is no historical law that polite manners and 'justice' shall conquer. In history there is always the question of *whose* manners and *whose* justice. A rising social class and a new order of society have got to break through the old moral codes just as they must break through the old economic and political institutions. Naturally, from the point of view of the old, they are monsters. If they win, they take care in due time of manners and morals.

This implies that literally anything can become right or wrong if the dominant class of the movement so wills it. It ignores the fact that certain rules of conduct have to be observed if human society is to hold together at all. Burnham, therefore, was unable to see that the crimes and follies of the Nazi régime *must* lead by one route or another to disaster. So also with his new-found admiration for Stalinism. It is too early to say in just what way the Russian régime will destroy itself. If I had to make a prophecy, I should say that a continuation of the Russian policies of the last fifteen years – and internal and external policy, of course, are merely two facets of the same thing – can only lead to a war conducted with atomic bombs, which will make Hitler's invasion look like a tea-party. But at any rate, the Russian régime will either democratize itself, or it will perish. The huge, invincible, everlasting slave empire of which Burnham appears to dream will not be established, or, if established, will not endure, because slavery is no longer a stable basis for human society.

One cannot always make positive prophecies, but there are times when one ought to be able to make negative ones. No one could have been expected to foresee the exact results of the Treaty of Versailles, but millions of thinking people could and did foresee that those results would be bad. Plenty of people, though not so many in this case, can foresee that the results of the settlement now being forced on Europe will also be bad. And to refrain from admiring Hitler or Stalin – that, too, should not require an enormous intellectual effort. But it is partly a moral effort. That a man of Burnham's gifts should have been able for a while to think of Nazism as something rather admirable, something that could and probably would build up a workable and durable social order, shows what damage is done to the sense of reality by the cultivation of what is now called 'realism'.

Polemic, No. 3, May

Politics vs. Literature: An Examination of *Gulliver's Travels*

In *Gulliver's Travels* humanity is attacked, or criticized, from at least three different angles, and the implied character of Gulliver himself necessarily changes somewhat in the process. In Part I he is the typical eighteenth-century voyager, bold, practical and unromantic, his homely outlook skilfully impressed on the reader by the biographical details at the beginning, by his age (he is a man of forty, with two children, when his adventures start), and by the inventory of the things in his pockets, especially his spectacles, which make several appearances. In Part II he has in general the same character, but at moments when the story demands it he has a tendency to develop into an imbecile who is capable of boasting of 'our noble Country, the Mistress of Arts and Arms, the Scourge of France' etc etc, and at the same time of betraying every available scandalous fact about the country which he professes to love. In Part III he is much as he was in Part I, though, as he is consorting chiefly with courtiers and men of learning, one has the impression that he has risen in the social scale. In Part IV he conceives a horror of the human race which is not apparent, or only intermittently apparent, in the earlier books, and changes into a sort of unreligious anchorite whose one desire is to live in some desolate spot where he can devote himself to meditating on the goodness of the Houyhnhnms. However, these inconsistencies are forced upon Swift by the fact that Gulliver is there chiefly to provide a contrast. It is necessary, for instance, that he should appear sensible in Part I and at least intermittently silly in Part II, because in both books the essential manoeuvre is the same, i.e. to make the human being look ridiculous by imagining him as a creature six inches high. Whenever Gulliver is not acting as a stooge there is a sort of continuity in his character, which comes out especially in his resourcefulness and his observation of physical detail. He is much the same kind of person, with the same prose style, when he bears off the warships of Blefuscu, when he rips open the belly of the monstrous rat, and when he sails away upon the ocean in his frail coracle made from the skins of Yahoos. Moreover, it is difficult not to feel that in his shrewder moments Gulliver is simply Swift himself, and there is at least one incident in which Swift seems to be venting his private grievance against contemporary society. It will be remembered that when the Emperor of Lilliput's palace catches fire, Gulliver puts it out by urinating on it. Instead of being congratulated on his presence of mind, he finds that he has committed a capital offence by making water in the precincts of the palace, and

> I was privately assured, that the Empress, conceiving the greatest Abhorrence of what I had done, removed to the most distant Side of the Court, firmly resolved that those buildings should never be repaired for her Use; and, in the Presence of her chief Confidents, could not forbear vowing Revenge.

According to Professor G. M. Trevelyan (*England under Queen Anne*), part of the reason for Swift's failure to get preferment was that the Queen was scandalized by *A Tale of a Tub* – a pamphlet in which Swift probably felt that he had done a great service to the English Crown, since it scarifies the Dissenters and still more the Catholics while leaving the Established Church alone. In any case no one would deny that *Gulliver's Travels* is a rancorous as well as a pessimistic book, and that especially in Parts I and III it often descends into political partisanship of a narrow kind. Pettiness and magnanimity, republicanism and authoritarianism, love of reason and lack of curiosity, are all mixed up in it. The hatred of the human body with which Swift is especially associated is only dominant in Part IV, but somehow this new preoccupation does not come as a surprise. One feels that all these adventures, and all these changes of mood, could have happened to the same person, and the inter-connection between Swift's political loyalties and his ultimate despair is one of the most interesting features of the book.

Politically, Swift was one of these people who are driven into a sort of perverse Toryism by the follies of the progressive party of the moment. Part I of *Gulliver's Travels,* ostensibly a satire on human greatness, can be seen, if one looks a little deeper, to be simply an attack on England, on the dominant Whig Party, and on the war with France, which – however bad the motives of the Allies may have been – did save Europe from being tyrannized over by a single reactionary power. Swift was not a Jacobite nor strictly speaking a Tory, and his declared aim in the war was merely a moderate peace treaty and not the outright defeat of England. Nevertheless there is a tinge of quislingism in his attitude, which comes out in the ending of Part I and slightly interferes with the allegory. When Gulliver flees from Lilliput (England) to Blefuscu (France) the assumption that a human being six inches high is inherently contemptible seems to be dropped. Whereas the people of Lilliput have behaved towards Gulliver with the utmost treachery and meanness, those of Blefuscu behave generously and straightforwardly, and indeed this section of the book ends on a different note from the all-round disillusionment of the earlier chapters. Evidently Swift's animus is, in the first place, against *England.* It is 'your Natives' (i.e. Gulliver's fellow countrymen) whom the King of Brobdingnag considers to be 'the most pernicious Race of little odious Vermin that Nature ever suffered to crawl upon the surface of the Earth', and the long passage at the end, denouncing colonization and foreign conquest, is plainly aimed at England, although the contrary is elaborately stated. The Dutch, England's allies and target of one of Swift's most famous pamphlets, are also more or less wantonly attacked in Part III. There is even what sounds like a personal note in the passage in which Gulliver records his satisfaction that the various countries he has discovered cannot be made colonies of the British Crown:

> The *Houyhnhnms,* indeed, appear not to be so well prepared for War, a Science to which they are perfect Strangers, and especially against missive Weapons. However, supposing myself to be a Minister of State, I could never give my advice for invading them ... Imagine twenty thousand of them breaking into the midst of an *European* army, confounding the Ranks, overturning the Carriages, battering the Warriors' Faces into Mummy, by terrible Yerks from their hinder Hoofs ...

Considering that Swift does not waste words, that phrase, 'battering the warriors' faces into mummy', probably indicates a secret wish to see the invincible armies of the Duke of Marlborough treated in a like manner. There are similar touches elsewhere. Even the country mentioned in Part III, where 'the Bulk of the People consist, in a Manner, wholly of Discoverers, Witnesses, Informers, Accusers, Prosecutors, Evidences, Swearers, together with their several subservient and subaltern Instruments, all under the Colours, the Conduct, and Pay of Ministers of State', is called Langdon, which is within one letter of being an anagram of England. (As the early editions of the book contain misprints, it may perhaps have been intended as a complete anagram.) Swift's *physical* repulsion from humanity is certainly real enough, but one has the feeling that his debunking of human grandeur, his diatribes against lords, politicians, court favourites, etc have mainly a local application and spring from the fact that he belonged to the unsuccessful party. He denounces injustice and oppression, but he gives no evidence of liking democracy. In spite of his enormously greater powers, his implied position is very similar to that of the innumerable silly-clever Conservatives of our own day – people like Sir Alan Herbert, Professor G. M. Young, Lord Elton, the Tory Reform Committee or the long line of Catholic apologists from W. H. Mallock onwards: people who specialize in cracking neat jokes at the expense of whatever is 'modern' and 'progressive', and whose opinions are often all the more extreme because they know that they cannot influence the actual drift of events. After all, such a pamphlet as *An Argument to prove that the Abolishing of Christianity* etc is very like 'Timothy Shy' having a bit of clean fun with the Brains Trust, or Father Ronald Knox exposing the errors of Bertrand Russell. And the ease with which Swift has been forgiven – and forgiven, sometimes, by devout believers – for the blasphemies of *A Tale of a Tub* demonstrates clearly enough the feebleness of religious sentiments as compared with political ones.

However, the reactionary cast of Swift's mind does not show itself chiefly in his political affiliations. The important thing is his attitude towards science, and, more broadly, towards intellectual curiosity. The famous Academy of Lagado, described in Part III of *Gulliver's Travels,* is no doubt a justified satire on most of the so-called scientists of Swift's own day. Significantly, the people at work in it are described as 'Projectors', that is, people not engaged in disinterested research but merely on the look-out for gadgets which will save labour and bring in money. But there is no sign – indeed, all through the book there are many signs to the contrary – that 'pure' science would have struck Swift as a worth-while activity. The more serious kind of scientist has already had a kick in the pants in Part II, when the 'Scholars' patronized by the King of Brobdingnag try to account for Gulliver's small stature:

> After much Debate, they concluded unanimously that I was only *Relplum Scalcath,* which is interpreted literally, *Lusus Naturae;* a Determination exactly agreeable to the modern philosophy of *Europe,* whose Professors, disdaining the old Evasion of *occult Causes,* whereby the followers of *Aristotle* endeavoured in vain to disguise their Ignorance, have invented this wonderful Solution of all Difficulties, to the unspeakable Advancement of human Knowledge.

If this stood by itself one might assume that Swift is merely the enemy of *sham* science. In a number of places, however, he goes out of his way to proclaim the uselessness of all learning or speculation not directed towards some practical end:

> The Learning of (the Brobdingnagians) is very defective, consisting only in Morality, History, Poetry, and Mathematics, wherein they must be allowed to excel. But, the last of these is wholly applied to what may be useful in Life, to the Improvement of Agriculture, and all mechanical Arts; so that among us it would be little esteemed. And as to Ideas, Entities, Abstractions, and Transcendentals, I could never drive the least Conception into their Heads.

The Houyhnhnms, Swift's ideal beings, are backward even in a mechanical sense. They are unacquainted with metals, have never heard of boats, do not, properly speaking, practise agriculture (we are told that the oats which they live upon 'grow naturally'), and appear not to have invented wheels.[1] They have no alphabet, and evidently have not much curiosity about the physical world. They do not believe that any inhabited country exists beside their own, and though they understand the motions of the sun and moon, and the nature of eclipses, 'this is the utmost Progress of their *Astronomy*'. By contrast, the philosophers of the flying island of Laputa are so continuously absorbed in mathematical speculations that before speaking to them one has to attract their attention by flapping them on the ear with a bladder. They have catalogued ten thousand fixed stars, have settled the periods of ninety-three comets, and have discovered, in advance of the astronomers of Europe, that Mars has two moons – all of which information Swift evidently regards as ridiculous, useless and uninteresting. As one might expect, he believes that the scientist's place, if he has a place, is in the laboratory, and that scientific knowledge has no bearing on political matters:

> What I . . . thought altogether unaccountable, was the strong Disposition I observed in them towards News and Politics, perpetually enquiring into Public Affairs, giving their judgements in Matters of State, and passionately disputing every Inch of a Party Opinion. I have, indeed, observed the same Disposition among most of the Mathematicians I have known in *Europe,* though I could never discover the least Analogy between the two Sciences; unless those People suppose, that, because the smallest Circle hath as many Degrees as the largest, therefore the Regulation and Management of the World require no more Abilities, than the Handling and Turning of a Globe.

Is there not something familiar in that phrase 'I could never discover the least analogy between the two sciences'? It has precisely the note of the popular Catholic apologists who profess to be astonished when a scientist utters an opinion on such questions as the existence of God or the immortality of the soul. The scientist, we are told is an expert only in one restricted field: why should his opinions be of value in any other? The implication is that theology is just as much an exact science as, for instance, chemistry, and that the priest is also an expert whose conclusions on certain subjects must be accepted. Swift in effect makes the same claim for the politician, but he goes one better in that he will not allow the scientist – either the 'pure' scientist or the *ad hoc* investigator – to be a useful person in his own line. Even if he had not written Part III of

[1] Houyhnhnms too old to walk are described as being carried in 'sledges' or in 'a kind of vehicle, drawn like a sledge'. Presumably these had no wheels. [Author's footnote.]

Gulliver's Travels, one could infer from the rest of the book that, like Tolstoy and like Blake, he hates the very idea of studying the processes of Nature. The 'Reason' which he so admires in the Houyhnhnms does not primarily mean the power of drawing logical inferences from observed facts. Although he never defines it, it appears in most contexts to mean either common sense – i.e. acceptance of the obvious and contempt for quibbles and abstractions – or absence of passion and superstition. In general he assumes that we know all that we need to know already, and merely use our knowledge incorrectly. Medicine, for instance, is a useless science, because if we lived in a more natural way, there would be no diseases. Swift, however, is not a simple-lifer or an admirer of the Noble Savage. He is in favour of civilization and the arts of civilization. Not only does he see the value of good manners, good conversation, and even learning of a literary and historical kind, he also sees that agriculture, navigation and architecture need to be studied and could with advantage be improved. But his implied aim is a static, incurious civilization – the world of his own day, a little cleaner, a little saner, with no radical change and no poking into the unknowable. More than one would expect in anyone so free from accepted fallacies, he reveres the past, especially classical antiquity, and believes that modern man has degenerated sharply during the past hundred years.[1] In the island of sorcerers, where the spirits of the dead can be called up at will:

> I desired that the Senate of *Rome* might appear before me in one large Chamber, and a modern Representative in Counterview, in another. The first seemed to be an Assembly of Heroes and Demy-Gods, the other a Knot of Pedlars, Pick-pockets, Highwaymen, and Bullies.

Although Swift uses this section of Part III to attack the truthfulness of recorded history, his critical spirit deserts him as soon as he is dealing with Greeks and Romans. He remarks, of course, upon the corruption of imperial Rome, but he has an almost unreasoning admiration for some of the leading figures of the ancient world:

> I was struck with profound Veneration at the Sight of *Brutus,* and could easily discover the most consummate Virtue, the greatest Intrepidity and Firmness of Mind, the truest Love of his Country, and general Benevolence for mankind, in every Lineament of his Countenance ... I had the Honour to have much Conversation with *Brutus,* and was told, that his Ancestor *Junius, Socrates, Epaminondas, Cato* the younger, *Sir Thomas More,* and himself, were perpetually together: a *Sextumvirate,* to which all the Ages of the World cannot add a seventh.

It will be noticed that of these six people only one is a Christian. This is an important point. If one adds together Swift's pessimism, his reverence for the past, his incuriosity and his horror of the human body, one arrives at an attitude common among religious reactionaries – that is, people who defend an

[1] The physical decadence which Swift claims to have observed may have been a reality at that date. He attributes it to syphillis, which was a new disease in Europe and may have been more virulent than it is now. Distilled liquors, also, were a novelty in the seventeenth century and must have led at first to a great increase in drunkenness. [Author's footnote.]

unjust order of society by claiming that this world cannot be substantially improved and only the 'next world' matters. However, Swift shows no sign of having any religious beliefs, at least in any ordinary sense of the words. He does not appear to believe seriously in life after death, and his idea of goodness is bound up with republicanism, love of liberty, courage, 'benevolence' (meaning in effect public spirit), 'reason' and other pagan qualities. This reminds one that there is another strain in Swift, not quite congruous with his disbelief in progress and his general hatred of humanity.

To begin with, he has moments when he is 'constructive' and even 'advanced'. To be occasionally inconsistent is almost a mark of vitality in Utopia books, and Swift sometimes inserts a word of praise into a passage that ought to be purely satirical. Thus, his ideas about the education of the young are fathered on to the Lilliputians, who have much the same views on this subject as the Houyhnhnms. The Lilliputians also have various social and legal institutions (for instance, there are old age pensions, and people are rewarded for keeping the law as well as punished for breaking it) which Swift would have liked to see prevailing in his own country. In the middle of this passage Swift remembers his satirical intention and adds, 'In relating these and the following Laws, I would only be understood to mean the original Institutions, and not the most scandalous Corruptions into which these people are fallen by the degenerate Nature of Man': but as Lilliput is supposed to represent England, and the laws he is speaking of have never had their parallel in England, it is clear that the impulse to make constructive suggestion, has been too much for him. But Swift's greatest contribution to political thought, in the narrower sense of the words, is his attacks, especially in Part III, on what would now be called totalitarianism. He has an extraordinarily clear prevision of the spy-haunted 'police State', with its endless heresy-hunts and treason trials, all really designed to neutralize popular discontent by changing it into war hysteria. And one must remember that Swift is here inferring the whole from a quite small part, for the feeble governments of his own day did not give him illustrations ready-made. For example, there is the professor at the School of Political Projectors who 'shewed me a large Paper of Instructions for discovering Plots and Conspiracies', and who claimed that one can find people's secret thoughts by examining their excrement:

> Because Men are never so serious, thoughtful, and intent, as when they are at Stool, which he found by frequent Experiment: for in such Conjectures, when he used merely as a Trial to consider what was the best Way of murdering the King, his Ordure would have a Tincture of Green; but quite different when he thought only of raising an Insurrection, or burning the Metropolis.

The professor and his theory are said to have been suggested to Swift by the – from our point of view – not particularly astonishing or disgusting fact that in a recent State Trial some letters found in somebody's privy had been put in evidence. Later in the same chapter we seem to be positively in the middle of the Russian purges:

> In the Kingdom of Tribnia, by the Natives called Langdon ... the Bulk of the People consist, in a Manner, wholly of Discoverers, Witnesses, Informers, Accusers, Prosecutors Evidences, Swearers ... It is first

> agreed, and settled among them, what suspected Persons shall be accused of a Plot: Then, effectual Care is taken to secure all their Letters and Papers, and put the Owners in Chains. These papers are delivered to a Sett of Artists, very dexterous in finding out the mysterious Meanings of Words, Syllables, and Letters ... Where this Method fails, they have two others more effectual, which the Learned among them call *Acrostics* and *Anagrams. First,* they can decypher all initial Letters into political Meanings: Thus, N shall signify a Plot, B a Regiment of Horse, L a Fleet at Sea: Or, *Secondly,* by transposing the Letters of the Alphabet in any suspected Paper, they can lay open the deepest Designs of a discontented Party. So, for Example, if I should say in a Letter to a Friend, *Our Brother Tom has just got the Piles,* a skilful Decypherer would discover that the same Letters, which compose that Sentence, may be analysed in the following Words: *Resist – a Plot is brought Home – The Tour.*[1] And this is the anagrammatic Method.

Other professors at the same school invent simplified languages, write books by machinery, educate their pupils by inscribing the lessons on a wafer and causing them to swallow it, or propose to abolish individuality altogether by cutting off part of the brain of one man and grafting it on to the head of another. There is something queerly familiar in the atmosphere of these chapters, because, mixed up with much fooling, there is a perception that one of the aims of totalitarianism is not merely to make sure that people will think the right thoughts, but actually to make them *less conscious.* Then, again, Swift's account of the Leader who is usually to be found ruling over a tribe of Yahoos, and of the 'favourite' who acts first as a dirty-worker and later as a scapegoat, fits remarkably well into the pattern of our own times. But are we to infer from all this that Swift was first and foremost an enemy of tyranny and a champion of the free intelligence? No: his own views, so far as one can discern them, are not markedly liberal. No doubt he hates lords, kings, bishops, generals, ladies of fashion, orders, titles and flummery generally, but he does not seem to think better of the common people than of their rulers, or to be in favour of increased social equality, or to be enthusiastic about representative institutions. The Houyhnhnms are organized upon a sort of caste system which is racial in character, the horses which do the menial work being of different colours from their masters and not interbreeding with them. The educational system which Swift admires in the Lilliputians takes hereditary class distinctions for granted, and the children of the poorest class do not go to school, because 'their Business being only to till and cultivate the Earth ... therefore their Education is of little Consequence to the Public'. Nor does he seem to have been strongly in favour of freedom of speech and the press, in spite of the toleration which his own writings enjoyed. The King of Brobdingnag is astonished at the multiplicity of religious and political sects in England, and considers that those who hold 'opinions prejudicial to the public' (in the context this seems to mean simply heretical opinions), though they need not be obliged to change them, ought to be obliged to conceal them: for 'as it was Tyranny in any Government to require the first, so it was Weakness not to enforce the second'. There is a subtler indication of Swift's own attitude in the manner in which Gulliver leaves the land of the Houyhnhnms. Intermittently, at least, Swift was a kind

[1] Tower. [Author's footnote.]

of anarchist, and Part IV of *Gulliver's Travels* is a picture of an anarchistic society, not governed by law in the ordinary sense, but by the dictates of 'Reason', which are voluntarily accepted by everyone. The General Assembly of the Houyhnhnms 'exhorts' Gulliver's master to get rid of him, and his neighbours put pressure on him to make him comply. Two reasons are given. One is that the presence of this unusual Yahoo may unsettle the rest of the tribe, and the other is that a friendly relationship between a Houyhnhnm and a Yahoo is 'not agreeable to Reason or Nature, or a Thing ever heard of before among them'. Gulliver's master is somewhat unwilling to obey, but the 'exhortation' (a Houyhnhnm, we are told, is never *compelled* to do anything, he is merely 'exhorted' or 'advised') cannot be disregarded. This illustrates very well the totalitarian tendency which is implicit in the anarchist or pacifist vision of society. In a society in which there is no law, and in theory no compulsion, the only arbiter of behaviour is public opinion. But public opinion, because of the tremendous urge to conformity in gregarious animals, is less tolerant than any system of law. When human beings are governed by 'thou shalt not', the individual can practise a certain amount of eccentricity: when they are supposedly governed by 'love' or 'reason', he is under continuous pressure to make him behave and think in exactly the same way as everyone else. The Houyhnhnms, we are told, were unanimous on almost all subjects. The only question they ever *discussed* was how to deal with the Yahoos. Otherwise there was no room for disagreement among them, because the truth is always either self-evident, or else it is undiscoverable and unimportant. They had apparently no word for 'opinion' in their language, and in their conversations there was no 'difference of sentiments'. They had reached, in fact, the highest stage of totalitarian organization, the stage when conformity has become so general that there is no need for a police force. Swift approves of this kind of thing because among his many gifts neither curiosity nor good nature was included. Disagreement would always seem to him sheer perversity. 'Reason,' among the Houyhnhnms, he says, 'is not a Point Problematical, as with us, where men can argue with Plausibility on both Sides of a Question; but strikes you with immediate Conviction; as it must needs do, where it is not mingled, obscured, or discoloured by Passion and Interest.' In other words, we know everything already, so why should dissident opinions be tolerated? The totalitarian society of the Houyhnhnms, where there can be no freedom and no development, follows naturally from this.

We are right to think of Swift as a rebel and iconoclast, but except in certain secondary matters, such as his insistence that women should receive the same education as men, he cannot be labelled 'left'. He is a Tory anarchist, despising authority while disbelieving in liberty, and preserving the aristocratic outlook while seeing clearly that the existing aristocracy is degenerate and contemptible. When Swift utters one of his characteristic diatribes against the rich and powerful, one must probably, as I said earlier, write off something for the fact that he himself belonged to the less successful party, and was personally disappointed. The 'outs', for obvious reasons, are always more radical than the 'ins'.[1] But the most essential thing in Swift is his inability to believe that life –

[1] At the end of the book, as typical specimens of human folly and viciousness, Swift names 'a Lawyer, a Pickpocket, a Colonel, a Fool, a Lord, a Gamester, a Politician, a Whoremaster, a Physician, an Evidence, A Suborner, an Attorney, a Traitor, or the like'. One sees here the irresponsible violence of the powerless. The list lumps together those who break the conventional code, and those who keep it. For instance, if you automatically

ordinary life on the solid earth, and not some rationalized, deodorized version of it – could be made worth living. Of course, no honest person claims that happiness is *now* a normal condition among adult human beings; but perhaps it *could* be made normal, and it is upon this question that all serious political controversy really turns. Swift has much in common – more, I believe, than has been noticed – with Tolstoy, another disbeliever in the possibility of happiness. In both men you have the same anarchistic outlook covering an authoritarian cast of mind; in both a similar hostility to science, the same impatience with opponents, the same inability to see the importance of any question not interesting to themselves; and in both cases a sort of horror of the actual process of life, though in Tolstoy's case it was arrived at later and in a different way. The sexual unhappiness of the two men was not of the same kind, but there was this in common, that in both of them a sincere loathing was mixed up with a morbid fascination. Tolstoy was a reformed rake who ended by preaching complete celibacy, while continuing to practise the opposite into extreme old age. Swift was presumably impotent, and had an exaggerated horror of human dung: he also thought about it incessantly, as is evident throughout this works. Such people are not likely to enjoy even the small amount of happiness that falls to most human beings, and, from obvious motives, are not likely to admit that earthly life is capable of much improvement. Their incuriosity, and hence their intolerance, spring from the same root.

Swift's disgust, rancour and pessimism would make sense against the background of a 'next world' to which this one is the prelude. As he does not appear to believe seriously in any such thing, it becomes necessary to construct a paradise supposedly existing on the surface of the earth, but something quite different from anything we know, with all that he disapproves of – lies, folly, change, enthusiasm, pleasure, love and dirt – eliminated from it. As his ideal being he chooses the horse, an animal whose excrement is not offensive. The Houyhnhnms are dreary beasts – this is so generally admitted that the point is not worth labouring. Swift's genius can make them credible, but there can have been very few readers in whom they have excited any feeling beyond dislike. And this is not from wounded vanity at seeing animals preferred to men; for, of the two, the Houyhnhnms are much liker to human beings than are the Yahoos, and Gulliver's horror of the Yahoos, together with his recognition that they are the same kind of creature as himself, contains a logical absurdity. This horror comes upon him at his very first sight of them. 'I never beheld,' he says, 'in all my Travels, so disagreeable an Animal, nor one against which I naturally conceived so strong an Antipathy.' But in comparison with what are the Yahoos disgusting? Not with the Houyhnhnms, because at this time Gulliver has not seen a Houyhnhnm. It can only be in comparison with himself, i.e. with a human being. Later, however, we are to be told that the Yahoos *are* human beings, and human society becomes insupportable to Gulliver because all men are Yahoos. In that case why did he not conceive his disgust of humanity earlier? In effect we are told that the Yahoos are fantastically different from men, and yet are the same. Swift has overreached

---

condemn a colonel, as such, on what grounds do you condemn a traitor? Or again, if you want to suppress pickpockets, you must have laws, which means that you must have lawyers. But the whole closing passage, in which the hatred is so authentic, and the reason given for it so inadequate, is somehow unconvincing. One has the feeling that personal animosity is at work. [Author's footnote.]

himself in his fury, and is shouting at his fellow creatures: 'You are filthier than you are!' However, it is impossible to feel much sympathy with the Yahoos, and it is not because they oppress the Yahoos that the Houyhnhnms are unattractive. They are unattractive because the 'Reason' by which they are governed is really a desire for death. They are exempt from love, friendship, curiosity, fear, sorrow and – except in their feelings towards the Yahoos, who occupy rather the same place in their community as the Jews in Nazi Germany – anger and hatred. 'They have no Fondness for their Colts or Foles, but the Care they take, in educating them, proceeds entirely from the Dictates of *Reason*.' They lay store by 'Friendship' and 'Benevolence', but 'these are not confined to particular Objects, but universal to the whole Race'. They also value conversation, but in their conversations there are no differences of opinion, and 'nothing passed but what was useful, expressed in the fewest and most significant Words'. They practise strict birth control, each couple producing two offspring and thereafter abstaining from sexual intercourse. Their marriages are arranged for them by their elders, on eugenic principles, and their language contains no word for 'love', in the sexual sense. When somebody dies they carry on exactly as before, without feeling any grief. It will be seen that their aim is to be as like a corpse as is possible while retaining physical life. One or two of their characteristics, it is true, do not seem to be strictly 'reasonable' in their own usage of the word. Thus, they place a great value not only on physical hardihood but on athleticism, and they are devoted to poetry. But these exceptions may be less arbitrary than they seem. Swift probably emphasizes the physical strength of the Houyhnhnms in order to make clear that they could never be conquered by the hated human race, while a taste for poetry may figure among their qualities because poetry appeared to Swift as the antithesis of science, from his point of view the most useless of all pursuits. In Part III he names 'Imagination, Fancy, and Invention' as desirable faculties in which the Laputan mathematicians (in spite of their love of music) were wholly lacking. One must remember that although Swift was an admirable writer of comic verse, the kind of poetry he thought valuable would probably be didactic poetry. The poetry of the Houyhnhnms, he says:

> must be allowed to excel (that of) all other Mortals; wherein the Justness of their Similes, and the Minuteness, as well as exactness, of their Descriptions, are, indeed, inimitable. Their Verses abound very much in both of these; and usually contain either some exalted Notions of Friendship and Benevolence, or the Praises of those who were Victors in Races, and other bodily Exercises.

Alas, not even the genius of Swift was equal to producing a specimen by which we could judge the poetry of the Houyhnhnms. But it sounds as though it were chilly stuff (in heroic couplets, presumably), and not seriously in conflict with the principles of 'Reason'.

Happiness is notoriously difficult to describe, and pictures of a just and well-ordered society are seldom either attractive or convincing. Most creators of 'favourable' Utopias, however, are concerned to show what life could be like if it were lived more fully. Swift advocates a simple refusal of life, justifying this by the claim that 'Reason' consists in thwarting your instincts. The Houyhnhnms, creatures without a history, continue for generation after generation to live prudently, maintaining their population at exactly the same level, avoiding all passion, suffering from no diseases, meeting death indifferently, training up their young in the same principles – and all for what? In order that the same process may continue indefinitely. The notions that life here and now is worth living, or that it could be made worth living, or that it must be sacrificed for some future good, are all absent. The dreary world of the Houyhnhnms was about as good a Utopia as Swift could construct, granting that he neither believed in a 'next world' nor could get any pleasure out of certain normal activities. But it is not really set up as something desirable in itself, but as the justification for another attack on humanity. The aim, as usual, is to humiliate Man by reminding him that he is weak and ridiculous, and above all that he stinks; and the ultimate motive, probably, is a kind of envy, the envy of the ghost for the living, of the man who knows he cannot be happy for the others who – so he fears – may be a little happier than himself. The political expression of such an outlook must be either reactionary or nihilistic, because the person who holds it will want to prevent society from developing in some direction in which his pessimism may be cheated. One can do this either by blowing everything to pieces, or by averting social change. Swift ultimately blew everything to pieces in the only way that was feasible before the atomic bomb – that is, he went mad – but, as I have tried to show, his political aims were on the whole reactionary ones.

From what I have written it may have seemed that I am *against* Swift, and that my object is to refute him and even to belittle him. In a political and moral sense I am against him, so far as I understand him. Yet curiously enough he is one of the writers I admire with least reserve, and *Gulliver's Travels*, in particular, is a book which it seems impossible for me to grow tired of. I read it first when I was eight – one day short of eight, to be exact, for I stole and furtively read the copy which was to be given me next day on my eighth birthday – and I have certainly not read it less than half a dozen times since. Its fascination seems inexhaustible. If I had to make a list of six books which were to be preserved when all others were destroyed, I would certainly put *Gulliver's Travels* among them. This raises the question: what is the relationship between agreement with a writer's opinions, and enjoyment of his work?

If one is capable of intellectual detachment, one can *perceive* merit in a writer whom one deeply disagrees with, but *enjoyment* is a different matter. Supposing that there is such a thing as good or bad art, then the goodness or badness must reside in the work of art itself – not independently of the observer, indeed, but independently of the mood of the observer. In one sense, therefore, it cannot be true that a poem is good on Monday and bad on Tuesday. But if one judges the poem by the appreciation it arouses, then it can certainly be true, because appreciation, or enjoyment, is a subjective condition which cannot be commanded. For a great deal of his waking life, even the most cultivated person has no aesthetic feelings whatever, and the power to have aesthetic feelings is very easily destroyed. When you are frightened, or hungry, or are suffering from toothache or seasickness, *King Lear* is no better from your point of view than *Peter Pan*. You may know in an intellectual sense that it is better, but that is simply a fact which you remember: you will not *feel* the merit of *King Lear* until you are normal again. And aesthetic judgement can be upset just as disastrously – more disastrously, because the cause is less readily recognized – by political or moral disagreement. If a book angers, wounds or alarms you, then you will not enjoy it, whatever its merits may be. If it seems to you a really pernicious book, likely to influence other people in some undesirable way, then you will probably construct an aesthetic theory to show that it *has* no merits. Current literary criticism consists quite largely of this kind of dodging to and fro between two sets of standards. And yet the opposite process can also happen: enjoyment can overwhelm disapproval, even though one clearly recognizes that one is enjoying something inimical. Swift, whose world-view is so peculiarly unacceptable, but who is nevertheless an extremely popular writer, is a good instance of this. Why is it that we don't mind being called Yahoos, although firmly convinced that we are *not* Yahoos?

It is not enough to make the usual answer that of course Swift was wrong, in fact he was insane, but he was 'a good writer'. It is true that the literary quality of a book is to some small extent separable from its subject-matter. Some people have a native gift for using words, as some people have a naturally 'good eye' at games. It is largely a question of timing and of instinctively knowing how much emphasis to use. As an example near at hand, look back at the passage I quoted earlier, starting 'In the Kingdom of Tribnia, by the Natives called Langdon'. It derives much of its force from the final sentence: 'And this is the anagrammatic Method.' Strictly speaking this sentence is unnecessary, for we have already seen the anagram deciphered, but the mock-solemn repetition, in which one seems to hear Swift's own voice uttering the words, drives home the idiocy of the activities described, like the final tap to a nail. But not all the power and simplicity of Swift's prose, nor the imaginative effort that has been able to make not one but a whole series of impossible worlds more credible than the majority of history books – none of this would enable us to enjoy Swift if his world-view were truly wounding or shocking. Millions of people, in many countries, must have enjoyed *Gulliver's Travels* while more or less seeing its anti-human implications: and even the child who accepts Parts I and II as a simple story gets a sense of absurdity from thinking of human beings six inches high. The explanation must be that Swift's world-view is felt to be *not* altogether false – or it would probably be more accurate to say, not false all the time. Swift is a diseased writer. He remains permanently in a depressed mood which in most people is only intermittent, rather as though someone suffering from jaundice or the after-effects of influenza should have the energy to write books. But we all know that mood, and something in us responds to the expression of it. Take, for instance, one of his most characteristic works, 'The Lady's Dressing Room': one might add the kindred poem, 'Upon a Beautiful Young Nymph Going to Bed'. Which is truer, the viewpoint expressed in these poems, or the viewpoint implied in Blake's phrase, 'The naked female human form divine'? No doubt Blake is nearer the truth, and yet who can fail to feel a sort of pleasure in seeing that fraud, feminine delicacy, exploded for once? Swift falsifies his picture of the whole world by refusing to see anything in human life except dirt, folly and wickedness, but the part which he abstracts from the whole does exist, and it is something which we all know about while shrinking from mentioning it. Part of our minds – in any normal person it is the dominant part – believes that man is a noble animal and life is worth living: but there is also a sort of inner self which at least intermittently stands aghast at the horror of existence. In the queerest way, pleasure, and disgust are linked together. The human body is beautiful: it is also repulsive and ridiculous, a fact which can be verified at any swimming pool. The sexual organs are objects of desire and also of loathing, so much so that in many languages, if not in all languages, their names are used as words of abuse. Meat is delicious, but a butcher's shop makes one feel sick: and indeed all our food springs ultimately from dung and dead bodies, the two things which of all others seem to us the most horrible. A child, when it is past the infantile stage but still looking at the world with fresh eyes, is moved by horror almost as often as by wonder – horror of snot and spittle, of the dogs' excrement on the pavement, the dying toad full of maggots, the sweaty smell of grown-ups, the hideousness of old men, with their bald heads and bulbous noses. In his endless harping on disease, dirt and deformity, Swift is not actually inventing anything, he is merely leaving something out. Human behaviour, too, especially in politics, is as he describes it, although it contains other more important factors which he refuses to admit. So far as we can see, both horror and pain are necessary to the continuance of life on this planet, and it is therefore open to pessimists like Swift to say: 'If horror and pain must always be with us, how can life be significantly improved?' His attitude is in effect the Christian attitude, minus the bribe of a 'next world' – which, however, probably has less hold upon the minds of believers than the conviction that this world is a vale of tears and the grave is a place of rest. It is, I am certain, a wrong attitude, and one which could have harmful effects upon behaviour; but something in us responds to it, as it responds to the gloomy words of the burial service and the sweetish smell of corpses in a country church.

It is often argued, at least by people who admit the importance of subject-matter, that a book cannot be 'good' if it expresses a palpably false view of life. We are told that in our own age, for instance, any book that has genuine literary merit will also be more or less 'progressive' in tendency. This ignores the fact that throughout history a similar struggle between progress and reaction has been raging, and that the best books of any one age have always been written from several different viewpoints, some of them palpably more false than others. In so far as a writer is a propagandist, the most one can ask of him is that he shall genuinely believe in what he is saying, and that it shall not be something blazingly silly. Today, for example, one can imagine a good book being written by a Catholic, a Communist, a Fascist, a Pacifist, an Anarchist, perhaps by an old-style Liberal or an ordinary Conservative: one cannot imagine a good book being written by a spiritualist, a Buchmanite or a member of the Ku Klux Klan. The views that a writer holds must be compatible with sanity, in the medical sense, and with the power of continuous thought: beyond that what we ask of him is talent, which is probably another name for conviction. Swift did not possess ordinary wisdom, but he did possess a terrible intensity of vision, capable of picking out a single hidden truth and then magnifying it and distorting it. The durability of *Gulliver's Travels* goes to show that, if the force of belief is behind it, a world-view which only just passes the test of sanity is sufficient to produce a great work of art.

Polemic, No. 5, September–October 1946

How the Poor Die

In the year 1929 I spent several weeks in the Hôpital X, in the fifteenth *arrondissement* of Paris. The clerks put me through the usual third-degree at the reception desk, and indeed I was kept answering questions for some twenty minutes before they would let me in. If you have ever had to fill up forms in a Latin country you will know the kind of questions I mean. For some days past I had been unequal to translating Réaumur into Fahrenheit, but I know that my temperature was round about 103, and by the end of the interview I had some difficulty in standing on my feet. At my back a resigned little knot of patients, carrying bundles done up in coloured handkerchiefs, waited their turn to be questioned.

After the questioning came the bath – a compulsory routine for all newcomers, apparently, just as in prison or the workhouse. My clothes were taken away from me, and after I had sat shivering for some minutes in five inches of warm water I was given a linen nightshirt and a short blue flannel dressing-gown – no slippers, they had none big enough for me, they said – and led out into the open air. This was a night in February and I was suffering from pneumonia. The ward we were going to was 200 yards away and it seemed that to get to it you had to cross the hospital grounds. Someone stumbled in front of me with a lantern. The gravel path was frosty underfoot, and the wind whipped the nightshirt round my bare calves. When we got into the ward I was aware of a strange feeling of familiarity whose origin I did not succeed in pinning down till later in the night. It was a long, rather low, ill-lit room, full of murmuring voices and with three rows of beds surprisingly close together. There was a foul smell, faecal and yet sweetish. As I lay down I saw on a bed nearly opposite me a small, round-shouldered, sandy-haired man sitting half naked while a doctor and a student performed some strange operation on him. First the doctor produced from his black bag a dozen small glasses like wine glasses, then the student burned a match inside each glass to exhaust the air, then the glass was popped on to the man's back or chest and the vacuum drew up a huge yellow blister. Only after some moments did I realize what they were doing to him. It was something called cupping, a treatment which you can read about in old medical text-books but which till then I had vaguely thought of as one of those things they do to horses.

The cold air outside had probably lowered my temperature, and I watched this barbarous remedy with detachment and even a certain amount of amusement. The next moment, however, the doctor and the student came across to my bed, hoisted me upright and without a word began applying the same set of glasses, which had not been sterilized in any way. A few feeble protests that I uttered got no more response than if I had been an animal. I was very much impressed by the impersonal way in which the two men started on me. I had never been in the public ward of a hospital before, and it was my first experience of doctors who handle you without speaking to you, or, in a human sense, taking any notice of you. They only put on six glasses in my case, but after doing so they scarified the blisters and applied the glasses again. Each glass now drew out about a dessert-spoonful of dark-coloured blood. As I lay down again, humiliated, disgusted and frightened by the thing that had been done to me, I reflected that now at least they would leave me alone. But no, not a bit of it. There was another treatment coming, the mustard poultice, seemingly a matter of routine like the hot bath. Two slatternly nurses had already got the poultice ready, and they lashed it round my chest as tight as a strait jacket while some men who were wandering about the ward in shirt and trousers began to collect round my bed with half-sympathetic grins. I learned later that watching a patient have a mustard poultice was a favourite pastime in the ward. These things are normally applied for a quarter of an hour and certainly they are funny enough if you don't happen to be the person inside. For the first five minutes the pain is severe, but you believe you can bear it. During the second five minutes this belief evaporates, but the poultice is buckled at the back and you can't get it off. This is the period the onlookers most enjoy. During the last five minutes, I noted a sort of numbness supervenes. After the poultice has been removed a waterproof pillow packed with ice was thrust beneath my head and I was left alone. I did not sleep and to the best of my knowledge this was the only night of my life – I mean the only night spent in bed – in which I have not slept at all, not even a minute.

During my first hour in the Hôpital X, I had had a whole series of different and contradictory treatments, but this was misleading, for in general you got very little treatment at all, either good or bad, unless you were ill in some interesting and instructive way. At five in the morning the nurses came round, woke the patients and took their temperatures, but did not wash them. If you were well enough you washed yourself, otherwise you depended on the kindness of some walking patient. It was generally patients, too, who carried the bed-bottles and the grim bed-pan, nicknamed *la casserole*. At eight breakfast arrived, called army-fashion *la soupe*. It was soup, too, a thin vegetable soup with slimy hunks of bread floating about in it. Later in the day the tall, solemn, black-bearded doctor made his rounds, with an *interne* and a troop of students following at his heels. but there were about sixty of us in the ward and it was evident that he had other wards to attend to as well. There were many beds past which he walked day after day, sometimes followed by imploring cries. On the other hand if you had some disease with which the students wanted to familiarize themselves you got plenty of attention of a kind. I myself, with an exceptionally fine specimen of a bronchial rattle, sometimes had as many as a dozen students queueing up to listen to my chest. It was a very queer feeling – queer, I mean, because of their intense interest in learning their job, together with a seeming lack of any perception that the patients were human beings. It is strange to relate, but sometimes as some young student stepped forward to take his turn at manipulating you he would be actually tremulous with excitement, like a boy who has at last got his hands on some expensive piece of machinery. And then ear after ear – ears of young men, of girls, of Negroes – pressed against your back, relays of fingers solemnly but clumsily tapping, and not from any one of them did you get a word of conversation or a look direct in your face. As a non-paying patient, in the uniform nightshirt, you were primarily *a specimen*, a thing I did not resent but could never quite get used to.

After some days I grew well enough to sit up and study the surrounding patients. The stuffy room, with its narrow beds so close together that you could easily touch your neighbour's hand, had every sort of disease in it except, I suppose, acutely infectious cases. My right-hand neighbour was a little red-haired cobbler with one leg shorter than the other, who used to announce the death of any other patient (this happened a number of times, and my neighbour was always the first to hear of it) by whistling to me, exclaiming '*Numéro 43!*' or whatever it was and flinging his arms above his head. This man had not much wrong with him, but in most of the other beds within my angle of vision some squalid tragedy or some plain horror was being enacted. In the bed that was foot to foot with mine there lay, until he died (I didn't see him die – they moved him to another bed), a little weazened man who was suffering from I do not know what disease, but something that made his whole body so intensely sensitive that any movement from side to side, sometimes even the weight of the bed-clothes, would make him shout out with pain. His worst suffering was when he urinated, which he did with the greatest difficulty. A nurse would bring him the bed-bottle and then for a long time stand beside his bed, whistling, as grooms are said to do with horses, until at last with an agonized shriek of '*Je pisse!*' he would get started. In the bed next to him the sandy-haired man whom I had seen being cupped used to cough up blood-streaked mucus at all hours. My left-hand neighbour was a tall, flaccid-looking young man who used periodically to have a tube inserted into his back and astonishing quantities of frothy liquid drawn off from some part of his body. In the bed beyond that a veteran of the war of 1870 was dying, a handsome old man with a white imperial, round whose bed, at all hours when visiting was allowed, four elderly female relatives dressed all in black sat exactly like crows, obviously scheming for some pitiful legacy. In the bed opposite me in the further row was an old bald-headed man with drooping moustaches and greatly swollen face and body, who was suffering from some disease that made him urinate almost incessantly. A huge glass receptacle stood always beside his bed. One day his wife and daughter came to visit him. At the sight of them the old man's bloated face lit up with a smile of surprising sweetness, and as his daughter, a pretty girl of about twenty, approached the bed I saw that his hand was slowly working its way from under the bed-clothes. I seemed to see in advance the gesture that was coming – the girl kneeling beside the bed, the old man's hand laid on her head in his dying blessing. But no, he merely handed her the bed-bottle, which she promptly took from him and emptied into the receptacle.

About a dozen beds away from me was *numéro 57* – I think that was his number – a cirrhosis of the liver case. Everyone in the ward knew him by sight because he was sometimes the subject of a medical lecture. On two afternoons a week the tall, grave doctor would lecture in the ward to a party of students, and on more than one occasion old *numéro 57* was wheeled on a sort of trolley into the middle of the ward, where the doctor would roll back his nightshirt, dilate with his fingers a huge flabby protuberance on the man's belly – the diseased liver, I suppose – and explain solemnly that this was a disease attributable to alcoholism, commoner in the wine-drinking countries. As usual he neither spoke to his patient nor gave him a smile, a nod or any kind of recognition. While he talked, very grave and upright, he would hold the wasted body beneath his two hands, sometimes giving it a gentle roll to and fro, in just the attitude of a woman handling a rolling-pin. Not that *numéro 57* minded this kind of thing. Obviously he was an old hospital inmate, a regular exhibit at lectures, his liver long since marked down for a bottle in some pathological museum. Utterly uninterested in what was said about him, he would lie with his colourless eyes gazing at nothing, while the doctor showed him off like a piece of antique china. He was a man of about sixty, astonishingly shrunken. His face, pale as vellum, had shrunken away till it seemed no bigger than a doll's.

One morning my cobbler neighbour woke me up by plucking at my pillow before the nurses arrived. '*Numéro 57!*' – he flung his arms above his head. There was a light in the ward, enough to see by. I could see old *numéro* 57 lying crumpled up on his side, his face sticking out over the side of the bed, and towards me. He had died some time during the night, nobody knew when. When the nurses came they received the news of his death indifferently and went about their work. After a long time, an hour or more, two other nurses marched in abreast like soldiers, with a great clumping of sabots, and knotted the corpse up in the sheets, but it was not removed till some time later. Meanwhile, in the better light, I had had time for a good look at *numéro* 57. Indeed I lay on my side to look at him. Curiously enough he was the first dead European I had seen. I had seen dead men before, but always Asiatics and usually people who had died violent deaths. *Numéro* 57's eyes were still open, his mouth also open, his small face contorted into an expression of agony. What most impressed me however was the whiteness of his face. It had been pale before, but now it was little darker than the sheets. As I gazed at the tiny, screwed-up face it struck me that this disgusting piece of refuse, waiting to be carted away and dumped on a slab in the dissecting room, was an example of 'natural' death, one of the things you pray for in the Litany. There you are, then, I thought, that's what is waiting for you, twenty, thirty, forty years hence: that is how the lucky ones die, the ones who live to be old. One wants to live, of course, indeed one only stays alive by virtue of the fear of death, but I think now, as I thought then, that it's better to die violently and not too old. People talk about the horrors of war, but what weapon has man invented that even approaches in cruelty some of the commoner diseases? 'Natural' death, almost by definition, means something slow, smelly and painful. Even at that, it makes a difference if you can achieve it in your own home and not in a public institution. This poor old wretch who had just flickered out like a candle-end was not even important enough to have anyone watching by his deathbed. He was merely a number, then a 'subject' for the students' scalpels. And the sordid publicity of dying in such a place! In the Hôpital X the beds were very close together and there were no screens. Fancy, for instance, dying like the little man whose bed was for a while foot to foot with mine, the one who cried out when the bed-clothes touched him! I dare say *Je pisse!* were his last recorded words. Perhaps the dying don't bother about such things – that at least would be the standard answer: nevertheless dying people are often more or less normal in their minds till within a day or so of the end.

In the public wards of a hospital you see horrors that you don't seem to meet with among people who manage to die in their own homes, as though certain diseases only attacked people at the lower income levels. But it is a fact that you would not in any English hospitals see some of the things I saw in the Hôpital X. This business of people just dying like animals, for instance, with nobody standing by, nobody interested, the death not even noticed till the morning – this happened more than once. You certainly would not see that in England, and still less would you see a corpse left exposed to the view of the other patients. I remember that once in a cottage hospital in England a man died while we were at tea, and though there were only six of us in the ward the nurses managed things so adroitly that the man was dead and his body removed without our even hearing about it till tea was over. A thing we perhaps underrate in England is the advantage we enjoy in having large numbers of well-trained and rigidly-disciplined nurses. No doubt English nurses are dumb enough, they may tell fortunes with tea-leaves, wear Union Jack badges and keep photographs of the Queen on their mantelpieces, but at least they don't let you lie unwashed and constipated on an unmade bed, out of sheer laziness. The nurses at the Hôpital X still had a tinge of Mrs Gamp about them, and later, in the military hospitals of Republican Spain, I was to see nurses almost too ignorant to take a temperature. You wouldn't, either, see in England such dirt as existed in the Hôpital X. Later on, when I was well enough to wash myself in the bathroom, I found that there was kept there a huge packing-case into which the scraps of food and dirty dressings from the ward were flung, and the wainscottings were infested by crickets.

When I had got back my clothes and grown strong on my legs I fled from the Hôpital X, before my time was up and without waiting for a medical discharge. It was not the only hospital I have fled from, but its gloom and bareness, its sickly smell and, above all, something in its mental atmosphere stand out in my memory as exceptional. I had been taken there because it was the hospital belonging to my *arrondissement*, and I did not learn till after I was in it that it bore a bad reputation. A year or two later the celebrated swindler, Madame Hanaud, who was ill while on remand, was taken to the Hôpital X, and after a few days of it she managed to elude her guards, took a taxi and drove back to the prison, explaining that she was more comfortable there. I have no doubt that the Hôpital X was quite untypical of French hospitals even at that date. But the patients, nearly all of them working men, were surprisingly resigned. Some of them seemed to find the conditions almost comfortable, for at least two were destitute malingerers who found this a good way of getting through the winter. The nurses connived because the malingerers made themselves useful by doing odd jobs. But the attitude of the majority was: of course this is a lousy place, but what else do you expect? It did not seem strange to them that you should be woken at five and then wait three hours before starting the day on watery soup, or that people should die with no one at their bedside, or even that your chance of getting medical attention should depend on catching the doctor's eye as he went past. According to their traditions that was what hospitals were like. If you are seriously ill, and if you are too poor to be treated in your own home, then you must go into hospital, and once there you must put up with harshness and discomfort, just as you would in the army. But on top of this I was interested to find a lingering belief in the old stories that have now almost faded from memory in England – stories, for instance, about doctors cutting you open out of sheer curiosity or thinking it funny to start operating before you were properly 'under'. There were dark tales about a little operating room said to be situated just beyond the bathroom. Dreadful screams were said to issue from this room. I saw nothing to confirm these stories and no doubt they were all nonsense, though I did see two students kill a sixteen-year-old boy, or nearly kill him (he appeared to be dying when I left the hospital, but he may have recovered later) by a mischievous experiment which they probably could not have tried on a paying patient. Well within living memory it used to be believed in London that in some of the big hospitals patients were killed off to get dissection subjects. I didn't hear this tale repeated at the Hôpital X, but I should think some of the men there would have found it credible. For it was a hospital in which not the methods, perhaps, but something of the atmosphere of the nineteenth century had managed to survive, and therein lay its peculiar interest.

During the past fifty years or so there has been a great change in the relationship between doctor and patient. If you look at almost any literature before the later part of the nineteenth century, you find that a hospital is popularly regarded as much the same thing as a prison, and an old-fashioned, dungeon-like prison at that. A hospital is a place of filth, torture and death, a sort of antechamber to the tomb. No one who was not more or less destitute would have thought of going into such a place for treatment. And especially in the early part of the last century, when medical science had grown bolder than before without being any more successful, the whole business of doctoring was looked on with horror and dread by ordinary people. Surgery, in particular, was believed to be no more than a peculiarly gruesome form of sadism, and dissection, possible only with the aid of body-snatchers, was even confused with necromancy. From the nineteenth century you could collect a large horror-literature connected with doctors and hospitals. Think of poor old George III, in his dotage, shrieking for mercy as he sees his surgeons approaching to 'bleed him till he faints'! Think of the conversations of Bob Sawyer and Benjamin Allen, which no doubt are hardly parodies, or the field hospitals in *La Débâcle* and *War and Peace*, or that shocking description of an amputation in Melville's *Whitejacket*! Even the names given to doctors in nineteenth-century English fiction, Slasher, Carver, Sawyer, Fillgrave and so on, and the generic nickname 'sawbones', are about as grim as they are comic. The anti-surgery tradition is perhaps best expressed in Tennyson's poem, 'The Children's Hospital', which is essentially a pre-chloroform document though it seems to have been written as late as 1880. Moreover, the outlook which Tennyson records in this poem had a lot to be said for it. When you consider what an operation without anaesthetics must have been like, what it notoriously *was* like, it is difficult not to suspect the motives of people who would undertake such things. For these bloody horrors which the students so eagerly looked forward to ('A magnificent sight if Slasher does it!') were admittedly more or less useless: the patient who did not die of shock usually died of gangrene, a result which was taken for granted. Even now doctors can be found whose motives are questionable. Anyone who has had much illness, or who has listened to medical students talking, will know what I mean. But anaesthetics were a turning-point, and disinfectants were another. Nowhere in the world, probably, would you now see the kind of scene described by Axel Munthe in *The Story of San Michele*, when the sinister surgeon in top-hat and frock-coat, his starched shirtfront spattered with blood and pus, carves up patient after patient with the same knife and flings the severed limbs into a pile beside the table. Moreover, national health insurance has partly done away with the idea that a working-class patient is a pauper who deserves little consideration. Well into this century it was usual for 'free' patients at the big hospitals to have their teeth extracted with no anaesthetic. They didn't pay, so why should they have an anaesthetic – that was the attitude. That too has changed.

And yet every institution will always bear upon it some lingering memory of its past. A barrack-room is still haunted by the ghost of Kipling, and it is difficult to enter a workhouse without being reminded of *Oliver Twist*. Hospitals began as a kind of casual ward for lepers and the like to die in, and they continued as places where medical students learned their art on the bodies of the poor. You can still catch a faint suggestion of their history in their characteristically gloomy architecture. I would be far from complaining about the treatment I have received in any English hospital, but I do know that it is a sound instinct that warns people to keep out of hospitals if possible, and especially out of the public wards. Whatever the legal position may be, it is unquestionable that you have far less control over your own treatment, far less certainty that frivolous experiments will not be tried on you, when it is a case of 'accept the discipline or get out'. And it is a great thing to die in your own bed, though it is better still to die in your boots. However great the kindness and the efficiency, in every hospital death there will be some cruel, squalid detail, something perhaps too small to be told but leaving terribly painful memories behind, arising out of the haste, the crowding, the impersonality of a place where every day people are dying among strangers.

The dread of hospitals probably still survives among the very poor and in all of us it has only recently disappeared. It is a dark patch not far beneath the surface of our minds. I have said earlier that, when I entered the ward at the Hôpital X, I was conscious of a strange feeling of familiarity. What the scene reminded me of, of course, was the reeking, pain-filled hospitals of the nineteenth century, which I had never seen but of which I had a traditional knowledge. And something, perhaps the black-clad doctor with his frowsy black bag, or perhaps only the sickly smell, played the queer trick of unearthing from my memory that poem of Tennyson's, 'The Children's Hospital', which I had not thought of for twenty years. It happened that as a child I had had it read aloud to me by a sick-nurse whose own working life might have stretched back to the time when Tennyson wrote the poem. The horrors and sufferings of the old-style hospitals were a vivid memory to her. We had shuddered over the poem together, and then seemingly I had forgotten it. Even its name would probably have recalled nothing to me. But the first glimpse of the ill-lit, murmurous room, with the beds so close together, suddenly roused the train of thought to which it belonged, and in the night that followed I found myself remembering the whole story and atmosphere of the poem, with many of its lines complete.

Now, November 1946

Riding Down from Bangor

The reappearance of *Helen's Babies*,[1] in its day one of the most popular books in the world – within the British Empire alone it was pirated by twenty different publishing firms, the author receiving a total profit of £40 from a sale of some hundreds of thousands or millions of copies – will ring a bell in any literate person over thirty-five. Not that the present edition is an altogether satisfactory one. It is a cheap little book with rather unsuitable illustrations, various American dialect words appear to have been cut out of it, and the sequel, *Other People's Children*, which was often bound up with it in earlier editions, is missing.

[1] *Helen's Babies* by John Habberton, first published in 1876.

Still, it is pleasant to see *Helen's Babies* in print again. It had become almost a rarity in recent years, and it is one of the best of the little library of American books on which people born at about the turn of the century were brought up.

The books one reads in childhood, and perhaps most of all the bad and good bad books, create in one's mind a sort of false map of the world, a series of fabulous countries into which one can retreat at odd moments throughout the rest of life, and which in some cases can even survive a visit to the real countries which they are supposed to represent. The pampas, the Amazon, the coral islands of the Pacific, Russia, land of birch-tree and samovar, Transylvania with its boyars and vampires, the China of Guy Boothby, the Paris of du Maurier – one could continue the list for a long time. But one other imaginary country that I acquired early in life was called America. If I pause on the word 'America', and, deliberately putting aside the existing reality, call up my childhood vision of it, I see two pictures – composite pictures, of course, from which I am omitting a good deal of the detail.

One is of a boy sitting in a whitewashed stone schoolroom. He wears braces and has patches on his shirt, and if it is summer he is barefooted. In the corner of the schoolroom there is a bucket of drinking water with a dipper. The boy lives in a farm-house, also of stone and also whitewashed, which has a mortgage on it. He aspires to be President, and is expected to keep the woodpile full. Somewhere in the background of the picture, but completely dominating it, is a huge black Bible. The other picture is of a tall, angular man, with a shapeless hat pulled down over his eyes, leaning against a wooden paling and whittling at a stick. His lower jaw moves slowly but ceaselessly. At very long intervals he emits some piece of wisdom such as 'A woman is the orneriest critter there is, 'ceptin' a mule', or 'When you don't know a thing to do, don't do a thing'; but more often it is a jet of tobacco juice that issues from the gap in his front teeth. Between them those two pictures summed up my earliest impression of America. And of the two, the first – which, I suppose, represented New England, the other representing the South – had the stronger hold upon me.

The books from which these pictures were derived included, of course, books which it is still possible to take seriously, such as *Tom Sawyer* and *Uncle Tom's Cabin,* but the most richly American flavour was to be found in minor works which are now almost forgotten. I wonder, for instance, if anyone still reads *Rebecca of Sunnybrook Farm,* which remained a popular favourite long enough to be filmed with Mary Pickford in the leading part. Or how about the 'Katy' books by Susan Coolidge (*What Katy Did at School,* etc), which, although girls' books and therefore 'soppy', had the fascination of foreignness? Louisa M. Alcott's *Little Women* and *Good Wives* are, I suppose, still flickeringly in print, and certainly they still have their devotees. As a child I loved both of them, though I was less pleased by the third of the trilogy, *Little Men.* That model school where the worst punishment was to have to whack the schoolmaster, on 'this hurts me more than it hurts you' principles, was rather difficult to swallow.

Helen's Babies belonged in much the same world as *Little Women,* and must have been published round about the same date. Then there were Artemus Ward, Bret Harte, and various songs, hymns and ballads, besides poems dealing with the civil war, such as 'Barbara Fritchie' ('"Shoot if you must this old grey head. But spare your country's flag," she said') and 'Little Gifford of Tennessee'. There were other books so obscure that it hardly seems worth mentioning them, and magazine stories of which I remember nothing except that the old homestead always seemed to have a mortgage on it. There was also *Beautiful Joe,* the American reply to *Black Beauty,* of which you might just possibly pick up a copy in a sixpenny box. All the books I have mentioned were written well before 1900, but something of the special American flavour lingered on into this century in, for instance, the Buster Brown coloured supplements, and even in Booth Tarkington's 'Penrod' stories, which will have been written round about 1910. Perhaps there was even a tinge of it in Ernest Thompson Seton's animal books (*Wild Animals I Have Known,* etc), which have now fallen from favour but which drew tears from the pre-1914 child as surely as *Misunderstood* had done from the children of a generation earlier.

Somewhat later my picture of nineteenth-century America was given greater precision by a song which is still fairly well known and which can be found (I think) in the *Scottish Students' Song Book.* As usual in these bookless days I cannot get hold of a copy, and I must quote fragments from memory. It begins:

Riding down from Bangor
On an Eastern train,
Bronzed with weeks of hunting
In the woods of Maine –
Quite extensive whiskers,
Beard, moustache as well –
Sat a student fellow,
Tall and slim and swell.

Presently an aged couple and a 'village maiden', described as 'beautiful, petite', get into the carriage. Quantities of cinders are flying about, and before long the student fellow gets one in the eye: the village maiden extracts it for him, to the scandal of the aged couple. Soon after this the train shoots into a long tunnel, 'black as Egypt's night'. When it emerges into the daylight again the maiden is covered with blushes, and the cause of her confusion is revealed when

There suddenly appeared
A tiny little ear-ring
In that horrid student's beard!

I do not know the date of the song, but the primitiveness of the train (no lights in the carriage, and a cinder in one's eye a normal accident) suggests that it belongs well back in the nineteenth century.

What connects this song with books like *Helen's Babies* is first of all a sort of sweet innocence – the climax, the thing you are supposed to be slightly shocked at, is an episode with which any modern piece of naughty-naughty would *start* – and, secondly, a faint vulgarity of language mixed up with a certain cultural pretentiousness. *Helen's Babies* is intended as a humorous, even a farcical book, but it is haunted all the way through by words like 'tasteful' and 'ladylike', and it is funny chiefly because its tiny disasters happen against a background of conscious gentility. 'Handsome, intelligent, composed, tastefully dressed, without a suspicion of the flirt or the languid woman of fashion about her, she awakened to the utmost my every admiring sentiment' – thus is the heroine described, figuring elsewhere as 'erect, fresh, neat, composed, bright-eyed, fair-faced, smiling and observant'. One gets beautiful glimpses of a now-vanished world in such remarks as: 'I believe you arranged the floral decorations at St Zephaniah's Fair last winter, Mr Burton? 'Twas the most tasteful display of the season.' But in spite of the occasional use of ''twas' and other archaisms – 'parlour' for sitting-room, 'chamber' for bedroom, 'real' as an adverb, and so forth – the book does not 'date' very markedly, and many of its admirers imagine it to have been written round about 1900. Actually it was written in 1875, a fact which one might infer from internal evidence, since the hero, aged twenty-eight, is a veteran of the civil war.

The book is very short and the story is a simple one. A young bachelor is prevailed on by his sister to look after her house and her two sons, aged five and three, while she and her husband go on a fortnight's holiday. The children drive him almost mad by an endless succession of such acts as falling into ponds, swallowing poison, throwing keys down wells, cutting themselves with razors, and the like, but also facilitate his engagement to 'a charming girl, whom, for about a year, I had been adoring from afar'. These events take place in an outer suburb of New York, in a society which now seems astonishingly sedate, formal, domesticated and, according to current conceptions, un-American. Every action is governed by etiquette. To pass a carriage full of ladies when your hat is crooked is an ordeal; to recognize an acquaintance in church is ill-bred; to become engaged after a ten days' courtship is a severe social lapse. We are accustomed to thinking of American society as more crude, adventurous and, in a cultural sense, democratic than our own, and from writers like Mark Twain, Whitman and Bret Harte, not to mention the cowboy and Red Indian stories of the weekly papers, one draws a picture of a wild anarchic world peopled by eccentrics and desperadoes who have no traditions and no attachment to one place. That aspect of nineteenth-century America did of course exist, but in the more populous eastern States a society similar to Jane Austen's seems to have survived longer than it did in England. And it is hard not to feel that it was a better kind of society than that which arose from the sudden industrialization of the later part of the century. The people in *Helen's Babies* or *Little Women* may be mildly ridiculous, but they are uncorrupted. They have something that is perhaps best described as integrity, or good morale, founded partly on an unthinking piety. It is a matter of course that everyone attends church on Sunday morning and says grace before meals and prayers at bedtime: to amuse the children one tells them Bible stories, and if they ask for a song it is probably 'Glory, glory Hallelujah'. Perhaps it is also a sign of spiritual health in the light literature of this period that death is mentioned freely. 'Baby Phil', the brother of Budge and Toddie, has died shortly before *Helen's Babies* opens, and there are various tear-jerking references to his 'tiny coffin'. A modern writer attempting a story of this kind would have kept coffins out of it.

English children are still americanized by way of the films, but it would no longer be generally claimed that American books are the best ones for children. Who, without misgivings, would bring up a child on the coloured 'comics' in which sinister professors manufacture atomic bombs in underground laboratories while Superman whizzes through the clouds, the machine-gun bullets bouncing off his chest like peas, and platinum blondes are raped, or very nearly, by steel robots and fifty-foot dinosaurs? It is a far cry from Superman to the Bible and the woodpile. The earlier children's books, or books readable by children, had not only innocence but a sort of native gaiety, a buoyant, carefree feeling, which was the product, presumably, of the unheard-of freedom and security which nineteenth-century America enjoyed. That is the connecting link between books so seemingly far apart as *Little Women* and *Life on the Mississippi*. The society described in the one is subdued, bookish and home-loving, while the other tells of a crazy world of bandits, gold mines, duels, drunkenness and gambling hells: but in both one can detect an underlying confidence in the future, a sense of freedom and opportunity.

Nineteenth-century America was a rich, empty country which lay outside the main stream of world events, and in which the twin nightmares that beset nearly every modern man, the nightmare of unemployment and the nightmare of State interference, had hardly come into being. There were social distinctions, more marked than those of today, and there was poverty (in *Little Women*, it will be remembered, the family is at one time so hard up that one of the girls sells her hair to the barber), but there was not, as there is now, an all-prevailing sense of helplessness. There was room for everybody, and if you worked hard you could be certain of a living – could even be certain of growing rich: this was generally believed, and for the greater part of the population it was even broadly true. In other words, the civilization of nineteenth-century America was capitalist civilization at its best. Soon after the civil war the inevitable deterioration started. But for some decades, at least, life in America was much better fun than life in Europe – there was more happening, more colour, more variety, more opportunity – and the books and songs of that period had a sort of bloom, a childlike quality. Hence, I think, the popularity of *Helen's Babies* and other 'light' literature, which made it normal for the English child of thirty or forty years ago to grow up with a theoretical knowledge of racoons, woodchucks, chipmunks, gophers, hickory trees, water-melons and other unfamiliar fragments of the American scene.

Tribune, 22 November 1946

Lear, Tolstoy and the Fool

Tolstoy's pamphlets are the least-known part of his work, and his attack on Shakespeare[1] is not even an easy document to get hold of, at any rate in an English translation. Perhaps, therefore, it will be useful if I give a summary of the pamphlet before trying to discuss it.

Tolstoy begins by saying that throughout life Shakespeare has aroused in him 'an irresistible repulsion and tedium'. Conscious that the opinion of the civilized world is against him, he has made one attempt after another on Shakespeare's works, reading and rereading them in Russian, English and German; but 'I invariably underwent the same feelings: repulsion, weariness and bewilderment'. Now, at the age of seventy-five, he has once again reread the entire works of Shakespeare, including the historical plays, and

[1] *Shakespeare and the Drama*. Written about 1903 as an introduction to another pamphlet, *Shakespeare and the Working Classes*, by Ernest Crosby. [Author's footnote.]

> I have felt with even greater force, the same feelings – this time, however, not of bewilderment, but of firm, indubitable conviction that the unquestionable glory of a great genius which Shakespeare enjoys, and which compels writers of our time to imitate him and readers and spectators to discover in him non-existent merits – thereby distorting their aesthetic and ethical understanding – is a great evil, as is every untruth.

Shakespeare, Tolstoy adds, is not merely no genius, but is not even 'an average author', and in order to demonstrate this fact he will examine *King Lear*, which, as he is able to show by quotations from Hazlitt, Brandes and others, has been extravagantly praised and can be taken as an example of Shakespeare's best work.

Tolstoy then makes a sort of exposition of the plot of *King Lear*, finding it at every step to be stupid, verbose, unnatural, unintelligible, bombastic, vulgar, tedious and full of incredible events, 'wild ravings', 'mirthless jokes', anachronisms, irrelevancies, obscenities, worn-out stage conventions and other faults both moral and aesthetic. *Lear* is, in any case, a plagiarism of an earlier and much better play, *King Leir*, by an unknown author, which Shakespeare stole and then ruined. It is worth quoting a specimen paragraph to illustrate the manner in which Tolstoy goes to work. Act III, Scene 2 (in which Lear, Kent and the Fool are together in the storm) is summarized thus:

> Lear walks about the heath and says words which are meant to express his despair: he desires that the winds should blow so hard that they (the winds) should crack their cheeks and that the rain should flood everything, that lightning should singe his white head, and the thunder flatten the world and destroy all germs 'that make ungrateful man'! The fool keeps uttering still more senseless words. Enter Kent: Lear says that for some reason during this storm all criminals shall be found out and convicted. Kent, still unrecognized by Lear, endeavours to persuade him to take refuge in a hovel. At this point the fool utters a prophecy in no wise related to the situation and they all depart.

Tolstoy's final verdict on *Lear* is that no unhypnotized observer, if such an observer existed, could read it to the end with any feeling except 'aversion and weariness'. And exactly the same is true of 'all the other extolled dramas of Shakespeare, not to mention the senseless dramatized tales, *Pericles, Twelfth Night, The Tempest, Cymbeline, Troilus and Cressida*'.

Having dealt with *Lear* Tolstoy draws up a more general indictment against Shakespeare. He finds that Shakespeare has a certain technical skill which is partly traceable to his having been an actor, but otherwise no merits whatever. He has no power of delineating character or of making words and actions spring naturally out of situations, his language is uniformly exaggerated and ridiculous, he constantly thrusts his own random thoughts into the mouth of any character who happens to be handy, he displays a 'complete absence of aesthetic feeling', and his words 'have nothing whatever in common with art and poetry'. 'Shakespeare might have been whatever you like,' Tolstoy concludes, 'but he was not an artist.' Moreover, his opinions are not original or interesting, and his tendency is 'of the lowest and most immoral'. Curiously enough, Tolstoy does not base this last judgement on Shakespeare's own utterances, but on the statements of two critics, Gervinus and Brandes.

According to Gervinus (or at any rate Tolstoy's reading of Gervinus) 'Shakespeare taught... that one *may be too good,*' while according to Brandes 'Shakespeare's fundamental principle... is that *the end justifies the means.*' Tolstoy adds on his own account that Shakespeare was a jingo patriot of the worst type, but apart from this he considers that Gervinus and Brandes have given a true and adequate description of Shakespeare's view of life.

Tolstoy then recapitulates in a few paragraphs the theory of art which he had expressed at greater length elsewhere. Put still more shortly, it amounts to a demand for dignity of subject-matter, sincerity, and good craftsmanship. A great work of art must deal with some subject which is 'important to the life of mankind', it must express something which the author genuinely feels, and it must use such technical methods as will produce the desired effect. As Shakespeare is debased in outlook, slipshod in execution and incapable of being sincere even for a moment, he obviously stands condemned.

But here there arises a difficult question. If Shakespeare is all that Tolstoy has shown him to be, how did he ever come to be so generally admired? Evidently the answer can only lie in a sort of mass hypnosis, or 'epidemic suggestion'. The whole civilized world has somehow been deluded into thinking Shakespeare a good writer, and even the plainest demonstration to the contrary makes no impression, because one is not dealing with a reasoned opinion but with something akin to religious faith. Throughout history, says Tolstoy, there has been an endless series of these 'epidemic suggestions' – for example, the Crusades, the search for the Philosopher's Stone, the craze for tulip growing which once swept over Holland, and so on and so forth. As a contemporary instance he cites, rather significantly, the Dreyfus Case, over which the whole world grew violently excited for no sufficient reason. There are also sudden short-lived crazes for new political and philosophical theories, or for this or that writer, artist or scientist – for example, Darwin, who (in 1903) is 'beginning to be forgotten'. And in some cases a quite worthless popular idol may remain in favour for centuries, for 'it also happens that such crazes, having arisen in consequence of special reasons accidentally favouring their establishment, correspond in such a degree to the views of life spread in society, and especially in literary circles, that they are maintained for a long time'. Shakespeare's plays have continued to be admired over a long period because 'they corresponded to the irreligious and immoral frame of mind of the upper classes of his time and ours'.

As to the manner in which Shakespeare's fame *started,* Tolstoy explains it as having been 'got up' by German professors towards the end of the eighteenth century. His reputation 'originated in Germany, and thence was transferred to England'. The Germans chose to elevate Shakespeare because, at a time when there was no German drama worth speaking about and French classical literature was beginning to seem frigid and artificial, they were captivated by Shakespeare's 'clever development of scenes' and also found in him a good expression of their own attitude towards life. Goethe pronounced Shakespeare a great poet, whereupon all the other critics flocked after him like a troop of parrots, and the general infatuation has lasted ever since. The result has been a further debasement of the drama – Tolstoy is careful to include his own plays when condemning the contemporary stage – and a further corruption of the prevailing moral outlook. It follows that 'the false glorification of Shakespeare' is an important evil which Tolstoy feels it his duty to combat.

This, then, is the substance of Tolstoy's pamphlet. One's first feeling is that in describing Shakespeare as a bad writer he is saying something demonstrably untrue. But this is not the case. In reality there is no kind of evidence or argument by which one can show that Shakespeare, or any other writer, is 'good'. Nor is there any way of definitely proving that – for instance – Warwick Deeping is 'bad'. Ultimately there is no test of literary merit except survival, which is itself merely an index to majority opinion. Artistic theories such as Tolstoy's are quite worthless, because they not only start out with arbitrary assumptions, but depend on vague terms ('sincere', 'important' and so forth) which can be interpreted in any way one chooses. Properly speaking one cannot *answer* Tolstoy's attack. The interesting question is: why did he make it? But it should be noticed in passing that he uses many weak or dishonest arguments. Some of these are worth pointing out, not because they invalidate his main charge but because they are, so to speak, evidence of malice.

To begin with, his examination of *King Lear* is not 'impartial', as he twice claims. On the contrary, it is a prolonged exercise in misrepresentation. It is obvious that when you are summarizing *King Lear* for the benefit of someone who has not read it, you are not really being impartial if you introduce an important speech (Lear's speech when Cordelia is dead in his arms) in this manner: 'Again begin Lear's awful ravings, at which one feels ashamed, as at unsuccessful jokes.' And in a long series of instances Tolstoy slightly alters or colours the passages he is criticizing, always in such a way as to make the plot appear a little more complicated and improbable, or the language a little more exaggerated. For example, we are told that Lear 'has no necessity or motive for his abdication', although his reason for abdicating (that he is old and wishes to retire from the cares of state) has been clearly indicated in the first scene. It will be seen that even in the passage which I quoted earlier, Tolstoy has wilfully misunderstood one phrase and slightly changed the meaning of another, making nonsense of a remark which is reasonable enough in its context. None of these misreadings is very gross in itself, but their cumulative effect is to exaggerate the psychological incoherence of the play. Again, Tolstoy is not able to explain why Shakespeare's plays were still in print, and still on the stage, two hundred years after his death (*before* the 'epidemic suggestion' started, that is); and his whole account of Shakespeare's rise to fame is guesswork punctuated by outright mis-statements. And again, various of his accusations contradict one another: for example, Shakespeare is a mere entertainer and 'not in earnest', but on the other hand he is constantly putting his own thoughts into the mouths of his characters. On the whole it is difficult to feel that Tolstoy's criticisms are uttered in good faith. In any case it is impossible that he should fully have believed in his main thesis – believed, that is to say, that for a century or more the entire civilized world had been taken in by a huge and palpable lie which he alone was able to see through. Certainly his dislike of Shakespeare is real enough, but the reasons for it may be different, or partly different, from what he avows; and therein lies the interest of his pamphlet.

At this point one is obliged to start guessing. However, there is one possible clue, or at least there is a question which may point the way to a clue. It is: why did Tolstoy, with thirty or more plays to choose from, pick out *King Lear* as his especial target? True, *Lear* is so well known and has been so much praised that it could justly be taken as representative of Shakespeare's best work: still, for the purpose of a hostile analysis Tolstoy would probably choose the play he disliked most. Is it not possible that he bore an especial enmity towards this particular play because he was aware, consciously or unconsciously, of the resemblance between Lear's story and his own? But it is better to approach this clue from the opposite direction – that is, by examining *Lear* itself, and the qualities in it that Tolstoy fails to mention.

One of the first things an English reader would notice in Tolstoy's pamphlet is that it hardly deals with Shakespeare as a poet. Shakespeare is treated as a dramatist, and in so far as his popularity is not spurious, it is held to be due to tricks of stagecraft which give good opportunities to clever actors. Now, so far as the English-speaking countries go, this is not true. Several of the plays which are most valued by lovers of Shakespeare (for instance, *Timon of Athens*) are seldom or never acted, while some of the most actable, such as *A Midsummer Night's Dream*, are the least admired. Those who care most for Shakespeare value him in the first place for his use of language, the 'verbal music' which even Bernard Shaw, another hostile critic, admits to be 'irresistible'. Tolstoy ignores this, and does not seem to realize that a poem may have a special value for those who speak the language in which it was written. However, even if one puts oneself in Tolstoy's place and tries to think of Shakespeare as a foreign poet it is still clear that there is something that Tolstoy has left out. Poetry, it seems, is *not* solely a matter of sound and association, and valueless outside its own language-group: otherwise, how is it that some poems, including poems written in dead languages, succeed in crossing frontiers? Clearly a lyric like 'Tomorrow is Saint Valentine's Day' could not be satisfactorily translated, but in Shakespeare's major work there is something describable as poetry that can be separated from the words. Tolstoy is right in saying that *Lear* is not a very good play, as a play. It is too drawn-out and has too many characters and sub-plots. One wicked daughter would have been quite enough, and Edgar is a superfluous character: indeed it would probably be a better play if Gloucester and both his sons were eliminated. Nevertheless, something, a kind of pattern, or perhaps only an atmosphere, survives the complications and the *longueurs*. *Lear* can be imagined as a puppet show, a mime, a ballet, a series of pictures. Part of its poetry, perhaps the most essential part, is inherent in the story and is dependent neither on any particular set of words, nor on flesh-and-blood presentation.

Shut your eyes and think of *King Lear*, if possible without calling to mind any of the dialogue. What do you see? Here at any rate is what I see: a majestic old man in a long black robe, with flowing white hair and beard, a figure out of Blake's drawings (but also, curiously enough, rather like Tolstoy), wandering through a storm and cursing the heavens, in company with a Fool and a lunatic. Presently the scene shifts, and the old man, still cursing, still understanding nothing, is holding a dead girl in his arms while the Fool dangles on a gallows somewhere in the background. This is the bare skeleton of the play, and even here Tolstoy wants to cut out most of what is essential. He objects to the storm, as being unnecessary, to the Fool, who in his eyes is simply a tedious nuisance and an excuse for making bad jokes, and to the death of Cordelia, which, as he sees it, robs the play of its moral. According to Tolstoy, the earlier play, *King Leir*, which Shakespeare adapted

> terminates more naturally and more in accordance with the moral demands of the spectator than does Shakespeare's: namely, by the King of the Gauls conquering the husbands of the elder sisters, and by Cordelia, instead of being killed, restoring Leir to his former position.

In other words the tragedy ought to have been a comedy, or perhaps a melodrama. It is doubtful whether the sense of tragedy is compatible with belief in God: at any rate, it is not compatible with disbelief in human dignity and with the kind of 'moral demand' which feels cheated when virtue fails to triumph. A tragic situation exists precisely when virtue does *not* triumph but when it is still felt that man is nobler than the forces which destroy him. It is perhaps more significant that Tolstoy sees no justification for the presence of the Fool. The Fool is integral to the play. He acts not only as a sort of chorus, making the central situation clearer by commenting on it more intelligently than the other characters, but as a foil to Lear's frenzies. His jokes, riddles and scraps of rhyme, and his endless digs at Lear's high-minded folly, ranging from mere derision to a sort of melancholy poetry ('All thy other titles thou hast given away; that thou wast born with'), are like a trickle of sanity running through the play, a reminder that somewhere or other, in spite of the injustices, cruelties, intrigues, deceptions and misunderstandings that are being enacted here, life is going on much as usual. In Tolstoy's impatience with the Fool one gets a glimpse of his deeper quarrel with Shakespeare. He objects, with some justification, to the raggedness of Shakespeare's plays, the irrelevancies, the incredible plots, the exaggerated language: but what at bottom he probably most dislikes is a sort of exuberance, a tendency to take – not so much a pleasure, as simply an interest in the actual process of life. It is a mistake to write Tolstoy off as a moralist attacking an artist. He never said that art, as such, is wicked or meaningless, nor did he even say that technical virtuosity is unimportant. But his main aim, in his later years, was to narrow the range of human consciousness. One's interests, one's points of attachment to the physical world and the day-to-day struggle, must be as few and not as many as possible. Literature must consist of parables, stripped of detail and almost independent of language. The parables – this is where Tolstoy differs from the average vulgar puritan – must themselves be works of art, but pleasure and curiosity must be excluded from them. Science, also, must be divorced from curiosity. The business of science, he says, is not to discover what happens, but to teach men how they ought to live. So also with history and politics. Many problems (for example, the Dreyfus Case) are simply not worth solving, and he is willing to leave them as loose ends. Indeed his whole theory of 'crazes' or 'epidemic suggestions', in which he lumps together such things as the Crusades and the Dutch passion of tulip growing, shows a willingness to regard many human activities as mere ant-like rushings to and fro, inexplicable and uninteresting. Clearly he could have no patience with a chaotic, detailed, discursive writer like Shakespeare. His reaction is that of an irritable old man who is being pestered by a noisy child. 'Why do you keep jumping up and down like that? Why can't you sit still like I do?' In a way the old man is in the right, but the trouble is that the child has a feeling in its limbs which the old man has lost. And if the old man knows of the existence of this feeling, the effect is merely to increase his irritation: he would make children senile, if he could. Tolstoy does not know, perhaps, just *what* he misses in Shakespeare, but he is aware that he misses something, and he is determined that others shall be deprived of it as well. By nature he was imperious as well as egotistical. Well after he was grown up he would still occasionally strike his servant in moments of anger, and somewhat later, according to his English biographer, Derrick Leon, he felt 'a frequent desire upon the slenderest provocation to slap the faces of those with whom he disagreed'. One does not necessarily get rid of that kind of temperament by undergoing religious conversion, and indeed it is obvious that the illusion of having been reborn may allow one's native vices to flourish more freely than ever, though perhaps in subtler forms. Tolstoy was capable of abjuring physical violence and of seeing what this implies, but he was not capable of tolerance or humility, and even if one knew nothing of his other writings, one could deduce his tendency towards spiritual bullying from this single pamphlet.

However, Tolstoy is not simply trying to rob others of a pleasure he does not share. He is doing that, but his quarrel with Shakespeare goes further. It is the quarrel between the religious and the humanist attitudes towards life. Here one comes back to the central theme of *King Lear,* which Tolstoy does not mention, although he sets forth the plot in some detail.

Lear is one of the minority of Shakespeare's plays that are unmistakably *about* something. As Tolstoy justly complains, much rubbish has been written about Shakespeare as a philosopher, as a psychologist, as a 'great moral teacher', and what not. Shakespeare was not a systematic thinker, his most serious thoughts are uttered irrelevantly or indirectly, and we do not know to what extent he wrote with a 'purpose' or even how much of the work attributed to him was actually written by him. In the Sonnets he never even refers to the plays as part of his achievement, though he does make what seems to be a half-ashamed allusion to his career as an actor. It is perfectly possible that he looked on at least half of his plays as mere pot-boilers and hardly bothered about purpose or probability so long as he could patch up something, usually from stolen material, which would more or less hang together on the stage. However, that is not the whole story. To begin with, as Tolstoy himself points out, Shakespeare has a habit of thrusting uncalled-for general reflections into the mouths of his characters. This is a serious fault in a dramatist but it does not fit in with Tolstoy's picture of Shakespeare as a vulgar hack who has no opinions of his own and merely wishes to produce the greatest effect with the least trouble. And more than this, about a dozen of his plays, written for the most part later than 1600, do unquestionably have a meaning and even a moral. They revolve round a central subject which in some cases can be reduced to a single word. For example, *Macbeth* is about ambition, *Othello* is about jealousy, and *Timon of Athens* is about money. The subject of *Lear* is renunciation, and it is only by being wilfully blind that one can fail to understand what Shakespeare is saying.

Lear renounces his throne but expects everyone to continue treating him as a king. He does not see that if he surrenders power, other people will take advantage of his weakness: also that those who flatter him the most grossly, i.e. Regan and Goneril, are exactly the ones who will turn against him. The moment he finds that he can no longer make people obey him as he did before, he falls into a rage which Tolstoy describes as 'strange and unnatural', but which in fact is perfectly in character. In his madness and despair, he passes through two moods which again are natural enough in his circumstances, though in one of them it is probable that he is being used partly as a mouthpiece for Shakespeare's own opinions. One is the mood of disgust in which Lear repents, as it were, for having been a king, and grasps for the first time the rottenness of formal justice and vulgar morality. The other is a mood of impotent fury in which he wreaks imaginary revenges upon those who have wronged him. 'To have a thousand with red burning spits Come hissing in upon 'em!', and:

It were a delicate stratagem to shoe
A troop of horse with felt: I'll put't in proof;
And when I have stol'n upon these sons-in-law,
Then kill, kill, kill, kill, kill!

Only at the end does he realize, as a sane man, that power, revenge and victory are not worth while:

No, no, no, no! Come, let's away to prison . . .
. . . . and we'll wear out,
In a wall'd prison, packs and sects of great ones
That ebb and flow by the moon.

But by the time he makes this discovery it is too late, for his death and Cordelia's are already decided on. That is the story, and, allowing for some clumsiness in the telling, it is a very good story.

But is it not also curiously similar to the history of Tolstoy himself? There is a general resemblance which one can hardly avoid seeing, because the most impressive event in Tolstoy's life, as in Lear's was a huge and gratuitous act of renunciation. In his old age he renounced his estate, his title and his copyrights, and made an attempt – a sincere attempt, though it was not successful – to escape from his privileged position and live the life of a peasant. But the deeper resemblance lies in the fact that Tolstoy, like Lear, acted on mistaken motives and failed to get the results he had hoped for. According to Tolstoy, the aim of every human being is happiness, and happiness can only be attained by doing the will of God. But doing the will of God means casting off all earthly pleasures and ambitions, and living only for others. Ultimately, therefore, Tolstoy renounced the world under the expectation that this would make him happier. But if there is one thing certain about his later years, it is that he was *not* happy. On the contrary, he was driven almost to the edge of madness by the behaviour of the people about him, who persecuted him precisely *because* of his renunciation. Like Lear, Tolstoy was not humble and not a good judge of character. He was inclined at moments to revert to the attitudes of an aristocrat, in spite of his peasant's blouse, and he even had two children whom he had believed in and who ultimately turned against him – though, of course, in a less sensational manner than Regan and Goneril. His exaggerated revulsion from sexuality was also distinctly similar to Lear's. Tolstoy's remark that marriage is 'slavery, satiety, repulsion' and means putting up with the proximity of 'ugliness, dirtiness, smell, sores', is matched by Lear's well-known outburst:

But to the girdle do the gods inherit,
Beneath is all the fiends;
There's hell, there's darkness, there's the sulphurous pit,
Burning, scalding, stench, consumption, etc etc.

And though Tolstoy could not foresee it when he wrote his essay on Shakespeare, even the ending of his life – the sudden unplanned flight across country, accompanied only by a faithful daughter, the death in a cottage in a strange village – seems to have in it a sort of phantom reminiscence of *Lear*.

Of course, one cannot assume that Tolstoy was aware of this resemblance, or would have admitted it if it had been pointed out to him. But his attitude towards the play must have been influenced by its theme. Renouncing power, giving away your lands, was a subject on which he had reason to feel deeply. Probably, therefore, he would be more angered and disturbed by the moral that Shakespeare draws than he would be in the case of some other play – *Macbeth*, for example – which did not touch so closely on his own life. But what exactly *is* the moral of *Lear*? Evidently there are two morals, one explicit, the other implied in the story.

Shakespeare starts by assuming that to make yourself powerless is to invite an attack. This does not mean that *everyone* will turn against you (Kent and the Fool stand by Lear from first to last), but in all probability *someone* will. If you throw away your weapons, some less scrupulous person will pick them up. If you turn the other cheek, you will get a harder blow on it than you got on the first one. This does not always happen, but it is to be expected, and you ought not to complain if it does happen. The second blow is, so to speak, part of the act of turning the other cheek. First of all, therefore, there is the vulgar, common-sense moral drawn by the Fool: 'Don't relinquish power, don't give away your lands.' But there is also another moral. Shakespeare never utters it in so many words, and it does not very much matter whether he was fully aware of it. It is contained in the story, which, after all, he made up, or altered to suit his purposes. It is: 'Give away your lands if you want to, but don't expect to gain happiness by doing so. Probably you won't gain happiness. If you live for others, you must live *for others*, and not as a roundabout way of getting an advantage for yourself.'

Obviously neither of these conclusions could have been pleasing to Tolstoy. The first of them expresses the ordinary, belly-to-earth selfishness from which he was genuinely trying to escape. The other conflicts with his desire to eat his cake and have it – that is, to destroy his own egoism and by so doing to gain eternal life. Of course, *Lear* is not a sermon in favour of altruism. It merely points out the results of practising self-denial for selfish reasons. Shakespeare had a considerable streak of worldliness in him, and if he had been forced to take sides in his own play, his sympathies would probably have lain with the Fool. But at least he could see the whole issue and treat it at the level of tragedy. Vice is punished, but virtue is not rewarded. The morality of Shakespeare's later tragedies is not religious in the ordinary sense, and certainly is not Christian. Only two of them, *Hamlet* and *Othello*, are supposedly occurring inside the Christian era, and even in those, apart from the antics of the ghost in *Hamlet*, there is no indication of a 'next world' where everything is to be put right. All of these tragedies start out with the humanist assumption that life, although full of sorrow, is worth living, and that Man is a noble animal – a belief which Tolstoy in his old age did not share.

Tolstoy was not a saint, but he tried very hard to make himself into a saint, and the standards he applied to literature were other-worldly ones. It is important to realize that the difference between a saint and an ordinary human being is a difference of kind and not of degree. That is, the one is not to be regarded as an imperfect form of the other. The saint, at any rate Tolstoy's kind of saint, is not trying to work an improvement in earthly life: he is trying to bring it to an end and put something different in its place. One obvious expression of this is the claim that celibacy is 'higher' than marriage. If only, Tolstoy says in effect, we would stop breeding, fighting, struggling and enjoying, if we could get rid not only of our sins but of everything else that binds us to the surface of the earth – including love, in the ordinary sense of caring more for one human being than another – then the whole painful process would be over and the Kingdom of Heaven would arrive. But a normal human being does not want the Kingdom of Heaven: he wants life on earth to continue. This is not solely because he is 'weak', 'sinful' and anxious for a 'good time'. Most people get a fair amount of fun out of their lives, but on balance life is suffering, and only the very young or the very foolish imagine otherwise. Ultimately it is the Christian attitude which is self-interested and hedonistic, since the aim is always to get away from the painful struggle of earthly life and find eternal peace in some kind of Heaven or Nirvana. The humanist attitude is that the struggle must continue and that death is the price of life. 'Men must endure Their going hence, even as their coming hither: Ripeness is all' – which is an un-Christian sentiment. Often there is a seeming truce between the humanist and the religious believer, but in fact their attitudes cannot be reconciled: one must choose between this world and the next. And the enormous majority of human beings, if they understood the issue, would choose this world. They do make that choice when they continue working, breeding and dying instead of crippling their faculties in the hope of obtaining a new lease of existence elsewhere.

We do not know a great deal about Shakespeare's religious beliefs, and from the evidence of his writings it would be difficult to prove that he had any. But at any rate he was not a saint or a would-be saint: he was a human being, and in some ways not a very good one. It is clear, for instance, that he liked to stand well with the rich and powerful, and was capable of flattering them in the most servile way. He is also noticeably cautious, not to say cowardly, in his manner of uttering unpopular opinions. Almost never does he put a subversive or sceptical remark into the mouth of a character likely to be identified with himself. Throughout his plays the acute social critics, the people who are not taken in by accepted fallacies, are buffoons, villains, lunatics or persons who are shamming insanity or are in a state of violent hysteria. *Lear* is a play in which this tendency is particularly well marked. It contains a great deal of veiled social criticism – a point Tolstoy misses – but it is all uttered either by the Fool, by Edgar when he is pretending to be mad, or by Lear during his bouts of madness. In his sane moments Lear hardly ever makes an intelligent remark. And yet the very fact that Shakespeare had to use these subterfuges shows how widely his thoughts ranged. He could not restrain himself from commenting on almost everything, although he put on a series of masks in order to do so. If one has once read Shakespeare with attention, it is not easy to go a day without quoting him, because there are not many subjects of major importance that he does not discuss or at least mention somewhere or other, in his unsystematic but illuminating way. Even the irrelevancies that litter every one of his plays – the puns and riddles, the lists of names, the scraps of reportage like the conversation of the carriers in *Henry IV*, the bawdy jokes, the rescued fragments of forgotten ballads – are merely the products of excessive vitality. Shakespeare was not a philosopher or a scientist, but he did have curiosity: he loved the surface of the earth and the process of life – which, it should be repeated, is *not* the same thing as wanting to have a good time and stay alive as long as possible. Of course, it is not because of the quality of his thought that Shakespeare has survived, and he might not even be remembered as a dramatist if he had not also been a poet. His main hold on us is through language. How deeply Shakespeare himself was fascinated by the music of words can probably be inferred from the speeches of Pistol. What Pistol says is largely meaningless, but if one considers his lines singly they are magnificent rhetorical verse. Evidently, pieces of resounding nonsense ('Let floods o'erswell, and fiends for food howl on', etc.) were constantly appearing in Shakespeare's mind of their own accord, and a half-lunatic character had to be invented to use them up. Tolstoy's native tongue was not English, and one cannot blame him for being unmoved by Shakespeare's verse, nor even, perhaps, for refusing to believe that Shakespeare's skill with words was something out of the ordinary. But he would also have rejected the whole notion of valuing poetry for its texture – valuing it, that is to say, as a kind of music. If it could somehow have been proved to him that his whole explanation of Shakespeare's rise to fame is mistaken, that inside the English-speaking world, at any rate, Shakespeare's popularity is genuine, that his mere skill in placing one syllable beside another has given acute pleasure to generation after generation of English-speaking people – all this would not have been counted as a merit to Shakespeare, but rather the contrary. It would simply have been one more proof of the irreligious, earthbound nature of Shakespeare and his admirers. Tolstoy would have said that poetry is to be judged by its meaning, and that seductive sounds merely cause false meanings to go unnoticed. At every level it is the same issue – this world against the next: and certainly the music of words is something that belongs to this world.

A sort of doubt has always hung round the character of Tolstoy, as round the character of Gandhi. He was not a vulgar hypocrite, as some people declared him to be, and he would probably have imposed even greater sacrifices on himself than he did, if he had not been interfered with at every step by the people surrounding him, especially his wife. But on the other hand it is dangerous to take such men as Tolstoy at their disciples' valuation. There is always the possibility – the probability, indeed – that they have done no more than exchange one form of egoism for another. Tolstoy renounced wealth, fame and privilege; he abjured violence in all its forms and was ready to suffer for doing so; but it is not so easy to believe that he abjured the principle of coercion, or at least the *desire* to coerce others. There are families in which the father will say to his child, 'You'll get a thick ear if you do that again,' while the mother, her eyes brimming over with tears, will take the child in her arms and murmur lovingly, 'Now, darling, *is* it kind to Mummy to do that?' And who would maintain that the second method is less tyrannous than the first? The distinction that really matters is not between violence and non-violence, but between having and not having the appetite for power. There are people who are convinced of the wickedness both of armies and of police forces, but who are nevertheless much more intolerant and inquisitorial in outlook than the normal person who believes that it is necessary to use violence in certain circumstances. They will not say to somebody else, 'Do this, that and the other or you will go to prison,' but they will, if they can, get inside his brain and dictate his thoughts for him in the minutest particulars. Creeds like pacifism and anarchism, which seem on the surface to imply a complete renunciation of power, rather encourage this habit of mind. For if you have embraced a creed which appears to be free from the ordinary dirtiness of politics – a creed from which you yourself cannot expect to draw any material advantage – surely that proves that you are in the right? And the more you are in the right, the more natural that everyone else should be bullied into thinking likewise.

If we are to believe what he says in his pamphlet, Tolstoy had never been able to see any merit in Shakespeare, and was always astonished to find that his fellow writers, Turgenev, Fet and others, thought differently. We may be sure that in his unregenerate days Tolstoy's conclusion would have been: 'You like Shakespeare – I don't. Let's leave it at that.' Later, when his perception that it takes all sorts to make a world had deserted him, he came to think of Shakespeare's writings as something dangerous to himself. The more pleasure people took in Shakespeare, the less they would listen to Tolstoy. Therefore nobody must be *allowed* to enjoy Shakespeare, just as nobody must be allowed to drink alcohol or smoke tobacco. True, Tolstoy would not prevent them by force. He is not demanding that the police shall impound every copy of Shakespeare's works. But he will do dirt on Shakespeare, if he can. He will try to get inside the mind of every lover of Shakespeare and kill his enjoyment by every trick he can think of, including – as I have shown in my summary of his pamphlet – arguments which are self-contradictory or even doubtfully honest.

But finally the most striking thing is how little difference it all makes. As I said earlier, one cannot *answer* Tolstoy's pamphlet, at least on its main counts. There is no argument by which one can defend a poem. It defends itself by surviving, or it is indefensible. And if this test is valid, I think the verdict in Shakespeare's case must be 'not guilty'. Like every other writer, Shakespeare will be forgotten sooner or later, but it is unlikely that a heavier indictment will ever be brought against him. Tolstoy was perhaps the most admired literary man of his age, and he was certainly not its least able pamphleteer. He turned all his powers of denunciation against Shakespeare, like all the guns of a battleship roaring simultaneously. And with what result? Forty years later, Shakespeare is still there, completely unaffected, and of the attempt to demolish him nothing remains except the yellowing pages of a pamphlet which hardly anyone has read, and which would be forgotten altogether if Tolstoy had not also been the author of *War and Peace* and *Anna Karenina*.

Polemic, No. 7, March 1947

Such, Such Were the Joys[1]

ONE

Soon after I arrived at St Cyprian's (not immediately, but after a week or two, just when I seemed to be settling into the routine of school life) I began wetting my bed. I was now aged eight, so that this was a reversion to a habit which I must have grown out of at least four years earlier.

Nowadays, I believe, bed-wetting in such circumstances is taken for granted. It is a normal reaction in children who have been removed from their homes to a strange place. In those days, however, it was looked on as a disgusting crime which the child committed on purpose and for which the proper cure was a

[1] In the version of this piece already published in the United States, St Cyprian's was called 'Crossgates'. Other old boys writing of the school followed Cyril Connolly and called it 'St Wulfric's', the name it was first given in *Enemies of Promise*. The text printed here is of Orwell's original typescript, but the names of his school fellows and the assistant masters have been changed.

beating. For my part I did not need to be told it was a crime. Night after night I prayed, with a fervour never previously attained in my prayers, 'Please God, do not let me wet my bed! Oh, please God, do not let me wet my bed!', but it made remarkably little difference. Some nights the thing happened, others not. There was no volition about it, no consciousness. You did not properly speaking *do* the deed: you merely woke up in the morning and found that the sheets were wringing wet.

After the second or third offence I was warned that I should be beaten next time, but I received the warning in a curiously roundabout way. One afternoon, as we were filing out from tea, Mrs W——, the Headmaster's wife, was sitting at the head of one of the tables, chatting with a lady of whom I knew nothing, except that she was on an afternoon's visit to the school. She was an intimidating, masculine-looking person wearing a riding-habit, or something that I took to be a riding-habit. I was just leaving the room when Mrs W—— called me back, as though to introduce me to the visitor.

Mrs W—— was nicknamed Flip, and I shall call her by that name, for I seldom think of her by any other. (Officially, however, she was addressed as Mum, probably a corruption of the 'Ma'am' used by public schoolboys to their housemasters' wives.) She was a stocky square-built woman with hard red cheeks, a flat top to her head, prominent brows and deep-set, suspicious eyes. Although a great deal of the time she was full of false heartiness, jollying one along with mannish slang ('*Buck* up, old chap!' and so forth), and even using one's Christian name, her eyes never lost their anxious, accusing look. It was very difficult to look her in the face without feeling guilty, even at moments when one was not guilty of anything in particular.

'Here is a little boy,' said Flip, indicating me to the strange lady, 'who wets his bed every night. Do you know what I am going to do if you wet your bed again?' she added, turning to me. 'I am going to get the Sixth Form to beat you.'

The strange lady put on an air of being inexpressibly shocked, and exclaimed 'I-should-*think*-so!' And here there occurred one of these wild, almost lunatic misunderstandings which are part of the daily experience of childhood. The Sixth Form was a group of older boys who were selected as having 'character' and were empowered to beat smaller boys. I had not yet learned of their existence, and I mis-heard the phrase 'the Sixth Form' as 'Mrs Form'. I took it as referring to the strange lady – I thought, that is, that her name was Mrs Form. It was an improbable name, but a child has no judgement in such matters. I imagined, therefore, that it was *she* who was to be deputed to beat me. It did not strike me as strange that this job should be turned over to a casual visitor in no way connected with the school. I merely assumed that 'Mrs Form' was a stern disciplinarian who enjoyed beating people (somehow her appearance seemed to bear this out) and I had an immediate terrifying vision of her arriving for the occasion in full riding kit and armed with a hunting-whip. To this day I can feel myself almost swooning with shame as I stood, a very small, round-faced boy in short corduroy knickers, before the two women. I could not speak. I felt that I should die if 'Mrs Form' were to beat me. But my dominant feeling was not fear or even resentment: it was simply shame because one more person, and that a woman, had been told of my disgusting offence.

A little later, I forget how, I learned that it was not after all 'Mrs Form' who would do the beating. I cannot remember whether it was that very night that I wetted my bed again, but at any rate I did wet it again quite soon. Oh, the despair, the feeling of cruel injustice, after all my prayers and resolutions, at once again waking between the clammy sheets! There was no chance of hiding what I had done. The grim statuesque matron, Margaret by name, arrived in the dormitory specially to inspect my bed. She pulled back the clothes, then drew herself up, and the dreaded words seemed to come rolling out of her like a peal of thunder:

'REPORT YOURSELF to the Headmaster after breakfast!'

I put REPORT YOURSELF in capitals because that was how it appeared in my mind. I do not know how many times I heard that phrase during my early years at St Cyprian's. It was only very rarely that it did not mean a beating. The words always had a portentous sound in my ears, like muffled drums or the words of the death sentence.

When I arrived to report myself, Flip was doing something or other at the long shiny table in the ante-room to the study. Her uneasy eyes searched me as I went past. In the study the Headmaster, nicknamed Sambo, was waiting. Sambo was a round-shouldered, curiously oafish-looking man, not large but shambling in gait, with a chubby face which was like that of an overgrown baby, and which was capable of good humour. He knew, of course, why I had been sent to him, and had already taken a bone-handled riding-crop out of the cupboard, but it was part of the punishment of reporting yourself that you had to proclaim your offence with your own lips. When I had said my say, he read me a short but pompous lecture, then seized me by the scruff of the neck, twisted me over and began beating me with the riding-crop. He had a habit of continuing his lecture while he flogged you, and I remember the words 'you dir-ty lit-tle boy' keeping time with the blows. The beating did not hurt (perhaps as it was the first time, he was not hitting me very hard), and I walked out feeling very much better. The fact that the beating had not hurt was a sort of victory and partially wiped out the shame of the bed-wetting. I was even incautious enough to wear a grin on my face. Some small boys were hanging about in the passage outside the door of the ante-room.

'D'you get the cane?'

'It didn't hurt,' I said proudly.

Flip had heard everything. Instantly her voice came screaming after me:

'Come here! Come here this instant! What was that you said?'

'I said it didn't hurt,' I faltered out.

'How dare you say a thing like that? Do you think that is a proper thing to say? Go in and REPORT YOURSELF AGAIN!'

This time Sambo laid on in real earnest. He continued for a length of time that frightened and astonished me – about five minutes, it seemed – ending up by breaking the riding-crop. The bone handle went flying across the room.

'Look what you've made me do!' he said furiously, holding up the broken crop.

I had fallen into a chair, weakly snivelling. I remember that this was the only time throughout my boyhood when a beating actually reduced me to tears, and curiously enough I was not even now crying because of the pain. The second beating had not hurt very much either. Fright and shame seemed to have anaesthetized me. I was crying partly because I felt that this was expected of me, partly from genuine repentance, but partly also because of a deeper grief which is peculiar to childhood and not easy to convey: a sense of desolate loneliness and helplessness, of being locked up not only in a hostile world but in a world of good and evil where the rules were such that it was actually not possible for me to keep them.

I knew that the bed-wetting was (a) wicked and (b) outside my control. The second fact I was personally aware of, and the first I did not question. It was possible, therefore, to commit a sin without knowing that you committed it, without wanting to commit it, and without being able to avoid it. Sin was not necessarily something that you did: it might be something that happened to you. I do not want to claim that this idea flashed into my mind as a complete novelty at this very moment, under the blows of Sambo's cane: I must have had glimpses of it even before I left home, for my early childhood had not been altogether happy. But at any rate this was the great, abiding lesson of my boyhood: that I was in a world where it was *not possible* for me to be good. And the double beating was a turning-point, for it brought home to me for the first time the harshness of the environment into which I had been flung. Life was more terrible, and I was more wicked, than I had imagined. At any rate, as I sat snivelling on the edge of a chair in Sambo's study, with not even the self-possession to stand up while he stormed at me, I had a conviction of sin and folly and weakness, such as I do not remember to have felt before.

In general, one's memories of any period must necessarily weaken as one moves away from it. One is constantly learning new facts, and old ones have to drop out to make way for them. At twenty I could have written the history of my schooldays with an accuracy which would be quite impossible now. But it can also happen that one's memories grow sharper after a long lapse of time, because one is looking at the past with fresh eyes and can isolate and, as it were, notice facts which previously existed undifferentiated among a mass of others. Here are two things which in a sense I remembered, but which did not strike me as strange or interesting until quite recently. One is that the second beating seemed to me a just and reasonable punishment. To get one beating, and then to get another and far fiercer one on top of it, for being so unwise as to show that the first had not hurt – that was quite natural. The gods are jealous, and when you have good fortune you should conceal it. The other is that I accepted the broken riding-crop as my own crime. I can still recall my feeling as I saw the handle lying on the carpet – the feeling of having done an ill-bred clumsy thing, and ruined an expensive object. *I* had broken it: so Sambo told me, and so I believed. This acceptance of guilt lay unnoticed in my memory for twenty or thirty years.

So much for the episode of the bed-wetting. But there is one more thing to be remarked. This is that I did not wet my bed again – at least, I did wet it once again, and received another beating, after which the trouble stopped. So perhaps this barbarous remedy does work, though at a heavy price, I have no doubt.

TWO

St Cyprian's was an expensive and snobbish school which was in process of becoming more snobbish, and, I imagine, more expensive. The public school with which it had special connections was Harrow, but during my time an increasing proportion of the boys went on to Eton. Most of them were the children of rich parents, but on the whole they were the un-aristocratic rich, the sort of people who live in huge shrubberied houses in Bournemouth or Richmond, and who have cars and butlers but not country estates. There were a few exotics among them – some South American boys, sons of Argentine beef barons, one or two Russians, and even a Siamese prince, or someone who was described as a prince.

Sambo had two great ambitions. One was to attract titled boys to the school, and the other was to train up pupils to win scholarships at public schools, above all at Eton. He did, towards the end of my time, succeed in getting hold of two boys with real English titles. One of them, I remember, was a wretched drivelling little creature, almost an albino, peering upwards out of weak eyes, with a long nose at the end of which a dewdrop always seemed to be trembling. Sambo always gave these boys their titles when mentioning them to a third person, and for their first few days he actually addressed them to their faces as 'Lord So-and-so'. Needless to say he found ways of drawing attention to them when any visitor was being shown round the school. Once, I remember, the little fair-haired boy had a choking fit at dinner, and a stream of snot ran out of his nose on to his plate in a way horrible to see. Any lesser person would have been called a dirty little beast and ordered out of the room instantly: but Sambo and Flip laughed it off in a 'boys will be boys' spirit.

All the very rich boys were more or less undisguisedly favoured. The school still had a faint suggestion of the Victorian 'private academy' with its 'parlour boarders', and when I later read about that kind of school in Thackeray I immediately saw the resemblance. The rich boys had milk and biscuits in the middle of the morning, they were given riding lessons once or twice a week, Flip mothered them and called them by their Christian names, and above all they were never caned. Apart from the South Americans, whose parents were safely distant, I doubt whether Sambo ever caned any boy whose father's income was much above £2,000 a year. But he was sometimes willing to sacrifice financial profit to scholastic prestige. Occasionally, by special arrangement, he would take at greatly reduced fees some boy who seemed likely to win scholarships and thus bring credit on the school. It was on these terms that I was at St Cyprian's myself: otherwise my parents could not have afforded to send me to so expensive a school.

I did not at first understand that I was being taken at reduced fees; it was only when I was about eleven that Flip and Sambo began throwing the fact in my teeth. For my first two or three years I went through the ordinary educational mill: then, soon after I had started Greek (one started Latin at eight, Greek at ten), I moved into the scholarship class, which was taught, so far as classics went, largely by Sambo himself. Over a period of two or three years the scholarship boys were crammed with learning as cynically as a goose is crammed for Christmas. And with what learning! This business of making a gifted boy's career depend on a competitive examination, taken when he is only twelve or thirteen, is an evil thing at best, but there do appear to be preparatory schools which send scholars to Eton, Winchester, etc without teaching them to see everything in terms of marks. At St Cyprian's the whole process was frankly a preparation for a sort of confidence trick. Your job was to learn exactly those things that would give an examiner the impression that you knew more than you did know, and as far as possible to avoid burdening your brain with anything else. Subjects which lacked examination-value, such as geography, were almost completely neglected, mathematics was also neglected if you were a 'classical', science was not taught in any form – indeed it was so despised that even an interest in natural history was discouraged – and even the books you were encouraged to read in your spare time were chosen with one eye on the 'English paper'. Latin and Greek, the main scholarship subjects, were what counted, but even these were deliberately taught in a flashy, unsound way. We never, for example, read right through even a single book of a Greek or Latin author: we merely read short passages which were picked out because they were the kind of thing likely to be set as an 'unseen translation'. During the last year or so before we went up for our scholarships, most of our time was spent in simply working our way through the scholarship papers of previous years. Sambo had sheaves of these in his possession, from every one of the major public schools. But the greatest outrage of all was the teaching of history.

There was in those days a piece of nonsense called the Harrow History Prize, an annual competition for which many preparatory schools entered. It was a tradition for St Cyprian's to win it every year, as well we might, for we had mugged up every paper that had been set since the competition started, and the supply of possible questions was not inexhaustible. They were the kind of stupid question that is answered by rapping out a name or a quotation. Who plundered the Begams? Who was beheaded in an open boat? Who caught the Whigs bathing and ran away with their clothes? Almost all our historical teaching was on this level. History was a series of unrelated, unintelligible but – in some way that was never explained to us – important facts with resounding phrases tied to them. Disraeli brought peace with honour. Clive was astonished at his moderation. Pitt called in the New World to redress the balance of the Old. And the dates, and the mnemonic devices! (Did you know, for example, that the initial letters of 'A black Negress was my aunt: there's her house behind the barn' are also the initial letters of the battles in the Wars of the Roses?) Flip, who 'took' the higher forms in history, revelled in this kind of thing. I recall positive orgies of dates, with the keener boys leaping up and down in their places in their eagerness to shout out the right answers, and at the same time not feeling the faintest interest in the meaning of the mysterious events they were naming.

'1587?'

'Massacre of St Bartholomew!'

'1707?'

'Death of Aurangzeeb!'

'1713?'

'Treaty of Utrecht!'

'1773?'

'Boston Tea Party!'

'1520?'

'Oo, Mum, please, Mum–'

'Please, Mum, please, Mum! Let me tell him, Mum!'

'Well! 1520?'

'Field of the Cloth of Gold!'

And so on.

But history and such secondary subjects were not bad fun. It was in 'classics' that the real strain came. Looking back, I realize that I then worked harder than I have ever done since, and yet at the time it never seemed possible to make quite the effort that was demanded of one. We would sit round the long shiny table, made of some very pale-coloured hard wood, with Sambo goading, threatening, exhorting, sometimes joking, very occasionally praising, but always prodding, prodding away at one's mind to keep it up to the right pitch of concentration, as one might keep a sloppy person awake by sticking pins into him.

'Go on, you little slacker! Go on, you idle, worthless little boy! The whole trouble with you is that you're bone and horn idle. You eat too much, that's why. You wolf down enormous meals, and then when you come here you're half asleep. Go on, now, put your back into it. You're not *thinking*. Your brain doesn't sweat.'

He would tap away at one's skull with his silver pencil, which, in my memory, seems to have been about the size of a banana, and which certainly was heavy enough to raise a bump: or he would pull the short hairs round one's ears, or, occasionally, reach out under the table and kick one's shin. On some days nothing seemed to go right, and then it would be: 'All right, then, I know what you want. You've been asking for it the whole morning. Come along, you useless little slacker. Come into the study.' And then whack, whack, whack, whack, and back one would come, red-wealed and smarting – in later years Sambo had abandoned his riding-crop in favour of a thin rattan cane which hurt very much more – to settle down to work again. This did not happen very often, but I do remember, more than once, being led out of the room in the middle of a Latin sentence, receiving a beating and then going straight ahead with the same sentence, just like that. It is a mistake to think such methods do not work. They work very well for their special purpose. Indeed, I doubt whether classical education ever has been or can be successfully carried on without corporal punishment. The boys themselves believed in its efficacy. There was a boy named Beacham, with no brains to speak of, but evidently in acute need of a scholarship. Sambo was flogging him towards the goal as one might do with a foundered horse. He went up for a scholarship at Uppingham, came back with a consciousness of having done badly, and a day or two later received a severe beating for idleness. 'I wish I'd had that caning before I went up for the exam,' he said sadly – a remark which I felt to be contemptible, but which I perfectly well understood.

The boys of the scholarship class were not all treated alike. If a boy were the son of rich parents to whom the saving of fees was not all-important, Sambo would goad him along in a comparatively fatherly way, with jokes and digs in the ribs and perhaps an occasional tap with the pencil, but no hair-pulling and no caning. It was the poor but 'clever' boys who suffered. Our brains were a gold-mine in which he had sunk money, and the dividends must be squeezed out of us. Long before I had grasped the nature of my financial relationship with Sambo, I had been made to understand that I was not on the same footing as most of the other boys. In effect there were three castes in the school. There was the minority with an aristocratic or millionaire background, there were the children of the ordinary suburban rich, who made up the bulk of the school, and there were a few underlings like myself, the sons of clergymen, Indian civil servants, struggling widows and the like. These poorer ones were discouraged from going in for 'extras' such as shooting and carpentry, and were humiliated over clothes and petty possessions. I never, for instance, succeeded in getting a cricket bat of my own, because 'Your parents wouldn't be able to afford it'. This phrase pursued me throughout my schooldays. At St Cyprian's we were not allowed to keep the money we brought back with us, but had to 'give it in' on the first day of term, and then from time to time were allowed to spend it under supervision. I and similarly-placed boys were always choked off from buying expensive toys like model aeroplanes, even if the necessary money stood to our credit. Flip, in particular, seemed to aim consciously at inculcating a humble outlook in the poorer boys. 'Do you think that's the sort of thing a boy like you should buy?' I remember her saying to somebody – and she said this in front of the whole school: 'You know you're not going to grow up with money, don't you? Your people aren't rich. You must learn to be sensible. Don't get above yourself.' There was also the weekly pocket-money, which we took out in sweets, dispensed by Flip from a large table. The millionaires had sixpence a week, but the normal sum was threepence. I and one or two others were only allowed twopence. My parents had not given instructions to this effect, and the saving of a penny a week could not conceivably have made any difference to them: it was a mark of status. Worse yet was the detail of the birthday cakes. It was usual for each boy, on his birthday, to have a large iced cake with candles, which was shared out at tea between the whole school. It was provided as a matter of routine and went on his parents' bill. I never had such a cake, though my parents would have paid for it readily enough. Year after year, never daring to ask, I would miserably hope that this year a cake would appear. Once or twice I even rashly pretended to my companions that this time I *was* going to have a cake. Then came tea-time, and no cake, which did not make me more popular.

Very early it was impressed upon me that I had no chance of a decent future unless I won a scholarship at a public school. Either I won my scholarship, or I must leave school at fourteen and become, in Sambo's favourite phrase 'a little office boy at forty pounds a year'. In my circumstances it was natural that I should believe this. Indeed, it was universally taken for granted at St Cyprian's that unless you went to a 'good' public school (and only about fifteen schools came under this heading) you were ruined for life. It is not easy to convey to a grown-up person the sense of strain, of nerving oneself for some terrible, all-deciding combat, as the date of the examination crept nearer – eleven years old, twelve years old, then thirteen, the fatal year itself! Over a period of about two years, I do not think there was ever a day when 'the exam', as I called it, was quite out of my waking thoughts. In my prayers it figured invariably: and whenever I got the bigger portion of a wishbone, or picked up a horseshoe, or bowed seven times to the new moon, or succeeded in passing through a wishing-gate without touching the sides, then the wish I earned by doing so went on 'the exam' as a matter of course. And yet curiously enough I was also tormented by an almost irresistible impulse *not* to work. There were days when my heart sickened at the labours ahead of me, and I stood stupid as an animal before the most elementary difficulties. In the holidays, also, I could not work. Some of the scholarship boys received extra tuition from a certain Mr Batchelor, a likeable, very hairy man who wore shaggy suits and lived in a typical bachelor's 'den' – booklined walls, overwhelming stench of tobacco – somewhere in the town. During the holidays Mr Batchelor used to send us extracts from Latin authors to translate, and we were supposed to send back a wad of work once a week. Somehow I could not do it. The empty paper and the black Latin dictionary lying on the table, the consciousness of a plain duty shirked, poisoned my leisure, but somehow I could not start, and by the end of the holidays I would only have sent Mr Batchelor fifty or a hundred lines. Undoubtedly part of the reason was that Sambo and his cane were far away. But in term-time, also, I would go through periods of idleness and stupidity when I would sink deeper and deeper into disgrace and even achieve a sort of feeble, snivelling defiance, fully conscious of my guilt and yet unable or unwilling – I could not be sure which – to do any better. Then Sambo or Flip would send for me, and this time it would not even be a caning.

Flip would search me with her baleful eyes. (What colour were those eyes, I wonder? I remember them as green, but actually no human being has green eyes. Perhaps they were hazel.) She would start off in her peculiar, wheedling, bullying style, which never failed to get right through one's guard and score a hit on one's better nature.

'I don't think it's awfully decent of you to behave like this, is it? Do you think it's quite playing the game by your mother and father to go on idling your time away, week after week, month after month? Do you *want* to throw all your chances away? You know your people aren't rich, don't you? You know they can't afford the same things as other boys' parents. How are they to send you to a public school if you don't win a scholarship? I know how proud your mother is of you. Do you *want* to let her down?'

'I don't think he wants to go to a public school any longer,' Sambo would say, addressing himself to Flip with a pretence that I was not there. 'I think he's given up that idea. He wants to be a little office boy at forty pounds a year.'

The horrible sensation of tears – a swelling in the breast, a tickling behind the nose – would already have assailed me. Flip would bring out her ace of trumps:

'And do you think it's quite fair to *us*, the way you're behaving? After all we've done for you? You *do* know what we've done for you, don't you?' Her eyes would pierce deep into me, and though she never said it straight out, I did know. 'We've had you here all these years – we even had you here for a week in the holidays so that Mr Batchelor could coach you. We don't *want* to have to send you away, you know, but we can't keep a boy here just to eat up our food, term after term. *I* don't think it's very straight, the way you're behaving. Do you?'

I never had any answer except a miserable 'No, Mum', or 'Yes, Mum,' as the case might be. Evidently it was *not* straight, the way I was behaving. And at some point or other the unwanted tear would always force its way out of the corner of my eye, roll down my nose, and splash.

Flip never said in plain words that I was a non-paying pupil, no doubt because vague phrases like 'all we've done for you' had a deeper emotional appeal. Sambo, who did not aspire to be loved by his pupils, put it more brutally, though, as was usual with him, in pompous language. 'You are living on my bounty' was his favourite phrase in this context. At least once I listened to these words between blows of the cane. I must say that these scenes were not frequent, and except on one occasion they did not take place in the presence of other boys. In public I was reminded that I was poor and that my parents 'wouldn't be able to afford' this or that, but I was not actually reminded of my dependent position. It was a final unanswerable argument, to be brought forth like an instrument of torture when my work became exceptionally bad.

To grasp the effect of this kind of thing on a child of ten or twelve, one has to remember that the child has little sense of proportion or probability. A child may be a mass of egoism and rebelliousness, but it has no accumulated experience to give it confidence in its own judgements. On the whole it will accept what it is told, and it will believe in the most fantastic way in the knowledge and powers of the adults surrounding it. Here is an example.

I have said that at St Cyprian's we were not allowed to keep our own money. However, it was possible to hold back a shilling or two, and sometimes I used furtively to buy sweets which I kept hidden in the loose ivy on the playing-field wall. One day when I had been sent on an errand I went into a sweet-shop a mile or more from the school and bought some chocolates. As I came out of the shop I saw on the opposite pavement a small sharp-faced man who seemed to be staring very hard at my school cap. Instantly a horrible fear went through me. There could be no doubt as to who the man was. He was a spy placed there by Sambo! I turned away unconcernedly, and then, as though my legs were doing it of their own accord, broke into a clumsy run. But when I got round the next corner I forced myself to walk again, for to run was a sign of guilt, and obviously there would be other spies posted here and there about the town. All that day and the next I waited for the summons to the study, and was surprised when it did not come. It did not seem to me strange that the headmaster of a private school should dispose of an army of informers, and I did not even imagine that he would have to pay them. I assumed that any adult, inside the school or outside, would collaborate voluntarily in preventing us from breaking the rules. Sambo was all-powerful; it was natural that his agents should be everywhere. When this episode happened I do not think I can have been less than twelve years old.

I hated Sambo and Flip, with a sort of shamefaced, remorseful hatred, but it did not occur to me to doubt their judgement. When they told me that I must either win a public-school scholarship or become an office boy at fourteen, I believed that those were the unavoidable alternatives before me. And above all, I believed Sambo and Flip when they told me they were my benefactors. I see now, of course, that from Sambo's point of view I was a good speculation. He sank money in me, and he looked to get it back in the form of prestige. If I had 'gone off', as promising boys sometimes do, I imagine that he would have got rid of me swiftly. As it was I won him two scholarships when the time came, and no doubt he made full use of them in his prospectuses. But it is difficult for a child to realize that a school is primarily a commercial venture. A child believes that the school exists to educate and that the schoolmaster disciplines him either for his own good, or from a love of bullying. Flip and Sambo had chosen to befriend me, and their friendship included canings, reproaches and humiliations, which were good for me and saved me from an office stool. That was their version, and I believed in it. It was therefore clear that I owed them a vast debt of gratitude. But I was *not* grateful, as I very well knew. On the contrary, I hated both of them. I could not control my subjective feelings, and I could not conceal them from myself. But it is wicked, is it not, to hate your benefactors? So I was taught, and so I believed. A child accepts the codes of behaviour that are presented to it, even when it breaks them. From the age of eight, or even earlier, the consciousness of sin was never far away from me. If I contrived to seem callous and defiant, it was only a thin cover over a mass of shame and dismay. All through my boyhood I had a profound conviction that I was no good, that I was wasting my time, wrecking my talents, behaving with monstrous folly and wickedness and ingratitude – and all this, it seemed, was inescapable, because I lived among laws which were absolute, like the law of gravity, but which it was not possible for me to keep.

THREE

No one can look back on his schooldays and say with truth that they were altogether unhappy.

I have good memories of St Cyprian's among a horde of bad ones. Sometimes on summer afternoons there were wonderful expeditions across the Downs to a village called Birling Gap, or to Beachy Head, where one bathed dangerously among the chalk boulders and came home covered with cuts. And there were still more wonderful mid-summer evenings when, as a special treat, we were not driven off to bed as usual but allowed to wander about the grounds in the long twilight, ending up with a plunge into the swimming bath at about nine o'clock. There was the joy of waking early on summer mornings and getting in an hour's undisturbed reading (Ian Hay, Thackeray, Kipling and H. G. Wells were the favourite authors of my boyhood) in the sunlit, sleeping dormitory. There was also cricket, which I was no good at but with which I conducted a sort of hopeless love affair up to the age of about eighteen. And there was the pleasure of keeping caterpillars – the silky green and purple puss-moth, the ghostly green poplar-hawk, the privet-hawk, large as one's third finger, specimens of which could be illicitly purchased for sixpence at a shop in the town – and, when one could escape long enough from the master who was 'taking the walk', there was the excitement of dredging the dew-ponds on the Downs for enormous newts with orange-coloured bellies. This business of being out for a walk, coming across something of fascinating interest and then being dragged away from it by a yell from the master, like a dog jerked onwards by the leash, is an important feature of school life, and helps to build up the conviction, so strong in many children, that the things you most want to do are always unattainable.

Very occasionally, perhaps once during each summer, it was possible to escape altogether from the barrack-like atmosphere of school, when Brown, the second master, was permitted to take one or two boys for an afternoon of butterfly hunting on a common a few miles away. Brown was a man with white hair and a red face like a strawberry, who was good at natural history, making models and plaster casts, operating magic lanterns, and things of that kind. He and Mr Batchelor were the only adults in any way connected with the school whom I did not either dislike or fear. Once he took me into his room and showed me in confidence a plated, pearl-handled revolver – his 'six-shooter', he called it – which he kept in a box under his bed. And oh, the joy of those occasional expeditions! The ride of two or three miles on a lonely little branch line, the afternoon of charging to and fro with large green nets, the beauty of the enormous dragonflies which hovered over the tops of the grasses, the sinister killing-bottle with its sickly smell, and then tea in the parlour of a pub with large slices of pale-coloured cake! The essence of it was in the railway journey, which seemed to put magic distances between yourself and school.

Flip, characteristically, disapproved of these expeditions, though not actually forbidding them. 'And have you been catching *little butterflies*?' she would say with a vicious sneer when one got back, making her voice as babyish as possible. From her point of view, natural history ('bug-hunting' she would probably have called it) was a babyish pursuit which a boy should be laughed out of as early as possible. Moreover it was somehow faintly plebeian, it was traditionally associated with boys who wore spectacles and were no good at games, it did not help you to pass exams, and above all it smelt of science and therefore seemed to menace classical education. It needed a considerable moral effort to accept Brown's invitation. How I dreaded that sneer of *little butterflies*! Brown, however, who had been at the school since its early days, had built up a certain independence for himself: he seemed able to handle Sambo, and ignored Flip a good deal. If it ever happened that both of them were away, Brown acted as deputy headmaster, and on those occasions, instead of reading the appointed lesson for the day at morning chapel, he would read us stories from the Apocrypha.

Most of the good memories of my childhood, and up to the age of about twenty, are in some way connected with animals. So far as St Cyprian's goes, it also seems, when I look back, that all my good memories are of summer. In winter your nose ran continually, your fingers were too numb to button your shirt (this was an especial misery on Sundays, when we wore Eton collars), and there was the daily nightmare of football – the cold, the mud, the hideous greasy ball that came whizzing at one's face, the gouging knees and trampling boots of the bigger boys. Part of the trouble was that in winter, after the age of about ten, I was seldom in good health, at any rate during term-time. I had defective bronchial tubes and a lesion in one lung which was not discovered till many years later. Hence I not only had a chronic cough, but running was a torment to me. In those days however, 'wheeziness', or 'chestiness', as it was called, was either diagnosed as imagination or was looked on as essentially a moral disorder, caused by overeating. 'You wheeze like a concertina,' Sambo would say disapprovingly as he stood behind my chair; 'You're perpetually stuffing yourself with food, that's why.' My cough was referred to as a 'stomach cough', which made it sound both disgusting and reprehensible. The cure for it was hard running, which, if you kept it up long enough, ultimately 'cleared your chest'.

It is curious, the degree – I will not say of actual hardship, but of squalor and neglect – that was taken for granted in upper-class schools of that period. Almost as in the days of Thackeray, it seemed natural that a little boy of eight or ten should be a miserable, snotty-nosed creature, his face almost permanently dirty, his hands chapped, his nails bitten, his handkerchief a sodden horror, his bottom frequently blue with bruises. It was partly the prospect of actual physical discomfort that made the thought of going back to school lie in one's breast like a lump of lead during the last few days of the holidays. A characteristic memory of St Cyprian's is the astonishing hardness of one's bed on the first night of term. Since this was an expensive school, I took a social step upwards by attending it, and yet the standard of comfort was in every way far lower than in my own home, or, indeed, than it would have been in a prosperous working-class home. One only had a hot bath once a week, for instance. The food was not only bad, it was also insufficient. Never before or since have I seen butter or jam scraped on bread so thinly. I do not think I can be imagining the fact that we were underfed, when I remember the lengths we would go in order to steal food. On a number of occasions I remember creeping down at two or three o'clock in the morning through what seemed like miles of pitch-dark stairways and passages – barefooted, stopping to listen after each step, paralysed with about equal fear of Sambo, ghosts and burglars – to steal stale bread from the pantry. The assistant masters had their meals with us, but they had somewhat better food, and if one got half a chance it was usual to steal left-over scraps of bacon rind or fried potato when their plates were removed.

As usual, I did not see the sound commercial reason for this underfeeding. On the whole I accepted Sambo's view that a boy's appetite is a sort of morbid growth which should be kept in check as much as possible. A maxim often repeated to us at St Cyprian's was that it is healthy to get up from a meal feeling as hungry as when you sat down. Only a generation earlier than this it had been common for school dinners to start off with a slab of unsweetened suet pudding, which, it was frankly said, 'broke the boys' appetites'. But the underfeeding was probably less flagrant at preparatory schools, where a boy was wholly dependent on the official diet, than at public schools, where he was allowed – indeed, expected – to buy extra food for himself. At some schools, he would literally not have had enough to eat unless he had bought regular supplies of eggs, sausages, sardines, etc; and his parents had to allow him money for this purpose. At Eton, for instance, at any rate in College, a boy was given no solid meal after midday dinner. For his afternoon tea he was given only tea and bread and butter, and at eight o'clock he was given a miserable supper of soup or fried fish, or more often bread and cheese, with water to drink. Sambo went down to see his eldest son at Eton and came back in snobbish ecstasies over the luxury in which the boys lived. 'They give them fried fish for supper!' he exclaimed, beaming all over his chubby face. 'There's no school like it in the world.' Fried fish! The habitual supper of the poorest of the working class! At very cheap boarding schools it was no doubt worse. A very early memory of mine is of seeing the boarders at a grammar school – the sons, probably, of farmers and shopkeepers – being fed on boiled lights.

Whoever writes about his childhood must beware of exaggeration and self-pity. I do not want to claim that I was a martyr or that St Cyprian's was a sort of Dotheboys Hall. But I should be falsifying my own memories if I did not record that they are largely memories of disgust. The overcrowded, underfed, underwashed life that we led *was* disgusting, as I recall it. If I shut my eyes and say 'school', it is of course the physical surroundings that first come back to me: the flat playing-field with its cricket pavilion and the little shed by the rifle range, the draughty dormitories, the dusty splintery passages, the square of asphalt in front of the gymnasium, the raw-looking pinewood chapel at the back. And at almost every point some filthy detail obtrudes itself. For example, there were the pewter bowls out of which we had our porridge. They had overhanging rims, and under the rims there were accumulations of sour porridge, which could be flaked off in long strips. The porridge itself, too, contained more lumps, hairs and unexplained black things than one would have thought possible, unless someone were putting them there on purpose. It was never safe to start on that porridge without investigating it first. And there was the slimy water of the plunge bath – it was twelve or fifteen feet long, the whole school was supposed to go into it every morning, and I doubt whether the water was changed at all frequently – and the always-damp towels with their cheesy smell: and, on occasional visits in the winter, the murky sea-water of the local Baths, which came straight in from the beach and on which I once saw floating a human turd. And the sweaty smell of the changing-room with its greasy basins, and, giving on this, the row of filthy, dilapidated lavatories, which had no fastenings of any kind on the doors, so that whenever you were sitting there someone was sure to come crashing in. It is not easy for me to think of my schooldays without seeming to breathe in a whiff of something cold and evil-smelling – a sort of compound of sweaty stockings, dirty towels, faecal smells blowing along corridors, forks with old food between the prongs, neck-of-mutton stew, and the banging doors of the lavatories and the echoing chamber-pots in the dormitories.

It is true that I am by nature not gregarious, the WC and dirty-handkerchief side of life is necessarily more obtrusive when great numbers of human beings are crushed together in a small space. It is just as bad in an army, and worse, no doubt, in a prison. Besides, boyhood is the age of disgust. After one has learned to differentiate, and before one has become hardened – between seven and eighteen, say – one seems always to be walking the tight-rope over a cesspool.

Yet I do not think I exaggerate the squalor of school life, when I remember how health and cleanliness were neglected, in spite of the hoo-ha about fresh air and cold water and keeping in hard training. It was common to remain constipated for days together. Indeed, one was hardly encouraged to keep one's bowels open, since the only aperients tolerated were castor oil or another almost equally horrible drink called liquorice powder. One was supposed to go into the plunge bath every morning, but some boys shirked it for days on end, simply making themselves scarce when the bell sounded, or else slipping along the edge of the bath among the crowd, and then wetting their hair with a little dirty water off the floor. A little boy of eight or nine will not necessarily keep himself clean unless there is someone to see that he does it. There was a new boy named Hazel, a pretty, mother's darling of a boy, who came a little while before I left. The first thing I noticed about him was the beautiful pearly whiteness of his teeth. By the end of that term his teeth were an extraordinary shade of green. During all that time, apparently, no one had taken sufficient interest in him to see that he brushed them.

But of course the differences between home and school were more than physical. That bump on the hard mattress, on the first night of term, used to give me a feeling of abrupt awakening, a feeling of: 'This is reality, this is what you are up against.' Your home might be far from perfect, but at least it was a place ruled by love rather than by fear, where you did not have to be perpetually on your guard against the people surrounding you. At eight years old you were suddenly taken out of this warm nest and flung into a world of force and fraud and secrecy, like a gold-fish into a tank full of pike. Against no matter what degree of bullying you had no redress. You could only have defended yourself by sneaking, which, except in a few rigidly defined circumstances, was the unforgivable sin. To write home and ask your parents to take you away would have been even less thinkable, since to do so would have been to admit yourself unhappy and unpopular, which a boy will never do. Boys are Erewhonians: they think that misfortune is disgraceful and must be concealed at all costs. It might perhaps have been considered permissible to complain to your parents about bad food, or an unjustified caning, or some other ill-treatment inflicted by masters and not by boys. The fact that Sambo never beat the richer boys suggests that such complaints were made occasionally. But in my own peculiar circumstances I could never have asked my parents to intervene on my behalf. Even before I understood about the reduced fees, I grasped that they were in some way under an obligation to Sambo, and therefore could not protect me against him. I have mentioned already that throughout my time at St Cyprian's I never had a cricket bat of my own. I had been told this was because 'your parents couldn't afford it'. One day in the holidays, by some casual remark, it came out that they had provided ten shillings to buy me one: yet no cricket bat appeared. I did not protest to my parents, let alone raise the subject with Sambo. How could I? I was dependent on him, and the ten shillings was merely a fragment of what I owed him. I reailize now, of course, that it is immensely unlikely that Sambo had simply stuck to the money. No doubt the matter had slipped his memory. But the point is that I assumed that he had stuck to it, and that he had a right to do so if he chose.

How difficult it is for a child to have any real independence of attitude could be seen in our behaviour towards Flip. I think it would be true to say that every boy in the school hated and feared her. Yet we all fawned on her in the most abject way, and the top layer of our feelings towards her was a sort of guilt-stricken loyalty. Flip, although the discipline of the school depended more on her than on Sambo, hardly pretended to dispense strict justice. She was frankly capricious. An act which might get you a caning one day might next day be laughed off as a boyish prank, or even commended because it 'showed you had guts'. There were days when everyone cowered before those deep-set, accusing eyes, and there were days when she was like a flirtatious queen surrounded by courtier-lovers, laughing and joking, scattering largesse, or the promise of largesse ('And if you win the Harrow History Prize I'll give you a new case for your camera!'), and occasionally even packing three or four favoured boys into her Ford car and carrying them off to a teashop in town, where they were allowed to buy coffee and cakes. Flip was inextricably mixed up in my mind with Queen Elizabeth, whose relations with Leicester and Essex and Raleigh were intelligible to me from a very early age. A word we all constantly used in speaking of Flip was 'favour'. 'I'm in good favour,' we would say, or 'I'm in bad favour.' Except for the handful of wealthy or titled boys, no one was permanently in good favour, but on the other hand even the outcasts had patches of it from time to time. Thus, although my memories of Flip are mostly hostile, I also remember considerable periods when I basked under her smiles, when she called me 'old chap' and used my Christian name, and allowed me to frequent her private library, where I first made acquaintance with *Vanity Fair*. The high-water mark of good favour was to be invited to serve at table on Sunday nights when Flip and Sambo had guests to dinner. In clearing away, of course, one had a chance to finish off the scraps, but one also got a servile pleasure from standing behind the seated guests and darting deferentially forward when something was wanted. Whenever one had the chance to suck up, one did suck up, and at the first smile one's hatred turned into a sort of cringing love. I was always tremendously proud when I succeeded in making Flip laugh. I have even, at her command, written *vers d'occasion*, comic verses to celebrate memorable events in the life of the school.

I am anxious to make it clear that I was not a rebel, except by force of circumstances. I accepted the codes that I found in being. Once, towards the end of my time, I even sneaked to Brown about a suspected case of homosexuality. I did not know very well what homosexuality was, but I knew that it happened and was bad, and that this was one of the contexts in which it was proper to sneak. Brown told me I was 'a good fellow', which made me feel horribly ashamed. Before Flip one seemed as helpless as a snake before the snake-charmer. She had a hardly-varying vocabulary of praise and abuse, a whole series of set phrases, each of which promptly called forth the appropriate response. There was '*Buck* up, old chap!', which inspired one to paroxysms of energy; there was 'Don't *be* such a fool!' or, 'It's path*et*ic, isn't it?', which made one feel a born idiot; and there was 'It isn't very straight of you, is it?', which always brought one to the brink of tears. And yet all the while, at the middle of one's heart, there seemed to stand an incorruptible inner self who knew that whatever one did – whether one laughed or snivelled or went into frenzies of gratitude for small favours – one's only true feeling was hatred.

FOUR

I had learned early in my career that one can do wrong against one's will, and before long I also learned that one can do wrong without ever discovering what one has done or why it was wrong. There were sins that were too subtle to be explained, and there were others that were too terrible to be clearly mentioned. For example, there was sex, which was always smouldering just under the surface and which suddenly blew up into a tremendous row when I was about twelve.

At some preparatory schools homosexuality is not a problem, but I think that St Cyprian's may have acquired a 'bad tone' thanks to the presence of the South American boys, who would perhaps mature a year or two earlier than an English boy. At that age I was not interested, so I do not actually know what went on, but I imagine it was group masturbation. At any rate, one day the storm suddenly burst over our heads. There were summonses, interrogations, confessions, floggings, repentances, solemn lectures of which one understood nothing except that some irredeemable sin known as 'swinishness' or 'beastliness' had been committed. One of the ringleaders, a boy named Horne, was flogged, according to eye-witnesses, for a quarter of an hour continuously before being expelled. His yells rang through the house. But we were all implicated, more or less, or felt ourselves to be implicated. Guilt seemed to hang in the air like a pall of smoke. A solemn, black-haired imbecile of an assistant master, who was later to be a Member of Parliament, took the older boys to a secluded room and delivered a talk on the Temple of the Body.

'Don't you realize what a wonderful thing your body is?' he said gravely. 'You talk of your motor-car engines, your Rolls-Royces and Daimlers and so on. Don't you understand that no engine ever made is fit to be compared with your body? And then you go and wreck it, ruin it – for life!'

He turned his cavernous black eyes on me and added sadly:

'And you, whom I'd always believed to be quite a decent person after your fashion – you, I hear, are one of the very worst.'

A feeling of doom descended upon me. So I was guilty too. I too had done the dreadful thing, whatever it was, that wrecked you for life, body and soul, and ended in suicide or the lunatic asylum. Till then I had hoped that I was innocent, and the conviction of sin which now took possession of me was perhaps all the stronger because I did not know what I had done. I was not among those who were interrogated and flogged, and it was not until the row was well over that I even learned about the trivial accident that had connected my name with it. Even then I understood nothing. It was not till about two years later that I fully grasped what that lecture on the Temple of the Body had referred to.

At this time I was in an almost sexless state, which is normal, or at any rate common, in boys of that age; I was therefore in the position of simultaneously knowing and not knowing what used to be called the Facts of Life. At five or six, like many children, I had passed through a phase of sexuality. My friends were the plumber's children up the road, and we used sometimes to play games of a vaguely erotic kind. One was called 'playing at doctors', and I remember getting a faint but definitely pleasant thrill from holding a toy trumpet, which was supposed to be a stethoscope, against a little girl's belly. About the same time I fell deeply in love, a far more worshipping kind of love than I have ever felt for anyone since, with a girl named Elsie at the convent school which I attended. She seemed to me grown up, so I suppose she must have been fifteen. After that, as so often happens, all sexual feelings seemed to go out of me for many years. At twelve I knew more than I had known as a young child, but I understood less, because I no longer knew the essential fact that there is something pleasant in sexual activity. Between roughly seven and fourteen, the whole subject seemed to me uninteresting and, when for some reason I was forced to think of it, disgusting. My knowledge of the so-called Facts of Life was derived from animals, and was therefore distorted, and in any case was only intermittent. I knew that animals copulated and that human beings had bodies resembling those of animals: but that human beings also copulated I only knew, as it were, reluctantly, when something, a phrase in the Bible, perhaps, compelled me to remember it. Not having desire, I had no curiosity, and was willing to leave many questions unanswered. Thus, I knew in principle how the baby gets into the woman, but I did not know how it gets out again, because I had never followed the subject up. I knew all the dirty words, and in my bad moments I would repeat them to myself, but I did not know what the worst of them meant, nor want to know. They were abstractly wicked, a sort of verbal charm. While I remained in this state, it was easy for me to remain ignorant of any sexual misdeeds that went on about me, and to be hardly wiser even when the row broke. At most, through the veiled and terrible warnings of Flip, Sambo and all the rest of them, I grasped that the crime of which we were all guilty was somehow connected with the sexual organs. I had noticed, without feeling much interest, that one's penis sometimes stands up of its own accord (this starts happening to a boy long before he has any conscious sexual desires), and I was inclined to believe, or half-believe, that *that* must be the crime. At any rate, it was something to do with the penis – so much I understood. Many other boys, I have no doubt, were equally in the dark.

After the talk on the Temple of the Body (days later, it seems in retrospect: the row seemed to continue for days), a dozen of us were seated at the long shiny table which Sambo used for the scholarship class, under Flip's lowering eye. A long, desolate wail rang out from a room somewhere above. A very small boy named Ronalds, aged no more than about ten, who was implicated in some way, was being flogged, or was recovering from a flogging. At the sound, Flip's eyes searched our faces, and settled upon me.

'*You see*,' she said.

I will not swear that she said 'You see what you have done,' but that was the sense of it. We were all bowed down with shame. It was *our* fault. Somehow or other we had led poor Ronalds astray: *we* were responsible for his agony and his ruin. Then Flip turned upon another boy named Heath. It is thirty years ago, and I cannot remember for certain whether she merely quoted a verse from the Bible, or whether she actually brought out a Bible and made Heath read it; but at any rate the text indicated was: 'Whoso shall offend one of these little ones that believe in me, it were better for him that a millstone were hanged about his neck, and that he were drowned in the depth of the sea.'

That, too, was terrible. Ronalds was one of these little ones, we had offended him; it were better that a millstone were hanged about our necks and that we were drowned in the depth of the sea.

'Have you thought about that, Heath – have you thought what it means?' Flip said. And Heath broke down into snivelling tears.

Another boy, Beacham, whom I have mentioned already, was similarly overwhelmed with shame by the accusation that he 'had black rings round his eyes'.

'Have you looked in the glass lately, Beacham?' said Flip. 'Aren't you ashamed to go about with a face like that? Do you think everyone doesn't know what it means when a boy has black rings round his eyes?'

Once again the load of guilt and fear seemed to settle down upon me. Had *I* got black rings round my eyes? A couple of years later I realized that these were supposed to be a symptom by which masturbators could be detected. But already, without knowing this, I accepted the black rings as a sure sign of depravity, *some* kind of depravity. And many times, even before I grasped the supposed meaning, I have gazed anxiously into the glass, looking for the first hint of that dreaded stigma, the confession which the secret sinner writes upon his own face.

These terrors wore off, or became merely intermittent, without affecting what one might call my official beliefs. It was still true about the madhouse and the suicide's grave, but it was no longer acutely frightening. Some months later it happened that I once again saw Horne, the ringleader who had been flogged and expelled. Horne was one of the outcasts, the son of poor middle-class parents, which was no doubt part of the reason why Sambo had handled him so roughly. The term after his expulsion he went on to Eastbourne College, the small local public school, which was hideously despised at St Cyprian's and looked on as 'not really' a public school at all. Only a very few boys from St Cyprian's went there, and Sambo always spoke of them with a sort of contemptuous pity. You had no chance if you went to a school like that: at the best your destiny would be a clerkship. I though of Horne as a person who at thirteen had already forfeited all hope of any decent future. Physically, morally and socially he was finished. Moreover I assumed that his parents had only sent him to Eastbourne College because after his disgrace no 'good' school would have him.

During the following term, when we were out for a walk, we passed Horne in the street. He looked completely normal. He was a strongly-built, rather good-looking boy with black hair. I immediately noticed that he looked better than when I had last seen him – his complexion, previously rather pale, was pinker and that he did not seem embarrassed at meeting us. Apparently he was not ashamed either of having been expelled, or of being at Eastbourne College. If one could gather anything from the way he looked at us as we filed past, it was that he was glad to have escaped from St Cyprian's. But the encounter made very little impression on me. I drew no inference from the fact that Horne, ruined in body and soul, appeared to be happy and in good health. I still believed in the sexual mythology that had been taught me by Sambo and Flip. The mysterious, terrible dangers were still there. Any morning the black rings might appear round your eyes and you would know that you too were among the lost ones. Only it no longer seemed to matter very much. These contradictions can exist easily in the mind of a child, because of its own vitality. It accepts – how can it do otherwise? – the nonsense that its elders tell it, but its youthful body, and the sweetness of the physical world, tell it another story. It was the same with Hell, which up to the age of about fourteen I officially believed in. Almost certainly Hell existed, and there were occasions when a vivid sermon could scare you into fits. But somehow it never lasted. The fire that waited for you was real fire, it would hurt in the same way as when you burnt your finger, and *for ever*, but most of the time you could contemplate it without bothering.

FIVE

The various codes which were presented to you at St Cyprian's – religious, moral, social and intellectual – contradicted one another if you worked out their implications. The essential conflict was between the tradition of nineteenth-century asceticism and the actually existing luxury and snobbery of the pre-1914 age. On the one side were low-church Bible Christianity, sex puritanism, insistence on hard work, respect for academic distinction, disapproval of self-indulgence: on the other, contempt for 'braininess', and worship of games, contempt for foreigners and the working class, an almost neurotic dread of poverty, and, above all, the assumption not only that money and privilege are the things that matter, but that it is better to inherit them than to have to work for them. Broadly, you were bidden to be at once a Christian and a social success, which is impossible. At the time I did not perceive that the various ideals which were set before us cancelled out. I merely saw that they were all, or nearly all, unattainable, so far as I was concerned, since they all depended not only on what you did but on what you *were*.

Very early, at the age of only ten or eleven, I reached the conclusion – no one told me this, but on the other hand I did not simply make it up out of my own head: somehow it was in the air I breathed – that you were no good unless you had £100,000. I had perhaps fixed on this particular sum as a result of reading Thackeray. The interest on £100,000 would be £4,000 a year (I was in favour of a safe 4 per cent), and this seemed to me the minimum income that you must possess if you were to belong to the real top crust, the people in the country houses. But it was clear that I could never find my way into that paradise, to which you did not really belong unless you were born into it. You could only *make* money, if at all, by a mysterious operation called 'going into the City', and when you came out of the City, having won your £100,000, you were fat and old. But the truly enviable thing about the top-notchers was that they were rich while young. For people like me, the ambitious middle class, the examination-passers, only a bleak, laborious kind of success was possible. You clambered upwards on a ladder of scholarships into the Civil Service or the Indian Civil Service, or possibly you became a barrister. And if at any point you 'slackened' or 'went off' and missed one of the rungs in the ladder, you became 'a little office boy at forty pounds a year'. But even if you climbed to the highest niche that was open to you, you could still only be an underling, a hanger-on of the people who really counted.

Even if I had not learned this from Sambo and Flip, I would have learned it from the other boys. Looking back, it is astonishing how intimately, intelligently snobbish we all were, how knowledgeable about names and addresses, how swift to detect small differences in accents and manners and the cut of clothes. There were some boys who seemed to drip money from their pores even in the bleak misery of the middle of a winter term. At the beginning and end of the term, especially, there was naively snobbish chatter about Switzerland, and Scotland with its ghillies and grouse moors, and 'my uncle's yacht', and 'our place in the country', and 'my pony' and 'my pater's touring car'. There never was, I suppose, in the history of the world a time when the sheer vulgar fatness of wealth, without any kind of aristocratic elegance to redeem it, was so obtrusive as in those years before 1914. It was the age when crazy millionaires in curly top-hats and lavender waistcoats gave champagne parties in rococo house-boats on the Thames, the age of diabolo and hobble skirts, the age of the 'knut' in his grey bowler and cutaway coat, the age of *The Merry Widow*, Saki's novels, *Peter Pan* and *Where the Rainbow Ends*, the age when people talked about chocs and cigs and ripping and topping and heavenly, when they went for divvy week-ends at Brighton and had scrumptious teas at the Troc. From the whole decade before 1914 there seems to breathe forth a smell of the more vulgar, un-grown-up kinds of luxury, a smell of brilliantine and *crème-de-menthe* and soft-centred chocolates – an atmosphere, as it were, of eating everlasting strawberry ices on green lawns to the tune of the Eton Boating Song. The extraordinary thing was the way in which everyone took it for granted that this oozing, bulging wealth of the English upper and upper-middle classes would last for ever, and was part of the order of things. After 1918 it was never quite the same again. Snobbishness and expensive habits came back, certainly, but they were self-conscious and on the defensive. Before the war the worship of money was entirely unreflecting and untroubled by any pang of conscience. The goodness of money was as unmistakable as the goodness of health or beauty, and a glittering car, a title or a horde of servants was mixed up in people's minds with the idea of actual moral virtue.

At St Cyprian's, in term-time, the general bareness of life enforced a certain democracy, but any mention of the holidays, and the consequent competitive swanking about cars and butlers and country houses, promptly called class distinctions into being. The school was pervaded by a curious cult of Scotland, which brought out the fundamental contradiction in our standard of values. Flip claimed Scottish ancestry, and she favoured the Scottish boys, encouraging them to wear kilts in their ancestral tartan instead of the school uniform, and even christened her youngest child by a Gaelic name. Ostensibly we were supposed to admire the Scots because they were 'grim' and 'dour' ('stern' was perhaps the key word), and irresistible on the field of battle. In the big schoolroom there was a steel engraving of the charge of the Scots Greys at Waterloo, all looking as though they enjoyed every moment of it. Our picture of Scotland was made up of burns, braes, kilts, sporrans, claymores, bagpipes and the like, all somehow mixed up with the invigorating effects of porridge, Protestantism and a cold climate. But underlying this was something quite different. The real reason for the cult of Scotland was that only very rich people could spend their summers there. And the pretended belief in Scottish superiority was a cover for the bad conscience of the occupying English, who had pushed the Highland peasantry off their farms to make way for the deer forests, and then compensated them by turning them into servants. Flip's face always beamed with innocent snobbishness when she spoke of Scotland. Occasionally she even attempted a trace of Scottish accent. Scotland was a private paradise which a few initiates could talk about and make outsiders feel small.

'You going to Scotland this hols?'

'Rather! We go every year.'

'My pater's got three miles of river.'

'My pater's giving me a new gun for the twelfth. There's jolly good black game where we go. Get out, Smith! What are you listening for? You've never been in Scotland. I bet you don't know what a blackcock looks like.'

Following on this, imitations of the cry of a blackcock, of the roaring of a stag, of the accent of 'our ghillies', etc etc.

And the questionings that new boys of doubtful social origin were sometimes put through – questionings quite surprising in their mean-minded particularity, when one reflects that the inquisitors were only twelve or thirteen!

'How much a year has your pater got? What part of London do you live in? Is that Knightsbridge or Kensington? How many bathrooms has your house got? How many servants do your people keep? Have you got a butler? Well, then, have you got a cook? Where do you get your clothes made? How many shows did you go to in the hols? How much money did you bring back with you?' etc etc.

I have seen a little new boy, hardly older than eight, desperately lying his way through such a catechism:

'Have your people got a car?'

'Yes.'

'What sort of car?'

'Daimler.'

'How many horse-power?'

(Pause, and leap in the dark.) 'Fifteen.'

'What kind of lights?'

The little boy is bewildered.

'What kind of lights? Electric or acetylene?'

(A longer pause, and another leap in the dark.) 'Acetylene.'

'Coo! He says his pater's car's got acetylene lamps. They went out years ago. It must be as old as the hills.'

'Rot! He's making it up. He hasn't got a car. He's just a navvy. Your pater's a navvy.'

And so on.

By the social standards that prevailed about me, I was no good, and could not be any good. But all the different kinds of virtue seemed to be mysteriously interconnected and to belong to much the same people. It was not only money that mattered: there were also strength, beauty, charm, athleticism and something called 'guts' or 'character', which in reality meant the power to impose your will on others. I did not possess any of these qualities. At games, for instance, I was hopeless. I was a fairly good swimmer and not altogether contemptible at cricket, but these had no prestige value, because boys only attach importance to a game if it requires strength and courage. What counted was football, at which I was a funk. I loathed the game, and since I could see no pleasure or usefulness in it, it was very difficult for me to show courage at it. Football, it seemed to me, is not really played for the pleasure of kicking a ball about, but is a species of fighting. The lovers of football are large, boisterous, nobbly boys who are good at knocking down and trampling on slightly smaller boys. That was the pattern of school life – a continuous triumph of the strong over the weak. Virtue consisted in winning: it consisted in being bigger, stronger, handsomer, richer, more popular, more elegant, more unscrupulous than other people – in dominating them, bullying them, making them suffer pain, making them look foolish, getting the better of them in every way. Life was hierarchical and whatever happened was right. There were the strong, who deserved to win and always did win, and there were the weak, who deserved to lose and always did lose, everlastingly.

I did not question the prevailing standards, because so far as I could see there were no others. How could the rich, the strong, the elegant, the fashionable, the powerful, be in the wrong? It was their world, and the rules they made for it must be the right ones. And yet from a very early age I was aware of the impossibility of any *subjective* conformity. Always at the centre of my heart the inner self seemed to be awake, pointing out the difference between the moral obligation and the psychological *fact*. It was the same in all matters, worldly or other-worldly. Take religion, for instance. You were supposed to love God, and I did not question this. Till the age of about fourteen I believed in God, and believed that the accounts given of him were true. But I was well aware that I did not love him. On the contrary, I hated him, just as I hated Jesus and the Hebrew patriarchs. If I had sympathetic feelings towards any character in the Old Testament, it was towards such people as Cain, Jezebel, Haman, Agag, Sisera: in the New Testament my friends, if any, were Ananias, Caiaphas, Judas and Pontius Pilate. But the whole business of religion seemed to be strewn with psychological impossibilities. The Prayer Book told you, for example, to love God and fear him: but how could you love someone whom you feared? With your private affections it was the same. What you *ought* to feel was usually clear enough, but the appropriate emotion could not be commanded. Obviously it was my duty to feel grateful towards Flip and Sambo; but I was not grateful. It was equally clear that one ought to love one's father, but I knew very well that I merely disliked my own father, whom I had barely seen before I was eight and who appeared to me simply as a gruff-voiced elderly man forever saying 'Don't.' It was not that one did not want to possess the right qualities or feel the correct emotions, but that one could not. The good and the possible never seemed to coincide.

There was a line of verse that I came across not actually while I was at St Cyprian's, but a year or two later, and which seemed to strike a sort of leaden echo in my heart. It was: 'The armies of unalterable law.' I understood to perfection what it meant to be Lucifer, defeated and justly defeated, with no possibility of revenge. The schoolmasters with their canes, the millionaires with their Scottish castles, the athletes with their curly hair – these were the armies of unalterable law. It was not easy, at that date, to realize that in fact it *was* alterable. And according to that law I was damned. I had no money, I was weak, I was ugly, I was unpopular, I had a chronic cough, I was cowardly, I smelt. This picture, I should add, was not altogether fanciful. I was an unattractive boy. St Cyprian's soon made me so, even if I had not been so before. But a child's belief in its own shortcomings is not much influenced by facts. I believed, for example, that I 'smelt', but this was based simply on general probability. It was notorious that disagreeable people smelt, and therefore presumably I did so too. Again, until after I had left school for good I continued to believe that I was preternaturally ugly. It was what my schoolfellows had told me, and I had no other authority to refer to. The conviction that it was *not possible* for me to be a success went deep enough to influence my actions till far into adult life. Until I was about thirty I always planned my life on the assumption not only that any major undertaking was bound to fail, but that I could only expect to live a few years longer.

But this sense of guilt and inevitable failure was balanced by something else: that is, the instinct to survive. Even a creature that is weak, ugly, cowardly, smelly and in no way justifiable still wants to stay alive and be happy after its own fashion. I could not invert the existing scale of values, or turn myself into a success, but I could accept my failure and make the best of it. I could resign myself to being what I was, and then endeavour to survive on those terms.

To survive, or at least to preserve any kind of independence, was essentially criminal, since it meant breaking rules which you yourself recognized. There was a boy named Johnny Hale who for some months oppressed me horribly. He was a big, powerful, coarsely handsome boy with a very red face and curly black hair, who was forever twisting somebody's arm, wringing somebody's ear, flogging somebody with a riding-crop (he was a member of the Sixth Form), or performing prodigies of activity on the football field. Flip loved him (hence the fact that he was habitually called by his Christian name) and

Sambo commended him as a boy who 'had character' and 'could keep order'. He was followed about by a group of toadies who nicknamed him Strong Man.

One day, when we were taking off our overcoats in the changing-room, Hale picked on me for some reason. I 'answered him back', whereupon he gripped my wrist, twisted it round and bent my forearm back upon itself in a hideously painful way. I remember his handsome, jeering red face bearing down upon mine. He was, I think, older than I, besides being enormously stronger. As he let go of me a terrible, wicked resolve formed itself in my heart. I would get back on him by hitting him when he did not expect it. It was a strategic moment, for the master who had been 'taking' the walk would be coming back almost immediately, and then there could be no fight. I let perhaps a minute go by, walked up to Hale with the most harmless air I could assume, and then, getting the weight of my body behind it, smashed my fist into his face. He was flung backwards by the blow, and some blood ran out of his mouth. His always sanguine face turned almost black with rage. Then he turned away to rinse his mouth at the washing-basins.

'*All right!*' he said to me between his teeth as the master led us away.

For days after this he followed me about, challenging me to fight. Although terrified out of my wits, I steadily refused to fight. I said that the blow in the face had served him right, and there was an end of it. Curiously enough he did not simply fall upon me there and then, which public opinion would probably have supported him in doing. So gradually the matter tailed off, and there was no fight.

Now, I had behaved wrongly, by my own code no less than his. To hit him unawares was wrong. But to refuse afterwards to fight knowing that if we fought he would beat me – that was far worse: it was cowardly. If I had refused because I disapproved of fighting, or because I genuinely felt the matter to be closed, it would have been all right; but I had refused merely because I was afraid. Even my revenge was made empty by that fact. I had struck the blow in a moment of mindless violence, deliberately not looking far ahead and merely determined to get my own back for once and damn the consequences. I had had time to realize that what I did was wrong, but it was the kind of crime from which you could get some satisfaction. Now all was nullified. There had been a sort of courage in the first act, but my subsequent cowardice had wiped it out.

The fact I hardly noticed was that though Hale formally challenged me to fight, he did not actually attack me. Indeed, after receiving that one blow he never oppressed me again. It was perhaps twenty years before I saw the significance of this. At the time I could not see beyond the moral dilemma that is presented to the weak in a world governed by the strong: Break the rules, or perish. I did not see that in that case the weak have the right to make a different set of rules for themselves; because, even if such an idea had occurred to me, there was no one in my environment who could have confirmed me in it. I lived in a world of boys, gregarious animals, questioning nothing, accepting the law of the stronger and avenging their own humiliations by passing them down to someone smaller. My situation was that of countless other boys, and if potentially I was more of a rebel than most, it was only because, by boyish standards, I was a poorer specimen. But I never did rebel intellectually, only emotionally. I had nothing to help me except my dumb selfishness, my inability – not, indeed, to despise myself, but to *dislike* myself – my instinct to survive.

It was about a year after I hit Johnny Hale in the face that I left St Cyprian's for ever. It was the end of a winter term. With a sense of coming out from darkness into sunlight I put on my Old Boy's tie as we dressed for the journey. I well remember the feeling of that brand-new silk tie round my neck, a feeling of emancipation, as though the tie had been at once a badge of manhood and an amulet against Flip's voice and Sambo's cane. I was escaping from bondage. It was not that I expected, or even intended, to be any more successful at a public school that I had been at St Cyprian's. But still, I was escaping. I knew that at a public school there would be more privacy, more neglect, more chance to be idle and self-indulgent and degenerate. For years past I had been resolved – unconsciously at first, but consciously later on – that when once my scholarship was won I would 'slack off' and cram no longer. This resolve, by the way, was so fully carried out that between the ages of thirteen and twenty-two or three I hardly ever did a stroke of avoidable work.

Flip shook hands to say good-bye. She even gave me my Christian name for the occasion. But there was a sort of patronage, almost a sneer, in her face and in her voice. The tone in which she said goodbye was nearly the tone in which she had been used to say *little butterflies*. I had won two scholarships, but I was a failure, because success was measured not by what you did but by what you *were*. I was 'not a good type of boy' and could bring no credit on the school. I did not possess character or courage or health or strength or money, or even good manners, the power to look like a gentleman.

'Good-bye,' Flip's parting smile seemed to say; 'it's not worth quarrelling now. You haven't made much of a success of your time at St Cyprian's, have you? And I don't suppose you'll get on awfully well at a public school either. We made a mistake, really, in wasting our time and money on you. This kind of education hasn't much to offer to a boy with your background and your outlook. Oh, don't think we don't understand you! We know all about those ideas you have at the back of your head, we know you disbelieve in everything we've taught you, and we know you aren't in the least grateful for all we've done for you. But there's no use in bringing it all up now. We aren't responsible for you any longer, and we shan't be seeing you again. Let's just admit that you're one of our failures and part without ill-feeling. And so, good-bye.'

That at least was what I read into her face. And yet how happy I was, that winter morning, as the train bore me away with the gleaming new silk tie (dark green, pale blue and black, if I remember rightly) round my neck! The world was opening before me, just a little, like a grey sky which exhibits a narrow crack of blue. A public school would be better fun than St Cyprian's, but at bottom equally alien. In a world where the prime necessities were money, titled relatives, athleticism, tailor-made clothes, neatly-brushed hair, a charming smile, I was no good. All I had gained was a breathing-space. A little quietude, a little self-indulgence, a little respite from cramming – and then, ruin. What kind of ruin I did not know: perhaps the colonies or an office stool, perhaps prison or an early death. But first a year or two in which one could 'slack off' and get the benefit of one's sins, like Doctor Faustus. I believed firmly in my evil destiny, and yet I was acutely happy. It is the advantage of being thirteen that you can not only live in the moment, but do so with full consciousness, foreseeing the future and yet not caring about it. Next term I was going to Wellington. I had also won a scholarship at Eton, but it was uncertain whether there would be a vacancy, and I was going to Wellington first. At Eton you had a room to yourself – a room which might even have a fire in it. At Wellington you had your own cubicle, and could make yourself cocoa in the evenings. The privacy of it, the grown-upness! And there would be libraries to hang about in, and summer afternoons when you could shirk games and mooch about the countryside alone, with no master driving you along. Meanwhile there were the holidays. There was the ·22 rifle that I had bought the previous holidays (the Crackshot, it was called, costing twety-two and sixpence), and Christmas was coming next week. There were also the pleasures of overeating. I thought of some particularly voluptuous cream buns which could be bought for twopence each at a shop in our town. (This was 1916, and food-rationing had not yet started.) Even the detail that my journey-money had been slightly miscalculated, leaving about a shilling over – enough for an unforeseen cup of coffee and a cake or two somewhere on the way – was enough to fill me with bliss. There was time for a bit of happiness before the future closed in upon me. But I did know that the future was dark. Failure, failure, failure – failure behind me, failure ahead of me – that was by far the deepest conviction that I carried away.

SIX

All this was thirty years ago and more. The question is: Does a child at school go through the same kind of experiences nowadays?

The only honest answer, I believe, is that we do not with certainty know. Of course it is obvious that the present-day *attitude* towards education is enormously more humane and sensible than that of the past. The snobbishness that was an integral part of my own education would be almost unthinkable today, because the society that nourished it is dead. I recall a conversation that must have taken place about a year before I left St Cyprian's. A Russian boy, large and fair-haired, a year older than myself, was questioning me.

'How much a year has your father got?'

I told him what I thought it was, adding a few hundreds to make it sound better. The Russian boy, neat in his habits, produced a pencil and a small notebook and made a calculation.

'My father has over two hundred times as much money as yours,' he announced with a sort of amused contempt.

That was in 1915. What happened to that money a couple of years later, I wonder? And still more I wonder, do conversations of that kind happen at preparatory schools now?

Clearly there has been a vast change of outlook, a general growth of 'enlightenment', even among ordinary, unthinking middle-class people. Religious belief, for instance, has largely vanished, dragging other kinds of nonsense after it. I imagine that very few people nowadays would tell a child that if it masturbates it will end in the lunatic asylum. Beating, too, has become discredited, and has even been abandoned at many schools. Nor is the underfeeding of children looked on as a normal, meritorious act. No one now would openly set out to give his pupils as little food as they could do with, or tell them that it is healthy to get up from a meal as hungry as you sat down. The whole status of children has improved, partly because they have grown relatively less numerous. And the diffusion of even a little psychological knowledge has made it harder for parents and schoolteachers to indulge their aberrations in the name of discipline. Here is a case, not known to me personally, but known to someone I can vouch for, and happening within my own lifetime. A small girl, daughter of a clergyman, continued wetting her bed at an age when she should have grown out of it. In order to punish her for this dreadful deed, her father took her to a large garden party and there introduced her to the whole company as a little girl who wetted her bed: and to underline her wickedness he had previously painted her face black. I do not suggest that Flip and Sambo would actually have done a thing like this, but I doubt whether it would have much surprised them. After all, things do change. And yet –!

The question is not whether boys are still buckled into Eton collars on Sunday, or told that babies are dug up under gooseberry bushes. That kind of thing is at an end, admittedly. The real question is whether it is still normal for a schoolchild to live for years amid irrational terrors and lunatic misunderstandings. And here one is up against the very great difficulty of knowing what a child really feels and thinks. A child which appears reasonably happy may actually be suffering horrors which it cannot or will not reveal. It lives in a sort of alien under-water world which we can only penetrate by memory or divination. Our chief clue is the fact that we were once children ourselves, and many people appear to forget the atmosphere of their own childhood almost entirely. Think for instance of the unnecessary torments that people will inflict by sending a child back to school with clothes of the wrong pattern, and refusing to see that this matters! Over things of this kind a child will sometimes utter a protest, but a great deal of the time its attitude is one of simple concealment. Not to expose your true feelings to an adult seems to be instinctive from the age of seven or eight onwards. Even the affection that one feels for a child, the desire to protect and cherish it, is a cause of misunderstanding. One can love a child, perhaps, more deeply than one can love another adult, but it is rash to assume that the child feels any love in return. Looking back on my own childhood, after the infant years were over, I do not believe that I ever felt love for any mature person, except my mother, and even her I did not trust, in the sense that shyness made me conceal most of my real feelings from her. Love, the spontaneous, unqualified emotion of love, was something I could only feel for people who were young. Towards people who were old – and remember that 'old' to a child means over thirty, or even over twenty-five – I could feel reverence, respect, admiration or compunction, but I seemed cut off from them by a veil of fear and shyness mixed up with physical distaste. People are too ready to forget the child's *physical* shrinking from the adult. The enormous size of grown-ups, their ungainly, rigid bodies, their coarse, wrinkled skins, their great relaxed eyelids, their yellow teeth, and the whiffs of musty clothes and beer and sweat and tobacco that disengage from them at every movement! Part of the reason for the ugliness of adults, in a child's eyes, is that the child is usually looking upwards, and few faces are at their best when seen from below. Besides, being fresh and unmarked itself, the child has impossibly high standards in the matter of skin and teeth and complexion. But the greatest barrier of all is the child's misconception about age. A child can hardly envisage life beyond thirty, and in judging people's ages it will make fantastic mistakes. It will think that a person of twenty-five is forty, that a person of forty is sixty-five, and so on. Thus, when I fell in love with Elsie I took her to be grown-up. I met her again, when I was thirteen and she, I think, must have been twenty-three; she now seemed to me a middle-aged woman, somewhat past her best. And the child thinks of growing old as an almost obscene calamity, which for some mysterious reason will never happen to itself. All who have passed the age of thirty are joyless grotesques, endlessly fussing about things of no importance and staying alive without, so far as the child can see, having anything to live for. Only child life is real life. The schoolmaster who imagines that he is loved and trusted by his boys is in fact mimicked and laughed at behind his back. An adult who does not seem dangerous nearly always seems ridiculous.

I base these generalizations on what I can recall of my own childhood outlook. Treacherous though memory is, it seems to me the chief means we have of discovering how a child's mind works. Only by resurrecting our own memories can we realize how incredibly distorted is the child's vision of the world. Consider this, for example. How would St Cyprian's appear to me now, if I could go back, at my present age, and see it as it was in 1915? What should I think of Sambo and Flip, those terrible, all-powerful monsters? I should see them as a couple of silly, shallow, ineffectual people, eagerly clambering up a social ladder which any thinking person could see to be on the point of collapse. I would no more be frightened of them than I would be frightened of a dormouse. Moreover, in those days they seemed to me fantastically old, whereas – though of this I am not certain – I imagine they must have been somewhat younger than I am now. And how would Johnny Hale appear, with his blacksmith's arms and his red, jeering face? Merely a scruffy little boy, barely distinguishable from hundreds of other scruffy little boys. The two sets of facts can lie side by side in my mind, because those happen to be my own memories. But it would be very difficult for me to see with the eyes of any other child, except by an effort of the imagination which might lead me completely astray. The child and the adult live in different worlds. If that is so, we cannot be certain that school, at any rate boarding school, is not still for many children as dreadful an experience as it used to be. Take away God, Latin, the cane, class distinctions and sexual taboos, and the fear, the hatred, the snobbery and the misunderstanding might still all be there. It will have been seen that my own main trouble was an utter lack of any sense of proportion or probability. This led me to accept outrages and believe absurdities, and to suffer torments over things which were in fact of no importance. It is not enough to say that I was 'silly' and 'ought to have known better'. Look back into your own childhood and think of the nonsense you used to believe and the trivialities which could make you suffer. Of course my own case had its individual variations, but essentially it was that of countless other boys. The weakness of the child is that it starts with a blank sheet. It neither understands nor questions the society in which it lives, and because of its credulity other people can work upon it, infecting it with the sense of inferiority and the dread of offending against mysterious, terrible laws. It may be that everything that happened to me at St Cyprian's could happen in the most 'enlightened' school, though perhaps in subtler forms. Of one thing, however, I do feel fairly sure, and that is that boarding schools are worse than day schools. A child has a better chance with the sanctuary of its home near at hand. And I think the characteristic faults of the English upper and middle classes may be partly due the the practice, general until recently, of sending children away from home as young as nine, eight or even seven.

I have never been back to St Cyprian's. Reunions, old boys' dinners and such-like leave me something more than cold, even when my memories are friendly. I have never even been down to Eton, where I was relatively happy, though I did once pass through it in 1933 and noted with interest that nothing seemed to have changed, except that the shops now sold radios. As for St Cyprian's, for years I loathed its very name so deeply that I could not view it with enough detachment to see the significance of the things that happened to me there. In a way, it is only within the last decade that I have really thought over my schooldays, vividly though their memory has always haunted me. Nowadays, I believe, it would make very little impression on me to see the place again, if it still exists. (I remember hearing a rumour some years ago that it had been burnt down.) If I had to pass through Eastbourne I would not make a detour to avoid the school: and if I happened to pass the school itself I might even stop for a moment by the low brick wall, with the steep bank running down from it, and look across the flat playing field at the ugly building with the square of asphalt in front of it. And if I went inside and smelt again the inky, dusty smell of the big schoolroom, the rosiny smell of the chapel, the stagnant smell of the swimming bath and the cold reek of the lavatories, I think I should only feel what one invariably feels in revisiting any scene of childhood: How small everything has grown, and how terrible is the deterioration in myself! But it is a fact that for many years I could hardly have borne to look at it again. Except upon dire necessity I would not have set foot in Eastbourne. I even conceived a prejudice against Sussex, as the county that contained St Cyprian's, and as an adult I have only once been in Sussex, on a short visit. Now, however, the place is out of my system for good. Its magic works no longer, and I have not even enough animosity left to make me hope that Flip and Sambo are dead or that the story of the school being burnt down was true.

Written by May 1947

Writers and Leviathan

The position of the writer in an age of State control is a subject that has already been fairly largely discussed, although most of the evidence that might be relevant is not yet available. In this place I do not want to express an opinion either for or against State patronage of the arts, but merely to point out that *what kind* of State rules over us must depend partly on the prevailing intellectual atmosphere: meaning, in this context, partly on the attitude of writers and artists themselves, and on their willingness or otherwise to keep the spirit of liberalism alive. If we find ourselves in ten years' time cringing before somebody like Zhdanov, it will probably be because that is what we have deserved. Obviously there are strong tendencies towards totalitarianism at work within the English literary intelligentsia already. But here I am not concerned with any organized and conscious movement such as Communism, but merely with the effect, on people of goodwill, of political thinking and the need to take sides politically.

This is a political age. War, Fascism, concentration camps, rubber truncheons, atomic bombs, etc are what we daily think about, and therefore to a great extent what we write about, even when we do not name them openly. We cannot help this. When you are on a sinking ship, your thoughts will be about sinking ships. But not only is our subject-matter narrowed, but our whole attitude towards literature is coloured by loyalties which we at least intermittently realize to be non-literary. I often have the feeling that even at the best of times literary criticism is fraudulent, since in the absence of any accepted standards whatever – any *external* reference which can give meaning to the statement that such and such a book is 'good' or 'bad' – every literary judgement consists in trumping up a set of rules to justify an instinctive preference. One's real reaction to a book, when one has a reaction at all, is usually 'I like this book' or 'I don't like it', and what follows is a rationalization. But 'I like this book' is not, I think, a non-literary reaction; the non-literary reaction is 'This book is on my side, and therefore I must discover merits in it.' Of course, when one praises a book for political reasons one may be emotionally sincere, in the sense that one does feel strong approval of it, but also it often happens that party solidarity demands a plain lie. Anyone used to reviewing books for political periodicals is well aware of this. In general, if you are writing for a paper that you are in agreement with, you sin by commission, and if for a paper of the opposite stamp, by omission. At any rate, innumerable controversial books – books for or against Soviet Russia, for or against Zionism, for or against the Catholic Church, etc – are judged before they are read, and in effect before they are written. One knows in advance what reception they will get in what papers. And yet, with a dishonesty that sometimes is not even quarter-conscious, the pretence is kept up that genuinely literary standards are being applied.

Of course, the invasion of literature by politics was bound to happen. It must have happened, even if the special problem of totalitarianism had never arisen, because we have developed a sort of compunction which our grandparents did not have, an awareness of the enormous injustice and misery of the world, and a guilt-stricken feeling that one ought to be doing something about it, which makes a purely aesthetic attitude towards life impossible. No one, now, could devote himself to literature as single-mindedly as Joyce or Henry James. But unfortunately, to accept political responsibility now means yielding oneself over to orthodoxies and 'party lines', with all the timidity and dishonesty that that implies. As against the Victorian writers, we have the disadvantage of living among clear-cut political ideologies and of usually knowing at a glance what thoughts are heretical. A modern literary intellectual lives and writes in constant dread – not, indeed, of public opinion in the wider sense, but of public opinion within his own group. As a rule, luckily, there is more than one group, but also at any given moment there is a dominant orthodoxy, to offend against which needs a thick skin and sometimes means cutting one's income in half for years on end. Obviously, for about fifteen years past, the dominant orthodoxy, especially among the young, has been 'left'. The key words are 'progressive', 'democratic' and 'revolutionary', while the labels which you must at all costs avoid having gummed upon you are 'bourgeois', 'reactionary' and 'Fascist'. Almost everyone nowadays, even the majority of Catholics and Conservatives, is 'progressive', or at least wishes to be thought so. No one, so far as I know, ever describes himself as a 'bourgeois', just as no one literate enough to have heard the word ever admits to being guilty of antisemitism. We are all of us good democrats, anti-Fascists, anti-imperialist, contemptuous of class distinctions, impervious to colour prejudice, and so on and so forth. Nor is there much doubt that the present-day 'left' orthodoxy is better than the rather snobbish, pietistic Conservative orthodoxy which prevailed twenty years ago, when the *Criterion* and (on a lower level) the *London Mercury* were the dominant literary magazines. For at the least its implied objective is a viable form of society which large numbers of people actually want. But it also has its own falsities which, because they cannot be admitted, make it impossible for certain questions to be seriously discussed.

The whole left-wing ideology, scientific and Utopian, was evolved by people who had no immediate prospect of attaining power. It was, therefore, an extremist ideology, utterly contemptuous of kings, governments, laws, prisons, police forces, armies, flags, frontiers, patriotism, religion, conventional morality, and, in fact, the whole existing scheme of things. Until well within living memory the forces of the Left in all countries were fighting against a tyranny which appeared to be invincible, and it was easy to assume that if only *that* particular tyranny – capitalism – could be overthrown, Socialism would follow. Moreover, the Left has inherited from Liberalism certain distinctly questionable beliefs, such as the belief that the truth will prevail and persecution defeats itself, or that man is naturally good and is only corrupted by his environment. This perfectionist ideology has persisted in nearly all of us, and it is in the name of it that we protest when (for instance) a Labour government votes huge incomes to the King's daughters or shows hesitation about nationalizing steel. But we have also accumulated in our minds a whole series of unadmitted contradictions, as a result of successive bumps against reality.

The first big bump was the Russian Revolution. For somewhat complex reasons, nearly the whole of the English Left has been driven to accept the Russian régime as 'Socialist', while silently recognizing that its spirit and practice are quite alien to anything that is meant by 'Socialism' in this country. Hence there has arisen a sort of schizophrenic manner of thinking, in which words like 'democracy' can bear two irreconcilable meanings, and such things as concentration camps and mass deportations can be right and wrong simultaneously. The next blow to the left-wing ideology was the rise of Fascism, which shook the pacifism and internationalism of the Left without bringing about a definite restatement of doctrine. The experience of German occupation taught the European peoples something that the colonial peoples knew already, namely, that class antagonisms are not all-important and that there is such a thing as national interest. After Hitler it was difficult to maintain seriously that 'the enemy is in your own country' and that national independence is of no value. But though we all know this and act upon it when necessary, we still feel that to say it aloud would be a kind of treachery. And finally, the greatest difficulty of all, there is the fact that the Left is now in power and is obliged to take responsibility and make genuine decisions.

Left governments almost invariably disappoint their supporters because, even when the prosperity which they have promised is achievable, there is always need of an uncomfortable transition period about which little has been said beforehand. At this moment we see our own Government, in its desperate economic straits, fighting in effect against its own past propaganda. The crisis that we are now in is not a sudden unexpected calamity, like an earthquake, and it was not caused by the war, but merely hastened by it. Decades ago it could be foreseen that something of this kind was going to happen. Ever since the nineteenth century our national income, dependent partly on interest from foreign investments, and on assured markets and cheap raw materials in colonial countries, had been extremely precarious. It was certain that, sooner or later, something would go wrong and we should be forced to make our exports balance our imports: and when that happened the British standard of living, including the working-class standard, was bound to fall, at least temporarily. Yet the left-wing parties, even when they were vociferously anti-imperialist, never made these facts clear. On occasion they were ready to admit that the British workers had benefited, to some extent, by the looting of Asia and Africa, but they always allowed it to appear that we could give up our loot and yet in some way contrive to remain prosperous. Quite largely, indeed, the workers were won over to Socialism by being told that they were exploited, whereas the brute truth was that, in world terms, they were exploiters. Now, to all appearances, the point has been reached when the working-class living-standard *cannot* be maintained, let alone raised. Even if we squeeze the rich out of existence, the mass of the people must either consume less or produce more. Or am I exaggerating the mess we are in? I may be, and I should be glad to find myself mistaken. But the point I wish to make is that this question, among people who are faithful to the Left ideology, cannot be genuinely discussed. The lowering of wages and raising of working hours are felt to be inherently anti-Socialist measures, and must therefore be dismissed in advance, whatever the economic situation may be. To suggest that they may be unavoidable is merely to risk being plastered with those labels that we are all terrified of. It is far safer to evade the issue and pretend that we can put everything right by redistributing the existing national income.

To accept an orthodoxy is always to inherit unresolved contradictions. Take for instance the fact that all sensitive people are revolted by industrialism and its products, and yet are aware that the conquest of poverty and the emancipation of the working class demand not less industrialization, but more and more. Or take the fact that certain jobs are absolutely necessary and yet are never done except under some kind of coercion. Or take the fact that it is impossible to have a positive foreign policy without having powerful armed forces. One could multiply examples. In every such case there is a conclusion which is perfectly plain but which can only be drawn if one is privately disloyal to the official ideology. The normal response is to push the question, unanswered, into a corner of one's mind, and then continue repeating contradictory catchwords. One does not have to search far through the reviews and magazines to discover the effects of this kind of thinking.

I am not, of course, suggesting that mental dishonesty is peculiar to Socialists and left-wingers generally, or is commonest among them. It is merely that acceptance of *any* political discipline seems to be incompatible with literary integrity. This applies equally to movements like Pacifism and Personalism, which claim to be outside the ordinary political struggle. Indeed, the mere sound of words ending in -ism seems to bring with it the smell of propaganda. Group loyalties are necessary, and yet they are poisonous to literature, so long as literature is the product of individuals. As soon as they are allowed to have any influence, even a negative one, on creative writing, the result is not only falsification, but often the actual drying-up of the inventive faculties.

Well, then what? Do we have to conclude that it is the duty of every writer to 'keep out of politics'? Certainly not! In any case, as I have said already, no thinking person can or does genuinely keep out of politics, in an age like the present one. I only suggest that we should draw a sharper distinction than we do at present between our political and our literary loyalties, and should recognize that a willingness to *do* certain distasteful but necessary things does not carry with it any obligation to swallow the beliefs that usually go with them. When a writer engages in politics he should do so as a citizen, as a human being, but not *as a writer*. I do not think that he has the right, merely on the score of his sensibilities, to shirk the ordinary dirty work of politics. Just as much as anyone else, he should be prepared to deliver lectures in draughty halls, to chalk pavements, to canvass voters, to distribute leaflets, even to fight in civil wars if it seems necessary. But whatever else he does in the service of his party, he should never write for it. He should make it clear that his writing is a thing apart. And he should be able to act co-operatively while, if he chooses, completely rejecting the official ideology. He should never turn back from a train of thought because it may lead to a heresy, and he should not mind very much if his unorthodoxy is smelt out, as it probably will be. Perhaps it is even a bad sign in a writer if he is not suspected of reactionary tendencies today, just as it was a bad sign if he was not suspected of Communist sympathies twenty years ago.

But does all this mean that a writer should not refuse to be dictated to by political bosses, but also that he should refrain from writing *about* politics? Once again, certainly not! There is no reason why he should not write in the most crudely political way, if he wishes to. Only he should do so as an individual, an outsider, at the most an unwelcome guerrilla on the flank of a regular army. This attitude is quite compatible with ordinary political usefulness. It is reasonable, for example, to be willing to fight in a war because one thinks the war ought to be won, and at the same time to refuse to write war propaganda. Sometimes, if a writer is honest, his writings and his political activities may actually contradict one another. There are occasions when that is plainly undesirable: but then the remedy is not to falsify one's impulses, but to remain silent.

To suggest that a creative writer, in a time of conflict, must split his life into two compartments, may seem defeatist or frivolous: yet in practice I do not see what else he can do. To lock yourself up in an ivory tower is impossible and undesirable. To yield subjectively, not merely to a party machine, but even to a group ideology, is to destroy yourself as a writer. We feel this dilemma to be a painful one, because we see the need of engaging in politics while also seeing what a dirty, degrading business it is. And most of us still have a lingering belief that every choice, even every political choice, is between good and evil, and that if a thing is necessary it is also right. We should, I think, get rid of this belief, which belongs to the nursery. In politics one can never do more than decide which of two evils is the lesser, and there are some situations from which one can only escape by acting like a devil or a lunatic. War, for example, may be necessary, but it is certainly not right or sane. Even a General Election is not exactly a pleasant or edifying spectacle. If you have to take part in such things – and I think you do have to, unless you are armoured by old age or stupidity or hypocrisy – then you also have to keep part of yourself inviolate. For most people the problem does not arise in the same form, because their lives are split already. They are truly alive only in their leisure hours, and there is no emotional connection between their work and their political activities. Nor are they generally asked, in the name of political loyalty, to debase themselves as workers. The artist, and especially the writer, is asked just that – in fact, it is the only thing that politicians ever ask of him. If he refuses, that does not mean that he is condemned to inactivity. One half of him, which in a sense is the whole of him, can act as resolutely, even as violently if need be, as anyone else. But his writings, in so far as they have any value, will always be the product of the saner self that stands aside, records the things that are done and admits their necessity, but refuses to be deceived as to their true nature.

Written [March] 1948

Reflections on Gandhi

Saints should always be judged guilty until they are proved innocent, but the tests that have to be applied to them are not, of course, the same in all cases. In Gandhi's case the questions one feels inclined to ask are: to what extent was Gandhi moved by vanity – by the consciousness of himself as a humble, naked old man, sitting on a praying-mat and shaking empires by sheer spiritual power – and to what extent did he compromise his own principles by entering into politics, which of their nature are inseparable from coercion and fraud? To give a definite answer one would have to study Gandhi's acts and writings in immense detail, for his whole life was a sort of pilgrimage in which every act was significant. But this partial autobiography, which ends in the nineteen-twenties, is strong evidence in his favour, all the more because it covers what he would have called the unregenerate part of his life and reminds one that inside the saint, or near-saint, there was a very shrewd, able person who could, if he had chosen, have been a brilliant success as a lawyer, an administrator or perhaps even a businessman.

At about the time when the autobiography[1] first appeared I remember reading its opening chapters in the ill-printed pages of some Indian newspaper. They made a good impression on me, which Gandhi himself, at that time, did not. The things that one associated with him – homespun cloth, 'soul forces' and vegetarianism – were unappealing, and his medievalist programme was obviously not viable in a backward, starving, overpopulated country. It was also apparent that the British were making use of him, or thought they were making use of him. Strictly speaking, as a Nationalist, he was an enemy, but since in every crisis he would exert himself to prevent violence – which, from the British point of view, meant preventing any effective action whatever – he could be regarded as 'our man'. In private this was sometimes cynically admitted. The attidue of the Indian millionaires was similar. Gandhi called upon them to repent, and naturally they preferred him to the Socialists and Communists who, given the chance, would actually have taken their money away. How reliable such calculations are in the long run is doubtful; as Gandhi himself says, 'in the end deceivers deceive only themselves'; but at any rate the gentleness with which he was nearly always handled was due partly to the feeling that he was useful. The British Conservatives only became really angry with him when, as in 1942, he was in effect turning his non-violence against a different conqueror.

But I could see even then that the British officials who spoke of him with a mixture of amusement and disapproval also genuinely liked and admired him, after a fashion. Nobody ever suggested that he was corrupt, or ambitious in any vulgar way, or that anything he did was actuated by fear or malice. In judging a man like Gandhi one seems instinctively to apply high standards, so that some of his virtues have passed almost unnoticed. For instance, it is clear even

[1] *The Story of my Experiments with Truth* by M. K. Gandhi, translated from the Gujarati by Mahadev Desai.

from the autobiography that his natural physical courage was quite outstanding: the manner of his death was a later illustration of this, for a public man who attached any value to his own skin would have been more adequately guarded. Again, he seems to have been quite free from that maniacal suspiciousness which, as E. M. Forster rightly says in *A Passage to India*, is the besetting Indian vice, as hypocrisy is the British vice. Although no doubt he was shrewd enough in detecting dishonesty, he seems wherever possible to have believed that other people were acting in good faith and had a better nature through which they could be approached. And though he came of a poor middle-class family, started life rather unfavourably, and was probably of unimpressive physical appearance, he was not afflicted by envy or by the feeling of inferiority. Colour feeling, when he first met it in its worst form in South Africa, seems rather to have astonished him. Even when he was fighting what was in effect a colour war he did not think of people in terms of race or status. The governor of a province, a cotton millionaire, a half-starved Dravidian coolie, a British private soldier, were all equally human beings, to be approached in much the same way. It is noticeable that even in the worst possible circumstances, as in South Africa, when he was making himself unpopular as the champion of the Indian community, he did not lack European friends.

Written in short lengths for newspaper serialization, the autobiography is not a literary masterpiece, but it is the more impressive because of the commonplaceness of much of its material. It is well to be reminded that Gandhi started out with the normal ambitions of a young Indian student and only adopted his extremist opinions by degrees and, in some cases, rather unwillingly. There was a time, it is interesting to learn, when he wore a top-hat, took dancing lessons, studied French and Latin, went up the Eiffel Tower, and even tried to learn the violin – all this with the idea of assimilating European civilization as thoroughly as possible. He was not one of those saints who are marked out by their phenomenal piety from childhood onwards, nor one of the other kind who forsake the world after sensational debaucheries. He makes full confession of the misdeeds of his youth, but in fact there is not much to confess. As a frontispiece to the book there is a photograph of Gandhi's possessions at the time of his death. The whole outfit could be purchased for about £5, and Gandhi's sins, at least his fleshly sins, would make the same sort of appearance if placed all in one heap. A few cigarettes, a few mouthfuls of meat, a few annas pilfered in childhood from the maidservant, two visits to a brothel (on each occasion he got away without 'doing anything'), one narrowly escaped lapse with his landlady in Plymouth, one outburst of temper – that is about the whole collection. Almost from childhood onwards he had a deep earnestness, an attitude ethical rather than religious, but, until he was about thirty, no very definite sense of direction. His first entry into anything describable as public life was made by way of vegetarianism. Underneath his less ordinary qualities one feels all the time the solid middle-class businessmen who were his ancestors. One feels that even after he had abandoned personal ambition he must have been a resourceful, energetic lawyer and a hard-headed political organizer, careful in keeping down expenses, an adroit handler of committees and an indefatigable chaser of subscriptions. His character was an extraordinarily mixed one, but there was almost nothing in it that you can put your finger on and call bad, and I believe that even Gandhi's worst enemies would admit that he was an interesting and unusual man who enriched the world simply by being alive. Whether he was also a lovable man, and whether his teachings can have much value for those who do not accept the religious beliefs on which they are founded, I have never felt fully certain.

Of later years it has been the fashion to talk about Gandhi as though he were not only sympathetic to the western left-wing movement, but were even integrally part of it. Anarchists and pacifists, in particular, have claimed him for their own, noticing only that he was opposed to centralism and State violence and ignoring the other-worldly, anti-humanist tendency of his doctrines. But one should, I think, realize that Gandhi's teachings cannot be squared with the belief that Man is the measure of all things, and that our job is to make life worth living on this earth, which is the only earth we have. They make sense only on the assumption that God exists and that the world of solid objects is an illusion to be escaped from. It is worth considering the disciplines which Gandhi imposed on himself and which – though he might not insist on every one of his followers observing every detail – he considered indispensable if one wanted to serve either God or humanity. First of all, no meat eating, and if possible no animal food in any form. (Gandhi himself, for the sake of his health, had to compromise on milk, but seems to have felt this to be a backsliding.) No alcohol or tobacco, and no spices or condiments, even of a vegetable kind, since food should be taken not for its own sake, but solely in order to preserve one's strength. Secondly, if possible, no sexual intercourse. If sexual intercourse must happen, then it should be for the sole purpose of begetting children and presumably at long intervals. Gandhi himself, in his middle thirties, took the vow of *bramahcharya*, which means not only complete chastity but the elimination of sexual desire. This condition, it seems, is difficult to attain without a special diet and frequent fasting. One of the dangers of milk drinking is that it is apt to arouse sexual desire. And finally – this is the cardinal point – for the seeker after goodness there must be no close friendships and no exclusive loves whatever.

Close friendships, Gandhi says, are dangerous, because 'friends react on one another' and through loyalty to a friend one can be led into wrong-doing. This is unquestionably true. Moreover, if one is to love God, or to love humanity as a whole, one cannot give one's preference to any individual person. This again is true, and it marks the point at which the humanistic and the religious attitudes cease to be reconcilable. To an ordinary human being, love means nothing if it does not mean loving some people more than others. The autobiography leaves it uncertain whether Gandhi behaved in an inconsiderate way to his wife and children, but at any rate it makes clear that on three occasions he was willing to let his wife or a child die rather than administer the animal food prescribed by the doctor. It is true that the threatened death never actually occurred, and also that Gandhi – with, one gathers, a good deal of moral pressure in the opposite direction – always gave the patient the choice of staying alive at the price of committing a sin: still, if the decision had been solely his own, he would have forbidden the animal food, whatever the risks might be. There must, he says, be some limit to what we will do in order to remain alive, and the limit is well on this side of chicken broth. This attitude is perhaps a noble one, but, in the sense which – I think – most people would give to the word, it is inhuman. The essence of being human is that one does not seek perfection, that one *is* sometimes willing to commit sins for the sake of loyalty, that one does not push asceticism to the point where it makes friendly intercourse impossible, and that one is prepared in the end to be defeated and broken up by life, which is the inevitable price of fastening one's love upon other human individuals. No doubt alcohol, tobacco and so forth are things that a saint must avoid, but sainthood is also a thing that human beings must avoid. There is an obvious retort to this, but one should be wary about making it. In this yogi-ridden age, it is too readily assumed that 'non-attachment' is not only better than a full acceptance of earthly life, but that the ordinary man only rejects it because it is too difficult: in other words, that the average human being is a failed saint. It is doubtful whether this is true. Many people genuinely do not wish to be saints, and it is probable that some who achieve or aspire to sainthood have never felt much temptation to be human beings. If one could follow it to its psychological roots, one would, I believe, find that the main motive for 'non-attachment' is a desire to escape from the pain of living, and above all from love, which, sexual or non-sexual, is hard work. But it is not necessary here to argue whether the other-worldly or the humanistic ideal is 'higher'. The point is that they are incompatible. One must choose between God and Man, and all 'radicals' and 'progressives', from the mildest Liberal to the most extreme Anarchist, have in effect chosen Man.

However, Gandhi's pacifism can be separated to some extent from his other teachings. Its motive was religious, but he claimed also for it that it was a definite technique, a method, capable of producing desired political results. Gandhi's attitude was not that of most western pacifists. *Satyagraha,* first evolved in South Africa, was a sort of non-violent warfare, a way of defeating the enemy without hurting him and without feeling or arousing hatred. It entailed such things as civil disobedience, strikes, lying down in front of railway trains, enduring police charges without running away and without hitting back, and the like. Gandhi objected to 'passive resistance' as a translation of *Satyagraha*: in Gujarati, it seems, the word means 'firmness in the truth'. In his early days Gandhi served as a stretcher-bearer on the British side in the Boer war, and he was prepared to do the same again in the war of 1914–18. Even after he had completely abjured violence he was honest enough to see that in war it is usually necessary to take sides. He did not – indeed, since his whole political life centred round a struggle for national independence, he could not – take the sterile and dishonest line of pretending that in every war both sides are exactly the same and it makes no difference who wins. Nor did he, like most western pacifists, specialise in avoiding awkward questions. In relation to the late war, one question that every pacifist had a clear obligation to answer was: 'What about the Jews? Are you prepared to see them exterminated? If not, how do you propose to save them without resorting to war?' I must say that I have never heard, from any western pacifist, an honest answer to this question, though I have heard plenty of evasions, usually of the 'you're another' type. But it so happens that Gandhi was asked a somewhat similar question in 1938 and that his answer is on record in Mr Louis Fischer's *Gandhi and Stalin.* According to Mr Fischer Gandhi's view was that the German Jews ought to commit collective suicide, which 'would have aroused the world and the people of Germany to Hitler's violence'. After the war he justified himself: the Jews had been killed anyway, and might as well have died significantly. One has the impression that this attitude staggered even so warm an admirer as Mr Fischer, but Gandhi was merely being honest. If you are not prepared to take life, you must often be prepared for lives to be lost in some other way. When, in 1942, he urged non-violent resistance against a Japanese invasion, he was ready to admit that it might cost several million deaths.

At the same time there is reason to think that Gandhi, who after all was born in 1869, did not understand the nature of totalitarianism and saw everything in terms of his own struggle against the British Government. The important point here is not so much that the British treated him forbearingly as that he was always able to command publicity. As can be seen from the phrase quoted above, he believed in 'arousing the world', which is only possible if the world gets a chance to hear what you are doing. It is difficult to see how Gandhi's methods could be applied in a country where opponents of the régime disappear in the middle of the night and are never heard of again. Without a free press and the right of assembly, it is impossible not merely to appeal to outside opinion, but to bring a mass movement into being, or even to make your intentions known to your adversary. Is there a Gandhi in Russia at this moment? And if there is, what is he accomplishing? The Russian masses could only practise civil disobedience if the same idea happened to occur to all of them simultaneously, and even then, to judge by the history of the Ukraine famine, it would make no difference. But let it be granted that non-violent resistance can be effective against one's own government, or against an occupying power: even so, how does one put it into practice internationally? Gandhi's various conflicting statements on the late war seem to show that he felt the difficulty of this. Applied to foreign politics, pacifism either stops being pacifist or becomes appeasement. Moreover the assumption, which served Gandhi so well in dealing with individuals, that all human beings are more or less approachable and will respond to a generous gesture, needs to be seriously questioned. It is not necessarily true, for example, when you are dealing with lunactics. Then the question becomes: Who is sane? Was Hitler sane? And is it not possible for one whole culture to be insane by the standards of another? And, so far as one can gauge the feelings of whole nations, is there any apparent connection between a generous deed and a friendly response? Is gratitude a factor in international politics?

These and kindred questions need discussion, and need it urgently, in the few years left to us before somebody presses the button and the rockets begin to fly. It seems doubtful whether civilization can stand another major war, and it is at least thinkable that the way out lies through non-violence. It is Ghandi's virtue that he would have been ready to give honest consideration to the kind of question that I have raised above; and, indeed, he probably did discuss most of these questions somewhere or other in his innumerable newspaper articles. One feels of him that there was much that he did not understand, but not that there was anything that he was frightened of saying or thinking. I have never been able to feel much liking for Gandhi, but I do not feel sure that as a political thinker he was wrong in the main, nor do I believe that his life was a failure. It is curious that when he was assassinated, many of his warmest admirers exclaimed sorrowfully that he had lived just long enough to see his life work in ruins, because India was engaged in a civil war which had always been foreseen as one of the by-products of the transfer of power. But it was not in trying to smooth down Hindu-Moslem rivalry that Gandhi had spent his life. His main political objective, the peaceful ending of British rule, had after all been attained. As usual, the relevant facts cut across one another. On the one hand, the British did get out of India without fighting, an event which very few observers indeed would have predicted until about a year before it happened. On the other hand, this was done by a Labour Government, and it is certain that a Conservative Government, especially a government headed by Churchill, would have acted differently. But if, by 1945, there had grown up in Britain a large body of opinion sympathetic to Indian independence, how far was this due to Gandhi's personal influence? And if, as may happen, India and Britain finally settle down into a decent and friendly relationship, will this be partly because Gandhi, by keeping up his struggle obstinately and without hatred, disinfected the political air? That one even thinks of asking such questions indicates his stature. One may feel, as I do, a sort of aesthetic distaste for Gandhi, one may reject the claims of sainthood made on his behalf (he never made any such claim himself, by the way), one may also reject sainthood as an ideal and therefore feel that Gandhi's basic aims were anti-human and reactionary: but regarded simply as a politician, and compared with the other leading political figures of our time, how clean a smell he has managed to leave behind!

Partisan Review, January 1949

TITLES IN THIS SERIES:

Eric Ambler
The Mask of Dimitrios
Passage of Arms
The Schirmer Inheritance
Journey into Fear
The Light of Day
Judgment on Deltchev

John le Carré
The Spy Who Came in from the Cold
Call for the Dead
A Murder of Quality
The Looking-Glass War
A Small Town in Germany

Raymond Chandler*
Farewell My Lovely
The Lady in the Lake
Playback
The Long Goodbye
The High Window
The Big Sleep

Joseph Conrad
Lord Jim
The Nigger of the 'Narcissus'
Typhoon
Nostromo
The Secret Agent

Catherine Cookson
The Round Tower
The Fifteen Streets
Feathers in the Fire
A Grand Man
The Blind Miller

Catherine Cookson
The Mallen Streak
The Girl
The Gambling Man
The Cinder Path
The Invisible Cord

Monica Dickens
One Pair of Hands
The Happy Prisoner
Mariana
Kate and Emma
One Pair of Feet

F. Scott Fitzgerald*
The Great Gatsby
Tender is the Night
This Side of Paradise
The Beautiful and Damned
The Last Tycoon

Ian Fleming
Dr. No
Thunderball
Goldfinger
On Her Majesty's Secret Service
Moonraker
From Russia, With Love

C. S. Forester
The Ship
Mr. Midshipman Hornblower
The Captain from Connecticut
The General
The Earthly Paradise
The African Queen

E. M. Forster
Where Angels Fear to Tread
The Longest Journey
A Room with a View
Howards End
A Passage to India

Fourteen Great Plays*

John Galsworthy
The Forsyte Saga:
The Man of Property
In Chancery To Let
A Modern Comedy:
The White Monkey
The Silver Spoon Swan Song

Erle Stanley Gardner
Perry Mason in the Case of the Gilded Lily
The Daring Decoy
The Fiery Fingers
The Lucky Loser
The Calendar Girl
The Deadly Toy
The Mischievous Doll
The Amorous Aunt

Richard Gordon
Doctor in the House
Doctor at Sea
Doctor at Large
Doctor in Love
Doctor in Clover
The Facemaker
The Medical Witness

Graham Greene
The Heart of the Matter
Stamboul Train
A Burnt-out Case
The Third Man
Loser Takes All
The Quiet American
The Power and the Glory

Ernest Hemingway*
For Whom the Bell Tolls
The Snows of Kilimanjaro
Fiesta
The Short Happy Life of Francis Macomber
Across the River and into the Trees
The Old Man and the Sea

Georgette Heyer
These Old Shades
Sprig Muslin
Sylvester
The Corinthian
The Convenient Marriage

Franz Kafka*
The Trial
America
In the Penal Settlement
Metamorphosis
The Castle
The Great Wall of China
Investigations of a Dog
Letter to his Father
The Diaries 1910-1923

Rudyard Kipling
The Jungle Book
The Second Jungle Book
Just So Stories
Puck of Pook's Hill
Stalky and Co.
Kim

D. H. Lawrence
Sons and Lovers
St. Mawr
The Fox
The White Peacock
Love among the Haystacks
The Virgin and the Gipsy
Lady Chatterley's Lover

D. H. Lawrence
Women in Love
The Ladybird
The Man Who Died
The Captain's Doll
The Rainbow

Norah Lofts
Jassy
Bless This House
Scent of Cloves
How Far to Bethlehem?

Robert Ludlum*
The Scarlatti Inheritance
The Osterman Weekend
The Matlock Paper
The Gemini Contenders

Thomas Mann*
Death in Venice
Tristan
Tonio Kröger
Doctor Faustus
Mario and the Magician
A Man and His Dog
The Black Swan
Confessions of Felix Krull, Confidence Man

W. Somerset Maugham
Cakes and Ale
The Painted Veil
Liza of Lambeth
The Razor's Edge
Theatre
The Moon and Sixpence

W. Somerset Maugham
Sixty-five Short Stories

Ed McBain*
Cop Hater
Give the Boys a Great Big Hand
Doll
Eighty Million Eyes
Hail, Hail, the Gang's All Here!
Sadie When She Died
Let's Hear it for the Deaf Man

James A. Michener*
The Source
The Bridges at Toko-Ri
Caravans
Sayonara

George Orwell
Animal Farm
Burmese Days
A Clergyman's Daughter
Coming up for Air
Keep the Aspidistra Flying
Nineteen Eighty-Four

Jean Plaidy
St. Thomas's Eve
Royal Road to Fotheringay
The Goldsmith's Wife
Perdita's Prince

Nevil Shute
A Town Like Alice
Pied Piper
The Far Country
The Chequer Board
No Highway

Georges Simenon
Ten Maigret Stories

Wilbur Smith
When the Lion Feeds
The Diamond Hunters
Eagle in the Sky
Gold Mine
Shout at the Devil

John Steinbeck*
The Grapes of Wrath
The Moon is Down
Cannery Row
East of Eden
Of Mice and Men

Mary Stewart
The Crystal Cave
The Hollow Hills
Wildfire at Midnight
Airs Above the Ground

Evelyn Waugh
Decline and Fall
Black Mischief
A Handful of Dust
Scoop
Put Out More Flags
Brideshead Revisited

H. G. Wells
The Time Machine
The Island of Dr. Moreau
The Invisible Man
The First Men in the Moon
The Food of the Gods
In the Days of the Comet
The War of the Worlds

Morris West
The Devil's Advocate
The Second Victory
Daughter of Silence
The Salamander
The Shoes of the Fisherman

Dennis Wheatley
The Devil Rides Out
The Haunting of Toby Jugg
Gateway to Hell
To the Devil – A Daughter

John Wyndham
The Day of the Triffids
The Kraken Wakes
The Chrysalids
The Seeds of Time
Trouble With Lichen
The Midwich Cuckoos

***Not currently available in Canada for copyright reasons**